AND TECHNOLOGY PROGRAM

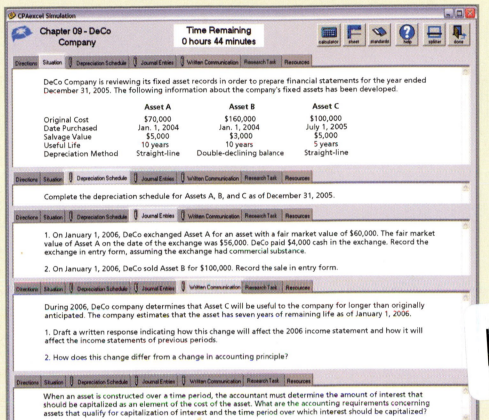

CPA-Adapted Problems and Simulations are offered through a partnership with Efficient Learning Systems. The simulations are reproduced at the end of each chapter and can be worked manually or online by accessing CPAexcel™. Also available are 300 AICPA-licensed exam questions to help prepare students for the Uniform CPA Examination.

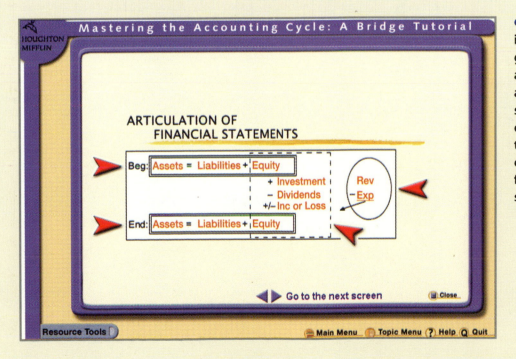

e-Study CD with Bridge Tutorial is designed to "bridge" the widening gap between introductory financial accounting and intermediate accounting. The Bridge Tutorial supports Chapter 1, the review chapter. It emphasizes accounting transactions, reviews the debit-credit mechanism, and provides a foundation for preparing financial statements.

INTERMEDIATE ACCOUNTING

SECOND EDITION

Intermediate Accounting
Financial Reporting and Analysis

Second Edition

Curtis L. Norton
Northern Illinois University

Michael A. Diamond
University of Southern California

Donald P. Pagach
North Carolina State University

Houghton Mifflin Company   Boston   New York

Publisher: *George Hoffman*
Senior Sponsoring Editor: *Ann West*
Senior Development Editor: *Margaret Kearney*
Editorial Assistant: *Alison McGonagle*
Project Editor: *Patricia English*
Editorial Assistant: *Brett Pasinella*
Art and Design Manager: *Gary Crespo*
Senior Photo Editor: *Jennifer Meyer Dare*
Composition Buyer: *Chuck Dutton*
Senior Designer: *Henry Rachlin*
Manufacturing Coordinator: *Florence Cadran*
Marketing Manager: *Mike Schenk*
Marketing Associate: *Kathleen Mellon*

Cover image: © Shigeru Tanaka/Photonica

PHOTO CREDITS: p. 2, AP/Wide World; p. 56, AP/Wide World Photos; p. 100, © Larry Kolvoord/The Image Works; p. 150, AP/Wide World Photos; p. 194, © Jack Kurtz/The Image Works; p. 252, © AFP/Getty Images; p. 300, © James Leynse/Corbis; p. 348, AP/Wide World Photos; p. 398, AP/Wide World Photos; p. 452, AP/Wide World Photos; p. 496, © Erik Freeland/Corbis; p. 544, © Rebecca Cook/Reuters/Corbis; p. 584, AP/Wide World Photos; p. 636, © Joe Raedle/Getty Images; p. 694, © Kim Kulish/Corbis; p. 752, © Tim Boyle/Getty Images; p. 810, AP/Wide World Photos; p. 858, © Free Agents Limited/Corbis; p. 906, AP/Wide World Photos.

Printed in the U.S.A.

Library of Congress Control Number: 2005935740

Instructor's exam copy:
ISBN 13: 978-0-618-72185-6
ISBN 10: 0-618-72185-1

For orders, use student text ISBNs:
ISBN 13: 978-0-618-56814-7
ISBN 10: 0-618-56814-X

23456789-WEB-10 09 08 07

ABOUT THE AUTHORS

Curtis L. Norton has been a professor at Northern Illinois University (NIU) in DeKalb, Illinois, since 1976 and has specialized in teaching Intermediate Accounting during those years. He earned his Ph.D. from Arizona State University in 1976, his M.B.A. from the University of South Dakota, and his B.S. from Jamestown College, North Dakota. His list of publications include articles in *The Accounting Review, Accounting Horizons, The Journal of Accounting Education, Journal of Accountancy, Journal of Corporate Accounting, Journal of the American Taxation Association, CPA Journal,* and many others. He also has been the co-author of two textbooks for introductory financial accounting. In 1988–1989, Professor Norton received the University Excellence in Teaching Award, the highest university-wide teaching recognition at NIU. For many years, he has taught in NIU's CPA Review Program. His consulting activities include developing training programs for public accounting firms, governmental agencies, banks, other companies, and advising firms on financial accounting policy issues. Professor Norton is a member of the American Accounting Association and the Financial Executives Institute.

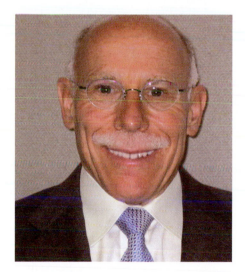

Michael A. Diamond served for 10 years as Vice President and Executive Vice Provost of the University of Southern California before rejoining the faculty of the USC Leventhal School of Accounting in July 2005. Prior to his Provost's Office appointments, Michael Diamond served as dean of the Leventhal School of Accounting and director of the school's SEC and Financial Reporting Institute from July 1987 through March 31, 1994. Professor Diamond is a leader in the accounting education reform movement. Because of his direction, the Leventhal School of Accounting at the University of Southern California is recognized as the pacesetter in accounting education change. Professor Diamond has lectured throughout the United States, Europe, and Asia on business and accounting education innovation. His articles have appeared in the *Harvard Business Review, Accounting Horizons,* and the *Journal of Accounting.* Professor Diamond served as president of the American Accounting Association from August 1998 to August 1999. He has taught at California State University, Los Angeles, and has been a visiting professor at the University of California, Berkeley and the University of California, Los Angeles. He also has taught in executive education programs for a number of international accounting firms as well as Fortune 500 companies. Professor Diamond is the recipient of the California Society of CPAs Faculty Excellence Award for 1993 and was named as one of the "Top100 Most Influential People in Accounting" in both the fall 1997 and 1998 issues of *Accounting Today.*

Donald P. Pagach is currently an associate professor at North Carolina State University. He received his bachelor's and master's degrees from the University of Wisconsin–Madison and his doctorate from Florida State University. Articles by Professor Pagach have appeared in the *Journal of Accounting Research, Contemporary Accounting Research, Decision Sciences, Issues in Accounting Education,* and other professional and academic journals. These articles have examined financial analyst forecasts and market microstructure issues. Professor Pagach is a member of the American Accounting Association and American Institute of Certified Public Accountants. He has been named an Outstanding Teacher and been inducted into the Academy of Outstanding Teachers at North Carolina State University.

BRIEF CONTENTS

CONTENTS

CHAPTER 3

The Income Statement and Comprehensive Income Disclosures 100

CHAPTER 8

Inventory 348

CHAPTER 9

Operating Assets: Acquisition, Cost Allocation, Impairment, and Disposal 398

CHAPTER 10 Intangible Assets 452

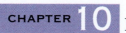

PART **III** Financial Instruments and Liabilities 495

CHAPTER **11** Investments: Debt and Equity Securities 496

CHAPTER **12** Current Liabilities and Contingencies 544

CHAPTER 13

Accounting for Long-Term Liabilities: Bonds and Notes Payable 584

CHAPTER 14

Accounting for Leases 636

CHAPTER 15

Pensions and Postretirement Plans 694

CHAPTER 16

Accounting for Income Taxes 752

PART **IV** Stockholders' Equity and Cash Flows 809

PREFACE

Measured transition. Progression. Change. Now more than ever, the role of the accountant has expanded well beyond basic recording and reporting functions. Accounting professionals lead businesses and communicate with peers in the financial community. They analyze complex financial statements and interpret the implications of business transactions and industry events.

This changing role places new demands on accountants—they need to think critically and to understand the "why" of accounting as well as the "how." Today's accounting professionals are users and interpreters of financial information as well as preparers of this information. As this change permeates the profession, a similar transition must occur in the education of the accountant. As educators, we must not only arm students with a solid understanding of procedural accounting and its underlying concepts, but also ensure that they are equipped to communicate, analyze, think critically, interpret financial events and transactions, and make important business decisions.

The first edition of *Intermediate Accounting: Financial Reporting and Analysis* was developed to achieve the following goals:

- Present the core body of knowledge and skills necessary to enable students to be outstanding professionals in a changing and complex accounting and global business environment

- Facilitate a careful, measured transition to an intermediate course that continues to provide solid procedural and technical content but also incorporates effective analysis and decision-making components

- Reflect current business practices and place students in work-authentic business situations to prepare them for successful professional careers

- Introduce accounting controversies, ethical issues, and real business dilemmas to foster critical thinking, judgment, and decision-making skills

- Present a text that is both pedagogically sound and engaging to read

- Support the use of today's technologies in preparing students for the global business environment

Based on the positive response to our first edition, we believe we have achieved these goals. With this second edition, we continue to update and describe new standards in financial accounting—and at the same time offer students a measured, balanced approach that focuses on the uses of financial information for analysis and decision making. Throughout the revision process, we listened carefully to reviewer and adopter comments to be sure that our book would provide instructors and students with the most current and relevant content available.

PRESENTS THE CORE BODY OF KNOWLEDGE AND SKILLS NECESSARY FOR PROFESSIONAL SUCCESS

Every day, the body of knowledge required of the intermediate accounting student expands. Ongoing statements, pronouncements, and opinions from the FASB, AICPA, IASB, SEC, and other influential bodies add complexities to the already weighty subject matter. Most accounting faculty state that the number one challenge in teaching intermediate accounting is dealing with this ever-growing body of knowledge. We keep hearing how students are getting lost in the myriad rules and procedures in encyclopedic texts. We worry that they are losing sight of the big picture of a financial event.

"I WAS PLEASED AND SURPRISED BY THE CONCISENESS OF THE TEXT AND THE SKILL IN PRESENTING COMPLEX ISSUES IN A MEANINGFUL AND CONCISE MANNER WITHOUT OVERLOAD OF TECHNICAL AND VERBAL DETAIL."
David Law,
Youngstown State University

We believe it is possible to provide students with a core body of knowledge and a solid coverage of necessary procedural details, yet offer a streamlined approach that is more conceptual in nature. Students, after all, are more likely to remember concepts than to remember rules and procedures that are always changing. By presenting a balance of concepts and procedures, we have designed an approach that will enable students to "learn to learn" by helping them understand the "why" of accounting as well as the "how." Thus, while we present traditional financial preparation issues, we do so within the context of a user orientation by discussing analysis and valuation issues beyond those currently available in standard intermediate accounting texts.

In addition to developing students' technical proficiencies, the text is designed to develop skills critical to lifelong learning. Specifically, the text advances critical thinking, fosters the development of valuable communication and spreadsheet skills, and emphasizes analysis and decision making as a means of developing the competencies required by professional accountants and business managers. Our text, then, presents a core body of knowledge and skills as verified through extensive market research with academics as well as practitioners. Its coverage is distinguished in the following ways:

- *Review of the accounting process.* Chapter 1, which is supported by the Bridge Tutorial CD-ROM, presents a basic review of the accounting process and the financial statements. The Bridge Tutorial CD-ROM is designed to reinforce a basic understanding of the accounting cycle and can be used as a review tool to prepare students to move into intermediate accounting in a seamless manner.

- *Integrated coverage of the statement of cash flows.* We introduce the statement of cash flows in Chapter 5 in order to support the integration of cash flows throughout the text. Because students receive a basic understanding of this important statement early in the course, they are able to comprehend discussions of cash flows in subsequent chapters. In addition, the text ends with a "capstone" chapter on this topic: Chapter 19, "Revisiting the Statement of Cash Flows." This approach not only enables students to recognize the importance of the cash flow statement as they progress through the course, but it also allows them to see the relationship of cash flows to the accrual amounts reflected in the other financial statements and consider the ever-widening gap between accrual and cash amounts.

- *Coverage of earnings quality and earnings management.* Understanding the nuances of earnings quality and earnings management is critical to the success of the accounting professional as a business adviser and ethical practitioner. Chapter 3 introduces these concepts and demonstrates how accounting policy plays a vital role in earnings presentation. Earnings management issues related to accounting estimates, pensions, timing of revenue recognition, and deferred taxes are also covered in Chapters 6, 15, and 16.

- *Coverage of revenue recognition.* Revenue recognition is introduced in Chapter 6. Because the basics of the income statement and the balance sheet are presented in Chapters 3 and 4, students are ready to connect the elements of each statement and apply revenue recognition concepts to issues such as long-term construction contracts and installment sales.

- *Coverage of investments.* Consistent with the logical flow of balance sheet items, investments are presented in Chapter 11. This coverage has become increasingly important as a result of the movement toward market value recognition.

- *Coverage of long-term liabilities.* Long-term liabilities are covered in Chapters 13 through 16 and are organized to align with the order of their appearance on the balance sheet. This presentation helps students see the logical progression of items—from current liabilities to long-term liabilities, then onward to leases, pensions, and deferred taxes.

- *Emerging accounting issues.* Recognizing the importance and timeliness of industry events, we introduce emerging accounting issues, as appropriate, within the text chapters. We also plan on updating the Instructor Website on a regular basis to include emerging accounting issues, releases of new accounting standards, and business events and legislation that will enrich the educational experience.

"THE TEXT HAS AN EXCELLENT INTEGRATION OF CASH FLOWS WITHIN EACH CHAPTER AND APPEARS TO INCLUDE A THOROUGH REVIEW OF BASIC CASH FLOWS EARLY IN THE TEXT."
Diane Tanner,
University of North Florida

"OVERALL THIS HAS THE POTENTIAL TO BE A GREAT TEXTBOOK. I ESPECIALLY LIKE THE INTEGRATION OF CASH FLOW CONSIDERATIONS IN THE CHAPTERS."
Patrick Fort,
University of Alaska

REFLECTS RECENT CHANGES TO ACCOUNTING STANDARDS AND BUSINESS PRACTICES

The Second Edition of *Intermediate Accounting* has been updated to reflect the latest pronouncements from the FASB and other standard-setting bodies. Current accounting standards have been fully integrated to ensure all data, examples, and end-of-chapter assignments are current and accurate. This includes:

- A major update to Chapter 2 on the hierarchy of GAAP reflecting the new FASB exposure draft, "The Hierarchy of Generally Accepted Accounting Principles." The discussion of ethics and self-regulation in the accounting profession was also expanded in this chapter.

- Significant changes to Chapter 3 regarding *SFAS 154*, "Accounting Changes and Error Corrections," which was issued in May 2005 and replaces *APB Opinion No. 20.*

- Revisions in Chapter 9 to accommodate a new treatment for changes in accounting principles involving depreciation methods in *SFAS 154*, and for modification of the accounting for nonmonetary exchanges, based on *SFAS 153.*

- A new paragraph on permanent impairment in Chapter 11, and clarification of the discussion of amortizing trading debt securities.

- Modification for FASB progress on debt/equity distinction in Chapter 13.

- Major changes to Chapter 18 because of stock options and the new pronouncement, *SFAS 123R.* A brief explanation of the "intrinsic method" has been retained to explain past practice, but the text has been shifted to reflect the "fair value" method now required by the FASB.

In addition, many of the companies featured in the chapter openers have been replaced to highlight recent events and trends in business accounting. For instance, the chapter opener on Transmeta in Chapter 10, "Intangible Assets," has been replaced with Nike. The discussion focuses on Nike's purchase of Converse, whose main assets were intangibles resulting from Converse's "retro" style comeback. The chapter opener on Microsoft in Chapter 17, "Stockholders' Equity," was retained, but the material was rewritten to reflect a major change in the company's dividend policy. Disney's financial statements, which appear in the opener and text of Chapter 18, "Dilutive Securities and Earnings per Share," were updated.

FOCUSES ON THE USES OF FINANCIAL INFORMATION FOR ANALYSIS AND DECISION MAKING

The text uses actual published financial statements to convey a broader knowledge of business and to provide a context for analysis and decision making. Whereas traditional courses generally have a basic preparer orientation, this text introduces a user perspective based on the knowledge and use of actual financial statements. Students are challenged to analyze financial transactions, review the financial statements of real businesses, and reflect on current business events. We achieve this in the following ways:

- *Financial Reporting Cases.* A Financial Reporting Case designed to expose students to current business and industry practices, competitive strategies, and reporting considerations opens each chapter. Each case features a real business, a reporting or analysis issue, and questions to stimulate thinking about the chapter concepts. For example, the Financial Reporting Case in Chapter 11 examines the investment strategies that Intel uses. In Chapter 18, the Financial Reporting Case discusses the dilutive effects of stock options on stockholders' equity for Disney shareholders.

- *Real financial statements.* Most chapters introduce two or more companies, generally competitors within the same market or industry, and use the financial statements of these companies to demonstrate reporting techniques, analysis comparisons, and conceptual issues. For example, in Chapter 9, excerpts from the financial statements of

"I FEEL THAT INTERMEDIATE COURSES WILL HAVE TO TRANSFORM THEMSELVES INTO MORE RESEARCH, ANALYSIS, AND COMMUNICATIONS COURSES RATHER THAN JUST PROCEDURES. THIS IS GOING TO BE A VERY DIFFICULT TRANSITION FOR US. AS THE FIRST STEP IN THIS TRANSITION, A BOOK THAT EMPHASIZES RESEARCH AND FASB WILL BE A TREMENDOUS BENEFIT OVER BOOKS THAT DO NOT."
Joanne Duke,
San Francisco State University

Lowe's and Home Depot illustrate the presentation and analysis of operating assets. In Chapter 17, students review selected reports from Microsoft and Nike as they study stock splits, treasury stock, analysis of stockholders' equity, and dividends.

● *Focused sections on analysis and decision making.* Most chapters include a dedicated section on analysis as it pertains to the chapter's financial reporting topics. Integration of analysis techniques and interpretations adds a critical dimension to the understanding of the business environment. For example, learning how to record and report long-term liabilities is the first step, but understanding how a company's debt level can be used to assess its solvency and leverage will take students to a more advanced professional level.

● *End-of-chapter problems and cases with skill-based components.* Exercises, problems, and cases at the end of each chapter challenge students to look beyond the numbers and demonstrate a conceptual understanding of the issues. Although many of the problems and cases require students to prepare statements and solve problems based on quantitative data, the problems also include skills-based components requiring students to exercise communication, analysis, research, critical thinking, and decision-making skills.

REFLECTS CURRENT BUSINESS PRACTICES, INCLUDING INTERNATIONAL PRACTICES

It is no secret that students connect to learning that reflects their experiences in the business world. In this text, we integrate business financial statements, business scenarios, and industry comparisons to provide a rich context for the chapter topics. Unlike other texts, where business data are relegated to boxed features, our text integrates these elements throughout the text because we believe they are an integral part of the learning process.

Likewise, we also integrate our discussion of international accounting institutions and standards into the text discussion. These discussions, identified with the icon INTERNATIONAL 🌐, provide a framework for understanding the differences in accounting practices outside the United States, consistent with the FASB's movement toward eliminating these differences. These discussions will also help students understand the implications of international reporting with such critical thinking questions as this one in Chapter 2: "As a potential investor who is comparing the financial performance of a U.S.-based company with that of a company based in Switzerland, what issues are you likely to face? How might you deal with any significant accounting differences between these two companies?"

INTRODUCES ACCOUNTING CONTROVERSIES AND ETHICAL DILEMMAS

We believe it is necessary to stress the heightened importance of the accountant's ethical responsibility. Few would have envisioned the corporate scandals of the past decade and resulting public scrutiny of the accounting profession. It is evident knowledge of accounting procedures is not enough. In this text, we challenge students to consider the ethical responsibilities of the profession. What is a corporation's responsibility? Is earnings management ethical? Do off-balance-sheet disclosures "fairly present" information? The following activities, content, and features flex critical thinking, judgment, and decision-making skills:

● *Critical thinking questions.* Critical thinking questions throughout the chapter motivate active reading, stimulate comprehension, and raise students' awareness of current business issues. The questions may also be used to stimulate classroom discussion. For example, in Chapter 2, one of the critical thinking questions asks students to consider what consequences for investors and creditors might result if acceptable accounting practices were not clearly defined, regulated, and enforced? In Chapter 11, another critical thinking question asks students to consider how companies might generate income from debt securities. (Suggested responses are provided in the *Instructor's Resource Manual,* which is available on the HMClassPrep™ with HMTesting CD-ROM and on the Instructor Website.)

- *Ethical decision-making model.* In Chapter 2, an ethical decision-making model provides students with a framework for both individual and corporate ethical decision making. The discussion includes an annotated case example that serves as a model for answering the end-of-chapter ethics cases.

- *Dedicated chapter sections on ethics.* Rather than relegate the discussion of ethics to boxed examples, we include section topics that focus on accounting and business practices involving ethical considerations. All are identified with the icon ETHICS ⚖ .

- *Point/Counterpoint presentations.* Throughout the text, Point/Counterpoint essays present contrasting points of view on controversial accounting issues as expressed by prominent accounting and financial professionals. Students will explore divergent viewpoints on such issues as the impact of stock option expensing, off-balance-sheet financing, rules-based standards versus principles-based standards, internally generated intangibles, and earnings management. Each Point/Counterpoint concludes by inviting students to take a position and/or do follow-up research on the issues.

- *End-of-chapter cases.* The cases at the end of each chapter place students in the role of decision maker, communicator, researcher, or analyst, challenging them to read the details of a business scenario, interpret financial data, and consider issues of ethics and corporate responsibility.

PRESENTS A STRAIGHTFORWARD PEDAGOGICAL FRAMEWORK

Knowing that financial accounting involves detailed, complex data and technical jargon, we have made every attempt to present the material in a student-friendly manner by introducing abstract concepts in the context of real business situations. In addition, we have incorporated numerous visual elements—diagrams, charts, and other illustrative examples—to make the material more real and engaging for students. The following pedagogical devices are designed to support learning in each chapter:

- *Learning objectives.* Each chapter opens with a series of learning objectives (LOs) that preview the key material that students will study. The LOs also appear in the margin next to the material they cover and appear with the end-of-chapter summaries, exercises, problems, and cases. In addition, the LOs are used to link the text material to each of the various student and instructor ancillaries, thus providing a well-integrated learning system.

- *Illustrations and figures.* Illustrations and figures appear throughout each chapter to reinforce and visually illuminate important concepts, procedures, and financial reporting methods. Illustrations include drawings, charts, tables, and hypothetical financial statements created by the authors. Figures are actual financial statements and other excerpts from the annual reports of real companies.

- *Critical thinking questions.* As students launch into new topics within the chapter discussions, critical thinking questions appear in the text margin to help stimulate thought on new ideas and concepts. These questions (described earlier) will challenge students to think about the "why" of accounting as they learn the "how."

- *Check your understanding questions.* A series of review questions follows each major chapter section, allowing students to test their comprehension of the material before moving on to new concepts in the chapter. These questions also serve as an excellent review device for students preparing for exams. Suggested responses to the review questions appear at the end of each chapter.

- *Summary by learning objective.* The chapter summary acts as a capstone for student learning and provides a quick review of key chapter concepts.

- *Key terms.* Key terms appear in blue the first time they are introduced in the text discussion. They also appear in the margin, along with brief definitions. Key terms are

"PROBABLY THE TWO MOST DISTINCT FEATURES ARE THE CRITICAL THINKING QUESTIONS . . . AND THE ADDITIONAL FEATURES OF THE PROBLEMS ASKING FOR AREAS SUCH AS COMMUNICATION, CRITICAL THINKING, AND ANALYSIS. I WOULD SERIOUSLY CONSIDER ADOPTING THE TEXT. THE TEXT WOULD BE AMONG MY TOP RANKING INTERMEDIATE TEXTS."
Russell Briner,
University of Texas, San Antonio

listed at the end of each chapter, and a full glossary of terms and definitions is provided on the Student CD-ROM and on the Student Website.

● *End-of-chapter assignments.* Each chapter provides a comprehensive set of assignment materials, including exercises, problems, and cases that are designed to reinforce students' understanding of the chapter concepts. While several of the problems require students to prepare partial financial statements and related note disclosure, many also focus on how to value the financial statement items. All have been rigorously class-tested and triple-checked for accuracy and clarity.

   • *Skills-based components.* All problems and cases in the end-of-chapter materials include components that require students to analyze financial reports or transactions, communicate orally and in writing about business events, research real business reporting, exercise their decision-making abilities, or utilize spreadsheet applications to complete problem assignments.

   • *CPA-adapted simulations.* To prepare students for the Uniform CPA examination, we have included in the end-of-chapter materials simulations that mirror the skills required in the *new* electronic CPA exam. Students will practice researching and interpreting standards, exercising judgment, preparing reports, drawing conclusions, and communicating financial information. The simulations can be done online or manually.

● *Additional Web activities.* The supporting *Intermediate Accounting* website provides a wealth of additional skills-based activities, including the following:

> **"I'M VERY PLEASED TO SEE CPA-ADAPTED PROBLEMS AND SIMULATIONS THAT STUDENTS WILL HAVE TO FACE ON THE NEW COMPUTER-BASED CPA EXAM."**
> *Charles Russo,*
> *Bloomsburg State University*

Web Activity	Skill(s)
Interpreting the Accounting Standards: critical thinking activities centered on a standard or opinion mentioned in the text, with links to information or a summary of the standard for research and interpretation purposes	Research, communication, analysis
Extending the Global Focus: extension activities requiring research on an international topic discussed in the chapter	Research, communication
Extending the Ethics Discussion: scenarios that require students to conduct research in considering ethical dilemmas	Communication, decision making, critical thinking
Annual Report Projects: projects related to the annual report of Coca-Cola, Inc.	Research, critical thinking, analysis, communication
Career Snapshots: activities that require students to perform online research regarding career paths in accounting	Research, communication
Mastering the Spreadsheet: additional spreadsheet activities based on the end-of-chapter problems	Spreadsheets

These activities are designed to motivate active learning, reinforce the text materials, and provide students with ample opportunities to apply their knowledge and to develop skills that are critical for lifelong learning and their professional development.

SUPPORTS THE TECHNOLOGIES USED IN BUSINESS TODAY

Technology is a driving force behind business growth and accounting education today. As an example, the environment of accounting changed dramatically when the CPA examination was moved to a computer-based format. Students preparing for or taking the exam must now be able to work online, access databases, and use spreadsheets and other technologies critical to business practice. Although we believe that the goals of this text and the goals of an intermediate accounting class go well beyond preparation for the CPA examination, we also believe that an intermediate accounting text must provide the necessary tools for preparing students for the exam. Therefore, we have developed an integrated text and technology program that is designed to prepare students for the practice of accounting. We support the use of technology in the following ways:

FOR THE STUDENT

- *Bridge Tutorial.* This tutorial, available on the Student CD-ROM, was designed to "bridge" the widening gap between introductory financial accounting and intermediate accounting. The Bridge Tutorial may be used for a stand-alone or "bridge" course or be assigned at the beginning of an intermediate accounting course. Created through the joint efforts of introductory and intermediate accounting authors and instructors, the Bridge Tutorial is designed to prepare students to move into the intermediate course in a seamless manner, thus reducing the number of class periods required for a review of financial accounting. The Bridge Tutorial supports Chapter 1, the review chapter. It emphasizes accounting transactions, reviews the debit-credit mechanism, and provides a foundation for preparing financial statements.

- *Spreadsheet exercises.* Students gain experience in using and applying spreadsheet applications through each chapter's end-of-chapter assignments. Additional "Mastering the Spreadsheet" activities are available on the Student Website at **www.college.hmco.com/ accounting/students**.

- *CPA-adapted problems and simulations.* Through a partnership with Efficient Learning Systems, students of instructors who request the CPAexcel passkey package can access CPAexcel, an online CPA exam review course. Offering approximately 300 AICPA-licensed exam questions and 25 CPA exam simulations (19 of which are reproduced at the ends of the text chapters), CPAexcel enables students to acquire the skills required of candidates preparing for the new Uniform CPA exam.

- *ACE practice tests.* Students can self-check their mastery of chapter topics and prepare for exams with the Student CD-ROM or the Student Website using Houghton Mifflin's popular ACE interactive quizzing program.

- *Eduspace® powered by Blackboard®.* This Web-enabled homework system is designed to allow students to complete text assignments online, submit them electronically, and receive immediate feedback on their answers.

- *Online tutoring from SMARTHINKING®.* Students are provided with access to personalized online tutoring through use of "e-structors" (online tutors) during typical homework hours.

- *Electronic working papers.* These Excel-formatted forms are tied directly to the text assignments and allow students to print the forms and complete them manually or to enter data electronically.

- *Student CD-ROM.* This CD-ROM includes the Bridge Tutorial (described earlier), along with ACE practice tests, a glossary of key terms, and a set of check figures for each of the end-of-chapter problems.

- *Student Website.* Students can reinforce their learning experience with a variety of online activities, problems, readings, research tools, and additional assessment materials available on the Student Website at **www.college.hmco.com/accounting/students**. Included are:
  - Interpreting the Accounting Standards
  - Extending the Global Focus
  - Extending the Ethics Discussion
  - ACE Practice Tests
  - Flashcards
  - Glossary

"**THE BRIDGE CD SHOULD BE A BIG HELP IN RELEARNING THE ACCOUNTING CYCLE. I WOULD NOT USE THE CD IN CLASS. RATHER, I WOULD LEAVE IT TO THE STUDENT TO USE AT HOME AS NECESSARY TO REVIEW OR RELEARN MATERIAL FROM INTRODUCTORY ACCOUNTING.**"
K. K. Raman,
University of North Texas

- Mastering the Spreadsheet
- Career Snapshots
- Annual Report Project
- Check Figures for Text Problems
- PowerPoint Presentations

FOR THE INSTRUCTOR

We also offer the following supplements to support instructors:

- *Instructor's Resource Manual.* This valuable resource includes chapter lecture outlines, suggested responses to the text critical thinking questions, and suggested answers to the text Point/Counterpoint features. There is an assignment matrix for each chapter categorizing the exercises, problems, and cases by learning objective, level of difficulty, and estimated completion time. These materials are provided on the Instructor's HMClass Prep™ with HMTesting CD-ROM, described below.

- *Solutions Manual.* Solutions for all chapter questions, exercises, problems, and cases are offered in print and electronic formats. The electronic solutions are available on the HMClassPrep with HMTesting CD-ROM and on the Instructor's Website.

- *Test bank.* The test bank includes over 2,000 multiple-choice questions, computational questions, exercises, and problems. A comprehensive exam for each of the four parts of the text is also provided. The computerized test bank is on the HMClassPrep with HMTesting CD-ROM. A printed version is also available.

- *HMClassPrep with HMTesting CD-ROM.* This easy-to-use CD-ROM for instructors includes all the components of the *Instructor's Resource Manual* (discussed earlier) along with the computerized test bank, PowerPoint presentations, and electronic solutions for all text exercises, problems, and cases.

- *Instructor Website.* This valuable resource center provides access to an array of teaching resources and activities to extend the textbook experience. Teaching resources, as previously described, include the *Instructor's Resource Manual,* the *Solutions Manual,* PowerPoint Presentations, FASB updates and other announcements on emerging issues, and a wealth of additional Web activities, all to be found in a password-protected site at **www.college.hmco.com/accounting/instructors**.

- *Eduspace powered by Blackboard.* This Web-enabled online homework system allows students to complete text assignments online, submit them electronically, and receive immediate feedback. It also reduces homework grading time for instructors.

- *Blackboard Course Cartridges and WebCT e-Packs.* These cartridges and e-packs provide instructors with flexible, efficient, and creative ways to present Internet-based learning materials and manage distance learning courses. Resources include the computerized test bank, ACE Practice Tests, PowerPoint slides, the *Instructors' Resource Manual,* and Excel solutions for the text exercises, problems and cases. Instructors may also make use of an electronic grade book, along with other functionality.

- *Wall Street Journal.* Students whose instructors have adopted the *Wall Street Journal* version of *Intermediate Accounting* will receive, packaged with their textbook, a registration card for a print and online subscription to the *Journal.* This package is designed to keep instructors and students on top of accounting news and changes.

ATTENTION AND COMMITMENT TO ACCURACY

Intermediate Accounting: Financial Reporting and Analysis has undergone several accuracy reviews throughout its development. The text chapters—both the chapter content and the end-of-chapter exercises, problems, and cases—were triple-checked, with an accuracy review in the book's draft stage, following copyediting, and at the final proof stage. Likewise, the solutions to the exercises, problems, and cases were carefully checked at all stages of development.

The ancillary programs, particularly the test bank, ACE self-quizzes, and PowerPoint slides, have been checked by professional accuracy reviewers for content and computational errors. Although no text, even ones in later editions, can be absolutely free of errors, we believe we have taken appropriate (in fact, extraordinary) measures to ensure accuracy across the text and ancillary program.

We could not have done this alone, and we therefore wish to thank the countless number of reviewers and accuracy checkers, as follows.

REVIEWERS AND ACCURACY CHECKERS

Charlene Abendroth, *California State University, Hayward*
Noel Addy, *Mississippi State*
Alex Ampadu, *University of Buffalo*
Matthew Anderson, *Michigan State University*
Ervin Black, *Brigham Young University*
Tiffany Bortz, *University of Texas, Dallas*
Elizabeth Briggs, *Louisiana State University*
Russell Briner, *University of Texas, San Antonio*
Gyan Chandra, *Miami University of Ohio*
Laura DeLaune, *Louisiana State University*
Joanne Duke, *San Francisco State University*
John Elfrink, *Central Missouri State University*
Alan Falcon, *Loyola Marymount*
Patrick Fort, *University of Alaska, Anchorage*
Steven Grossman, *Texas A&M University*
Lyle Hicks, *Danville Area Community College*
Kathy Horton, *College of DuPage*
Richard Houston, *University of Alabama*
M. Zafar Iqbal, *California Polytechnic State University*
Marianne James, *California State University, Los Angeles*
Lynn Johnson, *California State University, Stanislaus*
Kris Jones, *Southeastern Louisiana University*
Janet Kimbrell, *Oklahoma State University*
Florence Kirk, *State University of New York College at Oswego*
Ellen Landgraf, *Loyola University, Chicago*
Cathy Larson, *Middlesex Community College*
David Law, *Youngstown State University*

Philip Lewis, *Northern Kentucky University*
Gary Luoma, *University of South Carolina, Columbia*
Susan Lynn, *University of Baltimore*
Daphne Main, *University of New Orleans*
LuAnn Mangold, *Pittsburg State University*
Wilda Meixner, *Southwest Texas State University*
Paul Miller, *University of Colorado, Colorado Springs*
Emeka Ofobike, *University of Akron*
Anne Oppegard, *Augustana College*
Stephen Owusu-Ansah, *University of Texas, PanAmerican*
Catherine Craycrafte Plante, *University of New Hampshire*
Andrew Potts, *University of Southern Maine*
Jacqueline Power, *Texas A&M International University*
Mary Ann Prater, *Clemson University*
Kris K. Raman, *University of North Texas*
Robert Rambo, *University of Southern Mississippi*
Sara Reiter, *State University of New York, Binghamton*
Vernon Richardson, *University of Kansas*
Robert Rouse, *College of Charleston*
Charles Russo, *Bloomsburg State University*
Rafal Szwejkowski, *University of Texas, Dallas*
Diane Tanner, *University of North Florida*
Wayne Thomas, *Oklahoma State, Norman*
Richard Turpin, *University of Tennessee, Chattanooga*
David Weiner, *University of San Francisco*
Mary Jeanne Welsh, *La Salle University, Philadelphia*
Christian Wurst, *Temple University*
Joni Young, *University of New Mexico*

ADVISORY BOARD MEMBERS

We also wish to acknowledge and thank the many individuals who joined our Advisory Board and participated in a number of development activities, including market surveys, focus groups, workshops, and in-depth interviews. We apologize to anyone we may have overlooked or whose affiliations may have changed.

Charlene Abendroth, *California State University, Hayward*
Sunita Ahlawat, *College of New Jersey*
Nelson Alino, *Benedict College*
Marie Archambault, *Marshall University*
B. J. Ballanco, *University of New Orleans*
Homer Bates, *University of North Florida*
Jim Bates, *Mountain Empire Community College*
Leslie Bauman, *Minnesota West Community & Technical College, Granite Falls*
Terry Bechtel, *Northwestern State University of Louisiana*

Joseph Bentley, *Bunker Hill Community College*
Angela Blackwood, *Belmont Abbey College*
Phyllis Bloom, *Nazareth College*
Rodney Boydstun, *Ohio Valley College*
Doris Brooks, *University of Guam*
C. James Buckley, *Mesa State College*
Kurt Buerger, *Angelo State University*
Rose Marie L. Bukics, *Lafayette College*
Tammie Burkhart, *Concordia University*
Suzanne Busch, *California State University, Hayward*

Roberta Cable, *Pace University*

Jane Campbell, *Kennesaw State University*

Linda Campbell, *Siena Heights University*

Charles Carslaw, *University of Nevada, Reno*

Ted Chapman, *Ottawa University*

Raymond Chen, *California State University, Northridge*

Alan Cherry, *Loyola Marymount University*

David Ching, *Los Angeles Harbor College*

Anna Cianci, *University of Florida*

Douglas Cloud, *Pepperdine University*

Diane Clugston, *Cambria-Rowe Business College*

Hugh Cole, *Bluefield College*

Joe Colgan, *Fort Lewis College*

David Collins, *Bellarmine University*

Carol Coman, *California Lutheran University*

Teresa Conover, *University of North Texas*

Margaret Conway, *Kingsborough Community College*

William Cooper, *North Carolina A & T State University*

John Corless, *California State University, Sacramento*

Richard Cummings, *Benedictine College*

David Dahlberg, *College of St. Catherine*

Robert Darville, *Shorter College*

Julianne Davies, *Eastern Michigan University*

Larry Davis, *Southwest Virginia Community College*

Vaun Day, *Southwestern Oklahoma State University*

Dan Deines, *Kansas State University*

William Dent, *University of Texas, Dallas*

Robert DePasquale, *Saint Vincent College*

Douglas deVidal, *University of Texas, Austin*

Lee Dexter, *Moorhead State University*

Aurora Dolores, *East Los Angeles College*

Ben Doran, *Iowa State University*

Roger Dufresne, *Northern Essex Community College*

James Duncan, *Ball State University*

Linda Duvall, *Sam Houston State University*

Thomas Dyckman, *Cornell University*

Lawrence Eaton, *Gateway Technical College*

John Elfrink, *Central Missouri State University*

Joseph Fairchild, *Henderson State University*

William Faulk, *Northwestern Michigan College*

Ehsan Feroz, *University of Minnesota, Duluth*

Mary Flanigan, *Longwood College*

Brenda Flores, *University of Southern California*

Lou Fowler, *Missouri Western State College*

Joel Frazier, *DeVry University, Pomona*

Daniel Fulks, *Transylvania University*

Joseph Galante, *Millersville University*

Julie Gentile, *Glendale Community College*

Frank Gersich, *Monmouth College*

Christopher Gilbert, *Glendale Community College*

Jay Gordon, *Norwich University*

Janet Grange, *Chicago State University*

Gloria Grayless, *Sam Houston State University*

Vicki Greshik, *Jamestown College*

Krishan Gupta, *University of Massachusetts, Dartmouth*

Abo Habib, *Minnesota State University*

Dan Hall, *East Central College*

Mary Harston, *St. Mary's University*

LaRee Hartman, *Butte College*

Hassan Hefzi, *California State Polytechnic University, Pomona*

Kenneth Henry, *Florida International University*

James Higgins, *Holy Family College*

Rebecca Hook, *Greenville Technical College*

Kathy Horton, *College of DuPage*

Marsha Huber, *Otterbein College*

Candie Humphrey, *University of Dubuque*

Jim Hurley, *Winona State University*

M. Zafar Iqbal, *California Polytechnic State University*

Alicia Jackson, *Tuskegee University*

Judy Jager, *Pikes Peak Community College*

Marianne James, *California State University, Los Angeles*

Scott Jervis, *San Francisco State University*

Fred Jex, *Macomb Community College*

Gun-Ho Joh, *San Diego State University*

James Johnson, *Louisiana Technical University*

Tom Jones, *DeVry University*

Mark Kaiser, *State University of New York, Plattsburgh*

Jane Kaplan, *Drexel University*

Philip Kintzele, *Central Michigan University*

Yolanda Kirk, *University of Southern California*

David Knight, *Borough of Manhattan Community College*

Michael Krause, *LeMoyne College*

Meg Costello Lambert, *Oakland Community College*

Sandra Lang, *McKendree College*

David Law, *Youngstown State University*

Michael Layne, *Nassau Community College*

Patsy Lee, *University of Texas, Arlington*

Lydia Leporte, *Tidewater Community College*

Brian Leventhal, *University of Illinois, Chicago*

Marc Levine, *Queens College*

Joseph Lipari, *Montclair State University*

Ellen Lippman, *University of Portland*

Danny Litt, *University of California, Los Angeles*

Ted Lynch, *Hocking College*

Daphne Main, *University of New Orleans*

Jimmy Martin, *University of Montevallo*

Roger Martin, *University of Virginia*

Danny Matthews, *Midwestern State University*

Susan Matz Milstein, *Western Maryland College*

Robert Maurer, *Central College*

Florence McGovern, *Bergen County Community College*

Barbara Merino, *University of North Texas*

Jeanne Miller, *Cypress College*

Josephine Miller, *Mercer County Community College*

Janette Moody, *The Citadel*

Kate Mooney, *St. Cloud State University*

Joseph Moran, *College of DuPage*

Paula Morris, *Kennesaw State University*

Paul Mueller, *Western Nevada Community College*

Brock Murdoch, *California State University, Chico*

Tim Murphy, *Diablo Valley College*
Mark Myring, *Ball State University*
Ashok Nataranan, *California State Polytechnic University, Pomona*
Siva Nathan, *Georgia State University*
Margaret O'Brien, *Dakota State University*
Joseph Onyeocha, *South Carolina State University*
Anne Oppegard, *Augustana College*
Robert O'Toole, *Crafton Hills College*
Hong Pak, *California State Polytechnic University, Pomona*
Jane Park, *California State University, Los Angeles*
Ronald Pawliczek, *Boston College*
Roy Pentilla, *Lansing Community College*
Jacqueline Perry, *West Virginia University Institute of Technology*
Judy Peterson, *Monmouth College*
Timothy Peterson, *Gustavus Adolphus College*
A. Lee Phillips, *University of Kansas*
Andrew Piltz, *Rocky Mountain College*
Dennis Plezek, *Waukesha Country Technical College*
J. Marion Posey, *Pace University*
Andrew Potts, *University of Southern Maine*
Mary Ann Prater, *Clemson University*

Claire Purvis, *California State University, San Bernadino*
Vinita Ramaswamy, *University of St. Thomas*
Deanna Ramsey, *Midway College*
James Reburn, *Samford University*
Sara Reiter, *State University of New York, Binghamton*
Patricia Rinke, *Grand View College*
Waymond Rodgers, *University of California, Riverside*
Julie Rosenblatt, *Delaware Technical Community College*
Gerald Rosenfeld, *Robert Morris College*
John Rossi, *Moravian College*
Ralph Rumble, *Kankakee Community College*
John Sanders, *University of Southern Maine*
Lewis Shaw, *Suffolk University*
Adrianne Slaymaker, *Ferris State University*
Mark Soczek, *Washington University, St. Louis*
Beverly Soriano, *Framingham State College*
Kan Sugandh, *DeVry University, Pomona*
Viceola Sykes, *South Carolina State University*
Kathy Terrell, *University of Central Oklahoma*
Vicki Vorrell, *Cuyahoga Community College*
William Wilcox, *Bradley University*
Suzanne Wright, *Pennsylvania State University*

ANCILLARY PREPARERS

We are also grateful to those who worked diligently with us in preparing the many ancillaries and Web activities to support the text and technology program. Because of their efforts, we believe we have a strong, integrated learning system. In particular, we recognize and thank:

Charlene Abendroth, *California State University, Hayward*
Stan Chu, *Borough of Manhattan Community College*
Laura DeLaune, *Louisiana State University*
John Elfrink, *Central Missouri State University*
Marianne James, *California State University, Los Angeles*

Ed Julius, *California Lutheran University*
Michael Krause, *LeMoyne College*
Gail Mestas, *New Mexico State University*
Charles Russo, *Bloomsburg State University*
Diane Tanner, *University of North Florida*

OTHER ACKNOWLEDGMENTS

The authors gratefully acknowledge the members of the Houghton Mifflin team and their very significant contributions to this project. Bonnie Binkert's vision and enthusiastic support were instrumental during the development of the first edition and have continued through the second. Ann West has been our leader for the second edition and has managed all aspects of the process with a skill, enthusiasm, and professionalism that the authors sincerely appreciate. Margaret Kearney spent countless hours editing, advising, and monitoring all phases of the project. Henry Rachlin created the simple yet elegant design we wanted for the book. Todd Berman and Mike Schenk implemented the strategy for a successful launch of our text. Cynthia Fostle had a clear vision of the project, and her editing skills were greatly needed to refine the authors' work. Cathy Larson scrutinized the proofs looking for calculation errors and other inadvertent inconsistencies. Patricia English coordinated the production process for the second edition. Finally, the authors want to give special recognition to Jeri Condit, who was able to combine her accounting skills and editorial and publishing background in a unique way. This project would not have been possible without her talent, skills, and hard work. This truly was a team effort, and the authors want to thank all of the team members.

Financial Concepts and Financial Statements

Making business decisions requires information. Accounting is an information system that measures, records, and communicates financial information to a variety of users. In Part One, you will review the concepts and techniques that are fundamental to an accounting system and examine the components of each financial statement. Using the data communicated through the financial statements and disclosures, you will learn how analysis techniques are used to assess the financial health of a business.

1 Accounting Foundations
In this chapter, you will review the set of activities known as the accounting cycle, examine the components of the four primary financial statements, and consider the concepts and assumptions that support each statement.

2 Financial Reporting: The Cornerstone of a Market Economy
This chapter provides a detailed look at the purposes of financial reporting, the standards and standard setters that play a role in the current financial environment, and the importance of generally accepted accounting principles.

3 The Income Statement and Comprehensive Income Disclosures
The measurement of income is critical to determining the viability of a business. In Chapter 3, the reporting formats for the income statement and its components are presented, along with the treatment of nonrecurring items, comprehensive income, and the use of the income statement for analysis purposes.

4 The Balance Sheet
The balance sheet defines the financial position of a company. In Chapter 4, you will study the measurement and recording of balance sheet items and gain insight into the transactions that affect the statement of changes in stockholders' equity. Tools like benchmarking, percentage analysis, horizontal analysis, and ratio analysis, which are employed to give users perspective on the performance and condition of a business, are introduced as well.

5 The Statement of Cash Flows and Other Significant Financial Disclosures
In this chapter, you will survey the structure of the statement of cash flows and learn how cash is used in or generated from operating, financing, and investing activities. Using information gleaned from this statement, you will learn how to evaluate the performance and prospects of one company or to compare companies in the same industry. In addition, other significant financial disclosures, such as accounting policies, segments, the auditors' report, and interim reports, are discussed.

1

Accounting Foundations

LEARNING OBJECTIVES

After studying this chapter, you should be able to:

Section A

LO1 Identify the elements of the balance sheet and discuss four key concepts that underlie the balance sheet.

LO2 Identify the elements of the income statement and discuss six key concepts that underlie the income statement.

LO3 Summarize the contents of the statement of changes in stockholders' equity and the statement of cash flows.

Section B

LO4 Explain how the accounting equation forms the basis of double-entry accounting.

LO5 Outline the steps in the accounting cycle.

FINANCIAL REPORTING CASE

KEEPING SCORE: CONFIDENCE IN QUALCOMM NUMBERS

CEO Irwin Jacobs is responsible for fairly representing the financial position of QUALCOMM, a world leader in communication technology. What would you want to know before investing in this company?

QUALCOMM Profits? Cash flow? Assets? Invoices? Ledgers? Do you wonder how all these components fit together? A system of accounting can organize all of them into a language that conveys an understandable measure of performance and financial condition in business. Just as pro tennis player Serena Williams keeps score during each match she plays, business owners must measure and score their own performance. Accounting provides the necessary rules for keeping score. Certain basic financial reports—the balance sheet, income statement, statement of changes in stockholders' equity, and statement of cash flows—are used to present the score to interested parties.

If you were interested in investing in a company like QUALCOMM Inc., a world leader in communication technology, you might first examine its financial statements for information about the company's financial condition. While accounting systems vary from company to company, common procedures and principles prevail. But how can you be sure that QUALCOMM's statements were prepared in accordance with generally accepted practices? The auditors' report is key to the integrity of a firm's financial statements. Examine the following auditors' report, or report of independent accountants, for QUALCOMM Inc.

QUALCOMM

REPORT OF INDEPENDENT ACCOUNTANTS

To the Board of Directors and Stockholders of QUALCOMM Incorporated

In our opinion, the accompanying consolidated balance sheets and the related consolidated statements of operations, of cash flows and of stockholders' equity present fairly, in all material respects, the financial position of QUALCOMM Incorporated and its subsidiaries (the "Company") at September 30, 2003 and 2002, and the results of their operations and their cash flows for each of the three years in the period ended September 30, 2003 in conformity with accounting principles generally accepted in the United States of America. These financial statements are the responsibility of the Company's management; our responsibility is to express an opinion on these financial statements based on our audits. We conducted our audits of these statements in accordance with auditing standards generally accepted in the United States of America, which require that we plan and perform the audit to obtain reasonable assurance about whether the financial statements are free of material misstatement. An audit includes examining, on a test basis, evidence supporting the amounts and disclosures in the financial statements, assessing the accounting principles used and significant estimates made by management, and evaluating the overall financial statement presentation. We believe that our audits provide a reasonable basis for our opinion.

As discussed in Note 1 to the consolidated financial statements, the Company adopted Statement of Financial Accounting Standard No. 142, "Goodwill and Other Intangible Assets," during the year ended September 30, 2003, and the Company changed its method of recognizing revenue and adopted Statement of Financial Accounting Standard No. 133, "Accounting for Derivative Instruments and Hedging Activities," during the year ended September 30, 2001.

PricewaterhouseCoopers LLP

PRICEWATERHOUSECOOPERS LLP
San Diego, California
November 3, 2003

As you can see, the auditors' report presents the auditors' opinion that the company's statements were prepared in accordance with "accounting principles generally accepted in the United States of America." It is the adherence to established standards, in both form and substance, that has been and must continue to be the basis for investor confidence and for the ultimate success of our market economy.

In Section A of this chapter, you will review the basic financial statements, their elements, and the concepts underlying each statement. In Section B, you will review how business transactions are analyzed and recorded. As you recall the standard steps of the accounting cycle, remember that these are the important building blocks for a solid understanding of financial reporting.

BRIDGE TUTORIAL

As you study this chapter, use the activities and demonstration problems on the Bridge Tutorial CD-ROM to strengthen your understanding of the accounting foundation topics presented in this chapter. Look for the Bridge Tutorial icon in the margin for relevant review and assessment opportunities. To assess your knowledge of these accounting foundation topics now, take the **Pre-test** offered on the CD-ROM.

EXAMINING THE CASE

1. Name the four financial statements that are routinely audited by firms like PricewaterhouseCoopers.

2. As a potential investor, what value do you think the auditors' report provides?

3. What is the significance of the statement by PricewaterhouseCoopers that QUALCOMM's financial statements are in conformity with generally accepted accounting principles in the United States?

4. What do you think PricewaterhouseCoopers means when it says that the financial statements are the responsibility of management?

SECTION A

The Four Financial Statements

Accounting is an information system that measures, processes, and communicates information, primarily financial in nature, about an identifiable entity for the purpose of making economic decisions. Financial statements are the principal means through which firms communicate their financial position and the results of their business activities to interested users, such as present and potential investors and creditors. The four primary financial statements are the balance sheet, the income statement, the statement of changes in stockholders' equity, and the statement of cash flows. They are the products of the **accounting cycle**, which is the set of activities involved in analyzing business events, collecting and processing information related to those events, and summarizing that information in the four financial statements. The first section of this chapter reviews the purposes of the financial statements, the elements that the statements contain, and the basic accounting concepts that underlie the preparation of the statements. The second section of the chapter reviews the steps in the accounting cycle.

THE BALANCE SHEET

The **balance sheet**, sometimes called the *statement of financial position*, provides information about the financial position of a company at a specific point in time. The elements in this statement are assets, liabilities, and owners' (or stockholders') equity.

⟩ ASSETS

Assets, the economic resources of a firm, "are probable future economic benefits obtained or controlled by a particular entity as a result of past transactions or events."[1] The critical phrases in this definition are "owned or controlled" and "probable future economic benefits." For something to be considered an asset, the firm must control its use, but legal title to the asset is not necessary. A good example of an asset controlled by a company without legal title to it is a truck purchased by a firm and financed through a bank loan. Until the loan is paid off, the bank usually keeps legal title to the truck. Nonetheless, because the firm that purchased the truck has the right to control its use, the truck is considered an asset of the firm, not of the bank. In addition, an asset must provide probable future benefits to the firm, and those benefits must be measurable. Accountants recognize that a certain degree of uncertainty regarding potential benefits is expected and that the duration and value of these benefits can only be estimated. For example, the firm will benefit from the truck's use for several years, but the exact number of years is difficult to predict. Assets are distinguished from expenses in that assets have economic benefits that remain available for future use. In contrast, expenses are the benefits that have been used up in the current period.

⟩ LIABILITIES

Liabilities, the economic obligations of a firm, are "probable future sacrifices of economic benefits arising from present obligations of a particular entity to transfer assets or perform services to other entities in the future as a result of past transactions or events."[2] This definition parallels that of assets. There must be a current obligation that requires the firm to give up or use its assets or to perform a service. This

---

accounting an information system that measures, processes, and communicates information, primarily financial in nature, about an identifiable entity for the purpose of making economic decisions

accounting cycle the set of activities involved in analyzing business events, collecting and processing information related to those events, and summarizing that information in the four financial statements

LO1 Identify the elements of the balance sheet and discuss four key concepts that underlie the balance sheet.

balance sheet a financial statement that provides information about the financial position of a company at a specific point in time

assets the economic resources of a firm; probable future economic benefits obtained or controlled by a particular entity as a result of past transactions or events

▦ *Critical Thinking: If financial statements were not presented in commonly accepted formats, what problems might arise for financial statement users?*

liabilities the economic obligations of a firm; probable future sacrifices of economic benefits arising from present obligations of a particular entity to transfer assets or perform services to other entities in the future as a result of past transactions or events

---

1 "Elements of Financial Statements," *Statement of Financial Accounting Concepts No. 6* (Stamford, Conn.: Financial Accounting Standards Board, December 1985), par. 25.

2 *SFAC No. 6*, par. 35.

obligation must stem from a past transaction. Again, the concept of uncertainty comes into play; the obligation does not have to be certain but only probable. For example, consider what happens when General Motors (GM) sells an automobile with a 50,000-mile warranty. A past transaction, a sale, has occurred, and that sale will most likely obligate General Motors to make repairs free of charge at some future time while the car is under warranty. The obligation is certain because at the time of the sale GM agreed to make necessary warranty repairs. The kind and number of repairs are uncertain, but GM can estimate their costs based on past experience. Thus, when a sale takes place, General Motors must recognize the warranty obligation as a liability and estimate the future costs that could cause an outflow of assets.

▶ OWNERS' EQUITY (OR STOCKHOLDERS' EQUITY)

owners' equity the residual interest in the assets of an entity that remains after deducting the liabilities; known as **stockholders' equity** for a corporation

Owners' equity is the "residual interest in the assets of an entity that remains after deducting its liabilities."[3] For a corporation, owners' equity is called **stockholders' equity** and consists of the capital invested by the owners (capital or common stock and other paid-in capital) and the retained earnings of the business resulting from its cumulative profitable operations less any dividends issued. Investments by owners increase the equity of a business because the owners contribute assets in exchange for an ownership stake, or equity position, in the firm. When investors buy capital stock that has been newly issued by a company, they contribute cash or other assets to the firm.[4] A company's equity is also increased when its operations are profitable. Distributions to owners in the form of cash or property, called dividends, decrease the company's equity because the company's assets are distributed to the owners. When a company declares and issues a cash dividend to stockholders, its overall value decreases because its net assets are reduced.

Financial Accounting Standards Board (FASB) the private-sector organization that establishes generally accepted accounting principles in the United States with input from businesses, CPAs, accounting firms, the financial community, government entities, and the AICPA

American Institute of Certified Public Accountants (AICPA) the national organization representing certified public accountants

generally accepted accounting principles (GAAP) conventions, rules, and procedures that guide the preparation of financial statements by either law, regulation, or custom

The elements of the balance sheet, summarized in Illustration 1.1, are defined by the **Financial Accounting Standards Board (FASB)**, the private-sector organization that establishes generally accepted accounting principles in the United States with input from businesses, certified public accountants (CPAs), accounting firms, the financial community, academia, government entities, and the **American Institute of Certified Public Accountants (AICPA)**, the national organization representing certified public accountants. **Generally accepted accounting principles (GAAP)** consist of conventions, rules, and procedures that guide the preparation of financial statements by either law, regulation, or custom. As better methods evolve or as circumstances change, these conventions and rules may be altered or amended.

Illustration 1.1

Elements of the Balance Sheet

Assets	Probable future economic benefits obtained or controlled by a particular entity as a result of past transactions or events
Liabilities	Probable future sacrifices of economic benefits arising from present obligations of a particular entity to transfer assets or perform services to other entities in the future as a result of past transactions or events
Owners' Equity	The residual interest in the assets of an entity that remains after deducting its liabilities
or Stockholders' Equity	The residual interest of the owners of a corporation; the capital invested by the owners and the retained earnings of the business resulting from its cumulative profitable operations less any dividends issued

---

3 *SFAC No. 6*, par. 49.

4 If the stock is purchased directly from another investor, the purchase is a transaction between two individuals. The firm is not involved, and it receives no additional assets.

classified balance sheet a financial statement format in which the assets and liabilities are categorized according to whether they are current or long-term

current assets cash and other assets that are reasonably expected to be realized in cash, sold, or consumed during the normal operating cycle or within one year from the balance sheet date, whichever is longer

operating cycle the period of time in which a company purchases merchandise inventory, sells the inventory for cash or credit, and collects cash from sales

operating assets tangible assets that a company uses to create revenue from operations

> **ILLUSTRATION: CRAMER CORPORATION BALANCE SHEET**

An example of a balance sheet, the balance sheet for Cramer Corporation, is presented in Illustration 1.2. Since the assets and liabilities are categorized according to whether they are current or not current (long-term), the balance sheet shown here is called a **classified balance sheet**.

> **CURRENT ASSETS** **Current assets** are cash and other assets that are reasonably expected to be realized in cash, sold, or consumed during the normal operating cycle or within one year from the balance sheet date, whichever is longer. A firm's **operating cycle** is the period of time in which a company purchases merchandise inventory, sells the inventory for cash or credit, and collects cash from sales. Most firms have operating cycles of less than one year. Examples of current assets include cash, marketable securities, accounts receivable, prepaid expenses, inventories, and supplies.

> **OPERATING ASSETS** Assets that will last beyond one year are generally grouped in a category called operating assets. **Operating assets** are the tangible assets that a company uses to create revenue from operations. This category, often called *property, plant, and equipment (PP&E)* as in Illustration 1.2, typically includes such long-term assets as land, buildings, and equipment. It may also include assets with account titles such as Furniture and Fixtures, Land Improvements, and Automobiles. Operating

Illustration 1.2

Balance Sheet

Cramer Corporation Balance Sheet December 31, 2005		
Assets		
Current assets		
Cash	$ 15,000	
Accounts receivable	45,000	
Inventories	74,000	
Supplies	2,500	
Prepaid expenses	3,500	
Total current assets		$140,000
Property, plant, and equipment		
Land	$100,000	
Buildings, net of accumulated depreciation of $50,000	250,000	
Equipment, net of accumulated depreciation of $16,000	80,000	430,000
Total assets		$570,000
Liabilities and Stockholders' Equity		
Current liabilities		
Accounts payable	$ 12,000	
Salaries payable	7,000	
Interest payable	5,000	
Short-term notes payable	50,000	
Total current liabilities		$ 74,000
Long-term notes payable		80,000
Total liabilities		$154,000
Stockholders' equity		
Capital stock, 10,000 shares issued and outstanding	$200,000	
Retained earnings	216,000	
Total stockholders' equity		416,000
Total liabilities and stockholders' equity		$570,000

assets may also be referred to as *tangible assets, long-term plant assets,* or something similar.

Although operating assets last longer than current assets, they gradually decline in usefulness as a result of age, wear and tear, or obsolescence. To account for this declining usefulness, the cost of an operating asset is spread out over the asset's estimated useful life, and a part of the cost is apportioned to each fiscal period as depreciation. The accumulated depreciation to date is subtracted from the original cost of the asset, and the net amount is shown on the balance sheet. For example, Cramer Corporation purchased a building for $300,000 and has recorded depreciation to date of $50,000. Thus, the net amount shown on the balance sheet is $250,000.

current liabilities economic obligations that are expected to be liquidated using current assets or refinanced by other current liabilities during the normal operating cycle or within one year of the balance sheet date, whichever is longer

CURRENT LIABILITIES **Current liabilities** are economic obligations that are expected to be liquidated using current assets or refinanced by other current liabilities during the normal operating cycle or within one year of the balance sheet date, whichever is longer. Cramer Corporation's current liabilities include accounts payable, salaries payable, interest payable, and short-term notes payable.

noncurrent liabilities economic obligations that a firm will pay over a term longer than one year; also called *long-term liabilities*

NONCURRENT LIABILITIES **Noncurrent liabilities** are economic obligations that a firm will satisfy over a term longer than one year. Also called *long-term liabilities,* they include such items as long-term notes payable and bonds payable. As you can see from Illustration 1.2, Cramer Corporation's balance sheet reflects one type of long-term liability: long-term notes payable of $80,000.

capital stock shares of ownership in a corporation

retained earnings undistributed accumulated earnings of the firm since its inception less dividends or other distributions to owners

dividends distributions to shareholders of cash or property that have been earned through profitable operations

STOCKHOLDERS' EQUITY Cramer Corporation's stockholders' equity of $416,000 consists of two elements: $200,000 of **capital stock**, or shares of ownership in the corporation, and $216,000 of **retained earnings**, which are the undistributed accumulated earnings of the firm since its inception less dividends or other distributions to owners. **Dividends** are distributions to shareholders of cash or property that have been earned through profitable operations. Dividends are not an expense; they are a reduction in stockholders' equity.

CONCEPTS UNDERLYING THE BALANCE SHEET

As part of its work in developing a conceptual framework for financial reporting, the FASB has identified a number of important concepts and assumptions that underlie the financial statements.[5] Four key concepts that are especially relevant to the balance sheet are

1. The economic entity assumption
2. The historical cost principle
3. The monetary unit assumption
4. The going concern assumption

economic entity assumption the idea that the accounting for one economic unit should be kept separate from the accounting for the owners of that economic unit and from the accounting for other economic units owned or controlled by others

THE ECONOMIC ENTITY ASSUMPTION The **economic entity assumption** is the idea that the accounting for one economic unit should be kept separate from the accounting for the owners of that economic unit and from the accounting for other economic units owned or controlled by others. This assumption is critical to understanding accounting processes because it identifies what should be measured and reported in the financial statements for a specific entity and what should not be measured and reported. In particular, it establishes that the economic resources and obligations measured and reported for a business firm should not be confused with the owners' economic resources and obligations. For example, an owner's automobile should not be listed as an asset of the business unless the business holds title to the

---

5 Over the years, accountants have used several terms to identify these important concepts, including *assumptions, principles,* and *concepts.* Such distinctions are not significant to this discussion.

automobile or controls its use. Similarly, the cash in an owner's personal account should not be combined with the Cash account of the business.

The other side of the economic entity assumption is also very important. If a firm actually owns or controls the assets or liabilities of another entity or has assumed significant risk associated with them, it must include those assets and liabilities in its financial reports. This became an important issue in accounting when firms like Enron tried to avoid reporting certain assets and liabilities by setting up separate legal entities that they claimed were separate economic entities. Ultimately, it became clear that Enron had assumed significant economic risk associated with those outside entities and that Enron's financial position could not be accurately assessed unless those entities' assets and liabilities were included in Enron's financial statements.

historical cost principle a concept that guides the valuation of assets and liabilities by stating that an asset or liability should be initially recorded at its original, or historical, cost

> **THE HISTORICAL COST PRINCIPLE** The **historical cost principle** guides the valuation of assets and liabilities by stating that an asset or liability should be initially recorded at its original, or historical, cost. Under this principle, an asset is first recorded at the value of what is given in exchange for it. For example, when a plot of land is purchased for cash, the historical cost of the land is simply the amount of cash that the buyer paid. The issue is more complicated when assets other than cash are involved. When cash is not exchanged, or when cash is exchanged in combination with other assets, the price is based on the fair value of what is given or what is received, whichever is more clearly determinable. For instance, if the land were exchanged for a small building, instead of being purchased for cash, accountants would need to determine the fair value of the building—the asset given up in the exchange. That value would then become the historical cost of the land received in the exchange. If for some reason it was impossible to determine the value of the building, the fair value of the land (the asset received in the exchange) would be used to record the transaction.

A liability is initially recorded at the equivalent cash value of what is received in exchange. As with assets, when cash is received, the application of the historical cost principle is straightforward. Assume that a firm borrows $1 million from the bank at 6 percent interest per year. The liability, a note payable, is recorded at the amount of cash received, $1 million. As we will see in later chapters, valuing a liability becomes more complicated if assets other than cash are received in the exchange or if the interest is not stated or is well below current interest rates.

The use of historical costs has several important implications for financial reporting. Although historical costs are easier to verify than current values and are thus more reliable, they may not be as relevant to the users of financial statements. A balance sheet based on historical cost will not provide information about the current, or market, value of a firm's assets and liabilities. Many users believe that current values, although often less reliable than historical costs, are more relevant to decision making. Because of this perceived need by users, many of the more recent FASB standards require the use (or at least the disclosure) of current values for some of the assets and liabilities listed on the balance sheet.

If it is impossible to determine the historical cost of a potential asset or if the potential economic benefits of that asset cannot be measured, a different treatment is required. In such cases, the potential asset does not meet the accounting criteria for recognition and is not shown on the balance sheet. This applies to many internally generated assets, such as good management or loyal customers. While we know that good management has long-term economic benefits to a firm, there is no reasonable way to measure its historical cost or its future economic benefits. Therefore, you will not see an asset called Good Management on the balance sheet of any firm.

monetary unit assumption the concept that currency is an appropriate unit of measure for assessing the value of a firm in financial reporting

> **THE MONETARY UNIT ASSUMPTION** Closely related to the historical cost principle is the monetary unit assumption. The **monetary unit assumption** is the concept that currency is an appropriate unit of measure for assessing the value of a firm in financial reporting. In most economic environments, this assumption ignores inflation and presumes that a dollar (or any other currency) used to purchase an asset 20 years ago has the same value as a dollar used to purchase an asset today. The mone-

Critical Thinking:
Accounting conventions limit the recognition of assets to those that meet specific criteria. In what ways do these conventions limit the usefulness of financial statements?

going concern assumption the presumption that in the absence of evidence to the contrary, a firm will continue to operate indefinitely

LO2 Identify the elements of the income statement and discuss six key concepts that underlie the income statement.

income statement a financial statement that provides information about the amount of net income earned by a firm over a stated period of time by detailing the revenues earned and the expenses incurred during the period

net income (net loss) the amount that remains when all recognized expenses and losses are subtracted from all revenues and gains

revenues inflows or other enhancements of the assets of an entity or settlements of its liabilities (or a combination of both) from delivering or producing goods, rendering services, or carrying out other activities that constitute the entity's ongoing major or central operations

tary unit is considered to be stable. As a result, historical costs, as well as other values that may appear on the balance sheet, are shown in historical dollars, not dollars adjusted for changes in price levels. Even though we know that monetary values do not remain constant, assuming a stable monetary unit provides a baseline that analysts can use in making their own inflation adjustments. In the United States, where inflation (changes in general price levels) has been mild, assuming a stable monetary unit does not create many problems for analysts and other users of financial statements. However, in countries where hyperinflation is the norm, adjustments for changing price levels are difficult to make and the outcomes are less coherent.

❱ **THE GOING CONCERN ASSUMPTION** The **going concern assumption** is the presumption that in the absence of evidence to the contrary, a firm will operate indefinitely. This assumption underlies the use of historical costs in financial reports. The assumption that a firm will continue in business means that the firm must depreciate long-term assets over their useful lives, recognize revenue in the period in which it is earned, and value assets based on their expected future cash flows rather than on their liquidation values. If we knew that a firm was going out of business, we would use the liquidation value of its assets instead of using historical costs to value them.

THE INCOME STATEMENT

The **income statement** provides information about the amount of net income earned by a firm over a stated period of time by detailing the revenues earned and the expenses incurred during that period. Income statements are prepared at least annually and usually more often, such as quarterly or monthly. **Net income** (or **net loss**) is the amount that remains when all recognized expenses and losses are subtracted from all revenues and gains. Illustration 1.3 shows the income statement for our sample company, Cramer Corporation. Keep in mind that the balance sheet provides information about the financial position of a company at a specific point in time, whereas the income statement covers a period of time and thus is considered a change statement.

❱ **REVENUES AND EXPENSES**
In its *Statement of Financial Accounting Concepts No. 6*, the FASB defines revenues, expenses, gains, and losses. According to the FASB, **revenues** are "inflows or other

Illustration 1.3

Income Statement

Cramer Corporation Income Statement For the Year Ended December 31, 2005		
Revenues		
Sales	$1,200,000	
Interest revenue	10,000	
Gain on sale of equipment	25,000	
Total revenues		$1,235,000
Expenses		
Cost of goods sold	$ 810,000	
Salaries expense	200,000	
Office and general expenses	80,000	
Depreciation expense	50,000	
Interest expense	15,000	
Total expenses		1,155,000
Net income		$ 80,000

Critical Thinking: *What elements might you expect to find on an income statement for a not-for-profit organization such as a university? Would there likely be an element called* net income?

expenses outflows or using up of assets or incurrences of liabilities (or a combination of both) from delivering or producing goods, rendering services, or carrying out other activities that constitute the entity's ongoing major or central operations

gains increases in equity (net assets) from peripheral or incidental transactions of an entity and from all other transactions and other events and circumstances affecting the entity except those that result from revenues or investments by owners

losses decreases in equity (net assets) from peripheral or incidental transactions of an entity and from all other transactions and other events and circumstances affecting the entity except those that result from expenses or distributions to owners

enhancements of the assets of an entity or settlements of its liabilities (or a combination of both) from delivering or producing goods, rendering services, or carrying out other activities that constitute the entity's ongoing major or central operations."[6] A firm receives revenues when it sells goods or services related to its core operating activities. Revenues usually result in inflows of assets to the firm. For example, when Orchids by Hausermann sells a shipment of orchids to a florist, it receives either an account receivable (a promise to pay) or cash. The sale is recognized regardless of whether it is on account or for cash. The key is that by making the sale, Hausermann enhances its assets.

In some cases, revenues can be generated from the performance of a service that was originally recorded as a liability. For example, assume that Orchids by Hausermann sold a two-year subscription to its Surprise-a-Month Club. The day the sale took place, Hausermann acquired a liability to perform a future service—that is, to deliver an orchid to the subscriber each month for two years. As orchids are delivered over the next two years, that liability is reduced and revenue is recognized, probably monthly, but at least yearly.

Expenses are "outflows or other using up of assets or incurrences of liabilities (or a combination of both) from delivering or producing goods, rendering services, or carrying out other activities that constitute the entity's ongoing major or central operations."[7] According to this definition, expenses, like revenues, are associated with the core activities of an enterprise, but unlike revenues, expenses result in outflows of the firm's net assets. Common examples of expenses, as shown in Cramer Corporation's income statement in Illustration 1.3, are cost of goods sold, salaries expense, and interest expense.

❯ GAINS AND LOSSES

Gains are "increases in equity (net assets) from peripheral or incidental transactions of an entity and from all other transactions and other events and circumstances affecting the entity except those that result from revenues or investments by owners." **Losses** are "decreases in equity (net assets) from peripheral or incidental transactions of an entity and from all other transactions and other events and circumstances affecting the entity except those that result from expenses or distributions to owners."[8] Incidental or peripheral activities are normal activities of a firm that do not involve the firm's core activities. For example, if a manufacturer of paper products sells equipment that it previously used to manufacture shopping bags, the sale is considered a peripheral activity. Any difference between the net selling price and the cost basis of the asset is considered a gain or loss. Note that Cramer Corporation recorded a gain on the sale of equipment in its income statement in Illustration 1.3. The company's core business activity is making and selling MP-3 players, so selling the equipment that it used in developing the players is a peripheral activity. The gain or loss is the difference between the book value of the equipment (its historical cost less any accumulated depreciation to date) and the amount of cash received. For reporting purposes, gains are listed with revenues and losses are listed with expenses. The elements of the income statement as defined by the FASB are summarized in Illustration 1.4.

❯ CONCEPTS UNDERLYING THE INCOME STATEMENT

The six important concepts that underlie the income statement are

1. The periodicity assumption
2. Accrual accounting
3. The revenue recognition principle
4. The matching principle
5. Conservatism
6. Full disclosure

---

6 *SFAC No. 6,* par. 78.

7 *SFAC No. 6,* par. 80.

8 *SFAC No. 6,* pars. 82, 83.

Illustration 1.4

Elements of the Income Statement

Revenues	Inflows or other enhancements of the assets of an entity or settlements of its liabilities (or a combination of both) from delivering or producing goods, rendering services, or carrying out other activities that constitute the entity's ongoing major or central operations
Expenses	Outflows or other using up of assets or incurrences of liabilities (or a combination of both) from delivering or producing goods, rendering services, or carrying out other activities that constitute the entity's ongoing major or central operations
Gains	Inflows or other enhancements of the assets of an entity or settlements of its liabilities (or a combination of both) from peripheral or incidental activities of the firm, those not directly related to its core operations
Losses	Outflows or other using up of assets or incurrences of liabilities (or a combination of both) from peripheral or incidental activities of the firm, those not directly related to its core operations

periodicity assumption the view that it is meaningful to measure a firm's activities in terms of arbitrary time periods even though the firm's life is considered to be indefinite; also called *time period assumption*

❱ **THE PERIODICITY ASSUMPTION**   The **periodicity assumption** (or *time period assumption*) is the view that it is meaningful to measure a firm's activities in terms of arbitrary time periods even though the firm's life is considered to be indefinite. Note that a firm's operating cycle may differ from these arbitrary time periods. It is impossible to know exactly how profitable a firm has been until it is liquidated. However, the users of financial statements cannot wait until the end of a firm's life to make investment and credit decisions. Thus, public companies issue quarterly and yearly financial statements to provide information to interested users. The preparation of those periodic financial statements requires accountants to make estimates and judgments about events that were only partially completed at the end of the reporting period.

To illustrate the need for periodic financial statements, let's assume that when Cramer Corporation was organized, individuals invested $200,000 in exchange for capital stock (see the balance sheet in Illustration 1.2). Thus, the company started with one asset—cash of $200,000. Now let's fast-forward 25 years and assume that Cramer Corporation decides to go out of business. After it sells all its assets and pays all its liabilities, it has $1,200,000 in cash remaining. No dividends were issued during the company's life. We can say that over its lifetime, Cramer Corporation made a cumulative profit of $1,000,000, or $1,200,000 less the initial investment of $200,000. Stockholders, managers, and creditors, of course, needed an understanding of how much the company was earning along the way. Therefore, financial statements were prepared at the end of each accounting period to measure and report the firm's activity. To assign the profit to each year the company was in business and to generate financial statements each period, a variety of assumptions must be made about how revenue is earned, how assets are used, and how costs are incurred. Of necessity, those assumptions are based on estimates that reflect the judgment of the firm's accountants and outside auditors.

cash basis of accounting the practice of recording revenues when cash is received and recording expenses when cash is paid

accrual accounting the practice of recording transactions and other events and circumstances in the period in which they occur rather than in the period in which cash or some other form of payment is received or paid

❱ **ACCRUAL ACCOUNTING**   While some small businesses use the **cash basis of accounting**—the practice of recording revenues when cash is received and recording expenses when cash is paid—this simple approach to accounting does not meet the needs of most complex business transactions. In addition, financial statements prepared using the cash basis do not conform to generally accepted accounting principles. The acceptable method, **accrual accounting**, is the practice of recording transactions and other events and circumstances in the period in which they occur rather than in the period in which cash or some other form of payment is received or paid. Accrual accounting is probably the most fundamental concept underlying generally accepted accounting principles.

accrual the recognition of a revenue or an expense that has occurred but that has not yet been recorded in the accounting records

An **accrual** is the recognition of a revenue or an expense that has occurred but that has not yet been recorded in the accounting records. In effect, revenue has been earned, but the cash has not yet been collected, or an expense has been incurred, but the cash has not yet been paid. The following are examples of accruals:

● Recognizing an amount owed by a customer to the firm as revenue before cash is actually collected

● Recognizing an amount owed by the firm to a creditor as an expense before payment is actually made

deferral the postponement of the recognition of an expense that has already been paid or of a revenue that has already been received

A **deferral** is the postponement of the recognition of an expense that has already been paid or of a revenue that has already been received. Items that would require deferral include

● The prepayment of an expense (a prepaid asset)

● The receipt of a deposit for work to be performed in the future (a liability)

The advance payment of cash does not result in the immediate recognition of the expense. Instead, the costs are accumulated in a prepaid asset account and expensed as used. Similarly, when cash is received as a deposit for future work, no revenue is recognized until the work is performed. The cash received in advance is shown as a liability. Accruals and deferrals will be discussed in more detail later in this chapter.

recognition the process of formally recording an item in the accounting records

revenue recognition principle the assertion that revenue should be recognized when the amount and timing of revenue are reasonably determinable and the earnings process is complete or virtually complete

realization the conversion of noncash assets or claims to cash

❱ **THE REVENUE RECOGNITION PRINCIPLE** The revenue recognition principle governs *when* revenue should be recognized and thus recorded in the accounting records. **Recognition** is the process of formally recording an item in the accounting records. Under the **revenue recognition principle**, revenue should be recognized (recorded) when two criteria are met:

1. The amount and timing of revenue are reasonably determinable (revenue is realized or realizable).

2. The earnings process is complete or virtually complete (revenue has been earned).

Realization is the conversion of noncash assets or claims to cash, such as when inventory is sold for cash or on account.

In most cases, the sale of a product or the performance of a service is the point at which revenue is recognized. The firm has done what it is in business to do, sell a product or perform a service (criterion 2), and the amount of the asset received—cash or an account receivable—is known with a high degree of certainty (criterion 1).

matching principle the concept that expenses should be reported in the same accounting period as the revenues to which they are related

❱ **THE MATCHING PRINCIPLE** The critical principle behind accrual accounting is the matching principle. The **matching principle** holds that expenses should be reported in the same accounting period as the revenues to which they are related. It is under the matching principle that such practices as the depreciation of plant, equipment, and other operating assets are justified. When an asset is depreciated, its cost is recognized over the periods during which it contributes to revenue generation, thus matching the revenues produced by the asset with the expenses of using it in business operations.

conservatism the principle that requires a prudent reaction to uncertainty to try to ensure that the uncertainty and risks inherent in business situations are adequately considered

❱ **CONSERVATISM** Conservatism is an important principle that guides the valuation of assets and liabilities and influences the recognition of revenues and expenses and gains and losses. **Conservatism**, according to the FASB, is "a prudent reaction to uncertainty to try to ensure that the uncertainty and risks inherent in business situations are adequately considered."[9] Thus, conservatism requires accountants, when

---

9 "Qualitative Characteristics of Accounting Information," *Statement of Financial Accounting Concepts No. 2* (Stamford, Conn.: Financial Accounting Standards Board, May 1980), glossary.

faced with a choice, to select the accounting method that is least likely to overstate net income and the financial position of the firm. In practice, this means that losses are anticipated, but gains are generally not recorded until a transaction occurs.

One result of conservatism is that many assets are measured on the balance sheet at the lower of cost or market. For example, if the current value of a firm's inventory falls below its cost, the inventory is written down to the lower value and shown at that amount on the balance sheet. However, if the inventory's current value is greater than its cost, the increase in value is generally not recognized until an actual sale takes place. Statements issued by the FASB contain many instances in which conservatism requires assets to be written down if their value falls below their cost or the value that could be realized through the operations of the business. However, there are now more instances in which the FASB requires certain assets to be marked to market—that is, valued at their market value, regardless of whether that value is above or below their cost.

full disclosure the principle that requires that financial statements and related notes include any information that is significant or material enough to change the decisions of financial statement users

❱ FULL DISCLOSURE   The principle of **full disclosure** requires that financial statements and related notes include any information that is significant or material enough to change the decisions of financial statement users. Because today's business organizations are extremely complex, it is impossible to disclose within the body of their financial statements all the information that investors and creditors need in order to make informed decisions. Thus, details of complicated transactions, such as leases, interest swaps, and stock options, are usually disclosed in the notes to the financial statements and sometimes in other places in the annual report. The notes to the financial statements may also describe and provide useful measures of items that are not shown or recognized in the body of the financial statements. For example, a note might inform users of an important event that took place after the date of the financial statements that will affect future financial statements, such as the loss of a major customer.

LO3 Summarize the contents of the statement of changes in stockholders' equity and the statement of cash flows.

statement of changes in stockholders' equity a financial statement that summarizes the adjustments to stockholders' equity over an accounting period; known as the retained earnings statement for small corporations

THE STATEMENT OF CHANGES IN STOCKHOLDERS' EQUITY

The **statement of changes in stockholders' equity** (or, for small corporations, the *retained earnings statement*) summarizes the adjustments to stockholders' equity over an accounting period. Stockholders' equity accounts include capital or common stock accounts, other paid-in capital accounts, and retained earnings. The beginning balance of retained earnings is increased by net income and decreased by a net loss and issuance of dividends. Illustration 1.5 presents the statement of changes in stockholders' equity for Cramer Corporation.

Illustration 1.5

Statement of Changes in Stockholders' Equity

	Capital Stock	Retained Earnings	Total Stockholders' Equity
Cramer Corporation **Statement of Changes in Stockholders' Equity** **For the Year Ended December 31, 2005**			
Balance, January 1, 2005	$200,000	$136,000	$336,000
Net income for the year ended December 31, 2005		80,000	80,000
Balance, December 31, 2005	$200,000	$216,000	$416,000

Note that the net income for the year ended December 31, 2005, is the same as that shown on the income statement in Illustration 1.3. Also, note that total stockholders' equity at December 31, 2005, is $416,000, which is the same figure shown on the balance sheet in Illustration 1.2.

THE STATEMENT OF CASH FLOWS

statement of cash flows a financial statement that shows the amount of cash collected and paid out by a firm over an accounting period for operating activities, investing activities, and financing activities

Critical Thinking: What critical information do you think the statement of stockholders' equity and the statement of cash flows provide that is not found on the income statement or the balance sheet?

The fourth financial statement, the **statement of cash flows**, shows the amount of cash collected and paid out by a firm over an accounting period. Like the income statement and the statement of changes in stockholders' equity, it covers a period of time, so it too is a change statement. The statement of cash flows consists of three sections: cash flows from operating activities, cash flows from investing activities, and cash flows from financing activities. The sum of these three sections equals the change in cash for the reporting period. For example, if cash increases by $10,000, the statement of cash flows explains where that increase came from—whether from business operations, the issuance of more debt, a combination of the two, or from other transactions such as owner contributions. The statement also shows how much cash the firm used to purchase major assets, such as land and buildings. The statement of cash flows supplies important information that helps investors evaluate a firm's operations and activities. The statement of cash flows for Cramer Corporation is shown in Illustration 1.6.

Cash flows from operations start with net income for the year ($80,000). Net income must then be adjusted for the items it includes that do not affect cash flows. In Cramer's case, depreciation expense of $50,000 reduced net income but did not cause a cash outflow. The cash outflow took place when the item being depreciated was purchased. Thus, the $50,000 is added back to net income. The gain of $25,000 on the sale of equipment must be subtracted from net income to determine cash flows from operations. The transaction related to this sale is shown in the section labeled "Cash Flows from Investing Activities." The result of these two adjustments is that net cash provided from operations equals $105,000.

During the year, Cramer Corporation used cash of $175,000 to purchase a new building and increased its cash by $38,000 when it issued a long-term note payable. As a result of all these transactions, including cash flows from operations, cash increased by $8,000 during the year. When that $8,000 is added to the beginning cash balance of $7,000, the ending cash balance is $15,000. As you can see, this is the same amount of cash reported on the balance sheet in Illustration 1.2.

Illustration 1.6

Statement of Cash Flows

Cramer Corporation
Statement of Cash Flows
For the Year Ended December 31, 2005

Cash Flows from Operating Activities		
Net income	$ 80,000	
Add (subtract) noncash items:		
Depreciation	50,000	
Gain on sale of equipment	(25,000)	
Net cash provided from operations		$105,000
Cash Flows from Investing Activities		
Sale of equipment	$ 40,000	
Purchase of building	(175,000)	
Net cash used by investing activities		(135,000)
Cash Flows from Financing Activities		
Issuance of long-term notes payable		38,000
Increase in cash for the year		$ 8,000
Cash balance at January 1, 2005		7,000
Cash balance at December 31, 2005		$ 15,000

BRIDGE TUTORIAL

For a review of the concepts presented in this section, click on the menu item "The Financial Statements" and complete all of the questions and the Demonstration Problem and Internet Assignment.

CHECK YOUR UNDERSTANDING

1. What three primary elements are found on the balance sheet?

2. What underlying principle presumes that a business will continue to operate indefinitely? What does this mean for the definition of *assets*?

3. Which financial statements are considered "change" statements? Why?

4. Which financial statement provides information about the financial position of a business at a specific point in time?

5. Describe how cash-basis and accrual accounting differ.

6. List the three primary sections of the statement of cash flows.

7. Describe the principle of conservatism as it relates to the practice of accounting.

SECTION B

LO4 Explain how the accounting equation forms the basis of double-entry accounting.

The Double-Entry Accounting System and the Accounting Cycle

Most companies today use some form of computerized accounting system. It may be as simple as a program purchased at a local office supply store that will run on any PC or Mac, or as complex as a customized component integrated into a firm's enterprise-resource-planning system. No matter how simple or how complex the system is, its basis is the double-entry accounting process developed in the fourteenth century. **Double-entry accounting** is the process of recording the dual effect of every business transaction.

double-entry accounting the process of recording the dual effect of every business transaction

THE ACCOUNTING EQUATION

The **accounting equation**, which is the foundation for double-entry accounting and thus for the four financial statements, can be stated as follows:

accounting equation Assets = Liabilities + Owners' Equity (Stockholders' Equity); the foundation for double-entry accounting and thus for the four financial statements

$$\text{Assets} = \text{Liabilities} + \text{Owners' Equity (Stockholders' Equity)}$$

As mentioned earlier, owners' equity is called stockholders' equity for a corporation. Because this book focuses on the corporate form of organization, we will use the term *stockholders' equity* rather than *owners' equity* from this point on. When stockholders' equity is used, the accounting equation can be expanded as follows to include paid-in capital (an all-inclusive name for capital stock and other paid-in capital items) and retained earnings:

Critical Thinking: The basic accounting equation dictates that the sum of a firm's equity and liabilities should equal its assets. Consider your own personal equity, liabilities, and assets. How might they be reflected in the basic accounting equation?

$$\text{Assets} = \text{Liabilities} + \text{Paid-in Capital} + \text{Retained Earnings}$$

$$\text{Assets} = \text{Liabilities} + \text{Capital Stock} + \text{Other Paid-in Capital} + \text{Retained Earnings}$$

Retained earnings can also be expanded to include revenues, which increase retained earnings; expenses, which decrease retained earnings; and dividends, which decrease retained earnings:

$$\text{Assets} = \text{Liabilities} + \text{Capital Stock} + \text{Other Paid-in Capital} + \text{Retained Earnings}$$
$$+ \text{Revenues} - \text{Expenses} - \text{Dividends}$$

Illustration 1.7

Accounting Equation Relationships

Assets =	Liabilities +	Stockholders' Equity	
• Current assets (such as Cash, Receivables, Inventory) • Operating assets • Investments • Intangible assets • Other assets	• Current liabilities (such as Accounts Payable, Short-Term Notes Payable) • Noncurrent liabilities	• Contributed capital from owners (such as Capital Stock)	• Earned capital from operations (Retained Earnings = Accumulated Net Income less Distributions to Owners)

account the basic unit in accounting, used to systematically record and summarize amounts from similar transactions

The accounting equation expresses an *equality*, which means that the left side of the equation must always equal the right side of the equation. Each item on each side of the accounting equation is represented by an individual **account**, the basic unit in accounting, which is used to systematically record and summarize amounts from similar transactions. For example, if an account on the left side of the equation is increased, either another account on the left side must be decreased or an account on the right side must be increased. As stated earlier, the process of recording the dual effect that each economic transaction has on the accounting equation is called double-entry accounting. Sometimes a combination of increases and decreases occurs in double-entry accounting, but the equality of the accounting equation is always maintained. Illustration 1.7 illustrates the relationships among the elements in the accounting equation using typical accounts found in a business.

REVIEW OF DEBIT AND CREDIT RULES

chart of accounts a listing of all the accounts in the general ledger

ledger a book or an electronic file that contains all of a company's accounts, arranged by account number and title; also called the *general ledger*

T-account a visual representation of an account, used to illustrate its activity

debit (DR) an entry on the left side of an account

credit (CR) an entry on the right side of an account

An accounting system has a separate account for each asset, liability, and component of stockholders' equity. Each firm maintains a **chart of accounts**, which is a listing of all the accounts in the ledger. The **ledger**, also called the *general ledger,* is a book or an electronic file that contains all of a company's accounts, arranged by account number and title.

A **T-account** is the simplest way to illustrate the activity in the accounts of the general ledger. An entry on the left side of an account is called a **debit (DR)**. A **credit (CR)** is an entry on the right side of an account.

Account Title	
Debit	Credit

According to the double-entry system of accounting developed in the fourteenth century by Luca Pacioli, an Italian mathematician and Franciscan friar, each account is governed by certain rules for debits and credits:

● *For assets:* An increase is recorded on the left side of an account and a decrease is recorded on the right side of an account.

● *For liabilities and stockholders' equity accounts:* An increase is recorded on the right side of an account and a decrease is recorded on the left side of an account.

Thus, for every entry on the left side of an account (an increase in an asset account or a decrease in a liability or stockholders' equity account), there must be a corresponding entry on the right side of an account (a decrease in an asset account or an increase in a liability account or stockholders' equity account). This maintains the equality of the accounting equation.

Illustration 1.8

Rules for Debiting and Crediting Accounts

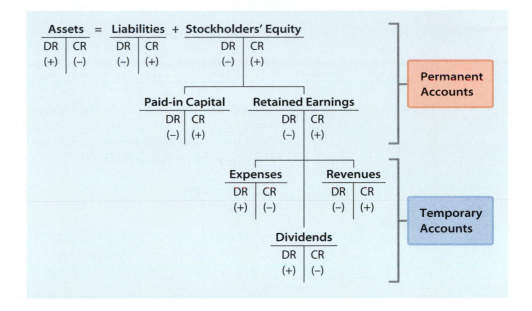

When the accounting equation is expanded to include revenues and expenses, the same rules apply. Revenues increase retained earnings, so increases in revenues are recorded as credits. Expenses decrease retained earnings, so increases in expenses are recorded as debits. Dividends decrease retained earnings and thus are recorded as debits. Keep in mind, however, that dividends are distributions of assets to the owners of a corporation—not expenses.

The T-accounts in Illustration 1.8 summarize the rules for debiting and crediting an account.

permanent accounts asset, liability, and stockholders' equity accounts (including Capital Stock, Paid-in Capital, and Retained Earnings) with balances that continue from one accounting period to the next and reflect the actual amounts in those accounts at any point in time

temporary accounts accounts that are used to record changes in retained earnings; their balances are periodically closed into retained earnings

Note that the accounts listed in the top two levels of Illustration 1.8 are often referred to as **permanent accounts**. Those asset, liability, and stockholders' equity accounts (including Capital Stock, Paid-in Capital, and Retained Earnings) have balances that continue from one accounting period to the next and reflect the actual amounts in those accounts at any point in time. The third and fourth levels—expenses, revenues, and dividends—are referred to as **temporary accounts**. Those accounts are used to record changes in retained earnings, and their balances are periodically closed into retained earnings. Temporary accounts must be maintained separately from retained earnings to generate the specific information about revenues and expenses that is needed to prepare financial statements. However, once the statements are prepared, the temporary accounts are zeroed out and their effects are transferred to the Retained Earnings account so that the next period's revenues and expenses can be determined.

The following examples illustrate how the rules of debit and credit are applied to specific transactions.

1. Land is purchased for $300,000 cash. One asset (cash) is exchanged for another asset (land). Thus, two asset accounts are involved. The Land account is increased (a debit), and the Cash account is decreased (a credit). The T-accounts appear as follows:

Cash		Land	
	300,000	300,000	
	—	+	
	decrease	increase	
	credit	debit	

2. A bank loan for $500,000 is obtained. In this case, an asset (cash) is received in exchange for a liability (a note payable). The Cash account is increased (a debit), and the Notes Payable account is also increased (a credit).

Cash			Notes Payable	
500,000				500,000
+				+
increase				increase
debit				credit

3. A $10,000 sale is made for cash. The increase in the Cash account, as before, is shown by a debit. The temporary revenue account Sales is also increased. Because sales ultimately increase retained earnings and increases in retained earnings are credits, the sale is recorded as a credit.

Cash			Sales	
10,000				10,000
+				+
increase				increase
debit				credit

ILLUSTRATION: KETTLE AND WOLF, INC.

In the rest of this chapter, we will utilize the transactions of Kettle and Wolf, Inc. to illustrate the accounting cycle. We will examine how each transaction affects the accounting equation. Then we will work through each step of the accounting cycle.

Nancy Wolf and John Kettle have decided to start an Internet newsletter for college students called *Kettle and Wolf*. They plan to sell one-year subscriptions that will entitle subscribers to view 12 monthly issues of the newsletter on a members-only website. They have produced the first month's edition and are ready to begin their business. The transactions for their first month of business, September 2006, are shown in Illustration 1.9.

Now that you have reviewed the transactions for the month, examine the effects of each transaction in Illustration 1.10. For example, Illustration 1.10 shows that on September 1, when John and Nancy each invested $5,000 in cash to start their business, the Cash account increased by $10,000 (a debit) and the Common Stock account increased by $10,000 (a credit). Note that after all the transactions for the month have been recorded, the accounting equation is still in balance. Assets total $27,000, and liabilities of $15,000 plus stockholders' equity of $12,000 also total $27,000.

As you can see, while these transactions affect a variety of accounts, the equality of the accounting equation is maintained throughout.

BRIDGE TUTORIAL

For a review of the concepts presented in this section, click on the menu item "The Double-Entry Accounting System" and complete the questions found under "The Accounting Equation" and "Review of Debits and Credits."

Illustration 1.9

Transactions for September 2006—Kettle and Wolf, Inc.

(1) On September 1, 2006, Nancy and John form a corporation by filing with the State of Illinois, and they each invest $5,000 in the business in exchange for common stock.

(2) On September 1, the company signs a note at the local bank for $3,000 due in two years at 12 percent annual interest.

(3) On September 1, the company purchases a computer for $3,000 cash.

(4) On September 1, office supplies are purchased on account for $1,000.

(5) On September 1, the company pays $4,800 for a website to be used for the next 24 months.

(6) On September 15, 800 newsletters are sold for $3 each as one-month trial subscriptions.

(7) On September 20, the company sells 1,000 one-year subscriptions (at $12 each) for access to the website. One-half of the payments are collected now, with the remainder due October 1, 2006.

(8) On September 30, the firm pays for the office supplies purchased on September 1.

(9) On September 30, monthly salaries of $200 each are paid to the firm's only two employees, the owners Nancy and John.

Illustration 1.10

Transaction Analysis for September 2006—Kettle and Wolf, Inc.

Transactions	Debits (DR) = Assets =	Credits (CR) + Liabilities +	Credits (CR) + Stockholders' Equity
(1) Nancy and John start their firm by each investing $5,000 in exchange for common stock	Cash +$10,000 *Debit*		Common Stock +$10,000 *Credit*
(2) The company borrows $3,000 at the local bank	Cash +$3,000 *Debit*	Long-Term Notes Payable +$3,000 *Credit*	
(3) The company purchases a computer for $3,000 cash	Computer Equipment +$3,000 *Debit* Cash −$3,000 *Credit*		
(4) Office supplies of $1,000 are purchased on account	Office Supplies +$1,000 *Debit*	Accounts Payable +$1,000 *Credit*	
(5) A website is purchased for $4,800	Prepaid Website +$4,800 *Debit* Cash −$4,800 *Credit*		
(6) The company sells 800 one-month trial subscriptions for $3 each	Cash +$2,400 *Debit*		Subscription Revenue + $2,400* *Credit*
(7) The company sells 1,000 one-year subscriptions for $12 each, one-half for cash and one-half on account	Cash +$6,000 *Debit* Accounts Receivable +$6,000 *Debit*	Unearned Revenue +$12,000† *Credit*	
(8) The company pays for the office supplies purchased on September 1	Cash −$1,000 *Credit*	Accounts Payable −$1,000 *Debit*	
(9) Salaries of $400 are paid	Cash −$400 *Credit*		Salaries Expense −$400‡ *Debit*
Totals	**$27,000** =	**$15,000** +	**$12,000**

* The sale of the trial subscriptions generates revenue, which is an increase to retained earnings and thus is shown in the Stockholders' Equity column.
† The revenue from the one-year subscriptions will be earned over the 12-month period and thus is initially recorded in a liability account, Unearned Revenue.
‡ The salaries are an expense of the month, which decreases retained earnings. Thus they are shown in the Stockholders' Equity column.

LO5 Outline the steps in the accounting cycle.

■■■ *Critical Thinking: Today almost all steps in the accounting cycle are completed electronically. What benefits and risks does this present for financial statement preparers and users?*

THE ACCOUNTING CYCLE

As mentioned earlier, the accounting cycle is the set of activities involved in analyzing business events, collecting and processing information related to those events, and summarizing that information in the four financial statements. It consists of seven steps, which are described in this section and summarized in Illustration 1.11. We will use a manual accounting system to examine the accounting cycle. Of course, many companies prepare journal entries and financial statements electronically, in which case many of the steps shown here are performed simultaneously, occur behind the scenes, or are even omitted. Nonetheless, reviewing the procedures for a manual system will help you understand how financial statements are ultimately constructed from the basic information contained in source documents.

Illustration 1.11

The Accounting Cycle

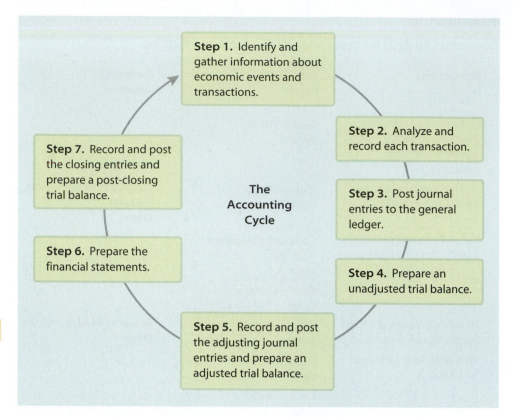

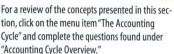

BRIDGE TUTORIAL

For a review of the concepts presented in this section, click on the menu item "The Accounting Cycle" and complete the questions found under "Accounting Cycle Overview."

▶ STEP 1: IDENTIFY AND GATHER TRANSACTION INFORMATION

source document written evidence that supports a transaction, such as a sales invoice, purchase order, or sales receipt

Step 1 of the accounting cycle is the use of source documents to gather information about transactions and other economic events that affect the assets, liabilities, and stockholders' equity of a firm. A **source document** is written evidence that supports a transaction. Typical source documents include sales invoices, purchase orders, receipts from asset purchases or sales, and computer printouts that summarize the electronic transactions for the period.

Transactions are often classified as either external or internal. External transactions involve an outside entity, such as when a firm purchases a piece of equipment. Internal transactions result from events within the firm itself. For example, depreciation, the allocation of an asset's cost over the time period of its use, is an internal transaction. The source document for an internal transaction might be a memo or, in this case, a depreciation schedule. In these examples, the external transaction took place when the asset was purchased; the internal transaction occurred when the firm recognized depreciation.

▶ STEP 2: ANALYZE EACH TRANSACTION AND RECORD IT IN A JOURNAL

journalize to record a transaction in a journal by adjusting at least two accounts

journal a book or an electronic file in which transactions are recorded chronologically

general journal an all-purpose journal that can be used to record any type of transaction

specialized journal a book or electronic file that is used to record a specific type of business transaction

Once a transaction has been identified, it must be quantified (measured) and then analyzed for its effect on specific account balances. That is, the accountant must determine what dollar amounts and accounts are involved. For example, if a sale took place, the accountant identifies the dollar amount to be recorded and whether the sale was for cash or on account. Once the particulars of a transaction are understood, the transaction must be **journalized**—that is, recorded in a journal by adjusting at least two accounts. A **journal** is a book or an electronic file in which transactions are recorded chronologically. A **general journal** is an all-purpose journal that can be used to record any type of transaction. A firm will often also have a number of **specialized journals**, each of which is used to record a single type of transaction. For example, a sales journal is a specialized journal in which all sales transactions are recorded. Throughout this book we will use only general journal entries to illustrate transactions.

As transactions are journalized, the equality of the accounting equation is maintained by ensuring that the debits (*increases* in assets or *decreases* in liabilities or stockholders' equity) equal the credits (*increases* in liabilities or stockholders' equity or *decreases* in assets). For example, if, on July 1, 2005, a firm purchases a plot of land for $300,000 cash, the journal entry will be recorded as follows:

Date	Account Title and Explanation	Post. Ref.	Debit	Credit
2005				
July 1	Land	500	300,000	
	Cash	100		300,000
	To record the purchase of land for			
	cash			

The general journal provides columns for the date, the account titles and an explanation of the transaction, a posting reference (showing the account number to which the account will be posted), debits, and credits. The conventional method of recording a journal entry is first to write the debited accounts and amounts, each on a separate line. On the next lines, indent and write the credited accounts and amounts. In the sample entry, the asset account Land is increased (debited) and the asset account Cash is decreased (credited). After the transaction is recorded, a description is noted so that if it is necessary to refer to the transaction at a later date, the details will be available. The posting reference column is used after the account is posted to the ledger. In subsequent illustrative journal entries, we will use dates only when they are necessary to clarify the transaction, and we will omit the posting reference column.

To illustrate how different transactions are recorded, the transactions for Kettle and Wolf (Illustration 1.9) are presented in journal entry form here.

(1) On September 1, 2006, Nancy and John form a corporation by filing with the State of Illinois, and they each invest $5,000 in exchange for common stock.

Cash	10,000	
Common Stock		10,000
To record the issuance of common stock in exchange for		
cash		

This transaction is an exchange of common stock for cash. Cash is increased (a debit because it is an increase in an asset account), and Common Stock is also increased (a credit because it is an increase in a stockholders' equity account).

(2) On September 1, the company signs a note at the local bank for $3,000 due in two years at 12 percent annual interest.

Cash	3,000	
Long-Term Notes Payable		3,000
To record the issuance of a long-term note payable in		
exchange for cash		

This transaction is a receipt of cash in exchange for a note payable. Cash is increased (a debit) and Long-Term Notes Payable is increased (a credit because it is an increase in a liability account).

(3) On September 1, the company purchases a computer for $3,000 cash.

Computer Equipment	3,000	
Cash		3,000
To record the purchase of a computer for cash		

This transaction is an exchange of one asset (cash) for another asset (a computer).

(4) On September 1, office supplies are purchased on an open account for $1,000.

Supplies	1,000	
Accounts Payable		1,000
To record the purchase of supplies on credit		

This transaction records the increase in an asset account, Office Supplies (a debit), and an increase in a liability account, Accounts Payable (a credit).

(5) On September 1, the company pays $4,800 for a website to be used for the next 24 months.

Prepaid Website	4,800	
Cash		4,800
To record the payment for website services to be used over the next 24 months		

This transaction involves two asset accounts, Prepaid Website, which is increased by a debit, and Cash, which is decreased by a credit.

(6) On September 15, 800 newsletters are sold for $3 each as one-month trial subscriptions.

Cash	2,400	
Subscription Revenue		2,400
To record the sale of 800 one-month trial subscriptions		

This transaction involves the recognition of revenue earned from the sale of 800 trial newsletter subscriptions. Cash is increased, a debit, and Subscription Revenue is increased, a credit. Revenues increase Retained Earnings, which is a stockholders' equity account that is increased by credits.

(7) On September 20, the company sells 1,000 one-year subscriptions (at $12 each) for access to the website. One-half of the payments are collected now, with the remainder due October 1, 2006.

Cash	6,000	
Accounts Receivable	6,000	
Unearned Revenue		12,000
To record the sale of 1,000 one-year subscriptions, to be earned over the next 12 months		

compound entry a journal entry that records a transaction involving more than two accounts

The sale of one-year subscriptions results in a **compound entry**, a journal entry that records a transaction involving more than two accounts. Two asset accounts, Cash and Accounts Receivable, are increased by debits. A liability account, Unearned Revenue, is increased by a credit. The amount in the Unearned Revenue account reflects Kettle and Wolf's obligation to perform a service, the delivery of the newsletter. No revenue is recognized as of September 20 because the company has yet to perform any services. As the services are provided each month, the firm will recognize a portion of the revenue. This recognition process is discussed later in the chapter.

(8) On September 30, the firm pays for the office supplies purchased on September 1.

Accounts Payable	1,000	
Cash		1,000
To record payment for supplies purchased on account		

This transaction involves a decrease in Cash, a credit, to recognize the cash paid on the account payable. The decrease in Accounts Payable is recorded by a debit.

BRIDGE TUTORIAL

For a review of the concepts presented in this section, click on the menu item "The Accounting Cycle" and complete the questions found under "Step 1: Identify and Gather Transaction Information" and "Step 2: Analyze Each Transaction and Record It in a Journal."

(9) On September 30, monthly salaries of $200 each are paid to the firm's only two employees, the owners Nancy and John.

Salaries Expense	400	
Cash		400
To record payment of salaries		

This transaction involves the recognition of salaries expense. Salaries Expense is increased by a debit; Cash is decreased by a credit.

▶ STEP 3: POST JOURNAL ENTRIES TO THE LEDGER

posting the process of transferring transaction information from the journal to the individual accounts in the general ledger

The entries in an accounting journal record the economic events for a firm chronologically, much as the entries in a personal journal record notable events for an individual. To keep track of how transactions affect individual accounts, the changes must be recognized in those accounts. **Posting** is the process of transferring transaction information from the journal to the individual accounts in the general ledger. In a manual system, posting is done periodically—daily, weekly, or monthly, depending upon the number and complexity of the transactions. Today ledgers are usually electronic files that record individual account balances as part of a computerized accounting information system. The general ledger software maintains the current balances of all the accounts that will appear on the firm's financial statements. Postings are often made at the same time the journal entry is recorded. For both computerized and manual systems, the balance of an account is the difference in dollars between debits and credits. For assets, the normal account balance is on the debit side, and for liabilities and stockholders' equity, the normal account balance is on the credit side.

subsidiary ledger a ledger that contains a group of related accounts, the total balance of which must equal the balance of the corresponding controlling account in the general ledger

Some accounts are listed in subsidiary ledgers. A **subsidiary ledger** contains a group of related accounts, the total balance of which must equal the balance of the corresponding controlling account in the general ledger. For example, a subsidiary ledger might contain a separate account for each creditor to which a firm owes money. The total of those accounts must equal the controlling Accounts Payable account in the general ledger. Or a subsidiary ledger might contain an account for each customer who owes the firm money. The total of those accounts must equal the controlling Accounts Receivables account in the general ledger.

Illustration 1.12 presents Kettle and Wolf's T-accounts after all the September transactions have been posted.

▶ STEP 4: PREPARE AN UNADJUSTED TRIAL BALANCE

trial balance a report that compares the total debit and credit balances in the ledger to check that they are equal

A **trial balance** is a comparison of the total debit and credit balances in the ledger to check that they are equal. Trial balances may be prepared anytime postings are made to the individual ledger accounts to ensure that there are no mechanical errors and thus to verify that the total of the debit balances equals the total of the credit balances. It is important to note that a trial balance will not ensure that the correct accounts were used. For example, if a debit were erroneously posted to the asset account Equipment instead of to the asset account Land, debits would still equal credits, but the individual totals in the two asset accounts would be incorrect.

unadjusted trial balance a report prepared before adjusting entries are made to ensure that the total debit balances and credit balances are equal

adjusted trial balance a report prepared after adjusting entries have been made to ensure that the total debit balances and credit balances are equal

post-closing trial balance a report prepared after the closing entries have been made to ensure that the accounts are still in balance

In a manual system, three different types of trial balances are usually prepared: an unadjusted trial balance, an adjusted trial balance, and a post-closing trial balance. The **unadjusted trial balance** is prepared before adjusting entries are made, the **adjusted trial balance** is prepared after adjusting entries but before closing entries, and the **post-closing trial balance** is prepared after closing entries. The post-closing trial balance ensures that the total debit balances equal the total credit balances and that all temporary accounts have been closed.

These three trial balances correspond to the times when posting takes place in a manual system. Today, because accounting software is programmed to ensure that journal entries balance, mathematical and posting errors are extremely unlikely, and therefore separate trial balances may not be prepared. The unadjusted trial balance for Kettle and Wolf, Inc. at September 30 is shown in Illustration 1.13.

Illustration 1.12

Balanced T-Accounts, September 2006

Cash			
9/1	10,000	3,000	9/1
9/1	3,000	4,800	9/1
9/15	2,400	1,000	9/30
9/20	6,000	400	9/30
	21,400	9,200	
9/30			
bal.	**12,200**		

Accounts Receivable		
9/20	6,000	

Prepaid Website	
9/1	4,800

Supplies	
9/1	1,000

Computer Equipment	
9/1	3,000

Accounts Payable			
9/30	1,000	1,000	9/1
9/30			
bal.		**0**	

Unearned Revenue		
	12,000	9/20

Long-Term Notes Payable		
	3,000	9/1

Common Stock		
	10,000	9/1

Retained Earnings

Subscription Revenue		
	2,400	9/15

Salaries Expense	
9/30	400

Illustration 1.13

Unadjusted Trial Balance

Kettle and Wolf, Inc.
Unadjusted Trial Balance
September 30, 2006

Account Title	Debits	Credits
Cash	$12,200	
Accounts Receivable	6,000	
Prepaid Website	4,800	
Supplies	1,000	
Computer Equipment	3,000	
Accounts Payable		$ 0
Unearned Revenue		12,000
Long-Term Notes Payable		3,000
Common Stock		10,000
Retained Earnings		0
Subscription Revenue		2,400
Salaries Expense	400	
Totals	$27,400	$27,400

BRIDGE TUTORIAL

For a review of the concepts presented in this section, click on the menu item "The Accounting Cycle" and complete the questions found under "Step 3: Post Journal Entries to the Ledger" and "Step 4: Prepare an Unadjusted Trial Balance."

adjusting entries entries made to record the financial effects of transactions that cover more than one accounting period and to make the estimates, corrections, and other changes necessary to bring the accounts to their actual balances

> **STEP 5: RECORD AND POST ADJUSTING ENTRIES AND PREPARE AN ADJUSTED TRIAL BALANCE**

The next step in the accounting cycle, recording and posting adjusting entries, is performed just before closing the books and preparing the financial statements for the period. **Adjusting entries** are made for two reasons: (1) to record the financial effects of transactions and events that cover more than one accounting period, and (2) to

Illustration 1.14

Accruals and Deferrals

Accruals	Deferrals
Accrued revenue: an amount that has been earned but for which cash has not yet been received (a revenue)	**Deferred revenue:** cash that has been received before the related revenue has been earned (a liability)
Example: Interest has been earned on a loan but will not be received until the following period.	*Example:* The company receives cash from a customer in one period for a service that will not be performed until the next period.
Accrued expense: a cost that has been incurred but for which payment has not yet been made (an expense)	**Deferred expense:** cash that has been paid before the related expense has been incurred (an asset)
Example: The company incurred salaries expense in one period, but it will not pay the employees until the next period.	*Example:* A firm has paid for an insurance policy that will continue in effect over several future periods.

make the estimates and other changes necessary to bring the accounts to their true balances. The adjustments ensure that all revenues earned in the current period are recognized in that period and that all expenses incurred in the current period are recognized in that period. Accrual accounting, the matching principle, and the revenue recognition principle are the key concepts behind adjusting entries. Recall that under accrual accounting, revenues and expenses must be recognized in the period in which they are earned or incurred regardless of when the actual cash flows take place. That is because often cash (or some other asset) is received or paid in one period, but the transaction that generated or used the cash affects several periods. Under the matching principle, revenues and their related expenses should be reported in the same accounting period. In most cases, a firm must make adjusting entries for several accounts to ensure that revenues and expenses are matched and are thus reported in the same period.

Determining how to allocate revenues and expenses among accounting periods requires accountants to exercise judgment. For example, when a piece of equipment is purchased, its useful life usually extends several years beyond the year of purchase. To match revenues and expenses, the company will depreciate the equipment—a process that requires the accountant to estimate both the life of the asset in light of how it will be used and any value that the asset may have at the end of its life.

Most adjustments are classified as either accruals or deferrals. An accrual is recognized when an economic event occurs *before* cash is exchanged. **Accrued revenue** is an amount that has been earned but for which cash has not been received as of the end of the accounting period. Thus, both a receivable account and a revenue account are involved. **Accrued expense** is an amount that has been incurred but for which cash has not been paid as of the end of the accounting period. Thus, both a payable account and an expense account are involved. A deferral is recognized when cash is exchanged *before* an economic event occurs. **Deferred revenue** is cash that has been received before the related revenue has been earned. Deferred revenue is often referred to as *unearned income.* Thus, both a liability account and a revenue account are involved. **Deferred expense** is cash that has been paid before the related expense has been incurred. Deferred expense is often referred to as a *prepaid expense.* Thus, both an asset account and an expense account are involved. Accruals and deferrals are reviewed in Illustration 1.14.

Adjusting entries recognize the revenues and expenses associated with accruals and deferrals, and they adjust the associated balance sheet accounts.

❯ ACCRUED REVENUE Adjusting entries must be made for accrued revenues to ensure that all revenues for the period are recorded in that period, even though the related cash may not be received until the next period. For example, assume that Kinglet Company bills its customers at the end of each month for services rendered. At the end of the accounting cycle, the company reviews its accounting records to ensure that all its customers have been billed for work performed up to the date of the

accrued revenue an amount that has been earned but for which cash has not been received as of the end of an accounting period

accrued expense an amount that has been incurred but for which cash has not been paid as of the end of an accounting period

deferred revenue cash that has been received before the related revenue has been earned; also known as *unearned income*

deferred expense cash that has been paid before the related expense has been incurred; also known as a *prepaid expense*

financial statements. The review indicates that service revenue of $5,000 was earned but had not been recorded as of the end of the period. The necessary adjusting entry is recorded as follows:

Accounts Receivable	5,000	
Service Revenue		5,000
To record revenue earned but not recorded		

An accrual of revenue always involves the recording of an asset, usually a receivable. Thus, although this type of transaction is usually referred to as accrued revenue, it may also be called an *accrued asset*. Other common examples of accrued revenues are interest revenue that has been earned but not received as of the end of the accounting period and rent revenue that has been earned but not yet received.

❯ ACCRUED EXPENSE   Adjusting entries must also be made for expenses that have been incurred during the period but have not yet been paid. For example, assume that at the end of the accounting period, payroll records indicate that Kinglet Company owes its employees $2,000 for time they have worked but for which they have not yet been paid. The adjusting entry is recorded as follows:

Wages and Salaries Expense	2,000	
Wages and Salaries Payable		2,000
To record wages and salaries owed to employees		

The accrual of an expense always involves the recording of a liability. This type of transaction is usually referred to as an accrued expense but may also be called an *accrued liability*. Other common examples of accrued expenses include interest that is owed but has not been paid as of the end of the period and utilities that have been used but have not been paid for as of the end of the period.

❯ DEFERRED REVENUE   Deferred revenue occurs when a firm receives cash or other assets prior to earning the revenue associated with the transaction. Advance deposits and professional retainers are typical deferred revenues. A deferral requires careful analysis because the adjusting entry depends upon how the cash transaction was originally recorded. For example, suppose that on July 1, 2006, Kinglet Company was paid $6,000 in advance (commonly called a retainer) to perform accounting services evenly over a two-year period beginning on July 1, 2006, and ending on June 30, 2008. On July 1, 2006, the $6,000 could be recorded in an unearned revenue (liability) account:

Cash	6,000	
Unearned Revenue		6,000
To record the receipt of cash prior to earning revenue		

At the end of the reporting period, for example on December 31, 2006, the portion of the revenue that has been earned must be recorded as income of the current period. In this case, the amount earned is $1,500 ($6,000 ÷ 24 months × 6 months), and the adjusting entry is recorded as follows:

Unearned Revenue	1,500	
Service Revenue		1,500
To record the revenue earned in the current period		

This entry reduces the liability account Unearned Revenue from its original amount of $6,000 to the correct year-end balance of $4,500. As a result, the $4,500 of unearned revenue to be earned in future periods is shown as a liability on the December 31, 2006, balance sheet, and the $1,500 that was earned during the period is shown as revenue on the income statement.

However, the July 1, 2006, transaction could have been recorded differently. Although either method of recording this transaction is correct, some accountants prefer the following treatment. Suppose that the retainer was initially recorded entirely in the Service Revenue account:

Cash	6,000	
Service Revenue		6,000
To record the receipt of cash prior to earning revenue		

In this case, on December 31, 2006, the portion of the revenue that remains unearned must be recognized as a liability. The amount unearned is $4,500 ($6,000 ÷ 24 months × 18 months), and the adjusting entry is recorded as follows:

Service Revenue	4,500	
Unearned Revenue		4,500
To record the revenue not earned in the current period		

This adjusting entry reduces the Service Revenue account by $4,500 to bring the balance to the actual amount earned, $1,500. Note that in both cases the amounts presented on the financial statements are the same. The $4,500 of unearned revenue that remains at the end of the period is shown on the December 31, 2006, balance sheet, and the $1,500 that was earned during the period is shown as revenue or income on the income statement.

❱ DEFERRED EXPENSE   A deferred expense results when cash has been paid before the related expense has been incurred. Supplies and prepaid expenses are good examples of deferred expenses. Such items are assets that will benefit both the period in which they are purchased and future periods. For example, suppose that on January 1, 2006, Kinglet Company purchased a three-year insurance policy for $3,000. As before, the nature and amount of the adjusting entry depend on how the purchase was initially recorded. Let's assume that when the insurance was purchased, the entire amount was recorded in the asset account Prepaid Insurance. The entry on January 1, 2006, is recorded as follows:

Prepaid Insurance	3,000	
Cash		3,000
To record the purchase of insurance that will benefit several periods		

When adjusting entries are made before preparing the annual financial statements on December 31, 2006, the account Prepaid Insurance must be reduced because one-third of the insurance has been used, or has expired. The adjusting entry on that date is recorded as follows:

Insurance Expense	1,000	
Prepaid Insurance		1,000
To recognize the expiration of prepaid insurance		

The amount of prepaid insurance that remains at the end of the period ($2,000) is shown on the December 31, 2006, balance sheet, and the amount that was used up during the period ($1,000) is shown as an expense on the income statement. In the next year, 2007, another $1,000 of prepaid insurance will be written off to expense, and in 2008, the final $1,000 will be written off.

However, the January 1, 2006, transaction could have been recorded differently. Suppose that the company had initially used the following entry to record the entire amount as expense:

Insurance Expense	3,000	
Cash		3,000
To record the purchase of insurance that will benefit several periods		

In this case, when adjusting entries are prepared on December 31, 2006, the account Insurance Expense must be reduced because two-thirds of the insurance remains as a prepaid asset. The adjusting entry on that date is recorded as follows:

Prepaid Insurance	2,000	
Insurance Expense		2,000
To recognize prepaid insurance		

Note that in both cases the amounts on the financial statements for Prepaid Insurance and Insurance Expense are the same. Thus the amount of prepaid insurance that remains at the end of the period ($2,000) is shown on the December 31, 2006, balance sheet, and the amount that was used up during the period ($1,000) is shown as an expense on the income statement. There is no right or wrong method of recording the initial transaction or the necessary adjustment. Either approach can be used as long as the corresponding adjusting entries are made at the end of the period.

Other Examples of Deferred Expenses. There are many other assets whose costs must be allocated to the several periods that they benefit. For example, when supplies are purchased, they are recorded as prepaid assets, and as they are used over several periods, the benefits from them are systematically recognized as expenses. Perhaps the most common deferral is depreciation expense. Assume that at the beginning of 2007 Sora Corporation purchases a large piece of equipment for $100,000. The firm estimates that this equipment has a useful life of five years and that it will have no value at the end of its useful life. When the equipment is purchased, it is recorded as follows:

Equipment	100,000	
Cash		100,000
To record the purchase of equipment for cash		

Because the equipment will benefit the company over the five years of its useful life, its cost must be systematically allocated to those years. If the cost of the asset is divided equally over the five years of its useful life (referred to as *straight-line depreciation*), annual depreciation expense is $20,000 ($100,000 ÷ 5 years).[10] The entry at December 31, 2007, to record one year of depreciation expense is

Depreciation Expense	20,000	
Accumulated Depreciation—Equipment		20,000
To record annual depreciation expense for equipment		

Note that when the annual depreciation expense is recorded, the asset account Equipment is not reduced. Rather, the account Accumulated Depreciation—Equipment is credited. Accumulated Depreciation—Equipment is a contra-asset account with a normal credit balance that is offset against its companion asset account, Equipment, on the balance sheet. An account that is offset against, or deducted from, another account is called a **contra account**; in this case, Accumulated Depreciation—Equipment is specifically a contra-asset account. The use of a contra account allows the original cost of the asset to be retained in the asset account Equipment. As a result, the original cost of the equipment is always available in the firm's records.

contra account an account that is offset against, or deducted from, another account

---

10 As will be discussed in Chapter 9, there are other methods of depreciation that do not allocate an asset's cost equally over its life.

The two accounts appear on the balance sheet at December 31, 2007, as follows:

Equipment	$100,000
Less: Accumulated Depreciation (to date)	20,000
Equipment (net)	$ 80,000

At December 31, 2008, a year later, the Equipment account will still have a balance of $100,000, but the Accumulated Depreciation—Equipment account will have a balance of $40,000. A net amount of $60,000 will be shown on the balance sheet. The income statement will show depreciation expense of $20,000 for the years ended December 31, 2007, and December 31, 2008, as well as for each of the next three years.

) ADDITIONAL ADJUSTMENTS At the end of the period, other adjustments often need to be made that do not easily fall into the categories of accruals or deferrals. For instance, estimates of future events that affect the current period's financial statements must be made. A good example is the estimate for bad debt expense. It is highly unlikely that a company will be able to collect all the accounts receivable it generates through sales on account. However, when sales are made, it may be difficult to predict which specific accounts will not be collectible in the future. Thus, the bad debt expense related to the current year's sales cannot be known for certain and can only be estimated. To illustrate, assume that from past experience Sora Corporation knows that ultimately it will not collect 2 percent of all sales made on account. During the current year, 2007, $500,000 of credit sales were made, so the company might estimate that $10,000 ($500,000 × 0.02) of the sales will not be collected. Because that expense is related to 2007 sales, it must be recognized in 2007, and the following entry is made:

Bad Debt Expense	10,000	
Allowance for Uncollectible Accounts		10,000
To record uncollectible accounts expense for the year		

Allowance for Uncollectible Accounts is a contra-asset account similar to the Accumulated Depreciation account and is netted against Accounts Receivable on the balance sheet. It is only when a specific account is determined to be uncollectible that Accounts Receivable is reduced, or credited; the debit is to Allowance for Uncollectible Accounts. Chapter 7 provides more detail on the various methods used to estimate bad debt expense.

Other expenses that may need to be estimated at the end of the period are warranty expense, pension costs, and postretirement benefits. In addition, the accountant analyzes the firm's accounts to make sure that all transactions have been accounted for, that any changes in value required by generally accepted accounting principles have been recorded, and that other events that might cause changes in the firm's accounts have been recorded. Any necessary changes are usually made during the adjustment process.

) ILLUSTRATION: KETTLE AND WOLF, INC. Recall that the unadjusted trial balance for Kettle and Wolf, Inc. was presented in Illustration 1.13. It will be revised to reflect the following adjusting entries, which must be made at September 30 to reflect all activity during the month.

● One month of accrued interest on the $3,000 long-term note payable at 12 percent must be recognized.

Interest Expense	30	
Interest Payable		30
To record interest expense for the current period:		
$3,000 × 0.12 × 1 / 12		

- One month of depreciation for the computer purchased on September 1 must be recorded. It is estimated that the computer will last for two years and will have no residual value. The purchase price was $3,000.

Depreciation Expense	125	
Accumulated Depreciation—Equipment		125
To record depreciation expense for the period:		
($3,000 − $0) / 24 months		

- The supplies used during the month must be recognized. At September 30, $900 of supplies remain. A purchase of $1,000 was originally recorded in the asset account Office Supplies. The adjusting entry records the expense and reduces the asset account by the amount used, or $100.

Supplies Expense	100	
Supplies		100
To record the use of supplies in the current period:		
$1,000 − $900 = $100		

- The monthly website expense must be recognized. The entire cost of the website ($4,800) was originally recorded in the asset account Prepaid Website. This account must be reduced to reflect one month's usage, or 1/24 of the cost.

Website Expense	200	
Prepaid Website		200
To record the website expense for the current period:		
$4,800 / 24 months		

- One month of revenue from the one-year subscriptions must be recognized. Kettle and Wolf sold $12,000 worth of one-year subscriptions and must recognize 1/12 of that total in the current month. At the time of the sale, the $12,000 was recorded in the liability account Unearned Revenue. This account must be reduced to reflect the revenue earned during the period. For simplicity, one month of revenue is recognized even though the subscriptions were sold on September 20.

Unearned Revenue	1,000	
Subscription Revenue		1,000
To record the subscription revenue earned for the current		
period: $12,000 / 12 months		

The T-accounts for Kettle and Wolf appear in Illustration 1.15. Note that the adjusting entries are highlighted.

Illustration 1.15

Adjusted T-Accounts, September 2006

Cash			
9/1	10,000	3,000	9/1
9/1	3,000	4,800	9/1
9/15	2,400	1,000	9/30
9/20	6,000	400	9/30
	21,400	9,200	
9/30			
bal.	**12,200**		

Accounts Receivable		
9/20	6,000	

Prepaid Website			
9/1	4,800		9/30
		200 adj.	
9/30			
bal.	**4,600**		

Supplies			
9/1	1,000		9/30
		100 adj.	
9/30			
bal.	**900**		

Computer Equipment			Accumulated Depreciation—Equipment		
9/1	3,000				9/30
				125	**adj.**

Accounts Payable				Unearned Revenue			
9/30	1,000	1,000	9/15	9/30		12,000	9/20
9/30				**adj.**	**1,000**		
bal.	**0**			9/30			
				bal.	**11,000**		

Long-Term Notes Payable			Interest Payable		
	10,000	9/1			9/30
				30	**adj.**

Common Stock			Retained Earnings	
	10,000	9/1		

Subscription Revenue				Salaries Expense		
		2,400	9/15	9/30	400	
			9/30			
		1,000	**adj.**			
			9/30			
		3,400	**bal.**			

Interest Expense			Depreciation Expense		
9/30			9/30		
adj.	**30**		**adj.**	**125**	

Supplies Expense			Website Expense		
9/30			9/30		
adj.	**100**		**adj.**	**200**	

BRIDGE TUTORIAL

For a review of the concepts presented in this section, click on the menu item "The Accounting Cycle" and complete the questions found under "Step 5: Record and Post Adjusting Entries and Prepare an Adjusted Trial Balance."

Now that the adjusting entries have been posted, the adjusted trial balance can be prepared, as shown in Illustration 1.16.

▶ STEP 6: PREPARE FINANCIAL STATEMENTS

Once the adjusted trial balance is completed, the income statement, statement of changes in stockholders' equity, balance sheet, and statement of cash flows can all be prepared. The income statement should be prepared first, since the balance sheet and statement of changes in stockholders' equity rely on the net income or loss amount. The preparation of financial statements is fully discussed in Chapters 3, 4, and 5.

▶ **THE INCOME STATEMENT**   The income statement provides information about the net income that a firm produced over a stated period of time by detailing the revenues earned and the expenses incurred. Illustration 1.17 shows the income statement for Kettle and Wolf, Inc. The expenses are listed in order of decreasing magnitude. They could also be listed in other ways, such as alphabetically. During the month of September, the firm's net income amounted to $2,545.

▶ **THE STATEMENT OF CHANGES IN STOCKHOLDERS' EQUITY**   The statement of changes in stockholders' equity (or, for small corporations, the retained earnings statement) summarizes the adjustments to stockholders' equity over the accounting period. Illustration 1.18 presents the statement of changes in stockholders' equity for Kettle and Wolf for the month ended September 30, 2006.

Illustration 1.16

Adjusted Trial Balance

Kettle and Wolf, Inc.
Adjusted Trial Balance
September 30, 2006

Account Title	Debits	Credits
Cash	$12,200	
Accounts Receivable	6,000	
Prepaid Website	4,600	
Supplies	900	
Computer Equipment	3,000	
Accumulated Depreciation—Equipment		$ 125
Accounts Payable		0
Unearned Revenue		11,000
Interest Payable		30
Long-Term Notes Payable		3,000
Common Stock		10,000
Retained Earnings		0
Subscription Revenue		3,400
Salaries Expense	400	
Interest Expense	30	
Depreciation Expense	125	
Supplies Expense	100	
Website Expense	200	
Totals	$27,555	$27,555

Illustration 1.17

Income Statement

Kettle and Wolf, Inc.
Income Statement
For the Month Ended September 30, 2006

Revenues		
Subscription revenue		$3,400
Expenses		
Salaries expense	$400	
Website expense	200	
Depreciation expense	125	
Supplies expense	100	
Interest expense	30	
Total expenses		855
Net income		$2,545

❭ **THE BALANCE SHEET**   The newly adjusted ending balance of retained earnings, which is contained in the statement of changes in stockholders' equity, is used to prepare the balance sheet, or statement of financial position. The classified balance sheet for Kettle and Wolf is shown in Illustration 1.19. Note that the ending balance in stockholders' equity at September 30 is the amount shown on the statement of changes in stockholders' equity in Illustration 1.18.

❭ **THE STATEMENT OF CASH FLOWS**   The statement of cash flows, the fourth financial statement, reconciles the reported net income for the year with the change in cash for the year. As mentioned earlier, the statement of cash flows has three sections: cash flows from operating activities, cash flows from investing activities, and cash flows from financing activities. The sum of those three sections equals the change in cash for the reporting period.

Illustration 1.18

Statement of Changes in Stockholders' Equity

Kettle and Wolf, Inc.
Statement of Changes in Stockholders' Equity
For the Month Ended September 30, 2006

	Common Stock	Retained Earnings	Total Stockholders' Equity
Balance, September 1, 2006	$ 0	$ 0	$ 0
Issuance of common stock	10,000		10,000
Net income for the month ended September 30, 2006		2,545	2,545
Balance, September 30, 2006	$10,000	$2,545	$12,545

Illustration 1.19

Balance Sheet

Kettle and Wolf, Inc.
Balance Sheet
September 30, 2006

Assets

Current assets		
Cash	$12,200	
Accounts receivable	6,000	
Prepaid website	4,600	
Supplies	900	
Total current assets		$23,700
Computer equipment, net of accumulated depreciation of $125		2,875
Total assets		$26,575

Liabilities and Stockholders' Equity

Current liabilities		
Unearned revenue	$11,000	
Interest payable	30	
Total current liabilities		$11,030
Long-term notes payable		3,000
Total liabilities		$14,030
Stockholders' equity		
Common stock	$10,000	
Retained earnings	2,545	
Total stockholders' equity		12,545
Total liabilities and stockholders' equity		$26,575

The statement of cash flows for Kettle and Wolf is shown in Illustration 1.20. Note that because this is the first month of operations, the firm started with no cash. Cash of $12,200 was provided through operations, the issuance of a note payable, and the issuance of stock. At the end of the period, the cash balance was $12,200, the same amount that is shown on the balance sheet in Illustration 1.19. The cash flows from operations represent cash-basis income. That is, this is the income that will be reported if revenues are recognized when cash is received regardless of when the revenues are earned, and expenses are recognized when they are paid in cash regardless of which accounting periods are benefited. Thus, the purchase of a website for $4,800 represents a cash-basis expense, whereas the accrual-basis expense for the website is only $200, the amount recognized for website usage in the month of September (as shown previously in the journal entry recording this expense).

Illustration 1.20

Statement of Cash Flows

Kettle and Wolf, Inc. Statement of Cash Flows For the Month Ended September 30, 2006		
Cash Flows from Operating Activities		
Net income		$ 2,545
Add (subtract) noncash items:		
Depreciation		125
Changes in current asset and current liability accounts:		
Increase in accounts receivable		(6,000)
Increase in prepaid website		(4,600)
Increase in supplies		(900)
Increase in unearned revenue		11,000
Increase in interest payable		30
Cash provided by operations		$ 2,200
Cash Flows from Investing Activities		
Purchase of computer		(3,000)
Cash Flows from Financing Activities		
Issuance of long-term note payable	$ 3,000	
Issuance of common stock	10,000	
Net cash flows from financing activities		13,000
Increase in cash for the year		$12,200
Cash balance at September 1, 2006		0
Cash balance at September 30, 2006		$12,200

❱ **FINANCIAL STATEMENT ARTICULATION** Kettle and Wolf's four financial statements systematically interrelate, or articulate. During September, the amount of the firm's net assets changed. Those changes are explained by the income statement and the statement of cash flows. The firm's net income of $2,545 for the month increased its net assets (assets minus liabilities) by the same amount. After the September 1 investment by the owners, the firm's net assets consisted of $10,000 in cash. At the end of the month, net assets consisted of $12,545, with the increase coming from the month's net income of $2,545.

BRIDGE TUTORIAL

For a review of the concepts presented in this section, click on the menu item "The Accounting Cycle" and complete the questions found under "Step 6: Prepare Financial Statements" and the Demonstration Problem and Internet Assignment.

STEP 7: PREPARE AND POST CLOSING ENTRIES AND PREPARE A POST-CLOSING TRIAL BALANCE

Recording and posting the closing entries is the final step in the accounting cycle. As noted earlier, there are two types of accounts: permanent (also called *real*) and temporary (also called *nominal*). **Closing entries** zero out the temporary accounts at the end of the current cycle so that a new cycle may begin. For example, to measure the revenues for a specific period, the revenue accounts need to begin with a clean slate, or zero balance. They need to be wiped clean, or closed, so that revenues for the next accounting cycle can be measured. Likewise, all expense accounts need to be closed. Temporary accounts are closed by transferring their balances to the permanent account Retained Earnings. If dividends have been issued during the period by debiting a Dividends account, this Dividends account must be closed to Retained Earnings. If the original debit was directly to the Retained Earnings account, then no closing entry is necessary. Assuming that a Dividends account is used, four closing entries are typically required to:

closing entries entries that zero out the temporary accounts at the end of the current accounting cycle so that a new cycle may begin

1. Close all revenue accounts to a new, but temporary, holding account called Income Summary.

2. Close all expense accounts to the Income Summary account.

3. Close the Income Summary account to Retained Earnings.

4. Close the Dividends account to Retained Earnings.

It is possible to shorten the process by closing revenue and expense accounts directly to Retained Earnings, without using the holding account Income Summary. In reality, closing entries are made only once, at year end, but for the sake of illustration, we will make them at the end of Kettle and Wolf's first month of operations. The closing entries for Kettle and Wolf are illustrated below.

Subscription Revenue	3,400	
Income Summary		3,400
To close Revenue account to Income Summary		

Income Summary	855	
Salaries Expense		400
Interest Expense		30
Depreciation Expense		125
Supplies Expense		100
Website Expense		200
To close expense accounts to Income Summary		

Income Summary	2,545	
Retained Earnings		2,545
To close Income Summary to Retained Earnings		

After these entries are posted, all revenue and expense accounts will have a zero balance and the Retained Earnings account will have been updated to show the effect of the month's net income of $2,545. The final amount transferred to Retained Earnings is the net income of the period (the difference between all of the revenue and gain accounts and all of the expense and loss accounts). If Kettle and Wolf had declared and distributed dividends during the month and recorded this in the Dividends account, this account would also be closed to the Retained Earnings account by debiting Retained Earnings and crediting Dividends. As a final check, a post-closing trial balance is prepared (see Illustration 1.21). That trial balance

Ilustration 1.21

Post-Closing Trial Balance

Kettle and Wolf, Inc.
Post-Closing Trial Balance
September 30, 2006

Account Title	Debits	Credits
Cash	$12,200	
Accounts Receivable	6,000	
Prepaid Website	4,600	
Supplies	900	
Computer Equipment	3,000	
Accumulated Depreciation—Equipment		$ 125
Accounts Payable		0
Unearned Revenue		11,000
Interest Payable		30
Long-Term Notes Payable		3,000
Common Stock		10,000
Retained Earnings		2,545
Totals	$26,700	$26,700

includes only balance sheet, or permanent, accounts because the income statement, or temporary, accounts have been closed into Retained Earnings.

BRIDGE TUTORIAL

For a review of the concepts presented in this section, click on the menu item "The Accounting Cycle" and complete the questions, Demonstration Problem, and Internet Assignment found under "Step 7: Prepare and Post Closing Entries and Prepare a Post-Closing Trial Balance."

CHECK YOUR UNDERSTANDING

1. Under the rules of debit and credit in a double-entry accounting system, describe the change represented by a debit to an asset account, to a liability account, and to a stockholders' equity account.

2. Describe the difference between a permanent account and a temporary account.

3. List the steps in the accounting cycle.

4. What is the purpose of posting?

5. Why are adjusting entries needed?

6. If a firm owes $2,200 to its employees at the end of an accounting period for work performed but not yet paid for, what journal entry should be recorded?

7. Describe the four basic closing entries required at the end of an accounting period.

Revisiting the Case

KEEPING SCORE: CONFIDENCE IN QUALCOMM NUMBERS

1. Auditors routinely review the balance sheet, the income statement (or statement of operations), the statement of cash flows, and the statement of changes in stockholders' equity.

2. The auditor's report provides a degree of assurance to the potential investor that the financial statements were prepared in accordance with generally accepted accounting principles and that commonly accepted procedures and practices were followed.

3. When financial statements are prepared in conformity with GAAP, users of financial statements can more readily rely on the validity and accuracy of the numbers reported, and thus can make informed investment and analysis decisions.

4. Though an auditor reviews the financial statements of a company for adherence to GAAP, the ultimate responsibility for the statements' accuracy and reliability rests with company management, not with the auditing group.

SUMMARY BY LEARNING OBJECTIVE

SECTION A

LO1 Identify the elements of the balance sheet and discuss four key concepts that underlie the balance sheet.

The balance sheet, sometimes referred to as the *statement of financial position*, provides information about the financial position of a company at a specific point in time. The primary elements of the balance sheet are assets, the economic resources of a firm; liabilities, the economic obligations of a firm; and owners' (or stockholders') equity, the residual interest in the assets of an entity that remains after deducting its liabilities. The four key concepts that underlie the balance sheet are (1) the economic entity assumption, which is the idea that the accounting for one economic unit should be kept separate from the accounting for the owners of that economic unit and from the accounting for other economic units owned or controlled by others; (2) the historical cost principle, which guides the valuation of assets and liabilities by stating that an asset or liability should be initially recorded at its original, or historical, cost; (3) the monetary unit assumption, which is the concept that currency is an appropriate unit of measure for assessing the value of a firm in financial reporting; and (4) the going concern assumption, which is the presumption that in the absence of evidence to the contrary, a firm will continue to operate indefinitely.

LO2 Identify the elements of the income statement and discuss six key concepts that underlie the income statement.

The income statement provides information about the amount of net income earned by the firm over a stated period of time by detailing the revenues earned and the expenses incurred. The primary elements of an income statement are revenues and expenses and gains and losses. Six important concepts underlie the income statement. They are (1) the periodicity assumption (or *time period assumption*), which is the belief that it is meaningful to measure a firm's activities in terms of arbitrary time periods even though the firm's life is considered to be indefinite; (2) accrual accounting, which is the practice of recording transactions and other events and circumstances in the period in which they occurred rather than in the period in which cash or some other form of payment is received or paid; (3) the revenue recognition principle, which is the concept that revenue should be recognized (recorded) when the amount and timing of that revenue are reasonably determinable (revenue is realized or realizable) and when the earnings process is complete or virtually complete (revenue is earned); (4) the matching principle, which holds that revenues should be reported in the same accounting period as the expenses to which they are related; (5) conservatism, which is a prudent reaction to uncertainty to try to ensure that the uncertainty and risks inherent in business situations are adequately considered; and (6) full disclosure, which requires that the financial statements and related notes include any information that is significant or material enough to change the decisions of users of financial statements.

LO3 Summarize the contents of the statement of changes in stockholders' equity and the statement of cash flows.

The statement of changes in stockholders' equity (or, for small corporations, the *retained earnings statement*) summarizes the adjustments to stockholders' equity over an accounting period. Stockholders' equity accounts include Capital or Common Stock accounts, Other Paid-in Capital accounts, and Retained Earnings. The beginning balance of Retained Earnings is increased by net income and decreased by a net loss and payment of dividends. Investments by stockholders increase the Capital Stock and Other Paid-in Capital accounts.

The statement of cash flows shows the amount of cash collected and paid out by a firm over an accounting period. It consists of three sections: cash flows from operating activities, cash flows from investing activities, and cash flows from financing activities. The net total of those three sections equals the change in cash for the reporting period.

SECTION B

LO4 Explain how the accounting equation forms the basis of double-entry accounting.

The accounting equation, Assets = Liabilities + Stockholders' Equity, expresses an equality. To maintain the equality between the left and right sides of the equation, at least two accounts must be adjusted for each transaction recorded. The process of recording the dual effect that each economic transaction has on the accounting equation is called double-entry accounting. Each item on each side of the accounting equation is represented by an individual account, the basic unit in accounting, which is used to systematically record and summarize amounts from similar transactions. An entry on the left side of an account is called a debit (DR). A debit represents an increase in an asset account, but a decrease in a liability or stockholders' equity account. A credit (CR) is an entry on the right side of an account. A credit represents a decrease in an asset account, but an increase in a liability or stockholders' equity account. When the equality of the accounting equation is preserved, debits always equal credits.

LO5 Outline the steps in the accounting cycle.

The accounting cycle is the set of activities involved in analyzing business events, collecting and processing information related to those events, and summarizing that information in the four financial statements. There are seven steps in the accounting cycle: (1) identify and gather transaction information; (2) analyze and record each transaction; (3) post the journal entries to the general ledger; (4) prepare an unadjusted trial balance; (5) record and post adjusting journal entries and prepare an adjusted trial balance; (6) prepare the financial statements; and (7) record and post closing entries and prepare a post-closing trial balance.

KEY TERMS

SECTION A

accounting (p. 4)
accounting cycle (p. 4)
accrual (p. 12)
accrual accounting (p. 11)
American Institute of Certified Public Accountants (AICPA) (p. 5)
assets (p. 4)
balance sheet (p. 4)
capital stock (p. 7)
cash basis of accounting (p. 11)
classified balance sheet (p. 6)
conservatism (p. 12)
current assets (p. 6)
current liabilities (p. 7)
deferral (p. 12)
dividends (p. 7)

economic entity assumption (p. 7)
expenses (p. 10)
Financial Accounting Standards Board (FASB) (p. 5)
full disclosure (p. 13)
gains (p. 10)
generally accepted accounting principles (GAAP) (p. 5)
going concern assumption (p. 9)
historical cost principle (p. 8)
income statement (p. 9)
liabilities (p. 4)
losses (p. 10)
matching principle (p. 12)
monetary unit assumption (p. 8)
net income (net loss) (p. 9)

noncurrent liabilities (p. 7)
operating assets (p. 6)
operating cycle (p. 6)
owners' equity (p. 5)
periodicity assumption (p. 11)
realization (p. 12)
recognition (p. 12)
retained earnings (p. 7)
revenue recognition principle (p. 12)
revenues (p. 9)
statement of cash flows (p. 14)
statement of changes in stockholders' equity (p. 13)
stockholders' equity (p. 5)

SECTION B

account (p. 16)
accounting equation (p. 15)
accrued expense (p. 25)
accrued revenue (p. 25)
adjusted trial balance (p. 23)
adjusting entries (p. 24)
chart of accounts (p. 16)
closing entries (p. 34)
compound entry (p. 22)
contra account (p. 28)

credit (CR) (p. 16)
debit (DR) (p. 16)
deferred expense (p. 25)
deferred revenue (p. 25)
double-entry accounting (p. 15)
general journal (p. 20)
journal (p. 20)
journalize (p. 20)
ledger (p. 16)
permanent accounts (p. 17)

post-closing trial balance (p. 23)
posting (p. 23)
source document (p. 20)
specialized journal (p. 20)
subsidiary ledger (p. 23)
T-account (p. 16)
temporary accounts (p. 17)
trial balance (p. 23)
unadjusted trial balance (p. 23)

EXERCISES

SECTION A

LO1, 2   **EXERCISE 1-1   Concepts Underlying Financial Statements**

Listed below are concepts that underlie the financial statements.

A. Periodicity

B. Monetary unit

C. Economic entity

D. Going concern

E. Historical cost

F. Revenue recognition

G. Full disclosure

H. Matching

Required: Identify which concept best relates to the statements that follow.

1. It is appropriate to use a financial measure of profit to assess the value of a firm for financial reporting purposes.

2. Business activity can be measured in terms of an arbitrary time period.

3. When the earnings process is virtually complete and the amount and timing of revenue can be determined, this principle applies.

4. It is assumed that a company will continue to operate.

5. The accounting for the economic units belonging to a firm is separate from the accounting for the economic units belonging to the firm's owners.

6. Under this assumption, most assets and liabilities are valued at their original cost.

7. Information that is significant or material enough to change the decision of a user of financial statements should be provided.

8. Expenses should be reported in the same period as the related revenues.

LO1 **EXERCISE 1-2   Understanding the Balance Sheet**

Armstrong Company's accountant is having trouble preparing the balance sheet for the firm at December 31, 2005, and provides you with the following data:

Cash	$35,000
Notes Payable (due in 2 years)	9,000
Accounts Receivable	20,000
Retained Earnings	?
Inventory	50,000
Accounts Payable	18,000
Supplies	4,000
Interest Payable	3,000
Capital Stock	40,000

Required: Prepare a classified balance sheet for the company for December 31, 2005.

LO1 **EXERCISE 1-3   Understanding Balance Sheet Concepts**

BB, Inc. recently opened for business as a small-computer repair store. The owner, Bonnie, invested $50,000 of her own funds to start the business. The firm received from **Microsoft Corporation** a picture of Bill Gates with the note, *Good Luck, Bonnie,* to display in the window. The company also purchased a lottery ticket for $10, hoping to win the $50 million jackpot. The company received an invoice from the local newspaper for $100 for newspapers delivered to the previous occupant of the store. Finally, Bonnie decided that the firm needed a new piece of high-tech equipment, which the firm purchased used for $5,000 in cash; new equipment would have cost $8,000.

Required: Which of these items should be listed as assets, liabilities, or stockholders' equity on the balance of the PC repair store? At what amounts? Explain your reasoning.

LO1, 2 **EXERCISE 1-4   Recognition of Balance Sheet and Income Statement Transactions**

Dean, Inc. is a political consulting firm, and a summary of certain of the firm's April transactions is listed below.

A. The firm collected $50,000 in April on accounts receivable generated from services billed in February and March.

B. The owner of the firm, H. Dean, felt that the firm needed additional funds and arranged a line of credit with the local bank for $100,000. Dean anticipates that the firm will not have to draw on any of these funds until midsummer, when business generally slows.

C. Cash received in April from April billings was $25,000.

D. Dean, Inc. declared and a paid a $1,000 dividend during April.

E. Dean, Inc. billed an additional $10,000 of fees for work done in April.

F. The firm pays each month's rent on the last day of the previous month and thus received an invoice in April for its May rent of $5,000 and paid it in April.

G. The firm received and paid its April utility bill of $600.

H. Several years ago, Dean, Inc. had purchased a small plot of land next to its current location in anticipation of constructing its own building. However, in April, the firm decided instead to sell the land, which had cost it $100,000, for $120,000. Dean, Inc. received $25,000 in cash and a receivable for the rest.

Required: State which of these events and what amounts would be recorded on Dean, Inc.'s income statement for April.

LO1, 2   **EXERCISE 1-5**   **Accounting Concepts**

Each of the situations described below involves an accounting concept. There may be more than one concept for each situation.

A. The treasurer of AXEL, Inc. was concerned about the financial picture of the firm and did not feel it was necessary to list in the firm's financial statements its interest in some oil drilling partnerships. The treasurer reasoned that the firm had made no actual investment in the partnerships, but did acknowledge that the firm actually controls the partnerships through its influence on their boards of directors.

B. Legacy Airlines, Inc., after many years of profitable operations, has incurred five years of huge losses and has seen its stockholders' equity turn negative. Given changes in the industry, the future of the airline is debatable.

C. Eric is the sole owner of a small advertising business. Because there are no other owners, he often uses the firm's cash to pay his own personal expenses. He reasons that it is okay to record these on the firm's books, as he does not need to report to anybody else.

D. Old Camera, Inc. had been a very successful retail camera store specializing in 35-millimeter cameras. The owners were convinced that digital cameras would never replace film cameras and thus carried very few digital cameras. One of the firm's suppliers of film cameras, Sigma, Inc., recently announced that it was stopping production of film cameras because of extremely slow sales. Old Camera, Inc. has an inventory of these film cameras from Sigma that cost $140,000; the cameras are currently probably worth only half that amount.

E. Alpha Beta's year end is June 30. Close to year end, it entered into an agreement to sell one of its major divisions. The papers were signed on June 30, but the actual transaction does not become effective until sometime in August because of the time needed for due diligence. The CFO of Alpha Beta has decided not to report the sale in June, as no funds have changed hands and the outcome of the due diligence is not known.

Required: Identify the accounting concept or concepts involved in each of these scenarios.

LO3   **EXERCISE 1-6**   **Understanding the Statement of Changes in Stockholders' Equity**

The following account balances are provided for Williams & Associates, Inc. for the year ended December 31, 2005:

	Jan. 1, 2005	Dec. 31, 2005
Common Stock	$350,000	$450,000
Preferred Stock	200,000	200,000
Retained Earnings	195,000	266,000

Required: Using the information above, present the statement of changes in stockholders' equity for the year ended December 31, 2005. Assume that no dividends were paid.

LO3   **EXERCISE 1-7**   **Understanding the Statement of Cash Flows**

The following transactions occurred during the month of June 2005 for Trident Company:

A. Depreciation of $880 was charged for a company transport truck.

B. The company purchased a new warehouse for $40,000 that will be used to store its products prior to sale.

C. The company recorded a loss on sale of warehouse equipment of $16,000.

The company reported net income of $76,000 for the month of June. The Cash account balance was $24,000 and $76,880 at June 1 and June 30, respectively.

Required: Using the information provided, present a statement of cash flows for June. Assume that no other relevant transactions took place during the month.

LO1, 2   **EXERCISE 1-8**   **Applying the Concepts Underlying Financial Statements**

Some of the concepts that underlie the financial statements are listed below.

A. Monetary unit

B. Economic entity

C. Historical cost

D. Revenue recognition

E. Periodicity

F. Matching

G. Full disclosure

Required: Identify which concept is involved in each of the following business scenarios. More than one concept may be involved in each scenario.

1. Rachel Woo, an accountant for Partovi Co., records the firm's equipment at its historical value and depreciates the equipment each period as it deteriorates with age.

2. Ratcliff Enterprises receives an order, along with payment, for 700 of its hand-made rocking chairs in May. The company recognizes revenue from the payment over the months of May, June, and July as the chairs are made and delivered.

3. TradeTek Industries has been charged in a class action lawsuit for product defects that have posed hazards to its customers in 2005. When the company issues its 2005 annual report, the class action lawsuit is disclosed in the notes.

SECTION B

LO4, 5   **EXERCISE 1-9   Record Transactions and Post to T-Accounts**

The following transactions occurred during January 2005 for Sunshine Company. Sunshine Company owns motor scooters and rents them to customers:

Jan. 1   Issued 1,000 shares of capital stock in exchange for $10,000 in cash.
 1   Purchased ten motor scooters for cash at a cost of $1,000 each.
 1   Borrowed $5,000 from the bank in exchange for a one-year note payable with an annual percentage rate (APR) of 10 percent.
 12   Paid $1,000 for gas and oil supplies. Sunshine expects that these supplies will be used over the next few months.
 13   Paid $600 for a one-year insurance policy covering January through December of 2005.
 31   Paid $3,000 in wages for the month of January.
 31   Rented motor scooters during January for $9,000, of which $6,000 was received as cash and the balance on account.

Required: Prepare journal entries for these transactions and post to T-accounts. Assume that the opening balances for all accounts are zero.

LO4, 5   **EXERCISE 1-10   Adjusting Entries and Posting to T-Accounts**

Use the transactions from Exercise 1-9 to complete this exercise. The following additional information is provided:

A. Sunshine Company determined that the motor scooters will be used for two years and will have zero residual value. Recognize depreciation for the month of January using the straight-line method.

B. Recognize interest expense for the month of January.

C. Sunshine determined that it has used $800 of the gas and oil supplies in January.

D. Recognize the insurance expense for the month of January.

E. Sunshine determined that it owes its employees $200 in wages for January.

Required: Prepare appropriate adjusting entries and post to T-accounts.

LO4, 5   **EXERCISE 1-11   Income Statement**

Use the information given in Exercises 1-9 and 1-10 for Sunshine Company.

Required: Prepare an income statement for Sunshine Company for January 2005.

LO4, 5   **EXERCISE 1-12   Balance Sheet**

Use the information in Exercises 1-9, 1-10, and 1-11 for Sunshine Company.

Required: Prepare a balance sheet for Sunshine Company at January 31, 2005.

LO5   EXERCISE **1-13**   **Closing Entries**

Use the information in Exercises 1-9 and 1-10 for Sunshine Company.

Required: Prepare closing entries for Sunshine Company for the month of January 2005.

LO4, 5   EXERCISE **1-14**   **Record Journal Entries**

Peak Computer Rentals rents computers and components to students in the Amherst, Massachusetts area. The company uses the accrual method of accounting. The following transactions occurred in March 2005:

Mar.   1   Peak Computer Rentals is established when Pat Brown files for incorporation in the Commonwealth of Massachusetts and receives common stock in exchange for $2,000 cash.

     1   Purchased 25 laptop computers for $576 each in cash from Micro Suppliers. Each laptop has an estimated useful life of two years with no residual value.

     1   Paid $700 in rent for the month of March using check no. 101.

     5   Paid $60 for a one-year business license using check no. 102.

   30   Earned $15,000 in rental fees for the month of March, received in cash.

   30   Paid wages of $1,500 for the month of March.

Required: Prepare journal entries for the transactions listed above. Assume that all accounts have beginning balances of zero.

LO4, 5   EXERCISE **1-15**   **Adjusting Entries and Income Statement**

Refer to the information in Exercise 1-14.

Required:

1. Are adjusting entries needed? If so, prepare adjusting entries for the month of March.
2. Prepare the income statement for Peak Computer Rentals for the month of March.

LO5   EXERCISE **1-16**   **Elements**

Financial statements contain accounts that can each be classified as one of the financial statement elements: asset, liability, stockholders' equity, revenue, or expense. For example, the Cash account is classified as an asset.

Required: Assign each item below to an element category.

1. Accounts receivable
2. Accounts payable
3. Common stock
4. Retained earnings
5. Depreciation expense
6. Inventory
7. Gain on sale of used equipment
8. Wages incurred for the current period
9. Allowance for uncollectible accounts
10. Interest payment on money owed
11. Receipt of rent on a building we own
12. Payment of rent for a future month to a third party

LO4, 5   EXERCISE **1-17**   **Record and Post Journal Entries**

The following transactions occurred during August 2005 for Central Park Rentals, Inc.:

Aug.   1   Wrote check no. 430 for the month's rent, $500.

     5   Wrote check no. 431 for the part-time desk clerk's salary, $260.

     5   Received $500 from a client for equipment rental, receipt no. 220.

     6   Wrote check no. 432 to pay the electricity bill, $79.

   12   Received $200 on a client's account.

   13   Customers rented equipment for $250 on account.

   19   Purchased two new canoes from Adventure Outfitters for a total of $490 on account.

The account balances on July 31, 2005, were as follows:

Cash	$12,566
Accounts Receivable	1,200
Accounts Payable	900
Equipment	16,500

Required: Record appropriate journal entries for each August transaction, then post each entry to the appropriate general ledger accounts.

LO5 **EXERCISE 1-18   Closing Entries**

Assume the following account balances for Donne Tractor Co. as of December 31, 2005:

Cash	$17,000
Equipment	7,500
Accumulated Depreciation—Equipment	1,600
Utilities Expense	300
Salaries Expense	3,500
Depreciation Expense	700
Tractor Inventory	29,000
Accounts Payable	11,160
Sales	29,000
Cost of Goods Sold	18,000
Insurance Expense	600
Retained Earnings	43,040

Required: Prepare closing entries for Donne Tractor at December 31, 2005.

LO4, 5 **EXERCISE 1-19   Analysis of the Accounting Equation and Stockholders' Equity**

XCB was formed 15 years ago to produce profiles of business executives for cable financial and business channels. When the firm was formed, its stockholders invested $800,000. Subsequent investments by the owners totaled another $300,000. During its 15-year existence, the company has been extremely profitable, and its total assets have grown to $3,500,000 at December 31, 2006. At that same time, the firm's total liabilities were only $750,000.

Required:

1. Assume that no dividends have been paid during the firm's existence. What is the amount of retained earnings at December 31, 2006?
2. Prepare the stockholders' equity section of the balance sheet at December 31, 2006.

LO4, 5 **EXERCISE 1-20   Understanding the Balance Sheet and the Income Statement**

Backus, Inc. markets accounting software to small and medium-sized businesses. The accounts listed below have the following December 31, 2005 balances:

Sales	$1,000,000
Cost of Goods Sold	?
Gain on Sale of Land	50,000
Salaries Expense	75,000
Marketing Expenses	30,000
Rent Expense	60,000
Cash	35,000
Accounts Receivable	55,000
Inventory	120,000
Land	?
Accounts and Short-Term Notes Payable	60,000
Salaries Payable	20,000

| Capital Stock | 125,000 |
| Retained Earnings, January 1, 2005 | 75,000 |

Required: Assume that all the firm's accounts are listed. Also assume that the net income for 2005 is $245,000.

1. Prepare an income statement for the year ended December 31, 2005.
2. Prepare a balance sheet at December 31, 2005.

PROBLEMS

SECTION A

LO1, 2   **PROBLEM 1-1**   **Financial Statement Concepts**

Below are several scenarios depicting the concepts underlying accounting information.

A. DuraStain acquired several acres of land for $600,000 from a company that had been forced into bankruptcy. The land was appraised shortly thereafter at $800,000, so the company reported the land at $800,000.

B. DuraStain acquired several acres of land for $600,000 from a company that had been forced into bankruptcy. The land was appraised shortly thereafter at $800,000, so the company reported a gain of $200,000.

C. DuraStain waits to recognize revenue until customers pay the amounts that they owe.

D. DuraStain allocates the cost of equipment over the accounting periods in which the equipment is used in earning revenue.

E. DuraStain was sure it would experience a loss from a hurricane that destroyed most of the company's warehouse, and so it recognized a loss on its current-year income statement, even though the insurance appraiser had not yet determined the exact loss.

F. DuraStain reported information in the financial statement notes about commitments it had made with suppliers.

Required: Indicate the accounting concept that applies to each case scenario and whether the concept was violated or followed. For each concept violated, indicate the proper treatment.

Analyze: Describe the implications of the accounting for land in situation (A) above.

LO1, 4   **PROBLEM 1-2**   **The Accounting Equation and Income**

Double Co. was incorporated on January 1, 2005, with $100,000 from the issuance of stock and borrowed funds of $120,000. During the first year of operations, revenue totaled $900,000 and expenses totaled $775,000. On December 15, Double Co. declared and paid a $110,000 cash dividend to its shareholders. Also during the year, additional stock was issued for $150,000.

Required:

1. Determine the amount of accounting income.
2. Determine the amount of change in stockholders' equity that occurred from January 1 to December 31, 2005.

Analyze: Why are the amounts in (1) and (2) different?

LO1, 2   **PROBLEM 1-3**   **Financial Statement Concepts**

Below are several scenarios depicting the assumptions underlying accounting information.

A. Because a pest control company was to fumigate the donut shop manager's apartment on Tuesday, the manager brought his dog to work with him. At lunchtime, the manager gave the dog two dozen donuts that could have been sold to customers.

B. A company reports its earnings annually to its shareholders.

C. Though inflation is a big factor in the cost of acquiring inventory items, a company reports inventory at the original cost paid.

D. Because the manager of a manufacturing plant intended to sell the parts division after three years, the accountant depreciated the new parts warehouse over three years with no residual value.

E. The owner's personal car was included among the assets on the balance sheet of his business.

F. All the amounts on a company's financial statements were reported in U.S. dollars.

Required: Indicate the concept that applies to each scenario and state whether the concept was violated or followed. Justify your answer.

Analyze: Explain why the accounting records are not adjusted for the effects of inflation.

LO1, 2 **PROBLEM 1-4** **Financial Statement Concepts**

Select the best answer for the following multiple-choice questions:

1. Which of the following concepts relates to cost allocation?

    a. Going concern   c. Revenue recognition
    b. Monetary unit   d. Matching

2. The process of reporting an item in the financial statements of an entity is

    a. allocation.   c. conservatism.
    b. matching.   d. recognition.

3. Which of the following is an essential characteristic of an asset?

    a. The claims to an asset's benefits must be owned by the enterprise.
    b. An asset is tangible.
    c. An asset is obtained at a cost.
    d. An asset provides future benefits.

Analyze: The practice of recording adjusting entries for accruals and deferrals helps accountants adhere to which underlying concept?

LO1, 2 **PROBLEM 1-5** **Elements and Concepts**

The FASB's conceptual framework identifies the elements of financial statements and various assumptions, principles, and constraints that guide financial reporting. Several descriptions of these terms are listed in the left column below, while several terms are listed in the right column.

Concept Statement Definitions	Terms
1. The idea that revenues should be reported in the same accounting period as the expenses to which they are related	A. Recognition
2. Increases in net assets from peripheral transactions affecting an entity	B. Full disclosure
3. The process of converting noncash resources and rights into cash or claims to cash	C. Losses
4. A prudent reaction to uncertainty	D. Revenues
5. The process of formally recording an item in the financial statements of an entity after it has met reporting criteria	E. Periodicity
6. The requirement that the financial statements and notes contain any information that is material enough to change the decisions of users	F. Conservatism
7. Inflows or other enhancements of the assets of an entity or settlements of its liabilities from delivering or producing goods, rendering services, or carrying on other activities that constitute the entity's ongoing operations	G. Gains

8. Outflows or other using up of assets or incurrences of liabilities	H. Net Income
9. The belief that it is meaningful to measure a firm's activities in terms of arbitrary time periods even though the firm's life is considered to be indefinite	I. Expenses
	J. Realization
	K. Matching

Required: For each of the items listed in the first column, select the best answer from the list of terms. Terms may be used once, more than once, or not at all. (CPA adapted)

Analyze: If an accountant chooses to value a building at its market value rather than its lower original cost, which principle has been violated?

SECTION B

LO4, 5 **PROBLEM 1-6 Comprehensive Accounting Cycle**

On September 1, 2005, Kelly Randolf and Paul Simple started a comic book industry newsletter called *Comic Times*. They produced the first month's edition during September. The following transactions occurred during their first month of operations:

Sept. 1 Comic Times, Inc. was formed when Kelly and Paul filed with the State of California and each received common stock in exchange for $10,000 in cash.

1 Applied for a loan with a bank and signed a note for $5,000 due in two years, at a 12 percent annual percentage rate.

1 Purchased a computer for $4,000 cash.

1 Purchased office supplies on account with Rapid Supplies for $1,500.

1 Paid $2,400 for a website to be used for the next two years (24 months).

1 Sold 1,800 one-year subscriptions for cash at $12 each.

30 Sold 400 more one-year subscriptions for cash at $12 each. These subscriptions begin on October 1.

30 Paid for the office supplies purchased on September 1 from Rapid Supplies.

30 Paid $200 for utilities for the month of September.

30 Paid Kelly and Paul a salary of $400 each for the month of September.

30 Declared and paid a total dividend of $160.

The following additional information is provided concerning the adjusting entries necessary at the end of September:

A. Interest is accrued at the end of each month.

B. The computer is estimated to last for two years and to have no residual value.

C. At the end of September, office supplies are counted and there are $1,200 of supplies on hand.

D. The website expense is recognized monthly.

E. Revenue is recognized in the period earned.

Required:

1. Journalize the September transactions. (Omit explanations.)

2. Journalize adjusting entries for September. Use September 30 as the date for each adjusting entry.

3. Prepare an income statement for Comic Times, Inc. for the month of September.

4. Prepare a statement of changes in stockholders' equity for the month of September.

5. Prepare a balance sheet for Comic Times, Inc. as of September 30, 2005.

Analyze: Total expenses are what percentage of total revenues for the month of September?

LO4, 5 **PROBLEM 1-7 Comprehensive Accounting Cycle**

On September 1, 2007, Nancy Wolf and John Kettle are ready to begin another year of operations for their Web newsletter. The newsletter is updated monthly and can be viewed during the year. The company had the following balances on August 31, 2007:

Cash	$10,000
Office Supplies	400
Computer Equipment	5,100
Accumulated Depreciation—Computer Equipment	1,700
Retained Earnings	3,800
Common Stock	10,000

The following transactions have taken place during the period from September 1, 2007, through August 31, 2008 (12 months):

Sept. 1   Applied for a loan with a bank and signed a note for $10,000 due August 31, 2008, at a 10 percent annual percentage rate.
1   Purchased office supplies for $2,000 on account.
1   Paid $2,000 for a website design and hosting service to be used for the next two years (24 months).
1   Sold 2,000 one-year subscriptions for cash at $12 each.
1   Paid two years of rent on office space for $3,000.
Dec. 1   Sold 4,000 one-year subscriptions for cash at $12 each.
Mar. 1   Sold 500 one-year subscriptions for cash at $12 each.
Aug. 31   Paid the bank loan in full, including interest.
31   Paid Nancy and John a salary of $10,000 each.
31   Declared and paid total dividends of $1,000.

Information concerning adjusting entries as of August 31, 2008 is as follows:

A. Utility bills received but not yet paid total $1,000.

B. The computer equipment was purchased on September 1, 2006, and is estimated to last three years and have no residual value. The company uses straight-line depreciation.

C. At the end of August, office supplies remaining on hand total $200.

D. Rent expense is recognized at the end of each accounting year.

E. Website expense is recognized at the end of each accounting year.

F. Revenue earned is recognized at the end of each accounting year.

Required:

1. Journalize the above transactions (omit explanations).

2. Journalize adjusting entries at August 31, 2008.

3. Prepare an income statement for Kettle and Wolf, Inc. for the year ended August 31, 2008.

4. Prepare a statement of changes in stockholders' equity for the year ended August 31, 2008.

5. Prepare a balance sheet for Kettle and Wolf, Inc. as of August 31, 2008.

Analyze: By what amount did total assets change in the fiscal year ended August 31, 2008?

Spreadsheet: Use a spreadsheet to prepare an income statement for Kettle and Wolf, Inc. for the year ended August 31, 2008.

LO5   PROBLEM 1-8   Cash- and Accrual-Basis Income Statements

Tami Shepler, a veterinarian, keeps the accounting records for her veterinary clinic on a cash basis. During 2005, clients paid $625,000 in fees, of which $4,200 were payments in advance for surgical procedures. At December 31, 2004, clients still owed $25,000, compared to $20,000 owed at December 31, 2005. Shepler paid expenses for 2005 amounting to $445,000. In addition, the clinic had $5,200 of invoices that were not paid at December 31, 2005, and $3,100 that were not paid as of the beginning of 2005.

Required:

1. Calculate the following amounts for Shepler Veterinary Clinic for the year ended December 31, 2005:

    a. Accrual-basis revenue   c. Accrual-basis expenses
    b. Cash-basis revenue   d. Cash-basis expenses

2. Prepare a comparative income statement for Shepler for the year ended December 31, 2005, using separate columns for cash-basis accounting and accrual-basis accounting.

Analyze: Why is the accrual accounting system considered the most accurate measure of the performance of a business operation?

LO5 **PROBLEM 1-9   Transaction Analysis and Accrual-Basis Expenses**
Dockley, Inc. began operations on May 1, 2005, and incurred the following transactions during May. Dockley uses straight-line depreciation.

A. Issued 600 shares of common stock for $21,000 cash.

B. Purchased office furniture with a five-year life for $7,000 by signing a four-year, 6 percent note for $6,000 and paying $1,000 in cash. Interest is due annually on April 30. Dockley estimates the furniture's residual value will be $1,000 at the end of its life.

C. Paid wages of $5,300 to employees.

D. Rented office space by paying rent totaling $4,000 for May and June.

E. Acquired merchandise from suppliers costing $12,400. As of May 31, $1,400 of this amount was still not paid.

F. Wages for the last week of May totaled $1,600, to be paid on June 4.

Required: Determine the amount of accrual-basis expenses for May 2005.

Analyze: For each transaction that does not affect expenses, indicate why not.

LO4 **PROBLEM 1-10   Analyzing Transactions**
Presented below are several accounts from the financial statements of AdCom, Inc., a multimedia advertising company, for the year ended May 31, 2005.

1. Cash
2. Accounts Receivable
3. Office Furniture
4. Accounts Payable
5. Common Stock
6. Retained Earnings
7. Dividends
8. Sales
9. Selling/Administrative Expenses
10. Interest Expense

Required: Each of these accounts has been assigned a number; use these numbers as answers for the transactions described below. Show the effect on the elements of the accounting equation by entering the account number(s) in the blank spaces under the respective accounting equation elements and indicate whether the entry for that account is a debit or a credit. The first transaction is completed for you.

	Assets =	Liabilities +	Stockholders' Equity	+ Revenue	− Expense
A. The company issues capital stock.	1 Debit		5 Credit		
B. The company purchases filing cabinets and desks on account.					
C. Payment is made for the office furniture purchased in item (B).					
D. Advertising services are sold to clients on account.					
E. Payment is received from the clients on account in item (D).					

	Assets = Liabilities +	Stockholders' Equity	+ Revenue − Expense
F. The company pays cash for the current month's rent.			
G. Customers pay cash for services rendered.			

Analyze: List the temporary accounts for AdCom, Inc. Why are these accounts considered temporary accounts?

LO4, 5   PROBLEM 1-11   Adjusting Entries

Office Shop Company has a fiscal year end of December 31. The company records adjusting entries only at year end. The company has provided information concerning transactions that occurred to aid in the year-end adjusting process.

A. Office Shop Company acquired equipment at a cost of $18,000 in 2000. The equipment is expected to be useful for 10 years and to have a $2,000 residual value.

B. The company paid its annual property insurance; the policy was effective May 1, 2005. The entire cost of $12,000 was debited to Prepaid Insurance when paid.

C. During 2005, the company collected $98,000 for services not yet performed. The balance in the Unearned Service Fees account at December 31, 2004 was $9,000. At the end of 2005, the amount still unearned is $2,500.

D. As of December 31, 2005, employees have earned wages amounting to $5,600, which will be paid on January 7, 2006.

E. At December 31, 2005 and 2004, the physical count of supplies on hand totaled $150 and $230, respectively. During 2005, the company purchased $2,000 of supplies on account, although only $1,800 had been paid for by the end of the year.

Required: Prepare adjusting entries necessary at December 31, 2005.

Analyze: How much would income be overstated or understated if Office Shop failed to recognize these adjustments? Consider each adjustment individually.

Communicate: Assume that you are training a new accounting clerk for Office Shop Company. In a memo to the new clerk, describe why adjusting entries are necessary.

LO4, 5   PROBLEM 1-12   Adjusting Entries and Partial Balance Sheet

DJ Dooby, Inc. is a distributor of pet foods in south Florida. DJ Dooby adjusts its accounts only at the end of its fiscal period, December 31. The account balances that follow were taken from DJ Dooby's unadjusted trial balance for the year ended December 31, 2005.

Accounts	Debit	Credit
Prepaid Insurance	$ 3,600	
Office Supplies	6,540	
Salaries Expense	97,300	
Customer Deposits		$32,500
Accounts Receivable	17,000	
Prepaid Advertising	12,000	

Selected information is provided to aid you in determining what adjustments are necessary for DJ Dooby at December 31, 2005.

A. The amount of insurance expired during the year is $2,200.

B. Office supplies purchased during the year totaled $6,200. A physical count at year end determined that $120 of supplies were on hand at December 31, 2005.

C. As of December 31, 2005, employees had earned $1,500 in salaries but had not yet been paid.

D. At December 31, customers still owed $23,000 to DJ Dooby, for purchases they made during the year.

E. Cash collections from customers during 2005 were $362,000. Total revenue for 2005 was $350,000. At year end, $7,000 of cash collected from customers was still unearned.

F. The company signed a 12-month advertising contract and paid $12,000 for it on June 1, 2005; the contract period began immediately.

Required:

1. Record all adjustments necessary at December 31, 2005.

2. Prepare a partial balance sheet showing the current assets and current liabilities that would be reported for DJ Dooby, Inc. at December 31, 2005.

3. How does the matching principle relate to accrual accounting?

Analyze: By what net amount do the accrual entries affect net income for the period?

LO5   PROBLEM 1-13   **Cash- and Accrual-Basis Income**

Digger Depot sells garden tools. The company has provided the following information for June 2005:

Cash sales to customers during June	$230,000
Costs incurred in June to be paid in July	26,000
Cash expenses paid during June	160,000
Costs deferred to July but paid for in June	21,000
Customers billed in June for work performed; payment due in July	32,000

Required: Answer the following questions:

1. How much will Digger Depot report as total expenses on its accrual-basis income statement?

2. How much will it report as total expenses on its cash-basis income statement?

3. What amount is reported for accounts receivable as of June 30, 2005, for Digger Depot under the accrual-basis system? Under the cash-basis system?

4. Prepare comparative income statements for Digger Depot for June 2005 under both accrual- and cash-basis accounting.

Analyze: Under which system, cash or accrual, will Digger Depot report more total liabilities? Explain.

LO4, 5   PROBLEM 1-14   **Financial Statement Calculations**

Reitvald Enterprises reports the following *selected* account balances at the end of 2005:

Dividends	$ 6,600
Utilities Payable	300
Accounts Payable	700
Dividends Payable	4,400
Prepaid Insurance	250
Customer Deposits	600
Cash	2,500
Retained Earnings, Jan. 1, 2004	5,000
Bonds Payable, due Dec. 31, 2005	4,000
Equipment	10,000
Accumulated Depreciation—Equipment	1,100
Administrative Expenses	9,800
Delivery Expense	100
Selling Expenses	1,500
Accounts Receivable	900
Common Stock, 1,500 shares	3,000

Sales Revenue	82,800
Cost of Goods Sold	67,100
Allowance for Doubtful Accounts	50

Required: Answer the following questions:

1. How much are current liabilities at December 31, 2005?

2. Suppose net income amounts to $4,300 for 2005. How much has Reitvald earned since it began operations that has not actually been distributed as dividends?

3. Given the assumptions in part 2, prepare a statement of changes in stockholders' equity for 2005 for Reitvald Enterprises.

4. Which accounts are contra accounts?

Analyze: By what percentage did total stockholders' equity change during fiscal year 2005?

LO4, 5 **PROBLEM 1-15** **Adjusting and Closing Entries**
Use the accounts provided in Problem 1-14.

Required:

1. Based on these accounts, prepare closing entries for Reitvald Enterprises for 2005.

2. Draw a T-account for the Retained Earnings account and post all closing entries to this account.

Communicate: Explain the purpose and importance of closing. What role does a post-closing trial balance play in the accounting process?

Analyze: Based on the selected accounts provided, what net income is reported for 2005?

LO4, 5 **PROBLEM 1-16** **Adjusting and Closing Entries**
Cana Company's accounts reflected the following selected balances at the end of 2005 just prior to closing:

Service Revenue	$82,000	Land	$17,000
Salaries Expense	21,000	Depreciation Expense	3,000
Accumulated Depreciation—		Retained Earnings	12,000
Equipment	13,000	Accounts Receivable	20,000
Rent Expense	7,000	Prepaid Rent	2,000
Salaries Payable	1,000	Accounts Payable	4,000

Required:

1. Identify the accounts that would probably have been affected by an adjusting entry. Indicate what adjustment would have been made and the effect it had on the accounts.

2. Prepare closing entries for Cana Company for 2005.

Analyze: If service revenue for the prior year was $65,000, by what percentage did service revenue increase in 2005?

LO4, 5 **PROBLEM 1-17** **Adjusting Entries and Financial Statement Amounts**
Information concerning events that occurred during 2005 for Severt, Inc. is provided. Assume a year end of December 31.

Required: For each item, answer the question. The items are independent.

1. On March 1, 2005, Severt, Inc. loaned $10,000 to another company on a 12 percent, one-year note. Prepare the adjusting entry required at December 31, 2005.

2. Insurance totaling $3,600 represents a two-year policy beginning on October 1, 2004, for which Severt paid cash on October 1. How much expense will Severt report for 2005 as a result of this transaction?

3. The wages payable on Severt's balance sheet at January 1, 2005, and December 31, 2005, were $54,000 and $51,000, respectively. The amount of wages on the income statement for 2005 was $842,000. Determine the amount of wages Severt paid during the year.

4. Severt, Inc. pays weekly advertising fees of $7,500 every Friday for a five-day week ending on the Friday of payment. In 2005, December 31 was on a Wednesday. How much will Severt report as advertising payable at December 31, 2005?

5. On July 1, 2005, Severt purchased equipment costing $90,000, paying $30,000 in cash and signing a one-year, 8 percent note payable for the balance. It is estimated that the equipment will have a residual value of $8,000 and a 10-year useful life. How much depreciation should Severt recognize during 2005?

Analyze: Use the information in part 5. How much interest payable should Severt recognize at December 31, 2005?

LO5 PROBLEM **1-18 Adjusting Entries**
On January 1, 2005, Armstrong Educational Consulting had these account balances:

Office Supplies	$14,600	Salaries Payable	18,000
Rent Expense	24,000	Unearned Consulting Revenue	15,000

The Rent Expense account balance represents two remaining years of rent that was paid in advance on January 1, 2005. When originally paid, the prepaid rent was recorded in the Rent Expense account. Unearned consulting revenue of $15,000 at January 1, 2005 was the result of a twelve-month contract that Armstrong Educational Consulting signed on October 1, 2004. During 2005, the following summary transactions related to these and certain other accounts occurred:

A. Salaries: All salaries owed as of January 1, 2005 were paid. Salaries earned and paid during 2005 amounted to $150,000. Salaries unpaid as of December 31, 2005 amounted to $17,000.

B. Office Supplies: During the year, additional office supplies of $35,000 were purchased on account. The account was paid in full before the end of 2005. The firm follows the policy of recording the purchase originally in the Office Supplies Expense account. At December 31, 2005, $5,000 of supplies remain on hand.

C. Rent: Rent expense and prepaid rent must be recognized at December 31, 2005.

D. Unearned Consulting Revenue: The current consulting contract expired at the end of its term. However, on September 1, 2005 Armstrong Educational Consulting signed a new contract with another client for $36,000 and received that amount in cash. The contract has a six-month term. The company's policy is to record the entire revenue when received in the Consulting Revenue account.

E. Note Receivable: On March 1, 2005, Armstrong Educational Consulting made a loan to a key employee to secure that individual's employment at the firm. The note, for $150,000, was fully payable in a lump sum plus interest (6 percent) in two years.

Required:

1. Prepare the necessary entries, without explanations, to record the summary transactions during the year.

2. Assuming that the company prepares financial statements annually, make the necessary adjusting entries for these accounts at December 31, 2005.

3. State the correct balances in each of the relevant accounts as of December 31, 2005.

CASES

LO1, 2, 3 RESEARCH CASE **1-1 QUALCOMM Financial Data**
The auditors' report for **QUALCOMM, Inc.** was discussed in the Financial Reporting Case at the beginning of this chapter. Using the Internet, locate the 2003 QUALCOMM, Inc. financial statements and answer the following questions.

Required:

1. What amount of total assets did the company report for the year ended September 30, 2003?

2. What sources of revenue did the company list on its statement of operations?

3. What amount of cash dividends were paid to stockholders in 2003?

4. Using the Internet, locate the 2004 QUALCOMM, Inc. financial statements and review the Report of the Independent Accountants. In what ways, if any, does this report differ from the one in 2003? What is the significance of the changes, if any?

LO1, 2   **COMMUNICATION CASE 1-2   Need for Accounting Information**
You are the accounting manager for Michelman's Mulch, Inc. Shortly after beginning work with the company, Earle Traynham, the new CEO, asked to meet with you. He questioned the costs incurred by the accounting department during the past year.

"The budget for the accounting department exceeds that of all the other support services of the company combined. I think this is a good place to cut expenses," stated Earle. "I don't think we need financial statements every quarter. No one ever reads them anyway! The company has done well over the past few years, so there is no need to have financial reports issued so frequently. I would like the accounting department to issue financial statements every other year instead of quarterly. We can then eliminate several of the accounting positions and reduce departmental costs by 30 percent. Please have your report detailing which positions you plan to cut to me by next week."

You disagree with the CEO's assessment and believe that frequent financial reporting is critical to investors.

Required: Prepare a memo response to the CEO from the accounting manager giving your views on the issue and how his request relates to GAAP. Support your comments using concepts from this chapter. Do not suggest alternatives to reduce costs.

LO1, 2   **ANALYSIS CASE 1-3   Accrual Accounting**
Cloran Industries is preparing to issue GAAP accrual-basis financial statements for the first time, in conjunction with applying for a line of credit with Wachovia Bank. Cloran Industries manufactures DVD display stands for DVD retailers. The company had previously used the cash basis of accounting for all of its management reporting needs. Jan Scott, the controller, is concerned that several types of transactions may need special attention during the conversion process, including the following:

A. The company bills its customers as soon as an order is received from a customer. Shipments occur about 10 days after the receipt of an order.

B. Cloran prepays its property liability insurance for the factory and headquarters two months in advance of the coverage date.

C. Cloran does not pay some of the invoices it receives from suppliers until the month after the invoice is received.

Required: Briefly explain how each of these items should be accounted for under accrual-basis accounting.

LO1, 2   **CRITICAL THINKING CASE 1-4   Revenue Recognition**
As controller of Techniques Factory, you are currently performing the annual closing process. You are concerned with the implications of the following scenario:

Techniques Factory has accrued revenue during 2004 for delivery of 80 stereo systems to Circuit Town, scheduled for January 3, 2005. Management justifies this accrual because the order was intended to be delivered on the last business day of 2004; however, United Parcel Service was overwhelmed with shipments and pushed the delivery to the next business day, which fell in 2005. The total value of the inventory involved is $35,000. In the past, Circuit Town has been known to return unsold merchandise frequently. However, management believes that January sales events should prevent this from happening. The company has a line of credit with a local bank. Communications with the bank have indicated that the bank will not extend the credit line beyond 2004 unless Techniques Factory shows adequate profitability for 2004. A calculation of the impact of the accrual indicates that Techniques will report a $300 loss for the year if the order is not accrued.

Required: Discuss the factors to be considered in recognizing revenue. Do you think revenue should be recognized in 2004 in this situation?

ON THE WEB

BRIDGE TUTORIAL

Once you have completed this chapter, assess your knowledge of the accounting foundations topics by taking the **Post-test** offered on the CD-ROM.

The following exercises, activities, and problems are available on the *Intermediate Accounting* website. Use these resources to reinforce your understanding of the topics presented in this chapter.

- CPA-Adapted Simulations
- Interpreting the Accounting Standards
- Extending the Global Focus
- Mastering the Spreadsheet
- Career Snapshots
- Annual Report Project

- ACE Practice Tests
- Flashcards
- Glossary
- Check Figures for Text Problems
- PowerPoint Presentations

SOLUTIONS: CHECK YOUR UNDERSTANDING

SECTION A (p. 15)

1. Assets, liabilities, and stockholders' equity (or owners' equity).

2. Going concern assumption.

3. Income statement, statement of changes in stockholders' equity, and statement of cash flows. Each of these statements presents financial data over a period of time rather than at a point in time.

4. Balance sheet.

5. Cash-basis accounting is the practice of recording revenues when cash is received and recording expenses when cash is paid. Accrual accounting records transactions and other events in the period in which they occurred rather than in the period in which cash or some other form of payment is received or paid.

6. Cash flows from operating activities, cash flows from investing activities, and cash flows from financing activities.

7. Conservatism requires accountants, when faced with a choice, to select the accounting method that is least likely to overstate net income and the financial position of the firm. It is a prudent reaction to uncertainty to try to ensure that the uncertainty and risks inherent in business situations are adequately considered.

SECTION B (p. 36)

1. A debit to an asset account represents an increase; a debit to a liability account represents a decrease; a debit to a stockholders' equity account represents a decrease.

2. Permanent accounts are asset, liability, and stockholders' equity accounts (including Capital Stock, Paid-in Capital, and Retained Earnings) that have balances that continue from one accounting period to the next and reflect the actual amounts in those accounts at any point in time. Temporary accounts are closed at the end of each accounting period and are used to record changes in retained earnings.

3. Step 1: Identify and gather information about economic events and transactions. Step 2: Analyze and record each transaction. Step 3: Post journal entries to the general ledger. Step 4: Prepare an unadjusted trial balance. Step 5: Record and post adjusting journal entries and prepare an adjusted trial balance. Step 6: Prepare the financial statements. Step 7: Record and post closing entries and prepare a post-closing trial balance.

4. The purpose of posting is to keep track of how transactions affect individual accounts. Posting is the process of transferring transaction information from the journal to the individual accounts in the general ledger.

5. Adjusting entries are needed to record the financial effects of transactions and events that cover more than one accounting period and to make the estimates and other changes necessary to bring the accounts to their actual balances.

6. Debit to Salaries Expense $2,200; credit to Salaries Payable $2,200.

7. Close all revenue accounts to Income Summary. Close all expense accounts to Income Summary. Close the Income Summary account to Retained Earnings. Close the Dividends account to Retained Earnings.

CPA-ADAPTED SIMULATION

This simulation asks you to complete various tasks related to a company's annual financial statements. If your instructor has signed up for CPAexcel™, you can do the work online at www.cpaexcel.com/hmco. You may also do the simulation manually.

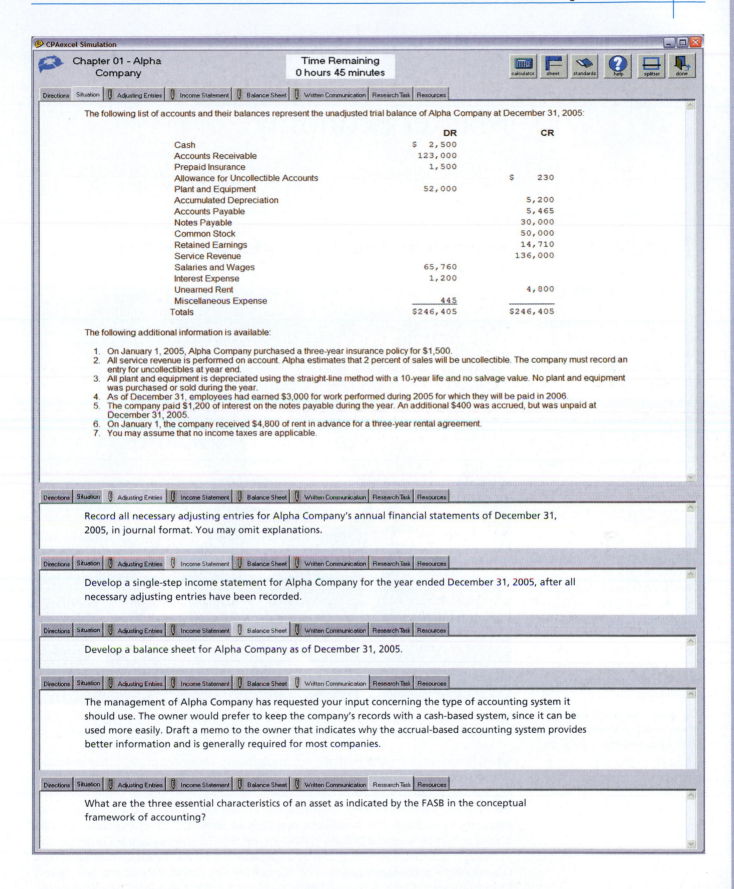

CPAexcel Simulation

Chapter 01 - Alpha Company

Time Remaining
0 hours 45 minutes

calculator | sheet | standards | help | splitter | done

Directions | Situation | Adjusting Entries | Income Statement | Balance Sheet | Written Communication | Research Task | Resources

The following list of accounts and their balances represent the unadjusted trial balance of Alpha Company at December 31, 2005:

	DR	CR
Cash	$ 2,500	
Accounts Receivable	123,000	
Prepaid Insurance	1,500	
Allowance for Uncollectible Accounts		$ 230
Plant and Equipment	52,000	
Accumulated Depreciation		5,200
Accounts Payable		5,465
Notes Payable		30,000
Common Stock		50,000
Retained Earnings		14,710
Service Revenue		136,000
Salaries and Wages	65,760	
Interest Expense	1,200	
Unearned Rent		4,800
Miscellaneous Expense	445	
Totals	$246,405	$246,405

The following additional information is available:

1. On January 1, 2005, Alpha Company purchased a three-year insurance policy for $1,500.
2. All service revenue is performed on account. Alpha estimates that 2 percent of sales will be uncollectible. The company must record an entry for uncollectibles at year end.
3. All plant and equipment is depreciated using the straight-line method with a 10-year life and no salvage value. No plant and equipment was purchased or sold during the year.
4. As of December 31, employees had earned $3,000 for work performed during 2005 for which they will be paid in 2006.
5. The company paid $1,200 of interest on the notes payable during the year. An additional $400 was accrued, but was unpaid at December 31, 2005.
6. On January 1, the company received $4,800 of rent in advance for a three-year rental agreement.
7. You may assume that no income taxes are applicable.

Directions | Situation | Adjusting Entries | Income Statement | Balance Sheet | Written Communication | Research Task | Resources

Record all necessary adjusting entries for Alpha Company's annual financial statements of December 31, 2005, in journal format. You may omit explanations.

Directions | Situation | Adjusting Entries | Income Statement | Balance Sheet | Written Communication | Research Task | Resources

Develop a single-step income statement for Alpha Company for the year ended December 31, 2005, after all necessary adjusting entries have been recorded.

Directions | Situation | Adjusting Entries | Income Statement | Balance Sheet | Written Communication | Research Task | Resources

Develop a balance sheet for Alpha Company as of December 31, 2005.

Directions | Situation | Adjusting Entries | Income Statement | Balance Sheet | Written Communication | Research Task | Resources

The management of Alpha Company has requested your input concerning the type of accounting system it should use. The owner would prefer to keep the company's records with a cash-based system, since it can be used more easily. Draft a memo to the owner that indicates why the accrual-based accounting system provides better information and is generally required for most companies.

Directions | Situation | Adjusting Entries | Income Statement | Balance Sheet | Written Communication | Research Task | Resources

What are the three essential characteristics of an asset as indicated by the FASB in the conceptual framework of accounting?

CHAPTER TWO

Financial Reporting: The Cornerstone of a Market Economy

FINANCIAL REPORTING CASE

SIGNING OF THE SARBANES-OXLEY ACT OF 2002

Representative Michael Oxley (left) and Senator Paul Sarbanes announce the signing of the Sarbanes-Oxley Act, sending a message to corporate leaders and the accounting profession.

When President George W. Bush signed the Sarbanes-Oxley Act of 2002, the landscape of the accounting profession and external financial reporting changed forever. While accounting professionals have demonstrated decades of reputable professionalism, the individual actions of a few unethical individuals have affected the profession significantly. In addition, the fraudulent practices of some U.S. chief executive officers (CEOs) and chief financial officers (CFOs) forced the U.S. Congress, the Securities and Exchange Commission (SEC), and the president to take unprecedented action. Questionable accounting practices in companies like Enron, WorldCom, and Qwest Communications included overstating earnings, booking expenses as investments, and hiding debt. As a result, businesses and the accounting profession are subject to more oversight and regulation than at any other time in history.

The East Room
10:15 A.M. EDT
July 30, 2002

THE PRESIDENT: Thank you very much. Welcome to the White House, and welcome to this historic occasion.

My administration pressed for greater corporate integrity. A united Congress has written it into law. And today I sign the most far-reaching reforms of American business practices since the time of Franklin Delano Roosevelt. This new law sends very clear messages that all concerned must heed. This law says to every dishonest corporate leader: you will be exposed and punished; the era of low standards and false profits is over; no boardroom in America is above or beyond the law.

This law says to honest corporate leaders: your integrity will be recognized and rewarded, because the shadow of suspicion will be lifted from good companies that respect the rules.

This law says to corporate accountants: the high standards of your profession will be enforced without exception; the auditors will be audited; the accountants will be held to account.

This law says to shareholders that the financial information you receive from a company will be true and reliable, for those who deliberately sign their names to deception will be punished.

This law says to workers: we will not tolerate reckless practices that artificially drive up stock prices and eventually destroy the companies, and the pensions, and your jobs.

Today, we are taking practical steps to encourage honest enterprise in our nation. Under this law, CEOs and chief financial officers must personally vouch for the truth and fairness of their companies' disclosures. Those financial disclosures will be broader and better for the sake of shareholders and investors.

For the first time, the accounting profession will be regulated by an independent board. This board will set clear standards to uphold the integrity of public audits, and have the authority to investigate abuses and discipline offenders. And auditing firms will no longer be permitted to provide consulting services that create conflicts of interest.

It is now my honor to sign the Sarbanes-Oxley Act of 2002.[1]

As the accounting industry makes the transition into a new era, the development of financial reporting standards is more important than ever. Participants in the development of these standards include players from both the public and the private sector—all of them keenly interested in the efficient functioning of our market economy.

EXAMINING THE CASE

1. Based on this excerpt from President Bush's remarks, what primary message is the Sarbanes-Oxley Act intended to send to the accounting profession and to corporate leaders?

2. What types of questionable accounting practices led to the signing of the Sarbanes-Oxley Act?

3. The Sarbanes-Oxley Act includes provisions regarding conflicts of interest for auditing firms. What types of situations do you think might cause conflicts of interest for an accounting professional?

---

1 Press release, "President Bush Signs Corporate Corruption Bill," The White House, July 30, 2002.

LO1 Describe the economic and regulatory purposes of financial reporting.

Critical Thinking: What circumstances in your personal life have required the reporting of financial data? For what purpose were the data required? What business events can you describe that might require financial reporting?

The Economic and Regulatory Purposes of Financial Reporting

Present and potential investors and creditors, federal and state governments, unions, employee groups, and a variety of other organizations need reliable and timely financial information to guide them in their investment and business decisions. This drives the economic demand for financial information. Many government agencies require financial information to enforce the regulations for which they are responsible. This drives the regulatory need for financial information.

THE ECONOMIC DEMAND FOR FINANCIAL INFORMATION

The efficient functioning of a market economy like that in the United States and many other parts of the world depends on the production of reliable and relevant financial information about the firms in which individuals and institutions may invest. Investors give up the present use of resources, usually cash, in return for an uncertain flow of future cash receipts. They need financial information to help them make informed and rational choices among investing opportunities. When investors have more financial information, they can assess future cash flows with greater certainty. Therefore, if firms want to attract affordable capital, it is in their best interest to supply reliable financial information to the market.

Financial reporting, including the preparation and dissemination of financial statements and related data, has evolved and continues to evolve to meet the needs of the investing public. Published financial reports are one of the primary sources of data for financial analysis, and determining and ensuring the quality of the information in those reports is fundamental to the capital allocation process.

Privately held firms, even though their stock is not publicly traded and they are thus exempt from certain regulatory requirements, also need to produce reliable external financial reports. For example, creditors require reliable financial information about a firm before they will lend it money, and suppliers need reliable financial information about a firm before they will extend it credit for purchases.

Although investors and creditors are usually considered the most significant external users of financial information, many other parties also need the information contained in financial reports and thus have a substantial stake in accounting standards. For example, employees may require financial information for labor contract negotiations, and customers might seek financial information to assess whether a company will be able to back up its product warranty over time.

The controversies surrounding the financial troubles and ultimate bankruptcies at **US Airways** and **United Airlines** in 2002 provide insight into the extensive range of groups that depend on reported financial information. Negotiations over labor costs were critical for both airlines as they tried to restructure. Engine suppliers such as **General Electric** and plane manufacturers such as **Boeing** and **Airbus** have important stakes in the financial health of the airlines. The traveling public also has a clear interest in the companies' financial fortunes. From a business perspective, safe, reliable, and efficient travel is essential; on a personal level, many individuals stand to lose valuable frequent flyer miles if the airlines cease operations.

The need for external reporting is not restricted to profit-seeking corporations. Not-for-profit organizations and government agencies also publish financial information to hold managers and elected officials accountable for their actions. Reports on the receipt and use of donations and tax revenues are published to enable interested parties to assess how efficiently not-for-profit and government organizations are being managed.

Managers also use financial information for a variety of internal purposes—assessing the performance of a division or segment, considering the purchase of assets,

management accounting the process of producing financial information for internal purposes

financial accounting the process of providing financial information for investors, creditors, and other external parties

or planning future growth, to name a few. **Management accounting** is the process of producing financial information for internal purposes, whereas **financial accounting** is the process of providing financial information for investors, creditors, and other external parties. Regardless of whether management or financial accounting is involved, all users of financial information demand accurate and practical information that will help them make informed decisions.

University students also have an important stake in financial information. Whether you are attending a private or a public university, you are likely to be interested in the tuition and room and board charges and how those charges reflect the cost of providing high-quality education. The financial health of the institution you are attending is critical to its ability to meet your educational needs. Many public and private universities make their financial statements available to the public.

THE REGULATORY DEMAND FOR FINANCIAL INFORMATION

Securities and Exchange Commission (SEC) an agency created by Congress to regulate the securities market and protect public investors from fraud or inadequate financial disclosures

The economic demand for financial information is driven by the needs of current and potential investors and creditors. There is also a regulatory demand for financial information—that is, certain government entities require financial reporting. The **Securities and Exchange Commission (SEC)** was created by Congress to regulate the securities market and protect public investors from fraud or inadequate financial disclosures. This government body requires publicly traded firms to submit a variety of reports that provide significant financial information. The Internal Revenue Service (IRS), another government agency, requires financial reporting to enable it to enforce its tax codes. Other federal bodies, such as the Federal Energy Regulatory Commission and the Federal Trade Commission, use financial information in promulgating their regulations. State and local governments and agencies use financial information in a variety of ways, including the awarding of franchises to cable companies and other telecommunication firms. In 2002 and 2003, hearings were held by the State of California and the Federal Energy Regulatory Commission concerning over $9 billion in alleged overcharges by various utility companies. Financial information was at the heart of the hearings, with extremely high stakes for all involved.

CHECK YOUR UNDERSTANDING

1. Explain how financial accounting differs from management accounting.

2. Identify several users that generate the economic demand for external financial reporting. Why are these groups interested in financial data?

3. Describe the government agencies that require financial reporting to perform their regulatory duties.

LO2 Identify the groups that establish accounting standards and describe their roles in the standard-setting process.

Sarbanes-Oxley Act legislation enacted to protect shareholders and the general public from accounting errors and fraudulent business practices; also known as the Public Company Accounting Reform and Investor Protection Act

Setting Accounting Standards: A Public-Private Partnership

The setting of accounting standards in the United States is a complex process that involves both the private and the public sector. The cases of fraudulent financial reporting that occurred in the early 2000s focused the attention of the public and Congress on how accounting standards are set and implemented. As noted in the Financial Reporting Case at the beginning of this chapter, the **Sarbanes-Oxley Act**, also known as the *Public Company Accounting Reform and Investor Protection Act,* was enacted to protect shareholders and the general public from accounting errors and fraudulent business practices. The act is administered by the SEC and introduces new regulatory requirements into an already complex standard-setting process. The

Illustration 2.1

Groups That Influence GAAP

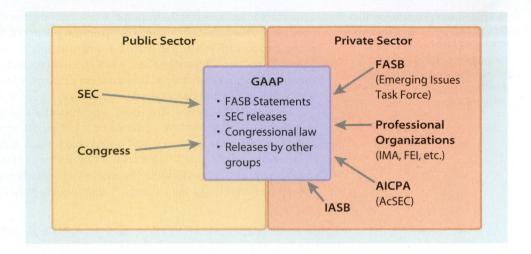

primary participants in setting standards in the United States are the SEC, the Financial Accounting Standards Board (FASB), and the American Institute of Certified Public Accountants (AICPA). However, other organizations influence the process, including some outside the United States. All these groups issue various standards, reports, bulletins, and positions that, taken together, constitute what is known as **generally accepted accounting principles (GAAP)**—the conventions, rules, and procedures that guide the preparation of financial statements by either law, regulation, or custom. Illustration 2.1 provides an overview of the groups that influence GAAP. These groups will be discussed in the sections that follow.

generally accepted accounting principles (GAAP) conventions, rules, and procedures that guide the preparation of financial statements by either law, regulation, or custom

Critical Thinking: Why do you think the setting of accounting standards has been referred to as a political process? What groups have significant interests in this process?

THE PUBLIC-SECTOR STANDARD SETTER: THE SECURITIES AND EXCHANGE COMMISSION

In reaction to the great stock market crash of 1929, Congress enacted the Securities Act of 1933 and the Securities Exchange Act of 1934, the latter of which established the Securities and Exchange Commission (SEC). The SEC regulates U.S. securities markets through powers granted by Congress and has the authority to set accounting and reporting standards. This agency, headquartered in Washington, D.C., has five commissioners, four divisions, and eighteen offices throughout the United States. Although the size of its staff has grown in recent years, the SEC, with just over 3,000 employees, is a small organization by federal agency standards. The SEC's five commissioners are appointed by the president with the advice and consent of the Senate. The commissioners' terms last five years and are staggered so that one commissioner's term ends in June of each year. To limit partisanship, no more than three commissioners may belong to the same political party. The president also designates one of the commissioners as chairperson, the SEC's top executive. Legislation in the early 2000s strengthened the SEC's oversight authority and provided it with significantly more resources. Of course, actual year-to-year funding depends on the president's budget and congressional authorizations.

The main function of the SEC is to regulate the capital markets so that public investors are protected from fraud or inadequate disclosures about the financial position and performance of public firms. The SEC requires publicly traded companies (companies whose stock is traded on an exchange and that are required to be listed with the SEC) to follow generally accepted accounting principles, to be audited by an independent certified public accountant (CPA), and to follow the SEC rules on corporate disclosure. From time to time, the SEC issues Staff Accounting Bulletins and Financial Reporting Releases (FRR), which contain accounting rules and other reporting requirements. The SEC website (www.sec.gov) offers a host of information, including SEC filings by publicly traded firms, new SEC rules, proposed SEC rules, and public statements made by SEC officials.

Public Company Accounting Oversight Board a five-member body created by the Sarbanes-Oxley Act that is responsible for establishing standards relating to the preparation of audit reports, conducting inspections of accounting firms, and conducting investigations and disciplinary proceedings and imposing appropriate sanctions

Although the SEC has the legal authority to set accounting principles and standards, in the past it deferred to agencies in the private sector to set standards. However, the Sarbanes-Oxley Act of 2002 significantly changed the SEC's role in setting accounting standards. The provisions of that act established the **Public Company Accounting Oversight Board** under the auspices of the SEC. The board has five full-time members appointed by the SEC, and among its responsibilities and duties are to

● Establish or adopt by rule auditing, quality control, ethics, independence, and other standards relating to the preparation of audit reports by the issuers of those reports

● Conduct inspections of accounting firms

● Conduct investigations and disciplinary proceedings, and impose appropriate sanctions[2]

Most important, from the perspective of external financial reporting, the oversight board is required to cooperate on an ongoing basis with designated professional groups of accountants and any advisory groups convened in connection with standard setting. The board can, to the extent it determines appropriate, adopt standards proposed by those groups, but it also has the authority to amend, modify, repeal, or reject any suggested standards. Although the SEC has always had the power to veto any standards set by other groups, the Sarbanes-Oxley Act makes that power explicit and sets up the expectation that the SEC will exercise it as needed.

The Public Company Accounting Oversight Board was first organized in 2002, but the SEC met with considerable controversy in selecting its first chair. Finally, after several false starts, William J. McDonough, the long-time president of the Federal Reserve Bank of New York, was selected as the initial chair.

PRIVATE-SECTOR STANDARD SETTERS

The American Institute of Certified Public Accountants and the Financial Accounting Standards Board are the two primary private-sector accounting-standard setters in the United States. Other professional organizations, investor groups, and the business community also influence the process.

▶ AMERICAN INSTITUTE OF CERTIFIED PUBLIC ACCOUNTANTS

American Institute of Certified Public Accountants (AICPA) the national organization representing certified public accountants; along with the FASB, one of the two primary private-sector accounting-standard setters in the United States

Committee on Accounting Procedure (CAP) a committee of the AICPA that set accounting standards until 1959, when it was replaced by the Accounting Principles Board (APB)

Accounting Principles Board (APB) a committee of the AICPA that set accounting standards from 1959 to 1973

The **American Institute of Certified Public Accountants (AICPA)**, first established in 1887 as the American Institute of Accountants, is the national organization representing certified public accountants. Until 1973, the AICPA was the private-sector organization that was responsible for setting accounting standards and principles. It did so through two committees. The first of these was the **Committee on Accounting Procedure (CAP)**, which set standards until 1959, when it was replaced by another AICPA committee, the **Accounting Principles Board (APB)**. Both the CAP and the APB functioned on a part-time basis. The APB issued 31 Accounting Principles Board Opinions from 1959 to 1973, when it was disbanded as a result of questions about its independence from the profession and its lack of full-time members and staff. Because all members of the CAP and the APB were CPAs, many individuals outside the profession contended that the groups' rulings were biased in favor of CPAs in the auditing profession and their clients. Other users of financial statements, such as regulators and investors, questioned the APB's independence because its members served only part-time and often continued to work for their former full-time employers. The APB's inability to develop a coherent structure for its opinions was also of concern. Nonetheless, unless the pronouncements of the APB have been specifically replaced by

---

2 According to the act, the board is to have five financially literate members, appointed for five-year terms. Two of the members must be or must have been certified public accountants, and the remaining three must not be and must not have been CPAs. The chair may be held by one of the CPA members, provided that he or she has not been engaged as a practicing CPA for five years.

subsequent standards (as is often the case), they are considered generally accepted accounting principles.

The AICPA continues to have influence in the standard-setting process, including the setting of auditing standards. The AICPA contributes to standard setting through its **Accounting Standards Executive Committee (AcSEC)**, which advises the FASB on agenda items and provides guidance to AICPA members on issues that have not yet been addressed by FASB standards. The AICPA also issues various practice bulletins, industry guides, and statements of position, all of which are part of the large body of accounting knowledge, standards, and regulations that is accepted as GAAP.

> ## FINANCIAL ACCOUNTING STANDARDS BOARD

The **Financial Accounting Standards Board (FASB)** was created in 1973 and is the current private-sector board that develops accounting principles and standards. It was organized as an independent organization with full-time board members and an appropriate staff to overcome some of the perceived independence problems of the APB and to establish a more professional organization for standard setting in the United States. As noted earlier, only the SEC has the legal authority to issue accounting standards for publicly traded firms, but since 1973, the SEC has looked to the FASB and other bodies to perform that function.[3] Of course, now, with the creation of the new Public Company Accounting Oversight Board, the SEC may be pressured into taking a more active role in standard setting than in the past.

> ### THE MISSION AND COMPOSITION OF THE FASB
The mission of the Financial Accounting Standards Board is to establish and improve standards of financial accounting and reporting for the guidance and education of the public, including preparers, auditors, and other users of financial information. The FASB accomplishes this mission in a variety of ways, but most importantly through the issuance of Statements of Financial Accounting Standards, Statements of Financial Accounting Concepts, and various interpretations and technical bulletins. The **Statements of Financial Accounting Standards (SFASs)** are a series of statements issued by the FASB that outline the accounting and reporting requirements for particular accounting issues. The **Statements of Financial Accounting Concepts (SFACs)** are a series of statements that outline the fundamental objectives and concepts established by the FASB to form a cohesive framework and serve as tools for solving existing and emerging accounting problems. In 1984, the FASB established the **Emerging Issues Task Force (EITF)** as a separate body to consider and resolve emerging issues. This task force develops and distributes EITF Issues, which are part of GAAP. If the EITF is unable to reach a consensus on an important emerging issue, that issue may be put on the FASB's agenda.

The FASB consists of seven full-time members who are required to sever all connections with the firms or institutions that they served prior to joining the board. Members come from diverse backgrounds, but all must possess knowledge of accounting, finance, and business and be concerned for the public interest in matters of financial accounting and reporting. Each board member is appointed for a five-year term and is eligible for reappointment to one additional five-year term. A change in the way the FASB is funded has resulted from the Sarbanes-Oxley Act. The FASB used to be funded through the efforts of the Financial Accounting Foundation, the body that oversees the FASB and appoints members to it. However, now the FASB must be funded by annual accounting support fees paid by the issuers of financial statements. Senator Christopher Dodd stated in the *Congressional Record* on July 25, 2002, that "having FASB now be compensated for and paid for from public money and not relying on the largess and generosity of the accounting industry to receive compensation will make a significant difference in establishing accounting rules and procedures."[4]

Accounting Standards Executive Committee (AcSEC) a committee of the AICPA that advises the FASB on agenda items and provides guidance to AICPA members on issues that have not yet been addressed by FASB standards

Financial Accounting Standards Board (FASB) the private-sector organization that establishes generally accepted accounting principles in the United States

Statements of Financial Accounting Standards (SFASs) a series of statements issued by the FASB that outline the accounting and reporting requirements for particular accounting issues

Statements of Financial Accounting Concepts (SFACs) a series of statements that outline the fundamental objectives and concepts established by the FASB to form a cohesive framework and serve as tools for solving existing and emerging accounting problems

Emerging Issues Task Force (EITF) a separate body established by the FASB to consider and try to resolve emerging issues

---

3 On several occasions, however, the SEC and even Congress have become directly involved in the handling of particular issues, such as the investment tax credit and, more recently, stock options.

4 *Congressional Record*, 107th Cong., 2nd sess., 2002, 148, pp. S7350–S7365.

Illustration 2.2

Participants and Their Contributions in the Standard-Setting Process

Participants	Significant Pronouncements
U.S. Congress	Laws
Securities and Exchange Commission (SEC)	Staff Accounting Bulletins (SABs)
	Financial Reporting Releases (FRRs)
Financial Accounting Standards Board (FASB)	Statements of Financial Accounting Standards (SFASs)
	Statements of Financial Accounting Concepts (SFACs)
	Interpretations
	Technical bulletins
	Emerging Issues Task Force issues
	Implementation guides
American Institute of Certified Public Accountants (AICPA)	Accounting Research Bulletins (ARBs)
	Accounting Principles Board Opinions (APBs)
	Industry Audit and Accounting Guides
	AICPA Statements of Position
	Accounting Standards Executive Committee Practice Bulletins
International Accounting Standards Board (IASB)	International Financial Reporting Standards (IFRS)
	International Accounting Standards (IASs)
Institute of Management Accountants (IMA)	Various publications—not authoritative
Financial Executives International (FEI)	Various publications—not authoritative

Institute of Management Accountants (IMA) an organization devoted primarily to management accounting and financial management that reports on professional opinions in its publications and also contributes to the standard-setting process by researching issues that it deems important to its constituency

Financial Executives International (FEI) a professional association for senior financial executives that provides peer networking opportunities, emerging issues alerts, personal and professional development, and advocacy services to chief financial officers, controllers, treasurers, tax executives, and finance and accounting professors

The FASB plays an important role in the standard-setting process, but it can continue in that role only as long as the public has confidence in its ability to be unbiased and efficient. The public must also continue to believe that the process allows all interested parties to be heard when a new standard is under consideration. The financial reporting failures that made headlines in 2001 and 2002 severely diminished the public's confidence in the FASB. The FASB is working hard to restore that confidence. The actual process that the FASB uses to develop accounting standards is discussed later in this chapter.

> **OTHER U.S. STANDARD-SETTING BODIES**

The **Institute of Management Accountants (IMA)**, an organization devoted primarily to management accounting and financial management, reports on professional opinions in its publications and also contributes to the standard-setting process by researching issues that it deems important to its constituency. The **Financial Executives International (FEI)**, a professional association for senior financial executives, provides peer networking opportunities, emerging issues alerts, personal and professional development, and advocacy services to chief financial officers, controllers, treasurers, tax executives, and finance and accounting professors. The FASB invites all interested parties, including the AICPA, IMA, and FEI, to comment on its current projects.

Illustration 2.2 outlines the groups within the United States that develop accounting standards and contribute to GAAP. Under the leadership of the SEC and the FASB, all these groups play a significant role.

1. Identify and describe the private-sector group that is most influential in the setting of accounting standards.

2. What types of accounting literature make up GAAP? Where does each type of literature originate?

3. What role does the SEC play in standard setting?

LO3 Describe the environment in which international accounting standards are set and identify the functions of the International Accounting Standards Board.

INTERNATIONAL

International Accounting Standards Board (IASB) an independent, privately funded body based in London that is committed to the development of a single set of international accounting standards

International Accounting Standards (IAS) accounting standards issued by the International Accounting Standards Committee between 1997 and 2002

International Financial Reporting Standards (IFRS) accounting standards issued by the International Accounting Standards Board

Critical Thinking: As a potential investor who is comparing the financial performance of a U.S.-based company with that of a company based in Switzerland, what issues are you likely to face? How might you deal with any significant accounting differences between these two companies?

An International Standard Setter: The IASB

With the emergence of a new global economy, the need for international accounting standards is increasingly critical. Multinational firms raise capital from investors around the world, and the shares of those companies are often traded both in New York and on international stock exchanges in London, Paris, Toronto, and other cities. The international movement of capital has driven the need for international accounting standards so that financial statements will be transparent regardless of where a firm is incorporated. Although a single set of international accounting standards is unlikely to be established anytime in the near future, standards that are more similar are emerging. This is due, in part, to the growing influence of the International Accounting Standards Board.

The **International Accounting Standards Board (IASB)** is an independent, privately funded, accounting-standard-setting body based in London. Board members come from nine countries and have a variety of functional backgrounds. According to its mission statement, "The Board is committed to developing, in the public interest, a single set of high quality, understandable and enforceable global accounting standards that require transparent and comparable information in general purpose financial statements. In addition, the Board cooperates with national accounting standard setters to achieve convergence in accounting standards around the world."[5] Although the ultimate goal may be to have a single set of global standards, such unity will probably not be achieved in the near future. The IASB's umbrella organization, the International Accounting Standards Committee (IASC), issued 41 **International Accounting Standards (IAS)** between 1997 and 2002. The IASB endorsed these standards and issues standards of its own, called **International Financial Reporting Standards (IFRS)**. Convergence, an intermediate goal, does not imply a single uniform set of accounting standards throughout the world, but rather a decrease in the amount of diversity that now exists. That goal is certainly more achievable.

Many stock exchanges, with the notable exception of those in the United States and Canada, accept International Accounting Standards for cross-border listings. Many countries already endorse International Accounting Standards as their own, either without amendment or with minor additions or deletions. In June 2000, the European Commission issued a communication proposing that all listed companies in the European Union (EU) be required to prepare their consolidated financial statements using International Accounting Standards. Already, both inside and outside the EU, many leading companies have stated that they prepare their financial reports in accordance with International Accounting Standards.

International Accounting Standards are also very important in developing countries and in other countries that do not have a national standard-setting body or that lack the resources to develop their own accounting standards. The development of accounting standards is costly, and it is not economically efficient for every country to have its own process for developing its own unique standards.

5 International Accounting Standards Board, Mission Statement, available at: www.iasb.org.uk. Accessed 5/10/03.

THE NEED FOR A SINGLE SET OF STANDARDS

cost of capital the cost of raising funds through either the issuance of debt, such as bonds, or the issuance of equity, such as common stock

At present, external financial reports are based on principles and procedures that may vary widely from country to country, and sometimes even within a country. Accounting reports, therefore, can lack comparability, one of the essential qualities of financial information. When financial reports from different countries are prepared according to different standards, investment analysts and other users of financial information incur extra costs to analyze and understand the data. The differing standards may also lead to errors in interpretation. Because of these difficulties in financial analysis, competition among the capital markets of the world may be impaired, and companies may incur higher costs of capital. (The **cost of capital** is the cost of raising funds through either the issuance of debt, such as bonds, or the issuance of equity, such as common stock.) Moreover, the credibility of accounting and of accounting reports suffers if differing national standards force a company to report different profit numbers in different countries for the same transactions.

The amount of cross-border financing, securities trading, and direct investment is enormous. For example, according to the Bureau of Economic Analysis, foreign-owned assets in the United States totaled over $8.5 trillion at the end of 2002, and U.S.-owned assets abroad totaled over $6.4 trillion.[6] Thus, the need for a single set of standards (or at least a set of comparable standards) for recognizing and measuring assets, liabilities, and income is urgent. Many members of the financial community hope that eventually all companies, including those in the United States, that publicly sell securities to investors will follow the IASB standards, although that is unlikely to happen in the near future. Fortunately, initial steps are being taken, as the FASB and IASB announced in a joint press release:

> The Financial Accounting Standards Board (FASB) and International Accounting Standards Board (IASB) have issued a *Memorandum of Understanding* marking a significant step toward formalizing their commitment to the convergence of U.S. and international accounting standards. The agreement follows the decisions recently reached by both Boards to add a joint short-term convergence project to their active agendas. The joint short-term convergence project will require both Boards to use their best efforts to propose changes to U.S. and international accounting standards that reflect common solutions to certain specifically identified differences.[7]

CHECK YOUR UNDERSTANDING

1. Why are international accounting standards important?

2. Describe the mission of the IASB.

LO4 Explain how accounting standards are set in actual practice.

Critical Thinking: What consequences for potential and current investors and creditors might result if acceptable accounting practices were not clearly defined, regulated, and enforced?

Standard Setting in Practice: An Economic and Political Process

As discussed earlier, the SEC and the FASB are the primary public and private participants in the standard-setting process in the United States. The IASB has significant authority in the rest of the world and influences U.S. standards. With the passage of the Sarbanes-Oxley Act in 2002, the SEC is expected to play a more dominant role in standard setting, especially in North America. According to that act, the SEC is

---

6 U.S. Department of Commerce, Bureau of Economic Analysis, news release, June 30, 2003.

7 Joint press release of the FASB and IASB, "FASB and IASB Agree to Work Together Toward Convergence of Global Accounting Standards," London, October 29, 2002.

Step	Explanation
1. **Problem identification**	The Emerging Issues Task Force identifies a reporting issue and places it on the FASB's agenda.
2. **Appointment of a task force**	A task force is appointed to advise the Board on the important issues.
3. **Research and analysis**	The FASB's technical staff researches the issue and examines IASB statements.
4. **Discussion memorandum (DM)**	A DM describing the issue is written and distributed to interested parties.
5. **Public response**	Public hearings are held to discuss the issue and possible solutions to the issue.
6. **Exposure draft (ED)**	The proposed solution to the issue is written and distributed to interested parties.
7. **Public response**	Written responses to the proposed solution are considered, and, if necessary, the proposed solution is modified.
8. **Issuance of the Statement of Financial Accounting Standards**	Four of the seven FASB members must approve a statement before it is issued.

authorized to recognize as generally accepted any accounting principles that are established by a standard-setting body that meets the bill's criteria. According to these criteria, the body should

- Be a private entity

- Be governed by a board of trustees (or equivalent body), the majority of whom are not or have not been associated with a public accounting firm for the past two years

- Be funded in a manner similar to the oversight board

- Have adopted procedures to ensure prompt consideration of changes in accounting principles by a majority vote

- Consider, when adopting standards, the need to keep them current and the extent to which international convergence of standards is necessary and appropriate

Despite its expanded role, the SEC continues to look to the FASB to set accounting standards. As outlined in Illustration 2.3, the FASB has established a set of procedures that must be followed before it issues an authoritative standard. Once an issue has been identified by the Emerging Issues Task Force and placed on the FASB's agenda, a task force is appointed to review the issue and work with the FASB staff to conduct research on it. A discussion memorandum is then issued, and public response is encouraged. After digesting that response, the FASB issues an exposure draft, invites additional public response, and finally issues an actual statement.

TIMELINESS OF STANDARD SETTING

Because the FASB's process for setting accounting standards involves a number of steps and calls for input from various parties, critics of this process find fault with the length of time needed to develop standards, given the fast-changing business environment. Under the FASB's system of due process, anyone may comment on a proposed statement before it is issued. Groups like the AICPA have significant influence on the FASB as it develops its standards. Further, because board meetings are open and public response to proposed standards is solicited, the investing public also has a voice in the development of FASB standards.

The FASB's perceived role in the Enron scandal during 2001 and 2002 added fuel to the criticism of the organization's standard-setting process. At that time, Enron was the central figure in the crisis of confidence that affected many large, high-profile public companies. The FASB was condemned by many in Congress and the investment community for taking too long to address the issues of special-purpose entities and off-balance-sheet liabilities—issues that eventually forced Enron into bankruptcy and caused investors, employees, and suppliers to lose millions of dollars. Off-balance-sheet financing had been discussed at the FASB for many years, but it was only after Enron's bankruptcy that the FASB made progress in resolving that important problem.

Since that time, the FASB has carried out an internal restructuring to speed up the standard-setting process. The Financial Accounting Foundation, which appoints the members of the FASB, changed the FASB's voting process to require a simple majority vote for the issuance of an accounting standard. Previously, affirmative votes from five of the board's seven members were required to adopt a standard, but now only four votes are needed. This is likely to make it easier to adopt new standards, especially those that are controversial.

COMPLEXITY OF ACCOUNTING STANDARDS

Not only has the FASB sometimes taken 10 or 20 years to promulgate an important accounting standard, but the resulting standard is often extremely complex and detailed. Complex rules are difficult for investors to understand. Complexity also allows executives to argue that if a particular accounting treatment is not disallowed, they should be able to use it. Robert Herdman, former SEC chief accountant, offered the following statement regarding FASB standards:

> Additionally, over the last few years, certain FASB standards have been rule-based, as opposed to principle-based. Rule-based accounting standards provide extremely detailed rules that attempt to contemplate virtually every application of the standard. This encourages a check-the-box mentality to financial reporting that eliminates judgments from the application of reporting. . . . Rule-based standards make it more difficult for preparers and auditors to step back and evaluate whether the overall impact is consistent with the objectives of the standard. . . . An ideal accounting standard is one that is principle-based and requires financial reporting to reflect the economic substance, not the form of the transaction.[8]

The FASB is responding to such criticisms and is considering the development of more principle-based standards like those that are commonly issued by the IASB. According to Harvey Pitt, former chairperson of the SEC, in 2002, "Eliminating check-the-box accounting will also put the U.S. more in sync with the rest of the world, where International Accounting Standards that rely far more on principles are rapidly being adopted."[9] Many critics consider *Statements of Financial Accounting Standards No. 141,* "Business Combinations," and *No. 142,* "Goodwill and Other Intangible Assets," to be steps in the right direction.

CHECK YOUR UNDERSTANDING

1. Describe the steps that the FASB takes before issuing a substantive accounting standard.

2. What criticisms have been levied against the FASB process for standard setting?

---

8 Robert Herdman, "Testimony Concerning the Roles of the SEC and FASB in Establishing GAAP," May 14, 2002.

9 "FASB: Rewriting the Book on Bookkeeping," *Business Week Online,* May 20, 2002, available at: **www.businessweek.com/magazine/content/02_20/b3783094.htm.** Accessed 04/05/04.

point ▶◀ counterpoint

Rules-Based or Principles-Based Accounting

the controversy Is U.S. GAAP one of the most important innovations in the history of our capital markets? This set of standardized accounting rules enabled investors to compare and contrast the performance of companies and to trust in reliable and consistent financial information. Or did it? Did the voluminous and complex set of rules encourage some companies to find the loopholes, manipulate the system, and ignore the spirit of the standards? With so many cases of accounting manipulations in the news, the FASB has been prompted to reassess its approach to accounting-standards setting and to move from a rules-based approach to a broader principles-based approach. Participants on both sides of the controversy agree that a trustworthy system of accounting standards is imperative in reestablishing the confidence of the investment community.

▶point

Donald Nicolaisen
chief accountant, SEC

on the point:

- **Harvey Pitt**
  former chairman of the SEC

- **Hank Paulson**
  chairman of the board and CEO of Goldman Sachs

- **Sir David Tweedie**
  chairman of the IASB

- **Robert Herz**
  FASB chairman

- **Robert Herdman**
  former SEC chief accountant

▶ **Shifting to a principles-based accounting system would improve the timeliness of standards issuance and the transparency of financial reporting.**

The ideal accounting standard is one that reflects substance, not form. Proponents of a principles-based accounting system believe that this approach would bring the big picture back into focus by lessening the dependence on fine distinctions and splitting hairs around particular rules. Principles-based standards provide general guidance on concepts instead of case-by-case rules. Donald Nicolaisen, Chief Accountant at the SEC, characterizes the system as having fewer rules and greater use of competent professional judgment."[1] Proponents argue that this type of system would not allow for Enron-type financial engineering, in which complex transactions are undertaken to get around specific rules-based accounting standards.

In testimony before the U.S. Senate Committee on Banking, Housing, and Urban Affairs in 2002, Harvey L. Pitt, then chairman of the SEC, said:

> Much of FASB's recent guidance has become rule-driven and complex. . . . This emphasis on detailed rules instead of broad principles has contributed to delays in issuing timely guidance. Additionally, because the standards are developed based on rules, and not broad principles, they are insufficiently flexible to accommodate future developments in the marketplace. This has resulted in accounting for unanticipated transactions that is less transparent and less consistent with the basic underlying principles that should apply.[2]

In accord with Pitt, proponents claim that standards issued under a principles-based approach would be less complex, take less time to be issued, cover a broader range of transactions, and produce more transparent financial statements.

In a speech to the National Press Club in June 2002, Henry M. Paulson, Jr., chairman and CEO of The Goldman Sachs Group, Inc. called for reform within the U.S. financial system to restore public confidence in business principles and practices. He desires a convergence of the U.S. system with the more principle-based European system, incorporating the best from both models.[3] Sir Edward Tweedie, the chairman of the IASB, also encourages this shift of U.S. standard setting, stating, "We favour an

1 Ramona Dzinkowski, "SEC's New Chief Accountant Weighs the Issues," Financial Management Network Online, Jan. 5, 2004, available at **www.fmnonline.com/publishing/article.cfm?article_id=761**. Accessed 6/23/04.

2 "Principles-Based Approach to Standard Setting," October 21, 2002, FASB proposal, available at **www.fasb.org**. Accessed 06/24/04.

3 "Goldman Sachs Chairman Hank Paulson Calls for Action to Restore Investor Confidence," Goldman Sachs website press release, available at **www.gs.com/our_firm/media_center/articles/press_release_2002_article_918630.html**. Accessed June 5, 2002.

approach that requires the company and its auditor to take a step back and consider whether the accounting suggested is consistent with the underlying principle. . . . We hope that a clear statement of the underlying principles will allow companies and auditors to deal with those situations without resorting to detailed rules."[4]

◄ counterpoint

Randall Vitray

accounting-consultant partner, PricewaterhouseCoopers LLP

on the counterpoint:

• Many practicing **auditors, accountants,** and **business law attorneys**

• **J. Edward Ketz**

professor, Pennsylvania State University

◄ **The current rules-based accounting system is already based on powerful principles and provides comparability and consistency in financial reporting.**

On the counterpoint, opponents claim that a shift to principles-based accounting solves nothing. Compared to a rules-based system, a principles-based system relies even more heavily on judgment calls and is more susceptible to manipulation, based on the needs and goals of company managers. J. Edward Ketz, associate professor of accounting at the Smeal College of Business, Pennsylvania State University states, "After all, a principles-based approach requires people who have principles. Given the events of the past year or so, that presumption is tenuous at best."[5] He contends that corporate transactions have grown increasingly complex and that therefore the accounting rules must follow suit. Randall Vitray, an accounting-consultant partner in PricewaterhouseCoopers LLP and a consultant to the FASB, says, "It makes life simpler for us auditors to have black-and-white, clear, objective guidelines we can show our clients and not debate with them what these guidelines mean."[6]

In response to the call for a more principles-based system, those who support the current system argue that U.S. GAAP is already built on seven broad and powerful principles: (1) historical cost, (2) objectivity or verifiability, (3) revenue recognition, (4) matching, (5) consistency, (6) full disclosure, and (7) relevance or fair value. These underlying principles require companies to present financial statements in a form that is not misleading, regardless of whether the specifics of the rules are followed. Controversy around this system may not be a problem with the rules-based system itself but more a crisis of ethics and the strong pressures that corporate managers are under to meet performance objectives.

Those who support a rules-based approach agree that the system may have become too "rules-centric," yet auditors, clients, and lawyers continue to demand clear instructions and reporting guidance. Supporters fear that a shift to a principles-based system would decrease transparency and lessen the amount of detail currently seen in financial reporting. A rules-based system provides more consistency in application and aids in comparability of statements between companies.

Take a Position　Assume that you are the senior accountant responsible for preparing your corporation's annual report. Would you prefer a rules-based or a principles-based system? Describe the challenges of both approaches.

Research　Locate the proposal "Principles-Based Approach to U.S. Standard Setting" published by the FASB on October 21, 2002 on the organization's website. Describe the two main differences outlined in this proposal between setting accounting standards under a principles-based system and under the existing accounting standards.

---

4 Speech delivered before the Committee on Banking, Housing and Affairs of the U.S. Senate at the hearing "Accounting and Investor Protection Issues Raised by Enron and Other Public Companies: International Accounting Standards and Necessary Reforms to Improve Financial Reporting." Washington, D.C., February 14, 2002.

5 J. Edward Ketz, "Principles-Based Standards," Smart Pros.com, available at **http://accounting.smartpros.com/x36098.xml.** Accessed 6/23/04.

6 Cassell Bryan-Low and Carrick Mollenkamp "'Off the Books' Cleanup Turns Out to Be Tough," *Wall Street Journal,* January 13, 2003.

LO5 Summarize the authoritative hierarchy of generally accepted accounting principles.

🔳 *Critical Thinking: Given that several entities issue interpretations, statements, and opinions on accounting practices, how do you think the accountant selects the appropriate authoritative rule for application?*

The Hierarchy of GAAP

Accountants refer to generally accepted accounting principles as the set of accounting rules and methods that have substantial authoritative support. However, because several agencies and organizations are involved in issuing accounting pronouncements, it is sometimes difficult to know which accounting rules are the most authoritative. Actually, Congress is the highest authority because it can set accounting policy through legislation. Historically, Congress has been hesitant to become involved, but recent accounting controversies have renewed its interest in accounting standards in such areas as stock options, pensions, and off-balance-sheet financing. Within the federal framework, the SEC is charged by Congress with overseeing accounting-standard setting. Although Congress could technically issue GAAP by legislation, SEC pronouncements (Staff Accounting Bulletins) are usually the highest level of authority and supersede any other source of GAAP for U.S. firms that are publicly traded.

The Statement on Auditing Standards (SAS) No. 69, "The Meaning of 'Present Fairly in Conformity with Generally Accepted Accounting Principles' in the Independent Auditor's Report," currently defines the hierarchy of GAAP. As shown in Illustration 2.4, the most authoritative bodies of literature are FASB Standards and Interpretations, APB Opinions, and AICPA Accounting Research Bulletins. If an issue is not covered by those sources, other accounting literature such as FASB Technical Bulletins should be consulted. Recently, however, both the FASB and the AICPA have issued exposure drafts that signal an important shift in thinking. The FASB exposure draft, "The Hierarchy of Generally Accepted Accounting Principles," moves the responsibility for the GAAP hierarchy for nongovernmental entities from the auditing literature *(SAS No. 69,* for example) to the accounting literature. The current FASB exposure draft does not make changes in the GAAP hierarchy but does anticipate future changes that would reduce the number of levels of accounting literature under the GAAP hierarchy to just two: authoritative and nonauthoritative, with all the authoritative literature compiled into what will be known as *The Codifcation.* The current exposure draft also addresses the role of the FASB Concept Statements in the GAAP hierarchy. The anticipated changes to *SAS No. 69* will make it consistent with the FASB's position as detailed in the exposure draft.

THE IMPORTANCE OF TRANSPARENCY IN FINANCIAL REPORTING

Since the financial reporting scandals of the early 2000s, it has become more evident that accurate, timely, and reliable financial reporting is critical to U.S. capital markets, and indeed to the entire world economy. Without reliable accounting standards, efficient capital markets cannot exist. Accounting standards developed by standard setters must ensure **transparency** in financial reporting—that is, the availability of relevant financial information about a company that is understandable to investors and other market participants. Transparency in reporting accomplishes the following:

transparency the availability of relevant financial information about a company that is understandable to investors and other market participants

- Enables investors, creditors, and the market to evaluate an entity
- Increases confidence in the fairness of U.S. markets
- Is fundamental to corporate governance because it enables boards of directors to evaluate management's effectiveness and to take early corrective actions, when necessary, to address deterioration in the financial condition of companies[10]

---

10 Robert K. Herdman, "Testimony Concerning the Roles of the SEC and the FASB in Establishing GAAP," May 14, 2002.

Illustration 2.4

Hierarchy of Sources of GAAP

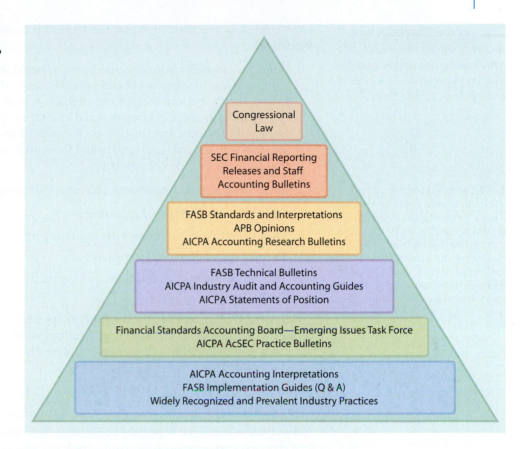

It is impossible to overstate the crucial role that high-quality generally accepted accounting principles play in transparent financial reporting. Standard setters throughout the world will continue to be pressured to provide accounting standards that lead to transparent financial reporting. Such standards provide a common language for all accountants and a benchmark for accounting and reporting by all companies.

The Securities and Exchange Commission requires all publicly listed companies to follow U.S. generally accepted accounting principles. Thus, when a U.S. auditing firm states that the financial statements it has audited are in conformity with generally accepted accounting principles, it means that those statements comply with the standards included in Illustration 2.4. In many other countries, the primary sources of GAAP are the standards issued by the International Accounting Standards Board.

CHECK YOUR UNDERSTANDING

1. Define transparency as it relates to financial reporting.

2. Identify three benefits of transparency in financial reporting.

3. List the three most authoritative sources of GAAP from the private sector.

LO6 Discuss the FASB's conceptual framework for financial reporting, including the objectives of financial reporting and the qualitative characteristics of accounting information.

The FASB's Conceptual Framework for Financial Reporting

The Accounting Principles Board was criticized for its failure to develop a conceptual framework to guide the development of its opinions. Because both the FASB and the IASB recognized this shortcoming, one of their initial goals was to create a conceptual framework to serve as a basis for the standards they developed. The

Critical Thinking: *As a user of financial statements, can you describe two critical qualities that the statements must have in order for you to find them useful?*

FASB's conceptual framework the frame of reference that serves as a basis for the standards the FASB develops; it addresses (1) the objectives of financial reporting, (2) the qualitative characteristics of accounting information, (3) the elements of financial statements, and (4) the environmental assumptions, principles, and constraints that guide financial reporting

FASB's mission statement includes the following comments regarding a conceptual framework:

> Concepts are useful in guiding the Board in establishing standards and in providing a frame of reference, or conceptual framework, for resolving accounting issues. The framework will help to establish reasonable bounds for judgment in preparing financial information and to increase understanding of, and confidence in, financial information on the part of users of financial reports. It also will help the public to understand the nature and limitations of information supplied by financial reporting.[11]

The **FASB's conceptual framework** addresses four issues:

1. The objectives of financial reporting
2. The qualitative characteristics of accounting information
3. The elements of financial statements
4. The environmental assumptions, principles, and constraints that guide financial reporting

Illustration 2.5 depicts how the four components of the framework relate to and support one another. The elements of financial statements and the guiding assumptions and principles behind those elements were discussed in Chapter 1.

THE OBJECTIVES OF FINANCIAL REPORTING

In November 1978, the FASB issued *Statement of Financial Accounting Concepts No. 1*, "Objectives of Financial Reporting by Business Enterprises." The objectives outlined in that statement address the information needs of external users, who depend on corporate management for the information they need to make informed decisions. The three objectives identified in *Statement of Financial Accounting Concepts No. 1* are to:

1. Provide information that is useful to present and potential investors, creditors, and other users in making rational investment, credit, and similar decisions. Implied in this objective is the idea that information should be *useful* to users who have a reasonable understanding of business and economic activities.

2. Provide information that will help present and potential investors, creditors, and other users to assess the amounts, timing, and uncertainty of prospective cash receipts from dividends or interest, as well as the proceeds from the sale, redemption, or maturity of securities or loans related to their investment in the firm. Implied in this objective is that information should help the investor *forecast future cash flows.*

3. Provide information about the economic resources of an enterprise, which are the sources, direct or indirect, of future cash inflows; about the claims to those resources, which are the sources, direct or indirect, of future cash outflows; and about the effects of transactions, events, and circumstances that can cause changes in resources and claims to those resources. Implied in this objective is that information should help investors *do fundamental analysis* of the assets, liabilities, and business activities of the firm for a given period of time.[12]

With these objectives in mind, the FASB concluded that the accounting profession should develop general-purpose financial statements that a "broad class of decision-makers could use in predicting the ability of an enterprise to generate future cash flows."[13]

---

11 "A Mission for Neutral Statements," *FASB Facts* (Norwalk, Conn.: FASB, 1973).

12 "Objectives of Financial Reporting by Business Enterprises," *Statement of Financial Accounting Concepts No. 1* (Stamford, Conn.: FASB, 1978).

13 Ibid., par. 28.

Illustration 2.5

FASB's Conceptual Framework

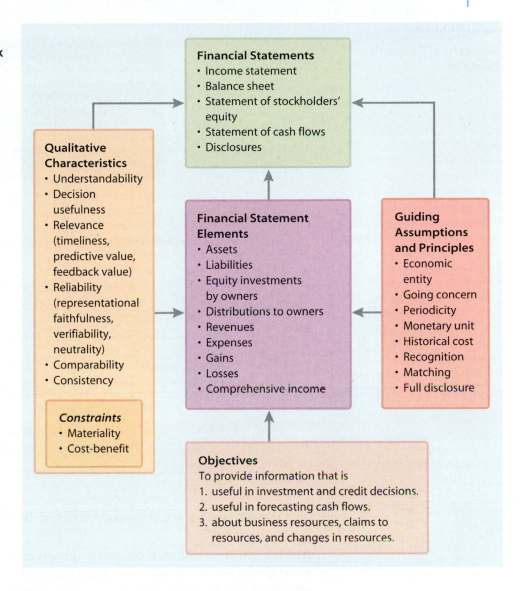

Financial Statements
- Income statement
- Balance sheet
- Statement of stockholders' equity
- Statement of cash flows
- Disclosures

Qualitative Characteristics
- Understandability
- Decision usefulness
- Relevance (timeliness, predictive value, feedback value)
- Reliability (representational faithfulness, verifiability, neutrality)
- Comparability
- Consistency

Constraints
- Materiality
- Cost-benefit

Financial Statement Elements
- Assets
- Liabilities
- Equity investments by owners
- Distributions to owners
- Revenues
- Expenses
- Gains
- Losses
- Comprehensive income

Guiding Assumptions and Principles
- Economic entity
- Going concern
- Periodicity
- Monetary unit
- Historical cost
- Recognition
- Matching
- Full disclosure

Objectives
To provide information that is
1. useful in investment and credit decisions.
2. useful in forecasting cash flows.
3. about business resources, claims to resources, and changes in resources.

THE QUALITATIVE CHARACTERISTICS OF ACCOUNTING INFORMATION

In 1980, the FASB issued *Statement of Financial Accounting Concepts No. 2*, "Qualitative Characteristics of Accounting Information," which links the objectives of financial reporting with the qualities that make financial information useful. Illustration 2.6 shows a hierarchy of those qualities as they pertain to the objectives of financial reporting.[14] Each element of the hierarchy will be discussed in the following pages. Note that users of financial statements are at the top of the hierarchy. They are assumed to have the ability to understand general-purpose financial statements.

Two user-specific qualities of accounting information are understandability and decision usefulness. Information has **understandability** if sophisticated users are able to perceive its significance in decision making. Clearly, financial information that users cannot understand is of little use, and the costs of preparing and disseminating such information will exceed the benefits. Information has **usefulness** if it will be of value to users in making investment, credit, and other decisions. Because decision usefulness is such a crucial quality, the FASB developed a hierarchy of qualities to explain it.

understandability the quality of information that enables sophisticated users to perceive its significance in decision making

usefulness the quality of information that makes it of value to users in making investment, credit, and other decisions

---

14 "Qualitative Characteristics of Accounting Information," *Statement of Financial Accounting Concepts No. 2* (Stamford, Conn.: FASB, 1980), Figure 1, p. 20.

Illustration 2.6

Hierarchy of Accounting Qualities

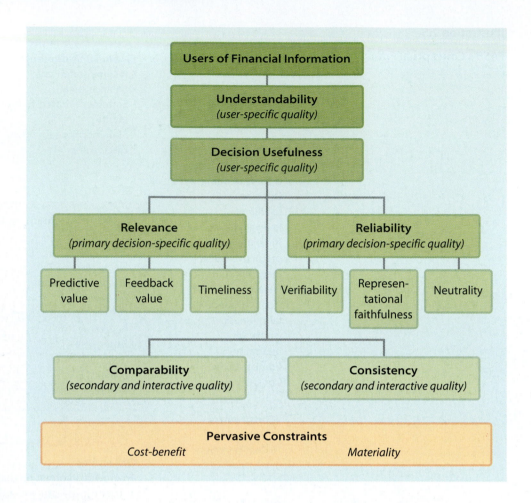

THE PRIMARY DECISION-SPECIFIC QUALITIES OF ACCOUNTING INFORMATION

The two primary qualities of decision usefulness are relevance and reliability. Imagine these qualities are being situated along a continuum, as depicted in Illustration 2.7. At one end is relevance, and at the other end is reliability. A continuum is a good analogy because most accounting information does not fall at either extreme, but rather is at some place in the middle. There are, however, some cases in which information is both relevant and reliable. Before the FASB issues a new standard, it must weigh both qualities in terms of decision makers' needs. In some cases, reliability is more important than relevance; in other cases, relevance takes priority.

RELEVANCE Information has **relevance** when it is capable of making a difference in users' decisions by enabling them to make predictions about the future or confirm or correct expectations. Information is relevant if it is timely and has both predictive value and feedback value. Financial information has **predictive value** if it helps users

relevance the primary quality of information that means that the information is capable of making a difference in users' decisions by enabling them to make predictions about the future or confirm or correct expectations; the ingredients of relevance are timeliness, feedback value, and predictive value

predictive value an ingredient of relevance; the trait of helping users make forecasts

Illustration 2.7

Decision-Useful Information in Financial Reporting

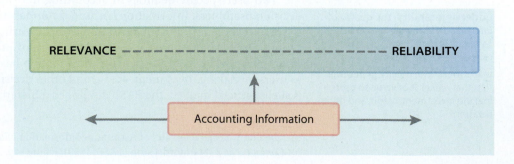

feedback value an ingredient of relevance; the trait of helping users confirm or correct previous expectations

timeliness an ingredient of relevance; the trait of being available to users soon enough to affect their decisions

make forecasts, and it has **feedback value** if it helps users confirm or correct previous expectations.

Information has **timeliness** when it is available to users soon enough to affect their decisions. Companies constantly enter into business transactions that may affect their financial capacities. If information about these transactions and events is not disclosed on a timely basis, that information is of little use (and perhaps could be harmful) to investors. In the past, investors relied on quarterly financial reports and newspaper articles to obtain timely information. However, as information is being generated with greater speed, it is absorbed into the financial markets at an increasing rate. The SEC now asks companies that have meetings with the press or with analysts to hold them online (or in some other public forum) so that all interested parties may obtain the information simultaneously. The speed with which investors can communicate and trade from computers, wireless phones, and other electronic devices has dramatically boosted the speed with which information translates into stock price changes. As a result, information about a company's stock price can quickly lose its timeliness and thus its relevance.

To illustrate relevance, consider again the building that Vireo Company purchased for $2 million five years ago. If an investor is evaluating the future prospects of Vireo Company, how relevant is the historical purchase price of $2 million? Many users of financial statements contend that the building's current value is timelier than the historical cost and thus is more relevant to forecasting the firm's future prospects. However, the current value may be less reliable because it probably can't be verified with the same degree of certainty as the historical cost. Furthermore, different individuals are likely to take different approaches to measuring current value. Some might base their estimates on the appraised value of the building, whereas others might use the recent sales price of a similar building in the same neighborhood.

reliability the primary quality of information that means that the information is reasonably free from error and bias and represents what it claims to represent; information that is reliable has representational faithfulness, verifiability, and neutrality

representational faithfulness an ingredient of reliability; the trait of faithfully describing what is or what happened

verifiability an ingredient of reliability; the trait of enabling different measurers to agree that information measures what it claims to measure

neutrality an ingredient of reliability; a lack of bias in the measurement process and a lack of intent to influence behavior or achieve a desired result

❱ **RELIABILITY**   At the other end of the continuum in Illustration 2.7 is reliability. Information has **reliability** when it is reasonably free from error and bias and, in fact, represents what it claims to represent. The ingredients of the reliability of information are representational faithfulness, verifiability, and neutrality.

Information has **representational faithfulness** when it faithfully describes what is or what happened. It has **verifiability** when different measurers agree that the information measures what it claims to measure. Verifiability implies consensus in obtaining a given result. Thus, information is verifiable if several measurers using the same methods would arrive at the same result. The less the uncertainty inherent in information, the more verifiable it is.

Information has **neutrality** when there is no bias in the measurement process and no intent to influence behavior or achieve a desired result. For example, if a company slanted its accounting with the goal of presenting an unduly favorable impression of its operations, the resulting information would not be neutral. Neutrality is an important goal in standard setting to ensure that accounting rules do not favor one group or industry and impose a greater burden on the rest.

For example, most accountants believe that historical costs have reliability. If Vireo Company purchased a building five years ago for $2 million, that amount is verifiable and represents what the firm in fact paid for the building. Because source documents are available, the cost of the transaction and the neutrality of the information can be determined. It is very likely that different users looking at those source documents would come to the same conclusion about the historical cost. However, it is less likely that the same users would agree on the current market value of the building.

In developing standards, the FASB and other standard setters may sometimes make trade-offs between reliability and relevance. The debate surrounding the use of fair values on the balance sheet for certain assets and liabilities is an example. Clearly, historical costs are more reliable, but they are not as relevant as fair values. Many of the recently issued standards contain elements of fair values, indicating that the FASB is sensitive to this trade-off.

The FASB introduced another variation on the trade-off between reliability and relevance when it issued Concept Statement No. 7 in 2000. This statement provides a framework for governing the use of future cash flows and present value as a basis for the measurement of assets and liabilities at the time of initial recognition or later when a fresh-start measurement is required. The concept statement notes that most accounting measurements use an observable marketplace-determined amount, such as cash received or paid, current cost, or current market value, to measure the initial cost of an asset or liability. This is because these measures are both relevant and reliable. There are, however, times when estimated future cash flows must be used as the basis for measuring an asset or liability. In the past, these cash flows have been estimated as a single number discounted at an appropriate interest rate. As the statement notes, "accounting applications of present value have typically used a single set of estimated cash flows and a single interest rate."[15]

Concept Statement No. 7 introduces a new idea, however, one that may be more useful, but less reliable. This idea is the *expected cash flow approach*, "which differs from the traditional approach by focusing on explicit assumptions about the range of possible estimated cash flows and their respective probabilities."[16] By introducing the idea of assigning probabilities to estimated future cash flows, the FASB felt that it was improving the usefulness and relevance of the resulting accounting measurements. This is inherently a subjective process, however, and many feel that when applied in actual FASB statements, it will further tilt the scale away from reliability toward relevance and make financial statement measurements more subjective.

THE SECONDARY AND INTERACTIVE QUALITIES OF ACCOUNTING INFORMATION

comparability a secondary quality of information; the trait of being measured and reported in the same way across enterprises or enabling users to identify similarities and differences among sets of information

Comparability and consistency are two secondary qualities of decision usefulness that interact with relevance and reliability to contribute to the value of information. Information has **comparability** when it is measured and reported in the same way across enterprises or when users can identify similarities and differences among sets of information. For example, financial information from Nightjar Corporation and Avocet, Inc. will be comparable if the two companies have used the same accounting rules to prepare their financial statements. Lack of comparability is one of the key problems that analysts encounter when they are evaluating financial statements that are prepared under GAAP of different countries. In many cases, the principles and standards are so different that the financial data are not comparable and thus are of limited value in decision-making endeavors.

consistency a secondary quality of information; the trait that results when a firm applies the same accounting rules across time

Information has **consistency** when a firm applies the same accounting rules across time. Consistency allows users to compare a firm's current financial results with its financial results from other periods.

THE ROLE OF CONSERVATISM

Chapter 1 introduced the accounting concept of conservatism, defined as "the prudent reaction to uncertainty to try to ensure that the uncertainty and risks inherent in business situations are adequately considered." Interestingly, conservatism is not included in the hierarchy of accounting qualities outlined by the FASB in Illustration 2.6 on page 74. In *Statement of Accounting Concepts No. 2*, the board states, "Nothing has yet been said about conservatism, a convention that many accountants believe to be appropriate in making accounting decisions."[17]

The board was concerned that conservatism was being used to deliberately and consistently understate net assets and profits, and that this could not be considered a

---

15 "Using Cash Flow Information and Present Value in Accounting Measurements," *Statement of Financial Accounting Concepts No. 2* (Stamford, Conn.: FASB, 2000), highlights.

16 *Concept Statement No. 7*, highlights.

17 "Qualitative Characteristics of Accounting Information," *Statement of Financial Accounting Concepts No. 2* (Stamford, Conn.: FASB, 1980), par. 91.

virtue, to use the FASB's word. The deliberate understatement of net assets in one period often leads to the overstatement of net assets in a future period, thus artificially smoothing earnings. The board ends its discussion of conservatism in *Statement of Accounting Concepts No. 2* with the following important statement:

> The Board emphasizes that any attempt to understate results consistently is likely to raise questions about reliability and integrity of information about those results and will probably be self-defeating in the long run. That kind of reporting, however well-intentioned, is not consistent with the desirable characteristics described in this Statement.[18]

This view of conservatism certainly represents a change from the older traditional view that understatement of net assets was somehow a virtue. As noted in Chapter 1, we can expect this current view of conservatism to continue to work its way into new FASB and IASB statements.

▶ PERVASIVE CONSTRAINTS IN FINANCIAL REPORTING

cost-benefit criterion the FASB constraint establishing that when the costs of preparing and communicating financial information are greater than its benefits to users, that information need not be disclosed or communicated

materiality the FASB constraint having to do with a threshold for recognition; having the capacity to affect the decisions a user makes

The FASB identifies two constraints on financial reporting. The first is the **cost-benefit criterion**, the requirement that benefits must exceed costs. The FASB will not require the preparation of financial information if the costs of producing and communicating that information exceed its perceived benefits to users. This constraint compels the FASB to compare the economic cost of requiring firms to apply a new standard with the economic benefit that the new information provides to users—a difficult process at best. The second constraint is a threshold for recognition called materiality. Information has **materiality** if it has the capacity to affect users' decisions. The cost-benefit and materiality constraints are related. If the cost of producing and disseminating a piece of information exceeds its benefits, that information is not likely to be material to a decision. Because judgments about materiality are highly subjective, the FASB allows each firm to determine whether specific information is material. If a firm determines that information that is typically disclosed is not material to its situation, it need not disclose that information.

What is material for one firm may not be material for another. Assume, for example, that **General Motors** purchases a computer for $2,000. The absolutely correct way to account for the computer is to consider it an asset, give it a useful life (such as three years), and depreciate it over that useful life. However, because the cost of doing the accounting would exceed the benefits of the resulting information, General Motors would probably expense the entire $2,000 in the year of purchase. Given the huge size of General Motors, it is unlikely that expensing the computer rather than depreciating it would affect the decision of a potential investor or creditor. However, for a small firm, such as the fictitious Kettle and Wolf, Inc., the $2,000 is material. In such cases, the computer should be recorded as an asset and depreciated over its useful life.

Materiality is often defined as a percentage of total assets or revenues, such as 5 percent of assets or 3 percent of revenues. However, these are rules of thumb; there is no one best or correct measure of materiality. Given that the determination of materiality can be subjective, the SEC has issued several statements to guide firms in reaching a decision. Nevertheless, defining materiality remains one of the most subjective issues facing accountants, auditors, and users of financial statements.

THE CONCEPTUAL FRAMEWORK IN TRANSITION

Since the FASB's first Concept Statement was issued in 1978, the economic environment within the United States and worldwide has changed dramatically. As a result, both the FASB and the IASB have begun a new joint agenda project to revisit their conceptual frameworks. According to the project managers:

---

18 Ibid., par. 96.

A common goal of the FASB and IASB, shared by their constituents, is for their standards to be "principles-based." To be principles-based, standards cannot be a collection of conventions, but rather must be rooted in fundamental concepts. For standards on various issues to result in coherent financial accounting reporting, the fundamental concepts need to constitute a framework that is sound, comprehensive, and internally consistent. Without the guidance provided by an agreed-upon framework, standard setting ends up being based on individual concepts developed by each member of the standard-setting body.[19]

Robert H. Herz, the current chairman of the FASB, believes that although the conceptual framework has served standard setters well, improvements are needed. In a speech to the American Accounting Association in 2005, Hertz noted that improvements are needed in six areas:

1. More clearly distinguishing liabilities from equity
2. Resolving the unit of account (aggregation, linkage, segregation)
3. Clarifying control in the definition of assets
4. Determining which measurement attribute(s) to use
5. Defining the reporting entity
6. Clarifying disclosure and display of accounting information

As the FASB and IASB jointly review and revise their conceptual frameworks, we can expect that these issues will be addressed in the spirit of converging accounting standards.

CHECK YOUR UNDERSTANDING

1. What is the purpose of the FASB's conceptual framework?
2. What is meant by relevance in financial reporting?
3. What are the two primary user-specific qualities of accounting information?
4. What constraints on financial reporting have been identified by the FASB?

LO7 Explain the importance of self-regulation and ethics to the accounting profession.

ETHICS

The Accounting Profession: Self-Regulation and Ethics

For decades, the accounting profession prided itself in its ability to regulate itself through the strong efforts of the AICPA, its code of professional conduct, and a culture of independence from its clients. This pride was well deserved, given that public opinion polls consistently showed the accounting profession (and CPAs) to be among the most respected professions in the country.

A cornerstone of the profession's self-regulation has been the AICPA's Code of Professional Conduct. This code, which defines the minimum level of professional responsibility and conduct, applies to all AICPA members who are in the practice of accounting. It consists of two sections: (1) the principles and (2) the rules. As stated in the introduction to the code, "the Principles provide the framework for the Rules, which govern the performance of professional services by members."[20] Figure 2.1 presents the code's six principles that guide the behavior of CPAs.

---

19 Halsey G. Bullen and Kimberly Crook, "Revisiting the Concepts," (Stamford, Conn.: FASB, May 2005).

20 AICPA, *Code of Professional Conduct*, introduction, available at: www.aicpa.org. The entire code can be found at this website.

Figure 2.1

AICPA Code of Professional Conduct: Principles of Professional Conduct

- In carrying out their responsibilities as professionals, members should exercise sensitive professional and moral judgments in all their activities.
- Members should accept the obligation to act in a way that will serve the public interest, honor the public trust, and demonstrate commitment to professionalism.
- To maintain and broaden public confidence, members should perform all professional responsibilities with the highest sense of integrity.
- A member should maintain objectivity and be free of conflicts of interest in discharging professional responsibilities. A member in public practice should be independent in fact and appearance when providing auditing and other attestation services.
- A member should observe the profession's technical and ethical standards, strive continually to improve competence and the quality of services, and discharge professional responsibility to the best of the member's ability.
- A member in public practice should observe the Principles of the Code of Professional Conduct in determining the scope and nature of services to be provided.

The section of the code on independence states that CPAs are expected to maintain independence from their clients both in fact and in appearance. This means that the auditor and the auditing firm must not have a direct or indirect financial interest in the client and must do nothing to undermine the perception of outside users that the individual or the firm has no interest in the outcome of the audit or the financial performance of the client. Independence both in fact and in appearance is crucial because external users must rely on the judgments of auditors and other outside accountants. This confidence can be achieved only if these judgments are free from client influence.

To maintain their independence, auditors are not allowed to have even the smallest financial interest in their clients. Of course, the troublesome question that arises is whether an auditor or auditing firm can be independent of a client that pays the audit or other professional fees. This is even more difficult to determine when the auditing firm receives a much higher fee for non-audit services, such as consulting, than it receives for the audit. The discrepancy between the high fees that many accounting firms earned from non-audit services and the more modest fees they earned from auditing caused many regulators to question the independence of accounting firms. Today, the Sarbanes-Oxley Act regulates non-audit work by CPA firms.

ETHICAL DECISION MAKING

Ethical behavior requires commitment beyond a few rules of conduct. No ethics code or set of written rules can apply to all situations that might arise in the business world today. Making ethical decisions requires the ability to make distinctions between competing choices and to understand the consequences of each choice. Decision makers must be able to evaluate complex, vague, or incomplete facts and to implement the final decision effectively. Most of all, ethical decision making requires a framework of principles that can be relied on and a model for applying these principles to problems.

A number of ethical decision-making models can be used to analyze ethical dilemmas. The model presented in Illustration 2.8 is one that may be used to consider the ethical cases presented in this text. As you can see, it is important to first gather all relevant facts and clearly define the ethical problem. After listing all the parties affected by the decision, identify the personal and work-related values, such as honesty, fairness, accountability, and respect, that should be considered. Next, list all potential courses of action that might be taken. Step 5 requires a system for prioritizing the importance of the stakeholders, values, and consequences involved in the situation. Finally, the ethical decision maker must choose a course of action and implement the decision.

Accountants play a major role in the operation, management, and development of business. In doing so, they can face many ethical dilemmas. The accountant's opinions,

Illustration 2.8

Ethical Decision-Making Model

1. Define the problem and gather all necessary facts.
2. List all parties who may be affected by the decision.
3. List all values and principles that should be reflected in the decision.
4. List all possible alternative actions that could be taken.
5. Choose and prioritize:
   a. Which party do you believe is most important in this situation?
   b. Which value do you believe is the highest value in this situation?
   c. Which of the likely consequences do you believe will cause the greatest good or the least harm?
   d. Prioritize a, b, and c to determine which is the most important consideration in this situation.
6. Make the decision based on the above factors.

practices, and behaviors directly affect how the company is viewed and how the profession, in turn, is assessed. In general, the ethically trained accountant should focus on the following goals:

- Avoid harm to stockholders.
- Optimize the interests of the public.
- Adhere to universal standards of what is right.
- Respect the human rights of all.

The benefits of ethical behavior are numerous. When individuals and businesses act in ethical ways, new wealth is created for society. When financial reporting is ethical, the public can have confidence in the data provided and make informed investment decisions. In turn, greater capital funding is available for growth and productivity, yielding strong and healthy economies.

❯ **ETHICAL DECISION MAKING ILLUSTRATED** To illustrate the process involved in ethical decision making, consider the following hypothetical situation.

Elle Wenar, CPA, has worked for a large public accounting firm as an auditor for the past seven years and has been senior lead auditor for the last three years. She has traveled extensively throughout the United States performing audits of financial statements. One of her most recent assignments was conducted from February through April at Supro Quality Manufacturing in Michigan. She recently decided to leave the accounting firm because of the extensive travel and overtime required, which conflicted with her family responsibilities.

She received an offer from Supro Quality Manufacturing, her previous audit client, to join its accounting staff as management accounting specialist. During the interview, she was told that she would be in charge of implementing a new inventory management system, which was expected to take one year. After the implementation was complete, she would be offered the position of controller, since the current controller was planning to relocate at that time.

Two weeks after Elle joined the firm, the chief financial officer (CFO), Megan Neuman, asked Elle to review and revise reports relating to the upcoming financial statement audit. Megan explained that the current controller was absent for a few days due to a family emergency. Despite some misgivings, Elle reviewed and revised the reports. During the next few days, Elle was again asked to consult on financial reporting issues related to the upcoming audit. A week later, Elle learned that the controller had been granted emergency leave for the next three months. The CFO asked Elle to delegate some of her inventory management duties to her staff so that she could continue to work on audit issues. Megan also expressed her appreciation for Elle's participation and suggested that this process would help Elle prepare for next year, when she will officially take the controller position.

Take another look at the ethical decision-making model presented in Illustration 2.8. The model may be used as a basis for consideration of the issues as follows:

1. *Define the problem and gather all necessary facts.* Elle faces an issue of independence in regard to her duties with Supro Quality Manufacturing and the upcoming audit. She has been asked to perform the duties of a controller, a position that is incompatible with the provisions of the Sarbanes-Oxley Act of 2002. According to this act, she cannot hold the position of controller for one year after having performed the audit for this company.

2. *List all parties who may be affected by the decision.* The parties affected by the situation are Elle, Supro Quality Manufacturing, and Supro's stockholders. In addition, the accounting profession at large is judged by the actions of its members, so the perception of the integrity of the profession may be affected.

3. *List all values and principles that should be reflected in the decision.* Elle is likely to consider her values related to honesty, compliance with the law, and integrity. Her principles as an accounting professional dictate that she must be unbiased and independent in fact and in appearance.

4. *List all possible alternative actions that could be taken.* Elle can take one or more of the following actions:

   a. She can choose to speak to the CFO and convince her that she cannot perform the duties of the controller because of her prior audit services.

   b. She can refuse to perform these duties and insist that someone else take the audit responsibilities.

   c. She can speak to the audit committee about her concerns.

   d. She can quit her job.

   e. She can continue to perform the duties of the controller.

5. *Choose and prioritize:*

   a. *Which party do you believe is most important in this situation?* Though identification of the most important party is often difficult, Elle should consider the professional and ethical duties of her profession and the interests of the stockholders of the company in this situation.

   b. *Which value do you believe is the highest value in this situation?* Honesty and compliance with the law are both highly important in this situation.

   c. *Which of the likely consequences do you believe will cause the greatest good or the least harm?* If Elle were to continue the audit responsibilities, the consequences could include harm to the perception of her professionalism, to the reliability of the audit process, and to the trust of the company's investors. Though she risks offending her superiors if she refuses the audit responsibilities, the greatest good can be achieved through an ethical audit process.

   d. *Prioritize a, b, and c to determine which is the most important consideration in this situation.* In this situation, Elle is likely to consider compliance with the law to be the most important consideration.

6. *Make the decision based on the above factors.* Elle should refuse to perform the duties of the controller, as dictated by the rules of independence within the Sarbanes-Oxley Act. If she cannot convince the CFO that she cannot perform these duties, she should resign her position.

Ethical cases are presented in each chapter's end-of-chapter assignments. While the model presented in Illustration 2.8 can be used as a general framework as you evaluate the ethical consequences of various accounting and business situations, you may also wish to consider accounting standards, legislation, and generally accepted accounting practices that may play a role in each situation.

LEGAL, REGULATORY, AND PROFESSIONAL REFORMS

Questions of independence plagued the accounting profession and stirred public concern in the early 2000s. As a result, the profession was thrust into the spotlight. Nonetheless, by mid-2002, with the passage of the Sarbanes-Oxley Act, significant reforms began, both within the profession and within the regulatory agencies that provide oversight to the profession. The most important provisions of the Sarbanes-Oxley Act include the following:

- Establish a new regulatory body, the Public Company Accounting Oversight Board, to oversee auditors of public companies.
- Redefine the relationship between auditors and their clients.
- Place direct responsibility for the audit relationship on audit committees.
- Establish new disclosure requirements for issuers of financial statements.
- Require CEOs and CFOs to certify the truthfulness of financial disclosures.
- Ban most loans to corporate officers and directors.
- Restrict certain transactions by executive officers and directors.
- Hold the CEO and CFO responsible for restatements due to misconduct.
- Impose new obligations and responsibilities on audit committees.
- Impose new rules of professional responsibility on lawyers and analysts.
- Stiffen a variety of criminal penalties and enforcement measures for securities-related offenses.

In addition to establishing the new Public Company Accounting Oversight Board, the Sarbanes-Oxley Act, as a way of strengthening auditor independence in fact and in perception, redefined the relationship between auditors and their clients by barring auditors from providing certain services to their clients. Under the act, an accounting firm cannot provide the following services at the same time that it is performing audit services:

- Bookkeeping and services related to accounting records and financial statements
- Design and implementation of financial information systems
- Valuation services
- Actuarial services
- Internal audit outsourcing services
- Management functions or human resource services
- Broker/dealer or investment banking services
- Legal services
- Any other services that the board determines are impermissible

The act does not prevent an accounting firm from providing tax services to an audit client so long as the services are approved by the client's board of directors or are small in scope (amounting to less than 5 percent of total revenues paid to the firm by the client).

The act also requires that the lead audit partner and the reviewing partner rotate off the audit every five years. In addition, in response to the criticism that many individuals who had worked on a firm's audit later became employees of that firm, the act prohibits a company's CEO, controller, CFO, chief accounting officer, or any person in an equivalent position from having been employed by the company's audit firm during the one-year period preceding the audit. All these provisions are aimed at increasing the actual and perceived independence of the auditing firm and the audit personnel.

Another key provision of the act requires CEOs and CFOs to submit statements to the SEC vouching for the truth and fairness of their firms' financial disclosures. When you read through the annual report of a public company today, you will see such a statement by the CEO and CFO. (An example of top management's certification of financial statements appears in Chapter 5.)

The AICPA also moved quickly to institute reforms in response to the changing regulatory environment. The following comment was made by the 2002–2003 chair of the AICPA:

> The Sarbanes-Oxley Act is a major step forward on the path to reform. But the real work to restore our profession's reputation as a steadfast guardian of the public trust is more personal. That work will be done by each and every one of us in this room during the course of fulfilling our daily responsibilities. The members of the AICPA—both corporate accountants and outside auditors— will be the ones who ultimately determine whether the reforms contained in the new law succeed or fail.[21]

CHECK YOUR UNDERSTANDING

1. What is the purpose of the AICPA Code of Professional Conduct?

2. If you were a CPA engaged in audit work for publicly traded companies, describe several ways in which the Sarbanes-Oxley Act would affect you.

3. Identify three types of activities that an accountant may not perform for a client if the accountant is also performing audit services for that client.

Revisiting the Case

SIGNING OF THE SARBANES-OXLEY ACT OF 2002

1. The Sarbanes-Oxley Act is intended to send the message to corporate leaders and to the accounting profession that integrity and high standards are to be expected and rewarded, and dishonesty and reckless practices will not be tolerated. The act seeks a higher level of scrutiny and regulation of accounting practices and ethical corporate governance.

2. High-profile cases involving overstatement of earnings, hiding debt, and booking expenses as investments led to the signing of the Sarbanes-Oxley Act.

3. Examples of conflicts of interest for accountants might include the accountant who acts both as a business adviser (consultant) and as an auditor, the accountant who holds a financial interest in his or her audit client, and the accountant who acts as an auditor for a previous employer.

---

21 William F. Ezzell, "Upholding the Public Trust," remarks prepared for delivery by the chairman of the board of the American Institute of Certified Public Accountants to the 2002 AICPA National Conference on Current Securities and Exchange Commission [SEC] Developments, December 12, 2002.

SUMMARY BY LEARNING OBJECTIVE

LO1 Describe the economic and regulatory purposes of financial reporting.

The efficient functioning of a market economy depends on the production of relevant and reliable financial information about the firms in which individuals and institutions invest. Although investors and creditors are considered the most significant external users of financial information, many other parties also need the information contained in financial reports, including managers, union negotiators, customers, voters, and students.

Government entities also require financial reporting. The Securities and Exchange Commission demands that publicly traded firms submit a variety of financial reports and adhere to generally accepted accounting principles. In addition, the SEC requires these companies to have their financial information certified annually by an independent certified public accountant so that investors can have confidence in that information. The Internal Revenue Service requires financial reporting to enable it to enforce its tax codes. Other federal bodies, such as the Federal Energy Regulatory Commission and the Federal Trade Commission, use financial information in promulgating their regulations, and state and local governments and agencies use financial information in a variety of ways, including in awarding franchises and contracts.

LO2 Identify the groups that establish accounting standards and describe their roles in the standard-setting process.

The setting of accounting standards in the United States is a complex process involving both the private and the public sector. The primary participants in setting standards in the United States are the Securities and Exchange Commission, the Financial Accounting Standards Board (FASB), and the American Institute of Certified Public Accountants (AICPA). These groups and others issue various standards, reports, bulletins, and positions that, taken together, contribute to the development of generally accepted accounting principles (GAAP)—the set of accounting standards that by either law, regulation, or custom guide the preparation of financial statements.

LO3 Describe the environment in which international accounting standards are set and identify the functions of the International Accounting Standards Board.

As the world's economy has become truly global, accounting standards have followed suit. Multinational firms raise capital from investors around the world and often trade their shares on international stock exchanges in London, Paris, Toronto, and other locations. The international movement of capital has driven the need for international accounting standards to ensure that financial statements will be transparent regardless of the country in which a firm is incorporated. Although the development of a single set of international accounting standards is a distant dream, accounting standards from different countries are showing more convergence. This is due, in part, to the growing influence of the International Accounting Standards Board, an independent, privately funded accounting-standard-setting body based in London. The IASB's members come from nine countries and have a variety of functional backgrounds.

LO4 Explain how accounting standards are set in actual practice.

Today, the SEC and the FASB are the two primary participants in the standard-setting process in the United States. The IASB has significant authority in the rest of the world and influences U.S. standards. With the passage of the Sarbanes-Oxley Act, the SEC is expected to play a more dominant role. However, most standard setting is actually done by the FASB with the implicit approval of the SEC. The FASB is a private board of seven members that represent different constituencies in the business, government, and academic sectors. The FASB follows a system of due process before issuing a new accounting standard. That system begins with identification of a problem and proceeds through research of the issue, distribution of a discussion memorandum presenting the issue and proposed solutions, public hearings, distribution of a proposed solution, and consideration of the public response. The final draft of the statement is issued if it is approved by four of the seven FASB members.

LO5 Summarize the authoritative hierarchy of generally accepted accounting principles.

The SEC is charged by Congress with overseeing the setting of accounting standards and issuing SEC pronouncements; this is the highest level of authority, superseding any other source of GAAP for publicly traded U.S. firms. The *Statement on Auditing Standards No. 69* establishes levels of authoritative support for the various accounting pronouncements. The most authoritative bodies of literature are FASB Standards and Interpretations, APB Opinions, and AICPA Accounting Research Bulletins. If an issue is not covered by one of those sources, accounting literature such as FASB Technical Bulletins, AICPA Industry Audit and Accounting Guides, International Accounting Standards, or AICPA Statements of Position should be consulted.

LO6 Discuss the FASB's conceptual framework for financial reporting, including the objectives of financial reporting and the qualitative characteristics of accounting information.

The FASB's conceptual framework addresses four issues: the objectives of financial reporting; the qualitative characteristics of accounting information; the elements of financial statements; and the environmental assumptions, principles, and constraints that guide financial reporting. The objectives of financial reporting are to provide information that is useful to decision makers; to provide information about the amount and timing of a company's cash flows; and to provide information about the resources, claims to resources, and changes in those items over the reporting period.

Statement of Financial Accounting Concepts No. 2 links the objectives of financial reporting with the qualities that make financial information useful. The two user-specific qualities are understandability and decision usefulness. To be useful in decision making, information must be both relevant and reliable, two qualities that the FASB must weigh whenever it issues a new standard. Information is reliable if it has representational faithfulness, verifiability, and neutrality, and it is relevant if it is timely and has both feedback value and predictive value. Two secondary qualities, comparability and consistency, interact with relevance and reliability to contribute to the usefulness of information. The two pervasive constraints on financial reporting are the cost-benefit criterion and materiality.

LO7 Explain the importance of self-regulation and ethics to the accounting profession.

For decades, the accounting profession prided itself on its ability to regulate itself through the strong efforts of the AICPA, its code of professional conduct, and a culture of independence from its clients. Nonetheless, in the early 2000s, the profession was rocked by news of questionable accounting practices within influential companies across all industries. By mid-2002, with the passage of the Sarbanes-Oxley Act, significant reforms began within the profession and within the regulatory agencies that provide oversight to the profession. As a result, the profession has redoubled its efforts at self-regulation; the cornerstone of this self-regulation is the AICPA's Code of Professional Conduct. This code, which defines the minimum level of professional responsibility and conduct, consists of two sections: (1) the principles and (2) the rules, with the section on independence being one of the most critical.

KEY TERMS

Accounting Principles Board (APB) (p. 61)
Accounting Standards Executive Committee (AcSEC) (p. 62)
American Institute of Certified Public Accountants (AICPA) (p. 61)
Committee on Accounting Procedure (CAP) (p. 61)
comparability (p. 76)
consistency (p. 76)
cost-benefit criterion (p. 77)
cost of capital (p. 65)
Emerging Issues Task Force (EITF) (p. 62)
FASB's conceptual framework (p. 72)
feedback value (p. 75)
financial accounting (p. 59)

Financial Accounting Standards Board (FASB) (p. 62)
Financial Executives International (FEI) (p. 63)
generally accepted accounting principles (GAAP) (p. 60)
Institute of Management Accountants (IMA) (p. 63)
International Accounting Standards (IAS) (p. 64)
International Accounting Standards Board (IASB) (p. 64)
International Financial Reporting Standards (IFRS) (p. 64)
management accounting (p. 59)
materiality (p. 77)
neutrality (p. 75)
predictive value (p. 74)

Public Company Accounting Oversight Board (p. 61)
relevance (p. 74)
reliability (p. 75)
representational faithfulness (p. 75)
Sarbanes-Oxley Act (p. 59)
Securities and Exchange Commission (SEC) (p. 59)
Statements of Financial Accounting Concepts (SFACs) (p. 62)
Statements of Financial Accounting Standards (SFASs) (p. 62)
timeliness (p. 75)
transparency (p. 70)
understandability (p. 73)
usefulness (p. 73)
verifiability (p. 75)

EXERCISES

LO2 **EXERCISE 2-1** **Standard Setting**

The setting of accounting standards in the United States is a complex process involving both the private and the public sector.

Required: Answer the following questions in complete sentences:

1. What is the FASB?

2. What role does the FASB play in our financial markets?

3. What role does the SEC play in standard setting?

4. Do you think the U.S. government should take over the primary role in standard setting? Explain your answer.

LO1,6 **EXERCISE 2-2** **Objectives of Accounting**

In November 1978, the FASB issued *Statement of Financial Accounting Concepts No. 1,* "Objectives of Financial Reporting by Business Enterprises."

Required: Describe the objectives of financial reporting in your own words.

LO6 **EXERCISE 2-3** **Qualitative Characteristics**

In 1980, the FASB issued *Statement of Financial Accounting Concepts No. 2,* "Qualitative Characteristics of Accounting Information."

Required: Identify the qualitative characteristics and explain their purpose.

LO6 **EXERCISE 2-4** **Relevance and Reliability**

The two primary qualities of decision usefulness are relevance and reliability.

Required:

1. Discuss relevance. What are the ingredients of relevance?

2. Discuss reliability. What are the ingredients of reliability?

3. Compare relevance and reliability. Which is more important? Discuss your answer.

LO5 **EXERCISE 2-5** **Sources of GAAP**

Accountants refer to generally accepted accounting principles as the set of accounting rules and methods that have substantial authoritative support. Types of pronouncements from various organizations appear below:

A. AICPA Statements of Position

B. FASB Implementation Guides

C. AICPA Industry Audit and Accounting Guides

D. FASB Standards

E. FASB Interpretations

F. AICPA Accounting Research Bulletins

G. AICPA Accounting Interpretations

H. AICPA AcSEC Practice Bulletins

I. APB Opinions

J. FASB Technical Bulletins

K. Congressional law

L. SEC Staff Accounting Bulletins

Required: Categorize each of these types of pronouncements in the appropriate hierarchical position according to numbers 1–6 below:

1. Highest level of GAAP

2. Second highest level of GAAP

3. Third level of GAAP

4. Fourth level of GAAP

5. Fifth level of GAAP

6. Lowest level of GAAP

LO7   **EXERCISE 2-6   Sarbanes-Oxley Act**

The Sarbanes-Oxley Act, as a way of strengthening auditor independence in fact and in perception, redefined the relationship between auditors and their clients by barring auditors from providing certain services to their clients. A list of services that may be provided by accountants and auditors appears below.

A. Bookkeeping services related to accounting records and financial statements

B. Design and implementation of financial information systems

C. Valuation services

D. Investment banking services

E. Actuarial services

F. Internal audit outsourcing services

G. Audits of financial statements

H. Management functions or human resource services

I. Broker/dealer services

J. Legal services

Required: Identify which of these activities may not be performed for a client if an accountant is also performing audit services for that client.

LO1   **EXERCISE 2-7   The Demand for Financial Information**

Accounting information is used by a variety of interested parties. Financial accounting meets the needs of some of these parties; management accounting is used to meet the needs of other groups.

Required: For each of the following groups of users or individuals, indicate whether financial reporting (F) or management reporting (M) meets this group's needs.

1. Employees

2. Manufacturing managers

3. Creditors

4. Chief financial officer

5. Suppliers

6. Taxpayers

7. Analysts

8. Investors

9. Customers

LO2   **EXERCISE 2-8   Standard Setters in the United States**

A variety of organizations contribute to the setting of accounting standards in the United States.

Required: For each of the following organizations, indicate whether it is a private-sector organization or a public-sector entity.

1. SEC

2. AICPA

3. FASB

4. Congress

5. FEI

LO3   **EXERCISE 2-9   International Accounting Standards**

The IASB is an independent, privately funded body that is committed to the development of a single set of enforceable global accounting standards.

Required: What is the EU's position regarding the use of IASB standards? Are companies within the EU required to use those standards?

LO4 **EXERCISE 2-10** **Setting Accounting Standards**

According to the Sarbanes-Oxley Act, the SEC is authorized to recognize generally accepted accounting principles if they are established by a body that meets certain criteria.

Required: Which of the items listed below are among the criteria that such a body must meet?

1. The body must be a public entity.
2. The body must be funded in a similar manner to the oversight board.
3. The body must be governed by a board whose members have been associated with a public accounting firm within the last two years.
4. The body must have adopted procedures to ensure prompt consideration of changes in accounting principles by a majority vote.

LO4 **EXERCISE 2-11** **Standard-Setting Process**

The FASB follows a set of procedures when it issues an authoritative standard.

Required: Read each of the statements below and indicate whether the statement is a true (T) or a false (F) reflection of FASB procedure.

1. The FASB appoints a task force to identify important reporting issues.
2. A discussion memorandum is issued after public hearings are held.
3. The issuance of a new standard requires a unanimous vote.
4. The FASB's process of standard issuance has been praised for its timeliness.
5. Public response is invited after both the discussion memorandum and the exposure draft.

LO7 **EXERCISE 2-12** **Independence of the CPA**

CPAs are expected to maintain independence from their clients both in fact and in appearance.

Required: Identify the situations listed below that jeopardize the CPA's independence.

1. An auditor for Miller Manufacturing also works as the company's business consultant.
2. Francis Properties employs Jack Clark, CPA, to conduct its annual audit. Jack lives in the same neighborhood as the owner of Francis Properties.
3. William Bennett is hired as the CPA for Lights Fantastic. He also owns stock in this publicly traded company.
4. Maureen Sellers provides legal and auditing services to Rand Balloon Company.

LO6 **EXERCISE 2-13** **Qualitative Characteristics of Accounting Information**

Statement of Financial Accounting Concepts No. 2 is used to guide accountants as they ascertain the qualitative characteristics of accounting information.

Required: Identify the qualitative characteristic of accounting information that is best described in each scenario below. (Do not list relevance and reliability.)

1. Schroeder Technologies has used the FIFO depreciation method since it began operations in 1998.
2. The financial statements of Redline Corporation have been audited by an independent auditing firm.
3. Lack's Motors reported revenues of $150,000 on its income statement. The company's internal sales reports reflect the same amount.
4. Power Depot issues its annual report one month after its year end.

LO7 **EXERCISE 2-14** **Principles of Professional Conduct**

The AICPA's six principles of professional conduct are presented in Figure 2.1, on page 79.

Required: For each situation listed below, indicate the principle that has been violated or followed.

1. The CPAs of King, Brant, and Riley regularly attend classes and workshops on new tax law and accounting practices.
2. In the course of an audit, a CPA learns that the company's president has filed for personal bankruptcy. The action does not affect the finances of the business. The CPA mentions the bankruptcy to a colleague.
3. A CPA performs an audit for a company owned by her husband.

LO6   **EXERCISE 2-15**   **Qualitative Characteristics**

Statement of Financial Accounting Concepts No. 2, "Qualitative Characteristics of Accounting Information," links the objectives of financial reporting with the qualities that make financial information useful. The list below contains several definitions of some of the qualitative characteristics.

A. It is measured and reported in the same way across enterprises.
B. This is the threshold for recognition.
C. It is perceived by sophisticated users as significant in decision making.
D. The same accounting rules are applied across time.
E. It is reasonably free from error and bias and represents what it claims to represent.
F. It faithfully describes what is or what happened.
G. Different measurers agree that the information measures what it claims to measure.
H. It helps users confirm or correct previous expectations.
I. It increases the likelihood that users will correctly forecast the outcome of past or present events.
J. It is available to users soon enough to affect their decisions.

Required:

1. For each of the items listed, name the quality that it describes.
2. What constraints have been identified in financial reporting?
3. Explain the constraints.

Critical Thinking: Why is materiality difficult to apply?

Analyze: Describe how the amount reported for an asset like equipment might be deemed reliable.

LO2, 4   **EXERCISE 2-16**   **Standard Setting**

Accounting standard setting involves the following primary players:

    SEC

    FASB

    AICPA

    Congress

The following roles are carried out by the previously listed standard setters:

A. Has the legal authority to prescribe accounting principles
B. Sets auditing standards
C. Regulates capital markets
D. Establishes and improves standards of financial accounting for the guidance and education of the public
E. Attempts to protect investors from fraud
F. Defines the terms on which accounting standards are based
G. Can veto accounting standards set by other groups
H. Has the highest level of GAAP authority under the FASB standards
I. Creates the most authoritative level of GAAP

Required: For each role listed, identify which of the four players in the standard-setting process is most likely to fill that role. Some roles may be taken on by more than one player.

Communicate: Prepare an oral presentation in which you describe the actual standard-setting process that is practiced today. Include your thoughts on the obstacles you see in the current process, if any.

LO6 **EXERCISE 2-17** **Objectives and Elements**

The financial statements, which are designed to meet the needs of external users, focus on the three objectives of financial reporting prescribed in the FASB's *Statement of Financial Accounting Concepts No. 1*.

Required: Identify which specific financial statements you think correlate with each of the three objectives. Support your answers.

LO6 **EXERCISE 2-18** **Relevance and Reliability**

Below are several scenarios depicting the primary qualities of accounting information.

A. The company uses historical cost on its balance sheet for plant asset purchases.

B. The actual cost of inventory on hand matches the amount that appears on the balance sheet.

C. The results of operations for 2003 were presented to the board of directors within two weeks after the company's year end.

D. Because the balance sheet indicated that the company had very little cash on hand, the bank assumed that the company could not repay an additional short-term loan.

E. The bank account balance reconciled to the cash amount on the balance sheet.

F. The creditors extended additional credit to the company, given its past history of reporting very little outstanding debt.

G. An outside appraiser concurred with the cost basis of the donated asset.

H. Both auditors agreed that the amount shown as revenue on the income statement was accurate.

I. Though management was certain that it would win the lawsuit, the accountant did not report a receivable for the amount the company thought it would win.

J. Because profits were based on current inventory prices, the investors used the gross profit margin as an indicator of future gross profit rates.

Required: For each scenario, decide whether the quality of relevance or that of reliability more closely applies. Why is it important that information have both of these qualities?

LO5, 6 **EXERCISE 2-19** **Concepts and Hierarchy** (CPA adapted)

The Statements of Financial Accounting Concepts serve accounting-standard-setting bodies as a framework for GAAP. Multiple-choice questions pertaining to these concepts and the hierarchy of GAAP appear below.

1. What are the Statements of Financial Accounting Concepts intended to establish?

   a. Generally accepted accounting principles in financial reporting by business enterprises

   b. The meaning of "present fairly in accordance with generally accepted accounting principles"

   c. The objectives and concepts for use in developing standards of financial accounting and reporting

   d. The hierarchy of sources of generally accepted accounting principles

2. According to the FASB conceptual framework, the objectives of financial reporting for business enterprises are based on

   a. generally accepted accounting principles.

   b. reporting on management's stewardship.

   c. the need for conservatism.

   d. the needs of users of the information.

3. According to the FASB conceptual framework, the usefulness of providing information in financial statements is subject to the constraint of

   a. consistency.   c. reliability.
   b. cost-benefit.   d. representational faithfulness.

4. According to the FASB conceptual framework, which of the following relates to both relevance and reliability?

   a. Comparability   c. Verifiability
   b. Feedback value   d. Timeliness

5. In the hierarchy of generally accepted accounting principles, APB Opinions have the same authority as AICPA

   a. Statements of Position.   c. Issues Papers.
   b. Industry Audit and Accounting Guides.   d. Accounting Research Bulletins.

6. According to *Statement of Financial Accounting Concepts No. 2*, which of the following is (are) neutrality an ingredient of?

	Reliability	Relevance
a.	Yes	Yes
b.	Yes	No
c.	No	Yes
d.	No	No

Required: Select the best answer for each question.

LO7 **EXERCISE 2-20   Challenges of the Accounting Profession**
The Sarbanes-Oxley Act is one of the most significant changes in the accounting profession that has ever been mandated.

Required:

1. List the major changes that the Sarbanes-Oxley Act has created in the accounting profession.

2. One provision of the Sarbanes-Oxley Act requires CEOs and CFOs to submit statements to the SEC. What is the nature of these statements? Why was this requirement included in the Sarbanes-Oxley Act?

CASES

LO2 **CRITICAL THINKING CASE 2-1   Standard-Setting Groups**
The FASB has been setting accounting standards since 1973.

Required:

1. How important is the FASB to the efficient operations of capital markets? Why?

2. Do you think the makeup of the FASB adequately represents the users of financial statements and the public in general? Explain your answer.

LO3 **RESEARCH CASE 2-2   International Accounting Standards**
The Internet provides helpful information about the current status of International Accounting Standards (IAS).

Required: Visit the International Accounting Standards Board website at **www.iasb.org.uk** and answer the following questions:

1. Has the IASB issued any new statements recently? If so, briefly describe the issue(s) addressed by the new statement(s).

2. How does the United States (the SEC and the FASB) currently view International Accounting Standards?

3. In your opinion, how close is the United States to adopting International Accounting Standards as a permitted form of GAAP for listing purposes?

LO3 RESEARCH CASE **2-3** **International Accounting**

According to the FASB's website (**www.fasb.org**), the Financial Accounting Standards Board strongly and actively supports the internationalization of accounting standards. Almost every FASB project is a matter of interest to some other country or to the International Accounting Standards Board. The FASB's obligation to its domestic constituents demands that it attempt to narrow the range of difference between U.S. standards and those of other countries. The board and the staff participate in many international liaison activities with different standard setters around the world.

Required:

1. Discuss the current activities of the FASB in supporting the internationalization of accounting standards. Research this issue on the FASB's website (**www.fasb.org**), the IASB's website (**www.iasb.org.uk**), and recent articles in the press.

2. List the topics that are different in U.S. GAAP and those standards currently being proposed by the IASB.

LO7 ETHICS CASE **2-4** **Challenges of the Accounting Profession**

 ETHICS

Linda Kroon recently received her CPA certification and began work as the senior staff accountant for Ralley Enterprises on March 1. As she was preparing to close the books at the quarter end and prepare the financial statements for that period, her boss, the company controller, asked her to record a journal entry for $800,000 in sales to Ryan Company on account. He said he'd just received a phone call from Ryan Company's account manager with the details. Linda asked for the documentation to support the entry and was told that the documentation would probably arrive in the next few weeks. "Those sales guys, they never get their paperwork in on time. I realize that you're new here, but our team does a lot of verbal sales commitments with customers," the controller told Linda. "Plus our sales are really down this quarter. This entry will help our bottom line." Linda feels uncomfortable about the request to record this transaction.

Required:

1. What ethical considerations exist in this situation?
2. List the parties who may be affected by Linda's decision.
3. What personal and professional values should Linda consider?
4. List the alternative actions that Linda might take.
5. Which party's interest should have the highest priority in this situation?
6. What course of action should Linda take?

LO7 ETHICS CASE **2-5** **Audit Services**

 ETHICS

Irma Smith is the CFO of Kataska Inc., a small public company. For the past six years, the company's financial statements have been audited by Knight, Rogers & Tanner, a regional public accounting firm. Irma and the accounting staff have developed a good working relationship with the audit staff, and Irma has developed a friendship with Maria Rogers, one of the public accounting firm's partners. Currently, Kataska is planning a major expansion. The expansion project will require the extensive use of outside information technology and human resource consulting. The company is also planning to outsource its entire internal audit function. Irma is currently seeking an appropriate accounting firm for the consulting and the internal audit project.

Maria Rogers is the partner in charge of the consulting division of Knight, Rogers & Tanner. She is urging her friend Irma to award the consulting contract to Knight, Rogers & Tanner and to also engage that firm as its internal auditor. Irma knows that the provisions of the Sarbanes-Oxley Act of 2002 prohibit accounting firms from performing both auditing and consulting services for the same client. Thus, if Kataska hires Knight, Rogers & Tanner as its internal auditor and consultant, it will have to engage a new firm to perform the audits of its financial statements.

Irma has been asked to make a recommendation to the company's CEO and board of directors. She believes that a new audit firm that was unfamiliar with the company would be likely to charge a higher fee and would require a great deal of assistance from the company's accounting staff. Thus, she is convinced that the company's current auditor, Knight,

Rogers & Tanner, will perform the best and least expensive audit. At the same time, she knows that Knight, Rogers & Tanner would prefer the higher-profit consulting and internal audit contract to the lower-profit and higher-risk audit engagement. She would like to help her friend obtain the consulting contract.

Required:

1. Why do you think the Sarbanes-Oxley Act of 2002 prohibits auditors of financial statements from performing internal audit or consulting services for the same client?
2. What are the problems and issues faced by the CFO?
3. Who will be affected by the decision made by the CFO?
4. What values and principles are likely to influence the decision?
5. What alternative actions can the CFO take?
6. a. Which party's interest is most important?
    b. Which values and principles are most important?
    c. Which of the possible consequences will do the most good or cause the least harm?
    d. Which consideration is most important?
7. If you were in Irma's position, what would you recommend to the CEO and the board of directors?

LO6, 7   **ETHICS CASE 2-6   The Timing of Revenue Recognition**

ETHICS

Bert Comp is the service department manager of a division of Sunly Corporation, a distributor of major household appliances. When Bert became manager of the service department three years ago, it was operating at a deficit. However, during the past three years, Bert has been able to improve the financial performance of the department by reducing expenses on purchases of appliance parts.

During the first week of January 2005, Kurt Newman, the division manager, reviews the performance reports for Bert's department. After comparing the department's actual performance to its budget for last year, Kurt notices that the costs incurred by the service department are $25,000 lower than budgeted. He is concerned that the division's cost budget will be reduced next year if the costs incurred by any of the departments are lower than budgeted.

The next day, Kurt informs Bert that he has ordered equipment for $25,000 from a supplier who happens to be a friend of his family. He tells Bert that the supplier will back-date the invoice and shipping documents to December 31, 2004. Kurt points out that this will help the department keep its cost budget intact and will also help the supplier, who appreciates the additional revenue for the 2004 reporting period. Bert, who completed numerous accounting courses in college, knows that this is a violation of generally accepted accounting principles. When the invoice arrives, Bert will have to verify receipt of the equipment and submit the paperwork to the accounting department.

Required:

1. What are the problems and issues that Bert faces?
2. Who will be affected by the decision that Bert must make?
3. What values and principles are likely to influence his decision?
4. What alternative actions are available to Bert?
5. a. Whose interest is most important in this decision?
    b. Which values and principles are most important in this decision?
    c. Which of the possible consequences will do the most good or cause the least harm?
    d. Which of the considerations identified in a, b, and c is most important?
6. What would you do if you were Bert?

LO1, 2   **CRITICAL THINKING CASE 2-7   Regulatory Issues and Fraud**

With the signing of the Sarbanes-Oxley Act of 2002, President George W. Bush made the following statement about the new law: "The law says to corporate accountants: the high standards of your profession will be enforced without exception; the auditors will be audited; the accountants will be held to account." Read the following article, which appeared in the *New York Times* on February 2, 2002.

Two, Three, Many?[22]
by Paul Krugman

Here's a scary question: How many more Enrons are out there?

Even now the conventional wisdom is that Enron was uniquely crooked. O.K., other companies have engaged in "aggressive accounting," the art form formerly known as fraud. But how likely is it that other major companies will turn out, behind their imposing facades, to be little more than pyramid schemes? Alas, it's all too likely. I can't tell you which corporate icons will turn out to be made of papier-mâché, but I'd be very surprised if we don't have two, three, even many Enrons in our future.

Why do I say this? Like any crime, a pyramid scheme requires means, motive and opportunity. Lately all three have been there in abundance.

Means: We now know how easily a company that earns a modest profit, or even loses money, can dress itself up to create the appearance of high profitability. Just the simple trick of paying employees not with straight salary, which counts as an expense, but with stock options, which don't, can have a startling effect on a company's reported profits. According to the British economist Andrew Smithers, in 1998 Cisco reported a profit of $1.35 billion; if it had counted the market value of the stock options it issued as an expense, it would have reported a loss of $4.9 billion. And stock options are only one of a panoply of techniques available to make the bottom line look artificially good.

Motive: The purpose of inflating earnings is, of course, to drive up the price of the stock. But why do companies want to do that?

One answer is that a high stock price helps a company grow; it makes it easier to raise money, to acquire other companies, to attract employees and so on. And no doubt most managers have puffed up their stock out of a genuine desire to make their companies grow. But as we watch top executives walk away rich while the companies they ran collapse (there are cases worse than Enron; the founder of Global Crossing has apparently walked away from bankruptcy with $750 million), it's clear that we should also think about the incentives of the managers themselves. Ask not what a high stock price can do for your company; ask what it can do for your personal bottom line.

Not incidentally, a high stock price facilitates the very accounting tricks that companies use to create phantom profits, further driving up the stock price. It's Ponzi time!

But what about opportunity? A confluence of three factors in the late 1990's opened the door for financial scams on a scale unseen for generations.

First was the rise of the "new economy." New technologies have, without question, created new opportunities and shaken up the industrial order. But that creates the kind of confusion in which scams flourish. How do you know whether a company has really found a highly profitable new-economy niche or is just faking it?

Second was the stock market bubble. As Robert Shiller pointed out in his book "Irrational Exuberance," a rising market is like a natural Ponzi scheme, in which each successive wave of investors generates gains for the last wave, making everything look great until you run out of suckers. What he didn't point out, but now seems obvious, is that in such an environment it's also easy to run deliberate pyramid schemes. When the public believes in magic, it's springtime for charlatans.

And finally, there was (and is) a permissive legal environment. Once upon a time, the threat of lawsuits hung over companies and auditors that engaged in sharp accounting practices. But in 1995 Congress, overriding a veto by Bill Clinton, passed the Private Securities Litigation Reform Act, which made such suits far more difficult. Soon accounting firms, the companies they audited and the investment banks that sold their stock got very cozy indeed.

And here too one must look not only at the motives of corporations, but at the personal motives of executives. We now know that Enron managers gave their

---

22 Paul Krugman, "Two, Three, Many?" *New York Times*, February 2, 2002.

investment bankers—not their investment banks but the individual bankers—an opportunity to invest in the shell companies they used to hide debt and siphon off money. Wanna bet that similar deals didn't take place at many other firms?

I hope that Enron turns out to be unique. But I'll be very surprised.

Required:

1. Reread the remarks by President Bush found in the Financial Reporting Case at the beginning of this chapter. What did President Bush mean by "the auditors will be audited"? Who will audit them?

2. What role do you think personal greed plays in accounting fraud? Explain.

LO2   **RESEARCH CASE 2-8   Standard Setters**

Both private and public organizations have a role in the accounting standard-setting process in the United States. Each organization has specific responsibilities; however, the SEC has a responsibility to Congress and the president as the ultimate standard setter and enforcement authority.

Required:

1. Briefly describe the roles of the SEC, FASB, and AICPA, and each organization's primary responsibility as it relates to setting accounting standards.

2. Visit the SEC's website at **http://www.sec.gov/**. Access the "What We Do" section.

   a. What is the mission of the SEC?
   b. What type of violations does the SEC investigate?

LO6   **ANALYSIS CASE 2-9   Qualitative Characteristics of Accounting Information**

The consolidated statement of earnings and the consolidated statements of financial position for **Tootsie Roll Industries, Inc.** appear below and on the next page.

Required:

1. Find the 2002 annual report for Tootsie Roll at **www.tootsie.com** and review the notes to the financial statements. Using the statements below and the notes in the annual report, give an example of how Tootsie Roll uses the qualitative characteristics of (a) comparability and (b) consistency in presenting its financial information.

2. Which qualitative characteristics are most important to ensure that financial information is transparent? Explain.

Tootsie Roll

Tootsie Roll Industries, Inc. and Subsidiaries
Consolidated Statement of Earnings
(in thousands except per share data)

	For the year ended December 31,		
	2003	**2002**	**2001**
Net sales	$392,656	$393,185	$391,755
Cost of goods sold	222,547	222,204	217,897
Gross margin	170,109	170,981	173,858
Selling, marketing and administrative expenses	77,756	75,751	77,376
Amortization of intangible assets	—	—	3,778
Earnings from operations	92,353	95,230	92,704
Other income, net	5,594	5,458	8,083
Earnings before income taxes	97,947	100,688	100,787
Provision for income taxes	32,933	34,300	35,100
Net earnings	$ 65,014	$ 66,388	$ 65,687
Earnings per share	$ 1.26	$ 1.25	$ 1.23
Average common and class B common shares outstanding	51,784	53,070	53,464

Tootsie Roll

Tootsie Roll Industries, Inc. and Subsidiaries
Consolidated Statement of Financial Position

Assets (in thousands)	December 31, 2003	December 31, 2002
Current Assets:		
Cash and cash equivalents	$ 84,084	$105,507
Investments	86,961	40,737
Accounts receivable trade, less allowances of $1,970 and $2,005	18,131	22,686
Other receivables	3,076	4,073
Inventories:		
Finished goods and work-in-process	28,969	26,591
Raw materials and supplies	17,117	17,054
Prepaid expenses	4,416	3,819
Deferred income taxes	951	4,481
Total current assets	243,705	224,948
Property, Plant and Equipment, at cost:		
Land	8,265	8,297
Buildings	44,960	43,948
Machinery and equipment	206,697	196,706
	259,922	248,951
Less—Accumulated depreciation	130,759	120,082
Total property, plant, and equipment	129,163	128,869
Other Assets:		
Goodwill	38,151	38,151
Trademarks	79,348	79,348
Investments	112,431	116,501
Split dollar officer life insurance	62,499	58,263
Total other assets	292,429	292,263
Total assets	$665,297	$646,080

Liabilities and Shareholders' Equity

	December 31, 2003	December 31, 2002
Current Liabilities:		
Accounts payable	$ 11,947	$ 12,505
Dividends payable	3,589	3,579
Accrued liabilities	38,834	35,825
Income taxes payable	8,517	11,187
Total current liabilities	62,887	63,096
Noncurrent Liabilities:		
Deferred income taxes	22,631	19,654
Postretirement health care and life insurance benefits	9,302	8,151
Industrial development bonds	7,500	7,500
Deferred compensation and other liabilities	26,396	20,939
Total noncurrent liabilities	65,829	56,244
Shareholders' Equity:		
Common stock, $.69–4/9 par value—120,000 and 120,000 shares authorized—34,082 and 34,248, respectively, issued	23,668	23,783
Class B common stock, $.69–4/9 par value—40,000 and 40,000 shares authorized—17,145 and 16,759, respectively, issued	11,906	11,638
Capital in excess of par value	357,922	355,658
Retained earnings, per accompanying statement	156,786	148,705
Accumulated other comprehensive earnings (loss)	(11,709)	(11,052)
Treasury stock (at cost)—56 shares and 55 shares, respectively	(1,992)	(1,992)
Total shareholders' equity	536,581	526,740
Total liabilities and shareholders' equity	$665,297	$646,080

ON THE WEB

The following exercises, activities, and problems are available on the *Intermediate Accounting* website. Use these resources to reinforce your understanding of the topics presented in this chapter.

- CPA-Adapted Simulations
- Interpreting the Accounting Standards
- Extending the Global Focus
- Extending the Ethics Discussion
- Mastering the Spreadsheet
- Career Snapshots
- Annual Report Project
- ACE Practice Tests
- Flashcards
- Glossary
- Check Figures for Text Problems
- PowerPoint Presentations

SOLUTIONS: CHECK YOUR UNDERSTANDING

The Economic and Regulatory Purposes of Financial Reporting (p. 59)

1. Management accounting is the process of producing financial information for internal purposes; financial accounting is the process of providing information for investors, creditors, and other external parties.

2. Potential and current investors have an interest in financial data so that they may make informed investment decisions. Creditors require financial data in order to decide whether to extend credit to the requesting company or to alter existing credit arrangements. Employees may require financial data to aid in contract negotiations.

3. The IRS requires financial data from individuals and businesses so that it can enforce the U.S. tax code. The SEC requires financial data from all publicly traded companies to protect public investors from fraud or inadequate financial disclosures.

Setting Accounting Standards: A Public-Private Partnership (p. 64)

1. The FASB is the most influential standard-setting body in the private sector. Its mission is to establish and improve standards of financial accounting and reporting for the public, including preparers, auditors, and other users of financial information.

2. Laws from Congress; SABs and FRRs from the SEC; SFASs, SFACs, Interpretations, Technical Bulletins, EITFs, and Implementation Guides from the FASB; ARBs, APBs, Industry Audit and Accounting Guides, Statements of Position, and Practice Bulletins from the AICPA; IFRSs and Interpretations from the IASB are part of GAAP. Publications from the IMA and FEI are not authoritative.

3. While the SEC has the legal authority to set accounting principles and standards, in the past it has deferred to the FASB and the private sector on this activity. The Sarbanes-Oxley Act of 2002 significantly changed the SEC's role in setting accounting standards. That act established the Public Company Accounting Oversight Board under the auspices of the SEC. The board can, to the extent it determines appropriate, adopt standards proposed by advisory groups, but it also has the authority to amend, modify, repeal, or reject any suggested standards.

An International Standard Setter: The IASB (p. 65)

1. International accounting standards are important because they would provide comparability between the financial statements of different countries. A decrease in the diversity of accounting standards that now exists will help achieve the goal of convergence.

2. The IASB seeks to develop a single set of high-quality, understandable, and enforceable global accounting standards that will provide transparent and comparable information in general-purpose financial statements. In addition, the board works with national accounting standard setters to achieve convergence in accounting standards around the world.

Standard Setting in Practice: An Economic and Political Process (p. 67)

1. Once an issue has been identified by the Emerging Issues Task Force and placed on the FASB's agenda, a task force is appointed to review the issue and work with the FASB staff to conduct research. A discussion memorandum is then issued, and public response is encouraged. After digesting that response, the FASB issues an exposure draft, invites additional public response, and finally issues an actual statement.

2. Critics contend that the amount of time that the FASB takes to study an accounting issue and release a statement is too long to meet users' needs given the fast-changing business environment.

The Hierarchy of GAAP (p. 71)

1. Transparency in financial reporting means that relevant and understandable financial information about a company is available to investors and other market participants.

2. Transparency in reporting enables investors, creditors, and the market to evaluate an entity; increases confidence in the fairness of U.S. markets; and is fundamental to corporate governance because it enables boards of directors to evaluate management's effectiveness and to take early corrective actions, when necessary.

3. The three most authoritative sources of GAAP from the private sector are FASB Standards, APB Opinions, and AICPA Accounting Research Bulletins.

The FASB's Conceptual Framework for Financial Reporting (p. 78)

1. The FASB's conceptual framework provides a frame of reference for resolving accounting issues. It helps establish reasonable bounds for judgment in preparing financial information and increases understanding of, and confidence in, financial information on the part of users of financial reports.

2. Information has relevance when it is capable of making a difference in users' decisions by enabling them to make predictions about the future or confirm or correct expectations. Information is relevant if it is timely and has both predictive value and feedback value.

3. Understandability and decision usefulness are the two user-specific qualities of accounting information.

4. The FASB has identified two constraints on financial reporting. The first is the cost-benefit criterion, the requirement that benefits must exceed costs. The second is a threshold for recognition called materiality. Information has materiality if it has the capacity to affect users' decisions.

The Accounting Profession: Self-Regulation and Ethics (p. 83)

1. The AICPA Code of Professional Conduct defines the minimum level of professional responsibility and conduct and applies to all AICPA members who are in the practice of accounting.

2. Auditors are now governed by the Public Company Accounting Oversight Board. The direct responsibility for the audit relationship now rests with the audit committee. Auditors should be aware of new disclosure requirements. They should also be careful not to perform other accounting services for the audit client that would place their independence in jeopardy.

3. Answers may include: bookkeeping and other services related to accounting records and financial statements; design and implementation of financial information systems; valuation services; actuarial services; internal audit outsourcing services; management functions or human resource services; broker/dealer or investment banking services; and legal services.

CPA-ADAPTED SIMULATION

This simulation asks you to complete various tasks related to a company's annual financial statements. If your instructor has signed up for CPAexcel™, you can do the work online at www.cpaexcel.com/hmco. You may also do the simulation manually.

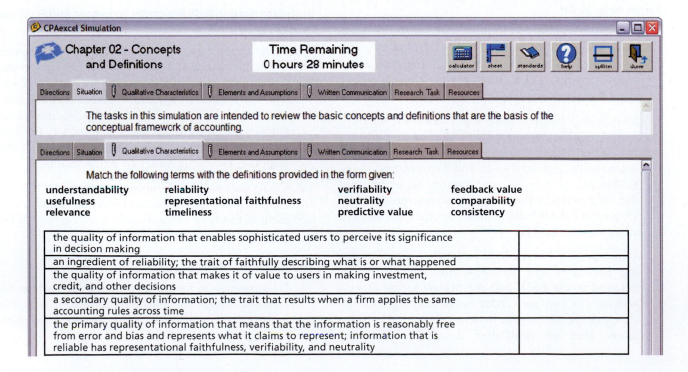

Definition	
the primary quality of information that means that the information is capable of making a difference in users' decisions by enabling them to make predictions about the future or confirm or correct expectations; the ingredients of relevance are timeliness, feedback value, and predictive value	
an ingredient of reliability; the trait of enabling different measurers to agree that information measures what it claims to measure	
an ingredient of reliability; a lack of bias in the measurement process and a lack of intent to influence behavior or achieve a desired result	
an ingredient of relevance; the trait of being available to users soon enough to affect their decisions	
an ingredient of relevance; the trait of helping users confirm or correct previous expectations	
a secondary quality of information; the trait of being measured and reported in the same way across enterprises or enabling users to identify similarities and differences among sets of information	
an ingredient of relevance; the trait of helping users make forecasts	

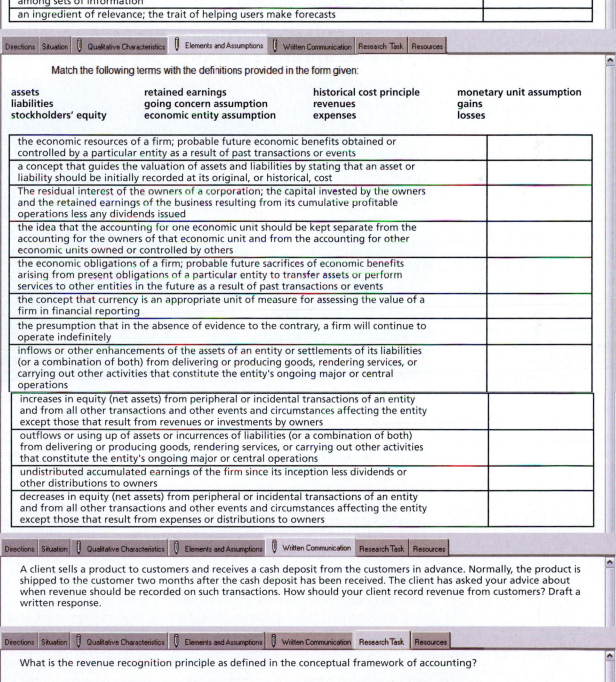

Directions | Situation | Qualitative Characteristics | Elements and Assumptions | Written Communication | Research Task | Resources

Match the following terms with the definitions provided in the form given:

assets	retained earnings	historical cost principle	monetary unit assumption
liabilities	going concern assumption	revenues	gains
stockholders' equity	economic entity assumption	expenses	losses

Definition	
the economic resources of a firm; probable future economic benefits obtained or controlled by a particular entity as a result of past transactions or events	
a concept that guides the valuation of assets and liabilities by stating that an asset or liability should be initially recorded at its original, or historical, cost	
The residual interest of the owners of a corporation; the capital invested by the owners and the retained earnings of the business resulting from its cumulative profitable operations less any dividends issued	
the idea that the accounting for one economic unit should be kept separate from the accounting for the owners of that economic unit and from the accounting for other economic units owned or controlled by others	
the economic obligations of a firm; probable future sacrifices of economic benefits arising from present obligations of a particular entity to transfer assets or perform services to other entities in the future as a result of past transactions or events	
the concept that currency is an appropriate unit of measure for assessing the value of a firm in financial reporting	
the presumption that in the absence of evidence to the contrary, a firm will continue to operate indefinitely	
inflows or other enhancements of the assets of an entity or settlements of its liabilities (or a combination of both) from delivering or producing goods, rendering services, or carrying out other activities that constitute the entity's ongoing major or central operations	
increases in equity (net assets) from peripheral or incidental transactions of an entity and from all other transactions and other events and circumstances affecting the entity except those that result from revenues or investments by owners	
outflows or using up of assets or incurrences of liabilities (or a combination of both) from delivering or producing goods, rendering services, or carrying out other activities that constitute the entity's ongoing major or central operations	
undistributed accumulated earnings of the firm since its inception less dividends or other distributions to owners	
decreases in equity (net assets) from peripheral or incidental transactions of an entity and from all other transactions and other events and circumstances affecting the entity except those that result from expenses or distributions to owners	

Directions | Situation | Qualitative Characteristics | Elements and Assumptions | Written Communication | Research Task | Resources

A client sells a product to customers and receives a cash deposit from the customers in advance. Normally, the product is shipped to the customer two months after the cash deposit has been received. The client has asked your advice about when revenue should be recorded on such transactions. How should your client record revenue from customers? Draft a written response.

Directions | Situation | Qualitative Characteristics | Elements and Assumptions | Written Communication | Research Task | Resources

What is the revenue recognition principle as defined in the conceptual framework of accounting?

The Income Statement and Comprehensive Income Disclosures

LEARNING OBJECTIVES

After studying this chapter, you should be able to:

LO1 Distinguish between the economic and accounting definitions of income.

LO2 Discuss the differences between a single-step income statement and a multiple-step income statement and list the elements each format contains.

LO3 Identify recurring and nonrecurring items and report them on the income statement.

LO4 Explain the concept of earnings per share and describe how EPS is reported on the income statement.

LO5 Define comprehensive income and discuss the required disclosures.

LO6 Use five basic measures to analyze an income statement.

LO7 Summarize the issues related to quality of earnings.

FINANCIAL REPORTING CASE

DELL DELIVERS DOMINO'S PIZZA AND WIDENS OVERALL MARKET-SHARE LEAD

CEO Michael Dell is proud of his company's global reach and operating results (which outperform the industry), as reported in the income statement of Dell Computer Corporation.

Dell When Domino's Pizza was searching for an integrated computer solution to avoid downtimes for its popular Internet and interactive TV ordering service, it turned to Dell for servers, monitors, desktop computers, and operating systems. By the end of 2004, Domino's Pizza had adopted Dell technologies in 100 percent of its stores. Success stories like this one keep Dell at the top of its game, building and customizing products and services to satisfy a range of customer requirements. Dell's climb in the marketplace is attributed to its focus on delivering the best possible customer experience by selling standards-based products and services directly to customers.

Whereas many of its competitors experienced sluggish growth in 2004, Dell achieved its best-ever quarterly operating results in the six-months ended August 1, 2004, and widened the company's overall global market-share lead. Total product shipments in the company's fiscal second quarter of 2004 were up 19 percent from a year earlier. This growth rate was sharply faster than the rest of the industry. In addition, as you can see in Dell's condensed consolidated statement of operations on the next page, the company saw a 20.4 percent increase in revenue for the six months ended August 1, 2004, as compared to the same period in 2003. Note that even with

Dell

Dell Computer Corporation
Condensed Consolidated Statement of Operations
(in millions; unaudited)

	Six Months Ended		% Growth Rates
	July 30, 2004	August 1, 2003	Yr. to Yr.
Net revenue	$23,246	$19,310	20.4%
Cost of revenue	19,039	15,784	20.6%
Gross margin	4,207	3,526	19.3%
Selling, general and administrative	1,999	1,648	21.3%
Research, development and engineering	236	227	4.2%
Total operating expenses	2,235	1,875	19.2%
Operating income	1,972	1,651	19.4%
Investment and other income, net	95	90	6.1%
Income before income taxes	2,067	1,741	18.7%
Income tax provision	537	522	2.8%
Net income	$ 1,530	$ 1,219	25.6%

increases in cost of revenue and selling, general and administrative expenses, the company still reported an even more impressive operating income increase of 19.4 percent.

Companies like Dell prepare income statements, often called statements of operations, at various times throughout the year to inform stockholders of their quarterly and annual performance. As shown by the example given here, such a statement can offer comparative elements so that investors can analyze the company's growth (or lack thereof) for different periods of time. The format of Dell's statement of operations, with such categories as net revenue, gross margin, operating expenses, operating income, and net income, is typical of most income statements prepared by U.S. companies.

EXAMINING THE CASE

1. Why do you think operating income is shown as a separate line item from net income?

2. If you were considering an investment in Dell Computer Corporation, how would you describe the company's performance based on the information presented in the statement of operations?

3. What general categories would you expect to see on an income statement for a U.S. company?

LO 1 Distinguish between the economic and accounting definitions of income.

Critical Thinking: In your personal life, how do you measure your income? Is this measurement the result of specific transactions? Explain.

The Economic and Accounting Definitions of Income

N et income is one of the most meaningful figures that a firm reports. Present and potential investors and creditors, management, and other interested users all focus on net income as a significant measure of a firm's past performance and an indication of its future prospects. Thus, the application of generally accepted accounting principles to determining and measuring net income is, and will continue to be, of critical importance.

Income, as a general concept, relates to whether an enterprise is better off at the end of a period than it was at the beginning of the period, apart from any capital contributions or withdrawals by its owners. It indicates whether an enterprise, through its operations or other events, has increased its net assets or owners' equity. Central to the determination of net income is the definition and measurement of the events that cause net assets to increase and whether those events should be included in net income.

DIFFERING MEASURES OF INCOME: AN ILLUSTRATION

To consider the various ways in which income may be measured, assume that at the beginning of the current year you paid $100,000 to purchase a plot of land on which you expected to build a home. At the end of the year, a real estate developer approaches you and wants to purchase the land from you for $150,000. During the year, price levels increased by 4 percent as a result of inflation. Although you had originally planned to hold on to the land, you decide that you should not pass up a good opportunity, and you agree to sell. As summarized in Illustration 3.1, the income resulting from this scenario may be calculated in three ways:

1. One measure of income is simply the difference between the land's selling price and its cost ($150,000 − $100,000 = $50,000). This is how accountants typically measure net income.

2. Another way to measure income is to take into account the change in price level caused by inflation. Because of inflation, the land's cost of $100,000 at the beginning of the year is equivalent to an adjusted cost of $104,000 ($100,000 × 1.04) at the end of the year. When that adjusted cost is deducted from the sales price of $150,000, the resulting income is $46,000, rather than the $50,000 previously calculated. The second figure is lower because $4,000 of the previously calculated income is the result of an inflation-based general increase in prices rather than a specific increase in the value of the land. Under U.S. GAAP, such adjustments in price level are not considered significant and are not accounted for.

3. Still another measure of the income from the sale is based on how much better off you really are if you need to replace that plot of land with another plot on which to build your home. If the replacement cost (the cost to purchase a similar plot of land in a similar location) is the same $150,000 that you sold your land for, are you

Illustration 3.1

Income Measurement Methods

1	2	3
Selling Price − Purchase Price	Selling Price − Adjusted Cost	Selling Price − Replacement Cost
$150,000 − $100,000 = $50,000	$150,000 − $104,000 = $46,000	$150,000 − $150,000 = $0

any better off after the sale than you were before? Under this measure of income, the answer is no because you must spend your entire proceeds to replace the land you sold.

THE ECONOMIC APPROACH TO DETERMINING NET INCOME

holding gain an increase in value that occurs while an asset is being held

economic income a change in net wealth due to a change in the current value of an asset

Now let's assume that you did not sell the land at the end of the year, but instead held on to it as you had originally planned. Did you have any income from the holding gain of $50,000? A **holding gain** is an increase in value that occurs while an asset is being held. From an economic perspective, the answer is yes, if income is defined as a change in net wealth due to a change in the current value of an asset—in this case, land. This perspective is the basis of **economic income**. In a more general sense, any increase in the current value of a firm's net assets (not counting capital contributions and withdrawals) is its economic income for the period. The drawback to the economic income approach is that because no actual transaction has taken place, it is difficult to measure an asset's fair market value in an objective and verifiable way that users can rely upon.

THE ACCOUNTING APPROACH TO DETERMINING NET INCOME

transaction-based income net income derived from all business transactions, determined by subtracting all recognized expenses and losses from all recognized revenues and gains; also called *accounting-based income*

Another way to determine net income is to focus on the actual business transactions of an enterprise. This is the approach most commonly applied under GAAP and the approach Dell Computer used to determine that its net income for the six months ended August 1, 2003 was $1,219 million. **Transaction-based income** (or *accounting-based income*) is the net income that a firm derives from all of its business transactions; it is determined by subtracting all recognized expenses and losses from all recognized revenues and gains. Increases in the market values of assets and liabilities are not always recognized under the transaction approach because they are considered holding gains and do not arise from actual transactions, such as sales. However, in some cases, a decline in the current value of an asset to below its historical cost is recognized as a result of the concept of conservatism. Under the transaction-based approach, net income is defined as follows:

$$\text{Net Income} = \text{Revenues} - \text{Expenses} + \text{Gains} - \text{Losses}$$

The relationship between the balance sheet (representing the historical costs of the net assets at the beginning and end of the period) and net income as determined on the income statement is shown in Illustration 3.2. A firm starts the accounting period with the group of net assets presented on the balance sheet at that date. During the period, the firm enters into various revenue and expense transactions, which are summarized on the income statement for the period. The firm may also enter into capital transactions that either increase net assets (for example, stock issues) or decrease net assets (dividends declared). When the capital transactions are combined with the income statement transactions, the result is the group of net assets at the end of the period, which is presented on the balance sheet at that date. The balance sheet at

Illustration 3.2

Relationship Between the Balance Sheet and the Income Statement

Historical cost of net assets at the beginning of the period		Income statement transactions during the period		Capital contributions and withdrawals during the period		Historical cost of net assets at the end of the period
	+ −		+ −		=	

the end of the period is the result of the external transactions that occurred during the period. As you will see, there are multiple internal transactions that will also affect the balance sheet. Nonetheless, this approach is primarily a transaction-based approach.

ACCRUAL ACCOUNTING

Accrual accounting is the foundation for determining net income under generally accepted accounting principles. As discussed in Chapter 1, accrual accounting dictates that transactions and other events and circumstances are recorded in the period in which they occur rather than in the period in which cash or some other form of payment is received or paid. Accrual accounting is based on the matching principle and the revenue recognition principle. (Recall that the matching principle holds that expenses should be recognized in the same period as the revenues to which they are related. The revenue recognition principle states that revenue should be recognized when the amount and timing of that revenue are reasonably determinable and the earnings process is complete or virtually complete.)

In light of these principles, GAAP is primarily transaction-based. That is, an actual transaction must occur, and it must be measured and recorded using historical costs and under the principles of accrual accounting. However, in an increasing number of cases, the FASB is turning to a more economic-based approach using current values. As you progress through this book, you will see that some of the latest Statements of Financial Accounting Standards issued by the FASB use current values and recognize changes in those values before a transaction actually occurs.

> **CHECK YOUR UNDERSTANDING**
>
> 1. Describe the difference between economic income and accounting-based income.
>
> 2. On which financial statement should revenue and expense transactions be summarized?
>
> 3. Name the principle that holds that expenses should be recognized in the same period as the revenues to which they are related.

LO 2 Discuss the differences between a single-step income statement and a multiple-step income statement and list the elements each format contains.

income statement a financial statement that provides information about the amount of net income earned by a firm over a stated period of time by detailing the revenues earned and the expenses incurred during the period

🧩 *Critical Thinking: If you were to prepare an income statement for your personal finances for the current month, what items would you list? How would you organize or categorize the items on the statement?*

The Income Statement: Elements and Reporting Formats

The **income statement** provides information about the amount of net income earned by a firm over a stated period of time by detailing the revenues earned and the expenses incurred during that period. Income statements are prepared at least annually and usually more often, such as quarterly or monthly. Net income (or net loss) is determined by subtracting all expenses and losses from all revenues and gains. The FASB's definitions of the four elements of the income statement—revenues, expenses, gains, and losses—are summarized in Illustration 3.3.

Potential and current investors and creditors need information to help them assess the amounts, certainty, and timing of future cash flows. The income statement, although historically based, is essential to making such assessments. To be most effective, the income statement must provide enough detail to help users distinguish the components of income that are likely to continue in the future and thus are ongoing from those that are more transitory and thus are one-time events. Therefore, two significant issues that arise are (1) how to organize the income statement based on the amount of detail presented and (2) how to disclose and differentiate among the various components of income.

Illustration 3.3

The Elements of the Income Statement[1]

Revenues	Inflows or other enhancements of the assets of an entity or settlements of its liabilities (or a combination of both) from delivering or producing goods, rendering services, or carrying out other activities that constitute the entity's ongoing major or central operations
Expenses	Outflows or other using up of assets or incurrences of liabilities (or a combination of both) from delivering or producing goods, rendering services, or carrying out other activities that constitute the entity's ongoing major or central operations
Gains	Inflows or other enhancements of the assets of an entity or settlements of its liabilities (or a combination of both) from peripheral or incidental activities of the firm, not directly related to its core operations
Losses	Outflows or other using up of assets or incurrences of liabilities (or a combination of both) from peripheral or incidental activities of the firm, not directly related to its core operations

INCOME STATEMENT FORMATS

There are two basic income statement formats that have developed over time and are considered acceptable: the single-step format and the multiple-step format. However, because firms have some discretion in the way they present their income statements, published income statements are often hybrids of the two formats. Although the single-step and multiple-step formats differ in the amount of detail provided and how various types of revenues and expenses are grouped, the two approaches must yield the same net income for a given company. The revenue and expense groupings on the income statement are based on the difference between operating and nonoperating activities.

operating activities activities undertaken by management in the course of running a business

Operating activities are activities undertaken by management in the course of running a business. On the income statement for Dell Computer Corporation shown at the beginning of the chapter, the expenses related to operating activities are cost of revenue and operating expenses, which include selling, general, and administrative expenses and research, development, and engineering expenses.

nonoperating activities activities that are not central to the revenue-producing pursuits of a firm

Nonoperating activities are activities that are not central to the revenue-producing pursuits of a firm. Gains or losses on the sale of assets used in the business and interest revenue and expense result from nonoperating activities.

❯ THE SINGLE-STEP FORMAT

single-step income statement an income statement in which all revenues and gains are placed in one category, and all expenses and losses are placed in another category

In a **single-step income statement**, all revenues and gains are placed in one category, and all expenses and losses are placed in another category. The difference between the two categories is the income or loss before income taxes. Net income is determined by deducting income taxes and other items, such as discontinued operations, extraordinary items, and changes in accounting principles, from the income or loss before income taxes. Usually, no distinction is made between items related to operating activities and items related to nonoperating activities. The single-step method of reporting operating income offers simplicity and is favored by many corporations. Figure 3.1 shows the single-step consolidated statement of operations (another name for the income statement) for **Hewlett-Packard Company**.

In the Hewlett-Packard statement, interest and other income is shown as a separate item below earnings from operations, as is gains (losses) on investments and early distinguishment of debt. In some single-step income statements, however, interest

---

1 "Elements of Financial Statements," *Statement of Financial Accounting Concepts No. 6* (Stamford, Conn.: FASB, 1985), pars. 78–89.

Figure 3.1

Single-Step Income Statement

Hewlett-Packard

Hewlett-Packard Company and Subsidiaries
Consolidated Statements of Operations
(In millions)

	For the fiscal years ended October 31		
	2004	**2003**	**2002**
Net revenue:			
Products	$64,127	$58,826	$45,878
Services	15,389	13,768	10,390
Financing income	389	467	320
Total net revenue	79,905	73,061	56,588
Costs and expenses:			
Cost of products	48,359	43,619	34,127
Cost of services	11,791	10,031	7,477
Financing interest	190	208	189
Research and development	3,506	3,651	3,368
Selling, general and administrative	11,024	11,012	8,763
Amortization of purchased intangible assets	603	563	402
Restructuring charges	114	800	1,780
Acquisition-related charges	54	280	701
In-process research and development charges	37	1	793
Total costs and expenses	75,678	70,165	57,600
Earnings (loss) from operations	4,227	2,896	(1,012)
Interest and other, net	35	21	52
Gains (losses) on investments and early distinguishment of debt	4	(29)	(75)
Dispute settlement	(70)	—	14
Earnings (loss) before taxes	4,196	2,888	(1,021)
Provision for (benefit from) taxes	699	349	(118)
Net earnings (loss)	$ 3,497	$ 2,539	$ (903)

income and other nonoperating income items, such as gains on sales of operating assets, would be included in the revenues section, and interest expense and nonoperating expense items, such as losses on sales of operating assets, are included in the costs and expenses section. In practice, many variations of the basic single-step format are used.

multiple-step income statement
a more complex form of income statement that clearly divides operating and nonoperating items

❯ THE MULTIPLE-STEP FORMAT

A **multiple-step income statement** is a more complex form of income statement that clearly divides operating and nonoperating items. Most companies that use the multiple-step format do so to provide more detailed information about their operations and the expenses involved in supporting these operations. Therefore, the operating section of a multiple-step income statement itemizes net sales; cost of goods sold (sometimes called cost of revenue, as in the Dell statement); gross profit on sales (sometimes called gross margin on sales), obtained by subtracting cost of goods sold from net sales; selling, general, and administrative expenses; and other operating income and expenses. The nonoperating section contains such categories as net interest revenue or expense (interest revenue and expense are often netted against each another) and any other nonoperating revenues and expenses (often shown net).

A complete multiple-step income statement would be very detailed, with several categories representing individual areas of expenses. Companies that publish a multiple-

Figure 3.2

Multiple-Step Income Statement

Sun Microsystems   **Consolidated Statements of Operations**
(in millions)

| | Fiscal Years Ended June 30 | | |
	2004	2003	2002
Net revenues:			
Products	$ 7,355	$ 7,793	$ 9,093
Services	3,830	3,641	3,403
Total net revenues	11,185	11,434	12,496
Cost of sales:			
Cost of sales—products	4,290	4,342	5,506
Cost of sales—services	2,379	2,150	2,074
Total cost of sales	6,669	6,492	7,580
Gross margin	4,516	4,942	4,916
Operating expenses:			
Research and development	1,926	1,837	1,832
Selling, general and administrative	3,317	3,329	3,806
Restructuring charges	344	371	517
Impairment of goodwill and other intangible assets	49	2,125	6
Purchased in-process research and development	70	4	3
Total operating expenses	5,706	7,666	6,164
Operating loss	(1,190)	(2,724)	(1,248)
Loss on equity investments, net	(64)	(84)	(99)
Interest income	137	166	243
Interest expense	(37)	(43)	(58)
Gain (loss) on marketable debt securities	(6)	32	114
Settlement income	1,597	—	—
Income (loss) before income taxes	437	(2,653)	(1,048)
Provision (benefit) for income taxes	825	776	(461)
Net loss	(388)	$(3,429)	$ (587)

step income statement usually use a condensed format, such as the one from **Sun Microsystems** shown in Figure 3.2. Though this format differs only slightly from that of the Hewlett-Packard statement in Figure 3.1, note that cost of sales and gross margin are shown separately.

Regardless of which reporting format is used, under GAAP, the information in an income statement must help investors and other users distinguish between income derived from ongoing activities and income derived from one-time events.

CHECK YOUR UNDERSTANDING

1. Describe the difference between revenues and gains.

2. Why is it important to distinguish components of income that are ongoing from those that are one-time events?

3. List the two basic income statement formats.

4. Describe the format of the multiple-step income statement and explain why a firm might choose this format.

LO 3 Identify recurring and non-recurring items and report them on the income statement.

Recurring and Nonrecurring Items

E ach year a firm is likely to enter into a variety of transactions that affect net income. Most of these transactions are related to ongoing operating activities, such as sales, cost of sales, administrative and operating expenses, interest income and expense, and gains or losses on sales of operating assets. Transactions that are related to the normal, ongoing operations of a firm are called **recurring items**. The amount on the income statement labeled "Income from continuing operations" reflects the net effect of these normal, ongoing operations.

recurring items transactions related to the normal, ongoing operations of a firm

A firm may also engage in transactions that are unusual, infrequent, or unrelated to its usual operations. Transactions of this kind are often referred to as **nonrecurring items** and are reported separately on the income statement. Prior to year-end 2005, they included discontinued operations, extraordinary items, and the cumulative effect of a change in accounting principle. However, the FASB recently issued *Statement No. 154*, "Accounting Changes and Error Corrections," which changes how the cumulative effect of a change in accounting principle is reported. *SFAS No. 154* now requires retrospective application to a prior period's financial statements. This pronouncement represents a major change in reporting standards for accounting changes, and is discussed later in this section.

nonrecurring items transactions that are unusual, infrequent, or unrelated to the usual operations of a business and are reported separately on the income statement

🧩 *Critical Thinking: If a business experiences a major loss as a result of an earthquake or a flood, how do you think this item is disclosed on the income statement?*

The distinction between recurring and nonrecurring items plays a critical role in assessing a firm's future cash flows. Recurring items—the normal revenues and expenses associated with running the business—are expected to occur in each accounting period. Thus, cash flows from recurring items can be expected to continue into the future with some constancy. In contrast, nonrecurring items usually result from one-time events, and the cash flows from such items are not expected to continue. Therefore, when analysts evaluate a firm's future prospects, they treat the effects of cash flows from nonrecurring items differently from the effects of recurring items.

REPORTING DISCONTINUED OPERATIONS

When a part of a business is discontinued or is being held for sale, the results of the reclassification and any gain or loss resulting from the disposal must be disclosed as a nonrecurring item on the income statement and presented separately after income from continuing operations. Because such situations are complicated, the FASB has spent a considerable amount of time and effort defining what constitutes a discontinued operation and how such items should be reported on the income statement.

In August 2001, the FASB issued *SFAS No. 144*, "Accounting for the Impairment or Disposal of Long-Lived Assets," which broadened the definition of discontinued operations and changed the method of calculating the resulting gain or loss. In previous pronouncements, the FASB had used the concept of a "segment of a business" (that is, a subsidiary, a division, or a department whose assets and operations are clearly distinguished from the firm's other assets and operations) as the guideline for determining what should be included in discontinued operations. For example, if a shoe manufacturer operated a chain of retail shoe stores, those stores could be viewed as a separate segment. As the board reviewed the issue, it became concerned that other asset groups that are disposed of but "are not reported separately in discontinued operations because they are not segments of business could have a significant effect on the ongoing operations of a business."[2] *SFAS No. 144* now includes assets that are defined as a component of an entity to take into account such asset groups. A **component of an entity** is defined as operations and cash flows that can be clearly distinguished, operationally and for financial reporting purposes, from the rest of the entity. Under this

component of an entity operations and cash flows that can be clearly distinguished, operationally and for financial reporting purposes, from the rest of the entity

---

2 "Accounting for the Impairment or Disposal of Long-Lived Assets," *Statement of Financial Accounting Standards No. 144* (Stamford, Conn.: FASB, 2001), par. B102.

Figure 3.3

Excerpts from Consolidated Statement of Earnings and Related Note on Discontinued Operations

IBM

Consolidated Statement of Earnings
(in millions)

For year ended December 31:	Notes	2004	2003	2002
Income from Continuing Operations Before Income Taxes		$12,028	$10,874	$ 7,524
Provision for income taxes	P	3,580	3,261	2,190
Income from Continuing Operations		8,448	7,613	5,334
Discontinued Operations:				
Loss from discontinued operations	C	18	30	1,755
Net Income		$ 8,430	$ 7,583	$ 3,579

Note C
Summarized selected financial information for the discontinued operations as follows:
(dollars in millions)

For the year ended December 31:		2004		2003		2002*
Revenue	$	—	$	—	$	1,946
Loss before income taxes	$	29	$	29	$	2,037
Income tax expense/(benefit)		(11)		1		(282)
Loss from discontinued operations	$	18	$	30	$	1,755

*At closing, the company incurred a significant U.S. tax charge of approximately $248 million related to the repatriation of divestiture proceeds from certain countries with low tax rates. This amount was included in the income tax benefit line item of discontinued operations.

discontinued operation a component of an entity that has been eliminated from the ongoing operations of the firm and in whose operations the firm will not have any significant continuing involvement

definition, a component of an entity may be a reportable segment, a reporting unit, a subsidiary, or an asset group.

A component of an entity that is classified as being held for sale or that has been disposed of is presented as a **discontinued operation** if (1) the operations and cash flows of the component will be (or have been) eliminated from the ongoing operations of the entity and (2) the entity will not have any significant continuing involvement in the operations of the component.[3] Once a firm has concluded that it has a component of an entity that qualifies as a discontinued operation, it must report both the revenues or losses from operations of that component plus any gain or loss on its disposal separately from income from continuing operations, net of tax, as shown in Figure 3.3.

As you can see in the excerpt from the **IBM** consolidated statement of earnings, the highlighted line item "Loss from discontinued operations" is shown at $18 million in 2004 and $30 million in 2003. These amounts are presented net of tax, as indicated in the accompanying note, in accordance with *SFAS No. 144*.

Our example assumes that the component of an entity that met the definition of a discontinued operation was actually disposed of during the period. That may not always be the case; the assets that make up the component may be being held for sale but may not yet have been disposed of. In such a situation, *SFAS No. 144* requires that the long-lived assets held for sale be measured at the lower of their carrying amount or their fair value less cost to sell. Thus, if an asset's fair value less the cost to sell it is below

3 "Accounting for the Impairment or Disposal of Long-Lived Assets," *Statement of Financial Accounting Standards No. 144* (Stamford, Conn.: FASB, 2001), pars. 41–42.

its carrying amount, the asset must be written down to the lower amount and a loss must be recognized even before the actual sale or disposal takes place. Moreover, once assets are classified as held for sale, they are no longer depreciated or amortized. When an actual sale takes place, any gain or loss that was not recognized in prior income statements must be recognized. Ultimately, the gain or loss on the actual disposal is combined with any results of operations related to the component of the entity to be sold and stated net of tax.

To illustrate, in 2003, **ConAgra** foods committed to a plan to sell its chicken business. Pilgrim's Pride was identified as the buyer, and the plan called for the sale to be completed in the summer of 2003. According to the note in the financial statements for 2003, the company recognized an impairment charge of $69.4 million (net of an income tax benefit of $42.6 million, meaning the actual impairment charge before taxes was $112 million). This impairment charge reduced the carrying amount of the chicken business's goodwill to zero. It also reflected a reduction in the carrying value of the long-lived assets of the chicken business to their fair market value, less cost to sell. The net result of this impairment and the loss on operations of the chicken business was a reported loss from discontinued operations, net of tax, of $69.2 million. The income statement and the relevant note from the 2003 annual report of ConAgra are shown in Figure 3.4.

REPORTING EXTRAORDINARY ITEMS

An **extraordinary item** is an unusual, infrequent, and material item that must be reported separately from the results of continuing operations. The AICPA defines the three key characteristics in the definition as follows:

extraordinary item an unusual, infrequent, and material item that must be reported separately from the results of continuing operations

- *Unusual*: possessing a high degree of abnormality and unrelated to the ordinary activities of the firm, taking into account the environment in which the firm operates

- *Infrequent*: not expected to recur in the foreseeable future, taking into account the environment in which the firm operates

- *Material*: large enough to make a difference in an investor's decision[4]

All three characteristics must be present for an item to be reported as extraordinary. On the income statement, extraordinary items are reported net of taxes. They follow discontinued operations, if that item exists.

Whether an item is extraordinary depends upon the nature of a firm's operations. The same event may be considered ordinary for one company but extraordinary for another. For example, flooding may be an ordinary event for companies located along the Mississippi River, but it would probably be an extraordinary event for a company located in a desert. The type of industry and the geographic area in which the company is located contribute to the determination of what is extraordinary.

Normally occurring items, such as write-offs of receivables, foreign currency exchange gains or losses, or the effects of a labor strike, are not considered extraordinary or nonrecurring and are included in the determination of income from continuing operations. According to *Statement of Financial Accounting Standards No. 145*, an early extinguishment of debt occurs when a firm repays its debt early, most likely because of favorable changes in interest rates. If the debt is extinguished for more than its carrying value, a loss occurs, and if it is extinguished for less than its carrying value, a gain occurs. Previously, *SFAS No. 4* required that such gains or losses be shown as

---

4 "Reporting the Results of Operations," *Opinions of the Accounting Principles Board No. 30* (New York: AICPA, 1973), par. 20.

Figure 3.4

Consolidated Statement of Operations

ConAgra

**ConAgra Foods, Inc. and Subsidiaries
Consolidated Statements of Earnings**

	For the fiscal years ended May		
Dollars in millions except per share amounts	**2003**	**2002**	**2001**
Net sales	$19,839.2	$25,473.0	$25,060.5
Costs and expenses			
Cost of goods sold	16,016.3	21,495.6	21,288.3
Selling, general and administrative expenses	2,308.4	2,423.1	2,274.0
Interest expense, net	276.3	401.1	422.5
	18,601.0	24,319.8	23,984.8
Income from continuing operations before equity method investment earnings, income taxes and cumulative effect of changes in accounting	1,238.2	1,153.2	1,075.7
Equity method investment earnings	37.9	27.2	19.5
Income tax expense	436.0	445.3	412.8
Income from continuing operations before cumulative effect of changes in accounting	840.1	735.1	682.4
Income (loss) from discontinued operations, net of tax	(69.2)	49.9	.1
Cumulative effect of changes in accounting*	3.9	(2.0)	(43.9)
Net income	$ 774.8	$ 783.0	$ 638.6
Earnings per share—basic			
Income from continuing operations before cumulative effect of changes in accounting income (loss) from discontinued operations	$ 1.59	$ 1.39	$ 1.33
	(.13)	.09	—
Cumulative effect of changes in accounting	.01	—	(.09)
Net income	$ 1.47	$ 1.48	$ 1.24
Earnings per share—diluted			
Income from continuing operations before cumulative effect of changes in accounting income (loss) from discontinued operations	$ 1.58	$ 1.38	$ 1.33
	(.13)	.09	—
Cumulative effect of changes in accounting	.01	—	(.09)
Net income	$ 1.46	$ 1.47	$ 1.24

The accompanying notes are an integral part of the consolidated financial statements.

*Published prior to the adoption of *SFAS No. 154.*

2. DISCONTINUED OPERATIONS

Summary results of operations of the chicken business included within discontinued operations are as follows:

	2003	2002	2001
Net sales	$2,213.3	$2,298.1	$2,181.1
Cost of goods sold	2,132.1	2,129.7	2,103.0
Selling, general and administrative expenses	80.5	86.7	77.2
Interest expense	.4	.4	.8
Long-lived asset impairment charge	112.0	—	—
Income (loss) before income taxes	(111.7)	81.3	.1
Income tax (expense) benefit	42.5	(31.4)	—
Income (loss) from discontinued operations, net of tax	$ (69.2)	$ 49.9	$ .1

extraordinary items. However, *SFAS No. 145* rescinds that requirement, and gains and losses on early extinguishment of debt are now shown as part of income from continuing operations. The board's reasoning is that debt extinguishments are often routine, recurring transactions and do not meet the definition of extraordinary items as described in *APB Opinion No. 30*.[5] This issue is discussed in more detail in Chapter 13. The result of this change in reporting standards means that fewer instances of extraordinary items are likely to be disclosed.

When an item is unusual but does not meet the criteria for extraordinary items, it must be included in the calculation of income from continuing operations. Depending upon the item's materiality, it may or may not be presented as a separate line item. For example, a restructuring charge resulting from a reorganization is normally displayed separately from other operating expenses, but it is still a part of income from continuing operations.

REPORTING ACCOUNTING CHANGES

In some situations management may decide or be required to make an accounting change. An **accounting change** is a global term used to describe three types of changes: (1) a switch or change in accounting principle that is either decided by management or mandated by the FASB or SEC, (2) a modification or change in an accounting estimate, or (3) a change in reporting entity. (A change in reporting entity is a more advanced topic that is not discussed in this text.) A correction of an error in previously issued financial statements, while not an accounting change, is in many respects treated in a similar manner. Error corrections are not reflected in the current period's income, but are reported as a prior period adjustment by restating prior period financial statements. Illustration 3.4 details the different types of accounting changes.

As previously mentioned, in May 2005, the FASB issued *SFAS No. 154*, "Accounting Changes and Error Corrections," which significantly altered the reporting standards for accounting changes, especially those for changes in accounting principles. Under the previous standards, *APB Opinion No. 20*, most voluntary changes in accounting principles were recognized by including in the net income of the period of the change a separate line item on the income statement called *cumulative effect of change in accounting principle*. *SFAS No. 154* now requires retrospective application of changes in accounting principles to prior period financial statements, unless it is impracticable to determine the period-specific effects of the change on prior periods.

In terms of a change in accounting principle, **retrospective application** means the application of a different accounting principle to one or more previously issued financial statements, or to the financial statement at the beginning of the period, as if that principle had always been used. What this means is that when a firm changes from one principle to another, it must restate the prior period financial statements to reflect that change as if it were in effect at the time the statements were issued.

Interestingly, *SFAS No. 154* moves U.S. GAAP closer to international accounting standards. According to the FASB, this new standard is the result of a broader effort to improve the comparability of cross-border financial reporting by working with the IASB toward the development of a single set of high-quality standards. FASB board member Michael Crooch noted, "This is one example of where the Board concluded that the IASB requirements result in better financial reporting. We were able to make meaningful improvements in U.S. GAAP while converging with the IASB."[6]

---

accounting change a global term used to describe three types of changes: (1) a switch or change in accounting principle that is either decided by management or mandated by the FASB or SEC, (2) a modification or change in an accounting estimate, or (3) a change in reporting entity

retrospective application the application of a different accounting principle to one or more previously issued financial statements, or to the financial statement at the beginning of the period, as if that principle had always been used

---

5 "Rescission of FASB Statements No. 4, 44, and 64, Amendment of FASB Statement No. 13, and Technical Corrections," *Statement of Financial Accounting Standards No. 145* (Norwalk, Conn.: FASB, 2002), par. A4.

6 Washington Society of CPAs, Short Form, "FASB Issues Accounting Standard That Improves the Reporting of Accounting Changes as Part of Convergence Effort with IASB," June 15, 2005.

Illustration 3.4

Types of Accounting Changes

Type of Change	Description / Explanation	Examples
Change in accounting principle	Switch from one generally accepted accounting principle to another generally accepted accounting principle	• Adoption of a new FASB standard • Change in depreciation method • Change in inventory costing method • Change in the way revenue is recognized, such as a switch from the percentage-of-completion method to the completed-contract method
a. Change in accounting estimate	Modification of accounting estimates as a result of new information or experience	• Change in the parameters of depreciation, such as useful life or residual value • Change in calculating expense estimates, such as bad debts and warranties
b. Change in accounting estimate effected by a change in accounting principle	Change in accounting principle that is inseperable from the effect of a related change in principle	• A change in depreciation methods, as from an accelerated method to the straight-line method
Change in reporting entity	A change that results in financial statements that, in effect, are those of a different reporting entity	• Presenting consolidated or combined financial statements in place of financial statements of individual entities • Changing the entities included in combined financial statements

❯ CHANGE IN ACCOUNTING PRINCIPLE

change in accounting principle a change from one generally accepted accounting principle to another generally accepted accounting principle when two or more generally accepted accounting principles apply or when the accounting principle formerly used is no longer accepted

As noted in Illustration 3.4, a **change in accounting principle** is a change from one generally accepted accounting principle to another generally accepted accounting principle when two or more generally accepted accounting principles apply or when the accounting principle formerly used is no longer accepted. For example, a change in inventory methods, a change in accounting for construction contracts, or a change mandated by a new reporting standard are examples of a change from one generally accepted accounting principle to another generally accepted principle. Further, a change in the method of applying an accounting principle is also considered a change in accounting principle.

Under the new *SFAS No. 154*, "Accounting Changes and Error Corrections," a change in depreciation method is no longer considered a change in accounting principle; it is a change in accounting *estimate* brought about by a change in accounting principle. As we will see, this determination is significant.

Consistent with prior pronouncements, *SFAS No. 154* clearly notes that a presumption exists that once a particular statement is adopted, it should not be changed in accounting for transactions of similar types. However, when a change in principle is made by an entity, that change must be accounted for through retrospective application of the new accounting principle to all prior periods, unless it is impracticable to do so. As stated in *SFAS No. 154*:

- The cumulative effect of the change to the new accounting principle on periods prior to those presented shall be reflected in the carrying amounts of assets and liabilities as of the beginning of the first period presented.

- An offsetting adjustment, if any, shall be made to the opening balance of retained earnings (or other appropriate components of equity or net assets in the statement of financial position) for that period.

To illustrate the application of this new standard, assume that Arrington Company decides at the beginning of 2007 to adopt the FIFO method of inventory valuation.[7] Since its inception in 2005, the company has used the LIFO method but has maintained records that are adequate to apply the FIFO method retrospectively. In addition, the following information is available:

Date	Inventory Determined by LIFO Method	Inventory Determined by FIFO Method	Cost of Sales Determined by LIFO Method	Cost of Sales Determined by FIFO Method
1/1/2005	$ 0	$ 0	$ 0	$ 0
12/31/2005	100	80	800	820
12/31/2006	200	240	1,000	940
12/31/2007	320	390	1,130	1,100

For each year, sales are $3,000, and selling, general, and administrative expenses are $1,000. The condensed income statements for 2006 and 2005 for Arrington Company are shown below.

	2006	2005
Sales	$3,000	$3,000
Cost of goods sold	1,000	800
Selling, general, and administrative expenses	1,000	1,000
Income before profit sharing and income taxes	1,000	1,200

In 2007, the company presents comparative 2007 and 2006 financial statements. The 2006 income statement must be restated to reflect the retrospective application of FIFO. The 2007 statement is also prepared using the FIFO method. This means that when the 2006 statement is revised, the cost of goods sold must be reduced from $1,000 to $940, with a corresponding increase of $60 in income before profit sharing and income taxes to $1,060, as shown in the condensed statements below:

	2007	2006 As Adjusted
Sales	$3,000	$3,000
Cost of goods sold	1,100	940
Selling, general, and administrative expenses	1,000	1,000
Income before profit sharing and income taxes	900	1,060

---

7 This example is based on the illustration provided by the FASB in *Statement No. 154*.

SFAS No. 154 also requires full disclosure of this change in the notes to the financial statements, including identification of line items (inventory, cost of goods sold, and net income, for example) in the financial statements that were affected by the change.

❯ CHANGE IN ACCOUNTING ESTIMATES

change in accounting estimate a modification to an accounting estimate resulting from new information or experience

The new FASB standard differentiates between a change in *accounting estimate* and a change in *accounting estimate effected by a change in accounting principle*. A **change in accounting estimate** is a modification to an accounting estimate resulting from new information or experience. These changes—for example, a change in the manner in which uncollectible accounts are estimated or a change in the useful life of a depreciable asset—are a normal part of running a business and are not given special treatment unless they are material. They have the effect of adjusting the carrying amount of an existing asset or liability or altering the subsequent accounting for existing or future assets or liabilities.

change in accounting estimate effected by a change in accounting principle a change in accounting estimate that is inseparable from and brought about by the effect of a related change in accounting principle

A **change in accounting estimate effected by a change in accounting principle** is a change in accounting estimate that is inseparable from and brought about by the effect of a related change in accounting principle. The most common example of this type of change is a change in the method of depreciation, amortization, or depletion for long-lived, nonfinancial assets.[8] Accounting for both of these accounting changes is discussed next.

❯ **EXAMPLE OF CHANGE IN ACCOUNTING ESTIMATE**   Prospectively changing the estimated life of a long-lived asset for depreciation purposes is a common example of a change in estimate. A new depreciation schedule is calculated, and the new depreciation expense incorporating the change is recorded as part of the current period's depreciation expense.

For example, assume that a piece of equipment was purchased for $60,000 and has a residual value of $5,000. At the time it was placed in service, it was given an estimated life of five years, and straight-line depreciation was used to depreciate it. After it had been used for two years, management decided that the asset still had a remaining life of four years, so the estimated useful life was changed to six years. Based on the straight-line method, the remaining undepreciated base of $33,000 (net book value at the end of 2005 of $38,000, less the $5,000 estimated residual value) would then be depreciated over the new remaining four-year life of the asset. As shown below, $8,250 ($33,000 ÷ 4 years) is recognized as depreciation in each of the remaining years.

Year	Acquisition Cost	Depreciation per Year	Accumulated Depreciation	Net Book Value
2004	$60,000	$11,000	$11,000	$49,000
2005	60,000	11,000	22,000	38,000
2006	60,000	8,250	30,250	29,750
2007	60,000	8,250	38,500	21,500
2008	60,000	8,250	46,750	13,250
2009	60,000	8,250	55,000	5,000

---

8 Under the previous standard, *APB Opinion No. 20,* these types of changes were called "changes in accounting principles" and were accounted for by determining their cumulative effect, which was shown as a separate item on the income statement.

It is important to keep in mind that this is a change in estimate, not the correction of an error. Acting on new information, management revised its original estimate of the useful life of the equipment; the original estimate was not an error that had to be corrected. As a result, depreciation from prior years that has already been recorded is not changed. The change in depreciation is made prospectively (that is, in future years)—in this case, in 2006 through 2009. Because no catch-up adjustment is made, a change in accounting estimate does not require retrospective adjustment.

❯ EXAMPLE OF CHANGE IN ACCOUNTING ESTIMATE EFFECTED BY A CHANGE IN ACCOUNTING PRINCIPLE (DEPRECIATION METHODS) *SFAS No. 154* made a significant change in the standard for reporting these types of changes. Under the previous standard, *APB Opinion No. 20*, these types of changes were called "changes in accounting principles" and were accounted for by determining their cumulative effect, which was shown as a separate item on the income statement. Now, according to *SFAS No. 154*, a change in depreciation method must be accounted for as a change in estimate. Thus, a change from an accelerated method of depreciation to the straight-line method would be accounted for in the same way as a change in estimate of useful lives, as shown in the previous example. However, because an actual change in principle is involved, a change in depreciation method is seen as a change in estimate inseparable from a change in principle. What this means is that the change must be justified as being preferable to the previously existing method, whereas such a justification is not needed for other changes in estimates, such as the estimate of useful lives of these long-lived assets.

For example, assume that at the beginning of 2003, a research laboratory company paid $220,000 for a large neutron microscope that has a useful life of ten years and no residual value. Initially, the lab decided to use an accelerated method of depreciation for the microscope. The resulting depreciation is shown in the schedule below.

Year	Accelerated Depreciation
2003	$ 40,000
2004	36,000
2005	32,000
2006	28,000
Total	$136,000

The net book value of the neutron at the end of 2006 is $84,000:

Cost of neutron microscope	$220,000
Cumulative amount of accelerated depreciation	136,000
Net book value of neutron	$ 84,000

In 2007, the laboratory decides to change from the accelerated method of depreciation to the straight-line method. As a result, depreciation expense for 2007 and each year thereafter is now $14,000 (the straight-line amount of $84,000 ÷ 6 years). Because this change is related to a change in principle, *SFAS No. 154* requires that the laboratory company in our example disclose (1) the nature and reason for the change in principle and why the newly adopted principle is preferable, (2) the method of applying the change, and (3) any other indirect effects of the change.

Keep in mind that the items in Illustration 3.4 (changes in accounting principle, both types of changes in accounting estimates and corrections) are all disclosed in the income statement to the extent they occurred during the year. The changes in accounting principles are shown by retrospective changes to prior financial statements. Both types of changes in estimates are included in the determination of current and future period's income from continuing operations, and error corrections are reflected through changes in retained earnings and preparation of new corrected statements, as necessary.

INTRAPERIOD INCOME TAX ALLOCATION

intraperiod income tax allocation the practice of relating income tax expense to the specific item or event that caused the tax

The practice of relating income tax expense to the specific item or event that caused the tax is called **intraperiod income tax allocation**. The amount of income tax related to income from continuing operations should be identified, but the nonrecurring items (discontinued operations and extraordinary items) are all presented net of the tax effects. A firm's total income tax expense does not change as a result of intraperiod tax allocation. The allocation simply allows users of financial statements to identify which portion of the taxes relates to operating activities and which portion relates to other activities.

INTERNATIONAL STANDARDS RELATED TO THE INCOME STATEMENT

INTERNATIONAL

Just as there are slightly different formats for income statements prepared by companies in the United States, there are different formats for income statements prepared by companies abroad. Nonetheless, the basic presentation of income statements based on international standards is very similar to that of income statements based on U.S. GAAP. Figure 3.5 shows the consolidated income statement for **Slovnaft, a.s.**, a large international integrated oil company based in the Slovak Republic. This statement is prepared in accordance with international accounting standards. As you can see, the format differs slightly from the GAAP formats discussed previously.

One of the more interesting differences in financial reporting standards related to the income statement involves the accounting for discontinued operations and extraordinary items. The reporting for these items depends on how standard setters define them, and those definitions vary from country to country. In addition, the International Accounting Standards Board (IASB) has recently proposed significant changes in its standards for reporting and disclosing extraordinary items.

Across the world, determining what constitutes an extraordinary item has always been controversial. David Tweedie, the chair of the IASB in 2003, declared that "extraordinary items in company accounts should become as rare as Martians walking through the streets." He was voicing a view, shared in the wider business community, that the use of extraordinary items allows companies to distort their financial figures. According to Tweedie, "the term has all but been eliminated in U.K. GAAP, and now exists only as a theoretically possible classification."[9]

Notwithstanding Tweedie's and others' concerns, international accounting standards currently allow for the separate disclosure of extraordinary items in a manner similar (but not identical) to U.S. standards. Under the provisions of *International Accounting Standard No. 8*, extraordinary items are "income or expenses that arise from events or transactions that are clearly distinct from the ordinary activities of the enterprise and therefore are not expected to recur frequently or regularly." This statement goes on to note that "such extraordinary items are rare and beyond management control. Examples are expropriation of assets and effects of natural disasters."[10] Interestingly, under U.S. GAPP, the losses sustained from Hurricane Katrina in August 2005 would probably not be considered extraordinary, whereas under international standards, this same natural disaster would be considered an extraordinary event.

---

9 Ben McLannahan, "Getting the Martians off the Street," CFO.com, November 1, 2001.

10 "Net Profit or Loss for the Period, Fundamental Errors and Changes in Accounting Policies," *International Accounting Standards No. 8* (London: IASB, 1983), summary page.

Figure 3.5

Consolidated Income Statement

Slovnaft, a.s.

Slovnaft, a.s.
Consolidated Income Statement

(in millions of Slovak crowns)	Notes	Year ended 31 December 2003	Year ended 31 December 2002
Net Sales	18	67,296	65,317
Other operating income		343	476
Total operating revenues		**67,639**	**65,793**
Raw material costs (incl. goods for resale and net of work performed by the Group enterprise and capitalised)		(51,526)	(50,480)
Personnel expenses	20	(2,906)	(2,438)
Depreciation, amortization and impairment	18, 26	(3,512)	(3,610)
Value of services used		(3,578)	(4,406)
Change in inventories of finished goods and work in progress		108	77
Capitalised own production		9	10
Other operating expenses		(3,402)	(1,982)
Total operating expenses		**(64,807)**	**(62,829)**
Operating profit	18, 26	**2,832**	**2,964**
Share of profits of equity consolidated undertakings	21	35	87
Net finance revenues	22	648	1,141
Profit before taxation	23	**3,515**	**4,192**
Income tax expense	23	(1,131)	(1,160)
Profit after taxation		**2,384**	**3,032**
Minority interest	12	**(10)**	**22**
Net income	24	**2,374**	**3,054**
Earnings per share (SKK per share)	24	**115.1**	**148.0**

The IASB is now reexamining the issue of what constitutes an extraordinary item. In a recent draft that proposes revisions in 12 of its 34 active standards, the IASB recommends eliminating the concept of extraordinary items from *IAS No. 8* and prohibiting the presentation of income and expense items as extraordinary items in the income statement and the notes. If the IASB prohibits the use of extraordinary items, this will put pressure on the FASB to do likewise. Many financial statement users agree with Tweedie that the use of extraordinary items allows companies to distort their financial figures by making artificial distinctions subject to rather loose definitions. One could argue that if the details of material transactions are fully disclosed, it should make little difference how these transactions are actually classified in the financial statements. This debate continues, and although the term "extraordinary item" is not commonly used, it may still be found on the income statements of a few U.S. companies.[11]

---

11 *Accounting Trends and Techniques—2001* (New York: AICPA) indicates that of 600 companies surveyed, only 78 reported extraordinary items. Of those companies, 70 were reporting the extinguishments of debt. Since debt extinguishments are no longer automatically an extraordinary item, there will be very few companies that report extraordinary items in the future.

LO 4 Explain the concept of earnings per share and describe how EPS is reported on the income statement.

earnings per share (EPS) the amount of earnings associated with each common share of a firm's stock

Critical Thinking: *Why would it be important for you as a stockholder to understand the nature of any outstanding financial contracts that allow for conversion to common stock?*

Reporting Earnings per Share

Earnings per share (EPS), the amount of earnings associated with each share of a firm's common stock, is shown on all income statements, regardless of format. Basic earnings per share for a firm's net income is calculated as follows:

$$EPS = \frac{\text{Net Income} - \text{Preferred Stock Dividends}}{\text{Weighted-Average Number of Common Shares Outstanding}}$$

EPS is important because it indicates, on a per share basis, the income of the current period for both the recurring and the nonrecurring items that are associated with the common shareholders' ownership interest. *Statement of Financial Accounting Standards No. 128* requires that EPS be reported for the following items:

- Income from continuing operations
- Discontinued operations
- Extraordinary items
- Net income

basic EPS a figure that relates net income to the firm's outstanding common stock

diluted EPS a figure that relates net income to the maximum possible number of shares of common stock if all possibly dilutive financial contracts, such as stock options, were converted to common stock

In some situations, two forms of EPS must be reported. **Basic EPS** relates net income to the firm's outstanding common stock. **Diluted EPS** relates net income to the maximum possible number of shares of common stock if all possibly dilutive financial contracts, such as stock options, were converted to common stock. Those contracts, if converted or assumed to be converted, will decrease earnings per share because the denominator of the ratio will increase (the number of shares outstanding is assumed to have been increased). For example, if a company had outstanding stock options, the related shares would not be included in the denominator for basic EPS but would be included for diluted EPS. Other examples of possibly dilutive securities are convertible preferred stock and convertible bonds, which can be exchanged for common stock. The related shares are not included in the basic EPS calculation but are included in the diluted EPS calculation. Calculating earnings per share can be quite intricate when a firm has a complicated capital structure. Such calculations are explained in more detail in Chapter 18.

Figure 3.6 presents excerpts from Citigroup Inc.'s consolidated statement of income for the years 2002 through 2004. As you can see, basic and diluted earnings per share are presented at the bottom of the statement for three categories—income from continuing operations, income from discontinued operations, and cumulative effect of accounting change. Note that earnings per share for the cumulative effect of accounting change is presented because of the previous requirements of *APB Opinion No. 20*, which required separate income statement presentation of these items. This is no longer the case under *SFAS No.154*, so this EPS item would not be separately disclosed in future years.

Figure 3.6

Excerpt from Consolidated Statement of Earnings

Citigroup

Citigroup Inc. and Subsidiaries
CONSOLIDATED STATEMENT OF INCOME

In millions of dollars, except per share amounts	Year Ended December 31		
	2004	**2003**	**2002**
Net income	$17,046	$17,853	$15,276
Basic earnings per share			
Income from continuing operations	$ 3.15	$ 3.38	$ 2.53
Income from discontinued operations, net	0.17	0.11	0.47
Cumulative effect of accounting change, net	—	—	(0.01)
Net income	$ 3.32	$ 3.49	$ 2.99
Weighted average common shares outstanding	5,107.2	5,093.3	5,078.0
Diluted earnings per share			
Income from continuing operations	$ 3.09	$ 3.31	$ 2.48
Income from discontinued operations, net	0.17	0.11	0.47
Cumulative effect of accounting change, net	—	—	(0.01)
Net income	$ 3.26	$ 3.42	$ 2.94
Adjusted weighted average common shares, outstanding	5,207.4	5,193.6	5,166.2

CHECK YOUR UNDERSTANDING

1. How is basic earnings per share calculated?

2. What is diluted earnings per share?

LO 5 Define comprehensive income and discuss the required disclosures.

Critical Thinking: *If a company holds marketable securities and those securities experience a change in value, how do you think this gain or loss is reported?*

comprehensive income the change in equity of a business enterprise during a period from transactions and other events and circumstances from non-owner sources

Comprehensive Income

The discussion thus far has focused on transactions that are considered components of net income under GAAP. However, from time to time the FASB has required firms to recognize certain transactions that bypass the income statement and thus are not included as part of net income. Those items were usually reported in the balance sheet as separate components of stockholders' equity. Nonetheless, the FASB has always felt that they were really part of a broader form of income called **comprehensive income**, which is defined in *Statement of Financial Accounting Concepts No. 6* as follows:

> The change in equity of a business enterprise during a period from transactions and other events and circumstances from non-owner sources. It includes all changes in equity during a period except those resulting from investments by owners and distributions to owners.[12]

Changes in equity can result from the basic operation of a business or from changes in the current business environment, such as fluctuations in the value of securities and real estate.

---

12 "Elements of Financial Statements," *Statement of Financial Accounting Concepts No. 6* (Norwalk, Conn.: FASB, 1985), par. 70.

In 1997, the FASB further refined the definition of comprehensive income by noting that it includes both net income as defined by accrual accounting principles and other components, including the following:

- Unrealized gains and losses on marketable securities held in the available-for-sale portfolio (discussed in Chapter 11)

- Unrealized gains and losses resulting from foreign currency translations that occur when foreign subsidiaries' financial statements are converted into U.S. dollars for the purpose of consolidation

- Amounts that are the result of recording the minimum pension obligation (discussed in Chapter 15)

Under *Statement of Financial Accounting Standards No. 130,* "Reporting Comprehensive Income," the effects of these and similar transactions that are primarily derived from events external to the firm are *not* included in what is considered traditional net income. Rather, the effects of these transactions are to be recorded in a special owners' equity account called Other Comprehensive Income. For example, an increase in the market value of marketable securities classified as available for sale is recognized as follows:

Marketable Securities Available for Sale	xx (increase in asset value)
Other Comprehensive Income	xx (increase in equity)

The Other Comprehensive Income account is not included in net income but is included in stockholders' equity.

According to *SFAS No. 130,* the components of comprehensive income may be reported in the following ways:

- A single statement in which net income and other comprehensive income are added together to obtain total comprehensive income

- Two statements, with net income reported in one statement and comprehensive income reported in the other statement

- Part of the statement of changes in stockholders' equity

Most firms have decided not to prepare a single statement of net income and other comprehensive income or two separate statements. Instead, they present the information as part of their statement of changes in stockholders' equity.[13] Figure 3.7 presents an excerpt from **Cisco Systems**'s Consolidated Statements of Shareholders' Equity. Note the highlighted column labeled Accumulated Other Comprehensive Income (Loss). A change in unrealized gain on investment of $352 million, net of tax, is reflected.

Figure 3.8 presents an excerpt from the Notes to Consolidated Financial Statements related to comprehensive income, taken from Cisco Systems's annual report of July 26, 2003. As you can see, the change in net unrealized gains and losses on investment is presented before and after the applicable tax effect.

CHECK YOUR UNDERSTANDING

1. What special owners' equity account is used to record the effects of transactions derived from events external to the firm?

2. According to *SFAS No. 130,* how may the components of comprehensive income be reported?

---

13 According to *Accounting Trends and Techniques—2001* (New York: AICPA), 76 percent of firms surveyed in 2000 chose to report the elements of other comprehensive income as part of the statement of changes in stockholders' equity.

Figure 3.7

Excerpt from Consolidated Statements of Shareholders' Equity

Cisco Systems

Cisco Systems
Consolidated Statements of Shareholders' Equity
(In millions)

	Shares of Common Stock	Common Stock and Additional Paid-In Capital	Retained Earnings	Accumulated Other Comprehensive Income (Loss)	Total Shareholders' Equity
BALANCE AT JULY 27, 2002	7,303	$ 20,950	$ 7,733	$ (27)	$ 28,656
Net income	—	—	3,578	—	3,578
Change in unrealized gains and losses on investments, net of tax	—	—	—	352	352
Other	—	—	—	29	29
Comprehensive income					3,959
Issuance of common stock	68	578	—	—	578
Repurchase of common stock	(424)	(1,232)	(4,752)	—	(5,984)
Tax benefits from employee stock option plans	—	132	—	—	132
Purchase acquisitions	51	557	—	—	557
Amortization of deferred stock-based compensation	—	131	—	—	131
BALANCE AT JULY 26, 2003	6,998	$ 21,116	$ 6,559	$ 354	$ 28,029

Figure 3.8

Notes to Consolidated Financial Statements: Comprehensive Income

Cisco Systems

Cisco Systems
Notes to Consolidated Financial Statements: Comprehensive Income

The components of comprehensive income (loss), net of tax, are as follows (in millions):

Years Ended	July 26, 2003	July 27, 2002	July 28, 2001
Net income (loss)	$3,578	$1,893	$(1,014)
Other comprehensive income (loss):			
Change in unrealized gains and losses on investments	502	215	(5,765)
Tax effect	(150)	9	1,953
Change in unrealized gains and losses on investments, net of tax	352	224	(3,812)
Other	29	24	7
Total	$3,959	$2,141	$(4,819)

LO 6 Use five basic measures to analyze an income statement.

ANALYSIS 🔍

🧩 *Critical Thinking: What types of managerial decisions might be made based on an analysis of income statement figures?*

Analyzing the Income Statement

F inancial statement analysis gives external users insights into a firm's history that enable them to forecast the firm's future prospects. It also helps managers evaluate the company's performance, look for favorable or unfavorable trends, and spot potential problem areas. The income statement is critical to financial analysis because its information is used in forecasting future earnings and cash flows. Analysts and investors pay close attention to forecasted earnings because earnings are related to stock prices. And creditors, such as banks and bondholders, are interested in forecasted cash flows because cash flows indicate a firm's ability to repay both short- and long-term debt.

Whereas thorough financial analysis requires data from both the income statement and the balance sheet, the following five measures are based solely on income statement data: gross profit, gross profit percentage, operating margin, operating margin percentage, and profit margin on sales.

As a means of illustrating how these measures are calculated and interpreted, we will use Dell Computer Corporation's consolidated statements of income, which are presented in Figure 3.9.

Figure 3.9

Consolidated Statements of Income

Dell

Dell Inc.
Consolidated Statements of Income
(in millions, except per share amounts)

	Fiscal Year Ended		
	January 28, 2005	January 30, 2004	January 31, 2003
Net revenue	$49,205	$41,444	$35,404
Cost of revenue	40,190	33,892	29,055
Gross margin	9,015	7,552	6,349
Operating expenses:			
Selling, general and administrative	4,298	3,544	3,050
Research, development and engineering	463	464	455
Total operating expenses	4,761	4,008	3,505
Operating income	4,254	3,544	2,844
Investment and other income, net	191	180	183
Income before income taxes	4,445	3,724	3,027
Income tax provision	1,402	1,079	905
Net income	$ 3,043	$ 2,645	$ 2,122
Earnings per common share:			
Basic	$ 1.21	$ 1.03	$ 0.82
Diluted	$ 1.18	$ 1.01	$ 0.80
Weighted average shares outstanding:			
Basic	2,509	2,565	2,584
Diluted	2,568	2,619	2,644

GROSS PROFIT AND GROSS PROFIT PERCENTAGE

gross profit the amount that a firm earns before operating expenses

Gross profit and gross profit percentage help financial statement users and management understand how well a firm is running its core operations. **Gross profit** (Net Sales − Cost of Sales) is the amount that a firm earns before operating expenses are considered. (Dell uses the term *gross margin* instead of gross profit.) Dell's gross profit for the fiscal year ended January 28, 2005, is $9,015 million ($49,205 million − $40,190 million). Note that Dell uses the term "cost of revenue" rather than "cost of sales," but they are the same thing. **Gross profit percentage** (Gross Profit ÷ Net Sales) indicates the amount (expressed as a percentage) of gross profit that a firm earns on each dollar of sales. Dell's gross profit percentage for the fiscal year ended January 28, 2005 is 18.3 percent ($9,015 million ÷ $49,205 million). What this means is that for each dollar of sales, Dell's average cost of product sold is $.817 ($1.00 − $.183) and its gross profit is $.183.

gross profit percentage gross profit divided by net sales; the amount (expressed as a percentage) of gross profit earned on each dollar of sales

OPERATING MARGIN (OR OPERATING INCOME) AND OPERATING MARGIN PERCENTAGE (OR OPERATING INCOME PERCENTAGE)

operating margin (or *operating income*) the amount the firm generates after operating expenses and cost of sales

Operating margin (or *operating income*) (Net Sales − [Cost of Sales + Operating Expenses]) indicates the amount the firm generates after operating expenses and cost of sales. **Operating margin percentage** (or *operating income percentage*) is a firm's operating margin divided by net sales, indicating how much operating margin is generated on each dollar of sales. Note that operating margin is calculated before financial and investment income and expenses (interest and investment revenue) are taken into consideration, as these are the result of financing rather than operating decisions.

operating margin percentage (or *operating income percentage*) operating income divided by net sales; the amount of operating income generated by each dollar of sales

Returning to the Dell example, the firm's operating margin for the fiscal year ended January 28, 2005, is $4,254 million ($49,205 million − [$40,190 million + $4,761 million]). Its operating margin percentage is 8.65 percent ($4,254 million ÷ $49,205 million). This means that for each dollar of sales, Dell earns 8.65 cents of operating margin.

PROFIT MARGIN ON SALES

profit margin on sales the amount of net income earned on each dollar of sales

Profit margin on sales is the amount of net income earned on each dollar of sales and is calculated by dividing net income by net sales. For fiscal year 2005, Dell's profit margin on sales is 6.18 percent ($3,043 million ÷ $49,205 million). This means that Dell earns 6.18 cents on each dollar of sales.

Illustration 3.5 summarizes this chapter's financial measures and their formulas.

LIMITATIONS ON THE USE OF FINANCIAL STATEMENT RATIOS

Taken alone, no financial ratio is particularly significant to either external or internal users. Ratios must be compared over time (across fiscal years) so that trends can be evaluated and changes noted. They must also be compared across firms in the same industry. For example, how does Dell's profit margin on sales compare to the profit margins of its competitors, such as IBM? In addition, it is often difficult to fully understand a firm's financial condition merely by examining its published financial reports. Clearly, not all the information necessary to gain a thorough understanding of a firm's past performance and future prospects is presented in the financial statements and related notes. After all, financial statement data are highly summarized, and given the complexity of many companies' operations, ratios based on such data can be mislead-

Illustration 3.5

Income Statement Measures

Measure	Formula
Gross profit	Net Sales − Cost of Sales
Gross profit percentage	Gross Profit ÷ Net Sales
Operating margin (or operating income)	Net Sales − (Cost of Sales + Operating Expenses)
Operating margin percentage (or operating income percentage)	Operating Margin (or Operating Income) ÷ Net Sales
Profit margin on sales	Net Income ÷ Net Sales

ing. For example, **Time Warner**, the multimedia giant, operates businesses as diverse as movie production, 24-hour news broadcasting, magazine publishing, and subscription Internet service, yet the results of all its activities are combined into a single set of consolidated financial statements. Those financial statements could be used to calculate many ratios, but how meaningful would the ratios be in isolation? This is one of the reasons the FASB requires firms to disclose certain data related to operating components. Those requirements are discussed in Chapter 5.

CHECK YOUR UNDERSTANDING

1. If a firm reports $985,000 in net sales and $289,000 in gross profit, what is the firm's gross profit percentage?

2. Why are items like interest expense and investment revenue excluded from operating income?

3. If Company A reports a profit margin on sales of 5.7 percent and Company B reports 7.2 percent, which company is performing better with regard to this measurement alone? Why?

LO 7 Summarize the issues related to quality of earnings.

quality of earnings the extent to which current earnings are useful in predicting future earnings and cash flows

🧩 *Critical Thinking: Describe the accounting factors that you think might affect how earnings are calculated and reported. How would these factors affect your ability to understand the financial performance of a company?*

The Quality of Reported Earnings Information

Perhaps the most significant variable in financial statement analysis is the quality of earnings that underlies reported net income. One of the primary purposes of financial reporting is to help current and potential investors and creditors forecast a firm's future earnings and cash flows. **Quality of earnings** is the extent to which current earnings are useful in predicting future earnings and cash flows. Quality of earnings reflects the degree of conservatism applied in the determination of a company's reported earnings. If reported earnings are based on conservative accounting principles, similar earnings are more likely to continue into the future than if less conservative principles are used. Indicators of high earnings quality include, but are not limited to, the following:

1. Conservative revenue recognition methods

2. Quick write-off of acquisition goodwill and other intangibles

3. Transparent and adequate disclosures

4. Limited use of off-balance-sheet financing techniques

5. Use of conservative assumptions for postretirement benefit obligations

6. Limited presence of nonrecurring items (restructuring charges, asset impairments, discontinued operations, extraordinary items, changes in accounting principles, and changes in estimates) in net income[14]

ATTRIBUTES OF QUALITY OF EARNINGS

Determining the quality of earnings is essential in assessing the probability that a firm will be able to sustain its current cash flows and increase them in the future. Among the warning signs of poor quality of earnings are operating earnings that include transitory transactions (one-time transactions that are not expected to continue) and the use of accounting principles and accounting estimates that artificially inflate earnings. For example, net income might include a number of nonrecurring items classified as extraordinary or the cumulative effect of changes in accounting principles in a period when the firm incurred a loss from continuing operations.

Management's choice of accounting methods also affects earnings quality. For example, the inventory method chosen, such as LIFO rather than FIFO, might result in higher profits under some circumstances and lower profits under other circumstances. The use of accelerated depreciation enables a firm to record larger amounts of depreciation expense in the earlier years of an asset's life than does the use of straight-line depreciation, which results in a constant amount of depreciation over an asset's lifetime.

❯ EARNINGS MANAGEMENT

earnings management the use of accounting information, principles, and standards that have been purposefully selected to smooth out ups and downs in earnings

Another influence on quality of earnings is **earnings management**, which is the use of accounting information, principles, or standards that have been purposefully selected to smooth out ups and downs in earnings, or, in Arthur Levitt's words, "to satisfy consensus earnings estimates and project a smooth earnings path."[15] There is evidence indicating that managers prefer to report earnings that are moving smoothly on an upward trajectory rather than earnings that fluctuate, because they believe that investors shy away from unpredictable investments.

Because accountants must constantly make estimates and choose between acceptable accounting methods, some degree of earnings management can probably be found in most financial statements. For example, using straight-line depreciation provides stable depreciation charges over a number of years. Among other techniques for smoothing earnings are the shrewd timing of asset sales and the selection of favorable accounting practices and estimates.

ETHICS ⚖️

❯ EARNINGS MANAGEMENT AND ETHICAL CONSIDERATIONS
Income statements that result from earnings management may contain information that could mislead analysts and cause them to reach erroneous conclusions. The practice has taken on a very negative connotation, as companies may sometimes use questionable or even fraudulent accounting that is outside GAAP to manipulate earnings. The extent of earnings management is now a concern to regulators and the investment community. When earnings management is extreme, or, more importantly, when fraudulent or questionable practices are used, the investing public may be misled into believing that current earnings will persist into the future.

For example, management may take actions to reduce the current year's earnings in a way that will allow earnings to be increased in future periods. One way to accomplish this is to create reserves that will be used to artificially inflate net income at a later date. These are often referred to as cookie jar reserves because they allow a company to

---

14 Adapted from the AICPA call for papers on its Quality of Earnings Project.

15 "SEC's Levitt Addresses Illusions," *Journal of Accountancy,* December 1978, p. 12.

stash away earnings for future use. Cookie jar reserves involve losses or write-downs of assets for unspecified or unwarranted purposes. When a company recognizes a loss or takes a write-down earlier than usual, it is able to report higher earnings in future years. Future earnings are increased because when an asset's value has been written down, or reduced, the depreciation expense recognized each year following the write-down will be lower. As a result, investors could be misled into believing that the higher earnings are real and that the company can sustain this inflated performance in the future.

❯ PERSISTENCE OF EARNINGS

persistence of earnings the predictability that earnings have when the components of net income can be expected to remain stable from year to year

Another factor that helps investors to forecast future performance is persistence of earnings. **Persistence of earnings** is the predictability that earnings have when the components of net income can be expected to remain fairly stable from year to year. For example, most selling and administrative expenses are recurring components of net income and should be fairly predictable from period to period. Thus, they would contribute to persistence of earnings. In contrast, gains or losses that are classified as extraordinary are one-time events and do not contribute to persistence of earnings. When analysts and other users of financial statements forecast future earnings, they want their predictions to be as realistic as possible, so they focus primarily on persistent, or repeating, elements of net income.

FRAUDULENT REPORTING PRACTICES

The late 1990s and early 2000s saw many cases of earnings management and other practices that were not based on legitimate accounting choices or management decisions. As a result, the quality of earnings of many U.S. companies was perceived as having decreased significantly. Even some traditional, or low-tech, companies engaged in such fraudulent reporting. For example, in May 2001, the Securities and Exchange Commission charged five former **Sunbeam** executives, including chairman and chief executive Al Dunlap, with massive accounting fraud that ultimately pushed the firm into bankruptcy. According to the SEC, Dunlap, a corporate turnaround specialist known as Chainsaw Al, and other top executives at Sunbeam used accounting tricks to inflate the company's stock. Sunbeam announced at least $60 million in bogus earnings in 1997, the SEC said. The deception worked for a time, though: Sunbeam's market capitalization hit $5 billion when its stock reached a high of $52 a share in March 1998.

The SEC said that Sunbeam created cookie jar reserves in late 1996, when it stashed funds to inflate its income in 1997 and falsely create the picture of a rapid financial turnaround. Sunbeam allegedly made the financial reports even brighter in 1997 by recognizing revenue on sales that did not meet accounting standards. According to the SEC, Sunbeam offered discounts and other incentives to encourage customers to buy products sooner than usual, a practice known as channel stuffing, but it failed to disclose that the near-term surge in revenue would come at the expense of future results.[16] Sunbeam is still in business but is operating in bankruptcy.

Unfortunately, Sunbeam is not the only company to have engaged in earnings management practices that actually amounted to fraudulent financial reporting. Continuing into the early 2000s, some of America's largest companies—**Microsoft**, **Qwest Communications**, **Time Warner**, **Global Crossing**, **WorldCom**, and **Enron**—had either unintentionally or, often, intentionally misused accounting practices. Many of the cases of fraudulent financial reporting centered on purposefully incorrect revenue recognition practices.

---

16 Judith Burns, "SEC Sues Ex-Sunbeam Exec Dunlap, Alleges Financial Fraud," Dow Jones Newswires, May 15, 2001.

point ►◄ counterpoint

Earnings Management

the controversy Earnings management. Some believe it is an age-old business practice entirely within the scope of generally accepted accounting principles used to smooth the peaks and dips of earnings. Others consider it a fraudulent activity with the intent of misleading investors. The controversy exists in the gray area in between these extremes. Earnings management is legal to a point, but often it is difficult to tell just where that point is. High-profile court cases involving Enron and WorldCom have contributed to the perception that companies have used questionable and sometimes unlawful accounting practices to manipulate the appearance of their financial health. Studies have shown that companies manage earnings in order to reduce taxes, to increase executive compensation, to avoid violations of debt agreements, and to temporarily boost stock prices.

Although it is commonly agreed that the practice of earnings management has existed in the business world for some time, corporate officers have been under increasing pressure to deliver earnings numbers that meet the projections of management. Failure to meet revenue predictions, even by a penny, can send a company's stock into a tailspin and has landed company executives on the unemployment line. Companies often achieve a healthy earnings snapshot through the use of various accounting maneuvers, some fully within the scope of GAAP and others involving a stretching and misinterpretation of the spirit of these principles.

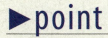point

Arthur Levitt

former SEC Chairman

on the point:

- **David M. Blitzer**
  S&P's chief investment strategist

►**Earnings management has become a prevalent and fraudulent method by which companies manipulate earnings and mislead investors.**

Former SEC Chairman Arthur Levitt expressed his concern regarding earnings management in a speech at the New York University Center for Law and Business on September 28, 1998 with the sentiment "earnings reports reflect the desires of management rather than the underlying financial performance of the company."[1] He stated that earnings management might be likened to "mismanagement" and that it results from companies exploiting the flexibility in accounting principles that allows financial reporting to keep pace with innovations in the economic and business environment. Some companies select accounting options that obscure management's decisions rather than shed light on them. The following five categories of earnings management techniques were identified as the most misused and misrepresented in financial reporting:

(1) *restructuring charges*—taking large charges for planned restructuring in order to clean up a balance sheet

(2) *acquisition accounting*—allocating large chunks of a purchase price to "in-process" R&D in order that they may be written off immediately; a one-time charge that boosts earnings drastically

(3) *recognition of reserves*—the use of "cookie jar" reserves when times are lean, improving a flailing income level

(4) *materiality*—the use of small "immaterial" adjustments to alter the overall earnings picture

(5) *revenue recognition*—recognizing revenue before the earnings process is complete

David M. Blitzer, S&P's chief investment strategist, holds that "the use of creative earnings measures has grown and grown and grown to the point where it has really got-

---

1 "The Numbers Game," remarks by Chairman Arthur Levitt, SEC. Delivered at the NYU Center for Law and Business, New York, September 28, 1998.

ten out of hand."[2] The use of fancy accounting footwork leads to financial statements that are not based on solid operational earnings but rather reflect management's ideal financial representation, resulting in questions about the overall quality of earnings.

◀ counterpoint

Paul Rosenfield

CPA and former director of the AICPA Accounting Standards Division

on the counterpoint:

- **Professor Robert Sterling**
  accounting theoretician
- **Walter Shuetze**
  former SEC chief accountant
- **William U. Parfet**
  FEI member and chairman and CEO of MPI Research, Inc.

◀Earnings management is driven by concepts central to GAAP and can be used in legal and ethical ways to create stable financial performance.

Within the scope of GAAP, companies have considerable discretion in reporting earnings. Judgment calls and estimation are involved. Paul Rosenfield, former director of the AICPA Accounting Standards Division, contends that GAAP itself supports the smoothing out of the peaks and valleys of earnings through concepts like realization and allocation. Over the years, leaders in accounting have viewed the current design of GAAP as a means to smooth the variations in actual business cycles. Accounting theoretician Professor Robert Sterling stated, "The purpose of allocation is to make the empirical phenomena appear to be smooth regardless of the actual variations." University of Alabama Professor Thomas A. Lee said that allocations are "designed to produce smoothed income flows." Former SEC chief accountant Walter Shuetze said that allocation is used to manage earnings to smooth "the hills and valleys of change."[3] Therefore, many purport that the very underpinnings of GAAP actually serve to drive the practice of earnings management.

The subtle smoothing of earnings through selling an asset at a key time or adjusting the valuation of another asset is characterized as simply good business management. In addition, many observers say that a certain amount of earnings management is good for both stockholders and the company. This is based on the belief that companies should make operating decisions that propel long-term performance by sometimes deferring spending or taking one-time charges that benefit the future.[4]

Many well-known and respected companies have been known to massage financial presentations to support a steady progression of earnings. For example, Reader's Digest Association Inc. became more optimistic about the number of customers who would pay their bills on time in 2001, thus adjusting its collection estimate and gaining approximately 16¢ a share on its stock price. Although there are certainly examples of companies who have stepped over the ethical line in their practices of earnings management, there are many that contend that their accounting practices are legal, ethical, and make the most of earnings—as all companies are in business to do.

Take a Position If you were an investor in Reader's Digest Association, Inc. and knew that the value of your stock had appreciated due to an adjustment of a collection estimate rather than an increase in operational income, how would you view this event? Explain how this earnings management technique affected the value of your stock.

Research Using an online business magazine or newspaper, locate a recent article pertaining to earnings management within a U.S. company. Prepare a written report that summarizes the details of the case. In this situation, do you believe the company has engaged in ethical earnings management practices? Explain your answer.

---

2 Nanette Byrnes and David Henry, "Confused About Earnings?" *Business Week,* November 26, 2001. Accessed 03/01/04 at Business Week Online, **http://www.businessweek.com/magazine/content/01_48/b3759001.htm.**

3 Paul Rosenfield , "What Drives Earnings Management?" *Journal of Accountancy*, October 2000. Accessed 03/01/04 at **http://www.aicpa.org/pubs/jofa/oct2000/opinion.htm.**

4 James R. Duncan, "Twenty Pressures to Manage Earnings," *The CPA Journal,* July 2001. Accessed 03/01/04 at **http://www.nysscpa.org/cpajournal/2001/0700/features/f073201.htm.**

In this chapter, we discussed the general rules for preparing the income statement. In subsequent chapters, we examine in greater depth how the elements of the income statement, such as revenues and expenses, are valued and reported. As noted earlier in the chapter, analysts evaluate the elements of net income for reliability, or degree of earnings management, even if a firm is correctly applying generally accepted accounting principles. They know that a high quality of earnings enhances the predictive value of their assessments of a firm's future cash flows. The remaining chapters in this book discuss accounting choices with an emphasis on earnings quality and earnings persistence.

CHECK YOUR UNDERSTANDING

1. Describe the concept of earnings management.

2. How do conservative accounting practices affect the quality of earnings?

3. Explain why persistence of earnings is important to quality of earnings.

Revisiting the Case

DELL DELIVERS DOMINO'S PIZZA AND WIDENS OVERALL MARKET-SHARE LEAD

1. It is important to measure income from operations separately from income generated from one-time or nonrecurring events and from income tax provisions.

2. Positive indicators of performance shown in the statement of operations include increases in net revenue, gross margin, and net income.

3. Net revenue, gross margin, operating expenses, operating income, and net income are general categories presented on the income statements for most U.S. companies.

SUMMARY BY LEARNING OBJECTIVE

LO1 Distinguish between the economic and accounting definitions of income.

Economic income is the change in net wealth that results from a change in the current value of an asset. In a general sense, any increase in the current value of a firm's net assets (not counting capital contributions and withdrawals) is its economic income for the period. The drawback to the economic income approach is that because no actual transaction has taken place, it is difficult to measure an asset's fair market value in an objective and verifiable way that users can rely upon. Transaction-based income (or accounting-based income) is the net income that a firm derives from all of its business transactions; it is determined by subtracting all recognized expenses and losses from all recognized revenues and gains. This is the approach most commonly applied under GAAP. Under the transaction-based approach, Net Income = Revenues − Expenses + Gains − Losses.

LO2 Discuss the differences between a single-step income statement and a multiple-step income statement and list the elements each format contains.

In a single-step income statement, all revenues and gains are placed in one category, and all expenses and losses are placed in another category. The difference between the two categories is the income or loss before income taxes. Net income is determined by deducting income taxes and other items, such as discontinued operations, extraordinary items, and changes in accounting principles, from the income or loss before income taxes. Usually, no distinction is made between items related to operating activities and items related to nonoperating activities. The single-step method of reporting operating income offers simplicity and is generally favored by most corporations.

A multiple-step income statement is a more complex form of income statement that is clearly divided into operating and nonoperating sections. Most companies that use the multiple-step format do so to provide more detailed information about their operations and the expenses involved in financing them. Therefore, the operating section of a multiple-step income statement itemizes net sales; cost of goods sold; gross profit on sales; selling, general, and administrative expenses; and other operating income and expenses. The nonoperating section contains such categories as net interest revenue or expense and other expense.

LO3 Identify recurring and non-recurring items and report them on the income statement.

Three income statement items require special and separate disclosure: discontinued operations, extraordinary items, and accounting changes.

- A component of an entity that is classified as being held for sale or that has been disposed of is presented as a discontinued operation if the operations and cash flows of the component will be (or have been) eliminated from the ongoing operations of the entity and if the entity will not have any significant continuing involvement in the operations of the component. Both the operations of a discontinued operation and any gain or loss on its disposal should be shown separately from income from continuing operations.

- An extraordinary item is an unusual, infrequent, and material item that must be reported separately from the results of continuing operations. Whether an item is extraordinary depends upon the nature of a firm's operations. On the income statement, extraordinary items are reported net of taxes. They follow discontinued operations, if that item exists.

- An *accounting change* is a global term used to describe three types of changes: (1) a switch or change in accounting principle that is either decided by management or mandated by the FASB or SEC, (2) a modification or change in an accounting estimate, or (3) a change in reporting entity. A correction of an error in previously issued financial statements is not an accounting change but is treated in many respects in a similar manner. In May 2005, the FASB issued *Statement No. 154,* "Accounting Changes and Error Corrections," which significantly changed the reporting standards for accounting changes, especially those for changes in accounting principles. *SFAS No. 154* now requires retrospective application to prior periods' financial statements of changes in accounting principles, unless it is impracticable to determine the period-specific effects of the change on prior periods. The new FASB standard differentiates between a change in accounting estimate and a change in accounting estimate effected by a change in accounting principle.

LO4 Explain the concept of earnings per share and describe how EPS is reported on the income statement.

Earnings per share (EPS) is the amount of earnings associated with each share of a firm's common stock. It is shown on all income statements, regardless of format. *SFAS No. 128* requires that EPS be reported for income from continuing operations, discontinued operations, extraordinary items, cumulative effects of a change in accounting principle, and net income. In many situations, two forms of EPS must be reported. Basic EPS relates net income to the number of shares of common stock outstanding. Diluted EPS relates net income to the maximum possible number of shares of common stock if all possibly dilutive financial contracts, such as stock options, were converted to common stock. The formula to calculate basic EPS is net income minus preferred stock dividends divided by the weighted-average number of common shares outstanding.

LO5 Define comprehensive income and discuss the required disclosures.

Comprehensive income is the change in the equity of a business enterprise during a period from transactions and other events and circumstances from non-owner sources. It includes both net income as defined by accrual accounting principles and other components, such as unrealized gains and losses on marketable securities held in the available-for-sale portfolio, unrealized gains and losses resulting from foreign currency translations that occur when foreign subsidiaries' financial statements are converted into U.S. dollars for the purpose of consolidation, and unrealized gains and losses resulting from changes in interest-rate assumptions when estimating pension obligations. Under *SFAS No. 130,* the effects of these and similar transactions that are primarily derived from events external to the firm are not included in what is considered traditional net income. Rather, they are recorded in a special owners' equity account called Other Comprehensive Income. That account is not included in net income but is included in stockholders' equity. Most firms report comprehensive income as part of their statement of changes in stockholders' equity.

LO6 Use five basic measures to analyze an income statement.

- Gross profit (Net Sales − Cost of Sales) is the amount that a firm earns before administrative expenses are considered.

- Gross profit percentage (Gross Profit ÷ Net Sales) is the amount of gross profit that a firm earns on each dollar of sales.

- Operating margin (or operating income) [Net Sales − (Cost of Sales + Operating Expenses)] is the amount of margin the firm generates after cost of sales and operating expenses.

- Operating margin percentage (or operating income percentage) [Operating Margin (or operating income) ÷ Net Sales] is the amount of operating margin that a firm earns on each dollar of sales.

- Profit margin on sales (Net Income ÷ Net Sales) is the amount of net income that a firm earns on each dollar of sales.

LO7 Summarize the issues related to quality of earnings.

Quality of earnings is the extent to which current earnings are useful in predicting future earnings and cash flows. Determining the quality of earnings is essential in assessing the probability that a firm will be able to sustain its current cash flows and increase them in the future. Among the warning signs of poor quality of earnings are operating earnings that include transitory transactions and the use of accounting principles and accounting estimates that artificially inflate earnings. Management's choice of accounting methods affects earnings quality, as does earnings management, which is the use of accounting information, principles, or standards that have been purposefully selected to smooth out ups and downs in earnings. Another factor that helps investors to forecast future performance is persistence of earnings, the predictability that earnings have when the components of net income can be expected to remain fairly stable from year to year.

KEY TERMS

accounting change (p. 112)
basic EPS (p. 119)
change in accounting principle (p. 113)
change in accounting estimate (p. 115)
change in accounting estimate effected by a change in accounting principle (p. 115)
component of an entity (p. 108)
comprehensive income (p. 120)
diluted EPS (p. 119)
discontinued operation (p. 109)

earnings management (p. 126)
earnings per share (EPS) (p. 119)
economic income (p. 103)
extraordinary item (p. 110)
gross profit (p. 124)
gross profit percentage (p. 124)
holding gain (p. 103)
income statement (p. 104)
intraperiod income tax allocation (p. 117)
multiple-step income statement (p. 106)
nonoperating activities (p. 105)

nonrecurring items (p. 108)
operating activities (p. 105)
operating margin (p. 124)
operating margin percentage (p. 124)
persistence of earnings (p. 127)
profit margin on sales (p. 124)
quality of earnings (p. 125)
recurring items (p. 108)
retrospective application (p. 112)
single-step income statement (p. 105)
transaction-based income (p. 103)

EXERCISES

LO2   EXERCISE 3-1   **Multiple-Step Income Statement**
As the accountant for Travis Boots, Inc., you have gathered the following information to prepare the year-end financial statements at December 31, 2005:

Boot Sales	$893,000
Accessories Sales	225,335
Advertising Expense	19,055
Utilities Expense	16,335
Cost of Goods Sold	226,774
Interest Expense on Bonds	15,000
Sales Salaries Expense	205,003
Insurance Expense	4,455
Depreciation Expense	1,100
Income Taxes	275,000

Required: Prepare a multiple-step income statement for Travis Boots, Inc.

LO3   EXERCISE 3-2   Reporting Nonrecurring Items

Over the years, Global Company has saved money by not buying hail insurance for its vans. When damage occurs, Global either pays for repairs or sells the damaged vans for salvage and then replaces them. The last hailstorm that caused damage occurred in mid-2004. During 2005, hail damaged several of Global Company's vans. Hailstorms had inflicted similar damage to the vans in the past. The vans that were damaged during 2005 were sold for less than their carrying amount. The loss was material.

Required: Indicate how and where Global Company should report the hail damage on its financial statements.

LO3   EXERCISE 3-3   Reporting Extraordinary Items

O'Hare Company had the following transactions during 2005:

A. $1,200,000 pretax loss on foreign currency exchange as a result of a major unexpected devaluation by a foreign government

B. $500,000 pretax loss from discontinuing the operations of a division

C. $800,000 pretax loss on equipment damaged by a hurricane. This was the first hurricane to strike in O'Hare's area. O'Hare also received $1,000,000 from its insurance company to replace a damaged building with a carrying value of $300,000 that was destroyed by the hurricane.

O'Hare pays a marginal tax rate of 35 percent.

Required: What amount should O'Hare report on its 2005 income statement as an extraordinary loss, net of tax? Show how the extraordinary items are reported on O'Hare's 2005 income statement.

LO3   EXERCISE 3-4   Extraordinary Items

Burt Company incurred the following loss and realized the following gain during 2005:

A. A $50,000 loss as the result of an unanticipated strike by its employees

B. A $25,000 gain as the result of the early extinguishment of bonds payable

Burt's income tax rate for 2005 was 30 percent.

Required: What amount should be reported as an extraordinary gain or loss for Burt Company?

LO2, 3   EXERCISE 3-5   Income from Operations and Nonrecurring Items

During 2005, Fine Steel Co. had $300,000 of income from continuing operations before taxes and before the following unusual financial events:

A. Bonds payable were retired during 2005, five years before the scheduled maturity, resulting in a $260,000 gain. Fine frequently retires bonds early when interest rates decline significantly.

B. The company's steel-forming segment suffered $255,000 in losses as a result of hurricane damage. This was the fourth similar loss sustained in a five-year period at this location.

C. A segment (considered a component) of Fine's operations, steel transportation, was sold at a net loss of $350,000. This was Fine's first divestiture of one of its operating components.

Fine's income tax rate is 30 percent.

Required:

1. What amount of gain (loss) should be reported as a component of income from continuing operations in 2005?

2. What amount should be disclosed as the gain (loss) from extraordinary items in 2005?

LO3 **EXERCISE 3-6 Discontinued Operations**
On January 1, 2005, the board of directors of Mars Manufacturing, Inc. committed to a plan to discontinue its Venus division (considered a component) in 2006. Venus's 2005 operating loss was $1,400,000, and at that time the division's net assets were approximately equal to their carrying value. Venus's 2006 operating loss was $500,000, and in 2006 Venus's facilities were sold at an actual loss of $300,000. Mars's effective income tax rate is 30 percent.

Required:

1. In its 2005 income statement, what amount should Mars report as a loss from discontinued operations?

2. In its 2006 income statement, what amount should Mars report as a loss from discontinued operations?

LO3 **EXERCISE 3-7 Discontinued Operations**
On January 1, 2006, Dove Corporation approved a plan to dispose of a component of its business in 2006. The operating loss for the component was $800,000. The assets of the component were sold on October 15, 2006, at a $1,500,000 loss. Dove pays a marginal tax rate of 30 percent.

Required: Show how Dove should report the discontinued component on its income statement for the year ended December 31, 2006.

LO3 **EXERCISE 3-8 Discontinued Operations**
On July 1, 2005, Thyme Corporation approved a formal plan to sell its herbal division, considered a component of the business. The sale will occur in the first three months of 2006. The division had an operating loss of $400,000 for the first six months of 2005 and expects an operating loss of $700,000 for the period from July 1 to December 31, 2005. At December 31, 2005, Thyme also estimated that it will incur a $200,000 loss in 2006 prior to the time of the actual sale. The company also estimated that at December 31, 2005, the fair value of the division's net assets will be $12,000,000, significantly below their carrying value of $20,000,000. The company's effective tax rate is 40 percent.

Required:

1. Determine the amount of gain or loss that Thyme should report for discontinued operations for the year ended December 31, 2005.

2. Assuming that during 2006 the division was sold for $11,000,000 and the actual operating loss of the division up to the time of sale was $250,000, determine the amount of gain or loss that Thyme should report for discontinued operations for the year ended December 31, 2006.

LO2, 3 **EXERCISE 3-9 Multiple-Step Income Statement with Nonrecurring Items**
The trial balance of Sube Corporation for the year ended December 31, 2005, included the items listed below. Income from continuing operations before income taxes and before the

effects of these items was calculated at $30,000. All amounts provided are before income taxes. The company has a 30 percent income tax rate.

- A gain of $5,000 from the early retirement of bonds payable.
- An uninsured fire loss in the amount of $7,000. Losses from fires have never occurred in the past.
- A loss in the amount of $1,500 related to the write-down of obsolete inventory.
- A gain of $1,000 related to the sale of a subsidiary company. The subsidiary was engaged in the pipe fabrication business, and Sube Corporation has no other operations in that business. Operations related to the subsidiary for the current year amounted to a $4,000 loss.

Required:

1. Calculate income from continuing operations for Sube Corporation for the year ended December 31, 2005.
2. Complete the income statement in multiple-step format beginning with income from continuing operations as calculated in question 1.
3. What differences would be apparent if the income statement in question 2 had been prepared using a single-step format?

LO3   **EXERCISE 3-10   Recurring and Nonrecurring Items**

The following terms and phrases relate to items found on the income statement.

Term	Phrase
1. Discontinued operations	A. Modification to an accounting estimate that is inseperable from and brought about by the effect of a related change in accounting principle
2. Change in estimate effected by a change in accounting principle	B. A figure that includes all the recurring operating transactions that affect income
3. Income from continuing operations	C. Losses from damage due to the eruption of a supposedly extinct volcano
4. Extraordinary items	D. A component of an entity that is classified as being held for sale or that has been disposed of
5. Change in estimate	E. A modification to an accounting estimate resulting from new information or experience

Required: Match each item in the Term column with the item in the Phrase column that is most closely related to it.

LO4   **EXERCISE 3-11   Earnings per Share**

The following information appeared in Coleman Company's accounting records as of December 31, 2005:

8% Preferred Stock, $2 par value, 30,000 shares authorized	$ 60,000
Additional Paid-in Capital—Preferred Stock	106,000
Common Stock, $1 par value, 50,000 shares authorized	30,000
Additional Paid-in Capital—Common Stock	625,000

On March 31, 2005, 4,000 shares of common stock were issued. Net income was $84,000 for the year ended December 31, 2005.

Required:

1. Calculate basic earnings per share for Coleman. (*Hint:* You must calculate the number of shares issued.)
2. Briefly describe how diluted EPS differs from basic earnings per share.

LO2, 4   EXERCISE 3-12   **Multiple-Step Income Statement and EPS**

Melia Meals began operations in 2002. Its income tax rate is 30 percent. Information from Melia Meals's December 31, 2005, accounting records follows:

Sales	$840,000	Selling Expenses	$120,000
Cost of Sales	380,000	Dividends Declared and Paid	50,000
Extraordinary Loss	45,000	Capital Stock, $2 par value	40,000
Interest Expense	12,000	Loss on Sale of Plant Asset	14,000
Interest Revenue	5,000	Administrative Expenses	90,000

Required: Prepare a multiple-step income statement for the year ended December 31, 2005, including earnings per share.

LO2, 4, 5   EXERCISE 3-13   **Combined Multiple-Step and Comprehensive Income Statement and EPS**

Waterloo Corp. prepared the following partial list of accounts and balances for the year ended December 31, 2005. All amounts are in thousands.

Sales Revenue	$420	Cash	$ 26
Administrative Expenses	42	Selling Expenses	51
Accounts Receivable	36	Common Stock, $1 par	50
Unrealized Gain from Investments, net	4	Prepaid Insurance	3
Foreign Currency Translation Loss, net	9	Dividends	14
Income Tax Expense	2	Cost of Sales	290

Required: Using the information presented, prepare a combined income and comprehensive income statement using the multiple-step format for Waterloo Corp. for the year ended December 31, 2005, including EPS.

LO1   EXERCISE 3-14   **Economic and Accounting Measures of Income**

Central to the determination of net income is the definition and measurement of the events that cause net assets to increase and whether those events should be included in the determination of net income.

Required: Identify whether each statement below defines economic income or accounting-based income.

1. Measures any increase in the current value of a firm's net assets (not counting capital contributions and withdrawals)
2. Focuses on the actual transactions of a business
3. Measured by subtracting all recognized expenses and losses from recognized gains and revenues
4. Transaction-based income
5. Measures income as a change in net wealth

LO4   EXERCISE 3-15   **Earnings per Share Presentation**

Rockwood Company has 100,000 shares of common stock outstanding during 2005. The following items were reported on the income statement dated December 31, 2005:

Income from continuing operations	$89,000
Loss from discontinued operations	14,000
Extraordinary gain	27,000

All amounts are net of tax. The company has no preferred stock and has not issued any dividends.

Required: Prepare the 2005 EPS presentation for Rockwood Company.

LO5   EXERCISE 3-16   **Presentation of Comprehensive Income**
Central Market's accounts reflect the following balances:

	June 30, 2004	June 29, 2005
Shares of common stock	225,000	?
Common stock and additional paid-in capital	$ 980,000	$1,110,330
Retained earnings	1,899,020	1,930,360
Accumulated other comprehensive income	56,000	?

The company issued 20,000 shares of common stock in August of 2004. Central Market recognized the increase in the value of its available-for-sale marketable securities of $76,000 in January 2005 as other comprehensive income.

Required: Prepare a statement of stockholders' equity for Central Market, including other comprehensive income. Assume no dividends were declared during the current fiscal year.

LO6   EXERCISE 3-17   **Income Statement Analysis**
Kyle Industries reported net sales of $24,003,404 for the year ended October 31, 2005. Cost of sales for the period was $16,300,566, and operating expenses were $4,110,000.

Required: Management has asked you to compute how much operating income is generated for each dollar of sales.

LO6   EXERCISE 3-18   **Income Statement Analysis**
CrossFire Technologies reported net income of $25,450 and net sales of $230,000 for the year ended December 31, 2005. Cost of sales was $172,550.

Required: CrossFire Technologies wishes to compare its gross profit percentage and its profit margin on sales with those of its competitor, Wildfire Industries. During this same period, Wildfire released the following figures: 5.5 percent profit margin; 11 percent gross profit percentage.

1. Compute the gross profit percentage and profit margin on sales for CrossFire.
2. For these two measurements, how does CrossFire compare to Wildfire?

LO7   EXERCISE 3-19   **Quality of Earnings**
The quality of earnings is the extent to which current earnings are useful in predicting future earnings and cash flows.

Required: Which items below are indicators of high earnings quality?
1. Conservative revenue recognition methods
2. Frequent appearance of nonrecurring charges in net income
3. Frequent changes in accounting methods, such as the inventory valuation method
4. Transparent and adequate disclosures
5. Use of conservative assumptions for items like postretirement benefit obligations

PROBLEMS

LO2   PROBLEM 3-1   **Multiple-Step and Single-Step Income Statement**
Phoenix Corporation sells widgets. It provided the following information for its year ended December 31, 2005:

Selling Expenses	$ 10,000	Net Sales	$500,000
Administrative Expenses	20,000	Cost of Sales	300,000
Interest Income	2,000	Rent Revenue	100,000
Interest Expense	5,000	Income Taxes	35% rate

Required:

1. Prepare an income statement in good form using the multiple-step format.

2. Prepare an income statement in good form using the single-step format.

Communicate: Phoenix's CEO asks for your advice as to which format is preferable. In a memo to the CEO, describe each format's usefulness and limitations.

Analyze: If Phoenix Corporation wishes to focus on decreasing its cost of sales over the next few years, which format would be more helpful in analyzing the company's progress?

LO2   **PROBLEM 3-2**   **Income Statement Format**

Rainy Days Corporation began business in 2002 by opening a retail store selling rain gear for sports events. Its effective income tax rate is 35 percent. Its general ledger shows the following amounts (in millions) as of December 31, 2005:

Sales Revenue	$100,000
Depreciation Expense	10,000
Cost of Goods Sold	40,000
Selling Expenses	1,000
Restructuring Expense	500
Administrative Expenses	2,000
Interest Income	20
Interest Expense	40
Loss due to early repayment of bonds payable	1,000
Loss from discontinued operations	1,200
Warranty Expense	10
Unexpected loss due to labor strike	30

Required: Prepare an income statement for 2005 in good form using the single-step format.

Analyze: What is Rainy Days Corporation's gross profit for the period?

Spreadsheet: Using a spreadsheet, prepare a single-step income statement for 2005.

LO3, 4   **PROBLEM 3-3**   **Classification on the Income Statement**

The following are independent cases relating to Strong Corp.'s transactions during 2005:

A. Material losses to a warehouse located one mile from the Mississippi River caused by the flooding of the river.

B. Material losses to office space owned in downtown Chicago caused by the flooding of the underground deep tunnel in Chicago.

C. Foreign currency translation losses resulting from the consolidation of Strong's foreign subsidiary with its U.S. parent.

D. A material loss related to the early extinguishment of $20 million in bonds payable.

E. Strong Corp. decided on January 1 to sell off a major business component. The gain related to the sale was $2 million.

F. Strong Corp. decided to close its factory in Dayton, Ohio. The loss related to the sale of the factory was $3 million.

G. Strong Corp. incurred a $12 million adjustment related to prior periods as a consequence of adopting a new FASB standard.

H. Strong Corp. recognized a $6 million expense related to corporate restructuring costs.

I. Strong Corp. changed its method of accounting for depreciation of long-lived assets. As a result, an additional $3 million in expenses is recognized for the previous years.

Required: Indicate whether each item should be considered part of income from continuing operations (CO), a discontinued operation (DO), an extraordinary item (EX), or a change in accounting principle (AP), or reported in other comprehensive income (OCI).

Analyze: Are companies required to report EPS for items E and F? Why?

LO3   PROBLEM 3-4   **Income Statement with Discontinued Operations**

The following is a condensed statement of income for Norton Corporation for the two years ended December 31, 2006 and 2005.

	2006	2005
Net sales	$20,000,000	$18,000,000
Cost of goods sold	12,000,000	10,000,000
Gross profit	$ 8,000,000	$ 8,000,000
Operating expenses	4,000,000	4,000,000
Operating income	$ 4,000,000	$ 4,000,000
Gain from discontinued operations	1,200,000	—
Income before income taxes	$ 5,200,000	$ 4,000,000
Income taxes	1,820,000	1,400,000
Net income	$ 3,380,000	$ 2,600,000

On June 1, 2005, Norton entered into an agreement to sell one of its separate operating divisions. The sale was completed in January of 2006 at a price of $4,000,000. As a result of the sale, Norton reported a gain of $1,200,000. The division's contribution before tax each year, all of which was included in the income amounts reported above, was as follows:

	Net Sales	Cost of Goods Sold	Net Loss
2006	$1,000,000	$1,300,000	$ 300,000 loss
2005	4,200,000	5,900,000	1,700,000 loss

Assume an income tax rate of 35 percent.

Required: Prepare a revised comparative statement of income for 2006 and 2005, assuming that the sale meets the reporting requirements for discontinued operations.

Spreadsheet: Using a spreadsheet, prepare the revised comparative statements of income for 2006 and 2005.

LO3, 5   PROBLEM 3-5   **Classification of Income Statement Items**

In your position as assistant to the controller of New Corporation, you have been asked to classify the following 2005 transactions for income statement presentation in the company's 2005 annual report:

A. The method of depreciation has been changed from an accelerated method to straight-line depreciation, and the adjustment is material.

B. An error in calculating depreciation in 2003 was discovered, and the amount is material.

C. New Corporation's Ohio factory sustained material losses as a result of a labor strike.

D. One of New Corporation's divisions keeps a large inventory of livestock. Because of an outbreak of hoof-and-mouth disease, the government ordered that the entire inventory be destroyed and burned. The amount of the loss was material.

E. Because of antiquated machinery, the plant in Michigan was closed. New Corporation plans to refit the machinery sometime in the future. Expenses related to the closure were material.

F. The estimated life of the machinery at the Iowa plant was changed from six remaining years to two years.

G. New Corporation entered into a contract to buy raw materials for the next twelve months at $4.00/lb. The market price of the raw material has just dropped to $3.50/lb. New Corporation estimates that it will have to pay $3 million more than market price because of the purchase commitment.

H. Because of the slowing economy, New Corporation now estimates that bad debts will probably be 1 percent of sales, rather than the 0.5 percent recognized in past years.

I. New Corporation has decided to sell its Internet subsidiary because of disappointing operating results. New Corporation sells the subsidiary for a loss of $2 million. The operating loss related to the subsidiary was $300,000 for the year.

J. Because of the strong U.S. dollar, the foreign currency translation loss resulting from the consolidation of the Australian subsidiary was material.

Required: Indicate the financial statement and section in which each of these transactions should be classified and reported.

Analyze: Why does the proper classification of nonrecurring and recurring items affect an analyst's ability to forecast future cash flows?

LO2, 3, 5 **PROBLEM 3-6** **Multiple-Step Income Statement, Comprehensive Income**

Civil Corporation manufactures paint at its plant in the Arizona desert, where floods are both unusual and infrequent. The company has a 30 percent income tax rate. It provided the following selected information from its accounting records for 2005:

Retained Earnings, January 1, 2005	$60,000
Cash dividends declared	6,000
Gain realized from insurance proceeds for flood damage before income taxes	4,000
Income from continuing operations	54,000
Unrealized gain from available-for-sale investments before income taxes	16,000
Prior years' effect of a change from straight-line to accelerated depreciation before income taxes	10,000

Required:

1. Using a multiple-step format, prepare an income statement beginning with income from continuing operations for the year ended December 31, 2005. If an income statement for December 31, 2004 was prepared, how would it be affected by these transactions?

2. Prepare a statement of comprehensive income for 2005.

3. Describe the two other options a company may use to report comprehensive income. Which of the three options do most companies use?

4. Why are comprehensive income items not reported as part of the traditional income statement?

Analyze: By what percentage did income change as a result of the extraordinary items and accounting changes?

LO3 **PROBLEM 3-7** **Reporting Discontinued Operations**

Freedman Corporation owns three soap manufacturing plants, two nightclubs, and a chain of department stores. Income from continuing operations for the Freedman Corporation for 2005 totaled $1,200,000. On July 1, 2005, Freedman's board of directors voted to sell the nightclub component of its business. Freedman will have no significant involvement in the operations of the nightclubs after the sale, but will continue operations to minimize costs until the clubs are sold. The income tax rate is 30 percent.

A. As of the company's fiscal year end, December 31, 2005, the company believes it has found a potential buyer for the nightclubs, with a March 15, 2006, anticipated sale date. The best estimate of a selling price will yield a $200,000 loss, which is the amount by which the carrying value of the net assets exceeded their fair market value.

B. The company realized an actual operating loss from nightclub operations from January 1, 2005, through July 1, 2005, amounting to $600,000.

C. The company realized a small operating profit for the division from July 1, 2005, through December 31, 2005, totaling $350,000.

D. The company estimated a loss from nightclub operations from January 1, 2006, through March 15, 2006, totaling $400,000.

E. On March 15, 2006, the division was sold at an actual loss of $200,000, and as previously estimated, the losses through March 15, 2006, totaled $400,000.

Required:

1. Does this sale qualify for discontinued operations treatment? Why or why not?

2. Assume that the disposal meets the discontinued operations reporting criteria. Show how the amounts would be reported in Freedman's income statement for the year ending December 31, 2005.

3. Why are discontinued operations reported separately from the operating results of the period?

4. Calculate the gain or loss on discontinued operations that Freedman would report for 2006.

Analyze: If the company reported an actual loss on the sale of $500,000 rather than $200,000, how would this be reported in 2005 and 2006? Why?

LO3, 5   **PROBLEM 3-8   Comprehensive Problem with Nonrecurring Items**

For the year ended December 31, 2005, Glisson Corporation tentatively reported income from continuing operations before taxes of $500,000. Glisson has a 30 percent income tax rate. The additional information that follows *has not* been recorded in the accounts.

A. An internal auditor discovered that the company omitted the amortization of intangible assets during 2003. The amount of amortization should have been $30,000.

B. The company is located in Mobile, Alabama. During the year, a hurricane tore through the area. Losses from flood damage were not covered by the company's property damage insurance and amounted to $200,000. Hurricanes are considered infrequent in this area and are unusual.

C. The company's employees went on strike for six weeks in June of 2005. Revenues would have been $80,000 more had the strike not occurred.

D. In 2005, Glisson sold equipment (plant assets) for $40,000. The equipment had originally cost $80,000 and had a book value on the date of sale of $21,000.

E. During 2005, the company changed its method of accounting for inventories from FIFO to weighted-average. The bookkeeper used the FIFO method during the current year. Had the weighted-average method been used during the current year, inventories reported on the balance sheet would have been $10,000 larger. Cost of goods sold related to the fiscal periods of 2004 and prior would have been $22,000 greater.

F. Glisson's accounts include $15,000 as Unrealized Holding Gain from Available-for-Sale Investments at December 31, 2005, and $12,000 at December 31, 2004. The effects of the gain amounts were not included in the tentative income from continuing operations before income taxes, since the bookkeeper was unsure of the proper reporting.

Required:

1. Calculate the amount that should be reported on Glisson's income statement as income from continuing operations for the year ended December 31, 2005.

2. How much should be reported for the year ended December 31, 2005, as extraordinary gains or losses?

3. Name the specific items for which Glisson must apply intraperiod tax allocation for reporting purposes.

Communicate: Why is intraperiod tax allocation required for reporting purposes?

Analyze: Suppose Glisson's actual net income for the year ended December 31, 2005, is $90,000. Calculate the amount of comprehensive income.

LO2, 3, 4   **PROBLEM 3-9   Income Statement with Nonrecurring Items and EPS**

Traynham Corporation began operations during 2000 by issuing common stock for $50,000 and preferred stock for $120,000. On April 1, 2005, Traynham issued another 1,000 shares of its common stock. During December of 2005, Traynham paid dividends of $.50

per share to both common and preferred stockholders. The following amounts were taken from Traynham Corporation's financial statements for the year ended December 31, 2005:

Sales	$900,000	Extraordinary loss from volcano	$ 40,000
Error correction	15,000	Operating expenses	260,000
Preferred stock, 10,000 shares	50,000	Cumulative effect of change	
Common stock, $3 par value	12,000	in accounting principle	44,000
Cost of goods sold	460,000		

The company provided the following other information:

A. The loss from the volcano eruption was not covered by the company's insurance policy.

B. The cumulative effect is the amount of depreciation adjustment for prior years as a result of changing from accelerated to straight-line depreciation.

C. The error correction adjusts for the omission of property taxes expense during 2003.

D. The company's income tax rate is 30 percent.

Required:

1. Prepare a multiple-step income statement for Traynham Corporation for 2005, including basic earnings per share amounts.

2. Why must companies disclose earnings per share on the income statement?

Analyze: Why are preferred dividends subtracted in calculating earnings per share?

LO1, 5 **PROBLEM 3-10** **Comprehensive Income and Economic Income**

Peters Company had net income of $50,000 in 2005 and pays income tax at a rate of 30 percent. The company provided the following before income tax amounts for 2005:

Unrealized gain on sale of available-for-sale securities	$ 5,000
Foreign currency translation loss adjustment	4,000
Dividends declared and paid	7,000
Loss on bond retirement	20,000
Interest revenue	2,000

Required:

1. Prepare a separate statement of comprehensive income for 2005.

2. For each item on Peters Company's list that does not appear directly on the statement of comprehensive income, describe how it is reported in the financial statements.

Communicate: Explain the concept of economic income as it applies to comprehensive income.

Analyze: As an investor, would you view the items listed on the statement of comprehensive income as being favorable to your earnings per share?

LO3, 6 **PROBLEM 3-11** **Income Calculations, Operating Margin, Profit Margin**

Gill Corp. operates a health clinic in Kansas. It reported sales of $400,000 and income from continuing operations before income taxes of $80,000 during 2005. Throughout the year, it had 500 shares of common stock outstanding. Gill Corp. has a 30 percent tax rate. The additional information given below refers to events that occurred during 2005 and *has not* been included in the accounts unless specifically stated.

A. In 2005, Gill Corp. sold an x-ray machine for $15,600. The equipment had a book value of $12,600.

B. Gill listed these items in its trial balance as of December 31, 2005: Cumulative effect of change in accounting principle, $5,000 credit; Interest expense, $4,000.

C. Gill paid $12,000 of estimated income taxes during the year.

D. Gill incurred repair costs of $40,000 related to damage resulting from flying debris caused by tornadoes. The company has experienced tornado damage to its property during each of the past five years.

Required:

1. Calculate the correct amount of income from continuing operations for Gill Corp. for the year ended December 31, 2005.
2. Calculate net income for the year ended December 31, 2005.

Analyze: Calculate the company's operating margin percentage and its profit margin. What information do these calculations provide? What other information is needed to adequately evaluate these ratios?

LO3   **PROBLEM 3-12   Discontinued Operations Reporting and Disclosures**

On August 17, 2005, Carter, Inc. decided to sell its radio subsidiary. A buyer has been found, and the sale is scheduled to close on June 1, 2006. The income tax rate is 30 percent. Income from continuing operations before income taxes was $80,000. Carter has a calendar year end. Pertinent data regarding the operations of the radio subsidiary are as follows:

Loss from operations from January 1 to August 17, 2005	$100,000
Realized loss from operations from August 17 to December 31, 2005	20,000
Estimated loss from operations from January 1, 2006, to June 1, 2006	40,000
Estimated loss on sale of subsidiary due to impairment of the net assets	50,000

Required:

1. What assets fall under *SFAS No. 144*'s definition for inclusion as discontinued operations?
2. Show how the results of discontinuing the radio subsidiary will be reported by Carter on its income statement for 2005. Prepare the note disclosure related to the discontinued operations.

Critical Thinking: Why are discontinued operations differentiated from other operations?

Analyze: If the estimated loss on the sale of the radio subsidiary due to impairment of the net assets were $90,000 instead of $50,000, what amount would be reported as the loss on disposal of the discontinued business?

LO3, 4, 6   **PROBLEM 3-13   Preparation of Income Statement with Nonrecurring Items and EPS**

The bookkeeper for Bulushi Sushi prepared the company's income statement for the year ended December 31, 2005, but omitted the following transactions. The company's income statement showed income before income taxes totaling $42,000. Throughout 2005, 1,000 shares of common stock were outstanding. The company has no preferred stock.

A. A loss of $500 from the early retirement of bonds payable.
B. An uninsured fire loss in the amount of $700. Fire losses are considered unusual for Bulushi Sushi, since it holds a quarterly fire safety training class for its employees. In fact, no fire losses have ever occurred.
C. A loss in the amount of $150 related to the write-down of obsolete inventory.
D. A loss in the amount of $200 from the sale of land to the city. The city expropriated the land for future highway construction.
E. A loss of $1,000 related to the sale of a subsidiary company. The subsidiary was engaged in the pipe fabrication business, and Bulushi Sushi has no other operations in that business. This loss is considered immaterial.
F. An increase of $300 in expense resulting from a change in depreciation method. Bulushi Sushi changed from straight-line to accelerated depreciation.

Required: Prepare the income statement for 2005, beginning with income from continuing operations before income taxes of $42,000. The company has a 30 percent income tax rate. (*Hint:* EPS is part of the income statement.)

Analyze: If net sales were $85,000 and cost of sales was $29,000, what is Bulushi Sushi's profit margin on sales? How much is Bulushi Sushi's gross profit? How do these results differ in terms of the information each provides?

LO3, 4 PROBLEM **3-14** **Analysis of Recurring and Nonrecurring Items**

Several financial statement components are presented below.

A. Loss on the closing of travel offices because of the decline of travel to the Far East as a result of the outbreak of the SARS virus.

B. Write-down of Beanie Babies inventory because of an unexpected decline in demand.

C. A reduction in the useful life of the company's packaging machines as a result of the development of new technology.

D. Loss resulting from foreign currency translation adjustment related to an unexpected currency devaluation by China.

E. Costs incurred related to an employee strike. The company has never experienced any strikes in twenty years of operations.

F. Discovery by the accountant that depreciation expense for equipment had not been recognized two years ago.

Required: Indicate the proper reporting of each event listed and justify why the reporting you select is appropriate.

Analyze: Why does GAAP exclude some items from operating income?

CASES

LO7 COMMUNICATIONS CASE **3-1** **Earnings Announcements and Disclosure**

Happy Days Corporation has reported steadily increasing sales each year for the past five years. Circulation from magazine sales has increased 20 percent per year on average for the past five years, and advertising revenue has grown correspondingly. The analysts have placed a buy recommendation on the company's publicly traded stock, expecting this sales growth to continue.

The treasurer of Happy Days, Joseph Smith, is discussing the firm's annual report, which is currently being prepared, with the CFO of the firm. Both agree that given the slowdown in the economy and the probability that a recession is looming, next year's sales will probably not grow at the 20 percent rate seen in the past. They agree that a conservative estimate would be to see Happy Days hold its market share but not grow at all in the next year. In addition, there are already signs that advertising revenues will be lower next year, as advertising budgets are being reduced because of the economic slowdown. Management is discussing how to disclose this forecast for the next year.

Smith thinks that since the economy may pick up and sales may continue to grow at the 20 percent annual pace, the company should not say anything about the anticipated slowdown in sales. "After all," he says, "once the announcement is made, our stock price is sure to fall." Since Happy Days is planning to issue stock next month, Smith argues that the company should not announce expected earnings until after the stock has been issued.

Sally Ride, CFO, is concerned about investor relations. She feels that although the stock price may temporarily fall if the expected earnings are announced, investors will reward the company later for being forthcoming concerning earnings expectations in that the quality of earnings will be perceived as high. She argues that the earnings announcement for the next period should be made as soon as possible, and before the new stock is issued.

Required: From the perspective of an outside consultant, write a memo to Stan Days, CEO, advising him when the earnings announcement should be made. Discuss the pros and cons of immediate disclosure and make a recommendation.

LO6, 7 RESEARCH CASE **3-2** **Analyzing Earnings**

Dell competes in a technology sector with companies like **Sun Microsystems** and **Hewlett-Packard**. Each company's financial data for the current period is offered on its website.

Required: Locate the most recent financial statements for Dell, Sun Microsystems, and Hewlett-Packard. Calculate the gross profit, operating margin, and profit margin on sales for each company for the period. Based on these calculations alone, what assumptions can you make about each company's performance as compared to that of its competitors?

LO7

ETHICS

ETHICS CASE 3-3   Earnings Management

Jane Gluck is the accounting manager for Ossar Corporation. During 2005, Ossar plans to expand its operations, which it will finance by issuing $10 million in bonds. The CFO wants to ensure that the income statement shows a trend of increasing profits so that the bond issue can be sold at a favorable price. Currently, 60 percent of Ossar's assets consist of depreciable assets that are depreciated over an average useful life of ten years using the double-declining-balance method. To improve Ossar's net income in the coming years, the CFO is considering changing the depreciation method to straight-line for all depreciable assets. He is also considering changing the estimate of useful life, since it would be accounted for prospectively according to GAAP. As Jane is preparing the financial statements for 2005, the CFO informs her that he would like her to change the estimated useful life to 11 years for all depreciable assets and switch to straight-line depreciation. He reminds her to make the proper financial statement disclosures. What should Jane do?

Required:

1. Is Jane facing an ethical problem? If so, describe the issue.
2. List the parties affected by the decision.
3. What values or principles play a role in this decision?
4. Describe alternative actions that Jane might consider.
5. Which of these actions will cause the greatest good or the least harm?
6. Describe the action that you believe Jane should take.
7. How would the actions suggested by the CFO be regarded by investors?

LO7

ETHICS

ETHICS CASE 3-4   Corporate Expansion and Ethical Decision-Making

In 2003, **Dell Computers** decided to significantly expand one of its current business segments—the service division. Compared to its major competitors, Dell lagged behind its rivals with respect to the percentage of its revenue derived from service contracts. Because service typically yields a higher gross margin than computer equipment sales does, this expansion effort may have a dramatic effect on the company's bottom line and may improve its profit margin, which has declined from 8.3 percent to 6.4 percent during the past few years.[17]

As companies like Dell plan such an expansion, several issues must be considered. First, Dell services only the computers it sells. Thus, its potential for service revenue is intrinsically limited to the amount of computers it sells. Second, Dell relies on independent contractors to respond to its customers' calls for service. Although the use of independent contractors requires less financial commitment in regard to employee benefits, the company has less control over quality of performance, reliability, and customer satisfaction.

This new attention to its service division creates risks and opportunities that will require that Dell make decisions about how it allocates resources. The allocation of resources for promotions, salaries, staffing, and administration will influence the financial outcome reflected on the income statement. In the short-term, Dell may be faced with increased costs and expenditures to establish and stabilize the service expansion, which would negatively affect its net income. It is safe to assume that many managers involved in the decision-making process likely own stock in the company through either outright purchases or employee stock option programs. Companies like Dell often face decisions that involve sacrificing short-term profits for the potential of long-term benefits.

Required:

1. Conceptually, how do you think service revenue differs from sales revenue? What are the accounting implications?
2. What are the problems and issues faced by the decision makers at Dell?
3. Who will be affected by the decision to expand the service division?
4. What values and principles will influence this decision?
5. What alternative actions might the decision makers at Dell take?

---

17 "Dell Pins Hopes on Services to Boost Profit," *Wall Street Journal*, Nov. 11, 2003.

6. Whose interests are most important in this decision?

7. If you were a decision maker at Dell, what would you do?

LO7 CRITICAL THINKING CASE **3-5** **Earnings Management versus Fraud**

The following excerpt was taken from the SEC's *Accounting and Auditing Enforcement Release No. 1966*, published on March 2, 2004.[18] The release details how the former CFO of **WorldCom** fraudulently manipulated earnings of the company for a period of several years:

> Rather than disclose WorldCom's true financial condition and suffer the resulting decline in the company's share price, from approximately September 2000 through June 2002, Sullivan engaged in a scheme that fraudulently concealed WorldCom's true operational and financial results. The scheme involved improperly manipulating WorldCom's reported revenue, expenses, net income, earnings before interest, taxes, depreciation and amortization (EBITDA), and earnings per share.

Required:

1. What is earnings management?

2. How do you think earnings management and fraudulent reporting are distinguished?

3. In your opinion, what arguments might WorldCom use in defense of the company's actions to claim that the accounting was considered earnings management as opposed to fraud in light of the fact that the CFO did not embezzle any assets of the company? Justify your answer.

LO6 ANALYSIS CASE **3-6** **Income Statement Measures**

Profitability analysis is an important analytical tool in evaluating the overall performance of a given company, including financial institutions such as banks. The income statement information that follows is for two large banks, **Bank of America** and **Sun Trust Banks, Inc.**, for the years ended December 31, 2003, 2002, and 2001.

Bank of America

Bank of America Corporation

PERIOD ENDING	31-Dec-03	31-Dec-02	31-Dec-01
Total Revenue	$49,006,000	$46,012,000	$53,116,000
Cost of Revenue	4,908,000	5,434,000	8,886,000
Gross Profit	44,098,000	40,578,000	44,230,000
Operating Expenses			
Selling General and Administrative	19,910,000	18,218,000	19,831,000
Non Recurring	—	(630,000)	—
Others	3,056,000	4,195,000	5,165,000
Operating Income or Loss	21,132,000	18,795,000	19,234,000
Income from Continuing Operations			
Earnings Before Interest And Taxes	21,132,000	18,795,000	19,234,000
Interest Expense	5,271,000	5,804,000	9,117,000
Income Before Tax	15,861,000	12,991,000	10,117,000
Income Tax Expense	5,051,000	3,742,000	3,325,000
Net Income From Continuing Ops	10,810,000	9,249,000	6,792,000
Net Income	10,810,000	9,249,000	6,792,000
Preferred Stock And Other Adjustments	(4,000)	—	(5,000)
Net Income Applicable To Common Shares	$10,806,000	$ 9,249,000	$ 6,787,000

---

18 SEC Accounting and Auditing Enforcement Release No. 1966, March 2, 2004; available at: **http://www.sec.gov/litigation/litreleases/lr18605.htm**. Accessed on 4/10/04.

Sun Trust Banks

Sun Trust Banks, Inc.

PERIOD ENDING	31-Dec-03	31-Dec-02	31-Dec-01
Total Revenue	$7,249,355	$7,636,960	$8,441,470
Cost of Revenue	771,631	1,117,296	1,812,385
Gross Profit	6,477,724	6,519,664	6,629,085
Operating Expenses			
Selling General and Administrative	3,400,616	3,326,270	3,113,538
Non Recurring	—	15,998	—
Others	491,062	579,880	281,238
Operating Income or Loss	2,586,046	2,597,516	3,234,309
Earnings Before Interest And Taxes	2,586,046	2,597,516	3,234,309
Interest Expense	676,908	774,192	1,214,589
Income Before Tax	1,909,138	1,823,324	2,019,720
Income Tax Expense	576,841	491,515	650,501
Net Income From Continuing Ops	1,332,297	1,331,809	1,369,219
Extraordinary Items	—	—	6,318
Net Income	$1,332,297	$1,331,809	$1,375,537

Required: Evaluate and interpret these analysis measurements for Bank of America and Sun Trust Banks for 2003: (1) operating margin percentage, (2) gross margin percentage.

LO3   CRITICAL THINKING CASE 3-7   Discontinued Operations

Carlton Inns is a regional operator of extended-stay suites. For 2003, its revenue was $240 million and its total assets were $320 million. Its business segments include laundry and dry cleaning service for all its hotels. This segment is managed by a vice president who also solicits outside customers. (In 2003, outside sales were 30 percent of total business sales of $4 million). All accounting and overhead are tracked separately for budget and financial reporting purposes, although they are consolidated at quarter and year end. Management is preparing to outsource its laundry and dry cleaning service to another vendor and dispose of this unit sometime during 2004.

Required: Evaluate how management would account for the disposal of its laundry and dry cleaning service. Justify your response.

LO3   RESEARCH CASE 3-8   Accounting Estimate versus an Accounting Error

Deloitte and Touche, one of the Big 4 public accounting firms, provides information for its clients on its website, IAS Plus, found at **www.iasplus.com**.

Required: Locate the Standards section of the website and read the overview of *International Accounting Standard No. 8*, "Accounting Policies, Changes in Accounting Estimates and Errors." Identify the disclosures necessary under International Accounting Standards for (1) accounting principle changes and (2) accounting estimate changes. How is *SFAS No. 154* similar or dissimilar to *IAS No. 8?*

ON THE WEB

The following exercises, activities, and problems are available on the *Intermediate Accounting* website. Use these resources to reinforce your understanding of the topics presented in this chapter.

- CPA-Adapted Simulations
- Interpreting the Accounting Standards
- Extending the Global Focus
- Extending the Ethics Discussion
- Mastering the Spreadsheet
- Career Snapshots
- Annual Report Project
- ACE Practice Tests
- Flashcards
- Glossary
- Check Figures for Text Problems
- PowerPoint Presentations

SOLUTIONS: CHECK YOUR UNDERSTANDING

The Economic and Accounting Definitions of Income (p. 104)

1. Any increase in the current value of a firm's net assets (not counting capital contributions and withdrawals) is considered to be economic income for the period. Economic income is not necessarily based on transactions, but rather is based on changes, for example, in the fair market value of the company's assets. Accounting-based income is the net income that a firm derives from all of its business transactions; it is determined by subtracting all recognized expenses and losses from all recognized revenues and gains.

2. Revenue and expense transactions are summarized on the income statement.

3. The matching principle holds that expenses should be recognized in the same period as the revenues to which they are related.

The Income Statement: Elements and Reporting Formats (p. 107)

1. Revenues are generated from a company's ongoing major central operations, while gains are realized from peripheral or incidental activities.

2. It is important to distinguish ongoing revenue from one-time events so that investors and managers can project the firm's future performance.

3. Single-step and multiple-step formats.

4. The multiple-step format includes operating and nonoperating sections. The operating section itemizes net sales; cost of goods sold; gross profit on sales; selling, general, and administrative expenses; and other operating income and expenses. The nonoperating section contains categories like net interest revenue or expense and other expense.

Recurring and Nonrecurring Items (p. 119)

1. When determining what should be included as a discontinued operation, consider whether the operations and cash flows of the component will be (or have been) eliminated from the ongoing operations of the entity and whether the entity will have any significant continuing involvement in the operations of the component.

2. The three key characteristics that define an extraordinary item are its unusual nature, its infrequency, and its materiality.

3. *SFAS No. 154* requires retrospective application to prior periods' financial statements of changes in accounting principles, unless it is impracticable to determine the period-specific effects of the change on prior periods. The new FASB standard differentiates between a change in accounting estimate and a change in accounting estimate effected by a change in accounting principle. A change in accounting estimate is a modification to an accounting estimate resulting from new information or experience.

These changes are a normal part of running a business and are not given special treatment unless material. A change in accounting estimate effected by a change in accounting principle is a change in accounting estimate that is inseparable from the effect of a related change in accounting principle. The most common example of this type of change is a change in the method of depreciation, amortization, or depletion for long-lived, nonfinancial assets. These changes require additional disclosures.

Reporting Earnings per Share (p. 120)

1. The calculation is net income minus preferred stock dividends divided by weighted-average number of common shares outstanding.

2. Diluted earnings per share is a form of EPS that relates net income to the maximum possible number of shares of common stock if all possibly dilutive financial contracts, such as stock options, were converted to common stock.

Comprehensive Income (p. 121)

1. The Other Comprehensive Income account is used to record the effects of transactions derived from events external to the firm.

2. According to *SFAS No. 130*, the components of comprehensive income may be reported in the following ways:

   • A single statement in which net income and other comprehensive income are added together to obtain total comprehensive income
   • Two statements, with net income reported in one statement and comprehensive income reported in the other statement
   • Part of the statement of changes in stockholders' equity

Analyzing the Income Statement (p. 125)

1. The gross profit percentage is 29.3 percent.

2. Interest expense and investment revenue are the result of financing activities, not operating activities.

3. Company B earns $.072 of profit on every dollar of sales, while Company A earns only $.057 per dollar of sales. Therefore Company B is performing better with regard to this measurement.

The Quality of Reported Earnings Information (p. 130)

1. Earnings management is the use of accounting information, principles, or standards that have been purposefully selected to smooth out ups and downs in earnings.

2. Conservative accounting practices increase the quality of earnings because with these practices, estimates and projections are not inflated or overstated.

3. Persistence of earnings is important to investors' confidence in quality of earnings, since it means that earnings will be fairly predictable from year to year.

CPA-ADAPTED SIMULATION

This simulation asks you to complete various tasks related to a compny's annual financial statements. If your instructor has signed up for CPAexcel™, you can do the work online at **www.cpaexcel.com/hmco**. You may also do the simulation manually.

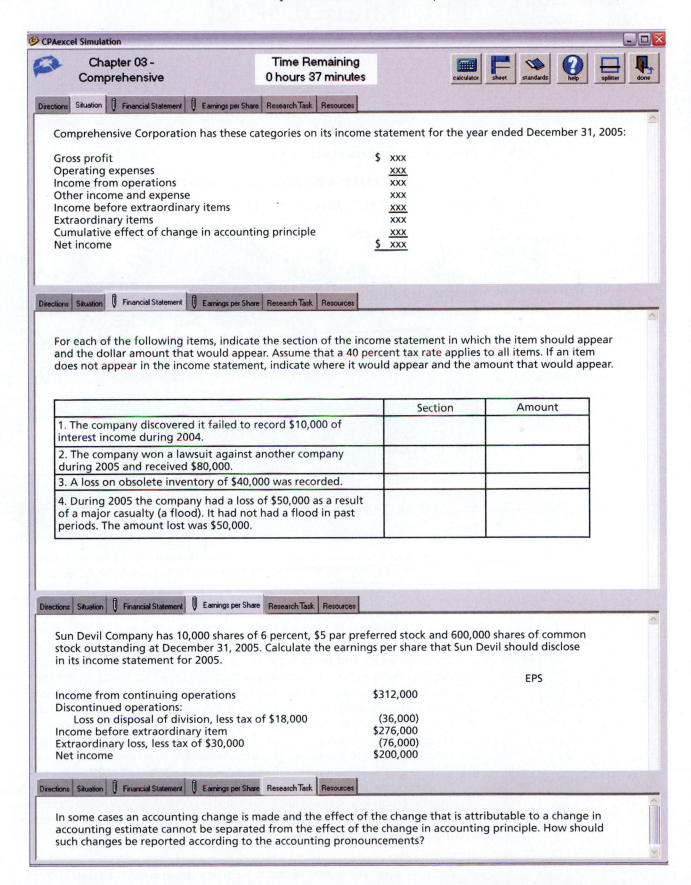

CPAexcel Simulation

Chapter 03 – Comprehensive

Time Remaining
0 hours 37 minutes

calculator | sheet | standards | help | splitter | done

Directions | Situation | Financial Statement | Earnings per Share | Research Task | Resources

Comprehensive Corporation has these categories on its income statement for the year ended December 31, 2005:

Gross profit	$ xxx
Operating expenses	xxx
Income from operations	xxx
Other income and expense	xxx
Income before extraordinary items	xxx
Extraordinary items	xxx
Cumulative effect of change in accounting principle	xxx
Net income	$ xxx

For each of the following items, indicate the section of the income statement in which the item should appear and the dollar amount that would appear. Assume that a 40 percent tax rate applies to all items. If an item does not appear in the income statement, indicate where it would appear and the amount that would appear.

	Section	Amount
1. The company discovered it failed to record $10,000 of interest income during 2004.		
2. The company won a lawsuit against another company during 2005 and received $80,000.		
3. A loss on obsolete inventory of $40,000 was recorded.		
4. During 2005 the company had a loss of $50,000 as a result of a major casualty (a flood). It had not had a flood in past periods. The amount lost was $50,000.		

Sun Devil Company has 10,000 shares of 6 percent, $5 par preferred stock and 600,000 shares of common stock outstanding at December 31, 2005. Calculate the earnings per share that Sun Devil should disclose in its income statement for 2005.

		EPS
Income from continuing operations	$312,000	
Discontinued operations:		
Loss on disposal of division, less tax of $18,000	(36,000)	
Income before extraordinary item	$276,000	
Extraordinary loss, less tax of $30,000	(76,000)	
Net income	$200,000	

In some cases an accounting change is made and the effect of the change that is attributable to a change in accounting estimate cannot be separated from the effect of the change in accounting principle. How should such changes be reported according to the accounting pronouncements?

The Balance Sheet

FINANCIAL REPORTING CASE

LOWE'S COMPANIES, INC. BUILDS ASSETS BEYOND THE BALANCE SHEET

The average shopper or investor might not be aware that Lowe's was named America's Most Admired Specialty Retailer and ENERGY STAR Retail Partner of the Year, since good management practices are rarely reflected on a company's balance sheet.

Lowe's While Lowe's was named America's Most Admired Specialty Retailer in 2003 by *Fortune* and ENERGY STAR Retail Partner of the Year in 2003 and 2004, you won't find these accolades listed on the company's balance sheet as an asset. The number two U.S. home improvement chain serves approximately nine million customers a week at more than 1,125 stores in 49 states. Lowe's consolidated balance sheets (opposite) are one of the four primary financial statements issued by all public companies in the United States and abroad. While the balance sheet reports assets like inventory, cash, accounts receivable, and operating assets, it does not include intangible assets like good management practices. Instead, it primarily gives historically based amounts, which are viewed by many as being more reliable.

In a new economy that is brimming with knowledge-based companies whose important intangible assets are not valued and reported, many academics and financial analysts are questioning the traditional approach to balance sheet preparation under GAAP. According to Professor Baruch Lev of New York University,

> Twenty-first-century business enterprises are fast changing; involved in complex networking joint ventures, partnerships, and other related entities;

Lowe's

Lowe's Companies, Inc.
Consolidated Balance Sheets

(In Millions, Except Par Value Data)	January 28, 2005	% Total	January 30, 2004 As Restated (Note 2)	% Total
Assets				
Current Assets:				
Cash and Cash Equivalents (Note 1)	$ 642	3.0%	$ 913	4.9%
Short-Term Investments (Note 4)	171	0.8	711	3.8
Accounts Receivable—Net (Notes 1 and 5)	9	—	146	0.8
Merchandise Inventory (Note 1)	5,982	28.2	4,584	24.4
Deferred Income Taxes (Note 15)	95	0.5	62	0.3
Other Assets	75	0.4	106	0.6
Total Current Assets	**6,974**	**32.9**	**6,522**	**34.8**
Property, Less Accumulated Depreciation (Notes 6 and 7)	13,911	65.6	11,819	63.0
Long-Term Investments (Note 4)	146	0.7	169	0.9
Other Assets (Note 7)	178	0.8	241	1.3
Total Assets	**$ 21,209**	**100.0%**	**$ 18,751**	**100.0%**
Liabilities and Shareholders' Equity				
Current Liabilities:				
Current Maturities of Long-Term Debt (Note 9)	$ 630	3.0%	77	0.4%
Accounts Payable	2,687	12.7	2,212	11.8
Accrued Salaries and Wages	386	1.8	335	1.8
Other Current Liabilities (Note 7)	2,016	9.5	1,576	8.4
Total Current Liabilities	**5,719**	**27.0**	**4,200**	**22.4**
Long-Term Debt, Excluding Current Maturities (Notes 9, 10 and 13)	3,060	14.4	3,678	19.6
Deferred Income Taxes (Note 15)	736	3.5	594	3.2
Other Long-Term Liabilities	159	0.7	63	0.3
Total Liabilities	**9,674**	**45.6**	**8,535**	**45.5**
Shareholders' Equity (Note 12):				
Preferred Stock—$5 Par Value, none issued	—	—	—	—
Common Stock—$.50 Par Value;				
Shares Issued and Outstanding				
January 28, 2005 774				
January 30, 2004 787	387	1.8	394	2.1
Capital in Excess of Par	1,514	7.1	2,247	12.0
Retained Earnings	9,634	45.5	7,574	40.4
Accumulated Other Comprehensive Income	—	—	1	—
Total Shareholders' Equity	**11,535**	**54.4**	**10,216**	**54.5**
Total Liabilities and Shareholders' Equity	**$ 21,209**	**100.0%**	**$ 18,751**	**100.0%**

and derive their value and growth primarily from intangible assets (patents, brands, know-how, unique organizational designs).

The traditional accounting system and its major product—publicly released financial reports—essentially reflect past transactions (sales, purchases, borrowing, etc.) only, and recognize physical and financial assets (plant and equipment, securities) to the exclusion of most intangible assets. Such narrowly based, backward-looking corporate reports are ill-suited to provide the information needed by investors, creditors, and policy makers (e.g., for national accounting measurements).[1]

---

1 Baruch Lev, "The Reform of Corporate Reporting and Auditing," testimony before the House of Representatives Committee on Energy and Commerce, February 6, 2002.

Given these concerns, the changing face of business presents new and unique challenges for today's accounting systems.

EXAMINING THE CASE

1. What obstacles can you describe to the reporting of assets like good management practices or "know-how" on a company's balance sheet?

2. Based on its January 28, 2005 balance sheet, which asset category contains the majority of Lowe's total assets?

3. What types of "assets" often contribute to a company's growth, but are not reflected on its balance sheet?

LO 1 **Identify the elements of the balance sheet and state the recognition and measurement criteria for those elements.**

balance sheet a financial statement that provides information about the financial position of a company at a specific point in time

▓ *Critical Thinking: Explain why assets and liabilities are different from revenues and expenses.*

assets the economic resources of a firm; probable future economic benefits obtained or controlled by a particular entity as a result of past transactions or events

liabilities the economic liabilities of a firm; probable future economic sacrifices of benefits arising from present obligations of a particular entity to transfer assets or provide services to other entities in the future as a result of past transactions or events

equity the residual interest in the assets of an entity that remains after deducting the liabilities; known as **stockholders' equity** for a corporation

market value the amount at which an asset could be bought or sold in a current arm's-length transaction other than a forced liquidation or sale; also called *current value* or *fair value*

The Balance Sheet: Elements and Issues

The **balance sheet** provides information about the financial position of a company at a specific point in time. This statement is also sometimes called the *statement of financial position*. Over the last 50 years, the standards relating to the recognition, measurement, and valuation of various balance sheet items have evolved as standard setters have responded to the needs of investors. As you will see, the result is, in some ways, a statement in transition—one that reflects a mixture of recognition, measurement, and valuation criteria.

THE ACCOUNTING EQUATION AND THE BALANCE SHEET

The balance sheet follows the form of the accounting equation: Assets = Liabilities + Owners' Equity (or Stockholders' Equity). It defines the financial position of a firm according to the FASB's definition of the elements of the accounting equation. Recall from Chapter 1 the following components of the accounting equation:

- *Assets:* the economic resources of a firm; probable future economic benefits obtained or controlled by a particular entity as a result of past transactions or events

- *Liabilities:* the economic liabilities of a firm; probable future economic sacrifices of benefits arising from present obligations of a particular entity to transfer assets or provide services to other entities in the future as a result of past transactions or events

- *Equity:* the residual interest in the assets of an entity that remains after deducting the liabilities; known as **stockholders' equity** for a corporation[2]

Assets are the resources a firm owns or controls and uses in conducting its business. They are obtained through either exchange for other assets, the borrowing of money to purchase them (liabilities), owner contributions, or earnings that the firm has generated (equity).

Assets and liabilities are reported on the balance sheet at their original, or historical, cost. Many of a firm's assets and liabilities may have a market value that differs from their historical cost. **Market value**, also called *current value* or *fair value*, is the amount at which an asset could be bought or sold in a current arm's-length transaction other than a forced liquidation or sale. However, historical costs are used because they are more easily determined, more objective, and thus, in the view of many, more reliable than market values. Furthermore, the going concern assumption presumes that a firm will continue to operate into the foreseeable future and thus that it will consume

2 "Elements of Financial Statements of Business Enterprises," *Statement of Financial Accounting Concepts No. 6* (Stamford, Conn.: FASB, 1985), pars. 25, 35, 49.

the benefits from its assets (except for inventories) through their use rather than through their sale.

The balance sheet is dated as of the last day in the firm's reporting period and is considered a snapshot, or picture, of the financial position of the firm as of that date. The notes and related disclosures are considered an integral part of the balance sheet because they describe the accounting methods used and the assumptions made in calculating the reported amounts. In today's disclosure environment, it is not unusual for the notes and related disclosures to run well over ten pages, far more than the space needed for the four primary financial statements.

Throughout this chapter, **Home Depot, Inc.,** a competitor of Lowe's, will be used to illustrate how the balance sheet of a large publicly traded company is presented. Home Depot is a leading retail outlet for building materials and home improvement, lawn, and garden products, with over 1,100 stores throughout the United States, Canada, and Mexico. Figure 4.1 shows the company's consolidated balance sheets at January 30, 2005, and February 1, 2004.

CLASSIFICATION OF BALANCE SHEET ELEMENTS

In general, the elements of the balance sheet are grouped according to the following reporting conventions:

- Assets are classified as *current* or *noncurrent*. Current assets are typically listed in decreasing order of liquidity, or ability to be converted into cash, and include items like cash, short-term investments, receivables, and inventory. The noncurrent assets are grouped into the following categories:

   Investments and funds

   Operating assets (also called property, plant, and equipment)

   Intangible assets

   Other assets

- Liabilities are classified as *current* or *noncurrent*, with the latter category usually being called long-term liabilities. Liabilities are presented according to time to maturity or due date. Those obligations that are expected to come due first are usually listed first, and those with the most distant due dates are listed last.

- Owners' or stockholders' equity items are listed in order of permanence. Contributed capital accounts, which change the least, are listed first, and accumulated other comprehensive income appears last. The following categories are often used:

   Contributed capital, such as capital stock, paid-in capital in excess of par value, and other contributed or donated capital

   Retained earnings

   Other equity adjustment accounts, such as accumulated other comprehensive income

Sometimes an item's intended use is more important for classification purposes than its nature. For example, a fund that is intended to be used to settle a long-term debt when that debt matures will be classified as a noncurrent asset, even though the fund itself may be very liquid or easily convertible to cash. Because the fund is not intended to be used to settle current liabilities, it is not classified as a current asset.

As you will see, these conventions are general guidelines; there is no single standard format for a balance sheet. Industry practices and characteristics play an important role. Thus, the balance sheet for a retail company like Home Depot is likely to look different from the balance sheet of a utility company such as Pacific Gas and Electric or a bank such as Wells Fargo. Moreover, balance sheets prepared under U.S. GAAP may look different from balance sheets prepared under GAAP of another nation or international accounting standards.

Figure 4.1

Consolidated Balance Sheets

Home Depot

The Home Depot, Inc. and Subsidiaries
Consolidated Balance Sheets

amounts in millions, except per share data	January 30, 2005	February 1, 2004
ASSETS		
Current Assets:		
Cash and Cash Equivalents	$ 506	$ 1,103
Short-Term Investments	1,659	1,749
Receivables, net	1,499	1,097
Merchandise Inventories	10,076	9,076
Other Current Assets	450	303
Total Current Assets	14,190	13,328
Property and Equipment, at cost:		
Land	6,932	6,397
Buildings	12,325	10,920
Furniture, Fixtures and Equipment	6,195	5,163
Leasehold Improvements	1,191	942
Construction in Progress	1,404	820
Capital Leases	390	352
	28,437	24,594
Less Accumulated Depreciation and Amortization	5,711	4,531
Net Property and Equipment	22,726	20,063
Notes Receivable	369	84
Cost in Excess of the Fair Value of Net Assets Acquired, net of accumulated amortization of $56 at January 30, 2005 and $54 at February 1, 2004	1,394	833
Other Assets	228	129
TOTAL ASSETS	$38,907	$34,437
LIABILITIES AND STOCKHOLDERS' EQUITY		
Current Liabilities:		
Accounts Payable	$ 5,766	$ 5,159
Accrued Salaries and Related Expenses	1,055	801
Sales Taxes Payable	412	419
Deferred Revenue	1,546	1,281
Income Taxes Payable	161	175
Current Installments of Long-Term Debt	11	509
Other Accrued Expenses	1,578	1,210
Total Current Liabilities	10,529	9,554
Long-Term Debt, excluding current installments	2,148	856
Other Long-Term Liabilities	763	653
Deferred Income Taxes	1,309	967
STOCKHOLDERS' EQUITY		
Common Stock, par value $0.05; authorized: 10,000 shares; issued 2,385 shares at January 30, 2005 and 2,373 shares at February 1, 2004; outstanding 2,185 shares at January 30, 2005 and 2,257 shares at February 1, 2004	119	119
Paid-In Capital	6,650	6,184
Retained Earnings	23,962	19,680
Accumulated Other Comprehensive Income	227	90
Unearned Compensation	(108)	(76)
Treasury Stock, at cost, 200 shares at January 30, 2005 and 116 shares at February 1, 2004	(6,692)	(3,590)
Total Stockholders' Equity	24,158	22,407
TOTAL LIABILITIES AND STOCKHOLDERS' EQUITY	$38,907	$34,437

CURRENT ASSETS

current assets cash and other assets that are reasonably expected to be realized in cash, sold, or consumed during the normal operating cycle or within one year from the balance sheet date, whichever is longer

operating cycle the period of time in which a company purchases merchandise inventory, sells the inventory for cash or credit, and collects cash from sales

monetary assets assets that are easily converted into fixed amounts of cash

nonmonetary assets assets that are not convertible into a fixed amount of cash

Current assets are cash and other assets that are reasonably expected to be realized in cash, sold, or consumed during the normal operating cycle or within one year from the balance sheet date, whichever is longer. As discussed in Chapter 1, a firm's **operating cycle** is the period of time in which a company purchases merchandise inventory, sells the inventory for cash or credit, and collects cash from sales. For example, to stock its shelves, Home Depot purchases various home improvement items from vendors on account. The company sells those items either for cash, through credit cards, or perhaps through its own accounts receivable. It collects cash from the open accounts—with luck, within 30 days—and pays cash to its vendors to settle its open accounts payable. Illustration 4.1 depicts this process. Most likely, Home Depot's operating cycle is fairly short, especially when compared to that of **Boeing** as it manufactures and sells a 777 airplane. For convenience, most companies use one year as their operating cycle because their cash-to-cash cycle is actually less than one year.

Current assets are usually listed in decreasing order of liquidity, or ability to be converted into cash. Cash and other **monetary assets** (assets that are easily converted into fixed amounts of cash), such as receivables, are listed first, followed by **nonmonetary assets** (assets that are not convertible into a fixed amount of cash), such as inventories and prepaid expenses. The current asset and current liability sections of Home Depot's consolidated balance sheets are shown in Figure 4.2.

Home Depot lists as its current assets cash and cash equivalents; short-term investments; receivables, net; merchandise inventories; and other current assets. Monetary assets are measured at their expected cash equivalents. Thus, as Home Depot states in the notes to its financial statements, short-term investments are shown at fair value as of the date of the balance sheet. Receivables are shown net of any estimated uncollectible accounts. Consequently, the stated dollar amount of these assets is their net realizable value, or expected cash equivalent.

Because Home Depot is a retailer, merchandise inventories are the most significant current asset on its balance sheet. As a nonmonetary asset, inventories are carried at the lower of their historical cost based on an accepted inventory costing method (such as FIFO, LIFO, or average cost) or market. The item "other current assets" includes a mixture of assets that individually are not material or need not be disclosed. Home Depot's Notes to Consolidated Financial Statements provide information about the accounting policies for certain current assets, as shown in Figure 4.3.

Illustration 4.1

The Operating Cycle for a Merchandising Business

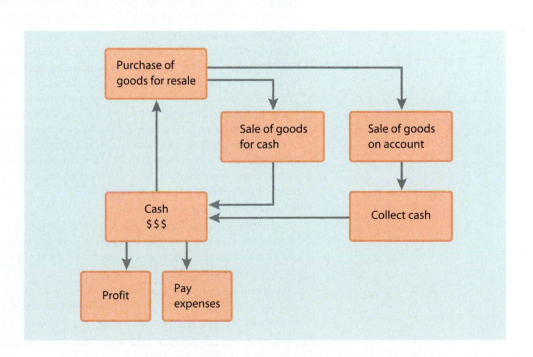

Figure 4.2

Current Asset and Current Liability Sections of Consolidated Balance Sheets

Home Depot

The Home Depot, Inc. and Subsidiaries
Current Asset and Current Liability Sections of Consolidated Balance Sheets

amounts in millions, except per share data	January 30, 2005	February 1, 2004
ASSETS		
Current Assets:		
Cash and Cash Equivalents	$ 506	$ 1,103
Short-Term Investments	1,659	1,749
Receivables, net	1,499	1,097
Merchandise Inventories	10,076	9,076
Other Current Assets	450	303
Total Current Assets	14,190	13,328
LIABILITIES AND STOCKHOLDERS' EQUITY		
Current Liabilities:		
Accounts Payable	$ 5,766	$ 5,159
Accrued Salaries and Related Expenses	1,055	801
Sales Taxes Payable	412	419
Deferred Revenue	1,546	1,281
Income Taxes Payable	161	175
Current Installments of Long-Term Debt	11	509
Other Accrued Expenses	1,578	1,210
Total Current Liabilities	10,529	9,554

Figure 4.3

Excerpts from Notes to Consolidated Financial Statements—2004 Home Depot Annual Report

Home Depot

Cash Equivalents

The Company considers all highly liquid investments purchased with maturities of three months or less to be cash equivalents. The Company's Cash and Cash Equivalents are carried at fair market value and consist primarily of high-grade commercial paper, money market funds, U.S. government agency securities and tax-exempt notes and bonds.

Short-Term Investments

Short-Term Investments are primarily auction rate securities. The interest rates on these securities are typically reset to prevailing market rates every 35 days or less, and in all cases every 90 days or less, but have longer stated maturities. Short-Term Investments are classified as available-for-sale, and changes in the fair value are included in Accumulated Other Comprehensive Income (Loss), net of applicable taxes in the accompanying Consolidated Financial Statements. Prior to the end of fiscal 2004, the Company classified auction rate securities in Cash and Cash Equivalents. Prior period information was reclassified, including the impact on Cash Flow from Investing Activities, to conform to the current year presentation. There was no impact on Net Earnings or Cash Flow from Operating Activities as a result of the reclassification.

Accounts Receivable

The Company's valuation reserve related to accounts receivable was not material as of January 30, 2005 and February 1, 2004. The Company has an agreement with a third-party service provider who manages the Company's private label credit card program and directly extends credit to customers.

Merchandise Inventories (partial)

The majority of the Company's Merchandise Inventories are stated at the lower of cost (first-in, first-out) or market, as determined by the retail inventory method....

CURRENT LIABILITIES

current liabilities economic obligations that are expected to be liquidated using current assets or refinanced by other current liabilities during the normal operating cycle or within one year of the balance sheet date, whichever is longer

Current liabilities are economic obligations that are expected to be liquidated using current assets or refinanced by other current liabilities during the normal operating cycle or within one year of the balance sheet date, whichever is longer. Based on this definition, the portion of long-term debt that is due in the current period is classified as a current liability. Each year, any installments on long-term debt that are due in the current year are reclassified as current. When the maturity date on long-term debt falls in the current period, the entire amount of that long-term debt is reclassified as current. Short-term obligations expected to be refinanced on a long-term basis can be excluded from current liabilities only if a firm intends to refinance them on a long-term basis and can demonstrate its ability to consummate the refinancing.[3] This standard was put in place to ensure that firms do not arbitrarily reclassify current debt as long-term.

Home Depot lists accounts payable, accrued salaries and related expenses, sales taxes payable, deferred revenue, income taxes payable, current installments of long-term debt, and other accrued expenses as current liabilities. All of these except deferred revenue are monetary, meaning that they will be discharged through cash payments or by incurring other monetary current liabilities. Current liabilities are shown on the balance sheet at their historical cost—in this case, the amount of cash required to discharge them.

Deferred revenue arises because Home Depot occasionally receives payment before ownership of merchandise has passed or before a service has been performed. This liability is usually discharged not by a payment of cash but through the delivery of the merchandise or the performance of the service.

NONCURRENT ASSETS

noncurrent assets assets whose benefits are expected to be realized or used up over more than one year or the normal operating cycle

Noncurrent assets are assets whose benefits are expected to be realized or used up over more than one year or the normal operating cycle. They are often separated into the following categories: long-term investments; operating assets (or property, plant, and equipment); intangible assets; deferred charges; and other, if necessary. Figure 4.4 shows the noncurrent asset section of Home Depot's consolidated balance sheets.

▶ OPERATING ASSETS (PROPERTY, PLANT, AND EQUIPMENT)

This category lists the tangible assets that a firm uses to create revenue from operations. These assets are sometimes referred to as *fixed assets, capital assets,* or *property, plant, and equipment.* Operating assets that are currently not in use are reclassified as other assets. Operating assets are tangible in that they have physical substance. In capital-intensive industries and those that manufacture products, they are a firm's primary revenue-producing assets.

amortization a general term that refers to the periodic write-off of the cast of intangible assets over their useful lives

Operating assets are carried at their acquisition cost less accumulated depreciation and amortization. Accumulated Depreciation is a contra account associated with tangible operating assets. It is reported as a separate account so that information about both the original cost of the assets and the amount of depreciation to date will be available. **Amortization** is a general term that refers to the periodic write-off of the cost of intangible assets such as patents or trademarks over their useful life. By convention, intangible assets are shown net of any amortization to date; a separate accumulated amortization account is usually not maintained. Land is usually carried at cost and not depreciated because it has an unlimited life.

Under current GAAP, when an impairment in value occurs, the asset is written down to reflect its fair value.[4] As mentioned earlier, *fair value,* another term for *market*

---

3 "Classification of Short-Term Obligations Expected to Be Refinanced," *Statement of Financial Accounting Standards No. 6* (Stamford, Conn.: FASB, 1975).

4 "Accounting for the Impairment or Disposal of Long-Lived Assets," *Statement of Financial Accounting Standards No. 144* (Norwalk, Conn.: FASB, 2001).

Figure 4.4

Noncurrent Asset Section of Home Depot's Consolidated Balance Sheets

Home Depot

The Home Depot, Inc. and Subsidiaries
Noncurrent Asset Section of Consolidated Balance Sheets

amounts in millions, except per share data	January 30, 2005	February 1, 2004
Property and Equipment, at cost:		
Land	6,932	6,397
Buildings	12,325	10,920
Furniture, Fixtures and Equipment	6,195	5,163
Leasehold Improvements	1,191	942
Construction in Progress	1,404	820
Capital Leases	390	352
	28,437	24,594
Less Accumulated Depreciation and Amortization	5,711	4,531
Net Property and Equipment	22,726	20,063
Notes Receivable	369	84
Cost in Excess of the Fair Value of Net Assets Acquired, net of accumulated amortization of $56 at January 30, 2005 and $54 at February 1, 2004	1,394	833
Other Assets	228	129

---

impairment a decrease in the value of an asset as a result of rapid technological advances, intense domestic and global competition, or changes in market demand

depletion the periodic allocation of the costs of natural resources

lease a contractual agreement in which the owner of property (the lessor) allows another party (the lessee) to use the property for a stated period of time in exchange for specified payments

capital lease a financial arrangement in which the lessee assumes most of the risk and rewards of ownership; thus the asset is recorded as an asset and related liability on the lessee's balance sheet

operating lease a financial arrangement in which the lessee does not assume the risk and rewards of ownership; thus the asset and its related liability are not recorded on the lessee's balance sheet

value, is the amount at which an asset could be bought or sold in a current arm's-length transaction other than a forced liquidation or sale.[5] An **impairment** is a decrease in the value of an asset as a result of rapid technological advances, intense domestic and global competition, or changes in market demand. Under conservative accounting, such a loss of value is shown in the period in which it occurs.

Operating assets can include natural resources for some companies, such as those in the oil and gas, timber, and mineral mining industries. Natural resources are usually reported at cost less accumulated depletion to date, unless a permanent impairment in value is determined. **Depletion** is the periodic allocation of the costs of natural resources. Just as the benefits from operating assets such as plant and equipment are used up, the benefits from natural resources such as oil are lost as the resources are extracted from the ground.

▶ LEASES

A **lease** is a contractual agreement in which the owner of property (the lessor) allows another party (the lessee) to use the property for a stated period of time in exchange for specified payments. A **capital lease** is a financial arrangement in which the lessee assumes most of the risk and rewards of ownership; thus the asset is recorded as an asset and related liability on the lessee's balance sheet. In contrast, the payments for an **operating lease,** a financial arrangement in which the lessee does not assume the risk and rewards of ownership (and thus the asset and its related liability are not recorded on the lessee's balance sheet), are reported as rent expense. The FASB has issued a number of accounting standards related to accounting for leases (see Chapter 14).

Operating leases have created a controversy involving off-balance-sheet financing. **Off-balance-sheet financing** occurs when a firm enters into transactions that obligate it to make future payments, but those payments are not recorded as actual liabilities at their present value. Instead, the monthly payments are recorded and expensed as

---

5 Ibid., par. 22.

off-balance-sheet financing a form of financing that occurs when a firm enters into transactions that obligate it to make future payments, but does not record the payments as actual liabilities at their present value; instead, the monthly payments are recorded and expensed as incurred

incurred. Although such transactions are disclosed in the notes to the financial statements, they are referred to as off-balance-sheet because they are not shown on the face of the balance sheet and their amounts are not included in total assets or total liabilities. Critics of this method hold that as a result, the balance sheet does not adequately reflect the true financial position of the company.

Home Depot leases many of its stores, some with capital leases and others with operating leases. As you can see from Figure 4.4, Home Depot reported capital leases of $390 million at January 30, 2005. The related liabilities are shown in both the current liabilities and long-term debt sections of the balance sheet. Those lease transactions are also described in considerable detail in the notes to the financial statements.

❱ INTANGIBLE ASSETS

intangible assets long-term assets that have no physical substance but that have value based on rights, privileges, or advantages coming to or belonging to the owner

goodwill an intangible asset that is recognized only when one company purchases another company; it represents the premium that a purchaser pays over the fair value of an acquired company's identifiable net assets

Intangible assets are long-term assets that have no physical substance but that have value based on rights, privileges, or advantages coming to or belonging to the owner. Their future benefits are often uncertain. Examples include trademarks, patents, copyrights, and franchises. **Goodwill**, an intangible asset that is recognized only when one company purchases another company, represents the premium that a purchaser pays over the fair value of an acquired company's identifiable net assets. On Home Depot's balance sheet, goodwill that resulted from purchases of other companies is reflected as "Cost in Excess of the Fair Value of Net Assets Acquired." The changes made to the accounting standards for goodwill in late 2001 significantly affected the balance sheets and income statements of many firms. Essentially, since 2001, a company can no longer amortize goodwill that resulted from paying more than fair value for the tangible or identifiable net assets of an acquired company. Prior standards required that such goodwill be amortized on a straight-line basis over a maximum of 40 years. Now, companies must perform an impairment test at the end of each year. If the test shows that the fair value of a reporting unit associated with goodwill is less than its carrying value, the impaired goodwill must be immediately written off against income in the current period.[6] The remaining goodwill is not amortized.

A firm's valuation of intangible assets depends on the type of intangible asset and whether the assets were acquired from others or created internally. Intangible assets are recorded at cost when they are acquired from others, and those that have a definite life, such as a patent or a trademark, are amortized over either their useful life or their legal life, whichever is shorter. Thus, a patent or a copyright purchased from another firm is carried at cost less accumulated amortization. Other intangibles, such as goodwill, are now considered to have an indefinite life and are not amortized.

The costs of internally created intangible assets are usually expensed in the period in which they are incurred. Because there is no verifiable way through an external purchase to measure the future economic benefits of an internally generated intangible asset, from an accounting perspective no asset is recorded. Accounting for research and development costs is a good example of how internally generated intangible assets are treated under current GAAP. *Statement of Financial Accounting Standards No. 2,* "Accounting for Research and Development Costs," requires that all research and development expenditures be expensed in the period in which they occur. This treatment does not allow for the capitalization of research and development costs incurred in the development of productive intangible assets, such as patents. (When costs are capitalized, an asset account is debited and then amortized over the asset's useful life.) Instead, the reported value of a patent typically reflects only the legal costs associated with filing for the patent and protecting it in court. For example, if a pharmaceutical company spends hundreds of millions of dollars on researching and developing a potential cancer drug, it must expense those costs in the periods in which they are incurred; it cannot accumulate them in an asset account. If the drug is eventually approved by the Federal Drug Administration, the firm's only costs that would appear

---

6 "Goodwill and Other Intangible Assets," *Statement of Financial Accounting Standards No. 142* (Norwalk, Conn.: FASB, 1995).

on the balance sheet as an intangible asset would be those related to obtaining a patent on it. If the drug is never approved, its costs have already been expensed.

LONG-TERM INVESTMENTS

Investments and funds set aside for long-term use and therefore not available to settle current liabilities are included in noncurrent assets. Examples include long-term notes receivable (see Figure 4.1); long-term investments in other companies' equity or debt that are not intended to be sold in the current period; investments in subsidiaries, including notes receivable from subsidiaries; funds set aside for use in the future, such as bond-retirement funds; cash surrender values of life insurance policies carried by the company; and investments in assets that are not currently being used in operations.

Investments and funds are normally carried at their fair value, with certain exceptions. Investments in bonds that management intends to hold to maturity are carried at their amortized cost, which means that any discount or premium is amortized over the life of the bond. Investments in equities of other companies in which the firm has a "significant influence" but over which it does not have legal or actual control are carried at cost and adjusted periodically for changes in the book equities of those companies.[7] Assets that are not currently used in operations, such as undeveloped land, are carried at cost unless there is an impairment in value. When an impairment in value occurs, the asset is written down to its fair value and the loss is recognized in that period.

OTHER ASSETS

This category is used when an asset does not fit into any other category. For example, a closed factory and equipment that is not currently used in operations would be considered other assets. However, care should be used when identifying other assets. If an asset has lost its productive value, it should be carefully evaluated for a permanent impairment in value and written off.

The "other asset" category might also contain **deferred charges**, which result from prepayments whose benefits will extend over a period of years from the time of incurrence and are carried forward to be expensed in future years. An example of a deferred charge might be rent paid in advance for a span of years; it is considered an asset until the rent is actually due.

NONCURRENT LIABILITIES

Liabilities are the economic obligations of a firm. A balance sheet usually has two categories of liabilities: current liabilities and noncurrent liabilities. We discussed current liabilities earlier, so we will now focus on noncurrent, or long-term, liabilities.

Noncurrent liabilities, or *long-term liabilities,* are economic obligations that a firm will pay over a period longer than one year. Examples of noncurrent liabilities are bonds payable, mortgage payable, long-term notes payable, pension obligations, capital lease obligations, minority interest, and long-term deferred taxes. The current portion of long-term debt, or the amount due in the next year, is reclassified as a current liability. Long-term liabilities are carried on the balance sheet at the present value of the future principal and interest payments. The discount rate is the effective yield (not the stated, or coupon, rate) at the time the debt was issued. The noncurrent liability section of Home Depot's consolidated balance sheets is shown in Figure 4.5.

In addition to long-term debt and other long-term liabilities, Home Depot reported $1,309 million in deferred income taxes in this section of the balance sheet at January 30, 2005. In some cases, the method that companies use to compute net income under the Internal Revenue Code for income taxes may be different from the method used for GAAP reporting purposes. Often this can result in reported tax expense that is higher than what will actually be paid to the IRS (Income Taxes

deferred charges assets that result from prepayments whose benefits will extend over a period of years from the time of incurrence and are carried forward to be expensed in future years

noncurrent liabilities economic obligations that a firm will pay over a period longer than one year; also called *long-term liabilities*

For a review on the time value of money and present value calculations, refer to Appendix A.

---

7 Chapter 11, "Investments: Debt and Equity Securities," discusses the valuation of long-term investments in more detail.

Figure 4.5

Noncurrent Liability Section of Consolidated Balance Sheets

Home Depot

The Home Depot, Inc. and Subsidiaries
Noncurrent Liability Section of Consolidated Balance Sheets

amounts in millions, except per share data	January 30, 2005	February 1, 2004
Long-Term Debt, excluding current installments	2,148	856
Other Long-Term Liabilities	763	653
Deferred Income Taxes	1,309	967

Payable). This difference is recorded as a liability, Deferred Income Taxes. It is a liability because, at some point, the difference will turn around and have the opposite effect, increasing taxable income vis-à-vis GAAP net income, and thus the Deferred Income Taxes account will be decreased. Deferred taxes will be covered in detail in Chapter 16.

Given that investors and creditors have a keen interest in a firm's liquidity and solvency, extensive disclosures about debt are required in the notes to the financial statements. Such information helps users of financial statements understand a firm's present and future cash needs and its ability to borrow more money if needed. Detailed information in the notes to Home Depot's financial statements describe the company's long-term debt, including interest rates, due dates, market values, and the method used to estimate those values.

STOCKHOLDERS' EQUITY

Stockholders' equity is the equivalent of owners' equity for a corporation. It consists of contributed capital and retained earnings.

▶ CONTRIBUTED CAPITAL

contributed capital the owners' investments in a business; also called *paid-in-capital*

Contributed capital (or *paid-in capital*) is the owners' investments in a business. For a sole proprietorship, the owner's contributed capital is recorded in a capital account that bears the owner's name, such as Monica Chavez-Silva, Capital. The earnings of the firm will increase the owner's capital account, and distributions to the owner will decrease it. Partnerships have a separate capital account for each partner, and those accounts are increased by the firm's earnings in accordance with the partnership agreement and decreased by partners' withdrawals.

capital stock shares of ownership in a corporation

Investors exchange cash or other assets for **capital stock**, or shares of ownership in a corporation. The purchase of capital stock increases both the assets and the equity of the corporation. The corporation is required to state the par value (if any) of the stock, the number of shares authorized by the corporate charter, the number of shares actually issued to date, and the number of shares outstanding (shares that have been issued and are still in circulation). If capital stock has a par or stated value, another account, Additional Paid-in Capital, is commonly used to record amounts in excess of par that were paid for the stock.

common stock capital stock that carries voting rights and entitles owners to a share in the firm's profits through dividends, if any are issued

preferred stock capital stock that has preference over common stock in terms of dividends and in liquidation but usually does not carry voting rights

Capital stock may be divided into two classes: common and preferred. **Common stock** carries voting rights and entitles owners to a share in the firm's profits through dividends, if any are issued. **Preferred stock** has preference over common stock in terms of dividends and in liquidation but usually does not carry voting rights. The stockholders' equity section of Home Depot's consolidated balance sheets is shown in Figure 4.6.

▶ RETAINED EARNINGS

retained earnings the accumulated earnings of a firm since its inception less dividends or other distributions to owners

Corporations classify their earnings separately from their contributed capital accounts. **Retained earnings** are the accumulated earnings of a firm since its inception less the

Figure 4.6

Stockholders' Equity Section of Consolidated Balance Sheets

Home Depot

The Home Depot, Inc. and Subsidiaries
Stockholders' Equity Section of Consolidated Balance Sheets

amounts in millions, except per share data	January 30, 2005	February 1, 2004
STOCKHOLDERS' EQUITY		
Common Stock, par value $0.05; authorized: 10,000 shares; issued 2,385 shares at January 30, 2005 and 2,373 shares at February 1, 2004; outstanding 2,185 shares at January 30, 2005 and 2,257 shares at February 1, 2004	119	119
Paid-In Capital	6,650	6,184
Retained Earnings	23,962	19,680
Accumulated Other Comprehensive Income	227	90
Unearned Compensation	(108)	(76)
Treasury Stock, at cost, 200 shares at January 30, 2005 and116 shares at February 1, 2004	(6,692)	(3,590)
Total Stockholders' Equity	24,158	22,407

dividends or other distributions it makes to owners. Retained earnings can be made a permanent part of contributed capital if the firm declares a stock dividend. A stock dividend reduces retained earnings and increases contributed capital, a topic that is discussed further in Chapter 17.

▶ ACCUMULATED OTHER COMPREHENSIVE INCOME

As discussed in Chapter 3, the FASB requires that an enterprise classify items of other comprehensive income by their nature in a financial statement and display the accumulated balance of other comprehensive income separately from retained earnings and additional paid-in capital in the equity section of the balance sheet. The beginning and ending balances of accumulated other comprehensive income must be reconciled in a schedule or notes to explain the changes in the balance from year to year. The relevant note in Home Depot's 2004 annual report says:

> Comprehensive income includes Net Earnings adjusted for certain revenues, expenses, gains and losses that are excluded from Net Earnings under generally accepted accounting principles. Examples include foreign currency translation adjustments and unrealized gains and losses on certain derivatives.

The next-to-last line item in Figure 4.6, unearned compensation, reports the cost of shares issued under Home Depot's employee stock purchase and option plans. The last item in Figure 4.6 is treasury stock. **Treasury stock** is a stock that has been issued by a corporation and reacquired at a later date. Under current standards, treasury stock is not shown as an asset on the balance sheet but is a debit item under stockholders' equity.

Each of the balance sheet items and the measurement criteria for them that we have discussed is presented in Illustration 4.2.

treasury stock a stock that has been issued by a corporation and reacquired at a later date.

INTERNATIONAL STANDARDS FOR THE PRESENTATION OF BALANCE SHEETS

INTERNATIONAL 🌐   International standards for balance sheet recognition, measurement, and valuation are similar in most respects to U.S. GAAP. According to *International Accounting Standard*

Illustration 4.2

Balance Sheet Elements and Measurement Criteria

Balance Sheet Element	Measurement Criteria
Assets	
Current assets	Net realizable value (monetary assets) or lower of historical cost or market (nonmonetary assets)
Investments and funds	Fair market value
Operating assets (property, plant, and equipment)	Net book value (historical cost less depreciation to date); reduced to fair value if impaired
Intangible assets	Net book value (historical cost less amortization to date); reduced to fair value if impaired; special rules apply to goodwill
Other assets	Historical cost (normally)
Liabilities	
Current liabilities	Historical cost—the amount of the original liability or the amount of cash needed to discharge the liability
Long-term liabilities	Discounted present value of future principal and interest payments at the yield at the time they were issued
Stockholders' Equity	
Paid-in capital	Historical cost
Retained earnings	Net accumulated earnings less cumulative dividends distributed
Other Balance Sheet Items	Measurement criteria vary with the nature of the item

No. 7, the International Accounting Standards Board requires that financial statements include a balance sheet, an income statement, a statement showing changes in equity, a cash flow statement, and accounting policies and explanatory notes. As in U.S. statements, the following items must be clearly identified: the financial statements, the reporting enterprise, whether the statements are for the enterprise or for a group, the date or period covered, the reporting currency, and the level of precision of the currency (such as thousands or millions). There is a presumption that financial statements will be prepared at least annually. Companies are also encouraged to present a financial review by management that describes and explains the main factors of and influences on financial performance, sources of funding, risk management policies, and strengths and resources whose value is not reflected in the balance sheet.

Whereas the format of U.S. balance sheets is usually consistent, you will see more variations in the format of non-U.S. balance sheets. Formats might include

● Separation of current assets from noncurrent assets and current liabilities from noncurrent liabilities (the most common format in the United States)

● Presentation of assets and liabilities in order of liquidity (or in reverse order of liquidity), without distinguishing between current and noncurrent items

● Net asset presentation (assets minus liabilities)

● Long-term financing approach, used in the United Kingdom and elsewhere (Fixed Assets + Current Assets − Short-Term Payables = Long-Term Debt + Equity)

Consolidation requirements are similar to those of U.S. standards. When a parent company has subsidiaries, the IASB requires that the financial statements of the subsidiaries be combined with those of the parent if the parent has control of the

Figure 4.7

BMW Group Balance Sheets

BMW

BMW Group
Group and Sub-Group Balance Sheets at 31 December

Assets in euro million	Group 2004	Group 2003	Industrial operations[1] 2004	Industrial operations[1] 2003	Financial operations[1] 2004	Financial operations[1] 2003
Intangible assets	3,758	3,200	3,739	3,181	19	19
Property, plant and equipment	10,724	9,708	10,703	9,688	21	20
Financial assets	769	607	750	593	19	14
Leased products	7,502	6,697	221	225	9,450	8,293
Non-current assets	**22,753**	**20,212**	**15,413**	**13,687**	**9,509**	**8,346**
Inventories	6,467	5,693	6,458	5,686	9	7
Trade receivables	1,868	2,257	1,820	2,191	48	66
Receivables from sales financing	25,054	21,950	—	—	25,054	21,950
Other receivables	6,474	7,184	4,817	4,829	3,084	3,545
Marketable securities	1,832	1,857	1,832	1,857	—	—
Cash and cash equivalents	2,128	1,659	1,997	1,247	131	412
Current assets	**43,823**	**40,600**	**16,924**	**15,810**	**28,326**	**25,980**
Deferred tax assets	**296**	**175**	**191**	**120**	**−1,012**	**−873**
Prepayments	**543**	**488**	**125**	**166**	**418**	**322**
Total assets	**67,415**	**61,475**	**32,653**	**29,783**	**37,241**	**33,775**
Total assets adjusted for asset backed financing transactions	**63,146**	56,487	—	—	**32,972**	28,787

Equity and liabilities in euro million	Group 2004	Group 2003	Industrial operations[1] 2004	Industrial operations[1] 2003	Financial operations[1] 2004	Financial operations[1] 2003
Subscribed capital	**674**	674				
Capital reserves	**1,971**	1,971				
Revenue reserves	**14,501**	12,671				
Accumulated other equity	**371**	834				
Equity	**17,517**	**16,150**	**14,647**	**13,534**	**3,613**	**3,298**
Pension provisions	2,703	2,430	2,680	2,410	23	20
Other provisions	6,769	6,321	6,376	6,008	441	356
Provisions	**9,472**	**8,751**	**9,056**	**8,418**	**464**	**376**
Debt	30,483	27,449	1,466	1,288	29,017	26,161
Trade payables	3,376	3,143	3,070	2,740	306	403
Other liabilities	2,395	2,634	1,606	1,811	2,216	2,013
Liabilities	**36,254**	**33,226**	**6,142**	**5,839**	**31,539**	**28,577**
Deferred tax liabilities	**2,596**	**2,501**	**1,800**	**1,592**	**601**	**777**
Deferred income	**1,576**	**847**	**1,008**	**400**	**1,024**	**747**
Total equity and liabilities	**67,415**	**61,475**	**32,653**	**29,783**	**37,241**	**33,775**
Total equity and liabilities adjusted for asset backed financing transactions	**63,146**	56,487	—	—	**32,972**	28,787

[1] before consolidation of transactions between the sub-groups

subsidiaries. Control is presumed when the parent acquires more than half of the voting rights of the enterprise. Even when the parent does not hold more than one-half of the voting rights, control may be evidenced in certain circumstances.

The **BMW Group**'s balance sheet, which is prepared under international accounting standards, is shown in Figure 4.7. Note that assets and liabilities are presented in reverse order of liquidity, a format rarely used by U.S. companies.

> **CHECK YOUR UNDERSTANDING**
>
> 1. How are current assets usually listed on the balance sheet?
> 2. What type of accounts would commonly be found in the current liabilities section of the balance sheet?
> 3. Explain the concept of off-balance-sheet financing.
> 4. How are operating assets valued on the balance sheet?
> 5. Describe the balance sheet classification formats allowed by international accounting standards.

LO 2 Describe the elements of the statement of changes in stockholders' equity.

statement of changes in stockholders' equity a financial statement that summarizes the transactions that affected stockholders' equity over an accounting period

Critical Thinking: What information does the statement of changes in stockholders' equity provide to potential investors that is different from that provided by the balance sheet?

The Statement of Changes in Stockholders' Equity

The **statement of changes in stockholders' equity** (or, for small corporations, the *retained earnings statement*) summarizes the transactions that affected stockholders' equity over an accounting period. It is a crucial statement because in today's financial environment, public companies continue to devise new and complex financial transactions aimed at raising capital from new sources, and information about those transactions is critical to financial statement users. In addition, the use of stock options to attract and retain key employees continues to grow—another transaction that is reflected on this statement. Consequently, almost all public companies prepare some version of a statement of changes in stockholders' equity (sometimes called *a statement of stockholders' equity*).

The components of stockholders' equity usually include common stock, paid-in capital (the amount the corporation received from the issuance of common stock above the stock's par or stated value), preferred stock (if authorized and issued), retained earnings, and treasury stock (if purchased by the corporation). Given the new requirements regarding the disclosure of comprehensive income items (discussed in Chapter 3), many firms include comprehensive income as part of their statement of changes in stockholders' equity. Events and transactions that cause changes in stockholders' equity may include net income, currency translations, purchases of treasury stock, issuance of common stock, issuance of cash dividends, and realized losses or gains on derivative instruments.

A statement of stockholders' equity for Home Depot, Inc. is presented in Figure 4.8. It shows the types of transactions that affected stockholders' equity between February 3, 2002, and January 30, 2005. As you can see, retained earnings is affected by net income and the issuance of dividends in each year. Users can identify activities such as issuance of common stock under an employee stock purchase plan and repurchase of treasury stock by the company from the entries in the applicable columns. Note that the company repurchased shares of treasury stock during each of the reported fiscal years.

Figure 4.8

Consolidated Statements of Stockholders' Equity and Comprehensive Income

Home Depot

The Home Depot, Inc. and Subsidiaries
Consolidated Statements of Stockholders' Equity and Comprehensive Income

amounts in millions, except per share data	Common Stock Shares	Amount	Paid-In Capital	Retained Earnings	Accumulated Other Comprehensive Income (Loss)[1]	Unearned Compensation	Treasury Stock Shares	Amount	Total Stockholders' Equity	Comprehensive Income[2]
BALANCE, FEBRUARY 3, 2002	2,346	$117	$5,412	$12,799	$(220)	$(26)	—	$ —	$18,082	
Net Earnings	—	—	—	3,664	—	—	—	—	3,664	$3,664
Shares Issued Under Employee Stock Plans	16	1	366	—	—	(40)	—	—	327	
Tax Effect of Sale of Option Shares by Employees	—	—	68	—	—	—	—	—	68	
Translation Adjustments	—	—	—	—	109	—	—	—	109	109
Realized Loss on Derivative	—	—	—	—	29	—	—	—	29	18
Stock Options, Awards and Amortization of Restricted Stock	—	—	12	—	—	3	—	—	15	
Repurchase of Common Stock	—	—	—	—	—	—	(69)	(2,000)	(2,000)	
Cash Dividends ($0.21 per share)	—	—	—	(492)	—	—	—	—	(492)	
Comprehensive Income										$3,791
BALANCE, FEBRUARY 2, 2003	2,362	$118	$5,858	$15,971	$ (82)	$(63)	(69)	$(2,000)	$19,802	
Net Earnings	—	—	—	4,304	—	—	—	—	4,304	$4,304
Shares Issued Under Employee Stock Plans	11	1	249	—	—	(26)	—	—	224	
Tax Effect of Sale of Option Shares by Employees	—	—	24	—	—	—	—	—	24	
Translation Adjustments	—	—	—	—	172	—	—	—	172	172
Stock Options, Awards and Amortization of Restricted Stock	—	—	53	—	—	13	—	—	66	
Repurchase of Common Stock	—	—	—	—	—	—	(47)	(1,590)	(1,590)	
Cash Dividends ($0.26 per share)	—	—	—	(595)	—	—	—	—	(595)	
Comprehensive Income										$4,476
BALANCE, FEBRUARY 1, 2004	2,373	$119	$6,184	$19,680	$ (90)	$(76)	(116)	$(3,590)	$22,407	
Net Earnings	—	—	—	5,001	—	—	—	—	5,001	$5,001
Shares Issued Under Employee Stock Plans	12	—	340	—	—	(54)	—	—	286	
Tax Effect of Sale of Option Shares by Employees	—	—	26	—	—	—	—	—	26	
Translation Adjustments	—	—	—	—	137	—	—	—	137	137
Stock Options, Awards and Amortization of Restricted Stock	—	—	100	—	—	22	—	—	122	
Repurchase of Common Stock	—	—	—	—	—	—	(84)	(3,102)	(3,102)	
Cash Dividends ($0.325 per share)	—	—	—	(719)	—	—	—	—	(719)	
Comprehensive Income										$5,138
BALANCE, JANUARY 30, 2005	2,385	$119	$6,650	$23,962	$ 227	$(108)	(200)	$(6,692)	$24,158	

(1) Balance of January 30, 2005 consists primarily of foreign currency translation adjustments.
(2) Components of Comprehensive Income are reported net of related income taxes.

LO 3 Summarize the tools used by financial analysts, including percentage analysis, horizontal analysis, ratio analysis, and benchmarking.

ANALYSIS

Critical Thinking: How might you go about analyzing your personal assets and liabilities for this year as compared to last year? How about your total assets as compared to your total liabilities? What value would these measurements have for the assessment of your financial condition?

percentage analysis the expression of each item on a financial statement in a given period as a proportion of a base figure; also known as *vertical analysis*

horizontal analysis a method of analysis that compares data from two or more time periods; often called *trend analysis*

Tools for Balance Sheet Analysis

Throughout this book, we emphasize both the preparation and the analysis of financial statements. From the investor's perspective, the purpose of financial statement analysis is to use a company's past performance to predict its future prospects. As discussed in Chapter 3, net income, or earnings, is the key to a company's long-term performance. Without earnings and the associated cash flow, a company cannot pay its operating expenses and debts, expand its operations, or pay dividends. Therefore, most analyses are directed toward understanding a company's earnings. Nonetheless, analysts also want to know how liquid a company is, how much debt it has, how it is using leverage, and how efficiently it uses its assets to generate revenues. Such questions can be addressed through balance sheet analysis.

Keep in mind that analyzing one year's balance sheet in isolation is not particularly informative. The analysis gains greater meaning when a company's current balance sheet is compared to its balance sheets from prior periods and when those balance sheets are compared to the balance sheets of similar companies. Percentage and horizontal analyses assist in comparing key items over time, and financial ratios allow comparisons among companies of various sizes by scaling them all to the same size.

PERCENTAGE ANALYSIS

Percentage analysis, also known as *vertical analysis*, is the expression of each item on a financial statement in a given period as a proportion of a base figure. For example, each line item on the balance sheet is divided by total assets (or by total liabilities plus stockholders' equity). Thus, each element on the balance sheet is expressed as a percentage of the whole, and changes in the percentage represented by each element can be analyzed over time. Percentage analysis also allows for easy comparisons among companies. Percentage analysis can also be applied to an income statement, in which case individual items are expressed as a percentage of sales.

HORIZONTAL ANALYSIS

Horizontal analysis is a method of analysis that compares data from two or more time periods. This type of analysis, often called *trend analysis,* helps investors see trends over time, such as increases in sales from one period to another or over a five-year period. Those trends can then be compared to the trends of other companies in similar industries. The data may be compared on either an absolute or a percentage basis to examine how balance sheet or income statement elements have changed over time. Percentages are derived by computing the difference between two accounts from one period to another and dividing the difference by the figure from the earlier period. Figure 4.9 provides both percentage and horizontal analyses for Home Depot's fiscal year 2004 balance sheet. The Percent of Total Assets columns give the percentage analysis for fiscal years 2004 and 2003. The Percent Change for the Year column gives the horizontal analysis, indicating the change from fiscal year 2003 to 2004.

Figure 4.9

Percentage and Horizontal Analyses Based on Condensed Balance Sheets

Home Depot

The Home Depot, Inc. and Subsidiaries
Percentage and Horizontal Analyses Based on Condensed Balance Sheets

(amounts in millions)	FY 2004	Percent of Total Assets	FY 2003	Percent of Total Assets	Percent Change for the Year
Assets					
Cash and Cash Equivalents	$ 506	1.30%	$ 1,103	3.20%	−54.13%
Short-Term Investments	1,659	4.26%	1,749	5.08%	−5.15%
Receivables, net	1,499	3.85%	1,097	3.19%	36.65%
Merchandise Inventory	10,076	25.90%	9,076	26.36%	11.02%
Other Current Assets	450	1.16%	303	0.88%	48.51%
Total Current Assets	$14,190	36.47%	$13,328	38.70%	6.47%
Net Property and Equipment	22,726	58.41%	20,063	58.26%	13.27%
Other Assets	1,991	5.12%	1,046	3.04%	90.34%
Total Assets	$38,907	100.00%	$34,437	100.00%*	12.98%
Liabilities					
Accounts Payable	$ 5,766	14.82%	$5,159	$ 14.98%	11.77%
Other Current Liabilities	4,752	12.21%	3,886	11.28%	22.29%
Current Installment of Long-Term Debt	11	0.03%	509	1.48%	−97.84%
Total Current Liabilities	$10,529	27.06%	$9,554	27.74%	10.21%
Long-Term Debt	2,148	5.52%	856	2.49%	150.93%
Other Long-Term Liabilities	763	1.96%	653	1.90%	16.85%
Deferred Income Taxes	1,309	3.36%	967	2.81%	35.37%
Total Stockholders' Equity	24,158	62.09%	22,407	65.07%	7.81%
Liabilities and Stockholders' Equity	$38,907	100.00%	$34,437	100.00%*	12.98%

* Difference due to rounding.

As you can see, the percentage analysis (or vertical analysis) presented in the Percent of Total Assets column for fiscal year 2004 shows that current assets make up 36.47 percent of total assets, while long-term debt amounts to 5.52 percent of total assets. The horizontal analysis helps statement users identify how assets, liabilities, and stockholders' equity have changed from fiscal year 2003 to fiscal year 2004. For example, Home Depot holds 6.47 percent more current assets in 2004 than in 2003.

RATIO ANALYSIS

ratio analysis a method of financial analysis in which meaningful relationships between the components of the financial statements are shown

Ratio analysis is a method of financial analysis in which meaningful relationships between the components of the financial statements are shown. Such an analysis can indicate potential problems for a company and is often used to identify items that need further investigation and explanation. A ratio is a numerical relationship between the amounts or sizes of two things and may be expressed in a variety of ways: as a percentage, a fraction, a "times" figure, a number of days, a rate, or just a number. Ratio analysis is widely used to evaluate four aspects of a firm's operations: liquidity, leverage, activity, and profitability.

▶ LIQUIDITY RATIOS

liquidity ratios measurements of financial data that help analysts assess a firm's ability to meet its financial obligations in the short term

Liquidity ratios help analysts assess a firm's ability to meet its financial obligations in the short term. Maintaining short-term liquidity is a critical objective of a company's management. A firm's inability to meet its current debts, either its operating payables or its current maturities of long-term debt, can quickly lead to defaults and perhaps even bankruptcy. The most common liquidity measurements are the following:

- *Current ratio* (compares the amount of all current assets to the amount of current liabilities)

- *Quick ratio* (compares only the most liquid of current assets to the amount of current liabilities)

- *Working capital* (indicates the current assets on hand that can be used to continue business operations)

These three ratios will be discussed in detail in Chapter 7.

❯ LEVERAGE RATIOS

leverage ratios financial analysis measurements that provide data about the long-term solvency of a firm

Leverage ratios provide data about the long-term solvency of a firm. They indicate the level of risk that an individual assumes when that individual invests in a company's debt or equity. Because interest must be paid on debts and debts must be paid off at maturity, a firm must generate sufficient cash in both the short term and the long term to satisfy its creditors. Common leverage ratios include the following:

- *Total liabilities to total assets* (shows what percentage of a company's total assets has been financed by creditors)

- *Total debt to total equity* (measures a company's debt exposure and the amount of assets supplied by the stockholders relative to those supplied by the creditors)

- *Times interest earned* (measures a company's ability to meet its interest payments as they come due by comparing income with interest expense)

These ratio measurements will be discussed in Chapter 13.

❯ ACTIVITY RATIOS

activity ratios financial analysis measurements that are used to assess the efficiency with which a firm uses its assets

Activity ratios are used to assess the efficiency with which a firm uses its assets. There are three commonly used ratios in this category:

- *Accounts receivable turnover ratio* (measures how quickly a firm collects its accounts receivable)

- *Inventory turnover ratio* (measures the number of times inventory is sold during the year)

- *Asset turnover ratio* (measures asset efficiency, or how much in total assets a firm must have to generate its sales)

These ratios enable analysts to evaluate how well a firm is managing its inventory, its accounts receivable (and credit policy), and its total assets relative to its earnings. The accounts receivable turnover, the inventory turnover, and the asset turnover ratios are discussed in Chapters 7, 8, and 9, respectively.

❯ PROFITABILITY RATIOS

profitability ratios financial analysis measurements used to examine how successful a firm is in using its operating processes and resources to earn income

Profitability ratios are used to examine how successful a firm is in using its operating processes and resources to earn income. Commonly used profitability ratios include the following:

- *Operating margin percentage* (indicates how much operating income is generated by each dollar of sales)

- *Profit margin on sales* (indicates how much net income is earned on each dollar of sales)

Illustration 4.3

Summary of Financial Ratios

Category	Purpose	Examples
Liquidity	Used to assess a firm's ability to meet its financial obligations in the short term	Current ratio, quick ratio, working capital
Leverage	Provide data about the long-term solvency of a firm	Total liabilities to total assets, total debt to total equity, times interest earned
Activity	Used to assess the efficiency with which a firm uses its assets	Accounts receivable turnover ratio, inventory turnover ratio, asset turnover ratio
Profitability	Used to examine how successful a firm is in using its operating processes and resources to earn income	Operating margin percentage, profit margin on sales, return on total assets, return on stockholders' equity

- *Return on total assets* (indicates how well management is using its assets)

- *Return on stockholders' equity* (indicates how much income was earned on each dollar invested by a common stockholder)

As you recall, operating margin percentage and profit margin on sales were discussed in Chapter 3. Return on total assets and return on stockholders' equity are discussed in Chapter 13.

A summary of the four categories of financial ratios is presented in Illustration 4.3. The calculation and interpretation of specific ratios will be discussed throughout the textbook.

BENCHMARKING TOOLS

benchmarking comparing one company's financial results with results from other companies or with an industry average

Benchmarking is comparing one company's financial results with results from other companies or with an industry average. One useful benchmarking tool, EdgarScan, is provided online by PricewaterhouseCoopers. EdgarScan is an interface to the SEC's EDGAR database that pulls filings from the SEC's servers and formats the data into Excel spreadsheets to assist in analysis. One of EdgarScan's tools compares a user-selected company to others in its industry and assigns a number indicating the company's rank on a specific ratio or data point, with 1 being the top ranking. Figure 4.10 shows a sample of the benchmarking information supplied by EdgarScan based on Home Depot, Inc.'s fiscal year 2004 annual report (10-K). Notice that in most categories, Home Depot receives a superior ranking (1) relative to other dealers in retail lumber and other building materials.

A number of free and subscription service firms provide comparative and other useful information about public companies. Hoover's Online is one example. It is a subscription-based service that provides comprehensive profiles, in-depth financials, full lists of key people and competitors, competitive analysis, advanced searching, and downloadable contact information.

Figure 4.10

Benchmarking Report

Sample EdgarScan Benchmarking Report, The Home Depot, Inc.*

Item	Value (millions)	Rank
Cash	506	1
Receivables	1,499	1
Inventory	10,076	1
Current Assets	14,190	1
Accounts Payable	5,766	1
Current Liabilities	1,578	1
Long-Term Debt	2,148	1
Total Debt	2,159	1
Net Sales	73,094	1
Cost of Goods Sold	48,664	1
Interest Expense	70	1
Operating Income	7,926	1
Net Income	5,001	1
Receivables Turnover	48.762	1
Asset Turnover Ratio	2.122	2
Current Ratio	1.348	2
Net Income Growth	0.162	3

* EdgarScan, available at **http://edgarscan.pwcglobal.com/servlets/getCompanyDetail?Name=** HOME+DEPOT+INC. Accessed 8/23/05.

CHECK YOUR UNDERSTANDING

1. What type of ratio might be used to assess the efficiency with which a firm uses its assets?

2. Describe the purpose of the use of liquidity ratios.

3. What method of analysis is used to compare data from two or more time periods?

4. If the managers of a grocery store chain compare the company's or the chain's financial data to the financial data from a competitor's chain, what type of analysis are they using?

5. Describe the difference between horizontal and vertical analysis.

LO 4 Discuss the limitations of a balance sheet prepared under GAAP.

Limitations of Balance Sheet Information

Users who understand the conventions that underlie the preparation of the balance sheet will find that it contains a great deal of valuable information about a company and its ongoing prospects. Nonetheless, to make the best use of a balance sheet, users must also recognize that it is a historically based document that is limited

Critical Thinking: If a company has been recognized for its ongoing stellar management practices, do you think that company should be allowed to list this recognition as an asset on its balance sheet? Explain your reasoning.

by the criteria used to recognize assets and liabilities, by the way those items are measured and valued, and by the very nature of financial statements based on principles of historical cost, conservatism, and objectivity.

As business continues to evolve from the well-entrenched industrial model to a more knowledge-based model, the criticism of traditional accounting has increased, and many critics question whether current GAAP can ever adequately reflect the true nature of the new types of business. At the beginning of this chapter, we quoted Professor Baruch Lev's testimony before the House of Representatives, in which he described the changing face of business and the challenges that those changes create for today's accounting system. Lev went on to note that the following business activities are missing from historical financial reports, especially the balance sheet prepared under GAAP:[8]

- *Networking activities.* Today's corporations conduct more and more of their business through networking activities. These include alliances, marketing activities, special-purpose entities, and partnerships, many of which are not currently recognized on the balance sheet as either assets or liabilities. For example, **Dell**'s leadership in the personal computer industry is based on its ability to harness the activities and manufacturing skills of its suppliers rather than on its own ability to manufacture components.

- *Unexecuted obligations.* Firms have a variety of obligations to and contractual arrangements with suppliers, alliance partners, and others that are ignored in historically based statements, even though those arrangements give rise to future obligations. For example, an unexecuted obligation arises when an airline agrees to a future purchase of airplanes from Boeing or **Airbus**. At the time of the agreement, no money is exchanged, and the arrangement has yet to be executed. Nonetheless, it is a major transaction that commits both the manufacturer and the purchaser to significant future actions.

- *Intangible assets.* As discussed earlier, some intangible assets that provide future benefits to a firm are not recognized under current GAAP because the benefits are difficult to measure reliably or cannot be verified. Current accounting principles regard assets like good management or research and development as expenses, as though they will not provide any future benefits. According to Lev and others, that approach produces serious biases in corporate balance sheets and income statements.

- *Risk exposure.* Businesses engage in many activities that expose them to financial and operating risks. Although the FASB has tried to force the disclosure of risks associated with innovative financial instruments, balance sheets make little mention of possible risks associated with interest-rate changes, foreign exchange rate changes, fluctuations in commodity prices, or even changes in the economic or political conditions of countries in which companies operate.

Traditional financial reporting has always opted for reliability over relevance. This trade-off has served the investing public well over the years. However, as the nature of business changes, accounting policy setters must continue to revisit this trade-off as they develop standards to meet the needs of twenty-first-century knowledge-based companies and investors. Indeed, in recent years, the FASB and the IASB have revisited many of their standards, have made significant changes, and are contemplating additional changes to make GAAP more and more relevant to today's financial statement users.

---

8 Baruch Lev, "The Reform of Corporate Reporting and Auditing," testimony before the House of Representatives Committee on Energy and Commerce, February 6, 2002.

Revisiting the Case

LOWE'S COMPANIES, INC. BUILDS ASSETS BEYOND THE BALANCE SHEET

1. The valuation of an intangible item like good management or "know-how" is difficult or impossible to estimate or calculate. Inclusion of these types of items on the balance sheet could lead to inflation of the company's worth and lessen investors' confidence in financial statements.

2. Lowe's January 28, 2005, balance sheet reflects a value of $13,911 million for its property, less accumulated depreciation—its largest asset.

3. Companies often experience growth and success as a result of factors like technological know-how, unique organizational designs, good management, partnerships with successful entities, and long-standing branding efforts, even though these "assets" are not reflected on the balance sheet, a historically based financial statement.

SUMMARY BY LEARNING OBJECTIVE

LO1 Identify the elements of the balance sheet and explain the recognition and measurement criteria for those elements.

The balance sheet reports the financial position of a firm using the elements of the accounting equation: Assets = Liabilities + Owners' Equity (Stockholders' Equity). The elements of the balance sheet are classified according to their nature and intended use. Assets are classified as either current or noncurrent. Current assets are generally listed in decreasing order of liquidity, or ability to be converted into cash. Noncurrent assets are grouped into the following categories: investments and funds; property, plant, and equipment; intangible assets; and other assets. Liabilities are classified as either current or noncurrent (long term). The liabilities are presented according to time to maturity or due date, with obligations that are expected to come due first being listed first and those with the latest due dates being listed last. Stockholders' equity items are listed in order of permanence. Contributed capital accounts, which change the least, are listed first, and accumulated other comprehensive income appears last. The following categories are used: contributed (paid-in) capital, such as capital stock, paid-in capital in excess of par value, and other contributed or donated capital; retained earnings; and other equity adjustment accounts, such as accumulated other comprehensive income.

The elements of the balance sheet are initially recorded at their historical cost. At the balance sheet date, monetary assets are shown at their net realizable value, and most nonmonetary assets are shown at the lower of their cost or market value, adjusted for any accumulated depreciation or amortization. Current liabilities are shown at the amount of cash necessary to discharge the liability, and long-term liabilities are shown at the present value of their future principal and interest payments.

LO2 Describe the elements of the statement of changes in stockholders' equity.

The statement of changes in stockholders' equity provides information on the sources of the changes in stockholders' equity over an accounting period. Common elements found on a statement of changes in stockholders' equity may include net income, currency translations, purchases of treasury stock, issuance of common stock, issuance of cash dividends, and realized losses or gains on derivative instruments.

LO3 Summarize the tools used by financial analysts, including percentage analysis, horizontal analysis, ratio analysis, and benchmarking.

Percentage analysis, also known as vertical analysis, is the expression of each item on a financial statement in a given period as a proportion of a base figure. For example, each line item on the balance sheet is divided by total assets (or by total liabilities plus stockholders' equity). Horizontal analysis is a method of analysis that compares data from two or more time periods. This type of analysis, often called *trend analysis,* helps investors see trends over time, such as increases in sales from one period to another or over a five-year period. Ratio analysis is a method of financial analysis in which meaningful relationships between the components of the financial statements are shown. Ratio analysis is widely used to evaluate four aspects of a firm's operations: liquidity, leverage, activity or turnover of assets, and profitability. Benchmarking is comparing one company's financial results with results from other companies or with an industry average.

LO4 Discuss the limitations of a balance sheet prepared under GAAP.

The balance sheet is a historically based financial statement that is limited by the criteria used to recognize assets and liabilities, by the way those items are measured and valued, and by the very nature of financial statements based on principles of conservatism and objectivity. As business continues to evolve from an industrial model to a more knowledge-based model, the criticism of traditional accounting is increasing. A number of items related to today's business activities are missing from balance sheets prepared under GAAP. These include networking activities, unexecuted obligations, intangible assets, and risk exposure. Traditional financial reporting has always opted for reliability over relevance, a trade-off that has served the investing public well over the years. However, recognizing the need to keep up with the times, the FASB and the IASB have revisited many of their standards, have made significant changes, and are contemplating additional changes to make GAAP more relevant to today's financial statement users.

KEY TERMS

activity ratios (p. 169)
amortization (p. 157)
assets (p. 152)
balance sheet (p. 152)
benchmarking (p. 170)
capital lease (p. 158)
capital stock (p. 161)
common stock (p. 161)
contributed capital (p. 161)
current assets (p. 155)
current liabilities (p. 157)
deferred charges (p. 160)
depletion (p. 158)

equity (p. 152)
goodwill (p. 159)
horizontal analysis (p. 167)
impairment (p. 158)
intangible assets (p. 159)
lease (p. 158)
leverage ratios (p. 169)
liabilities (p. 152)
liquidity ratios (p. 168)
market value (p. 152)
monetary assets (p. 155)
noncurrent assets (p. 157)
noncurrent liabilities (p. 160)

nonmonetary assets (p. 155)
off-balance-sheet financing (p. 158)
operating cycle (p. 155)
operating lease (p. 158)
percentage analysis (p. 167)
preferred stock (p. 161)
profitability ratios (p. 169)
ratio analysis (p. 168)
retained earnings (p. 161)
statement of changes in stockholders' equity (p. 165)
stockholders' equity (p. 152)
treasury stock (p. 162)

EXERCISES

LO1   **EXERCISE 4-1   Account Classification**

Selected accounts appear below:

Cash and Cash Equivalents

Long-Term Debt, due in 4 years

Accumulated Other Comprehensive Income

Net Sales

Cost of Merchandise Sold

Selling and Administrative Expenses

Income Taxes Payable

Other Accrued Expenses

Short-Term Investments

Current Installments of Long-Term Debt

Buildings, net of accumulated depreciation

Furniture, Fixtures, and Equipment, net of accumulated depreciation

Leasehold Improvements, net of amortization

Bonds Payable, due in 2 years

Patents

Long-Term Investments

Notes Receivable, due in 12 months

Cost in Excess of the Fair Value of Net Assets Acquired

Common Stock

Additional Paid-in Capital

Retained Earnings

Required: Place each of these accounts into one of the following categories:

Current assets (CA)

Noncurrent assets (NA)

Current liabilities (CL)

Noncurrent liabilities (NL)

Stockholders' equity (SE)

Income statement accounts (ISA)

LO1   EXERCISE 4-2   Accounting Equation Elements

Scooter, Inc. reported the following information at December 31, 2005:

Long-term debt	$15,800	Property, plant, and equipment	$34,000
Current assets	14,500	Current liabilities	11,300
Retained earnings	4,600		

Required:

1. Determine the amount of common stock.

2. How much is total stockholders' equity at the end of the year?

LO1   EXERCISE 4-3   Balance Sheet Classifications

The accounts for Reality Inc. are listed below:

A. Unearned Revenue

B. Allowance for Uncollectible Accounts

C. Inventories

D. Current Installments of Long-Term Debt

E. Prepaid Insurance

F. Loss from Sale of Equipment

G. Interest Receivable

H. Wages Payable

I. Cash (checking account)

J. Deferred Subscription Revenue

The following list contains potential balance sheet classifications for Reality's accounts:

CA	Current assets	CL	Current liabilities
IF	Investments and funds	LTL	Long-term liabilities
PPE	Property, plant, and equipment	PIC	Paid-in capital
INT	Intangible assets	OCI	Other comprehensive income
OA	Other assets	RE	Retained earnings

Required: Indicate which balance sheet classification is the most appropriate for reporting each account by selecting the appropriate balance sheet element abbreviation. If the account is reported on the income statement rather than the balance sheet, indicate that fact with an IS. Assume all items are material.

LO2   **EXERCISE 4-4   Stockholders' Equity**

The following information was provided by Fido Corporation for 2006:

Net income for 2006	$4,600
Cash dividend declared and paid in 2006	3,900

Fido determined the balances of the following accounts as of December 31, 2006:

Common Stock	$ 800
Additional Paid-in Capital	3,000
Cash	3,700
Sales Revenue	46,000

The balance of Retained Earnings on December 31, 2005, was $1,540. During 2006, 1,000 shares of $.10 par value common stock were issued for $500. The company had no comprehensive income items at December 31, 2005; however, an unrealized loss from an investment in available-for-sale securities totaling $200 (net of tax) was recognized during 2006.

Required: Prepare a statement of changes in stockholders' equity for the year ended December 31, 2006, assuming that Fido Corporation discloses comprehensive income as part of its statement of stockholders' equity.

LO2   **EXERCISE 4-5   Statement of Changes in Stockholders' Equity**

Zukierski Zest Company provided the following selected accounts from its accounting records as of December 31, 2006 and 2005:

	Dec. 31, 2006	Dec. 31, 2005
Additional Paid-in Capital	$78,000	$48,000
Retained Earnings	?	32,000
Foreign Currency Translation Loss, net	(2,000)	(6,000)
Unrealized Gain from Available-for-Sale Securities, net	5,000	4,000
Common Stock, par value $.50	12,000	10,000

The following additional information is provided concerning these accounts:

A. The company declared and paid cash dividends of $43,000 on December 28, 2006.

B. The company issued 4,000 shares of its common stock on July 1, 2006.

C. Net income was $65,000 for 2005 and $46,000 for 2006.

D. 40,000 shares of common stock are authorized.

E. The comprehensive income items are net of income taxes.

Required:

1. Prepare the statement of changes in stockholders' equity for the year ended December 31, 2006.

2. How does the stockholders' equity section of Zukierski Zest Company's balance sheet differ from the statement of changes in stockholders' equity for the year ended December 31, 2006?

LO3   **EXERCISE 4-6   Horizontal Analysis**

Macey, Inc. released the following balance sheets as of December 31, 2005 and 2006.

Macey, Inc.
Consolidated Balance Sheets
December 31, 2006 and 2005

	2006	2005
Assets		
Current assets:		
Cash	$ 90,000	$ 56,000
Accounts receivable	45,000	85,000
Less allowance for uncollectible accounts	(12,000)	(19,000)
Notes receivable	22,000	22,000
Inventories	120,000	130,000
Total current assets	$265,000	$274,000
Investments	320,000	280,000
Property, plant, and equipment, net	89,000	72,000
Total assets	$674,000	$626,000
Liabilities and Stockholders' Equity		
Current liabilities:		
Accounts payable	$ 14,000	$ 12,000
Salaries payable	14,000	18,000
Current maturities of long-term debt	17,500	18,500
Total current liabilities	$ 45,500	$ 48,500
Long-term liabilities:		
Notes payable	$ 60,000	$120,000
Bonds payable	200,000	200,000
Total long-term liabilities	$260,000	$320,000
Stockholders' equity		
Common stock, no par, 800,000 shares authorized, 100,000 shares issued and outstanding	$200,000	$200,000
Retained Earnings	168,500	57,500
Total stockholders' equity	$368,500	$257,500
Total liabilities and stockholders' equity	$674,000	$626,000

Required:

1. Calculate the percentage change at December 31, 2006, for each of the following line items:

   a. Total assets
   b. Total stockholders' equity
   c. Total long-term liabilities
   d. Total current liabilities

2. Based on the changes you indicated in question 1, what is your assessment of the company's financial position at December 31, 2006, as compared to December 31, 2005?

LO3   **EXERCISE 4-7   Financial Analysis**

Several descriptions related to financial analysis terminology follow.

A. A category of ratios used to assess the efficiency with which a firm uses its assets; includes the accounts receivable turnover ratio, the inventory turnover ratio, and the asset turnover ratio

B. Comparing one company's financial results with results from other companies or with an industry average

C. A method of financial analysis that compares data from two or more time periods; also called *trend analysis*

D. A category of ratios that provide data about the long-term solvency of a firm; includes total liabilities to total assets and times interest earned

E. A category of ratios that helps analysts to assess a firm's ability to meet its financial obligations in the short term; includes the current ratio and the quick ratio

F. The expression of each item on a financial statement in a given period as a proportion of a base figure

G. A category of ratios used to examine how successful a firm is in using its operating processes and resources to earn income

Required: Identify the financial analysis tool described in each of the items listed.

LO3 **EXERCISE 4-8   Benchmarking**

Walsh Company released the following amounts from its 2005 financial statements. Industry averages are presented alongside each Walsh amount.

	Walsh Company	Industry Averages
Sales	$65,000,000	$50,000,000
Net income	2,400,000	2,200,000
Profit margin on sales	12%	11.4%
Gross profit percentage	58%	55%
Return on total assets	11%	12%

Required: The controller has asked you to benchmark the company's profitability against the industry. Justify your analysis.

LO4 **EXERCISE 4-9   Limitations of the Balance Sheet**

Companies often have various business activities that do not appear on the balance sheet under current GAAP.

Required: Identify two types of events or occurrences that should be disclosed along with a company's financial statements in order to comply with a very strict sense of conservatism. Justify your response.

LO1 **EXERCISE 4-10   Classified Balance Sheet**

Refer to the accounts provided in Exercise 4–1.

Required: Prepare a classified balance sheet using the accounts listed in Exercise 4–1. No monetary amounts are required.

LO1 **EXERCISE 4-11   Elements of the Balance Sheet**

The terms in the first list below relate to elements found on the balance sheet. The second list contains phrases and definitions related to the terms in the first list.

1. Operating lease
2. Impairment
3. Goodwill
4. Depletion
5. Capital lease

A. An intangible asset that is recognized only when one company purchases another company; represents the premium that a purchaser pays over the fair value of an acquired company's identifiable net assets

B. The periodic allocation of the costs of natural resources

C. A short-term or cancelable lease in which the risk of ownership lies with the lessor

D. A long-term lease in which the risk of ownership lies with the lessee and whose terms resemble a purchase or sale on installment; must be capitalized on the balance sheet

E. A decrease in the value of an asset as a result of rapid technological advances, intense domestic and global competition, or changes in market demand

Required: Match each term in the first list with the corresponding phrase or definition from the second list.

LO1   **EXERCISE 4-12   Balance Sheet Preparation**
The account balances for Bridge Corporation at December 31, 2005, are as follows.

	Debits	Credits
Cash	$ 225,000	
Land	375,000	
Equipment	142,000	
Accumulated Depreciation—Equipment		$ 22,000
Long-Term Investment in Stock	35,000	
Short-Term Notes Payable		75,000
Bonds Payable		150,000
Common Stock ($10 par)		300,000
Preferred Stock		50,000
Retained Earnings		298,930
Additional Paid-in Capital		19,000
Accounts Receivable	14,000	
Inventories	173,430	
Dividends Payable		22,000
Selling Expenses	51,000	
Administrative Expenses	27,000	
Cost of Goods Sold	58,000	
Sales		120,000
Interest Expense	14,500	
Long-Term Notes Payable		58,000
Totals	$1,114,930	$1,114,930

Required: Prepare a balance sheet for Bridge Corporation at December 31, 2005. You may ignore income taxes.

LO3   **EXERCISE 4-13   Analysis of Balance Sheet Items**
Your boss at Tipper Companies is concerned about the company's ability to meet its operating payables and its current maturities of long-term debt.

Required: In a memo to your boss, outline the types of analysis measurements that you could perform in order to address her concerns.

LO3   **EXERCISE 4-14   Percentage Analysis of the Balance Sheet**
CalKing Skateboard Company's balance sheet as of August 31, 2005, appears on the next page.

Required: After performing a selected percentage analysis of the balance sheet based on total assets, answer the following questions:

1. Which asset makes up 46.8 percent of total assets?

2. What percentage of total assets is represented by net property and equipment?

3. What percentage of total liabilities and stockholders' equity is represented by retained earnings?

CalKing Skateboard Company
Balance Sheet
August 31, 2005

Assets

Current assets		
Cash		$ 90,000
Accounts receivable	$180,000	
Less allowance for doubtful accounts	40,000	140,000
Notes receivable		70,000
Merchandise inventories		425,000
Prepaid insurance		20,000
Total current assets		$745,000
Noncurrent assets		
Property and equipment:		
Land	$ 30,000	
Buildings	55,000	
Equipment	18,000	
	$103,000	
Less accumulated depreciation	20,000	
Net property and equipment		83,000
Patent		80,000
Total assets		$908,000

Liabilities and Stockholders' Equity

Current liabilities		
Accounts payable		$ 27,000
Sales salaries payable		4,000
Current maturities of long-term debt		9,500
Total current liabilities		$ 40,500
Long-term liabilities		
Notes payable		60,000
Stockholders' equity		
Common stock, no par, 300,000 shares		
authorized, 175,000 shares outstanding	$450,000	
Retained earnings	357,500	
Total stockholders' equity		807,500
Total liabilities and stockholders' equity		$908,000

4. The management of CalKing has expressed a goal of keeping total liabilities at no more than 10 percent of total assets. Has the company reached this goal? Explain.

LO2 **EXERCISE 4-15   Statement of Changes in Stockholders' Equity**

Randolph Properties reported the following account balances at December 31, 2004 and 2005:

	2004	2005
Common Stock	$500,500	$760,000
Additional Paid-in Capital	95,600	124,000
Treasury Stock	0	75,000
Accumulated Other Comprehensive Income	28,000	39,000
Retained Earnings	375,500	?

The company paid dividends of $35,700 during the year and reported a net loss of $25,400. Other comprehensive income in this period resulted from an unrealized gain from a foreign currency translation.

Required: Prepare a statement of changes in stockholders' equity for Randolph Properties.

LO1   **EXERCISE 4-16   Measurement of Balance Sheet Items**
A list of items commonly found on the balance sheet appears below:

A. Monetary assets

B. Nonmonetary assets

C. Investments and funds

D. Intangible assets

E. Long-term liabilities

F. Paid-in capital

G. Current liabilities

H. Operating assets

Required: For each method of measurement listed below, identify the item or items on the balance sheet (A–H) that are appropriate to that measurement.

1. Measured at historical cost

2. Measured at net realizable value

3. Measured at fair market value

4. Measured at lower of cost or market

5. Measured at discounted present value of future principal and interest payments at the yield at time of issue

6. Measured at the historical cost less depreciation or amortization to date

LO4   **EXERCISE 4-17   Balance Sheet Limitations**
The selected transactions and events listed below occurred at Spry Technologies during 2005:

A. Spry conducted meetings with Plainview Software in which the designs, marketing strategies, and functionality of a new technology that will revolutionize the way business uses the Internet were discussed. An arrangement was made for a mid-2006 launch of the product.

B. The company declared and paid dividends to its preferred stockholders.

C. Spry operates one of its manufacturing divisions in Mexico. Recent political changes in that country make the continuation of this division questionable in the coming year. In the event of closure, costs are unknown.

D. The company issued 40,000 shares of its common stock.

E. The company was recognized by *Good Business* magazine as the "Top IT Company" of 2005. Management believes this publicity will increase sales substantially next year.

F. The company signed a long-term note payable for $450,000.

Required: Identify the transactions or events in this list that affect the balance sheet or statement of changes in stockholders' equity. Identify the transactions that will not appear on the face of either statement.

PROBLEMS

LO1, 3, 4   **PROBLEM 4-1   Accounting Equation and Elements**
Barrie Corporation reported the following information at December 31, 2005, in thousands:

Long-term debt	$600	Property, plant, and equipment	$1,460
Retained earnings	?	Common stock	470
Current assets	320	Current liabilities	280

Required: Determine the totals of the three elements of the accounting equation.

Analyze: If Barrie Corporation's current ratio is 1.14 and the industry average is 2.0, how liquid is Barrie compared to the industry?

Communicate: What are the limitations of a historically based balance sheet? Why does GAAP still require the historical cost measurement on many of the assets presented?

LO2 PROBLEM 4-2 **Statement of Changes in Stockholders' Equity**
The following amounts were taken from Paperline, Inc.'s accounts.

Retained Earnings, January 1, 2005	$16,000
Unrealized Loss from Available-for-Sale Securities, net of tax, January 1, 2005	8,000
Unrealized Loss from Available-for-Sale Securities, net of tax, December 31, 2005	3,000
Net income for the year ended December 31, 2005	70,000
Additional Paid-in Capital, January 1, 2005 balance	92,000
Prior period adjustment before income tax	15,000
Common Stock, $3 par value, January 1, 2005 balance	12,000
Cash dividends declared and paid during 2005	11,000

The company issued 3,000 shares of its common stock for $45,000 during 2005. The prior period adjustment made during 2005 is from depreciation that was inadvertently omitted during 2002. The company has a 30 percent income tax rate.

Required: Use a columnar format to prepare a statement of changes in stockholders' equity for Paperline, Inc. for the year ended December 31, 2005. Include comprehensive income as a component.

Analyze: By what net amount did the Retained Earnings account change during 2005? What transactions or events affected the balance?

Spreadsheet: Use a spreadsheet application to prepare the statement of changes in stockholders' equity for Paperline, Inc.

LO1 PROBLEM 4-3 **Classifying Accounts as Balance Sheet Elements**
The bookkeeper for Peters Corporation needs your help in classifying selected accounts into one of the following balance sheet elements:

CA	Current assets		CL	Current liabilities
IF	Investments and funds		LTL	Long-term liabilities
PPE	Property, plant, and equipment		PIC	Paid-in capital
INT	Intangible assets		OCI	Other comprehensive income
OA	Other assets		RE	Retained earnings

The company's accounts are listed below:

A. Research and Development Costs

B. Undeveloped Land (not being used)

C. Merchandise Inventories

D. Current Installments of Long-Term Debt

E. Accumulated Depletion

F. Unrealized Loss from Available-for-Sale Investments

G. Accrued Interest on 2-year Note Receivable

H. Construction in Progress

I. Cash Surrender Value of Life Insurance

J. Copper Ore Mines

K. Preferred Stock

L. Goodwill

M. Cash Equivalents

N. Accrued Salaries Payable

O. Unexpired Insurance Expense

P. Unearned Subscription Revenue

Q. Investment in Subsidiary

R. Deferred Revenues

S. Finished Goods

T. Bond Retirement Fund

Required: For each account listed, indicate its classification on the balance sheet by selecting the abbreviation of the appropriate section from the list of balance sheet elements provided. Indicate contra accounts by using the label "contra" along with the abbreviation of the appropriate section. For any account that does not appear on the balance sheet, use X.

Analyze: While there are general conventions for preparing the balance sheet, why do you think there is no single standard required format under international GAAP?

LO1, 3   PROBLEM 4-4   **Balance Sheet Calculations, Ratio Analysis**
Selected information for Blackburn, Inc. for 2006 and 2005 is presented below:

	2006	2005
Total liabilities balance as of December 31	$230,000	$180,000
Retained earnings balance as of December 31	55,000	62,000
Net income	?	42,000
Cash dividends paid	56,000	20,000
Cash dividends declared	61,000	18,000
Additional paid-in capital balance as of December 31	150,000	150,000
Common stock balance as of December 31	24,000	24,000

Required:

1. Calculate total stockholders' equity at December 31, 2005.

2. Calculate total assets as of December 31, 2006. (*Hint:* Use the accounting equation.)

Analyze: What kind of ratio analysis would help determine how efficiently Blackburn uses its assets?

LO3   PROBLEM 4-5   **Trend Analysis**
Mr. Barfield, the CEO of Barfield Hardware and Building Supplies, Inc., has asked you to perform a trend analysis from 2005 to 2006. He has e-mailed you the balance sheets provided below as of December 31, 2006 and 2005.

	December 31, 2006	December 31, 2005
Assets		
Current assets		
Cash	$ 21,000	$ 41,000
Accounts receivable	23,000	18,000
Notes receivable	40,000	40,000
Inventories	19,000	12,000
Prepaid expenses	8,000	2,000
Total current assets	$111,000	$113,000
Plant assets, net	120,000	134,000
Total assets	$231,000	$247,000
Liabilities and Stockholders' Equity		
Current liabilities		
Accounts payable	$ 30,000	$ 45,000
Other accruals	12,000	8,000
Total current liabilities	$ 42,000	$ 53,000
Long-term liabilities	122,000	136,000
Total liabilities	$164,000	$189,000
Stockholders' equity		
Capital stock	25,000	20,000
Retained earnings	42,000	38,000
Total liabilities and stockholders' equity	$231,000	$247,000

Required: Perform a trend analysis from 2005 to 2006, indicating the percentage change for each line item on the balance sheet.

Communicate and Analyze: Write a short memo to Mr. Barfield with your analysis of the changes that warrant further investigation.

LO1, 2   PROBLEM 4-6   **Statement of Changes in Stockholders' Equity and Balance Sheet**

The bookkeeper for Wilson Electrical provided the following selected accounts and balances as of December 31, 2005 and 2004:

	2005	2004
Cash Dividends Payable	$ 28,000	$18,000
Additional Paid-in Capital	102,000	60,000
Retained Earnings	163,000	45,000
Foreign Currency Translation Gain/(Loss)	62,000	78,000
Unrealized Gain/(Loss) from Available-for-Sale Securities	(3,000)	12,000
Common Stock, par value, $1.00	19,000	16,000

Additional information concerning the accounts follows:

A. Cash dividends of $28,000 were declared on December 15, 2005, payable January 15, 2006.

B. The company issued 3,000 shares of its common stock on July 1, 2005.

C. Net income was $142,000 for 2004 and $146,000 for 2005.

D. There are 100,000 shares of common stock authorized.

E. The comprehensive income items are net of income tax.

Required:

1. Prepare the stockholders' equity section of Wilson Electrical's balance sheet at December 31, 2005.

2. Prepare the statement of changes in stockholders' equity for the year ended December 31, 2005.

Analyze: What is the difference between the information provided in the statement of changes in stockholders' equity and that provided in the stockholders' equity section of the balance sheet? How do the dates on the two statements reflect this?

LO1   PROBLEM 4-7   **Classifying and Describing Balance Sheet Elements**

The bookkeeper for Manasis Corporation needs your help in classifying selected accounts into one of the following balance sheet elements:

CA	Current assets
IF	Investments and funds
PPE	Property, plant, and equipment
INT	Intangible assets
OA	Other assets
CL	Current liabilities
LTL	Long-term liabilities
PIC	Paid-in capital
OCI	Other comprehensive income
RE	Retained earnings

The company's accounts are listed below:

A. Additional Paid-in Capital

B. Land (used as a parking lot)

C. Prepaid Property Taxes

D. Current Portion of Long-Term Mortgage

E. Accumulated Depreciation

F. Unrealized Gain from Available-for-Sale Securities

G. Gain on Sale of Equipment

H. Deferred Subscription Revenue

I. Sales Taxes Payable

J. Patents

Required: For each account listed, indicate its classification on the balance sheet by selecting the abbreviation of the appropriate section from the list of balance sheet elements provided. Indicate contra accounts by using the label "contra" along with the abbreviation of the appropriate section. For any account that does not appear on the balance sheet, use X. Describe the nature of each balance sheet account using your knowledge of what transactions cause the account to increase.

Analyze: Is Deferred Subscription Revenue considered monetary? Why or why not?

LO1, 4   **PROBLEM 4-8   Measurement of Balance Sheet Elements**

Watson Widgets provided the following list of accounts from its balance sheet:

Accounts Receivable

Notes Receivable

Merchandise Inventories

Prepaid Expenses

Cash Dividends Payable

Additional Paid-in Capital

Buildings

Long-Term Mortgage Payable

Common Stock

Required: Indicate how each of the accounts listed is measured.

Analyze: What limitations exist as a result of using historical cost to measure assets on the balance sheet? Which items might be missing from historical cost financial reports?

LO1   **PROBLEM 4-9   Measurement of Balance Sheet Elements**

Balance sheet items are measured differently based on the nature of the specific element. Possible measurements are

A. Par value

B. Present value of cash flows

C. Fair value at balance sheet date

D. Lower of cost or market

E. Net realizable value

F. Historical cost

G. Current cost of replacement

H. Amount payable when due

I. Original cost less accumulated depletion

J. Original cost less accumulated amortization

K. Original cost less accumulated depreciation

The following accounts were taken from the balance sheet of DriFast, Inc.:

1. Common Stock

2. Copyrights

3. Coal Deposits

4. Land (in use)

5. Property, Plant, and Equipment

6. Accounts Receivable

7. Bonds Payable (maturing in 6 months)

8. Trade Accounts Payable

9. Note Payable (due in 2 years)

10. Mortgage Receivable

11. Investment in General Motors' stock

12. Merchandise Inventory

Required: Use the code letters (A–L) for the measurement valuations to identify the most probable measurement method for each balance sheet item (1–12) listed. You may use some items more than once and some not at all.

Analyze: When an impairment of an asset has occurred, how is the asset valued?

LO1 PROBLEM 4-10 **Classifying and Measuring Balance Sheet Elements**

Elements of the balance sheet are listed below:

CA	Current assets
IF	Investments and funds
PPE	Property, plant, and equipment
INT	Intangible assets
OA	Other assets
CL	Current liabilities
LTL	Long-term liabilities
PIC	Paid-in capital
OCI	Other comprehensive income
RE	Retained earnings

The selected accounts for the company are as follows:

1. Accrued Interest on Long-Term Bonds Payable

2. Allowance for Uncollectible Accounts

3. Prepaid Insurance

4. Salaries Payable

5. Three-Year Note Receivable (matures in 1 month)

6. Investment in Mutual Fund

7. Treasury Stock

8. Cash Equivalents

9. Accumulated Depletion

10. Oil Reserves

11. Goodwill

12. Land (held for speculation)

13. Raw Materials

14. Investment in Public Company Stock

15. Deposit Paid to Utility Company (to be refunded at end of service period)

Required:

1. For each account listed, indicate its balance sheet classification by selecting the abbreviation of the appropriate section from the list of balance sheet elements provided. Indicate contra accounts by using the label "contra" along with the abbreviation of the appropriate section. For any account that does not appear on the balance sheet, use X.

2. State the most probable measurement valuation for each account.

Analyze: What controversy surrounds the recording of operating leases? What method of recording would provide transparency in reporting?

LO3   **PROBLEM 4-11**   **Percentage Analysis**

Mr. Media, the CEO of Media Time, Inc., has asked you to provide some financial analysis for 2005 and 2006. The company's balance sheets as of December 31, 2006 and 2005 are as follows.

	December 31, 2006	December 31, 2005
Assets		
Current assets		
Cash	$ 21,000	$ 41,000
Accounts receivable	23,000	18,000
Notes receivable	40,000	40,000
Inventories	19,000	12,000
Prepaid expenses	8,000	2,000
Total current assets	$111,000	$113,000
Plant assets, net	120,000	134,000
Total assets	$231,000	$247,000
Liabilities and Stockholders' Equity		
Current liabilities		
Accounts payable	$ 30,000	$ 45,000
Other accruals	12,000	8,000
Total current liabilities	$ 42,000	$ 53,000
Long-term liabilities	122,000	136,000
Total liabilities	$164,000	$189,000
Stockholders' equity		
Capital stock	25,000	20,000
Retained earnings	42,000	38,000
Total liabilities and stockholders' equity	$231,000	$247,000

Required: Complete a percentage analysis for Media Time, Inc.

Analyze: Provide a short memo to Mr. Media outlining any pertinent findings.

CASES

LO1   **CRITICAL THINKING CASE 4-1**   **International Accounting**

According to *International Accounting Standard No. 7*, the International Accounting Standards Board requires that financial statements include a balance sheet, an income statement, a statement showing changes in equity, a cash flow statement, and accounting policies and explanatory notes.

Required:

1. Describe the balance sheet classification formats allowed by *IAS No. 7*. How do these compare to reporting requirements under U.S. GAAP?

2. According to the Securities and Exchange Commission, only U.S. GAAP is permitted for firms that are publicly listed in the United States. Do you agree with this policy? Why or why not?

LO3   RESEARCH CASE 4-2   **Benchmarking and Ratio Analysis**

It is important for investors and analysts to understand how one company's performance and financial condition compares to those of other companies in the same industry. The "Benchmarking Assistant" tool found at EdgarScan **http://edgarscan.pwcglobal.com/ servlets/edgarscan**) provides valuable comparative data for most U.S. companies.

Required:

1. Use the "Benchmarking Assistant" on EdgarScan to compare the following financial ratios and measurements for Staples, Inc. and Office Depot for the three fiscal years given. After selecting **Staples** and **Office Depot** on the "Companies" tab, click the "Graph" tab and select the following financial data from the pull-down menu. Remember to select "3" and "2002" from the pull-down list of "Years" for which financial data are to be displayed. Prepare a spreadsheet containing the amounts displayed, using the format of the table that follows.

2. If you were a potential investor, which company would you favor? Why?

Measurement	Year	Staples	Office Depot
Current ratio	2000		
	2001		
	2002		
Quick ratio	2000		
	2001		
	2002		
Liabilities to assets	2000		
	2001		
	2002		
Inventory turnover ratio	2000		
	2001		
	2002		
Asset turnover ratio	2000		
	2001		
	2002		

LO3   ANALYSIS CASE 4-3   **Financial Analysis**

Lowe's is a do-it-yourself hardware and building supplies store. The company's consolidated balance sheets as of January 28, 2005 and January 30, 2004 are presented in the Financial Reporting Case at the beginning of this chapter.

Required: Prepare a table showing percentage changes over these two fiscal periods to identify how the following items have changed: total current assets, total assets, total current liabilities, and total stockholders' equity.

LO1   ETHICS CASE 4-4   **Classifying Accounts Receivables**

ETHICS

Adele Braun is the accounts receivable manager at Macheni Company, a wholesaler of kitchen appliances. One of Macheni's new customers, Albert, Inc., recently placed a major order. The merchandise has been delivered, and the receivable, which represents approximately 40 percent of the company's accounts receivable balance, is still outstanding at the end of the fiscal year. Adele knows that the president of Macheni is a personal friend of the owner of Albert, Inc. and negotiated the sale with the owner. She also has been informed that while the sales contract specifies that the receivable is due in full in February of the upcoming year, the president has informally negotiated a longer payment period with the customer. In fact, about half of the receivable is expected to be collected in 16 months.

At the beginning of January, prior to the issuance of the previous year's financial statements, Adele is surprised to learn that the entire receivable has been classified as a short-term receivable. She decides to speak to the controller and the vice president of Macheni about the informal agreement that significantly extended the due date for half of Albert, Inc.'s receivable. The vice president replies that according to the company's president, the customer may pay within the next few months. Adele feels uneasy about this response, but the vice president dismisses her concerns and tells her not to spend any more time on this issue.

Required:

1. What is the accounting issue that the accounts receivable manager is concerned about?
2. What will be the effect on the financial statements if the entire receivable is classified as short-term? What ratios will be affected?
3. What is the ethical issue faced by the accounts receivable manager?
4. Who will be affected by the decision to classify the receivable as short-term?
5. What values and principles are likely to influence the decision?
6. What alternative actions can the accounts receivable manager take?
7. a. Whose interests are most important?
   b. Which values and principles are most important?
   c. Which of the possible consequences will do the most good or cause the least harm?
   d. Which consideration is most important?
8. What would you do if you were Adele?

LO3

 ETHICS

ETHICS CASE 4-5   The Effect of Expansion

In an effort to expand its market share, **Lowe's** has undertaken an extensive expansion project to add a significant number of new stores in the U.S. market. This expansion project will heighten its competition with **Home Depot**, the largest home improvement retail business and Lowe's primary competitor. The opening of new stores carries both benefits and risks.

This expansion strategy has added a significant amount of new assets to the company's balance sheet and provides the potential for increased earnings and a higher growth rate. As a result of the expansion, Lowe's revenues and profits have increased, and it has outperformed its competitor in terms of growth rate. [9]

Lowe's strategy also carries risk associated with the additional debt required to finance the expansion, which affects key analysis measurements. For the year ended October 31, 2003, Lowe's return on assets was 10.33 percent and its return on equity was 20.22 percent. In comparison, its competitor's return on assets was 12.23 percent and its return on equity was 19.27 percent. Lowe's debt to equity ratio, a key indicator of risk exposure, has risen to 38.1 percent. In comparison, Home Depot's debt to equity ratio is only 6.1 percent. [10]

Whereas expansion financed by borrowing funds at favorable rates may preserve and potentially enhance the return to stockholders, a higher asset base may slow growth, reduce the return on assets, or expose the owners of the company to risk. As explained in this chapter, the return on assets is typically viewed as an indicator of how well a company is managing and utilizing its assets.

---

9 Mary Ellen Lloyd, "Lowe's 2nd-Period Net Rose 28% with Weather, Marketing Cited," *Wall Street Journal*, August 19, 2003, p. B12.

10 Ratios obtained from **http://finance.yahoo.com**. Accessed 03/15/04.

Suppose you were the CEO of a company like Lowe's and additional expansions are pending. Assume that your primary competitor is also expanding, increasing the competitive pressure in the market segment. Suppose that you have just learned that your company's return on assets has decreased. You fear that further expansion could further decrease this measurement, yet you have been promised additional compensation if the expansion is successful. You also wonder how much risk exposure your stockholders are comfortable with.

Required:

1. What are the issues that should be considered in this situation?

2. What parties will be affected by your decision?

3. How could the return on assets decrease even if revenue and income are increasing?

4. What are your potential courses of action?

5. Would you recommend scaling back the expansion project to preserve the company's returns? Should compensation issues affect your decision?

LO1 **RESEARCH CASE 4-6   Off-Balance-Sheet Financing**
Since the passage of the Sarbanes-Oxley Act of 2002, regulatory agencies and private organizations that promulgate accounting standards have targeted past abuses that have caused financial failures, including those of Enron and WorldCom. One of the most common abuses was off-balance-sheet financing. **Coca-Cola** has also encountered off-balance-sheet considerations with regard to its bottlers and other related entities.

Required:

1. Visit the Investopedia website at **www.investopedia.com**. How does Investopedia define off-balance-sheet financing? How might off-balance-sheet financing items be considered a limitation of the balance sheet?

2. Locate the 2003 and 2004 10-K annual reports for Coca-Cola. Read the Management's Discussion and Analysis sections. What off-balance-sheet financing does Coca-Cola disclose?

LO1, 3, 4 **CRITICAL THINKING CASE 4-7   Asset Measurement**
With the acquisition of **Time Warner** by **AOL** in 1999, one of the largest "soft" assets ever to exist was created—AOL recorded an intangible asset, goodwill, from that transaction of $128 billion. Later, in January 2003, AOL Time Warner issued a news release that discussed how, under the new FASB requirements, the company had written off almost $100 billion of that balance as a result of goodwill impairment.[11]

Required:

1. What is goodwill?

2. What measurement criteria are used to report goodwill on the balance sheet?

3. Why do you think the value of an asset could fall this much in such a short period of time?

LO3 **ANALYSIS CASE 4-8   Horizontal Analysis and SIC Codes**
Rob's Warehouse Junction is a national discount chain of waterbed and mattress retailers. The company reported revenue of $40 million for 2003 with $1.2 million in net income, and is expected to have revenue of $45 million for 2004 with $2.0 million of net income. Rob's CFO, Harry Mullins, has asked you to determine the "best" furniture operators in standard industrial classification (SIC) 5712. This is the SIC in which Rob's Warehouse Junction falls. Harry would like to see how Rob's Warehouse Junction compares against the benchmark companies in terms of operating revenue, net income, and total assets for 2003.

---

11 Stephen Taub, "AOL Time Warner Reports $100 Billion Loss," CFO.com, January 30, 2003, available at: www.cfo.com/article/1,5309,8737%7C%7CA%7C93%7C,00.html. Accessed 4/20/04.

Required:

Use PricewaterhouseCoopers' Edgarscan website, found at **http://edgarscan.pwcglobal. com/servlets/edgarscan**. Select the link "Standard Industrial Classifications" and then select SIC code 5712.

1. Determine which company is the highest rated in the categories that Harry has requested.

2. Prepare a vertical or percentage analysis of the company with the largest amount of total assets for 2003 and 2002. What trends are evident?

LO4   **CRITICAL THINKING CASE 4-9   Human Capital**

Starbucks Coffee has become a phenomenon as a result of its growth over the last two decades. The creation of urban community gathering spots for coffee lovers has wowed Wall Street and Main Street alike. The Starbucks logo has become a widely recognized icon in current urban culture.

Required:

1. Two keys to Starbucks' success are its management team and its logo. Can either of these be reported as an asset under GAAP? Why or why not?

2. Suppose management were to recognize the value of the two "assets" mentioned in question 1, with a corresponding increase in revenue. What concepts would be violated as a result?

ON THE WEB

The following exercises, activities, and problems are available on the *Intermediate Accounting* website. Use these resources to reinforce your understanding of the topics presented in this chapter.

- CPA-Adapted Simulations
- Interpreting the Accounting Standards
- Extending the Global Focus
- Extending the Ethics Discussion
- Mastering the Spreadsheet
- Career Snapshots
- Annual Report Project
- ACE Practice Tests
- Flashcards
- Glossary
- Check Figures for Text Problems
- PowerPoint Presentations

SOLUTIONS: CHECK YOUR UNDERSTANDING

The Balance Sheet: Elements and Issues (p. 165)

1. Current assets are usually listed in decreasing order of liquidity, or ability to be converted into cash.

2. Accounts payable, accrued salaries and related expenses, sales taxes payable, deferred revenue, income taxes payable, current installments of long-term debt, and other accrued expenses are found in the current liabilities section of the balance sheet.

3. Off-balance-sheet financing occurs when a firm enters into transactions that obligate it to make future payments, but those payments are not recorded as actual liabilities at their present value. Instead, the monthly payments are recorded and expensed as incurred.

4. Operating assets are carried at acquisition cost less accumulated depreciation.

5. The following formats are allowed: (1) Separation of current assets from noncurrent assets and of current liabilities from noncurrent liabilities (the most common format in the United States); (2) presentation of assets and liabilities in order of liquidity (or in reverse order of liquidity), without distinguishing between current and noncurrent items; (3) net asset presentation (assets minus liabilities); (4) long-term financing approach.

The Statement of Changes in Stockholders' Equity (p. 167)

1. The activities reflected in the statement of changes in stockholders' equity over an accounting period might

include net income or loss, currency translations, purchases of treasury stock, issuance of common stock, issuance of cash dividends, and realized losses or gains on derivative instruments.

2. Total stockholders' equity increased by $2,605 million. Net earnings of $4,304 million had the largest impact.

Tools for Balance Sheet Analysis (p. 171)

1. Activity ratios may be used to assess the efficiency with which a firm uses its assets.

2. Liquidity ratios help analysts assess a firm's ability to meet its financial obligations in the short term.

3. Horizontal analysis is used to compare data from two or more time periods.

4. They are using benchmarking to compare the financial data of one company to those of another company in the same industry.

5. Horizontal analysis compares data for the same line items on a financial statement from different periods. Vertical (or percentage) analysis compares one line item to a base item on a financial statement.

Limitations of Balance Sheet Information (p. 173)

1. The principles of historical cost, conservatism, and objectivity limit the usefulness of balance sheet information for knowledge-based businesses.

2. Risks associated with interest-rate changes, foreign exchange rate changes, fluctuations in commodity prices, and changes in the economic or political conditions of countries in which companies operate are types of risk that are not reflected on the balance sheet.

3. Investors may be interested in unexecuted obligations because the company may have made commitments to significant future actions that will require expenditures or capital funding.

CPA-ADAPTED SIMULATION

This simulation asks you to complete various tasks related to a company's annual financial statements. If your instructor has signed up for CPAexcel™, you can do the work online at **www.cpaexcel.com/hmco**. You may also do the simulation manually.

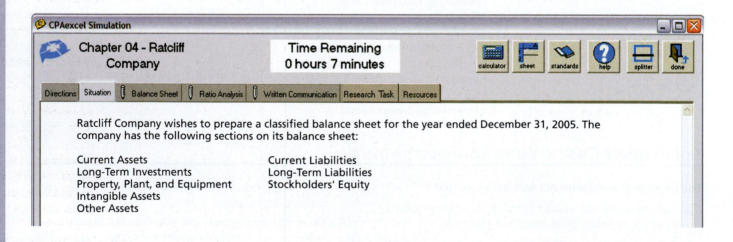

Directions | Situation | Balance Sheet | Ratio Analysis | Written Communication | Research Task | Resources

Classification Task

For each of the following accounts, indicate the section of the balance sheet in which it should appear, and indicate whether the normal balance of the account is a debit or credit.

	Section of the Balance Sheet	Normal Balance Debit or Credit
1. Advances received from customers		
2. Advances to suppliers		
3. Accrued interest on investments		
4. Allowance for Doubtful Accounts		
5. Accumulated Depreciation		
6. Accrued Salaries and Wages		
7. Capital in Excess of Par		
8. Customers' accounts with credit balances		
9. Dividends Payable		
10. Treasury Stock		

Directions | Situation | Balance Sheet | Ratio Analysis | Written Communication | Research Task | Resources

Assume that Ratcliff Company has the following financial information on its December 31 balance sheet:

Current assets

Cash and equivalents $2,852
Receivables, net $1,097
Inventories $9,400

Current liabilities

Accounts payable $5,160
Accrued liabilities $1,000
Tax payable $500

Additional information: Inventories at January 1: $9,000
Receivables at January 1: $12,000
Cost of goods sold: $27,000
Sales revenue: $115,000

Determine the following:

Current ratio:	
Quick ratio:	
Working capital:	
Inventory turnover ratio:	
Receivables turnover ratio:	

Directions | Situation | Balance Sheet | Ratio Analysis | Written Communication | Research Task | Resources

On December 31, 2005, Ratcliff Company borrowed $500,000 from a bank. The note matures in 2010. Equal payments of principal are due annually, and 10 percent interest is also paid annually, beginning on December 30, 2006. Land valued at $300,000 was used as collateral for the loan.

Draft a written response that explains what amounts should be in the current asset and current liability sections of the balance sheet of December 31, 2005. Also, indicate what additional disclosures should be made by Ratcliff pertaining to the loan.

Directions | Situation | Balance Sheet | Ratio Analysis | Written Communication | Research Task | Resources

In some cases, a long-lived asset must be tested to determine whether the amount that has been recorded for the asset is recoverable. This is referred to as a test of the impairment of the long-lived asset. According to the accounting pronouncements, what events or circumstances require a company to test for the impairment of an asset?

CHAPTER FIVE

The Statement of Cash Flows and Other Significant Financial Disclosures

FINANCIAL REPORTING CASE

AMAZON.COM FOCUSES ON GENERATING CASH FLOWS, NOT EARNINGS OR EARNINGS PER SHARE

Founder Jeff Bezos reveals through the company's financial statements how Amazon.com survived the dot-com "bust" and reached a major milestone in generating positive cash flows.

Amazon.com Jeff Bezos, the founder of Amazon.com, is clear about the company's focus on generating cash flows. The following excerpt is from his letter to stockholders in the firm's 2004 annual report:

Our ultimate financial measure, and the one we most want to drive over the long term, is free cash flow per share.

Why not focus first and foremost, as many do, on earnings, earnings per share, or earnings growth? The simple answer is that earnings don't directly translate into cash flows, and shares are worth only the present value of their future cash flows, not the present value of their future earnings. Future earnings are a component—but not the only important component—of future cash flow per share. Working capital and capital expenditures are also important, as is future share dilution.

Though some may find it counterintuitive, a company can actually impair shareholder value in certain circumstances by growing earnings. This happens when the capital investments required for growth exceed the present value of the cash flow derived from those investments.

Amazon.com

AMAZON.COM, INC.
CONSOLIDATED STATEMENTS OF CASH FLOWS
(in thousands)

Years Ended December 31,

	2004	2003	2002
CASH AND CASH EQUIVALENTS, BEGINNING OF PERIOD	$1,102,273	$738,254	$540,282
OPERATING ACTIVITIES:			
Net income (loss)	588,451	35,282	(149,132)
Adjustments to reconcile net income (loss) to net cash provided by operating activities:			
Depreciation of fixed assets, including internal-use software and website development, and other amortization	75,724	75,558	82,274
Stock-based compensation	57,702	87,751	68,927
Other operating expense (income)	(7,964)	2,752	8,948
Gains on sale of marketable securities, net	(586)	(9,598)	(5,700)
Remeasurements and other	824	130,097	109,442
Non-cash interest expense and other	4,756	12,918	29,586
Deferred income taxes	(256,696)	931	(553)
Cumulative effect of change in accounting principle	—	—	(801)
Changes in operating assets and liabilities:			
Inventories	(168,896)	(76,786)	(51,303)
Accounts receivable, net and other current assets	(1,745)	1,616	(31,704)
Accounts payable	286,091	167,732	156,542
Accrued expenses and other current liabilities	(15,110)	(27,982)	3,800
Additions to unearned revenue	109,936	101,641	95,404
Amortization of previously unearned revenue	(106,886)	(111,740)	(135,466)
Interest payable	959	1,850	3,027
Net cash provided by operating activities	566,560	392,022	174,291
INVESTING ACTIVITIES:			
Sales and maturities of marketable securities and other investments	1,426,786	813,184	553,289
Purchases of marketable securities	(1,584,089)	(535,642)	(635,810)
Purchases of fixed assets, including internal-use software and website development	(89,133)	(45,963)	(39,163)
Proceeds from sale of subsidiary	—	5,072	—
Acquisition, net of cash acquired	(71,195)	—	—
Net cash (used in) provided by investing activities	(317,631)	236,651	(121,684)
FINANCING ACTIVITIES:			
Proceeds from exercise of stock options	60,109	163,322	121,689
Repayments of long-term debt, capital lease obligations	(157,401)	(495,308)	(14,795)
Net cash (used in) provided by financing activities	(97,292)	(331,986)	106,894
Foreign-currency effect on cash and cash equivalents	48,690	67,332	38,471
Net increase in cash and cash equivalents	200,327	364,019	197,972
CASH AND CASH EQUIVALENTS, END OF PERIOD	$ 1,302,600	$1,102,273	$738,254
SUPPLEMENTAL CASH FLOW INFORMATION:			
Fixed assets acquired under capital leases and other financing arrangements	$ 860	$ 2,677	$ 3,023
Cash paid for interest	107,604	119,947	111,589
Cash paid for income taxes	4,051	1,825	1,448

Cash flow statements often don't receive as much attention as they deserve. Discerning investors don't stop with the income statement.

Our Most Important Financial Measure: Free Cash Flow Per Share

Amazon.com's financial focus is on long-term growth in free cash flow per share.

Amazon.com's free cash flow is driven primarily by increasing operating profit dollars and efficiently managing both working capital and capital expenditures. We work to increase operating profit by focusing on improving all aspects of the customer experience to grow sales and by maintaining a lean cost structure.

To illustrate how the statement of cash flows can help investors better understand the financial position of a company, consider Amazon.com, probably the best-known e-retailer in the world. As you can see from the company's consolidated statements of cash flows for 2002–2004, the company reported a net loss in 2002, a small profit in 2003, and a more significant profit in 2004. However, the last two years, 2003 and 2004, the company generated cash flows from operating activities and increased its net cash and cash equivalents during all three years presented. In fact, enough cash was generated in 2004 from operations and other activities that Amazon.com was able to make significant repayments of long-term debt, capital lease obligations, and other debt in both 2003 and 2004.

Conversely, consider **General Electric**—one of America's oldest and consistently most profitable companies. Over the last few years, GE's operations have generated cash flows of between $30 and $36 billion per year, and the company reported net income of over $15 billion for the year ended December 31, 2003 and almost $17 billion for the year ended December 31, 2004. Thus, not only is GE profitable, but it is also able to generate cash for use in all aspects of its business.

EXAMINING THE CASE

1. What amount did Amazon.com report as net cash provided by operating activities for 2003 and 2004?

2. What type(s) of transactions provided cash flows from investing activities in 2003 and 2004?

3. How might investors and analysts interpret the cash flow trend as reflected on Amazon.com's consolidated statements of cash flows?

LO1 Explain the importance of the statement of cash flows.

statement of cash flows a financial statement that shows the amount of cash collected and paid out by a firm over an accounting period for operating activities, investing activities, and financing activities

H *Critical Thinking:* Do you think that the income statement and the balance sheet provide interested parties with adequate information about cash? Why? Why not?

The Importance of the Statement of Cash Flows

The **statement of cash flows** is a financial statement that shows the amount of cash collected and paid out by a firm over an accounting period for operating activities, investing activities, and financing activities. In determining cash flows from operating activities, the statement also reconciles a firm's reported net income for the year with its change in cash for the same accounting period.

The reconciliation of net income with the change in cash for the period is helpful in explaining why some growing companies experience net losses while still generating positive cash flows. For example, there are many instances in which net income (which is affected by various accruals and deferrals) does not provide a complete picture of a company's performance. As discussed in the Financial Reporting Case, Amazon.com sustained accounting-based net losses for 2002 but was able to generate positive cash flow from operating activities in 2002, 2003, and 2004. Many analysts and users see this as a precursor to a firm's ability to generate both net income and positive cash flows, as Amazon.com did by 2003.

In some instances, a company reports net income, yet its ongoing operations do not generate a positive cash flow. For example, **Advanced Digital Information Corporation (ADIC),** an information storage solutions company, reported net income of over $95 million in 2000. However, a close look at the company's statement of cash flows shows that operating activities actually *used* over $18 million in cash. The primary difference between the net income and the cash used in operations was a $97 million gain that the company recorded on the sale of securities. These securities transactions, while they increased net income, were not part of the company's primary operations and must be considered in this light when forecasting ADIC's future cash flows.

The statement of cash flows helps users identify the major activities, both operating and nonoperating, that occurred during the period. Although it is based on information that is already contained in the balance sheet and the income statement, the statement of cash flows provides valuable insights into the performance and prospects of a firm that cannot be gleaned from only those two statements. As a result, it allows users to analyze and forecast a firm's cash receipts and disbursements more accurately.

The overall usefulness of a statement of cash flows can be seen by looking at Figure 5.1, the consolidated statements of cash flows for **Home Depot, Inc.,** one of the companies we highlighted in the previous chapter. Note that Home Depot generated net cash flows from operating activities of $6,904 million in 2004, an indicator that the company's operating activities not only provide a net profit to the company, but also bring in positive cash flows. The company used cash for investing activities in 2004 of $4,479 million and used cash through its financing activities of $3,055 million. By reviewing the cash flows from the investing activities section, users can determine that the majority of the funds used for investing activities went toward long-term investments (offset by the proceeds from sales and maturities of investments) and, to a lesser extent, capital expenditures. As noted in the annual report, this increase was primarily the result of a large increase in capital expenditures to modernize stores and $727 million

Figure 5.1

Consolidated Statements of Cash Flows

Home Depot

THE HOME DEPOT, INC. AND SUBSIDIARIES
CONSOLIDATED STATEMENTS OF CASH FLOWS

	Fiscal Year Ended[1]		
amounts in millions	January 30, 2005	February 1, 2004	February 2, 2003
CASH FLOWS FROM OPERATING ACTIVITIES:			
Net Earnings	$5,001	$4,304	$3,664
Reconcilation Net Earnings to Net Cash Provided by Operating Activities:			
Depreciation and Amortization	1,319	1,076	903
Stock-Based Compensation Expense	125	67	15
Changes in Assets and Liabilities, net of the effecs of acquisitions:	(266)	25	(38)
(Increase) Decrease in Receivables, net	(266)	25	(38)
Increase in Merchandise Inventories	(849)	(693)	(1,592)
Increase in Accounts Payable, and Accrued Liabilities	917	790	1,394
Increase in Deferred Revenue	263	279	147
Increase (Decrease) in Income Taxes Payable	2	(27)	83
Increase in Deferred Income Taxes	319	605	173
Increase in Other Long-Term Liabilities	119	33	66
Other	(46)	86	(13)
Net Cash Provided by Operating Activities	6,904	6,545	4,802

(continued)

Figure 5.1, *continued*

Consolidated Statements of Cash Flows

	2005	2004	2003
CASH FLOWS FROM INVESTING ACTIVITIES:			
Capital Expenditures, net of $38, $47 and $49 of non-cash capital expenditures in fiscal 2004, 2003 and 2002, respectively	(3,948)	(3,508)	(2,749)
Purchase of Assets from Off-Balance Sheet Financing Arrangement	—	(598)	—
Payments for Businesses Acquired, net	(727)	(215)	(235)
Proceeds from Sales of Businesses, net	—	—	22
Proceeds from Sales of Property and Equipment	96	265	105
Purchases of Investments	(25,890)	(38,649)	(38,367)
Proceeds from Sales and Maturities of Investments	25,990	38,534	38,623
Net Cash Used in Investing Activities	(4,479)	(4,171)	(2,601)
CASH FLOWS FROM FINANCING ACTIVITIES:			
Proceeds from Long-Term Borrowings, net of discount	995	—	1
Repayments of Long-Term Debt	(510)	(9)	—
Repurchase of Common Stock	(3,106)	(1,554)	(2,000)
Proceeds from Sale of Common Stock, net	285	227	326
Cash Dividends Paid to Stockholders	(719)	(595)	(492)
Net Cash Used in Financing Activities	(3,055)	(1,931)	(2,165)
(Decrease) Increase in Cash and Cash Equivalents	(630)	443	36
Effect of Exchange Rate Changes on Cash and Cash Equivalents	33	20	8
Cash and Cash Equivalents of Beginning of Year	1,103	640	596
Cash and Cash Equivalents at End of Year	$ 506	$ 1,103	$ 640
SUPPLEMENTAL DISCLOSURE OF CASH PAYMENTS MADE FOR:			
Interest, net of interest capitalized	$ 78	$ 70	$ 50
Income Taxes	$ 2,793	$ 2,037	$ 1,951

(1) Fiscal years ended January 30, 2005, February 1, 2004 and February 2, 2003 include 52 weeks.

to purchase (1) **White Cap**, a leading distributor of specialty hardware, tools, and materials, and (2) **Home Mart**, the second-largest home improvement retailer in Mexico. The statement of cash flows also reveals that the company used cash to repurchase common stock ($3,106 million), paid cash dividends of $719 million, and received proceeds from long-term borrowings of $995 million. These details related to cash flows are not readily available on either the balance sheet or the income statement, making the statement of cash flows a valuable tool for the investor and analyst.

> **CHECK YOUR UNDERSTANDING**
>
> 1. Describe the primary purpose of the statement of cash flows.
>
> 2. How can the statement of cash flows help analysts and investors in a way that the balance sheet or the income statement cannot?

LO2 Describe how the statement of cash flows is structured.

Critical Thinking: If you were to prepare a report on the sources and uses of your personal cash, how would you structure the statement? If you received cash from sources other than a paycheck from your job, would you categorize these receipts differently?

The Structure of the Statement of Cash Flows

The standards for the preparation of the statement are found in *Statement of Financial Accounting Standards No. 95*, "The Statement of Cash Flows." The format of the statement of cash flows is straightforward. The increases and decreases in cash and cash equivalents for the period are summarized in three main categories:

- Cash flows from operating activities
- Cash flows from investing activities
- Cash flows from financing activities

In addition, the effect of foreign currency translations on cash is disclosed, and the beginning and ending cash balances are reconciled. Any noncash transactions are disclosed in a separate schedule or in the notes to the statement.

cash equivalents highly liquid investments that are easily converted into cash

The statement of cash flows reconciles the balances of cash and cash equivalents at the end of the period from that at the beginning of the period. **Cash equivalents** are highly liquid investments that are easily convertible into cash. Usually, investments with original maturities of three months or less qualify as cash equivalents. Because they are close to maturity, the risk of any change in value is insignificant, and the transaction cost to convert these securities to cash is relatively insignificant. As a firm can easily switch back and forth between these investments and cash without loss of principal, cash equivalents are considered cash for the purposes of the statement of cash flows. The investments that are classified as cash equivalents are usually disclosed in the notes to the financial statements and are likely to include such items as commercial paper, certificates of deposits, U.S. government securities, and similar items.

cash flows from operating activities cash receipts and payments resulting from the operations of a firm's core business

Cash flows from operating activities are cash receipts and payments resulting from the operations of a firm's core business. These include cash receipts from sales and fee revenue, interest revenue, dividend revenue, and the sale of trading securities, and cash payments for inventory purchases, wages and salaries, operating expenses, tax expense, and interest expense. The FASB requires that interest revenue and expense be included in cash flows from operating activities, but on the income statement, they may be and often are omitted from the determination of income from operations. The FASB reasoned that even though interest revenue and interest expense are not normally included in the determination of operating income, they are included in the determination of net income and should therefore be classified as operating cash flows.

cash flows from investing activities cash receipts and payments resulting from a firm's long-term investments and disinvestments in productive assets, such as plant and equipment

Cash flows from investing activities are cash receipts and payments resulting from a firm's long-term investments and disinvestments in productive assets, such as plant and equipment. For most firms, cash payments for plant assets are common, as are purchases of marketable and longer-term securities. Investments in such assets are necessary because they provide the base of revenue production for most firms. Any proceeds from the sale of those productive assets are also included in cash flows from investing activities. Other common cash flows in this category are receipts from the sale of a component of an entity and the collection of a note receivable, as well as payments for the purchase of a business and the issuance of a note receivable for cash.

cash flows from financing activities cash receipts and payments related to liabilities and owners' equity (other than through operations)

Cash flows from financing activities are cash receipts and payments related to long-term liabilities and owners' equity (other than through operations). Financing activities that provide cash inflows to the firm include the issuance of debt securities, such as bonds, notes, and mortgages, and the issuance of equity securities, such as common or preferred stock. Among the most common financing activities that result in cash outflows are the repayment of debt securities, the repurchase of common stock (treasury stock), and the payment of dividends. Illustration 5.1 summarizes the classification of various cash receipts and payments on the statement of cash flows.

USING THE ACCOUNTING EQUATION TO UNDERSTAND THE STATEMENT OF CASH FLOWS

The accounting equation can be revised to reflect the information provided by the statement of cash flows. First, assume that all changes in account balances on the balance sheet are the result of a cash inflow or outflow. (Recall that significant noncash investing and financing transactions are not disclosed in the body of the statement, but are put in a separate schedule. Also recall that we are using the term *cash* to include both cash and cash equivalents.) Then evaluate the accounts on the balance sheet for changes that affected cash. To accomplish this, the accounting equation needs to be

Illustration 5.1

Classification of Cash Receipts and Payments on the Statement of Cash Flows

Cash Flows from Operating Activities	
Cash Receipts From	**Cash Payments For**
Sales, fee revenue	Inventory purchases
Interest revenue	Wages and salaries
Dividend revenue	Operating expenses
Sale of trading securities	Tax expense
	Interest expense

Cash Flows from Investing Activities	
Cash Receipts From	**Cash Payments For**
Sale of investment securities	Purchase of investment securities
Sale of plant assets	Purchase of plant assets
Sale of a component of an entity*	Purchase of a business
Collection of a note receivable	Issuance of a note receivable in exchange for cash

Cash Flows from Financing Activities	
Cash Receipts From	**Cash Payments For**
Issuance of debt securities	Repayment of debt securities
Issuance of equity securities	Repurchase of common stock (treasury stock)
	Payment of dividends

* *Component of an entity* is the term generally used by the FASB in recent standards to describe what used to be thought of as a business segment.

rearranged so that the balance sheet is viewed from the perspective of cash. Cash will be on the left side of the equation, and all the other balance sheet accounts will be on the right side. To illustrate, begin with the usual accounting equation:

$$\text{Assets} = \text{Liabilities} + \text{Stockholders' Equity}$$

When assets are defined as cash (and cash equivalents) + noncash assets, the accounting equation is rewritten as follows:

$$\text{Cash} + \text{Noncash Assets} = \text{Liabilities} + \text{Stockholders' Equity}$$

The accounting equation is again rewritten, this time with only cash on the left side:

$$\text{Cash} = \text{Liabilities} + \text{Stockholders' Equity} - \text{Noncash Assets}$$

When we evaluate the changes (represented as Δ) in the elements on the balance sheet, the change in cash is related to the changes in the other elements:

$$\Delta\, \text{Cash} = \Delta\, \text{Liabilities} + \Delta\, \text{Stockholders' Equity} - \Delta\, \text{Noncash Assets}$$

The application of the equation to specific balance sheet items is shown in Illustration 5.2. As the table shows, an increase in cash is related to an increase in liabilities, an increase in stockholders' equity, a decrease in noncash assets, or a mixture of these changes. For example, cash is increased when a company borrows money (an increase in debt), when it issues stock (an increase in stockholders' equity), or when it sells noncash assets (a reduction in noncash assets such as equipment or land). The reverse also holds true: cash is decreased when a company pays off debt (a reduction in

Illustration 5.2

Cash-Related Effects of Changes in Elements of the Balance Sheet

Δ Cash	=	Δ Liabilities	+	Δ Stockholders' Equity	−	Δ Noncash Assets	Example
Increase		Increase					Cash, Notes Payable
Increase				Increase			Cash, Common Stock
Increase						Decrease	Cash, Note Receivable
Decrease		Decrease					Cash, Accounts Payable
Decrease				Decrease			Cash, Retained Earnings (Dividends)
Decrease						Increase	Cash, Equipment

liabilities), buys back its own stock or pays dividends (a reduction in stockholders' equity), or purchases noncash assets (an increase in noncash assets).

> **CHECK YOUR UNDERSTANDING**
>
> 1. What three main sections of the statement of cash flows are used to categorize changes in cash and cash equivalents?
>
> 2. List three potential transactions that would result in cash outflows categorized as financing activities on the statement of cash flows.
>
> 3. To find cash flows from financing activities, which accounts are evaluated?

LO3 **Prepare a statement of cash flows.**

Critical Thinking: *"The statement of cash flows is the easiest of all the financial statements to prepare." Do you agree? Why or why not?*

Preparing the Statement of Cash Flows

This chapter discusses the purposes and uses of the statement of cash flows and presents an overview of how to prepare the statement of cash flows. You will find a more detailed discussion of the statement in Chapter 19. The statement of cash flows is often prepared after the income statement and balance sheet because much of the required data is drawn from those two statements. There are usually four steps in the preparation of this statement:

1. Determine the cash provided by or used in operating activities.

2. Determine the cash provided by or used in investing activities.

3. Determine the cash provided by or used in financing activities.

4. Determine the change (increase or decrease) in cash during the period and determine the ending balance of cash and cash equivalents.

We will use Amazon.com's statement of cash flows for the year ended December 31, 2004, to illustrate these four steps.

STEP 1: DETERMINE CASH FLOWS FROM OPERATING ACTIVITIES

Cash flows from operating activities are closely related to net income. Cash receipts from operating activities include cash collected from customers. Cash payments for operating activities include payments for inventory and operating expenses. Net income does not represent cash flow, however, so cash flows from operations must be reconciled with the net income reported for the period. This may be done by using either the indirect method or direct method of reporting cash flows from operations.

Figure 5.2

Operating Activities Section of the Statements of Cash Flows

Amazon.com

AMAZON.COM, INC.
OPERATING ACTIVITIES SECTION OF CONSOLIDATED STATEMENTS OF CASH FLOWS
(in thousands)

	Years Ended December 31,		
	2004	**2003**	**2002**
CASH AND CASH EQUIVALENTS, BEGINNING OF PERIOD	$1,102,273	$738,254	$540,282
OPERATING ACTIVITIES:			
Net income (loss)	588,451	35,282	(149,132)
Adjustments to reconcile net income (loss) to net cash provided by operating activities:			
Depreciation of fixed assets, including internal-use software and website development, and other amortization	75,724	75,558	82,274
Stock-based compensation	57,702	87,751	68,927
Other operating expense (income)	(7,964)	2,752	8,948
Gains on sale of marketable securities, net	(586)	(9,598)	(5,700)
Remeasurements and other	824	130,097	100,442
Non-cash interest expense and other	4,756	12,918	29,586
Deferred income taxes	(256,696)	931	(553)
Cumulative effect of change in accounting principle	—	—	(801)
Changes in operating assets and liabilities:			
Inventories	(168,896)	(76,786)	(51,303)
Accounts receivable, net and other current assets	(1,745)	1,616	(31,704)
Accounts payable	286,091	167,732	156,542
Accrued expenses and other current liabilities	(15,110)	(27,982)	3,800
Additions to unearned revenue	109,936	101,641	95,404
Amortization of previously unearned revenue	(106,886)	(111,740)	(135,466)
Interest payable	959	1,850	3,027
Net cash provided by operating activities	566,560	392,022	174,291

❯ THE INDIRECT METHOD

indirect method a method of calculating cash flows from operating activities in which net income is adjusted for items that do not affect cash flows

In the United States, the indirect method is more commonly used to calculate cash flows from operating activities. Under the **indirect method**, net income is adjusted for items that *do not* affect cash flows, including depreciation, amortization, depletion, gains, losses, and changes in current assets and current liabilities. When the indirect method is used, net income, as determined in the income statement, is listed first. Net income is then reconciled to net cash provided by or used in operations by making the adjustments for noncash items such as those listed above.

For illustrative purposes, the operating activities section of Amazon.com's consolidated statements of cash flows is presented in Figure 5.2.

Amazon.com used the following process to calculate cash flows from operations for 2004 using the indirect method:

● Amazon.com's net income of $588,451 thousand is the starting point in determining net cash provided by operating activities.

● Amazon.com must make adjustments for three types of noncash transactions that are included in the determination of net income but are not included in the determination of cash flows from operating activities. The first type is *operating transactions that increased or decreased net income but had no cash flow effect,* such as the cumulative effect of an accounting change and depreciation, amortization, and other noncash items. For example, depreciation reduces net income but involves no cash flows;

it is just an allocation of an asset's cost to current and future accounting periods. The cash outflow took place in the period in which the asset was paid for and was shown at that time as an addition to property and equipment in the investing activities category. Remember, when depreciation expense is recorded, the Depreciation Expense account is debited and the Accumulated Depreciation account for the asset is credited. As you can see, no cash is involved in this entry. Amazon.com made the following adjustments to net income for operating activities:

- ▶ It added back $75,724 thousand for noncash charges of depreciation and amortization.
- ▶ It added back stock-based compensation of $57,702 thousand because this did not affect cash in the current period, but was recorded as an expense.
- ▶ It added back a remeasurement charge of $824 thousand. This had to do with a set of complicated Euro-denominated notes that had to be remeasured to current value, resulting in a noncash loss.
- ▶ It added back noncash interest expense and other of $4,756 thousand.
- ▶ It subtracted other income of $7,964 thousand from net income to determine net cash provided by operating activities. This is because the firm earned other income that was included in income from operations and thus net income, but the source was not directly related to operations as defined for the statement of cash flows. Thus, it must be subtracted from net income.
- ▶ The single largest item for fiscal year 2004 was the adjustment for deferred income taxes. Because Amazon.com was finally profitable, it started to use up the accumulated net operating losses it had for income taxes. This means that although Amazon.com's income before taxes was $355,870 thousand, it actually could use a tax benefit of $232,581 thousand (instead of having a tax expense it received a tax benefit), raising its net income to $588,451 thousand ($355,870 thousand plus the tax benefit of $232,581 thousand). Although this tax benefit increased net income, it did not result in any cash flow to the firm. Therefore, the $232,581 thousand plus some additional tax items that brought the total to $256,696 thousand had to be subtracted from net income.

● The second type of adjustment that must be made is for *nonoperating gains or losses that are included in net income.* That is, the effect of these gains and losses must be taken out of the reported net income or loss. This is because the total effect of the transaction that caused the gain or loss (the sale proceeds) is included in the investing activities category. To obtain cash flows from operating activities, gains are subtracted from net income, and losses are added to net income. To illustrate, assume that a firm sold a building for $1 million and recorded a gain on the sale of $200,000. (The historical cost of the building is $1,100,000 and accumulated depreciation to date is $300,000, yielding a net book value of $800,000.) The firm's net income for the period is $700,000. The gain of $200,000 is already included in net income and must be subtracted to determine cash flows from operating activities. This is because the total sales price for this transaction, $1 million, is included as "proceeds from the sale of a building" in the cash flows from investing activities category. This treatment ensures that the transaction is not counted twice. The best way to visualize this is to look at the journal entry that records this gain.

Cash	1,000,000	
Accumulated Depreciation—Building	300,000	
Gain on Sale of Building		200,000
Building		1,100,000

The cash inflow in this transaction is $1,000,000, and that total amount will be included in cash flows from investing activities; therefore, the effect of the $200,000 gain must be taken out of net income. From the perspective of the statement of cash flows, we are interested not in the gain or loss on the transaction (which affects the income statement), but in the total inflows from the transaction. Finally, if a firm has recorded a net loss for the period in the income statement, any gains on sales of assets serve to increase that loss when cash flows from operating activities are determined, while any losses on sales of assets serve to decrease the net loss when cash flows from operating activities are determined.

▶ In Amazon.com's case, the firm recorded a gain on the sale of marketable securities of $586 thousand. This gain must be subtracted from the reported net income, as the reported net income is higher than it otherwise would have been because of the inclusion of the gain on the sale of marketable securities. The entire cash flow effect of the sale is combined with the additional purchases and shown in the investing activities section as purchases of marketable securities in the amount of $1,584,089 thousand (see Amazon.com's statement of cash flows on page 195). Losses on the sale of assets such as these are handled in the opposite way. That is, the amount of the loss is added back to net income and the entire cash flow effect is then shown in the investing activities category.

● The third type of required adjustment is *the conversion of current asset and liability accounts, such as receivables and payables, from the accrual basis to the cash basis.* To understand how this conversion is accomplished, assume that a company had $1,500,000 in sales during the year, all on credit. The balance in Accounts Receivable grew from $187,500 at the beginning of the year to $220,000 at the end of the year. The $32,500 growth in accounts receivable represents sales that were recorded on the accrual basis but for which the cash was not collected as of year end. Therefore, the actual amount of sales for which cash was collected was $1,467,500, or accrual-basis sales of $1,500,000 less the growth in receivables of $32,500. Another way to look at this is to analyze the company's Accounts Receivable account:

Beginning balance in receivables	$ 187,500
Sales during the year	1,500,000
Total owed by customers	$1,687,500
Less ending balance in receivables	220,000
Cash collected from sales	$1,467,500

Included in net income are the total accrual-basis sales of $1,500,000. However, because cash-basis sales are $1,467,500, net income must be reduced by the difference of $32,500 (assuming all else is equal) to determine cash flows from operations. *In general, to determine cash flows from operations, any increase in a current asset account must be subtracted from net income, and any decrease in a current asset account must be added to net income.*

Current payables can be converted from an accrual basis to a cash basis through a similar analysis, although the effect of the changes is opposite to the effect of changes in current asset accounts. For example, if a firm's accounts payable increased during the year, its actual cash outflow was less than the related expense recorded in net income. Thus, accrual-basis expenses are higher than cash-basis expenses, and net income is lower than cash flow from operations. The increase in the payables account must be added to net income to determine cash flows provided by operations.

To illustrate, assume that a company has a beginning balance in its Salaries Payable account of $30,000. Salaries expense during the year amounted to $160,000, and the ending balance in Salaries Payable was $49,000. In this example, cash paid for salaries is $141,000, determined as follows:

Beginning balance in payable	$ 30,000
Salaries expense during period	160,000
Total salaries owed during period	$190,000
Less ending balance in payable	49,000
Actual salaries paid in cash	$141,000

In general, to determine cash flows from operations, any increase in a current payable account must be added to net income, and any decrease in a current payable account must be subtracted from net income.

Amazon.com made the following adjustments for changes in its operating assets and liabilities:

- Amazon.com's net accounts receivable and its other current assets increased by $1,745 thousand during the period. This increase serves to decrease the firm's net income when that figure is converted to cash flows from operating activities. In this case, accrual-basis revenues are lower than cash-basis revenues. The increase in inventories of $168,896 thousand is handled in the opposite way as the increase in receivables. By increasing its inventories during the year, Amazon.com actually purchased more goods than it sold. Thus cost of goods sold on a cash basis is actually greater than cost of goods sold on an accrual basis. This means that accrual-basis net income is higher (due to lower cost of goods sold) than cash flows from operations (which are lower due to higher cost of goods sold). Thus the increase in inventories reduces net income in the computation of cash flows provided by operations.

- The increase in accounts payable of $286,091 thousand was added back to net income, the effect being to increase net cash flows provided by operations by this amount. This is because an increase in a payable account causes the actual accrual-basis expense to be greater than the cash outflows. Amazon.com has elected to break out the actual increase in its unearned revenue account of $3,050 thousand between additions to unearned revenue of $109,936 thousand and amortization of previously unearned income of $106,886 thousand. The net effect must be added back to net income to determine net cash provided by operating activities, because the increase in the liability causes the firm's expense on an accrual basis to be greater than that on a cash basis. The decrease in Amazon.com's accrued expenses and other current liabilities of $15,110 thousand is handled in the same way. Finally, the increase in interest payable of $959 thousand must be added to accrual-basis net income to calculate cash flows provided by operations.

As a result of the adjustments, net cash from operating activities for 2004 is $566,560 thousand.

Compare Amazon.com's positive net cash provided by operating activities over the three-year period. Each year Amazon.com has significantly increased the cash generated from its operations—a very positive sign. In the Financial Reporting Case at the beginning of the chapter, recall what Jeff Bezos told stockholders about the company's ability to generate what he calls *free cash flows*. Bezos went on to say:

We have a cash generative operating cycle because we turn our inventory quickly, collecting payments from our customers before payments are due to suppliers. Our high inventory turnover means we maintain relatively low levels of investment in inventory—$480 million at year end on a sales base of nearly $7 billion.

The capital efficiency of our business model is illustrated by our modest investments in fixed assets, which were $246 million at year end or 4% of 2004 sales.

Free cash flow grew 38% to $477 million in 2004, a $131 million improvement over the prior year. We are confident that if we continue to improve customer experience—including increasing selection and lowering prices—and execute efficiently, our value proposition, as well as our free cash flow, will further expand.

❱ THE DIRECT METHOD

direct method a method of determining cash flows from operating activities in which each item on the income statement is converted from an accrual basis to a cash basis

As an alternative to the indirect method, in the **direct method**, cash flows from operating activities are determined by converting each item on the income statement from an accrual basis to a cash basis. In effect, a cash-basis income statement is prepared. Although the direct method is easier to read and understand than the indirect method, it is used by very few firms. In 2001, *Accounting Trends and Techniques* reported that of the 600 companies surveyed, only 8 used the direct method. Most companies in the United States use the indirect method because their accounting systems are more easily programmed for that method and it is easier to report.

Under the direct method, cash receipts from operations are listed first. Cash payments for operations are listed next, then subtracted from cash receipts from operations. The result is cash flows from operations, the same number derived by using the indirect method. Given that few companies actually keep their accounts on a cash basis, calculating cash flows from operations using the direct method basically requires converting accrual-basis current accounts to the cash basis. Chapter 19 provides a complete discussion of how that conversion is made. For illustrative purposes, Figure 5.3 shows the operating activities section of the statement of cash flows based on the direct method for **Tech Data Corporation**, a leading distributor of information- and logistics-management products.

In this financial statement, the actual activities that generate cash inflows and outflows from operations are listed separately (cash received from customers, cash paid to suppliers and employees, interest paid, and income taxes paid). The net result is shown as net cash provided by (used in) operating activities. As you can see, the format used to prepare the operating activities section differs from the one used by Amazon.com for the consolidated statements of cash flows on page 195, prepared using the indirect method. In the Amazon.com statement, the operating activities section begins with net income and is then adjusted by several items to calculate net cash provided by (used in) operations. There is no difference between the direct and indirect methods in determining cash flows from either investing or financing activities.

STEP 2: DETERMINE CASH FLOWS FROM INVESTING ACTIVITIES

Returning to our discussion of Amazon.com's 2004 statement of cash flows, the investing activities section is presented next. Cash flows from investing activities are related to the acquisition of operating assets and investments. They include cash receipts from the sale of operating assets such as property, plant, and equipment, and cash payments for the purchase of investments such as marketable securities. Sales and purchases of assets usually are not netted together but are reported separately. For example, cash received from the sale of marketable securities is often reported separately from cash paid for the purchase of marketable securities.

The investing activities section of Amazon.com's consolidated statements of cash flows is presented in Figure 5.4. As you can see, Amazon.com reported net cash used in investing activities in 2004 of $317,631 thousand, which consisted of the following elements:

- $1,426,786 thousand received from sales and maturities of marketable securities and other investments

- $1,584,089 thousand used for purchases of marketable securities

- $89,133 thousand used for purchases of fixed assets

- $71,195 thousand used for acquisitions

STEP 3: DETERMINE CASH FLOWS FROM FINANCING ACTIVITIES

After the investing activities section is prepared, cash flows from financing activities are determined. Cash flows from financing activities result from activities related to raising debt and equity capital. Outflows of cash resulting from financing activities might

Figure 5.3

Direct Method Used to Prepare the Operating Activities Section of the Statement of Cash Flows

Tech Data

TECH DATA COPRORATION
OPERATING ACTIVITIES SECTION OF STATEMENT OF CASH FLOWS

(in thousands)	Year ended January 31,		
	2005	**2004**	**2003**
Cash flows from operating activities:			
Cash received from customers	$19,745,283	$17,390,674	$15,897,728
Cash paid to suppliers and employees	(19,571,824)	(17,027,162)	(15,685,447)
Interest paid	(18,837)	(17,045)	(25,421)
Income taxes paid	(47,677)	(43,233)	(61,811)
Net cash provided by operating activities	106,945	303,234	125,049
Cash flows from investing activities:			
Acquisition of businesses, net of cash acquired	—	(203,010)	(1,125)
Disposition of subsidiaries, net of cash sold	—	—	(2,289)
Proceeds from sale of property and equipment	5,130	4,484	—
Expenditures for property and equipment	(25,876)	(31,278)	(26,276)
Software development costs	(17,899)	(21,714)	(32,862)
Net cash used in investing activities	(38,645)	(251,518)	(62,552)
Cash flows from financing activities:			
Proceeds from the issuance of common stock, net of related tax benefit	32,733	28,823	28,587
Net borrowings (repayments) on revolving credit loans	(11,319)	(138,039)	91,306
Principal payments on long-term debt	(9,214)	(1,492)	(301,227)
Net cash provided by (used in) financing activities	12,200	(110,708)	(181,334)
Effect of exchange rate changes on cash	5,755	10,602	18,101
Net increase (decrease) in cash and cash equivalents	86,255	(48,390)	(100,736)
Cash and cash equivalents at beginning of year	108,801	157,191	257,927
Cash and cash equivalents at end of year	$ 195,056	$ 108,801	$ 157,191
Reconciliation of net income (loss) to net cash provided by operating activities:			
Net income (loss)	$ 162,460	$ 104,147	$ (199,818)
Adjustments to reconcile net income (loss) to net cash provided by operating activities:			
Depreciation and amortization	55,472	55,084	49,849
Provision for losses on accounts receivable	13,268	29,214	31,243
Non-cash special charges	—	—	328,872
Loss on disposition of subsidiaries	—	—	5,745
Deferred income taxes	(3,616)	7,369	17,453
Changes in operating assets and liabilities, net of effects of acquisitions:			
Accounts receivable	(44,305)	(15,699)	159,256
Inventories	(119,999)	(140,203)	26,881
Prepaid and other assets	(32,193)	14,713	(18,256)
Accounts payable	55,849	300,350	(239,059)
Accrued expenses and other liabilities	20,009	(51,741)	(37,117)
Total adjustments	(55,515)	199,087	324,867
Net cash provided by operating activities	$ 106,945	$ 303,234	$ 125,049

Figure 5.4

Investing Activities Section of the Statements of Cash Flows

Amazon.com

AMAZON.COM
INVESTING ACTIVITIES SECTION OF CONSOLIDATED STATEMENTS OF CASH FLOWS
(in thousands)

	Years Ended December 31,		
	2004	**2003**	**2002**
INVESTING ACTIVITIES:			
Sales and maturities of marketable securities and other investments	$1,426,786	$813,184	$553,289
Purchases of marketable securities	(1,584,089)	(535,642)	(635,810)
Purchases of fixed assets, including internal-use software and website development	(89,133)	(45,963)	(39,163)
Proceeds from sale of subsidiary	—	5,072	—
Acquisition, net of cash acquired	(71,195)	—	—
Net cash provided by (used in) investing activities	($317,631)	$236,651	($121,684)

include the payment of dividends to stockholders, the repayment of the principal portion of debt (interest expense is classified as an operating activity), and the purchase of treasury stock.

As you can see from Figure 5.5, Amazon.com reported $97,292 thousand of net cash used in financing activities in 2004, which consisted of the following elements:

- $60,109 thousand received from the exercise of stock options

- $157,401 thousand used for the repayment of long-term debt, capital lease obligations, and other

STEP 4: DETERMINE THE CHANGE IN CASH AND THE ENDING BALANCE IN CASH AND CASH EQUIVALENTS

The cash flows from operating, investing, and financing activities and the effect of the gain or loss from foreign currency translation are all summarized in the final section of the statement of cash flows. When a company has operations in a foreign country, the net income or net loss from those operations must be translated into U.S. dollars. Because the value of the U.S. dollar fluctuates against most foreign currencies, the **foreign currency translation gain or loss** from these fluctuations is reported on the balance sheet as a component of accumulated other comprehensive income rather than on the income statement (see Chapter 3).

The cash balance will change as a result of those gains or losses, and the adjustment for the period is reported separately on the statement of cash flows, after the operating, investing, and financing activities sections.

Look again at Amazon.com's consolidated statements of cash flows in the Financial Reporting Case on page 195. Note that "foreign-currency effect on cash and cash equivalents" is disclosed after the operating, investing, and financing activities sections and amounts to $48,690 thousand in 2004.

To complete the statement of cash flows, the beginning cash balance is added to the total effect of operating, investing, and financing items and exchange rates, and the sum is listed as "cash and cash equivalents, end of period." The beginning and ending

foreign currency translation gain or loss a gain or loss resulting from fluctuations of the U.S. dollar against foreign currencies; reported on the balance sheet as a component of accumulated other comprehensive income

Figure 5.5

Financing Activities Section of the Statements of Cash Flows

Amazon.com

AMAZON.COM
FINANCING ACTIVITIES SECTION OF CONSOLIDATED STATEMENTS OF CASH FLOWS
(in thousands)

	Years Ended December 31,		
	2004	**2003**	**2002**
FINANCING ACTIVITIES:			
Proceeds from exercise of stock options	$ 60,109	$163,322	$121,689
Repayment of long-term debt, capital lease obligations, and other	(157,401)	(495,308)	(14,795)
Net cash (used in) provided by financing activities	$ 97,292	$(331,986)	$106,894

cash balances must correspond with the amounts reported on the balance sheet for the current and previous periods. In Amazon.com's case, there was a net increase in cash and cash equivalents of $200,327 thousand for the year ended December 31, 2004. The cash and cash equivalents balance at year end was $1,302,600 thousand.

SIGNIFICANT NONCASH INVESTING AND FINANCING ACTIVITIES AND OTHER REQUIRED DISCLOSURES

FASB *Statement No. 95* requires that companies make two sets of additional disclosures. The first requirement concerns disclosure of significant noncash items. For example, when an asset is acquired in exchange for stock or debt (or a combination of the two), a significant investing and financing activity has occurred and must be reported on a separate schedule or in the notes to the statement of cash flows, even though no actual cash flow took place. That information assists users in reconciling the changes in the balance sheet accounts with the cash flows reported in the statement of cash flows. Amazon.com reported one item in its 2004 annual report: fixed assets acquired under capital leases and other financing arrangements.

The second type of disclosure relates to the suggestion that companies report major classes of gross cash receipts and cash payments such as those found if the direct method was used in determining cash flows from operations. These are suggested disclosures, but *Statement No. 95* does require the disclosure of certain items such as interest and dividends received, interest paid, and income taxes paid. Amazon.com discloses cash paid for interest and cash paid for income taxes on its 2004 statement in the supplemental cash flow information section of the consolidated statements of cash flows (see page 195).

INTERNATIONAL REPORTING STANDARDS FOR THE STATEMENT OF CASH FLOWS

 INTERNATIONAL

In 1992, the International Accounting Standards Committee (IASC) issued *International Accounting Standard No. 7*, which guides the preparation of the statement of cash flows for firms using international accounting standards. The IASC's name was changed to the International Accounting Standards Board (IASB). Current IASB standards generally follow the provisions of the FASB's *Statement of Financial Accounting Standards*

No. 95. However, the IASB allows more discretion in how to report items such as interest paid or received and dividends paid or received, and in how tax expense is classified. The FASB classifies interest and dividends received from investments as operating activities, whereas the IASB allows firms to classify those items as either operating or investing cash flows. Similarly, the FASB classifies interest expense as an operating activity, even though the principal amount of the debt issued is classified as a financing activity. The IASB allows firms to classify interest expense as either an operating activity or a financing activity. The FASB classifies dividends paid to stockholders as a financing activity, whereas the IASB allows firms to classify dividends paid as either an operating activity or a financing activity. The FASB classifies tax expense as an operating activity. The IASB also classifies tax expense as an operating activity, unless the tax expense or benefit can be specifically identified with a financing or investing activity. For example, the tax effect of the sale of a discontinued component of an entity could be classified under investing activities. This increased flexibility is in line with the tendency of IASB standards to allow for more alternatives than U.S. standards. When comparing cash flow statements from different countries, it is important to keep this increased flexibility in mind and to note what items are considered operating, investing, and financing activities.

CHECK YOUR UNDERSTANDING

1. List the four steps in preparing the statement of cash flows.

2. Explain the difference between the direct and indirect methods of reporting cash flows from operations.

3. How are nonoperating gains included in net income treated on the statement of cash flows?

4. If a company's accounts payable increased during the period, how is the amount of the increase treated on the statement of cash flows?

LO4 Use the statement of cash flows to analyze a company's cash adequacy and its performance with regard to cash.

ANALYSIS

Critical Thinking: *If a company is profitable, can you assume that the company is generating enough cash from operations to sustain itself? Explain your answer.*

Analyzing the Statement of Cash Flows

The statement of cash flows, like the other primary financial statements, provides information that can be analyzed over time to obtain a better understanding of the past performance of a firm, as well as its future prospects. Information gleaned from this statement can also be effectively used to compare the performance and prospects of different firms in an industry and of different industries. There are several ratios based on cash flows from operating activities that are useful in this analysis. These ratios generally fall into two major categories: cash flow coverage (or adequacy) ratios and cash flow performance measures.

CASH FLOW COVERAGE (ADEQUACY) RATIOS

As we have noted, a firm's operating activities must, in the long run, be able to generate enough cash to meet the firm's needs, as there are always limits to the amount of funds that can be generated through debt and equity offerings. Several ratios have been developed to help users assess the amount of cash generated from operating activities. The four most common ratios include

- Cash debt coverage ratio
- Cash dividend coverage ratio

- Cash dividend payout ratio

- Cash interest coverage ratio

These ratios are based on cash provided by operating activities, and they provide a way to measure adequacy or liquidity.

To illustrate these cash flow coverage ratios, we will use the following 2003 financial data from **General Electric**. All data with the exception of common shares outstanding are in millions.

Cash flows from operating activities	$ 30,289
Cash interest payments	10,561
Cash tax payments	1,539
Operating income	15,589
Net income	15,002
Cash Dividends paid to shareholders	7,643
Average total assets	611,364
Average total debt	534,294
Average stockholders' equity	77,069*
Common stock—shares outstanding	10,063,120,000

*Included in average total equity is minority interests of $5,627.

Because the ratios that follow are aimed at determining the adequacy of cash, cash interest payments, cash tax payments, and dividends paid are used rather than their accrual-basis counterparts—interest expense, tax expense, and dividends declared. If the activities of a company are fairly stable, there will not be much difference between the cash-basis and the accrual-basis figures for these items. However, to the extent that a company is growing or shrinking cash flows, figures may lag or lead accrual-basis figures. Nonetheless, to be consistent both the numerator and denominator of the ratios are based on the cash flow figure, where appropriate.

▶ CASH DEBT COVERAGE RATIO

cash debt coverage ratio an analysis ratio that measures a firm's ability to repay both its short-term and long-term debt; calculated by dividing cash flows from operating activities by average total debt (current liabilities plus long-term debt)

The **cash debt coverage ratio** is calculated by dividing cash flows from operating activities by average total debt (current liabilities plus long-term debt). This ratio measures a firm's ability to repay both its short- and its long-term debt. In a sense, this ratio is an indicator of the financial risk of a firm. If the ratio is high, the firm faces less risk by generating cash flows to repay its debt. For General Electric, this ratio is computed as follows:

$$\text{Cash Debt Coverage Ratio} = \frac{\text{Cash Flows from Operating Activities}}{\text{Average Total Debt}}$$

$$= \frac{\$30,289}{\$534,294} = 0.057$$

Although GE is clearly a financially stable company, this is not a particularly high ratio. In part, this is because GE's financing arm, GE Capital Services, is included in GE's consolidated financial statements, and this entity holds a significant amount of debt.

▶ CASH DIVIDEND COVERAGE RATIO

cash dividend coverage ratio an analysis ratio that measures the ability of a firm to pay dividends at the current level or to increase dividends in the future; calculated by dividing cash flows from operating activities by total dividends paid

The **cash dividend coverage ratio** is calculated by dividing cash flows from operating activities by total dividends paid and measures the firm's ability to pay dividends at the current level or to potentially increase dividends in the future. The cash dividend coverage ratio for GE is calculated as shown on the next page.

$$\text{Cash Dividend Coverage Ratio} = \frac{\text{Cash Flows from Operating Activities}}{\text{Total Dividends Paid}}$$

$$= \frac{\$30,289}{\$7,643} = 3.96$$

This ratio indicates that GE is generating almost four times the amount of cash needed to cover its current dividends.

❱ CASH DIVIDEND PAYOUT RATIO

cash dividend payout ratio an analysis ratio that measures a firm's ability to make its dividend payments; calculated by dividing total dividends paid by cash flows from operating activities

The **cash dividend payout ratio** is calculated by dividing total dividends paid by cash flows from operating activities. The cash dividend payout ratio is the inverse of the cash dividend coverage ratio and is also a measure of a firm's ability to make its dividend payments. For GE, the ratio is calculated as follows:

$$\text{Cash Dividend Payout Ratio} = \frac{\text{Total Dividends Paid}}{\text{Cash Flows from Operating Activities}}$$

$$= \frac{\$7,643}{\$30,289} = 0.25$$

This calculation indicates that approximately 25 percent of cash flows from operating activities are used for dividends.

❱ CASH INTEREST COVERAGE RATIO

cash interest coverage ratio an analysis ratio that measures a firm's ability to meet its current interest payments; calculated by adding cash flows from operating activities to interest paid and taxes paid and dividing this total by cash interest payments

The **cash interest coverage ratio** is calculated by adding cash flows from operating activities to interest and taxes paid in cash, then dividing this total by cash interest payments. It is a measure of a firm's ability to meet its current interest payments. This ratio is similar to the times interest earned ratio discussed in Chapter 4, except that it is based on cash flows from operating activities rather than on net income. For General Electric, this ratio is computed as follows:

$$\text{Cash Interest Coverage Ratio} = \frac{\text{Cash Flows from Operating Activities} + \text{Interest Paid} + \text{Taxes Paid}}{\text{Cash Interest Payments}}$$

$$= \frac{\$30,289 + \$10,561 + \$1,539}{\$10,561} = 4.01$$

This ratio indicates that GE is generating cash flows before interest and taxes that are more than four times the amount of its interest payments. This ratio, together with the cash dividend coverage ratio of about the same amount, indicates that GE is generating more than enough cash flows from its operating activities to cover its annual interest and dividend payments.

CASH FLOW PERFORMANCE MEASURES

Information presented on the statement of cash flows can also be used to analyze the performance of a firm from a cash flow perspective. Five such performance measures are

- Cash flow return on assets
- Cash flow return on equity

- Cash flow per share
- Cash flow to operating income ratio
- Cash flow to net income ratio

▶ CASH FLOW RETURN ON ASSETS AND ON EQUITY

cash flow return on assets an analysis ratio that measures a firm's cash flow as a percentage of assets; calculated by dividing cash flows from operating activities before interest and taxes paid by average total assets for the period

cash flow return on equity an analysis ratio that measures whether stockholders are earning adequate cash flows from their investments; calculated by dividing cash flows from operating activities less any preferred dividends paid by average common stockholders' equity

Cash flow return on assets is calculated by dividing cash flows from operating activities before interest and taxes by average total assets for the period, while **cash flow return on equity** is calculated by dividing cash flows from operating activities less any preferred dividends by average common stockholders' equity. These ratios help users assess whether a firm is earning an adequate cash flow return on its net assets and whether stockholders are earning adequate cash flows from their investments. For GE, the cash flow return on assets and cash flow return on equity are calculated as follows:

$$\text{Cash Flow Return on Assets} = \frac{\text{Cash Flows from Operating Activities} + \text{Interest Paid} + \text{Taxes Paid}}{\text{Average Total Assets}}$$

$$= \frac{\$30,289 + \$10,561 + \$1,539}{\$611,364} = 0.069$$

$$\text{Cash Flow Return on Equity} = \frac{\text{Cash Flows from Operating Activities} - \text{Preferred Dividends Paid}}{\text{Average Common Stockholders' Equity}}$$

$$= \frac{\$30,289 - \$0^*}{\$77,069} = 0.393$$

*GE has no preferred stock and therefore no preferred dividends.

The cash return on equity is high because GE (and especially its finance subsidiary, GE Capital Services) is highly leveraged. A profitable highly leveraged company will generate high returns on equity, as most of the assets are provided not by the stockholders, but by the debt holders.

▶ CASH FLOW PER SHARE

cash flow per share an analysis calculation that measures how much cash flow is attributed to each share of stock issued; calculated by dividing cash flows from operating activities by the number of issued shares

Cash flow per share is calculated by dividing cash flows from operating activities by the number of issued shares. This measurement helps users understand how much cash flow is attributed to each share of stock issued. For GE, this ratio is calculated as follows:

$$\text{Cash Flow per Share} = \frac{\text{Cash Flows from Operating Activities}}{\text{Number of Issued Shares}} = \frac{\$30,289,000,000}{10,063,120,000} = 3.01$$

▶ CASH FLOW TO OPERATING INCOME AND CASH FLOW TO NET INCOME RATIOS

cash flow to operating income ratio an analysis ratio that measures the quality of earnings; calculated by dividing cash flows from operating activities by operating income

cash flow to net income ratio an analysis ratio that measures the quality of earnings; calculated by dividing cash flows from operating activities by net income

Operating income and net income, the results of accrual-based GAAP, must ultimately generate cash flows. Indicators of how closely income mirrors cash flows from operating activities are the **cash flow to operating income ratio** (cash flows from operating activities divided by operating income) and the **cash flow to net income ratio** (cash flows from operating activities divided by net income). Some analysts consider these ratios a measure of the quality of earnings. That is, the closer operating income and net income are to cash flows from operating activities, the higher the quality of earnings.

Using the data from GE, these ratios are calculated as follows:

$$\text{Cash Flow to Operating Income Ratio} = \frac{\text{Cash Flows from Operating Activities}}{\text{Operating Income}}$$

$$= \frac{\$30,289}{\$15,589} = 1.94$$

$$\text{Cash Flow to Net Income Ratio} = \frac{\text{Cash Flows from Operating Activities}}{\text{Net Income}}$$

$$= \frac{\$30,289}{\$15,002} = 2.02$$

These ratios indicate that not only is GE profitable, but its operations are generating significant amounts of cash flows—about twice the amount of operating income and net income.

TREND ANALYSIS

Examining the change in the cash provided by operating activities from the previous period to the current period can also offer financial statement users useful clues. For example, if the cash provided by operating activities declined significantly during the reporting period, it is important to determine the reason for the drop and to assess whether it may signal a future trend. If the cash provided by operating activities is negative (net cash is used by operations) and continues that way, the firm's ability to remain a going concern must be carefully evaluated.

> **CHECK YOUR UNDERSTANDING**
>
> 1. If a company reports $250,000 in net cash flows from operating activities and $210,000 in net income, what is the company's cash flow to net income ratio? How would you interpret this ratio?
>
> 2. If a company's average total debt is $52,940 and its cash flow from operating activities is $227,492, how would you interpret its ability to repay its debt?
>
> 3. Which ratio measures whether a firm is earning adequate cash flow on its net assets?

LO5 Identify additional significant financial disclosures required by GAAP and the SEC.

HI *Critical Thinking: Do you think that information about a company's business strategies, accounting policies, or changing relationships should be provided to the investment community? Explain your answer.*

accounting policies choices that management makes in its application of generally accepted accounting principles

Other Significant Financial Disclosures

In addition to the information in the four primary financial statements and their notes, a public corporation must disclose other information as part of its annual report or in filings with the SEC. The required disclosures include an explanation of significant accounting policies, reports by operating segment, discussion of subsequent events, Regulation FD disclosures, interim reports, an auditor's report, and management's reports.

SIGNIFICANT ACCOUNTING POLICIES AND RELATED NOTES

Accounting policies are the choices that management makes in its application of generally accepted accounting principles. There are alternative ways of measuring and recording transactions and events under GAAP, and management must decide which of these it will use. Management must also make many estimates in applying GAAP, and these can have material effects on the numbers reported in the financial statements. For those reasons, management must disclose the accounting choices and estimates used in the calculation and measurement of the elements of the financial statements. That information assists analysts and investors in understanding the financial statements and, in some cases, actually restating them to make them more comparable with those of other companies.

The summary of significant accounting policies should provide enough information to enable users to comprehend the numbers reported in the financial statements. This information includes, where applicable, the method used for inventory costing, depreciation methods, the amortization of intangibles, the basis of consolidation, foreign currency translation methods, and other specifics that are helpful to users.

A number of different accounting pronouncements require the inclusion of notes that add information to that already provided on the face of the financial statements. For example, a company must supply additional information about long-term debt so that users will know the interest rates and maturity dates for that debt and any significant issues related to it. Other notes to the financial statements provide details about leases, employee stock plans, employee benefit plans, earnings per share, taxes, commitments and contingencies, segment information, quarterly financial information, and subsequent events, if appropriate.

REPORTS BY OPERATING SEGMENT

In 1994, the American Institute of Certified Public Accountants (AICPA) Special Committee on Financial Reporting issued a report entitled "Improving Business Reporting—A Customer Focus." The committee was established in response to widespread frustration with the level of disclosure in financial statements. One of the areas identified for improvement was segment reporting. Segment reports under the original standards were considered too aggregated to be of much use. As a result of the committee's recommendations, the FASB issued *Statement of Financial Accounting Standards No. 131,* "Disclosures About Segments of an Enterprise and Related Information," which requires the disclosure of both income statement and balance sheet items for segments.

operating segment a business unit that engages in revenue-earning activities and incurs expenses, whose operating results are regularly reviewed by the chief operating officer to make operating decisions, and for which financial information is available

SFAS No. 131 identifies the following criteria for an **operating segment**:

1. One that engages in business activities to earn revenues and incur expenses

2. One whose operating results are regularly reviewed by the company's chief operating officer to make decisions about resources to be allocated to the segment and to assess its performance

3. One for which financial information is available[1]

An operating segment usually has a segment manager who reports directly to top management and not to another layer of management. This approach to identifying an operating segment is called the *management approach* because the classification of a unit depends on how the firm makes operating decisions and assesses performance.

Key information about a segment must be reported if *any* of the following three conditions is satisfied:

1. The segment's reported revenues (including sales to external customers and transfer sales within the company) are 10 percent or more of the combined revenues of all the company's reported operating segments.

2. The absolute amount of the segment's profit or loss is 10 percent or more of the greater of (a) the combined reported profits of all operating segments that did not

---

1 "Disclosures About Segments of an Enterprise and Related Information," *Statement of Financial Accounting Standards No. 131* (Norwalk, Conn.: FASB, 1997), par. 1.

Ilustratlon 5.3

Information Required for Reportable Operating Segments

General information	The company must identify how it is organized and what factors were used to identify its operating segments. It must describe the types of products and services from which each segment derives its revenues.
Information about profit (or loss)	The company must report the profit (or loss) for each reportable operating segment. Revenues, separated by external sales and intercompany sales; interest revenue and interest expense; and depreciation, depletion, and amortization expense are also required.
Information about assets	The company must report the assets of each reportable operating segment. The amount of total capital expenditures for additions to long-lived assets must be disclosed.
Reconciliation	The company must reconcile (1) the total of the reportable segments' revenues to total company revenues, (2) the total of the reportable segments' profit (or loss) to the company's pretax income from continuing operations, and (3) the total of the reportable segments' assets to the company's total assets. The revenues, profit (loss), and segment assets of the "all other" segment category must be included in the reconciliation.

report a loss or (b) the combined reported loss of all operating segments that did report a loss.

3. The segment's assets are 10 percent or more of the combined assets of all operating segments.

If an operating segment meets any of the three criteria, the company must report general information about its segments, information about each reported segment's profit or loss, information about its assets, and reconciling information, as detailed in Illustration 5.3.[2] The disclosures, which also include geographical information, can be quite detailed. Consider, for example, the excerpt from Amazon.com's 2004 annual report giving segment information that is shown in Figure 5.6. As you can see, Amazon.com reports on North America and International segments. Net sales, gross profit, operating income, and depreciation expense are provided for each segment.

SUBSEQUENT EVENTS

Because closing and auditing procedures can be time-consuming, financial statements are usually issued from a few weeks to as much as three months after a company's year end. Currently, the SEC requires that Form 10-K, the annual report to the agency, be filed within 60 days of a company's year end. Because of the lag in reporting data, companies are required to disclose any **subsequent events**, which are significant post-statement events that occur between the year-end date of the financial statements and the actual date the financial statements are issued. This time period is often referred to as the *interim period*. If an event occurred before the balance sheet date but was settled during this interim period, the financial statements must be revised before they are issued to reflect the financial effects of this event. This is because the actual event

subsequent events significant post-statement events that occur between the year-end date and the date the financial statements are issued

---

2 *SFAS No. 131.*

Figure 5.6

Excerpt on Segments—Amazon.com 2004 Annual Report

Amazon.com

	Year Ended December 31, 2004:		
	North America	**International**	**Consolidated**
Net sales	$3,847,344	$3,073,780	$6,921,124
Cost of sales	2,823,792	2,495,335	5,319,127
Gross profit	1,023,552	578,445	1,601,997
Direct segment operating expenses	702,676	409,158	1,111,834
Segment operating income	320,876	169,287	490,163
Stock-based compensation			57,702
Other operating income			(7,964)
Income from operations			440,425
Total non-operating expense, net			84,555
Benefit from income taxes, net			(232,581)
Net income			$ 588,451

Net sales shipped to customers outside of the U.S. represented approximately 49%, 43%, and 35% of net sales for 2004, 2003, and 2002. Net sales from *www.amazon.co.uk*, *www.amazon.de*, and *www.amazon.co.jp* each represented 10% or more of consolidated net sales in 2004, and net sales from *www.amazon.co.uk* and *www.amazon.de* each represented 10% or more of consolidated net sales in 2003 and 2002. Net fixed assets held in locations outside the U.S. were $57 million, $45 million, and $44 million at December 31, 2004, 2003, and 2002.

Total assets, by segment, reconciled to consolidated amounts were (in thousands):

	December 31,		
	2004	**2003**	**2002**
North America	$1,921,686	$1,276,300	$1,525,038
International	1,326,822	885,733	465,411
Consolidated	$3,248,508	$2,162,033	$1,990,449

Depreciation expense, by segment, was as follows (in thousands):

	North America	**International**	**Consolidated**
2004	$63,173	$11,490	$74,663
2003	59,558	10,186	69,744
2002	67,036	9,625	76,661

that caused the transaction occurred within the time period of the financial statements. A material lawsuit that originated prior to year end but was settled in the interim period is a good example of an event that requires revision of the financial statements. Often, however, significant post-statement events occur *after* the balance sheet date but *within* the interim period. These events, if material, must be fully disclosed in the notes to the financial statements. The actual statements, however, are not revised because the original triggering event did not occur within the financial statement period. Examples of subsequent events that require disclosure include the planned issuance of new debt or equity, spin-offs, contingent losses, and other occurrences that will have a material effect on the future results of operations.

REGULATION FD DISCLOSURES

Regulation FD an SEC regulation that requires that public companies make sure that disclosures that are intentionally made to analysts and certain other users are simultaneously disseminated to the public

In 2000, the SEC issued **Regulation FD**, which requires public companies to make sure that disclosures that are intentionally made to analysts and certain other users are simultaneously disseminated to the public. According to the SEC, the goal of Regulation FD is to ensure that all market participants have equal access to market-moving, material news. The regulation grew out of concern that some analysts and others were getting important information before the investing public. One of the results of Regulation FD is that more companies are webcasting their conference calls giving analysts quarterly results and earnings guidance. Current requirements also oblige companies to provide investors with adequate notice of when scheduled conference calls are to occur. According to a survey by the National Investor Relations Institute (NIRI), approximately 80 percent of companies provide such notice about a week in advance in a news release on the company's website. In addition, the survey found that 92 percent of NIRI member companies are webcasting their quarterly conference calls and that millions of investors are listening to the live calls.[3]

INTERIM REPORTING AND RELATED DISCLOSURE REQUIREMENTS

interim financial reports reports that cover a period of less than one year

Companies that are registered with the SEC are required to submit **interim financial reports**—reports that cover a period of less than one year. The SEC requires some companies to file Form 10-Q for quarterly financial disclosures. It also requires these companies to provide certain quarterly data in the notes to the annual report. Most companies produce quarterly or other interim financial reports and disseminate them to stockholders and other financial statement users as well.

While interim reports can provide timely information to users of financial statements, two opposing views on interim reporting periods have emerged. Some companies view each interim period as a separate accounting period. This approach is referred to as the **discrete view**. In this view, the results of operations should be determined in essentially the same way that they would be if the interim period were an annual period. Other companies hold that each interim period is an integral part of the larger annual accounting period. This **integral view** means that revenues and expenses are recognized on the same basis as they are for annual statements. For example, an expense that is incurred in a particular quarter should be recognized in that quarter, but if it affects future quarters, the expense should be allocated over those quarters.

discrete view a view on interim reporting periods that holds that the results of operations should be determined in essentially the same way that they would be if the interim period were an annual period

integral view a view on interim reporting periods that holds that revenues and expenses are recognized on the same basis as they are for annual statements

The Accounting Principles Board, which preceded the FASB, adopted the view that the interim period is an integral part of the annual accounting period. Thus, if a firm incurred a first-quarter, $5 million expense to buy TV advertising time during the Super Bowl in late January 2005, that expense should be allocated over all four quarters of the annual period. In contrast, if the first quarter were seen as a separate accounting period, the entire $5 million would be allocated to the first quarter. In both views, the $5 million is an expense of the year 2005. The debate is over when that expense should be recognized: Should it be spread evenly over all four quarters of 2005, or should the entire amount be recognized in the first quarter? The prevailing view is that it should be allocated over all four quarters. Other ongoing expenses that are subject to year-end adjustments, such as annual depreciation expense, should be estimated for the entire year and then allocated to the four quarters in some reasonable manner. Note that unusual items, like discontinued operations or extraordinary losses, should be reported separately in the interim period in which they occur.

❯ ADVANTAGES OF INTERIM REPORTING

Interim reports provide important and timely information to investors and other users of financial statements. Interim reports are essential in helping investors predict annual operating results, identify turning points in earnings trends, and evaluate management's performance. Further, because the information in quarterly reports is more timely, many users feel that it has more influence on a firm's stock price than the information contained in annual reports does, even though interim reports are not audited.[4]

---

3 Louis M. Thompson, Jr., "Guidance for Compliance with Regulation FD," Executive Alert, National Investor Relations Institute, September 10, 2001, available at: **www.niri.org/publications/alerts/ EA091001.cfm.** Accessed 5/12/03.

4 Adapted from Ernst & Young, *Quarterly Financial Reporting: A Guide for Financial Officers.*

❯ DISADVANTAGES OF INTERIM REPORTING

Although interim financial reporting offers clear benefits, it also has some disadvantages. For example, because of the relatively short time periods involved, accounting estimates and allocations are more arbitrary, and the resulting information is less reliable. It is difficult enough to allocate costs to a specific year, but the problem is compounded when the allocation period is three months or even less. In addition, a series of transactions may all occur in a particular quarter and have an abnormally strong impact on that period's financial statements.

❯ TREATMENT OF SPECIAL ITEMS IN INTERIM REPORTS

A number of special items require different treatment in interim reports. For example, in the first quarter of 2002, **AOL Time Warner** (as the company was then called) was forced to reevaluate the value of goodwill on its accounting records and wrote off $54 billion against earnings. This write-off was seen as a discrete event of that quarter, and the entire loss was recorded then. It was not allocated across all four quarters. Likewise, a discontinued operation or an extraordinary item is reported completely in the quarter in which the event occurred. Earnings per share calculations are based solely on the specific quarter in which they are reported.

❯ REQUIRED INTERIM DISCLOSURES

According to *APB Opinion No. 28*, publicly traded companies are required to disclose the following summarized interim financial data:

- Sales, income taxes, extraordinary items and unusual or infrequently occurring items, the cumulative effect of changes in accounting principles or estimates, and net income
- Earnings per share
- Seasonal revenue, costs, and expenses
- Significant changes in estimates for income tax expense
- Discontinued operations
- Contingent items
- Significant changes in financial position

Figure 5.7 shows how Amazon.com disclosed quarterly information in its 2004 annual report. Included are unaudited summarized data for net sales, gross profit, net income and its significant components, and earnings per share for 2004, 2003, and 2002.

THE AUDITOR'S REPORT

Publicly held companies are required to have their financial statements audited by CPAs, and most firms hire national or international CPA firms to do the job. The stockholders in a corporation vote to select the auditor because they rely on the auditor's findings when making their investment decisions. Private companies are commonly required to be audited as a condition of applying for credit or seeking debt financing. The auditor examines the firm's internal controls, books, records, and other evidence and expresses an opinion—the **auditor's report**—about whether the financial statements fairly present the firm's financial position, results of operations, and cash flows in accordance with generally accepted accounting principles.

The opinion expressed by the CPA firm usually takes one of four forms: unqualified opinion, qualified opinion, adverse opinion, or disclaimer of an opinion. An unqualified opinion indicates the highest degree of confidence in the presentation of the financial statements. A qualified opinion is expressed when the scope of the examination is restricted or when the statements do not fairly present the financial

auditor's report a statement issued by an independent auditor about whether the financial statements of a company fairly present the firm's financial position, results of operations, and cash flows in accordance with generally accepted accounting principles

Figure 5.7

Quarterly Information—Amazon.com 2004 Annual Report

Amazon.com

Note 14—QUARTERLY RESULTS (UNAUDITED)

The following tables contain selected unaudited statement of operations information for each quarter of 2004, 2003, and 2002. The following information reflects all normal recurring adjustments necessary for a fair presentation of the information for the periods presented. The operating results for any quarter are not necessarily indicative of results for any future period. Unaudited quarterly results were as follows (in thousands, except per share data):

	Year Ended December 31, 2004			
	Fourth Quarter	Third Quarter	Second Quarter	First Quarter
Net sales	$2,540,959	$1,462,475	$1,387,341	$1,530,349
Gross profit	544,466	355,651	341,046	360,834
Net income	346,688	54,147	76,480	111,136
Basic earnings per share (1)	$ 0.85	$ 0.13	$ 0.19	$ 0.28
Diluted earnings per share (1)	$ 0.82	$ 0.13	$ 0.18	$ 0.26
Shares used in computation of earnings (loss) per share:				
Basic	408,227	406,647	405,268	403,542
Diluted	425,034	424,777	424,678	424,519

	Year Ended December 31, 2003			
	Fourth Quarter	Third Quarter	Second Quarter	First Quarter
Net sales	$1,945,772	$1,134,456	$1,099,912	$1,083,559
Gross profit	426,837	285,821	273,928	270,582
Net income (loss)	73,154	15,563	(43,314)	(10,121)
Basic earnings (loss) per share (1)	$ 0.18	$ 0.04	$ (0.11)	$ (0.03)
Diluted earnings (loss) per share (1)	$ 0.17	$ 0.04	$ (0.11)	$ (0.03)
Shares used in computation of earnings (loss) per share:				
Basic	401,422	397,912	393,876	388,541
Diluted	425,214	422,802	393,876	388,541

	Year Ended December 31, 2002			
	Fourth Quarter	Third Quarter	Second Quarter	First Quarter
Net sales	$1,428,610	$ 851,299	$ 805,605	$ 847,422
Gross profit	335,159	216,167	218,167	223,125
Income (loss) before change in accounting principle	2,651	(35,080)	(93,553)	(23,951)
Cumulative effect of change in accounting principle	—	—	—	801
Net income (loss)	2,651	(35,080)	(93,553)	(23,150)
Basic and diluted earnings (loss) per share (1):				
Prior to cumulative effect of change in accounting principle	$ 0.01	$ (0.09)	$ (0.25)	$ (0.06)
Cumulative effect of change in accounting principle	—	—	—	—
	$ 0.01	$ (0.09)	$ (0.25)	$ (0.06)
Shares used in computation of earnings (loss) per share:				
Basic	383,702	379,650	376,937	373,031
Diluted	407,056	379,650	376,937	373,031

(1) The sum of quarterly per share amounts may not equal per share amounts reported for year-to-date periods. This is due to changes in the number of weighted-average shares outstanding and the effects of rounding for each period.

Figure 5.8

Auditor's Report—Amazon.com 2004 Annual Report

Amazon.com

REPORT OF ERNST & YOUNG LLP, INDEPENDENT AUDITORS

The Board of Directors and Stockholders
Amazon.com, Inc.

We have audited the accompanying consolidated balance sheets of Amazon.com, Inc. as of December 31, 2004 and 2003, and the related consolidated statements of operations, stockholders' deficit, and cash flows for each of the three years in the period ended December 31, 2004. Our audits also included the financial statement schedule listed at Item 15(a)(2). These financial statements and schedule are the responsibility of the Company's management. Our responsibility is to express an opinion on these financial statements and schedule based on our audits.

We conducted our audits in accordance with the standards of the Public Company Accounting Oversight Board (United States). Those standards require that we plan and perform the audit to obtain reasonable assurance about whether the financial statements are free of material misstatement. An audit includes examining, on a test basis, evidence supporting the amounts and disclosures in the financial statements. An audit also includes assessing the accounting principles used and significant estimates made by management, as well as evaluating the overall financial statement presentation. We believe that our audits provide a reasonable basis for our opinion.

In our opinion, the financial statements referred to above present fairly, in all material respects, the consolidated financial position of Amazon.com, Inc. at December 31, 2004 and 2003, and the consolidated results of its operations and its cash flows for each of the three years in the period ended December 31, 2004, in conformity with U.S. generally accepted accounting principles. Also, in our opinion, the related financial statement schedule, when considered in relation to the basic financial statements taken as a whole, presents fairly in all material respects the information set forth therein.

We also have audited, in accordance with the standards of the Public Company Accounting Oversight Board (United States), the effectiveness of Amazon.com, Inc.'s internal control over financial reporting as of December 31, 2004, based on criteria established in Internal Control-Integrated Framework issued by the Committee of Sponsoring Organizations of the Treadway Commission and our report dated February 24, 2005 expressed an unqualified opinion thereon.

/s/   ERNST & YOUNG LLP

Seattle, Washington
January 24, 2005,

position, results of operations, and cash flows because of a lack of conformity with GAAP or inadequate disclosure. A qualified opinion is poorly received by investors and regulators and is usually considered a red flag signaling impending trouble for the firm. Given those far-reaching consequences, executives are highly motivated to ensure that their firms' financial statements comply with GAAP and to cooperate with the auditors before the financial statements are issued. As a result, qualified opinions are rarely issued. An adverse opinion is expressed when the auditor finds that the exceptions to GAAP are so material that the financial statements are not fairly presented and therefore should not be relied upon. A disclaimer is issued when the information reviewed is so limited that the auditor cannot state an opinion about the financial statements. Figure 5.8 shows an auditor's unqualified opinion for Amazon.com's financial statements, taken from the company's annual report.

MANAGEMENT'S REPORTS

As part of its responsibility for preparing financial statements that fairly present the financial activities of the firm, management is required to prepare several reports that are included in the company's annual report. Two of the most significant reports are management's discussion and analysis and statements certifying certain aspects of the financial statements.

❯ MANAGEMENT'S DISCUSSION AND ANALYSIS

management's discussion and analysis (MD&A) the section of an annual report in which management presents information about the company's operations, liquidity, and capital resources as well as certain forward-looking information

The **management's discussion and analysis (MD&A)** section of an annual report presents information about the company's operations, liquidity, and capital resources. Because the MD&A is written by management, it reflects management's views, but it must still be consistent with the information contained in the audited financial statements. Management is required to identify favorable and unfavorable trends and the events and uncertainties that may affect those trends. Because estimates of events in the future are subject to change, management must also discuss risk factors, such as the effects of inflation and changing prices.

forward-looking information management's estimates concerning the future performance of the company

The MD&A not only discusses the results of operations but also provides **forward-looking information**, in the form of management's estimates concerning the future performance of the firm. Prior to 1995, companies were discouraged from providing forward-looking information because of the potential for lawsuits from investors who purchased stock based on management's estimates of future performance and suffered a loss when the predicted performance was not realized. To reduce

Figure 5.9

Amazon.com's Management Evaluation of Internal Controls, 2004

Amazon.com

Evaluation of Disclosure Controls and Procedures

We carried out an evaluation required by the 1934 Act, under the supervision and with the participation of our principal executive officer and principal financial officer, of the effectiveness of the design and operation of our disclosure controls and procedures, as defined in Rule 13a-15(e) of the 1934 Act, as of December 31, 2004. Based on this evaluation, our principal executive officer and principal financial officer concluded that, as of December 31, 2004, our disclosure controls and procedures were effective in timely alerting them to material information required to be included in our periodic SEC reports.

Management's Report on Internal Control over Financial Reporting

Management is responsible for establishing and maintaining adequate internal control over financial reporting, as defined in Rule 13a-15(f) of the 1934 Act. Management has assessed the effectiveness of our internal control over financial reporting as of December 31, 2004 based on criteria established in Internal Control-Integrated Framework issued by the Committee of Sponsoring Organizations of the Treadway Commission. As a result of this assessment, management concluded that, as of December 31, 2004, our internal control over financial reporting was effective in providing reasonable assurance regarding the reliability of financial reporting and the preparation of financial statements for external purposes in accordance with generally accepted accounting principles. Ernst & Young LLP has issued an attestation report on management's assessment of internal control over financial reporting, a copy of which is included in this annual report on Form 10-K.

Limitations on Controls

Management does not expect that our disclosure controls and procedures or our internal control over financial reporting will prevent or detect all error and fraud. Any control system, no matter how well designed and operated, is based upon certain assumptions and can provide only reasonable, not absolute, assurance that its objectives will be met. Further, no evaluation of controls can provide absolute assurance that misstatements due to error or fraud will not occur or that all control issues and instances of fraud, if any, within the Company have been detected.

Private Securities Litigation Reform Act (PSLRA) of 1995 a law intended to discourage frivolous lawsuits from being filed without deterring the filing of meritorious suits

safe harbor rule a rule that allows companies to make financial forecasts without fear of litigation

the number of lawsuits related to forward-looking information, the **Private Securities Litigation Reform Act (PSLRA) of 1995** was enacted after much debate, a presidential veto, and a congressional override. By enacting the PSLRA, Congress hoped, among other things, to discourage frivolous lawsuits from being filed without deterring the filing of meritorious suits. The PSLRA provides for a **safe harbor rule** that allows companies to make financial forecasts without fear of litigation.

TOP MANAGEMENT'S CERTIFICATION OF FINANCIAL STATEMENTS

To curb fraudulent financial reporting, the SEC and the provisions of the Sarbanes-Oxley Act now require a firm's CEO and CFO to certify that their firm's financial statements do not contain any misstatements. Figure 5.9 is an evaluation of Amazon.com's internal control structure by Amazon.com's management. In addition, the firm's auditor must give an opinion as to management's assessment that the particular firm maintained effective internal control over financial reporting based on criteria that was established by a special committee that developed an integrated framework for internal controls. Figure 5.10 is an evaluation of Amazon.com's internal controls by Ernst & Young LLP, the firm's auditor.

Figure 5.10

Ernst & Young's Management Evaluation of Amazon.com's Internal Controls, 2004

Amazon.com

Report of Ernst & Young LLP
Independent Registered Public Accounting Firm

The Board of Directors and Stockholders
Amazon.com, Inc.

We have audited management's assessment, included in the accompanying Management's Report on Internal Control over Financial Reporting, that Amazon.com, Inc. maintained effective internal control over financial reporting, as of December 31, 2004, based on criteria established in Internal Control-Integrated Framework issued by the Committee of Sponsoring Organizations of the Treadway Commission (the COSO criteria). Amazon.com, Inc.'s management is responsible for maintaining effective internal control over financial reporting and for its assessment of the effectiveness of internal control over financial reporting. Our responsibility is to express an opinion on management's assessment and an opinion on the effectiveness of the company's internal control over financial reporting based on our audit.

We conducted our audit in accordance with the standards of the Public Company Accounting Oversight Board (United States). Those standards require that we plan and perform the audit to obtain reasonable assurance about whether effective internal control over financial reporting was maintained in all material respects. Our audit included obtaining an understanding of internal control over financial reporting, evaluating management's assessment, testing and evaluating the design and operating effectiveness of internal control, and performing such other procedures as we considered necessary in the circumstances. We believe that our audit provides a reasonable basis for our opinion.

A company's internal control over financial reporting is a process designed to provide reasonable assurance regarding the reliability of financial reporting and the preparation of financial statements for external purposes in accordance with generally accepted accounting principles. A company's internal control over financial reporting includes those policies and procedures that (1) pertain to the maintenance of records that, in reasonable detail, accurately and fairly reflect the transactions and dispositions of the assets of the company; (2) provide reasonable assurance that transactions are recorded as necessary to permit preparation of financial statements in accordance with generally accepted accounting principles, and that receipts and expenditures of the company are being made only in accordance with authorizations of management and directors of the company; and (3) provide reasonable assurance regarding prevention or timely detection of unauthorized acquisition, use, or disposition of the company's assets that could have a material effect on the financial statements.

(continued)

Figure 5.10 *continued*

Ernst & Young's Management Evaluation of Amazon.com's Internal Controls, 2004

Because of its inherent limitations, internal control over financial reporting may not prevent or detect misstatements. Also, projections of any evaluation of effectiveness to future periods are subject to the risk that controls may become inadequate because of changes in conditions, or that the degree of compliance with the policies or procedures may deteriorate.

In our opinion, management's assessment that Amazon.com, Inc. maintained effective internal control over financial reporting as of December 31, 2004, is fairly stated, in all material respects, based on the COSO criteria. Also, in our opinion, Amazon.com, Inc. maintained, in all material respects, effective internal control over financial reporting as of December 31, 2004, based on the COSO criteria.

We have also audited, in accordance with the standards of the Public Company Accounting Oversight Board (United States), the consolidated balance sheets of Amazon.com, Inc. as of December 31, 2004 and 2003, and the related statements of operations, shareholders' deficit, and cash flows for each of the three years in the period ended December 31, 2004 of Amazon.com, Inc. and our report dated February 24, 2005 expressed an unqualified opinion thereon.

/s/ ERNST & YOUNG LLP

Seattle, Washington
February 24, 2005

CHECK YOUR UNDERSTANDING

1. What criteria must be met in order for a company to be required to report segment information in its annual report?

2. List two examples of subsequent events that should be reported in the notes to a company's financial statements.

3. Describe two views on interim reporting periods.

4. What is the purpose of the auditor's report?

Revisiting the Case

AMAZON.COM REPORTS POSITIVE CASH FLOWS FROM OPERATIONS

1. $566,560 thousand was reported as net cash provided by operating activities for 2004; $392,022 thousand was reported for 2003.

2. Sales and maturities of marketable securities and other investments provided cash flows from investing activities.

3. Answers will vary, but investors might surmise that the company has significantly improved its financial condition based on the increase in cash generated from operations, as well as generating net income for 2004 and 2003.

SUMMARY BY LEARNING OBJECTIVE

LO1 **Explain the importance of the statement of cash flows.**

By converting accrual-based net income to cash flows from operations and detailing the cash receipts and disbursements from operating, investing, and financing activities, the statement of cash flows adds valuable information to the historical data presented on the balance sheet and income statement. In addition, the statement of cash flows reconciles a firm's reported net income for the year with its change in cash for the same accounting period. As a result, users can more accurately analyze and forecast a firm's cash receipts and disbursements, thereby assessing its liquidity and flexibility.

LO2 Describe how the statement of cash flows is structured.

On the statement of cash flows, a firm's increases and decreases in cash and cash equivalents for the period are summarized in three main categories: cash flows from operating activities, cash flows from investing activities, and cash flows from financing activities. Cash flows from operating activities are cash receipts and payments resulting from the operations of a firm's core business, such as cash receipts from sales and fee revenue, wages and salaries, and operating expenses. Cash flows from investing activities are cash receipts and payments resulting from a firm's long-term investments and disinvestments in productive assets, such as plant and equipment. Cash flows from financing activities are cash receipts and payments related to long-term liabilities and stockholders' equity, including the issuance of bonds, the repurchase of common stock, and the payment of dividends. The effect of foreign currency translation on cash is disclosed, and the beginning and ending cash balances are reconciled. Any non-cash transactions are disclosed in a separate schedule or in the notes to the statement. Cash flows from investing activities are derived by evaluating changes in noncurrent assets. Cash flows from financing activities are derived by evaluating changes in non-current liabilities and stockholders' equity accounts other than changes in retained earnings due to net income or net loss for the period.

LO3 Prepare a statement of cash flows.

The statement of cash flows is usually prepared after the income statement and the balance sheet because much of the required data is drawn from those two statements. There are usually four steps in the preparation of this statement:

1. Determine the cash provided by or used in operating activities.

2. Determine the cash provided by or used in investing activities.

3. Determine the cash provided by or used in financing activities.

4. Determine the change (increase or decrease) in cash during the period and determine the ending balance of cash and cash equivalents.

Cash flows from operations must be reconciled with the net income reported for the period. This may be done by using either the indirect method or the direct method of reporting cash flows from operations. Under the indirect method, net income (or loss) is listed first and then reconciled to net cash provided by or used in operations. Under the direct method, items on the income statement are converted from an accrual basis to a cash basis. Any gain or loss from currency translation is reported separately on the statement of cash flows, after the operating, investing, and financing activities sections. The cash flows from operating, investing, and financing activities and the effect of the gain or loss from foreign currency translation are added together to arrive at the net increase or decrease in cash for the period. This is added to the beginning cash balance, and the sum is listed as the ending cash balance. The beginning and ending cash balances must correspond with the amounts reported on the balance sheet for the current and previous periods.

LO4 Use the statement of cash flows to analyze a company's cash adequacy and its performance with regard to cash.

The cash debt coverage ratio measures a firm's ability to repay its debt; it is calculated by dividing cash flows from operating activities by average total debt. The cash dividend coverage ratio helps users determine whether a company is generating enough cash from operations to cover its dividends. This ratio is calculated by dividing cash flows from operating activities by total dividends paid. The cash dividend payout ratio measures a firm's ability to make its dividend payments and is calculated by dividing total dividends paid by cash flows from operating activities. When assessing a firm's ability to meet current interest payments, the cash interest coverage ratio is used. Cash flows from operating activities are added to interest and taxes paid. Then this total is divided by cash interest payments.

Cash flow return on assets is calculated by dividing cash flows from operating activities before interest and taxes paid by average total assets for the period, and cash flow return on equity is calculated by dividing cash flows from operating activities less any preferred dividends paid by average common stockholders' equity. These ratios help users assess whether a firm is earning an adequate cash flow return on its net assets and whether stockholders are earning adequate cash flows from their investments. Cash flow per share is calculated by dividing cash flows from operating activities by the number of issued shares. This ratio helps users understand how much cash flow is attributed to each share of stock issued. Indicators of how closely net income mirrors cash flows from operating activities are the cash flow to operating income ratio (cash flows from operating activities divided by operating income) and the cash flow to net income ratio (cash flows from operating activities divided by net income).

LO5 Identify additional significant financial disclosures required by GAAP and the SEC.

In addition to the four primary financial statements and their notes, a public corporation must submit other information as part of its annual report or in filings with the SEC. The required submissions include an explanation of significant accounting policies and related notes; reports by operating segment; a discussion of subsequent events; interim reports; an auditor's report, which expresses an opinion about whether the financial statements are in accordance with GAAP; management's discussion and analysis, which explains the results of operations and future risks and trends; and certification of the financial statements by top management. Public companies must also comply with Regulation FD, which requires them to ensure that disclosures that are intentionally made to analysts and certain other users are simultaneously disseminated to the public.

KEY TERMS

accounting policies (p. 214)
auditor's report (p. 219)
cash debt coverage ratio (p. 211)
cash dividend coverage ratio (p. 211)
cash dividend payout ratio (p. 212)
cash equivalents (p. 199)
cash flow per share (p. 213)
cash flow return on assets (p. 213)
cash flow return on equity (p. 213)
cash flow to net income ratio (p. 213)
cash flow to operating income ratio (p. 213)

cash flows from financing activities (p. 199)
cash flows from investing activities (p. 199)
cash flows from operating activities (p. 199)
cash interest coverage ratio (p. 212)
direct method (p. 205)
discrete view (p. 218)
foreign currency translation gain or loss (p. 208)
forward-looking information (p. 222)

indirect method (p. 202)
integral view (p. 218)
interim financial reports (p. 218)
management's discussion and analysis (MD&A) (p. 222)
operating segment (p. 215)
Private Securities Litigation Reform Act (PSLRA) of 1995 (p. 223)
Regulation FD (p. 217)
safe harbor rule (p. 223)
statement of cash flows (p. 196)
subsequent events (p. 216)

EXERCISES

LO2, 3 **EXERCISE 5-1** **Operating Activities**

The following selected, nonordered financial information was taken from the records of Flowers, Inc. at December 31:

	2005	2004
Accounts Receivable	$12,000	$39,500
Inventories	16,000	31,000
Accounts Payable	32,000	21,300
Prepaid Insurance	700	2,000
Equipment	98,000	85,000
Accumulated Depreciation	17,000	18,000
Notes Payable	81,000	67,000
Common Stock	32,000	14,000
Dividends Payable	0	6,600
Additional Paid-in Capital	65,000	40,000
Retained Earnings	16,200	21,200

Flowers, Inc.
Income Statement
For the Year Ended December 31, 2005

Sales	$616,000
Sales returns	5,000
Net sales	$611,000
Cost of goods sold	434,000
Operating expenses (includes $8,000 of depreciation)	182,000
Loss on sale of equipment	6,000
Net income	$ 11,000

Additional information:

A. Equipment with a cost of $20,000 was sold for $5,000 during 2005. New equipment was purchased for cash.

B. The only other items affecting retained earnings in 2005 was net income for the period and dividends declared of $16,000. Dividends paid during the period were $22,600.

C. The company borrowed $14,000 from the bank.

D. New investors contributed cash and received stock in exchange.

Required:

1. How much cash was collected from customers during 2005?

2. How much cash was paid for operating expenses during 2005?

3. How much cash was paid to acquire inventories during 2005?

LO2, 3   **EXERCISE 5-2   Investing Activities**
Use the information provided in Exercise 5-1.

Required: Prepare the investing activities section of the statement of cash flows for 2005.

LO3   **EXERCISE 5-3   Financing Activities**
Use the information provided in Exercise 5-1.

Required: Prepare the financing activities section of the statement of cash flows for 2005.

LO3   **EXERCISE 5-4   Operating Activities**
Jasper Heavy Equipment presented its comparative financial data at December 31 as shown in the following table:

	2005	2004
Cash	$ 53,000	$ 42,000
Accounts receivable	311,000	252,000
Prepaid expenses	3,800	3,000
Inventory	850,000	1,021,000
Building and equipment	203,200	110,000
Accumulated depreciation	(60,000)	(51,000)
	$1,361,000	$1,377,000
Accounts payable	$ 76,000	$ 43,000
Dividends payable	161,000	88,000
Accrued expenses	201,000	302,000
Long-term note payable	312,000	352,000
Common stock	230,000	248,000
Additional paid-in capital	121,000	121,000
Retained earnings	260,000	223,000
Total liabilities and stockholders' equity	$1,361,000	$1,377,000

Additional information for the year 2005:

A. Equipment was purchased for $173,200 and was paid in cash. Other equipment costing $80,000 was sold at a $3,000 gain and was 60 percent depreciated at the time of sale.

B. Depreciation expense was recorded.

C. Net income was $110,000.

Required: Prepare the operating activities section of the statement of cash flows for 2005, using the indirect method.

LO2, 3 **EXERCISE 5-5** **Financing Activities**

Rogers Widgets, Inc. presents the following selected comparative financial data at December 31:

	Dec. 31, 2005	Dec. 31, 2004
Accounts Payable	$16,000	$43,000
Dividends Payable	82,000	88,000
Accrued Expenses	11,000	10,000
Common Stock	50,000	50,000
Additional Paid-in Capital	15,000	15,000
Retained Earnings	66,200	21,200

Additional information for 2005:

A. A cash dividend of $40,000 was declared.

B. Depreciation expense of $35,000 was recorded.

C. Net income was $85,000.

Required: Calculate dividends paid during 2005.

LO2, 3 **EXERCISE 5-6** **Financing Activities**

Kind Creatures, Inc. presented the following comparative financial data at December 31:

	Dec. 31, 2005	Dec. 31, 2004
Cash	$ 2,000	$ 4,000
Accounts receivable	14,000	12,000
Inventory	8,000	11,000
Building and equipment	14,000	8,000
Accumulated depreciation	(6,000)	(2,000)
	$32,000	$33,000
Accounts payable	$ 6,000	$ 6,000
Dividends payable	4,000	9,000
Common stock	5,000	4,000
Additional paid-in capital	9,000	8,000
Retained earnings	8,000	6,000
Total liabilities and stockholders' equity	$32,000	$33,000

Additional information for 2005:

A. Cash dividends declared were $3,000.

B. Common stock was issued to a new investor for cash.

C. Net income was $5,000.

Required: Prepare the financing activities section of the statement of cash flows for 2005.

LO3 **EXERCISE 5-7** **Investing Activities**

Caliper Restaurants presented the following selected comparative financial data at December 31:

	Dec. 31, 2005	Dec. 31, 2004
Cash	$?	$ 42,000
Accounts Receivable	31,000	32,000
Inventory	6,000	21,000
Equipment	165,000	167,500
Accumulated Depreciation	13,000	12,000

Additional information for 2005:

A. Only one equipment transaction occurred during 2005. One fryer with an original cost of $2,500 was sold, with a $300 loss on the sale.

B. Depreciation expense for the year was $2,200.

Required: Calculate the cash flows from the sale of the equipment.

LO2, 3 **EXERCISE 5-8   Cash Collected from Customers**

The following is selected financial information for Star Capps Distribution Company for 2005:

Sales	$110,000
Sales returns	5,000
Net sales	$105,000
Cost of goods sold	84,000
Operating expenses (includes $2,000 of depreciation)	17,000
Net income	$ 4,000

Additional information at December 31:

	2005	2004
Cash	$21,000	$42,000
Accounts Receivable	31,000	21,000
Retained Earnings	8,000	7,000

Required: Determine how much cash was collected from customers during 2005.

LO3 **EXERCISE 5-9   Operating Activities—Indirect Method**

Farmers Surplus Company presented the following comparative financial data at December 31:

	Dec. 31, 2005	Dec. 31, 2004
Cash	$ 10,000	$ 42,000
Accounts receivable	91,000	53,000
Building and equipment	300,000	200,000
Accumulated depreciation	60,000	51,000
Total assets	$341,000	$244,000
Accounts payable	$ 55,000	$ 21,000
Dividends payable	42,000	21,000
Common stock	110,000	110,000
Additional paid-in capital	60,000	60,000
Retained earnings	74,000	32,000
Total liabilities and stockholders' equity	$341,000	$244,000

Additional information for the year 2005:

A. Equipment costing $80,000 was sold at a $1,000 gain and was 30 percent depreciated at the time of sale.

B. Depreciation expense was recorded.

C. Net income was $75,000.

Required: In good form, prepare the operating activities section of the statement of cash flows for 2005 using the indirect method.

LO3 **EXERCISE 5-10 Statement of Cash Flows—Indirect Method**
Diaz Corporation presented the following selected financial information for the years 2004 and 2005 and balances at December 31, 2004 and 2005:

	2005	2004
Net income	$19,000	$22,000
Depreciation Expense	8,000	6,000
Cash	39,000	15,000
Accounts Receivable	11,000	9,000
Prepaid Insurance	2,000	1,000
Plant Assets, net	78,000	86,000
Accounts Payable	18,000	16,000
Notes Payable	42,000	44,000

Other than depreciation, there were no changes in plant assets during the year.

Required: Prepare the statement of cash flows for Diaz Corporation for 2005. Use the indirect method.

LO4 **EXERCISE 5-11 Cash Flow Statement Analysis**
The accountant for Mercury Carpets reported that the company's income statement for 2004 showed a net loss of $11,000. The accountant provided the following operating activities section of the company's statement of cash flows for 2005:

Mercury Carpets
Statement of Cash Flows—Operating Activities Section
For the Year Ended December 31, 2005

Net loss	($11,000)
Depreciation expense	6,500
Amortization of intangibles	4,000
Decrease in accounts receivable	6,500
Increase in inventories	(3,200)
Decrease in accounts payable	(500)
Decrease in other accrued expenses	(600)
Net cash flows provided by operating activities	$ 1,700

Mercury Carpet's average total debt outstanding for the past two years totaled $34,000. The total of interest and taxes paid for 2005 is $5,300, and the average total assets for the past two years is $70,000.

Required:

1. Would you be concerned about the company's ability to repay its debt? Explain why or why not.

2. Do you think the shareholders are receiving a fair return on the company's assets from a cash flow perspective? Justify your answer.

LO2, 4 **EXERCISE 5-12 Cash Flow Statement Analysis**
Diesel Repair Company has experienced challenges in the last two years related to attrition of controllers in the accounting department. As a result, the president of the company has struggled to obtain a regular analysis of the financial statements. A selection of the information for 2005 is as follows:

Net income	$65,000
Depreciation	11,000
Change in Current Assets (excluding cash)	(6,000)
Change in Current Liabilities	(12,000)
Interest Expense	12,000
Income Taxes Paid	38,000
Cash Interest Payments	18,000

Required: As the new controller, you have been asked to analyze key aspects of the company's cash flow. The following questions have been asked:

1. Determine the cash interest coverage ratio for the company.
2. With regard to the quality of earnings (determined via the calculation of the cash flow to net income ratio), how would you rate Diesel Repair Company?

LO5   **EXERCISE 5-13   Additional Disclosures Required by the SEC**

Jostlen Industries has four divisions that represent diverse manufacturing lines of business. Jostlen's CPA has questioned the CFO about whether Jostlen is currently complying with *SFAS No. 131*. The following is a recap of selected financial information for each division:

	Cass	Bat	Red	Stem
Revenue	$ 42,000	$112,000	$ 84,000	$16,000
Operating profit (loss)	(4,100)	12,000	6,000	500
Total assets	414,000	210,000	112,500	45,000

Required: If the company currently recognizes only Bat as an operating segment, is this correct according to *SFAS No. 131* or not?

LO1   **EXERCISE 5-14   Importance of the Statement of Cash Flows**

The statement of cash flows is one of the four required primary financial statements.

Required: Indicate whether the following statements are true (T) or false (F).

1. The statement of cash flows gives users an itemized accounting for the elements that make up net income.
2. The statement of cash flows helps users understand the difference between net income or loss and the change in cash for the period.
3. A company cannot generate positive cash flows from operations and report a net loss for the same period.
4. The statement of cash flows outlines the uses and sources of cash from three primary activities: operating, investing, and financing.
5. The statement of cash flows provides details on cash transactions that are not reflected on the balance sheet or the income statement.

LO4   **EXERCISE 5-15   Analysis of Cash Performance**

Lakeline Electric Co. is considering purchasing Raleigh Electric to increase its customer service area and increase its overall cash flows. The following information for the year ended December 31, 2005 was given to Lakeline for review as it considers the purchase.

Operating income	$1,500,345
Net income	980,020
Cash flows from operating activities	2,559,550
Cash flows from investing activities	180,000
Cash flows from financing activities	750,335

Required:

1. Compute Raleigh's cash flow to operating income ratio.
2. Compute Raleigh's cash flow to net income ratio.
3. What is your analysis of Raleigh's quality of earnings, based on these two ratios?

LO5 EXERCISE 5-16 **Financial Statement Disclosures**

In addition to the information in the four primary financial statements and their notes, a public corporation must disclose other pertinent information as part of its annual report or in filings with the SEC.

Required: Indicate whether the following statements regarding financial disclosures are true (T) or false (F).

1. The SEC requires that Form 10-K be filed within 90 days of a company's year end.

2. Companies are required to disclose any significant post-statement events that occur between the year-end date and the date on which the financial statements are issued.

3. Earnings per share data are not required in publicly traded companies' interim reports.

4. An unqualified opinion in the auditor's report indicates the lowest degree of confidence in the presentation of the financial statements.

5. The management's discussion and analysis section of an annual report reflects management's views on the company's operations, its liquidity, and its capital resources.

LO4 EXERCISE 5-17 **Analysis of Cash Flow Coverage**

As a potential investor in Blair Enterprises, Inc., you wish to investigate how the company has managed to cover its dividends to current stockholders. You gather the following data from the company's current annual report:

	2005	2004
Dividends paid	$ 56,500	$ 23,000
Cash flows from operating activities	256,700	350,050

Required:

1. What percentage of cash flows from operating activities was used for dividends in 2005? In 2004?

2. How would you characterize the company's ability to cover its current dividends in 2005? In 2004?

LO5 EXERCISE 5-18 **Required Financial Disclosures**

Publicly held companies are required to have their financial statements audited by a CPA and must include a certification of the financial statements by top management.

Required: Describe the role and importance of the auditor's report and the certification of financial statements by management as found in a company's annual report.

LO5 EXERCISE 5-19 **Disclosure of Subsequent Events**

Janice Johnson was hired at BeeBop Records on February 9, 2005, as the senior staff accountant. The company is in the process of preparing the financial statements for the year ended December 31, 2004. The statements will be released on February 28, 2005. In reviewing the company's records, she found the following details:

A. A letter from BeeBop's attorney arrives on February 15, 2005. The letter references a pending lawsuit in which BeeBop is accused of copyright infringement by Randy Buckle, a country-western songwriter. The attorney has negotiated a settlement of $1.2 million, to be paid to Mr. Buckle in 2006 and 2007.

B. As a result of repeated errors in shipments to TipTop Music, BeeBop Records has lost its distribution contract with TipTop. TipTop, one of BeeBop's major customers, has informed BeeBop that it will no longer carry artists on the BeeBop label.

C. The company experienced a loss of $2.3 million on the sale of a business segment on February 20, 2005.

Required: Describe how each event would be reflected in the financial statements and related notes to be issued on February 28, 2005.

LO2 EXERCISE 5-20 **Classification of Cash Flows**

The following types of transactions affect cash flows and would therefore be reported on a statement of cash flows:

A. Cash payment for inventory

B. Cash receipt from the sale of investment securities

C. Issuance of capital stock

D. Payment of dividends to stockholders

E. Purchase of a plant asset

F. Cash payment for wages

G. Cash received for sales

H. Collection of a note receivable

Required: For each of these items, indicate the appropriate classification on the statement of cash flows: operating activities (OA), investing activities (IA), or financing activities (FA).

PROBLEMS

LO2, 3, 4   **PROBLEM 5-1   Cash Flows; Operating Activities Using the Indirect Method**

The following selected, nonordered account balances were taken from Boucherie, Inc.'s balance sheets at December 31:

	2005	2004
Accounts Receivable	$42,000	$39,500
Inventories	28,600	31,000
Accounts Payable	19,000	21,300
Income Taxes Payable	13,000	5,000
Prepaid Insurance	700	2,000
Other Accrued Expenses	1,000	1,600
Equipment	59,000	69,000
Accumulated Depreciation	16,400	28,000
Notes Payable	46,000	67,000
Common Stock	32,000	14,000
Dividends Payable	3,000	6,600
Additional Paid-in Capital	65,000	40,000
Retained Earnings	32,800	21,200

Boucherie, Inc. reported the following operating results for 2005:

Sales	$525,000
Sales returns	5,000
Net sales	$520,000
Cost of goods sold	317,000
Operating expenses (includes $4,400 of depreciation)	112,000
Loss on sale of equipment	2,000
Income tax expense	28,000
Net income	$ 61,000

Additional information:

A. All merchandise is purchased on account.

B. Equipment with a cost of $25,000 was sold for $7,000 during 2005. New equipment was purchased for cash. Equipment costing $15,000 was acquired by issuing common stock worth the same amount and having a par value of $2,000.

C. Additional stock was sold for cash.

D. The only items affecting retained earnings in 2005 were net income and cash dividends declared of $49,400.

E. No new loans were acquired in 2005.

Required:

1. How much cash was collected from customers during 2005?
2. How much cash was paid for inventory during 2005?
3. How much cash was paid for income taxes during 2005?
4. How much cash was paid for operating expenses during 2005?
5. Based on your calculations in questions 1 through 4, what are the net cash flows from operating activities for 2005?
6. In good form, prepare the operating activities section of the statement of cash flows, using the indirect method.

Critical Thinking: Why do you think the indirect method of preparing the statement of cash flows is more commonly used by companies than the direct method?

Analyze: What is the company's cash flow to net income ratio for 2005?

LO2, 3   **PROBLEM 5-2**   **Financing Activities**

The following selected, nonordered account balances and net income were taken from Torre, Inc.'s financial statements at December 31:

	2005	2004
Prepaid Insurance	$ 700	$ 2,000
Other Accrued Expenses	1,000	1,600
Equipment	59,000	69,000
Accumulated Depreciation	16,400	28,000
Notes Payable	46,000	67,000
Common Stock	32,000	14,000
Dividends Payable	8,000	15,000
Income Taxes Payable	10,000	6,000
Additional Paid-in Capital	65,000	40,000
Retained Earnings	32,800	21,200
Net Income	64,000	42,000
Depreciation Expense	4,400	3,400

Additional information:

A. Equipment with a cost of $25,000 was sold for $7,000 at a loss of $2,000 during 2005.
B. New equipment was purchased for cash.
C. No new loans were acquired in 2005.
D. Torre issued common stock for cash during the year.
E. The only items affecting retained earnings in 2005 were cash dividends declared of $52,400 and net income.

Required: In good form, prepare the financing activities section of the statement of cash flows for 2005.

Analyze: How would the financing activities section of the statement of cash flows differ if Torre, Inc. had issued stock in exchange for the new equipment instead of paying cash? Explain.

Spreadsheet: Prepare the financing activities section of the statement of cash flows using a spreadsheet application.

LO2, 3   **PROBLEM 5-3**   **Cash Equivalents; Operating Activities Using the Indirect Method**

Pens Galore, Inc. provided the following selected balance sheet accounts at December 31 and income statement accounts for the years 2004 and 2005.

Balance Sheet	2005	2004
Accounts Receivable	$ 36,000	$ 42,000
Accounts Payable	28,000	25,000
Certificates of Deposit	12,000	4,000
Patent	15,000	16,000
Equipment	160,000	140,000
Accumulated Depreciation	30,000	34,000
Cash	21,000	25,000
Note Payable, due in 2006	48,000	20,000
Retained Earnings	65,000	40,000

Income Statement	2005	2004
Net sales	$420,000	$400,000
Cost of goods sold	280,000	272,000
Patent amortization expense	1,000	1,000
Gain (loss) on sale of equipment	1,800	(400)
Interest expense	9,600	7,600
Other operating expenses, including depreciation	84,000	90,000
Net income	$ 47,200	$ 29,000

Additional information:

A. Equipment with a cost of $21,000 and a book value of $3,000 was sold during 2005. Additional equipment was purchased.

B. Information on the certificates of deposit follows:

  • $4,000, 120-day CD dated and acquired November 15, 2004
  • $12,000, 90-day CD that matures on January 4, 2006

Required:

1. How much should Pens Galore, Inc. report as "net increase or decrease in cash and cash equivalents" for 2005?

2. What disclosures must Pens Galore make pertaining to its cash equivalents?

3. Prepare the operating activities section of the statement of cash flows for 2005, using the indirect method. (*Hint:* You must calculate depreciation expense.)

Analyze: Suppose Pens Galore purchased a $20,000, 90-day certificate of deposit (CD) on March 16, 2005, and received cash from the same CD when it matured on June 15, 2005. How would this transaction be reported in the statement of cash flows? Why would it be reported in that way?

Research: Locate the investor relations section of the BIC website (**www.bicworld.com**). Find the 2002 statement of cash flows. Does BIC use the direct or the indirect method when preparing its statement of cash flows? What amount of net cash from operating activities was reported in 2002?

LO2, 3, 4   **PROBLEM 5-4   Operating, Investing, and Financing Activities; Analysis**
Kravat Company provided the following selected, nonordered balance sheet accounts at December 31 and income statement accounts for the years 2004 and 2005:

	2005	2004
Accumulated Depreciation	$350,000	$450,000
Building	720,000	620,000
Dividends Payable	10,000	8,000
Retained Earnings	400,000	300,000
Common Stock	42,000	30,000
Additional Paid-in Capital	98,000	34,000
Depreciation Expense	47,000	46,000
Mortgage Payable	360,000	0
Gain on Sale of Building	20,000	30,000

During 2005, Kravat Company sold a building with a book value of $40,000 and an original cost of $280,000. During the same year, Kravat purchased a building by signing a mortgage for $360,000 and paying the balance in cash. Kravat declared dividends of $50,000 and reported net income totaling $150,000 on its income statement during 2005. Kravat's net increase in cash flows for 2005 (the total on its statement of cash flows) was $3,000.

Required:

1. Prepare the investing activities section of the statement of cash flows for the year ended December 31, 2005.

2. Prepare the financing activities section for the year ended December 31, 2005.

3. Determine the amount of cash flows from operating activities for 2005. (*Hint:* Because you don't have all the information needed to create the operating activities section, you will have to look at the other totals you know on the statement of cash flows.)

Analyze: Comment on Kravat's sources and uses of cash flows for 2005. In your opinion, what are the long-term prospects for Kravat Company if it continues the same trend of cash flows?

LO3 **PROBLEM 5-5** **Cash Flow Amounts**

Manning Corp. provided the following selected, nonordered balance sheet accounts at December 31 and income statement accounts for the year 2005:

	2005	2004
Accounts Receivable	$ 36,000	$30,000
Inventories	22,000	25,000
Accounts Payable	39,000	35,000
Salaries Payable	1,000	2,000
Equipment	60,000	40,000
Accumulated Depreciation	12,000	16,000
Notes Payable	0	50,000
Common Stock	40,000	10,000
Dividends Payable	8,000	15,000
Additional Paid-in Capital	125,000	20,000
Retained Earnings	38,000	20,000

Net sales	$430,000
Cost of goods sold	300,000
Depreciation expense	8,000
Other operating expenses	84,000
Gain on sale of equipment	2,000
Net income	$ 40,000

The accounting records revealed the following additional information:

A. Equipment with a cost of $15,000 and a book value of $3,000 was sold for $5,000 during 2005. New equipment was purchased.

B. Common stock with a par value of $13,000 was issued to a lender in exchange for the payoff of the principal of the note payable due during 2005. No new funds were borrowed during the year.

C. The only items affecting retained earnings in 2005 were net income and cash dividends declared.

Required:

1. What amount of cash was collected from customers during 2005?

2. What amount was paid for purchases of merchandise during 2005?

3. What amount was paid to acquire equipment during 2005?

4. What amount was the stock issued for during 2005?

5. What amount was paid for dividends during 2005?

Analyze: Why is a company's net income different from its net cash flow for the same period?

LO2, 4   PROBLEM 5-6   **Transaction Classification, International Accounting Comparison**

Patel, Inc., a health and fitness club, completed the following transactions during 2005:

A. Purchased computer equipment for cash

B. Issued preferred stock to investors.

C. Paid employee salaries and wages.

D. Purchased treasury stock.

E. Received dividends from a stock investment.

F. Issued common stock to acquire a building.

G. Recorded depreciation expense for the year.

H. Paid interest on bonds payable.

I. Declared cash dividends.

J. Repaid a bank loan.

K. Received interest on a note receivable.

L. Accrued salaries at year end.

M. Purchased a copyright.

N. Received payments from credit sales.

Patel, Inc. uses the direct method to prepare the operating activities section of its statement of cash flows.

Required:

1. Classify transactions A through N according to how they should be presented on Patel's statement of cash flows by selecting the appropriate cash flow effect from the list below.

    Inflow from operating activity

    Outflow from operating activity

    Inflow from investing activity

    Outflow from investing activity

    Inflow from financing activity

    Outflow from financing activity

    Noncash investing and financing activity

    Not reported on the statement of cash flows under the direct method

2. Which items would be reported differently under International Accounting Standards? Indicate how these items should be reported under the IAS guidelines.

Analyze: Is the cash balance affected if a company conducts operations in a foreign country but prepares its financial statements according to U.S. GAAP? Why or why not?

LO2, 3   PROBLEM 5-7   **Cash Flow Calculations; Reconciliation**

Short Corp. provided the following selected balance sheet accounts at December 31 and income statement accounts for the years 2004 and 2005:

	2005	2004
Accounts Receivable	$ 65,800	$ 59,400
Accounts Payable	49,000	51,300
Sales Revenue	754,000	780,000
Cost of Goods Sold	326,000	310,000
Sales Discounts	7,800	7,600
Customer Advance Deposits	25,000	14,000
Income Taxes Payable	3,900	3,500
Inventories	22,000	27,000
Income Tax Expense	34,200	35,000

Short uses accounts payable for inventory acquisitions only. Net income for 2005 was $68,000.

Required:

1. How much should Short report as cash collected from customers?

2. How much should be reported as cash paid for inventory?

3. Prepare a reconciliation of net income to cash flows from operating activities for 2005.

Communicate: For each item in question 4 that is added to or subtracted from net income, indicate why this adjustment was necessary.

Analyze: How much should be reported as cash paid for income taxes?

LO2, 3 **PROBLEM 5-8** **Reporting Sale of Plant Asset on Statement of Cash Flows; Adjustments**

Styling Company uses the indirect method of preparing the statement of cash flows. During 2005, Styling Company sold a machine that cost $52,000 and had a book value of $35,000 for $25,000. During the same year, Styling purchased a new machine with a cash payment of $80,000. Net income for 2005 is $30,000. The balance sheet accounts at December 31 and income statement accounts for the years 2004 and 2005 follow:

	2005	2004
Cash	$ 35,000	$ 32,000
90-day Treasury Bill	40,000	55,000
Interest Expense	4,300	2,600
Income Tax Expense	40,400	61,200
4-Month Certificate of Deposit, matures Jan. 8, 2006	25,000	0
Machine	353,000	325,000
Accumulated Depreciation	93,000	78,000

Required:

1. Determine the net increase or decrease in cash and cash equivalents for 2005.

2. Prepare the investing activities section of Styling Company's statement of cash flows for 2005.

3. Show how the items related to the machines will be reported in the operating activities section of Styling Company's statement of cash flows for 2005, using the indirect method.

Communicate: Assume you are training a new accounting clerk who has never prepared a statement of cash flows. Explain the adjustments that you made to net income to arrive at net cash flows from operating activities.

Analyze: By what percentage did Styling Company's cash and cash equivalents change in 2005?

LO2, 3 **PROBLEM 5-9** **Indirect Method, Foreign Currency Translation Gain**

The following data are taken from the accounts of Cox Company at December 31:

	2005	2004
Cash	$85,000	$61,000
Accounts Receivable	25,000	24,000
Foreign Currency Translation Gain	5,000	2,000
Accounts Payable	10,000	12,500
Inventory	20,000	22,100
60-Day Certificate of Deposit	20,000	15,000

During 2005, Cox paid $65,000 in dividends, recognized a loss of $11,000 on the sale of machinery used in production, and recognized $21,000 of depreciation expense for the year. Net income reported by Cox Company totaled $110,000.

Required:

1. Calculate Cox's cash flows from operating activities for 2005, using the indirect method.

2. Calculate the amount that Cox would report as "Net increase/decrease in cash and cash equivalents" for the year ended December 31, 2005.

Communicate: Cox Company has conducted business in Mexico only for the past two years. Explain how the foreign currency translation should be reported.

Analyze: What amount of foreign currency translation gain should be reported on the statement of cash flows?

LO1, 2, 3, 4   **PROBLEM 5-10   Direct Method; Usefulness of Statement of Cash Flows**

Jugalusi Corporation has provided the following information concerning its financial activities during 2005:

Cash and cash equivalents balance:	
Dec. 31, 2004	$ 12,000
Dec. 31, 2005	29,000
Cash paid for equipment	25,000
Cash borrowed by signing a 2-year note payable	40,000
Foreign currency translation loss	(5,000)
Cash paid to purchase treasury stock	30,000
Accepted note receivable from a customer in exchange for merchandise	10,000
Cash paid for dividends	50,000
Cash paid for interest on bonds	4,000
Cash paid for operating expenses	82,000
Cash paid for merchandise	116,000
Interest received	2,000
Net income	44,000
Cash paid for note interest expense	3,000
Gain on sale of equipment	1,000
Cash received from issuance of bonds	80,000
Depreciation expense	15,000
Cash received from customers	210,000
Sales revenue recognized	220,000

Required: Prepare a statement of cash flows for Jugalusi Corporation for the year ended December 31, 2005, using the direct method. (*Hint:* You will not use all items.)

Critical Thinking: What is the purpose of the statement of cash flows? Why is it important to understand a company's cash position?

Analyze: Calculate and interpret Jugalusi Corporation's cash flow to net income ratio. Assume that the ratios for Jugalusi's closest competitors are 1.2 and 0.975.

LO5   **PROBLEM 5-11   Segment Reporting**

First Corp. and its divisions are engaged in manufacturing operations. The data that follow pertain to the industries in which operations were conducted for the year ended December 31, 2005.

Segment	Identifiable Assets	Revenue	Profit/Loss
Bill	$12,000,000	$1,850,000	$22,000,000
Hillary	8,000,000	1,400,000	(17,000,000)
George	6,000,000	1,200,000	12,500,000
Laura	3,000,000	550,000	3,500,000
Ronald	4,250,000	275,000	(2,000,000)
Nancy	1,500,000	225,000	(3,000,000)
Totals	$34,750,000	$5,500,000	$16,000,000

Required:

1. Which segments are considered reportable under *SFAS No. 131*?

2. What information should First Corp. report for each segment that is considered reportable?

Critical Thinking: *SFAS No. 131* indicates that companies should disclose information for up to 10 operating segments, but no more. Why do you think this requirement exists?

Analyze: Why do you think some companies might resist segment reporting?

LO5 **PROBLEM 5-12   Segment Reporting**

Information pertaining to five industry segments has been identified by Latski Company:

Segment	Total Revenue	Operating Profit (Loss)	Identifiable Assets
A	$ 220,000	$200,000	$ 850,000
B	50,000	(110,000)	150,000
C	90,000	26,000	60,000
D	100,000	(15,000)	200,000
E	540,000	159,000	120,000
Totals	$1,000,000	$260,000	$1,380,000

Required: Indicate which of these segments are considered reportable under GAAP.

Analyze: What is meant by the management approach to segment reporting?

LO5 **PROBLEM 5-13   Subsequent Events**

The following events occurred in the post–balance sheet period, shortly after Dargon Parts's 2004 year end. Dargon's annual report was issued on February 3, 2005. All amounts are material.

A. On January 15, 2005, the market value of Dargon stock dropped 10 percent.

B. On January 4, 2005, $3.2 million of five-year bonds were issued.

C. Dargon's employees staged a walkout on February 1, 2005, as a result of a stalemate in union wage negotiations. Operations ceased immediately and were not expected to begin again until April. Dargon estimated that $10 million in revenue would be lost as a result.

D. On January 31, 2005, an investigation by the State of Florida Revenue Department revealed that income taxes relating to 2002 should be an additional $800,000.

Required: For each transaction, identify the type of accounting and/or disclosure required of Dargon in its financial statements for the fiscal year ended December 31, 2004. Provide justification for your answer.

Analyze: What timing issue makes identifying and reporting post–balance sheet events necessary? Explain.

LO5   **PROBLEM 5-14   Interim Reporting**

The events listed here occurred during 2004 for Peters, Inc. The company issues quarterly financial statements for each of its fiscal periods ended March 31, June 30, and September 30. Full financial statements are issued in its annual reporting at December 31.

A. On January 1, 2004, Peters, Inc. paid property taxes amounting to $64,000 on its plant for the calendar year 2004.

B. On July 31, Peters recognized an extraordinary loss due to a fire in one of its warehouses. The fire caused $500,000 of damage; however, $440,000 was covered by insurance.

C. During each month of the year, Peters paid salaries amounting to $6,000. Because of the timing of pay periods during December, however, Peters paid only $4,000 during December 2003. An additional $2,000 was accrued on December 31, 2004, and was paid on January 2, 2005.

D. On April 1, 2004, Peters completed its annual painting of the fences that surround its warehouse facility. The cost was $16,000, which was $2,000 more than the previous year's annual painting cost on April 1, 2003. The annual painting lasts for one year.

Required: For each transaction, identify the amount that should be reported during each of the company's quarterly reporting periods by completing the chart that follows.

Transaction	First Quarter	Second Quarter	Third Quarter	Fourth Quarter
A.				
B.				
C.				
D.				

Critical Thinking: Why do you think companies registered with the SEC are required to submit quarterly reports?

Analyze: Are your answers for A through D based on an integral or discrete view? Explain.

CASES

LO1   **CRITICAL THINKING CASE 5-1   Importance of the Statement of Cash Flows**

The accountant for Mercury Carpets reported that the company's income statement for 2004 showed a net loss of $11,000. The accountant provided the following operating activities section of the company's statement of cash flows for 2004.

Mercury Carpets
Statement of Cash Flows—Operating Activities Section
For the Year Ended December 31, 2004

Net loss	($11,000)
Depreciation expense	6,500
Amortization of intangibles	4,000
Decrease in accounts receivable	6,500
Increase in inventories	(3,200)
Decrease in accounts payable	(500)
Decrease in other accrued expenses	(600)
Net cash flows provided by operating activities	$ 1,700

Required: You have been asked to assist the president in determining the implications of this important section of the statement of cash flows. The president has questioned how the company can have both a net loss of $11,000 and a positive operating cash flow of $1,700. Explain how this might be possible.

LO2 COMMUNICATIONS CASE 5-2   **Structure of the Statement of Cash Flows**

The statement of cash flows for Primedia, Inc. for the four quarters ending June 30, 2003, appears below. Assume that you are the senior audit manager from Primedia's independent CPA firm.

Primedia, Inc.
Statement of Cash Flows

Period Ending	June 30, 2003	Mar. 31, 2003	Dec. 31, 2002	Sept. 30, 2002
(000s omitted)				
Net Income (loss)	$88,904	($20,247)	($72,889)	($352,605)
Operating Activities, Cash Flows Provided By or Used In				
Depreciation	—	—	304,661	—
Adjustments to net income	(57,913)	34,609	(180,028)	372,844
Changes in accounts receivable	—	—	43,162	—
Changes in liabilities	—	—	(79,610)	—
Changes in inventories	—	—	8,826	—
Changes in other operating activities	(25,559)	(21,514)	13,730	2,094
Total Cash Flow from Operating Activities	5,432	(7,152)	37,852	22,333
Investing Activities, Cash Flows Provided By or Used In				
Capital expenditures	(12,180)	(8,986)	(11,759)	(8,276)
Investments	1,140	(132)	(597)	(2,614)
Other cash flows from investing activities	180,268	(2,142)	111,934	41,405
Total Cash Flows from Investing Activities	169,228	(11,260)	99,578	30,515
Financing Activities, Cash Flows Provided By or Used In				
Dividends paid	(11,394)	(11,527)	(11,527)	(12,016)
Sale or purchase of stock	(15,047)	(3,751)	(98)	642
Net borrowings	(145,389)	37,825	(125,315)	(41,322)
Other cash flows from financing activities	(905)	(1,038)	(704)	(980)
Total Cash Flows from Financing Activities	(172,735)	21,509	(137,644)	(53,676)
Effect of exchange rate changes	—	—	—	—
Change in Cash and Cash Equivalents	$ 1,925	$ 3,097	($ 214)	($ 828)

Required: As the senior audit manager, you have been asked to answer certain questions regarding the company's financial statements. During your presentation to the audit committee, you are asked to explain the implications of the company's cash flows. In particular, the committee is interested in the fact that cash flow from investing activities exceeds cash flow from operating activities in the most recent quarter. Prepare a response that speaks to this issue. Be sure to address any items that seem unusually large.

LO2   **ANALYSIS CASE 5-3   Preparation of the Statement of Cash Flows**

Manny Enterprises, Inc., a producer of orange juice in Florida, has experienced both profitable and unprofitable operations in recent years. The following table reflects Manny's operating results for the last two years:

Operating Statement	Year Ended 2005	Year Ended 2004
Net produce revenues	$420,000	$375,000
Cost of produce sold	336,000	298,000
Other operating expenses	94,000	62,000
Net income/(loss)	(10,000)	15,000

For the year ended 2005, Accounts Payable increased from $10,000 to $15,000, and Accounts Receivable increased from $6,000 to $12,000.

Required: Use the accounting equation format given here to illustrate the effects of the changes in the company's operating cash flows between 2004 and 2005, assuming that no significant changes occurred in the company's other balance sheet accounts for the same period.

$$\Delta \text{ Cash} = \Delta \text{ Liabilities} + \Delta \text{ Stockholders' Equity} - \Delta \text{ Noncash Assets}$$

LO4   **ETHICS CASE 5-4   Cash Flow Analysis and Quality of Earnings**

ETHICS

Robert Schulze and his family recently relocated from a large metropolitan city to a small community in the Midwest. They had decided to move because the cost of living would be lower and because they were attracted by the idea of a smaller, more child-friendly community. Robert, a CPA, interviewed for a position with Salzig, Inc., a regional manufacturing company, and was offered the position of accounting manager. Prior to accepting the offer, Robert reviewed the company's financial statements. He noticed that net income, earnings per share, and return on assets had increased steadily during the past few years. He also noticed that the company had a healthy cash balance and an acceptable current ratio. However, Robert noticed that during the past two years, operating cash flows had decreased while income had increased. He calculated the ratio of cash flows from operating activities to net income and found that during the past three years, the ratio had decreased from 1.3 to 0.95 to 0.75. Based on this trend, Robert wondered whether the company was using aggressive accounting policies to maintain income growth. These findings concerned Robert, and he wondered whether he should reconsider accepting the offer. He was aware that the job market in this small community was tight, and that there would be few positions better than the one that Salzig was offering.

Required:

1. Why do Robert's analysis findings concern him?
2. If Robert were to take this position, what ethical considerations might he face?
3. When companies use aggressive accounting methods to support earnings trends, who are the affected parties?
4. What would you do if you were Robert?

LO4   **RESEARCH CASE 5-5   Cash Flow Adequacy**

An excerpt from the statement of cash flows for **Boca Resorts** for the six months ended December 31, 2003 and 2002, is presented on the next page. Key figures from the company's 2002 and 2003 income statements are also provided.

Required:

1. During which period did Boca Resorts perform better in terms of GAAP earnings? During which period did Boca Resorts perform better in terms of cash flows?
2. Calculate the cash debt coverage ratio for Boca Resorts for the six-month period ended 2003 if average total debt was $209,145,000. Should management be concerned? Does the time period covered by the financial information presented affect your analysis? If so, how?

Boca Resorts

(000s omitted)	6 months ended	
	12/31/2003	**12/31/2002**
Operating activities:		
Net loss	($ 7,981)	($ 9,403)
Adjustments to reconcile net loss to net cash provided by operating activities:		
Depreciation	20,108	18,020
Non-cash compensation expense	453	163
Impairment loss on land parcel	0	2,396
Gain on sale of land parcel	0	(2,291)
Loss on early retirement of debt	0	149
Benefit for deferred income taxes	(4,995)	(5,887)
Changes in operating assets and liabilities		
Accounts receivable	1,512	4,334
Other assets	(2,213)	2,075
Accounts payable and accrued expenses	(3,513)	(4,942)
Deferred revenue and other liabilities	6,039	9,392
Net liabilities of discontinued operations	(29)	(467)
Net cash provided by operating activities	$ 9,381	$ 13,539
Revenue	$119,931	$113,338
Operating income	(2,640)	(4,289)
Income (loss) from continuing operations	(12,976)	(15,290)
Net income (loss)	(7,981)	(9,403)

3. Locate Boca Resorts' 10-K *annual* report filed with the SEC for 2003. Recalculate the cash debt coverage ratio for the 2003 fiscal year. Comment on the change in Boca Resorts' debt coverage from 2002.

LO4   CRITICAL THINKING CASE 5-6   **Cash Flow Adequacy and Performance Analysis**

Assume that you are the manager of the loan department at Wachovia National Bank. The controller of **United Parcel Service** has asked for an increase in the company's line of credit. You are concerned that UPS may have too much debt and may not be able to make principal and interest payments when they are due. A portion of UPS's interim financial statements for the nine months ended September 30, 2003 and 2002, appears below and on the opposite page.

UPS

Selected amounts from Income Statements: (in millions of dollars)	Nine Months Ended September 30	
	2003	**2002**
Operating income	$4,445	$4,096
Interest expense	94	121
Income taxes expense	1,031	1,096

Required:

1. Calculate the debt coverage and interest coverage ratios for UPS for 2003.

2. Calculate the cash flow to operating income ratio and the cash flow to net income ratio for UPS for the periods ended September 30, 2003 and 2002.

3. Evaluate UPS's cash flow adequacy and quality of earnings. Would you grant an increase in UPS's line of credit? Justify your response.

UPS

Partial Statements of Cash Flows
(in millions of dollars)

	Nine Months Ended September 30	
	2003	2002
Cash flows from operating activities:		
Net income	$2,042	$1,680
Adjustments to reconcile net income to net cash from operating activities:		
Depreciation and amortization	1,162	1,086
Postretirement benefits	60	104
Deferred taxes, credits and other	81	80
Stock award plans	394	361
Loss on investments	54	12
Loss on disposal of assets	8	26
Impairment of goodwill	—	72
Changes in assets and liabilities:		
Accounts receivable	12	328
Other current assets	(48)	492
Prepaid pension costs	(275)	(91)
Accounts payable	196	98
Accrued wages and withholdings	316	344
Dividends payable	(212)	(212)
Income taxes payable	365	(79)
Other current liabilities	5	210
Net cash from operating activities	$4,160	$4,511
Cash Paid During the Period For:		
Interest	$ 126	$ 190
Income taxes	1,097	1,416

UPS

Partial Balance Sheets
Liabilities & Shareowners' Equity
(in millions of dollars)

	Sept. 30, 2003	Sept. 30, 2002
Current Liabilities:		
Current maturities of long-term debt and commercial paper	$ 645	$ 1,107
Accounts payable	2,118	1,908
Accrued wages & withholdings	1,714	1,084
Income taxes payable	357	19
Dividends payable	—	212
Other current liabilities	1,229	1,225
Total Current Liabilities	$ 6,063	$ 5,555
Long-Term Debt	3,425	3,495
Accumulated Postretirement Benefit Obligation, Net	1,311	1,251
Deferred Taxes, Credits & Other Liabilities	3,843	3,601
Total liabilities	$14,642	$13,902

LO4 ANALYSIS CASE 5-7 **Evaluating Ratios Relative to Cash Flows**

Target Corporation's statements of cash flows from its 2003 annual report are as follows.

Target

Target Corporation
Statements of Cash Flows

(millions)	2003	2002	2001
Operating activities			
Net earnings	$1,841	$1,654	$1,368
Reconciliation to cash flow:			
Depreciation and amortization	1,320	1,212	1,079
Bad debt provision	532	460	230
Deferred tax provision	249	248	49
Loss on disposal of fixed assets, net	54	67	52
Other non-cash items affecting earnings	11	159	160
Changes in operating accounts providing/(requiring) cash:			
Accounts receivable	(744)	(2,194)	(1,193)
Inventory	(583)	(311)	(201)
Other current assets	(255)	15	(91)
Other assets	(196)	(174)	(178)
Accounts payable	764	524	584
Accrued liabilities	57	(21)	29
Income taxes payable	91	(79)	124
Other	19	30	—
Cash flow provided by operations	3,160	1,590	2,012
Investing activities			
Expenditures for property and equipment	(3,004)	(3,221)	(3,163)
Increase in receivable-backed securities	—	—	(174)
Proceeds from disposals of property and equipment	85	32	32
Other	—	—	(5)
Cash flow required for investing activities	(2,919)	(3,189)	(3,310)
Financing activities			
Decrease in notes payable, net	(100)	—	(808)
Additions to long-term debt	1,200	3,153	3,250
Reductions of long-term debt	(1,172)	(1,071)	(793)
Dividends paid	(237)	(218)	(203)
Repurchase of stock	—	(14)	(20)
Other	26	8	15
Cash flow (used)/provided by financing activities	(283)	1,858	1,441
Net (decrease)/increase in cash and cash equivalents	(42)	259	143
Cash and cash equivalents at beginning of year	758	499	356
Cash and cash equivalents at end of year	$ 716	$ 758	$ 499

Required:

1. Review the operating section of the statement of cash flows. Calculate the cash flow to net income ratio for 2002 and 2003.

2. Identify two important observations about the change in the cash flow to net income ratio from 2002 to 2003. Explain.

3. On which one item did Target spend the majority of its cash?

4. Summarize the nature of the activities from which Target received its cash and on which it used its cash during the 2003 fiscal year.

LO5 CRITICAL THINKING CASE **5-8** **Subsequent Events**

Jab Company, a small publicly traded company, produces various types of sunscreen for drugstores to sell under their own generic and name brands. The president of Jab, Mike Ditcoff, is proud of the quality of the sunscreen that Jab produces and is convinced that its quality is unsurpassed by its competitors' products. He feels confident that sunscreen will continue to contribute to the company's 30 percent annual growth rate.

One of Jab's most popular products is a new PABA blend of sunscreen. However, a recent problem with the quality of the product has surfaced. Several customers have made complaints that are likely to generate a class action lawsuit: they say that the product has caused serious skin problems in the form of rashes that produce localized pain and discoloration of the skin. Upon further investigation, Jab's managers discovered that a production run in December that was shipped in January was contaminated with an industrial-grade acid-cleaning compound. The entire production run was shipped to one customer, A&D Drug Stores, and represented a $2 million sales order. A&D is one of Jab's largest customers, providing 25 percent of Jab's total revenue on an ongoing basis. On February 15, 2005, 45 days before Jab was to file its 2004 annual report with the SEC, A&D notified Jab that it was likely to cease doing business with Jab in the future.

Required:

As the filing date for the 2004 10-K report approaches, Carl Rant, the controller, has asked you to evaluate the situation and determine if any disclosure is necessary in the 2004 annual report. Write a short memo to Carl, explaining what accounting for these events is necessary. Be sure to provide information on any necessary accruals and/or disclosures by Jab Company.

LO5 RESEARCH CASE **5-9** **Significant Accounting Policies**

The summary of significant accounting policies should provide enough information to enable users to comprehend the numbers reported in the financial statements.

Required:

Locate Target Corporation's most recent annual report at **www.target.com** and answer the following questions:

1. Name Target Corporation's operating segments. On what basis does Target Corporation determine its segments?

2. For the most recent year, which of Target Corporation's operating segments created the largest amount of revenues? Which segment created the largest income before taxes?

3. Over what period of time does Target Corporation depreciate its fixtures and equipment? What method of depreciation does Target use?

4. What method of accounting for inventories does Target use?

5. Who is the auditor for Target Corporation?

ON THE WEB

The following exercises, activities, and problems are available on the *Intermediate Accounting* website. Use these resources to reinforce your understanding of the topics presented in this chapter.

- CPA-Adapted Simulations
- Interpreting the Accounting Standards
- Extending the Global Focus
- Extending the Ethics Discussion
- Mastering the Spreadsheet
- Career Snapshots

- Annual Report Project
- ACE Practice Tests
- Flashcards
- Glossary
- Check Figures for Text Problems
- PowerPoint Presentations

SOLUTIONS: CHECK YOUR UNDERSTANDING

The Importance of the Statement of Cash Flows (p. 198)

1. The statement of cash flows reports the amount of cash collected and paid out by a firm over a specified period. It reconciles reported net income or loss with the change in cash for the period.

2. The income statement and balance sheet are prepared using an accrual basis and do not help investors and analysts see how much actual cash was generated and used. The statement of cash flows adjusts all accrual entries to a cash basis and helps users understand what actual cash inflows and outflows occurred.

The Structure of the Statement of Cash Flows (p. 201)

1. Cash flows from operating activities, cash flows from investing activities, and cash flows from financing activities.

2. Payment of dividends, repurchase of common stock, and retirement of debt securities.

3. Noncurrent liabilities and stockholders' equity accounts (excluding changes in retained earnings due to net income or loss).

Preparing the Statement of Cash Flows (p. 210)

1. The four steps are: (1) determine the cash provided by or used in operating activities; (2) determine the cash provided by or used in investing activities; (3) determine the cash provided by or used in financing activities; (4) determine the change (increase or decrease) in cash during the period and compute the ending balance of cash and cash equivalents.

2. Under the indirect method, net income is adjusted for items that do not affect cash flows, including depreciation, amortization, depletion, gains, losses, and changes in current assets and current liabilities. With the direct method, each item on the income statement is adjusted from the accrual basis to the cash basis.

3. Gains are subtracted from net income.

4. The increase is added to net income.

Analyzing the Statement of Cash Flows (p. 214)

1. 1.19; this indicates a high quality of earnings because net income is not diluted by a large amount of accruals or deferrals.

2. The cash debt coverage ratio would be 4.3:1, indicating a strong ability to repay debt.

3. Cash flow return on assets.

Other Significant Financial Disclosures (p. 224)

1. Key information about a segment must be reported if *any* of the following three conditions is satisfied: (1) the segment's reported revenues (including sales to external customers and transfer sales within the company) are 10 percent or more of the combined revenues of all the company's reported operating segments; (2) the absolute amount of its profit or loss is 10 percent or more of the greater of (a) the combined reported profits of all operating segments that did not report a loss or (b) the combined reported loss of all operating segments that did not report a loss; or (3) its assets are 10 percent or more of the combined assets of all operating segments.

2. Significant business combinations, issuance of new debt, or occurrences that will have a material effect on operations.

3. The discrete view of interim periods holds that each interim period should be treated as a separate accounting period. The integral view holds that each interim period is an integral part of the larger annual accounting period.

4. The auditor's report expresses an opinion about whether the financial statements fairly present the firm's financial position, results of operations, and cash flows in accordance with generally accepted accounting principles.

CPA-ADAPTED SIMULATION

This simulation asks you to complete various tasks related to a company's annual financial statements. If your instructor has signed up for CPAexcel™, you can do the work online at **www.cpaexcel.com/hmco**. You may also do the simulation manually.

CPAexcel Simulation

Chapter 05 – Fever
Company

Time Remaining
0 hours 43 minutes

calculator   sheet   standards   help   splitter   done

Directions | Situation | Statement Preparation | Cash Flows | Written Communication | Research Task | Resources

Fever Company reported the following amounts on its balance sheets at the end of 2005 and 2004:

	12/31/05	12/31/04
Assets		
Cash	$20,200	$12,500
Accounts receivable (net)	5,000	3,000
Inventories	2,000	10,000
Plant assets (net)	33,000	38,000
Long-term investments	27,000	24,000
Total	$97,200	$87,500
Liabilities and Stockholders' Equity		
Accounts payable	$10,100	$3,000
Mortgage payable	24,000	32,000
Common stock	49,000	43,400
Retained earnings	14,100	9,100
Total	$97,200	$87,500

Additional data:

   a. Dividends declared and paid: $4,500.
   b. No accounts receivable were written off. No purchase or sales of plant assets occurred.
   c. Long-term investments purchased during the year: $3,000.

Directions | Situation | Statement Preparation | Cash Flows | Written Communication | Research Task | Resources

Prepare the statement of cash flows for Fever Company for 2005 using the indirect method.

Directions | Situation | Statement Preparation | Cash Flows | Written Communication | Research Task | Resources

Indicate whether the following items would appear in the operating, investing, or financing activities section of a statement of cash flows when using the indirect method. Also, indicate whether the items would be added or deducted within the category.

	Section	Increase or decrease
1. Depreciation expense		
2. Loss on sale of plant assets		
3. Increase in Accounts Receivable		
4. Increase in Accounts Payable		
5. Payment of dividend		
6. Payment of wages		
7. Purchase of equipment for cash		
8. Payment received on a note receivable		
9. Issuance of a note		
10. Dividend revenue		

Directions | Situation | Statement Preparation | Cash Flows | Written Communication | Research Task | Resources

1. Explain the difference between the terms cash and cash equivalents. Which should be reflected on the statement of cash flows?

2. A company borrows money with a long-term loan and makes annual interest and principal payments. Indicate what the effect will be on the statement of cash flows and what sections of the statement would be affected.

3. Which method of presenting cash-flow information (direct or indirect) is required by GAAP? Does the FASB have a preference for one or the other?

4. How are dividends received classified in the statement of cash flows?

Directions | Situation | Statement Preparation | Cash Flows | Written Communication | Research Task | Resources

Some companies wish to enhance their cash flow disclosures by reporting an amount referred to as cash flow per share. What is the official stance of the FASB on the reporting of a cash flow per share amount?

The Measurement of Income and Assets

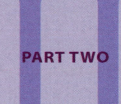

The appropriate measurement and recognition of revenue is critical to accounting for the performance of a business. The "bottom line," as reflected in the income statement, is significantly affected by decisions concerning how and when to record revenue. In Part Two, you will learn how revenue recognition decisions affect financial reporting and thus the perception of a company's success. Equally important, the valuation of a company's assets lays a financial foundation for the representation of that company's balance sheet position. In Part Two, you will also learn how the appropriate valuation of assets like cash, receivables, inventories, operating assets, and intangible assets is accomplished and how to analyze the financial statement disclosures of such assets in order to understand more about the financial health of a company.

CHAPTER SIX

Revenue Recognition

FINANCIAL REPORTING CASE

AIG INSURANCE FORCED TO RESTATE EARNINGS

Maurice (Hank) Greenberg, the former CEO of AIG, leaves a meeting with authorities investigating his role in the accounting scandal that shook his company and the insurance industry.

AIG American International Group, Inc. (AIG) is one of the nation's largest insurance and financial services companies. In May 2005, AIG announced that after an extensive internal audit, the company was restating its financial statements for the years ended December 31, 2003, 2002, 2001, and 2000. The news release stated that "AIG's prior financial statements for those periods and its previously announced unaudited financial results for the year and quarter ended December 31, 2004 should therefore no longer be relied upon."[1]

These adjustments were necessary because of accounting fraud, including improper revenue recognition. More significantly, these misrepresentations took place with the knowledge of senior management. AIG's auditor made the following statement in its internal controls report:

Control environment: Certain of AIG's controls within its control environment were not effective to prevent certain members of senior management, including the former Chief Executive Officer and former Chief Financial Officer, from having the ability, which in certain instances was utilized, to override certain controls and effect certain transactions and accounting

1 AIG, News Release, May 1, 2005.

AIG

CONSOLIDATED STATEMENT OF INCOME
Year Ended December 31, 2003

(in millions, except per share amounts)	Previously Reported	Adjustments	As Restated	Percent Change
Revenues:				
Premiums and other considerations	$55,226	$(346)	$54,880	(0.6)%
Net investment income	16,596	(1,128)	15,468	(6.8)
Realized capital gains (losses)	(1,433)	813	(620)	—
Other revenues	10,914	(1,196)	9,718	(11.0)
Total revenues	81,303	(1,857)	79,446	(2.3)
Benefits and expenses:				
Incurred policy losses and benefits	46,390	(245)	46,145	(0.5)
Insurance acquisition and other operating expenses	21,005	641	21,646	3.1
Total benefits and expenses	67,395	396	67,791	0.6
Income before income taxes, minority interest and cumulative effect of accounting changes	13,908	(2,253)	11,655	(16.2)
Income Taxes				
Current	3,407	(621)	2,786	(18.2)
Deferred	857	(240)	617	(28.0)
	4,264	(861)	3,403	(20.2)
Income before minority interest and cumulative effect of accounting changes	9,644	(1,392)	8,252	(14.4)
Minority interest	(379)	127	(252)	—
Income before cumulative effect of accounting changes	9,265	(1,265)	8,000	(13.7)
Cumulative effect of accounting changes, net of tax	9	—	9	—
Net income	$9,274	$(1,265)	$ 8,009	(13.6)%

entries. In certain of these instances, such transactions and accounting entries appear to have been largely motivated to achieve desired accounting results and were not properly accounted for in accordance with GAAP.[2]

In its 2004 annual report, AIG restated both its 2003 and 2002 financial statements. A summary of these restatements for 2003 appears above.

Revenue is usually the largest single item in the financial statements. Determining the timing and amount of revenue often involves subtle judgments that are open to differing interpretations. Yet, studies indicate that revenue recognition is one of the single largest issues requiring the restatement of financial statements. Consequently, issues involving revenue recognition are among the most important—and the most difficult—that standard setters and accountants face.

EXAMINING THE CASE

1. By what total amount were AIG's revenues overstated in 2003? Do you consider this amount material to previously stated 2003 results?

2. By what total amount was AIG's net income overstated in 2003? Do you consider this amount material to previously stated 2003 results?

3. The compensation of many corporate executives is tied to their ability to *deliver earnings* and meet or exceed the expectations of analysts. As an investor, how do you view this practice?

---

2 AIG, 2004 Annual Report.

LO 1 Explain the conceptual issues and timing criteria guiding revenue recognition.

revenues inflows or other enhancements of the assets of an entity or settlements of its liabilities (or a combination of both) from delivering or producing goods, rendering services, or carrying out other activities that constitute the entity's ongoing major or central operations

expenses outflows or other using up of assets or incurrences of liabilities (or a combination of both) from delivering or producing goods, rendering services, or carrying out other activities that constitute the entity's ongoing major or central operations

recognition the act of recording revenues or expenses

revenue recognition principle the concept that revenue should be recognized (and recorded) when two criteria are met: (1) the amount and timing of revenue can be reasonably determined (revenue is realized or realizable), and (2) the earnings process is complete or virtually complete (revenue is earned)

Critical Thinking: Describe how you think the timing of revenue recognition can affect a company's bottom line.

Conceptual Issues Guiding Revenue Recognition

When *Statement of Financial Concepts No. 6* was issued in 1986, the FASB defined revenues and expenses according to the accounting practices at that time. **Revenues** were defined as inflows or other enhancements of the assets of an entity or settlements of its liabilities (or a combination of both) from delivering or producing goods, rendering services, or carrying out other activities that constitute the entity's ongoing major or central operations. **Expenses** were defined as outflows or other using up of assets or incurrences of liabilities (or a combination of both) from delivering or producing goods, rendering services, or carrying out other activities that constitute the entity's ongoing major or central operations. According to these definitions, revenues and expenses are associated with a firm's core activities and are usually described as inflows or outflows of net assets as a result of operating activities.

As discussed in Chapters 1 and 3, under accrual accounting, revenues and expenses are recognized in the period in which the event occurs rather than in the period in which cash or some other form of payment is received or paid by the firm. The matching principle underlies accrual accounting and requires that revenues and related expenses be reported together in the same accounting period. The *act* of recording revenues or expenses is referred to as **recognition**. Two issues that are at the heart of revenue recognition are *when* revenues should be recognized and *how much* revenue should be recognized. Under the **revenue recognition principle**, revenue should be recognized (and recorded) when two criteria are met:

1. The amount and timing of revenue can be reasonably determined (revenue is realized or realizable).

2. The earnings process is complete or virtually complete (revenue is earned).

In most cases, adherence to these two criteria leads to recognition of revenue at the time of sale rather than at the time cash is collected. The sale is considered complete when the product or service is delivered, which is an essential aspect of accrual accounting. The sale signifies that the earnings process is complete; by making a sale, the firm has done what it is in business to do. In addition, at the time of the sale, the amount and timing of revenue can be reasonably determined because the firm has received either cash or a claim to cash, such as an account receivable. However, as we will see throughout the chapter, sometimes a sale does not meet the criteria for revenue recognition, and so revenue is recognized at other times during the earnings process.

EVOLVING REVENUE RECOGNITION GUIDANCE

The broad guidelines for revenue recognition require a great deal of judgment on the part of accountants and auditors. Since the issuance of *Statement of Financial Concepts No. 6*, "Elements of Financial Statements," the accounting profession has released various types of detailed implementation guidance that are applicable to specific transactions and industries in an attempt to deal with the ambiguities of revenue recognition. The FASB notes that the revenue recognition guidance currently in the authoritative literature "has been developed largely on an ad hoc basis and issued in numerous pronouncements having differing degrees of authority." The FASB has included revenue recognition on its active projects list and will develop a new statement to address the various issues. In doing so, the "Board decided that the revenue recognition statement would (a) eliminate inconsistencies in the existing authoritative literature and accepted practices, (b) fill the voids that have emerged in revenue recognition guidance in recent years, and (c) provide guidance for addressing issues that arise in the future."[3] This FASB project was initiated in 2002 and will take some time to complete.

---

3 "Project Updates, Revenue Recognition," FASB, December 2, 2002.

Throughout the 1990s, the SEC was also concerned about lax revenue recognition criteria and the ways in which many firms applied them. Therefore, in December 1999, the SEC issued *Staff Accounting Bulletin (SAB) No. 101*, which stated that if a revenue transaction falls within the scope of specific guidance, that guidance should be followed. To cover situations in which guidance is lacking, the bulletin reaffirmed the definition of revenue and the criteria for revenue recognition issued by the FASB in *Statement of Financial Accounting Concepts No. 5,* "Recognition and Measurement in Financial Statements of Business Enterprises," which states that "an entity's revenue-earning activities involve delivering or producing goods, rendering services, or other activities that constitute its ongoing major or central operations, and revenues are considered to have been earned when the entity has substantially accomplished what it must do to be entitled to the benefits represented by the revenues." That is, revenue should not be recognized until it is realized or realizable and has been earned. Relying upon an AICPA pronouncement regarding software revenue recognition, the SEC in *SAB No. 101* made the more general statement that revenue is realized or realizable and earned when all of the following four criteria have been met:

1. Persuasive evidence of an arrangement exists (a bill of sale, for example).

2. Delivery has occurred or services have been rendered (the revenue-producing activity has been completed).

3. The seller's price is fixed and determinable (not contingent on future events).

4. Collectibility is reasonably assured (the buyer has the resources to pay).[4]

As noted by Lynn Turner, the chief accountant of the SEC when *SAB No. 101* was issued, "The general framework and foundation for *SAB 101* could not be simpler—it is based on the commonsense notion that revenue on a sale should not be recognized until the seller has fulfilled its obligations to the buyer under the sale arrangement."[5] Nonetheless, actually applying this commonsense framework has caused innumerable problems for firms, their managers, and the accounting profession.

The FASB seems to be moving away from the realization and earnings approach to revenue recognition, which is at the heart of *SFAC No. 5.* According to the latest FASB Project Update, "the Board is pursuing an approach that focuses on changes in assets and liabilities (consistent with the definition of revenues in Concepts Statement 6) and is not overridden by tests on the notions of realization and completion of the earnings process presented in Concepts Statement 5."[6] As this project moves forward, we can expect significant changes in the concept and perhaps the practices of revenue recognition and measurement.

CHALLENGES IN REVENUE RECOGNITION

In today's economy, firms enter into a variety of transactions that ultimately involve revenue recognition. These range from barter transactions and software swaps to long-term construction contracts and long-term installment sales. Identifying when revenue is realized or realizable and has been earned often involves judgments that must be made by a firm's management and confirmed by its outside auditors. One way to approach the issue is to consider the level of certainty associated with the ultimate receipt of the revenues. That is, when does the receipt of cash or claims to cash become certain enough for the company to recognize the revenue associated with the transac-

---

4 "Revenue Recognition in Financial Statements," *Staff Accounting Bulletin No. 101* (Washington, D.C.: SEC, 1999).

5 Remarks by Lynn E. Turner, chief accountant, U.S. Securities and Exchange Commission, at the University of Southern California's SEC and Financial Reporting Institute (Los Angeles, May 31, 2001).

6 "Project Updates, Revenue Recognition," FASB, August 19, 2005.

Illustration 6.1

Potential Points of Revenue Recognition in the Earnings Process

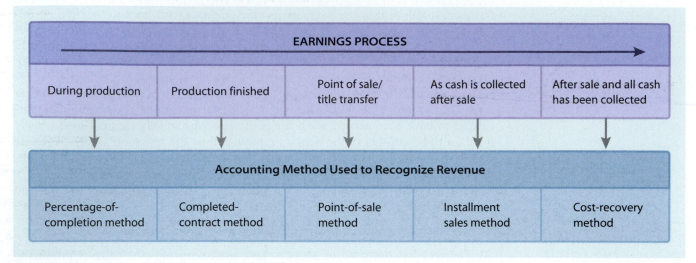

tion? Revenue may be recognized at different points in the earnings cycle, from production of goods and services to cash collection. For example, revenue may be recognized during or at the completion of production, at the point of sale, during or after the cash collection process, or after the right-of-return period has expired. Illustration 6.1 is an overview of the various points of revenue recognition in the earnings process.

CHECK YOUR UNDERSTANDING

1. Under the revenue recognition principle, when should revenue be recognized and recorded?

2. What entities have issued guidance on the topic of revenue recognition?

3. List the four criteria for revenue recognition outlined by *SAB No. 101*.

LO 2 **Account for revenue transactions at the point of sale and discuss the related issues.**

point of sale the point at which legal title passes to the buyer

Critical Thinking: *If you were to sell your car to a friend, at what point would you recognize revenue from the sale? Explain why you have chosen this point of recognition. Would your answer change if you allowed your friend to return the car to you within 30 days if he wasn't satisfied?*

Revenue Recognition at the Point of Sale

For most companies, revenue is recognized at the **point of sale**, which is the point at which legal title passes to the buyer. In most cases, legal title passes at the point of delivery. The point of sale is key because most often, that is when all four of the revenue recognition criteria identified in *SAB No. 101* are met.

Assume that Green Darner Company made a sale on account of $500,000. The following entry is recorded at the point of sale to recognize the revenue:

Accounts Receivable	500,000	
Sales		500,000

When Green Darner collects the cash, it will debit Cash and credit Accounts Receivable. Of course, if the original sale had been for cash, the company would have debited Cash rather than Accounts Receivable.

SALES WHEN THE RIGHT OF RETURN EXISTS

right of return the permission a seller gives to a buyer to return a purchase for a refund

Sales returns are common in most businesses. Many firms give buyers a **right of return**, which is permission to return a purchase for a refund. Since the return of goods will wipe out the benefit of the original sale, the seller must meet certain criteria before it can recognize revenue when a right of return exists. The FASB, in *SFAS No. 48*, identified the following criteria for recognizing revenues from products that have a right of return:[7]

- The amount of future returns can be reasonably estimated.

- The transaction has a fixed or determinable sales price.

- No contingent obligations are related to the sale.

- The buyer has the economic wherewithal independent of the seller to complete the sale.

For most products sold by retailers and other firms, the right of return causes few problems. In most cases, even though a formal right of return exists, revenue is still recognized at the point of delivery because, based on past experience, the amount of such returns can be estimated and matched against the sales of the same period.

To illustrate, assume a customer returns a treadmill he originally purchased on credit for $1,000. At the time of the return, the company records the following entry:

Sales Returns and Allowances	1,000	
Accounts Receivable		1,000

The Sales Returns and Allowances account (sometimes just called Sales Returns) is a contra-revenue account that is subtracted from sales to derive net sales. The use of a separate contra account makes it easier to keep track of returns.

In certain industries, like catalog retailing, sales returns can be significant. In such cases, if potential returns can be estimated, a company establishes an Allowance for Sales Returns account in the same period as the related sales take place. To illustrate, assume that at year end 2005 the Kur Catalog Co. estimates that $40,000 of its current year's sales will be returned during the next year. At the end of 2005, Kur will make an adjusting entry to record the estimated sales returns for the coming year.

2005 Year-End Adjusting Entry		
Sales Returns and Allowances	40,000	
Allowance for Sales Returns and Allowances		40,000

The year-end adjusting entry debits Sales Returns and Allowances and credits the contra-asset account Allowance for Sales Returns and Allowances. This account is similar to the Allowance for Uncollectible Accounts account.

During 2006, the company actually receives $37,000 in returns. As it receives these returns, it will make individual entries to record them. When a specific customer returns merchandise, the Allowance account is debited and the actual customer's Account Receivable account is credited. For illustrative purposes, however, the entries for 2006 are shown as one summary entry at the end of the year.

2006 Summary Entry to Record Actual Returns		
Allowance for Sales Returns and Allowances	37,000	
Accounts Receivable		37,000

When sales returns cannot be reasonably estimated or when other criteria of *SFAS No. 48* are not met, revenue should not be recognized at the point of sale, but should be deferred until the uncertainties have been resolved. For example, recognition may be deferred until the right-of-return period has expired or until sufficient evidence exists

---

7 "Revenue Recognition When the Right of Return Exists," *Statement of Financial Accounting Standards No. 48* (Stamford, Conn.: FASB, 1981).

to permit an estimate of sales returns. For instance, assume that Ebony Jewelwing Publishers ships the latest novel by a famous author to bookstores under a right-of-return policy that permits the stores to return all copies that they cannot sell within six months. Once Ebony Jewelwing collects sufficient evidence about how well the book is selling, it can estimate the number of returns and recognize revenue before the right-of-return period expires. If the company cannot gather sufficient evidence to make an estimate of returns, it cannot recognize revenue until the right-of-return period expires.

In some cases, companies may choose to recognize the revenue from sales but reduced by the amount of expected returns. In the notes to its financial statements, **Monsanto**, a global provider of agricultural products, explains its revenue recognition policies as follows:

> Revenues from all branded seed sales are recognized when the title to the products is transferred, at which time the goods are deemed to have been delivered. When the right of return exists in the company's seed business, sales revenues are reduced at the time of sale to reflect expected returns. In order to estimate the expected returns, management analyzes historical returns, economic trends, market conditions, and changes in customer demand.
>
> Revenues for agricultural chemical products are recognized when title to the products is transferred and the goods are deemed delivered to customers. The company recognizes revenue on products it sells to distributors when, according to the terms of the sales agreements, delivery has occurred, performance is complete, no right of return exists, and pricing is fixed or determinable at the time of sale.[8]

UNCOLLECTIBLE ACCOUNTS

There will always be some customers who are unable to pay their accounts. The amount of such uncollectible accounts needs to be recognized in the same period as the sales took place. To do this, the amount is estimated and then recognized by an entry that debits Bad Debt Expense and credits the contra-asset account Allowance for Uncollectible Accounts.[9] The following adjusting entry is recorded to estimate uncollectible accounts at the end of the accounting period:

Year-End Adjusting Entry		
Bad Debt Expense	12,000	
Allowance for Uncollectible Accounts		12,000

On the date that a customer's account receivable is deemed uncollectible, the following entry is recorded:

Write-off During the Year		
Allowance for Uncollectible Accounts	800	
Accounts Receivable (J. Smith)		800

SALES OF SERVICES

The previous examples of revenue recognition pertained to sales of products. However, in our service- and knowledge-based economy, increasing amounts of revenue are generated through the sale of services, such as those provided by consulting firms, law firms, and other organizations of professionals and by companies like health clubs that

---

8 Monsanto 2004 10K, Note 2, "Significant Accounting Policies, Revenue Recognition," p. 69.

9 The procedures used to estimate bad debt expense are discussed in detail in Chapter 7.

furnish services to members or subscribers. For the most part, revenue is recognized in proportion to the services rendered and the expenses incurred in performing those services. This is called the **proportional-performance method**. Given the long-term nature of some service contracts, revenue is recognized as services are performed. When a service contract specifies the acts to be performed, the revenue (and cost) per act can be calculated and recognized as the services are supplied. When a contract does not specify the number or kind of acts to be performed, revenue is recognized over the contract term using the straight-line method.

> **proportional-performance method** the recognition of service revenue in proportion to the services rendered and the expenses incurred in performing the services

Costs incurred as a result of long-term service contracts are defined as initial direct costs, direct costs, or indirect costs. The initial direct costs are allocated over the performance period in proportion to the revenue recognized for that period. Direct costs can be matched with the services provided and are therefore expensed as incurred. Indirect costs are also expensed as incurred, since they do not provide any future benefit.

If there is one specific, final event that results in the culmination of the earnings process, it is not appropriate to recognize revenue on a proportional basis. Such cases require the use of the **completed-performance method**, in which recognition of revenues and related expenses is deferred until a final event occurs. For example, companies in the moving and storage industry use the completed-performance method because the delivery of the goods is the most significant event in the earnings process, even though other events, such as packing and transporting, take place earlier in the process.

> **completed-performance method** an approach to revenue recognition in which service revenues and related expenses are not recognized until a final event occurs

---

CHECK YOUR UNDERSTANDING

1. If a company experiences a high level of product returns, what entry can be made to estimate potential returns?

2. If sales returns cannot be reasonably estimated or if the criteria of *SFAS No. 48* are not met, how should revenue be recognized?

3. Explain the methods by which revenues generated from the sale of services may be accounted for.

Revenue Recognition During Production or Before Delivery

> **LO 3** Account for revenue transactions during production and before delivery.
>
> *Critical Thinking: Why do you think a shipbuilder might choose to recognize revenue while construction is in process?*

In some industries, the point of sale is not the appropriate point in the earnings cycle to recognize revenue because revenue is earned over a long period of time (construction contracts), at the end of production (certain agricultural products), or over the period during which the cash is collected (certain installment sales). In this section, we will consider revenue recognized during the production cycle.

REVENUE RECOGNITION DURING THE PRODUCTION CYCLE

> **percentage-of-completion method** an approach to revenue recognition for long-term construction contracts in which revenue is recognized as it is earned over the period of the contract

Certain companies enter into construction contracts involving production that takes place over a long period of time. For example, commercial buildings, cruise ships, and military equipment such as aircraft usually take more than a year to build. If the amount and timing of the receipts are known and if the costs can be reasonably estimated, revenue can be recognized as it is earned over the period of the construction contract. This is known as the **percentage-of-completion method**. If costs cannot be reasonably estimated or if the timing of the receipts is uncertain, revenue recognition

completed-contract method an approach to revenue recognition for long-term construction contracts in which revenue is not recognized until the project has been completed

(and the resulting gross profit) should be deferred until the project has been completed. This is known as the **completed-contract method**.

▶ PERCENTAGE-OF-COMPLETION METHOD

Use of the percentage-of-completion method enables a firm to recognize revenue, along with construction costs and gross profit, while a project is in progress. This method is preferable to the completed-contract method because it relates revenue flows more closely to the actual earnings process. For example, consider a company that builds a cruise ship that will take three years to complete. During all three years, as the ship is being constructed, the firm is earning revenue. It would be a distortion to recognize no revenue for the first two years and then the total revenue in the last year. By using the percentage-of-completion method, the company can recognize and record revenue in proportion to the progress of the ship's construction.

Under the percentage-of-completion method, the revenues recognized each year are based on the following formula:

$$\text{Revenue Recognized in Current Period} = \text{Contract Price} \times \frac{\text{Costs Incurred to Date}}{\text{Estimated Total Costs}}$$

$$- \text{ Previously Recognized Revenue on the Contract}^*$$

*Subject to limitations on losses.

Construction costs are recognized as they are incurred by debiting the Construction-in-Progress account, much the way costs are accumulated in an inventory account. Gross profit is the difference between the revenue recognized for the period and the construction costs incurred for the period. However, whenever a net loss is projected for a project, the entire amount of the net loss is recognized immediately in that period.

For example, assume that Vulcan Construction Company signs a contract with the city of Hilo on January 1, 2006, to build a highway up the mountain to a volcano. The contract price is $3,000,000, and construction costs are estimated to be $2,500,000. The highway is expected to be completed by December 31, 2008. The city of Hilo will make three equal annual cash payments of $1,000,000. By 2007, actual costs have climbed to $2,600,000, which is $100,000 above the total estimated costs of $2,500,000. (In construction contracts, actual costs will rarely be the same as estimated costs.) Vulcan's revenues and costs for the highway project are as follows:

	2006	2007	2008
Costs incurred to date	$1,200,000	$2,000,000	$2,600,000
Estimated future costs to complete	1,300,000	600,000	—
Billings to date	1,000,000	2,000,000	3,000,000
Cash collections to date	1,000,000	2,000,000	3,000,000

Based on these data, the gross profit recognized for 2006, 2007, and 2008 is calculated as follows:

1. Calculate the percent completed based on costs incurred to date and the estimated total cost of the project:

$$\frac{\text{Costs Incurred to Date}}{(\text{Costs Incurred to Date} + \text{Estimated Future Costs to Complete})}$$

2006 $1,200,000 \div ($1,200,000 + $1,300,000) = 0.480$, or 48.0%
2007 $2,000,000 \div ($2,000,000 + $600,000) = 0.769$, or 76.9%
2008 $2,600,000 \div $2,600,000 = 1.00$, or 100.0%

2. Calculate the estimated total gross profit on the contract by comparing the contract price with the latest estimate of total costs:

   2006 $3,000,000 - $2,500,000 = $500,000$ estimated total gross profit
   2007 $3,000,000 - $2,600,000 = $400,000$ estimated total gross profit
   2008 $3,000,000 - $2,600,000 = $400,000$ actual gross profit*

*At the end of 2008, the contract is completed, so total costs and actual gross profits earned are known.

3. Calculate the estimated gross profit earned to date by multiplying the percentage-of-completion ratio calculated in step 1 by the estimated gross profit calculated in step 2:

   2006 $0.480 \times $500,000 = $240,000$
   2007 $0.769 \times $400,000 = $307,600$
   2008 $1.000 \times $400,000 = $400,000$

4. Calculate the amount of estimated gross profit to recognize in each of the three years by calculating each year's incremental gross profit. This is done by subtracting any gross profit earned in previous periods from the gross profit earned to date:

   2006 $240,000 - $0 = $240,000$
   2007 $307,600 - $240,000 = $67,600$
   2008 $400,000 - $307,600 = $92,400$

The journal entries to record costs incurred, gross profit recognized, billings, and collections for each of the three years of the contract are shown in Illustration 6.2. Note that two alternatives are given for recording the estimated gross profit on the contract. In the first, the gross profit is recorded on a net basis as determined under the percentage-of-completion method. That is, only the 2006 gross profit of $240,000 is recorded. Thus, in 2006, the entry is a debit to Construction in Progress (the account in which the contract costs and the gross profit are accumulated) and a credit to Profit on Long-Term Construction Contract. The other method shows the total revenue recognized (for example, $1,440,000 in 2006), the estimated expenses related to those revenues ($1,200,000 in 2006), and the resulting gross profit of $240,000.

The transactions related to the Hilo highway construction project will be reported in Vulcan's 2006 through 2008 financial statements as shown in Illustration 6.3.

Note that on the balance sheet, the asset account Construction in Progress is reported net of Billings on Construction in Progress. In a sense, the amount in the account Construction in Progress in Excess of Billings represents the construction company's net investment in the construction project. If the cumulative balance of the Billings on Construction in Progress account were higher than the cumulative balance in the Construction in Progress account, the net amount would be reported as a current liability. This is similar to billing a client before work is done, which would typically be recorded as unearned revenue.

❯ COMPLETED-CONTRACT METHOD

When a long-term construction contract exists but total costs cannot be reasonably estimated, the completed-contract method should be used. The entries to record a project using the completed-contract method are essentially the same as the entries for the percentage-of-completion method, except that the estimated gross profit is not recorded until the project is complete and has been accepted by the client, and the total

Illustration 6.2

Journal Entries, Percentage-of-Completion Method

Journal Entries	2006		2007		2008	
1. Record costs incurred for the year:						
Construction in Progress (Inventory)	1,200,000		800,000		600,000	
Accounts Payable, Cash, Salaries Payable, etc.		1,200,000		800,000		600,000
2. Record billings sent to city of Hilo:						
Accounts Receivable	1,000,000		1,000,000		1,000,000	
Billings on Construction in Progress		1,000,000		1,000,000		1,000,000
3. Record cash collected from city of Hilo:						
Cash	1,000,000		1,000,000		1,000,000	
Accounts Receivable		1,000,000		1,000,000		1,000,000
4a. Record profit recognized for the year:						
Construction in Progress	240,000		67,600		92,400	
Profit on Long-Term Construction Contract		240,000		67,600		92,400
4b. Alternative method of recording gross profit:						
Construction in Progress (gross profit recognized)*	240,000		67,600		92,400	
Construction Costs	1,200,000		800,000		600,000	
Construction Revenue		1,440,000		867,600		692,400
5. Record completion of contract and close out accounts:						
Billings on Construction in Progress	No entry		No entry		3,000,000	
Construction in Progress						3,000,000

*(Contract Price × Costs Incurred to Date ÷ Estimated Total Costs) − Revenue Previously Recognized

costs are known. Thus, all gross profit is deferred to the last period; the periods during construction will not show any gross profit.

Assume that Vulcan Construction Company accounts for the Hilo highway project using the completed-contract method instead of the percentage-of-completion method. The first three journal entries, to record construction costs, billings, and cash collections, are the same. However, there is no journal entry to recognize gross profit for the year. The entry to recognize the completion of the project is made in the final year, 2008, and is recorded as follows:

Billings on Construction in Progress	3,000,000	
Construction in Progress		2,600,000
Profit on Long-Term Construction Project		400,000

This entry closes out the Billings on Construction in Progress and Construction in Progress accounts and records the gross profit on the contract, which is the difference between those two accounts. Under the completed-contract method, the accounts will appear in Vulcan Construction Company's financial statements as shown in Illustration 6.4.

Note that under the completed-contract method, as under the percentage-of-completion method, the Construction in Progress account is reported net of Billings on Construction in Progress. If the cumulative balance of the Billings on Construction in

Illustration 6.3

Financial Statements, Percentage-of-Completion Method

Vulcan Construction Company
Extracts Related to Hilo Highway Construction Project

Income Statement

	2006	2007	2008
Revenue from long-term contracts	$1,440,000	$ 867,600	$ 692,400
Construction costs	(1,200,000)	(800,000)	(600,000)
Gross profit	$ 240,000	$ 67,600	$ 92,400

Statement of Cash Flows

	2006	2007	2008
Cash Flows from Operating Activities			
Cash collected on long-term contracts	$1,000,000	$1,000,000	$1,000,000
Cash payments for construction costs*	(1,200,000)	(800,000)	(600,000)
Net cash	($ 200,000)	$ 200,000	$ 400,000

*Assume all costs are paid in cash when the expense is recognized.

Balance Sheet

	2006	2007	2008
Current Assets:			
Construction in progress	$1,440,000	$2,307,600	$ 0
Less: Billings on construction in progress	(1,000,000)	(2,000,000)	0
Construction in progress in excess of billings	$ 440,000	$ 307,600	$ 0

Illustration 6.4

Financial Statements, Completed-Contract Method

Vulcan Construction Company
Extracts Related to Hilo Highway Construction Project

Income Statement

	2006	2007	2008
Revenue from long-term contracts	$ 0	$ 0	$3,000,000
Construction costs	0	0	(2,600,000)
Gross profit	$ 0	$ 0	$ 400,000

Statement of Cash Flows

	2006	2007	2008
Cash Flows From Operating Activities			
Cash collected on long-term contracts	$1,000,000	$1,000,000	$1,000,000
Cash payments for construction costs*	(1,200,000)	(800,000)	(600,000)
Net cash	($ 200,000)	$ 200,000	$ 400,000

*Assume that all costs are paid in cash when the expense is recognized.

Balance Sheet

	2006	2007	2008
Current Assets:			
Construction in progress	$1,200,000	$2,000,000	$ 0
Less: Billings on construction in progress	(1,000,000)	(2,000,000)	0
Construction in progress in excess of billings	$ 200,000	$ 0	$ 0

Illustration 6.5

Recognition of Gross Profit, Percentage-of-Completion Method versus Completed-Contract Method

Year	Percentage-of-Completion Method	Completed-Contract Method
2006	$240,000	$ 0
2007	67,600	0
2008	92,400	400,000
Total gross profit	$400,000	$400,000

Progress account were higher than the cumulative balance of the Construction in Progress account, the net amount would be reported as a current liability.

The amount of gross profit recognized under the percentage-of-completion method and the completed-contract method will be the same, but it will be recognized at different points in time. Illustration 6.5 summarizes the timing of gross profit recognized under both methods for Vulcan Construction Company.

Most companies engaged in long-term contracts use the percentage-of-completion method for financial reporting because it results in more uniform recognition of earnings over the contract period and provides the best matching of revenues, expenses, and effort. However, many companies use the completed-contract method for tax purposes because it enables them to defer payment of income taxes.

ACCOUNTING FOR CONSTRUCTION CONTRACTS WHEN A LOSS IS ANTICIPATED

In accounting for construction contracts, estimated total costs often differ from actual costs. If a company estimates that it will incur a loss on a long-term contract, it should immediately recognize that loss in full once it becomes evident. This treatment is in line with conservative accounting, under which losses are recognized immediately, but gains are never recorded until a transaction occurs.

To illustrate the accounting for a construction contract on which a loss is anticipated, assume that Vulcan Construction Company's actual costs on the Hilo highway construction project ($3,000,000 contract price) were as follows:

	2006	2007	2008
Costs incurred to date	$1,200,000	$2,600,000	$3,100,000
Estimated future costs to complete project	1,300,000	600,000	—
Billings to date	1,000,000	2,000,000	3,000,000
Cash collections to date	1,000,000	2,000,000	3,000,000

▶ PERCENTAGE-OF-COMPLETION METHOD

Under the percentage-of-completion method, the gross profit recognized in each year is based on the ratio of costs incurred to date to the most recent estimate of total contract costs. However, losses are recognized in full using the latest cost estimate. Given these data, the gross profit (loss) for 2006, 2007, and 2008 is determined as follows:

1. Calculate the percentage-of-completion gross profits or losses to be recognized based on the ratio of costs incurred to date and the estimated total costs of the project (costs incurred to date plus remaining costs to complete) multiplied by estimated gross profit. If a net loss is estimated, the entire net loss is recognized, as well as any previously recognized gross profit.

   a. In 2006 (the first year of the contract), an overall gross profit is estimated. Use the following formulas to recognize the gross profit:

$$\frac{\text{Costs Incurred to Date}}{\text{Estimated Total Costs of the Project}} = \text{Estimated Gross Profit Percentage}$$

$$\frac{\$1,200,000}{\$1,200,000 + \$1,300,000} = 48\% \text{ of estimated gross profit}$$

$$(\text{Contract Price} - \text{Estimated Total Costs of the Project}) \times \text{Estimated Gross Percentage} = \begin{matrix}\text{Gross Profit}\\\text{Recognized in}\\\text{Current Year}\end{matrix}$$

$$(\$3,000,000 - \$2,500,000) \times 0.48 = \$240,000 \text{ gross profit recognized}$$
for 2006

b. In 2007, it is estimated that the contract will result in a loss ($3,000,000 − $3,200,000). The amount of the loss must be recognized in full: $200,000 plus the amount previously recognized as income, $240,000, equals a loss of $440,000 for 2007.

c. In 2008, Vulcan is able to determine that it has suffered an actual total loss on the contract of $100,000, or the total contract price of $3,000,000 less the total costs of $3,100,000. Because Vulcan has already recognized a net loss of $200,000 on this project (the $240,000 gross profit in 2006 plus the $440,000 loss in 2007), $100,000 is recovered as income in 2008. The combination of the $240,000 gross profit in 2006, the $440,000 loss in 2007, and the $100,000 gross profit in 2008 results in the actual loss of $100,000 on the contract.

The journal entries required to record costs incurred, gross profit (loss) recognized, billings, and collections for each of the three years are shown in Illustration 6.6.

Illustration 6.6

Journal Entries to Record Profit (Loss), Percentage-of-Completion Method

	2006		2007		2008	
1. Record costs incurred for the year:						
Construction in Progress (Inventory)	1,200,000		1,400,000		500,000	
Accounts Payable, Cash, Salaries Payable, etc.		1,200,000		1,400,000		500,000
2. Record billings sent to city of Hilo:						
Accounts Receivable	1,000,000		1,000,000		1,000,000	
Billings on Construction in Progress		1,000,000		1,000,000		1,000,000
3. Record cash collected from city of Hilo:						
Cash	1,000,000		1,000,000		1,000,000	
Accounts Receivable		1,000,000		1,000,000		1,000,000
4. Record profit recognized for the year:						
2006: Construction in Progress	240,000					
Profit on Long-Term Construction Project		240,000				
2007: Loss on Long-Term Construction Project			440,000			
Construction in Progress				440,000		
2008: Construction in Progress					100,000	
Profit on Long-Term Construction Project						100,000
5. Record completion of contract and close out of accounts:						
Billings on Construction in Progress	No entry		No entry		3,000,000	
Construction in Progress						3,000,000

Illustration 6.7

Balance Sheet, Percentage-of-Completion Method

	2006	2007	2008
Vulcan Construction			
Extract Related to Hilo Highway Construction Project			
Balance Sheets			
Current Assets:			
Construction in progress	$1,440,000	$2,400,000	$3,000,000
Less: Billings on construction in progress	(1,000,000)	(2,000,000)	(3,000,000)
Construction in progress in excess of billings (asset)	$ 440,000	$ 400,000	$ 0

The accounts will appear as depicted in Illustration 6.7 in the balance sheets for 2006, 2007, and 2008.

▶ COMPLETED-CONTRACT METHOD

Under the completed-contract method, the loss on the project should be recognized when it becomes evident—in this case, during 2007. By the end of 2007, Vulcan estimates that it will incur costs of $3,200,000 (actual costs of $2,600,000 plus $600,000 estimated future costs) against a contract price of only $3,000,000. In this case, the entire $200,000 loss is recognized in 2007. During 2008, it is determined with certainty that the actual loss is only $100,000, so Vulcan can recognize $100,000 of gross profit in 2008 to close out the contract with a net $100,000 loss (the $200,000 loss in 2007 less the $100,000 gross profit in 2008).

CONSTRUCTION CONTRACT DISCLOSURES

A company must disclose its method of revenue recognition for long-term contracts in the notes to its financial statements and/or in management's discussion and analysis of operations. **Heico Corporation**'s disclosures about revenue recognition and long-term construction contracts are shown in Figure 6.1. Heico Corporation is principally engaged in the design, manufacture, and sale of aerospace, defense, and electronics-related products and services.

As you can see, Heico Corporation uses point-of-sale, completed-contract, and percentage-of-completion methods of revenue recognition, depending on the individual contract at hand.

CHECK YOUR UNDERSTANDING

1. Describe the difference between the percentage-of-completion method and the completed-contract method of revenue recognition.

2. What items need to be known in order to use the percentage-of-completion method of revenue recognition?

3. Radiant Corporation signs a contract to install a new lighting system throughout the capitol building for the state of Texas. The contract price is $150,000, and construction costs are estimated to be $112,000. The state of Texas has agreed to make two payments of $75,000 over the two-year life of the contract. During the first year of the contract, costs of $60,000 were incurred and estimated total costs are still $112,000. What revenue should be recognized in the first year if Radiant uses the percentage-of-completion method?

Figure 6.1

Revenue Recognition Disclosure

Heico

Heico Corporation
Notes to Consolidated Financial Statements
For the years ended October 31, 2004, 2003 and 2002

Revenue recognition

Revenue is recognized on an accrual basis, primarily upon shipment of products and the rendering of services. Revenue from certain fixed price contracts for which costs can be dependably estimated is recognized on the percentage-of-completion method, measured by the percentage of costs incurred to date to estimated total costs for each contract. Revisions in cost estimates as contracts progress have the effect of increasing or decreasing profits in the period of revision. For fixed price contracts in which costs cannot be dependably estimated, revenue is recognized on the completed-contract method. A contract is considered complete when all costs except insignificant items have been incurred or the item has been accepted by the customer. The aggregate effects of changes in estimates relating to inventories and/or long-term contracts did not have a significant effect on net income or diluted net income per share in fiscal 2004, 2003 or 2002. Revenues earned from rendering services represented less than 10% of consolidated net sales for all periods presented.

Long-term contracts

Accounts receivable and accrued expenses and other current liabilities include amounts related to the production of products under fixed-price contracts exceeding terms of one year. Revenues are recognized on the percentage-of-completion method for certain of these contracts, measured by the percentage of costs incurred to date to estimated total costs for each contract. This method is used because management considers costs incurred to be the best available measure of progress on these contracts. Revenues are recognized on the completed-contract method for certain other contracts. This method is used when the Company does not have adequate historical data to ensure that estimates are reasonably dependable.

Contract costs include all direct material and labor costs and those indirect costs related to contract performance, such as indirect labor, supplies, tools, repairs, and depreciation costs. Selling, general and administrative costs are charged to expense as incurred. Provisions for estimated losses on uncompleted contracts are made in the period in which such losses are determined. Variations in actual labor performance, changes to estimated profitability and final contract settlements may result in revisions to cost estimates and are recognized in income in the period in which the revisions are determined.

The asset, "costs and estimated earnings in excess of billings" on uncompleted percentage-of-completion contracts, included in accounts receivable, represents revenues recognized in excess of amounts billed. The liability, "billings in excess of costs and estimated earnings," included in accrued expenses and other current liabilities, represents billings in excess of revenues recognized on contracts accounted for under either the percentage-of-completion method or the completed-contract method. Billings are made based on the completion of certain milestones as provided for in the contracts.

LO 4 Account for revenue transactions at the end of production but prior to delivery.

🧩 *Critical Thinking: If transfer of title is an important criterion with regard to revenue recognition, why do you think it is acceptable in some cases to recognize revenue after production is complete, but before delivery has been accomplished?*

Revenue Recognized at the End of Production but Prior to Delivery

In certain industries, revenue is recognized when production is complete, even though this is before the product is actually delivered. For example, when an agricultural crop is harvested or when precious minerals have been mined, the activities required to earn revenue are substantially complete. That is, the critical event in the earnings process is not the sale, but the harvesting of the crop or the mining of the minerals. For example, once a bushel of wheat has been harvested, threats such as drought, insect infestation, and disease are mitigated. Further, because most agricultural products are sold in large markets that are relatively uninfluenced by individual sales (i.e., the conditions for perfect competition in the economic sense exist), the individual farmer can sell the entire crop at the time of harvest at well-established market prices. Thus, the conditions for revenue recognition are met. If the farmer decides to hold the wheat, he or she is speculating on future price changes, and the income or loss from this speculation should be accounted for separately.

completed-production method
an approach to revenue recognition, used in industries such as agriculture and mining, in which revenue is recognized upon completion of the production process, assuming that the market price of the commodity is stable and that the units produced are homogeneous

Under the **completed-production method** of revenue recognition, revenue is recognized upon completion of the production process, assuming that the market price of the commodity is stable and that the units produced are homogeneous, or similar to other units produced. Although this method of revenue recognition is industry-specific and not very widespread, a brief example follows.

Assume that Colina Farms, a grower of barley, harvests 5,000 bushels on December 15, 2005. At this time, the market price of barley is $2.20 per bushel and the cost to produce each bushel of barley is $.85. On this date, Colina Farms sells 3,000 bushels for cash and decides to hold the other 2,000 bushels, as it expects the price to increase after year end. At December 31, the market price has indeed increased to $2.40 per bushel, but when Colina actually sells the remaining 2,000 bushels on January 10, 2006, the price has decreased to $2.34 per bushel. Colina Farms first makes an entry to record the cost to grow and harvest all 5,000 bushels of barley:

| Dec. 15 | Inventory (5,000 × $.85) | 4,250 | |
| | Cash, Accounts Payable, etc. | | 4,250 |

This entry is followed by the entry to record the sale of 3,000 bushels of barley:

| Dec. 15 | Cash (3,000 bushels × $2.20) | 6,600 | |
| | Revenue from Production of Barley | | 6,600 |

Next, the company records the costs associated with that sale as follows:

| Dec. 15 | Cost of Goods Sold (3,000 bushels × $.85) | 2,550 | |
| | Barley Inventory | | 2,550 |

Colina Farms also recognizes revenue on the remaining 2,000 bushels of barley that it has harvested but has not sold (this is critical to the completed-production method). Revenue is recognized at the market price less the cost to produce the barley, in this case, $1.35 per bushel ($2.20 − $0.85), because the bushels have been harvested—the critical event in the earnings process.

Dec. 15	Barley Inventory		
	[2,000 bushels × ($2.20 − $.85)]	2,700	
	Revenue from Production of Barley		2,700

Because Colina Farms has decided to hold the remaining 2,000 bushels of barley, it has really decided to speculate on future prices, and the accounting records must reflect the gains or losses on this speculation. At December 31, the following entry is made to reflect the price increase from $2.20 to $2.40 per bushel:

Dec. 31	Barley Inventory		
	[2,000 bushels × ($2.40 − $2.20)]	400	
	Holding Gain on Barley Held for Sale		400

Finally, when the 2,000 bushels are actually sold on January 10, 2006, at $2.34 per bushel, Colina Farms must recognize a holding loss of $120, or the difference between the $2.40 per bushel market price at December 31 and the $2.34 per bushel market price on the date when the barley is actually sold. The entry is recorded as follows:

Jan. 10	Cash (2,000 bushels × $2.34)	4,680	
	Holding Loss on Barley		
	[2,000 × ($2.40 − $2.34)]	120	
	Barley Inventory (2,000 bushels × $2.40)		4,800

No sales revenue is recognized, as the revenue related to all 5,000 bushels was recognized on December 15, 2005, when the barley was harvested. Under the completed-production method, the total net gain of $7,030 from these transactions is divided between two components (revenue from harvesting and holding or speculation gains and losses) and between two years as follows:

1. Net revenue in December (market price less cost
   of production, or $2.20 − $.85) for 5,000 bushels $6,750
2. Increase in value of 2,000 bushels held at year end   400
   Total net gain from transactions in 2005 $7,150
3. Decrease in value of 2,000 bushels sold on
   January 10, 2006   (120)
   Total for 2005 and 2006 $7,030

Under the normal method of recording revenues at the time of sale, Colina Farms would recognize income of $4,050 [3,000 × ($2.20 − $.85)] from the sale of 3,000 bushels in 2005 and income of $2,980 [2,000 × ($2.34 − $.85)] from the sale of 2,000 bushels in 2006. The net of $7,030 over the two years is the same as under the completed-production method; it is just allocated and described differently.

CHECK YOUR UNDERSTANDING

1. Explain how revenue is recognized under the completed-production method.

2. Why is the completed-production method especially suitable for companies that sell agricultural crops or mined resources?

LO 5 Account for revenue transactions after delivery and during cash collection.

Critical Thinking: *Can you identify types of sales that present more of a collection risk? How might this risk affect revenue recognition?*

Revenue Recognition After Delivery and During Collection of Cash

There are occasions when it is appropriate to delay the recognition of revenue until the cash from the transaction is actually received. These situations occur when there are significant uncertainties concerning the ultimate collection of the cash from the sale. These uncertainties are usually caused by long cash collection periods combined with a distinct possibility of uncollectible accounts or of the product's being returned. In most circumstances, these uncertainties can be reasonably estimated, and normal accounting procedures are used to match revenues and expenses. However, when the uncertainties are sufficiently significant, alternative revenue recognition policies may be utilized. These include the installment sales method and the cost-recovery method.

INSTALLMENT SALES METHOD

installment sale a sale in which the seller allows the buyer to pay for a purchase with a series of payments over a period of time

An **installment sale** is a sale in which the seller allows the buyer to pay for a purchase with a series of payments over a period of time. Often the seller retains title to the merchandise until it is paid for in full. For example, in retailing, installment sales are used for products like furniture, appliances, or farming equipment. The sale of unimproved

Illustration 6.8

Revenue Recognition Using the Installment Sales Method

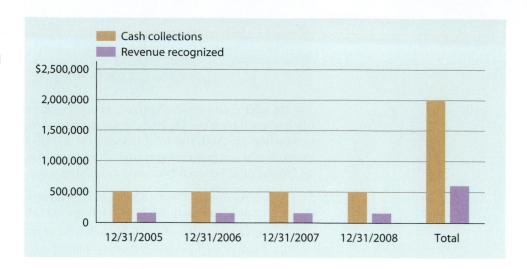

installment sales method an approach to revenue recognition that recognizes both the revenue and the cost of sales proportionately as cash is collected; used when collection of installment payments is uncertain

land is another situation in which installment sales are common. Sometimes the collection of cash on an installment sale takes place over several years. In such situations, the seller cannot be certain that the total amount due will be paid, and the risk of noncollection increases with the length of the collection period. Because the cash flows are uncertain, the **installment sales method** of revenue recognition is used. This method recognizes both the revenue and the cost of sales proportionately as the cash is collected. The gross profit recognized in each period (revenue – cost of sales) depends on both the gross profit percentage for the period's sales (gross profit/sales of the item for the year) and the amount of cash collected in that period.

Illustration 6.8 shows the revenue recognition flows based on the sale of land for $2,000,000 with an original cost of $1,400,000. The receivable is paid in four equal installments of $500,000 (this example assumes no interest). The gross profit on the contract is $600,000 ($2,000,000 – $1,400,000), and the gross profit percentage is 30 percent ($600,000 ÷ $2,000,000). Each year, 30 percent of the $500,000 received (or $150,000) is recognized as profit for the year. At the end of the four-year period, all the $600,000 gross profit has been recognized. The concept is very similar to revenue recognition in the percentage-of-completion method, except that recognition on installment sales is delayed until the cash is received. Under the percentage-of-completion method, revenue is recognized not as the cash is received, but as the work is performed.

The installment sales method is favored for tax purposes because it defers taxes to future periods. At one point in the late 1990s, Congress disallowed the use of the installment sales method for tax purposes, but it later reinstated it.

The Cal Land Sales Company uses the installment sales method to recognize revenue on the land it sells on credit. Assume that in 2004 and 2005, the company had the installment sales and cash collections shown in Illustration 6.9. The company will recognize the gross profits on those installment sales by making the journal entries shown in Illustration 6.10. In 2004, Cal Land recognizes $160,000 of the $800,000 in gross profit, with the remaining $640,000 deferred to future years, when cash will be collected. In 2005, Cal Land recognizes gross profit of $334,000 from two sets of installment sales: $180,000 from the 2005 cash collections on 2004 installment sales at a gross profit percentage of 40 percent and $154,000 from 2005 cash collections on 2005 installment sales.

The balance sheet shows the installment receivables less the deferred gross profit. Thus, at the end of 2004, the balance sheet accounts appear as follows:

Installment receivables	$1,600,000
Less: Deferred gross profit	640,000
Net installment receivables	$ 960,000

Illustration 6.9

Sales and Cash Collection Report, Installment Sales Method

Cal Land Sales Company

	2004	2005
Installment sales	$2,000,000	$2,200,000
Cost of installment sales	1,200,000	1,430,000
Gross profit	$ 800,000	$ 770,000
Gross profit percentage	40%	35%
Cash collections:		
On 2004 sales	$ 400,000	$ 450,000
On 2005 sales	—	$ 440,000
Gross profit recognized:		
On 2004 sales	$ 160,000*	$ 180,000**
On 2005 sales	—	154,000†
Total gross profit recognized per year	$ 160,000	$ 334,000
Total gross profit deferred per year	$ 640,000	$1,076,000‡

* (0.40 × $400,000)   † (0.35 × $440,000)
** (0.40 × $450,000)   ‡ ($640,000 − $180,000) + ($770,000 − $154,000)

The deferred gross profit of $640,000 is the difference between the original total deferral of $800,000 and the $160,000 gross profit recognized in 2004. The total deferred gross profit at the end of 2005 of $1,076,000 is equal to the remaining 2004 gross profit ($640,000 − $180,000) plus the 2005 deferred gross profit of $616,000 ($770,000 − $154,000).

The realized gross profit recognized is usually presented as a line item on the income statement with a reconciliation of deferred gross profit in the notes. Many accountants report the Deferred Gross Profit account as a current liability on the balance sheet, although the FASB states in *SFAC No. 6* that "no matter how it is displayed in financial statements, deferred gross profit on an installment sale is conceptually an

Illustration 6.10

Journal Entries for Installment Sales

	2004		2005	
Record Installment Sales:				
Installment Receivables for 2004 Sales	2,000,000			
Installment Receivables for 2005 Sales			2,200,000	
Inventory		1,200,000		1,430,000
Deferred Gross Profit		800,000		770,000
Record Cash Collections:				
Cash	400,000		890,000	
Installment Receivables—2004 Sales		400,000		450,000
Installment Receivables—2005 Sales				440,000
Recognize Gross Profit for Cash Collected:				
Deferred Gross Profit	160,000*		334,000†	
Realized Gross Profit on Installment Sales (from Prior Periods)		160,000		334,000

*($800,000 ÷ $2,000,000) = 0.40 × $400,000 = $160,000
†{[($770,000 ÷ $2,200,000) = 0.35 × $440,000 = $154,000] + (0.40 × $450,000 = $180,000)} = $334,000

Illustration 6.11

Summary of Revenue Recognition Methods

Point in Earnings Cycle	Example	Recognition Criteria	Accounting Method
During production	Construction of buildings	Ability to estimate current and future receipts and construction costs	Percentage of completion (can estimate future receipts and costs) or completed contract (cannot estimate future receipts and costs)
At the end of production	Certain agricultural and mining products	Crop is harvested or mineral is mined and price is established by market	Completed production
At the point of sale	Most retail and wholesale sales transactions	Earnings process is complete and amount and timing of revenue are reasonably determined	Sale
As cash is collected	Sales of land involving long-term collections	Gross profit is recognized as cash is collected on the installment basis	Installment sales
After all cash is collected	Sales of land when collection of cash is not assured	Revenue is not recognized until enough cash has been received to cover the asset's cost	Cost recovery

asset valuation—that is, a reduction of an asset."[10] Thus, the Deferred Gross Profit account may be reflected as a contra-receivable on the balance sheet. At this point, either presentation is acceptable according to GAAP, and both are found in practice. Many companies with installment sales sell their receivables to a bank or factor, and thus do not report them on their financial statements.

When a company allows a customer to pay in installments, it usually adds a finance charge to the unpaid balance. This interest component is not included in the recognized gross profit on installment sales. Rather, the FASB requires that the interest component of the cash payments collected be disclosed separately as interest revenue.

COST-RECOVERY METHOD

The cost-recovery method is used to recognize revenue from installment sales when the collection of payments is so highly uncertain that even the installment sales method is not feasible. Under the **cost-recovery method**, revenue is not recognized until enough cash has been collected to cover the cost of the product that was sold. Then, as more cash installments are made, the gross profit is recognized. This is a very conservative approach and is only used in rare situations.

cost-recovery method a method of revenue recognition that is used when the collection of installment payments is so highly uncertain that revenue is not recognized until enough cash has been collected to cover the cost of the product that was sold

---

10 "Elements of Financial Statements," *Statement of Financial Accounting Concepts No. 6* (Stamford, Conn.: FASB, 1985), par. 234.

SUMMARY OF REVENUE RECOGNITION METHODS

In reality, the earnings process of most firms is continuous. However, as a practical matter, accountants must pick a specific point within that continuous process at which to recognize and record the revenue. The point that is selected is where the earnings process is essentially complete and the amount and timing of the revenues can be reasonably determined. This point differs depending on the type of industry and the specific nature of the sale. Illustration 6.11 summarizes the most common points at which the criteria are most clearly met and indicates the corresponding revenue recognition method.

CHECK YOUR UNDERSTANDING

1. If a company sells a product to a consumer and allows a series of payments over time, how can revenues be recognized?

2. What accounts are affected when recording an initial installment sale transaction under the installment sales method?

3. When using the installment sales method, how are revenues recognized?

4. Why is the cost-recovery method used in certain sales situations?

LO 6 Recognize transactions that present challenging revenue recognition issues and identify how quality of earnings is affected.

Critical Thinking: What types of sales transactions can you identify that might add complications to the timing of revenue recognition? Consider the types of sales transactions that you have participated in over the past year.

Challenging Revenue Recognition Issues

Throughout this chapter, various revenue recognition standards and recording methods have been discussed. However, as noted earlier, revenue recognition is not always a straightforward issue. Determining the timing and amount of revenue often involves subtle judgments that are open to differing interpretations. For typical retail and wholesale activities, the criteria for revenue recognition at the point of sale are easy to apply. However, when transactions like swaps, barters, exchanges, or consignments occur, it becomes more difficult to apply those criteria with any consistency. Let's now look at these criteria in more detail and discuss some relevant real-world examples.

THE SEC'S *STAFF ACCOUNTING BULLETIN* No. 101

In *SAB No. 101*, the SEC provides the following additional guidance for applying each of the revenue recognition criteria discussed earlier in this chapter.

1. *Persuasive evidence of an arrangement exists (a bill of sale, for example).* From the SEC's perspective, binding purchase orders or online authorizations constitute documentation of a sales arrangement. However, the SEC notes that when customers cannot sign the agreement by the end of the accounting period, the sale should be considered a transaction of the next period, even if the product is delivered prior to the end of the period. Sometimes a customer and seller will enter into a side agreement that effectively amends the master contract or agreement. Side agreements could include cancellation, termination, or other provisions that affect revenue recognition. When this occurs, companies should ensure that appropriate policies, procedures, and internal controls exist and are properly documented so as to provide reasonable assurances that sales transactions, including those affected by side agreements, are properly accounted for in accordance with generally accepted accounting principles. The existence of a subsequently executed side agreement may also be an indicator that the original agreement was not final and revenue recognition was not appropriate. For example, a side agreement

may say that the seller will repurchase inventory after a period of time, which will void the sale.

2. *Delivery has occurred or services have been rendered (the revenue-producing activity has been completed).* Once delivery has occurred, the customer takes title to the goods and assumes the risk of ownership, indicating that a sale has taken place. Typically this occurs when a product is delivered to the customer's delivery site (if the terms of the sale are "FOB destination") or when a product is shipped to the customer (if the terms are "FOB shipping point"). However, problems arise if a transaction is a consignment, a financing, or some other arrangement for which revenue recognition is not appropriate. If title to the goods has passed but the substance of the arrangement is not a sale, the consigned inventory should be reported separately from other inventory in the consignor's financial statements as "inventory consigned to others" or another appropriate caption.

3. *The seller's price to the buyer is fixed and determinable.* This means that the price is not contingent on future events.

4. *Collectibility is reasonably assured (the buyer has the resources to pay).* This criterion is involved in layaway sales. Although collectibility may be reasonably assured, a company should not recognize revenue from sales made under its layaway program until delivery of the merchandise to the customer. Until then, the amount of cash received should be recognized as a liability under the title "deposits received from customers for layaway sales" or a similarly descriptive caption. Because the company retains the risks of ownership of the merchandise, receives only a deposit from the customer, and does not have an enforceable right to the remainder of the purchase price, the company should not recognize any revenue upon receipt of the cash deposit. The logic here is that until the customer picks up the inventory, the company must defer recognition of the sale because the collection of the remainder is unenforceable.

The SEC has listed many other concerns related to improper revenue recognition in *Staff Accounting Bulletin No. 101,* "Revenue Recognition in Financial Statements," which is available on its website.

REVENUE RECOGNITION ISSUES IN THE REAL WORLD

In the last few years, the growth of Internet and business-to-business commerce has complicated the following issues related to revenue recognition:

- What is a sale?

- When has a sale occurred?

- What amount of revenue has been generated?

In the industrial economy of the last part of the twentieth century, such issues were not particularly significant, but they have become the heart of accounting controversies in the last five years. Three of the more interesting issues surround sales that are recorded gross versus net, barter transactions, and capacity swaps.

▶ RECORDING GROSS VERSUS NET REVENUES: PRICELINE.COM

Revenue recognition at **Priceline.com** presents an interesting question regarding the measurement of revenues. Priceline.com sells travel products to consumers through a name-your-own-price bidding system. For example, assume that you wish to purchase an airplane ticket from Los Angeles to Miami to attend the Orange Bowl. To use Priceline.com, you would go to its website, identify your travel dates, and specify the price you are willing to pay. Priceline.com would then see if any of its suppliers will

Figure 6.2

Merchant Revenues and Merchant Cost of Revenues— Priceline.com

Priceline.com

Name Your Own Price® Services: Merchant revenues and related cost of revenues are derived from transactions where we are the merchant of record and, among other things, select suppliers determine the price to be paid by the customer. We recognize such revenue and costs if and when we accept and fulfill the customer's non-refundable offer. Merchant revenues and cost of merchant revenues include the selling price and cost, respectively, of the travel services and are reported on a gross basis. Pursuant to the terms of our hotel service, our hotel suppliers are permitted to bill us for the underlying cost of the service during a specified period of time. In the event that we are not billed by our hotel supplier within the specified time period, we reduce our cost of revenues by the unbilled amounts. In very limited circumstances, we make certain customer accommodations to satisfy disputes and complaints. We accrue for such estimated losses and classify the resulting expense as adjustments to merchant revenue and cost of merchant revenues or the allowance for doubtful accounts, as appropriate.

Travelweb: Merchant revenues for Travelweb are derived from transactions where customers use the Travelweb service to purchase hotel rooms from hotel suppliers at rates which are subject to contractual arrangements. Charges are billed to customers at the time of booking and are included in Deferred Merchant Bookings until the customer completes his or her stay. Such amounts are generally refundable upon cancellation prior to stay, subject to cancellation penalties in certain cases. Merchant revenues and accounts payable to the hotel supplier are recognized at the conclusion of the customer's stay at the hotel. Travelweb records the difference between the selling price and the cost of the hotel room as merchant revenue.

agree to that price. According to Priceline.com, this distribution system benefits both the customer and the supplier (seller). As the company notes in its 2004 annual report:

> Sellers use our *Name Your Own Price®* demand collection system as a revenue management tool to generate incremental revenue without disrupting their existing distribution channels or retail pricing structures. We require consumers to be flexible with respect to brands and product features. As a result, our *Name Your Own Price®* system does not reveal sellers' brands to customers prior to the consummation of a transaction, thereby protecting their brand integrity. This shielding of brand identity and price enables sellers to sell products and services at discounted prices without cannibalizing their own retail sales by publicly announcing discount prices and without competing against their own distributors.

Assume that you bid $500 for your trip from Los Angeles to Miami and that one of Priceline's airline partners accepts that price. Priceline then pays the airline $460 for your ticket and earns a net of $40 on your transaction. From an accounting perspective, what revenue has Priceline earned, and when should it be recorded? Should the company record a gross revenue of $500 with a cost of sales of $460? Or should Priceline record only the net revenue of $40?

Priceline.com has adopted the view that it should record the full amount of the agreed-upon ticket price as revenue ($500 in this case) and then record a cost of sales for what it must pay the airline ($460 in this case). This approach is shown in Figure 6.2, a note to the company's 2004 financial statements.

In addition to *Name Your Own Price®*, Priceline.com has another service called *Travelweb*. This is a different service in which Priceline.com acts as a facilitator between the customer and the supplier. In this situation, as shown in Figure 6.2, Priceline only records the difference between the selling price and the cost of the hotel room as merchant revenue.

Management's rationale for recording the gross amount is that the company takes ownership of the items it resells rather than receiving a fee or commission. A sales price has been agreed upon, and the sale is final because the customer has agreed to purchase the ticket if the bid is accepted. Thus, the criteria for revenue recognition have been met. To Priceline's way of thinking, the fact that it purchased a ticket from an airline, took the risks of ownership associated with that ticket, and then sold it to a customer entitles it to record the total price of the ticket as revenue. The counterargument, of course, is that Priceline is merely the facilitator of the transaction and that the only revenue it earns is a commission based on the difference between the selling price to the customer and the ticket cost, or $40 in our example.

The dollar amounts are significant. According to Priceline's financial statements, for the year ended December 31, 2004, the company's merchant revenues were $872,994 million, and the cost of those revenues was $714,822 million, providing a gross margin of $158,172 million and a gross margin percentage of 18.2 percent. Imagine how different the financial statements would look if Priceline showed $158,172 million as revenue.

▶ RECORDING ELECTRONIC ADVERTISING REVNUE: GOOGLE

In spite of the Internet bubble in the early 2000s, e-business and e-advertising have flourished over the last few years. Businesses such as **eBay**, **Yahoo!**, and **Google** have become everyday names in our daily lives. An interesting revenue recognition question arises as to how companies such as these should recognize the advertising revenue they receive from Internet users who access the sites of their advertisers.

To illustrate this point, let's take a look at how Google, Inc., one of the Internet success stories of this era, recognizes revenue from the advertising on its website. Google's advertising revenues for the year ended December 31, 2004, were almost $3.2 billion (interestingly, the cost of the revenues was only about $1.5 billion). Google has several types of advertising programs such as Google AdWords and Google AdSense. Figure 6.3 is an excerpt from Google's 2004 annual report that details how it recognizes revenue from these advertising programs.

Figure 6.3

Revenue Recognition Policies—Google

Google

Revenue Recognition. In the first quarter of 2000, the Company introduced its first advertising program through which it offered advertisers the ability to place text-based ads on Google web sites targeted to users' search queries. Advertisers paid the Company based on the number of times their ads were displayed on users' search results pages and the Company recognized revenue at the time these ads appeared. In the fourth quarter of 2000, the Company launched Google AdWords, an online self-service program that enables advertisers to place text-based ads on Google web sites. AdWords advertisers originally paid the Company based on the number of times their ads appeared on users' search results pages. In the first quarter of 2002, the Company began offering AdWords exclusively on a cost per click basis, so that an advertiser pays the Company only when a user clicks on one of its ads. The Company recognizes as revenue the fees charged advertisers each time a user clicks on one of the text-based ads that are displayed next to the search results on Google web sites. Effective January 1, 2004, the Company offered a single pricing structure to all of its advertisers based on the AdWords cost per click model.

Google AdSense is the program through which the Company distributes its advertisers' text-based ads for display on the web sites of the Google Network members. In accordance with Emerging Issues Task Force ("EITF") Issue No. 99 19, *Reporting Revenue Gross as a Principal Versus Net as an Agent,* the Company recognizes as revenues the fees it receives from its advertisers. This revenue is reported gross primarily because the Company is the primary obligor to its advertisers.

Figure 6.4

Revenue Recognition Press Release—Qwest Communications

Qwest

DENVER, Oct. 28/PRNewswire-FirstCall/—Qwest Communications International Inc. (NYSE: Q-News) today announced that, in consultation with its auditor KPMG LLP ("KPMG"), it has completed its analysis and concluded that for accounting purposes it will treat sales of optical capacity assets (commonly known as "IRUs") for cash as operating leases and recognize the revenue from these assets over the life of the IRUs. The company has concluded that its policies and practices for determining the value of the various elements of the fees earned in connection with the sales of optical capacity assets for cash did not support the accounting treatment. As a result, the company concluded that it should defer the $531 million of revenue previously recognized on such sales over the life of the underlying agreements.

This announcement relates to optical capacity asset transactions recorded in periods following the merger of Qwest and U S WEST, Inc. ("U S WEST") on June 30, 2000. Approximately $1.48 billion in total revenue was recognized in these periods from all IRU transactions and, as previously announced, is made up of the $950 million from exchanges of optical capacity assets and the $531 million from sales of optical capacity assets for cash. As previously announced, the company will reverse the $950 million in revenues and related costs ($685 million and $265 million in 2001 and 2000, respectively) related to the exchange transactions. Of the $531 million of revenue that the company announced today will be deferred, $331 million and $200 million of sales of optical capacity assets were recognized in 2001 and 2000, respectively. The company historically accounted for sales of optical capacity assets for cash based on accounting policies approved by its previous auditor, Arthur Andersen LLP ("Andersen").

❯ RECORDING CAPACITY SWAPS: QWEST COMMUNICATIONS

As the telecommunications industry mushroomed in the mid-1990s and then began to quickly collapse, more companies entered into capacity swaps. Those companies would swap or sell excess capacity to other companies and then record revenues and associated expenses from the swaps. However, no cash changed hands, and the swaps did not change the firms' economic situations. This led to questions about whether revenue should be recorded for the swaps, and, if so, how much.

Qwest Communications, a large telecommunications company with headquarters in Denver, Colorado, used swaps as part of its business practices. The SEC opened an informal investigation into Qwest's accounting treatment of sales and swaps of optical capacity assets (optical telecommunication lines) and the sale of equipment to customers from which Qwest bought Internet services or to which it contributed equity financing. Such transactions contributed revenues of over $1.48 billion in 2000 and 2001. The company also started its own investigation into those matters. As a result of its investigation, Qwest determined that it had, in fact, not followed proper accounting methods. In response, it reversed $950 million of revenues and expenses related to swaps of optical capacity assets and deferred the recognition of revenue from cash sales of those assets. The company issued a press release on the situation, shown in Figure 6.4.

We started our discussion by saying that the sale is the most common point of revenue recognition, and indeed it is. However, as our economy has become increasingly service- and technology-driven, it has become more and more difficult to determine when a sale has in fact taken place, the amount of revenue associated with that sale, and over what period of time the revenue should be recognized. Guidance from the FASB, AICPA, and SEC has helped, but it is management's responsibility to make the ultimate judgments, and it is the accounting profession's obligation to ensure that those judgments are within the realm of GAAP.

ETHICS AND QUALITY OF EARNINGS

ETHICS

Applying guidance from the SEC, AICPA, and FASB in a transparent and conservative manner increases a firm's quality of earnings. A company must disclose its revenue recognition policies in the notes to its financial statements, as illustrated by various examples throughout this chapter. A clearly stated revenue policy increases the transparency of the reported results and enhances the readability and understandability of the financial statements. Confusing or unclear statements about revenue recognition make it difficult for financial statement users to fully understand a firm's operations and may be a red flag concerning the quality of earnings.

Financial statement users expect firms to apply conservatism in selecting the appropriate method of revenue recognition. The more conservative the method selected, the higher the quality of earnings. As we have seen, a number of large, high-profile companies, such as **AIG**, have been known to select revenue recognition policies that accelerated the recognition of revenues or led to the reporting of inflated revenues. Many of these companies have been asked to restate their financial reports to reflect appropriate revenue recognition policies. According to Huron Consulting Group, revenue recognition was the second leading cause of restatements in 2003.[11] Although the application of inappropriate revenue recognition policies may sometimes be an oversight or misuse of facts, fraud and unethical intentions are often at the core of such situations. Financial officers and managers may be prompted to develop revenue recognition policies that do not reflect the best interests of the stockholders and that overstate earnings.

The nature of a company's sales also affects its quality of earnings. Clearly, cash sales provide the highest quality of earnings, whereas swaps and barters provide a substantially lower quality of earnings. When two companies swap services, revenue is recognized, but cash is not increased. If a firm produces most of its revenues from swaps, it will have a hard time paying its bills and staying in business because, for a business to be sustainable, increases in revenues must ultimately correspond to increases in cash provided by operations.

CHECK YOUR UNDERSTANDING

1. Why is it important for financial statement users to understand revenue recognition methods?

2. If a company trades advertising space online with another company, how should revenue from this barter transaction be recognized?

3. If a company engages in layaway sales, how should revenue from these sales be recognized?

LO 7 Describe the current status and future direction of international standards on revenue recognition.

INTERNATIONAL

International Issues Related to Revenue Recognition

Revenue recognition issues and controversies are not limited to the United States. Currently, no common standards for revenue recognition exist among the countries associated with the International Accounting Standards Board (IASB). Recognizing the important need for such standards, the Accounting Standards Board of Great Britain noted:

---

11 "Study: Reserve Accounting Leading Cause of Restatements in 2003," SmartPros.com, January 14, 2004. Available at: **http://accounting.smartpros.com/x42122.xml**. Accessed 2/27/04.

Critical Thinking: *What obstacles might exist for an analyst who wishes to compare the revenue data for a U.S.-based manufacturing company with those for a similar manufacturer based in Germany?*

The recognition and measurement of revenue are of fundamental importance to proper financial reporting. Individual companies within the same sector can, at present, have different accounting policies, leading to marked variations in the timing of revenue recognition, and hence profit. Revenue recognition has been one of the concerns at the heart of the recent debate over aggressive earnings management.

With the exception of the requirements for long-term contracts in *SSAP 9 'Stocks and long-term contracts,'* there is at present no accounting standard in the UK and the Republic of Ireland that contains specific requirements for how revenue is to be defined and recognised. Faced with difficult questions over revenue recognition, different companies have found different answers, and practices have developed that are in some respects inconsistent from one industry to another and within a single industry.[12]

Given the importance of this issue and the need for convergence of accounting standards, the IASB has joined the FASB in a high-priority project on revenue recognition. According to the IASB, the objectives of the joint project are to

1. Develop a comprehensive set of principles for revenue recognition in order to eliminate the inconsistencies in the existing authoritative literature and accepted practices, fill the voids that have emerged in revenue recognition in recent years, and provide guidance for addressing issues that arise in the future.

2. Amend the conceptual guidance with respect to the potential inconsistencies related to revenue recognition, for example, the potential inconsistencies between the revenue recognition criteria and the definition of liabilities.

3. Converge the conceptual and authoritative guidance of the IASB and FASB with respect to revenue recognition.

> **CHECK YOUR UNDERSTANDING**
>
> 1. Describe the ramifications of varying revenue recognition policies as described by the Accounting Standards Board of Great Britain.
>
> 2. What are the IASB's objectives regarding revenue recognition standards?

Revisiting the Case

AIG INSURANCE FORCED TO RESTATE EARNINGS

1. Revenues were overstated by $1,857 million. The major components of the adjustment were in net investment income and other revenues. The percentage decreases in these amounts were 6.8 and 11.0, respectively. Most investors would consider these amounts material.

2. Net income for 2003 was overstated by $1,265 million, which represented a decrease of 13.6 percent, an amount most investors would consider material.

3. Because compensation is closely tied to the financial performance of a company, managers might be tempted to push earnings toward analysts' earnings expectations.

---

12 "ED Amendment to FRS 5 'Reporting the Substance of Transactions': Revenue Recognition," Accounting Standards Board. Available at: **www.asb.org.uk/publications/publicationproject. cfm?upid=147**. Accessed 10/21/03.

SUMMARY BY LEARNING OBJECTIVE

LO1 Explain the conceptual issues and timing criteria guiding revenue recognition.

Revenues are recognized when persuasive evidence of an arrangement exists, delivery has occurred or services have been rendered, the seller's price to the buyer is fixed or determinable, and collectibility is reasonably assured. In essence, revenues are recognized when they are earned and realized (cash is collected) or realizable (collection is reasonably certain).

LO2 Account for revenue transactions at the point of sale and discuss the related issues.

For most companies and for most transactions, revenue is normally recognized at the point of sale because that is the point at which all of the revenue recognition criteria are met. Those criteria are the following: (1) there is evidence of a sales arrangement (a bill of sale), (2) delivery has occurred or services have been rendered (the revenue-producing activity has been completed), (3) the price to the buyer is fixed or determinable (not contingent on future events), and (4) collectibility is reasonably assured (the buyer has the resources to pay). If any of these conditions are uncertain, revenue should not be recognized at the point of sale, but should be deferred until these uncertainties have been reasonably resolved.

LO3 Account for revenue transactions during production and before delivery.

Certain companies enter into construction contracts involving production that takes place over a long period of time. If the amount and timing of the receipts are known and if the costs can be reasonably estimated, revenue can be recognized as it is earned over the period of the construction contract (the percentage-of-completion method). If costs cannot be reasonably estimated or if the timing of the receipts is uncertain, revenue recognition (and the resulting gross profit) should be deferred until the project has been completed (the completed-contract method).

LO4 Account for revenue transactions at the end of production but prior to delivery.

In certain industries, revenue is recognized when production is complete, even though this is before the product is actually delivered. Under the completed-production method of revenue recognition, revenue is recognized upon completion of the production process, assuming that the market price of the commodity is stable and that the units produced are homogeneous, or similar to other units produced. This method of revenue recognition is industry-specific and not very widespread.

LO5 Account for revenue transactions after delivery and during cash collection.

Sometimes it is appropriate to delay the recognition of revenue until the cash from the transaction is actually received. These situations occur when there are significant uncertainties surrounding the ultimate collection of the cash from the sale. These uncertainties are usually caused by extended cash collection periods combined with a significant possibility of uncollectible accounts or of the product or item's being returned. In most circumstances, these uncertainties can be reasonably estimated and normal accounting procedures are used to match revenues and expenses. However, when the uncertainties are sufficiently significant, alternative revenue recognition policies are utilized. These include the installment sales method and the cost-recovery method.

LO6 Recognize transactions that present challenging revenue recognition issues and identify how quality of earnings is affected.

In *SAB No. 101,* the SEC tried to provide more guidance for applying the criteria for revenue recognition and, as noted previously, focused on the following criteria:

1. Persuasive evidence of an arrangement exists (a bill of sale, for example).

2. Delivery has occurred or services have been rendered (the revenue-producing activity has been completed).

3. The seller's price to the buyer is fixed and determinable (not contingent on future events).

4. Collectibility is reasonably assured (the buyer has the resources to pay).

Revenue that is properly recognized is considered sustainable, whereas revenue that is recognized too soon is often inflated and subsequently revised downward. Determining whether revenues have been recognized properly is an important determinant in assessing the quality of a company's earnings. The revenue recognition policy should be clearly stated in the notes to the financial statements and should be transparent to the users.

LO7 **Describe the current status and future direction of international standards on revenue recognition.**

Revenue recognition issues are not limited to the United States. In fact, the controversies that are being debated in the United States are also being debated in other countries. Currently, no common standards for revenue recognition exist among the countries associated with the International Accounting Standards Board (IASB). Given the importance of this issue and the need for convergence of accounting standards, the IASB has joined the FASB in a high-priority project on revenue recognition.

KEY TERMS

completed-contract method (p. 260)
completed-performance method (p. 259)
completed-production method (p. 268)
cost-recovery method (p. 272)

expenses (p. 254)
installment sale (p. 269)
installment sales method (p. 270)
percentage-of-completion method (p. 259)
point of sale (p. 256)

proportional-performance method (p. 259)
recognition (p. 254)
revenue recognition principle (p. 254)
revenues (p. 254)
right of return (p. 256)

EXERCISES

LO1, 3   **EXERCISE 6-1   Percentage-of-Completion Method**
Wind and Water Energy Company hired Smith Construction Corporation to build a new building for its operations. Smith agreed to build the plant for $1,200,000, and Wind and Water Energy agreed to pay Smith $300,000 on January 1 and July 1 for two years, beginning July 1, 2006. Smith estimates that it will incur total costs of $950,000 to complete construction. The following details exist at December 31, 2006:

Costs incurred to date	$400,000
Estimated costs to complete	550,000
Billings to date	300,000
Collections to date	300,000

Required:

1. Calculate the amount of income that Smith should recognize for 2006, using the percentage-of-completion method.

2. Prepare the journal entries for the costs incurred, billings, collections, and income recognized on this job for 2006.

LO1, 3   **EXERCISE 6-2   Percentage-of-Completion Method**
Refer to the information provided in Exercise 6–1. Smith Construction Corporation completes the new building for Wind and Water Energy Company in 2008. The details for 2007 and 2008 follow:

	12/31/2007	12/31/2008
Costs incurred to date	$850,000	$ 950,000
Estimated costs to complete	150,000	—
Billings to date	900,000	1,200,000
Collections to date	900,000	1,200,000

Required:

1. Calculate the amount of income Smith will recognize on this project in 2007.

2. Calculate the amount of income Smith will recognize on this project in 2008.

3. Prepare the journal entries to record the income recognized for 2007 and 2008.

LO1, 3 **EXERCISE 6-3 Completed-Contract Method**

Refer to Exercises 6-1 and 6-2. Assume that Smith Construction Corporation cannot estimate total costs when beginning this project for Wind and Water Energy Company. As a result, Smith will use the completed-contract method of income recognition.

Required:

1. Prepare the journal entries that Smith would make to record the costs, billings, and collections for this project for 2006.

2. Prepare the journal entries that Smith would make to record the costs, billings, and collections for this project for 2007.

3. Prepare the journal entries that Smith would make to record the costs, billings, and collections for this project for 2008.

LO1, 3 **EXERCISE 6-4 Percentage-of-Completion Method**

Happy Construction Company uses the percentage-of-completion method when total construction costs can be estimated. Happy is building a road for Payne County for $2,000,000 with the following details:

	12/31/2004	12/31/2005
Costs incurred during the year	$ 900,000	$ 850,000
Estimated costs to complete	800,000	—
Billings to date	1,000,000	2,000,000
Collections to date	900,000	1,800,000

Required:

1. How much income will Happy recognize in 2004?

2. How much income will Happy recognize in 2005?

3. Show how this job will be reported on the balance sheet at the end of 2004. Indicate the name(s) of the account(s) and how each amount is classified and reported.

LO1, 3 **EXERCISE 6-5 Percentage-of-Completion Method**

Sad Construction Company uses the percentage-of-completion method when total construction costs can be estimated. Sad is building an office building for Porter Company for $10,000,000 with the following details:

	12/31/2004	12/31/2005	12/31/2006
Costs incurred to date	$2,000,000	$3,500,000	$ 6,500,000
Estimated costs to complete	6,000,000	4,500,000	1,500,000
Billings to date	6,000,000	8,000,000	10,000,000
Collections to date	3,000,000	5,500,000	10,000,000

Required:

1. Prepare all journal entries for 2004 that Sad should make for this job.

2. Prepare all journal entries for 2005 that Sad should make for this job.

LO5 **EXERCISE 6-6 Installment Sales**

Kimbrell Company sells household appliances to customers and allows customers to make installment payments on their purchases. The following information is from Kimbrell's accounting records for 2004 and 2005:

	2004	2005
Installment sales	$500,000	$600,000
Cost of goods sold	350,000	390,000
Cash collections on 2004 sales	360,000	140,000
Cash collections on 2005 sales	—	370,000

Required:

1. Using the installment sales method of revenue recognition, calculate how much income Kimbrell will recognize in 2004.

2. Using the installment sales method of revenue recognition, calculate how much income Kimbrell will recognize in 2005.

3. Prepare the journal entries to record the sales, cash collection, and income for 2004 and 2005.

LO5   **EXERCISE 6-7   Cost-Recovery Method**
Use the information given in Exercise 6-6.

Required:

1. Under what circumstances would it be appropriate for Kimbrel to use the cost recovery method of revenue recognition rather than the installment sales method?

2. Under the cost recovery method, how much income, if any, would Kimbrel recognize in 2004?

LO1, 2, 4   **EXERCISE 6-8   Various Methods of Revenue Recognition**
Elgin Soybean Farms, Inc. produced 50,000 bushels of soybeans in 2004. The selling price at the time of production was $3.10 per bushel. During 2004, Elgin sold 20,000 bushels at $3.10 per bushel. Elgin collected half of the cash for the sale in 2004 and half of the cash in 2005. Depreciation on farm equipment and other production costs were $2.60 per bushel.

Required:

1. Assume that Elgin recognizes income when the soybeans are harvested. What amount of income will Elgin recognize for 2004?

2. Assume that Elgin recognizes income at the point of sale. What amount of income will Elgin recognize for 2004?

LO5   **EXERCISE 6-9   Installment Sales Method**
Vast Land Sales reported the following data for its undeveloped property sales for 2004, 2005, and 2006:

	2004	2005	2006
Sales	$300,000	$330,000	$360,000
Cost of goods sold	180,000	191,400	212,400
Operating expenses	50,000	60,000	70,000
Cash collections:			
On 2004 sales	100,000	100,000	100,000
On 2005 sales	—	110,000	110,000
On 2006 sales	—	—	120,000

Required: Calculate how much gross profit and income Vast Land Sales will recognize in 2004, 2005, and 2006, assuming that the installment sales method is used.

LO2   **EXERCISE 6-10   Right of Return**
Mile High Recording Studio sells CDs to various retail outlets. Mile High shipped the following CD units at $5.00 each in the first half of 2004:

January	100 units
February	300 units
March	250 units
April	200 units
May	330 units
June	210 units
Total	1,390 units

Required:

1. Assume that Mile High has a no-return policy. Prepare the journal entry to record the sale of the units for the six-month period.

2. Assume that Mile High allows returns within 90 days. Mile High estimates that 4 percent of the units sold will be returned. Assume that 50 units were returned on account by the end of the period. Prepare the journal entries to record the sale of the units and the returns for the period.

3. Assume that Mile High allows returns within 90 days, but is unable to estimate the amount of returns for any given period. Returns are expected to be substantial, and 140 units have been returned on account for the period. Prepare the journal entries to record the sale of the units and the returns for the period.

LO1, 6   EXERCISE 6-11   Consignments and Quality of Earnings

Jay, Inc. is a New Jersey–based public company that manufactures men's ties and bowties for national distribution. Jay has recently been struggling to hold its market share because of increased competition from large fashion designers that have outsourced manufacturing to Asian countries where labor costs are lower. Jay has recently signed a partner agreement with Grads R Us, a large regional retail tuxedo rental company. The substance of the agreement is that Jay will ship large orders of ties to Grads R Us that will be made available to customers who rent tuxedos for events such as graduation and weddings. The agreement specifies that once a tie has been rented four times, Grads R Us must purchase the tie and pay the invoice amount. This usually takes anywhere from four to eight months.

Required:

1. Do you believe Jay should recognize the revenue upon delivery to Grads R Us? Why or why not?

2. What journal entry should Jay record when it ships 200 ties to Grads R Us? The selling price is $6 each, and the cost is $2.50 each.

LO1   EXERCISE 6-12   Revenue Recognition

BVD Co. rented a machine to Les Co. on January 1, 2004, for two years. The annual rental is $84,000. Additionally, on January 1, 2004, Les Co. paid $30,000 to BVD Co. as a one-time rental fee. BVD required an additional $12,000 as a security deposit that is refundable at the end of the rental period.

Required:

1. How much revenue should BVD recognize during 2004 as a result of the transactions relating to the rental?

2. Identify the revenue recognition criteria and explain how these concepts apply to the rental agreement for BVD.

LO2   EXERCISE 6-13   Right of Return

Candle Enterprises, a catalog retailer of candles and gifts, records sales of $900,000 on account during 2005. Over the past six years, sales returns have averaged 4 percent of annual sales. During 2006, customers returned a total of $30,000 in merchandise.

Required:

1. Record the journal entry for sales on account for 2005.

2. Record the adjustment for estimated sales returns at year end for 2005.

3. Record the journal entry for actual returns during 2006.

LO4   EXERCISE 6-14   Completed-Production Method

Fresh Masters grows and harvests a variety of vegetable products for the national grocery chain Main Street Markets, as well as for other small grocery stores in Texas and Oklahoma. On July 31, 2005, Fresh Masters harvests 20,000 bushels of corn. The market price on that date is $2.00 per bushel. The cost to produce each bushel is $1.25. Fresh Masters sells 15,000 bushels to Main Street Markets that day and holds the remaining 5,000 bushels to sell in the first few weeks of August. The company hopes that the market price for corn will increase to $2.25 per bushel. The fiscal year for Fresh Masters ends on July 31. When Fresh Masters sells its remaining corn inventory on August 10 to Troy Groceries, the market price is $2.10 per bushel.

Required:

1. Record the revenues and costs associated with the sale to Main Street Markets.
2. Record the journal entry to recognize any revenue accruals on July 31.
3. Record the journal entry to recognize the gain or loss from speculation on the price of corn.
4. Record the journal entry for the actual sale to Troy Groceries in August.

LO5   **EXERCISE 6-15   Installment Sales Method**

Trademark Designs reported the following data for its sales in 2005, 2006, and 2007:

	2005	2006	2007
Sales	$800,000	$800,000	$1,000,000
Cost of goods sold	560,000	610,000	645,000
Operating expenses	50,000	70,000	90,000
Cash collections:			
On 2005 sales	200,000	200,000	200,000
On 2006 sales	—	200,000	200,000
On 2007 sales	—	—	250,000

Required: Calculate how much gross profit and income Trademark Designs will recognize in 2005, 2006, and 2007, assuming that the installment sales method is used.

LO3   **EXERCISE 6-16   Gross Profit and the Percentage-of-Completion Method**

Broad Construction Company uses the percentage-of-completion method when total construction costs can be estimated. Broad is building a warehouse facility for Kellog Company for $30,000,000 with the following details:

	12/31/2004	12/31/2005	12/31/2006
Costs incurred to date	$12,000,000	$20,000,000	$24,000,000
Estimated costs to complete	10,000,000	3,000,000	—

Required: Calculate the estimated total gross profit on the contract as of December 31, 2004, 2005, and 2006.

LO6   **EXERCISE 6-17   Revenue Recognition for Goods on Consignment**

Trailer Trade manufactures horse and utility trailers. The trailers are sold via consignment through retail trailer stores nationwide. Trailer Trade holds title to the product until final sale and delivery to an end customer. Trailer Trade ships two trailers to Motor World in Gulfport, Mississippi, for $18,500 each in 2004. The cost to manufacture each was $12,000. Both trailers were sold and delivered to customers by Motor World in 2005 for $22,500 each.

Required:

1. When should Trailer Trade recognize the sale of a trailer?
2. What amount of revenue should be recognized by Motor World in 2005 for these trailers?
3. What revenue should be recognized by Trailer Trade in 2005 for these trailers?

LO7   **EXERCISE 6-18   Revenue Recognition International Standards**

Revenue recognition issues continue to be a challenge to both U.S. and international companies.

Required: Describe the importance of the convergence of revenue recognition accounting standards among all countries. Explain the objectives of the joint project between the IASB and the FASB on revenue recognition.

PROBLEMS

LO3   **PROBLEM 6-1   Percentage-of-Completion Method with Gross Profits for Three Years**

Janice Construction Company uses the percentage-of-completion method when total construction costs can be estimated. Janice is building an office building for TK Company for $20,000,000 with the following details:

	12/31/2004	12/31/2005	12/31/2006
Costs incurred to date	$8,000,000	$10,000,000	$14,000,000
Estimated costs to complete	6,000,000	4,000,000	—
Billings to date	8,000,000	16,000,000	20,000,000
Collections to date	6,000,000	12,000,000	18,000,000

Required:

1. Calculate the estimated total gross profit on the contract as of December 31, 2004, 2005, and 2006.

2. Calculate the percentage of completion for 2004, 2005, and 2006.

3. Calculate the amount of income (loss) that Janice will recognize for 2004, 2005, and 2006.

4. Prepare all journal entries related to this project for Janice Construction Company for all three years.

5. How will this project be reported on the balance sheets for 2004, 2005, and 2006?

Analyze: Explain the revenue recognition theory behind the percentage-of-completion method.

LO3   **PROBLEM 6-2   Percentage-of-Completion Method with Reduced Gross Profits**

George Construction Company uses the percentage-of-completion method when total construction costs can be estimated. George is building an office building for James Company for $20,000,000 with the following details:

	12/31/2004	12/31/2005	12/31/2006
Costs incurred to date	$8,000,000	$16,000,000	$18,000,000
Estimated costs to complete	6,000,000	3,000,000	—
Billings to date	8,000,000	16,000,000	20,000,000
Collections to date	6,000,000	12,000,000	18,000,000

Required:

1. Calculate the estimated total gross profit on the contract as of December 31, 2004, 2005, and 2006.

2. Calculate the percentage of completion for 2004, 2005, and 2006.

3. Calculate the amount of income (loss) George will recognize for 2004, 2005, and 2006.

4. Prepare all journal entries related to this project for all three years.

5. How will this project be carried on the balance sheets for 2004, 2005, and 2006?

Analyze: How does a fluctuating estimated gross profit affect revenue recognition when the percentage-of-completion method is used?

Spreadsheet: Use a spreadsheet application to perform the calculations and present your answers for questions 1, 2, 3, and 5.

LO3 PROBLEM 6-3 **Percentage-of-Completion Method with Losses; Completed-Contract Method**

Thomas Construction Company uses the percentage-of-completion method when total construction costs can be estimated. Thomas is building an office building for LM Company for $20,000,000 with the following details:

	12/31/2004	12/31/2005	12/31/2006
Costs incurred to date	$8,000,000	$16,000,000	$22,000,000
Estimated costs to complete	8,000,000	8,000,000	—
Billings to date	8,000,000	16,000,000	20,000,000
Collections to date	6,000,000	12,000,000	18,000,000

Required:

1. Calculate the estimated total gross profit on the contract as of December 31, 2004, 2005, and 2006.

2. Calculate the percentage of completion for 2004, 2005, and 2006.

3. Calculate the amount of income (loss) that Thomas will recognize for 2004, 2005, and 2006.

4. Prepare all journal entries related to this project for Thomas Construction Company for all three years.

5. How will this project be carried on the balance sheets for 2004, 2005, and 2006?

Analyze: Assume that Thomas uses the completed-contract method of revenue recognition. How much income (loss) will Thomas recognize for 2004, 2005, and 2006?

LO5 PROBLEM 6-4 **Installment Sales Method**

The following information is for JK Company, which began its operations in 2004:

	2004	2005
Installment sales	$1,500,000	$1,800,000
Gross profit percentage	30%	28%
Cash collections during 2005:		
From 2004 installment sales	$375,000	$750,000
From 2005 installment sales		500,000

Required: Prepare the journal entries to record the sales, inventory cost, deferred gross profit, and gross profit recognized on 2004 and 2005 sales and cash collections.

Analyze: Why is the installment method favored for income tax purposes?

LO5 PROBLEM 6-5 **Cost-Recovery Method**

Elizabeth Energy Company sold an idle plant to Ruth Power Company for $2,500,000 on January 1, 2004. On this date, the plant had a depreciated cost of $2,000,000. Ruth paid $500,000 in cash and signed a 10 percent note for the balance, to be paid in equal installments of $630,942 per year over the next four years. Payments are made on December 31 of each year. Since there is no reasonable basis for estimating the collectibility of the note, Elizabeth accounts for the note under the cost-recovery method. The payments were received on time as follows:

Date	Payment	Interest	Principal	Balance
1/1/04				$2,000,000
12/31/04	$630,942	$200,000	$430,942	1,569,058
12/31/05	630,942	156,906	474,036	1,095,022
12/31/06	630,942	109,502	521,440	573,582
12/31/07	630,942	57,360	573,582	—

Required: Prepare a schedule showing the sale of the facility, the receipt of the note and cash on the date of sale, the deferred income, cash collections, and revenue recognized over the cash collection period.

Analyze: What overall percentage of interest did Elizabeth Energy Company earn on the $2,000,000 installment receivable?

LO2   **PROBLEM 6-6   Proportional-Performance Method of Revenue Recognition**

Sammy Consulting Company has several long-term contracts to provide consulting services. Sammy uses the proportional-performance method to recognize revenue. Sammy sells three-year contracts for $3,000 in advance to provide services over the three-year period. Any unused portion of the contract is refundable. Each contract requires Sammy to perform IT services a total of 90 times and to perform HR services a total of 30 times. The contribution to revenue for each IT and each HR performance is equal. At the beginning of 2004, 500 contracts were sold with the following data:

	Costs	Performance in 2004	Performance in 2005	Performance in 2006
Initial direct costs	$9,000			
Direct cost per IT service	$15.00			
Direct cost per HR service	$20.00			
IT services provided		12,000	15,000	18,000
HR services provided		4,000	5,000	6,000

Required:

1. When should Sammy recognize revenue on these contracts? At their inception? During performance? When performance is complete? Why?

2. Prepare the company's condensed income statements for 2004, 2005, and 2006.

Analyze: Assume that the $3,000 per contract was nonrefundable. Would your answer to question 1 change? Why or why not?

Spreadsheet: Use a spreadsheet application to prepare the condensed income statements for 2004, 2005, and 2006.

LO1, 2, 4, 5   **PROBLEM 6-7   Alternative Methods of Revenue Recognition**

ProFarma, a progressive farming company, produced 20,000 bushels of wheat in 2004, its first year of operations. During 2004, ProFarma sold 12,000 bushels of the wheat for $3.00 per bushel and collected 80 percent of the selling price for the wheat sold; the balance will be collected in two equal installments over the next two years. The market price of the wheat at December 31, 2004, is $3.10 per bushel. Additional information for ProFarma's 2004 operations is as follows:

Production costs per bushel	$.60
Depreciation on farm equipment	$5,000
Administrative costs	$10,000
Selling costs per bushel (paid at time of sale)	$.09

Required:

1. Determine ProFarma's income for 2004 using the completed-production method.

2. Determine ProFarma's income for 2004 using the point-of-sale method.

3. Determine ProFarma's income for 2004 using the installment sales method.

Analyze: Comment on which method you think ProFarma should use, and why.

LO6   **PROBLEM 6-8   Revenue Recognition for Goods on Consignment**

Great Lakes Company manufactures fishing boats. The boats are sold through third-party dealers on a consignment basis. The consignment agreement indicates that Great Lakes is to hold title to the boats until final sale and delivery to the customer. Dealers can return unsold boats by paying shipping costs and a financing fee of $250 per boat per month for the time the inventory was held. The cost charged to the dealers for each boat is $50,000. Great Lakes's cost of manufacturing the boats is $38,500 per boat. Great Lakes shipped 60 boats to All Seasons Fishing Boats, a dealer, during 2004. As of December 31, 2004, all but 10 boats had been sold by All Seasons Fishing Boats and delivered to customers. All Seasons Fishing Boats sells the boats to customers for $53,000 each.

Required:

1. When should Great Lakes recognize the sale of the boats? Why?

2. When should All Seasons Fishing Boats recognize the sale? Why?

3. Prepare a schedule showing 2004 revenues, cost of goods sold, and gross profit for Great Lakes.

4. Prepare a schedule showing 2004 revenues, cost of goods sold, and gross profit for All Seasons Fishing Boats.

5. How should All Seasons report the unsold boats on hand at December 31, 2004?

Analyze: At what amount should Great Lakes report the unsold boats shipped to All Seasons?

LO1, 2, 3, 4, 5 **PROBLEM 6-9   Alternative Revenue Recognition Methods**

The four points in time of revenue recognition are as follows:

A. Point of sale

B. During production

C. At completion of production

D. As cash is collected

1. In 2004, Sonta Devco began construction work under a three-year contract for $400,000. Sonta Devco uses the percentage-of-completion method for financial accounting purposes.

2. AT Publications distributes textbooks to college bookstores. Bookstores have the right to return unsold texts to AT for a full refund within two months of the date of purchase. AT is not able to estimate returns or collectibility of the amounts owed by the bookstores.

3. Copper Company was organized to explore for and mine copper and sell it to dealers. During the year, Copper Company discovered and mined 80,000 tons of copper. The copper had a current trading price on December 31, 2004, of $240 per ton. Copper plans to sell the copper in 2005 to five dealers that it has sold to in the past.

4. MegaShip began production of cruise ships during 2004. Each ship takes four years to complete. MegaShip has contracted with buyers for its ships and is assured of the collectibility of the receivables. MegaShip is able to estimate its costs and has a fixed contract price of $892 million for each ship. MegaShip has not implemented a cost control system, so it is not able to estimate its level of completion accurately.

Required: Select the revenue recognition alternative from the list given that most appropriately reflects the proper recognition of income according to GAAP. Briefly justify your selection for each. You may use each alternative more than once or not at all.

Analyze: What benefit is derived when revenue recognition is postponed?

LO1, 2, 5 **PROBLEM 6-10   Alternative Revenue Recognition Methods**

Mims Company manufactures computer memory devices. During 2004, Mims manufactured 50 devices at a cost of $2,000 each. Each device has a selling price of $6,000. During 2004, Mims sold 40 devices to customers for a 20 percent down payment, with the balance to be paid in 24 equal monthly payments of $200 on the first day of each month beginning November 1, 2004. All amounts due were collected in a timely manner.

Required: Calculate the amount of income to be recognized for 2004 if revenue is recognized at the point of sale.

Analyze: As it relates to recognizing revenue during production and recognizing revenue as cash is collected, describe the difference between realization and recognition.

LO1, 3, 5 **PROBLEM 6-11   Alternative Revenue Recognition Methods**

During 2004, Spinelli Enterprises entered into a contract for $800,000 with a customer and began construction on a yacht with an estimated cost of $480,000. Spinelli completed the yacht and delivered it to the customer during 2006. Other information as of December 31, 2004, is as follows:

Year	Customer Payments	Cost Incurred During Each Year
2004	$300,000	$216,000
2005	400,000	90,000
2006	100,000	174,000

Required:

1. How much income would Spinelli Enterprises report during 2004 if revenue is recognized during production?

2. Assume the same facts as before, but now assume that the yacht was delivered and all costs were incurred during 2004. How much income should Spinelli Enterprises report during 2004 if revenue is recognized under the installment sales method?

3. Determine the amount to be reported on the statement of cash flows under the methods used in questions 1 and 2. Explain why these amounts are different or the same.

Analyze: Would the method used in question 1 or that used in question 2 result in a higher income tax liability?

LO3 **PROBLEM 6-12   Percentage-of-Completion Method**

Restropo Construction Company uses the percentage-of-completion method of accounting. In 2004, Restropo began work on contract 86, which provided for a contract price of $1,800,000 and an estimated cost of $1,600,000. Other details are as follows:

	2004	2005	2006
Costs incurred during the year	$ 400,000	$ 925,000	$525,000
Estimated costs to complete, as of December 31	1,200,000	500,000	—
Billings during the year	420,000	1,080,000	300,000
Collections during the year	350,000	1,000,000	350,000

Required: Compute the amount of income or loss to be recognized in 2004, 2005, and 2006.

Analyze: Why is the percentage of the job that has been completed ignored when a contract loss occurs?

LO1, 2, 5 **PROBLEM 6-13   Alternative Revenue Recognition Methods**

During 2004, which was its first year of operations, Clark Company engaged in the following transactions:

A. Built 45 widgets at a cost of $43,400 each.

B. On November 1, sold 38 of the widgets for $62,000 each. The customers agreed to pay $6,200 per month for 10 months on the last day of each month, beginning November 30, until the total was paid in full.

C. Received the two installment payments expected for each widget sold.

Required: Determine how much gross profit should be recognized for 2004 under each of the following timings of revenue recognition:

1. Point of sale

2. As cash is received, using the installment method

Analyze: Under what conditions is the point-of-sale method the better choice for recognizing revenue?

LO1, 2, 3 **PROBLEM 6-14 Alternative Revenue Recognition Methods**

Hensel, Inc. began work in 2004 on a contract for $6,300,000. Other data are as follows:

	2004	2005
Costs to date	$2,700,000	$4,300,000
Estimated costs to complete	1,800,000	—
Billings to date	2,000,000	6,300,000
Collections to date	1,600,000	5,400,000

Required:

1. If Hensel recognizes revenue during production, how much gross profit will it recognize during 2004?

2. If Hensel recognizes revenue using the completed-contract method, how much gross profit will be recognized in 2004 and 2005?

Analyze: What role does the level of certainty play with regard to revenue recognition?

LO1, 3 **PROBLEM 6-15 Revenue Recognition During Production**

Garbonzo Construction Company uses the percentage-of-completion method of accounting. In 2004, Garbonzo began work on contract 34, which provided for a contract price of $2,000,000. Other details are as follows:

	2004	2005
Costs incurred to date	$ 300,000	$1,525,000
Estimated cost to complete, as of December 31	1,200,000	—
Billings during the year	320,000	1,480,000
Collections during the year	300,000	1,500,000

Required:

1. Compute the amount of income or loss to be recognized in 2004 and 2005.

2. What amounts should Garbonzo report on its balance sheet at December 31, 2004, for this contract?

Analyze: Why is this method of revenue recognition preferred to the point-of-sale method for this construction contract?

LO1, 2, 5, 7 **PROBLEM 6-16 Revenue Recognition Alternatives**

Peak Appliances manufactures refrigerators. During 2004, Peak manufactured 30 refrigerators at a cost of $600 each. Each has a selling price of $1,000. During 2004, the company sold 25 refrigerators to customers for a 10 percent down payment ($100), with the balance to be paid in nine equal monthly payments of $100 beginning September 1, 2004. All amounts due were collected in a timely manner.

Required:

1. Calculate the amount of gross profit to be recognized for 2004 under the following revenue recognition alternatives:
   a. Revenue is recognized at the point of sale.
   b. Revenue is recognized under the installment sales method.
   c. Revenue is recognized under the cost-recovery method.

2. What disclosure must a company make with respect to its revenue recognition policies? Why is this necessary?

3. Peak Appliances is considering moving its operations to the United Kingdom and will present its financial statements in accordance with GAAP and IAS. What challenges will this move present for Peak's accountants?

Critical Thinking: How does conservatism affect revenue recognition? What impact does the use of a conservative method have on the quality of earnings?

Analyze: If the board of directors of Peak Appliances inquired as to the method that would yield the greatest gross profit for the period, how would you respond?

CASES

LO1,6 RESEARCH CASE **6-1** **Revenue Recognition**

In 2001, **Global Crossing Ltd.** was completing its 100,000-mile fiber-optic network. In the spring of 2001, Global Crossing Ltd. recorded the following transaction:

> EPIK Communications Inc. paid $40 million for the right to divert some of its telephone and data traffic through Global Crossing's Latin America fiber routes. At the same time, Global spent $40 million for the unspecified future use of EPIK's facilities, which include a 1,850-mile fiber network linking Atlanta and Miami. Global recorded the purchase from EPIK as a capital expenditure (asset) while recording the sale to EPIK as revenue. As of February 13, 2002, Global has not found a use for the asset purchased from EPIK. This "swap of capacity" was investigated by the SEC and the FBI in 2002 as to whether the revenue recognized on the swap was falsely inflated.[13]

Required:

1. Do a Web search on the SEC's and the FBI's investigation of improper revenue recognition by Global Crossing Ltd. Has there been any resolution of this issue?

2. Find Global Crossing Ltd.'s financial statements for 2001. What would net income and EPS have been if Global Crossing had not recognized the $40 million swap as revenue?

3. How do you think swaps such as these should be accounted for? Why?

LO1,6 ETHICS CASE **6-2** **Revenue Recognition**

ETHICS

In 2000, **Enron Corp.** and **Blockbuster Inc.** joined forces by announcing that they would soon be allowing consumers across America to choose from among thousands of movies, including hot new features, which would be sent via telephone lines to their TVs at home. Within months of signing the deal, Enron set up an affiliated partnership, code-named Project Braveheart. Enron obtained a $115.2 million investment in the partnership from CIBC World Markets, the investment-banking arm of **Canadian Imperial Bank of Commerce** in Toronto. In return, CIBC received a promise of almost all earnings from Enron's share of the venture for the first 10 years. The partnership had no separate staff and no assets other than Enron's stake in the venture with Blockbuster, which was barely getting off the ground in late 2000. In exchange for its $115.2 million investment, CIBC was supposed to receive 93 percent of Braveheart's cash flow for 10 years. But Enron made the investment in the embryonic partnership more attractive by promising to repay CIBC the full value of its investment if the partnership failed to be profitable.

Enron reported $110.9 million in profits from Braveheart in the fourth quarter of 2000 and the first quarter of 2001.[14]

Required:

1. Discuss the appropriateness of recognizing revenue by "selling" a contract to provide movies via telephone lines sometime in the future. If Enron had not "sold" this contract, how should it have recognized the revenue from the contract?

2. Enron guaranteed the $115.2 million from CIBC in the event that Braveheart was not profitable. How should a guarantee such as this be reported?

---

13 Adapted from Dennis K. Berman and Deborah Solomon, "Optical Illusion? Accounting Questions Swirl," *Wall Street Journal*, February 13, 2002.

14 Adapted from Rebecca Smith, "Blockbuster Deal Shows Enron's Inclination to All-Show, Little Substance Partnerships," *Wall Street Journal*, January 17, 2002. Available at: **http://online.wsj.com/article_print/0,4287,SB1011217368129907240,00.html**. Accessed 2/27/04.

LO1,6   FINANCIAL REPORTING CASE 6-3   Revenue Recognition

Both Google and Yahoo! receive considerable revenues from advertising through their websites. The revenue recognition policies that Google currently uses are discussed in this chapter.

Required:

1. Using the Internet, obtain and review the 2004 financial statements from Google and Yahoo! Be sure to review the management discussion and analysis section and the notes to the financial statements.

   a. Compare the total revenues each company receives from advertising as well as the type of advertising revenues they earn.

   b. Compare each company's current revenue recognition policies. Have these policies changed over time? Review the article "Yahoo, Google and Internet Math," by Scott Thurm and Kevin Delaney (*Wall Street Journal,* May 10, 2004). Comment on the content of this article.

   c. Discuss the differences between recognizing *gross amounts* and *net amounts.* Review the accounting literature (FASB, AICPA, and SEC) and explain, in your view, when each method is most appropriate.

   d. Compare the amount of net income each company earned during 2004. To what extent do these differences, if any, in revenue recognition policies affect your comparison of the financial performance of the two companies?

2. The price of Google's stock at the time of its IPO was $85. At what price is it currently trading? At what price is Yahoo! currently trading and what was its estimated price at the time of Google's IPO? As a potential investor, which company (or both) might you consider investing in? Why?

LO1   CRITICAL THINKING CASE 6-4   Timing of Revenue Recognition

Blockbuster Inc. has for at least two years utilized a program that has seemed to bring it some success. The following is an excerpt from a promotion regarding the release of *Pirates of the Caribbean: Curse of the Black Pearl*:

> ***Pirates of the Caribbean: The Curse of the Black Pearl* Pre-order Bundle**
> BLOCKBUSTER® members can pre-buy *Pirates of the Caribbean* on DVD or VHS and seven (7) movie (DVD or VHS) rentals for a set price plus tax by December 1, 2003 at a participating BLOCKBUSTER® store. Price may vary by store. The movie rentals are redeemable for one (1) free movie rental the week of the date of purchase and for 6 consecutive weeks following the week from the date of purchase at the same participating store location where this pre-order bundle is purchased. Limit one (1) rental redeemed per week. All 7 movie rentals must be placed on the BLOCKBUSTER® membership account number used to purchase the pre-order bundle. Weeks begin on Monday and end on Sunday. Your movie rentals will automatically be added to your BLOCKBUSTER® membership account, may not be transferred and must be used at the same store where you purchased the movie. Any week(s) skipped cannot be later redeemed and shall be forfeited. If you purchased the movie on Sunday, the first movie rental must be redeemed that day or will be forfeited. This offer is not valid with any other discounts or offers including any price match guarantee. Rental offer excludes game and equipment rentals. Membership rules apply for rental. Purchaser responsible for all applicable taxes and extended viewing fees associated with these rentals. If purchaser rents multiple movies when redeeming these rentals, credit will be applied to the highest rental price. These rentals will *not* count as paid rentals towards BLOCKBUSTER Rewards® benefits. Prices may vary. The release date of the movie is subject to change. You must pick up your VHS or DVD at the store location where purchased. Actual value of Pirates of the Caribbean movie and rental card package depends upon customer's use of movie rental card, actual rental price and location of store.[15]

15 Excerpt from the Blockbuster.com website. © 2003 Blockbuster Inc. All rights reserved.

Assume that the price for this program is $29.99. The regular price of the DVD is $21.99, and each rental is $4.25.

Required: What revenue recognition issues are posed by this program? Specifically address the amount that Blockbuster should recognize and the timing of the recognition.

LO1, 3

ETHICS

ETHICS CASE 6-5   Timing the Recognition of Revenues

Andy Merchant is the cost accountant at Baumann Company, a midsize construction contractor. Two years ago, Baumann accepted a three-year construction project that was expected to result in $1 million of income. At the end of the second year, the company estimated that the project was about 70 percent complete. The company had recognized revenue and cost of goods sold for the first two years of the project, resulting in reported income of $300,000 for the first year and preliminary reported income of $400,000 for the second year. At the beginning of the third year, before the final financial statements have been prepared, a major problem in the construction of the building has been discovered. The company has mistakenly constructed a type of roof that is not permitted, given the angle of the structure. This problem will require major rework and incur additional costs.

Andy conducted a cost analysis to determine the additional rework cost and estimates that the project will yield a total profit of only $200,000 instead of the previously estimated $1,000,000. He immediately communicated this information to the project manager. The project manager responded that he believes that some of the materials in the faulty roof can be reused and that this will mitigate the reduction in income. He wants to wait and see how much of the material can be salvaged before changing the cost and profit estimate. Andy recommended that this new estimate be used and that the profit for the second year be reversed. The project manager indicated that he would speak to the company's controller regarding this issue. A week later, Andy learned from his friend in the accounting department that the preliminary financial statements still show a profit of $400,000 for the current year and $300,000 for the prior year.

Required:

1. What is the proper accounting treatment for this new estimate?
2. What are the problems and issues faced by the accountant?
3. Who will be affected by the accountant's decision?
4. What values and principles are likely to influence his decision?
5. What alternative actions can the accountant take?
6. a. Of the parties you listed in question 3, whose interest is most important?
   b. Of the values and principles you listed in question 4, which is the most important?
   c. Of the actions you listed in question 5, which will do the most good or cause the least harm?
   d. Which consideration is most important?
7. What would you do?

LO6

ETHICS

ETHICS CASE 6-6   Financial Misstatements

In April of 2002, the SEC charged **Xerox** with fraud, alleging that management accelerated revenue recognition on leased equipment by more than $3 billion over a four-year period. After settling the charges by agreeing to a $10 million fine, the company restated its financial statements from 1997 to 2001.[16]

After Xerox settled with the SEC in 2002, its stock fell to an all-time low of $4.20 per share. While the stock price has since recovered to $14.74 at April 2, 2004, the company is still struggling to regain investors' confidence. In an effort to do so, Xerox has initiated changes in its corporate governance by centralizing the company's accounting function within the chief accountant's office and adding an independent (outside) director to its board of directors.

---

16 Craig Schneider, "Xerox: New Lease on Life," *CFO.com*, October 24, 2003. Available at: **http://www.cfo.com/Article?article=10882**. Accessed 4/5/04.

Suppose you are working as a junior staff accountant at a company like Xerox. You have just completed your accounting degree, and you are enthusiastic about your professional career. Through discussions with other staff accountants, you become aware that the company may be recognizing revenue too early, and thus overstating income. You have discussed the issue with your immediate supervisor, but he has dismissed your concerns, stating that the company's top accountants, its auditors, and the audit committee are comfortable with the revenue recognition policy.

Required:

1. What are the ethical issues that you face?
2. Why does it matter if a company recognizes revenue too early if, over a number of years, the total revenue recognized is correct?
3. Who will be affected by any decision you make on this issue?
4. What values and principles are likely to influence your decision?
5. What alternative actions might you take?
6. What would you do?

LO2 RESEARCH CASE 6-7 Departures from GAAP

With the increased regulatory enforcement actions by the SEC and the recent emphasis on independent audits, managers of companies must thoroughly evaluate critical accounting policies and determine whether those policies are appropriate and in accordance with GAAP. The following press release by **NDCHealth** was released on April 1, 2004:

> **NDC Health Delays Fiscal Third Quarter Results**
> ATLANTA, April 1 /PRNewswire-FirstCall/—NDCHealth Corporation (NYSE: *NDC*) today announced that it will delay release of its 2004 fiscal third quarter financial results and the conference call previously scheduled for April 1 and April 2, 2004, respectively. This decision was prompted by the company's initiation of a review concerning practices and procedures relating to the timing of revenue recognition of sales to the value-added reseller channel in its physician business unit. The physician systems business historically has constituted approximately 8% of the company's total revenue and 6.5% of its total operating income. NDCHealth will release its results as soon as its review is completed.[17]

Required: Locate the 2004 second-quarter 10-Q SEC filing for NDCHealth Corporation on the company's website. Review Note 1 in the report. Explain the accounting policies used by the company for revenue recognition. What two operating segments does the company have? What primary sources of revenue does the company have?

LO1, 2 CRITICAL THINKING CASE 6-8 Recognition at Point of Sale

Read the following revenue recognition note from **Intel Corporation**'s 2003 Form 10-K filed with the SEC.

> ### *Intel*   Revenue Recognition
>
> The company recognizes net revenue when the earnings process is complete, as evidenced by an agreement with the customer, transfer of title and acceptance, if applicable, as well as fixed pricing and probable collectibility. Because of frequent sales price reductions and rapid technology obsolescence in the industry, sales made to distributors under agreements allowing price protection and/or right of return are deferred until the distributors sell the merchandise. Shipping charges billed to customers are included in net revenue, and the related shipping costs are included in cost of sales.

---

17 PRNewswire, FirstCall. NDCHealth Corporation. "NDCHealth Delays Fiscal Third Quarter Results" (April 1, 2004), available at: **www.prnewswire.com/cgi-bin/microstories.pl?ACCT= 603950 &TICK=NDC&STORY=/www/story/04-01-2004/0002139137&EDATE=Apr+1, +2004**. Accessed 4/9/04.

Required:

1. What aspect of revenue recognition might cause Intel to defer recognizing revenue on sales to certain distributors?

2. Which criterion of *SAB No. 101* is most challenging to Intel?

LO3 ANALYSIS CASE **6-9**   **Percentage-of-Completion Method**

Boeing Company's 2003 annual report reported "Advances in Excess of Related Costs" in the amount of $3,464 million and $3,123 million, respectively, for its fiscal years ended December 31, 2003 and 2002. The information that follows is taken from its financial statement notes.

Boeing   **Note 1 – Summary of Significant Accounting Policies**

Revenue Recognition

Contract accounting is used predominately by the segments within Integrated Defense Systems (IDS). The majority of business conducted in these segments is performed under contracts with the U.S. Government and foreign governments that extend over a number of years. Contract accounting involves a judgmental process of estimating the total sales and costs for each contract, which results in the development of estimated cost of sales percentages. For each sale contract, the amount reported as cost of sales is determined by applying the estimated cost of sales percentage to the amount of revenue recognized.

Note 8 – Inventories

Inventories at December 31 consisted of the following:

	2003	2002
Long-term contracts in progress	$10,117	$ 9,790
Commercial aircraft programs	6,448	7,379
Commercial spare parts, used aircraft, general stock materials and other, net of reserves	2,707	2,713
	19,272	19,882
Less advances and progress billings	(13,934)	(13,698)
	$ 5,338	$ 6,184

Total costs of products during 2003 were $43,862 million and total sales were $50,485 million.

Required:

1. Determine the gross profit rate for 2003.

2. Based on the information provided, prepare summary journal entries to recognize costs, profit, billings, and completion of the contracts. Be sure you consider the beginning and ending balances of the applicable accounts.

LO1 CRITICAL THINKING CASE **6-10**   **Earnings Management Versus Fraud**

Yang Products had a banner year in 2004. During 2005, this specialty garden hose manufacturer was challenged to meet sales projections that had been promised in an earnings forecast to Wall Street at the beginning of the year. As of December 15, the executives were making serious efforts to find a way to ensure that actual sales exceeded $30 million. As of December 29, the estimate of sales to date was $29.8 million. Unfortunately, the specialty hardware stores that represent almost 95 percent of Yang's customer base had preordered most of their inventory requirements through the spring of 2006. Making $200,000 in sales in the last three days of the year was critical for the president and the CFO, whose bonuses and stock options demanded that sales, related earnings, and the corresponding stock price achieve estimates. Fortunately, a last-minute phone call on December 31 came in with a $200,000 order. Though the customer asked to have the order shipped on March 1, the president was able to entice the customer to accept the order for shipment immediately by offering a 15 percent discount. Other customers were not offered this discount.

Required: Should Yang Products be able to recognize the sale made at year-end during 2005? Justify your response.

ON THE WEB

The following exercises, activities, and problems are available on the *Intermediate Accounting* website. Use these resources to reinforce your understanding of the topics presented in this chapter.

- CPA-Adapted Simulations
- Interpreting the Accounting Standards
- Extending the Global Focus
- Extending the Ethics Discussion
- Mastering the Spreadsheet
- Career Snapshots
- Annual Report Project
- ACE Practice Tests
- Flashcards
- Glossary
- Check Figures for Text Problems
- PowerPoint Presentations

SOLUTIONS: CHECK YOUR UNDERSTANDING

Conceptual Issues Guiding Revenue Recognition (p. 256)

1. Under the revenue recognition principle, revenue should be recognized (and recorded) when two criteria are met:
   - The amount and timing of revenue can be reasonably determined (revenue is realized or realizable).
   - The earnings process is complete or virtually complete (revenue is earned).

2. The AICPA, FASB, and SEC have issued guidance on the topic of revenue recognition.

3. *SAB No. 101* stated that revenue is realized or realizable and earned when all of the following four criteria are met:
   - Persuasive evidence of an arrangement exists (a bill of sale, for example).
   - Delivery has occurred or services have been rendered (the revenue-producing activity has been completed).
   - The seller's price to the buyer is fixed and determinable (not contingent on future events).
   - Collectibility is reasonably assured (the buyer has the resources to pay).

Revenue Recognition at the Point of Sale (p. 259)

1. If a company experiences a high level of product returns, the following entry can be made to estimate potential returns: debit Sales Returns and Allowances, credit Allowance for Sales Returns and Allowances.

2. If sales returns cannot be reasonably estimated or if other criteria of *SFAS No. 48* are not met, revenue should not be recognized at the point of sale, but should be deferred until the uncertainties have been resolved.

3. The proportional-performance method and the completed-performance method may be used to account for sales of services.

Revenue Recognition During Production or Before Delivery (p. 266)

1. The percentage-of-completion recognizes gross profit on the construction contract as work is done, represented by costs incurred to date. The completed-contract method delays the recognition of gross profit until the completion of the contract, when all facts are known for sure. The percentage-of-completion method is used if the amount and timing of the receipts are known and if the costs can be reasonably estimated. Revenue is recognized as it is earned over the period of the construction contract. If costs cannot be reasonably estimated or if the timing of the receipts is uncertain, revenue recognition (and the resulting gross profit) should be deferred until the project has been completed, using the completed-contract method.

2. Amount of receipts, timing of receipts, and estimated costs need to be known in order to use the percentage-of-completion method.

3. $60,000/$112,000 = 53.6 percent complete; $150,000 − $112,000 = $38,000 estimated total gross profit; $38,000 × 53.6% = $20,368 revenue recognized in the first year.

Revenue Recognized at the End of Production but Prior to Delivery (p. 269)

1. Under the completed-production method of revenue recognition, revenue is recognized upon completion of

the production process, assuming that the market price of the commodity is stable and that the units produced are homogeneous, or similar to other units produced.

2. When an agricultural crop has been harvested or when precious minerals have been mined, the activities required to earn revenue are substantially complete. The price of such resources can be easily determined, and therefore the completed-production method is suitable.

Revenue Recognition After Delivery and During Collection of Cash (p. 273)

1. The installment sales method can be used (it recognizes both the revenue and the cost of sales proportionately as the cash is collected). If collection of payments is highly uncertain, the cost-recovery method may be used.

2. Debit Installment Receivables, credit Installment Sales Revenue.

3. Revenues are recognized proportionately as cash payments are received.

4. This method is used in situations where the collection of payments is so highly uncertain that it would not be prudent to recognize revenues until enough cash has been collected to cover the cost of the product sold.

Challenging Revenue Recognition Issues (p. 278)

1. It is important for financial statement users to understand revenue recognition methods because the use of different methods can result in drastically different revenue amounts within the same industry.

2. Under GAAP, barter transactions should be recorded at fair value. Specifically, advertising from barter transactions should be recognized only when a company has an established history of earning cash from the sale of the same space. In such cases, the value is based on similar cash transactions that occurred within six months prior to the barter transactions.

3. A company should not recognize revenue from sales made under its layaway program until delivery of the merchandise to the customer. Until then, the amount of cash received should be recognized as a liability with the title of "deposits received from customers for layaway sales" or a similarly descriptive caption.

International Issues Related to Revenue Recognition (p. 279)

1. Different revenue recognition policies can lead to marked variations in profit and inconsistencies from one industry to another and within an industry.

2. According to the IASB, the objectives of the new joint project with the FASB are to develop a comprehensive set of principles for revenue recognition, fill the voids that have emerged in revenue recognition in recent years, provide guidance for addressing issues that arise in the future, amend the conceptual guidance with respect to the potential inconsistencies related to revenue recognition, and converge the conceptual and authoritative guidance of the IASB and FASB with respect to revenue recognition.

CPA-ADAPTED SIMULATION

This simulation asks you to complete various tasks related to a comany's annual financial statements. If your instructor has signed up for CPAexcel™, you can do the work online at **www.cpaexcel.com/hmco**. You may also do the simulation manually.

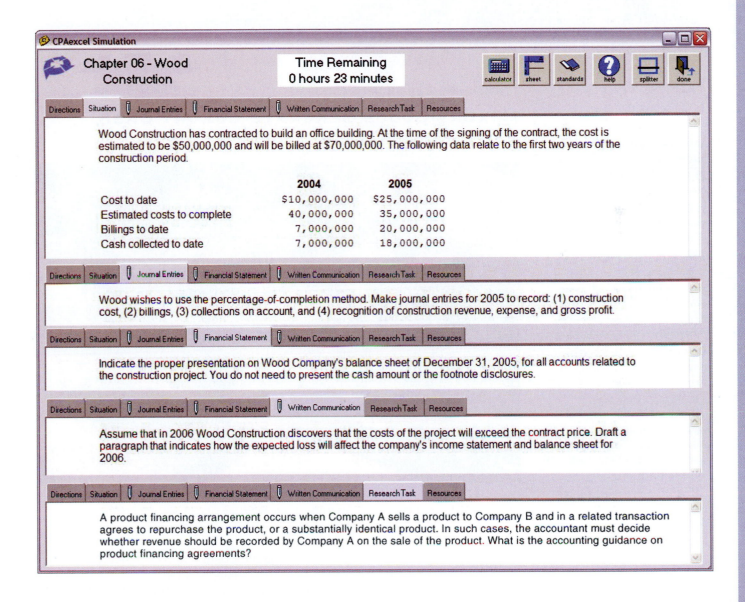

CPAexcel Simulation

Chapter 06 – Wood Construction

Time Remaining
0 hours 23 minutes

calculator | sheet | standards | help | splitter | done

Directions | Situation | Journal Entries | Financial Statement | Written Communication | Research Task | Resources

Wood Construction has contracted to build an office building. At the time of the signing of the contract, the cost is estimated to be $50,000,000 and will be billed at $70,000,000. The following data relate to the first two years of the construction period.

	2004	2005
Cost to date	$10,000,000	$25,000,000
Estimated costs to complete	40,000,000	35,000,000
Billings to date	7,000,000	20,000,000
Cash collected to date	7,000,000	18,000,000

Directions | Situation | Journal Entries | Financial Statement | Written Communication | Research Task | Resources

Wood wishes to use the percentage-of-completion method. Make journal entries for 2005 to record: (1) construction cost, (2) billings, (3) collections on account, and (4) recognition of construction revenue, expense, and gross profit.

Directions | Situation | Journal Entries | Financial Statement | Written Communication | Research Task | Resources

Indicate the proper presentation on Wood Company's balance sheet of December 31, 2005, for all accounts related to the construction project. You do not need to present the cash amount or the footnote disclosures.

Directions | Situation | Journal Entries | Financial Statement | Written Communication | Research Task | Resources

Assume that in 2006 Wood Construction discovers that the costs of the project will exceed the contract price. Draft a paragraph that indicates how the expected loss will affect the company's income statement and balance sheet for 2006.

Directions | Situation | Journal Entries | Financial Statement | Written Communication | Research Task | Resources

A product financing arrangement occurs when Company A sells a product to Company B and in a related transaction agrees to repurchase the product, or a substantially identical product. In such cases, the accountant must decide whether revenue should be recorded by Company A on the sale of the product. What is the accounting guidance on product financing agreements?

7

Cash and Receivables

FINANCIAL REPORTING CASE

LUXURY GOODS GENERATE LUXURY CASH FOR COACH

Coach, whose handbags and accessories have become some of the most sought after in the world, has generated record levels of cash because its operations are efficient and profitable.

Coach Over the past few years, leather handbags and accessories from Coach have become some of the most sought-after luxury goods in the world. Coach's management transformed the company by building on its classic styles and adding new products and categories that included new materials and new styles. Sales growth of Coach-branded goods has been over 30 percent in 2003 and 2004 and has led to record levels of net income.

Coach is able to generate this level of cash because its operations are efficient and profitable. In 2004, the company reported a gross profit percentage of 72 percent, and Coach's operating activities generated $448.6 million of cash. This financial strength provides Coach's management with more flexibility when deciding on future expansion, store openings, store renovations, and international expansion. In fact, Coach has generated so much cash from operations that the company disclosed in the management discussion and analysis section of its 2004 annual report

Coach

2004 QUARTERLY DATA FOR COACH, INC.
PARTIAL BALANCE SHEET DATA

(amounts in thousands, except share data)

ASSETS	Quarter 4 07/03/04	Quarter 3 03/27/04	Quarter 2 12/27/03	Quarter 1 09/27/03
Cash and cash equivalents	$262,720	$445,343	$372,775	$255,357
Short-term investments	171,723	0	0	0
Trade accounts receivable	61,180	84,668	101,420	65,972
Allowance for accounts receivable	−5,456	−6,011	−6,968	−6,113
Inventories	161,913	153,834	157,226	176,794
Other current assets	53,536	46,978	51,548	37,431
Total current assets	$705,616	$724,812	$676,001	$529,441

that "During fiscal 2004, Coach began investing in marketable securities with maturities greater than 90 days in order to maximize the rate of return on investments.[1]"

While Coach's future remains bright, one challenge that its management continues to face is the seasonal nature of its business. Because Coach products are commonly given as gifts, sales spike during Coach's second fiscal quarter, which includes the months of November and December. As you can see from the 2004 quarterly balance sheet data provided, Coach builds up its inventory during its first fiscal quarter. During the company's second quarter, inventory is sold and accounts receivable build up. In the third and fourth quarters, accounts receivable are collected, resulting in an increase in cash and short-term investments. Then the cycle begins again.

Coach's management carefully examines sales trends, cash, accounts receivable, and inventory levels throughout the year, and the company continues to strive for achieving higher levels of sales growth in nonholiday quarters in order to smooth out seasonal fluctuations.

EXAMINING THE CASE

1. What factors led to Coach's experiencing record levels of cash?
2. Why did Coach decide to invest excess cash in short-term marketable securities?
3. What effect does seasonality have on a company's cash and accounts receivable balances?

---

1 Coach, Inc., 2004 Annual Report.

LO 1 Identify items classified as cash and cash equivalents.

Forms of Cash

CASH AND CASH EQUIVALENTS

cash bank deposits, currency and coins, and checks received from customers

cash equivalents highly liquid investments that are easily convertible into cash; usually grouped with cash on the balance sheet

Critical Thinking: *Why do you think cash is often referred to as the lifeblood of a business?*

The asset section of every balance sheet begins with cash and cash equivalents. **Cash** includes bank deposits, currency and coins, and checks received from customers. If a company has cash denominated in foreign currency units, those amounts are translated into U.S. dollar equivalents. Because cash is a monetary asset, the translation is based on the rate of exchange that is in effect on the balance sheet date. **Cash equivalents**, highly liquid investments that are easily convertible into cash, are usually grouped with cash on the balance sheet.

Figure 7.1 presents an excerpt from **Coach**'s consolidated balance sheets at July 3, 2004 and June 28, 2003. As you can see, the company reported $262,720 thousand in cash and cash equivalents at July 3, 2004.

Companies must set policies concerning which items will be considered cash equivalents. Most companies include money market accounts and certificates of deposit, commercial paper, and U.S. Treasury bills that have a term of 90 days or less at their date of purchase. These short-term investments must be reported at their fair market value, not their face value. For example, in its annual report, Coach discloses the following information about its cash equivalents:

> CASH AND CASH EQUIVALENTS Cash and cash equivalents consist of cash balances and highly liquid investments with a maturity of less than 90 days.

RESTRICTED CASH

restricted cash material amounts of cash set aside from regular cash for specific purposes

Restrictions on cash may be imposed internally by management in the form of express intentions to earmark a certain amount of cash for a specific purpose. Companies may set aside cash for dividends, facility expansions, or other uses. Such material amounts set aside for specific purposes are considered **restricted cash** and are segregated from regular cash for reporting purposes. These restricted funds are classified as current assets or long-term assets, depending on the intended date of their use.

❯ COMPENSATING BALANCES

Also excluded from the cash balance is any portion of an account to which the company is denied unlimited access. For example, when a financial institution extends a

Figure 7.1

Balance Sheet

Coach	Coach, Inc. EXCERPT FROM CONSOLIDATED BALANCE SHEETS		
(amounts in thousands, except share data)		**July 3, 2004**	June 28, 2003
ASSETS			
Cash and cash equivalents		**$262,720**	$229,176
Short-term investments		**171,723**	—
Trade accounts receivable, less allowances of $5,456 and $6,095, respectively		**55,724**	35,470
Inventories		**161,913**	143,807
Deferred income taxes		**34,521**	21,264
Prepaid expenses and other current assets		**19,015**	18,821
Total current assets		**705,616**	448,538

Figure 7.2

Restricted Cash

TruServ

TruServ Corporation, 2002 10-K Form
Restricted Cash

Restricted cash consisted of the following at December 31:

($ in thousands)	2002	2001
Letters of credit	$11,691	$11,392
Proceeds from sale of assets available for debt reduction by the collateral agent	39	10,906
Lockbox cash management deposit requirements	4,025	4,000
Redeemable (subordinated) notes	—	1,746
Escrow	—	1,031
	$15,755	$29,075

compensating balance a minimum amount that a financial institution requires a company to keep in its account as part of a credit-granting arrangement

loan to a company, it often requires the company to keep a minimum balance in its account, called a **compensating balance**, as part of the credit-granting agreement. The financial institution uses this amount as collateral for the loan. Since less money is actually available to the company than the amount stated on the loan agreement, the compensating balance results in a higher effective interest rate.

For example, assume that Zeta Technologies borrows $300,000 from NC National Bank and agrees to an interest rate of 8 percent. NC National Bank requires Zeta to keep $75,000 of the borrowed funds in an account that pays 3 percent interest. Although Zeta receives interest income on the compensating balance, the company has in effect borrowed only 75 percent of the total amount but is paying interest on the full amount. The company's effective interest rate would be computed as follows:

$$\frac{\text{Total Interest Cost}}{\text{Effective Amount Borrowed}} = \text{Effective Interest Rate}$$

$$\frac{(\$300,000 \times 8\%) - (\$75,000 \times 3\%)}{\$300,000 - \$75,000} = 9.67\%$$

A compensating balance is disclosed separately from cash and cash equivalents as either a current or a long-term asset, depending on the terms of the borrowing agreement that restricts the funds.

To illustrate how funds aside from regular cash may be reported, Figure 7.2 presents an excerpt from **TruServ Corporation**'s 10-K form filed with the SEC for the year ended December 31, 2002.

TruServ has restricted cash in the amount of $15,755,000 in 2002. These funds are restricted by letters of credit, proceeds from the sale of assets available for debt reduction by the collateral agent, and lockbox cash management deposit requirements.

CASH AND INTERNATIONAL OPERATIONS

 INTERNATIONAL

Many companies operate in a global marketplace and must therefore account for transactions in foreign currencies, which are not immediately converted to U.S. dollars. For example, a company may collect foreign currencies for sales and deposit these funds in a foreign bank until the funds are needed. Because the exchange rate between the foreign currency and the U.S. dollar may change over this holding period, the amount must be remeasured at each balance sheet date, and a foreign exchange gain or loss must be recognized.

To illustrate, assume that Monitor, Inc., a Florida-based company, received 100,000 Mexican pesos for a cash sale originally made on October 15, 2005. Monitor deposited the pesos in a Mexican bank, and the funds remained on deposit at December 31, 2005.

Assume that the exchange rates between the Mexican peso and the U.S. dollar were as follows:

October 15, 2005	1 peso = U.S. $.09
December 31, 2005	1 peso = U.S. $.11

As you can see, the peso has appreciated in value against the dollar over the holding period.

Monitor would record the cash sale on October 15 in U.S. dollars as follows:

Cash	9,000	
Sales		9,000

Because the exchange rate changed between the deposit of funds and the end of period balance sheet, Monitor should record a remeasurement gain or loss. On December 31, 2005, the Mexican pesos on deposit are remeasured based on the $.02 increase in exchange rates since the sale date. Monitor would record the remeasurements as follows:

Cash [100,000 × ($.11 − $.09)]	2,000	
Foreign Exchange Gain		2,000

The $2,000 gain would be credited to income. The gain represents the positive effect of holding Mexican pesos during a time when the currency was appreciating against the dollar.

CHECK YOUR UNDERSTANDING

1. List examples of items that would be classified as cash and cash equivalents on a balance sheet.

2. Explain the concept of a compensating balance and describe how such balances should be reported on the balance sheet.

3. What effect does a compensating balance requirement have on the interest rate on the corresponding loan?

LO 2 Explain why cash controls are important and describe the specific tools used to control and protect cash.

internal controls a system of procedures to protect and control cash and other assets

Critical Thinking: *What tools do you use to protect your personal cash and liquid assets?*

Cash Controls

C ash is a company's most liquid asset. Therefore, it is important to protect it from theft, loss, waste, and embezzlement. Every business must establish a system of procedures to protect cash and other assets, called **internal controls**. Though internal control systems vary from business to business, the following basic tools are often utilized to control and protect cash disbursements and cash receipts:

1. Limit the number of persons who handle cash.

2. Separate the accounting tasks involving cash between different employees.

3. Bond employees who handle cash or cash records.

4. Use a cash register and a safe.

5. Use a checking account to make all cash payments and to provide a separate record of all transactions.

6. Deposit cash receipts in the bank in a timely fashion, usually daily.

Because the use of a checking account will provide a separate record of all transactions, it is important that the bank statement be reconciled promptly when it is received to verify that the balance in the general ledger corresponds with the balance reflected on the bank statement.

RECONCILING THE BANK STATEMENT

At any point in time, there will be differences between the cash balance reported by the bank and the cash balance in the general ledger as a result of such things as cash deposits that have not been processed by the bank, outstanding checks, and errors. A **bank reconciliation** is a process by which an accountant determines whether and why there is a difference between the balance shown on the bank statement and the balance of the Cash account in the company's general ledger. The reconciliation ensures that after adjustments are taken into account, both the bank and the Cash ledger balance agree.

In reconciling the bank statement to the cash ledger balance, adjustments are examined to determine whether they affect the bank balance or the ledger balance. The following adjustments commonly affect the bank balance:

bank reconciliation a process by which an accountant determines whether and why there is a difference between the balance shown on the bank statement and the balance of the Cash account in the company's general ledger

- *Deposits in transit.* Deposits that have been received by the company and debited to the ledger account but have not yet been recognized by the bank should be added to the bank balance.

- *Outstanding checks.* Checks that have been written by the company and credited to the ledger account but have not yet been processed by the bank should be subtracted from the bank balance.

- *Errors.* Errors may require either additions to or subtractions from the bank balance. For example, if the bank mistakenly charged a fee to the company's account, the amount of the fee should be added back to the bank balance.

The following adjustments commonly affect the Cash balance in the ledger:

- *Direct collection of receivables.* Many banks collect companies' outstanding receivables directly and deposit the collections immediately. During a bank reconciliation, a company should add to its Cash ledger balance any direct deposits that it has not previously recorded.

- *Interest.* The company should add to its Cash ledger balance any interest received during the period that has not previously been recorded.

- *Direct charges and payments.* Many companies use automatic payments for regular expenses, such as rent and utilities. A company should subtract such amounts from the Cash ledger balance if they have not previously been recorded. In addition, any unrecorded bank charges should be subtracted from the ledger balance.

- *Errors.* Errors may result in either additions to or subtractions from the ledger balance. For example, if the company mistakenly recognized a deposit of $200 as $2,000, the $1,800 difference would need to be deducted from the Cash balance in the ledger.

- *Insufficient funds checks.* If the bank returns a customer's check because the customer's account lacked sufficient funds to cover the check, the company must adjust its ledger account by subtracting the insufficient funds check.

Whenever adjustments are made to the ledger account in a bank reconciliation, journal entries must be made to ensure that the amount in the ledger is the actual Cash

Illustration 7.1

Bank Reconciliation

Dogwood Corporation
Bank Reconciliation
For the Month Ended August 31, 2005

Balance per bank statement		$71,980
Add:		
Deposits in transit	$ 5,000	
Bank error	2,700	7,700
Subtract:		
Outstanding checks		(4,560)
Cash balance at August 31—adjusted		$75,120
Balance per ledger		$60,645
Add:		
Receivables collected	$16,500	
Interest Income	185	16,685
Subtract:		
Bank fees	$ (310)	
Returned check	(1,900)	(2,210)
Cash balance at August 31—adjusted		$75,120

balance. For example, if a bank returned a customer's insufficient funds check to a company along with its bank statement, the company would need to reduce its Cash balance to reflect the fact that the cash was never actually received and reinstate the customer's account receivable to show that the money is still owed. To illustrate the bank reconciliation process, review the following information regarding Dogwood Corporation.

❭ **EXAMPLE: DOGWOOD CORPORATION** On August 31, 2005, Dogwood Corporation's Cash account had a balance of $60,645. When the company's bank statement for the period ended August 31, 2005, arrived, it showed a balance of $71,980. To reconcile the balance in Dogwood's Cash account with the balance in its bank account, the company's controller, Rhodeshia Jordan, identified the following items requiring adjustment:

● The bank charged fees of $60 for the account.

● The bank collected two receivables for the company, one in the amount of $6,500 and the other in the amount of $10,000. The bank charged an additional fee of $250 for the collections.

● The bank returned a check in the amount $1,900 from a customer who did not have sufficient funds to pay.

● The bank statement showed that Dogwood earned $185 in interest during the month of August.

● At August 31, Dogwood had written eight checks that the bank had not yet cashed; the total of those checks was $4,560.

● On August 31, Dogwood deposited a customer's check for $5,000; this had not yet been recorded by the bank.

● The bank recorded one of Dogwood's bank deposits as $300 instead of $3,000. Rhodeshia had contacted the bank, and it was in the process of correcting its error.

Using this information, Rhodeshia prepared the bank reconciliation shown in Illustration 7.1. She then made the following journal entries to ensure that cash is properly stated at August 31, 2005:

Cash	16,500	
Accounts Receivable		16,500

Cash	185	
Interest Income		185

Miscellaneous Bank Expense	310	
Cash		310

Accounts Receivable	1,900	
Cash		1,900

After the entries are made, the balance in Dogwood's Cash account reflects the true cash balance of $75,120.

CHECK YOUR UNDERSTANDING

1. Describe the purpose of internal controls.

2. List common tools used by businesses to control and protect cash.

3. Describe three potential items that may cause a difference between the bank statement balance and the general ledger Cash account.

Classifying Receivables

LO 3 Define and identify different types of receivables.

receivables claims to money, goods, or services owed to a company by others

account receivable an amount owed by a customer for goods or services purchased in the normal course of business; also called a trade receivable

other receivables amounts due as a result of transactions that are not customer-related

notes receivable written contracts promising to pay specified amounts to a company on specified dates

promissory note a written and signed document specifying the payment dates, interest, and other terms of a note receivable to ensure that both parties perform

Critical Thinking: *What types of money, services, or assets are owed to you? How do you think these receivables affect your net worth?*

Receivables are claims to money, goods, or services owed to a company by others. The classification of a receivable on the balance sheet depends on when it is due and whom the receivable is from. If the receivable arises from the sale of goods or services on credit at the wholesale or the retail level in the normal course of business, it is classified as an **account receivable**. A number of companies also use the term *trade receivable* to describe amounts owed by customers or wholesale vendors. Amounts due as a result of transactions that are not customer-related are usually recognized as **other receivables**. Examples of other receivables include tax refund claims, insurance claims, and advances to employees. An account receivable or other receivable is typically backed by a sales invoice or some other simple agreement rather than by a contractual agreement and is expected to be paid within 30 to 90 days.

Many companies also record **notes receivable**, which are written contracts promising to pay specified amounts to the company on specified dates. A note receivable is backed by a **promissory note**, a written and signed document specifying the payment dates, interest, and other terms to ensure that both parties perform. A note receivable may result from a customer transaction or from some other kind of transaction, but because the transaction is formally documented, the amount owed is classified as a note receivable rather than a trade receivable or other receivable. This distinction informs the financial statement user that the company has more specific rights (for example, in the case of nonpayment) than it has with a trade or other receivable. A note receivable may be short-term or long-term, depending on its due date.

Figure 7.3 presents the asset section of Coach's consolidated balance sheets at July 3, 2004 and June 28, 2003. As you can see, the company reported $55,724 thousand of net receivables in the current asset section of the balance sheet at July 3, 2004. Current accounts receivables are typically due within one year of the balance sheet date.

Figure 7.3

Asset Section of Consolidated Balance Sheets

Coach

Coach, Inc.
ASSET SECTION OF CONSOLIDATED BALANCE SHEETS

(amounts in thousands, except share data)	July 3, 2004	June 28, 2003
ASSETS		
Cash and cash equivalents	$ 262,720	$229,176
Short-term investments	171,723	—
Trade accounts receivable, less allowances of		
$5,456 and $6,095, respectively	55,724	35,470
Inventories	161,913	143,807
Deferred income taxes	34,521	21,264
Prepaid expenses and other current assets	19,015	18,821
Total current assets	705,616	448,538
Property and equipment, net	148,524	118,547
Long-term investments	130,000	—
Deferred income taxes	—	9,112
Goodwill	13,605	13,009
Indefinite life intangibles	9,788	9,389
Other noncurent assets	21,125	19,057
Total assets	$1,028,658	$617,652

Although receivables are only a small portion of Coach's total assets, there are a number of important accounting issues relating to their classification, recognition, and valuation.

> **CHECK YOUR UNDERSTANDING**
>
> 1. Describe the difference between a note receivable and an account receivable.
>
> 2. List examples of receivables that would be classified as "other receivables."
>
> 3. What details do promissory notes generally specify?

LO 4 Demonstrate the appropriate accounting treatment to record and value accounts receivable.

Accounting for Accounts Receivable

RECORDING ACCOUNTS RECEIVABLE

Accounts receivable are recorded at an amount equal to the sales price agreed to by the customer, called the exchange price. For example, when Coach sells a handbag to a customer through its website in exchange for a promise to pay $125 within 30 days, Coach records an account receivable of $125 as follows:

Accounts Receivable	125	
Sales		125

The account receivable will be reduced when the customer pays or when it is determined that the amount will go uncollected.

CASH DISCOUNTS

Many companies encourage their customers to pay their bills quickly by offering them a **cash discount**, sometimes also referred to as a *sales discount*. For example, a company might state its payment terms as 3/10, net/30, which means that a 3 percent discount may be taken by customers who pay within 10 days and that the full balance is due within 30 days. If a customer pays quickly and takes the cash discount, the company will receive an amount that is less than the amount recorded for that account receivable.

Companies may record cash discounts using one of two methods: the gross method or the net method. Under the **gross method**, cash discounts that are not taken by customers are viewed as part of sales. Under the **net method**, sales revenues are considered to be the net amount, after the discount, and any discounts that are not taken are classified as interest income. Most companies employ the gross method, recording the full amount of the receivable as sales and accounting for the discount when payment is received, as illustrated in the following scenario.

On October 15, 2005, Catalpa Company made a sale of $200 to Juniper Corporation with payment terms of 2/10, net/30. Catalpa would record the sale in the following way:

Accounts Receivable	200	
Sales		200

If Catalpa receives Juniper's payment by October 25, 2005, Catalpa will make the following entry:

Cash	196	
Cash Discounts	4	
Accounts Receivable		200

The amount of the cash discount is calculated by multiplying the amount of the receivable by the discount rate: $200 \times 2\% = \$4$. The Cash Discounts account is a contra account; its balance is deducted from sales when preparing the income statement.

If Catalpa does not receive Juniper's payment within the 10-day discount period, Catalpa will make the following entry after payment is made:

Cash	200	
Accounts Receivable		200

VALUATION OF ACCOUNTS RECEIVABLE

When reporting receivables, most companies list a "net" amount on the balance sheet. This means that the receivables are reported at **net realizable value**, or the amount that the company expects to receive in cash at the time of collection. To arrive at net realizable value, the company deducts an estimate of future uncollectible accounts from the total of accounts receivable. Reducing the value of receivables to what management believes will actually be collected helps meet the financial reporting objective of providing accurate information about future cash inflows to the company. Receivables that mature within one year are usually reported at face value, while longer-term receivables should be reported at the present value of the cash to be received.

Critical Thinking: If a company offers a cash discount to customers who pay their accounts promptly, how do you think these cash discounts affect sales revenues?

cash discount a method of speeding cash collection by offering a price cut if an account is paid quickly; also called a *sales discount*

gross method an approach to recording cash discounts that views cash discounts that are not taken as part of sales

net method an approach to recording cash discounts that considers sales revenue to be the net amount, after the discount, and classifies any discounts that are not taken as interest income

net realizable value the amount that a company expects to receive in cash at the time of collection of accounts receivable; total accounts receivable less an estimate of future uncollectible accounts

THE ALLOWANCE METHOD

allowance method a way of accounting for bad debt by writing off an estimated amount in the period in which the related sales take place

An estimate for uncollectible accounts is created through an end-of-period adjusting entry that reduces the value of the asset and creates bad debt expense. Unless a company has an immaterial amount of uncollectible accounts, it must create an allowance account against which future uncollectible accounts can be charged. The use of the **allowance method** ensures that an estimated amount of bad debt expense is recognized in the period in which the related sales occur. The Bad Debt Expense account is debited and the Allowance for Uncollectible Accounts account is credited. Allowance for Uncollectible Accounts, a contra-asset account, is used to reduce accounts receivable. As a result, an expense is recognized in the accounting period in which the sale is recorded and not in a future period when a specific account receivable might actually be declared uncollectible.

Companies base their estimates of uncollectible receivables on past experience and forecasts of future business activity, utilizing one of these two common ways of estimating uncollectible accounts:

- Percentage-of-sales method
- Percentage-of-receivables method

percentage-of-sales method a technique for estimating uncollectible accounts based on a historically determined percentage of each period's credit sales; also called the *income statement approach*

THE PERCENTAGE-OF-SALES METHOD Under the **percentage-of-sales method**, the estimate of uncollectible accounts is based on a historically determined percentage of *each period's credit sales*. For example, if a company's experience indicates that uncollectible accounts average about 3 percent of total credit sales, an adjusting entry would be made at year end to expense 3 percent of that period's credit sales. If credit sales for the period were $520,000 and the company estimated that 3 percent would prove uncollectible, the end-of-period adjusting entry would be recorded as follows:

Bad Debt Expense	15,600	
Allowance for Uncollectible Accounts		15,600

It is important to recognize that the percentage-of-sales method focuses on the current year only; it does not consider the balance in the allowance account prior to the current year's adjusting entry. The percentage-of-sales method is often referred to as the *income statement approach.*

percentage-of-receivables method a way of estimating uncollectible accounts based on the assumption that a predictable percentage of the accounts receivable will not be collected; also called the *balance sheet approach*

THE PERCENTAGE-OF-RECEIVABLES METHOD Under the **percentage-of-receivables method**, the estimate of uncollectible accounts is based on a historically determined percentage of the *gross receivables*. The allowance account is then adjusted to equal this estimate of uncollectible accounts. Because the method emphasizes valuation of the receivables at net realizable value on the balance sheet, it is often referred to as the *balance sheet approach.*

In the percentage-of-receivables method, the balance in the Allowance for Uncollectible Accounts account is adjusted to reflect the current estimate of uncollectibles. For example, assume that prior to adjustment, Accounts Receivable has a balance of $350,000 and Allowance for Uncollectible Accounts has a credit balance of $5,200. If the company estimates that 5 percent of its accounts receivable will prove to be uncollectible, the following calculation is performed:

Amount estimated to be uncollectible: $350,000 × 5% = $17,500

Adjustment needed to bring the allowance account to $17,500	$17,500
Less: Credit balance in the allowance account	(5,200)
	$12,300

The adjusting journal entry would be recorded as follows:

Bad Debt Expense	12,300	
Allowance for Uncollectible Accounts		12,300

accounts receivable aging schedule a table that lists each customer's total accounts receivable balance and breaks down the total into categories based on the due date of each amount

In determining the percentage of uncollectible accounts receivable, many companies use an accounts receivable aging schedule. An **accounts receivable aging schedule** lists each customer's total accounts receivable balance and breaks down the total into categories based on the due date of each amount. For example, the aging schedule for Rage Jewelry Wholesale, shown in Illustration 7.2, divides each customer's balance into four categories: current, 1 to 30 days past due, 31 to 60 days past due, and over 60 days past due. The total for each category is then multiplied by a percentage that is assumed to be uncollectible. The aging method assumes that the longer a receivable remains outstanding, the less likely it is to be collected.

Based on its aging schedule, Rage Jewelry Wholesale estimates that $690 of its accounts receivable will be uncollectible. If it had a credit balance of $100 in Allowance for Uncollectible Accounts prior to the adjustment, it would record this entry:

Bad Debt Expense	590	
Allowance for Uncollectible Accounts		590

This adjustment would increase the allowance account to $690, the new estimated amount of uncollectible accounts.

Allowance for Uncollectible Accounts

	100	beg. bal.
	590	adj. entry
	690	end. bal.

Regardless of the method used to estimate uncollectibles, when a company decides to write off a specific account receivable, it will reduce Allowance for Uncollectible Accounts and remove the specific customer's account from Accounts Receivable. The journal entry will appear as follows:

Allowance for Uncollectible Accounts	xxx	
Accounts Receivable—Poplar, Inc.		xxx

Illustration 7.2

Accounts Receivable Aging Schedule

Rage Jewelry Wholesale
Accounts Receivable Aging Schedule
As of July 31, 2005

Customer Name	Total Accounts Receivable	Current	1–30 Days Past Due	31–60 Days Past Due	Over 60 Days Past Due
Graham Diamond Corp.	$ 3,500	$1,500	$1,000	$ 300	$ 700
Rubies by Raymond	1,900	1,700	200	—	—
Sapphire Store	1,200	600	600	—	—
Jenness, Inc.	2,500	900	1,600	—	—
Precious Pearls	2,000	1,100	500	400	—
Turquoise and Silver, Inc.	1,100	—	—	700	400
Olivia's Gold Store	2,200	2,200	—	—	—
Total	$14,400	$8,000	$3,900	$1,400	$ 1,100
Percentage expected to be uncollectible		× 1%	× 5%	× 10%	× 25%
Amount expected to be uncollectible		$ 80	$ 195	$ 140	$ 275

Illustration 7.3

Comparison of Allowance Methods

Allowance Method	Based On	Approach	Considers Previous Allowance Balance
Percentage-of-sales	Current-year sales	Income statement	No
Percentage-of-receivables	Net realizable value of accounts receivable	Balance sheet	Yes

It is important to remember that the write-off of a specific account receivable is not an expense of the period.

Illustration 7.3 provides a comparison of the percentage-of-sales and percentage-of-receivables methods.

❯ THE DIRECT WRITE-OFF METHOD

When it is impossible to estimate uncollectible accounts with reasonable accuracy or when uncollectible accounts are immaterial, companies may use the direct write-off method. Under the **direct write-off method**, no entries are made until a customer actually defaults on the account, at which time the uncollectible account receivable is written off to Bad Debt Expense. In this case, no allowance account is required.

For example, if Redbud Corp. had never had any uncollectible accounts and if Spruce, Inc., which owed $250, informed the company that it had gone bankrupt, Redbud would journalize the transaction as follows:

Bad Debt Expense	250	
Accounts Receivable—Spruce, Inc.		250

direct write-off method an approach to recording bad debt expense in which no entries are made until a customer actually defaults on the account, at which time the uncollectible account receivable is written off to Bad Debt Expense

CHECK YOUR UNDERSTANDING

1. If a company uses the gross method of recording cash discounts, what entry is made when a customer pays within the discount period?

2. What is the net realizable value of an account receivable, and how is this value determined?

3. If a company uses the percentage-of-sales method to estimate uncollectibles, how is the estimate calculated?

4. Describe how the direct write-off method differs from the allowance method.

LO 5 Demonstrate the appropriate accounting treatment to record notes receivable.

Recording Notes Receivable

As discussed earlier, notes receivable are supported by written contracts in which a party agrees to pay the company a specific amount, known as the principal, on a specific date. **Interest-bearing notes** have a stated rate of interest, requiring the party to pay the face value of the note plus interest. With **non-interest-bearing notes**, the interest, called the *discount*, is deducted in advance from the face value of the note. Notice that both types of notes actually do bear interest, despite the name of the latter type. The examples that follow illustrate how short-term notes are recorded.

interest-bearing note a note that carries a stated rate of interest, requiring the party to pay the face value of the note plus interest

non-interest-bearing note a note where interest (called the *discount*) is deducted in advance from the face value of the note

Critical Thinking: *Why do you think companies agree to accept notes receivable from their customers and clients?*

INTEREST-BEARING NOTES

A typical interest-bearing note receivable indicates that interest is to be paid at a stated percentage of the face amount of the note. Interest is calculated as follows:

$$\text{Face Amount} \times \text{Annual Interest Rate} \times \text{Time}$$

For example, Fly Fishing Suppliers agrees to accept a $4,000, 12-month, 10 percent note from Fishing Vacations Unlimited, a customer, on January 1, 2005. Interest is payable at maturity. Fly Fishing Suppliers would record the note as follows:

Notes Receivable	4,000	
Sales		4,000

When Fishing Vacations Unlimited pays the note on December 31, 2005, the following entry is recorded by Fly Fishing Suppliers:

Cash	4,400	
Interest Income ($4,000 × 10% × 12/12)		400
Notes Receivable		4,000

NON-INTEREST-BEARING NOTES

In some cases, a note receivable may be considered non-interest-bearing. Though these notes actually do bear interest, the interest (or discount) is deducted from the face amount of the note at the beginning of the transaction.

For example, assume that Linden Corp. sold a piece of equipment for $1,000 and received in exchange a 12-month non-interest-bearing note receivable with a discount rate of 10 percent. The discount on the note is calculated as follows:

$$\begin{array}{ccccccc} \text{Face Value} & \times & \text{Discount Rate} & \times & \text{Time} & = & \text{Discount} \\ \$1,000 & \times & 0.10 & \times & 12/12 & = & \$100 \end{array}$$

The company would record the transaction as follows:

Notes Receivable	1,000	
Discount on Notes Receivable		100
Sales		900

The amount credited to the Discount on Notes Receivable account is the difference between the note's face value and its present value. It is the effective interest that will be earned by holding the note until collection. The Discount on Notes Receivable account is a contra account to the Notes Receivable account.

At the end of the 12-month period, when the customer pays, Linden Corp. will make the following entry in its journal:

Cash	1,000	
Discount on Notes Receivable	100	
Interest Income		100
Notes Receivable		1,000

The discount on the note receivable is amortized to interest income over the life of the note. Because the note receivable is a negotiable instrument, the company recognizes the time value of money and records the transaction at its present value.

CHECK YOUR UNDERSTANDING

1. How is interest calculated on a typical interest-bearing note receivable?

2. How is the Discount on Notes Receivable account reported on the balance sheet?

3. Describe why a non-interest-bearing note yields less cash for the borrower.

LO 6 Explain the cash management tools and receivables financing arrangements that companies can use to obtain cash more quickly.

CASH FLOW

 Critical Thinking: Why do you think it is important for companies to turn accounts receivable into cash as quickly as possible?

assignment of accounts receivable a transaction in which a company uses its accounts receivable as collateral in support of a loan agreement

Cash Inflows and Receivables

Companies employ a number of techniques to accelerate the receipt of cash from accounts receivable. These techniques range from the simple use of lockboxes to complex financing agreements in which companies use their accounts receivable as collateral when borrowing money. Accounts receivables may be sold outright, or companies may choose to sell securities backed by their accounts receivable. The cash flows from customers are then used to make payments on the securities.

ASSIGNMENT OF RECEIVABLES

Firms often use their accounts receivable as collateral in a loan agreement. In this type of transaction, called **assignment of accounts receivable**, the accounts receivable serve much the same function as a car title in an automobile loan—they act as assurance that the borrower has adequate assets to pay off the debt. If the borrower fails to repay the debt in accordance with the loan agreement, the lender has the right to collect the receivables. Assigned receivables are accounted for in the same way as other receivables—the firm records cash collections, returns, and uncollectible accounts as usual. However, the firm's accounting records should include the following entry disclosing that its receivables are being used as collateral in a borrowing agreement:

Assigned Accounts Receivable	xxx	
Accounts Receivable		xxx

At the completion of the borrowing agreement, the journal entry would be reversed to show that the accounts receivable are no longer restricted in any way.

FACTORING AND SECURITIZATION

Many companies that extend credit to their customers face extended collection periods. Normally, companies that extend credit allow anywhere from 30 to 60 days for customers to pay. Such delays in payment can affect the creditor's working capital. For instance, assume that Sycamore Corp. has credit sales of $100,000 per month and that its customers pay off their accounts in an average of 45 days. As a result, at any point in time, Sycamore has accounts receivable representing one and a half months of credit sales, or $150,000, on its books. In effect, Sycamore is losing money because accounts receivable, unlike other assets, do not generate a return for the company. Two possible solutions for Sycamore are factoring and securitization.

factoring the transferring, or selling, of receivables to a third party, either with or without recourse

▶ FACTORING

Factoring is the transferring, or selling, of receivables to a third party. In factoring agreements, receivables are sold either with recourse or without recourse. When a company factors its receivables *with recourse,* the seller guarantees payment to the buyer even if some of the receivables are uncollectible. In this case, although the company has factored its receivables, it still has the risk of bad debts. In contrast, when a company factors its receivables *without recourse,* the buyer assumes the risk of bad debts and must take the loss if any accounts are uncollectible.

The parties to a factoring agreement must also determine how much will be paid for the accounts receivable. Factoring companies charge a fee for the transaction and usually withhold a percentage of the value to cover sales returns and allowances, cash discounts, and (for factoring with recourse) uncollectible accounts. At the completion of the factoring transaction, which usually covers a set time period, the factoring company compares the amount withheld to sales returns and allowances, cash discounts, and uncollectible accounts and either returns some of the withheld money to the seller or asks for an additional amount to cover the shortage.

❯ FACTORING WITHOUT RECOURSE   When a factoring transaction is without recourse, it is treated as an outright sale of the accounts receivable. For example, assume that Cottonwood Corporation factors $100,000 of accounts receivable to First Bank. First Bank charges an 8 percent fee for the transaction and withholds 10 percent in case of returns and allowances and cash discounts.

Cottonwood would make the following journal entries:

Cash	82,000	
Due from First Bank	10,000*	
Loss on Factoring Agreement	8,000†	
Accounts Receivable		100,000

* $100,000 × 10% = $10,000

† $100,000 × 8% = $8,000

Note that Cottonwood recognizes the factoring fee as a loss at the time the transaction is entered into. The amount withheld for returns and allowance and discounts is treated as an asset.

First Bank records the transaction as follows:

Accounts Receivable	100,000	
Payable to Cottonwood		10,000
Factoring Revenue		8,000
Cash		82,000

At the end of the factoring transaction, the two parties would reconcile the amount withheld with actual returns and allowances and discounts. For example, assume that customers returned $4,000 of goods and received allowances on $2,500 of goods. As a result, $6,500 of the accounts receivable were cancelled, and First Bank would pay Cottonwood only $3,500 of the $10,000 originally withheld. The two companies' journal entries would be as follows:

Cottonwood Corporation		
Sales Returns and Allowances	6,500	
Cash	3,500	
Due from First Bank		10,000

First Bank		
Payable to Cottonwood	10,000	
Cash		3,500
Accounts Receivable		6,500

) FACTORING WITH RECOURSE   Recall that when a company factors its receivables with recourse, it guarantees that the buyer will receive payment even if some of the receivables are uncollectible. Because the original owner of the receivables retains some of the risks of ownership, it is not always clear that a sale has occurred. Thus, for a factoring with recourse transaction to be considered a sale, the following strict conditions must be met:

- The transferred receivables must have been isolated from the seller, especially in the case of a seller who is declaring bankruptcy.

- The right to pledge or exchange the transferred receivables must be held only by the factor.

- The seller of the receivables must not maintain effective control over the transferred receivables through an agreement that allows for either mandatory repurchase or redemption of the assets prior to maturity.

If these conditions are met, a factoring agreement with recourse is accounted for in the same way as an agreement without recourse. If the transaction does not qualify as a sale, the seller must set up a contingency fund to cover any receivables that may not be paid and must account for the contingency as an obligation at the time the transaction is entered into.

For example, assume that Cottonwood Corporation factored its receivables to First Bank under the same terms mentioned earlier, except that the sale is done with recourse. Based on current market conditions, Cottonwood and First Bank agree that the recourse contingency has a fair value of $2,800. In this case, Cottonwood would record the transaction as follows:

Cash	82,000	
Due from First Bank	10,000	
Loss on Factoring Agreement	10,800	
Accounts Receivable		100,000
Recourse Contingency		2,800

The loss recognized by Cottonwood is calculated by comparing the amount of accounts receivable factored to the net proceeds received from First Bank:

Accounts receivable factored		$100,000
Cash received initially from First Bank	$82,000	
Amount due from First Bank	10,000	
Less recourse contingency	(2,800)	
Net proceeds from First Bank		89,200
Loss on factoring agreement		$ 10,800

As specific accounts receivable are determined to be uncollectible, the recourse contingency and amount due from First Bank are reduced. In addition, actual returns and allowances and any discounts also reduce the amount due from First Bank.

At the completion of the factoring agreement, if the recourse contingency is greater than the actual amount of uncollectible accounts, the loss that was initially recognized will be reduced. For example, if the final actual amount of uncollectible accounts is only $1,700, Cottonwood would make the following entry:

Recourse Contingency ($2,800 − $1,700)	1,100	
Loss on Factoring Agreement		1,100

Any amount remaining in the recourse contingency fund would be netted against the amount due from First Bank at the end of the agreement.

In contrast, if the actual amount of uncollectible accounts is greater than the initial loss contingency, Cottonwood would be required to pay First Bank additional money, which would increase the company's loss on the factoring agreement.

In its books, First Bank would initially record the transaction as follows:

Accounts Receivable	100,000	
Payable to Cottonwood		10,000
Factoring Revenue		8,000
Cash		82,000

Note that for the purchaser, a factoring agreement with recourse is recorded in the same way as a factoring agreement without recourse.

If a receivable is determined to be uncollectible, Cottonwood will pay First Bank the required amount and reduce its Recourse Contingency account accordingly. First Bank will recognize the cash received and decrease Accounts Receivable.

❱ SECURITIZATION

securitization the transfer of receivables, either individually or pooled, to a trust account in which investors may purchase shares that entitle them to receive cash as the receivables are paid

Securitization is the transfer of receivables, either individually or pooled, to a trust account in which investors may purchase shares that entitle them to receive cash as the receivables are paid. In most cases, companies that securitize receivables are large financial institutions, such as credit card companies, mortgage lenders, and leasing companies. However, almost any stream of receivables can be securitized, as demonstrated by the rock star David Bowie. In that securitization transaction, Bowie agreed to place his right to receive royalties into a trust, and investors could purchase shares in that trust that entitled them to receive the royalty payments. Based on Bowie's past history of record sales that generated royalty payments, investors could estimate what future royalty payments would be and then discount the cash flows to determine their present value. The securitization transaction would work as shown in Illustration 7.4.

Illustration 7.4

Securitization of Accounts Receivable

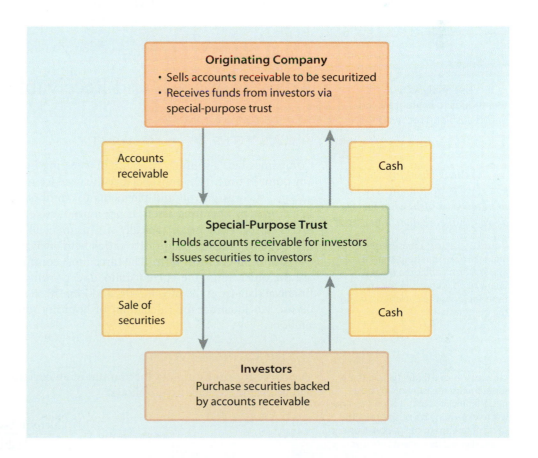

When a company securitizes its receivables, numerous investors participate in the transaction. As a result, a company can securitize much larger amounts than it can factor. In addition, securitization is often more cost-effective than factoring because the fees are lower.

LOCKBOXES

lockbox a method of speeding cash receipts in which a company rents a postal box to receive customer payments and gives its bank access to the box; the bank picks up the mail, opens the envelopes, copies the checks, and deposits the funds in the company's account

Many companies use payment lockboxes to accelerate cash collection. When a company uses a **lockbox**, it rents a postal box to receive customer payments and gives its bank access to the box. The bank picks up the mail, opens the envelopes, copies the checks, and deposits the funds in the company's account. Lockboxes provide two advantages: they ensure that checks are deposited quickly, so that interest income is earned as soon as possible, and they increase internal control over cash receipts.

PRIVATE-LABEL CREDIT CARDS

Many companies, such as **Amazon.com**, issue private-label credit cards to qualified customers. By offering customers the ability to charge purchases on their Amazon credit card, as opposed to a Visa or MasterCard, Amazon achieves a number of benefits, including lower transaction costs for credit card sales, more control over the customer relationship so that advertising and promotions can be better focused, and the ability to track customer buying habits and loyalty.

> **CHECK YOUR UNDERSTANDING**
>
> 1. Explain factoring with recourse. What conditions are required for this arrangement?
>
> 2. Describe the process of securitization.
>
> 3. How does the use of a lockbox accelerate cash collections?

Analysis of Cash and Receivables

LO 7 Use analysis techniques to evaluate a company's cash and receivables.

ANALYSIS

Critical Thinking: When you consider a company's ability to manage its cash, what factors do you think are most important?

liquidity ratios measurements of financial data that help analysts assess a firm's ability to meet its financial obligations in the short term; includes the current ratio and the quick ratio

ANALYSIS OF LIQUIDITY

Companies face a number of issues in assessing how much cash they should hold at any point in time. They must balance the need for holding cash to meet recurring obligations, such as payroll and payments to vendors, against the fact that cash, unlike inventories or operating assets, is not a productive asset for most companies. Cash in excess of recurring needs typically sits in financial accounts earning a low return. As discussed in Chapter 4, **liquidity ratios** help analysts assess a firm's ability to meet its obligations in the short term. The three most commonly used liquidity measurements are the quick ratio, the current ratio, and working capital. In the following section, financial data from the July 3, 2004, and June 28, 2003, Coach financial statements will be used to illustrate the calculation of liquidity ratios. Note that all amounts are in millions.

current ratio a liquidity ratio that is the standard measure of any business's financial health, it allows an analyst to determine if a business is able to meet its current obligations; current assets divided by current liabilities

▶ THE CURRENT RATIO

The **current ratio** compares the amount of all current assets to the amount of current liabilities and is calculated as follows:

$$\text{Current Ratio} = \frac{\text{Current Assets}}{\text{Current Liabilities}}$$

For Coach, the current ratios for the 2004 and 2003 financial statements were 3.88 and 2.78, respectively:

$$2004 \text{ Coach Current Ratio} = \frac{\$705{,}616}{\$181{,}938}$$

$$= \underline{3.88}$$

$$2003 \text{ Coach Current Ratio} = \frac{\$448{,}538}{\$161{,}461}$$

$$= \underline{2.78}$$

Coach's current ratio of 3.88 for 2004 means that at the end of that fiscal period the company had $3.88 of current assets for every $1.00 of current liabilities. This represents a strong financial position for Coach and suggests that the company should have adequate resources to meet its obligations. Normally, lenders, suppliers, and others who extend credit request that firms maintain a current ratio greater than 1. The 2004 current ratio shows almost a 40 percent increase over the 2003 current ratio. The increase occurred because of the large increase in Coach's short-term investments during the period, while most other current accounts grew at a steady pace. To further examine the strength or weakness of a company's financial ratios, it is important to compare them against similar-sized competitors. For example, the current ratio for **Kenneth Cole Productions**, a competitor of Coach, is 4.33.

》 THE QUICK RATIO

quick ratio a liquidity ratio that measures a company's ability to pay its short-term obligations from its most liquid assets and avoids the question of inventory valuation; cash and cash equivalents, short-term investments, and receivables divided by current liabilities

The **quick ratio** measures a company's ability to pay its short-term obligations from its most liquid assets and avoids the issue of inventory valuation by excluding inventory from the calculation. The quick ratio is determined by dividing cash and cash equivalents, short-term investments, and receivables by current liabilities:

$$\text{Quick Ratio} = \frac{\text{Cash} + \text{Short-Term Investments} + \text{Receivables}}{\text{Current Liabilities}}$$

The quick ratio for Coach changed significantly between 2004 and 2003. At July 3, 2004, Coach's quick ratio was 2.69:

$$2004 \text{ Coach Quick Ratio} = \frac{\$262{,}720 + \$171{,}723 + \$55{,}724}{\$181{,}938}$$

$$= \underline{2.69}$$

At June 28, 2003, Coach's quick ratio was 1.64:

$$2003 \text{ Coach Quick Ratio} = \frac{\$229{,}176 + 0 + \$35{,}470}{\$161{,}461}$$

$$= \underline{1.64}$$

Because inventories are such a significant component of current assets, their exclusion from the quick ratio has a significant effect—the quick ratio is typically smaller than the current ratio and for many companies less than 1.0. Given that cash, receivables, and even short-term investments do not usually earn a large return, companies prefer to hold only the minimum amount of cash, short-term investments, and receivables necessary to meet their ongoing needs. Removing inventory amounts still leaves Coach with a very healthy quick ratio of 2.69 in 2004. It is important to compare companies' ratios to competitors' and to previous fiscal periods. For example, Coach's quick ratio at the end of its 2000 fiscal year was only 0.44. The dramatic increase in the quick ratio from 2000 to 2004 demonstrates how well management at Coach has done in building up the company's cash and investment balances.

WORKING CAPITAL

working capital a liquidity measurement that indicates the amount of current assets available to continue business operations; current assets minus current liabilities

Working capital represents the amount of current assets that are required to fund a company's day-to-day operations. The traditional method of calculating working capital is to subtract current liabilities from current assets. This provides a measure of the dollar value of assets remaining or needed after paying off all liabilities due within one year. Holding greater amounts of working capital results in firms having more short-term financial flexibility.

$$2004 \text{ Coach Working Capital} = \$705{,}616 - \$181{,}938 = \$523{,}678$$

$$2003 \text{ Coach Working Capital} = \$448{,}538 - \$161{,}461 = \$287{,}077$$

One difficulty in interpreting working capital amounts is determining if the amount is adequate for the company. Because working capital is tied to a company's operating and investment activities, it is difficult to determine what level of working capital is optimal for a specific firm. Too little working capital is dangerous because it results in liquidity risk; however, an excess of working capital is also problematic because the excess working capital is not as productive as other operating assets.

THE DEFENSIVE RATIO

defensive ratio a liquidity ratio that measures the number of days a business could operate without obtaining any additional cash, investments, or receivables; cash and cash equivalents, short-term investments, and receivables divided by the company's average daily operating cash outflow

The defensive ratio is an additional ratio that managers use to examine their company's liquidity. The **defensive ratio** is calculated by dividing cash and cash equivalents, short-term investments, and receivables by the company's average daily operating cash outflow. Operating cash outflows are a firm's payments for salaries, purchases, and other operating requirements. The average daily operating cash outflow is based on those payments to employees and vendors over an extended time period. The defensive ratio measures the number of days a business could operate without obtaining any additional cash, investments, or receivables.

$$\text{Defensive Ratio} = \frac{\text{Cash} + \text{Investments} + \text{Receivables}}{\text{Average Daily Operating Cash Outflow}}$$

The defensive ratio is used to examine a company's liquidity over time, and its calculation requires access to internal accounting data.

ANALYSIS OF RECEIVABLES

When analyzing receivables, financial analysts calculate the accounts receivable turnover ratio and examine days in receivables to determine how well companies are managing their receivables.

THE ACCOUNTS RECEIVABLE TURNOVER RATIO

accounts receivable turnover ratio a measure of a company's ability to collect cash from its credit customers; net sales divided by average net accounts receivable

The **accounts receivable turnover ratio** measures a company's ability to collect cash from its credit customers. It is calculated as follows:

$$\text{Accounts Receivable Turnover Ratio} = \frac{\text{Net Sales}}{\text{Average Net Accounts Receivable}}$$

Theoretically, the numerator in this equation should include only credit sales, but this figure is not widely available to analysts. Thus, the net sales figure is most often used. Note that average net accounts receivable for the period (the denominator) is calculated by performing the following computation:

$$\text{Average Net Accounts Receivable} = \frac{\text{Beg. Net Accounts Receivable} + \text{End. Net Accounts Receivable}}{2}$$

To calculate the accounts receivable turnover ratio for Coach, use the following financial data. The company reported net sales of $1,321,106 thousand in 2004. Coach also reported the following account balances:

	July 3, 2004	June 28, 2003
(in thousands)		
Accounts receivable	$61,180	$41,565
Allowance for uncollectible accounts	(5,456)	(6,095)
Net accounts receivable	$55,724	$35,470

Average net accounts receivable is calculated as follows:

$$\frac{\$55,724 + \$35,470}{2} = \$45,597$$

The accounts receivable turnover ratio for Coach is calculated as follows:

$$\$1,321,106 \div \$45,597 = 28.97$$

This ratio tells analysts that, on average, receivables are collected 28.97 times during the fiscal period. A lower number would indicate a slower, and thus less favorable, collection rate, while a higher number would represent a faster, more favorable one.

DAYS IN RECEIVABLES

days in receivables the average number of days it takes a company to collect its accounts receivable; the number of days in the year (365) divided by the accounts receivable turnover ratio

Many analysts recast the turnover ratio in terms of **days in receivables**, which is the average number of days it takes a company to collect its accounts receivable. Days in receivables is calculated by dividing the number of days in the year, 365, by the accounts receivable turnover ratio:

$$\text{Days in Receivables} = \frac{365}{\text{Accounts Receivable Turnover Ratio}}$$

Based on the Coach accounts receivable turnover ratio calculated in the previous section, the days in receivables is expressed as follows:

$$\text{Days in Receivables} = \frac{365}{28.97} = 12.6 \text{ days}$$

Evaluating the trend in number of days in receivables over a period of years can reveal accounts receivable collection problems or management's success in collecting receivables in a timely manner. In addition, the days in receivable number must be evaluated in terms of a company's credit term and quality of accounts receivable.

> **CHECK YOUR UNDERSTANDING**
>
> 1. Which analysis ratio measures a company's ability to pay its short-term obligations from its most liquid assets and excludes inventory amounts?
>
> 2. If Company A has a current ratio of 2.5 and Company B has a current ratio of 1.3, which company demonstrates a stronger ability to cover its current liabilities with its current assets?
>
> 3. Describe how the accounts receivable turnover ratio is computed.

Revisiting the Case

LUXURY GOODS GENERATE LUXURY CASH FOR COACH

1. Coach is extremely profitable and efficient. Its gross profit margin is 72 percent, which has led to record levels of net income and cash.

2. Cash deposited with a financial institution normally earns a very low rate of return. Because Coach had a high level of cash, it was able to take a portion that was not immediately needed and invest it in short-term securities. These securities will earn a slightly higher return for Coach, but because they are short term, there will not be a high level of risk.

3. Coach faces much higher demand for its products during its second fiscal quarter. Because most of Coach's sales are on credit, the second quarter sees an increase in accounts receivable as sales peak. During the third and fourth quarters, the accounts receivable are collected, and cash and short-term investments replace accounts receivable on the balance sheet. The cash is then used to purchase inventory during the next quarter, and users see a buildup of inventory in the first quarter.

SUMMARY BY LEARNING OBJECTIVE

LO1 Identify items classified as cash and cash equivalents.

Cash includes bank deposits, currency and coins, and checks received from customers. Foreign currency units should be translated into U.S. dollar equivalents. Because cash is a monetary asset, the translation is based on the rate of exchange that is in effect on the balance sheet date. Cash equivalents, which are highly liquid investments that are easily convertible into cash, are usually grouped with cash on the balance sheet. Most companies include money market accounts and certificates of deposit, commercial paper, and U.S. Treasury bills that have a term of 90 days or less at their date of purchase as cash equivalents. Cash that is restricted by a loan agreement or other contractual agreement should be reported separately as restricted cash and should be classified as a current or long-term asset, depending on when the restriction will no longer be effective.

LO2 Explain why cash controls are important and describe the specific tools used to control and protect cash.

Every business must establish a system of internal controls to protect its cash and other assets. The following basic tools are often utilized: (1) Limit the number of persons who handle cash. (2) Separate the accounting tasks involving cash between different employees. (3) Bond employees who handle cash or cash records. (4) Use a cash register and a safe. (5) Use a checking account to make all cash payments and to provide a separate record of all transactions. (6) Deposit cash receipts in the bank in a timely fashion, usually daily. Since the use of a checking account will provide a separate record of all transactions, it is important that the bank statement be reconciled promptly when it is received to verify that the balance in the general ledger corresponds with the balance reflected on the bank statement.

LO3 Define and identify different types of receivables.

Receivables are claims to money, goods, or services owed to a company by others. If a receivable arises from the sale of goods or services on credit at the wholesale or the retail level in the normal course of business, it is classified as an account receivable, also known as a trade receivable. Amounts due as a result of transactions that are not customer-related are usually recognized as other receivables. An account receivable or other receivable is typically backed by a sales invoice or some other simple agreement rather than by a contractual agreement and is expected to be paid within 30 to 90 days. Notes receivable are written contracts promising to pay specified amounts to the company on specified dates.

LO4 Demonstrate the appropriate accounting treatment to record and value accounts receivable.

Accounts receivable are recorded at an amount equal to the sales price agreed to by the customer, called the exchange price. Companies that offer cash discounts, or discounts for payment of credit sales within a specified time period, may record these cash discounts using either the gross method or the net method. Under the gross method, cash discounts that are not taken by customers are viewed as part of sales. Under the net method, sales revenue is considered to be the net amount, after the discount, and any discounts that are not taken are classified as interest revenue. Receivables that mature within one year are usually reported at face value, while longer-term receivables should be reported at the present value of the cash to be received. In both cases, the receivables amount should be reported on the balance sheet net of the estimate of uncollectible accounts, or at net realizable value. The use of an allowance method like the percentage-of-sales method or the percentage-of-receivables method ensures that an estimated amount of uncollectible accounts expense is written off in the period in which the related sales occur. When it is impossible to estimate uncollectible accounts with reasonable accuracy or when uncollectible accounts are immaterial, companies may use the direct write-off method.

LO5 Demonstrate the appropriate accounting treatment to record notes receivable.

Notes receivable are supported by written contracts in which a party agrees to pay the company a specific amount, known as the principal, on a specific date. Interest-bearing notes have a stated rate of interest, requiring the party to pay the face value of the note plus interest. To record the initial note receivable transaction, Notes Receivable is debited and Sales is credited. When the note is paid, interest is recorded as interest income and the receivable is removed. With non-interest-bearing notes, the interest, called the *discount*, is deducted in advance from the face value of the note. The amount credited to the Discount on Notes Receivable account is the difference between the note's face value and its present value.

LO6 Explain the cash management tools and receivables financing arrangements that companies can use to obtain cash more quickly.

Companies may use their accounts receivable as collateral in support of a loan agreement, known as assignment of accounts receivable. If the borrower fails to repay the debt in accordance with the loan agreement, the lender has the right to collect the receivables. Factoring is the transferring, or selling, of receivables to a third party. In factoring agreements, receivables are sold either with recourse or without recourse. When a company factors its receivables with recourse, the seller guarantees payment to the buyer even if some of the receivables are uncollectible. In this case, although the company has factored its receivables, it still has the risk of bad debts. In contrast, when a company factors its receivables without recourse, the buyer assumes the risk of bad debts and must take the loss if any accounts are uncollectible. Securitization is the transfer of receivables, either individually or pooled, to a trust account in which investors may purchase shares that entitle them to receive cash as the receivables are paid. In an effort to accelerate cash collections, companies also often use lockboxes, where customer payments are sent directly to the bank and deposited in the company's account. The use of private-label credit cards reduces transaction costs and allows for better management of the customer relationship.

LO7 Use analysis techniques to evaluate a company's cash and receivables.

Liquidity ratios help analysts assess a firm's ability to meet its obligations in the short term. The three most commonly used liquidity measurements are the quick ratio, the current ratio, and working capital. The current ratio is calculated by dividing current assets by current liabilities. The quick ratio is calculated by dividing the sum of cash, investments, and receivables by current liabilities. Working capital is computed by subtracting current liabilities from current assets. In addition, some managers calculate the defensive ratio by dividing cash and cash equivalents, short-term investments, and receivables by the company's average daily operating cash outflow. In order to analyze a company's ability to collect cash from its credit customers, the accounts receivable turnover ratio (net sales divided by average net accounts receivable) is computed. Days in receivables is calculated by dividing the number of days in the year by the accounts receivable turnover ratio.

KEY TERMS

account receivable (p. 307)
accounts receivable aging schedule (p. 311)
accounts receivable turnover ratio (p. 320)
allowance method (p. 310)
assignment of accounts receivable (p. 314)
bank reconciliation (p. 305)
cash (p. 302)
cash discount (p. 309)
cash equivalents (p. 302)
compensating balance (p. 303)

current ratio (p. 318)
days in receivables (p. 321)
defensive ratio (p. 320)
direct write-off method (p. 312)
factoring (p. 314)
gross method (p. 309)
interest-bearing note (p. 312)
internal controls (p. 304)
liquidity ratios (p. 318)
lockbox (p. 318)
net method (p. 309)
net realizable value (p. 309)
non-interest-bearing note (p. 312)

notes receivable (p. 307)
other receivables (p. 307)
percentage-of-receivables method (p. 310)
percentage-of-sales method (p. 310)
promissory note (p. 307)
quick ratio (p. 319)
receivables (p. 307)
restricted cash (p. 302)
securitization (p. 317)
working capital (p. 320)

EXERCISES

LO7   **EXERCISE 7-1   Accounts Receivable Turnover**
The following appeared in Maynor Company's financial statements:

	December 31, 2005	December 31, 2004
Accounts receivable, net of uncollectibles of $2,300 and $2,100	$ 62,000	$ 50,000
Net sales	489,400	475,000

Required:

1. Calculate Maynor's accounts receivable turnover ratios for 2005.

2. If the norm for Maynor's industry is a turnover of 7.2, is Maynor's turnover ratio good or bad? What information is provided by this ratio?

LO1   **EXERCISE 7-2   Cash and Cash Equivalents**
Nortake Company has the following items in its general ledger as of December 31, 2004:

Petty cash fund	$ 500
Checking Account, Wachovia Bank	29,000
Postage Stamps (on hand)	600
Certificate of Deposit, Wachovia Bank	10,000
Savings Account, Federal Credit Union	13,000

The certificate of deposit is for three months and matures on January 14, 2005.

Required:

1. Prepare a partial balance sheet for Nortake Company at December 31, 2004.

2. List examples of items that would be classified as cash equivalents on a balance sheet.

LO4, 7   **EXERCISE 7-3   Receivable Transactions and Analysis**
The following appeared in Cenara Company's financial statements:

	December 31, 2005	December 31, 2004
Accounts receivable, net of uncollectibles of $10,100 and $9,900	$ 145,400	$ 136,300
Net sales	2,600,000	3,140,000

Of the company's sales, 98 percent are on account. The company estimates uncollectible receivables to be 0.5 percent of net credit sales.

Required:

1. Prepare summary journal entries to show the effects of these transactions during 2005:
   a. Sales
   b. Estimate of uncollectible accounts
   c. Write-off of uncollectible accounts
   d. Collection of receivables

2. Calculate how long it takes Cenara to collect its receivables for 2005. Explain what information this provides.

LO6   EXERCISE 7-4   Factoring and Assignments

The following independent transactions occurred during 2005:

A. Patel, Inc. has $400,000 of accounts receivables and estimates that 1 percent will not be collected. Patel agrees to transfer ownership rights to Household Finance. At any time Patel is financially able, it may repurchase the receivables, but it will still incur a 3 percent finance fee on the face amount of the receivables.

B. Cricket Company has $100,000 of accounts receivables. Cricket decides to use the receivables as collateral for a two-year, 8 percent commercial loan for $80,000 from Sun Bank.

Required:

1. What type of agreement has Patel entered into?
2. Record the transaction on Patel's books.
3. What type of agreement has Cricket Company entered into?
4. Record the transactions on Cricket's books.

LO6   EXERCISE 7-5   Factoring Receivables

On March 31, 2004, Grilliot Company factored $120,000 of its accounts receivable to Finance Factor, Inc. Grilliot guarantees payment of the receivables and estimates uncollectible accounts to be 4 percent of the amount owed. Grilliot transfers all rights of ownership to Finance Factor, Inc. The factor charged a 6 percent discount rate.

Required:

1. Is this transaction treated as a sale or as a liability? Justify your response.
2. Calculate the proceeds to be received from the factoring by Grilliot on March 31, 2004.
3. Record the factoring transaction for Grilliot Company.

LO1   EXERCISE 7-6   Cash Reporting

Stats Corporation's checkbook balance on December 31, 2005, was $63,400. In addition, Stats's accountant held the following items in the company safe on December 31:

A. Check payable to Stats Corporation, dated January 2, 2006, not included in the December 31 checkbook balance: $5,000.

B. Check payable to Stats Corporation for $2,300, deposited December 20 and included in the December 31 checkbook balance, but returned by the bank on December 30, stamped "NSF." The check was redeposited January 2, 2006, and cleared January 4, 2006.

C. Postage stamps received from mail-order customers, $23.

D. Check written by Stats Corporation to pay supplier, dated and recorded December 31, but not mailed until January 15, 2006, $800.

E. Stats has a compensating balance agreement with its bank for $20,000.

Required: Calculate the proper amount to be shown as cash on Stats's balance sheet at December 31, 2005. For any amount not used in calculating the cash amount, explain why.

LO6   EXERCISE 7-7   Factoring Without Recourse

On December 30, 2005, Cards Company sells $70,000 of its $80,000 in accounts receivable to a factor without recourse and receives cash less 3 percent withheld for possible returns and discounts. A 5 percent fee based on the gross amount of factored accounts receivable is charged by the finance company.

Required:

1. Prepare the entry to record this factoring transaction for Cards Company.
2. Show how the effects of the factoring will be reported on Cards Company's balance sheet at December 31, 2005.

LO4 EXERCISE 7-8 **Allowance Method**

Raspberry, Inc. had the following account balances related to its accounts for 2005:

Accounts Receivable, January 1, 2005	$ 45,000
Allowance for Uncollectible Accounts, January 1, 2005 (credit)	3,600
Sales during 2005	944,000
Cash collections from customers during 2005	923,000
Cash discounts taken by customers during 2005	2,500
Sales returns and allowances during 2005	2,000

Accounts that were deemed uncollectible during 2005 totaled $3,700. Raspberry uses the gross method of accounting for discounts. All accounts given have normal balances.

Required: Answer the following independent questions:

1. What method of accounting for uncollectible accounts does Raspberry use?
2. Raspberry estimates uncollectible accounts to be 0.4 percent of net sales. Create T-accounts and post the results of this estimate and the amounts provided in the problem. Calculate balances.
3. Calculate the amount of Bad Debt Expense to be reported, assuming that Raspberry estimates the amount to be $4,200 based on an aging schedule as of December 31, 2005.

LO5 EXERCISE 7-9 **Notes Receivable**

On June 1, 2005, Barder accepted a $10,000, 10-month, non-interest-bearing note in exchange for goods. On August 31, 2005, Barder accepted a $10,000, 10 percent, six-month note for cash.

Required:

1. Show your interest calculations for both notes. Twelve percent is a reasonable cost of borrowing for non-interest-bearing notes of this nature.
2. Show how the notes will appear on Barder's December 31, 2005, classified balance sheet.

LO6 EXERCISE 7-10 **Assignment of Receivables**

On January 1, 2005, Selvog, Inc. assigned $102,000 of receivables in order to borrow $88,000 on an eight-month, 8 percent note payable from a finance company. The finance company charges a 3 percent finance fee assessed on the assigned receivables.

Required:

1. How much in total will Selvog report on its income statement for its year ending June 30, 2005, as a result of the assignment?
2. What entry should be made to record receivables used as collateral?

LO6 EXERCISE 7-11 **Factoring with and Without Recourse: Seller**

On April 30 of the current year, Crass Company sold receivables with a carrying value of $320,000 to Dingle, Inc. at a 5 percent factor fee.

Required: Record the transactions at April 30 for Crass Company for the factoring transaction under each of the following scenarios:

1. The transfer was made without recourse, and the factor assumes all the risk associated with uncollectibility.

2. The transfer was made with recourse, and the parties agree that Crass will accept responsibility for uncollectible accounts, which are estimated at 2 percent (included in the 5 percent factor fee). This amount is withheld by Dingle. The parties also agree that the recourse contingency has a fair market value of $6,400.

LO6   **EXERCISE 7-12   Factoring with and Without Recourse: Factor**

On April 30 of the current year, Dingle, Inc. bought receivables with a carrying value of $320,000 from Crass Company and charged a 5 percent factor fee. On June 10, receivables worth $3,500 were deemed uncollectible.

Required:

1. Record the transactions at April 30 for Dingle, Inc. under each of the following scenarios:

   a. The transfer was made without recourse, and the factor assumes all the risk associated with uncollectibility.

   b. The transfer was made with recourse, and the parties agree that Crass will accept responsibility for uncollectible accounts, which are estimated at 2 percent (included in the 5 percent factor fee). This amount is withheld by Dingle.

2. Record the write-off of the receivables on June 10 by the factor.

LO1   **EXERCISE 7-13   Cash Reporting and Disclosure**

Elkins Movers has the following reconciled account balances in its general ledger as of December 31, 2005:

Petty Cash Fund	$ 4,000
Checking account, CitiBank	35,800
Six-month, 5 percent, certificate of deposit, CitiBank, matures January 31, 2006	10,000
Checking account, Garland Bank	14,600
90-day Treasury bill, matures March 31, 2006	14,400

Because Elkins has a $200,000 loan agreement with CitiBank, it must maintain at least 10 percent of the loan amount in its non-interest-bearing checking account as a compensating balance. Outstanding checks on the Citibank checking account total $2,400.

Required: Prepare a partial balance sheet for Elkins Movers at December 31, 2005, and all necessary disclosures. For any items not reported as cash and cash equivalents, indicate the proper reporting.

LO4   **EXERCISE 7-14   Accounts Receivable**

Santiago Company reported the following in its 2006 balance sheet:

	2006	2005
Cash and cash equivalents	$59,000	$54,000
Accounts receivable, net of uncollectibles of $4,100 and $4,300	83,000	82,000

The company reported sales totaling $880,000 for 2006. Customers returned goods totaling $2,000 during 2006 and received credit on their accounts. Customers took discounts for early payment totaling $4,800. Terms are 2/10, net/30. All accounts determined to be uncollectible during 2006 have been appropriately written off.

Required:

1. Briefly state how you know that Santiago uses the allowance method.

2. How much do customers owe Santiago Company at December 31, 2006?

3. How much is the net realizable value of receivables at December 31, 2006?

4. At the end of 2006, how much does Santiago think it will collect from its customers?

LO2   **EXERCISE 7-15**   **Bank Reconciliation**

The following information was assembled in order to prepare WDT Company's bank reconciliation for September 2005:

Balance per bank statement, September 30	$69,800
Customer payments collected by bank	1,240
Interest earned	140
Outstanding checks	3,540
Service charge	60
Deposit in transit	11,500
Balance per ledger, September 30	76,350

WDT's bookkeeper recorded one of its payments on account received from a customer as $560. The correct amount of $650 was recorded by the bank.

Required:

1. Prepare a bank reconciliation for WDT for September.
2. Record the transactions necessary to adjust the Cash account as a result of the reconciliation.
3. How much should WDT report for Cash in its balance sheet at September 30?

LO4   **EXERCISE 7-16**   **Accounts Receivable Transactions**

Bocca Bargains began May with $4,800 of accounts receivable. The following transactions occurred during May of 2005:

A. May 3, 2005: Sold merchandise costing $1,900 to Nole Corp., terms 3/10, net/30, for $3,200.

B. May 9, 2005: Sold merchandise costing $760 to Sem Corp., terms 2/15, net/30, for $1,800.

C. May 12, 2005: Received payment from Nole Corp. on account for merchandise sold May 3.

D. May 16, 2005: Granted a credit of $600 for merchandise returned by Sem Corp. originally sold on May 9. The cost of the merchandise returned was $240.

Bocca Bargains utilizes a perpetual inventory system.

Required: Compute gross profit for Bocca Bargains, using (1) the gross method of accounting for cash discounts and (2) the net method of accounting for cash discounts.

LO4   **EXERCISE 7-17**   **Uncollectible Accounts**

The following is key information concerning Jazzco, a wholesale fishing net distributor, as of December 31, 2005, prior to the close of the fiscal year. The following amounts are for unadjusted accounts.

Accounts Receivable	$ 420,000
Allowance for Uncollectible Accounts (credit)	36,000
Sales	1,800,000
Sales Returns and Allowances	65,000

Required:

1. Prepare the appropriate journal entries for each of the following independent events:
   a. The account of Kist Company, in the amount of $41,000, is determined to be uncollectible. It has not yet been written off.
   b. Jazzco estimates bad debt expense at 4 percent of net sales. Prepare the appropriate journal entries.
   c. Management wants to base the allowance on 8 percent of gross accounts receivable, after the write-off of the Kist Company account. Prepare the entry to record this transaction.

2. Of the methods used in question 1b and c, which method is the recommended method under GAAP? Why?

LO4   EXERCISE 7-18   Aging Schedule and Allowance Method

Summary information on the age of the customer accounts of Zippo Company as of May 31, 2005, is as follows:

Account Balances	Age in Days	Probability of Collection
$120,000	< 30 days	99%
114,000	31–60 days	92
50,000	61–90 days	75
30,000	91–120 days	60
5,000	> 120 days	10

The balance of the allowance account as of May 31 was a $400 debit balance after the write-off of $41,000 of uncollectible accounts.

Required:

1. Compute the required balance of the allowance account using the aging method.
2. Prepare the appropriate journal entry to adjust the allowance account.
3. How much will be reported as bad debt expense for the period?

PROBLEMS

LO4   PROBLEM 7-1   Receivables and the Allowance Method

Cast, Inc. reported the following amounts shortly before it made its year-end adjustments at June 30, 2005:

Sales	$425,000
Sales Returns and Allowances	9,000
Cash Discounts	5,000
Accounts Receivable	43,000
Allowance for Uncollectible Accounts (credit)	760

Required: Answer each of the following independent questions concerning Cast, Inc.:

1. Briefly state how you know that Cast uses the allowance method.
2. If Cast estimates that uncollectible accounts will be 1 percent of net sales, what adjustment amount is required?
3. If Cast estimates that uncollectible accounts will be 8 percent of gross accounts receivable, how much is bad debt expense for the year?
4. If Cast uses an aging schedule to estimate its uncollectible accounts and determines that $2,200 will probably not be collected, what is the net realizable value of the receivables at year end? What does this amount represent?
5. Show how the receivables in questions 2 and 3 would appear on Cast's June 30, 2005, balance sheet. Which method seems to present a more accurate balance sheet measurement? Justify your answer.

Analyze: What does the balance in Allowance for Uncollectible Accounts represent?

LO4, 7   PROBLEM 7-2   Receivables and the Allowance Method, Analysis

Popcorn Company's balance sheet showed the following at December 31, 2004 and 2005:

	2005	2004
Cash and cash equivalents	$134,000	$124,000
Accounts receivable, net of uncollectibles of $24,400 and $25,000	383,000	382,000

The company also reported the following amounts for 2005 on its income statement:

Sales	$5,000,000
Sales returns and allowances	11,200

All accounts that were determined to be uncollectible during the year ended December 31, 2005, have been appropriately written off. During 2005, this amount was $26,200. Popcorn Company's sales terms are 2/10, net/30. All sales are on account.

Required:

1. What method of accounting for uncollectible accounts does Popcorn Company use?
2. How much do customers owe Popcorn Company at December 31, 2005?
3. How much does Popcorn Company think its customers will actually pay at December 31, 2005?
4. How much bad debt expense did Popcorn Company report for 2005?
5. How many days does it take Popcorn Company to collect its receivables?

Analyze: Evaluate the ability of Popcorn's credit department to collect receivables.

LO4 **PROBLEM 7-3   Receivables, Allowance Method**

Locke Corporation provided the following amounts from its accounting records for the year ended December 31, 2005. Locke's cost of borrowing during 2005 was 12 percent.

Sales (all amounts are on account)	$480,000
Sales Returns and Allowances	3,000
Accounts Receivable, January 1, 2005	30,000
Accounts written off as uncollectible during 2005	10,000
Cash payments received from customers during 2005	465,000
Notes Receivable	42,000
Allowance for Uncollectible Accounts, January 1, 2005 (credit)	1,400

Estimated uncollectible accounts from the aging schedule at December 31, 2005, totaled $1,600. The note is for nine months, is non-interest-bearing, and is dated November 1, 2005.

Required:

1. Draw T-accounts for Accounts Receivable and Allowance for Uncollectible Accounts and post all transactions. Determine the balances of the two accounts at December 31, 2005.
2. Which approach does Locke use to estimate uncollectible accounts?
3. On December 31, 2005, Locke assigned $20,000 of its receivables and signed a 12 percent, $18,000 note. Locke was charged a finance fee of 1 percent of the accounts receivable assigned. Record the transactions to recognize the assignment.
4. Show how the accounts provided by Locke would appear on its balance sheet as of December 31, 2005.

Analyze: How much is bad debt expense for 2005?

LO2 **PROBLEM 7-4   Bank Reconciliation**

The following information was assembled by Sonoma Inc. in order to prepare its bank reconciliation:

Balance per bank statement, May 31	$11,800
Balance per ledger, May 31	13,160
Interest earned	40
Outstanding checks	200
Returned check	300
Deposit in transit	1,200

Sonoma's bookkeeper correctly recorded one of its deposits for $800, although the bank recorded only $700.

Required:

1. Prepare the bank reconciliation for Sonoma for May.
2. What is the dollar amount of the checks that have been recorded on the accounting records but have not yet posted on the bank statement? Why do these amounts exist?
3. Explain the returned check.
4. How much should Sonoma report on its balance sheet as cash at May 31?

Critical Thinking: Why are cash controls so important for businesses?

Analyze: What is the amount of Sonoma's net adjustment to its Cash account as a result of the reconciliation?

LO6   **PROBLEM 7-5   Financing with Receivables**

Given below are possible alternative accounting treatments for transferring receivables.

A. An assignment of receivables reported as a sale
B. A factoring of receivables reported as a liability (borrowing)
C. A factoring of receivables reported as a sale
D. An assignment of receivables reported as a borrowing

Required: For each transaction below, select the appropriate accounting treatment from the list. Justify your choice.

1. A company transferred its receivables to a factor with recourse. The transferred receivables cannot be reclaimed by the seller, the agreement has no repurchase or redemption clause, and the seller has no control over the transferred receivables.
2. A company used notes receivables as collateral on a loan and gave the lender the legal right to the receivables in satisfaction of the debt. Once the loan is paid, the right to receive any amount still owed by customers is transferred back to the debtor.
3. A company sold its receivables with recourse and agreed to surrender control of the future benefits from the receivables, although the transfer provision required a repurchase at the buyer's option if collectibility becomes a concern.
4. A company used accounts receivable as collateral on a loan.
5. A company sold its accounts receivable without recourse because it could not estimate the uncollectible accounts.
6. A company sold its receivables with recourse and agreed to surrender control of all future benefits from the receivables. The contract contained no repurchase agreement and no provision that allows the seller to reacquire the receivables. The buyer can pledge or sell the receivables to a third party.
7. A company sold its receivables with recourse to a factor and agreed to repurchase the receivables at the demand of the buyer.

Analyze: If a company wished to increase its liquidity, how could factoring be used to achieve this?

LO1, 2   **PROBLEM 7-6   Bank Reconciliation, Cash and Cash Equivalents**

The following amounts were taken from Price Enterprises' general ledger before year-end adjustments at June 30, 2006:

Checking Account	$13,500
Petty Cash	200
Money Market Savings Account	12,000
Four-month, 5 percent Certificate of Deposit (dated April 15, 2006)	20,000
Ninety-day, 4.5 percent U.S. Treasury Bill (dated May 31, 2006)	26,000
Change Fund	600
Postage Stamps	120

The change fund is used to stock the cash registers with coins and small bills at the beginning of operations each day. The bank has a 10-business-day rule on money market accounts that requires the company to notify the bank 10 business days prior to withdrawing funds. The decline in interest rates has caused the fair value of the Treasury bill to increase to $26,800. The proceeds of all interest-bearing investments will be received at maturity.

Price's accountant has assembled the following additional information concerning its checking account as of June 30, 2006:

Checking account balance per bank statement, 6/30/06	$11,650
Deposit in transit	3,900
Outstanding checks	2,750
Bank service charges for June	100
Return of customer's check for insufficient funds	600

On June 30, 2006, the accountant reimbursed the petty cash fund for the proper amount and properly recorded the reimbursement entry in the accounting records.

Required:

1. What amount should be reported as the reconciled balance of the checking account at June 30, 2006?

2. What amount should be reported on the balance sheet for cash at June 30, 2006?

3. What amount should be reported on the balance sheet for cash and cash equivalents at June 30, 2006? For any item listed that you did not include, explain why not.

4. Prepare any adjusting entries needed as a result of the bank reconciliation.

5. Prepare the current assets section of Price Enterprises' balance sheet at June 30, 2006, showing how the items given in this problem would be reported.

Analyze: If Price Enterprises reported current liabilities of $65,500 for the year ended June 30, 2006, compute the company's current ratio. How does this ratio compare to that of Price's competitor, which has a current ratio of 1.95?

LO4, 5 | **PROBLEM 7-7** **Notes and Accounts Receivable**

Comparative financial statements for the years ended December 31, 2005 and 2006, for EP Company reported the following information:

	2006	2005
Cash and cash equivalents	$29,000	$31,200
Accounts receivable, net of uncollectibles of $3,276 and $2,920	43,524	38,794
Notes receivable, net of discount of $2,600 and $3,400	34,000	54,000

EP Company has no investments and no other receivables. Sales during 2006, all of which were on account, amounted to $1,100,000. Customers returned $5,600 of items during the year. EP estimates uncollectibles at 7 percent. Bad debt expense for 2006 totaled $3,500. No new notes receivable were accepted during the year. A portion of the principal on the notes was collected during the year.

Required:

1. Determine the *gross amount* of accounts receivable for EP Company at December 31, 2006.

2. How much is the *net realizable value* of accounts receivable for EP Company at December 31, 2006? What does this amount represent?

3. How much interest income from the notes will EP Company report on its income statement for the year ended December 31, 2006? How much principal was repaid during the year?

4. Record the transactions that pertain to the receivables that occurred during 2006. *Hint:* You will have to work backwards in some cases to determine what occurred.

Analyze: What method of accounting for uncollectible accounts does EP use? What method of estimating uncollectibles does it use? Explain.

LO4, 5   **PROBLEM 7-8**   **Gross and Net Method; Notes Receivable Transactions**

Mart Company began business operations on June 1, 2004. The following transactions occurred during the remainder of 2004:

A. November 1, 2004: Sold merchandise to Page Corp., terms 1/10, net/30, for $10,000.

B. December 1, 2004: Accepted a six-month, 9 percent promissory note from Page Corp. in lieu of the accounts receivable balance owed.

C. December 10, 2004: Sold merchandise to Leaf Corp., terms 2/15, net/30, for $5,000.

D. December 22, 2004: Received payment in full from Leaf Corp. for the December 10 sale.

Mart Company utilizes a periodic inventory system. Notes of similar risk are offered at 9 percent in the market.

Required:

1. Prepare the journal entries for transactions A–D and prepare a partial income statement and balance sheet assuming that Mart uses the gross method of accounting for cash discounts.

2. Prepare the journal entries for transactions A–D and prepare a partial income statement and balance sheet assuming that Mart uses the net method of accounting.

3. How would the answers to questions 1 and 2 differ if the payment from Leaf Corp. was received on December 28 instead of December 22?

Analyze: For what purpose(s) might a company offer cash discounts?

LO4   **PROBLEM 7-9**   **Uncollectible Accounts**

Morris Corp. provided the following information at the end of 2004 concerning its activity and selected account balances:

Sales Revenue (all amounts are on account)	$900,000
Sales Returns and Allowances	8,000
Accounts Receivable, beginning of year	140,000
Accounts written off as uncollectible during 2004	9,600
Cash payments received from customers during 2004	924,000
Allowance for Uncollectible Accounts, 1/1/04 (credit)	8,000

Morris Corp. estimated its uncollectible accounts at $8,400 based on an aging schedule.

Required:

1. Determine the balance of the Accounts Receivable account at December 31, 2004.

2. Determine bad debt expense for 2004.

3. Calculate the net realizable value of accounts receivable at year end. Explain why the write-offs have no effect on the net realizable value of receivables.

Critical Thinking: Why are accounts receivable not valued at present value?

Analyze: Does the method Morris used to estimate uncollectible accounts focus more on matching or on proper asset valuation? Explain.

LO4, 7   **PROBLEM 7-10**   **Uncollectible Accounts, Turnover, and Liquidity**

During 2005, Laos, Inc. recognized sales of $1,500,000, of which 30 percent represented credit sales with terms 1/10, net/30. Discounts taken during 2004 totaled $900. Customers returned $14,000 of merchandise. Laos views net credit sales as the best indicator when calculating ratios that require sales. Returns are proportional to credit and cash sales. The following appeared on Laos, Inc.'s balance sheets at December 31, 2004 and 2005.

	2005	2004
Cash	$14,000	$15,100
Accounts receivables, net of uncollectibles of $4,540 and $4,480	71,540	68,620
Inventories	34,700	31,200
Accounts payable	46,000	24,000
Other accrued liabilities	24,000	22,600

Based on prior experience, Laos estimates a 1 percent bad debt rate on net credit sales.

Required:

1. How much bad debt expense did Laos recognize for 2005?
2. How much of the uncollectible accounts were written off during 2005?
3. How much is Laos's accounts receivable turnover ratio for 2005?
4. What are days in receivables at the end of 2005?
5. What information is provided by your calculations in questions 3 and 4?

Analyze: Calculate the current ratio and evaluate the change in Laos's liquidity from 2004 to 2005. Comment on your findings.

LO4 **PROBLEM 7-11 Uncollectible Accounts**

Soltry, Inc. had the following account balances immediately *before* adjustments at December 31, 2005:

Accounts Receivable	$ 23,400
Allowance for Uncollectible Accounts (debit)	200
Sales	823,500
Cash Discounts	2,700

Soltry wrote off $5,100 of accounts that were deemed uncollectible during the year (prior to the calculation of the balances given).

Required:

1. What method of accounting for uncollectible accounts does Soltry use? What evidence supports your answer?
2. Calculate the amount of bad debt expense that Soltry should report if it estimates uncollectible accounts to be 1 percent of net sales.
3. What is the net realizable value of the receivables immediately after Soltry estimates bad debts?

Analyze: Briefly state why the allowance method of accounting for bad debts is preferred over the direct write-off method.

LO4, 5 **PROBLEM 7-12 Accounts and Notes Receivable**

Dillinger Co.'s partial balance sheet at December 31, 2004 and 2005 is as follows:

	2005	2004
Accounts receivable, net of uncollectibles of $11,000 and $8,400	$311,000	$264,000
Notes receivable	140,000	60,000
Less: Discount on notes receivable	(3,200)	(0)

Required:

1. What is the net realizable value of accounts receivable at December 31, 2005?
2. A one-year note was acquired on July 1, 2005. Determine the interest rate on this note.
3. Prepare the entry to record the note acquired during the year and the year-end entry to accrue interest on the note acquired during the year. Assume that the note was from a customer in settlement of an account balance due.

4. How much did the company write off as uncollectible during 2005 if the bad debt expense recorded was $9,000?

Analyze: Explain how you know that Dillinger Co. issued a non-interest-bearing note during 2005.

LO4, 5   **PROBLEM 7-13   Accounts and Notes Receivables**

The following amounts appear in the accounting records of Rosenberg Corporation as of December 31, 2005. All uncollectibles relate to unassigned receivables.

Accounts Receivable	$161,000
Assigned Accounts Receivable	32,000
Notes Payable, 10 percent	25,000
Allowance for Uncollectible Accounts—balance on January 1, 2005 (credit)	5,800
Allowance for Uncollectible Accounts—adjusted balance on December 31, 2005 (credit)	6,600
Discount on Notes Receivable	800
Sales Returns and Allowances	3,400
Notes Receivable	20,000
Interest Receivable	1,040
Interest Income	2,600
Interest Expense	1,960

Additional information needed for adjustments and write-offs:

A. All accounts have normal balances, and all notes are due in less than one year.

B. As of the completion of operations on December 31, 2005, Rosenberg estimated that $6,600 of amounts owed would probably become uncollectible.

C. During the year, $6,200 of specific receivables were determined to be uncollectible and written off.

D. The assigned accounts receivable serve as general collateral for the 10 percent Notes Payable.

Required:

1. What method of estimating uncollectible accounts does Rosenberg use?

2. How do you know the answer to question 1?

3. Prepare the journal entry that Rosenberg made to write off the $6,200 of accounts that were deemed uncollectible.

4. Calculate the net realizable value of the *unassigned* accounts receivable at December 31, 2005.

5. Show how the accounts listed would appear on the balance sheet as of December 31, 2005.

Analyze: What percentage of receivables was allocated to the allowance account in 2005?

Critical Thinking: What is the nature of the Discount on Notes Receivable account?

Spreadsheet: Use a spreadsheet to prepare the partial balance sheet in question 5.

LO1, 2   **PROBLEM 7-14   Bank Reconciliation and Cash Reporting**

The following is information relating to a checking account provided by Garrett, Inc.:

Balance per bank, May 31, 2004	$11,800
Interest earned	23
Deposit made on May 30 that is not on bank statement	1,200
Outstanding checks	2,300
Bank fees charged	12

The company has the following additional information:

A. Garrett has a $300 petty cash account that was reimbursed on May 31. Just prior to reimbursement, the petty cash box contained $60 in cash and $236 of receipts. The reimbursement was properly recorded.

B. Enclosed with the bank statement was a returned check for $80 that Garrett had received from a customer and had originally deposited on May 29.

C. An electronic transfer for $750 that Garrett made from its checking account on May 31 to pay a supplier was not reflected on the bank statement because it was processed after closing hours. This amount was properly recorded in the accounting records.

D. Garrett held two certificates of deposit on May 31. The first was a $30,000, six-month CD with a maturity date of June 15. The other was a $10,000, 90-day CD dated May 15.

E. Garrett made a deposit during May for $670 and properly recorded it, although the bank recorded it as $770.

F. Garrett held a postdated check for $600 received from a customer on May 31, $42 of unused postage stamps, and a cash register change fund of $1,200 at the close of business on May 31.

Required:

1. Prepare a bank reconciliation for Garrett for the month of May. The balance per ledger is $9,919 on May 31.

2. What corrections must the *bank* make to Garrett's account? If none, state why not.

3. How much will Garrett report on its balance sheet as cash at May 31, 2004?

4. How much will Garrett report on its balance sheet as cash and cash equivalents at May 31, 2004?

5. Identify some important cash internal controls that businesses should employ.

Analyze: Describe the implications if the bank statement were not reconciled monthly.

LO3, 4 **PROBLEM 7-15** **Reporting Receivables**

The following accounts appear in the accounting records of Gottberg Corporation as of December 31, 2005. All accounts have normal balances, and all notes are due in less than one year. Based on an estimate, Gottberg determined that $5,100 of accounts were uncollectible.

Accounts Receivable	$45,000
Allowance for Uncollectible Accounts (credit)	4,400
Receivable from Officer	1,200
Notes Receivable	16,000
Assigned Accounts Receivable	21,000
Interest Accrued on Notes Receivable	600
Receivables with Credit Balances—Customers	400
Employee Receivables	1,800
Bad Debt Expense	5,100
Notes Payable (related to assigned accounts)	14,000
Discount on Notes Receivable	500
Interest Expense	1,650

Required:

1. What method of accounting for uncollectible accounts does Gottberg use?

2. What method of estimating uncollectible accounts does Gottberg use?

3. Which of the receivable accounts listed are not considered trade receivables? Explain.

4. In good form, prepare the current assets section of a classified balance sheet for Gottberg Corporation at December 31, 2005.

Analyze: Briefly indicate how you determined the answers to questions 1 and 2.

LO6 PROBLEM 7-16 **Assignment and Factoring of Receivables**

On January 31, 2005, Biddle, Inc. assigned $10,000 of receivables in order to borrow $7,000 on a six-month, 12 percent note payable from a finance company. The finance company charges a 5 percent finance fee based on receivables assigned. Through February, $2,000 of receivables were collected, and on February 28 they were remitted to the finance company as payment of accrued interest and principal on the loan.

Required:

1. How much does Biddle owe as a result of the assignment as of February 28, 2005?

2. What is the amount of receivables still being used as collateral at February 28, 2005?

3. What accounts and amounts would you report on the income statement for the year ended February 28, 2005, relative to these transactions and any related accruals?

4. What is the effect on liquidity when a company assigns its receivables?

Analyze: How does the practice of assigning receivables differ from factoring?

LO1, 2 PROBLEM 7-17 **Compensating Balance**

On October 1, 2004, Dollarama Company borrowed $100,000 from Wachovia Bank and agreed to an interest rate of 6 percent. The bank requires that Dollarama Company keep $50,000 of its borrowed funds in an account that pays 2 percent interest.

Required:

1. Calculate Dollarama Company's effective interest rate on its loan.

2. How should the company disclose its compensating balance?

Critical Thinking: For what purpose might a financial institution require a compensating balance?

Analyze: Is the compensating balance considered restricted cash? Why or why not?

LO7 PROBLEM 7-18 **Liquidity Analysis**

Provided below is partial balance sheet information for Zap, Inc. for its fiscal years 2004, 2005, and 2006.

Zap, Inc.
Partial Balance Sheet

	December 31		
	2006	2005	2004
Current Assets:			
Cash	$3,500	$2,500	$5,000
Accounts receivable	500	700	300
Inventory	1,200	4,500	2,100
Total current assets	$5,200	$7,700	$7,400
Current Liabilities:			
Accounts payable	$2,200	$3,100	$2,800
Wages payable	1,200	1,200	1,200
Total current liabilities	$3,400	$4,300	$4,000

The company's average daily operating cash outflow is $200 and $300 at December 31, 2005 and 2006.

Required:

1. Calculate Zap's current ratio at December 31, 2004, 2005, and 2006.

2. Calculate Zap's quick ratio at December 31, 2004, 2005, and 2006.

3. Calculate the amount of Zap's working capital at December 31, 2005 and 2006.

4. Calculate the amount of Zap's defensive ratio for 2005 and 2006.

Analyze: Evaluate Zap's liquidity trend. Are there issues that are cause for concern?

LO5 PROBLEM 7-19 **Notes Receivable**

On November 30, 2004, Lewinski Tie Company sold merchandise to Clinton Company, accepting a non-interest-bearing, $30,000, nine-month promissory note. Notes of similar risk carry an 8 percent rate. Both companies' fiscal years end on December 31.

Required:

1. Prepare the journal entries necessary to record the note on November 30 and to recognize interest on December 31, 2004, by Lewinski Tie Company.

2. Determine the book value of the note on Lewinski Tie Company's balance sheet at December 31, 2004.

3. Prepare a partial balance sheet for Lewinski Tie Company as of December 31, 2004, showing the note.

4. If Clinton were to pay off the debt on December 31, 2004, how much cash would Lewinski Tie Company receive?

5. What is the effective interest rate on the note?

6. How much will Lewinski Tie Company receive for the note at maturity?

Analyze: If the note was interest-bearing at 8 percent, how would your answer to question 6 change?

Critical Thinking: How do notes receivable differ from accounts receivable?

LO2 PROBLEM 7-20 **Bank Reconciliation**

The following information for Stinger Corporation reflects activity for the month of November 2004.

Balance per bank statement, November 30	$35,200
Cash account balance, November 1	19,000
Checks written during November not on bank statement:	
Check no. 400	450
Check no. 402	6,000
Check no. 404	8,800
Bank services charges unrecorded on books	50
Deposits on the bank statement	42,000
Deposits in transit at October 31	2,000
Checks outstanding at October 31 (that appear on the November bank statement)	14,000
Total deposits made for the month	45,000
Total checks written for the month	38,000
One returned check on the bank statement	1,000

Required:

1. Determine the Cash account balance at month end.

2. Prepare a bank reconciliation for the month of November 2004.

Analyze: How does a bank reconciliation act as an internal control for a company?

CASES

LO2 COMMUNICATION CASE 7-1 **Internal Control of Cash**

Zeg Utility Company's management has asked you, the company's CPA, to look closely at some of the controls surrounding the company's cash receipts as a result of some recent problems. The following describes the process by which cash is recorded: The mailroom clerk receives and opens all mail that comes in that is related to customers' remittances. The mailroom clerk looks up the account on the Accounts Receivable and Cash general ledger control accounts and posts the remittance. The mailroom clerk then hands the remittance package, with the general ledger entries, to the accounting supervisor, who compiles the deposit for the bank. Although the invoices to customers for their monthly utility bill specify payment by check or money order only, cash is frequently remitted for payment. When cash comes in, it is put in a drawer next to the accounting supervisor's desk until the balance reaches $5,000. This practice dates back to 1979, when the company was trying to reduce the costs of travel to the bank.

Required: Identify any deficiencies and make at least four recommendations to management concerning its internal controls. Provide the reasons that you believe these controls are necessary.

LO6   ANALYSIS CASE 7-2   **Securitization of Receivables**

The following excerpts were taken from **Sears, Roebuck and Co.**'s 2002 10-K report filed with the Securities and Exchange Commission:

Sears   SEARS, ROEBUCK AND CO.
Partial Consolidated Statements of Income

millions, except per common share data	2002	2001	2000
REVENUES			
Merchandise sales and services	$35,698	$35,755	$36,277
Credit and financial products revenues	5,668	5,235	4,571
Total revenues	41,366	40,990	40,848
COSTS AND EXPENSES			
Cost of sales, buying and occupancy	25,646	26,234	26,632
Selling and administrative	9,249	8,892	8,807
Provision for uncollectible accounts	2,261	1,866	884
Depreciation and amortization	875	863	839
Interest	1,143	1,415	1,248
Special charges and impairments	111	542	251
Total costs and expenses	39,285	39,812	38,661

Sears   SEARS, ROEBUCK AND CO.
Partial Consolidated Balance Sheets

millions, except per share data	2002	2001
ASSETS		
Current assets		
Cash and cash equivalents	$ 1,962	$ 1,064
Credit card receivables	32,595	29,321
Less allowance for uncollectible accounts	1,836	1,166
Net credit card receivables	30,759	28,155
Other receivables	863	658
Merchandise inventories	5,115	4,912
Prepaid expenses and deferred charges	535	458
Deferred income taxes	749	858
Total current assets	39,983	36,105

Sears

NOTE 1 - SUMMARY OF SIGNIFICANT ACCOUNTING POLICIES

Credit Card Receivables

Credit card receivables arise under revolving credit accounts used primarily to finance purchases. Sears Card products are typically available only on purchases of merchandise and services offered by the Company, whereas MasterCard is widely accepted by merchants outside the Company. Additional MasterCard product receivables are generated from balance transfers and cash advances. These accounts have various billing and payment structures, including varying minimum payment levels and finance charge rates and fees. Based on historical payment patterns, the full receivable balance will not be repaid within one year.

Credit card receivables are shown net of an allowance for uncollectible accounts. The allowance is an estimate of losses inherent in the portfolio (including current accounts, finance charges and credit card fee balances) as of the balance sheet date. The Company calculates the allowance using a model that analyzes factors such as bankruptcy filings, delinquency rates, historical charge-off patterns, recovery rates and other portfolio data. The Company's calculation is then reviewed by management to assess whether, based on economic events, additional analyses are required to appropriately estimate losses inherent in the portfolio.

The entire balance of an account is contractually delinquent if the minimum payment is not received by the payment due date. The Company's current credit processing system charges off an account automatically when a customer's number of missed monthly payments outstanding reaches eight; however, accounts may be charged off sooner in the event of customer bankruptcy. Bankrupt customer accounts are charged off 60 days after the first meeting of the creditors for a filing under Chapter 7 of the U.S. Bankruptcy Code and 90 days after the first meeting of the creditors for a filing under Chapter 13 of the U.S. Bankruptcy Code. All amounts collected on previously charged off accounts are included in recoveries for the determination of net charge-offs.

Accounting for Securitizations

On March 31, 2001, the Company adopted the requirements of SFAS No. 140, "Accounting for Transfers and Servicing of Financial Assets and Extinguishments of Liabilities", which superceded SFAS No. 125. Under SFAS No. 125, the Company's securitization transactions were accounted for as sales of receivables. SFAS No. 140 established new conditions for a securitization to be accounted for as a sale of receivables. Specifically, SFAS No. 140 changed the requirements for an entity to be a qualifying special purpose entity and modified under what conditions a transferor has retained effective control over transferred assets. The new standard became effective for transfers occurring after March 31, 2001.

The addition of previously uncommitted assets to the securitization trust in April 2001 required the Company to consolidate the securitization structure for financial reporting purposes on a prospective basis. Accordingly, the Company recorded on the balance sheet approximately $8.1 billion of previously unconsolidated securitized credit card receivables and related securitization borrowings in the second quarter of 2001. In addition, approximately $3.9 billion of assets were reclassified to credit card receivables from retained interest in transferred credit card receivables. The Company recognized incremental operating income of $40 million and $128 million in 2001 and 2000, respectively, from net securitization activity. The Company now accounts for securitizations as secured borrowings.

In connection with the consolidation of the securitization structure, the Company recognized a non-cash, pretax charge of $522 million in 2001 to establish an allowance for uncollectible accounts related to the receivables which were previously considered as sold or accounted for as retained interests in transferred credit card receivables.

(continued)

NOTE 3 - CREDIT CARD RECEIVABLES

A summary of the Company's credit card receivables at year-end is as follows:

Millions	2002	2001
Credit card receivables [1]		
Domestic	$30,766	$27,599
Sears Canada	1,797	1,682
	32,563	29,281
Other customer receivables	32	40
Total credit card receivables	$32,595	$29,321

[1]At December 28, 2002 and December 29, 2001, $23.8 billion and $16.1 billion, respectively, of credit card receivables were segregated in securitization trusts.

Summary of Securitization Process

Credit card securitizations are utilized as part of the Company's overall funding strategy. Sears sells certain of its credit card receivable balances to various subsidiaries that in turn transfer those balances to master trusts ("trusts"). The trusts then securitize the receivable balances by issuing certificates representing undivided interests in the trusts' receivables to both outside investors and to the Company (as a retained interest). These certificates entitle the holder to a series of scheduled cash flows under preset terms and conditions, the receipt of which is dependent upon cash flows generated by the related trusts' assets. In each securitization transaction, a Sears subsidiary has retained certain subordinated interests which serve as a credit enhancement to the certificates held by the outside investors. As a result, the credit quality of certificates held by outside investors is enhanced. However, the investors and the trusts have no recourse against the Company beyond the trust assets.

Required:

1. What was the amount that Sears originally committed to securitizations before the implementation of *SFAS No. 140*? Assume that no other amounts were transferred between December 29, 2001, and the date the amounts were consolidated. How does Sears account for the securitized receivables now?

2. In reference to Sears's recording of an allowance for uncollectible accounts, why was this necessary?

3. Examine Illustration 7.4 on page 317 of this chapter. Is the manner in which Sears records its securitizations consistent with this figure?

4. Why would a company such as Sears use securitization instead of factoring of its receivables?

LO7   ANALYSIS CASE 7-3   Financial Ratios

Balance sheet information for the **Walt Disney Company** for 2003, 2002, and 2001 appears on the next page.

Required:

1. Calculate the current ratio of the company for the years ending 2003 and 2002.

2. Calculate the amount of working capital for 2003 and 2002 for the company.

3. What is the accounts receivable turnover ratio for 2003? If the average turnover for the industry is 4.0, is Disney performing well in this area? Net sales for 2003 were $27,061 (in millions of dollars).

4. Comment on the company's liquidity position.

Disney

Walt Disney Company
Balance Sheet Information

Amounts in Thousands

PERIOD ENDING	30-Sep-03	30-Sep-02	30-Sep-01
Assets			
Current Assets			
Cash and Cash Equivalents	$ 1,583,000	$ 1,239,000	$ 618,000
Net Receivables	4,912,000	4,673,000	3,965,000
Inventory	1,271,000	697,000	671,000
Other Current Assets	548,000	1,240,000	1,775,000
Total Current Assets	8,314,000	7,849,000	7,029,000
Long Term Investments	1,849,000	1,810,000	2,061,000
Property Plant and Equipment	18,883,000	12,780,000	12,907,000
Goodwill	16,966,000	17,083,000	—
Intangible Assets	2,786,000	8,735,000	19,775,000
Other Assets	1,190,000	1,788,000	1,927,000
Total Assets	**$49,988,000**	**$50,045,000**	**$43,699,000**
Liabilities			
Current Liabilities			
Accounts Payable	$ 5,044,000	$ 5,173,000	$ 4,603,000
Short/Current Long Term Debt	2,457,000	1,663,000	829,000
Other Current Liabilities	1,168,000	983,000	787,000
Total Current Liabilities	8,669,000	7,819,000	6,219,000
Long-Term Debt	10,643,000	12,825,000	8,940,000
Other Liabilities	3,745,000	2,311,000	2,756,000
Deferred Long Term Liability Charges	2,712,000	3,211,000	2,730,000
Minority Interest	428,000	434,000	382,000
Total Liabilities	**26,197,000**	**26,600,000**	**21,027,000**
Stockholders' Equity			
Common Stock	12,154,000	12,107,000	12,096,000
Retained Earnings	13,817,000	12,979,000	12,171,000
Treasury Stock	(1,527,000)	(1,395,000)	(1,395,000)
Other Stockholders' Equity	(653,000)	(246,000)	(200,000)
Total Stockholders' Equity	**23,791,000**	**23,445,000**	**22,672,000**
Total Liabilities and Stockholders' Equity	**$49,988,000**	**$50,045,000**	**$43,699,000**

LO4

ETHICS

ETHICS CASE 7-4   Estimating Uncollectibles

Elisa Monterin is the accounts receivable manager at Kadrin Company, a wholesaler of office supplies. The company customarily extends 30 days of credit to its established customers. Under Elisa's diligent management, the accounts receivable department has been able to increase its collection rate significantly.

Because Elisa is very knowledgeable about receivables and holds an accounting degree, one of her duties is to estimate the expected uncollectible accounts. At the end of the current year, she created an aging of accounts receivables schedule, calculated an estimate of the uncollectible accounts, and communicated the estimate to Fred Maran, the company's controller. On the same day, Fred sent an e-mail to Elisa asking her to increase the percentage of estimated uncollectibles by 2 percent for each of the four "time outstanding" categories. Elisa knew that the accounts outstanding were those of customers who have historically paid their balances in full. Because she had recently implemented an enhanced screening process for new credit customers and because she had been successful in increasing the collection rate of existing receivables, she felt that the percentage should be reduced, not increased.

Fred did not agree and stated that the percentage increase that he had suggested was conservative and reflected the company's strong commitment to providing useful and conservative accounting information. He also stated that the company was negotiating with a number of new customers who were expected to purchase a large amount of inventory. He asserted that new customers are important for the continued growth of the company, but that they also increase the risk of uncollectibles. He further indicated that a reserve for next year would be advantageous to the company's financial results. Fred asked her to recalculate the uncollectible accounts expense utilizing the new percentage.

Required:

1. What is the accounting issue involved in this situation?
2. What is the ethical issue that Elisa faces?
3. Who will be affected by the decision that Elisa makes?
4. What values and principles are likely to influence her decision?
5. What alternative actions can she take?
6. What do you think Elisa should do?

LO4, 6

ETHICS

ETHICS CASE 7-5   Balancing Competing Objectives

Home Depot has been quite successful in managing its cash and building up a large cash balance. Home Depot's ability to manage its cash is evidenced by the company's ability to increase the days' payables outstanding and to increase its average accounts receivable balance by a significantly lower percentage than its sales. For fiscal 2002, days' payables outstanding increased to 42 days, from 34 days in fiscal 2001. The company states that the increase has been due to its efforts to move its payment terms to industry averages.[2] For the year ended February 2, 2003, the company reported net receivables of $1,072 million. These efforts have led to greater flexibility and a larger amount of available working capital.

In fiscal 2003, Home Depot intends to continue its plan to increase the number of retail stores it operates. These expansion plans come at a time when its chief competitor, **Lowe's**, has already taken significant steps to expand its own operations. In fact, as part of its expansion project, Lowe's opened 47 new stores in just one quarter alone, and increased its revenues by 20 percent and its income by 28 percent.[3] Many of Lowe's new stores are located in close proximity to Home Depot's stores. This sharply increases the competition faced by Home Depot.

Expansion carries both risks and rewards, and it increases the need for working capital. One of the methods that could be used to enhance sales and thus ensure the success of the expansion project is to relax the rigor of collection of accounts receivables and extend credit periods, thereby allowing customers longer periods of time to pay. However, less rigorous collection methods increase the risk of higher uncollectibles.

Suppose you are working for a company similar to Home Depot and are the executive responsible for sales at new stores. Your compensation plan includes a bonus for increasing quarterly sales. Assume that Randall Smith is in charge of accounts receivable collections for the new stores. He is planning to leave the company soon, and he wants to use his achievements in shortening collection periods to secure a new position. Suppose you believe that by relaxing credit terms and collection strategies, you could enhance sales. You also are aware that this strategy would be likely to result in higher uncollectibles and slower collections.

Required:

1. What are the issues that you face? What are the problems faced by the accounts receivable manager?
2. Who will be affected by the decision that you make?
3. What values and principles are likely to influence your decision?

---

2 Home Depot, Inc. 2002 Annual Report, p. 24.

3 Dan More, "Lowe's Cos. Posts 28% Rise in Net on Surging Sales," *Wall Street Journal*, February 24, 2004, p. B7.

4. What alternative actions should you consider?

5. What would you do?

6. How would relaxing credit and collection terms be likely to affect the company's balance sheet?

LO4   **COMMUNICATION CASE 7-6   Establishing an Allowance for Uncollectibles**

You recently started work as the staff accountant for Stainless, Inc., a new company that manufactures semiconductors. The company has been in operation for only a few months and is just beginning to ship its products to customers. Nonetheless, Stainless's investors are pressuring management to produce profits. In addition, a bonus program for managers has been established that is based on profits.

On December 27, the production manager ships a large order to a customer and sends you the paperwork so that the sale will be recognized in the current year. This sales order represents 25 percent of all the revenues for the year. In addition, the sale will allow the company to show a profit for the year. Interestingly, the customer is one that has been plagued with financial problems for a number of years and has recognized net losses in each of the last four years. Many of Stainless's customers are having financial difficulties as a result of the poor economy. Because Stainless is just starting to ship its products, it has never created an Allowance for Uncollectible Accounts account. The company's fiscal year end is December 31.

When you ask the chief financial officer about establishing an Allowance for Uncollectible Accounts account, he states that it is not necessary because all of the accounts receivables are with companies that are still in business.

Required:

1. Why would the chief financial officer prefer not to establish an Allowance for Uncollectible Accounts account?

2. Write a memo to the president of the company discussing why an allowance account is needed.

LO7   **ANALYSIS CASE 7-7   Receivables Analysis**

ANALYSIS

Snap-On Tools and **Black & Decker** are two of the largest global manufacturers of tools and related equipment. Snap-On Tools sells the majority of its products to professional users through a dealer network, whereas Black & Decker sells its products to individual home-improvement users through large stores like Lowe's and Home Depot. Sales and receivables data for the two manufacturers are provided here:

	2003	2002	2001
Snap-On Tools			
Sales	$2,233,200	$2,109,100	$2,095,700
Accounts receivable	591,800	597,400	612,400
Allowance for doubtful accounts	(45,000)	(41,200)	(39,600)
Black & Decker			
Sales	4,482,700	4,291,800	4,139,900
Accounts receivable	856,400	761,800	760,500
Allowance for doubtful accounts	(47,400)	(46,300)	(51,900)

Required:

1. Calculate the 2002 and 2003 accounts receivable turnover ratio and days in receivables for each company.

2. Why might these two companies have differences in their days in receivables?

LO6   **COMMUNICATION CASE 7-8   Managing Cash**

Pop Brands, Inc. has been extremely successful in the launch of a new product. The product has sold at a record pace, and as sales have increased, so has the company's accounts receivables balance. Because the company is growing at such a fast rate, it is experiencing a cash shortage. As the controller of the company, you need to find a way to obtain cash to improve the company's working capital position. The chief financial officer has asked you to provide an analysis of how the company could use assignment or factoring to obtain cash from its receivables more quickly. She is very interested in the financial statement effects of each of the methods.

Required: Write a memo to the chief financial officer in which you explain assignment and factoring transactions. In addition, discuss how each method would affect the financial statements.

LO1 **FINANCIAL REPORTING CASE 7-9** **Disclosure of Cash and Cash Equivalents**

The following information has been provided for Hill Company at December 31, 2005:

Checking account	$ 28,543
Savings account	194,521
Portion of savings account restricted by lockbox requirement	15,000
Portion of savings account restricted by compensating balance on loan agreement	50,000
Petty cash account	500
Investments in short-term (less than 60 days) government securities, maturing January 21, 2006	200,000

Required: Use the information provided to prepare the cash portion of the balance sheet at December 31, 2005, along with any note disclosures that may be needed.

LO3 **RESEARCH CASE 7-10** **Cash and Receivables**

The investor relations section of Lowe's website contains financial information that is useful to potential and current investors. Lowe's website is found at **www.lowes.com**.

Required: Locate the company's most recent annual report and answer the following questions:

1. What types of assets does Lowe's include in cash and cash equivalents?

2. For the most recent period, what was the gross amount of Lowe's accounts receivable and the allowance for doubtful accounts?

3. Does Lowe's accounts receivable asset include receivables from the Lowe's credit card? If not, who owns these credit card receivables?

ON THE WEB

The following exercises, activities, and problems are available on the *Intermediate Accounting* website. Use these resources to reinforce your understanding of the topics presented in this chapter.

- CPA-Adapted Simulations
- Interpreting the Accounting Standards
- Extending the Global Focus
- Extending the Ethics Discussion
- Mastering the Spreadsheet
- Career Snapshots
- Annual Report Project
- ACE Practice Tests
- Flashcards
- Glossary
- Check Figures for Text Problems
- PowerPoint Presentations

SOLUTIONS: CHECK YOUR UNDERSTANDING

Forms of Cash (p. 304)

1. Items classified as cash and cash equivalents include bank deposits; currency and coins; checks from customers; money market accounts; and certificates of deposit, commercial paper, and U.S. Treasury bills that have a term of 90 days or less from their date of purchase.

2. A compensating balance is an amount that a lender requires a borrower to keep in an account as part of a credit-granting agreement. The financial institution uses the amount as collateral on the loan. A compensating balance is disclosed separately from cash and cash equivalents as either a current or a long-term asset, depending on the terms of the borrowing agreement that restricts the funds.

3. A compensating balance increases the effective interest rate.

Cash Controls (p. 307)

1. A system of internal controls protects cash and other assets from loss, theft, and embezzlement.

2. Common tools used to protect and control cash include the following: limit the number of persons who handle cash; separate the accounting tasks involving cash between different employees; bond employees who handle cash or cash records; use a cash register and a safe; use a checking account to make all cash payments; deposit cash receipts in the bank in a timely fashion, usually daily; and reconcile the bank statement promptly.

3. Differences between the bank balance and the general ledger Cash account balance may be caused by deposits in transit, outstanding checks, bank errors, book errors, interest, direct charges or deposits, or insufficient funds checks.

Classifying Receivables (p. 308)

1. Notes receivable are backed by written contracts promising to pay specified amounts to the company on specified dates. Accounts receivable are not supported by such formal contracts but arise from the sale of goods or services on credit at the wholesale or the retail level in the normal course of business.

2. Other receivables might include tax refund claims, insurance claims, and advances to employees.

3. Promissory notes specify payment dates, interest, and other terms to ensure that both parties perform.

Accounting for Accounts Receivable (p. 312)

1. Debit Cash, debit Cash Discounts, credit Accounts Receivable.

2. The net realizable value is the actual amount that a company expects to receive in cash at the time of collection. To arrive at net realizable value, the company deducts an estimate of future uncollectible accounts from the total of accounts receivable.

3. The estimate is calculated by applying a historically determined percentage to the period's credit sales.

4. Under the direct write-off method, no entries are made until a customer actually defaults on payment, at which time the uncollectible account receivable is written off to Bad Debt Expense. Conversely, under the allowance method, an allowance account is established to offset the period's revenues with an estimated bad debt expense.

Recording Notes Receivable (p. 314)

1. Interest is calculated using the following formula: Face Amount $\times$ Annual Interest Rate $\times$ Fraction of the Annual Period

2. The Discount on Notes Receivable account is reported on the balance sheet as a contra account to the Notes Receivable account.

3. The interest (or discount) is deducted from the face amount at the beginning of the transaction, thereby yielding less cash for the borrower.

Cash Inflows and Receivables (p. 318)

1. Factoring is the transferring, or selling, of receivables to a third party. When a company factors its receivables with recourse, the seller guarantees payment to the buyer even if some of the receivables are uncollectible. The seller retains the risk of bad debts. The following conditions must be met: (1) The transferred receivables must have been isolated from the seller, especially in the case of a seller who is declaring bankruptcy. (2) The right to pledge or exchange the transferred receivables must be held only by the factor. (3) The seller of the receivables must not maintain effective control over the transferred receivables through an agreement that allows for either mandatory repurchase or redemption of the assets prior to maturity.

2. Securitization is the transfer of receivables, either individually or pooled, to a trust account in which investors may purchase shares that entitle them to receive cash as the receivables are paid.

3. Lockboxes ensure that checks are deposited quickly and interest income is earned as soon as possible.

Analysis of Cash and Receivables (p. 321)

1. The quick ratio measures a company's ability to pay its short-term obligations from its most liquid assets and excludes inventory amounts.

2. Company A's current ratio of 2.5 indicates that it has $2.50 in current assets for every $1 of current liabilities. Company B's current ratio indicates that it has only $1.30 in current assets for every $1 of current liabilities. Therefore, Company A has a stronger ability to meet its current liability obligations.

3. The accounts receivable turnover ratio is calculated by dividing net sales by average net accounts receivable.

CPA-ADAPTED SIMULATION

This simulation asks you to complete various tasks related to a company's annual financial statements. If your instructor has signed up for CPAexcel™, you can do the work online at **www.cpaexcel.com/hmco**. You may also do the simulation manually.

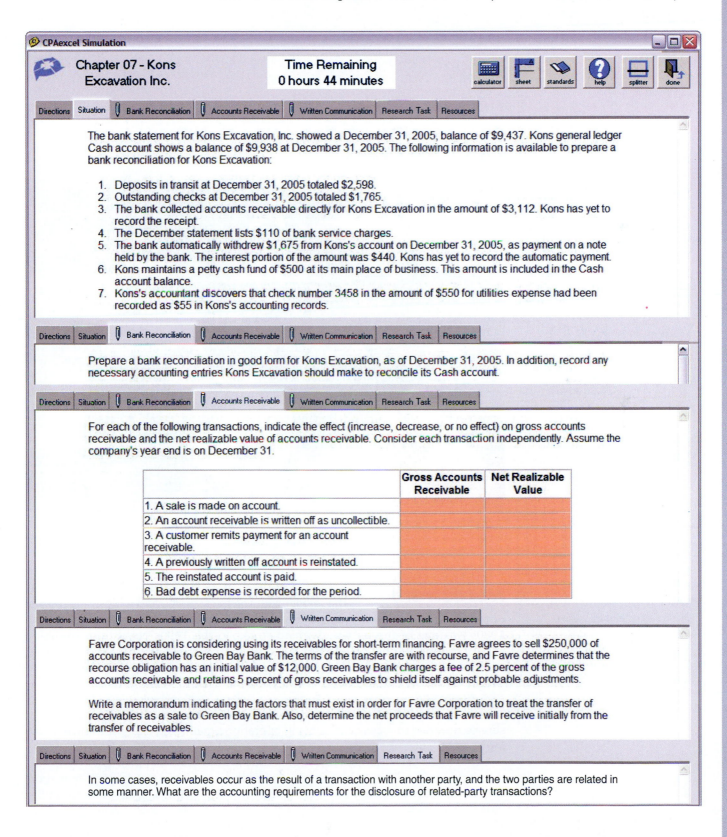

CPAexcel Simulation

Chapter 07 – Kons Excavation Inc.

Time Remaining
0 hours 44 minutes

calculator   sheet   standards   help   splitter   done

Directions   Situation   Bank Reconciliation   Accounts Receivable   Written Communication   Research Task   Resources

The bank statement for Kons Excavation, Inc. showed a December 31, 2005, balance of $9,437. Kons general ledger Cash account shows a balance of $9,938 at December 31, 2005. The following information is available to prepare a bank reconciliation for Kons Excavation:

1. Deposits in transit at December 31, 2005 totaled $2,598.
2. Outstanding checks at December 31, 2005 totaled $1,765.
3. The bank collected accounts receivable directly for Kons Excavation in the amount of $3,112. Kons has yet to record the receipt.
4. The December statement lists $110 of bank service charges.
5. The bank automatically withdrew $1,675 from Kons's account on December 31, 2005, as payment on a note held by the bank. The interest portion of the amount was $440. Kons has yet to record the automatic payment.
6. Kons maintains a petty cash fund of $500 at its main place of business. This amount is included in the Cash account balance.
7. Kons's accountant discovers that check number 3458 in the amount of $550 for utilities expense had been recorded as $55 in Kons's accounting records.

Directions   Situation   Bank Reconciliation   Accounts Receivable   Written Communication   Research Task   Resources

Prepare a bank reconciliation in good form for Kons Excavation, as of December 31, 2005. In addition, record any necessary accounting entries Kons Excavation should make to reconcile its Cash account.

Directions   Situation   Bank Reconciliation   Accounts Receivable   Written Communication   Research Task   Resources

For each of the following transactions, indicate the effect (increase, decrease, or no effect) on gross accounts receivable and the net realizable value of accounts receivable. Consider each transaction independently. Assume the company's year end is on December 31.

	Gross Accounts Receivable	Net Realizable Value
1. A sale is made on account.		
2. An account receivable is written off as uncollectible.		
3. A customer remits payment for an account receivable.		
4. A previously written off account is reinstated.		
5. The reinstated account is paid.		
6. Bad debt expense is recorded for the period.		

Directions   Situation   Bank Reconciliation   Accounts Receivable   Written Communication   Research Task   Resources

Favre Corporation is considering using its receivables for short-term financing. Favre agrees to sell $250,000 of accounts receivable to Green Bay Bank. The terms of the transfer are with recourse, and Favre determines that the recourse obligation has an initial value of $12,000. Green Bay Bank charges a fee of 2.5 percent of the gross accounts receivable and retains 5 percent of gross receivables to shield itself against probable adjustments.

Write a memorandum indicating the factors that must exist in order for Favre Corporation to treat the transfer of receivables as a sale to Green Bay Bank. Also, determine the net proceeds that Favre will receive initially from the transfer of receivables.

Directions   Situation   Bank Reconciliation   Accounts Receivable   Written Communication   Research Task   Resources

In some cases, receivables occur as the result of a transaction with another party, and the two parties are related in some manner. What are the accounting requirements for the disclosure of related-party transactions?

Inventory

FINANCIAL REPORTING CASE

IMPROVED INVENTORY SYSTEM PAYS OFF FOR NORDSTROM

Nordstrom's change to a more efficient perpetual inventory system played a role in increasing its net sales 29 percent from 2000 to 2004.

Nordstrom

For much of the century, Nordstrom Inc. was known as the retailer with the best service and widest selection of upscale merchandise in America. The company was founded in 1901, and in the 1980s was one of the best performing stocks. In the 1990s, Nordstrom stumbled against tough competition, as many customers moved to retailers that offered lower prices and less service. The company's stock price dropped from $44.81 in 1999 to $14.19 in late 2001. In addition, the company was slow to respond to fashion trends and did not know what merchandise was selling out and what was languishing. Nordstom, which had always concentrated on having beautiful stores and great service, now had to focus on improving operations, managing expenses, and improving inventory management.

One of the first changes Nordstrom made in 2001 was to implement a perpetual inventory system. This investment in technology provided Nordstrom's managers with better knowledge of what merchandise was selling, the amount of merchandise

Nordstrom

Nordstrom, Inc.
PARTIAL ELEVEN-YEAR STATISTICAL SUMMARY

(Dollars in thousands except square footage and per share amounts)

Fiscal Year	2004	2003	2002	2001	2000
Financial Position					
Customer accounts receivable, net	$ 580,397	$ 594,900	$ 606,861	$ 621,491	$ 649,504
Investment in asset backed securities	422,416	272,294	124,543	58,539	50,183
Merchandise inventories	917,182	901,623	953,112	888,172	945,687
Current assets	2,572,444	2,524,843	2,125,356	2,095,317	1,812,982
Current liabilities	1,341,152	1,122,559	925,978	986,587	950,568
Working capital	1,231,292	1,402,284	1,199,378	1,108,730	862,414
Working capital ratio	1.92	2.25	2.30	2.12	1.91
Land, buildings, and equipment, net	1,780,366	1,807,778	1,849,961	1,761,082	1,599,938
Long-term debt, inc. current portion	1,030,107	1,234,243	1,350,595	1,424,242	1,112,296
Debt/capital ratio	.3654	.4304	.4960	.5197	.4922
Shareholders' equity	1,788,994	1,634,009	1,372,864	1,316,245	1,233,445
Shares outstanding (in thousands)	135,665	138,377	135,444	134,469	133,798
Book value per share	13.19	11.81	10.14	9.79	9.22
Total assets	4,605,390	4,569,233	4,185,269	4,084,356	3,608,503
Operations					
Net sales	7,131,388	6,448,678	5,944,656	5,607,687	5,511,908
Gross profit	2,572,000	2,233,132	1,974,634	1,844,133	1,854,220

that was on hand at any point in time, and what trends might be developing for certain merchandise. The perpetual inventory system also allowed managers to concentrate on selling as much merchandise as possible at regular prices, which reduced the need for markdowns to clear out slower-moving goods.

How did the investment in a perpetual inventory system pay off for Nordstrom? As you can see from the data excerpted from the 11-year summary of operations from Nordstrom's annual report, inventory amounts actually decreased over the period 2000 to 2004, even though net sales increased 29 percent during that period. As Nordstrom's management stated in the management discussion and analysis section of its 2004 10K, "We maintained our inventory at levels consistent with the prior year, even though our sales and square footage grew in 2004. The overall improvements in merchandise management have generated higher margins on our inventory investments."[1]

Inventory levels play an important role in the analysis of a company's strategy. By examining a company's financial statements, a financial analyst can determine how efficiently the company is managing it resources. For example, financial analysts are interested in how long companies hold their inventories. Strong companies that sell items in high demand will have high inventory turnover, whereas companies that face weak demand due to changes in consumers' needs or tastes will have low inventory turnover.

In addition to determining the optimal level of inventory, determining the optimal mix of merchandise is another difficult task for retailers. Inventory managers must be careful to keep enough merchandise in stock so that if demand for a specific style increases, the store will not run out and lose sales. However, fashion trends are unpredictable, and overpurchasing the wrong style can lead to markdowns and decreased profits.

---

[1] Nordstrom Inc., Form 10-K, 04/08/2005.

EXAMINING THE CASE

1. What percentage of Nordstrom's current assets was composed of inventory in 2004? In 2003?

2. What challenges does Nordstrom's management face in determining the amount of inventory to hold at any point in time?

3. What are some things financial analysts look for when analyzing inventory?

LO1 Describe the purchasing and sales cycles and their effects on the financial statements.

inventory an asset a company holds and will ultimately sell to its customers

Critical Thinking: *Describe how you think the purchasing cycle for a retail department store differs from the purchasing cycle for a shipbuilder.*

The Purchasing and Sales Cycles

Inventory is an asset a company holds and will ultimately sell to its customers. In many cases, inventory is the largest current asset that a company holds. Thus, how a company manages, accounts for, and reports its inventory can significantly affect its financial statements. Manufacturing companies have three categories of inventory: raw materials, work in process, and finished goods. Merchandisers, in contrast, have only one category, the finished goods that are ready to be sold to customers. Whether a company holds raw materials, work in process, or finished goods in inventories, the same basic process and inventory measurement techniques are used. Therefore, to streamline this chapter's discussions, we will take the perspective of a merchandiser such as Nordstrom. To understand how inventory is reported in the financial statements, it is important to be familiar with the purchasing and sales cycles.

THE PURCHASING CYCLE

The purchasing cycle begins when a company decides to purchase an inventory item. To initiate the purchase, the company creates a purchase order and transmits it to the vendor. Depending on the order's shipping terms, the purchase will be entered into the accounting system either when the goods are shipped or when they are received. If the inventory is shipped FOB shipping point (FOB stands for "free on board"), the buyer pays the transportation costs and the purchase will be recorded when the inventory is shipped by the vendor. If the inventory is shipped FOB destination, the seller pays the transportation costs and the purchase will be recorded when the inventory is received by the purchaser. The FOB terms determine which company owns the goods during the shipping process and, more importantly, who would incur a loss if the goods were damaged or destroyed while being shipped.

For instance, if a company in Atlanta purchases goods from a vendor in San Diego and agrees to the shipping terms FOB Atlanta (destination), the company will record the purchase when the goods arrive at the company's Atlanta location. If the terms were FOB San Diego, the purchase would be recorded when the vendor shipped the goods from its San Diego location. The inventory item enters the accounting system and becomes a current asset at the time the company takes possession of it. The purchasing cycle results in assets being increased by the amount of the new inventory and either assets being decreased (if cash is paid) or liabilities being increased (if an account payable is created). When the company remits payment to the vendor, the purchasing cycle is complete. Illustration 8.1 summarizes the typical purchasing cycle.

THE SALES CYCLE

The sales cycle begins when a customer purchases an inventory item and the company records a sale. The sale of inventory has two effects on the financial statements. First, either the Cash or the Accounts Receivable account must be increased by the amount of the sale, and the Sales account must be increased by the same amount. Second, the cost of the sale must be recorded. The **cost of sales** is the amount that a company paid for the merchandise it sold during the period. Cost of sales is also sometimes called *cost*

cost of sales the amount that a company paid for the merchandise it sold during the period; also called *cost of goods sold*

Illustration 8.1

Purchasing Cycle

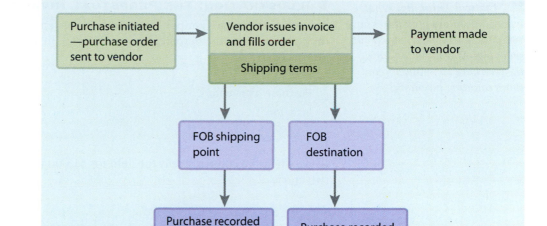

of goods sold. For a merchandiser, the cost of a sale is the cost of the inventory item sold to the customer, so the Inventory account must be decreased and the Cost of Sales account must be increased. The sales cycle is complete when payment for the purchase is received by the company.

The net effect of a sales transaction is that assets increase by the excess of the sales price over the cost of purchasing inventory. Sales revenues and expenses also increase, which ultimately will increase retained earnings by the same amount as assets.

CHECK YOUR UNDERSTANDING

1. If goods are purchased FOB shipping point, when does the purchaser record an increase in inventory?

2. Describe the kinds of inventories that a manufacturing business might hold.

3. What effects does the sale of an inventory item have on the accounting records?

LO2 Explain the differences between the perpetual inventory system and the periodic inventory system.

Recording Inventory

Inventory should initially be recorded at its full cost, which is its purchase price plus any related additional costs, such as shipping and handling, shipping insurance, taxes, and other direct costs of purchasing. Any purchase discounts should be deducted from the invoice price so that the inventory is recorded at its true cash cost.

SYSTEMS OF ACCOUNTING FOR INVENTORY

perpetual inventory system a system of accounting for inventory in which the Inventory account is adjusted each time inventory is purchased or sold

periodic inventory system a system of accounting for inventory in which the Inventory account is updated only at the end of each accounting period

When accounting for inventory, a company must decide how often it wants to update its Inventory account. There are two basic systems of accounting for purchases and sales of inventory, the perpetual system and the periodic system. Under the **perpetual inventory system**, the Inventory account is adjusted each time inventory is purchased or sold, so that the account is perpetually updated. Under the **periodic inventory system**, the Inventory account is adjusted only at the end of each accounting period. With the increased use of computerized accounting systems, more companies are recording purchases and sales on a perpetual basis. We illustrate both systems in this section, but we will focus on the perpetual system throughout the balance of the chapter.

Critical Thinking: *What types of inventory procedures have you noticed as you have been out shopping? At what point during the year have you noticed retail stores counting inventory?*

ILLUSTRATION: THE PERPETUAL INVENTORY SYSTEM

Assume that Vanya Company purchases an inventory item on account for $10. If the company uses the perpetual system to track inventory, it will make the following journal entry:

Purchase of Inventory		
Inventory	10	
Accounts Payable		10

Later, when the company sells the item for $15 on account, it will make the following two entries:

Sale of Inventory		
Accounts Receivable	15	
Sales		15
Cost of Sales	10	
Inventory		10

Under the perpetual system, the Inventory account is updated after both the purchase and the sale of inventory. Ideally, the Inventory account reflects the true value of inventory at any point in time. However, as a result of such factors as spoilage, breakage, and theft, the actual value of inventory may differ from the balance in the Inventory account. For this reason, a company must make a physical count of its inventory periodically and adjust its Inventory account accordingly.

ILLUSTRATION: THE PERIODIC INVENTORY SYSTEM

If Vanya Company uses the periodic system to track inventory, it will make the following journal entries when an inventory item is bought and sold:

Purchase of Inventory		
Purchases	10	
Accounts Payable		10
Sale of Inventory		
Accounts Receivable	15	
Sales		15

Under the periodic inventory system, the Inventory account will not be updated until the end of the period. At that time, a physical count (or estimate) of the ending inventory will be made, and the cost of sales can be determined using the following calculation:

$$
\begin{array}{l}
\quad \text{Beginning Inventory} \\
+ \; \text{Purchases} \\
\hline
\quad \text{Cost of Goods Available for Sale} \\
- \; \text{Ending Inventory} \\
\hline
\quad \text{Cost of Sales} \\
\hline
\end{array}
$$

Although both systems are acceptable, the perpetual system allows managers more control over inventory and provides more accurate information about inventory at any point in time.

LO3 Demonstrate the use of four methods of calculating inventory cost: specific identification; average cost; first-in, first-out; and last-in, first-out.

🧩 *Critical Thinking: What factors do you think businesses consider when choosing one inventory method over another?*

Costing Inventory

During an accounting period, most companies purchase inventory a number of times at a number of different prices. Because inventories can be very large and can turn over rapidly, it is not always practical or even possible to determine exactly which items were bought at which prices or exactly which items remain in inventory and which have been sold. Therefore, when deciding how to value its inventory, a company must select one of several common cost-flow assumptions. It is important to recognize that the inventory cost-flow assumption need not correspond to the way goods physically flow through the business. Nonetheless, the choice is crucial because applying the various cost-flow assumptions to the same purchase and sales data can result in dramatically different costs of sales and inventory amounts.

The four basic cost-flow assumptions are:

1. *Specific identification*—the assumption that the cost flow of inventory is the same as the physical flow of inventory

2. *Average cost*—the assumption that all inventory items have the same average cost

3. *First-in, first-out (FIFO)*—the assumption that the first inventory item purchased is the first item sold to customers

4. *Last-in, first-out (LIFO)*—the assumption that the last inventory item purchased is the first item sold to customers

Each cost-flow assumption forms the basis for a method of accounting for inventory. A company may choose to use any of these methods to account for its inventory, and it does not have to use the same method for all inventories. For example, in its 2002 annual report, **Chico's**, a women's clothing company, provided the information about its inventories presented in Figure 8.1. As you can see, the company uses FIFO for its raw materials inventory and LIFO for its finished goods inventory.

Figure 8.1

Inventories Disclosure

> ## Chico's
> **Excerpt from Chico's 2002 Annual Report**
> **INVENTORIES**
>
> Raw material inventories consisting of fabric of approximately $2,400,000 and $3,644,000 as of February 2, 2002, and February 3, 2001, respectively, are recorded at the lower of cost, using the first-in, first-out (FIFO) method, or market. All other inventories consist of finished clothing and accessories and are recorded at the lower of cost, using the last-in, first-out (LIFO) method, or market. Purchasing, distribution and design costs are expensed as incurred, and are included in the accompanying consolidated statements of income as a component of cost of sales.

Illustration 8.2

Inventory Records for Psyche Air-X Shoes

Shoe Warehouse Company: January 1 to 31, 2005					
Date	Transaction	Quantity (Pairs)	Cost per Pair	Price per Pair	Total
2005					
Jan. 1	Beginning inventory	25	$60		$ 1,500
3	Purchase	100	70		7,000
8	Sale	80		$125	10,000
10	Purchase	100	80		8,000
14	Sale	105		130	13,650
20	Purchase	100	90		9,000
28	Sale	75		133	9,975

To illustrate the different methods of accounting for inventory, the purchase and sales transactions presented in Illustration 8.2 for Shoe Warehouse will be used. Shoe Warehouse sells Psyche Air-X brand basketball shoes to the public. It opened in the month of January 2005 with 25 pairs of shoes in beginning inventory, each with a cost of $60, and subsequently made three purchases and three sales.

The following sections will discuss the four methods of accounting for inventory listed below using a perpetual system (inventory records to be maintained on a continuous basis).

- Specific identification method
- Average-cost method
- First-in, first-out method
- Last-in, first-out method

SPECIFIC IDENTIFICATION

specific identification method a method of accounting for inventory based on the assumption that each inventory item bought and sold can be matched with its actual cost

The **specific identification method** of accounting for inventory is based on the assumption that each inventory item bought and sold can be matched with its actual cost. With this approach, the Inventory account reflects the physical flow of goods. When an inventory item is sold, its actual cost is used to increase Cost of Sales and decrease Inventory. Ideally, this will result in an inventory amount that exactly matches the true cost of the inventory on hand. The specific identification method is ideal for a company that has low sales volume and can easily track its goods, such as a jeweler or an art gallery. However, for most companies, the specific identification method is not practical.

AVERAGE COST

average-cost method a method of accounting for inventory based on the assumption that the cost of an inventory item is the average of the costs of all goods available for sale at that point in time

The **average-cost method** of accounting for inventory assumes that the cost of an inventory item is the average of the costs of all goods available for sale at that point in time. The average-cost inventory method is well suited to companies that carry homogeneous inventory items, such as grocery stores and office supply stores. This method decreases the potential for income manipulation because units are assigned an average cost rather than a specific cost. Under the perpetual inventory system, the average-cost method requires that a new average cost be calculated after each purchase. A new average cost is determined by (1) summing the cost of the previous inventory balance and the cost of the new purchase and (2) dividing this total by the number of units on hand. This average cost is applied to all the units sold until the next purchase is made.

To illustrate, Shoe Warehouse would record the following series of journal entries for the inventory purchases and sales reflected in Illustration 8.2. The company records the first purchase of inventory as follows:

Jan. 3	Inventory	7,000	
	Cash		7,000

Before the next sale is made, a new average unit cost should be determined by making the following calculation:

Beginning inventory cost (25 pairs × $60) $1,500
January 3 purchase (100 pairs × $70)   7,000
$8,500 ÷ 125 = $68

Next, the January 8 sale of shoes is recorded using the new average cost per unit:

Jan. 8	Cash	10,000	
	Sales		10,000
	Cost of Sales (80 pairs × $68)	5,440	
	Inventory		5,440

After the first purchase and sale, Shoe Warehouse has 45 pairs of shoes in inventory that cost $68 per pair on average, for a total cost of $3,060. On January 10, the company records the following journal entry for the purchase of new inventory:

Jan. 10	Inventory (100 pairs × $80)	8,000	
	Cash		8,000

A new average cost is again computed:

Previous inventory cost (45 pairs × $68) $ 3,060
January 10 purchase (100 pairs × $80)   8,000
$11,060 ÷ 145 = $76.28

The sale on January 14 is recorded as follows, using the new average unit cost:

Jan. 14	Cash	13,650	
	Sales		13,650
	Cost of Sales (105 pairs × $76.28)	8,009	
	Inventory		8,009

The balance of inventory is now 40 pairs at $76.28, or $3,051. Next, Shoe Warehouse purchases inventory items and records this entry:

Jan. 20	Inventory (100 pairs × $90)	9,000	
	Cash		9,000

After the purchase, a new average cost is again computed:

Previous inventory cost (40 pairs × $76.28) $ 3,051
January 20 purchase (100 pairs × $90)   9,000
$12,051 ÷ 140 = $86.08

Now the company records the sale of shoes on January 28 as follows:

Jan. 28	Cash	9,975	
	Sales		9,975
	Cost of sales (75 pairs × $86.08)	6,456	
	Inventory		6,456

Illustration 8.3

Average-Cost Method of Costing Inventory

Date	Purchases	Sales	Cost of Sales	Inventory Balance
2005 Jan. 1	Beginning balance			$25 \times \$60 = \underline{\$\ 1,500.00}$
Jan. 3	100 pairs $\times$ $70			$25 \times \$60 = \$\ 1,500.00$ $100 \times \$70 = \underline{\ 7,000.00}$
Updated average cost per unit = $8,500 ÷ 125 = $68.00				$\underline{\$\ 8,500.00}$
Jan. 8		80 pairs $\times$ $125 = $10,000	$80 \times \$68 = \$5,440$	$45 \times \$68 = \underline{\$\ 3,060.00}$
Jan. 10	100 pairs $\times$ $80			$45 \times \$68 = \$\ 3,060.00$ $100 \times \$80 = \underline{\ 8,000.00}$
Updated average cost per unit = $11,060 ÷ 145 = $76.28				$\underline{\$11,060.00}$
Jan. 14		105 pairs $\times$ $130 = $13,650	$105 \times \$76.28 = \$8,009$	$40 \times \$76.28 = \underline{\$\ 3,051.00}$
Jan. 20	100 pairs $\times$ $90			$40 \times \$76.28 = \$\ 3,051.00$ $100 \times \$90 = \underline{\ 9,000.00}$
Updated average cost per unit = $12,051 ÷ 140 = $86.08				$\underline{\$12,051.00}$
Jan. 28		75 pairs $\times$ $133 = $9,975	$75 \times \$86.08 = \$6,456$	$65 \times \$86.08 = \underline{\$\ 5,595.00}$

After the final purchase and sale for the month are recorded, Shoe Warehouse's ending inventory consists of 65 pairs of shoes, each at an average cost of $86.08, for a total of $5,595.

Shoe Warehouse's cost of inventory for the month of January under the average-cost method is summarized in Illustration 8.3. Shoe Warehouse sold 260 pairs of shoes, and its cost of sales was $19,905. Gross profit for January is $13,720 (sales of $33,625 less cost of sales of $19,905).

FIRST-IN, FIRST-OUT (FIFO)

first-in, first-out (FIFO) method
a method of costing inventories based on the assumption that the first inventory item to come into the business is the first item sold to the customer

The **first-in, first-out (FIFO) method** of accounting for inventory is based on the assumption that the first inventory item to come into a business is the first item sold to the customer. As a result, inventory is carried at more current costs and cost of sales consists of older costs. With a perpetual inventory system, the Inventory and Cost of Sales accounts are updated after each purchase and sale.

When FIFO is used to calculate the cost of sales, it is assumed that the shoes that are in inventory at the beginning of a period are the first sold. Again, refer to the sales and purchases in Illustration 8.2 for Shoe Warehouse. The following entry is made to record the first purchase of inventory on January 3:

Jan. 3	Inventory	7,000	
	Cash		7,000

For the January 8 sale, all 25 pairs of shoes in the beginning inventory are assumed to be sold first. In addition, 55 pairs from the January 3 purchase are assumed sold. To record the sale on January 8, the first 25 shoes are computed at $60 a pair, while $70 a pair is used for the next 55 pairs:

Jan. 8	Cash	10,000	
	Sales		10,000
	Cost of Sales [80 pairs: (25 × $60) +		
	(55 × $70)]	5,350	
	Inventory		5,350

After the first purchase and sale, Shoe Warehouse has 45 pairs of shoes in inventory that cost $70 per pair, for a total cost of $3,150. Next, the company records the purchase of 100 pairs of shoes on January 10:

Jan. 10	Inventory (100 pairs × $80)	8,000	
	Cash		8,000

To determine the cost of sales for the January 14 sale, it is assumed that the remaining 45 pairs from the January 3 purchase are sold. In addition, 60 pairs from the January 10 purchase are assumed sold. On January 14, the sale of 105 pairs is recorded as follows:

Jan. 14	Cash	13,650	
	Sales		13,650
	Cost of Sales [105 pairs: (45 pairs ×		
	$70) + (60 pairs × $80)]	7,950	
	Inventory		7,950

After the January 14 sale, inventory consists of 40 pairs of shoes that cost $80 per pair. The company records the purchase of inventory on January 20 and the sale on January 28 as follows, keeping in mind that the first units into the store are assumed to be the first units sold to customers:

Jan. 20	Inventory (100 pairs × $90)	9,000	
	Cash		9,000
28	Cash	9,975	
	Sales		9,975
	Cost of Sales [75 pairs: (40 pairs × $80)		
	+ (35 pairs × $90)]	6,350	
	Inventory		6,350

After the final purchase and sale for the month are recorded, Shoe Warehouse's ending inventory consists of 65 pairs of shoes costing $90 per pair, which results in a total of $5,850. In January, Shoe Warehouse sold 260 pairs of shoes; under the FIFO method, the company's cost of sales was $19,650, and its gross profit was $13,975. For a summarization of the FIFO method of costing inventory at Shoe Warehouse, refer to Illustration 8.4.

FIFO assumes that the first goods to come into a business are the first goods sold to customers. This results in ending inventory being valued at the most recent purchase prices. This is why analysts consider the FIFO value of inventory to be more consistent with the current replacement cost. However, because FIFO allocates the earliest purchases to the cost of sales, gross profit will be larger than it would be using current inventory costs. This occurs because although sales revenue is shown at current amounts, the cost of sales may include older and less costly inventory amounts, which exaggerates actual gross profit.

Illustration 8.4

FIFO Method of Costing Inventory

Date	Purchases	Sales	Cost of Sales	Inventory Balance
2005 Jan. 1	Beginning balance			25 × $60 = $ 1,500.00
Jan. 3	100 pairs × $70			25 × $60 = $ 1,500.00
				100 × $70 = 7,000.00
				$ 8,500.00
Jan. 8		80 pairs × $125 = $10,000	25 × $60 = $1,500	
			55 × $70 = $3,850	45 × $70 = $ 3,150.00
				$ 3,150.00
Jan. 10	100 pairs × $80			45 × $70 = $ 3,150.00
				100 × $80 = 8,000.00
				$11,150.00
Jan. 14		105 pairs × $130 = $13,650	45 × $70 = $3,150	
			60 × $80 = $4,800	40 × $80 = $ 3,200.00
				$ 3,200.00
Jan. 20	100 pairs × $90			40 × $80 = $ 3,200.00
				100 × $90 = 9,000.00
				$12,200.00
Jan. 28		75 pairs × $133 = $9,975	40 × $80 = $3,200	
			35 × $90 = $3,150	65 × $90 = $ 5,850.00
				$ 5,850.00

LAST-IN, FIRST-OUT (LIFO)

last-in, first-out (LIFO) method
a method of costing inventories based on the assumption that the last inventory item to come into the business is the first item sold to the customer

The **last-in, first-out (LIFO) method** of accounting for inventory assumes that the last inventory item to come into a business is the first item sold to the customer. As a result, cost of sales consists of more recent costs and inventory is valued at older costs. With a perpetual inventory system, the Inventory and Cost of Sales accounts are updated after each purchase and sale.

The following series of journal entries records the sales and purchases listed in Illustration 8.2 for Shoe Warehouse using the LIFO method of accounting for inventory. When the cost of sales is calculated under LIFO, it is assumed that the most recently purchased shoes are the first pairs sold. The purchase of inventory on January 3 and the sale on January 8 are recorded as follows:

Jan. 3	Inventory (100 pairs × $70)	7,000	
	Cash		7,000
Jan. 8	Cash	10,000	
	Sales		10,000
	Cost of Sales (80 pairs × $70)	5,600	
	Inventory		5,600

The 80 pairs of shoes that were sold on January 8 would be assumed to have come from the most recently purchased inventory. After that sale, the Shoe Warehouse has 45 pairs of shoes left in inventory. It has the 25 pairs from beginning inventory that cost $60 per pair and 20 pairs from its January 3 purchase that cost $70 per pair, for a total cost of $2,900. Next, the purchase of January 10 and the sale of January 14 are recorded as follows:

Jan. 10	Inventory (100 pairs × $80)	8,000	
	Cash		8,000
14	Cash	13,650	
	Sales		13,650
	Cost of Sales [105 pairs: (100 pairs × $80)		
	+ (5 pairs × $70)]	8,350	
	Inventory		8,350

After the January 14 sale, inventory consists of the 25 pairs of shoes from beginning inventory, valued at $60 per pair, and 15 pairs of shoes with a cost of $70 per pair. Next, the transactions of January 20 and 28 are recorded:

Jan. 20	Inventory (100 pairs × $90)	9,000	
	Cash		9,000
28	Cash	9,975	
	Sales		9,975
	Cost of Sales (75 pairs × $90)	6,750	
	Inventory		6,750

After the month's final purchase and sale are recorded, Shoe Warehouse's ending inventory consists of 65 pairs of shoes: 25 pairs at a cost of $60, 15 pairs at a cost of $70, and 25 pairs at a cost of $90, for a total of $4,800. For the month of January, Shoe Warehouse sold 260 pairs of shoes, and under the LIFO method, the company's cost of sales was $20,700 and its gross profit was $12,925. The LIFO method of costing inventory at the Shoe Warehouse is summarized in Illustration 8.5.

It is important to remember that LIFO is an assumption about cost flow, not physical flow. A company may have very old costs in its Inventory account, but that does not mean that its actual goods are old or out-of-date.

Because LIFO assumes that the last goods to come into a business are the first goods sold to customers, inventory will be understated relative to its replacement cost in times of rising prices. For example, if Shoe Warehouse wanted to replace the 65 pairs of shoes that it has in inventory at the end of January, it would most likely have to pay the most recent purchase price of $90 per pair, or $5,850, even though the shoes are valued at $4,800 on the company's January balance sheet. The $1,050 difference is a result of assuming that more recent purchases have been sold and that inventory consists of older and less expensive goods.

Under LIFO, the value of inventory does not reflect current cost, but the cost of sales is more current. Because LIFO assumes that the last goods to come into a business are the first goods sold to customers, the more recent purchases are reflected in the cost of sales.

COMPARISON OF COST OF SALES AND GROSS PROFIT UNDER LIFO AND FIFO

Because LIFO and FIFO are the most widely used inventory methods, it is important to understand their effects on financial statements. As noted earlier, the LIFO and

Illustration 8.5

LIFO Method of Costing Inventory

Date	Purchases	Sales	Cost of Sales	Inventory Balance
2005 Jan. 1	Beginning balance			25 × $60 = $ 1,500.00
Jan. 3	100 pairs × $70			25 × $60 = $ 1,500.00 100 × $70 = 7,000.00 $ 8,500.00
Jan. 8		80 pairs × $125 = $10,000	80 × $70 = $5,600	25 × $60 = $ 1,500.00 20 × $70 = 1,400.00 $ 2,900.00
Jan. 10	100 pairs × $80			25 × $60 = $ 1,500.00 20 × $70 = 1,400.00 100 × $80 = 8,000.00 $10,900.00
Jan. 14		105 pairs × $130 = $13,650	100 × $80 = $8,000 5 × $70 = $350	25 × $60 = $ 1,500.00 15 × $70 = 1,050.00 $ 2,550.00
Jan. 20	100 pairs × $90			25 × $60 = $ 1,500.00 15 × $70 = 1,050.00 100 × $90 = 9,000.00 $11,550.00
Jan. 28		75 pairs × $133 = $9,975	75 × $90 = $6,750	25 × $60 = $ 1,500.00 15 × $70 = 1,050.00 25 × $90 = 2,250.00 $ 4,800.00

Illustration 8.6

A Comparison of the Effects of Using LIFO Versus FIFO in the Financial Statements in Times of Rising Costs

Financial Statement	LIFO	FIFO
Balance Sheet		
Inventory	Lower	Higher
Statement of Cash Flows		
Cash flows from operations	Higher	Lower
Income Statement		
Cost of sales	Higher	Lower
Gross profit	Lower	Higher
Income tax expense	Lower	Higher
Net income	Lower	Higher

Illustration 8.7

Advantages and Disadvantages of the LIFO and FIFO Methods

LIFO		FIFO	
Advantages	*Disadvantages*	*Advantages*	*Disadvantages*
	Weaker correlation between inventory amount on balance sheet and current replacement cost	Stronger correlation between inventory amount on balance sheet and current replacement cost	
Closer match between earnings and current-cost income			Overstated earnings in comparison to current-cost income when prices are rising
Lower pretax earnings, which leads to lower tax payments			Higher pretax earnings, which leads to higher tax payments
	Lower reported net income for external financial reports	Higher reported net income for external financial reports	
	More complex record keeping	Easier record keeping	
	Risk of LIFO liquidation, which can lead to lost tax advantages and a larger than usual tax payment	No risk of LIFO liquidation	

FIFO inventory methods result in different ending inventory values and costs of sales during periods of changing prices. During inflationary periods, inventory values will be lower under LIFO than under FIFO. Because LIFO results in a lower inventory value, it also yields a higher cost of sales and a lower gross profit. Ultimately, a lower gross profit leads to a lower net income.

Given that the use of LIFO results in lower net income in times of rising prices, it is important to consider why any company would use that method. The answer is taxation. When a company reports lower income, it pays less taxes and has more after-tax cash. Consequently, the Internal Revenue Service requires that any company that uses LIFO for tax purposes also use LIFO for external financial reporting. However, those companies are allowed to report what inventory and net income would have been under an alternative inventory method in the notes to the financial statements.

The effects of the LIFO and FIFO methods on the financial statements when purchase costs are rising are summarized in Illustration 8.6, and the advantages and disadvantages of the two methods are summarized in Illustration 8.7.

CHECK YOUR UNDERSTANDING

1. List the four basic cost-flow assumptions used to account for inventories.

2. Which inventory method is based on the assumption that each inventory item bought and sold can be matched with its actual cost?

3. Which inventory method results in more recent costs of sales and older costs in inventory?

4. If a company seeks to lower its externally reported net income, would the use of FIFO or LIFO help to accomplish this goal? Why?

Choosing an Inventory Method

Managers must consider a number of factors when deciding which inventory cost-flow assumption to utilize. Some of the issues that may go into the managers' decision process are as follows:

- *What cost-flow assumption will be used for tax purposes?* The IRS requires firms that adopt LIFO for tax purposes to also use LIFO for financial reporting. LIFO companies may, however, report non-LIFO supplemental information in the footnotes.

- *Which cost-flow assumption will result in the most cash flow?* In times of rising prices, LIFO results in lower income and lower tax payments, which means that the company will have more cash left after paying taxes.

- *What cost-flow assumptions are the competitors using?* The choice of inventory method greatly affects a firm's financial results and ratios, so companies may want to choose methods equivalent to those of their competitors to make comparison easier.

- *Which cost-flow assumption is easiest to implement?* The LIFO method requires a large amount of additional record keeping compared to the other methods.

LO4 Discuss special issues related to using the LIFO inventory costing method.

Critical Thinking: *With regard to inventory valuation, why do you think LIFO results in more record keeping than other methods?*

Special LIFO Issues

The use of the LIFO inventory method causes older, less current values to be reported as inventory amounts, causing distortions in the financial statements. These distortions often call for reporting adjustments. LIFO can also be costly to employ, since it requires tracking each unit of inventory as it is purchased and sold. Companies may employ different inventory techniques to minimize these disadvantages of the traditional LIFO method.

THE LIFO RESERVE

LIFO reserve the difference between the value of inventory reported under LIFO and what the value would have been if the inventory had been reported at current cost

LIFO effect the change in a company's LIFO reserve from one period to another; this allows users of financial statements to estimate how the employment of LIFO affects cost of sales and earnings

Some companies use LIFO for tax and external reporting purposes, but base their internal decisions on the current cost of inventory. To make the comparison between LIFO and current cost, companies calculate a **LIFO reserve**, the difference between the value of inventory reported under LIFO and what the value would have been if the inventory had been reported at current cost. This LIFO reserve must be disclosed in the notes to the financial statements.

The **LIFO effect**, which is the change in the LIFO reserve from one period to another, enables users of financial statements to estimate how a company's employment of LIFO affects its cost of sales and its earnings. To adjust the LIFO cost of sales to a FIFO basis, the change in the LIFO reserve is subtracted from the LIFO cost of sales. If the LIFO reserve has increased over the accounting period, the cost of sales on a FIFO basis will be lower than the cost of sales on a LIFO basis. A lower cost of sales would result in an increase in pretax earnings.

Figure 8.2 presents the inventory note from **Tiffany and Co.**'s 2004 annual report. In both 2004 and 2003, the value of Tiffany's inventory as reported under LIFO was lower than the current cost. In addition, the LIFO reserve increased by $10,452,000 during the period, which would have resulted in higher income if the FIFO method had been used.

LIFO LIQUIDATION

Because inventory amounts under LIFO can consist of costs that are lower than current replacement costs, if inventory continues to grow period after period, the discrep-

Figure 8.2

Inventory Note

> ### *Tiffany*
> LIFO-based inventories at January 31, 2004 and 2003 represented 69% and 73% of inventories, net, with the current cost exceeding the LIFO inventory value by $30,587,000 and $20,135,000. The LIFO valuation method had the effect of decreasing earnings per diluted share by $0.05 for the year ended January 31, 2004, had no effect on earnings per diluted share for the year ended January 31, 2003 and had the effect of decreasing earnings per diluted share by $0.01 for the year ended January 31, 2002.

LIFO liquidation a situation that arises under the LIFO method if a period's ending inventory is lower than its beginning inventory; because older, less costly inventory has been sold, the cost of sales does not reflect current costs and gross profit is inflated

ancy between the LIFO value of the inventory and its replacement cost will also continue to grow. If a period's ending inventory is ever lower than its beginning inventory, it is assumed that older, less costly inventory has been sold. This is known as **LIFO liquidation**. The effect of a LIFO liquidation is that the cost of sales does not reflect current costs and gross profit is inflated. This leads to higher earnings, which is the opposite of the intended effect of the LIFO method.

For example, recall that under the LIFO method, Shoe Warehouse's inventory at the end of January consists of 65 pairs of shoes: 25 pairs valued at $60 per pair, 15 valued at $70 per pair, and 25 valued at $90 per pair. Assume that Shoe Warehouse purchases 25 more pairs at $100 per pair on February 3 and then sells all 90 pairs on February 7 at $135 per pair. The cost of sales for the period is computed as follows:

$$
\begin{array}{rcl}
25 \text{ pairs} \times \$60 &=& \$1,500 \\
15 \text{ pairs} \times \$70 &=& 1,050 \\
25 \text{ pairs} \times \$90 &=& 2,250 \\
25 \text{ pairs} \times \$100 &=& \underline{2,500} \\
&& \underline{\$7,300}
\end{array}
$$

Gross profit for the period would be computed as follows:

$$
\begin{array}{lcl}
\text{Sales (90 pairs} \times \$135) &=& \$12,150 \\
\text{Cost of sales} &=& \underline{7,300} \\
\text{Gross profit} &=& \underline{\$\ 4,850}
\end{array}
$$

The gross profit percentage for the period is $4,850 \div \$12,150 = 40\%$.

The question that needs to be examined is whether the 40 percent gross profit is consistent with current costs and selling prices. The company is currently paying $100 for each new inventory item and selling it for $135, which results in a 26 percent gross profit ($35/$135). However, because inventory decreased from 90 pairs to zero during the period, LIFO assumes that earlier purchases were sold. As a result, older costs are being matched with current sales prices, and gross profit is increased. If we examine the gross profit for each pair of shoes sold, we see that the gross profit percentage for old inventory items is much higher than that using current costs:

Inventory	Cost	Sales Price	Gross Profit	Gross Profit Percentage
25 pairs	$ 60	$135	$75	56%
15 pairs	70	135	65	48
25 pairs	90	135	45	33
25 pairs	100	135	35	26

When inventory levels decrease, older costs get associated with the cost of sales, resulting in a higher than normal gross profit per inventory item.

Figure 8.3

Earnings Announcement and LIFO Liquidations

Lancaster

Lancaster Colony Corporation (Nasdaq: LANC) today reported net earnings for its fiscal year ended June 30, 2002, reached $91,940,000 or $2.49 per basic and diluted share compared to $89,238,000, or $2.37 per basic and diluted share in the prior year. Net sales totaled $1,130,000,000, up three percent from sales of $1,093,000,000 in fiscal 2001.

Fiscal 2002 earnings also includes income of approximately $2 million after taxes from the **liquidation** of certain **LIFO** inventories carried at prior years' lower costs, while fiscal 2001 results include an after-tax charge of approximately $1 million for the cumulative effect of an accounting change.

For the fourth fiscal quarter ended June 30, 2002, net income reached a record high of $25,369,000, up 26 percent from $20,066,000 earned in the corresponding quarter a year ago. Included in the quarter's earnings was income of approximately $1.8 million after taxes, equivalent to approximately five cents per share, related to the **liquidation** of certain **LIFO** inventories carried at prior years' lower costs. Benefiting from the company's share repurchases, basic and diluted earnings per share reached 69 cents, an increase of 28 percent compared to 54 cents basic and diluted in the fourth quarter of fiscal 2001. Net sales reached a record fourth quarter high of $282 million, an increase of 11 percent above the $254 million reported in the fourth quarter last year.

To illustrate how companies present discussions of LIFO liquidations, refer to Figure 8.3. **Lancaster Colony Corporation** is a specialty foods manufacturer that uses LIFO.

INVENTORY POOLS

To reduce the problem of LIFO liquidation, companies employ a number of inventory techniques that make LIFO easier and less prone to LIFO liquidation. For example, most companies do not maintain inventory records for each inventory item. Instead, they track their entire inventory as a whole or break their inventory into pools of like items. For example, a sporting goods store may use four pools when accounting for its inventory: athletic shoes, athletic equipment, athletic apparel, and miscellaneous inventory.

The use of inventory pools lessens the danger of LIFO liquidation because a reduction in one inventory item within the pool is likely to be offset by an increase in another item within the pool. In addition, the discontinuation of a specific product or its replacement by a new version or model will not result in a LIFO liquidation. In the next section of the chapter, we discuss a variation of the standard LIFO method in which inventory is tracked in terms of dollars rather than physical objects.

DOLLAR-VALUE LIFO

dollar-value LIFO a method of accounting for inventory that is based on the assumption that inventory is a quantity of value rather than a quantity of physical goods; thus increases and decreases in inventory are measured in dollar amounts rather than in numbers of objects

The use of dollar-value LIFO can help companies avoid some of the problems associated with traditional LIFO. The **dollar-value LIFO** method of accounting for inventory is based on the assumption that inventory is a quantity of value rather than a quantity of physical goods. As a result, increases and decreases in inventory are measured in dollar amounts rather than in numbers of items. Dollar-value LIFO enables companies to include a broader range of goods in a single inventory pool. For example, a sporting goods company may group all athletic shoes, athletic equipment, and athletic apparel in one pool. When a greater variety of inventory items is included in a pool, there is less chance that a decline in one item will cause the entire pool to decline. In addition, dollar-value LIFO overcomes issues related to physical quantity by treating the inventory as a pool of dollars. The use of dollar-value LIFO enables accountants to manage the entire inventory valuation instead of worrying about units and product mix. For example, assume that Equipo Company has the categories of inventory shown below:

Item	Units (Pairs)	Unit Cost	Total Cost
High-priced basketball shoes	100	$100	$10,000
Medium-priced basketball shoes	500	50	25,000
Total inventory	600		$35,000

Under the traditional LIFO method, if the company decided to stop selling high-priced basketball shoes and carry only medium-priced brands, as the high-priced shoes were sold, that category of inventory would undergo a LIFO liquidation. However, under dollar-value LIFO, as long as the company maintained a shoe inventory with a value of at least $35,000, no LIFO liquidation would take place.

To avoid a LIFO liquidation, an equivalent dollar value of inventory in real dollars, or net of inflation, must be maintained. The equivalent amount is determined by applying a price index to each year's inventory value to determine whether inventory has increased or decreased in real dollars. To determine whether prices have changed, a company can use a general economic index such as the Consumer Price Index, published by the U.S. government; use a more specific industry index; or create its own price index. Most industries track how inflation is specifically affecting their operations and make that information available.

To see why it is important to address price changes, assume that a company begins the year with $100 of inventory, consisting of 10 units costing $10 per unit, and ends the year with $160 of inventory. Without information about what has happened to the cost per unit, it is impossible to tell whether the inventory quantity has increased. If the cost per unit has remained $10, inventory has increased to 16 units. If the cost per unit has increased to $20, inventory has decreased to 8 units.

To see how dollar-value LIFO works, assume that on January 1, 2004, when Komanda Company decides to start using dollar-value LIFO, it has beginning inventory of $35,000. When a company starts using dollar-value LIFO, the beginning inventory of that period is called the **base-year inventory**, and the base-year inventory price index is 100 percent. If the price index increases, prices are increasing, and if the price index decreases, prices are decreasing.

base-year inventory the beginning inventory of the period in which a company starts using dollar-value LIFO

If Komanda Company has an ending inventory of $42,000 at the end of 2004, the first question that needs to be addressed is whether inventory has increased or decreased in real dollars. Prices in Komanda's industry have increased from the base year, so that the industry price index is now 107 percent. To determine if Komanda's inventory has increased in real terms, the ending inventory amount is divided by the industry price index:

$$\frac{\text{Ending Inventory}}{\text{Price Index}} = \frac{\$42,000}{107\%} = \$39,252$$

Because the resulting number is higher than Komanda's base-year inventory, the company's inventory has actually increased by $4,252 during the year, and the increase is due to a growth in inventory rather than to price increases.

The next issue to be addressed is how much Komanda paid for the additional inventory it acquired during the period. Again the price index is used to adjust the new inventory to current-year dollars. This is accomplished by grouping inventory into layers, with the base year as the first layer and each year's increase in prices as a subsequent layer. The period's price index is used to determine the price increase, and that amount is added to the beginning inventory to arrive at the period's dollar-value LIFO ending inventory.

	Value in Base-Year Dollars (Used for Internal Purposes)	Price Index for the Period	Balance Sheet Value (Used for External Reporting)
Layer 1: Base-year inventory at January 1, 2004	$35,000	100%	$35,000
Layer 2: Inventory increase for 2004 in terms of price index	4,252	107	4,550
Dollar-value LIFO inventory at December 31, 2004	$39,252		$39,550

Komanda would report a balance sheet inventory amount of $39,550 at December 31, 2004.

At the end of 2005, Komanda Company has an inventory balance of $48,000, and because prices have increased during the period, the price index is now 125 percent. In terms of base-year prices, the inventory would have a value of $38,400:

$$\frac{\text{Ending Inventory}}{\text{Price Index}} = \frac{\$48,000}{125\%} = \$38,400$$

Given that inventory at the end of 2004 was valued at $39,252 in base-year dollars, the value of inventory at the end of 2005, when considered in terms of base-year dollars, has decreased. No inventory was added during 2005, so the price index in effect for the period would not be considered when valuing the ending inventory.

	Value in Base-Year Dollars (Used for Internal Purposes)	Price Index for the Period	Balance Sheet Value (Used for External Reporting)
Layer 1: Base-year inventory at January 1, 2004	$35,000	100%	$35,000
Layer 2: Inventory increase for 2004 in terms of price index	3,400	107	3,638
Layer 3: Inventory increase for 2005 in terms of price index	0	125	0
Dollar-value LIFO inventory at December 31, 2005	$38,400		$38,638

Note that for consistency with the last-in, first-out assumption, the most recently added layer of inventory, layer 2, is adjusted to show the 2005 decrease in value.

At the end of 2006, Komanda Company has an inventory balance of $55,000, and prices have again increased, so that the price index is now 130 percent. In terms of base-year prices, the company's inventory would have a value of $42,308:

$$\frac{\text{Ending Inventory}}{\text{Price Index}} = \frac{\$55,000}{130\%} = \$42,308$$

Komanda Company's inventory has increased from the previous year, when the ending inventory value was $38,400 in base-year dollars. The $3,908 of inventory added in 2006 is multiplied by the 2006 price index of 130 percent when determining the ending inventory value.

	Value in Base-Year Dollars (Used for Internal Purposes)	Price Index for the Period	Balance Sheet Value (Used for External Reporting)
Layer 1: Base-year inventory at January 1, 2004	$35,000	100%	$35,000
Layer 2: Inventory increase for 2004 in terms of price index	3,400	107	3,638
Layer 3: Inventory increase for 2005 in terms of price index	0	125	0
Layer 4: Inventory increase for 2006 in terms of price index	3,908	130	5,080
Dollar-value LIFO inventory at December 31, 2006	$42,308		$43,718

The changes in inventory values result from the price increases that occurred each year and from applying each price increase only to the goods added to inventory during that year. The use of the dollar-value LIFO method yields an inventory value that is consistent with the LIFO assumption; however, it decreases the probability of a LIFO liquidation.

INTERNATIONAL

Accounting for inventory has long been a stumbling block in the effort to have international standards converge with GAAP standards. As part of its project to improve standards, the IASB has called for the elimination of the LIFO inventory method, with the only inventory option being FIFO. The IASB suggested the elimination of the LIFO method for two reasons:

1. Elimination of alternative methods

2. A belief that LIFO does not present a reliable representation of physical inventory flows

The IASB's decision to eliminate LIFO could lead U.S. standard setters to also decide to eliminate LIFO in order to reduce differences with international principles, or the decision could lead to more divergence between U.S. and international accounting standards.

In 2002, the European Union ruled that the consolidated financial statements of all companies with public shares listed on European markets must follow International Accounting Standards. This rule covers more than 7,000 companies. While the United States has not yet agreed to accept international standards, representatives from the United States are working with the IASB to help determine areas in which standards could be made consistent.

LO5 Use the gross profit method to estimate inventory cost.

Estimating Inventory

At times, a firm must estimate inventory totals: at interim dates, for example, or for a specific event, such as a merger. If it uses the perpetual inventory system, its Inventory account will contain an up-to-date total, but if it uses the periodic system, a current value for inventory will need to be estimated. One accepted method of estimating inventory cost is the **gross profit method**, which makes use of the traditional cost of sales formula. Remember that cost of sales can be stated as follows:

gross profit method a method of estimating inventory cost that makes use of the traditional cost of sales formula

Critical Thinking: *Why do you think it is important for a company to be able to assign a value to its inventory at any point in time during the fiscal year?*

Beginning Inventory
+ Purchases
_____
Cost of Goods Available for Sale
− Ending Inventory
_____
Cost of Sales
_____

The formula can be rearranged as follows to solve for ending inventory:

Beginning Inventory
+ Purchases
_____
Cost of Goods Available for Sale
− Cost of Sales
_____
Ending Inventory
_____

To calculate ending inventory, an estimate of the cost of sales must be obtained. Cost of sales can be estimated by examining a company's sales and its cost ratio. The **cost ratio**, which is the cost of an inventory item divided by its sales price, can be computed from a past income statement. For example, Nordstrom's income statement reveals that it had the following cost ratios (dollars are in millions):

cost ratio the cost of an inventory item divided by its sale price

	2004	2003
Cost of sales	$4,559	$4,216
Sales	$7,131	$6,449
Cost ratio	63.9%	65.4%

Knowing its cost ratio allows a firm to calculate its cost of sales and ending inventory at any point in time using beginning inventory, purchases, and sales for the period.

Assume that in the first quarter of 2005, Costello Corporation had beginning inventory of $3,425,000 and purchased an additional $16,875,000 of inventory during the period. In addition, Costello reported sales of $21,450,000 for the first quarter and has a cost ratio of 68 percent. Given this information, Costello's ending first-quarter inventory can be estimated using the following formula:

Beginning Inventory	$ 3,425,000
Purchases	16,875,000
Cost of Goods Available for Sale	$20,300,000
Estimated Cost of Sales ($21,450,000 × 68%)	(14,586,000)
Ending Inventory	$ 5,714,000

Even when companies are able to estimate their inventories, the SEC still requires that a physical count of inventory take place at least once a year.

CHECK YOUR UNDERSTANDING

1. How is the cost ratio computed?

2. How can the cost of sales formula be rearranged to solve for ending inventory?

LO6 Describe the impact of inventory errors on the financial statements.

Inventory Errors

Companies normally take a physical count of inventory at the end of each year to ensure that the recorded inventory amount is correct. However, errors can still enter into an inventory system, and these errors can create problems throughout the financial statements. This is because when an error occurs in the Inventory account, it creates errors not only in the current period's financial statements, but also in the next period's financial statements. These errors can occur whether a company is using a periodic or a perpetual inventory system.

To illustrate the effect of inventory errors, assume that a company miscounts its physical inventory at year end and believes that it has $25,000 of inventory rather than its real inventory of $27,000 (a $2,000 understatement). While this obviously creates an error in the balance sheet, it also creates an error in the income statement. Assume that the company reports the following information:

	Reported Amounts		Correct Amounts		Effect of Error
Sales		$105,000		$105,000	
Cost of sales:					
Beginning inventory	$25,000		$25,000		
Add purchases	60,000		60,000		
Cost of goods available for sale	$85,000		$85,000		
Less ending inventory	(25,000)		(27,000)		$2,000 understatement
Cost of sales		60,000		58,000	$2,000 overstatement
Gross profit		$ 45,000		$ 47,000	$2,000 understatement
Other expenses		(25,000)		(25,000)	
Income before income taxes		$ 20,000		$ 22,000	$2,000 understatement
Income tax expense (35%)		(7,000)		(7,700)	$2,000 × tax rate understatement
Net income		$ 13,000		$ 14,300	$2,000 × (1 - tax rate) understatement

If the company uses a periodic inventory system, the error would result in the company's calculating its cost of sales incorrectly because the incorrect ending inventory

Illustration 8.8

Counterbalancing of Inventory Errors over Two Years

	2005 INCOME STATEMENT			2006 INCOME STATEMENT		
	Reported Amounts	Correct Amounts	Effect of Error	Reported Amounts	Correct Amounts	Effect of Error
Sales	$105,000	$105,000		$125,000	$125,000	
Cost of sales						
Beginning inventory	$25,000	$25,000		$25,000	$27,000	$2,000 understatement
Add purchases	60,000	60,000		73,000	73,000	
Cost of goods available for sale	$85,000	$85,000		$98,000	$100,000	
Less ending inventory	(25,000)	(27,000)	$2,000 understatement	(32,000)	(32,000)	Correct
Cost of sales	60,000	58,000	$2,000 overstatement	66,000	68,000	$2,000 understatement
Gross profit	$ 45,000	$ 47,000	$2,000 understatement	$ 59,000	$ 57,000	$2,000 overstatement
Other expenses	(25,000)	(25,000)		(30,000)	(30,000)	
Income before income taxes	$ 20,000	$ 22,000	$2,000 understatement	$ 29,000	$ 27,000	$2,000 overstatement
Income tax expense (35%)	(7,000)	(7,700)	$2,000 × tax rate understatement	(10,150)	(9,450)	$2,000 × tax rate overstatement
Net income	$ 13,000	$ 14,300	$2,000 × (1 − tax rate) understatement	$ 18,850	$ 17,550	$2,000 × (1 − tax rate) overstatement

Net income for two periods as reported $31,850

Correct net income for two periods $31,850

amount would be subtracted when calculating the cost of sales. The error in ending inventory creates an error throughout the balance of the income statement. However, it is important to recognize that the $2,000 understatement does not create a $2,000 understatement in final net income because of income taxes. Assuming a tax rate of 35 percent and that the income tax has not been paid as of year end, the balance sheet would be misstated as follows:

Assets	**= Liabilities**	**+ Stockholders' Equity**
$2,000	= $2,000 × tax rate = $700	$2,000 × (1 − tax rate) = $1,300
Understated	Understated	Understated

Errors in inventory are counterbalanced when the previous period's ending inventory becomes the beginning inventory of the next period. This counterbalancing occurs because, while errors in ending inventory create errors in the same direction in net income, errors in beginning inventory cause opposite-direction errors in net income. As you can see in Illustration 8.8, the $2,000 understatement of ending inventory in 2005 would result in an understated net income in this period. In addition, 2006's beginning inventory would also be understated by $2,000, which would cause 2006's net income to be overstated. Assuming that there are no other errors in the income statement, total net income over the two periods would be correct. Net income as reported with misstated inventory amounts for the two years is $31,850, as is net income when the correct inventory amounts are used.

CHECK YOUR UNDERSTANDING

1. If a company miscounts ending inventory in a physical count and overestimates its inventory, what impact does this have on the current year's income before income taxes?

2. If a company understates ending inventory in 2005 and that inventory balance is carried forward to 2006 as beginning inventory, how is 2006 net income affected?

LO7 Explain why inventory may be valued at the lower of cost or market and apply that approach to inventory valuation.

lower-of-cost-or-market (LCM) rule the requirement that when the replacement cost of inventory falls below the original cost, the inventory must be written down to the lower value and a loss must be recorded

The Lower-of-Cost-or-Market Rule for Valuing Inventory

The first note to the financial statements usually provides information about the accounting procedures used for inventory. For example, Figure 8.4 presents the first note to the 2003 financial statements for **3M Corporation**.

As you can see, 3M Corporation states inventories at the lower of cost or market. Under the **lower-of-cost-or-market (LCM) rule**, when the market value of inventory falls below the original cost, the inventory must be written down to the lower value and a loss must be recorded. In this case, *market* is the cost to replace the inventory, either

Figure 8.4

Significant Accounting Policies

3M   **Excerpt from 2003 3M Corporation Annual Report**

NOTE 1   SIGNIFICANT ACCOUNTING POLICIES

INVENTORIES: Inventories are stated at lower of cost or market, with cost generally determined on a first-in, first-out basis.

Illustration 8.9

Inventory Valuation: Lower of Cost or Market

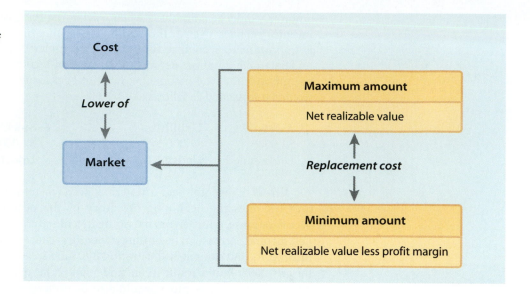

Critical Thinking: *If you were asked to assign a value to your personal assets, how might you determine this total value?*

by purchase or by reproduction. It refers to the market in which the inventory was purchased, not the market in which it is sold. The LCM rule reflects a conservative approach to accounting in that it requires inventory to be valued in a way that is least likely to overstate a firm's net income and financial position. It is similar to the allowance adjustment that ensures that accounts receivable are stated at net realizable value.

The biggest challenge in applying the lower-of-cost-or-market rule is determining the inventory's designated market value. Normally, the designated market value of an inventory item is its replacement cost, but sometimes that value needs to be adjusted.

For example, assume that Rockwood Co. purchases inventory at a cost of $100. This inventory sells for $125, yielding a 20 percent gross profit. If, at the end of the accounting period, the replacement cost of the inventory is $100 or more, the inventory will be recorded at its cost—in this case, $100.

However, a different approach is required when the value of inventory declines. A decline in value may occur because of new technologies or because of greater efficiency on the part of manufacturers. For instance, assume that at the end of the accounting period, the inventory's replacement cost has fallen to $80. Under the LCM rule, in most cases, the inventory would be recorded at its replacement cost because that cost would reflect the inventory's reduction in value. In order to decrease the inventory's value to its replacement cost, a loss must be recognized.

Sometimes a reduction in the replacement cost does not indicate a reduction in the inventory's utility. A maximum and minimum value limitation must then be considered. *Accounting Research Bulletin No. 43* designates the following criteria:

net realizable value of inventory the estimated selling price of inventory in the ordinary course of business less normal selling costs; the maximum possible market value of inventory when applying the lower-of-cost-or-market rule

net realizable value less profit margin the estimated selling price of inventory during the ordinary course of business less normal selling costs and a normal profit margin; the minimum possible market value of inventory when applying the lower-of-cost-or-market rule

The inventory's current replacement cost should not exceed the **net realizable value of inventory**, which is the estimated selling price of the inventory in the normal course of business less selling costs. It should not be less than the **net realizable value less profit margin**, or the estimated selling price of the inventory during the ordinary course of business less normal selling costs and a normal profit margin.

The relationship of these inventory values is shown in Illustration 8.9.

Returning to the Rockwood Co. example, assume that the inventory's replacement cost has decreased to $80 and that, in addition, its selling price less normal selling costs (net realizable value) has decreased from $125 to $105. Normally, the company requires a 25 percent gross profit margin on each sale, which would result in a net realizable value less profit margin of $78.75 [$105 − ($105 × 25%)]. The maximum amount that the designated market value could be is $105, which is net realizable

Illustration 8.10

Determining Final Values of Individual Inventory Items

Inventory Item	Inventory Cost	Replacement Cost	Net Realizable Value	Net Realizable Value Less Profit Margin	Designated Market Value	Inventory Loss
			Blue Corporal Company			
Personal digital assistants	$ 150	$ 85	$ 110	$100	$ 100	$50
MP3 players	70	80	120	75	80	None
Notebook computers	900	950	1,025	925	950	None
Personal computers	450	450	440	400	440	$10
Total inventory	$1,570				$1,570	0

value. Because the replacement cost of $80 falls between the maximum and minimum amounts, it is used as the designated market value when applying the lower-of-cost-or-market rule. Given that the inventory's designated market value is below its cost, the inventory must be reduced to its designated market value by recording a loss:

Loss Due to Market Value Decline of Inventory	20	
Inventory (or Inventory Allowance)		20

If replacement cost is above the maximum market value, net realizable value is treated as the designated market value when applying the lower-of-cost-or-market rule. If replacement cost is below the minimum market value, net realizable value less normal profit margin is treated as the designated market value when applying the lower-of-cost-or-market rule.

The maximum and minimum values ensure that the lower-of-cost-or-market rule is applied fairly across inventory by ensuring that losses are not taken in periods when, for instance, replacement cost declines without an equivalent decrease in selling price. For example, if the replacement cost of our sample inventory item decreases to $80 but the company can still sell the item for $125, the inventory has not suffered a decrease in utility and no loss would be recognized.

To better understand maximum and minimum market values, consider the case of Blue Corporal Company, a computer retailer that has a number of different computer items in its inventory at the end of the accounting period. For each item, Blue Corporal calculates the designated market value and compares it to the item's original cost to determine the lower of cost or market and see if there is an inventory loss. The final inventory values for Blue Corporal are shown in Illustration 8.10.

Note that the replacement cost for personal digital assistants is below the minimum possible market value (net realizable value less profit margin), so the designated market value must be the minimum value of $100. The company must report a loss of $50 on the personal digital assistants, which is equal to the item's cost of $150 less the designated market value of $100.

In contrast, the inventory costs for MP3 players typify the way businesses normally operate. The inventory cost for MP3 players is below the designated market value, so there is no need to record a loss.

The inventory of personal computers illustrates yet another possibility that may arise. The inventory cost of the personal computers is equal to the replacement cost. However, the net realizable value of $440 must be used as the designated market value, which results in a loss of $10.

The lower-of-cost-or-market rule ensures that losses on inventory are recognized in the period in which economic value was lost, not in the period in which the inventory is ultimately sold. The LCM adjustment is made at the end of the accounting period and prevents inventory from being overstated on the balance sheet.

A firm may apply the LCM rule to individual inventory items, categories of inventory, or the entire inventory. Applying the LCM rule to individual inventory items, as in the preceding example, is the most conservative approach because it does not allow losses on one inventory item to be offset by gains on other inventory items. For example, if Blue Corporal applied the LCM rule to its entire inventory, it would not have to report a loss, because the total inventory cost is equal to the total inventory's designated market value.

The main advantage of the LCM rule is that it requires a company to record a loss in the period in which the company suffers an economic loss in value, not in the period in which the company finally decides to sell the inventory item. In addition, the rule ensures that a company's inventory value is not overstated. However, these advantages may be outweighed by some of the problems created by the LCM rule. For example, the LCM rule creates an inconsistency in both the balance sheet and the income statement. For the balance sheet, the LCM rule will result in inventory's being carried at cost in some periods and being carried at market value in some periods. For the income statement, the LCM rule requires that a decrease in the value of inventory be recorded as a loss but does not require that an increase in value be recorded as a gain.

> **CHECK YOUR UNDERSTANDING**
>
> 1. What is the lower-of-cost-or-market rule?
>
> 2. When determining replacement costs for inventories, what maximum and minimum amounts must be considered?
>
> 3. When are losses on inventory value recorded?

LO8 Analyze inventory levels using financial ratios and other metrics.

ANALYSIS

HE *Critical Thinking: How do you think the analysis of inventory amounts might provide information regarding a company's efficiency?*

Analyzing Inventory

The analysis of inventory plays an important role in the assessment of a company's future prospects. As discussed earlier, a change in the amount of inventory can provide valuable information about future sales. However, without taking a deeper look at inventory, an analyst might reach the wrong conclusions. For example, an increase in inventory might mean either that managers expect future sales to grow or that past sales have been poor. To get a clearer picture of what is happening at a company, it is necessary to evaluate the efficiency and productivity of inventory. The inventory measurements that are most commonly examined are the inventory turnover ratio, days in inventory, and inventory yield.

INVENTORY TURNOVER RATIO AND DAYS IN INVENTORY

inventory turnover ratio a measure of how quickly inventory flows through a business and of management's effectiveness in controlling inventory; cost of sales divided by average inventory

The **inventory turnover ratio** is a measure of how quickly inventory flows through a business and of management efficiency. The higher this ratio is, the more effectively management is controlling inventory. The formulas for the inventory turnover ratio and days in inventory are as follows:

$$\text{Inventory Turnover Ratio} = \frac{\text{Cost of Sales}}{\text{Average Inventory}}$$

where

$$\text{Average Inventory} = \frac{\text{Beg. Inventory} + \text{End. Inventory}}{2}$$

days in inventory the average number of days that a company holds inventory before selling it; 365 divided by the inventory turnover ratio

The inventory turnover ratio can be converted into **days in inventory** to get a more intuitive measure of inventory velocity. That ratio indicates how many days, on average, a company holds inventory before selling it. The calculation to convert the inventory turnover ratio into days in inventory is as follows:

$$\text{Days in Inventory} = \frac{365}{\text{Inventory Turnover Ratio}}$$

To calculate the inventory turnover ratio for Nordstrom, use the following financial data. The company reported cost of sales of $4,559 million for the 2004 fiscal year. In addition, Nordstrom had the following account balances:

	2004	2003
	(in millions)	
Inventory	917	902

Average inventory for Nordstrom is calculated as follows:

$$\frac{\$917 + \$902}{2} = \$909.50$$

The inventory turnover ratio for Nordstrom would be:

$$\frac{\$4,559}{\$909.50} = 5.01$$

This results in a days in inventory of 73 days for Nordstrom ($365 \div 5.01 = 73$).

When comparing firms in terms of inventory turnover and days in inventory, it is important to make sure that all the firms being compared are using the same inventory costing method. In periods of rising inventory costs, companies that use LIFO will tend to have higher inventory turnover ratios and lower days in inventory than comparable firms that use FIFO. This occurs because LIFO allocates older purchases to inventory, whereas FIFO allocates more recent purchases to inventory.

INVENTORY YIELD

inventory yield a measure of the return on dollars invested in inventory, or the profitability of inventory; gross profit divided by average inventory

Another ratio, **inventory yield**, measures the return on dollars invested in inventory, or the profitability of inventory. The goal for a manager is to increase gross profits without increasing inventories. This is accomplished through successful inventory management. Inventory yield is calculated as follows:

$$\text{Inventory Yield} = \frac{\text{Gross Profit}}{\text{Average Inventory}}$$

Nordstrom reported $2,572 of gross profit in 2004 and had an average inventory of $909.50 million. This would result in an inventory yield of 2.83:

Illustration 8.11

Inventory Turnover and Inventory Yield

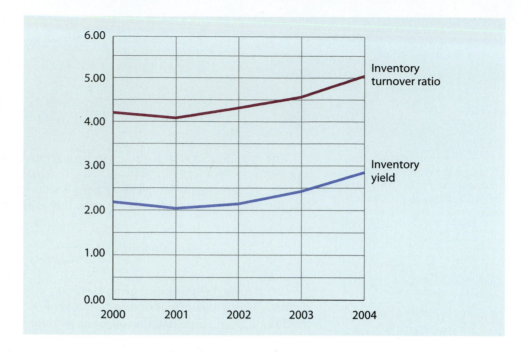

$$\text{Inventory Yield} = \frac{\$2,572}{\$909.50} = 2.83$$

Illustration 8.11 tracks the inventory turnover ratio and inventory yield for Nordstrom from 2000 to 2004. By implementing a perpetual inventory system and refocusing on inventory levels and product mix, the company was able to maintain inventory levels even though sales were increasing by almost 30 percent from 2000 to 2004.

CHECK YOUR UNDERSTANDING

1. What ratio(s) measure how quickly inventory flows through a business?

2. When comparing the inventory turnover ratio and days in inventory between companies, is it important that all companies use the same inventory costing method? Explain your answer.

3. If Atlas Manufacturing reported a gross profit of $490,000 in 2005 and an average inventory of $260,000 for that year, what is the company's inventory yield? Explain what this ratio measures.

Revisiting the Case

IMPROVED INVENTORY SYSTEM PAYS OFF FOR NORDSTROM

1. 2004: Inventory made up 35.6 percent of Nordstrom's current assets; 2003: inventory made up 35 percent of Nordstrom's current assets.

2. The challenge for all companies is to determine the optimal mix of products that will provide the greatest number of sales at the highest gross margins. Companies do not want to lose sales because they are out of stock; nor do they want to bear the cost of carrying excessive amounts of inventory that may end up not being sold.

3. Financial analysts want to examine if inventory is being sold quickly, so that the company does not have to resort to markdowns and sales to move inventory. However, analysts also want to ensure that a company has enough inventory in stock so that the company is not losing sales.

SUMMARY BY LEARNING OBJECTIVE

LO1 Describe the purchasing and sales cycles and their effects on the financial statements.

The purchasing cycle begins when a company decides to purchase an inventory item. To initiate the purchase, the company creates a purchase order and transmits it to the vendor. Depending on the order's shipping terms, the purchase will be entered into the accounting system either when the goods are shipped or when they are received. At that time, assets are increased by the amount of the new inventory and either assets are decreased (if cash is paid) or liabilities are increased (if an account payable is created). When the company remits payment to the vendor, the purchasing cycle is complete. The sales cycle begins when a customer purchases an inventory item and the company records a sale. The sale of inventory has two effects on the financial statements. First, either the Cash or the Accounts Receivable account must be increased by the amount of the sale, and the Sales account must be increased by the same amount. Second, the cost of the sale must be recorded and inventory must be reduced. The sales cycle is complete when the customer pays for the purchase. The net effect of a sales transaction is that assets increase by the excess of the sales price over the cost of purchasing inventory. Sales revenues and expenses also increase, which ultimately will increase retained earnings by the same amount as assets.

LO2 Explain the differences between the perpetual inventory system and the periodic inventory system.

Under the perpetual inventory system, the Inventory account is adjusted each time inventory is purchased or sold. Ideally, under the perpetual system, the Inventory account reflects the true value of inventory at any point in time. However, as a result of such factors as spoilage, breakage, and theft, the actual value of inventory may differ from the balance in the Inventory account. Consequently, a company must make a physical count of its inventory each year and adjust its Inventory account accordingly. Under the periodic inventory system, the Inventory account is adjusted only at the end of each accounting period. At that time, a physical count (or estimate) of the ending inventory is made. Although both systems are acceptable, the perpetual system allows managers more control over inventory and provides more information about inventory at any point in time.

LO3 Demonstrate the use of four methods of calculating inventory cost: specific identification; average cost; first-in, first-out; and last-in, first-out.

When deciding how to value its inventory, a company must select one of several common cost-flow assumptions. The choice is crucial because applying the different assumptions to the same purchase and sales data can result in dramatically different costs of sales and inventory amounts. The specific identification method is based on the assumption that each inventory item bought and sold can be matched with its actual cost. When an inventory item is sold, its actual cost is used to increase cost of sales and decrease inventory.

The average-cost method assumes that the cost of an inventory item is the average of the costs of all goods available for sale at that point in time. Under the perpetual inventory system, the average-cost method requires that a new average cost be calculated after each purchase. The first-in, first-out (FIFO) method is based on the assumption that the first inventory item to come into a business is the first item sold to the customer. Under FIFO, inventory is carried at more current costs and the cost of sales consists of older costs. Consequently, in times of rising prices, the FIFO value of inventory is more consistent with the current replacement cost. However, because FIFO allocates the earliest purchases to the cost of sales, gross profit will be larger than current inventory costs and sales would suggest. The last-in, first-out (LIFO) method assumes that the last inventory item to come into a business is the first item sold to the customer. Under LIFO, the cost of sales consists of more recent costs and inventory is valued at older costs. Consequently, when prices are increasing, the costlier purchases are reflected in the cost of sales.

LO4 Discuss special issues related to using the LIFO inventory costing method.

Because the LIFO inventory costing method values reported on the balance sheet may be lower than current costs, companies that use LIFO are required to provide additional information. That information, called the LIFO reserve, is the difference between the value of inventory reported under LIFO and what the value would have been if the inventory had been reported at current cost. The LIFO effect, which is the change in the LIFO reserve from one period to another, enables users of financial statements to estimate how a company's employment of LIFO affects its cost of sales and its earnings. A LIFO liquidation occurs if a period's ending inventory is lower than its beginning inventory. The effect of a LIFO liquidation is that the cost of sales does not reflect current costs and gross profit is inflated. This leads to higher earnings, which is the opposite of the intended effect of the LIFO method.

The use of dollar-value LIFO can help companies avoid some of the problems associated with traditional LIFO. Because the dollar-value LIFO method is based on the assumption that inventory is a quantity of value rather than a quantity of physical goods, changes in inventory are measured in dollar amounts rather than in numbers of objects. Dollar-value LIFO enables companies to include a broader range of goods in a single inventory pool, which decreases the possibility that a decline in one item will cause the entire pool to decline. In addition, the use of dollar-value LIFO enables accountants to manage the entire inventory valuation instead of worrying about units and product mix.

LO5 Use the gross profit method to estimate inventory cost.

The gross profit method enables companies to estimate inventory totals at interim dates or for a specific event, such as a merger. Under this method, ending inventory is determined by rearranging the traditional cost of sales formula as follows:

$$
\begin{aligned}
&\quad \text{Beginning Inventory} \\
+\ &\underline{\text{Purchases}} \\
&\quad \text{Cost of Goods Available for Sale} \\
-\ &\underline{\text{Cost of Sales}} \\
&\quad \underline{\underline{\text{Ending Inventory}}}
\end{aligned}
$$

Cost of sales can be estimated by examining a company's sales and its cost ratio. The cost ratio, which is the cost of an inventory item divided by its sales price, can be computed from a past income statement.

LO6 Describe the impact of inventory errors on the financial statements.

When an error occurs in the Inventory account, it creates errors not only in the current period's financial statements, but also in the next period's financial statements. These errors can occur whether a company is using a periodic or a perpetual inventory system. An understatement of ending inventory leads to an understatement of current-period net income. Conversely, an overstatement of ending inventory leads to an overstatement of current-period net income. Errors in inventory are counterbalanced when the previous period's ending inventory becomes the beginning inventory of the next period. This counterbalancing occurs because, while errors in ending inventory create errors in the same direction in net income, errors in beginning inventory cause opposite-direction errors in net income.

LO7 Explain why inventory may be valued at the lower of cost or market and apply that approach to inventory valuation.

Under the lower-of-cost-or-market (LCM) rule, when the market value of inventory falls below the original cost, the inventory must be written down to the lower value and a loss must be recorded. Normally, the designated market value of an inventory item is its replacement cost. However, a different approach is required when the value of inventory declines. Determination of the designated market value must consider two amounts in addition to the replacement cost—net realizable value (the maximum amount) and net realizable value less profit margin (the minimum amount). Then all three amounts—replacement cost, net realizable value, and net realizable value less profit margin—are considered, and the middle of the three amounts is compared to cost. The lower-of-cost-or-market rule ensures that losses on inventory are recognized in the period in which economic value was lost, not in the period in which the inventory is ultimately sold. The LCM adjustment is made at the end of the accounting period and prevents inventory from being overstated on the balance sheet.

LO8 Analyze inventory levels using financial ratios and other metrics.

The inventory turnover ratio is a measure of how quickly inventory flows through a business and of management efficiency. The higher this ratio is, the more effectively management is controlling inventory. The inventory turnover ratio can be converted into days in inventory to get a more intuitive measure of inventory velocity. That ratio indicates how many days, on average, a company holds inventory before selling it. Another ratio, inventory yield, measures the return on dollars invested in inventory, or the profitability of inventory. The goal for a manager is to increase gross profits without increasing inventories.

KEY TERMS

average-cost method (p. 354)
base-year inventory (p. 365)
cost of sales (p. 350)
cost ratio (p. 368)
days in inventory (p. 375)
dollar-value LIFO (p. 364)
first-in, first-out (FIFO) method
  (p. 356)
gross profit method (p. 368)
inventory (p. 350)

inventory turnover ratio (p. 374)
inventory yield (p. 375)
last-in, first-out (LIFO) method
  (p. 358)
LIFO effect (p. 362)
LIFO liquidation (p. 363)
LIFO reserve (p. 362)
lower-of-cost-or-market (LCM) rule
  (p. 371)

net realizable value less profit margin
  (p. 372)
net realizable value of inventory
  (p. 372)
periodic inventory system (p. 351)
perpetual inventory system (p. 351)
specific identification method
  (p. 354)

EXERCISES

LO1   **EXERCISE 8-1   Inventory Acquisition Cost**
Kit Barbeque Grills, Inc. determined that the invoice cost of its inventory at year end was $45,340; however, the following items were omitted from the calculation:

A. Cash discounts taken on two purchases totaling $430
B. Sales taxes paid on grills acquired to be resold, $150
C. Freight costs incurred by Kit to ship grills to its own place of business, $120
D. Freight costs incurred by Kit to ship grills to its customers, $450
E. Cost of assembling grills before they are sold to customers, $700
F. Salary of the clerk who ordered the grills from the supplier, $400
G. Cost of insurance during transit to acquire the grills, $20

Required: Determine which costs should be included as part of the cost of inventory and determine the final inventory cost. For each item that you determine is not part of inventory cost, indicate why not.

LO8   **EXERCISE 8-2   Analysis of Inventory**
Twine Mart has experienced fluctuations in income over the last two years. The gross profit percentage has increased from 24 percent in 2004 to 30 percent in 2005, while total sales have decreased from $200,000 to $170,000. Inventory reported on Twine Mart's balance sheet at the end of 2003, 2004, and 2005 totaled $12,000, $15,000, and $13,500, respectively.

Required:

1. Prepare a partial income statement for Twine Mart for 2004 and 2005 that reflects the amounts to be reported for sales, cost of sales, and gross profit.
2. Calculate the company's inventory turnover ratio for 2004 and 2005.
3. Are these changes favorable or not? Explain.

LO2, 3   **EXERCISE 8-3   Perpetual Inventory System**
Putnam Corporation, a wholesaler of men's clothing, uses the perpetual inventory system. The information on the following page relates to the company's suit inventory during its most recent month of operations, July 2005.

July	1	Beginning inventory	1,100 suits at $175 per suit
	3	Purchase	500 suits at $190 per suit
	7	Sale	300 suits at $260 per suit
	9	Sale	500 suits at $265 per suit
	11	Purchase	900 suits at $195 per suit
	17	Purchase	400 suits at $200 per suit
	24	Sale	700 suits at $255 per suit

Required:

1. Calculate the number of suits that Putnam has in ending inventory at the end of July.

2. Determine Putnam's ending inventory amount assuming that Putnam uses the LIFO method.

3. Determine Putnam's ending inventory amount assuming that Putnam uses the FIFO method.

LO3   **EXERCISE 8-4   Perpetual Inventory System and Gross Profit**

Refer to the information provided in Exercise 8-3.

Required:

1. Calculate Putnam's cost of sales and gross profit for the month of July assuming the company uses the LIFO method.

2. Calculate Putnam's cost of sales and gross profit for the month of July assuming the company uses the FIFO method.

LO3   **EXERCISE 8-5   Perpetual Inventory System**

Vanguard Incorporated uses a perpetual inventory system for tracking its inventory of lawnmowers. The following information relates to the company's inventory during its most recent month of operations, March 2005:

March	1	Beginning inventory	15 lawnmowers at $725 per unit
	2	Purchase	6 lawnmowers at $690 per unit
	5	Purchase	5 lawnmowers at $720 per unit
	7	Sale	12 lawnmowers at $1,260 per unit
	9	Purchase	5 lawnmowers at $765 per unit
	11	Sale	9 lawnmowers at $1,195 per unit
	17	Sale	5 lawnmowers at $1,200 per unit
	24	Purchase	10 lawnmowers at $855 per unit

Required:

1. Calculate the number of lawnmowers that Vanguard has in ending inventory at the end of March.

2. Determine Vanguard's ending inventory amount, cost of sales, and gross profit assuming that Vanguard uses the LIFO method.

3. Determine Vanguard's ending inventory amount, cost of sales, and gross profit assuming that Vanguard uses the FIFO method.

LO3   **EXERCISE 8-6   Average-Cost Method—Perpetual Inventory System**

Mein Zen Corp. provided the following inventory records for January:

Beginning inventory	15 units @ $1 each
January 12 purchase	20 units @ $2 each
January 14 sale	10 units
January 17 purchase	15 units @ $3 each
January 25 sale	30 units

Required: Calculate each of the following:

1. January 31 ending inventory using the perpetual average-cost method.
2. January cost of sales using the perpetual average-cost method.

LO1, 2   EXERCISE 8-7   Periodic Inventory Calculations

Adams, Inc. reported the following amounts from its accounting records for 2004:

Inventory, January 1, 2004	$ 12,400	Purchase Returns	$3,000
Transportation Out	1,000	Purchase Discounts	2,000
Purchases	140,000	Transportation In	6,000
Sales	245,000	Sales Returns	4,000

The physical count at the end of 2004 indicated that the inventory was $11,300.

Required:

1. Is the company using a periodic or a perpetual inventory system? Justify your response.
2. How much is the net cost of purchases?
3. How much is cost of goods available for sale?
4. How much is cost of sales?

LO3   EXERCISE 8-8   Comparison of Inventory Costing Methods

The four inventory costing methods are as follows:

SI—specific identification   AC—average cost
FIFO—first-in, first-out   LIFO—last-in, first-out

Various descriptions associated with the inventory costing methods are given in items A through L.

A. It tends to match current costs with current revenue.
B. It is closest to the physical flow of goods for most companies.
C. Inventory is valued at the oldest unit cost.
D. Inventory and cost of goods sold are valued at the same unit cost.
E. It can be manipulated by the choice of unit costs when items are sold.
F. It minimizes income taxes in periods of rising prices.
G. It causes income taxes to be minimized in periods of declining prices.
H. It is the most literal application of the physical flow of goods for a company.
I. Inventory is valued at the most recent unit cost.
J. It allows the company to have the most positive cash flow in periods of rising prices.
K. It provides the most current valuation on the balance sheet when prices are declining.
L. It tends to match current costs with current revenue.

Required: For each description in items A through L, select the proper inventory costing method, using the codes provided.

LO5   EXERCISE 8-9   Estimating Inventory

A fire destroyed most of the inventory of Office Stop's southside store on February 23, 2004. Inventory of $22,000 that was in transit to the location was the only part of the inventory that was not destroyed. This purchase of inventory had not been recorded at the date of the fire. The accountant kept the accounting records at her office and was able to provide the following information:

Inventory, January 1, 2004	$ 26,000
Purchases, January 1–February 22	530,000
Sales, January 1–February 22	800,000

The gross profit rate in past years has averaged 35 percent.

Required: Determine the amount of inventory lost in the fire. How is this amount reported in the company's financial statements?

LO8   **EXERCISE 8-10   Analysis of Inventory**

Clinton.com had cost of goods sold of $7,600 million in 2005 and $7,700 million in 2004. Its merchandise inventory was $1,866 million at the end of 2005 and $2,100 million at the end of 2004.

Required:

1. How many days did it take Clinton.com to sell its inventory during 2005?
2. What does the inventory turnover ratio measure?
3. Is a high inventory turnover better than a low turnover? Explain.

LO7   **EXERCISE 8-11   Lower of Cost or Market**

Rotunda Company carries three different types of inventory, which are listed here along with other relevant data. Rotunda uses the lower-of-cost-or-market method to value inventory.

Product	Cost	Profit Margin	Replacement Cost	Selling Price	Expected Selling Costs
A	$10	$3	$18	$24	$2
B	36	7	30	39	4
C	11	1	10	13	2

Required: Indicate whether the following statements are correct or incorrect. Provide support for your answers.

1. The minimum amount that the designated market value could be for product A is $19.
2. The designated market value for product C is $10.
3. The maximum amount that the designated market value could be for product B is $35.
4. Under the individual item approach, Product A should be reported on the balance sheet at $20.
5. Under the individual item approach, Product B should be reported on the balance sheet at $35.
6. Under the individual item approach, Product C should be reported on the balance sheet at its floor.

LO1, 2   **EXERCISE 8-12   Purchasing Inventory**

Raspberry Roads, Inc. is preparing its 2004 year-end financial statements. Prior to any adjustments, the general ledger Inventory account showed a cost of $42,000. The company uses a perpetual FIFO inventory method. The following information has been found relating to certain inventory transactions:

A. Goods belonging to a customer that have a cost of $2,000 and a selling price of $2,600 are being held in the warehouse. They were scheduled to be picked up by the customer on December 31; in fact, the customer picked up the goods on January 6. These goods are included in the $42,000 inventory amount at $2,000.

B. Goods costing $1,500 with a selling price of $2,800 were shipped to a customer on December 31, 2004, terms FOB destination. The goods are expected to arrive January 8. The goods have not been included in the $42,000 physical count.

Required: Calculate the proper inventory amount to be reported on Raspberry Roads's balance sheet at December 31, 2004.

LO8   **EXERCISE 8-13   Inventory Analysis**

Several accounts from Glover Corporation's adjusted trial balance are as follows:

	12/31/06	12/31/05
Cash	$ 60,000	$ 19,000
Inventory	32,000	31,000
Accounts Payable	18,000	16,000
Sales	200,000	185,000
Cost of Sales	435,000	424,000

Net income for 2006 amounted to $55,000. Accounts Payable was used for merchandise purchases only.

Required:

1. Calculate the cost of goods available for sale for the year ended December 31, 2006.
2. How much were purchases during 2006?
3. Calculate Glover's inventory turnover ratio for 2006.
4. How many days does it take Glover to sell inventory, on the average, during 2006?

LO6 **EXERCISE 8-14   Inventory Errors**

Charlotte Inc. uses an outside service to physically count its inventory at the end of each fiscal year. Because of a misunderstanding, the inventory team did not count the products in one of Charlotte's off-site warehouses. This resulted in an understatement of the company's actual 2005 ending inventory of $225,000 by $40,000. During 2005, Charlotte recorded sales of $1,450,000 and gross profit of $720,000. At the end of 2004, Charlotte recorded inventory of $175,000.

Required: Assuming that Charlotte recorded its inventory properly in the previous period, what effect will this error have on Charlotte's inventory turnover ratio and inventory yield measure?

LO4 **EXERCISE 8-15   Dollar-Value LIFO**

Barney Corporation adopted the dollar-value LIFO method of inventory valuation on December 31, 2004. Its inventory at that date was $22,000, and the relevant price index was 100 percent. Purchases during 2005 and 2006 totaled $560,000 and $630,000, respectively. Information regarding inventory is as follows:

Date	Inventory at Current Prices	Price Index
December 31, 2005	$25,300	110%
December 31, 2006	23,940	114

Required:

1. Calculate the ending inventory at December 31, 2006, under dollar-value LIFO.
2. If Barney used FIFO, at what amount would its inventory be reported on its December 31, 2005, balance sheet?

LO1,2 **EXERCISE 8-16   Inventory Transactions**

The following are account balances of Crater Corporation for December 31, 2006 and 2005:

	2006	2005
Cash	$ 35,500	$ 12,000
Inventory	17,000	15,000
Accounts Payable	24,000	20,000
Cost of Sales	682,000	640,000

Crater uses a perpetual inventory system. During 2006, $1,000 of purchase discounts were taken. Payment terms are net/30.

Required:

1. Determine how much Crater Corporation's purchases were during 2006.
2. Prepare the journal entries to show the purchase of inventory, assuming that 80 percent are on account, and the payment on account for 2006.

LO5   EXERCISE 8-17   **Estimating Inventory**

The following information was obtained from the accounting records of Raffle Company:

Sales (1/1/06–5/25/06)	$820,000
Inventory (1/1/06)	64,000
Purchases (1/1/06–5/25/06)	620,000
Gross profit percentage	25% of sales

On May 25, 2006, a fire occurred in Raffle Company's warehouse, destroying most of the inventory.

Required:

1. What is the approximate inventory loss as a result of the fire?
2. What is a cost ratio? How is it used in estimating ending inventory?

LO4   EXERCISE 8-18   **LIFO Reserve**

Monkey Zone, Inc. uses the LIFO method to determine inventory. The company bases most of its pricing decisions on the current cost of inventory, however. Provided below is information to determine Monkey Zone's ending inventory using the LIFO method and current cost:

Inventory Method	Ending Inventory—Product A	Ending Inventory—Product B
LIFO	3,000 units @ $3.90 each	1,500 units @ $1.50 each
Current Cost	3,000 units @ $4 each	1,500 units @ $2 each

Required:

1. Determine the LIFO reserve for Monkey Zone, Inc.
2. Explain the LIFO reserve.

LO6   EXERCISE 8-19   **Inventory Errors**

At the end of 2005, Madison Corporation mistakenly counted part of its inventory stored at an offsite warehouse twice. The inventory error resulted in Madison's recording ending inventory at $15,000 instead of the correct amount of $10,000. The company reported net income of $12,000. Madison has a tax rate of 35 percent.

Required: By what amount will Madison's 2005 gross profit and net income be misstated as a result of the error in counting inventory?

LO6   EXERCISE 8-20   **Inventory Errors**

The 2005 ending inventory of Raleigh Corporation is understated as a result of an error in a physical count. Determine how this error will affect the following items in Raleigh's 2005 and 2006 financial statements if it is not found.

Required: For each item, determine whether the amount in the financial statement is overstated or understated.

	2005	2006
Beginning inventory		
Ending inventory	Understated	
Cost of sales		
Gross profit		
Net income		

PROBLEMS

LO4   **PROBLEM 8-1   Dollar-Value LIFO**

At the end of 2004, Peters, Inc. adopted the dollar-value LIFO method, and the end-of-year inventory cost was calculated to be $15,000.

Year	Ending Inventory at Year-End Prices	Price Index
2005	$40,800	120%
2006	49,400	130

Required: Under the dollar-value LIFO method, calculate the value of the inventory at the end of 2006.

Analyze: Did Peters, Inc. incur a LIFO liquidation? Explain.

LO4   **PROBLEM 8-2   Dollar-Value LIFO and LIFO Liquidation**

Rasta Company adopted the dollar-value LIFO inventory method on December 31, 2005. Rasta's entire inventory constitutes a single pool. On December 31, 2005, the inventory was $150,000. Sales for the year amounted to $2,240,000. Inventory data for 2006 are as follows:

December 31, 2006, inventory at year-end prices	$231,000
Relevant price index at year end (base year 2005)	105%
Net purchases during the year	$1,892,000

Required:

1. Using the dollar-value LIFO method, calculate Rasta's inventory at December 31, 2006.
2. Calculate gross profit for the year ended December 31, 2006.

Analyze: What happens to inventory levels when the company experiences a LIFO liquidation? Explain how this might affect the company's profitability for 2006.

LO1, 2   **PROBLEM 8-3   Perpetual Inventory Transactions, Shipping Terms**

On December 31, 2005, Road Ring Company held $32,000 of merchandise inventory. During 2006, $270,000 in merchandise was purchased on account (and received) with credit terms of 1/15, net/45. In addition, Road Ring paid freight charges of $8,000 on inventory purchase deliveries. All discounts were taken (not allowed on freight). Purchases were all made FOB shipping point. In addition to the $270,000 of purchases during the year, there was $13,000 of merchandise in transit from vendors at year end that had not been paid for. Accounts payable decreased by $7,000 during the year from a beginning balance of $38,000 to an ending balance of $31,000. Cost of sales for the year was $280,000. Road Ring uses a perpetual inventory system.

Required:

1. Prepare journal entries for the inventory transactions incurred during 2006.
2. How much is ending inventory at December 31, 2006?

Analyze: What differences would there be if the goods had been shipped FOB destination? Would ending inventory be greater or less if the terms were FOB destination?

LO1, 2, 8   **PROBLEM 8-4   Periodic Inventory Calculations and Turnover**

Macy Gray, Inc. provided the following information:

Inventory (beg. balance)	$ 6,000	Sales	$95,000
Purchases Returns and Allowances	2,000	Transportation In	600
		Sales Returns and Allowances	2,000
Purchases	300,000	Purchase Discounts	140
Inventory (end. balance)	8,000		

Required:

1. How much is cost of sales?

2. What amount is reported on the balance sheet for inventory?

Analyze: Calculate the inventory turnover ratio for the year. Explain what information this provides managers for use in purchasing decisions.

LO3 **PROBLEM 8-5   Inventory Costing—LIFO and FIFO**

Red Tide Company provided the following information concerning sales and purchases of widgets for the month of May 2005:

Transactions	Units	Unit Cost	Total
Beginning inventory, May 1, 2005	10	$2	$ 20
Purchase, May 8	7	3	21
Sale, May 12 (sold at $12 each)	9		108
Purchase, May 19	7	4	28
Sale, May 30 (sold at $12 each)	6		72

Required: Calculate each of the following independent amounts:

1. Number of units available for sale at month end.

2. Amount of cost of sales under the perpetual LIFO method.

3. Amount of ending inventory under the perpetual average-cost method.

Analyze: What is the gross profit for May under the perpetual FIFO method?

LO3 **PROBLEM 8-6   Inventory Costing—LIFO and FIFO**

Gilligan, Inc. uses the perpetual inventory system for its only product, widgets. Gilligan provided the following information concerning sales and purchases for June 2004:

Transactions	Units	Unit Cost	Total
Beginning inventory, June 1, 2004	100	$1	$ 100
Sale, June 3 (sold at $10 each)	80		800
Purchase, June 17	125	3	375
Sale, June 28 (sold at $10 each)	130		1,300

Required:

1. How many units are available for sale?

2. How many units are in ending inventory?

3. Using FIFO, how much is cost of sales for June?

4. Using LIFO, how much is ending inventory to be reported on the balance sheet?

Analyze: What advantages exist for companies that use LIFO in periods of rising prices?

LO2, 3 **PROBLEM 8-7   Inventory Valuation**

Selected accounts and amounts appearing in the ledger of Rasputin Corp. for the year ended December 31, 2004, are listed here. The physical inventory count at that date was $23,000.

Inventory, January 1, 2003	$ 10,200	Purchases	$225,000
Selling and Administrative Expenses	95,600	Transportation In	4,700
Freight Out	12,500	Income Taxes Expense	22,000
Accounts Receivable	32,000	Sales Discounts	17,000
Sales	420,000	Purchase Discounts	4,000
Purchase Allowances	1,800	Sales Returns	7,200

Required:

1. Which inventory system does Rasputin use?

2. Which accounts would not be used if Rasputin used the perpetual inventory system?

3. How much will Rasputin report on its balance sheet for inventory at December 31, 2004?

4. Calculate cost of goods available for sale.

5. Calculate cost of sales.

Analyze: Why is the selection of a costing method important for companies?

LO4 **PROBLEM 8-8** **Inventory Costing Methods**

Cullen Company provided the following information concerning its inventory transactions for the month ending April 30, 2005:

Beginning inventory	8 @ $2	$ 16
April 7 purchase	20 @ $4	80
April 9 sale	25 @ $20	500
April 21 purchase	15 @ $6	90
April 24 sale	11 @ $20	220

Required:

1. Calculate the cost of sales under the perpetual FIFO method.

2. Calculate the ending inventory under the perpetual average-cost method.

3. Calculate the ending inventory under the perpetual LIFO method.

Analyze: Compare the effects on the financial statements of using the LIFO and FIFO methods of inventory costing.

LO2, 3 **PROBLEM 8-9** **Inventory Costing Methods**

Use the following data to answer the questions:

June	1	On hand, 20 units @ $4 each	$ 80
	5	Purchased 60 units @ $5 each	300
	12	Sold 35 units @ $20 each	700
	22	Purchased 70 units @ $6 each	420
	28	Sold 80 @ $20 each	1,600

Required:

1. How many units are in ending inventory at June 30?

2. Calculate cost of sales for June using a perpetual LIFO method.

3. Calculate ending inventory at June 30 using a perpetual FIFO method.

Analyze: Why do you think more companies have moved toward recording purchases and sales on a perpetual basis? What advantages does a perpetual system have?

LO3 **PROBLEM 8-10** **Inventory Costing Methods**

Billings Company uses a perpetual inventory system. The following data were available for the month of January 2005:

Beginning inventory: 10 units @ $2 each		$ 20
January 7: Purchase: 6 units @ $4 each		24
January 23: Purchase: 6 units @ $6 each		36
Sales during the month:		
January 15: 15 units @ $20 each		$300
January 30: 5 units @ $20 each		100

Required:

1. How many units are on hand at the end of January?

2. Calculate the amount of inventory to be reported on the balance sheet at January 31 using FIFO.

3. Calculate cost of sales for January using LIFO.

4. Calculate sales revenue for January.

5. How much is cost of goods available for sale for January?

Analyze: Under LIFO, does the cost of sales consist of more recent costs or older costs? Explain.

LO3 PROBLEM 8-11 **Inventory Costing**

Tripfield Company provided the following information concerning sales and purchases of widgets for the month of May 2005:

Transactions	Units	Unit Cost	Total
Beginning inventory, May 1, 2005	30	$1	$ 30
Purchase, May 6	35	2	70
Sale, May 12 (sold at $20 each)	48		960
Purchase, May 22	40	3	120
Sale, May 30 (sold at $20 each)	34		680

Required:

1. Calculate the number of units that are available for sale.
2. Calculate the number of units in ending inventory on May 31.
3. Calculate the cost of sales under the perpetual FIFO method.
4. Calculate the ending inventory under the perpetual average-cost method.
5. Calculate the ending inventory under the perpetual LIFO method.

Analyze: By what percentage did the inventory value change under the perpetual LIFO method in May?

LO4 PROBLEM 8-12 **Inventory Costing**

Pharisee Company uses a perpetual inventory system. Pharisee provided the following information concerning sales and purchases of widgets for the month of January 2005:

Transactions	Units	Unit Cost	Total
Beginning inventory, January 1, 2005	40	$1.25	$ 50
Purchase, January 4	50	2.00	100
Sale, January 12 (sold at $12 each)	40		480
Purchase, January 19	35	3.00	105
Sale, January 30 (sold at $12 each)	50		600

Required: Calculate each of the following:

1. The number of units available for sale and the number of units in ending inventory on January 31
2. Ending inventory under the LIFO method
3. Cost of sales under the average-cost method
4. Gross profit under the FIFO method

Analyze: Does the perpetual or the periodic inventory system adjust inventory levels in a more timely fashion?

LO5 PROBLEM 8-13 **Estimating Ending Inventory**

On August 21, 2004, Hurricane Curt damaged a warehouse used by Publix Groceries. The entire inventory was completely destroyed. The hurricane loss is both unusual and infrequent. The data below were salvaged:

Purchases, January 1 to August 21	$ 750,000
Gross sales, January 1 to August 21	1,600,000
Gross profit percentage on sales	15%
Inventory, January 1, 2004	936,400

Required:

1. Compute the estimated inventory loss as a result of the hurricane.

2. Show how the loss would be reported on Publix's income statement for the year ended August 31, 2004. Publix has a 30 percent income tax rate. (*Hint:* Recall how to report unusual and infrequent items.)

3. Can a company rely on estimates only for reporting ending inventory?

Analyze: If Publix reported sales of $1,395,000 and cost of sales of $1,268,000 in 2005, what is the company's cost ratio?

LO4   **PROBLEM 8-14   Dollar-Value LIFO**

Weiner Corporation adopted the dollar-value LIFO method of inventory valuation on December 31, 2004. Its inventory at that date was $21,000, and the relevant price index was 100 percent. Purchases during 2005 and 2006 totaled $635,000 and $680,000, respectively. Sales totaled $980,000 for 2005 and $990,000 for 2006. Information regarding inventory for 2005 and 2006 is as follows:

Date	Inventory at Current Prices	Price Index
December 31, 2005	$34,650	105%
December 31, 2006	50,400	112

Required:

1. Did prices rise or fall between 2005 and 2006? Briefly state how you know this.

2. Calculate the ending inventory at December 31, 2005 and 2006, under dollar-value LIFO.

3. Calculate cost of sales for the year ended December 31, 2006.

Analyze: How much would Wiener report as ending inventory at December 31, 2006, if it used the FIFO inventory method? Explain.

LO4   **PROBLEM 8-15   Dollar-Value LIFO**

At the end of 2004, Rand Company adopted the dollar-value LIFO method, and the end-of-year 2004 inventory cost was calculated to be $40,000.

Year	Ending Inventory at End-of-Year Prices	Price Index
2005	$50,600	110%
2006	43,200	120
2007	66,300	130

Required:

1. Under the dollar-value LIFO method, what is the value of the inventory at the end of 2007?

2. Assume the company purchased $950,000 of goods during 2007. Calculate cost of sales for 2007.

Analyze: Why might a company use dollar-value LIFO instead of regular LIFO?

LO7   **PROBLEM 8-16   Lower of Cost or Market**

Randal Company began its operations in early 2004. The normal profit margin is 20 percent of the selling price. Randal uses the lower-of-cost-or-market method to value inventory.

Product	Quantity	Cost	Replacement Cost	Expected Selling Price	Expected Selling Costs
A	10	$12	$11	$18	$3
B	20	22	24	25	4

Required:

1. What are the maximum and minimum designated market values for product A?

2. What is the amount of the designated market value for product B?

3. What is the lower of cost or market for product A?

4. What is the purpose of the lower-of-cost-or-market adjustment?

Analyze: What is the main advantage of the LCM rule?

CASES

LO1, 2, 8

ETHICS

ETHICS CASE 8-1   Inventory Acquisitions with LIFO

The manager of Mickel, Inc., which uses the LIFO method to account for inventory, called its supplier and asked that its inventory delivery scheduled for December 30 be deferred until January. Though the manager did not tell the supplier this, the goal was to report the costs of the older, lower-priced items that remained in inventory as cost of goods sold instead of those of the newer, more expensive inventory items that were on order. The manager was concerned that profit would be lower than usual unless something was done to increase it before the end of the year.

Required:

1. What is the effect of the deferral on income?

2. Why might the manager want to defer the acquisition?

3. Does the deferral violate GAAP?

4. Is the deferral ethical?

LO4   **ANALYSIS CASE 8-2   LIFO Issues**

Portions of the comparative financial statements and the Notes to the Financial Statements from the 2002 annual report of **Sears, Roebuck and Co.** follow.

Sears

SEARS, ROEBUCK AND CO.
Consolidated Statements of Income

millions, except per common share data	2002	2001	2000
REVENUES			
Merchandise sales and services	$35,698	$35,755	$36,277
Credit and financial products revenues	5,668	5,235	4,571
Total revenues	41,366	40,990	40,848
COSTS AND EXPENSES			
Cost of sales, buying and occupancy	25,646	26,234	26,632
Selling and administrative	9,249	8,892	8,807
Provision for uncollectible accounts	2,261	1,866	884
Depreciation and amortization	875	863	839
Interest	1,143	1,415	1,248
Special charges and impairments	111	542	251
Total costs and expenses	39,285	39,812	38,661
Operating income	2,081	1,178	2,187
Other income, net	372	45	36
Income before income taxes, minority interest and cumulative effect of change in accounting principle	2,453	1,223	2,223
Income taxes	858	467	831
Minority interest	11	21	49
Income before cumulative effect of change in accounting principle	1,584	735	1,343
Cumulative effect of a change in accounting for goodwill	(208)	—	—
NET INCOME	$ 1,376	$ 735	$ 1,343

Sears

SEARS, ROEBUCK AND CO.
Excerpt from Consolidated Balance Sheets

millions, except per share data	2002	2001
ASSETS		
Current assets		
Cash and cash equivalents	$ 1,962	$ 1,064
Credit card receivables	32,595	29,321
Less allowance for uncollectible accounts	1,836	1,166
Net credit card receivables	30,759	28,155
Other receivables	863	658
Merchandise inventories	5,115	4,912
Prepaid expenses and deferred charges	535	458
Deferred income taxes	749	858
Total current assets	39,983	36,105
Property and equipment		
Land	442	434
Buildings and improvements	6,930	6,539
Furniture, fixtures and equipment	5,050	5,620
Capitalized leases	557	544
Gross property and equipment	12,979	13,137
Less accumulated depreciation	6,069	6,313
Total property and equipment, net	6,910	6,824
Deferred income taxes	734	415
Goodwill	944	294
Tradenames and other intangible assets	704	—
Other assets	1,134	679
TOTAL ASSETS	$50,409	$44,317

Sears

SEARS, ROEBUCK AND CO.
Partial Consolidated Statements of Cash Flows

millions	2002	2001	2000
CASH FLOWS FROM OPERATING ACTIVITIES			
Net income	$1,376	$ 735	$1,343
Adjustments to reconcile net income to net cash provided by (used in) operating activities			
Depreciation and amortization	875	863	839
Cumulative effect of change in accounting principle	208	—	—
Provision for uncollectible accounts	2,261	1,866	884
Special charges and impairments	111	542	265
Gain on sales of property and investments	(347)	(21)	(19)
Income tax benefit on nonqualified stock options	24	14	3
Change in (net of acquisitions):			
Deferred income taxes	(203)	(190)	62
Retained interest in transferred credit card receivables	—	(759)	106
Credit card receivables	(4,833)	(810)	(199)
Merchandise inventories	45	610	(560)
Other operating assets	(56)	61	8
Other operating liabilities	34	(596)	(47)
Net cash (used in) provided by operating activities	(505)	2,315	2,685

Sears

NOTE 1 - SUMMARY OF SIGNIFICANT ACCOUNTING POLICIES

Merchandise Inventories

Approximately 89% of merchandise inventories are valued at the lower of cost or market, with cost determined using the retail inventory method ("RIM") under the last-in, first-out ("LIFO") cost flow assumption. To estimate the effects of inflation on inventories, the Company utilizes internally developed price indices.

The LIFO adjustment to cost of sales was a charge of $11 million in 2002, a charge of $25 million in 2001 and a credit of $29 million in 2000. If the first-in, first-out ("FIFO") method of inventory valuation had been used instead of the LIFO method, merchandise inventories would have been $602 and $591 million higher at December 28, 2002 and December 29, 2001, respectively.

Assume that Sears uses Accounts Payable for inventory purchases only.

Required:

1. How much of Sears's assets are tied up in inventory as of year end 2002?

2. What method does Sears use to cost its inventory?

3. How much inventory did Sears purchase during 2002?

4. Calculate the amount of the LIFO reserve at the company's year ends 2002 and 2001. Prepare the journal entry that would have been prepared by Sears to recognize the LIFO effect during 2002.

5. How much income would Sears have reported if it had used FIFO instead of LIFO?

6. Why do you think Sears chose LIFO instead of FIFO?

LO8

ANALYSIS

ANALYSIS CASE 8-3   Controlling the Inventory Turnover Ratio

Curt Neilson has worked as the accountant at Cell Technics Company for several years. The company has continually experienced growth in revenue that has required increases in the amount of inventory purchased so that goods would be available for customers. As a result, inventory levels have been increasing over the last few quarters, and cash has been required to pay the related liabilities. Cell Technics began to experience what the bank called an "inventory turnover problem." Keeping liquidity ratios in line to avoid violations of loan agreements is a priority for the company. There have been no substantial changes in other costs, so the only concern is inventory. Selected data from the past four quarters are as follows:

	12/31/04	9/30/04	6/30/04	3/31/04
Cash	$ 59,000	$ 78,000	$ 112,000	$ 134,000
Inventory	260,000	198,000	100,000	40,000
Accounts Payable	320,000	178,000	90,000	11,200
Sales	2,600,000	2,200,000	1,500,000	1,040,000
Cost of Sales	1,300,000	1,100,000	750,000	520,000

Since a violation of a bank agreement would cause the bank to demand repayment of the company's $800,000 loan, Curt Neilson has given you the task of evaluating the current inventory turnover ratio and preparing a proposal to bring the inventory to a quarterly turnover ratio of 7. Inventory at December 31, 2003 was $40,000.

Required: Prepare a short analysis of the company's inventory turnover ratio based on the data provided. Write a short report offering at least two suggestions for things the company can do to increase its inventory turnover ratio.

LO3, 4

ETHICS

ETHICS CASE 8-4   **Inventory Depletion**

Anna Smith is the account manager for Rants Corporation, a wholesaler of popular arts and crafts supplies. The company has been utilizing the LIFO inventory costing method since 1989, the year the company incorporated. Sales and income have increased at an average annual rate of 4 percent during the past eight years. However, for the current year, projections show that even though sales have increased, income will decrease by approximately 2 percent from the prior year. This decrease is caused primarily by an increase in the cost of merchandise and increases in employee benefits expenses. Because of competitive pressures, the company was unable to increase the prices of its merchandise significantly.

The company is planning to expand its business and add a new product line, gift baskets. Financing for this expansion is expected to come from the sale of additional shares of common stock. The president of the company, who has a degree in accounting as well as in finance, fears that a decrease in income will lower the sales price of the stock and thus the proceeds from the common stock sale. He suggests that the company lower its normal inventory levels and defer replenishing its inventory until next year. He expects that this action will allow the company to achieve its annual increase in income. Anna learned about this strategy at a recent staff meeting when the president asked her to emphasize the "efficiency" aspect of lowering inventory levels when she prepares the financial statement disclosures of the inventory depletion. She feels uncomfortable with an income increase that is achieved by depleting inventory.

Required:

1. What are the problems and issues faced by Anna?
2. Who will be affected by the decision she makes?
3. What values and principles are likely to influence her decision?
4. What alternative actions can Anna take?
5. a. Of the parties you listed in question 2, whose interest is most important?
   b. Of the values and principles you listed in question 3, which is most important?
   c. Of the alternatives you listed in question 4, which will do the most good or cause the least harm?
   d. As you review your answers to parts a, b, and c, which consideration is most important?
6. What would you do if you were Anna?

LO5

COMMUNICATION CASE 8-5   **Inventory Estimation**

One of your close friends owns a golf store that has just been robbed of its inventory of golf clubs and accessories. Your friend knows that you are taking an accounting course and asks your help in estimating the theft loss and writing a report for the insurance company. After speaking with your friend, you find that he has not yet taken a physical inventory and has only the following data available for you to estimate inventory:

Inventory—Beginning of the period (at cost)	$150,000
Additional purchases during the period (at cost)	310,000
Sales to customers during the period (at sales price)	295,000
Sales returns during the period (at sales price)	15,000

In addition, your friend states that the golf store has been selling golf inventory at approximately 25 percent of sales.

Required: To help your friend submit his insurance claim, prepare an estimate of the inventory loss along with a memo on how you arrived at your estimate. In addition, discuss what assumptions must be made in order to use the gross profit method.

LO7

COMMUNICATION CASE 8-6   **Lower-of-Cost-or-Market Method**

You have just been hired as an assistant controller by an electronics retailer that specializes in computer equipment. The company is finally becoming successful after a period of losses. At the end of the period, during your examination of inventory you discover that the company has a large number of X1000 computers that contain an older technology than the technology used in the X3000 computer. The X1000s cost $900 each, whereas your company is purchasing X3000s for $960 each. You ask the controller about writing down the X1000 inventory to lower of cost or market and are told that it is not necessary because any loss would be recognized when the X1000 computers are finally sold at a discount. In addition, the controller states that because inventory that increases in demand is not written up to its higher market value, it is inconsistent to write down inventory to its lower market value.

Required: Write a memo discussing the proper accounting treatment for the X1000 inventory and its affect on the current period's financial statement. Include in your discussion the reason for the lower-of-cost-or-market method and why the controller might not want to apply it.

LO8   ANALYSIS CASE 8-7   **Inventory Analysis**

Dell and **Gateway** are two of the world's largest sellers of computer and technology products and services. Both companies design, develop, manufacture, and service a wide range of technology products. Whereas both companies sell many of their computers through their websites and call centers, Gateway has opened a number of retail outlets. Selected financial information for the two companies appears below:

Dell, Inc. (in millions)

Fiscal Year Ended	2003	2002	2001
Sales	$41,444	$35,404	$31,168
Cost of Sales	33,892	29,055	25,661
Inventory	327	306	278

Gateway, Inc. (in millions)

Fiscal Year Ended	2003	2002	2001
Sales	$3,402	$4,171	$5,938
Cost of Sales	2,938	3,605	5,100
Inventory	114	89	120

Required:

1. For each company, calculate the inventory turnover ratio and days in inventory for 2003 and 2002.

2. What are the implications of the differences in the inventory ratios?

LO2, 3   FINANCIAL REPORTING CASE 8-8   **Inventory**

At the end of the fiscal year, you are asked to determine the inventory to be reported in Taser Incorporated's December 31, 2005, balance sheet. You are provided with the following information:

Physical inventory on hand (counted 12/31/2005)	$78,450
Goods sold F.O.B. destination (in transit at 12/31/2005, reported at cost)	2,890
Goods sold F.O.B. shipping point (in transit at 12/31/2005, reported at cost)	4,520
Office supplies	975
Goods purchased F.O.B. shipping point (in transit at 12/31/2005, reported at cost)	10,235

Required: Prepare a schedule showing the proper amount of inventory as of the end of the fiscal year end December 31, 2005.

LO2, 3   **RESEARCH CASE 8-9   Inventory Methods**

Caterpillar has been manufacturing construction and mining equipment, diesel and natural gas engines, and industrial gas turbines for more than 75 years. The company is one of the world's largest manufacturers of heavy equipment, with sales of more than $23 billion dollars per year.

Required: Go to the company's website (**http://www.caterpillar.com**), access the investor information area, and answer the following questions about the company:

1. What method does Caterpillar use to account for inventory?
2. As of the most recent balance sheet date, what was the total of Caterpillar's inventory? What made up Caterpillar's inventory?
3. What would Caterpillar's inventory amount have been if it had used the FIFO method to account for inventory?

ON THE WEB

The following exercises, activities, and problems are available on the *Intermediate Accounting* website. Use these resources to reinforce your understanding of the topics presented in this chapter.

- CPA-Adapted Simulations
- Interpreting the Accounting Standards
- Extending the Global Focus
- Extending the Ethics Discussion
- Mastering the Spreadsheet
- Career Snapshots
- Annual Report Project
- ACE Practice Tests
- Flashcards
- Glossary
- Check Figures for Text Problems
- PowerPoint Presentations

SOLUTIONS: CHECK YOUR UNDERSTANDING

The Purchasing and Sales Cycles (p. 351)

1. The purchaser records an increase in inventory when goods are shipped from the vendor.
2. Raw materials, work in process, and finished goods.
3. The sale of an inventory item increases assets by the difference between the sales price and the cost of purchasing the inventory. Also, sales revenue increases and expenses increase.

Recording Inventory (p. 353)

1. Debit Accounts Receivable or Cash; credit Sales. Debit Cost of Sales; credit Inventory.
2. The perpetual system adjusts inventory levels in a more timely fashion, as it updates the accounting records at each purchase and sale.
3. Beginning Inventory + Purchases = Cost of Goods Available for Sale − Ending Inventory = Cost of Sales.

Costing Inventory (p. 361)

1. Specific identification, average cost, FIFO, LIFO.
2. Specific identification.
3. LIFO.
4. LIFO would help during periods of rising prices. This is because the LIFO method associates more recent (and higher priced) inventory costs with cost of sales, which reduces income.

Special LIFO Issues (p. 368)

1. A LIFO reserve is the difference between the value of inventory reported under LIFO and what the value would have been if the inventory had been reported at current cost.
2. A LIFO liquidation occurs if a period's ending inventory is lower than its beginning inventory.
3. The dollar-value LIFO method of accounting for inventory is based on the assumption that inventory is a quantity of value rather than a quantity of physical goods. As a result, increases and decreases in inventory are measured in dollar amounts rather than in numbers of objects.

Estimating Inventory (p. 369)

1. The cost of an inventory item is divided by its sales price.
2. Beginning Inventory + Purchases = Cost of Goods Available for Sale − Cost of Sales = Ending Inventory.

Inventory Errors (p. 371)

1. Overstating inventory leads to an overstatement of income before income taxes in the current year.
2. An inventory understatement in 2005 will lead to a net income overstatement in 2006 if that balance is carried forward from one period to the next.

The Lower-of-Cost-or-Market Rule for Valuing Inventory (p. 374)

1. Under the lower-of-cost-or-market (LCM) rule, when the market value of inventory falls below the original cost, the inventory must be written down to the lower value and a loss must be recorded.

2. The inventory's current replacement cost should not exceed the net realizable value, which is the estimated selling price of the inventory in the normal course of business less selling costs. It should not be less than the net realizable value less profit margin, or the estimated selling price of the inventory during the ordinary course of business less normal selling costs and a normal profit margin.

3. Losses on inventory value are recognized in the period in which economic value is lost, not in the period in which the inventory is ultimately sold.

Analyzing Inventory (p. 376)

1. Inventory turnover ratio and days in inventory.

2. The same inventory costing method should be used so that the assignment of costs is comparable.

3. 1.88. This ratio measures the return on dollars invested in inventory.

CPA-ADAPTED SIMULATION

This simulation asks you to complete various tasks related to a company's annual financial statements. If your instructor has signed up for CPAexcel™, you can do the work online at **www.cpaexcel.com/hmco**. You may also do the simulation manually.

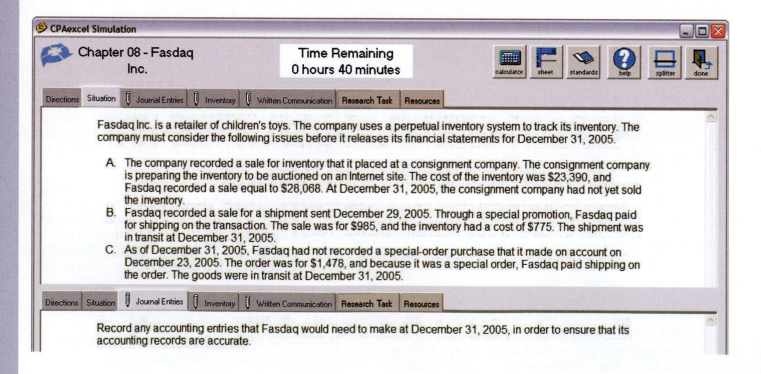

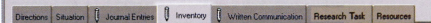

Directions | Situation | Journal Entries | Inventory | Written Communication | Research Task | Resources

For each of the following situations, determine the market value that should be used in carrying out the lower-of-cost-or-market comparison for inventory. In addition, determine if a loss should be recorded for the individual inventory item when applying the lower-of-cost-or-market rule directly to each item.

	Cost	Replacement Cost	Net Realizable Value	Normal Profit Margin	Market Value	Loss on Inventory Item
1. flat panel monitor	$475	$425	$510	$60		
2. PDA-455 personal digital assistant	$233	$260	$295	$40		
3. PF-987 combined fax-printer	$365	$365	$350	$0		
4. LP-355 laptop computer	$980	$1,070	$1,230	$100		
5. X-25 digital camera	$420	$415	$455	$50		
6. MP-67 MP3 player	$155	$130	$150	$15		

Directions | Situation | Journal Entries | Inventory | Written Communication | Research Task | Resources

One of your clients owns a men's clothing store that has been completely destroyed by a fire. Your client asks for your help in estimating the inventory loss and in writing a report for the insurance company. After speaking with your client, you find that she has not yet taken a physical inventory and has only the following data available for your estimation:

Inventory-beginning of the period (at cost)	$ 234,875
Additional purchases during the period (at cost)	1,230,000
Sales to customers during the period (at sales price)	1,238,450
Sales returns during the period (at sales price)	11,895

In addition, your client states that the clothing store has a normal gross profit margin of 25 percent.

To help your client submit her insurance claim, prepare an estimate of the inventory loss using the gross profit method, along with a memo on how you arrived at your estimate. In addition, discuss what assumptions must be made in order to use the gross profit method.

Directions | Situation | Journal Entries | Inventory | Written Communication | Research Task | Resources

The lower of cost or market method could be applied in several different ways. For example, it could be applied to each individual inventory item or to the total inventory as a group of items. What are the accounting guidelines concerning the proper application of the lower of cost or market method for inventory?

Operating Assets: Acquisition, Cost Allocation, Impairment, and Disposal

FINANCIAL REPORTING CASE

LOWE'S EXPANSION REQUIRES COMMITMENT TO NEW OPERATING ASSETS

As the second-largest retailer in the home improvement sector, Lowe's maintains wholesale supply outlets and retail stores that require significant operating assets.

Lowe's What does it take to be the second-largest retailer in the home improvement industry and the fourteenth-largest retailer in the United States? Lowe's Companies has achieved this status by aggressive expansion strategies and a commitment to earning the loyalty of its customers. Serving over 7 million do-it-yourself individual and commercial business customers, the company maintains wholesale supply outlets and retail units that require significant investments in property, including land, buildings, and equipment. Home improvement customers expect to shop in modern, clean, efficient retail outlets backed by extensive warehouse and distribution systems. To meet this need, Lowe's carries on an aggressive growth strategy. In 2004, the company operated 1,087 stores in 48 states and spent approximately $2.9 billion for new operating assets. As you can see from the excerpt from Lowe's consolidated balance sheet at January 28, 2005, the company reported total property, less accumulated depreciation, of over $13.9 billion, an amount that has grown rapidly over the years. In fact, the property category of Lowe's balance sheet represented more than 65 percent of total assets. In most cases, Lowe's finances the purchase of new operating assets with funds from operations and the issuance of debt.

Lowe's

Lowe's Companies
Asset Section of Consolidated Balance Sheets

(*In millions*)	January 28, 2005	% Total	January 30, 2004	% Total
Assets				
Current Assets:				
Cash and Cash Equivalents (Note 1)	$ 642	3.0%	$ 913	4.9%
Short-Term Investments (Note 4)	171	0.8	711	3.8
Accounts Receivable - Net (Notes 1 and 5)	9	—	146	0.8
Merchandise Inventory (Note 1)	5,982	28.2	4,584	24.4
Deferred Income Taxes (Note 15)	95	0.5	62	0.3
Other Assets	75	0.4	106	0.6
Total Current Assets	**6,974**	32.9	**6,522**	34.8
Property, Less Accumulated Depreciation (Notes 6 and 7)	13,911	65.6	11,819	63.0
Long-Term Investments (Note 4)	146	0.7	169	0.9
Other Assets (Note 7)	178	0.8	241	1.3
Total Assets	**$21,209**	100.0%	**$18,751**	100.0%

In Lowe's 2004 annual report, the notes to the financial statements present the following brief description of how the company's assets are recorded and depreciated:

Lowe's

Property and Depreciation Property is recorded at cost. Costs associated with major additions are capitalized and depreciated. Capital assets are expected to yield future benefits and have useful lives which exceed one year. The total cost of a capital asset generally includes all applicable sales taxes, delivery costs, installation costs and other appropriate costs incurred by the Company in the case of self-constructed assets. Upon disposal, the cost of properties and related accumulated depreciation are removed from the accounts with gains and losses reflected in earnings.

Depreciation is provided over the estimated useful lives of the depreciable assets. Assets are depreciated using the straight-line method. Leasehold improvements are depreciated over the shorter of their estimated useful lives or the term of the related lease....

As for any corporation holding many capital assets, the appropriate recording of the purchase of each asset and its depreciation over its estimated useful life has a significant bearing on both the income statement and the balance sheet of the company. As the company continues its expansion strategies, it must fund the purchase of new operating assets while tackling the challenges of a weak economy and price fluctuations in the home improvement market.

EXAMINING THE CASE

1. What net amount of property did Lowe's report at January 28, 2005?
2. How do you think Lowe's accounts for the use and deterioration of its operating assets?
3. As Lowe's opens new stores nationwide, what kinds of operating assets would you expect the company to purchase?
4. How does Lowe's typically fund the purchase of operating assets?
5. What method does Lowe's use to depreciate assets?

LO1 Identify the characteristics of operating assets.

operating assets tangible assets that a company uses to create operational revenue

Critical Thinking: *How do you think operating assets differ from current assets?*

Characteristics and Presentation of Operating Assets

In today's competitive marketplace, businesses like **Lowe's** carry out their growth strategies by investing significant amounts of money in **operating assets**, which are defined as the tangible assets that a company uses to create operational revenue; these assets are also called *property, plant, and equipment (PP&E), tangible assets,* or *long-term plant assets.* Although assets like land, buildings, and equipment are generally included as operating assets on the balance sheet, furniture and fixtures, land improvements, automobiles, natural resources, and construction in progress may also be included if they are purchased to create operational revenue.

CHARACTERISTICS OF OPERATING ASSETS

Companies purchase and maintain a wide variety of assets in the course of their operations, and they are often evaluated by investors on their effective use of these assets. To determine whether an asset should be considered an operating asset, follow these guidelines:

1. *Operating assets include only those assets that are presently being used in operations.* This does not mean that the asset must be continuously used in the firm's actual operations, but it must be management's intent that the asset be used in the normal course of business in producing revenue. Therefore, idle equipment and closed facilities are often categorized as "Other Assets" because they are not contributing to earnings. When an asset like land is not used for operating activities, it should be classified as "Investments," "Inventory," or "Other Assets," depending on management's intent for its future use. For example, many companies would normally categorize land as an operating asset, but a real estate company that buys land and subdivides it for purposes of resale should classify the land as "Inventory."

2. *Operating assets must have a useful life of more than one year.* Readers of financial statements assume that operating assets are long-term assets, purchased to yield revenues over a number of years. The assignment of costs to future periods is accomplished through depreciation charges, which will be discussed later in this chapter. Inventories or supplies should be excluded from the operating asset category and included in the current asset category because of the short-term nature of their use.

3. *Operating assets must have a physical existence.* That is, only tangible assets should be included in the operating assets or property, plant, and equipment category of the balance sheet. Intangible assets, or assets without a physical existence, should be placed in a separate category. (See Chapter 10 for a complete discussion of intangible assets.)

PRESENTATION OF OPERATING ASSETS

Once a company's operating assets have been properly identified, it is important for the company to disclose appropriate information regarding these assets in the financial statements and related notes. The nature and extent of the disclosures of operating assets on the balance sheet vary somewhat by company. *APB Opinion No. 12*[1] states that because of the significant nature of the depreciable assets, the following disclosures should be made in the financial statements or in the related notes:

---

1 "Omnibus Opinion," *Opinions of the Accounting Principles Board No. 12* (New York: AICPA, 1967).

Figure 9.1

Items Included in the Property Category

Lowe's

Lowe's Companies
NOTE 6 - Property and Accumulated Depreciation

Property is summarized by major class in the following table:

(*In millions*)	January 28, 2005	January 30, 2004
Cost:		
Land	$ 4,197	$ 3,635
Buildings	7,007	5,950
Equipment	5,405	4,355
Leasehold Improvements	1,401	1,133
Total Cost	18,010	15,073
Accumulated Depreciation and Amortization	(4,099)	(3,254)
Net Property	**$13,911**	**$11,819**

1. Depreciation expense for the period

2. Balances of major classes of depreciable assets, by nature or function, at the balance sheet date

3. Accumulated depreciation, either by major classes of assets or in total, at the balance sheet date

4. A general description of the method or methods used in computing depreciation with respect to major classes of assets

It is particularly important to note that some companies report property, plant, and equipment as a net amount on the balance sheet, with an accompanying note providing the disclosures required by *APB Opinion No. 12*. For example, the Lowe's balance sheet at January 28, 2005 presented earlier indicated the company had property, plant, and equipment net of accumulated depreciation of $13,911 million. The amount of the property, plant, and equipment net of accumulated depreciation is often referred to as the **book value** of the asset. That is, book value is measured as the original acquisition cost of the asset minus the total amount of accumulated depreciation on the asset since the date of purchase. Figure 9.1 provides the note to Lowe's financial statements with a breakdown of the items included in the property category.

book value the original acquisition cost of an asset minus the total amount of accumulated depreciation on the asset since the date of purchase

CHECK YOUR UNDERSTANDING

1. List items that are generally included in the operating asset category.

2. Describe three identifying characteristics of an operating asset.

3. What disclosures are required for depreciable assets?

LO2 Determine the cost basis for operating assets at acquisition.

acquisition cost all costs necessary to obtain an asset and prepare it for its intended use

capitalization the practice of adding costs to the value of an asset rather than expensing them

Costs at Acquisition

Operating assets are recorded at **acquisition cost**, which is defined as all costs necessary to obtain the asset and prepare it for its intended use. These costs are capitalized and make up the cost basis for that asset. The acquisition cost for an asset is also sometimes referred to as its *historical cost*. The **capitalization** of a cost is the practice of adding the cost to the value of the asset, rather than expensing it.

Critical Thinking: If a business purchases an asset like a building, then pays to have it inspected and refurbished to make it ready for use as a warehouse, how do you think this asset should be valued on the books of the business?

Operating assets are normally reported on the balance sheet at the amount of their acquisition cost minus accumulated depreciation. These amounts are not intended to reflect the fair market values of the assets, since management intends to hold such assets for long periods of time and use them in the productive process. For that reason, the acquisition cost is the most relevant attribute to measure. The acquisition cost of an operating asset is also used in determining the amount of depreciation. Depreciation is the allocation of the cost of an asset over its useful life in a systematic and rational manner. The following discussion outlines the types of costs commonly included in the cost basis of individual operating assets.

LAND

The acquisition cost of land commonly includes the purchase price, the assumption of unpaid taxes on the land, legal fees, surveying fees, costs of clearing and grading the land (preparing it for its intended use), and any special assessments for streets, water, or sewage improvements made by the local government. In order to determine whether a cost should be included as an acquisition cost, ask the following question: Could the land be realistically used without this expenditure (such as water or sewage line improvements)?

If the case can be made that these were necessary costs incurred in order to use the land, they may be capitalized as part of the cost of the land.

LAND IMPROVEMENTS

land improvements improvements made to land that have a limited life

Since land has an unlimited useful life, it is not depreciated. Therefore, any improvements made to land that have a limited life are referred to as **land improvements** and should be treated as separate assets that will be depreciated over their useful lives. Fences and roads on the land would be considered land improvements, since they need to be replaced periodically.

EQUIPMENT

As is the case for all operating assets, the acquisition cost of equipment includes all costs deemed necessary to acquire the asset and prepare it for its intended use. Of course, it is sometimes difficult to determine which costs were "necessary" and directly related to the acquisition decision. The acquisition cost of acquired equipment commonly includes the purchase price, taxes, shipping, insurance, installation, and testing costs of the equipment if those costs were necessary and directly related to the acquisition decision.

BUILDINGS

The acquisition cost of purchased buildings commonly includes the purchase price, commissions, property taxes, legal fees, and any necessary costs incurred to ready the asset for its intended use. With regard to buildings, particular care must be taken to measure and record the acquisition cost of the building as a distinct cost element, separate from that of the land or property that is associated with the building. Since the building is a depreciable asset and land is not depreciable, the two must be carefully delineated.

A common business situation is the purchase of land with an existing building on it. If the company's management intends, at the time of purchase, to remove the old building in preparation for constructing a new building, then the costs of the removal should be considered as part of the cost of the land rather than as costs associated with the new building.

ASSETS PURCHASED FOR A LUMP-SUM AMOUNT

It is quite common for a company to purchase several assets and pay a lump-sum amount for all of these assets. In these situations, it is necessary to determine the acquisition cost of each of the assets. This is particularly important when land is involved, since land is not depreciable, whereas the other assets acquired may be depreciable. The general rule in such lump-sum purchases is to allocate the purchase price among the assets using the proportion of the fair market value of all the assets that is represented by each asset's fair market value. Often, the fair market value of each individual asset must be established by independent appraisal, by reference to other similar assets, or by some other means.

For example, assume that Bucho Company purchased a factory building, the land that it is located on, and the equipment in the building. A lump-sum amount of $2,000,000 was paid. An independent appraisal established that the fair market values are $1,200,000, $300,000, and $900,000 for the building, land, and equipment, respectively. The acquisition cost of each asset is calculated as follows:

Building	$2,000,000 × ($1,200,000 ÷ $2,400,000) =	$1,000,000
Land	$2,000,000 × ($300,000 ÷ $2,400,000) =	250,000
Equipment	$2,000,000 × ($900,000 ÷ $2,400,000) =	750,000
Total		$2,000,000

In this example, the company must also consider the acquisition cost of each item of equipment to determine the applicable depreciation for each item. The total amount allocated to equipment should be allocated to each equipment item using the market values of the equipment in a manner similar to that illustrated here.

SELF-CONSTRUCTED ASSETS

self-constructed assets assets that are constructed by the company that intends to use them

Whereas some businesses may purchase operating assets from outside sources, others may choose to construct assets like buildings or warehouses themselves. Assets that are constructed by the company that intends to use them are called **self-constructed assets**. Since there is no purchase price, the company must tally the costs attributable to the asset to determine its cost basis. Labor, materials, and other direct costs will be added to the value of the asset as it is constructed. In addition, companies must consider the assignment of indirect costs like utilities, salaries, or taxes and of interest costs incurred during construction.

❯ OVERHEAD

If indirect overhead is included in acquisition costs and therefore added to the asset account, care must be taken to ensure that the amount capitalized does not exceed the market price, or bids received for the project. This application of conservatism requires that the project be valued at the lower of cost or market. The appropriate treatment of interest costs incurred for the construction of operating assets must also be considered.

LO3 Identify how to account for interest charges as part of the cost basis for self-constructed operating assets.

❯ INTEREST CAPITALIZATION

When accounting professionals identify the assignable costs for self-constructed assets, the treatment of interest costs varies. The following practices demonstrate various positions on the treatment of interest charges.

capitalization of interest the treatment of some portion of the interest incurred for the construction of an asset as part of the cost of the asset rather than as an expense

1. *Statement of Financial Accounting Standards No. 34,* "The Capitalization of Interest Cost," states that interest cost is an integral part of the cost of construction. Therefore, some portion of the interest incurred for the construction of an asset should be treated as part of the cost of the asset rather than as an expense. This procedure is referred to as the **capitalization of interest**.

INTERNATIONAL

Critical Thinking: *When businesses construct their own assets like buildings or warehouses, they often must finance the construction. Do you think the interest they pay on this construction should be included as part of the cost of the asset rather than being treated as an expense?*

qualifying assets certain assets for which interest may be capitalized, including self-constructed assets and inventory that is produced on a discrete, not a continuous, basis

avoidable interest the amount of interest that could have been avoided if a self-constructed asset project had not been undertaken

actual interest incurred the amount of interest on all debt in a company's capital structure

weighted-average expenditures the construction expenditures weighted by the amount of time that an interest cost could be incurred on those expenditures during the construction period

2. *International Accounting Standard 23*, issued by the International Accounting Standards Committee (IASC), forbids the capitalization of interest that is incurred during the construction of certain assets and states that all interest should be expensed.[2]

3. The Association of Financial Analysts recommends that interest be considered a financing cost and not added to the cost of self-constructed assets.

4. In the United States, the capitalization of interest in certain situations is required by GAAP. Interest may be included in the cost of construction for certain qualifying assets, over a stipulated time period, for time-weighted expenditures, and capitalized at a stipulated rate subject to certain constraints. To implement the approach required by GAAP, the following issues should be considered:

▸ *Issue 1. Does the asset qualify for interest capitalization?*
Qualifying assets include self-constructed assets such as machinery and buildings, and inventory that is produced on a discrete, not a continuous, basis, such as real estate projects. Interest may not be capitalized for inventories that are manufactured or produced on a repetitive basis, for assets that are currently being used, or for assets that are idle and are not undergoing activities to prepare them for use.[3]

▸ *Issue 2. Over what period can interest be capitalized?*
Interest may be capitalized only during the period of construction, which begins when three things occur: (1) expenditures related to the project have been made, (2) work on the project has begun, and (3) interest is being incurred. The period of interest capitalization ends when the work is virtually complete and the asset is placed into use or delivered.

▸ *Issue 3. What amount of interest may be capitalized?*
The amount of interest that can be capitalized is the portion that could have been avoided if the project had not been undertaken; this is known as the **avoidable interest**. The amount of interest that may be capitalized can be viewed as interest on the incremental amount of debt incurred (or not redeemed) to finance the project. Even if no new debt is incurred, the opportunity cost associated with maintaining current debt is considered incremental. However, the FASB ruling set as an upper limit on the amount of interest that can be capitalized the amount of **actual interest incurred**, or the amount of interest on all debt in the company's capital structure. Companies that do not have any debt in their capital structure are not allowed to capitalize any interest on a construction project. Therefore, the measurement of the amount of interest to be capitalized on a constructed asset can be stated as the amount of the avoidable interest that does not exceed the amount of actual interest incurred by a company during the period.

▸ **WEIGHTED-AVERAGE EXPENDITURES**   The avoidable interest calculation should be based on the **weighted-average expenditures**, which are defined as the construction expenditures weighted by the amount of time that an interest cost could be incurred on those expenditures during the construction period. Although *Statement of Financial Accounting Standards No. 34* does not require any particular weighting technique, the most exact weighting would require calculating the exact number of days involved. However, the number of months involved will be used for all capitalization of interest calculations in this chapter. The weighted-average amount of accumulated

---

2 "Borrowing Costs," *International Accounting Standard 23* (London: International Accounting Standards Committee, 1993).

3 "Capitalization of Interest Cost," *Statement of Financial Accounting Standards No. 34* (Stamford, Conn.: FASB, 1979), par. 10.

Illustration 9.1

Determining Interest Capitalization

Step 1: Determine the qualifying assets.
Step 2: Determine the weighted-average accumulated expenditures for the period.
Step 3: Determine whether specific borrowing exists. If so, use the interest rate on the specific borrowing. The weighted-average interest rate on all other debt should be used when average accumulated expenditures exceed the amount of specific borrowing.
Step 4: Determine the avoidable interest by applying the appropriate interest rate(s) to the weighted-average accumulated expenditures.
Step 5: Determine the amount of actual interest incurred.
Step 6: The amount of interest to be capitalized is the amount of avoidable interest, but not more than the actual interest incurred.

expenditures is calculated for each individual construction project undertaken by a company.

❯ **INTEREST RATES**   Once the weighted-average expenditures have been calculated, the amount of avoidable interest is calculated by multiplying the weighted-average expenditures by an interest rate. The rate chosen is based on the relationship between the weighted-average expenditures and the amounts borrowed specifically for construction.

1. If the weighted-average expenditures are less than or equal to the amounts borrowed to finance construction of the asset, the rate incurred on those specific borrowings is used. This is referred to as the rate on specific debt or specific borrowing.

2. If the weighted-average expenditures exceed the amount of the specific debt, an interest rate that represents a weighted-average interest rate for all other debt the company has, excluding the specific borrowing, must be used.

Finally, the amount of the avoidable interest must be compared to the actual amount of interest incurred by the company on all of its debt during the construction period. The amount of interest capitalized is the lesser of the avoidable interest or the actual interest incurred. Illustration 9.1 summarizes the steps involved in the capitalization of interest.

The amount of interest that is capitalized is treated as part of the acquisition cost of the asset and becomes part of the depreciable base of the asset in the same manner as any other portion of the acquisition cost. We will illustrate the concepts and calculations of interest capitalization with the following example.

❯ **INTEREST CAPITALIZATION ILLUSTRATED**   Assume that Sosa Company began to construct a machine for its own use on January 1, 2005, and completed the project on December 31 of the same year. The following costs were incurred on the indicated dates:

January 1	$1,000,000
July 1	2,000,000
October 1	2,000,000
December 31	1,000,000

In order to finance the construction, Sosa received a $2,000,000 loan from the bank on January 1 at an annual interest rate of 8 percent and allowed the bank to use the constructed asset as collateral for the loan. The company had the following loans throughout the year:

Loan from First National Bank	$2,000,000 at 12 percent interest
Loan from Resource Bank	$4,000,000 at 9 percent interest

Step 1: Determine the qualifying assets.

Because the machine will be constructed by Sosa Company and will benefit the company as a long-term revenue-producing asset, it is considered a qualifying asset.

Step 2: Determine the weighted-average accumulated expenditures for the period.

In order to calculate the amount of interest that should be capitalized on the construction project, Sosa must first calculate the weighted-average expenditures, as follows:

Jan. 1	$1,000,000 × 12/12 =	$1,000,000
July 1	2,000,000 × 6/12 =	1,000,000
Oct. 1	2,000,000 × 3/12 =	500,000
Dec. 31	1,000,000 × 0/12 =	0
Total weighted-average accumulated expenditures =		$2,500,000

Note that each expenditure is weighted by the amount of time between the point at which the expenditure occurred and the end of the construction period. The December 31 expenditure received a weighting of 0/12 because the expenditure occurred on the last day of the construction period, and therefore no interest cost was incurred.

Step 3: Determine whether specific borrowing exists. If so, use the interest rate on the specific borrowing. The weighted-average interest rate on all other debt should be used when average accumulated expenditures exceed the amount of specific borrowing.

For the first $2,000,000 of construction costs, the interest rate of 8 percent must be applied. In this case, however, we must also calculate the weighted-average interest rate on all other debt and use that rate for the remaining $500,000 of the construction costs. The weighted-average interest rate on other debt is calculated as follows:

$$\text{Weighted-Average Rate} = 12\% \times (\$2,000,000 \div \$6,000,000)$$
$$+ 9\% \times (\$4,000,000 \div \$6,000,000)$$
$$= 10\%$$

Step 4: Determine the avoidable interest by applying the interest rate to the weighted-average accumulated expenditures.

The amount of the avoidable interest is defined as the weighted-average accumulated expenditures multiplied by the appropriate interest rate. Therefore, the amount of avoidable interest is calculated as follows:

Avoidable Interest =	$2,000,000 × 8% =	$160,000
	500,000 × 10% =	50,000
		$210,000

Step 5: Determine the amount of actual interest incurred.

The amount of the actual interest incurred by Sosa during the year 2005 is computed as follows:

$$\text{Actual Interest} = \$2,000,000 \times 8\% = \$160,000$$
$$2,000,000 \times 12\% = 240,000$$
$$4,000,000 \times 9\% = \underline{360,000}$$
$$\$760,000$$

Step 6: The amount of interest to be capitalized is the amount of avoidable interest, but not more than the actual interest incurred.

In this example, the amount of interest to be capitalized is the avoidable interest, $210,000, since it is less than the actual interest incurred ($760,000).

The journal entries in 2005 to record the amounts involved may vary based on the company's methodology but would be similar to the following:

Machine	6,000,000	
Cash (or Accounts Payable)		6,000,000
To record the construction costs		

(*Note:* A separate entry would be made on the date of each expenditure.)

Interest Expense	760,000	
Cash		760,000
To record the interest on the loans		
(assume that interest is paid on December 31 for		
all of the loans)		

Machine	210,000	
Interest Expense		210,000
To record the capitalization of interest at the end		
of the accounting period		

Assume that the company will depreciate the machine over a 10-year life using the straight-line method with zero residual value. The entry to record depreciation on the machine in 2006 would be as follows:

Depreciation Expense	621,000	
Accumulated Depreciation—Machine		621,000

Note that the capitalization of interest is essentially a question of the timing of the expense. If the interest were not capitalized, an additional $210,000 of interest expense would be recorded in 2005. Because that interest is capitalized, the amount will become depreciation expense and will be charged over the life of the asset.

▶ IMPACT OF INTEREST CAPITALIZATION

The amount of interest capitalized by a U.S. company depends on its capital expenditures for construction during the time period examined and may vary somewhat from year to year. When a U.S. company capitalizes its interest costs instead of expensing them, two effects are realized:

1. The company will report higher earnings on its income statement.

2. The company will report higher operating assets as a result of the interest that has been added to the cost basis of the self-constructed asset.

 INTERNATIONAL

As noted earlier, firms following international accounting standards may not capitalize interest on constructed assets. This difference between GAAP in the United

States and the rules of the IASB has led to a lack of comparability between U.S. firms and foreign firms.

DONATED ASSETS

When assets are donated, the receiving company should determine the fair market value of the asset and record the amount received as revenue.[4] The fair market value should be considered to be the acquisition cost and therefore the basis for depreciation of the asset.

For example, assume that the city of Wheatland wishes to attract George Company and, as an inducement, donates the land for a factory site to the company. If the land has a fair market value of $800,000 at the time of the donation, George Company should record the following entry:

Land	800,000	
Revenue from Donation of Land		800,000

Because the actual acquisition cost (or historical cost) of the land is zero, this is an instance in which accountants deviate from the historical cost principle in order to provide more relevant information. Under *SFAS No. 116*, a firm must consider carefully when the donation should be recorded. A donation should be recorded if the actual transfer of the assets has occurred or if an *unconditional promise* to transfer assets in the future has been given. Further, if the donation is restricted, so that certain conditions must be met before it may be used, the asset and revenue are not recorded until those conditions are met.

CHECK YOUR UNDERSTANDING

1. What are acquisition costs?

2. How are operating assets normally reported on the balance sheet?

3. Describe how acquisition costs are determined if assets are purchased for a lump-sum amount.

4. If an asset is self-constructed and interest is capitalized in the current year, how are current-year net earnings affected?

5. For donated assets, what value should be recorded upon acquisition?

LO4 Describe and apply the common methods of depreciation.

Depreciation

Once a company has accounted for the acquisition of an operating asset, the appropriate allocation of the cost of the asset to the periods that will benefit from its use must be considered. **Depreciation** is the process of allocating the cost basis of an asset, less its estimated residual value, over the estimated useful life of the asset. The **residual value** is the estimated value of the asset at its retirement. Accumulated depreciation is recorded as a contra-asset to indicate the cumulative amount of depreciation taken for an asset or a class of assets. Although depreciating an

depreciation the process of allocating the cost basis of an asset, less its estimated residual value, over the estimated useful life of the asset

residual value the estimated value of the asset at its retirement

---

4 "Accounting for Contributions Received and Contributions Made," *Statement of Financial Accounting Standards No. 116* (Stamford, Conn.: FASB, 1993).

Critical Thinking: *Why do you think it is important for businesses to keep track of the value of their assets as those assets deteriorate or become outdated?*

asset reduces its book value to reflect its usage, it is not the same as marking the asset to fair market value. In most cases, the book value of the asset (cost less accumulated depreciation) is different than the fair market value of the asset. That is, accountants view depreciation as a process of cost allocation in order to accurately match the amount of revenue in a given period with the expense (depreciation) that was related to that revenue.

In theory, the depreciation method used should coincide with the decline in usefulness of the asset. In some cases, the decline in the usefulness of an asset occurs as a function of time. In other cases, the decline in the usefulness of the asset is related to other factors, such as technological obsolescence or usage patterns of the asset. A discussion of the most commonly used methods of depreciation follows.

STRAIGHT-LINE DEPRECIATION

straight-line depreciation a method of depreciation in which the same amount of depreciation is recorded in each time period over an asset's useful life

Straight-line depreciation is a method of depreciation in which the same amount of depreciation is recorded in each time period over an asset's useful life. Straight-line depreciation is the most commonly used method for financial reporting because it produces a constant charge to net income and assists managers in smoothing earnings over time. Before the value of the asset is allocated over the useful life of the asset, the residual value is subtracted from the cost basis of the asset. Straight-line depreciation is calculated as follows:

$$\text{Depreciation Expense per Period} = (\text{Cost Basis} - \text{Residual Value}) \div \text{Estimated Life}$$

To illustrate, assume that Mumta Company purchased an operating asset on January 1, 2004, with a cost basis of $30,000, an estimated residual value of $5,000, and a five-year life. The depreciation for the asset, using straight-line depreciation, is calculated in Illustration 9.2.

Review the Notes to Consolidated Financial Statements for **Home Depot Inc.** presented in Figure 9.2. Disclosures regarding the straight-line depreciation method along with information regarding asset types and estimated service lives are presented.

Illustration 9.2

Calculating Depreciation Using Straight-Line Depreciation

End of Year	Calculation: (Cost Basis − Residual Value) ÷ Years	Depreciation Expense	Accumulated Depreciation (A.D.)	Asset Book Value (Cost − A.D.)
2004	$25,000 ÷ 5 =	$5,000	$ 5,000	$25,000
2005	25,000 ÷ 5 =	5,000	10,000	20,000
2006	25,000 ÷ 5 =	5,000	15,000	15,000
2007	25,000 ÷ 5 =	5,000	20,000	10,000
2008	25,000 ÷ 5 =	5,000	25,000	5,000

Figure 9.2

Depreciation Notes

Home Depot

Notes to Consolidated Financial Statements: Home Depot Inc. 2004 Annual Report

DEPRECIATION AND AMORTIZATION The Company's Buildings, Furniture, Fixtures and Equipment are depreciated using the straight-line method over the estimated useful lives of the assets. Leasehold Improvements are amortized using the straight-line method over the life of the lease or the useful life of the improvement, whichever is shorter.

Illustration 9.3

Calculating Depreciation Using the Units-of-Production Method

End of Year	Calculation: (Cost Basis − Residual Value) ÷ Total Units	Depreciation Expense = Actual Units Produced × Net Cost per Unit	Accumulated Depreciation (A.D.)	Asset Book Value (Cost − A.D.)
2004	$25,000 ÷ 10,000 units = $2.50 per unit	2,000 × $2.50 = $5,000	$ 5,000	$25,000
2005	2.50 per unit	2,800 × $2.50 = 7,000	12,000	18,000
2006	2.50 per unit	1,700 × $2.50 = 4,250	16,250	13,750
2007	2.50 per unit	1,500 × $2.50 = 3,750	20,000	10,000
2008	2.50 per unit	2,000 × $2.50 = 5,000	25,000	5,000

UNITS-OF-PRODUCTION METHOD

units-of-production method an activity-based depreciation method in which depreciation is calculated using a variable unit that is related to the asset's estimated productive ability

Another commonly used depreciation method is the **units-of-production method** (also referred to as a *usage method* or an *activity-based method*). In this method, depreciation is calculated using a variable unit that is related to the asset's estimated productive ability. Theoretically, the units-of-production method is appropriate when the decline in the usefulness of an asset is a function of the *usage* of that asset, rather than a function of time.

An input variable or output variable may be used as a base for allocating the cost of the asset as it is actually being used. Service hours or labor hours may be used as a usage variable, or units of output produced may be used to allocate the cost of the asset. For example, assume that an operating asset purchased in 2004 at a cost of $30,000 has an estimated residual value of $5,000 and an expected total output capacity of 10,000 units. The depreciation schedule using the units-of-production method is calculated in Illustration 9.3.

ACCELERATED DEPRECIATION

As previously stated, depreciation is the process of allocating the cost basis of an asset, less its estimated residual value, over its estimated useful life. Accountants view depreciation as a process of cost allocation that is intended to accurately match the amount of revenue for a given period with the expense related to that revenue. In theory, the depreciation method used should coincide with the decline in usefulness of the asset. In some cases, more of this decline in usefulness occurs in the early years of the asset's life and less in the later years. In these cases, an **accelerated depreciation method** is appropriate. With accelerated methods, a greater amount of depreciation is taken in the early years of the life of the asset and a lesser amount in the later years. There are several different forms of accelerated depreciation, including the double-declining-balance method, that use a depreciation rate that is some multiple of the straight-line depreciation rate.

accelerated depreciation method any depreciation method in which greater amounts of depreciation are taken in the early years of an asset's life and lesser amounts are taken in the later years

▶ DOUBLE-DECLINING-BALANCE METHOD

double-declining-balance method an accelerated depreciation method in which depreciation is calculated at twice the straight-line rate

The most commonly used form of accelerated depreciation is the **double-declining-balance method**. With this method, depreciation is calculated at twice the straight-line rate. For example, if the estimated life of an asset is 10 years, the straight-line rate, expressed as a percentage, is 10 percent. The rate for purposes of calculating double-declining-balance depreciation would be twice the straight-line rate, or 20 percent. Two other aspects of this method should be noted:

1. The same rate is applied for each year, but the *balance* is decreased each year.

Illustration 9.4

Calculating Depreciation Using the Double-Declining-Balance Method

End of Year	Depreciation Expense	Accumulated Depreciation	Asset Book Value
2004	$30,000 × 40% = $12,000	$12,000	$18,000
2005	18,000 × 40% = 7,200	19,200	10,800
2006	10,800 × 40% = 4,320	23,520	6,480
2007	1,480*	25,000	5,000

*$6,480 − $5,000 residual.

2. The residual value of the asset is not deducted in calculating the amount to depreciate, but the asset should not be depreciated to an amount lower than its residual value.

To illustrate, assume that Olsen Company purchased an operating asset on January 1, 2004, with a cost basis of $30,000, an estimated residual value of $5,000, and a five-year life. The depreciation for the asset using the double-declining-balance method is calculated in Illustration 9.4.

Note that the amount of depreciation in 2007 is limited to the amount that reduces the asset to its salvage value. Thus, the amount of depreciation is $1,480 rather than $6,480 × 40 percent, or $2,592.

Accelerated methods of depreciation are not commonly used for financial reporting purposes. In most cases, companies prefer depreciation methods that result in an even amount of depreciation expense (this is sometimes referred to as smoothing of income). Straight-line depreciation allows a company to report a constant amount of expense across periods and may give investors the impression that the company's future income is easier to predict. That may be one of the reasons that many companies prefer the straight-line method of depreciation.

DEPRECIATION FOR INCOME TAX PURPOSES

It is important to understand that many companies use different methods of depreciation for financial reporting purposes and income tax purposes. For financial reporting purposes, the company's objective is to accurately reflect income by matching the depreciation expense to the revenues of the period. For income tax purposes, the company's objective is to minimize its tax burden by using the methods allowed by the income tax code.

Modified Accelerated Cost Recovery System (MACRS) an accelerated method of depreciation often used for income tax purposes in which depreciation is calculated based on the adjusted cost of the property, using a period of years set by law for all property of a specific type

The vast majority of companies use an accelerated method of depreciation for income tax purposes that is somewhat similar to the double-declining-balance method previously illustrated. Tax laws allow the use of a method known as the **Modified Accelerated Cost Recovery System (MACRS)**. This system computes depreciation based on the adjusted cost of the property and uses a period of years set by law for all property of a specific type. The amount of depreciation per year depends on the legally specified life of that class of asset; the percentages to be used are shown in Illustration 9.5.

The MACRS method allows for a larger amount of depreciation write-off in the early years of the asset and a lesser amount in later years. The income tax savings realized when this method is used make it a popular choice for tax purposes. Refer to the current year's tax code for more specific information.

DEPRECIATION AND PARTIAL PERIODS

The examples provided thus far have illustrated depreciation calculations for a full year of depreciation. That is, the assets in these examples have been purchased on January 1,

Illustration 9.5

MACRS Table for 3-, 5-, 7-, and 10-Year Classes of Property

Year	3-Year	5-Year	7-Year	10-Year
1	33.33%	20.00%	14.29%	10.00%
2	44.45	32.00	24.49	18.00
3	14.81	19.20	17.49	14.40
4	7.41	11.52	12.49	11.52
5		11.52	8.92	9.22
6		5.76	8.92	7.37
7			8.92	6.55
8			4.46	6.55
9				6.56
10				6.55
11				3.28

and the amount of depreciation for the year-end income statement has been calculated. It is important to consider the amount of depreciation that should be calculated when an asset is purchased at a time other than January 1. For some depreciation methods, additional complexities are introduced when depreciation is calculated for partial periods.

To avoid the complexities associated with partial-period depreciation, many companies establish a policy that allows them to treat all assets in a similar manner. For example, a company may indicate that a half-year of depreciation will be recorded on all assets in the year of acquisition and a half-year will be recorded in the year of sale. Alternatively, a company may indicate that a full year of depreciation will be recorded in the year of acquisition and zero in the year of sale. These policies are acceptable and are considered to be within generally accepted accounting principles provided that they are applied consistently from year to year for all depreciable assets.

CHECK YOUR UNDERSTANDING

1. Why are operating assets depreciated?

2. How is straight-line depreciation calculated?

3. Which depreciation method is referred to as a usage method?

4. Explain the double-declining-balance method of depreciation.

LO5 Explain how to identify and capitalize appropriate costs subsequent to operating asset acquisition.

Critical Thinking: What guidelines exist to determine whether a repair expenditure is capitalized? What role should materiality place in the decision to capitalize or expense?

Costs Subsequent to Acquisition

After an asset has been acquired and placed into use, expenditures for repairs, maintenance, additions, and improvements of the asset are likely to occur. With all such expenditures, the company must decide whether the costs involved should be capitalized (added to the value of the asset) or treated as an expense of the period in which the costs are incurred.

IDENTIFYING CAPITAL EXPENDITURES

Capital expenditures are those that are incurred in order to achieve greater benefits from an asset in the future. If an expenditure increases the future economic benefits of the asset, that expenditure should be capitalized. Thus, if an expenditure increases the useful life of the asset, increases the productivity of the asset, increases the quality of the asset's output, or allows the asset to operate at a lower cost, the expenditure should be added to the cost of the asset. If, however, the expenditure is incurred in order to maintain the asset in its normal operating condition, then the expenditure should be treated as an expense of the period and should not be capitalized.

CAPITALIZATION POLICIES

The capitalize-versus-expense decision can be difficult. Many companies establish a policy on this issue and use the principle of materiality as guidance. For example, it is allowable for a company to establish a policy that all expenditures less than a specified amount be treated as an expense. The policy must be applied in a consistent manner and should not be intended as a way of manipulating the company's income level.

IMPACT ON ASSET VALUE AND DEPRECIATION COSTS IF CAPITALIZED

Newly capitalized amounts become part of the depreciable basis of the asset. Therefore, the amount of depreciation recorded on the asset must be adjusted to reflect this higher basis. The useful life of the asset may also be extended, and this will affect the amount of depreciation that should be recognized each period.

For example, assume that Kori Company purchased a building on January 1, 2000, for $550,000. Initially, Kori depreciated the asset over a 10-year life, using straight-line depreciation and a residual value of $50,000. On January 1, 2004, Kori made a major renovation costing $420,000 to the building that substantially improved the building and extended its life by an additional six years. Assume that the residual value at the end of the building's life will continue to be $50,000.

Kori should treat the expenditure as a capital expenditure and make the following entry on January 1, 2004:

Building	420,000	
Cash (or Accounts Payable)		420,000

At the end of 2004, Kori should calculate the amount of depreciation for the year as follows:

Original cost	$550,000
Depreciation to beginning of 2004 [($500,000 ÷ 10 years) × 4 years]	200,000
Book value	$350,000
Plus: Capital expenditure	420,000
Less: Residual value	(50,000)
Depreciable amount	$720,000
Depreciation for year 2004 ($720,000 ÷ 12 years remaining)	$ 60,000

CHECK YOUR UNDERSTANDING

1. What criteria should be used to determine whether costs for repairs, maintenance, or additions to operating assets should be capitalized?

2. If capitalized improvements are made to an operating asset, does the useful life of the asset change? Explain.

Changes in Estimate and Changes in Principle

LO6 Describe the proper
accounting treatment when a
change in estimate or a change in
accounting principle is made.

Critical Thinking: *Do you
think it is important that management disclose to its investors
the fact that it has changed depreciation methods? Why or why not?*

Once a cost basis for an operating asset has been determined, a method of cost allocation is selected, and this method is usually used consistently throughout the asset's useful life. If the method of cost allocation is changed, this is considered to be a change in accounting principle. Also, the residual value of the asset and its useful life must be estimated. Changes in these estimates are allowed when new evidence becomes available to indicate that the original estimates are not accurate. These changes are known as changes in estimate.

CHANGE IN ESTIMATE

change in estimate a modification
to an accounting estimate resulting
from new information or experience

A **change in estimate** is defined as a modification to an accounting estimate resulting from new information or experience. Once these changes in estimate are made, a new depreciation schedule should be calculated and used from that time forward. Changes in estimate should be treated in a *prospective* manner. That is, the amount of depreciation of the asset should be altered for the year of the change and for future years. No retroactive restatements of past depreciation amounts are required for a change in estimate. However, if the change in estimate is considered material, it should be disclosed in the notes to the financial statements, along with the effect of the change on earnings per share.

For example, assume that Woody Company purchased an asset for $360,000 on January 1, 2000, and has depreciated the asset using a 10-year life and zero residual value. During 2004, a new technology is developed that will make the asset obsolete by the end of 2007. To calculate the depreciation for 2004, Woody should determine the remaining depreciable amount of the asset as $216,000 ($360,000 minus depreciation of $36,000 × 4 years). Depreciation for 2004 should be recorded as $54,000 ($216,000 ÷ 4 years remaining). The entry to record the 2004 depreciation should be as follows:

Depreciation Expense	54,000	
Accumulated Depreciation—Asset		54,000

The change in estimate should be reflected on the financial statements for the year of the change and for future years (this is referred to as *prospective treatment* of the change). Disclosures of changes in estimate are often not extensive, and readers of the financial statements must examine them carefully to determine whether such changes have affected the comparability of current and past statements, because net income and related per share amounts will be affected.

CHANGE IN ACCOUNTING PRINCIPLE

change in accounting principle a
change from one generally accepted
accounting principle to another generally accepted accounting principle

A **change in accounting principle** occurs when a company changes from one generally accepted accounting principle to another generally accepted accounting principle. For example, a company may change its method of depreciation when this is justified by changes in economic circumstances, by changes within its industry, or for other acceptable reasons.

For example, assume that Chandra Company purchased an asset on January 1, 2000, for $500,000 and has depreciated the asset for four years using an accelerated depreciation method, resulting in a total of $380,000 of accumulated depreciation. The asset has a 10-year life and zero residual value. At the beginning of 2004, Chandra changed to straight-line depreciation and is justified in making the change. Prior to 2006, the FASB required the "cumulative effect" of the change on prior periods to be reported as a separate item on the income statement in the year of the accounting change. The amount of the cumulative effect of the change in our example (assuming no income tax effect) is as follows:

Accumulated depreciation using the accelerated method	$380,000
Accumulated depreciation using the straight-line method ($500,000 ÷ 10 years) × 4 years	200,000
Cumulative effect	$180,000

Under the FASB rules prior to 2006, the amount of the cumulative effect should appear on the 2004 income statement as an addition to income in a separate section of the statement after extraordinary items.

In 2005, the FASB issued a standard that changed the manner in which accounting changes should be reported. Regarding changes in depreciation methods, the pronouncement took the view that the effect of the change in accounting *principle* is inseparable from the effect of the change in accounting *estimate*. As a result, it held that changes in depreciation methods "are considered changes in estimate for purposes of applying this Statement"[5] The standard is for accounting changes made in fiscal years beginning after December 31, 2005. Therefore, we will illustrate changes in depreciation methods as changes in estimates.

Refer to our previous example of Chandra Company. If the company used an accelerated method for four years, resulting in accumulated depreciation of $380,000, and then chose to change to the straight-line method at January 1, 2004, the company would calculate depreciation for 2004 as follows:

Original cost of the asset	$500,000
Less accumulated depreciation	380,000
Book value	$120,000
Less residual value	0
Remaining depreciable amount	$120,000

Depreciation Expense = $120,000 ÷ 6 years (remaining life of the asset) = $20,000

It should be noted that the one of the virtues of the treatment of changes in depreciation method as changes in estimate is simplicity. However, it does lead to a lack of comparability from period to period. In our example, the company recorded a much higher amount for depreciation in the years before the change than for the years after the change. Those who read financial statements should be careful in the analysis of companies that have had changes in depreciation methods.

CHECK YOUR UNDERSTANDING

1. How are changes in estimates treated in the accounting records?

2. If a company changes depreciation methods, what disclosures or entries should be made?

---

5 "Accounting Changes and Error Corrections: *Statement of Financial Accounting Standards No. 154* (Stamford, Conn.: FASB, December 15, 2003), par. 17.

LO7 Explain the accounting procedures related to the impairment of an operating asset.

Asset Impairment

In most cases, operating assets are stated on the balance sheet at historical cost amounts. That is, balance sheet amounts are stated at acquisition cost less accumulated depreciation and are not adjusted for fluctuations in the market values of the assets. In certain cases, however, it may become apparent that the value of an asset has decreased as a result of rapid technological advances, intense domestic and global competition, or changes in market demand. This is referred to as **impairment** of the asset. In such cases, it may be appropriate to record a loss on the asset and write the asset down to a more appropriate value on the balance sheet. When the value of an operating asset is *permanently* impaired, it must be examined for the possibility of loss recognition. Accountants must evaluate impairments carefully and determine what amount should be recorded as a loss.

impairment a situation in which the value of an asset has decreased as a result of rapid technological advances, intense domestic and global competition, or changes in market demand

Critical Thinking: *How do you think a company might account for a piece of its machinery becoming obsolete as a result of new technologies?*

DETERMINING IMPAIRMENT

According to *Statement of Financial Accounting Standards No. 144*, "Accounting for the Impairment or Disposal of Long-Lived Assets," long-lived assets must be examined at the end of every year for possible impairment using a two-step process.[6]

Step 1: Determine whether an impairment has occurred. An impairment loss is required when the undiscounted sum of estimated future cash flows from the asset is less than the book value of the asset. Therefore, the impairment test is

$$\text{Undiscounted Cash Flows} < \text{Book Value of the Asset}$$

Note that the impairment test requires a measure of all of the future cash flows associated with the asset but does not require a calculation of the *present value* of those cash flows. Instead, the amount of *undiscounted* cash flows is used as the impairment test. This was clearly a compromise position by the FASB in order to avoid the difficult questions associated with present value measurement and to appease many reporting firms that opposed this standard.

Step 2: If an impairment loss has occurred, calculate the amount of the loss. The impairment loss is measured as the difference between the fair value of the asset and the book value of the asset.

$$\text{Impairment Loss} = \text{Book Value of Asset} - \text{Fair Value of Asset}$$

The fair value of the asset is defined as the amount at which the asset could be sold in a transaction between willing parties. The best estimate of fair value is often the quoted market price in an active market. If quoted market prices are not available, the accountant should consider other valuation techniques, such as the market prices of similar assets and estimates based on the present value of estimated future cash flows from the asset.

ASSET IMPAIRMENT ILLUSTRATED

To illustrate the identification and calculation of asset impairment, review this example. Assume that Kruse Company owns a large piece of factory equipment as follows:

---

6 "Accounting for the Impairment or Disposal of Long-Lived Assets," *Statement of Financial Accounting Standards No. 144* (Stamford, Conn.: FASB, 2001).

Original cost	$1,000,000
Accumulated depreciation	500,000
Fair value	400,000

Because of technological changes, Kruse is concerned that the value of the asset has been permanently impaired. If the asset is retained in its present state, Kruse believes that it can be used to produce product worth $45,000 per year for the next 10 years. Therefore, the total amount of undiscounted cash flows equals $450,000. The impairment test reveals the following:

$$\text{Undiscounted Cash Flows (\$450,000)} < \text{Book Value (\$500,000)}$$

Therefore, an impairment loss has occurred and must be recognized. The amount of the impairment loss is calculated as follows:

$$\text{Impairment Loss} = \text{Book Value of Asset (\$500,000)} - \text{Fair Value of Asset (\$400,000)}$$

$$\text{Impairment Loss} = \$100,000.$$

Kruse should make the following entry to record the impairment:

Loss on Impairment	100,000	
Accumulated Depreciation—Equipment		100,000

Once the impairment has been recorded, the adjusted amount becomes the basis for depreciation of the asset. Thus, the book value of the asset is now $400,000, and that amount should be depreciated over the remaining life of the asset (10 years).

The evaluation of impairment losses should be conducted at the end of each accounting period. What should happen if the value of an asset increases after it has been written down because of an impairment? According to *SFAS No. 144*, once the asset has been written down, if the fair value subsequently increases, the asset may not be written back up. This again illustrates the conservative nature of the accounting discipline. Accountants are more willing to record losses on assets because of decreases in value than to record gains on assets resulting from increases in value.

DISCLOSURE OF IMPAIRMENT

When an impairment loss is recognized, it must be disclosed in the financial statements and the accompanying notes. The required disclosure should explain the impairment, the assumptions used in measuring the impairment, and the effect of the loss on any business segments. As a result of *SFAS No. 144*, many large companies have been required to evaluate their long-term operating assets carefully and consider whether those assets have become impaired. For example, Lowe's accounting policy regarding impairment of assets is depicted in Figure 9.3.[7]

IMPAIRMENT OF LONG-LIVED ASSETS

Remember that the accounting rules given in this section are intended for property, plant, and equipment that will be held for operating use. *SFAS No. 144* also provides guidance on accounting for operating assets that will be disposed of in the near term. Such assets should be reported at the lower of the book value or fair value of the assets less the costs to sell or dispose of the assets.

---

7 Lowe's 2004 Annual Report, p. 36.

Figure 9.3

Impairment of Long-Lived Assets

Lowe's

Lowe's Companies
NOTE 7—Impairment and Store Closing Costs

The company periodically reviews the carrying value of long-lived assets for potential impairment. When management commits to close or relocate a store location, or when there are indicators that the carrying value of a long-lived asset may not be recoverable, the company evaluates the carrying value of the asset in relation to its expected future cash flows. If the carrying value of the asset is greater than the expected future cash flows and the fair value of the asset is less than the carrying value, a provision is made for the impairment of the asset based on the excess of carrying value over fair value. The fair value of the assets is generally based on appraisals and the Company's historical experience. The provision for impairment is included in SG&A expense....

INTERNATIONAL

The IASC issued *International Accounting Standard No. 36,* "Impairment of Assets," requiring that a company recognize an impairment loss whenever the "recoverable value" of an asset is less than its book value.[8] Recoverable value is the higher of the anticipated selling price of the asset *or* the discounted future cash flows associated with the asset's use. The international standard used for asset impairment is more rigorous in that an impairment loss must be recognized when the discounted cash flows are less than book value. The IAS also allows a reversal of the impairment in later years if it is found that the asset is no longer impaired, whereas the FASB does not.

CHECK YOUR UNDERSTANDING

1. According to *SFAS No. 144,* what test is used to determine whether an impairment has occurred?

2. If an impairment has occurred, how is the loss calculated?

3. What disclosures are required for impairments of operating assets?

Disposal of Operating Assets

Operating assets are eventually sold, exchanged, abandoned, retired, or given up by involuntary conversion such as fire or theft. When these assets are disposed of, a gain or loss is recognized equal to the difference between the book value of the asset (cost − accumulated depreciation to date) and any amount received on its disposal.

For reporting purposes, gains and losses are normally reported "above the line" (before income from continuing operations). However, if the gain or loss is related to a disposition of a business segment, it will be reported "below the line" (after income from continuing operations and before extraordinary items). The sections that follow examine the accounting treatment for the sale, exchange, and retirement of operating assets.

LO8 Demonstrate the proper accounting treatment for the sale of operating assets.

SALE OF ASSETS FOR CASH

When the sale of a depreciable asset occurs, the asset must be removed from the accounts, and the amount of the gain or loss on the sale must be calculated and recorded. The amount of the gain or loss on sale can be determined as follows:

---

8 "Impairment of Assets," *International Accounting Standard No. 36* (London: International Accounting Standards Committee, 1998).

Critical Thinking: When a business sells an operating asset, where do you think the gain or loss on that transaction is reflected on the income statement?

Cash Proceeds from Sale − Book Value of Asset = Gain on Sale of Asset

Book Value of Asset − Cash Proceeds from Sale = Loss on Sale of Asset

To calculate the book value of the asset, depreciation must be calculated to the date of the sale. For example, assume that Phillips Company sold an asset on July 1, 2004, for $100,000. The asset had been purchased for $220,000 on January 1, 2000, and had been depreciated using the straight-line method, using a 10-year life and $20,000 residual value. If no depreciation has been recorded for 2004, Phillips should first record a half-year of depreciation as follows:

Depreciation Expense	10,000	
Accumulated Depreciation—Asset		10,000

Because the book value of the asset at the time of sale was $130,000 ($220,000 less accumulated depreciation of $90,000) and the sale proceeds were $100,000, a loss of $30,000 should be recorded as follows:

Cash	100,000	
Accumulated Depreciation—Asset	90,000	
Loss on Sale of Asset	30,000	
Asset		220,000

An amount recorded as a gain or loss on the sale of an asset is generally *not* classified as an extraordinary item on the income statement, but instead usually appears in the "Other Income or Expense" category of the income statement. In certain cases, however, the sale of an asset may be associated with a discontinued operation of the company and should be recorded and classified in accordance with *SFAS No. 144.*[9]

Companies may also dispose of assets in ways other than selling them for cash or other proceeds. For example, a company may simply retire or abandon an asset with no cash involved. In this case, the calculation of a loss should be consistent with the previous example except that no proceeds have been received.

LO9 Detail the accounting procedures involved in the exchange of nonmonetary operating assets.

nonmonetary exchange disposition of an asset by an exchange for another noncash asset

Critical Thinking: What steps would you take to determine whether a nonmonetary exchange has "commercial substance"? How does your decision affect the accounting for an exchange?

EXCHANGE OF ASSETS

Whereas some assets are disposed of by sale, others are disposed of by an exchange for another noncash asset, which is referred to as a **nonmonetary exchange**. In this case, the accounting rules derived from *FASB Statement 153* apply.[10] Accounting for this type of exchange depends on the nature of the exchange and the intent of the parties involved. These fundamental accounting questions must be answered:

1. Should a gain or loss be recorded when an asset is exchanged for another non-monetary asset?

2. Does the exchange complete the earnings process? That is, does the exchange have "commercial substance"?

3. What amount should be used to record the asset received as a result of the exchange?

▶ EXCHANGES THAT HAVE COMMERCIAL SUBSTANCE

In some cases, an exchange of assets is a completion of the earnings process. In such cases, the FASB has chosen to use the term **commercial substance**. An exchange has commercial substance if the entity's future cash flows are expected to change significantly

commercial substance an exchange of assets that results in a significant change in an entity's future cash flows

---

9 *SFAS No. 144.*

10 "Exchange of Nonmonetary Assets: An Amendment of APB No. 29," *Statement of Financial Accounting Standards No. 153* (Stamford, Conn.: FASB, 2004).

as a result of the exchange.[11] An exchange with commercial substance might involve the exchange of inventory for a building or the exchange of equipment for land. A gain or loss should be recorded on the exchange of dissimilar assets because the exchange results in the culmination of the earnings process in the same manner as if the asset had been exchanged for cash. The new asset (the asset received in the exchange) should be recorded at its fair market value. The fair market value is determined by the most objective measure of the value of either the asset acquired or the asset given up.

In some instances, an exchange of assets may include a small amount of cash (often referred to as *boot*) to compensate one party for any difference between the fair market values of the assets exchanged. The accounting rules for exchanges that involve commercial substance are applied even if the exchange involves a small amount of cash.

For example, assume that Atlantis Company and Beta Company exchange assets with the following characteristics:

Atlantis Company		Beta Company	
Original cost	$50,000	Original cost	$60,000
Accumulated depreciation	45,000	Accumulated depreciation	30,000
Fair market value	13,000	Fair market value	25,000

The two parties have agreed to exchange the assets, and the exchange is deemed to have commercial substance. Since Beta Company's asset has a higher fair market value, Atlantis Company has agreed to give Beta Company $12,000 cash in addition to the asset it currently holds.

In computing the amount of the gain or loss on nonmonetary exchanges, you should note that the amount of the gain or loss is not determined by whether a company is giving or receiving cash in the transaction. The amount of the gain or loss is determined as follows:

$$\text{Gain} = \text{Fair Market Value of Asset Given} - \text{Book Value of Asset Given}$$

or

$$\text{Loss} = \text{Book Value of Asset Given} - \text{Fair Market Value of Asset Given}$$

For Atlantis Company	For Beta Company
Gain = $13,000 − $5,000	Loss = $30,000 − $25,000
Gain = $8,000	Loss = $5,000

The amount recorded as the acquisition cost of the acquired asset should be the fair market value of the asset. The amount can also be expressed as

$$\text{Cost of Asset Acquired} = \text{Fair Market Value of Asset Given} \\ + \text{Cash Paid or} - \text{Cash Received}$$

In this case, Atlantis Company should record its acquired asset at $25,000, and Beta Company should record its acquired asset at $13,000. Thus, the companies should record the following transactions:

Atlantis Company		
Asset (New)	25,000	
Accumulated Depreciation—Asset	45,000	
Cash		12,000
Gain on Exchange of Asset		8,000
Asset (Old)		50,000

---

11 *SFAS No. 153*, par. 21.

Beta Company		
Asset (New)	13,000	
Accumulated Depreciation—Asset	30,000	
Cash	12,000	
Loss on Exchange of Asset	5,000	
Asset (Old)		60,000

❯ EXCHANGES LACKING COMMERCIAL SUBSTANCE

The accounting rules for nonmonetary exchanges must be modified somewhat if the exchange is lacking in commercial substance. These modifications also apply if an exchange is made to facilitate sales to a customer. For example, an auto dealer may exchange an auto in inventory with another dealer because a customer wants a particular color or style. If the exchange lacks commercial substance, the transaction should not be considered the completion of the earnings process, since the two parties have not altered or improved their position as a result of the exchange. The accounting rules for nonmonetary exchanges that lack commercial substance must be separated into three cases:

1. A loss is incurred.

2. A gain is realized and cash was given.

3. A gain is realized and cash was received.

❯ LACKING IN SUBSTANCE—LOSS When a loss is incurred on a nonmonetary exchange that lacks commercial substance, the accounting is the same as for exchanges that have commercial substance. A loss is recognized on the exchange regardless of whether the company was receiving cash or paying cash in the transaction. Because of the conservative nature of accounting, accountants tend to recognize losses more readily than they recognize gains.

Refer to Beta Company in the previous example. The company had an asset with a book value of $30,000 (original cost of $60,000 and accumulated depreciation of $30,000). The fair market value of the asset at the time of the exchange was $25,000. Therefore, a loss of $5,000 was incurred on the exchange. How would the accounting for Beta Company change if we assume that the exchange did not have commercial substance?

The accounting would be exactly the same as that previously described. The loss of $5,000 must be recorded, and the asset acquired in the transaction should be recorded at its fair market value. Thus the journal entry for Beta Company would be as follows:

Asset (New)	13,000	
Accumulated Depreciation—Asset	30,000	
Cash	12,000	
Loss on Exchange of Asset	5,000	
Asset (Old)		60,000

❯ LACKING COMMERCIAL SUBSTANCE—GAIN, PAYING CASH When a gain occurs on an exchange that lacks commercial substance, accountants take a more conservative approach. It is assumed that the exchange does not complete the earnings process. Therefore, when a gain occurs on such an exchange and the company is paying cash in the exchange transaction, *the amount of the gain is not recorded*. Because the gain on the transaction is not recorded, it is not possible to record the asset acquired in the exchange at its fair market value. The cost of the acquired asset can be stated as follows:

$$\text{Cost of Asset Acquired} = \text{Fair Market Value of Asset Received} - \text{Amount of Gain } not \text{ Recorded}$$

Alternatively, the cost of the asset acquired can be stated in terms of the book value of the asset given up in the exchange, as follows:

$$\text{Cost of Asset Acquired} = \text{Book Value of Asset Given} + \text{Cash Paid}$$

Refer to Atlantis Company in the previous example. The company had an asset with a book value of $5,000 (original cost of $50,000 and accumulated depreciation of $45,000). The fair market value of the asset at the time of the exchange was $13,000. Therefore, a gain of $8,000 was incurred on the exchange. How would the accounting for Atlantis Company change if we assume that the exchange was lacking in commercial substance?

Because the exchange lacks commercial substance and Atlantis Company paid cash in the transaction, the company should not record the gain of $8,000. The company should record the transaction as follows:

Asset (New)	17,000*	
Accumulated Depreciation—Asset	45,000	
Cash		12,000
Asset (Old)		50,000

*($25,000 − $8,000)

❯ **LACKING COMMERCIAL SUBSTANCE—GAIN, RECEIVING CASH** In the previous example, a gain is not recorded when the exchange of assets is accompanied by a payment of cash because the exchange does not complete the earnings process. In the next situation, an exchange lacking in commercial substance results in a gain and the company receives cash in the transaction. In this case, it is assumed that the company has completed the earnings process to the extent that cash was received in the exchange. Therefore, the portion of the gain that represents the extent to which cash was received should be recorded. The gain should be calculated and recorded as follows:

$$\text{Gain Recorded} = \text{Total Gain on Asset Given} \times [\text{Cash Received} \\ \div (\text{Cash Received} + \text{Fair Market Value of Asset Received})]$$

The value to be recorded for the asset received must also be considered in such an exchange. Because only a portion of the gain is recorded, the asset received cannot be recorded at its fair market value. Instead, the value of the asset received can be stated as

$$\text{Cost of Asset Acquired} = \text{Fair Market Value of Asset Received} \\ - \text{Amount of Gain } not \text{ Recorded}$$

As an example, consider Colby Company, which has the following asset:

Original cost	$50,000
Accumulated depreciation	45,000
Fair market value	10,000

Assume that Colby Company wishes to engage in an exchange with another company that has an asset with a fair market value of $8,000 and the exchange is lacking in commercial substance. As a result of the exchange, Colby Company will receive that asset plus cash in the amount of $2,000 in order to equal the fair market value of the asset that it will be giving in the exchange. Colby Company should calculate the total gain on the asset given up in the exchange as $5,000 (fair market value of $10,000 less the book value of $5,000). However, the portion of the gain that should be recorded in the transaction should be calculated as

$$\text{Gain Recorded} = \$5,000 \times [\$2,000 \div (\$2,000 + \$8,000)]$$

$$\text{Gain Recorded} = \$1,000$$

Illustration 9.6

Nonmonetary Exchanges

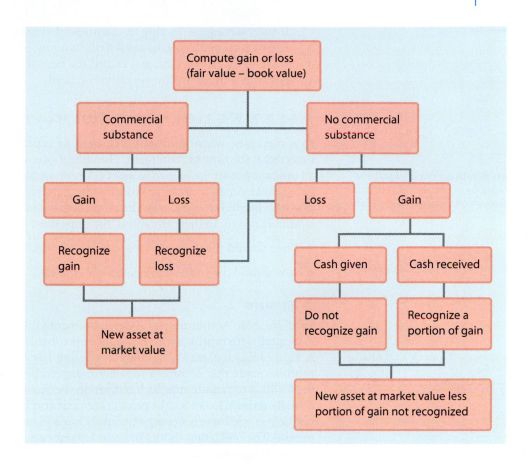

Colby Company should make the following entry to record the exchange of assets and the receipt of the cash:

Asset (New)	4,000*	
Accumulated Depreciation—Asset	45,000	
Cash	2,000	
Gain on Exchange of Asset		1,000
Asset (Old)		50,000

*($5,000 − $1,000)

▶ SUMMARY OF EXCHANGE RULES

Illustration 9.6 provides a flowchart that describes the rules for nonmonetary exchanges of similar and dissimilar assets. These rules can be summarized as follows:

1. Determine the fair market value of the asset(s) surrendered.

2. Compare the fair market value with the book value to determine whether there is a loss or a gain on the exchange.

3. Always recognize losses, whether or not the exchange has commercial substance.

4. If the exchange has commercial substance and there is a gain, recognize the gain on exchange and record the new asset at its fair market value.

5. If the exchange is lacking in commercial substance, there is a gain, and no cash is exchanged, defer recognition of the gain and record the new asset at the book value of the old asset.

6. If the exchange is lacking in commercial substance, there is a gain, and cash is paid, defer recognition of the gain and record the new asset at the book value of the old asset plus any cash paid.

7. If the exchange is lacking in commercial substance, there is a gain, and cash is received, recognize a gain equal to the amount of cash received divided by the total value of assets received, and record the new asset at its fair market value less the portion of the gain that was not recognized.

ASSET RETIREMENT OBLIGATIONS

asset retirement obligations
obligations or costs related to the disposition of an operating asset

In some cases, when an asset is removed or retired, there may be significant costs incurred at the time of retirement. The obligations or costs related to the disposition of an operating asset are known as **asset retirement obligations**. For example, an oil and gas company may incur large costs for the removal of an offshore oil rig. Companies that have landfills may face significant costs to restore a site to its natural state when the landfill is closed. In these situations, the important accounting questions are:

● When should the obligation for such costs be recognized?

● How should the costs be presented in a company's financial statements?

❱ TIMING

SFAS No. 143, "Accounting for Asset Retirement Obligations," established that the costs associated with retiring an asset should be recorded at the time a legal obligation arises. A legal obligation may arise from an existing law or statute, a written contract, or a promise made that conveys a reasonable expectation of performance.[12] The intent of the FASB is to require that such obligations be recorded many years before the asset is actually retired. However, the pronouncement also indicates that the obligation should not be recorded when a company simply has a plan to dispose of the asset and restore the site. The obligation should be recorded only when it meets the test to be considered a legal obligation.

❱ VALUATION

When an obligation is recognized, it should be recorded at its estimated fair value (present value of cash flows may be used to estimate fair value). In periods subsequent to recognition, the liability should be analyzed, and increases in the value of the liability should be recognized as an expense (decreases should be recognized as revenue). Changes in the value of the liability may occur because of two factors: (1) changes in the estimate of the amount to be incurred at retirement, or (2) the passage of time. The increase in the liability as a result of the passage of time is an interest component and is similar to the change in the value of any liability measured using present value techniques.

When a liability for asset retirement obligations is recognized, a corresponding amount must also be recognized for the asset that will be retired. This amount should be amortized as an expense from the time of recognition until the time of retirement, in a manner similar to depreciating the asset. The FASB does not require that a particular method of amortization be used provided that it is "systematic."

To illustrate, assume that Landfill Company determined on January 1, 2005, that an obligation existed related to a landfill that will be used for 10 additional years. Assume that the company has estimated the present value of the cash flows associated with the retirement to be $2,000,000 using an 8 percent discount rate. On January 1, 2005, the company should record the following entry:

Asset Retirement Costs	2,000,000	
Asset Retirement Obligation		2,000,000

Assume that the company has decided to amortize the costs associated with the asset using the straight-line method and that there has been no change in the estimated

---

12 "Accounting for Asset Retirement Obligations," *Statement of Financial Accounting Standards No. 143* (Stamford, Conn.: FASB, 2001).

amount of the cash flows related to the liability by year end. At December 31, 2005, the company should amortize the amount of $200,000 ($2,000,000 ÷ 10 years) as follows:

Asset Retirement Expense	200,000	
Asset Retirement Costs		200,000

The company should also record the change in the present value of the liability on December 31, 2005, as a result of the passage of time as follows:

Asset Retirement Interest Expense ($2,000,000 × 0.08)	160,000	
Asset Retirement Obligation		160,000

Thus, the asset and the liability will initially be equal, but will normally change at different rates. The asset amount will *decrease* in the periods subsequent to recognition because of amortization, while the liability will *increase* in future periods as the company approaches the time of retirement.

It should be noted that *SFAS No. 143* currently affects only companies in certain industries, such as nuclear energy, oil and gas, and landfills. However, as our society becomes more conscious of environmental issues, companies in many other industries may be asked to assume the costs associated with the retirement of assets.

CHECK YOUR UNDERSTANDING

1. How is a gain or loss on the sale of an asset classified on the income statement?

2. When a gain occurs on the exchange of assets where there is no commercial substance and the company is paying cash, how is the gain treated?

LO10 Describe and apply methods for analyzing operating assets.

Critical Thinking: *If you were considering investing in two firms like Home Depot and Lowe's, what factors do you think would be important in regard to each company's operating assets?*

Analysis and Cash Flow Issues

As financial statement users review the financial performance of a company, the ability to analyze its effective investment in and utilization of operating assets is key to understanding its long-term profitability potential.

THE IMPORTANCE OF OPERATING ASSETS

For companies that invest in equipment to manufacture products, operating assets are often the largest category of assets on the balance sheet. For retail companies, these assets can also represent a large percentage of total assets and contribute to the company's operating ability. For example, Figure 9.4 indicates that Home Depot has 58.4 percent ($22,726 million ÷ $38,907 million) of its total assets invested in Net Property and Equipment at January 30, 2005.

The operating asset category is also important for analysis purposes because of its impact on net income. Because manufacturing firms have a significant amount of capital invested in operating assets, the way in which the cost basis is determined and the allocation of those costs can have a significant effect on net income. For many firms, depreciation of operating assets is one of the largest costs affecting income. The management of the company must make important decisions regarding the life of the operating assets and the appropriate depreciation methods. The outcome of those decisions can have a material impact on the company's bottom line.

It is important that users of financial data understand the relationship of operating asset acquisition and cost allocation to income and cash flow. Since depreciation is not a use of cash, it is often one of the largest positive adjustments to net income on the statement of cash flows. Many analysts and readers of financial statements are placing increased emphasis on a company's cash flow as an indication of the "quality" of its earnings.

Figure 9.4

Consolidated Balance Sheets

Home Depot

Home Depot, Inc.
Consolidated Balance Sheets

(amounts in millions, except per share data)	January 30, 2005	February 1, 2004
ASSETS		
Current Assets:		
Cash and Cash Equivalents	$ 506	$ 1,103
Short-Term Investments	1,659	1,749
Receivables, net	1,499	1,097
Merchandise Inventories	10,076	9,076
Other Current Assets	450	303
Total Current Assets	14,190	13,328
Property and Equipment, at cost:		
Land	6,932	6,397
Buildings	12,325	10,920
Furniture, Fixtures and Equipment	6,195	5,163
Leasehold Improvements	1,191	942
Construction in Progress	1,404	820
Capital Leases	390	352
	28,437	24,594
Less Accumulated Depreciation and Amortization	5,711	4,531
Net Property and Equipment	22,726	20,063
Notes Receivable	369	84
Cost in Excess of the Fair Value of Net Assets Acquired, net of accumulated amortization of $56 at January 30, 2005 and $54 at February 1, 2004	1,394	833
Other Assets	228	129
TOTAL ASSETS	$38,907	$34,437

 ANALYSIS

ANALYSIS AND RATIOS

To analyze the performance of operating assets, it is important to determine how these assets contribute to the generation of sales and income.

▶ ASSET TURNOVER RATIO

asset turnover ratio a ratio that indicates how many dollars in sales are generated for each dollar invested in operating assets; calculated by dividing net sales by average net operating assets

A useful measure in the analysis of operating asset utilization is the **asset turnover ratio**, or *PP&E turnover*. The asset turnover ratio indicates how many dollars in sales are generated for each dollar invested in operating assets. The turnover on operating assets is calculated as follows:

$$\text{Asset Turnover Ratio} = \frac{\text{Net Sales}}{\text{Average Net Operating Assets}}$$

The average amount of net operating assets should be used in the denominator because sales are generated over a time period, and it is important to determine the amount of assets employed during that time period. Generally, the average is calculated as follows:

Illustration 9.7

Analyzing Operating Assets: Home Depot Versus Lowe's Companies (in thousands)

	Net Sales	Net Operating Assets Beginning Balance	Net Operating Assets Ending Balance	Net Operating Assets Average	Asset Turnover Ratio	Operating Income	Return on Operating Assets
Home Depot, 2004	$73,094,000	$20,063,000	$22,726,000	$21,394,500	3.42	$7,926,000	37.0%
Lowe's, 2004	36,464,000	12,229,000	14,235,000	13,232,000	2.76	3,712,000	28.1

$$\frac{(\text{Beginning Net Operating Assets} + \text{Ending Net Operating Assets})}{2} = \begin{array}{l}\text{Average Net} \\ \text{Operating} \\ \text{Assets}\end{array}$$

Illustration 9.7 shows the analysis of the operating assets of Home Depot and Lowe's for fiscal year 2004. As you can see, the analysis indicates that for 2004, Home Depot had a higher operating asset turnover ratio (3.42) than did Lowe's (2.76). Home Depot was able to produce more sales for each dollar of assets than Lowe's.

❱ RETURN ON OPERATING ASSETS

return on operating assets a measure showing the amount of operating income generated by the average dollar amount invested in operating assets; calculated by dividing operating income by average net operating assets

Although the relationship between sales and assets is an important measure of performance, a measurement of how assets affect operating income is especially critical. Efficient use of operating assets can be calculated using the **return on operating assets**. This ratio measures the amount of operating income generated by the average dollar amount invested in operating assets. It measures how efficiently a company is using its operating assets in producing income. The rate is especially important for highly capitalized firms, and less so for service firms. The return on operating assets is calculated as follows:

$$\frac{\text{Operating Income}}{\text{Average Net Operating Assets}} = \text{Return on Operating Assets}$$

Illustration 9.7 also analyzed the return on operating assets of Home Depot and Lowe's for fiscal year 2004. Again, Home Depot's results appear to be more favorable. Home Depot had a return on operating assets during 2004 of 37.0 percent, whereas Lowe's had a return of 28.1 percent.

❱ AVERAGE USEFUL LIFE OF OPERATING ASSETS

average useful life of operating assets a measurement of the age and composition of operating assets; calculated by dividing average operating assets by depreciation expense

As operating assets are analyzed, it is important to consider the age and composition of those assets. Several difficulties may arise in such an analysis. When comparing two firms in the same industry, it is difficult to see whether one firm has newer operating assets because of differences in depreciation schedules. One firm may estimate a higher residual value than another for similar assets, and one firm may estimate a longer useful life than the other for similar assets. Furthermore, one firm may use straight-line depreciation, while another may use an accelerated method of depreciation. To estimate the **average useful life of operating assets** for firms that use straight-line depreciation, use the following calculation:

$$\frac{\text{Average Operating Assets}}{\text{Depreciation Expense}} = \text{Average Useful Life}$$

Illustration 9.8

Analysis of Average Age and Useful Life: Lowe's Companies Versus Home Depot

Lowe's Companies, 2004		Home Depot 2004	
Average useful life of operating assets:		Average useful life of operating assets:	
Average operating assets	$16,541,500	Average operating assets	$26,515,500
Depreciation and amortization	920,000	Depreciation and amortization	1,319,000
Average useful life	17.98 years	Average useful life	20.15 years
Accumulated depreciation	4,099,000	Accumulated depreciation	5,711,000
Average age of assets	4.46 years	Average age of assets	4.33 years

To find depreciation expense, use the statement of cash flows. To calculate the average age of the assets, divide the amount of accumulated depreciation by the amount of depreciation expense for the most recent year.

$$\frac{\text{Accumulated Depreciation}}{\text{Depreciation Expense}} = \text{Average Age}$$

An analysis of the average useful life and average age of the assets of Home Depot and Lowe's is provided in Illustration 9.8.

The analysis indicates that Home Depot's assets have a slightly longer useful life (20.15 years versus 17.98 years), but the average age of the existing assets of the two companies is nearly equal at 4.46 and 4.33 years.

LO11 Explain how asset acquisition, disposal, and depreciation affect the statement of cash flows.

CASH FLOW $

 Critical Thinking:
Companies routinely acquire and dispose of operating assets each year. As an investor, why do you think it is important to be able to track these transactions?

PRESENTATION OF OPERATING ASSETS ON THE STATEMENT OF CASH FLOWS

Information about the operating assets is presented in two distinct sections of the statement of cash flows. When the indirect method for preparing the statement of cash flows is used, depreciation is presented in the operating activities section as an adjustment to the net income amount. Depreciation is not a cash flow item, so it must be added back in order to adjust the net income amount for all noncash items.

Information about the amount of assets purchased or sold during a period is presented in the investing activities section of the statement. In fact, for most companies, it is the most significant amount presented in that section. Figure 9.5 shows the operating activities and investing activities sections of the statement of cash flows for Lowe's for the periods ended January 28, 2005, January 30, 2004, and January 31, 2003.

Note that Lowe's had $920 million of depreciation and amortization during the year ended January 28, 2005, as indicated in the operating activities section of the statement. The company purchased or acquired $2,927 billion of fixed assets during the year, as indicated in the investing activities section.

ANALYSIS OF CASH AMOUNTS

Information on the statement of cash flows may be used to determine whether a company is investing wisely in new operating assets. A company that is experiencing financial difficulties may attempt to conserve cash by restricting the purchase of new operating assets. While this may give an initial positive impression to financial statement users and the measurement of return on assets may improve over the short term, such actions rarely lead to long-term profitability.

Figure 9.5

Consolidated Statements of Cash Flows

Lowe's

Lowe's Companies
Partial Consolidated Statements of Cash Flows
(In millions)

Years Ended On	January 28, 2005	January 30, 2004*	January 31, 2003*
Cash Flows From Operating Activities:			
Net Earnings	$2,176	$1,844	$1,491
Earnings from Discontinued Operations, Net of Tax	—	(15)	(12)
Earnings from Continuing Operations	2,176	1,829	1,479
Adjustments to Reconcile Net Earnings to Net Cash Provided By Operating Activities:			
Depreciation and Amortization	920	800	659
Deferred Income Taxes	109	157	221
Loss on Disposition/Writedown of Fixed and Other Assets	21	31	18
Stock-Based Compensation Expense	70	51	—
Tax Effect of Stock Options Exercised	33	31	29
Changes in Operating Assets and Liabilities:			
Accounts Receivable—Net	125	(16)	(9)
Merchandise Inventory	(1,389)	(648)	(357)
Other Operating Assets	31	(10)	(9)
Accounts Payable	475	421	202
Other Operating Liabilities	462	296	421
Net Cash Provided by Operating Activities from Continuing Operations	3,033	2,942	2,654
Cash Flows from Investing Activities:			
Decrease (Increase) in Short-Term Investments	690	86	(128)
Purchases of Long-Term Investments	(156)	(381)	(24)
Proceeds from Sale/Maturity of Long-Term Investments	28	193	—
Increase in Other Long-Term Assets	(14)	(95)	(33)
Fixed Assets Acquired	(2,927)	(2,345)	(2,336)
Proceeds from the Sale of Fixed and Other Long-Term Assets	122	45	44
Net Cash Used in Investing Activities from Continuing Operations	(2,257)	(2,497)	(2,477)

*As Restated (Note 2)

It is important to remember that the statement of cash flows indicates the amount of *cash* invested in operating assets during the period or the amount of *cash* received from the disposal of assets. It does not indicate the *cost* of the assets that were disposed of during the period. To determine that amount, you need to carefully consider how a disposal affects the total operating assets. For example, assume that Buell Company had the following amounts for 2004:

Cash flows from sale of equipment	$100,000
Loss on sale of equipment	10,000
Accumulated depreciation—equipment, January 1, 2004	50,000
Accumulated depreciation—equipment, December 31, 2004	60,000
Depreciation expense for 2004	40,000

We can determine the accumulated depreciation related to equipment sold during the period by analysis of the Accumulated Depreciation account as follows:

Accumulated Depreciation—Equipment

	50,000	beg. bal.
X = ?	40,000	depr. expense
	60,000	**end. bal.**

The amount for X represents the accumulated depreciation on the asset disposed of during the period, or $30,000.

The book value is calculated as follows:

$$\text{Loss on Sale} = \text{Book Value} - \text{Cash Received from Sale}$$
$$\$10,000 = X - \$100,000$$
$$X = \$110,000$$

The cost of the equipment sold is computed from the following equation:

$$\text{Book Value} = \text{Cost of Equipment} - \text{Accumulated Depreciation}$$

We can use this equation to calculate the cost of the equipment sold:

$$\$110,000 = X - \$30,000$$

Here, X represents the cost of the equipment sold during the period, or $140,000.

CHECK YOUR UNDERSTANDING

1. Describe how the asset turnover ratio is calculated. What does this ratio tell analysts or financial statement users?

2. Where are depreciation costs reflected on the statement of cash flows?

Revisiting the Case

LOWE'S EXPANSION REQUIRES COMMITMENT TO NEW OPERATING ASSETS

1. Lowe's reported $13.91 billion in net property at January 28, 2005.

2. Lowe's, like other companies, uses depreciation methods to account for the use or deterioration of its operating assets.

3. Buildings, land, equipment, machinery, transportation systems, computer systems, and furniture are a few of the types of operating assets that Lowe's may purchase when it opens new stores.

4. Lowe's typically uses funds from operations and debt issuance to purchase new operating assets.

5. Lowe's uses the straight-line method of depreciation.

SUMMARY BY LEARNING OBJECTIVE

LO1 Identify the characteristics of operating assets.

Operating assets, also called *property, plant, and equipment (PP&E)*, *tangible assets*, or *long-term plant assets*, are the tangible assets that a company uses to create operational revenue. Land, buildings, equipment, furniture and fixtures, land improvements, and construction in progress are generally included in this asset category. Only tangible assets that are actually being used in operations and that have a useful life of more than a year should be included in this category.

LO2 Determine the cost basis for operating assets at acquisition.

Operating assets are measured at acquisition cost or historical cost. Acquisition cost should include all costs necessary to acquire the asset and prepare it for its intended use. The acquisition cost of land should be measured separately from land improvements because land is not depreciable, whereas land improvements are depreciable. When a lump-sum purchase of assets occurs, the acquisition cost of each asset should be determined by the proportion of the total fair market value of all assets purchased in the transaction that it represents.

LO3 Identify how to account for interest charges as part of the cost basis for self-constructed operating assets.

Interest is capitalized as part of the acquisition cost only when a company is constructing an asset over time and only during the construction period. The amount of interest capitalized is based on the weighted-average accumulated expenditures for the period but may not be greater than the total interest incurred during the period. The interest rate used should be that for debt that is specifically related to the construction project. If the weighted-average accumulated expenditures exceed the specific debt, then the interest rate on the balance should reflect the interest on all other company debt.

LO4 Describe and apply the common methods of depreciation.

Depreciation is the process of allocating the original cost of an asset over its useful life. Theoretically, the method used should coincide with the decline in usefulness of the asset. Straight-line depreciation allocates the same amount of depreciation to each time period. The units-of-production method determines depreciation as a function of the amount of product or output that the asset will produce over its useful life. Accelerated depreciation methods, such as the double-declining-balance method, recognize a greater portion of the asset cost in the early years of the asset's life and a lesser portion in the later years.

LO5 Explain how to identify and capitalize appropriate costs subsequent to operating asset acquisition.

Costs that occur after the acquisition of the asset should be capitalized as part of the asset if the costs increase the life of the asset, the quality of the asset, or the productivity of the asset. If an amount is capitalized, this changes the depreciable basis of the asset and therefore the amount of depreciation in future periods. Expenditures that simply maintain the asset in its normal operating condition should be treated as expenses of the period rather than as capitalized costs.

LO6 Describe the proper accounting treatment when a change in estimate or a change in accounting principle is made.

A change in estimate occurs if a company changes the useful life or the residual value of a depreciable asset. A change in estimate should affect the current year and future years but does not affect past periods. A change in accounting principle occurs if a company changes the method of depreciation. Under a recent FASB statement, changes in depreciation methods should be treated as changes in estimates.

LO7 Explain the accounting procedures related to the impairment of an operating asset.

An asset should be considered permanently impaired if the book value of the asset exceeds the total undiscounted cash flows that the asset will produce in future periods. The amount of the impairment loss should be measured as the excess of the book value of the asset over its fair value, and this amount should be recorded as a loss or expense of the period. Generally, once an impairment loss has been recognized, the asset should not be written back up if the value of the asset increases in future periods.

LO8 Demonstrate the proper accounting treatment for the sale of operating assets.

Operating assets are eventually sold, exchanged, abandoned, or given up by involuntary conversion. A gain or loss equal to the difference between book value and the consideration received is recognized on disposal.

LO9 Detail the accounting procedures involved in the exchange of nonmonetary operating assets.

Accounting for nonmonetary exchanges of operating assets depends on whether the exchange has commercial substance. If the exchange does have commercial substance, the gain or loss on each asset is recognized, and the acquired asset is recorded at fair market value. If the exchange lacks commercial substance and a party has a loss at the time of the exchange, the accounting is the same as for dissimilar assets. If a gain occurs and the company paid any cash in the exchange, the gain is not recognized and the acquired asset is not recorded at fair market value. If a gain occurs and the company received cash in the exchange, a portion of the gain is recorded.

LO10 Describe and apply methods for analyzing operating assets.

The asset turnover ratio measures how many dollars in sales are generated for each dollar invested in operating assets. Return on operating assets indicates the rate of return on every dollar invested in operating assets. The average useful life and average age of the assets can also be computed and indicate the nature and composition of the operating assets.

LO11 Explain how asset acquisition, disposal, and depreciation affect the statement of cash flows.

Depreciation can be the biggest adjustment to net income in deriving cash flows from operating activities. Depreciation for the period is added back to net income (under the indirect method) as an adjustment to find operating cash flows. This adjustment is more significant for those companies with heavy investments in plant assets. The investing activities section of the statement of cash flows must also be analyzed to see if the company is investing more in operating assets than it is selling, and at what rate.

KEY TERMS

accelerated depreciation method (p. 410)
acquisition cost (p. 401)
actual interest incurred (p. 404)
asset retirement obligations (p. 424)
asset turnover ratio (p. 426)
average useful life of operating assets (p. 427)
avoidable interest (p. 404)
book value (p. 401)
capitalization (p. 401)
capitalization of interest (p. 403)

change in accounting principle (p. 414)
change in estimate (p. 414)
commercial substance (p. 419)
depreciation (p. 408)
double-declining-balance method (p. 410)
impairment (p. 416)
land improvements (p. 402)
Modified Accelerated Cost Recovery System (MACRS) (p. 411)

nonmonetary exchange (p. 419)
operating assets (p. 400)
qualifying assets (p. 404)
residual value (p. 408)
return on operating assets (p. 427)
self-constructed assets (p. 403)
straight-line depreciation (p. 409)
units-of-production method (p. 410)
weighted-average expenditures (p. 404)

EXERCISES

LO4 **EXERCISE 9-1** **Compute Depreciation**

A. Scott and Wells Company has an Accumulated Depreciation—Asset account with a balance of $22,000 on January 1, 2004, and a balance of $30,000 on December 31, 2004. There were no purchases or sales of depreciable assets during the period.

B. Buena Company has an Accumulated Depreciation—Asset account with a balance of $22,000 on January 1, 2004, and a balance of $30,000 on December 31, 2004. During the year, an asset with a book value of $6,000 was sold for $9,000. The original cost of the asset was $10,000 when it was purchased in 1999.

Required:

1. Calculate the amount of depreciation expense in scenario A for the year 2004.
2. Calculate the amount of depreciation expense in scenario B for the year 2004.

LO4, 8 **EXERCISE 9-2** **Depreciation Methods**

A. On July 1, 2003, Company A sold an asset for $400,000. The asset was purchased on January 1, 2000, for $600,000 and was depreciated on a straight-line basis with zero residual value and an estimated life of five years.

B. Assume the same facts as in scenario A, except that the company used the double-declining-balance method of depreciation.

Required:

1. For scenario A, calculate the gain or loss on the sale and record a journal entry for the sale of the asset.

2. For scenario B, calculate the gain or loss on the sale and record a journal entry for the sale of the asset.

LO8   **EXERCISE 9-3   Sale of Asset**

The accountant for Rambler Company gathered the following financial information:

	Dec. 31, 2004	Dec. 31, 2003
Equipment	$200,000	$290,000
Accumulated Depreciation—Equipment	50,000	60,000

Rambler's income statement for the year 2004 revealed the following accounts:

Depreciation Expense	$15,000
Loss on Sale of Equipment	12,000

There were no purchases of equipment during 2004.

Required:

1. Calculate the amount of cash received from the sale of equipment during the year.

2. Record a journal entry for the sale of equipment by Rambler Company.

LO11   **EXERCISE 9-4   Cash Flows from Sale of Asset**

Refer to the information in Exercise 9-3.

Required: What information related to the accounts in Exercise 9-3 would appear on Rambler's statement of cash flows for the year ended December 31, 2004? Provide the dollar amount of each item that would appear and the category of the cash flow statement in which the information would appear. Assume that Rambler uses the indirect method for the statement of cash flows. Net income for 2004 was $149,000.

LO8   **EXERCISE 9-5   Sale of Asset**

The accountant for Huskie Company gathered the following financial information:

	Dec. 31, 2004	Dec. 31, 2003
Equipment	$400,000	$480,000
Accumulated Depreciation	250,000	220,000

Huskie's income statement for the year ended December 31, 2004, revealed the following account:

Gain on Sale of Equipment	$30,000

There were no purchases of equipment during 2004. During the year, equipment with a book value of $60,000 was sold.

Required:

1. Calculate the amount of cash received from the sale of equipment during the year.

2. Record a journal entry for the sale of equipment by Huskie Company.

LO11   **EXERCISE 9-6   Cash Flows from Sale of Asset**

Refer to the information in Exercise 9-5.

Required: What information related to the accounts in Exercise 9-5 would appear on Huskie's statement of cash flows for the year ended December 31, 2004? Give the dollar amount of each item that would appear and the category of the cash flow statement in which the information would appear. Assume that Huskie uses the indirect method for the statement of cash flows. Net income for 2004 was $75,500.

LO4, 8 EXERCISE **9-7** **Depreciation and Gain or Loss**

Titan Co. purchased an asset for $130,000 on July 1, 2002. The life of the asset was estimated to be 10 years and the residual value, $10,000. The company also estimated that the asset would produce 240,000 units of output, with the output being distributed as follows: 30,000 units in 2002, 50,000 in 2003, and 20,000 in 2004 and each year thereafter.

Required:

1. Develop a depreciation schedule that indicates the amount of depreciation that will be recorded on the asset for the first five years under the straight-line method, the double-declining-balance method, and the units-of-production method.

2. Assume that the asset is sold for $60,000 on December 31, 2004. Calculate the gain or loss that will result under each of the methods.

LO4, 6 EXERCISE **9-8** **Depreciation and Change in Estimate**

Randall Company purchased an asset for $130,000 on January 1, 2004. The company estimated that the asset would have an eight-year life and its residual value would be zero.

Required:

1. Develop a depreciation schedule that indicates the amount of depreciation that will be recorded on the asset for the next eight years under the straight-line and double-declining-balance methods.

2. Assume that on January 1, 2006, the company discovers that the asset will become technologically obsolete in five years. Develop a depreciation schedule that indicates the amount of depreciation that will be recorded on the asset for the remaining five years under the straight-line and double-declining-balance methods.

LO4, 6 EXERCISE **9-9** **Depreciation and Change in Accounting Principle**

Powell Company purchased an asset for $130,000 on January 1, 2004. The company estimated that the life of the asset would be eight years and the residual value of the asset would be zero at the end of that time. Powell used the double-declining-balance method to depreciate the asset. On January 1, 2007, Powell changed to the straight-line method of depreciation. You may assume that the company is justified in making the accounting change and that there is no income tax applicable to the transaction. Treat changes in depreciation methods as changes in estimate.

Required:

1. Calculate the amount of depreciation that should be recorded in 2004, 2005, and 2006 using the double-declining balance method of depreciation.

2. Calculate the amount of depreciation that should be recorded in 2007 using the straight-line method.

3. Record all entries necessary for 2007, the year of the change in depreciation methods.

LO2 EXERCISE **9-10** **Acquisition Cost**

Hector Company purchased equipment on January 1, 2004. The equipment was installed on January 15, and its use began on January 30. The following amounts were expenditures related to the equipment (assume that all amounts are material):

Invoice price	$100,000
Discount of 2 percent taken for paying within 10 days	
Delivery charges	1,000
Setup costs	2,500
Repair of asset prior to installation	3,000
Costs of training employees to use the equipment	5,000
Increased electricity costs and ventilation costs for the new equipment	4,000
Costs of repair of the equipment, incurred on July 1	6,000
Direct materials costs for a base built for the equipment	5,400
Overhead costs for building a base for the equipment	3,600

Required: Calculate the total amount that should be considered the acquisition cost of the equipment for depreciation purposes.

LO2   EXERCISE 9-11   **Acquisition Cost**

A. The city of New Salem donated land to Stacy Company on January 1, 2004, as an inducement for Stacy to locate its plant in the city. In return, Stacy agreed to provide a minimum of 500 jobs and to maintain its plant for at least five years. An appraisal indicated that the value of the property at the time of the donation was $400,000.

B. In addition, on January 1, 2004, Stacy Company purchased several assets, including property adjacent to the donated land, for a lump-sum amount of $500,000 cash. An appraisal of the individual assets indicated the following fair market values:

Building	$250,000
Land	125,000
Equipment	120,000
Land improvements	25,000

Required: Determine the acquisition cost of the assets in these transactions and record the necessary journal entries.

LO9   EXERCISE 9-12   **Exchanges of Assets**

On January 1, 2005, AB Company and XY Company agree to exchange assets with the following characteristics:

	AB Company	XY Company
Original cost	$50,000	$60,000
Accumulated depreciation	30,000	40,000
Fair market value	24,000	30,000

AB Company has agreed to pay $6,000 cash to XY Company in the exchange.

Required:

1. Assume that the exchange of assets has commercial substance. Make the necessary journal entries to record the exchange for both parties.

2. Assume that the exchange of assets does not have commercial substance. Make the necessary journal entries to record the exchange for both parties.

LO9   EXERCISE 9-13   **Exchanges of Assets**

On January 1, 2005, CD Company and PQ Company agree to exchange assets with the following characteristics:

	CD Company	PQ Company
Original cost	$50,000	$60,000
Accumulated depreciation	30,000	50,000
Fair market value	34,000	30,000

PQ Company has agreed to pay $4,000 cash to CD Company in the exchange.

Required:

1. Assume that the exchange of assets has commercial substance. Make the necessary journal entries to record the exchange for both parties.

2. Assume that the exchange of assets does not have commercial substance. Make the necessary journal entries to record the exchange for both parties.

LO3   EXERCISE 9-14   **Capitalization of Interest**

Tucker Company began to construct an asset for its own use on January 1, 2005, and completed the construction on December 31 of that year. The amounts listed on the next page were expended during the construction process.

January 1	$1,000,000
March 1	500,000
July 1	400,000
October 1	800,000

Tucker Company did not take out a loan to finance the construction of the asset. Instead, the company issued stock for $2,000,000. As a result, the company did not have any specific borrowing for the construction project. The company had existing loans of $1,000,000 from First National Bank at an interest rate of 9 percent and $2,000,000 from Second National Bank at an interest rate of 11 percent; both these loans were acquired before January 1, 2005.

Required:

1. Calculate the amount of the weighted-average accumulated expenditures on the construction project for 2005.

2. Calculate the amount of the avoidable interest.

3. Calculate the amount of the actual interest incurred.

4. What is the amount of interest that should be capitalized for 2005?

LO3   **EXERCISE 9-15   Capitalization of Interest**

Teryl Company began to construct an asset for its own use on January 1, 2005, and completed the construction on December 31 of that year. The following amounts were expended during the construction process:

January 1	$1,000,000
March 1	900,000
July 1	400,000
October 1	800,000

To finance the construction of the asset, Teryl issued $1,000,000 in stock on January 1 and on the same date received a loan of $1,200,000 at 8 percent from Alpine Bank, using the constructed asset as collateral for the loan. In addition, the company had existing loans (both acquired before January 1, 2005) of $1,000,000 from First National Bank at an interest rate of 9 percent and $2,000,000 from Second National Bank at an interest rate of 11 percent.

Required:

1. Calculate the amount of the weighted-average accumulated expenditures on the construction project for 2005.

2. Calculate the amount of the avoidable interest.

3. Calculate the amount of the actual interest incurred.

4. What is the amount of interest that should be capitalized for 2005?

LO4, 7   **EXERCISE 9-16   Asset Impairment**

On January 1, 2001, Bubbers Company purchased equipment for $600,000. The company has used the straight-line depreciation method with an estimated life of 10 years and zero residual value. Because of technological changes in the industry, Bubbers is concerned that the value of the asset has permanently decreased and must determine whether the asset should be written down to a lower amount. Bubbers anticipates that it will continue to use the asset at operating capacity for its remaining life. On January 1, 2004, the company collected the following information concerning the asset:

Total cash flows produced by the asset during its remaining life	$380,000
Present value of the future cash flows	320,000
Fair market value of the asset	400,000
Cost of new asset with updated technology	700,000

Required:

1. Calculate the amount of impairment of the asset and record the necessary journal entry on January 1, 2004.

2. Calculate the amount of depreciation to be recorded on the annual income statement as of December 31, 2004.

3. Assume that on December 31, 2004, market conditions have changed markedly and the fair market value of the asset has rebounded to $440,000. Record any necessary entries on that date.

LO2, 3   **EXERCISE 9-17   Interest Capitalization and Cost Basis**

Early in 2005, Carter Corp. engaged Berthet, Inc. to design and construct a complete modernization of Carter's manufacturing facility. Construction began on June 1, 2005 and was completed on December 31, 2005. Carter made the following payments to Berthet, Inc. during 2005:

Date	Payment Amount
June 1, 2005	$2,400,000
September 30, 2005	7,800,000
December 31, 2005	4,000,000

To help finance the construction, Carter issued the following during 2005:

- $1,500,000, 10-year, 10 perent note payable issued on June 1, 2005, with interest payable annually on May 31

Other debt held by the company during 2005 was as follows:

- A $4,000,000, 12 percent note payable dated January 1, 2002, due January 1, 2010, with interest payable annually on January 1
- A 30-day, 9 percent loan dated July 1, 2005, in the amount of $1,000,000

Required:

1. Compute the amounts of each of the following:

   a. Weighted-average accumulated expenditures qualifying for capitalization of interest cost

   b. Avoidable interest

   c. Cost basis of the facility

2. How would the cost basis of the facility differ under *IAS 23*? Explain.

LO10   **EXERCISE 9-18   Analyzing Operating Assets**

Seguna Enterprises reported the following on its balance sheets at December 31, 2004, 2005, and 2006:

	December 31,		
	2006	2005	2004
Property, plant, and equipment, net of accumulated depreciation of $6,800, $5,600, and $5,400 respectively	$36,500	$35,300	$34,200

Seguna's income statement reported $12,400, $11,200, and $13,500 of net income for the years ended December 31, 2006, 2005, and 2004, respectively. Included in these amounts are net sales of $256,000, $235,000, and $220,000, and total depreciation expense of $3,300, $3,100, and $3,800, for the same years, respectively. Income taxes amounted to 30 percent of income before income taxes. A gain on the sale of equipment of $2,000 was reported during 2006.

Required:

1. Calculate Seguna Enterprise's PP&E turnover for 2006 and 2005. What information is provided by this calculation?

2. Calculate Seguna Enterprise's return on operating assets for 2006 and 2005. What information is provided by this calculation?

LO1, 2 **EXERCISE 9-19** **Cost Basis and Characteristics of Operating Assets**

Bateh Company purchased land as a factory site for $200,000. It paid legal fees of $3,000 for closing costs on the purchase. An additional $1,500 was paid for title insurance. Bateh paid $28,000 to tear down two old buildings on the land. Salvage was sold for $5,000. Architect's fees were $14,000 for design of the building, $6,000 for landscape (permanent) design, and $4,000 for design of parking lots. Liability insurance during construction cost $1,800. The contractor was paid $950,000 at the completion of the building. The city assessed a one-time fee for sewer hookup totaling $3,500. Qualifying interest costs during construction were $52,000.

Required:

1. Calculate the cost of the land that should be recorded by Bateh Company.

2. Calculate the cost of the building that should be recorded by Bateh Company.

3. What characteristics must exist to classify assets as operating assets? How does the estimate of useful life differ for land as compared to depreciable assets?

LO2, 5 **EXERCISE 9-20** **Cost Basis and Subsequent Expenditures**

On January 1, 2005, Brazee Company gave a one-year, 10 percent note for $165,000 to Beasley Company in exchange for a conveyor to be installed in its new facility. The conveyor has an estimated residual value of $60,000 at the date of the exchange, is expected to last for 10 years, and will be needed as long as the company is in existence. Brazee paid $3,000 to Carcello Company to install the conveyor and $5,000 to Pierce Insurance for the first two years of equipment insurance. On January 31, 2006, Brazee incurred $1,600 to perform routine maintenance on the conveyor. On June 30, 2006, Brazee incurred $32,000 to replace the hydraulic sliders in the conveyor with a new movement system that streamlined the production process significantly.

Required:

1. How much should be capitalized on January 1, 2005 as the cost of the conveyor to Brazee Company?

2. How are the costs incurred during 2006 accounted for? Justify your response conceptually. Do not provide calculations.

LO9 **EXERCISE 9-21** **Nonmonetary Exchanges**

Chapin Marley, a Midwest farmer, exchanged the following land parcels used for growing crops for new parcels in four independent exchanges that do not have commercial substance.

Exchange	Adjusted Basis of Old Parcel	FMV of New Parcel	Cash Given	Cash Received
1	$8,000	$18,000	$ 0	$ 0
2	8,000	18,000	6,000	0
3	8,000	18,000	12,000	0
4	8,000	18,000	0	6,000

Required:

1. For each exchange, determine how much gain or loss should be realized, how much should be recognized, and the amount of the basis in the new property acquired.

2. Why are some realized gains recognized and others deferred when businesses exchange assets?

PROBLEMS

LO4, 9 **PROBLEM 9-1   Depreciation and Exchange of Assets** (CPA adapted)
Portland Company uses straight-line depreciation for most of its depreciable assets. All assets are depreciated individually except manufacturing machinery, which is depreciated using the double-declining-balance method. During the year, Portland exchanged a delivery truck with Maine Company for a larger delivery truck. It paid cash equal to 10 percent of the larger truck's value.

Required:

1. How should Portland account for and report the truck exchange transaction assuming the exchange was lacking in commercial substance?

2. How should Portland have calculated the manufacturing machinery's annual depreciation expense in its first year of operation?

Critical Thinking: What factors should have influenced Portland's selection of the straight-line depreciation method?

Analyze: What would be the effect on depreciation expense of Portland's using the double-declining-balance method, rather than the straight-line method, for manufacturing machinery?

LO4, 6 **PROBLEM 9-2   Depreciation Methods and Change in Estimate**
The following data relate to the plant and equipment account of Slam Dunk Company, a manufacturer of sports equipment.

	Asset A	Asset B	Asset C
Original Cost	$35,000	$51,000	$80,000
Year Purchased	1999	2000	2002
Residual Value	$3,000	$3,000	$3,000
Useful Life	10 years	10 years	10 years
Depreciation Method	Straight-line	Straight-line	Double-declining-balance

In the year in which an asset is purchased, Slam Dunk does not record any depreciation. In the year in which an asset is retired, a full year's depreciation is recorded.

Required:

1. Calculate the total depreciation expense for calendar year 2004.

2. Calculate total accumulated depreciation as of December 31, 2004.

3. Before recording depreciation in 2004, assume that Slam Dunk decides that Asset B has a remaining life of three years. Prepare all entries necessary in 2004 to record depreciation expense and/or the revision in useful life for Asset B.

Analyze: Which method expenses higher amounts of depreciation in earlier years?

Research: Locate the current annual reports for **Reebok** and **Nike**. What methods of depreciation do these companies use?

LO3 **PROBLEM 9-3   Capitalization of Interest**
Consider the amount of interest that should be capitalized for the following two companies.
    Company A began construction of an asset for its own use on January 1, 2004, and completed the construction process on October 1, 2004. The amounts shown on the next page were expended during the construction process.

January 1	$1,000,000
July 1	2,000,000
October 1	2,400,000

Over the course of several years, Company A has been very profitable, and as a result, it does not have any existing debt. In 2001, the company had issued a very large block of stock, and the proceeds from that equity issuance, combined with available internal funds, were used to finance the construction. As a result, no interest was incurred.

Company B constructed the same asset and had the same expenditures as Company A on the same dates. However, Company B did not have liquid funds available and acquired a $3,000,000 loan at 8 percent interest to finance the construction. Company B has no other existing debt.

Required:

1. Calculate the amount of interest that should be capitalized by Company A and Company B.

2. Assume that both companies will use the straight-line method of depreciation with a 10-year life and zero residual value. Calculate the amount of depreciation that should be recognized by Company A and Company B for 2004.

Analyze: If the two companies have the same amount of revenue and all other expenses (other than interest and depreciation) are equal, which company will appear more profitable?

Communicate: Assume that you are an accountant for Company B. Write a memo to your boss explaining the accounting rules for capitalization of interest.

LO4, 10, 11   **PROBLEM 9-4   Depreciation Methods, Analysis, and Cash Flow**

A partial income statement for Bishop Company for the year ended December 31, 2004, is given here:

Sales	$12,000
Cost of sales	8,000
Gross profit	$ 4,000
Operating expenses	1,000
Depreciation expense	???
Income before income taxes	$???
Income tax expense (40%)	???
Net income	$???

On January 1, 2004, Bishop purchased a $5,000 asset with a 10-year life and zero residual value. Bishop is considering whether to use the straight-line or the double-declining-balance method of depreciation.

Required:

1. Complete the company's income statement assuming that Bishop uses the straight-line method.

2. Complete a second income statement assuming that the company uses the double-declining-balance method.

3. Assume that all of the company's sales and expenses are cash items (except for depreciation). Develop the operating activities section of the statement of cash flows using the direct method for each depreciation method.

Analyze: Calculate the asset turnover ratio for the company for each depreciation method. You may assume that the asset purchased in 2004 is the company's only operating asset.

Spreadsheet: Use a spreadsheet application to generate the statement of cash flows and the income statement using the straight-line depreciation method.

LO8, 11 **PROBLEM 9-5 Analysis and Cash Flow**

A note from the 2004 financial statements of NortCor is provided here, along with the relevant portions of the consolidated statement of cash flows for the year ended December 31, 2004.

Note 4. Property, Plant, and Equipment (amounts in thousands)

	Dec. 31, 2004	Dec. 31, 2003
Land and improvements	$ 69,626	$ 68,946
Buildings and improvements	313,624	313,058
Machinery and equipment	3,003,385	2,937,690
Construction in process and equipment deposits	293,287	78,073
	$3,679,922	$3,397,767
Less: Accumulated depreciation	1,488,583	1,300,689
	$2,191,339	$2,097,078

NortCor
Consolidated Statement of Cash Flows
For the Year Ended December 31, 2004
(amounts in thousands)

Operating activities:

Net earnings	$244,589
Adjustments:	
Depreciation	256,637
Deferred tax	10,600
Minority interests	85,651
Changes in:	
Accounts receivable	(94,518)
Inventories	(29,098)
Accounts payable	56,899
Federal income taxes	(23,634)
Other	97,708
Cash provided by operating activities	$604,834

Investing activities:

Capital expenditures	($374,717)
Disposition of operating assets	442
Cash used in investing activities	($374,275)

Required:

1. Assume that the only changes affecting the operating asset category were related to acquisitions, disposals, and depreciation. Calculate the original cost of the assets that were disposed of during 2004.

2. Calculate the accumulated depreciation related to assets that were disposed of during 2004.

3. Determine the amount of gain or loss that was recognized on the disposal of assets during 2004.

4. Reconstruct a summary journal entry to record the sale or disposal of assets during 2004.

Analyze: By what percentage did total gross operating assets change from 2003 to 2004?

LO10 **PROBLEM 9-6 Analysis and Ratios**

Refer to the information for NortCor in Problem 9-5.

Required:

1. NortCor's net sales for 2004 were $4,009,346. Calculate the asset turnover ratio.

2. NortCor's operating income for 2004 was $3,630,157. Calculate the return on operating assets.

3. Calculate the average useful life of the operating assets. NortCor uses the straight-line method of depreciation for all operating assets.

4. Calculate the average age of the assets.

Analyze: If NortCor's main competitor reported an operating asset turnover ratio of 2.1, how does NortCor compare?

Communicate: Draft a memo that explains what each of the ratios is intended to measure, what the ratios reveal about the age and composition of NortCor's operating assets, and whether the operating assets have been utilized efficiently.

LO4, 6, 9 PROBLEM 9-7 **Depreciation, Change in Estimate and Principle, Exchange**

Gates Company compiled the following information concerning its equipment:

A. Equipment A was purchased on January 1, 2001, at a cost of $260,000. The asset has been depreciated over an eight-year life using the straight-line method with an estimated residual value of $20,000. On January 1, 2004, the life of the asset was reviewed and it was determined that the remaining life of the asset, as of January 1, 2004, was four years.

B. Equipment B was purchased on January 1, 2001, at a cost of $300,000. The asset has been depreciated over a 10-year life using the double-declining balance method. On January 1, 2004, Gates adopted the straight-line method of depreciation for Equipment B. The estimated life of the asset was not altered, but the company estimated that the residual value of the asset would be $10,000 at the end of the asset's life.

C. Equipment C was purchased on January 1, 2002, at a cost of $400,000. The asset has been depreciated using the units-of-production method and zero residual value. The total estimated number of units to be produced by the equipment was 80,000. The number of units produced by the asset has been 20,000, 15,000, and 8,000 in 2002, 2003, and 2004, respectively.

D. Equipment D was purchased on January 1, 2002, at a cost of $360,000. The asset has been depreciated over a 10-year life using the straight-line method and zero residual value. On July 1, 2004, the fair market value of the asset was $290,000. At that time, the asset was exchanged for Equipment E, and $25,000 cash was received as boot in the exchange. The exchange did not alter the expected cash flows of the company. Equipment E will be depreciated over a six-year life using the straight-line method with zero residual value.

Required:

1. Record all necessary journal entries related to the Gates Company's equipment for the year 2004. You may assume that the company has a December 31 year end. You may also ignore income taxes.

2. Calculate the amounts related to equipment that should appear on the balance sheet as of December 31, 2004.

Analyze: What actual cash flows resulted from transactions A through D in 2004?

LO9 PROBLEM 9-8 **Exchanges**

Consider the following exchanges of nonmonetary assets.

A. Exchange with commercial substance:

Old equipment	$50,000
Accumulated depreciation	45,000
Fair market value	13,000
Cash	−12,000

B. Exchange lacking in commercial substance—same data as in A:

C. Exchange lacking in commercial substance:

Old equipment	$50,000
Accumulated depreciation	45,000
Fair market value	3,000
Cash	0

D. Exchange lacking in commercial substance:

Old equipment	$50,000
Accumulated depreciation	39,000
Fair market value	10,000
Cash	+2,000

E. Exchange lacking in commercial substance:

Old equipment	$50,000
Accumulated depreciation	45,000
Fair market value	10,000
Cash	+2,000
Fair market value of asset acquired	8,000

Required: Make the necessary journal entries to record the exchanges of assets. *Hint:* In all cases, you may assume that the total fair market value (asset + or − cash) given in the transaction equals the total received.

Analyze: What total gains and losses were reported for items A through E?

LO4, 9   **PROBLEM 9-9   Book Value and Exchange of Similar Assets**

Solano Company has a Web server used in its e-commerce operations that cost $120,000 on its purchase date of March 1, 2000. Solano has been depreciating the server over its estimated life of five years using straight-line depreciation with an estimated residual value of $12,000. On September 1, 2003, in an effort to downsize its operations, Solano traded in its old server for a smaller server that had a cash price of $40,000. As part of the exchange, Solano received $10,000 cash. Solano's fiscal period ends on December 31.

Required:

1. Calculate the book value of the old server on September 1, 2003, for Solano Company.

2. What rationale is used for determining whether an exchange of nonmonetary assets is the completion of the earning process?

3. Show the calculation of the amount of any realized gain or loss on the exchange for Solano Company assuming the exchange is lacking in commercial substance.

4. Show the calculation of the cost basis for the new server.

Analyze: For what conceptual reason is the amount you calculated in question 3 recognized or deferred?

LO4, 6   **PROBLEM 9-10   Calculating and Reporting an Accounting Change**

On January 1, 2007, Barnes Corp. changed from the straight-line method of depreciation to the double-declining-balance method for its machinery to more accurately recognize depreciation charges. The machinery was acquired on June 30, 2005, and its cost was $50,000, with a $6,000 residual value. The estimated useful life of the machinery was eight years. Barnes has a calendar fiscal period and a 30 percent income tax rate. Barnes reported $28,203 of income from continuing operations in 2007, before income taxes and before the effects of the accounting change and current-year depreciation.

Required:

1. Calculate the amount of depreciation expense for 2005 and 2006.

2. Calculate the depreciation expense for 2007 and the adjusted income from continuing operations for the year.

Analyze: Explain how to identify whether an accounting change is a change in accounting principle or a change in accounting estimate. Which type of change did Barnes Corp. incur?

LO4, 8, 11   **PROBLEM 9-11   Depreciation, Disposal, Cash Flows**

Cham Company purchased a truck on January 1, 2003, at a cash cost of $10,600. The estimated residual value was $400, and the estimated useful life was four years. The company uses straight-line depreciation. On March 31, 2005, the company sold the truck for $5,600 cash. Cham Company uses the indirect method to prepare the operating activities section of its statement of cash flows.

Required:

1. How much is total accumulated depreciation at March 31, 2005?

2. How much gain or loss will Cham recognize as a result of the sale of the truck?

3. Indicate what amounts related to the truck will be shown on Cham's statement of cash flows for the year ended December 31, 2005.

Analyze: How does the amount reported as a "gain or loss from the sale of the truck" differ from amounts reported as sales revenue?

LO4, 5   **PROBLEM 9-12   Depreciation Calculation, Subsequent Costs**

On March 31, 2004, Darden Company purchased a delivery truck for $30,000. The truck is expected to last six years with a $3,000 residual value. The company uses the straight-line method to depreciate its truck. On January 1, 2006, Darden paid $5,375 to purchase an automatic lift for the truck that enabled the company to load and unload more quickly. Assume that the company's accounting year ends on December 31.

Required:

1. Calculate depreciation expense for 2004.

2. Calculate depreciation expense for 2006.

Analyze: What options does Darden have in accounting for partial-period depreciation? Why might Darden prefer an alternative to computing partial-period depreciation on a monthly basis?

LO3   **PROBLEM 9-13   Interest Capitalization**

Perry Inc. contracted with Mixon Corp. to construct a production machine. Construction of the machine began on February 1, 2004, and was completed on November 30 of the same year. Amounts paid to the contractor during 2004 were as follows:

April 1	$240,000
June 1	500,000
November 1	360,000

Perry had the following obligations outstanding during 2004:

- A 5-year, 12 percent note payable securing company trucks dated December 1, 2000, for $360,000.
- A 12-month, 6 percent working capital loan dated June 1, 2004, for $120,000.

For construction purposes, Perry borrowed $350,000 on February 1 at 8 percent for two years.

Required:

1. Identify the beginning and ending dates of the capitalization period.

2. How much are the weighted-average accumulated expenditures?

3. How much is the weighted-average interest rate?

4. How much is avoidable interest? Why is this amount considered to be a cost of the constructed asset?

5. At what amount should the production machine be recorded in Perry's books at November 30?

Analyze: On what date will Perry begin depreciating the machine? Why?

LO1, 2, 5   **PROBLEM 9-14   Acquisition Costs, Costs Subsequent to Acquisition**
Hemingway Company had the following transactions during 2003:

A. Acquired machinery and a storage building for $2,000,000 cash. The appraised values of the machinery and the storage building were $1,500,000 and $1,000,000, respectively. How much should be debited to the Machinery account?

B. Performed periodic maintenance on old machinery at a cost of $2,800. How much should be capitalized as part of the machinery cost? Justify your response.

C. Acquired a tract of land and a building for $300,000. The land was appraised at $370,000, and the building was valued at $30,000. Hemingway did not want the building and rented a bulldozer to raze it, at a cost of $12,000. The salvaged materials were sold for $4,000 to a junk dealer. How much should be capitalized to the Land account?

D. Purchased a delivery truck for $24,000 cash that had a useful life of four years and a residual value of $500. Prior to using the truck, Hemingway installed storage compartments on the truck at a cost of $2,000 and had the truck painted with the company's trade name for $400. During the installation of the storage compartments, one of Hemingway's employees smashed his finger in the truck door, and Hemingway had to pay $150 in medical fees for the visit to the emergency room. How much should Hemingway capitalize to the Truck account?

E. After the storage building had been used for six months, it was remodeled so that supplies could be stored more efficiently. The cost was $60,000, but since cash flows were a concern, the amount was financed with a 9 percent, three-year note. What account should be debited, and why?

Required: Answer the questions for each independent transaction in items A through E. All amounts are material.

Analyze: For each cost in D that is not capitalized to the Truck account, indicate how that cost is accounted for.

LO1, 2, 5   **PROBLEM 9-15   Acquisition Costs, Costs Subsequent to Acquisition**
On January 1, 2001, Manning Corporation purchased land and a building for a total cash price of $280,000. Manning also paid $3,000 for surveying fees, $3,900 in legal fees related to the purchase, and $5,100 in property taxes for 1999 and 2000. Appraised values at the time of the purchase were: land, $80,000, and building, $240,000. Shortly after closing, the city assessed Manning a special one-time fee of $21,000 for streetlights, which the city will maintain. Manning paid a subcontractor $62,000 to pave a parking lot on the property.

Required:

1. Determine how much Manning will recognize as the cost of the land and the cost of the building as a result of the purchase.

2. Why is the cost of the land not depreciated?

Analyze: Suppose Manning had paid $340,000 to purchase the land and building instead of $280,000. How would the transaction be accounted for differently as a result?

LO4, 9   **PROBLEM 9-16   Exchange of Assets**
On March 31, 2003, Woodley Company traded in a forklift that had a book value of $15,000. Its cost was $40,000, and the fair market value is now $24,000. Woodley paid cash of $6,000 and received a new smaller forklift with a fair market value of $30,000. Woodley plans to use straight-line depreciation and a 10-year life for its new forklift, and estimates its residual value to be $1,250.

Required:

1. How much gain or loss will Woodley realize on the exchange assuming the exchange was lacking in commercial substance?
2. How much gain or loss should Woodley recognize (record) on the exchange? Why?
3. How much is recognized as the cost of the new forklift?

Analyze: If this exchange did have commercial substance, how would depreciation expense for 2004 differ? Respond conceptually and not with calculations.

LO3, 4, 7 PROBLEM 9-17 **Impairment, Interest, Depreciation**

On March 31, 2003, Graff Company arranged for Fales Company to construct a special machine. Fales began construction immediately. Fales Company did not require any payments until the day of completion, March 31, 2004. On that date, Graff paid Fales Company $500,000 and accepted delivery of the machine. Graff began depreciating the machine using straight-line depreciation over a 10-year life with no residual value. Graff did not obtain a construction loan, but it had a five-year note outstanding for the entire period in the amount of $800,000 that carried a 10 percent interest rate with interest payable annually on March 31. On March 31, 2006, a new electronic machine that was more efficient than Fales's machine was released by a competitor and was available at a lower cost. Graff estimates that its machine will generate $30,000 of cash flows per year. It now appears that Graff's machine has a market value of $140,000.

Required:

1. Identify the two steps that relate to impairment of operating assets.
2. Prepare any journal entry necessary to record the impairment of value on March 31, 2006.
3. Show the effect of the impairment on Graff's income statement for its year ended March 31, 2006.
4. Which accounting concept dictates how accounting for subsequent increases in value should be handled?

Analyze: When should a company evaluate impairment?

CASES

LO3 RESEARCH CASE 9-1 **Capitalization of Interest**

The information that appears at the top of the opposite page is from the financial statements of the cruise line company, **Carnival Corporation**.

Required:

1. What are the requirements for capitalization of interest?
2. On which assets does Carnival capitalize interest? Why does the company not capitalize interest on other assets in the operating asset category?
3. What was Carnival's total interest incurred for 2002? For 2001?
4. What would Carnival's interest expense be in 2002 if it did not capitalize interest? What other accounts would be affected?
5. What interest expense or income is reported in Carnival's current-year income statement?

LO7 CRITICAL THINKING CASE 9-2 **Impairment of Operating Assets**

Refer to the Carnival Corporation financial information in Case 9-1.

Required:

1. Explain the meaning of the impairment charge that appears in the consolidated statements of operations.

Carnival

Carnival Corporation
CONSOLIDATED STATEMENTS OF OPERATIONS
(in thousands)

	Years Ended November 30,	
	2002	**2001**
Revenues	$4,368,269	$4,535,751
Costs and Expenses		
Operating	2,311,919	2,468,730
Selling and administrative	611,948	618,664
Depreciation and amortization	382,343	372,224
Impairment charge	20,000	140,378
Loss (income) from affiliated operations, net	—	44,024
	3,326,210	3,644,020
Operating Income	1,042,059	891,731
Nonoperating (Expense) Income		
Interest income	32,140	34,255
Interest expense, net of capitalized interest	(110,740)	(120,692)
Other (expense) income, net	(4,080)	108,649
Income tax benefit (expense), net	56,562	12,257
	(26,118)	34,469
Net Income	$1,015,941	$ 926,200

Capitalized interest, primarily on our ships under construction, amounted to $39 million and $29 million in fiscal 2002 and 2001, respectively.

2. What amounts must be calculated to determine whether assets are impaired?

3. How is the amount of the impairment charge calculated?

4. Once assets have been written down because of an impairment charge, may they be written up again in future periods?

LO2, 5

ETHICS

ETHICS CASE 9-3   Capital Expenditures

The following excerpt from *Computer Technology Review* concerns the well-publicized scandal at **WorldCom** in 2002.

> By now, the details of the newest, and presumably largest, corporate accounting scandal are well known. The company, under the leadership of CEO Bernard Ebbers, hid billions in losses by apparently faking not only earnings reports but actual earnings statements.
>
> What the company did, according to investigators, is deceptively simple. It characterized basic expenses as capital investments, thereby limiting the company's apparent losses while at the same time raising its apparent gains. For example, when WorldCom needed to spend capital to, say, fix a segment of cut fiber line, this was booked as "capital spending" rather than as an expense. In this way, it could limit losses, which of course gives the appearance of more revenue. It appears that all earnings reports from 2001 and 2002 are in doubt—covering $3.8 billion—and investigators are expecting to find as much as a billion more dollars in hidden losses when balance sheets from 1999 and 2000 are examined.[13]

---

13 Joshua Piven, "Summer of Scandal," *Computer Technology Review* 22 (August 2001): 30–31.

Required:

1. What are the guidelines that determine whether an item is a capital expenditure or should be treated as an expense? Is judgment involved in determining whether an item is a capital expenditure?

2. What is the impact on the income statement and the balance sheet if items are treated as capital expenditures rather than expenses?

3. When WorldCom discovered the "hidden losses" of $3.8 billion, how should it have treated the amount? Is this considered a change in estimate?

LO4, 6

ETHICS ⚖

ETHICS CASE 9-4   Accounting for Operating Assets

Sarah Johnson is the assistant controller of Besser Corporation, a manufacturer of high-end consumer appliances. Sarah holds active CPA and CMA licenses, and is a member of the AICPA, the IMA, and the Maine State Board of Accountancy. While she is reviewing a draft of the company's financial statement notes for the upcoming reporting period, John Blau, the controller of Besser Corporation, enters her office and asks to see a copy of the draft financial statements. He then informs Sarah that some revisions are necessary with respect to property, plant, and equipment. These revisions consist of (1) changing the policy for capitalizing small tools, (2) changing from an accelerated method of depreciation to the straight-line method, and (3) lengthening the useful life of most of the manufacturing equipment. He asks her to recalculate earnings consistent with these changes.

Sarah decides that she will have to consider the issues. She speaks to the production line foreman regarding the manufacturing equipment and learns that as a result of unexpected technology changes, some of the main machinery that has a remaining depreciable life of three years will probably be replaced in two years. Thus, she determines that the estimated useful life should probably be shortened instead of lengthened, which would increase current-year depreciation significantly. She meets with John to discuss her findings and tells him that (1) the expensing policy for small tools had been in effect for many years and should not be changed, and (2) the useful life should be shortened, which would increase current-year depreciation expense by $150,000. She tells John her analysis indicates that even after changing to the straight-line method, depreciation expense would be higher than prior to those changes.

John reminds Sarah that raw material costs have increased during the current year, and he tells her that he feels it is important that the company report higher income to compensate for these costs. After considering this, Sarah suggests that they could ignore the change in useful life, since it was not certain that the machinery would be replaced in two years. She also reminds John that keeping the useful life unchanged would allow the company to record less depreciation expense, but she does not agree with the change in depreciation methods. John wishes to go further. He knows that analysts frequently ignore income from accounting changes. He argues that current operating income needs to be enhanced. He suggests that the company switch to straight-line for about half of the machinery and increase the useful life for the other half, thus increasing both operating income and net income.

As you can see, accounting for these long-term assets requires a considerable amount of judgment. It is also one of the areas that provides management with the highest degree of accounting flexibility.

Required:

1. What are the problems and issues that Sarah faces?
2. Who will be affected by the decision that Sarah makes?
3. What values and principles are likely to influence her decision?
4. What alternative actions can Sarah take?
5. Of the parties you listed in question 2, whose interest is most important?
6. Of the values and principles you listed in question 3, which value is most important?
7. Which of the possible consequences will do the most good or cause the least harm?
8. What do you think Sarah should do?

ON THE WEB

The following exercises, activities, and problems are available on the *Intermediate Accounting* website. Use these resources to reinforce your understanding of the topics presented in this chapter.

- CPA-Adapted Simulations
- Interpreting the Accounting Standards
- Extending the Global Focus
- Extending the Ethics Discussion
- Mastering the Spreadsheet
- Career Snapshots

- Annual Report Project
- ACE Practice Tests
- Flashcards
- Glossary
- Check Figures for Text Problems
- PowerPoint Presentations

SOLUTIONS: CHECK YOUR UNDERSTANDING

Characteristics and Presentation of Operating Assets (p. 401)

1. Land, buildings, and equipment are generally included as operating assets. Furniture and fixtures, land improvements, automobiles, natural resources, and construction in progress may also be categorized as operating assets on the balance sheet if they are purchased to create operational revenue.

2. Operating assets include only those assets that are presently being used in operations, that have a useful life of more than one year, and that have a physical existence.

3. Disclosures for depreciable assets should include the amount of depreciation expense for the period; the balances of major classes of depreciable assets, by nature or function, at the balance sheet date; the amount of accumulated depreciation, either by major classes of assets or in total, at the balance sheet date; and a general description of the method or methods used in computing depreciation with respect to major classes of assets.

Costs at Acquisition (p. 408)

1. Acquisition costs are all costs necessary to obtain the asset and prepare it for its intended use.

2. Operating assets are reported on the balance sheet at acquisition cost less accumulated depreciation.

3. If assets are purchased for a lump-sum amount, the purchase price should be allocated among the assets using the proportion of the fair market value of all the assets that is represented by each asset's fair market value.

4. Net earnings are increased in the current period if interest is capitalized on a self-constructed asset.

5. When an asset is donated, the receiving company should determine the fair value of the asset and record the amount received as revenue. The fair value should be considered the acquisition cost and therefore the basis for depreciation of the asset.

Depreciation (p. 412)

1. Operating assets are depreciated in an effort to match expenses with revenues and to write down the value of the asset as it declines in usefulness.

2. Straight-line depreciation is calculated as follows: Depreciation Expense per Period = (Cost Basis − Residual Value) ÷ Estimated Life.

3. The units-of-production method is referred to as a usage method.

4. The double-declining-balance method of depreciation is a method in which depreciation is calculated at twice the straight-line rate. The same rate is applied each period, but the book value of the asset is decreased each year.

Costs Subsequent to Acquisition (p. 413)

1. Capital expenditures are those incurred in order to achieve greater benefits in the future from an asset. If an expenditure increases the future economic benefits of the asset, the expenditure should be capitalized. If, however, the expenditure is incurred in order to maintain the asset in its normal operating condition, then the expenditure should be treated as an expense of the period and should not be capitalized.

2. In some cases, an improvement to an operating asset may increase its useful life. In such cases, depreciation should be recalculated based on the new life.

Changes in Estimate and Changes in Principle (p. 415)

1. Changes in estimate should be treated in a prospective manner. That is, the amount of depreciation of the asset should be altered for the year of the change and for future years. No retroactive restatements of past depreciation amounts are required for a change in estimate.

2. Under the previous accounting rule, if a company changes depreciation methods, the company must report the cumulative effect of the change on prior periods as a separate item on the income statement after extraordinary items. Under the new accounting rule, changes in depreciation methods should be treated as changes in estimate. The changes are not treated retroactively.

Asset Impairment (p. 418)

1. According to *SFAS No. 144*, an impairment loss has occurred when the undiscounted sum of estimated

future cash flows from the asset is less than the book value of the asset.

2. The impairment loss is calculated as the difference between the fair value of the asset and the book value of the asset.

3. When an impairment loss is recognized, it must be disclosed in the financial statements and the accompanying notes. The required disclosure should explain the impairment, the assumptions used in measuring the impairment, and the effect of the loss on any business segments.

Disposal of Operating Assets (p. 425)

1. Gains and losses on sales of assets are normally reported before income from continuing operations. However, if the gain or loss is related to the disposition of a business segment, it will be reported after income from continuing operations and before extraordinary items.

2. When a gain occurs on the exchange of assets that lack commercial substance and the company is paying cash in the exchange transaction, the amount of the gain is not recorded.

Analysis and Cash Flow Issues (p. 430)

1. The asset turnover ratio is calculated by dividing net sales by average net operating assets. It tells how many dollars in sales are generated for each dollar invested in operating assets.

2. Depreciation costs should be added back to net income in the operating activities section of the statement of cash flows when using the indirect method, since depreciation is not a true cash deduction.

CPA-ADAPTED SIMULATION

This simulation asks you to complete various tasks related to a company's annual financial statements. If your instructor has signed up for CPAexcel™, you can do the work online at **www.cpaexcel.com/hmco.** You may also do the simulation manually.

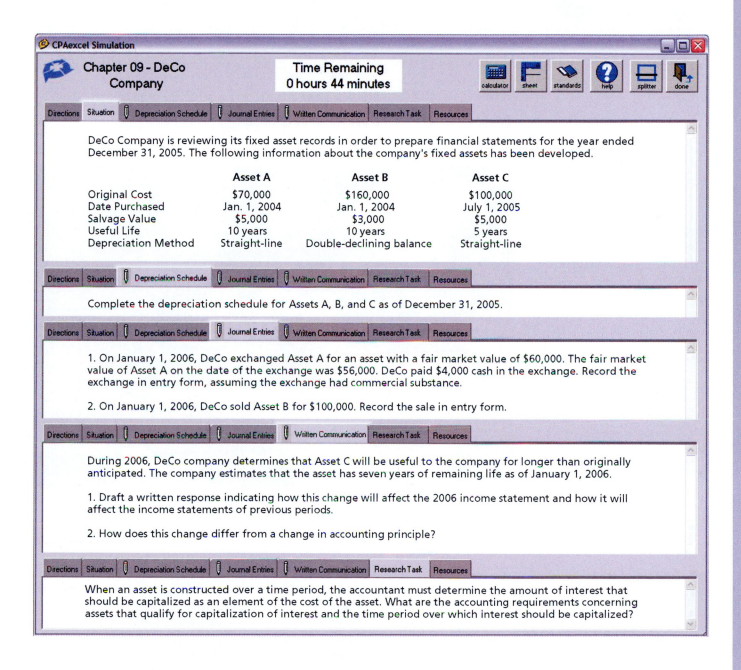

CPAexcel Simulation

Chapter 09 - DeCo Company

Time Remaining
0 hours 44 minutes

calculator | sheet | standards | help | splitter | done

Directions | Situation | Depreciation Schedule | Journal Entries | Written Communication | Research Task | Resources

DeCo Company is reviewing its fixed asset records in order to prepare financial statements for the year ended December 31, 2005. The following information about the company's fixed assets has been developed.

	Asset A	Asset B	Asset C
Original Cost	$70,000	$160,000	$100,000
Date Purchased	Jan. 1, 2004	Jan. 1, 2004	July 1, 2005
Salvage Value	$5,000	$3,000	$5,000
Useful Life	10 years	10 years	5 years
Depreciation Method	Straight-line	Double-declining balance	Straight-line

Directions | Situation | Depreciation Schedule | Journal Entries | Written Communication | Research Task | Resources

Complete the depreciation schedule for Assets A, B, and C as of December 31, 2005.

Directions | Situation | Depreciation Schedule | Journal Entries | Written Communication | Research Task | Resources

1. On January 1, 2006, DeCo exchanged Asset A for an asset with a fair market value of $60,000. The fair market value of Asset A on the date of the exchange was $56,000. DeCo paid $4,000 cash in the exchange. Record the exchange in entry form, assuming the exchange had commercial substance.

2. On January 1, 2006, DeCo sold Asset B for $100,000. Record the sale in entry form.

Directions | Situation | Depreciation Schedule | Journal Entries | Written Communication | Research Task | Resources

During 2006, DeCo company determines that Asset C will be useful to the company for longer than originally anticipated. The company estimates that the asset has seven years of remaining life as of January 1, 2006.

1. Draft a written response indicating how this change will affect the 2006 income statement and how it will affect the income statements of previous periods.

2. How does this change differ from a change in accounting principle?

Directions | Situation | Depreciation Schedule | Journal Entries | Written Communication | Research Task | Resources

When an asset is constructed over a time period, the accountant must determine the amount of interest that should be capitalized as an element of the cost of the asset. What are the accounting requirements concerning assets that qualify for capitalization of interest and the time period over which interest should be capitalized?

Intangible Assets

FINANCIAL REPORTING CASE

NIKE CASHES IN ON RETRO CONVERSE SHOES

The assets Nike received when it purchased Converse in 2003 were mostly in the form of intangible assets resulting from acquiring Converse's famed Chuck Taylor All-Star sneaker.

Nike For most of the century, the best-known basketball shoe manufacturer was Converse, Inc. However, in the 1980s, Nike began to outpace its former rival, and Converse began a downward slide. In 2002, Nike reported more than $10.7 billion dollars in revenue, whereas Converse reported a mere $205 million after having gone through numerous management teams and restructuring programs.

Nevertheless, Converse had something that Nike did not and that was the famed Chuck Taylor All-Star sneaker, one of the best-known and most authentic brands in the world. So, in July 2003, Nike purchased Converse. The purchase gave Nike access to a new product line just when "retro" sneakers were making a comeback. As Robert Toomey, a financial analyst covering the footwear industry, stated at the time of the acquisition, "Retro styling has come back strong, a lot stronger than I would have expected. Nike is always on the lookout for building their market share and strengthening their stable of products and brands."[1]

---

1 BBC News World Edition, "Nike Expands Trainer Empire," July 10, 2003, http://news.bbc.co.uk/2/hi/americas/3054777.stm.

Nike

**NOTES TO CONSOLIDATED
FINANCIAL STATEMENTS—(CONTINUED)**

The following table summarizes the Company's identifiable intangible assets balances as of May 31, 2004 and May 31, 2003:

	May 31, 2004			May 31, 2003		
	Gross Carrying Amount	Accumulated Amortization	Net Carrying Amount	Gross Carrying Amount	Accumulated Amortization	Net Carrying Amount
Amortized intangible assets:						
Patents	$27.9	$(11.9)	$ 16.0	$24.0	$(10.4)	$ 14.5
Trademarks	14.1	(11.5)	2.6	12.9	(10.6)	2.3
Other	17.0	(10.8)	6.2	7.5	(1.1)	6.4
Total	$59.0	$(34.2)	$ 24.8	$45.3	$(22.1)	$ 23.2
Unamortized intangible assets—						
Trademarks			$341.5			$ 95.0
Total			$366.3			$118.2

Tom Clarke, Nike's President of New Business Ventures, had this to say about the acquisition: "Converse is one of the strongest footwear brands in the world with great heritage and a long history of success. Converse shares our passion for sports and, together, Nike and Converse will generate even greater access to a dynamic consumer base."[2]

The assets that Nike received in the purchase of Converse were mostly in the form of intangible assets, representing the Converse trademarks and patents. In addition, Nike recognized goodwill associated with the purchase, representing the anticipated future benefits of the combination of Nike and Converse. Nike reported the details of the purchase of Converse in the notes to its 2004 Annual Report in the following manner:

Note 15—Acquisition

On September 4, 2003, the Company acquired 100 percent of the equity shares of Converse. Converse designs, distributes, and markets high performance and casual athletic footwear and apparel.

All assets and liabilities of Converse have been recorded in the Company's consolidated balance sheet based on their estimated fair values at the date of the acquisition. Identifiable intangible assets and goodwill relating to the purchase approximated $254.8 and $69.1 million, respectively. Identifiable intangible assets include $246.2 million for trademarks that have an indefinite life, and $8.6 million of other intangible assets that were amortized over nine months.... The pro forma effect of the acquisition on the combined results of operations was not significant.

The table above, which is from the notes of Nike's annual report, summarizes Nike's identifiable intangible assets balances as of May 31, 2004 and May 31, 2003. Nike's intangible assets are also reflected in the asset section of Nike's balance sheet, which appears on the next page.

Intangible assets, such as trademarks, patents, and long-standing customer relationships, can allow companies to increase their competitive advantage, develop new markets, and generate new revenue streams.

---

2 ESPN Sports Business, "Nike Hopes to Cash in on 'Retro' Converse," July 9, 2003, http://espn.go.com/sportsbusiness/news/2003/07091/1578731.html.

Nike, Inc.

CONSOLIDATED BALANCE SHEETS

	May 31, 2004	2003
	(In millions)	
ASSETS		
Current assets:		
Cash and equivalents	$ 828.0	$ 634.0
Short-term investments	400.8	—
Accounts receivable, less allowance for doubtful accounts of $95.3 and $81.9	2,120.2	2,083.9
Inventories (Note 2)	1,633.6	1,514.9
Deferred income taxes (Note 8)	165.0	221.8
Prepaid expenses and other current assets	364.4	332.5
Total current assets	5,512.0	4,787.1
Property, plant and equipment, net (Note 3)	1,586.9	1,620.8
Identifiable intangible assets, net (Note 4)	366.3	118.2
Goodwill (Note 4)	135.4	65.6
Deferred income taxes and other assets (Note 8)	291.0	229.4
Total assets	$7,891.6	$6,821.1

EXAMINING THE CASE

1. What challenges do companies face in protecting their intangible assets, such as the Nike Swoosh?

2. Where are intangible assets such as trademarks reported on a company's financial statements?

3. What challenges do you think accountants face when recognizing the value of an intangible asset such as a trademark?

LO 1 Identify the categories of intangible assets.

intangible assets assets that have no physical substance but do have a value based on rights, privileges, or advantages coming to or belonging to the owner

trademark a federally registered word, phrase, symbol, or design that identifies the source and quality of a particular good or service

patent an exclusive right granted by the federal government to make a specific product or use a specific process without competition for a specific period of time

copyright an exclusive right granted by the federal government to publish and sell literary, musical, or other artistic materials for a period of the author's life plus 70 years

The Nature of Intangible Assets

Although many assets of a business are tangible, like buildings, equipment, or financial instruments, some companies possess assets like trademarks, distinctive brands, or a secret manufacturing process. These **intangible assets** are assets that have no physical substance but do have a value based on rights, privileges, or advantages coming to or belonging to the owner. In many instances, these rights, privileges, or advantages are granted or protected by the government. For example, a **trademark** is a federally registered word, phrase, symbol, or design that identifies the source and quality of a particular good or service. Legal rights to a trademark exclude others from using the same trademark or one that is confusingly similar for an indefinite period of time. A **patent** is an exclusive right granted by the federal government to make a specific product or use a specific process without competition for a period of years. Utility patents, which are granted to anyone who invents, discovers, or improves a useful process or machine, expire 20 years from the date of filing. Design patents, which are granted to anyone who has invented a new, original, and ornamental design for a product, expire 14 years from grant. A **copyright** is an exclusive right granted by the federal government to publish and sell literary, musical, or other artistic materials for a period of the author's life plus 70 years.

Many companies invest heavily in developing and using intangible assets. These assets allow companies and individuals to own their creativity and innovation in the same way that they can own physical property. Thus, just as a company can control a machine that it produces, it can also control the design of that machine through a patent. The owner of an intangible asset can control and be rewarded for its use through licensing and royalty agreements that allow other companies to use the asset. Giving the owners of intangible assets control over their creations encourages further innovation, which ultimately benefits the economy. Software companies continue to develop new applications because they know that if they are successful, they will reap the rewards of their hard work, and their ideas will be protected from being stolen. Investments in intangible assets can range from pure research and development that results in patents or trademarks to the compilation and cultivation of customer lists and marketing information. In addition to developing intangible assets internally, many companies purchase or license intangible assets from other companies.

For accountants, the key question is how intangible assets should be measured and recorded. To provide guidance, *Statement of Accounting Standards No. 141,* "Business Combinations," identifies five basic categories of intangible assets:

1. Marketing-related intangible assets

2. Customer-related intangible assets

3. Artistic-related intangible assets

4. Contract-based intangible assets

5. Technology-based intangible assets

In the following sections, we will briefly examine some specific intangible assets included in each category. We will also discuss the time period over which these assets can be expected to provide value to their owners. This time period may be a limited period or an indefinite period, depending on the nature of the intangible asset.

MARKETING-RELATED INTANGIBLE ASSETS

marketing-related intangible assets assets that allow a company to promote itself or its products

Marketing-related intangible assets are assets that allow a company to promote itself or its products. Included in this group are such things as trademarks and trade names, package designs, Internet domain names, and noncompete agreements. These intangible assets are protected by legal standards that allow a company to sue if, for example, another company copies its product's packaging or design.

For instance, the **Hinckley Company** is a yacht builder that has developed a number of unique and widely copied boats. During 2001, Hinckley issued a statement saying that it would "address the problem of the growing number of copycat boats." The company contended that the proliferation of look-alike versions "threatens to erode the investment our owners have made in buying a Hinckley, as well as the significant investment the company has made in research and development, new production facilities, and marketing."[3] The boat builder did not contend that other companies were replicating its boats, but it argued that they were copying enough key elements to cloud the identity of its unique product.

Product design (or, in legal terms, trade dress) cases have involved the layout of a publication, the design of outdoor furniture, and the appearance of a sports car. In each case, the owners of the original product won the case.

useful life the length of time during which a long-term asset can be expected to perform its function

Marketing-related intangible assets typically have varying useful lives. The **useful life** of an asset is the length of time during which it can be expected to perform its function. For example, the right to a trademark never expires, so the asset has an indefinite useful life. The government provides trademark protection for 10 years, but

---

3 "Hinckley Warns Off Copycats," *Soundings Trade Only Today,* October 26, 2001.

companies may renew their applications indefinitely. On the other hand, noncompete agreements have useful lives equal to the length of the contractual agreement between the employee and the employer and therefore are considered to have a limited useful life.

CUSTOMER-RELATED INTANGIBLE ASSETS

customer-related intangible assets assets that provide benefits to a company by allowing it to sell, lease, or exchange information about its customers

Customer-related intangible assets provide benefits to a company by allowing it to sell, lease, or exchange information about its customers. Included in this category are customer lists, order backlogs, customer relationships, and contracts. The significant value of such intangibles is exemplified by the $3.35 million that **KB Toys** paid for the **eToys** trade name, logo, and e-mail services in 2001. The e-mail services included the right to contact former eToys customers with information about how to continue their online toy shopping by switching to KB Toys. Although the useful lives of customer-related intangible assets are not limited by regulatory or legal provisions, the useful life of a specific customer-related intangible asset is usually limited by its usefulness.

ARTISTIC-RELATED INTANGIBLE ASSETS

artistic-related intangible assets assets that are protected by copyrights granted by governments to the creators of original artistic works

Artistic-related intangible assets are assets that are protected by copyrights granted by governments to the creators of original artistic works. Copyright law protects a broad range of artistic works, from plays, operas, and ballets to images and photographs. The owners of copyrights are allowed the exclusive right to reproduce, copy, and perform their artistic works for profit. In the United States, copyrights continue for the life of the artist plus 70 years. When determining the useful life of an artistic-related intangible asset, however, a company must establish the number of years over which the intangible asset will provide benefits. That time period may be much shorter than the maximum allowable period of the artist's life plus 70 years.

The Internet has presented new challenges to entertainment companies that seek to protect the value of the copyrights on their artistic-related intangible assets. Because copyrighted material can easily be downloaded from the Internet without paying the usual fees, companies' revenue from such fees is steadily decreasing. For example, in 2003, **PricewaterhouseCoopers** estimated that 50 percent of a film's income came from DVD rentals and sales. However, as more movies are downloaded from the Internet, even though the movies are copyrighted, revenue from DVD rentals and sales will be more difficult to earn.

CONTRACT-BASED INTANGIBLE ASSETS

contract-based intangible assets assets that are based on legal agreements between two parties to perform specified duties

Contract-based intangible assets are assets that are based on legal agreements between two parties to perform specified duties. Among the assets that are included in this category are licensing and royalty contracts, construction permits, franchise agreements, employment contracts, and broadcast rights. In addition, timber, drilling, mineral, and water rights are considered contract-based intangible assets. The useful lives of intangible assets in this category are usually set forth in the contracts that create them.

For example, although **QUALCOMM** manufactures cell phone handsets, its other main source of revenue is licensing and royalty revenue from agreements allowing other companies to use the technology that it has developed. QUALCOMM developed code division multiple access (CDMA) cell phone technology, which works by converting speech into digital information that is then transmitted as a radio signal over a wireless network. CDMA became the leading wireless technology and was selected as the standard for the new third-generation (3G) wireless systems. Thus, wireless carriers that want to build or upgrade to 3G CDMA networks to provide more capacity for voice traffic and high-speed data capabilities must first sign licensing and royalty

Illustration 10.1

Five Categories of Intangible Assets

Intangible Assets	Attributes	Examples
Marketing-related intangible assets	Assets that allow a company to promote itself or its products	Trademarks, trade names, package designs, Internet domain names, and noncompete agreements
Customer-related intangible assets	Assets that provide benefits to a company by allowing it to sell, lease, or exchange information about its customers	Customer lists, order backlogs, customer relationships, and contracts
Artistic-related intangible assets	Assets that are protected by copyrights granted by governments to the creators of original artistic works	Copyrights
Contract-based intangible assets	Assets that represent legal agreements between two parties to perform specified duties	Licensing and royalty contracts, lease agreements, construction permits, franchise agreements, employment contracts, and broadcast rights
Technology-based intangible assets	Assets that represent technological change	Patents, trade secrets, computer databases, and software

agreements with QUALCOMM. Those licensing and royalty agreements generated over $830 million of revenue in 2003. If a company uses CDMA technology without signing an agreement, QUALCOMM may sue the company to protect its intangible asset.

TECHNOLOGY-BASED INTANGIBLE ASSETS

technology-based intangible assets assets derived from patents, trade secrets, computer databases, and software

Technology-based intangible assets are assets such as patents, trade secrets, computer databases, and software. They provide value to companies through either legal or contractual protection. In 2003, **Microsoft** recorded purchases of $306 million of intangible assets, $97 million of which were technology-based assets related to the acquisition of **Navision a/s** and **Rare, Ltd. Software**. Trade secrets and databases would normally be amortized over their useful lives. However, if no factors limit their useful lives, they may be considered to have an indefinite life.

The five categories of intangible assets are summarized in Illustration 10.1.

INTANGIBLE ASSETS AND ETHICS

ETHICS

Although intangible assets may take the form of customer relationships, superior management, or trade secrets, companies are becoming increasingly aware that their policies as ethical corporate citizens affect their ability to create more shareholder value in the long run. They realize that market perception, customer satisfaction, ethical behavior, brand identity, corporate governance, and corporate reputation play large roles in the building of intangible assets. **Telefonica**, the leading telecommunications company in the Spanish- and Portuguese-speaking markets, created an "Integrated Model of Corporate Reputation" with the aim of integrating the management of its intangible assets so that it would create more shareholder value in the long run.[4] The model focuses on variables that provide the foundation for a solid reputation in the business world: ethics, values, mission, vision, social responsibility, working practices, and corporate governance. Management of these variables provides a way for the company to build trust and strengthen the value of its corporate reputation.

CHECK YOUR UNDERSTANDING

1. List the five basic categories of intangible assets.

2. Provide three examples of a customer-related intangible asset.

3. How is the useful life of an artistic-related intangible asset determined?

LO 2 Value and amortize intangible assets.

🧩 *Critical Thinking: If your company developed a secret and highly effective new manufacturing process, how do you think a value would be assigned to that intangible asset?*

The Initial Measurement of Intangible Assets

How a company gains ownership of an intangible asset determines what costs are included in that asset's value. An intangible asset that a company creates itself is valued differently from an intangible asset that is purchased from an outside source. For example, when a company compiles a detailed customer list for its products, the costs of creating the list do not appear on the financial statements. However, if a company buys a customer list, it can record the cost of the list as an intangible asset.

The useful life of an intangible asset also depends on specific circumstances. Some intangible assets, such as pharmaceutical patents, have definite lives, whereas others, such as trademarks, have indefinite lives. Useful life plays a crucial role in amortization, the process of allocating the cost of an intangible asset to the periods the asset benefits.

VALUING INTANGIBLE ASSETS PURCHASED FROM AN OUTSIDE SOURCE

A purchased intangible asset is recorded at its acquisition cost plus any additional costs needed to prepare the asset for use. These additional costs may include legal and accounting costs, appraisal fees, and recording fees. If payment is made in shares of the company's stock, the market value of the shares at the time of the agreement serves as the asset's cost. For instance, Tech Company agreed to purchase Value Corp's patents and patent rights for $30 million cash plus shares of the company's stock valued at $10 million. If Tech Company had incurred an additional $1 million in legal fees to draw up the purchase contract, the company would have recorded the patents and patent rights as follows:

Patents and Patent Rights	41,000,000	
Cash (to Value Corp.)		30,000,000
Capital Stock		10,000,000
Cash (to Lawyers)		1,000,000

If several intangible assets are purchased together for one price, the cost is allocated among the assets based on their relative fair market values. If fair market values are not available, appraised values may be used. For example, assume that Block Corporation purchases a patent, a customer list, and construction permits from Circle Corporation for $380,000. Block Corporation estimates that the fair market values of the three intangible assets are as follows:

---

4 Telefonica Corporate Responsibility, available at: **www.telefonica.com**. Accessed 3/15/04.

Patent	$120,000
Customer list	200,000
Construction permits	80,000
Total fair market value	$400,000

The company determines the specific value of each intangible asset by dividing its fair market value by the total fair market value and multiplying by the purchase price:

$$\text{Patent} \qquad \frac{\$120,000}{\$400,000} \times \$380,000 = \$114,000$$

$$\text{Customer list} \qquad \frac{\$200,000}{\$400,000} \times \$380,000 = \$190,000$$

$$\text{Construction permits} \qquad \frac{\$80,000}{\$400,000} \times \$380,000 = \$76,000$$

Block would record the intangible assets as follows:

Patent	114,000	
Customer List	190,000	
Construction Permits	76,000	
Cash		380,000

VALUING INTANGIBLE ASSETS DEVELOPED INTERNALLY

For an intangible asset that is developed internally, the initial recording is quite different. The only costs that can be associated with this kind of intangible asset are direct costs, such as application fees, legal and accounting fees, and recording fees. Any costs incurred for research and development efforts are considered to be indirect costs and are expensed as incurred. **Research and development (R&D)** is the effort to discover new knowledge and to translate that knowledge into plans and designs for new or improved products, services, and processes. Assume that LaserX Corporation spent $5,000,000 in 2005 on researching and developing a new laser for eye surgery. The effort was successful, so LaserX paid $145,000 to a legal firm specializing in intellectual property to research and file a patent on the laser. When the patent came through, LaserX recorded the patent at its direct cost of $145,000 as follows:

Laser Patent	145,000	
Cash		145,000

research and development (R&D) efforts to discover new knowledge and to translate that knowledge into plans and designs for new or improved products, services, and processes

The research and development costs were not included because they are considered internal development costs.

Users of financial statements may wonder why acquired intangible assets are valued differently from internally developed intangible assets. When an intangible asset is purchased, the price at which it is recorded represents the fair market value of the research and development that went into its production. However, when an intangible asset is developed through an internal process, it is recorded at the cost of ensuring that it is legally protected. That could be, for example, the cost of filing a patent application. Internally developed intangible assets are valued differently because the results of research and development are uncertain and because it is difficult to assign specific costs to specific research and development projects. Although all research and development is undertaken with the hope of obtaining new and useful products, only a small percentage of exploratory projects actually succeed.

point ▶◀ counterpoint

Internally Generated Intangibles: To Book or Not to Book?

the controversy Imagine that your company has designed a supply-chain management system that brings customized inventory assortments to your national retail stores in record time and at minimum cost. Your customers are highly satisfied, and you have wowed the business world at large with your innovation. Can you record a value for this innovative supply-chain system on your balance sheet and call it an asset? At present, internally generated intangible assets are not valued and recorded on the balance sheet. A growing number of academics and practitioners believe that this position should change. Because items like intellectual property, innovative thinking, and branding are highly relevant in today's knowledge-based economy, many think these items deserve a spot on the balance sheet. Others oppose the practice, believing that the valuation of such items would be subjective at best and that including them on the balance sheet would decrease the comparability and reliability of the financial statement.

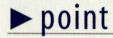 **point**

Baruch Lev

accounting and finance professor, New York University

on the point:

- **Holman and Kahn**
  accounting practitioners

- **Margaret Blair and Steven Wallman**
  The Brookings Institution, think tank

- **Bob Herz**
  partner at PricewaterhouseCoopers

▶ **The balance sheet should reflect internally generated intangibles because they are relevant assets in today's new economy.**

Baruch Lev, one of the most outspoken proponents of a system that recognizes intangibles on the balance sheet, believes that failure to do so damages the current reporting environment and undervalues the capital markets as a whole. He says, "The market value of S&P 500 companies is more than six times what's on their books. This means that for every $6.50 or so of market value, only $1 appears on the books."[1] He and others contend that exclusion of intangibles makes financial statements less useful than they could be because, for many corporations, they do not contain the complete picture.

The traditional accounting view that has precluded companies from including internally generated intangibles on the balance sheet also keeps these companies from leveraging these assets when attempting to entice investors and borrow capital. In addition, many academics and accounting practitioners agree that in an economy that is highly reliant on innovation, intellectual capital, and knowledge, companies that generate such assets should be allowed to record them.

Although proponents agree that valuation is tricky, they believe that this difficulty should not halt the effort to provide complete and relevant financial reports. In response to the opinion of those who feel that intangibles could be disclosed in the footnotes of an annual report and not included on the face of the balance sheet, Lev says, "You know that when something is put in a footnote, it is buried there forever. No one pays much attention to footnotes."[2]

---

1 Heather Baukney, "Intangible Assets: An Interview with Baruch Lev," ITWorld.com, 3/15/01, available at **www.itworld.com/Man/2817/CIO010315lev/**. Accessed 06/30/04.

2 Roundtable Comments, CRIW/NBER Conference Measuring Capital in the New Economy, April 2002, available at: **www.nber.org/books/CRIW02/lev_roundtable12-31-03.pdf**. Accessed on 6/30/04.

◀ counterpoint

Association for Financial Professionals

on the counterpoint:

- **Paul Rosenfield**
  CPA, former director of the AICPA Accounting Standards Division

- **Ernst & Young**

- **George Harrington**
  chief financial officer, IBM

- **Andrew Lennard**
  director of operations at the UK Accounting Standards Board

- **Michael Quinn**
  chief executive of Innovation Capital

◀ **The balance sheet must be based on reliable and comparable amounts. Thus, the nature of valuation of internally generated intangibles precludes them from being reflected on the balance sheet.**

In a letter to the FASB in September 2001, the Association of Financial Professionals expressed concern regarding a shift to valuation of intangibles on the balance sheet, stating, "Valuation of internally created assets would create a significant burden on auditors and preparers and may result in subjective and inconsistent data."[3] FASB Research Director Timothy S. Lucas agrees that there are significant measurement and definition problems. Many academics, like Paul B. W. Miller, professor of accounting at the University of Colorado, see the biggest problem in the valuation of intangibles to be the subjective judgments that would be necessary—something that accountants generally dislike.[4] Many companies worry that inaccurate measurement of intangibles would lead to more lawsuits and even greater investor mistrust.

In refutation of the idea that the balance sheet should contain a complete picture of the assets, liabilities, and equity of a company, many contend that information provided in financial reporting is only the starting point for understanding a company's performance, potential, and value. Andrew Lennard, director of operations at the UK Accounting Standards Board, believes that it is not necessary to *tell* analysts the value of a company.[5] Their job is to make this determination based on a variety of sources—financial statements being only one such source.

Take a Position   Imagine that you are an active participant in the investment community and that you review routinely the financial statements of the companies in which you invest. Do you believe that internally generated assets should be valued and reflected on the face of the balance sheet for publicly traded companies? Explain your position.

Research   Locate the 2003 annual report for Procter & Gamble on the company's website. What types of identifiable intangible assets does the company list in Note 4? What was the net value of total intangible assets with determinable lives at June 20, 2003? What was the net value of the company's trademarks with determinable lives at that date? What amount did the company spend in 2003 for research and development?

3 Comment Letter on FASB Project: Disclosures About Intangible Assets, Association of Finance Professionals, available at: **www.fasb.org/ocl/1123-001/9579.pdf**. Accessed on 7/1/04.

4 Neil Gross, "Valuing 'Intangibles' Is a Tough Job, but It Has to Be Done," BusinessWeek Online, available at: **www.businessweek.com/magazine/content/01_32/b3744008.htm**. Accessed on 7/2/04.

5 "Understanding Corporate Value: Managing and Reporting Intellectual Capital," Cranfield University School of Management, published by the Chartered Institute of Management Accountants, p. 24, available at: **www.valuebasedmanagement.net/articles_cima_understanding.pdf**. Accessed on 7/2/04.

INTERNATIONAL STANDARDS FOR INTERNALLY GENERATED INTANGIBLE ASSETS

 INTERNATIONAL

International accounting standards are in agreement with GAAP regarding the accounting for internally generated intangible assets. This has created a major issue for companies based in Australia, which is expected to adopt international standards in 2005. Australian accounting rules have long allowed companies to capitalize internally generated intangible assets, such as brand names and mastheads, at their current fair value. In addition, Australian rules allow for an upward revaluation of intangible assets when circumstances justify it, even if there is no market for the asset. International accounting-standard setters are pushing for requiring Australian firms to write off internally generated intangible assets prior to adopting international accounting standards. Australian firms are pushing for flexibility during the initial adoption period.

AMORTIZING INTANGIBLE ASSETS

amortization of intangibles the process of allocating the cost of an intangible asset to the periods that the asset benefits

As you will recall from the discussion of categories of intangible assets, some intangible assets have set useful lives, and others are expected to have indefinite useful lives. Under *Statement of Accounting Standards No. 142,* "Goodwill and Other Intangible Assets," only intangible assets with set useful lives are subject to amortization. **Amortization of intangibles** is the process of allocating the cost of an intangible asset to the periods that the asset benefits. It is analogous to depreciation for fixed assets. Assets with indefinite useful lives are not subject to amortization.

A number of factors are considered in determining the useful life of an intangible asset. First and foremost is the period over which the intangible asset is expected to generate cash flows. Other considerations include legal, regulatory, and contractual factors that limit the intangible asset's useful life; how the asset will be used; how long related assets will be useful; governmental and regulatory provisions; and economic factors such as obsolescence, competition, and demand. Some of those factors may suggest a shorter time period than the regulatory life of the asset.

residual value the estimated value of an asset at its retirement

The residual value of an intangible asset is assumed to be zero, unless there is a firm offer to purchase the asset sometime in the future or an existing market for the asset. **Residual value** is the estimated value of an asset at its retirement.

The amortization method should capture how the intangible asset is used up. Either an activity method or an accelerated method may be employed. If it is impossible to determine how the intangible asset will be used up, the straight-line method may be employed.

For example, assume that Davis Company purchases an Internet domain name from another company for $1,250,000 and spends another $200,000 on legal fees to register the name. Although Internet domain names have an indefinite life, Davis Company believes that, because of competition, the intangible asset will have a useful life of seven years. In addition, Davis has signed an agreement to sell the domain name to a third party in seven years for $50,000. Davis believes that the Internet domain name will provide equal benefits during each year of its seven-year life and chooses to amortize it on a straight-line basis. Thus, Davis would record the intangible asset on its balance sheet at $1,450,000 and would amortize $200,000 of its cost each year:

Amortization calculation:

$$\frac{\$1,450,000 - \$50,000}{7} = \$200,000$$

Amortization entry:

Amortization Expense	200,000	
Internet Domain Name		200,000

As you can see, Davis reduced the intangible asset directly instead of creating an accumulated amortization account.

If there is no limit on how long an intangible asset may be used, it is classified as an indefinite-life intangible asset. An **indefinite-life intangible asset** is expected to benefit a company for as long as the company is in business and thus is not subject to amortization. However, if at some point it is determined that the assumption of indefinite life is no longer valid, the company should begin to amortize the intangible asset.

indefinite-life intangible asset an intangible asset that is expected to benefit a company for as long as the company is in business and thus is not subject to amortization

---

CHECK YOUR UNDERSTANDING

1. If an intangible asset is purchased from an outside source, what amounts are included in its recorded value?

2. When several intangible assets are purchased for a lump-sum amount, how is the cost allocated?

3. What factors are considered when determining the useful life of an intangible asset?

LO 3 Identify and account for impairment of intangible assets.

impairment a decrease in the value of an asset as a result of rapid technological advances, intense domestic and global competition, or changes in market demand

Critical Thinking: What factors might lead to a decline in the value of an intangible asset?

Impairment of Intangible Assets

Like all assets, intangible assets are subject to the risk of economic and technological change. **Impairment** is a decrease in the value of an asset as a result of rapid technological advances, intense domestic and global competition, or changes in market demand. To see how an intangible asset can become impaired, consider the case of **Fox Broadcasting**. In 1998, Fox paid the **National Football League** $4.4 billion for the broadcast rights to football games for the following eight years. At that time, the U.S. economy was thriving, and Fox believed that it could earn back the large broadcast fees through advertising sales. However, in 2002 there was a steep decline in advertising throughout the entire economy, and Fox was forced to write down the value of the broadcast rights by $909 million.

When an intangible asset becomes impaired, it must be written down to its new fair market value. The evaluation of impairment often involves many hard-to-quantify factors. For example, when determining the future utility or value of an intangible asset, a company must estimate such things as future consumer demand, future sales prices, and the cost of providing the product or service affected by the intangible asset.

TESTING FOR IMPAIRMENT OF INTANGIBLE ASSETS

An intangible asset must be tested for impairment annually and at any time between annual tests when events or circumstances suggest that the value of the asset may have declined. Some of the events that may signal impairment and the need to test are operating losses, changes in the legal or regulatory environment, or a change in how the intangible asset is used. Testing for impairment consists of two basic steps:

1. Determine whether an impairment has occurred.

2. Calculate the amount of the impairment loss.

There is a slight difference in the way step 1 is performed for an intangible asset that is not being amortized and for an intangible asset that is being amortized.

▶ UNAMORTIZED INTANGIBLE ASSETS

To determine if an intangible asset that is not being amortized is impaired, you must compare the asset's fair value to its book value. The **book value of an intangible asset**

book value of an intangible asset the original acquisition cost of an intangible asset minus the total amount of accumulated amortization on the asset (in the case of an unamortized intangible asset, none)

is the original acquisition cost of an intangible asset minus the total amount of accumulated amortization on the asset (in the case of an unamortized intangible asset, none). If the asset's fair value is below its book value, an impairment loss equal to the difference should be recognized.

Given the uniqueness of intangible assets, the determination of fair value can be problematical. An asset's fair value is clear-cut if a reliable market price is available. However, when market prices for an unamortized intangible asset do not exist, the present value must be calculated. The asset's future cash flows must be estimated and discounted back to the current period. In situations in which it is difficult to determine specific future cash flows, a range of cash flows may be assumed.

For example, assume that Positron Corporation owns a trademark that is currently valued at $300,000. At the end of 2004, when preparing its annual impairment test, management discovers that because no quoted market prices are available for comparison, it needs to calculate the trademark's present value. In considering future cash flows, the company decides that there are two possibilities: a 75 percent chance that the trademark will provide enormous benefits and a 25 percent chance that the trademark will provide little benefit. The company's financial analysts prepare the following cash flow outlooks:

Scenario	2005 Cash Flows	2006 Cash Flows	2007 Cash Flows	2008 Cash Flows	2009 Cash Flows
Trademark is successful (75% chance)	$50,000	$100,000	$200,000	$50,000	$25,000
Trademark is not successful (25% chance)	$25,000	$ 15,000	$ 5,000	$ 0	$ 0

By multiplying each cash flow by its probability, the financial analysts suggest that the trademark can be expected to create the following cash flows:

	2005	2006	2007	2008	2009
Expected cash flows from trademark	(75% × $50,000) + (25% × $25,000) $43,750	(75% × $100,000) + (25% × $15,000) $78,750	(75% × $200,000) + (25% × $5,000) $151,250	(75% × $50,000) + (25% × $0) $37,500	(75% × $25,000) + (25% × $0) $18,750

The financial analysts then discount the expected future cash flows back to 2004 using an interest rate that the company believes is relevant to its business. Positron considers an interest rate of 10 percent to be appropriate, so the financial analysts calculate the present value of the trademark as follows:

2005	2006	2007	2008	2009	Present Value of Trademark*
$43,750	$78,750	$151,250	$37,500	$18,750	
× .9091	× .8264	× .7513	× .6830	× .6209	
$39,773 +	$65,079 +	$113,634 +	$25,613 +	$11,642 =	$255,741

*Refer to the present value tables in Appendix A.

Because the analysis yields a fair value of $255,741 and the trademark is currently on the balance sheet at $300,000, Positron needs to recognize an impairment loss. The loss, which is the difference between the current book value and the calculated fair value ($300,000 − $255,741), is recognized in the following manner:

Impairment Loss on Trademark	44,259	
Trademark		44,259

This reduces the value of the trademark to its current fair value of $255,741. Because the trademark is not being amortized, it will remain on the balance sheet at $255,741 unless it becomes further impaired.

❯ AMORTIZED INTANGIBLE ASSETS

Impairment tests are also required for intangible assets that are amortized. Management should perform impairment tests annually or whenever circumstances occur that could affect the future utility of an amortized intangible asset. Impairment tests ensure that an intangible asset is carried on the balance sheet at an amount that does not exceed the asset's recoverable amount. Once an impairment is recognized, it cannot be reversed.

The test for impairment of an amortized intangible asset is the same as the test for impairment of an operating asset. The first step is to determine whether an impairment has occurred, and, if it has, the second step is to calculate the amount of the impairment loss.

The occurrence of an impairment is established by comparing the intangible asset's book value with the net cash flows that the asset is expected to provide. In this step, the *cash flows do not have to be discounted* because we are trying to determine if the cost of the intangible asset can be recovered.

For example, assume that Techno Corporation owns a royalty agreement that it acquired in 2004 for $1,200,000. Techno determined that the royalty agreement had a six-year useful life with no residual value and has been amortizing the asset on a straight-line basis. At the end of 2006, the asset has been amortized for three years and has a book value of $600,000 [$1,200,000 − ($200,000 × 3)]. In its annual impairment test, Techno determines that the royalty agreement can be expected to generate the following net cash flows:

	2007	2008	2009
Expected net cash flows from royalty agreement	$300,000	$275,000	$250,000

Given that the expected net cash flows from the royalty agreement are $825,000 and the book value of the royalty agreement at the end of 2006 is $600,000, Techno Corporation would conclude that the royalty agreement is not impaired. It would remain on Techno's balance sheet at $600,000.

In contrast, assume instead that Techno Corporation forecasts the following net cash flows from its royalty agreement:

	2007	2008	2009
Expected net cash flows from royalty agreement	$200,000	$175,000	$150,000

In this case, the expected net cash flows of $525,000 from the royalty agreement are less than the book value of $600,000. Techno would conclude that the intangible asset is impaired and would proceed to the second step of the impairment test, determining the amount of impairment loss.

The impairment loss for an amortized intangible asset is calculated in the same way as the impairment loss for an unamortized intangible asset. The fair value of the intangible asset is calculated, and the impairment loss is equal to the amount by which the asset's book value exceeds its fair value.

The best indicator of an intangible asset's fair value is its market price. However, if no comparable market prices exist, the present value of future cash flows should be used as a measure of fair value.

If no comparable market price exists for Techno Corporation's royalty agreement, the company would use the present value approach to calculate the impairment loss. Assuming that Techno Corporation has a 10 percent interest rate, the present value of the future cash flows would be calculated as follows:

	2007	2008	2009	Total
Expected cash flows from royalty agreement	$200,000	$175,000	$150,000	
Present value factor*	× .9091	× .8264	× .7513	
Present value of cash flows	$181,820 +	$144,620 +	$112,695 =	$439,135

*Refer to the present value tables in Appendix A.

Techno would need to record an impairment loss on its royalty agreement equal to the difference between the asset's book value of $600,000 and its present value–based fair value of $439,135. The impairment loss would be recorded as follows:

Impairment Loss on Royalty Agreement	160,865	
Royalty Agreement		160,865

Because the royalty agreement's book value has been decreased, future amortization amounts must also be adjusted. If Techno continues to use the straight-line method of amortization, the 2007 amortization expense on the royalty agreement will be $146,378 ($439,135 divided by the three remaining years).

CHECK YOUR UNDERSTANDING

1. In determining whether an impairment has occurred for an unamortized asset versus an amortized asset, what different calculation is made?

2. What types of events might cause impairment of an intangible asset?

3. If an impairment has been identified for an amortized asset, what value is recorded as a loss?

LO 4 Value and account for goodwill.

goodwill an intangible asset that is recognized only when one company purchases another company; it represents the premium that a purchaser pays over the fair value of an acquired company's identifiable net assets

Goodwill

Goodwill, an intangible asset that is recognized only when one company purchases another company, represents the premium that a purchaser pays over the fair value of an acquired company's identifiable net assets. For example, imagine that Kedzie Company had net assets with a fair market value of $5,000 and that Montrose Company paid $8,000 to purchase those assets. The $3,000 that Montrose paid in excess of the fair market value of Kedzie's net assets is represented in accounting by the intangible asset goodwill. Factors like outstanding customer relations, superior management, or favorable location might contribute to a company's goodwill.

Critical Thinking: What is the component of goodwill that is perceived by the marketplace but not recorded by a company?

Goodwill represents the future benefits that are expected to be obtained from the assets acquired and the liabilities incurred. In *Statement of Financial Accounting Standards No. 141,* "Business Combinations," the FASB identifies the following two components of goodwill:

1. The fair value of the "going concern" element of the acquired entity's existing business. The going concern element represents the ability of an established business to earn a higher rate of return on an assembled collection of net assets than would be expected if those net assets had to be acquired separately. That value stems from the synergies of the net assets of the business, as well as from other benefits (such as factors related to market imperfections, including the ability to earn monopoly profits and barriers to market entry—either legal or because of transaction costs—by potential competitors).

2. The fair value of the expected synergies and other benefits from combining the acquiring entity's and the acquired entity's net assets and businesses. Those synergies and other benefits are unique to each combination, and different combinations would produce different synergies and, hence, different values.[5]

RECOGNIZING GOODWILL AT THE TIME OF PURCHASE

To illustrate how goodwill is recognized, assume that Hi-Tech Company purchases Wave Corporation to complete its product line. After examining Wave's operations and its balance sheet, presented in Illustration 10.2, Hi-Tech bids $1,200,000 for all of the stock of Wave Corporation.

As you can see from Wave's balance sheet, the company's net assets have a book value of $875,000 ($1,550,000 of assets less $675,000 of liabilities). Based on that figure, Hi-Tech paid a premium of $325,000 over the book value of Wave's net assets. That premium, however, is not the amount of goodwill resulting from this transaction. To calculate the proper amount of goodwill to recognize, Hi-Tech must calculate the premium paid over the fair market value of *identifiable net assets.*

After further examination of Wave's assets and liabilities, the accountant at Hi-Tech compiled a schedule comparing the accounting book values with fair market values, as shown in Illustration 10.3. The accountant also discovered two intangible assets that did not appear on Wave's balance sheet because they were internally created. These intangible assets were a customer list valued at $25,000 and a trademark valued at $75,000.

due diligence the process of examining and investigating the financial records and operating performance of a potential purchase

The process of examining and investigating the financial records and operating performance of a potential purchase is referred to as **due diligence**. The due diligence process allows a potential buyer to obtain private information about a company that it is looking to purchase.

The differences between book values and fair market values can result from numerous factors. For example, with accounts receivable, the purchasing company may believe that future bad debts will be greater than current estimates and therefore may value the accounts receivable at a lower amount. For operating assets, the use of accounting-based depreciation methods such as the straight-line or accelerated methods can cause book values and fair market values to diverge because such methods are not meant to capture the actual decreases in fair market value from period to period. A purchaser will also want to be certain that all liabilities are disclosed and accounted for.

For other intangible assets to be recognized at a merger, the FASB requires that they arise from a contractual or other legal right or be separable from the acquired

---

5 "Business Combinations," *Statement of Financial Accounting Standards No. 141* (Norwalk, Conn.: FASB, 2001), par. B102.

Illustration 10.2

Balance Sheet

Wave Corporation
Balance Sheet
June 30, 2005

Assets

Current assets		
Cash	$500,000	
Accounts receivable	150,000	
Inventory	100,000	
Total current assets		$ 750,000
Operating assets	$900,000	
Less: Accumulated depreciation	(250,000)	
Net operating assets		650,000
Other assets		150,000
Total assets		$1,550,000

Liabilities and Stockholders' Equity

Current liabilities		
Accounts payable	$225,000	
Accrued expenses	50,000	
Other current liabilities	100,000	
Total current liabilities		$ 375,000
Long-term debt		
Bonds payable		300,000
Total liabilities		$ 675,000
Stockholders' equity		
Common stock	$500,000	
Retained earnings	375,000	
Total stockholders' equity		875,000
Total liabilities and stockholders' equity		$1,550,000

Illustration 10.3

Book Values and Fair Market Values at Purchase Date— Wave Corporation

	At June 30, 2005	
	Book Values	*Fair Market Values*
Cash	$500,000	$ 500,000
Accounts receivable	150,000	140,000
Inventory	100,000	130,000
Net operating assets	650,000	700,000
Other assets	150,000	150,000
Accounts payable	(225,000)	(225,000)
Accrued expenses	(50,000)	(50,000)
Other current liabilities	(100,000)	(115,000)
Bonds payable	(300,000)	(300,000)
Customer list	0	25,000
Trademark	0	75,000
Net assets	$875,000	$1,030,000

company. An intangible asset is considered separable if it could be sold, rented, or leased independently of the company. The Wave trademark meets the contractual standard because trademarks are legally protected by the government. The customer list would have to meet the separability standard to be assigned a value at the time of purchase. In this example, we will assume that the customer list can be separated from Wave's other assets and that it is thus accounted for as an identified asset at the time of the purchase.

Hi-Tech is now able to assign a value to the goodwill acquired through the purchase of Wave. The company paid $1,200,000 for all of Wave's net assets, which resulted in a $170,000 premium over the net identifiable assets. That premium would represent goodwill.

Price paid by acquiring company, Hi-Tech	$1,200,000
Fair market value of identifiable net assets of acquired company	1,030,000
Goodwill resulting from purchase	$ 170,000

Recall that goodwill represents the ability of the acquiring company to earn a higher expected rate of return and the expected synergies and benefits from combining with the acquired company.

Hi-Tech's journal entry to record its acquisition of Wave would be as follows:

Cash	500,000	
Accounts Receivable	140,000	
Inventory	130,000	
Net Operating Assets	700,000	
Other Assets	150,000	
Customer List	25,000	
Trademark	75,000	
Goodwill	170,000	
Accounts Payable		225,000
Accrued Expenses		50,000
Other Current Liabilities		115,000
Bonds Payable		300,000
Cash		1,200,000

ACCOUNTING FOR GOODWILL AFTER RECOGNITION

Because goodwill is considered to have an indefinite life, it is not amortized. Instead, it is maintained on a company's books and tested for impairment annually and at any time between annual tests when a change in circumstances suggests that the factors that led to the recognition of goodwill, such as expected synergies or benefits, may no longer exist. Some circumstances that would require an additional impairment test would be expanded competition, a change in the regulatory and legal environment, or a loss of key employees.

To test for impairment, the same two basic steps are followed:

1. Determine whether an impairment has occurred.

2. If an impairment has occurred, measure the amount of impairment loss.

To determine whether goodwill is impaired, compare the book value to the fair market value. If the book value exceeds the fair value, an impairment loss is recognized. In the case of goodwill, the determination of fair market value is difficult because goodwill is a unique asset that does not have a unique standalone value. Its value can only be determined by examining how it creates value for the company.

Illustration 10.4

Reporting Units at Hi-Tech Company

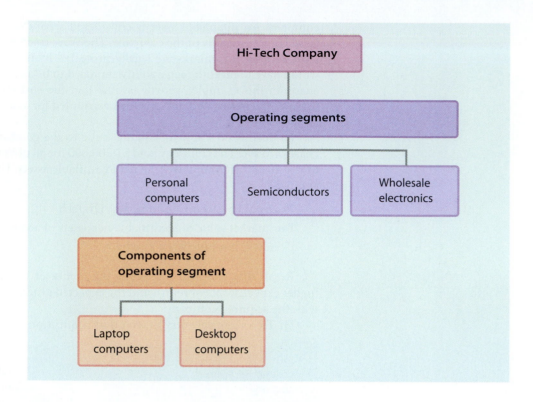

reporting unit an operating segment or a component of an operating segment that produces separate accounting information

Before the fair value of goodwill can be determined, the goodwill must be assigned to a reporting unit within the company. A **reporting unit** is either an operating segment or a component of an operating segment that produces separate accounting information. For example, as shown in Illustration 10.4, Hi-Tech Company has five reporting units. It has three operating segments that each report accounting results separately: personal computers, semiconductors, and wholesale electronics. In addition, the personal computer segment has two components, laptop computers and desktop computers, that also report separately. If Hi-Tech purchases Wave Corporation to benefit the semiconductor segment, the goodwill associated with the purchase will be assigned to that reporting unit. Tests for impairment of goodwill are made at the reporting unit level. Companies may have one or many reporting units.

Once a company has assigned goodwill to a reporting unit, it must perform the two-step impairment test. Both steps require that the fair value of the reporting unit be known. The fair value of a reporting unit is the amount for which the unit could be sold. This amount can be estimated by using present value techniques or by comparing the reporting unit to companies like it.

The reporting unit's estimated fair value is compared to its book value, including goodwill. If the fair value is greater than the book value, the goodwill is not impaired and remains on the financial statements. If the fair value is less than the book value, the goodwill is impaired and the amount of impairment must be measured.

For example, assume that Hi-Tech's semiconductor reporting unit has a book value of $7,500,000 after the purchased net assets of Wave Corporation are added to its balance sheet and that the unit's estimated fair value is $8,000,000. Because the unit's fair value is greater than its book value, the goodwill assigned to the unit is not impaired. However, if, as a result of increased competition, management estimated that the fair value of the semiconductor reporting unit was $7,000,000, the goodwill assigned to the reporting unit would be impaired.

implied fair value an amount determined by comparing the fair value of a unit to the fair value of the unit's net assets, excluding the reporting unit's goodwill; used in determining impairment of goodwill

The amount of goodwill impairment loss is determined by comparing the goodwill's book value to its implied fair value. The **implied fair value** of a reporting unit's goodwill is determined by comparing the fair value of the unit to the fair value of the unit's net assets, excluding the reporting unit's goodwill. If the implied fair value is greater than the book value, the amount of impairment is zero. However, if the implied fair value is less than the book value, the difference equals the amount of the impairment loss.

For example, if the estimated fair value of Hi-Tech's semiconductor reporting unit is $7,000,000 and the estimated fair value of the unit's net assets, excluding its goodwill, is $6,900,000, the implied fair value of goodwill is $100,000. However, recall that when Wave was first acquired, goodwill was recorded at $170,000. The $70,000 by which the book value of goodwill exceeds the implied fair value of goodwill is the amount of the impairment loss. That loss would be recorded by this journal entry:

Impairment Loss on Goodwill	70,000	
Goodwill		70,000

CHECK YOUR UNDERSTANDING

1. What is goodwill and when is it recognized?

2. If the fair value of a reporting unit is greater than the book value, what entry, if any, is required?

LO 5 Explain how to account for research and development costs.

Critical Thinking: Why do you think the FASB requires the immediate expensing of research and development costs?

Research and Development Costs

Each year U.S. businesses spend over $300 billion on research and development. As discussed earlier, research and development is the effort to discover new knowledge and to translate that knowledge into plans and designs for new or improved products, services, and processes. Sometimes the research and development process is successful and a patented product is created, a new trademark is recorded, or a copyright is granted. Other times—in fact, most of the time—research and development ends in failure.

The FASB defines research activities as searching or investigating for new knowledge, while development activities are the translation of research into a new product or process or a significant improvement to an existing product or process. Because of the difficulty of determining which research and development projects will result in future benefits, accounting standards require that all research and development costs be expensed as incurred.[6] This includes both direct costs, such as the salaries and benefits of personnel working on research and development, and allocated indirect costs. If research and development activities require the use of long-term fixed assets, the depreciation related to those assets is charged to Research and Development Expense. If, at a later date, the same long-term fixed assets are used in a different facet of the business, their depreciation will once again be charged to Depreciation Expense.

The requirement that all research and development expenditures be treated as expenses of the current period is quite conservative and can make the analysis of companies with extensive research and development activities difficult. For example, consider how the cost of sales for an automobile differs from the cost of sales for a new pharmaceutical drug. An automobile's cost of sales includes the costs of direct materials, direct labor, and an overhead allocation. The new drug's cost of sales also includes direct materials, direct labor, and an overhead allocation, but it does not include the expense incurred for research and development. Even though research and development is often the largest expenditure in bringing new drugs to market, because of accounting rules, it is never included in a drug's cost of sales.

---

6 "Accounting for Research and Development Costs," *Statement of Financial Accounting Standards No. 2* (Stamford, Conn.: FASB, 1974).

IN-PROCESS RESEARCH AND DEVELOPMENT

When a company that is performing research and development efforts is acquired, a challenging situation arises for the accountant who records the transaction. How much of the purchase price should be allocated to an intangible asset representing the research and development activities of the company being purchased? This intangible asset is called in-process research and development, and current accounting principles require that this asset be written off as an expense in the period of acquisition.

For example, assume that Health Corp. acquires a biotech research company for $10 million. The fair value of the net assets of the biotech company is only $1 million. Thus, accountants must determine how much of the $9 million excess is related to research and development activities that are being undertaken by the biotech company. The first step in valuing in-process research and development is to identify all acquired research and development projects. Accountants must estimate the value of the in-process research and development projects, which is usually done by calculating the present value of expected economic income. This value is then assigned to in-process research and development and written off immediately. Any remaining excess is allocated to goodwill. Accounting for in-process research and development has been controversial; critics have charged that by expensing in-process research and development immediately, companies are able to make their future earnings look much better.

> **CHECK YOUR UNDERSTANDING**
>
> 1. How are research and development costs treated in the accounting records of a business?
>
> 2. Describe examples of costs that might be considered research and development costs.

Revisiting the Case

NIKE CASHES IN ON RETRO CONVERSE SHOES

1. Companies must protect their intangible assets, just as if they were physical property. This requires ensuring that only authorized parties are using the assets and that contracts are being properly enforced.

2. Trademarks and other intangible assets normally appear in the long-term assets section of the balance sheet.

3. Accountants face the difficult challenge of forecasting the future expected benefits expected to be realized from owning the intangible asset. In addition, it is difficult to put a dollar measurement on the expected benefits.

SUMMARY BY LEARNING OBJECTIVE

LO1 Identify the categories of intangible assets.

The FASB has identified five basic categories of intangible assets. (1) Marketing-related intangible assets allow a company to promote itself or its products. (2) Customer-related intangible assets provide benefits to a company by allowing it to sell, lease, or exchange information about its customers. (3) Artistic-related intangible assets are protected by copyrights granted by governments to the creators of original artistic works. (4) Contract-based intangible assets are based on legal agreements between two parties to perform specified duties. (5) Technology-based intangible assets are assets such as patents, trade secrets, computer databases, and software.

LO2 Value and amortize intangible assets.

How a company gains ownership of an intangible asset determines what costs are included in that asset's value. When an intangible asset is purchased, it is recorded at its acquisition cost plus any additional costs needed to prepare it for use. These additional costs may include legal and accounting costs, appraisal fees, and recording fees. When an intangible asset is developed internally, the only costs that can be associated with it are direct costs, such as application fees, legal and accounting fees, and recording fees. Any costs incurred for research and development are considered indirect costs and are expensed as incurred.

Under current accounting rules, only intangible assets with set useful lives are amortized. The amortization method should capture how the intangible asset is used up. Either an activity method or an accelerated method may be employed. If it is impossible to determine how an intangible asset will be used up, the straight-line method is employed.

If there is no limit on how long an intangible asset may be used, it is classified as an indefinite-life intangible asset. Such an asset is expected to benefit a company for as long as the company is in business; thus, it is not subject to amortization.

LO3 Identify and account for impairment of intangible assets.

Impairment is a decrease in the value of an asset as a result of rapid technological advances, intense domestic and global competition, or changes in market demand. An intangible asset must be tested for impairment annually and at any time between annual tests when events or circumstances suggest that the value of the asset may have declined. When an intangible asset becomes impaired, it must be written down to its new fair market value.

How an intangible asset is tested for impairment depends on whether the asset is being amortized. To determine whether an intangible asset that is not being amortized is impaired, it is necessary to compare the asset's fair value to its book value. An impairment loss is recorded as a decrease in the book value of the intangible asset.

The test for impairment of an amortized intangible asset is the same as the test for impairment of an operating asset. The occurrence of an impairment is established by comparing the intangible asset's book value with the net cash flows that the asset is expected to provide. In this step, the cash flows do not have to be discounted. If an impairment has occurred, the amount of the loss is calculated in the same way as the impairment loss for an unamortized intangible asset. The loss is then recorded as a decrease in the book value of the asset. When the book value of an amortized intangible asset is decreased, future amortization amounts must also be adjusted.

LO4 Value and account for goodwill.

Goodwill represents the premium that a purchaser pays over the fair market value of an acquired company's identifiable net assets. Goodwill may be identified by comparing the book values of an acquired company's assets and liabilities with the corresponding fair market values. Goodwill may also result from internally generated intangible assets that do not appear on the financial statements but are discovered during due diligence. For other intangible assets to be recognized at a merger, the FASB requires that they arise from a contractual or other legal right or be separable from the acquired company.

Goodwill must be assigned to a reporting unit within the company. Because goodwill has an indefinite life, it is not depreciated. Instead, it is maintained on the company's books and tested for impairment annually and at any time between annual tests when a change in circumstances suggests that the factors that led to the recognition of goodwill may no longer exist. To test for impairment, the reporting unit's estimated fair value is compared to its book value, including goodwill. If the fair value is less than the book value, the goodwill is impaired and the amount of impairment loss must be determined. That is accomplished by comparing the goodwill's implied fair value to its book value. If the implied fair value is less than the book value, the difference equals the amount of the impairment loss.

LO5 Explain how to account for research and development costs.

Because of the difficulty of determining which research and development projects will result in future benefits, accounting standards require that all research and development costs be expensed as incurred. This includes direct costs, such as the salaries and benefits of personnel working on research and development, and allocated indirect costs. If research and development activities require the use of long-term fixed assets, the depreciation related to those assets is charged to Research and Development Expense. If, at a later date, the same long-term fixed assets are used in a different facet of the busin ess, their depreciation will once again be charged to Depreciation Expense.

KEY TERMS

amortization of intangibles (p. 462)
artistic-related intangible assets (p. 456)
book value of an intangible asset (p. 463)
contract-based intangible assets (p. 456)
copyright (p. 454)
customer-related intangible assets (p. 456)

due diligence (p. 467)
goodwill (p. 466)
impairment (p. 463)
implied fair value (p. 470)
indefinite-life intangible asset (p. 463)
intangible assets (p. 454)
marketing-related intangible assets (p. 455)
patent (p. 454)

reporting unit (p. 470)
research and development (R&D) (p. 459)
residual value (p. 462)
technology-based intangible assets (p. 457)
trademark (p. 454)
useful life (p. 455)

EXERCISES

LO1, 2 **EXERCISE 10-1   Patent Transactions**

Several years ago, Castle Company purchased a patent and has since been amortizing it on a straight-line basis over its estimated useful life. The company's comparative balance sheets contain the following item:

	December 31	
	2006	2005
Intangible Assets		
Patent, net of amortization, $124,000 and $108,000, respectively	$520,000	$430,000

Required:

1. How much amortization expense was recorded during 2006?

2. What is the original cost of the patent acquired during 2006? Over how many years has the original patent been amortized as of the end of 2005?

3. Into which of the five categories does this intangible fall? Explain why this category of asset can hold assets with either an indefinite or a definite life.

LO3 **EXERCISE 10-2   Impairment of Patent**

Caper Mills purchased a patent in 2004 at a cost of $600,000 and estimated that it would benefit the company over 10 years. Two years later, Caper determined that the expected net future cash flows that were related to the patent were $425,000, and the present value of the future cash flows was $325,000. As of year-end 2006, the book value of the patent is $440,000, and it is estimated that the fair value is $330,000.

Required:

1. Show that an impairment has occurred as of the end of 2006.

2. Determine the impairment loss.

3. Show the transaction that Caper Mills should record to recognize the loss.

LO1   **EXERCISE 10-3**   **Patent Categories**

The five basic categories of intangible assets as described in *Statement of Accounting Standards No. 141,* "Business Combinations," are as follows:

   A. Marketing-related intangible assets

   B. Customer-related intangible assets

   C. Artistic-related intangible assets

   D. Contract-based intangible assets

   E. Technology-based intangible assets

Required: For each of the intangible costs listed, indicate the applicable category.

   1. Licensing agreements

   2. Plays, operas

   3. Customer lists

   4. Royalty contracts

   5. Employment contracts

   6. Computer databases

   7. Images and photographs

   8. Package design

   9. Construction permits

   10. Patents

   11. Trade secrets

   12. Customer relationships

   13. Franchise agreements

   14. Noncompete agreements

   15. Order backlogs

   16. Broadcast rights

   17. Software

   18. Trade names

   19. Timber, drilling, mineral, and water rights

   20. Internet domain names

LO2   **EXERCISE 10-4**   **Valuation and Balance Sheet Presentation**

Sodilla purchased a patent on July 1, 2004, for $200,000. Sodilla estimated its productive life to be eight years, although its remaining legal life was 10 years. On July 1, 2005, Sodilla spent $14,000 in legal fees in defense of the patent and won the suit.

On January 1, 2005, Sodilla agreed to purchase an Internet domain name for $160,000 cash plus shares of Sodilla's stock valued at $320,000. Sodilla paid its attorney an additional $60,000 in legal fees to draw up the purchase contract. The domain name was registered through the end of 2008, although Sodilla believed it would benefit the company for at least 10 years.

Required:

   1. How much is the book value of the patent at Sodilla's year end on December 31, 2005?

   2. What amount should Sodilla capitalize for the Internet domain name?

   3. Prepare a partial balance sheet showing how the intangibles would be reported as of December 31, 2006.

LO1, 2, 3   **EXERCISE 10-5**   **Valuation and Impairment of Intangibles**

At the beginning of 2004, Lugnuts Corporation purchased a patent, a customer list, and construction permits from Wamsutta Corporation for $365,000. Lugnuts Corporation estimated the fair market values of the three intangible assets as shown on the next page.

Patent	$120,000
Customer list	200,000
Construction permits	80,000
Total fair market value	$400,000

Lugnuts estimated that the patent would benefit the company for five years and the customer list for three years. The construction permit expires at the end of 2008, so Lugnuts plans on beginning construction soon because the project is expected to take several years to build. The patent has a remaining legal life of eight years.

During the latter part of 2004, Lugnuts filed suit against a competitor for patent infringement. After $30,000 in legal fees, Lugnuts lost the suit in court on December 31, 2004. Lugnuts records adjustments at the end of its fiscal period on December 31.

Required:

1. How much should Lugnuts capitalize for each of the intangibles?

2. Identify the category in which each of the intangibles falls.

3. Prepare the transaction to properly account for the patent on December 31, 2004 as a result of the court settlement.

LO2, 5 | **EXERCISE 10-6   Intangible Costs**

Dingle Donuts engaged in the following transactions during 2004:

A. On July 1, 2004, Dingle paid Java Company $400,000 for the right to market a particular coffee product in its stores, using the Java name and logo in promotional material. The franchise runs for as long as Dingle is in business.

B. On August 1, 2004, Dingle spent $300,000 developing a new manufacturing process. On September 1, 2004, Dingle Donuts applied for a patent and paid $18,000 to its attorney to register it. Dingle assumes that the patent will be beneficial for 10 years, although its legal life is 17 years. On September 1, 2005, Dingle incurred costs of $51,000 for successfully defending its patent in an infringement suit.

Dingle Donuts determined that the cost of both intangibles was less than the expected future cash flows as of December 31, 2004, its fiscal year end.

Required:

1. How do the costs that are included in the value of an intangible asset developed internally differ from those included in the value of an intangible asset purchased from an outside source?

2. Determine the book value of each intangible asset as of December 31, 2005.

LO2 | **EXERCISE 10-7   Reporting Intangibles**

The following information is taken from the accounting records of Low-Carb Company for the years ended December 31, 2004 and 2005.

	Dec. 31, 2005	Dec. 31, 2004
Patents, net	$326,400	$324,000

On January 1, 2005, Low-Carb Company sold a patent for $125,000 that had an original cost of $84,000. It had been acquired on July 1, 2000, and was being amortized over 15 years. The company incurred costs of $45,000 for developing a new patent during 2005 and paid $95,000 to register the patent with the federal government. The patent was granted on October 1, 2005.

Required:

1. Draw a T-account beginning with the January 1, 2005 balance, and post all transactions incurred during 2005.

2. How much amortization did Low-Carb recognize during 2005?

3. Prepare all transactions recorded by Low-Carb during 2005 in connection with the patents.

LO5   **EXERCISE 10-8   R&D Costs**

Road Technologies manufactures and sells automobile tires. Because safety is a primary concern, the company spends a significant part of its budget researching and developing new safety features for the tires. During 2004, the company incurred the following costs related to a new tire tread pattern that decreases sliding in wet weather significantly:

A. $45,000 to research rubber densities

B. $55,000 to investigate a new process for molding the rubber into tires

C. $95,000 to translate the rubber density research into a new tire model

D. $120,000 to make significant improvements to an existing tire tread pattern

E. $240,000 for salaries and benefits of personnel working on research and development

F. $28,000 of depreciation related to plant assets costing $750,000 that were used in the development of tire safety

G. $12,000 to register the patent with the federal government

H. $40,000 to pay the attorneys for legal work in connection with the patent

Required:

1. Determine the total amount of costs that should be capitalized for 2005, based on the items listed. How will the other costs be reported?

2. Why do you think the FASB requires the immediate expensing of research and development costs?

LO1, 2, 5   **EXERCISE 10-9   Patents and R&D Costs**

The following are transactions engaged in by Mock Company during 2004:

A. March 31: Developed a new process for packaging products at a cost of $225,000. Paid $60,000 to register the patent.

B. September 30: Defended the patent in court and won. Legal costs amounted to $24,000. The legal life of the patent is 17 years. The company expects to earn revenue related to the process for a total of eight years.

C. June 1: Incurred engineering follow-through costs in an early phase of production amounting to $90,000. (The company still has not reached the stage of commercial feasibility.)

Required:

1. Which amounts are considered R&D costs?

2. Prepare the intangible assets section of the balance sheet for Mock Company at December 31, 2004.

LO4   **EXERCISE 10-10   Goodwill**

On July 1, 2004, Beyonce, Inc. purchased a subsidiary at a cost of $8,200,000. The subsidiary's balance sheet reported assets and liabilities totaling $12,900,000 and $8,200,000, respectively. The fair value of the assets exceeded the book value by $300,000. The book value of the liabilities equaled the fair value. The subsidiary is expected to produce profits for 40 years.

Required:

1. Determine how much goodwill Beyonce will record at acquisition.

2. What test must be performed on goodwill at least annually?

LO4 EXERCISE 10-11 **Goodwill**

Physics Company decided to expand by purchasing Chemistry Company on October 1, 2005. Chemistry Company's balance sheet amounts as of October 1, 2005, are as follows:

Cash	$ 200,000
Receivables	150,000
Inventory	100,000
Common stock	50,000
Operating assets	1,800,000
Accrued liabilities	300,000
Long-term debt	600,000
Retained earnings	780,000
Purchased trademark	180,000
Accumulated depreciation	700,000

An appraisal, to which the parties agreed, indicated that the fair market value of the inventory was $160,000 and that the fair market value of the operating assets was $1,230,000. The agreed-upon purchase price was $1,400,000, and Physics Company paid this amount in cash. At the end of 2006, Physics Company determined that the fair value of the unit's net assets totaled $1,350,000 and the unit's book value (excluding goodwill) on that date totaled $850,000.

Required:

1. Determine the amount of goodwill on the purchase date.

2. Does an impairment loss exist at December 31, 2006? Explain your answer.

LO2, 3 EXERCISE 10-12 **Reporting, Valuation, and Impairment**

The intangible assets section of Morgan Company's comparative balance sheets as of December 31, 2005 and 2004, is as follows:

	2005	2004
Intangible Assets		
Patents, net of amortization of $30,000 and $20,000, respectively	$230,000	$236,000
Trademark, net of amortization of $? and $20,000, respectively	375,000	400,000

One new patent was purchased on June 30, 2005, by issuing 400 shares of $10 par value common stock that was selling for $140 per share on the same date. The 2005 income statement disclosed a $44,000 loss on the impairment of a patent as a result of determining that one of the company's patents was worthless on January 1, 2005. No new trademarks were acquired during 2005.

Required:

1. How much is the original cost of the patents reported at December 31, 2004?

2. At what amount is the new patent capitalized on its acquisition date?

3. Calculate the cost of the patent written off in 2005.

4. Calculate trademark amortization expense for 2005.

5. If a portion of the book value of the patent is written down as a result of impairment of value at the end of 2005, what change is made in calculating future amortization amounts?

LO4 EXERCISE 10-13 **Intangible Asset Impairment**

During 2004, Krinkle purchased Wright Company for $800,000 and recorded a royalty agreement of $180,000 as part of the transaction. As of year end, the expected undiscounted future net cash flows from the royalty agreement are determined to be $280,000, with cash flows to occur equally over 10 years. A reasonable interest rate is 8 percent. This revised outlook is determined to be permanent in nature.

Required:

1. Show how you determine whether an impairment in value has occurred at December 31, 2004.
2. Why is impairment of unamortized intangibles often difficult to determine?

LO2   **EXERCISE 10-14   Reporting Intangibles**

Clasp Company purchased a patent several years ago. Since then, it has been amortizing the patent on a straight-line basis over its estimated useful life. The company purchased an additional patent during 2005. The company's comparative balance sheets contain the following item:

	December 31	
	2005	2004
Intangible Assets		
Patents, net of amortization of $25,000 and $20,000, respectively	$93,000	$88,000

Required:

1. How much amortization expense was recorded during 2005?
2. How much did the company spend on patent acquisitions during 2005?
3. Over how many years is the old patent being amortized?

LO3   **EXERCISE 10-15   Impairment of Value**

FKC Company spent two years developing a "secret recipe" for its roasted chicken. The cost included $1,200,000 for salaries of employees involved in developing the recipe, $300,000 for supplies, and other related development costs. On March 31, 2005, FKC paid $32,000 in legal and registration fees to register the recipe with the U.S. Patent and Trademark Office. FKC predicts that the intangible asset will have a useful life of no more than five years. FKC believes that the recipe will provide equal benefits during each year of its five-year life and chooses to amortize it on a straight-line basis.

Required:

1. When should FKC Company test its secret recipe patent for impairment? What events might signal impairment of the patent?
2. On December 31, 2005, FKC Company determined its secret recipe had a fair market value of $25,000. Has an impairment occurred? Justify your response.
3. Assume that no fair market value exists for the secret recipe. On December 31, 2005, FKC Company determined that competition may have caused the value of its secret recipe to decline. No clearly determinable fair value existed, however. Estimated future cash flows were determined by the sales department as follows:

2006	2007	2008	2009	2010
$10,000	$9,000	$8,000	$7,000	$6,000

FKC considers an interest rate of 6 percent to be appropriate. Has an impairment occurred? Justify your response.

LO4   **EXERCISE 10-16   Goodwill Valuation and Impairment Loss**

On April 16, 2003, **Pfizer Inc.** acquired Pharmacia for a purchase price of approximately $56 billion. Note 8A and a portion of Note 8B from Pfizer's 2003 annual report appear on the following page.

Pfizer

Note 8A: Goodwill

The changes in the carrying amount of goodwill by segment for the years ended December 31, 2003 and 2002 follow:

(millions of dollars)	Pharmaceutical	Consumer Healthcare	Animal Health	Other	Total
Balance December 31, 2001	$ 311	$ 833	$536	$ 9	$ 1,689
Impairment loss	—	—	(536)	—	(536)
Other*	51	(4)	—	—	47
Balance December 31, 2002	362	829	—	9	1,200
Pharmacia acquisition (preliminary)	18,548	1,714	77	108	20,447
Other*	581	72	1	5	659
Balance December 31, 2003	**$19,491**	**$2,615**	**$ 78**	**$122**	**$22,306**

*Primarily reflects the impact of foreign exchange.

In 2002, as a result of adopting *SFAS No. 142*, "Goodwill and Other Intangible Assets," we recorded a write-down of $536 million for the impairment provisions related to goodwill in our animal health business. The fair value of the animal health business was determined using discounted cash flows. This write-down, along with $29 million for impairment provisions related to identifiable intangible assets, was reported as a cumulative effect of a change in accounting principle as of the beginning of 2002 totaling $565 million ($410 million net of tax).

Portion of Note 8B: Allocation of Purchase Price

(millions of dollars)	
Estimated book value of net assets acquired	$ 8,795
Less: existing goodwill and other intangible assets	1,559
Tangible book value of net assets acquired	7,236
Remaining allocation:	
Increase assets to fair value	3,027
Record in-process research and development charge	5,052
Record identifiable intangible assets	37,220
Increase liabilities and accrued costs to fair value	(3,418)
Tax adjustments—provision due	(13,592)
Goodwill	20,447
Estimated purchase price	$ 55,972

The long-term asset section of Pfizer's comparative 2003 and 2002 balance sheets appears below.

Pfizer

(millions of dollars)	12-31-03	12-31-02
Long-term investments and loans	$ 6,142	$ 5,161
Property, plant and equipment, less accumulated depreciation	18,287	10,712
Goodwill	22,306	1,200
Identifiable intangible assets, less accumulated amortization	36,350	921
Other assets, deferred taxes and deferred charges	3,949	3,581

Required:

1. Based on the estimates provided, prepare the entries to record Pfizer's purchase of Pharmacia during 2003. Assume that the fair value of the net tangible assets acquired is $37,000,000,000 for assets and $29,764,000,000 for liabilities.

2. Prepare the entry to record the write-down to fair value during 2002 for Pfizer.

3. Why is the cost of goodwill not allocated over time?

LO5   **EXERCISE 10-17   Research and Development Costs**

According to the 2003 **Pfizer Inc. and Subsidiaries** 2003 annual report, **Pfizer Global Research and Development** boasts the industry's largest pharmaceutical R&D organization with an R&D budget for 2003 of $7.1 billion. Pfizer's R&D efforts have resulted in many discoveries that have resulted in numerous patents. The following costs were incurred by Pfizer during 2003:

A. Salaries and benefits of personnel working on research

B. Supplies used to develop new products

C. Depreciation of microscopes used in the discovery of new drugs

D. Engineering salaries (to develop designs for improved products)

E. Investigative trial study for experimental drug

F. Depreciation of machine to produce a newly developed product

G. Allocation of indirect overhead costs to wages of researchers; allocation is based on direct labor dollars

H. Cost to register patent on newly created drug

Required:

1. Identify which of the costs listed above should be reported as R&D expenses for the year.

2. Why are the costs of R&D expensed immediately?

LO1   **EXERCISE 10-18   Intangible Assets Categories**

Information taken from **Pfizer**'s 2003 annual report at December 31, 2003 and 2002 appears below.

Pfizer

in millions	Gross Carrying Amount		Accumulated Amortization	
As of December 31:	2003	2002	2003	2002
Developed technology rights	$32,289	$526	$(2,400)	$(72)
Trademarks	147	133	(88)	(72)
Brands	5,308	—	—	—
License agreements—unlimited life	288	—	—	—
Patents	33	33	(27)	(24)
License agreements—limited life	48	42	(13)	(25)
Trademarks	266	240	—	—
Customer contracts	149	—	(25)	—
Noncompete agreements	50	48	(46)	(39)

Required:

1. What is the cost of Pfizer's contract-based intangible assets at December 31, 2003?

2. Why are there two categories of license agreements and two categories of trademarks? (*Hint:* Look at the amounts of accumulated amortization.)

3. In which of the five categories of intangible assets do "noncompete agreements" fall? Explain.

4. What is the nature of "developed technology rights"?

LO4   **EXERCISE 10-19   Goodwill Valuation and Impairment**

On January 1, 2005, Outkast, Inc. paid $860,000 to purchase Speakerboxx, Inc. The balance sheet value and fair market value of Speakerboxx's net assets on that date were $710,000 and $735,000, respectively. The accountant discovered two internally created intangible assets that did not appear on Speakerboxx's balance sheet. These were a customer list valued at $55,000 and a noncompete agreement valued at $30,000. The customer list is separable; the noncompete agreement is not. Outkast amortizes its intangibles over 12 years. On December 31, 2006 and 2007, it was estimated that the reporting unit to which the goodwill related could be sold for $780,000 and $660,000, respectively. The reporting unit showed a book value of the net assets on December 31, 2006 and 2007 totaling $770,000 and $740,000, respectively.

Required:

1. How much will Outkast report as goodwill on its balance sheet at January 1, 2005 as a result of the acquisition?

2. Does an impairment exist at December 31, 2006 or 2007? If so, how much?

3. What is due diligence, and how does it affect the valuation of goodwill?

LO2   EXERCISE **10-20**   **Intangible Transactions and Reporting**

On June 30, 2004, Max Burgers gave 40,000 shares of its $1 par common stock for the following assets:

A. A recipe for secret sauce valued at $800,000

B. Sponsorship rights for the *Talent Scout* television show valued at $3,200,000.

Max Burgers's stock was selling at $90 per share on the date of the exchange. The sponsorship rights cover two seasons of network programming. The recipe is expected to benefit Max Burgers indefinitely.

On September 1, 2004, Max Burgers hired an advertising agency to develop advertising for the 30-second viewing slots in each of the weekly *Talent Scout* shows running from January through May of each year. The advertising agency was paid $1,400,000 for the advertising contract that was expected to create goodwill totaling $4,100,000 over a five-year period.

Required:

1. Prepare a partial balance sheet at June 30, 2005.

2. When accounting for amortization, a company has an option of crediting two different accounts. What two options exist?

PROBLEMS

LO1, 2, 4, 5   PROBLEM **10-1**   **Intangible Transactions**

The following information was provided by Signa Manufacturing concerning activity during its first year of business:

Jan. 1–Mar. 31, 2004	Signa incurred the following initial project costs: Engineering follow-through in an early phase of commercial production of $19,000; design, construction, and testing of pre-production prototypes and models of $137,000.
Mar. 31, 2004	Issued 100 shares of $10 par value common stock that was selling at $250 per share in exchange for data research services related to a new product.
Apr.–June 2004	Developed a new process for packaging products at a cost of $150,000. Paid $75,000 to register the patent on June 30, 2004.
Sept. 30, 2004	Defended the patent in court and lost. Legal costs amounted to $18,000. Economic benefit period of the patent is five years.
Nov. 1, 2004	Purchased a subsidiary at a cost of $3,200,000. The subsidiary's balance sheet reported assets and liabilities of $5,200,000 and $3,000,000, respectively. The fair value of the assets exceeded the book value by $500,000. The book value of the liabilities equaled the fair value.
Dec. 1, 2004	A trademark was purchased from a competitor for $20,000 cash down and a 10 percent note for $40,000, due at the end of one year. Signa estimates a three-year period of benefit from using the trademark.

Required: Prepare the intangible assets section of the balance sheet and a partial income statement showing the effects of these transactions for the year ended December 31, 2004.

Analyze: Why is goodwill not amortized?

LO3   PROBLEM **10-2**   **Impairment with Indefinite Life**

Snow Products, Inc. has excelled in the snowboard manufacturing industry. Its leading product, the X-1000, is the leading snowboard sold in Europe and the western United States. A patent was awarded in February 2003 for its unique design concepts, including its core and its carbon top design elements. Management has determined that the patent has an indefinite life. The patent has an original cost of $650,000.

As of December 31, 2004, Snow Products' controller is examining the value assigned to the patent because of certain developments in the snowboard industry. One development relates to claims by popular snowboard magazine editors that the X-1000 board has lost its technological advantage. Accordingly, impairment is now being considered as of the valuation date (2004). An outside industry expert has advised management that certain events could either greatly decrease or greatly increase the value of the product's patent. The following are the cash flows from the product that would result from each of those events:

	2005	2006	2007	2008	2009
Celebrity endorsement (35% chance)	$300,000	$200,000	$175,000	$125,000	$85,000
Testing suggests no advantage to new technology (40% chance)	150,000	75,000	50,000	45,000	20,000
Critics' award (25% chance)	400,000	300,000	250,000	150,000	75,000

Management uses an 8 percent interest rate in cost of capital decisions.

Required:

1. What specific event would most likely have triggered a need to determine if an impairment to this patent exists? Prepare an analysis to support your conclusion.
2. Determine whether an impairment exists as of December 31, 2004.
3. Prepare the journal entries associated with your evaluation, if applicable.

Analyze: How does accounting for intangibles with unlimited lives differ from accounting for those with limited lives?

LO3   PROBLEM **10-3**   **Impairment with Amortized Intangibles**

Harvesters Farm Equipment has enjoyed over 50 years of success with specialty tractors. Its smallest tractor, the Series 500, has been successful for over 10 years. The trademark slogan, "Series 500, all you'll ever need on a farm," has been a major reason for the success of that tractor. Management initially assigned that trademark a value of $400,000 with a 20-year life and no residual value. The net book value of the trademark as of the end of the current year, 2005, is $100,000 with five years remaining on the life. Management has been amortizing the trademark on a straight-line basis.

Management has asked a CPA firm, ABC Company, to assist it in evaluating whether any impairment of value has occurred in the trademark. The following information was supplied by the CFO to assist in that process:

	2006	2007	2008	2009	2010
Expected gross cash flows from trademark	$40,000	$35,000	$10,000	$5,000	$2,000

Required:

1. What is the first step in evaluating whether the trademark is impaired? Is there an impairment in the trademark?

2. If an impairment was determined in question 1, what is the impairment amount? Assume a cost of capital of 7 percent.

3. Prepare the journal entry for the impairment, if applicable.

Analyze: What is the conceptual reason that impairment losses must be recognized?

LO4 PROBLEM **10-4 Goodwill Valuation**

Colossal Industries consummated its fifth acquisition of the year just before its year end in 2004. Its acquisition of Smalltime Company is expected to increase earnings and aid its long-term strategy to be the world's leading producer of specialty magnets. The purchase price of $4 million is at a premium above net book value. More information on Smalltime as of December 31, 2004 follows:

	Book Value	Fair Value
Cash	$ 140,000	$ 140,000
Accounts receivable, net of allowances of $30,200 and $20,000, respectively	2,300,000	2,100,000
Inventories	350,000	360,000
Land	1,100,000	1,800,000
Accounts payable	46,000	38,000
Other accrued liabilities	24,000	25,000
Long-term debt	1,200,000	1,150,000
Other long-term liabilities	150,000	160,000
Not previously recorded:		
Customer list	0	300,000

Required:

1. What is the estimated amount of goodwill arising from this purchase?

2. Show the journal entries needed to record the purchase of Smalltime Company.

Analyze: Under the definition of goodwill, are there any assets that could be challenged as not being "separately identifiable"? Justify your answer.

LO4 PROBLEM **10-5 Goodwill Impairment**

Refer to the information provided in Problem 10-4. Assume that Smalltime Company was designated by Colossal's management as a separate reporting unit. The following amounts are taken from Smalltime's accounting records of December 31, 2006, two years after the acquisition:

	Book Value
Cash	$ 85,000
Accounts receivable, net of allowance of $34,200	650,000
Inventories	150,000
Land	1,800,000
Customer list	300,000
Goodwill	673,000
Accounts payable	16,000
Other accrued liabilities	85,000
Long-term debt	600,000
Other long-term liabilities	350,000

Required:

1. The fair value assigned to the Smalltime unit is $2,500,000 at December 31, 2006. Should Smalltime's management consider any impairment issues involving goodwill? Explain why or why not.

2. If an impairment exists, show the calculation of the impairment loss. Prepare any necessary journal entry.

Analyze: Explain the two components of goodwill as identified by the FASB. What does each represent?

LO1, 2   **PROBLEM 10-6   Intangible Assets**

Several transactions for Jared, Inc. are as follows:

A. January 1, 2005: Issued 100 shares of $30 par value common stock that was selling at $200 per share in exchange for engineering drawings related to potential product development.

B. May 30, 2005: Developed a new production process for products at a cost of $135,000. Costs of design, construction, and testing of pre-production prototypes and models totaled $65,000.

C. August 31, 2005: Paid $34,000 to register the patent (in item B), of which $3,800 was administrative costs. The patent has a 17-year legal life, but it is expected to benefit the company for 30 years.

D. October 1, 2005: Purchased Pharaoh Industries at a cost of $740,000. At the acquisition date, Pharaoh's balance sheet reported assets and liabilities of $4,000,000 and $3,800,000, respectively. The fair value of Pharaoh's assets totaled $4,200,000. The book value of its liabilities was $40,000 more than the fair value.

E. December 1, 2005: Incurred costs of $21,000 for the distribution of product samples, which is expected to produce income over the next three years.

Required:

1. Indicate the effect of each transaction on intangible assets.

2. Prepare the intangible assets section of the balance sheet at December 31, 2005.

3. How does the current accounting for research and development expenditures make the analysis of companies with extensive research and development activities difficult?

Analyze: Why does GAAP require different treatment for internally and externally developed intangible assets?

Critical Thinking: Why are research and development costs expensed when incurred?

LO2, 4, 5   **PROBLEM 10-7   Intangible Transactions**

The following transactions of Piper Industries occurred during 2004:

A. During 2004, the company developed a new process for packaging products at a cost of $120,000. On April 1, 2004, it paid $65,000 to register the packaging patent, which the company believes will produce profits for five years. Six months later, the company defended the patent in court and won. It paid the attorney another $13,500 in legal costs for the defense. The patent has a 17-year legal life.

B. On October 1, 2004, Piper purchased a subsidiary for $4,500,000. The subsidiary's balance sheet reported assets of $6,000,000 and liabilities of $2,600,000. The fair value of the acquired assets was $6,600,000. The book value of the liabilities equaled the fair value. Piper believes that the purchase will be profitable for at least 50 years.

Required: Prepare the intangible assets section of Piper's balance sheet at December 31, 2004.

Analyze: In what situations can a company recognize goodwill?

Critical Thinking: What role does ethics play in a company's ability to generate inherent goodwill?

LO1, 2, 4, 5 **PROBLEM 10-8   Intangible Transactions**
Consider the following 2004 transactions for Peppermint Company:

Jan. 1   Purchased a subsidiary at a cost of $4,060,000. The subsidiary's balance sheet reported assets and liabilities totaling $7,500,000 and $4,000,000, respectively. The fair value of the assets exceeds the book value by $300,000. The book value of the liabilities equals the fair value. The subsidiary is expected to produce profits for at least 50 years.

Feb. 28   Completed the development of a new process for packaging products at a cost of $225,000.

Mar. 31   Paid $30,000 to register the packaging patent. The legal life of the patent is 17 years, but the company expects future benefits to last only 5 years.

June 1   Incurred advertising costs for the new patent totaling $80,000. The company expects the advertising to generate customers for 10 years.

Dec. 31   Defended the patent in court and won. Legal costs amounted to $16,000.

Required: Prepare the intangible assets section of the balance sheet at December 31, 2004, for Peppermint Company.

Analyze: Why are acquired intangible assets valued differently from internally developed intangible assets?

LO2, 4, 5 **PROBLEM 10-9   Intangible Transactions**
The following transactions of Tassanee Industries occurred during 2005:

Jan. 1   Purchased a subsidiary at a cost of $2,600,000. The subsidiary's balance sheet reported assets and liabilities totaling $8,200,000 and $6,000,000, respectively. The fair value of the assets exceeded the book value by $100,000. The book value of the liabilities equaled the fair value. The subsidiary is expected to produce profits for at least 50 years.

Mar. 31   Developed a new process for packaging products at a cost of $225,000. Paid $50,000 to register the patent. On December 31, defended the patent in court and won. Legal costs amounted to $26,000. The legal life of the patent is 17 years, but the company expects future benefits to last only 5 years.

Required: Prepare the intangible assets section of the balance sheet at December 31, 2005.

Critical Thinking: Amortization is said to be analogous to depreciation for fixed assets. Explain.

Analyze: What factors affect the determination of a useful life over which to amortize intangibles?

CASES

LO4 **RESEARCH CASE 10-1   Impairment and Goodwill**
Goodwill is an important factor when evaluating a company's financial condition.

Required: Locate the accounting section of the Outsourcing Law website, at **www.outsourcinglaw.com/accounting.htm**. Click on the topic "Goodwill" and answer the following questions:

1. Describe why evaluation of impairment is necessary.

2. Describe the tests necessary for goodwill impairment.

3. What impact does impairment of goodwill have on share prices and financial condition? Explain why you think this impact occurs.

LO4 **CRITICAL THINKING CASE 10-2   Effects of Goodwill Accounting**
Statement of Financial Accounting Standards No. 142, "Goodwill and Other Intangible Assets," eliminates the amortization of goodwill and institutes an annual impairment test.

Required: Locate the Investopedia website, **www.taxopedia.com**. Use the site's search function to find the article "Lady Godiva Accounting Principles," by Rick Wayman. Answer the following questions:

1. Why does the author of the article believe that EPS will be boosted as a result of accounting for goodwill under *SFAS No. 142*? Recall that EPS is earnings per share, calculated by dividing net income by the weighted-average number of shares of stock outstanding.

2. Why does the author believe that not restating past results creates a problem?

3. Why do companies have the incentive to perform charge-offs upon the adoption of *SFAS No. 142*?

LO4   RESEARCH CASE **10-3**   **Research International Accounting for Goodwill**

Access the International Accounting Standards Board's website, **www.iasb.org**.

Required: Research the International Accounting Standards Board's website for the current international accounting standards for goodwill. Identify the differences that exist between accounting for goodwill under International Accounting Standards and under U.S. GAAP. What changes related to accounting for goodwill would you foresee for U.S. companies if the United States adopted International Accounting Standards?

LO4   ANALYSIS CASE **10-4**   **Goodwill Impairment**

Portions of the financial statements and related notes for **Sears, Roebuck and Co.**, taken from its 2002 annual report, follow.

Sears

SEARS, ROEBUCK AND CO.
Consolidated Balance Sheets

millions	2002	2001
ASSETS		
Current assets		
Cash and cash equivalents	$ 1,962	$ 1,064
Credit card receivables	32,595	29,321
Less allowance for uncollectible accounts	1,836	1,166
Net credit card receivables	30,759	28,155
Other receivables	863	658
Merchandise inventories	5,115	4,912
Prepaid expenses and deferred charges	535	458
Deferred income taxes	749	858
Total current assets	39,983	36,105
Property and equipment		
Land	442	434
Buildings and improvements	6,930	6,539
Furniture, fixtures and equipment	5,050	5,620
Capitalized leases	557	544
Gross property and equipment	12,979	13,137
Less accumulated depreciation	6,069	6,313
Total property and equipment, net	6,910	6,824
Deferred income taxes	734	415
Goodwill	944	294
Trade names and other intangible assets	704	—
Other assets	1,134	679
TOTAL ASSETS	$50,409	$44,317

Sears

Trade Names and Other Identifiable Intangible Assets

The identifiable intangible assets of the Company are primarily trade names acquired in business combinations. The Company adopted the provisions of Statement of Financial Accounting Standards ("SFAS") No. 142, "Goodwill and Other Intangible Assets", at the beginning of 2002. Under the provisions of SFAS No. 142, identifiable intangibles with finite lives are amortized and those with indefinite lives are not amortized. The estimated useful life of an identifiable intangible asset to the Company is based upon a number of factors including the effects of demand, competition and the level of maintenance expenditures required to obtain future cash flows. Prior to the start of 2002, the Company followed the provisions of Accounting Principles Board Opinion ("APB") No. 17, which required that all identifiable intangibles be amortized by systematic charges to income over the period expected to be benefited.

The Company tests identifiable intangible assets with an indefinite life for impairment, at a minimum on an annual basis, relying on a number of factors including operating results, business plans and projected future cash flows. Identifiable intangible assets that are subject to amortization are evaluated for impairment using a process similar to that used to evaluate other long-lived assets. The impairment test for identifiable intangible assets not subject to amortization consists of a comparison of the fair value of the intangible asset with its carrying amount. An impairment loss is recognized for the amount by which the carrying value exceeds the fair value of the asset.

Goodwill

Under the provisions of SFAS No. 142, goodwill is no longer amortized. Prior to the start of 2002, the Company followed the provisions of APB Opinion No. 17, which required that goodwill be amortized by systematic charges to income over the period expected to be benefited. That period ranged from 5 to 40 years.

NOTE 17—Implementation of New Accounting Standard

SFAS No. 145, "Rescission of FASB Statement No. 4, 44 and 64, Amendment of FASB Statement No. 13, and Technical Corrections", is effective for all financial statements issued on or after May 15, 2002. SFAS 145, eliminates Statement 4, which required all gains and losses from debt extinguishment to be aggregated, and if material, classified as an extraordinary item, net of tax. Under SFAS No. 145, debt extinguishments used as part of an entity's risk management strategy do not meet the criteria for classification as extraordinary items. The Company's adoption of SFAS No. 145 did not have an impact on the consolidated financial statements.

Effective at the beginning of 2002, the Company adopted SFAS No. 142, "Goodwill and Other Intangible Assets". Upon adoption of SFAS No. 142, goodwill amortization ceased. Goodwill is now subject to fair-value based impairment tests performed, at a minimum, on an annual basis. In addition, a transitional goodwill impairment test is required as of the adoption date. These impairment tests are conducted on each business of the Company where goodwill is recorded, and may require two steps. The initial step is designed to identify potential goodwill impairment by comparing an estimate of fair value for each applicable business to its respective carrying value. For those businesses where the carrying value exceeds fair value, a second step is performed to measure the amount of goodwill impairment in existence, if any.

The Company had approximately $371 million in positive goodwill and $77 million in negative goodwill recorded in its consolidated balance sheet at the beginning of 2002 as well as approximately $104 million in positive goodwill related to an equity method investment which is not subject to SFAS No. 142 impairment tests. The $77 million in negative goodwill was required to be recognized into income upon adoption of the Statement. The Company completed the required transitional goodwill impairment test in the first quarter of 2002 and determined that $261 million of goodwill recorded within the Company's Retail and Related Services segment, primarily related to NTB and Orchard Supply Hardware, was impaired under the fair value impairment test approach required by SFAS No. 142.

(continued)

The fair value of these reporting units was estimated using the expected present value of associated future cash flows and market values of comparable businesses where available. Upon adoption of the Statement, a $208 million charge, net of tax and minority interest, was recognized in the first quarter of 2002 to record this impairment as well as the recognition of negative goodwill and was classified as a cumulative effect of a change in accounting principle.

The following table presents the pro forma effect of the adoption of SFAS No. 142 on recent fiscal periods as if the change was applied at the beginning of the respective fiscal year:

millions, except earnings (loss) per common share	2001	2000
Reported net income	$ 735	$1,343
Add back:		
Negative goodwill amortization	(14)	(15)
Positive goodwill amortization	20	24
Pro forma net income	$ 741	$1,352

The changes in the carrying amount of goodwill as of December 28, 2002 are as follows:

Millions	Retail and Related Services	Credit and Financial Products	Corporate and other	Sears Canada	Total
Balance as of December 29, 2001	$291	$2	$61	$(60)	$294
Cumulative effect of adopting SFAS No. 142:					
Impairment loss recognized	(261)	—	—	—	(261)
Elimination of negative goodwill	—	—	—	77	77
Acquisition of Lands' End	834	—	—	—	834
Balance as of December 28, 2002	$864	$2	$61	$17	$944

The Company's policy is to test the realizability of goodwill as of the end of the fiscal year. The Company tested the realizability of the $944 million of goodwill as of December 28, 2002 resulting in no additional impairment being recorded.

Required:

1. What is goodwill?

2. Prepare the entry made by Sears, Roebuck and Co. to recognize the impairment of goodwill during 2002.

3. What is the nature of the two increases in goodwill during 2002?

LO1   **COMMUNICATION CASE 10-5   Intangible Asset Characteristics**

Imagine that you are a new employee of **Sears, Roebuck and Co.** and you are in charge of determining the proper valuation of assets on the balance sheet. As you review the 2002 annual report, you notice that Sears spends a considerable amount on advertising. The vice president of marketing has sent you an e-mail message asking, "Why are advertising costs not reported as intangible assets on the balance sheet?" The vice president points out that advertising messages affect customers' decisions to shop at Sears in the future, even though a particular advertisement might be published during the current week. The vice president's e-mail brought up a good point: "For instance, many customers don't need a new washing machine today; however, when the time comes to replace the family washer, a customer might remember Sears's washing machine advertisement and make the purchase at that time." You recall from your accounting classes that assets are economic resources with future benefits. In an effort to answer the vice president's question, you find the information that follows in the company's 2002 annual report.

Sears

Advertising and Direct Response Marketing

Costs for newspaper, television, radio and other media advertising are expensed the first time the advertising occurs. The total cost of advertising charged to selling, general and administrative expense was $1.8 billion in 2002 and $1.6 billion in each of 2001 and 2000.

Certain direct response advertising and solicitation costs are capitalized. Membership acquisition and renewal costs, which primarily relate to membership solicitations, are capitalized since such direct response advertising costs result in future economic benefits. Generally, such costs are amortized over the shorter of the program's life or five years, primarily in proportion to when revenues are recognized. For specialty catalogs, costs are amortized over the life of the catalog, not to exceed one year. When the carrying amount of such deferred direct advertising costs exceed the estimated future net revenues realized from such advertising, any excess is recorded as advertising expense of the current period. The consolidated balance sheets include deferred direct response advertising costs of $58 million and $57 million at December 28, 2002 and December 29, 2001, respectively. The current portion is included in prepaid expenses and deferred charges, while the long-term portion is included in other assets.

Required: Use what you know about intangible assets to explain to the vice president of marketing why advertising costs are not reported as intangible assets. Justify your response.

LO1, 2

 ETHICS

ETHICS CASE 10-6   The Life of Intangibles

Anna Manry recently joined Olsen Manufacturing Company as the chief accountant. While familiarizing herself with the company's accounting system and financial statements, Anna notices that the company's intangible assets represent a significant part of total assets. Several of the company's most significant intangible assets are trademarks. The company is amortizing these trademarks over 40 years. Anna is aware that some intangible assets should not be amortized if they have an indefinite life.

Anna realizes that the top trademarks may continue to benefit the company for a nearly unlimited number of years. Since she is anxious to help her new company improve its financial position, she considers suggesting to the chief financial officer (CFO) that the company's major trademarks could be reclassified as having an indefinite life, and thus the amortization expense would be eliminated. This would improve both the balance sheet and the income statement.

Required:

1. Are there any ethical considerations involved in this strategy?
2. Who will be affected by the decision to change to an indefinite life?
3. What alternative actions are available?
4. What would you do?

LO2, 5

 ETHICS

ETHICS CASE 10-7   Purchasing or Developing Assets

Transmeta Corporation is a developer and manufacturer of microprocessors for computers. During October 2003, Transmeta introduced its newest processor technology, the "Efficeon TM800." This new processor is expected to provide better performance and conserve battery power. Transmeta's stock rose from $1.50 to $5.51 a share during the months leading up to the introduction of its new chip. However, a few days after the introduction of the chip, Transmeta's stock price fell to $4.00 when it published its quarterly financial results. Apparently, investors were disappointed by Transmeta's revenue of $2.7 billion (significantly lower than expected), and the company's loss ($19 million even after excluding noncash charges).[7]

---

7 Bill Albert, "When Intel Isn't Inside," *Barron's,* October 20, 2003, pp. T1–T2.

In response, Transmeta may seek to increase its income by changing the way it develops new products. In the past, the company has incurred significant research and development costs by developing products internally. The company could choose to purchase technologies from external sources instead, thereby lowering its expenses and improving its reported income.

Required:

1. What ethical considerations are involved in this decision?
2. Who will be affected by the decision?
3. What values and principles are likely to influence the decision?
4. What alternative actions might the CFO take?
5. a. Whose interest is most important?
   b. Which values and principles are most important?
   c. Which of the possible consequences will do the most good or cause the least harm?
   d. Which consideration is most important?
6. If you were the chief financial officer of Transmeta, what would you do?

ON THE WEB

The following exercises, activities, and problems are available on the *Intermediate Accounting* website. Use these resources to reinforce your understanding of the topics presented in this chapter.

- CPA-Adapted Simulations
- Interpreting the Accounting Standards
- Extending the Global Focus
- Extending the Ethics Discussion
- Mastering the Spreadsheet
- Career Snapshots
- Annual Report Project
- ACE Practice Tests
- Flashcards
- Glossary
- Check Figures for Text Problems
- PowerPoint Presentations

SOLUTIONS: CHECK YOUR UNDERSTANDING

The Nature of Intangible Assets (p. 458)

1. (1) Marketing-related, (2) customer-related, (3) artistic-related (4) contract-based, and (5) technology-based.

2. Customer lists, order backlogs, and customer relationships are customer-related intangible assets.

3. The useful life of an artistic-related intangible asset is determined by establishing the number of years over which the intangible asset will provide benefits. That time period may be much shorter than the maximum allowable period of the artist's life plus 70 years.

The Initial Measurement of Intangible Assets (p. 463)

1. If an intangible asset is purchased from an outside source, the asset is recorded at its acquisition cost plus any additional costs needed to prepare the asset for use.

2. If several intangible assets are purchased for a lump-sum amount, the cost is allocated among the assets on the basis of their relative fair market values. If fair market values are not available, appraised values may be used.

3. In determining the useful life of an intangible asset, these factors are examined: the period over which the intangible asset is expected to generate cash flows; legal, regulatory, and contractual factors that limit the intangible asset's useful life; how the asset will be used; how long related assets will be useful; governmental and regulatory provisions; and economic factors such as obsolescence, competition, and demand.

Impairment of Intangible Assets (p. 466)

1. To determine the impairment of an unamortized asset, the fair value of the asset is compared to its book value. If market values do not exist, the asset's future cash flows are estimated and discounted back to the current period. In making this calculation for an amortized asset, cash flows do not have to be discounted.

2. Rapid technological advances, intense domestic and global competition, and changes in market demand are events that might cause the impairment of an intangible asset.

3. The impairment loss is equal to the amount by which the asset's book value exceeds its fair value.

Goodwill (p. 171)

1. Goodwill is an intangible asset that is recognized only when one company purchases another company; it represents the premium that a purchaser pays over the fair value of an acquired company's identifiable net assets.

2. If the fair value is greater than the book value, the goodwill is not impaired and remains on the financial statements. No entry is required.

Research and Development Costs (p. 472)

1. Research and development costs are expensed as incurred.

2. Research and development costs might include both direct costs, such as the salaries and benefits of personnel working on research and development, and allocated indirect costs, such as depreciation on fixed assets used in the R&D efforts.

CPA-ADAPTED SIMULATION

This simulation asks you to complete various tasks related to a company's annual financial statements. If your instructor has signed up for CPAexcel™, you can do the work online at **www.cpaexcel.com/hmco**. You may also do the simulation manually.

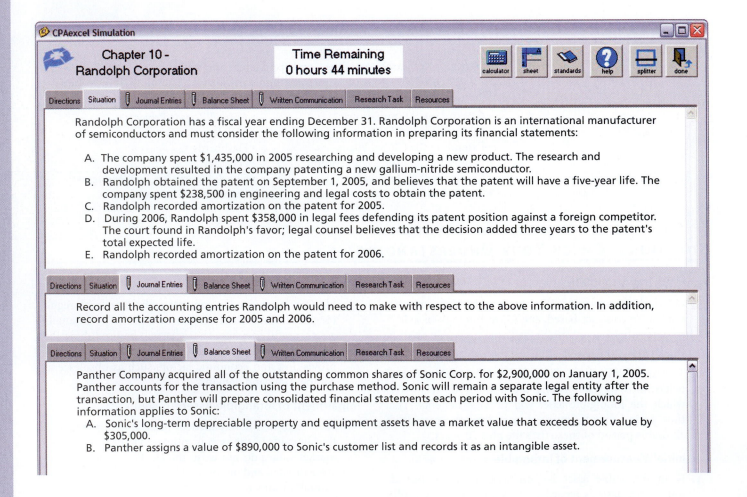

CPAexcel Simulation

Chapter 10 - Randolph Corporation

Time Remaining
0 hours 44 minutes

calculator | sheet | standards | help | splitter | done

Directions | Situation | Journal Entries | Balance Sheet | Written Communication | Research Task | Resources

Randolph Corporation has a fiscal year ending December 31. Randolph Corporation is an international manufacturer of semiconductors and must consider the following information in preparing its financial statements:

A. The company spent $1,435,000 in 2005 researching and developing a new product. The research and development resulted in the company patenting a new gallium-nitride semiconductor.
B. Randolph obtained the patent on September 1, 2005, and believes that the patent will have a five-year life. The company spent $238,500 in engineering and legal costs to obtain the patent.
C. Randolph recorded amortization on the patent for 2005.
D. During 2006, Randolph spent $358,000 in legal fees defending its patent position against a foreign competitor. The court found in Randolph's favor; legal counsel believes that the decision added three years to the patent's total expected life.
E. Randolph recorded amortization on the patent for 2006.

Directions | Situation | Journal Entries | Balance Sheet | Written Communication | Research Task | Resources

Record all the accounting entries Randolph would need to make with respect to the above information. In addition, record amortization expense for 2005 and 2006.

Directions | Situation | Journal Entries | Balance Sheet | Written Communication | Research Task | Resources

Panther Company acquired all of the outstanding common shares of Sonic Corp. for $2,900,000 on January 1, 2005. Panther accounts for the transaction using the purchase method. Sonic will remain a separate legal entity after the transaction, but Panther will prepare consolidated financial statements each period with Sonic. The following information applies to Sonic:
A. Sonic's long-term depreciable property and equipment assets have a market value that exceeds book value by $305,000.
B. Panther assigns a value of $890,000 to Sonic's customer list and records it as an intangible asset.

Information about Panther Company and Sonic Corporation's balance sheets at the acquisition date appears below:

Consolidated Financial Information
Panther Company and Sonic Corp.
January 1, 2005 Acquisition Date

	Panther	Sonic
Assets		
Current assets	$ 4,230,600	$1,330,000
Property and equipment less accumulated depreciation	6,900,000	945,000
Other long-term assets	345,000	–
Intangible asset-customer list	–	–
Goodwill	–	–
Total assets	$11,475,600	$2,275,000
Liabilities and Equities		
Current liabilities	$ 5,500,600	$1,670,000
Long-term liabilities	600,000	–
Shareholder's equity	5,375,000	605,000
Total liabilities and shareholder's equity	$11,475,600	$2,275,000

Prepare the journal entry Panther should make to record the purchase of Sonic.

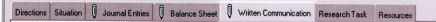

Delhomme Company owns the following intangible assets:

A. A copyright with a 10-year life purchased for $235,000 in 2003. The company is amortizing it using the straight-line method.
B. A customer list with an indefinite useful life purchased from an international competitor for $578,000.

Write a memorandum discussing how Delhomme should test each intangible asset for impairment at its balance sheet date.

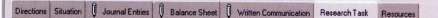

Often a company acquires equipment for a research and development project. In some cases the equipment may be used only for a particular research project. In other cases the equipment may have alternative future uses and may be used in other research projects. How should the cost of such equipment be recognized and reported?

Financial Instruments and Liabilities

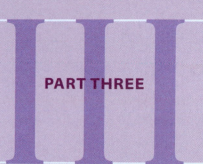

As businesses conduct operations and grow their enterprises, they must often use investment strategies to fund these activities and strengthen their financial condition. While some investments take the form of equity, like stock ownership, others take the form of debt. Companies may choose to gather funding from bonds or notes, or simply use credit extended by suppliers to pay for inventory or capital purchases. Part Three provides a look at current and long-term liabilities, investing activities, and accounting for income taxes.

11 Investments: Debt and Equity Securities
Chapter 11 provides a detailed look at the proper accounting treatment for various types of debt and equity securities and illustrates how financial statement disclosures may be used to analyze a company's investments.

12 Current Liabilities and Contingencies
Chapter 12 begins a five-chapter series on liabilities. We first examine current liabilities—how to identify them, how to properly account for them, and how to set up accruals and deferrals. Then the issues surrounding contingent liabilities are covered. You will also learn how to analyze current liabilities in order to better understand a company's financial position and how current liabilities affect a company's cash flows.

13 Accounting for Long-Term Liabilities: Bonds and Notes Payable
As we continue our examination of liabilities, Chapter 13 prepares you to identify long-term liabilities, properly account for bonds and notes payable, and use analysis techniques to examine the effect of long-term liabilities on the financial statements.

14 Accounting for Leases
In addition to debts that arise from bonds, notes, or short-term liabilities, companies also enter into lease agreements that produce liabilities. In this chapter, you will learn how to differentiate a capital lease from an operating lease and a direct financing lease from a sales-type lease, and how to account for each type of lease appropriately.

15 Pensions and Postretirement Plans
While companies certainly provide compensation to their employees in the form of a weekly or monthly paycheck, compensation may also be offered in the form of a pension plan, payable to employees after they retire. In this chapter, you will learn how to account for various types of pension plans and identify the appropriate financial disclosures for such plans.

16 Accounting for Income Taxes
Chapter 16 not only covers the determination, recording, and financial statement presentation of tax expenses and liabilities, but also describes why interperiod tax allocation is necessary and how these allocations affect cash flows. You will also learn how to use income tax disclosures in the financial statements and related notes to discern a company's quality of earnings.

CHAPTER ELEVEN

Investments: Debt and Equity Securities

FINANCIAL REPORTING CASE

INTEL'S CAPITAL INVESTMENT PROGRAM DOMINATES

Intel's investing activities are an integral part of the company's business strategy in launching new products like the Intel XScale chip, used in mobile phones.

Intel   Intel doesn't believe in putting all its eggs in one basket. Instead, the company strategically invests in technology, communication, and manufacturing companies worldwide, thereby influencing and dominating today's technology sector. The "Intel Capital" strategic investment program seeks to stimulate advances in computing and Internet technologies, while maximizing the financial returns to its investors. Intel has had this investment program for several years. AMD, one of Intel's major competitors, stated in its 2000 annual report, "Intel invests billions of dollars in, and as a result exerts influence over, many other technology companies. We expect Intel to continue to invest heavily in research and development, new manufacturing facilities and other technology companies, and to remain dominant."[1]

At the end of 2003, Intel had more than $8 billion invested worldwide and was considered one of the most active investors in the technology sector. Although the com-

---

1 AMD 2000 Annual Report, p. 21.

496

Intel

INTEL CORPORATION
PARTIAL CONSOLIDATED BALANCE SHEETS

December 27, 2003 and December 28, 2002

(In Millions)	2003	2002
Assets		
Current assets:		
Cash and cash equivalents	$ 7,971	$ 7,404
Short-term investments	5,568	3,382
Trading assets	2,625	1,801
Accounts receivable, net of allowance for doubtful		
accounts of $55 ($57 in 2002)	2,960	2,574
Inventories	2,519	2,276
Deferred tax assets	969	1,136
Other current assets	270	352
Total current assets	22,882	18,925
Property, plant and equipment, net	16,661	17,847
Marketable strategic equity securities	514	56
Other long-term investments	1,866	1,178
Goodwill	3,705	4,330
Other assets	1,515	1,888
Total assets	$47,143	$44,224

pany's investment portfolio performed well in the 1990s, the downturn of the stock market in 2001 required a shift in strategy. Since then, the company has transformed many of its investments into short-term holdings to avoid heavy fluctuations in earnings.

An excerpt from Intel's consolidated balance sheets at December 27, 2003 and December 28, 2002 appears above. As you can see, at December 27, 2003, the company reported short-term investments of $5,568 million and trading assets of $2,625 million. Included in these categories are investments like commercial paper, corporate bonds, and notes. In addition, the company had marketable strategic equity securities of $514 million.

EXAMINING THE CASE

1. By what percentage did Intel's short-term investments and trading assets change from 2002 to 2003?

2. Describe the advantages of Intel's capital investment program as you see them.

3. Which financial statement would reveal more about Intel's net cash flows from investing activities?

Investment Activities and Types of Securities

investing activities the acquisition and sale of long-term marketable securities and the making and collecting of loans

security an investment instrument issued by a corporation, government, or other organization that offers evidence of debt or of an equity investment

LO1 Describe three primary reasons why companies engage in investment activities.

Critical Thinking: Identify the potential benefits and risks that businesses and individuals face when conducting investing activities.

As indicated in the Financial Reporting Case about **Intel**, investments in securities can be an integral part of a company's business strategy. These **investing activities** involve the acquisition and sale of long-term marketable securities and the making and collecting of loans. Investments generally take the form of stocks or bonds, but certificates of deposit, mutual funds, and Treasury bills may also be included in this category. The term **security** is often also used to define investment instruments such as bond or stock certificates that offer evidence of a debt or an equity investment.

MOTIVATIONS FOR INVESTING ACTIVITIES

Although companies engage in investment activities for many reasons, motivations can be classified into the following primary categories:

1. *Management of excess cash and income generation.* The operations of some companies are cyclical in nature; they generate cash during "up cycles" that is later needed during "down cycles." These companies invest their excess cash in liquid investment vehicles for short periods of time. Their primary motivation is not to produce income but to manage their cash flows efficiently. Other companies may invest in order to generate a significant amount of income. Interest and dividend income from investments may be an important source of income, but it is seldom the primary focus of a company's operations. For that reason, this income is usually classified as other income on the income statement.

2. *Relationship development.* In some cases, a company may invest in the stock of another company in order to develop a continuing relationship with the investee. For example, a company may acquire stock in a supplier or lend money to a supplier in order to ensure a continued flow of a critical product. As indicated earlier, Intel actively develops many such relationships and influences the markets in its industry through such holdings.

3. *Control.* In some cases, a company may invest in another company in order to acquire ownership control of that company. The FASB has considered at length how control should be defined and how to account for such investments.[2] Control exists when a company owns a majority of the stock in the investee company and *may* exist in certain joint ventures and other business relationships. When control exists, the two entities must usually provide consolidated financial statements. The issues involved in consolidated statements are beyond the scope of this text and will not be addressed in this chapter.

INVESTMENT RISK

All investing activities involve a certain amount of risk because a known amount (cash) is surrendered in return for a future amount (interest or dividends) that is unknown. There are several types of risk involved with investing activities:

interest-rate risk the risk of changes in the fair value of the cash flows of an asset as a result of changes in the interest rate

currency risk the risk of changes in the value of an asset as a result of changes in foreign currency exchange rates

● **Interest-rate risk** is the risk of changes in the fair value of the cash flows of an asset as a result of changes in the interest rate.

● **Currency risk** is the risk of changes in the value of an asset as a result of changes in foreign currency exchange rates.

---

2 See the FASB project "Business Combinations" for a complete discussion of control relationships.

credit risk the risk that one party will fail to discharge its contractual obligations and thereby cause the other party to incur a loss

liquidity risk the risk that a loss may be incurred because an investment cannot be eliminated quickly

- **Credit risk** is the risk that one party will fail to discharge its contractual obligations and thereby cause the other party to incur a loss.

- **Liquidity risk** is the risk that a loss may be incurred because an investment cannot be eliminated quickly.[3]

Although all investing involves a certain amount of risk, companies should generally avoid investing based on speculation—that is, basing investment decisions on inconclusive evidence. This *unwarranted* level of risk is viewed negatively by investors, management, and boards of directors alike.

TYPES OF SECURITIES

debt securities securities that represent a creditor relationship with an enterprise

The FASB divides all investments into two types: debt securities and equity securities. **Debt securities** are those securities that represent a creditor relationship with an enterprise. The following are commonly considered debt securities:

- Bonds

- Loans

- Preferred stock that must be redeemed or that is redeemable at the option of the investor

- U.S. Treasury securities

- Municipal securities

- Corporate bonds

- Convertible debt

- Securitized instruments such as collateralized mortgage obligations[4]

equity securities securities that represent an ownership interest in an enterprise

Equity securities are defined as those securities that represent an ownership interest in an enterprise. The equity securities category commonly includes the following items:

- Common stock

- Preferred stock

- Warrants

- Rights

- Call options[5]

marketable equity securities stocks that have a readily determinable value

In some cases, equity investments may be called **marketable equity securities**. Marketable equity securities are stocks that have a readily determinable value. Usually, the fair market value of a stock can be determined because the stock is bought and sold on a stock exchange such as the New York Stock Exchange or the NASDAQ. To be precise, the accounting rules given in this chapter apply only in situations in which a fair market value can be determined. Because the fair market value of most equity securities can be determined in some manner, we will assume that this is the case in all subsequent discussions.

---

3 Definitions are from *Financial Instruments and Similar Items*, a special report of the Joint Working Group of Standard Setters (Stamford, Conn.: FASB, 2000).

4 "Accounting for Certain Investments in Debt and Equity Securities," *SFAS No. 115* (Stamford, Conn.: FASB, 1993), par. 137.

5 Ibid.

LO2 Describe the characteristics of held-to-maturity, trading, and available-for-sale securities.

Critical Thinking: *Can you describe different ways in which securities can generate income for the investor?*

held-to-maturity securities debt securities that the investing company has both the intent and the ability to hold to the maturity date

trading securities debt or equity securities that are bought principally for the purpose of selling them in the near term

available-for-sale securities investments that are not classified as trading or held-to-maturity; they may be intended for income generation, price appreciation, or other corporate purposes

CATEGORIES OF INVESTMENT SECURITIES

The accounting rules concerning the categorization of investments are provided in *SFAS No. 115* and several subsequent rulings. These accounting rules are based on the intent of corporate management in making the investment and the time period over which the company intends to maintain the investment. Investments can be classified into the following three categories: held-to-maturity, trading, and available-for-sale.

❯ HELD-TO-MATURITY SECURITIES

Held-to-maturity securities are debt securities that the investing company has both the *intent* and the *ability* to hold to the maturity date. It is assumed that debt in this category is held primarily for the interest income it produces. Company management *ordinarily* would not be led to sell such an investment in debt because of short-term fluctuations in interest-rate conditions or changes in the market value of the debt. The accounting rule does anticipate that certain drastic circumstances (changes in tax laws, a significant deterioration in the borrower's prospects, or a major business combination) would lead a company to sell debt securities in this category prior to their maturity date. Still, the intent of the FASB is clear: Securities that are classified as held-to-maturity should, in fact, be held to maturity unless isolated, unforeseen, or unusual circumstances occur.[6]

Note that only debt securities have a maturity date, and thus only debt securities can be classified as held-to-maturity. Equity securities cannot be held-to-maturity because stock does not have a maturity date.

❯ TRADING SECURITIES

Trading securities are defined as debt or equity securities that are bought principally for the purpose of selling them in the near term. This active and frequent buying and selling is used to generate profits from short-term differences in price.[7] Banks, financial institutions, brokers, and dealers hold sizable portfolios of trading securities. These companies buy and sell large numbers of securities on a frequent basis, and their intention is to profit from these activities.

❯ AVAILABLE-FOR-SALE SECURITIES

Available-for-sale securities are investments that are not classified as trading or held-to-maturity. In spite of the fact that this category may seem somewhat loosely defined, it is the largest category for most companies because of its flexibility. Securities in this category may be held for any period of time and may be intended for income generation, price appreciation, or other corporate purposes. As an example, Figure 11.1 provides information on Intel's available-for-sale securities as presented in its 2003 financial statement notes.

As you can see from Figure 11.1, Intel holds an available-for-sale portfolio with a cost of $15.66 billion and a market value of $15.71 billion as of December 27, 2003. A large portion of the portfolio consists of various types of debt securities, mostly commercial paper, which represents notes issued by other companies. These types of investments are likely to produce a stable, predictable income flow for the company. Note that the difference between cost and market value for debt securities (all of the items in Figure 11.1 except for preferred stock and marketable strategic equity securities) is minimal. The unrealized gain of $47 million for marketable strategic equity securities indicates a rise in stock prices since the time that some of the securities were purchased. The unrealized loss of $1 million for commercial paper indicates that the price of some securities declined since the time they were purchased.

---

6 Ibid., par. 8.

7 Ibid., par. 12.

Figure 11.1

Available-for-Sale Investments (in millions)

Intel

Intel's Available-for-Sale Investments at December 27, 2003

	Cost	Unrealized Gains	Unrealized Losses	Fair Value
Commercial paper	$ 9,948	$ —	$ (1)	$ 9,947
Bank time deposits	1,900	—	—	1,900
Loan participations	985	—	—	985
Corporate bonds	703	—	—	703
Floating rate notes	1,078	—	—	1,078
Preferred stock and other equity	224	9	—	233
Other debt securities	352	—	—	352
Marketable strategic equity securities	467	47	—	514
Total available-for-sale securities	$ 15,657*	$ 56	$ (1)	$ 15,712

*The available-for-sale investments are shown in several categories of the balance sheet, including $7,764 million treated as cash and cash equivalents.

Indicates that market value was higher than cost on some securities

Indicates that market value was lower than cost on some securities

CHECK YOUR UNDERSTANDING

1. Give three primary reasons that motivate businesses to engage in investing activities.

2. Explain the difference between debt securities and equity securities. Provide examples of each category.

Accounting for Debt Securities

Debt securities such as bonds or notes represent a creditor relationship with an enterprise. The categorization of such securities is critical to determining the appropriate accounting treatment. In addition, the following issues must be considered:

1. Should the securities be valued at original cost, amortized cost, or fair value on the balance sheet?

2. When bonds are purchased, the difference between the purchase price and the face value of the bonds represents a premium or discount. Should this premium or discount be amortized?

3. If securities are represented at fair value on the balance sheet, should the unrealized gains and losses from holding the securities be treated as income or as a portion of stockholders' equity? An **unrealized gain or loss** represents a change in the fair market value of the securities held. It is sometimes called a *holding gain or loss* because it is related to the securities that the company has not yet sold. We will assume that the changes in the market value of the securities are the result of "temporary" fluctuations. The Emerging Issues Task Force has issued a pronouncement concerning how to account for fluctuations that are "other than temporary." However, the FASB has suspended certain paragraphs of that pronouncement for further study. (*See EITF No. 03-01.*)

unrealized gain or loss a change in the fair market value of the securities held

Illustration 11.1

Accounting for Debt Securities

Type	Valuation	Amortize Premium or Discount?	Treatment of Unrealized Gain/Loss	Treatment of Realized Gain/Loss	Balance Sheet Presentation
Held-to-maturity	Amortized cost	Yes	Not applicable	On income statement	Long-term*
Available-for-sale	Fair value	Yes	Other comprehensive income	On income statement	Current and long-term†
Trading	Fair value	No	On income statement	Not reported ‡	Current

*Held-to-maturity securities are usually classified as long-term until the security is due within one year of the balance sheet date.

†The portion that will be due within one year should be classified as current; the remaining portion should be classified as long-term.

‡Because unrealized gains or losses are reported, it is not necessary to report the gain or loss at the time of sale. Some companies may choose to calculate the amount of realized gain or loss but must be careful to avoid double counting.

realized gain or loss the difference between the amortized cost as of the date of sale and the selling price of the securities

4. When bonds are sold, a realized gain or loss results. Should the realized gain or loss be included on the income statement? The **realized gain or loss** is the difference between the amortized cost as of the date of the sale and the selling price of the bonds.

Illustration 11.1 summarizes the appropriate accounting treatments for debt securities transactions to be discussed throughout the following pages.

HELD-TO-MATURITY DEBT SECURITIES

LO3 Demonstrate the proper accounting and reporting treatment for held-to-maturity debt securities.

When a company has both the *ability* and the *intent* to hold debt securities until the maturity date, the securities should be treated as part of the held-to-maturity security portfolio. The following guidelines should be used when accounting for held-to-maturity debt securities:

Critical Thinking: *If a company intends to hold an investment for a long period of time, rather than trade it quickly based on fluctuating prices, do you think these investments will be accounted for differently? If so, what accounting procedures would you expect to perform?*

- The cost of the investment is recognized at the *original* cost.

- Any discount or premium on these securities should be *amortized* over the time period from the date of purchase to the maturity date. If a bond is purchased for an amount greater than the face value of the bond, a premium results; it can be computed as follows:

$$\text{Purchase Price} - \text{Face Value} = \text{Premium}$$

- If a bond is purchased for an amount that is less than face value, a discount results; it can be computed as follows:

$$\text{Face Value} - \text{Purchase Price} = \text{Discount}$$

fair value the present market price of an investment

- The **fair value**, or present market price, of the investment in bonds is not reported if the intent is to hold the investment until its maturity date, since the fair market value of the debt at dates prior to maturity is not particularly relevant.

▶ RECORDING THE INVESTMENT

To illustrate, assume that on January 1, 2004, Milhorn Company purchases bonds of Tammy Company with a face value of $100,000 for $95,000. The bonds pay interest at

8 percent semiannually (4 percent per semiannual period) and are due in five years. On January 1, 2004, Milhorn Company should record the purchase of the bonds as follows:

Jan. 1, 2004		
Investment in Bonds—Held-to-Maturity	95,000	
Cash		95,000

The discount on the bonds can be calculated as follows:

$$\text{Face Value} - \text{Purchase Price} = \text{Discount}$$
$$\$100,000 - \$95,000 = \$5,000$$

▶ AMORTIZING A DISCOUNT OR PREMIUM

In this transaction, the Investment in Bonds—Held-to-Maturity account opens with an amount of $95,000. The discount represents additional interest income that Milhorn will receive in addition to the semiannual interest payments because the company lent $95,000 when the bond was purchased and will receive $100,000 when the bond is due. Thus, the discount should be *amortized* over the life of the bond. This involves an adjustment of the interest income earned by Milhorn. The process of amortizing a *discount* on a bond investment involves *increasing* the Investment in Bonds—Held-to-Maturity account and *increasing* the Interest Income account. Over the life of the bond, the amount of the discount will be reduced to zero and the amount of the Investment in Bonds—Held-to-Maturity account should be increased to the maturity value or face value.

A premium results when the buyer pays more than the face value of the bond at the time of purchase. The premium must be amortized over the life of the bond by *reducing* the Interest Income account and *reducing* the Investment in Bonds—Held-to-Maturity account. Amortizing a bond premium involves *decreasing* the Investment in Bonds—Held-to-Maturity account and *decreasing* Interest Income.

	Entry			Effect
Amortizing a discount	Investment in Bonds—			Increases interest
	Held-to-Maturity	xxx		income
	Interest Income		xxx	
Amortizing a premium	Interest Income	xxx		Decreases interest
	Investment in Bonds—			income
	Held-to-Maturity		xxx	

There are two methods available to amortize a premium or discount. In this chapter, we will illustrate the simpler method of amortization, the straight-line method, rather than the effective interest method. When the straight-line method is used, the amount of the adjustment to Interest Income is the same in each period. In the case of the Milhorn bond, the amount of the amortization is $500 per semiannual period ($5,000 ÷ 5 years × ½).

On July 1, 2004, when the first interest payment is received, Milhorn should record the following for receipt of the interest and amortization of the discount:

July 1, 2004		
Cash ($100,000 × 8% × ½ year)	4,000	
Investment in Bonds—Held-to-Maturity ($5,000 ÷		
5 years × ½)	500	
Interest Income ($4,000 + $500)		4,500

A similar entry should be made each semiannual period for five years. At December 31, 2004, the balance of the Investment in Bonds—Held-to-Maturity account should appear as follows:

**Investment in Bonds—
Held-to-Maturity**

1/1	95,000	
7/1	500	
12/31	500	
bal.	**96,000**	

The balance of the account should be reported on the December 31, 2004, balance sheet as a long-term investment.

LO4 Demonstrate the proper accounting and reporting treatment for available-for-sale debt securities.

amortized cost method a method of accounting for investments in which premiums or discounts are amortized over the life of the investment

Critical Thinking: *How do you think companies generate income from debt securities?*

AVAILABLE-FOR-SALE DEBT SECURITIES

Accounting for debt securities classified as available-for-sale is similar to that for held-to-maturity securities. The **amortized cost method**, in which premiums or discounts are amortized over the life of the investment, is used to account for the bonds. However, at the end of each reporting period, the bonds should be "marked to market." Thus, the fair market value of the bonds must be determined, and the bonds should be recognized at that amount on the balance sheet.

▶ ADJUSTING INVESTMENTS TO FAIR VALUE

Assume the same facts for Milhorn Company as in the previous example: Bonds of $100,000 face value are purchased on January 1, 2004, at $95,000. The bonds pay 8 percent interest semiannually (4 percent per semiannual period). As in the previous example, the purchase price of the bonds should be recorded as $95,000 and the following amortization and interest entry is recorded in each semiannual period:

Cash	4,000	
Investment in Bonds—Available-for-Sale	500	
Interest Income		4,500

Unlike what was done in the previous example, however, the market value of the bonds should be recognized at each reporting period. Assume, for example, that the market value of the bonds at December 31, 2004, is $96,700 and the difference between amortized cost and market value is as follows:

Date	Amortized Cost	Market Value	Adjustment Account
12/31/04	$96,000	$96,700	$700 Debit balance in adjustment account

Previous bal.	0
Entry	$700 Debit to adjustment account

As previously stated, the difference between amortized cost and market value represents an unrealized holding gain or loss. *SFAS No. 115* indicates that unrealized holding gains or losses on available-for-sale securities should be recognized but should not be included in the calculation of net income. Instead, unrealized holding gains and losses *that occurred during the current year* should be included in *other comprehensive income* on the statement of comprehensive income. At December 31, 2004, Milhorn should record the following to recognize the unrealized holding gain:[8]

---

8 *SFAS No. 115* does not require firms to use an adjustment account. Some firms may record the adjustments directly to the investment account. However, because using an adjustment account simplifies the accounting and maintains the amortized cost separately, we use it in all examples.

After these transactions, the balances of the accounts are as follows:

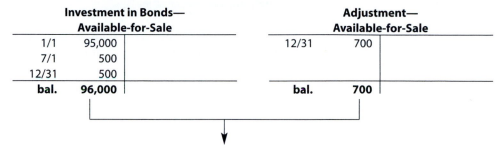

Investment in Bonds—Available-for-Sale		**Adjustment—Available-for-Sale**	
1/1	95,000	12/31	700
7/1	500		
12/31	500		
bal.	**96,000**	**bal.**	**700**

Balance sheet: Long-term investment $96,700

Unrealized Holding Gain—Equity		
	700	12/31
	700	**bal.**

Balance sheet: Stockholders' equity $700

❱ REPORTING AVAILABLE-FOR-SALE DEBT SECURITIES

Unrealized gains and losses on available-for-sale debt securities should be included as part of comprehensive income. Items that are not reported as part of the net income calculation but are reported as comprehensive income are referred to as *other comprehensive income*. Although there are other sources of comprehensive income, for most companies, the unrealized gain or loss on available-for-sale securities is a primary component.

The *balance* of the Unrealized Holding Gain—Equity account should be presented in the stockholders' equity section of the balance sheet. The Investment in Bonds—Available-for-Sale account and the related Adjustment—Available-for-Sale account should be included in the long-term investment portion of the balance sheet.

❱ TREATMENT OF A LOSS

The treatment of unrealized holding losses is similar to that for holding gains. An unrealized holding loss would exist if the market value were *less* than the amortized cost. Thus, the Adjustment—Available-for-Sale account would have a credit balance (a contra-asset account) and would be a reduction of the Investment in Bonds—Available-for-Sale account. The Unrealized Holding Loss—Equity account would have a debit balance.

❱ MARKET VALUE BEYOND THE FIRST YEAR

When investments are held for more than one year and the market value fluctuates in response to changing interest-rate conditions, it is important to reflect the appropriate value on the balance sheet. Assume that Milhorn continues to hold the bonds purchased on January 1, 2004, until December 31, 2005, and that the market value of the bonds at that time is $97,500. The difference between amortized cost and market value is as follows:

Date	Amortized Cost	Market Value		Adjustment Account	
12/31/05	$97,000	$97,500		$500	Debit balance in adjustment account
			Previous bal.	700	Debit
			Entry	($200)	Credit to adjustment account

Note the distinction between the *change* in the accounts and the *balance* of the accounts. The accounting entry should be based on the change in the accounts as follows:

Dec. 31, 2005		
Unrealized Holding Gain—Equity	200	
Adjustment—Available-for-Sale		200

The debit to the Unrealized Holding Gain—Equity account reduces the amount of unrealized holding gain. It may also be considered an unrealized holding loss. Essentially, Milhorn's position has changed as follows:

12/31/04 Market above cost ($96,700 − $96,000)	$700
12/31/05 Market above cost ($97,500 − $97,000)	500
Reduction of unrealized holding gain or unrealized holding loss	$200

The *change* in unrealized holding gains or losses is reported as other comprehensive income on the income statement in each period. However, for balance sheet purposes, the *balances* of the accounts are reported. The following illustrates how each account is represented on the balance sheet:

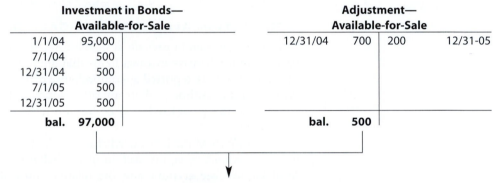

Balance sheet: Long-term investment $97,500

Unrealized Holding Gain—Equity			
12/31/05	200	700	12/31/04
		500	bal. → Balance sheet: Stockholders' equity $500

Note that our examples illustrate an investment in one security. In actual practice, the accounting for investments would be based on the entire portfolio of securities considered to be available-for-sale and would use the difference between the total amortized cost and the total market value of the portfolio of securities. This valuation of corporate assets can have a significant effect on earnings, again emphasizing the importance of proper categorization of securities.

SALE OF SECURITIES

When available-for-sale debt securities are sold prior to their maturity date, a gain or loss results; this is considered a realized gain or loss. The amount of the realized gain or loss is the *difference between the amortized cost as of the date of sale and the selling price of the bonds* and is presented on the income statement as part of other income.[9] In

---

9 Gains or losses for the investing company can be considered extraordinary only if they meet the criteria of being unusual in nature and infrequent in occurrence of *SFAS No. 4.*

calculating the amount of the realized gain or loss, it is not necessary to consider whether any portion of it has previously been considered an unrealized gain or loss for the security sold.

Continuing with the Milhorn Company example, assume that on January 1, 2006, the company sold the bonds it held in its available-for-sale portfolio for $99,000. The realized gain is calculated as follows:

Selling price	$99,000
Amortized cost at 1/1/06	97,000
Realized gain	$ 2,000

Milhorn should record the following entry at the time of sale:

Jan. 1, 2006		
Cash	99,000	
Investment in Bonds—Available-for-Sale		97,000
Realized Gain on Sale of Securities		2,000

In addition, the company should consider the balances that exist in the related accounts of Adjustment—Available-for-Sale and Unrealized Gain—Equity. In most cases, this would be done at the end of the period as an adjusting entry, but if there are no other securities in the portfolio, the balances of those accounts can be eliminated at the time of the sale. At December 31, 2006, the company would perform an analysis as indicated for the past periods:

Date	Amortized Cost	Market Value		Adjustment Account
12/31/06	$0	$0	$ 0	Debit balance in adjustment account
			Previous bal. 500	Debit
			Entry ($500)	Credit to adjustment account

In order to eliminate the balances of the Unrealized Holding Gain—Equity account and the Adjustment—Available-for-sale account, the following entry would be recorded:

Dec. 31, 2006		
Unrealized Holding Gain—Equity	500	
Adjustment—Available-for-Sale		500

The amount of the realized gain should appear on the income statement as part of other income as follows:

Other Income:

Realized gain on sale of securities $2,000

It is important to present the information on the sale of the securities in a way that does not "double-count" gains and losses on available-for-sale securities. In the example used here, the $500 amount was counted as income when the company was holding the securities because the unrealized gain was included as other comprehensive income on the statement of comprehensive income. As a result, the FASB requires that a reclassification adjustment be presented on the statement of comprehensive income in the year of sale for available-for-sale securities. The **reclassification adjustment** represents the amount that was treated as *unrealized* gain or loss in previous periods and is treated as *realized* gain or loss in the current period.

A statement of comprehensive income for Milhorn Company for 2006 would appear as shown on the following page.

reclassification adjustment the amount that was treated as unrealized gain or loss in previous periods and is treated as realized gain or loss in the current period

Net income		$xxx
Unrealized holding gains/losses during the year	$ 0	
Less: Reclassification adjustments for gains included in net income	(500)	(500)
Comprehensive income		$xxx

LO5 **Demonstrate the proper accounting and reporting treatment for debt securities held in the trading category.**

Critical Thinking: *Why do you think a company would invest in a security if it did not intend to hold it to its maturity date?*

TRADING DEBT SECURITIES

Investment in trading securities assumes that a firm's management intends to hold the debt for only a short period of time and to sell it prior to its maturity date. The following guidelines should be used when accounting for debt securities in the trading category:

- The cost of the investment is recognized at *original* cost.

- Any premium or discount is (usually) not amortized. Note that *SFAS 115* does not preclude amortization, but since trading securities are held for short time periods, we will assume no amortization.

- At the end of each reporting period, the fair market value is recognized and an unrealized gain or loss (a holding gain or loss) is recorded.

- An unrealized gain or loss on trading securities is treated as an income statement item in the period of the change in the fair market value of the debt, unlike unrealized gains or losses on available-for-sale securities.

▶ RECORDING THE INVESTMENT

To illustrate, assume that Milhorn Company purchased bonds of Tammy Company with a face value of $100,000 for $95,000 on January 1, 2004. The bonds pay interest at 8 percent semiannually (4 percent per semiannual period) and are due in five years. Milhorn has chosen to treat the bonds as trading securities. Therefore, the bonds will be recorded initially in the Investment in Bonds—Trading account at $95,000. The discount on the bonds will not be amortized because the company intends to hold the bonds for only a short period of time.

▶ RECORDING THE UNREALIZED GAIN OR LOSS

Assume that the fair market value of the bonds at December 31, 2004, has risen to $96,700 in response to changing interest-rate conditions. Milhorn should record the following transaction at that date:

Dec. 31, 2004		
Adjustment—Trading	1,700	
Unrealized Holding Gain—Income		1,700

At December 31, 2004, the account balances and financial statement treatment are:

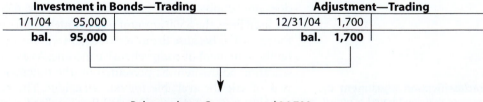

As you can see, $1,700 is reported as other income on the income statement.

▶ REPORTING TRADING DEBT SECURITIES

The Investment in Bonds—Trading account, net of the related Adjustment—Trading account, is reported as a current asset on the balance sheet. The Unrealized Holding Gain—Income account affects the calculation of net income in the case of Milhorn Company. Some reporting companies have expressed concern about the income volatility that is created when unrealized holding gains and losses are included. This is particularly true for companies with large holdings of trading securities, such as banks or brokers and securities dealers. Recent events in the stock and bond markets indicate that fair market values can fluctuate quite violently and may cause significant volatility in income for those companies.

▶ MARKET VALUE BEYOND THE FIRST YEAR

It is again important to consider the proper accounting when bonds are held beyond one year and their market value continues to fluctuate in response to changing interest-rate conditions. Assume that Milhorn continues to hold the bonds purchased on January 1, 2004, until December 31, 2005, and that the market value of the bonds is $97,500 at that time. The difference between cost and market value is as follows:

Date	Cost	Market Value	Difference	
12/31/05	$95,000	$97,500		$2,500
			Previous bal.	1,700
			Change	$ 800

The change in unrealized holding gains or losses is reported as income in each period. The balances of the accounts as of December 31, 2005, and the treatment of those accounts on the financial statements is as follows:

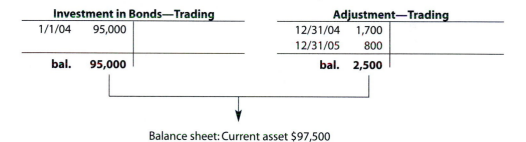

Investment in Bonds—Trading			Adjustment—Trading	
1/1/04	95,000		12/31/04	1,700
			12/31/05	800
bal.	**95,000**		**bal.**	**2,500**

Balance sheet: Current asset $97,500

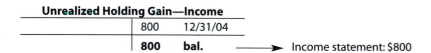

Unrealized Holding Gain—Income	
800	12/31/04
800	**bal.**

Income statement: $800

The differences in the treatment of unrealized holding gains on trading securities as opposed to those on available-for-sale securities are summarized in Illustration 11.2.

The exact placement of the Unrealized Holding Gain—Income account on the income statement depends upon the type of company that is engaging in the trading activities. If the company is a securities broker or dealer, securities transactions are the primary focus of its operations, and the unrealized gains or losses should be presented as revenue. If the company is not a broker or dealer, the amount of unrealized gain or loss should be presented as part of other income on the income statement.

▶ SALE OF SECURITIES

When trading securities are sold prior to their maturity date, a company may present the information concerning the loss or gain in one of two ways.

Illustration 11.2

Accounting for Available-for-Sale Debt Securities Versus Trading Debt Securities

	Accounts Reflected on Balance Sheet	Accounts Reflected on Income Statement
Available-for-sale debt securities	• Present asset account at fair value • Unrealized gains and losses presented as a stockholders' equity account named Unrealized Holding Gains and Losses—Equity	Interest presented as revenue
Trading debt securities	• Present asset account at fair value • Generally presented as current asset	• Interest presented as revenue • Unrealized holding gains and losses presented as income

1. *Unrealized gains or losses.* Since unrealized gains or losses on trading securities are treated as income as they arise, the company does not have an additional gain or loss at the time of sale. Essentially, the unrealized gain or loss has become a realized gain or loss because the security was sold. But the unrealized gain or loss has already been treated as an income statement item in previous periods, and so no additional gain or loss needs to be reported. If a company chooses to present only the unrealized gains or losses on the income statement, then it must be careful to record all unrealized gains or losses on the security up to the date of sale.

2. *Realized gains or losses.* Some companies may choose to present the amount of the realized gain or loss on the income statement. The amount of the realized gain or loss is the *difference between the original cost and the selling price of the bonds.* Companies and financial statement users may consider a presentation of the realized gains or losses important for several reasons. Most importantly, for income tax purposes, gains or losses on securities must be reported in the period of sale (when they become realized). Unrealized gains or losses are not reported for income tax purposes. Additionally, financial statement users may consider information about realized gains or losses to be important because they result from actual transactions, as opposed to being "paper gains and losses." If a company chooses to report realized gains or losses on trading securities on the income statement, it should be careful not to double-count the gains or losses. *Unrealized* gains and losses on trading securities are included in income at the end of each reporting period as market value changes. When *realized* gains or losses are reported, the amount of previously reported unrealized gains or losses must be deducted to prevent double counting.

CHECK YOUR UNDERSTANDING

1. How are available-for-sale debt securities presented on the balance sheet?

2. In accounting for available-for-sale debt securities, how are unrealized holding gains and losses that occurred during the current year treated on the income statement?

3. When trading securities are sold prior to their maturity date, describe the two ways in which the gain or loss may be presented.

Accounting for Equity Securities

The proper accounting for investments in equity securities depends on several factors. First, it is necessary to consider what percentage of the investee's stock the investing company owns. Second, it is necessary to consider management's intent in holding the stock and the length of time it intends to hold the stock as an investment. The accounting alternatives are portrayed in Illustration 11.3 and discussed in the following sections.

As indicated in Illustration 11.3, if a company owns 50 percent or more of the stock of another company, then the two companies are generally required to present consolidated statements. Business combinations and consolidated statements are the focus of advanced financial accounting classes, and these topics are not addressed in this chapter.

If a company owns from 20 to 50 percent of the stock of another company, the investor company is required to use an accounting method referred to as the equity method. The **equity method** is based on the assumption that if a company owns more than 20 percent of the stock of another company, it is able to exert "significant influence" over the operations of that company. Under the equity method, the amount of the investment is periodically adjusted for changes in the net assets of the investee. The stock of many corporations is quite widely held, so a stockholder with 20 percent ownership would probably be one of the largest and most influential stockholders of the company.

The accounting guidance regarding the equity method indicates that "significant influence" may exist even when ownership is less than 20 percent. To ascertain whether significant influence exists, consider voting rights at stockholders' meetings, membership on the board of directors, and other contracts or relationships between the investor and the investee.[10] When using the equity method, the investor company records income based on its percentage ownership of the investee. The accounting issues related to the equity method are covered in detail on the *Intermediate Accounting* website.

The following examples illustrate instances in which less than 20 percent of the stock is owned and the investor does not have significant influence over the activities of the investee. In these cases, the investor company must treat the investment as part of either the available-for-sale or the trading portfolio based on management's intent. Illustration 11.4 summarizes the accounting treatment and presentation issues for investments in equity securities.

equity method a method of accounting for equity investments in which the amount of the investment is periodically adjusted for changes in the net assets of the investee

Illustration 11.3

Accounting for Investments in Stock

Percent Ownership	Accounting Treatment
50% or more (control)	Present consolidated statements
20% to 50% (significant influence)	Use equity method
Less than 20%	Assess intent: • Available-for-sale—use market value • Trading—use market value

---

10 See "Criteria for Applying the Equity Method of Accounting for Investments in Common Stock," Interpretation to *SFAS No. 35.*

Illustration 11.4

Accounting for Equity Securities

Type	Valuation	Treatment of Unrealized Gain/Loss	Treatment of Realized Gain/Loss	Balance Sheet Presentation
Available-for-sale	Fair value	Other comprehensive income	On income statement	Current and long-term*
Trading	Fair value	On income statement	Not reported†	Current

*The portion that will be sold within one year should be classified as current. The remaining portion should be classified as long-term.

†Because unrealized gains or losses are reported, it is not necessary to report the gain or loss at the time of sale. Some companies may choose to calculate the amount of realized gain or loss but must be careful to avoid double-counting.

LO6 Demonstrate the proper accounting and reporting treatment for available-for-sale equity securities.

Critical Thinking: Why do you think certain securities are adjusted to fair market value at the end of each reporting period?

AVAILABLE-FOR-SALE EQUITY SECURITIES

When equity securities are purchased as an investment, they are initially recorded at cost. The cost of the securities should include any brokerage or transaction costs directly associated with the purchase. At the end of each reporting period, the fair market value is determined in order to "mark to market," or adjust the reported amount to fair market value. For example, assume that on January 1, 2004, Metcalf Company purchased 1,000 shares of Bert Company for $9.90 per share plus $100 of brokerage costs (a total of $10,000) and 1,000 shares of Ernie Company for $19.80 per share plus $200 of brokerage costs (a total of $20,000). The securities will be treated as available-for-sale. (Assume that these are the only securities in the portfolio.) At December 31, 2004, Metcalf Company determined the fair market value of the securities and the difference between cost and fair market value as follows:

Date		Cost	Market Value	Adjustment Account
12/31/04	Bert Co.	$10,000	$ 9,000	
	Ernie Co.	20,000	18,500	
		$30,000	$27,500	($2,500) Credit to adj. account
			Previous bal.	0
			Entry	($2,500) Credit to adj. account

At December 31, 2004, Metcalf should record the unrealized holding loss as follows:

Dec. 31, 2004		
Unrealized Holding Loss—Equity	2,500	
Adjustment—Available-for-Sale		2,500

The balances of the accounts as of December 31, 2004, and the treatment of those accounts on the financial statements are as follows:

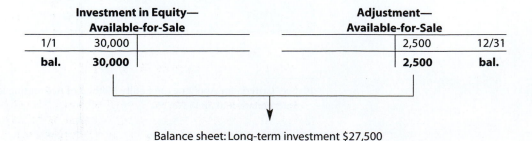

	Investment in Equity—Available-for-Sale			Adjustment—Available-for-Sale	
1/1	30,000			2,500	12/31
bal.	30,000			2,500	bal.

Balance sheet: Long-term investment $27,500

Unrealized Holding Loss—Equity

12/31	2,500
bal.	**2,500**

bal. 2,500 ——————➤ Balance sheet: Stockholders' equity ($2,500)

The unrealized holding loss on the available-for-sale securities that occurred during the current year should be treated as part of other comprehensive income on the statement of comprehensive income. Notice that unrealized holding losses or gains are based on the total difference between cost and market value for the portfolio, not on the difference for individual securities within the category. In subsequent periods, the *change* in unrealized gain or loss represents the change in the market value of the portfolio that occurred during the period. The *balance* of the Unrealized Holding Loss—Equity account represents the total difference between the cost and the market value of the portfolio. The balance of the Unrealized Holding Loss—Equity account should be presented in the stockholders' equity section of the balance sheet.

❱ SALE OF EQUITY SECURITIES

When available-for-sale equity securities are sold, a *realized* gain or loss should be recorded to represent the difference between the original cost of the stock and its selling price. Any brokerage costs or transaction costs should be deducted in determining the selling price of the stock. For example, assume that on January 1, 2005, Metcalf sells 1,000 shares of Bert Company stock for $9.10 per share and incurs brokerage costs of $100. A net amount of $9,000 is received. A realized loss of $1,000 has occurred and should be recorded as follows:

Jan. 1, 2005		
Cash	9,000	
Realized Loss on Sale of Securities	1,000	
Investment in Equity—Available-for-Sale		10,000

❱ REPORTING GAINS OR LOSSES

A realized loss, like that in the previous example, should appear on the income statement as part of other income as follows:

Other income:
Realized loss on sale of securities $1,000

The same double-counting issue that was previously discussed for debt securities exists for equity securities as well. It is necessary to present the information on the sale in a way that does not double-count the loss. In this example, the $1,000 loss was counted as income in 2004 when the company was holding the stock because it was included as other comprehensive income on the statement of comprehensive income. Therefore, a reclassification adjustment must be presented on the statement of comprehensive income in 2005. A statement of comprehensive income for Metcalf Company for 2005 would appear as follows:

Net income		$ xxx
Unrealized gains/losses during the year	$ xxx	
Plus reclassification adjustment for losses deducted from net income	1,000	1,000
Comprehensive income		$ xxx

LO7 Demonstrate the proper accounting and reporting treatment for equity securities held in the trading category.

TRADING EQUITY SECURITIES

When equity securities are purchased and considered to be part of the trading portfolio, they are initially recorded at cost. At the end of each reporting period, it is necessary to determine the fair market value of the stock and "mark to market" in a manner

Illustration 11.5

Presentation of Debt and Equity Securities in the Financial Statements

Type of Security	Balance Sheet Presentation	Income Statement Presentation
Held-to-maturity debt	• Amortized cost method • Long-term asset	Interest as revenue
Available-for-sale debt	• Fair value method • Unrealized holding gains and losses in stockholders' equity	Interest as revenue
Trading securities debt	• Fair value method • Current asset	• Interest as revenue • Unrealized holding gains and losses as income
Available-for-sale equity securities (less than 20%)	• Fair value method • Unrealized holding gains and losses in stockholders' equity	Dividends as income
Trading equity securities (less than 20%)	• Fair value method • Current asset	Unrealized holding gains and losses as income

Critical Thinking: When companies hold securities for short periods of time with the intent to trade them for quick gains, do you think the market values of these securities are important?

similar to that used for available-for-sale stock. However, if the stock is part of the trading portfolio, the unrealized gains and losses are treated as income and presented on the income statement.

To illustrate, assume the same facts as in the Metcalf example in the previous section except that the Bert Company and Ernie Company stocks will be held for only a short period and are therefore considered to be part of the trading portfolio. Remember that the costs of the Bert Co. and Ernie Co. stocks were $10,000 and $20,000, respectively. If the market values of the two stock holdings are $9,000 and $18,500 at December 31, 2004, then Metcalf should record the following entry at year end:

Dec. 31, 2004		
Unrealized Holding Loss—Income	2,500	
Adjustment—Trading		2,500

▶ REPORTING TRADING SECURITIES

An unrealized holding gain or loss on trading securities is treated as an income statement amount. The presentation of the account on the income statement depends on the type of company engaged in the trading activities. If the company is a securities broker or dealer, securities transactions are the primary focus of its operations, and the unrealized gains or losses are presented as revenue. If the company is not a broker or dealer, the amount of unrealized gain or loss should be presented as part of other income on the income statement. Because trading securities are those securities that management intends to hold for only a short period of time, the change in their market value is considered relevant information for investors and other financial statement users and should be included in the income statement. However, it is important to realize that such gains or losses are paper gains or losses. Some users of financial statements may place less importance on such gains and losses because an actual sale transaction has not yet occurred.

SUMMARY OF SECURITIES' PRESENTATION

A summary of the balance sheet and income statement presentation of investments in debt and equity securities is presented in Illustration 11.5.

CHECK YOUR UNDERSTANDING

1. What factors are used to determine whether one company has "significant influence" over another?

2. If a company owns between 20 and 50 percent of another company's stock, how should this investment be reported on the balance sheet?

3. When determining the original cost of an equity security, what costs might be included in this original valuation?

LO8 Explain how financial statement disclosures may be used to analyze investments.

ANALYSIS

🧩 *Critical Thinking: Based on the procedures and entries you have learned in this chapter, what details concerning a company's investment portfolio do you think should be provided to investors?*

Analysis of Investments

Financial statements and their related notes are provided to inform interested parties as to the financial status, business strategies, and accounting procedures of the company. As these statements are reviewed, users should investigate two important issues related to investing activities:

1. What information is provided about unrealized holding gains and losses?

2. Is there evidence of unfavorable practices used to enhance earnings, known as "gains trading"?

UNREALIZED HOLDING GAINS OR LOSSES

As investors review the financial statements of a company, it is important that they pay special attention to information about the estimated fair market value of the investment portfolio as compared to its historical cost. *SFAS No. 115* requires that these values be provided to investors. Prior to *SFAS No. 115*, an investment in securities was generally measured using either the historical cost method or the lower-of-cost-or-market method. When the historical cost method was used, neither the fair market value of the securities nor the unrealized holding gains or losses were evident. The use of fair market value for investments provides important information about holding gains that may be used to evaluate a company's investment portfolio and its investment strategy.

Figure 11.2 provides excerpts from Intel's note disclosures for available-for-sale securities at December 27, 2003, and December 28, 2002.

Figure 11.2

Unrealized Gains and Losses

Intel

		Gross Unrealized Gains	Gross Unrealized Losses	Estimated Fair Value
	Cost			
Total available-for-sale investments 12/28/2002	$11,786	$21	($2)	$11,805
Total available-for-sale investments 12/27/2003	15,657	56	(1)	15,712

Intel, Inc.
Unrealized Gains and Losses
December 27, 2003 and December 28, 2002
(in millions)

Intel's notes reveal a positive investment portfolio position at the end of 2002. While the cost of the investment securities was $11,786 million, the market value was $11,805 million. Unrealized holding gains of $21 million (and unrealized losses of only $2 million) indicate that the market value of the securities had increased significantly since the time of purchase. The position continued to be positive in 2003. At December 27, 2003, the cost of the portfolio had grown to $15,657 million and the market value had increased to $15,712. Unrealized holding gains had increased to $56 million, and there were $1 million of unrealized holding losses.

It is important for investors and analysts to consider the potential reasons for changes in the investment portfolio. In some cases, the changes may be due to changes in the prices of the stocks in the portfolio. Analysts must also consider whether there was a change in investment strategy, whether the types of securities in the portfolio were altered, and whether other industry factors contributed to the increase or decline in market value.

▶ FASB POSITION ON UNREALIZED GAINS AND LOSSES

As indicated in the preceding paragraphs, information about unrealized gains and losses can be important to investors and analysts. Interestingly, the FASB's position on the importance of fair value and unrealized holding gains is mixed. The conflicting opinions of the members of the FASB are evident in the following quote:

> Some Board members believe that measuring all investments in debt and equity at fair value in the financial statements is relevant and useful to present and potential investors, creditors, and others in making rational investment, credit, and similar decisions. . . . Other Board members are uncertain about the relevance of measuring those investments at fair value. Opponents challenge the subjectivity that may be necessary in estimating fair value.[11]

The approach taken by the FASB in *SFAS No. 115* reflects a compromise between the conflicting opinions of board members. Unrealized gains and losses on *trading* securities are treated as part of net income, while unrealized gains and losses on *available-for-sale* securities are not part of net income but are included in comprehensive income. Unfortunately, this may give the impression that unrealized gains or losses on available-for-sale securities are of lesser importance.

EVIDENCE OF GAINS TRADING AND ETHICS

ETHICS ⚖

gains trading selling securities in order to manage or manipulate earnings

Gains trading involves selling securities in order to manage (or manipulate) earnings. Prior to *SFAS No. 115*, it was possible to sell securities whose market value *exceeded* their cost and use the gain to increase earnings. Securities whose market value was *less than* their cost were not sold and continued to be part of the investment portfolio. In other words, companies would choose to sell their "performers" and hold their "losers." If this practice is continued over time, the quality of the investment portfolio is diminished through management's quest to increase earnings. If a corporate environment exerts extraordinary pressure on its management to achieve higher levels of reported earnings or ties compensation to achieving earnings goals, this may encourage managers to engage in gains trading in an effort to inflate earnings. The Office of the Comptroller of the Currency and the Federal Home Loan Bank Board had expressed concern about accounting for investment securities and the investment practices of banks and other financial institutions.[12]

One of the purposes of *SFAS No. 115* was to require the use of the fair market value method and thereby eliminate the gains-trading practices of investment managers. Unfortunately, *SFAS No. 115* does not completely eliminate the possibility of gains trading. It is still possible for a company to increase its earnings by selling

---

11 *SFAS No. 115*, pars. 39 and 42.

12 Ibid., par. 30.

securities that have increased in value. This is particularly true for stocks or bonds that are treated as part of the available-for-sale portfolio, since unrealized gains and losses on securities in that category are not treated as an element of net income. In fact, one dissenting member of the FASB stated:

> [The] conclusions do not alleviate the potential for volatility in reported earnings; rather they provide the opportunity for selective volatility—that is the volatility in reported earnings that results from the recognition of unrealized changes in fair value in earnings through selective sales of securities.[13]

However, although the potential for gains trading has not been completely eliminated, it should be significantly curtailed by the disclosure requirements of *SFAS No. 115*. For each category of securities, companies are required to disclose the aggregate fair value, gross unrealized holding gains, gross unrealized holding losses, and amortized cost. Companies are also required to disclose the proceeds from sales of available-for-sale securities and the gross realized gains and gross realized losses on those sales. If investors and other statement users analyze the note disclosures provided for investment securities, gains-trading activities can be detected.

CHECK YOUR UNDERSTANDING

1. What is gains trading?

2. Why do you think companies are now required to disclose fair market value and unrealized gains and losses on their investment portfolios?

LO9 Determine the cash flow impact of investment activities.

CASH FLOW $

Impact of Investments on Cash Flow

The manner in which investment transactions are recorded and classified has a variety of implications for the statement of cash flows. To locate disclosures for all securities transactions, statement users must look in several places on the statement of cash flows. Illustration 11.6 summarizes these disclosures, assuming use of the indirect method for the statement of cash flows.

Illustration 11.6

Treatment of Investments on the Statement of Cash Flows (Indirect Method)

Item or Account	Treatment
Unrealized gains on trading securities	Deducted in operating category
Unrealized losses on trading securities	Added in operating category
Unrealized gains on available-for-sale securities	Not presented*
Unrealized losses on available-for-sale securities	Not presented*
Realized gains on investments	Deducted in operating category
Realized losses on investments	Added in operating category
Purchases of available-for-sale and held-to-maturity securities	Deducted in investing category
Sales of available-for-sale and held-to-maturity securities	Added in investing category
Purchases of trading securities	Deducted in operating category
Sales of trading securities	Added in operating category

*Unrealized gains and losses are not included in net income, but are part of comprehensive income. Therefore, an adjustment to net income on the statement of cash flows is not necessary.

---

13 Ibid., par. 25.

UNREALIZED GAINS AND LOSSES

Unrealized gains and losses occur because of changes in the market value of an investment. Therefore, they are noncash items. If the unrealized gains or losses were included in the calculation of net income, as occurs with trading securities, they must be eliminated in the statement of cash flows. However, unrealized gains and losses on available-for-sale securities are not included in the calculation of net income. Rather, they are treated as other comprehensive income items. Since the statement of cash flows normally begins with the amount of net income, it is not necessary to adjust for unrealized gains and losses on available-for-sale securities.

REALIZED GAINS AND LOSSES

Realized gains and losses are included in net income. When the indirect method is used for the statement of cash flows, the amount of the gain or loss should appear as an adjustment to net income in the operating activities portion of the statement. Realized gains were added in calculating net income, so they should be deducted in determining the amount of cash generated from operating activities. Realized losses were deducted in calculating net income, so they should be added in determining the amount of cash generated from operating activities.

PURCHASES OR SALES OF SECURITIES

Cash flows that result from purchases or sales of available-for-sale or held-to-maturity securities should be presented in the investing activities category of the statement of cash flows. However, the FASB has taken the stance that cash flows that result from the purchase or sale of trading securities are more closely related to the normal operating activity of a company. Therefore, these amounts should be presented in the operating activities category of the statement of cash flows.[14]

Figure 11.3 presents the operating and investing sections of Intel's statement of cash flows for 2003. As you can see from the figure, Intel bought and sold a considerable amount of investments in 2003. The operating activities category reveals a loss on investments in equity securities of $283 million. This amount was added back to net income on the 2003 statement of cash flows, since no cash was actually lost. The operating activities section also indicates that Intel purchased trading assets of $511 million during 2003. The investing activities section reveals that the company purchased $11,662 of available-for-sale securities and sold $8,488 of available-for-sale securities during 2003.

The investing activities category reveals that Intel was quite active in managing its investment portfolio. This may have been the result of changing market conditions, but it may also have been linked to Intel's business strategy, referred to in the Financial Reporting Case at the beginning of this chapter, of making investments in other companies to form strategic business relationships.

ACCRUAL TO CASH ISSUES

As investors and analysts review financial data related to investment activities, the amount of interest income reported for the period can be easily found in the income statement. However, users may also be interested in the amount of *actual cash* received for interest during a period. To find this amount, it is necessary to convert from the accrual basis to the cash basis, starting with the interest income (an accrual number) and adjusting for all balance sheet accounts related to interest income.

---

14 Ibid., par. 18.

Figure 11.3

Statement of Cash Flows

Intel

Intel Corporation
Partial Consolidated Statements of Cash Flows

Three Years Ended December 27, 2003

(In Millions)	2003	2002	2001
Cash and cash equivalents, beginning of year	$ 7,404	$ 7,970	$ 2,976
Cash flows provided by (used for) operating activities:			
Net income	5,641	3,117	1,291
Adjustments to reconcile net income to net cash provided by operating activities:			
Depreciation	4,651	4,676	4,131
Impairment of goodwill	617	—	98
Amortization of goodwill	—	—	1,612
Amortization and impairment of intangibles and other acquisition-related costs	419	668	717
Purchased in-process research and development	5	20	198
Losses on equity securities, net	283	372	466
Loss on investment in Convera	—	—	196
Net loss on retirements and impairments of property, plant and equipment	217	301	119
Deferred taxes	391	110	(519)
Tax benefit from employee stock plans	216	270	435
Changes in assets and liabilities:			
Trading assets	(511)	(444)	898
Accounts receivable	(430)	30	1,561
Inventories	(245)	(26)	24
Accounts payable	116	(226)	(673)
Accrued compensation and benefits	276	107	(524)
Income taxes payable	(361)	175	(270)
Other assets and liabilities	230	(21)	(971)
Total adjustments	5,874	6,012	7,498
Net cash provided by operating activities	11,515	9,129	8,789
Cash flows provided by (used for) investing activities:			
Additions to property, plant and equipment	(3,656)	(4,703)	(7,309)
Acquisitions, net of cash acquired	(61)	(57)	(883)
Purchases of available-for-sale investments	(11,662)	(6,309)	(7,141)
Maturities and sales of available-for-sale investments	8,488	5,634	15,398
Other investing activities	(199)	(330)	(395)
Net cash used for investing activities	(7,090)	(5,765)	(330)

For example, assume that the income statement of Reiter Company indicates interest income of $90,000 for the year 2004. Also assume that the company had the following account balances at the beginning and end of the year:

Account	Beginning Balance	Ending Balance
Interest Receivable	$ 20,000	$ 35,000
Investment in Held-to-Maturity Bonds	240,000	200,000

The change in the Investment in Held-to-Maturity Bonds account may have had several causes. Assume that $10,000 of the change represents amortization of a premium on bonds purchased in a prior year and that the remaining change represents bonds sold at retirement date at their face value. Since amortization is a noncash transaction, the change in the account must be used to adjust the accrual amount of interest. Additionally, an increase in interest receivable of $15,000 indicates that interest has been recorded as income but has not been received. The amount of cash received for interest is computed as follows:

Accrual Amount	Cash Amount
Interest income	$90,000
Increase in interest receivable	(15,000)
Amortization of bond premium	10,000
Cash interest received	$85,000

All balance sheet accounts related to interest must be analyzed in order to determine the amount of interest received. For example, the Unearned Interest account may require analysis as well. In each case, it is the *change* in the account balance, rather than the ending balance, that is important in adjusting from the accrual amount of interest to the amount actually received in cash.

CHECK YOUR UNDERSTANDING

1. Why is amortization on bond investments considered an adjustment to net income in determining cash flows from operating activities?

2. Describe how a realized gain would appear on the statement of cash flows.

Revisiting the Case

INTEL'S CAPITAL INVESTMENT PROGRAM DOMINATES

1. Intel had $1,801 million in 2002 and $2,625 million in 2003 invested in trading assets, an increase of $824 million, or 46 percent. Short-term investments also increased from $3,382 million to $5,568 million, an increase of $2,186 million, or 65 percent, in 2003.

2. Intel's capital investment program allows the company to diversify its holdings, thereby lessening its risk if one sector were to perform poorly. The program also gives Intel increased control over several companies that have a direct impact on its products.

3. The statement of cash flows has a section that outlines inflows and outflows from all investing activities.

SUMMARY BY LEARNING OBJECTIVE

LO1 Describe three primary reasons why companies engage in investment activities.

Companies invest in securities for three primary reasons. Some companies invest in order to generate excess cash during up cycles to use in down cycles or to earn interest or dividend income to supplement their earnings. Other companies wish to develop continuing relationships with the companies in which they invest. Finally, a company may invest in order to have ownership control of another company.

LO2 Describe the characteristics of held-to-maturity, trading, and available-for-sale securities.

- Held-to-maturity securities are debt securities, such as bonds or notes, that the investing company has both the *intent* and the *ability* to hold to the maturity date. Debt in this category is held primarily for the interest income produced. Only debt securities have a maturity date, and thus only debt securities can be classified as held-to-maturity.

- Trading securities are defined as debt or equity securities that are bought principally for the purpose of selling them in the near term. With these investments, companies seek to generate profits from short-term differences in price.

- Available-for-sale securities are investments that are not classified as trading or held-to-maturity. Securities in this category may be held for any period of time and may be intended for income generation, price appreciation, or other corporate purposes.

LO3 Demonstrate the proper accounting and reporting treatment for held-to-maturity debt securities.

Debt securities that are included in the held-to-maturity portfolio are reported at amortized cost. Any premium or discount on the debt is amortized over the period from purchase date to maturity date. The market value of securities in this portfolio is not reported because management's intent is to hold the debt until maturity.

LO4 Demonstrate the proper accounting and reporting treatment for available-for-sale debt securities.

The amortized cost method is used initially to account for debt in the available-for-sale portfolio. At the end of each reporting period, however, the bonds are marked to market value. The unrealized gain or loss, representing the difference between the amortized cost and the market value, is not included in the calculation of net income but is included in other comprehensive income.

LO5 Demonstrate the proper accounting and reporting treatment for debt securities held in the trading category.

Debt in this portfolio is intended to be held for a short period of time. The cost method is initially used to account for debt in this portfolio. Premiums or discounts are not amortized because the debt will not be held for a long period of time. At the end of each reporting period, the bonds are marked to market value. In this case however, the unrealized gain or loss, representing the difference between the amortized cost and the market value, is included in the calculation of net income.

LO6 Demonstrate the proper accounting and reporting treatment for available-for-sale equity securities.

The equity securities in this portfolio are initially recorded at their acquisition cost. At the end of each reporting period, the stocks in the portfolio are marked to market value. The unrealized gain or loss, representing the difference between original cost and market value, is not included in the calculation of net income but is included in other comprehensive income.

LO7 Demonstrate the proper accounting and reporting treatment for equity securities held in the trading category.

The equity securities in this portfolio are initially recorded at their acquisition cost. At the end of each reporting period, the stocks in the portfolio are marked to market value. In this case, however, the unrealized gain or loss, representing the difference between the original cost and market value, is included in the calculation of net income.

LO8 Explain how financial statement disclosures may be used to analyze investments.

Disclosures related to the fair market value of a company's investment portfolio provide valuable information to financial statement users. Analysts and other statement users should consider the magnitude of unrealized holding gains and losses and assess the importance of investment activity as an element of a company's business strategy. The information on investments should also be used to determine whether the company has engaged in activities designed to manage or manipulate its earnings.

LO9 Determine the cash flow impact of investment activities.

Purchases and sales of trading securities are reported in the operating activities section of the statement, whereas purchases and sales of available-for-sale and held-to-maturity securities are reported in the investing activities section. Additionally, realized gains and losses on sales of all securities should be eliminated from the operating activities section because they are noncash items. Finally, amortization of premium or discount is also a noncash charge that must be eliminated in order to determine the amount of cash flows related to investments.

KEY TERMS

amortized cost method (p. 504)
available-for-sale securities (p. 500)
credit risk (p. 499)
currency risk (p. 498)
debt securities (p. 499)
equity method (p. 511)
equity securities (p. 499)

fair value (p. 502)
gains trading (p. 516)
held-to-maturity securities (p. 500)
interest-rate risk (p. 498)
investing activities (p. 498)
liquidity risk (p. 499)
marketable equity securities (p. 499)

realized gain or loss (p. 502)
reclassification adjustment (p. 507)
security (p. 498)
trading securities (p. 500)
unrealized gain or loss (p. 501)

EXERCISES

LO2, 3, 5, 6   **EXERCISE 11-1   Types of Investments**

The following investment scenarios occurred in 2005 for Nichols Company, Jen Ching Company, Montessi Company, and Piet Company:

1. Nichols Company believes that interest-rate conditions will change in a short period of time and has purchased bonds as an investment. As interest rates fall, bond prices will increase, and the company plans to sell the bonds in order to profit.

2. Jen Ching Company has received a loan for a construction project. A portion of the loan was used immediately to pay for construction costs. The remainder was invested in stock. The company will sell the stock when additional construction costs are incurred, but it does not anticipate selling the stock to profit from fluctuations in the stock market.

3. Montessi Company invests in bonds due in five years. The company normally holds bonds until they are due and does not plan to sell them before the due date unless major unforeseen interest-rate fluctuations occur.

4. Piet Company has purchased the stock of Jean Company in order to have a relationship with the company. At the present time, Piet owns less than 20 percent of the outstanding stock of Jean.

Required:

For the scenarios listed, indicate the security type (A, B, or C), treatment of gains or losses (D, E, or F), and classification (G or H), as listed in the following table.

Security Type
A   Held-to-maturity
B   Available-for-sale
C   Trading
Treatment of Gains and Losses
D   Unrealized gains and losses not recognized
E   Unrealized gains and losses recognized as other comprehensive income
F   Unrealized gains and losses recognized as income
Classification
G   Classified on the balance sheet as a current asset
H   Classified on the balance sheet as a long-term asset

LO3   **EXERCISE 11-2   Held-to-Maturity Debt Securities with a Premium**

On April 1, 2004, Smith Company purchased bonds issued by Lane Company. The bonds have a face value of $100,000, pay interest semiannually at 10 percent (5 percent per semiannual period) on October 1 and April 1, and mature in five years from the date of purchase. Smith purchased the bonds for $108,000, including $5,200 of brokerage costs. Smith's accounting year ends on December 31.

Required:

1. Assume that Smith Company intends to hold the bonds until their maturity date. Record the journal entry necessary on April 1, 2004, to acquire the bonds.

2. Record the journal entry necessary on October 1, 2004, to receive interest and amortize the premium.

3. Record the journal entry necessary on December 31, 2004, to accrue interest and amortize the premium.

4. Develop the proper balance sheet presentation of all accounts related to the bonds for the December 31, 2004 balance sheet.

LO3   **EXERCISE 11-3   Held-to-Maturity Debt Securities with a Discount**

On April 1, 2004, Ralph Company purchased bonds issued by Lane Company. The bonds have a face value of $100,000, pay interest semiannually at 10 percent (5 percent per semi-annual period) on October 1 and April 1, and mature in five years from the date of purchase. Ralph purchased the bonds for $94,000, including $5,200 of brokerage costs. Ralph's accounting year ends on December 31.

Required:

1. Assume that Ralph Company intends to hold the bonds until their maturity date. Record the journal entry necessary on April 1, 2004, to acquire the bonds.

2. Record the journal entry necessary on October 1, 2004, to receive interest and amortize the discount.

3. Record the journal entry necessary on December 31, 2004, to accrue interest and amortize the discount.

4. Develop the proper balance sheet presentation of all accounts related to the bonds for the December 31, 2004 balance sheet.

LO4   **EXERCISE 11-4   Available-for-Sale Debt Securities**

Refer to the Ralph Company purchase of bonds in Exercise 11-3. Assume that at the time of the purchase, Ralph Company management chooses to treat the bonds purchased as available-for-sale securities. There are no other securities in the available-for-sale portfolio, and the company has not previously held securities in that portfolio. Assume that on December 31, 2004, the fair market value of the bonds was $98,000.

Required:

1. What factors may have caused an increase in the market value of the bonds since the time they were purchased?

2. Record the necessary entry on December 31, 2004, to adjust the bonds to fair market value.

3. Develop the proper balance sheet presentation of all accounts related to the bonds for the December 31, 2004 balance sheet.

LO5   **EXERCISE 11-5   Trading Securities—Debt**

On April 1, 2004, Donne Company purchased bonds issued by Trident Company. The bonds have a face value of $100,000, pay interest semiannually at 10 percent (5 percent per semiannual period) on October 1 and April 1, and mature in five years from the date of purchase. Donne purchased the bonds for $94,000, including $5,200 of brokerage costs. Donne's accounting year ends on December 31. Donne Company intends to hold the bonds for a short period of time. This investment will be the only item in its trading securities portfolio, and the company has not previously had a trading securities portfolio. Assume that on December 31, 2004, the fair market value of the bonds was $98,000.

Required:

1. What factors may have caused an increase in the market value of the bonds since the time they were purchased?
2. Record the necessary entry on December 31, 2004, to adjust the bonds to fair market value.
3. Develop the proper balance sheet presentation of all accounts related to the bonds for the December 31, 2004 balance sheet.

LO6　EXERCISE 11-6　**Available-for-Sale Equity, Two Years**

Lambrecht Company began operations in 2004 after receiving a large bank loan. The company used a portion of the loan to fund its operations; the remainder was used to purchase stock as an investment. During 2004, the company purchased 100 shares of Decent Technology stock at $50 per share and 200 shares of IMB stock at $40 per share. The market value per share of the stock at December 31, 2004 and 2005, was as follows:

	2004 Fair Market Value	2005 Fair Market Value
Decent Technology	$54	$48
IMB	42	38

Required:

1. Assume that the two stock holdings are the only securities in the available-for-sale portfolio. Record the entries necessary to adjust the securities to market value at the end of 2004 and 2005.
2. Develop the proper balance sheet presentation of all accounts related to the stock investment for the balance sheets of December 31, 2004, and December 31, 2005.

LO7　EXERCISE 11-7　**Trading Securities—Equity, Two Years**

Refer to the facts presented in Exercise 11-6.

Required:

1. Assume that the two stock holdings are the only securities in the trading portfolio. Record the entries necessary to adjust the securities to market value at the end of 2004 and 2005.
2. Develop the proper balance sheet presentation of all accounts related to the stock investment for the balance sheets of December 31, 2004, and December 31, 2005.

LO9　EXERCISE 11-8　**Accrual to Cash for Interest**

Assume that the income statement of Duncan Company indicates interest income from investments in bonds of $100,000 for the year 2004. Also, assume that the company had the following account balances at the beginning and end of 2004:

Account	Beginning Balance	Ending Balance
Interest Receivable	$30,000	$15,000
Unearned Interest	10,000	30,000

You should also assume that the bonds were purchased at a premium and that $12,000 of premium was amortized during the year.

Required:

Determine the amount of cash received for interest during the year.

LO9　EXERCISE 11-9　**Cash to Accrual for Interest**

Assume that the Shaq Company has received cash from investments in bonds of $100,000 for the year 2004. Also, assume the company had the following account balances at the beginning and end of 2004:

Account	Beginning Balance	Ending Balance
Interest Receivable	$30,000	$15,000
Unearned Interest	10,000	30,000

The bonds were purchased at a discount, and $8,000 of the discount was amortized during the year.

Required:

Determine the amount of interest income on the accrual basis for the year.

LO8   **EXERCISE 11-10   Investments and Interest on Statement of Cash Flows**

Bulow Company has received cash interest from investments in bonds of $200,000 during 2004. The following items were among those presented in the operating activities section of the company's statement of cash flows for 2004:

Net income	$ 900,000
Adjustments to reconcile net income to cash:	
Depreciation	100,000
Realized gain on trading securities	(10,000)
Sale of trading securities	50,000
Unrealized gain on trading securities	(26,000)
Changes in assets and liabilities:	
Accounts receivable	(8,000)
Interest receivable	(7,000)
Unearned interest	6,000
Cash flows from operating activities	$1,005,000

Required:

1. Did the Interest Receivable and Unearned Interest accounts increase or decrease during the period?

2. Determine the amount of interest income reported on the accrual basis for the year 2004.

3. Assume that the balance of Trading Securities at January 1, 2004, was $400,000 and that cost was equal to market value at that time. Also, assume that no trading securities were purchased during the period. Determine the amount that should be reported for trading securities on the balance sheet at December 31, 2004.

LO1   **EXERCISE 11-11   Investing Activities**

Businesses engage in investing activities for a variety of reasons.

Required: Review the business situations in the following list. Indicate how investing activities might be used in each situation.

1. Drake's Ice Cream Emporium, Inc. has 28 locations nationwide, located in amusement parks and on beach boardwalks. The shops experience heavy traffic during the spring and summer, but little in the winter and fall. Therefore, Drake's sees a downturn in cash flows during the latter two seasons.

2. Media Enterprises develops website solutions, print brochures, and graphics for clients worldwide. It utilizes the services of freelance graphic artists, webmasters, and print shops. For most of its large corporate print jobs, Media uses Brown Printing, a publicly traded company. Last week, the print manager at Media was distraught to learn that Brown could not accept a large print job because it was already overbooked for the month.

3. Garbo Hair, Inc. operates 12 hair salons in California. Its competitor, Hollywood Designs, which is publicly traded on the New York Stock Exchange, operates 8 salons in the same shopping districts throughout California. Garbo Hair's CEO is concerned

that too many of its clients are switching to Hollywood Designs because of discounted prices and coupons.

LO1 **EXERCISE 11-12** **Types of Securities**

The FASB divides all investments into two types: debt securities and equity securities.

Required:

For each security listed here, indicate whether it is classified as a debt security (D) or as an equity security (E).

1. Corporate bond
2. Loan
3. Warrant
4. Call option
5. Common stock
6. Municipal security
7. Convertible debt
8. Collateralized mortgage
9. Preferred stock

LO2 **EXERCISE 11-13** **Classification of Securities; Treatment of Premiums or Discounts**

The proper classification of securities investments is important because of its effect on how premiums or discounts on the original purchase are treated.

Required: For the following investment situations, indicate how the securities should be classified and, for question 2, how any discount or premium is to be accounted for.

1. Treaty Oak Financial invests in common stock of Reliant Corporation, IBM, and Dell with the intent of selling it as soon as stock prices increase by at least $2 per share.
2. People Movers Inc. purchased bonds from Colleen Enterprises with a face value of $100,000 for $92,000. The bonds pay interest at 9 percent semiannually and are due in six years. The company has the ability and intent to hold the bonds until the maturity date.

LO3, 4, 5 **EXERCISE 11-14** **Valuation of Securities**

The classification of a security determines how it will be valued at year end for financial reporting purposes.

Required: Answer the following questions about the security transactions presented.

1. Silvercrest Company purchases a security for the held-to-maturity category in April of 2005 for $75,000. If the market value of the security at year end is $72,000, what is the carrying amount of the security on the balance sheet of December 31, 2005?
2. Klein Inc. sold an available-for-sale debt security in 2005 for $95,000. The security originally cost $110,000, and its amortized cost at the time of the sale was $90,000. What is the amount of realized gain or loss for this security?
3. Transitions Company purchased trading securities in 2005 for $45,000. At year end, the securities had a fair value of $48,000. What is the carrying value at year end?

LO4 **EXERCISE 11-15** **Accounting for Available-for-Sale Securities**

Shapeshift Company purchased corporate bonds of Hallow Enterprises at 98 (98 percent of face value) as an investment on January 1, 2005. The bonds have a face amount of $500,000, pay interest at 8 percent semiannually, and mature in 10 years. Shapeshift amortizes premiums or discounts using the straight-line method.

Required:

1. Record the journal entry for this purchase, classified as available-for-sale.
2. Record the receipt of interest and amortization of the discount at June 30, 2005.

LO6   **EXERCISE 11-16   Valuation of Available-for-Sale Securities**

Roberts Company purchased 500 shares of MicroMining stock at $26.50 per share and 300 shares of IDT stock at $95.45 per share during 2004. The market value per share at December 31, 2004 and 2005, was as follows:

	2004 Fair Market Value	2005 Fair Market Value
MicroMining	$28	$30
IDT	89	94

Required: Assume that the two stock holdings are the only securities in the available-for-sale portfolio. Record the entries necessary to adjust the securities to market value at the end of 2004 and 2005.

LO6   **EXERCISE 11-17   Sale of Securities**

Tailspin Technologies sold 500 shares of Plough Industries for $8.50 per share on December 31, 2005. A net amount of $4,250 was received. The original cost of the stock was $4,500, and Tailspin classifies these securities as available-for-sale.

Required:

1. Record the journal entry for the sale.
2. How is the gain or loss on this transaction reflected on the income statement?

LO9   **EXERCISE 11-18   Cash Flows and Investment Activities**

The manner in which investment transactions are recorded and classified has a variety of implications for the statement of cash flows.

Required: Match the items listed on the left with the appropriate treatment on the statement of cash flows on the right.

1. Trading securities, unrealized gain
2. Trading securities, initial purchase
3. Available-for-sale securities, unrealized loss
4. Sale of available-for-sale securities
5. Purchase of held-to-maturity securities

A. Deduct in operating activities section
B. Add in investing activities section
C. Not presented
D. Deduct in investing activities section

LO3, 4, 5   **EXERCISE 11-19   Investment in Debt Securities**

Cattle Company purchased bonds and prepared the following amortization schedule:

Date	Cash Received	Interest Income	Amortization	Carrying Value
10/1/04				$20,456
3/31/05	$1,161	$1,309	$148	20,604
9/30/05	1,161	1,319	158	20,762
3/31/06	1,161	1,329	168	20,930
9/30/06	1,161	1,339	178	21,108
3/31/07	1,161	1,351	190	21,298
9/30/07	1,161	1,363	202	21,500

The fair value of the bonds was $21,000 and $20,200 on March 31, 2005, and September 30, 2005, respectively. Cattle Company has a 30 percent income tax rate.

Required: Show the effects of the bonds and all related adjustments on Cattle's balance sheet at September 30, 2005, if the bonds are considered:

1. Held-to-maturity securities

2. Trading securities

3. Available-for-sale securities

LO6, 8, 9   **EXERCISE 11-20   Available-for-Sale Equity Disclosure**

Sharkley, Inc. reported the following information concerning its long-term equity investments in a note to its 2005 and 2004 financial statements.

Note 4—Investments in Marketable Securities

The following is a summary of long-term available-for-sale marketable securities at December 31, 2005 and 2004, and related unrealized gains and losses:

December 31, 2005 and December 31, 2004

Net of Tax Amounts	Cost	Gross Unrealized Gains	Gross Unrealized Losses	Fair Value
December 31, 2005	$14,560	$490	($ 120)	$14,930
December 31, 2004	7,640	200	(1,200)	6,640

The following table summarizes sales of available-for-sale securities for the years ended December 31, 2005 and 2004:

	2005	2004
Proceeds from sales	$5,600	$12,500
Gross realized gains	2,100	1,400
Gross realized losses	(700)	(900)

Required:

1. Show how Sharkley would present its investments on its December 31, 2005 balance sheet and the investing activities section of its 2005 statement of cash flows.

2. Is there evidence of gains trading? Explain.

LO6   **EXERCISE 11-21   Available-for-Sale Equity Investments**

During 2004, Comcity Corp. purchased stock for $40,000, plus an additional fee of $400 as broker's commission. The fair value of the stock at the end of 2004 was $41,000, and the fair value at the end of 2005 was $37,000. During January of 2006, Comcity sold the investment for $38,500. Comcity classified the investment as available-for-sale. The company's income tax rate is 30 percent.

Required:

1. How much will Comcity report as an unrealized gain or loss on its balance sheet at December 31, 2004?

2. How much will Comcity report as an unrealized gain or loss on its balance sheet at December 31, 2005?

3. How much will Comcity report as a realized gain or loss on its income statement during 2006 as a result of the sale?

4. How much will Comcity report as accumulated other comprehensive income on its balance sheet at December 31, 2005?

5. How much will Comcity report as other comprehensive income for the year ended December 31, 2005?

6. Describe the nature of investments reported as available-for-sale.

PROBLEMS

LO2, 3, 6, 7   **PROBLEM 11-1**   **Analysis of Investment Portfolio** (CPA adapted)

The following information pertains to Dyle, Inc.'s portfolio of investments for the year ended December 31, 2004:

	Cost	Fair Value 12/31/03	2004 Purchases	2004 Sales	Fair Value 12/31/04
Held-to-Maturity Securities					
Security ABC			$100,000		$95,000
Trading					
Security DEF	$150,000	$160,000			155,000
Available-for-Sale Securities					
Security GHI	190,000	165,000		$175,000	
Security JKL	170,000	176,000			160,000

Assume that Security ABC was purchased at par and assume that all declines in fair value are considered temporary.

Required:

1. What is the carrying amount of Security ABC at December 31, 2004?
2. What is the carrying amount of Security DEF at December 31, 2004?
3. What is the carrying amount of Security JKL at December 31, 2004?
4. What is the amount of realized gain or loss on Security GHI?
5. What is the amount of unrealized gain or loss to be reported on the 2004 income statement?
6. What is the amount of unrealized gain or loss to be reported at December 31, 2004, as a separate component of stockholders' equity?

Analyze: In determining the carrying amount, why are Securities DEF and JKL treated differently from Security ABC?

Communicate: If you were asked to determine the fair market value of securities that your company holds, describe how you would perform this task.

LO2, 6, 8   **PROBLEM 11-2**   **Analysis of AMD's Investment Performance**

Presented on the following page is a portion of the accounting policy note of **AMD Corp.**, one of Intel's competitors, as well as a portion of the note concerning its investment portfolio as of December 29, 2002.

AMD realized a net gain on the sales of available-for-sale securities of $5,334,000 for 2002 and a loss of $1,565,000 in 2001. The cash flow statement indicates proceeds from the sale of available-for-sale securities of $4,334,000 and purchases of available-for-sale securities of $4,465,000 during 2002.

Required:

1. What amounts should be reported on the income statement and balance sheet related to long-term investments for 2002? Assume that AMD developed a statement of comprehensive income for 2002. What amounts would be reported on this statement for 2002?
2. What amount should be reported on the balance sheet related to long-term investments for 2001?

AMD Corp.

INVESTMENTS: Currently, the Company classifies its securities as available-for-sale. These securities are reported at fair market value with the related unrealized gains and losses included in other comprehensive income (loss), net of tax, a component of stockholders' equity. Realized gains and losses and declines in the value of securities judged to be other than temporary are included in interest income and other, net.

Available-for-sale securities as of December 29, 2002, and December 30, 2001, were as follows:

(thousands)	Cost	Gross Unrealized Gains	Gross Unrealized Losses	Fair Market Value
2002 Long-term investments:				
Equity investments	$ 8,023	$ 988	$(1,126)	$ 7,885
2001 Long-term investments:				
Equity investments	$11,571	$8,257	$ (486)	$19,342

Analyze: Why do you think AMD classifies its securities reported here as available-for-sale?

LO2, 6, 8   **PROBLEM 11-3**   **Analysis of Microsoft's Investment Portfolio**

The following information is taken from the notes that accompany **Microsoft**'s annual report of June 30, 2003.

Microsoft

Year Ended June 30 (in millions)	2001	2002	2003
Net unrealized investment gains/(losses):			
Unrealized holding gains/(losses), net of tax effect of $(351) in 2001, $(955) in 2002, and $610 in 2003	(1,200)	(1,774)	1,132
Reclassification adjustment for (gains)/losses included in net income, net of tax effect of $(128) in 2001, $958 in 2002, and $60 in 2003	(260)	1,779	111

Required:

1. Microsoft classifies all equity investments as long-term assets. What is the amount of unrealized gains or losses for the year ended June 30, 2003?

2. In what category of the income statement would you expect the unrealized gains to be reported?

Analyze: What is the purpose of the reclassification adjustment of $111 million during the year?

LO2, 4, 5, 6, 7   **PROBLEM 11-4**   **Securities Held over Two Years**

Assume the following transactions and events occur over a two-year time period for Dayton Company. Dayton has not held investments prior to January 1, 2004, and has an annual accounting period that ends on December 31 of each year.

Jan. 1, 2004   Purchased bonds of Burrow Company as an investment. The bonds have a face amount of $800,000, pay interest at 8 percent semiannually (4 percent per semi-annual period), and mature in five years. Dayton purchased the bonds at 97. Burrow amortizes a premium or discount using the straight-line method at year end.

April 1, 2004	Purchased the stock of Ellie Company as an investment. Dayton purchased 1,000 shares at $75 per share plus brokerage costs of $250. The number of shares held by Dayton represents less than 20 percent of the Ellie Company stock outstanding.
June 1, 2004	Purchased the stock of Artie Company as an investment. Dayton purchased 900 shares at $100 per share plus brokerage costs of $300. The number of shares held by Dayton represents less than 20 percent of the Artie Company stock outstanding.
June 30, 2004	Received interest on the Burrow Company bonds.
Dec. 31, 2004	Received interest on the Burrow Company bonds. The market values of the securities as of December 31, 2004 were:

Burrow Company bonds	$770,000
Ellie Company stock	74,000
Artie Company stock	84,000

June 30, 2005	Received interest on the Burrow Company bonds.
July 15, 2005	Sold 500 shares of Ellie Company stock at $74 per share less brokerage costs of $100.
Dec. 31, 2005	Received interest on the Burrow Company bonds. The market values of the securities as of December 31, 2005 were:

Burrow Company bonds	$870,000
Ellie Company stock	42,000
Artie Company stock	92,000

Required:

1. Record all necessary transactions assuming that the securities are treated as available-for-sale. You may ignore income taxes in all transactions.

2. If the securities are treated as available-for-sale, what amounts will be reported on the balance sheets at December 31, 2004 and 2005, and in what categories will the amounts be reported?

3. Record all necessary transactions assuming that the securities are treated as trading securities.

Analyze: How is the balance of the Investment in Equity—Trading account at December 31, 2005 computed?

LO9   PROBLEM 11-5   **Cash Flows of Bond Investment**
Phillips Corporation had the following account balances for 2004:

Realized Gain on Sale of Securities	$ 8,000
Interest Income from Investment in Bonds	40,000
Interest Receivable, January 1, 2004	6,000
Interest Receivable, December 31, 2004	8,000
Unearned Interest, January 1, 2004	2,000
Unearned Interest, December 31, 2004	5,000
Investment in Bonds—Held-to-Maturity, January 1, 2004	470,000
Investment in Bonds—Held-to-Maturity, December 31, 2004	350,000

During 2004, the amount of discount amortization related to held-to-maturity bonds was $5,000. No bonds were purchased as an investment during the year.

Required:

1. Determine the amount of cash received from the sale of held-to-maturity bonds during the year.

2. Determine the amount of cash received from interest on investments in bonds during the year.

Analyze: By what amount did the Investment in Bonds—Held-to-Maturity account change in 2004?

LO2, 4, 6, 8   **PROBLEM 11-6   Analysis of the Investment Portfolio of Sun Microsystems**

The following excerpts are from the accounting policy note and the note concerning the investment portfolio of **Sun Microsystems** from the annual report for the year ended June 30, 2003.

Sun Microsystems

Investments in marketable debt securities consist primarily of corporate notes and bonds, asset and mortgage backed securities and U.S. government notes and bonds with original maturities beyond three months. At June 30, 2003 and 2002 all of Sun's marketable debt securities were classified as available-for-sale and were carried at fair market value.

Marketable Equity Securities

Investments in marketable equity securities consist of equity holdings in public companies. Marketable equity securities are initially recorded at cost upon acquisition and are classified as available-for-sale when there are no restrictions on Sun's ability to liquidate such securities within 12 months. Investments in marketable equity securities were $15 million and $18 million at June 30, 2003 and 2002, respectively. At June 30, 2003, all marketable equity investments were classified as available-for-sale and are included in Other non-current assets, net in the Consolidated Balance Sheet. Changes in the fair value of these securities are recognized in Accumulated other comprehensive income (loss), net of tax in the Consolidated Statements of Stockholders Equity. Net unrealized gains, net of tax, on marketable equity investments were $9 million, none, and $10 million at June 30, 2003, 2002 and 2001, respectively. Realized gains on marketable equity securities totaled $6 million, $3 million and $31 million in fiscal 2003, 2002 and 2001, respectively, and are recognized in Loss on equity investments, net in the Consolidated Statements of Operations. In addition, we review all marketable equity securities for other than temporary declines in fair value. We consider a marketable equity security to be other-than-temporarily impaired if, as of the end of any quarter, the carrying value of the investment has been greater than the market value for the last six consecutive months. This evaluation is performed on a quarterly basis. Based on our evaluation, if a security is considered to be other than temporarily impaired, an impairment charge is recognized in Loss on equity investments, net in the Consolidated Statements of Operations. For fiscal 2003, 2002 and 2001, $8 million, $23 million and $70 million were recorded as impairment charges related to marketable equity securities, respectively.

	2003			
	Cost	**Gross Unrealized Gains**	**Gross Unrealized Losses**	**Fair Value**
Corporate notes and bonds	$ 1,310	$ 17	$ —	$ 1,327
Asset and mortgage-based securities	1,252	12	(4)	1,260
U.S. government notes and bonds	1,124	7	(1)	1,130
Money market securities	1,473	—	—	1,473
State and local government debt	8	—	—	8
Total marketable securities	$ 5,167	$ 36	$ (5)	$ 5,198

Required:

1. What amount of unrealized gains and losses existed at June 30, 2003, on Sun Microsystems's corporate notes and bonds? In what category of the balance sheet would these amounts appear?

2. What amount of unrealized gains and losses existed at June 30, 2003, on Sun Microsystems's equity instruments?

3. In which of the financial statements would you find information about the unrealized gains and losses on the company's debt and equity securities? Which account in that statement would reveal the information?

4. In which of the financial statements would you find information about the realized gains and losses on the company's debt and equity securities? Which account in that statement would reveal the information?

Analyze: Characterize your assessment of Sun's investments in long-term marketable securities. Has the company improved its position since these investments were acquired? Explain your position.

LO1, 2, 6, 7, 8   **PROBLEM 11-7   Available-for-Sale and Trading Equity Securities over Two Years, Comprehensive Income**

On March 1, 2004, Wilson Corp. purchased 2,000 shares (15 percent) of $1 par value common stock of Hart Company for $18 per share. Wilson Corp. incurred broker's fees totaling $400 in connection with the purchase. Wilson has a December 31 year end. Wilson reports this investment as available-for-sale and does not have the ability to exercise significant influence over Hart Company's activities. Additional information:

A. Wilson properly accounted for the investments owned at December 31, 2004.

B. Hart Company reported net income of $90,000 and $60,000 for the years ended December 31, 2005 and 2004, respectively.

C. The financial news reported that on December 31, 2005, Hart Company trading closed at $18 per share and that on December 31, 2004, it closed at $19 per share.

D. Wilson Corp.'s net income for 2003 was $16,000.

E. The federal income tax rate is 30 percent.

Required:

1. At what dollar amount and in what section (be specific) of Wilson's December 31, 2005, balance sheet should the Hart investment be reported?

2. Show how the effects of appropriate year-end accounting will be reported in the stockholders' equity section of Wilson's balance sheet at December 31, 2005.

3. Prepare a separate statement of comprehensive income in good form for Wilson Corp. for 2005.

4. Specify how reporting on the balance sheet, income statement, and statement of comprehensive income for the year ended December 31, 2005, would have differed if the investment had been accounted for as a trading security instead of as available-for-sale. (Omit amounts.)

Analyze: Why do the majority of companies classify their securities as available-for-sale rather than trading?

LO3, 4, 8   **PROBLEM 11-8   Available-for-Sale and Held-to-Maturity Debt Securities, Comprehensive Income**

On January 1, 2004, Freedman, Inc. purchased $66,000 of five-year, 7.3 percent bonds from Locke Company dated January 1, 2004. The bonds pay interest annually on January 1. Freedman classified the bonds as available-for-sale. The bonds were selling at $67,320 and $65,746 at December 31, 2004 and 2005, respectively. Freedman has a 30 percent income tax rate. Freedman provides the following schedule for the bonds:

Date	Cash	Interest	Amortization	Book Value
Jan. 1, 2004				$59,245
Dec. 31, 2004	$4,818	$5,924	$1,106	60,351
Dec. 31, 2005	4,818	6,035	1,217	61,568
Dec. 31, 2006	4,818	6,157	1,339	62,907
Dec. 31, 2007	4,818	6,291	1,473	64,380
Dec. 31, 2008	4,818	6,438	1,620	66,000

Required:

1. Create a T-account for the investment and additional T-accounts for accounts used in the adjustment process. Post all transactions and related necessary adjustments to the T-accounts through December 31, 2005. Calculate and show the carrying value of the investment in the T-accounts at December 31, 2004 and 2005.

2. Prepare a partial balance sheet at December 31, 2005, for Freedman that reflects all aspects of the investment.

3. How much should Freedman report on its comprehensive income statement related to this investment for the year ended December 31, 2005?

Analyze: Identify what differences in Freedman's balance sheet at December 31, 2005, would result if these bonds were considered held-to-maturity instead of available-for-sale.

LO1, 2, 6, 7, 8 **PROBLEM 11-9 Trading and Available-for-Sale Equity Securities, Comprehensive Income**

Homer Company purchased equity securities during 2004. At December 31, 2005, Homer still owned two of these investments. Information about them is as follows:

Name	Date Acquired	Acquisition Cost	Fair Value at Dec. 31, 2004	Fair Value at Dec. 31, 2005	Dividends Received
Lisa Company, 9,000 common shares	3/1/04	$31,500	$26,000	$3.20 per share	Oct. 1, 2005: 15% stock dividend
Bart Company, 8,000 shares of preferred	11/30/05	$17,000	—	$15,800	Dec. 30, 2005: $780

A. Homer has no ability to influence management decisions at either company.

B. Homer acquired the Bart Company stock solely for short-term profits.

C. Homer has no idea how long it will hold the Lisa Company stock.

D. Homer has a 30 percent income tax rate.

E. Homer's net income *after* considering the effects of the investments is $5,016.

Required:

1. Show how these investments and the effects of any related adjustments will be reported on Homer Company's balance sheet as of December 31, 2005.

2. Prepare a statement of comprehensive income for the year ended December 31, 2005.

3. Assume that Homer Company sells 1,600 shares of its investment in Bart Company for $4 per share on January 1, 2006. Show the effect of this sale on Homer's income statement.

Spreadsheet: Use a spreadsheet application to make your calculations for question 1 and to prepare the statement of comprehensive income for question 2.

Analyze: As Homer Company's financial adviser, how would you characterize the status of these two equity securities at December 31, 2005?

LO2, 7, 8, 9 **PROBLEM 11-10 Trading Equity Securities, Cash Flows**

The following information is available for Nolan Company for the year ended December 31, 2005. All investments are equity securities.

Net income	$120,000
Trading securities reported at December 31, 2004	4,000
Realized loss on sale of trading securities	3,000
Cost of trading securities sold	10,000

Trading securities reported at December 31, 2005	$ 24,000
Unrealized gain arising during the period on trading securities	1,500
Balance at December 31, 2004, of Unrealized Holding Gain— Trading (before closing)	7,000
Cash dividends received/earned from trading investments	1,300

The income tax rate is 30 percent. Additional trading securities were acquired during 2005. Some trading investments were sold during December of 2005.

Required:

1. Calculate the amount at which Nolan sold the trading securities.

2. Indicate how the items should be presented in the operating activities section of the statement of cash flows for the year ended December 31, 2005, using the indirect method.

Analyze: How would your response to question 2 differ if this investment were classified as available-for-sale instead of trading? Respond conceptually.

LO1, 2, 6, 8   **PROBLEM 11-11   Equity Securities**

Kowkabany Company acquired 2,000 shares of Mills, Inc. common stock for $18,000 on November 30, 2004, and appropriately accounted for the investment for the year ended December 31, 2004. Kowkabany's income tax rate is 30 percent. Other information concerning the Mills, Inc. investment is as follows:

Fair Value 12/31/04	Fair Value 12/31/05	Dividends Received During 2005
$17,000	$10 per share	Nov. 1: Cash dividend, $.40 per share

A. Kowkabany is *not able* to exercise significant influence over Mills.

B. Kowkabany is unsure of its intended holding period for the Mills stock.

C. For the year ended December 31, 2005, Kowkabany's net income was $40,000 and Mills's net income was $50,000.

Required:

1. What two clues tell you that this investment falls under fair value accounting?

2. Into which classification of investment (under *SFAS No. 115*) will this investment be placed?

3. Prepare a partial balance sheet at December 31, 2005 and a partial income statement for Kowkabany Company for the year ended December 31, 2005.

Analyze: How does accounting for investments under *SFAS No. 115* help minimize gains trading as compared to the situation pre-*SFAS No. 115*?

LO1, 2, 6, 8, 9   **PROBLEM 11-12   Available-for-Sale Equity Securities, Cash Flows**

Perot Company purchased 1,200 common shares of Hillary Company common stock, representing a 4 percent interest, on November 1, 2005, for $40,000. In addition, Perot paid the broker $920 as commission on the trade. At the purchase date, the fair value of Hillary Company's net assets is $700,000. There is no difference between the book value and the fair value of Hillary's net assets. Perot intends to hold this investment until Hillary Company distributes its annual dividend during July of 2006. Perot is unable to influence Hillary Company's decision making. As of December 31, 2005, the stock was selling for $32 per share. On July 3, 2006, Perot received its expected cash dividend of $.45 per share. On July 8, 2006, Perot sold its investment in Hillary on the open market for $36 per share. Perot's income tax rate is 30 percent.

Required:

1. Prepare a partial balance sheet for Perot Company at December 31, 2005, reflecting the investment. Label statement classification(s) clearly.

2. How much should be reported on Perot's 2006 income statement as a result of the sale?

3. What amounts will Perot report on its 2006 statement of cash flows relative to the investment if the indirect method is used?

Analyze: If the investment in Hillary is Perot's only investment, would you say that Perot's investment portfolio is in a positive or a negative position at December 31, 2005? Identify any other concerns that investors might have. Justify your response.

LO2, 3, 6, 7, 8, 9 PROBLEM 11-13 **Available-for-Sale, Trading, and Held-to-Maturity Securities, Cash Flows**

Presented here is information from Dove, Inc. for the year ended December 31, 2005. All accounts have normal balances.

Dove, Inc.
Income Statement
For the Year Ended December 31, 2005

Sales	$820,000
Cost of sales	490,000
Gross profit	$330,000
Interest expense	(30,000)
Other operating expenses	(92,000)
Unrealized holding loss—trading securities	(4,000)
Realized gain from sale of trading securities	2,000
Realized gain from sale of available-for-sale securities	5,000
Dividend revenue	3,000
Interest revenue (includes $3,500 of bond discount amortization)	11,000
Income taxes	(80,000)
Net income	$145,000

Accounts and Balances	12/31/05	12/31/04
Investment in Equity—Trading	$61,500	$54,000
Adjustment—Trading	2,400 cr.	1,200 cr.
Investment in Bonds—Held-to-Maturity	171,500	175,000
Investment in Equity—Available-for-Sale	81,400	80,000
Adjustment—Available-for-Sale	4,200	1,800
Unrealized Holding Gain—Available-for-Sale Securities	4,200	1,800

During 2005, Dove purchased and sold trading securities several times. Total purchases cost $23,000. Dove sold available-for-sale securities with an original cost of $15,000. A $1,400 unrealized gain had previously been recognized for this investment. All acquisitions were for cash unless otherwise stated.

Required:

1. How much cash was paid to purchase available-for-sale securities during 2005?

2. How much cash was received from the sale of trading securities during 2005?

3. Show how the results of the investments would be reported on Dove's statement of cash flows for 2005 using the indirect method.

Analyze: What types of investing activities yield true cash flows?

LO1, 2, 6, 7, 8 PROBLEM 11-14 **Trading and Available-for-Sale Equity Securities, Comprehensive Income**

During 2004 and 2005, Roberts Company purchased a 15 percent equity investment in two corporations: Holt Company and Crowell Enterprises. The names, cost, and fair values at

December 31, 2004 and 2005, and the cash dividends received during each year are shown in the following table. Necessary adjustments were made according to GAAP during 2002. Roberts has an income tax rate of 30 percent.

Name	Acquisition Date	Acquisition Cost	Fair Value at 12/31/04	Fair Value at 12/31/05	Cash Dividends
Holt Company	4/30/04	$12,000	$11,000	$12,600	2004 = $400 2005 = $600
Crowell Enterprises	11/5/05	$14,000	NA	$15,200	2005 = $900

A. Roberts cannot exercise significant influence on either of these investments.

B. Roberts has not determined how long it will hold the Holt stock.

C. Roberts hopes to earn a short-term gain on the Crowell investment.

D. The stocks are both actively traded on Wall Street.

E. Roberts's net income for 2004 and 2005, respectively, was $70,000 and $30,000. Both Holt and Crowell reported $50,000 of net income during each year the investments were owned by Roberts.

Required:

1. If either or both of the investments must be accounted for in a certain category, identify the category. If category is not an issue, indicate why not.

2. Indicate the section of the balance sheet in which each investment will be reported by Roberts at December 31, 2005, and the respective dollar amount at which each investment should be valued.

3. Show the effects of the transactions provided and the related year-end accounting procedures as they will be reported in Roberts's multiple-step income statement for the year ended December 31, 2005, and in the stockholders' equity section of the balance sheet at December 31, 2005.

4. Prepare the complete statement of comprehensive income for the year ended December 31, 2005.

Analyze: At what conceptual asset *valuation* (no calculations) are these investments measured by Roberts?

LO3, 7, 9 **PROBLEM 11-15   Trading and Held-to-Maturity Securities, Cash Flows**
Burns Company reported $51,000 net income for the year ended December 31, 2005. The following transactions occurred during 2005:

A. Burns purchased $30,000 of 8 percent bonds for $32,000 on January 1, 2005. During 2005, one interest payment was received and $300 of amortization was recognized for the period. Burns accounted for the bond investment as held-to-maturity.

B. On December 29, 2005, Burns sold trading securities for $5,000 that had been acquired on December 4, 2005, at a cost of $4,200.

Required: Prepare a partial statement of cash flows for the year ended December 31, 2005, using the indirect method, that reflects only the transactions provided.

Analyze: Why are realized gains subtracted from net income in determining cash flows from operating activities? Why is amortization on bond investments considered an adjustment to net income in determining cash flows from operating activities?

LO1, 2, 3, 5, 9 **PROBLEM 11-16   Held-to-Maturity Securities, Available-for-Sale Debt Securities, Cash Flows**
Alabassi Company purchased $10,000 of 12 percent, five-year bonds on January 1, 2005, for $10,800. The company uses the straight-line method to amortize the premium. The bonds

were selling for $10,100 as of December 31, 2005. The bonds pay interest annually on December 31, and they mature on December 31, 2009.

Required:

1. Assume that this investment is accounted for as available-for-sale.

   a. At what amount would the bonds be reported on the balance sheet at December 31, 2005?
   b. In what balance sheet section would Alabassi report this investment?
   c. Name the two accounting adjustments that would be made at year-end.

2. Assume that this investment is accounted for as a held-to-maturity investment.

   a. At what amount would it be reported on Alabassi's balance sheet at December 31, 2005?
   b. How much should Alabassi report on its income statement for the year ended December 31, 2005? Specifically where will Alabassi report this amount?

Analyze: Why are fair value adjustments made for investments in available-for-sale debt securities when they are not made for held-to-maturity investments?

CASES

LO8   **RESEARCH CASE 11-1   Intel's Investment Gains**

The following excerpts are taken from a *Wall Street Journal* article concerning the treatment of investment gains by **Intel** in 2000:[15]

> Intel Corp.'s second-quarter earnings shot up 79%, although the results were muddied by a variety of special items and controversy over the chip maker's practice of including one-time gains from stock sales as part of its ordinary earnings. Intel's results include a variety of special items, the largest being a $2.1 billion net gain from the company's sale of securities from its investment portfolio. Intel also posted acquisition-related charges consisting of $394 million related to amortization of goodwill and $21 million for in-process research and development, as well as a previously announced $200 million charge to account for a recall of a defective memory component.
>
> Due to confusion wrought by the complex accounting, however, many analysts argued that comparing Intel's results to the consensus will be a useless exercise, particularly since the investment gains alone boosted results by roughly 15 cents a share on a post-split basis. The situation is "an unholy mess," said Drew Peck, an analyst at S.G. Cowen & Co. "Apples-to-apples comparisons will be very difficult."
>
> The common high-tech practice of treating investment gains as ordinary income has grown increasingly controversial, with some analysts and accountants arguing that it inflates companies' operating performance by rolling them together with one-time, non-repeatable securities gains. Last month, however, Intel abruptly announced that interest and "other" income, including capital gains, for the second quarter would rise to $2.3 billion, up from the $725 million it had previously forecast.

Intel's stock portfolio may be less of an issue in the future, however, particularly if the valuations of Internet stocks continue to decline. Between April 1 and July 1, in fact, the size of Intel's portfolio dropped to $7.5 billion from $10.8 billion, equally reflecting the sale of assets and a decline in equity values, Mr. Bryant said. Over the same period, Intel reported that unrealized gains in the portfolio dropped by nearly $3.2 billion.

---

15 David P. Hamilton, "Intel Says Net Jumped 79%; Analysts Upset," *Wall Street Journal*, July 19, 2000.

Required:

1. Locate Intel's income statement for 2000 online. In what category of the statement were the gains disclosed? Do the gains represent realized or unrealized amounts?

2. During 2001, Intel's investment performance changed, and the unrealized gains in the portfolio dropped by nearly $3.2 billion. Where would you find the *change* in the unrealized gains disclosed in the 2001 financial statements? Where would the total amount of unrealized gains on Intel's investment portfolio be reflected?

3. Do you believe that Intel followed proper accounting guidelines in its presentation of investment gains for 2000 and 2001? Why or why not?

4. Refer to the most recent financial statements available for Intel. What amount of realized and unrealized investment gains and losses are reported, and in what category of the statements are the amounts reported?

LO1, 6, 8

ETHICS

ETHICS CASE 11-2   Ethics of Gains Trading

Bill Worth is the CFO for a midsize company. He has analyzed the following equity holdings in the company's available-for-sale portfolio of investments as of December 1, 2004:

	Cost	Market Value
High Tech Co.	$900,000	$400,000
Telecom Co.	600,000	400,000
Flyer Co.	400,000	900,000

Bill is worried about the company's ability to meet its profit goal for the year. He is also concerned because the company has a performance plan that provides a bonus to the CFO and his staff if certain profit performance measures are met. As a result, Bill is considering selling the Flyer Co. stock before December 31 in order to meet the profit objectives.

Required:

1. What will be the impact on profitability if the Flyer Co. stock is sold? How will it affect the amount reported as comprehensive income?

2. Do you feel that Bill is operating in an ethical manner if he sells the stock in order to meet the profitability goals that have been established?

LO1

ETHICS

ETHICS CASE 11-3   Ethical Competition

The microprocessor industry is highly competitive and relies on constant product innovation. In the case of **Intel**, such innovations have helped the company achieve its position as the global industry leader, with more than 80 percent of the world market. Intel's financial investments in other companies also contribute to this market position, as the company works diligently to establish relationships with suppliers and customers. However, because of its market power and customer dependency, Intel may also exert influence without direct financial investment.

Over the years, Intel has been the target of several lawsuits alleging that Intel has used its power to engage in illegal competitive practices. In 1999, the FTC investigated a claim that Intel had tried to force clients to end patent infringement suits by threatening to discontinue providing them with technical information about its products. In its decision, the FTC firmly established that "a monopolist may not use its monopoly power to coerce or intimidate rivals from a full opportunity to compete in the marketplace."[16]

In 2003, **Advanced Micro Devices (AMD)** claimed that Intel had intimidated some of its clients so that they would not join the company during its launch of its new 64-bit computer chip.[17] Critics claim that Intel's practices have hurt not only its competitors, but also personal computer makers and users.

16 David Balto, "Protecting Competition from the Abuse of Monopoly Power: The Intel Case," *Computer Lawyer* 16(6/7), 1999, pp. 4–10.

17 Don Clark, "AMD Says Intel Intimidates Clients," *Wall Street Journal*, September 24, 2003, p. B3.

Required:

1. Do you think that a company should use its influence in the marketplace to preserve its market share?

2. Where is the line between building strong business relationships and using illegal or unethical sales tactics?

3. Suppose you were the CEO of Intel and you were responsible for setting policies regarding customer relations. How would you influence your customers to keep them from buying products from your competitors?

4. As you consider strategies to retain and win over customers, what role should the interests of your stockholders play? What is in the best interest of consumers?

LO2 COMMUNICATION CASE 11-4 **Classification of Investments**

As the controller for a medium-sized manufacturing company, you are responsible for accounting for your company's investments. The company routinely purchases investments as an alternative to holding cash in the bank. Bonuses are paid to executives based on the performance of the company, measured by net income. During the current year, the company's investments have done quite well, and at the end of the year the company will report a large unrealized holding gain. When the CEO sees your initial income statement for the period, he is perplexed to find that the unrealized holding gain is not reflected on the statement. He states that the investments were bought for trading purposes and that he expects you to make sure that the income statement shows the unrealized holding gains.

Required:

1. Why do you think the CEO wants the investments to be treated as trading securities?

2. Write a memo to the board of directors discussing the proper accounting for investments. Include in your memo your opinion of where the current period's unrealized holding gain should be shown on the financial statements.

LO5 FINANCIAL REPORTING CASE 11-5 **Recording Investments in Bonds**

Assume that you have been hired as the controller for Nathan Company and one of your duties is to account for the company's investment account. On January 1, 2005, Nathan Company purchased $200,000 of 8 percent bonds of Universal Co. for $208,203. The bonds were purchased to yield 7 percent interest. Interest is payable annually on December 31. The bonds mature on December 31, 2009.

Required:

1. Prepare the journal entry to record the purchase of bonds by Nathan Company on January 1. Assume that the bonds are classified as trading investments.

2. Prepare the journal entry to record the receipt of annual interest on December 31, 2005.

3. The fair value of the Universal bonds on December 31, 2005, was $207,000. Prepare any necessary adjusting entry needed by Nathan Company.

LO6 FINANCIAL REPORTING CASE 11-6 **Accounting for Equity Securities**

As the new chief accountant for Woods Corporation, you are responsible for accounting for the company's available-for-sale equity portfolio. At December 31, 2005, you are given the following information about Woods Corporation's available-for-sale portfolio:

Security	Cost	Fair Value	Unrealized Gain (Loss)
Els	$22,000	$23,000	$1,000
Singh	17,000	14,000	(3,000)
Stricker	8,500	15,000	6,500
Mickelson	29,000	35,000	6,000
Total	$76,500	$87,000	

The debit balance in the Adjustment—Available-for-Sale account at December 31, 2004, was $5,000. On February 12, 2006, Woods sold its Els shares for $24,500 less brokerage fees of $525. On May 15, 2006, Woods bought 200 shares of Toms Corp. for $95 per share plus brokerage fees of $800. Fair market values at the end of 2006 are as follows:

Singh	$12,500	Mickelson	$38,000
Stricker	14,000	Toms	23,000

Required:

1. Prepare the adjusting entry at the end of 2005.

2. Prepare the entries that Woods should make in February and May.

3. Prepare the adjusting entry at the end of 2006.

LO2, 8 **RESEARCH CASE 11-7** **Classification of Investments**

Berkshire Hathaway is a holding company that owns and operates a number of businesses, including operations in the insurance, apparel, building products, finance and financial products, flight services, and retail industries. The company's website can be found at **www.berkshirehathaway.com**.

Required:

Go to the company's website and access the company's most recent annual report in order to answer the following questions:

1. Berkshire Hathaway owns numerous investments. How does the company normally classify its investments?

2. What is the cost of the company's available-for-sale equity portfolio? What is its most recent market value?

3. What is Berkshire Hathaway's single most valuable equity investment?

4. For its most recent fiscal period, what amounts were reported for realized investment gains and losses?

LO2 **COMMUNICATION CASE 11-8** **Classification of Investments**

Assume that you are the controller for a profitable service company. The company has been increasing its cash balance over the past two fiscal years, and management has made a decision to start investing some of its excess cash in the stock of other companies. Management is concerned about how its investments will affect the company's net income, as it does not want to break its streak of 20 consecutive profitable quarters. Management asks you to write a memo detailing the company's potential investment guidelines. In the memo, address how investments should be classified on the balance sheet and how changes in value should be recognized. Management stresses that it wants investment guidelines that will avoid affecting the income statement as much as possible.

Required: Prepare a memo to the management of your company suggesting investment guidelines. In your memo, discuss how you think the investments should be recorded and how changes in their value will affect the balance sheet, the income statement, the statement of comprehensive income, and the statement of cash flows.

On the Web

The following exercises, activities, and problems are available on the *Intermediate Accounting* website. Use these resources to reinforce your understanding of the topics presented in this chapter.

- CPA-Adapted Simulations
- Interpreting the Accounting Standards
- Extending the Global Focus
- Extending the Ethics Discussion
- Mastering the Spreadsheet
- Career Snapshots
- Annual Report Project
- ACE Practice Tests
- Flashcards
- Glossary
- Check Figures for Text Problems
- PowerPoint Presentations

SOLUTIONS: CHECK YOUR UNDERSTANDING

Investment Activities and Types of Securities (p. 501)

1. Companies engage in investing activities in order to generate income or manage their excess cash, to develop relationships with companies in which they invest, or to acquire a controlling interest in another company.

2. Debt securities, like bonds or loans, are those securities that represent a creditor relationship with a business. Equity securities, like stocks or call options, are defined as those securities that represent an ownership interest in a company or enterprise.

Accounting for Debt Securities (p. 510)

1. The portion of available-for-sale debt securities that will be due within one year should be classified as a current asset on the balance sheet, while the remaining portion should be classified as a long-term asset.

2. Unrealized holding gains and losses *that occurred during the current year* should be treated as *other comprehensive income* on the statement of comprehensive income.

3. If a company treats unrealized gains or losses as income as they arise, it does not have an additional gain or loss at the time of sale. Some companies may choose to present the realized gain or loss on the income statement at the time of sale. In this case, the company must be careful not to double-count gains or losses on securities.

Accounting for Equity Securities (p. 515)

1. To ascertain whether significant influence exists, consider voting rights at stockholders' meetings, membership on the board of directors, and other contracts or relationships between the investor and the investee.

2. If a company owns between 20 and 50 percent of another company's stock, the investment should be reported using the equity method, recording income based on the investor's percentage ownership of the investee.

3. Brokerage costs, transaction fees, and stock costs will be included in the original valuation.

Analysis of Investments (p. 517)

1. Gains trading is selling securities in order to manage (or manipulate) earnings. In this practice, companies choose to sell their "performers" in order to increase earnings.

2. Prior to *SFAS No. 115*, companies used the historical cost method or the lower-of-cost-or-market method when measuring their investment portfolios. When the historical cost method was used, the investor had no way of knowing what unrealized gains or losses were occurring. The use of fair market values helps investors see holding gains or losses.

Impact of Investments on Cash Flow (p. 520)

1. Amortization on a bond investment is not a true cash outflow and therefore must be added back to or subtracted from the net income amount.

2. A realized gain would appear as a deduction from net income in the operating activities section of the statement of cash flows when using the indirect method.

CPA-ADAPTED SIMULATION

This simulation asks you to complete various tasks related to a company's annual financial statements. If your instructor has signed up for CPAexcel™, you can do the work online at **www.cpaexcel.com/hmco**. You may also do the simulation manually.

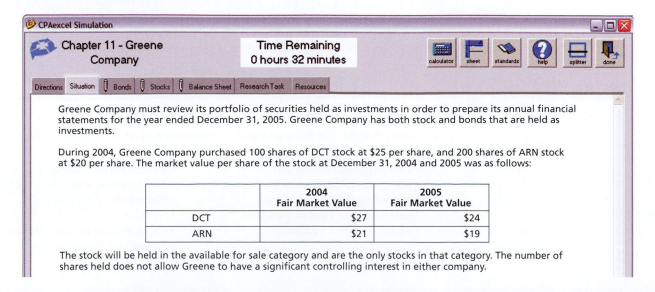

Greene Company must review its portfolio of securities held as investments in order to prepare its annual financial statements for the year ended December 31, 2005. Greene Company has both stock and bonds that are held as investments.

During 2004, Greene Company purchased 100 shares of DCT stock at $25 per share, and 200 shares of ARN stock at $20 per share. The market value per share of the stock at December 31, 2004 and 2005 was as follows:

	2004 Fair Market Value	2005 Fair Market Value
DCT	$27	$24
ARN	$21	$19

The stock will be held in the available for sale category and are the only stocks in that category. The number of shares held does not allow Greene to have a significant controlling interest in either company.

On October 1, 2005 Greene Company purchased bonds issued by LCA Company. The bonds have a face value of $100,000, pay interest semiannually at 8% (4% per semiannual period) on October 1 and April 1, and mature in five years from the date of purchase. Greene purchased the bonds for $94,000 including $2,400 of brokerage costs. Greene Company intends to hold the bonds for a short period of time and will include the investment as its only item in the trading securities portfolio. The company has not previously had a trading securities portfolio. Assume that on December 31, 2005, the fair market value of the bonds was $98,000.

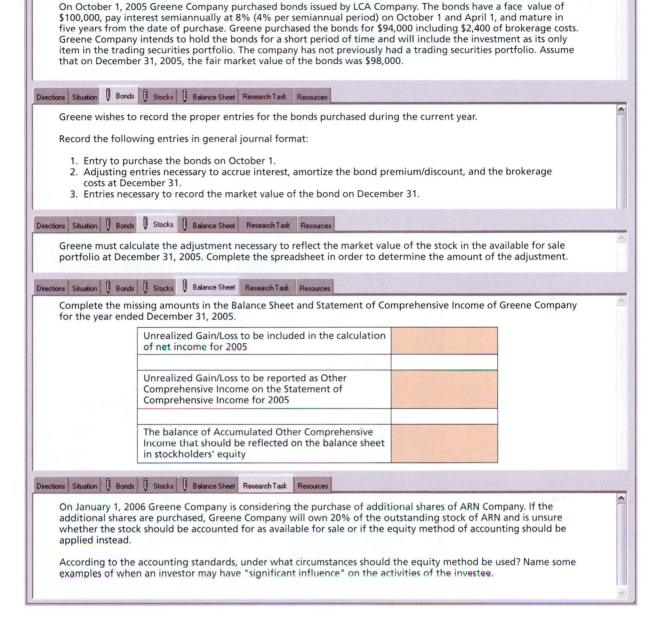

Directions | Situation | Bonds | Stocks | Balance Sheet | Research Task | Resources

Greene wishes to record the proper entries for the bonds purchased during the current year.

Record the following entries in general journal format:

1. Entry to purchase the bonds on October 1.
2. Adjusting entries necessary to accrue interest, amortize the bond premium/discount, and the brokerage costs at December 31.
3. Entries necessary to record the market value of the bond on December 31.

Directions | Situation | Bonds | Stocks | Balance Sheet | Research Task | Resources

Greene must calculate the adjustment necessary to reflect the market value of the stock in the available for sale portfolio at December 31, 2005. Complete the spreadsheet in order to determine the amount of the adjustment.

Directions | Situation | Bonds | Stocks | Balance Sheet | Research Task | Resources

Complete the missing amounts in the Balance Sheet and Statement of Comprehensive Income of Greene Company for the year ended December 31, 2005.

Unrealized Gain/Loss to be included in the calculation of net income for 2005	
Unrealized Gain/Loss to be reported as Other Comprehensive Income on the Statement of Comprehensive Income for 2005	
The balance of Accumulated Other Comprehensive Income that should be reflected on the balance sheet in stockholders' equity	

Directions | Situation | Bonds | Stocks | Balance Sheet | Research Task | Resources

On January 1, 2006 Greene Company is considering the purchase of additional shares of ARN Company. If the additional shares are purchased, Greene Company will own 20% of the outstanding stock of ARN and is unsure whether the stock should be accounted for as available for sale or if the equity method of accounting should be applied instead.

According to the accounting standards, under what circumstances should the equity method be used? Name some examples of when an investor may have "significant influence" on the activities of the investee.

CHAPTER TWELVE

Current Liabilities and Contingencies

FINANCIAL REPORTING CASE

FIRESTONE TIRE RECALL AFFECTS FORD'S CONTINGENT LIABILITIES

CEO Bill Ford was forced to disclose contingent liabilities associated with pending litigation against the Ford Motor Company.

Ford Ford Motor Company, one of the world's leading automobile manufacturers since the early 1900s, experienced a major bump in the road in the winter of 2000. A recall of Firestone tires, used as original equipment on the Ford Explorer, led to a significant number of personal injury and class action lawsuits against the company. Claims resulting from Explorer rollovers climbed to approximately $590 million, and additional litigation was expected from consumers demanding replacement of faulty Firestone tires.[1]

Ford's accounting professionals were required to examine the potential liabilities that might arise from these lawsuits and determine what amounts or disclosures

---

1 Anita Kumar, "Companies Warming to Settlements," *St. Petersburg Times*, May 20, 2001.

Ford

NOTE 16. Litigation and Claims

Various legal actions, governmental investigations and proceedings and claims are pending or may be instituted or asserted in the future against the Company and its subsidiaries, including those arising out of alleged defects in the Company's products; governmental regulations relating to safety, emissions and fuel economy; financial services; employment-related matters; dealer, supplier and other contractual relationships; intellectual property rights; product warranties; and environmental matters. Certain of the pending legal actions are, or purport to be, class actions. Some of the foregoing matters involve or may involve compensatory, punitive, or antitrust or other treble damage claims in very large amounts, or demands for recall campaigns, environmental remediation programs, sanctions, or other relief which, if granted, would require very large expenditures.

Litigation is subject to many uncertainties, and the outcome of individual litigated matters is not predictable with assurance. Reserves have been established by the Company for certain of the matters discussed in the foregoing paragraph where losses are deemed probable. It is reasonably possible, however, that some of the matters discussed in the foregoing paragraph for which reserves have not been established could be decided unfavorably to the Company or the subsidiary involved and could require the Company or such subsidiary to pay damages or make other expenditures in amounts or a range of amounts that cannot be estimated at December 31, 2000. The Company does not reasonably expect, based on its analysis, that such matters would have a material effect on future consolidated financial statements for a particular year, although such an outcome is possible.

should be noted within the company's financial statements. While these lawsuits were filed in 2000, the outcome would not be determined until 2001, creating potential liabilities, or *contingencies*, for which Ford might be responsible.

In addition, the company faced lawsuits filed by angry shareholders, who claimed that Ford had breached its fiduciary duties by failing to detect problems with the Firestone tires and with the stability of the Ford Explorer. The plaintiffs also claimed that they had purchased Ford stock at inflated prices based on Ford's misrepresentations and had been damaged when the price of the stock fell upon announcement of the tire recall.

The disclosure addressing the possibility of large expenditures related to these lawsuits appeared in Ford's 2000 annual report and is presented above.

An understanding of contingent liabilities is critical to accurate analysis of the current and future financial health of a company. Investors and analysts depend on accurate representation of a company's potential debts as they make investment decisions.

EXAMINING THE CASE

1. What events in 2000 required Ford to determine whether contingent liabilities should be recorded?

2. Based on the information in Note 16, was Ford able to estimate potential damages resulting from the lawsuits at year end?

3. How do you think the disclosure Ford made in Note 16 serves the interest of the company and the potential investor?

Current Liabilities

I f you have ever borrowed money from a friend or colleague and repaid the loan in a short period of time, then you have settled a current liability in your personal finances. As you recall from Chapter 1, **liabilities** are the economic obligations of a firm—the probable future sacrifices of economic benefits arising from present obligations of a particular entity to transfer assets or perform services to other entities in the future as a result of past transactions or events.

In a classified balance sheet, liabilities are classified as current or long-term. Current liabilities are the focus of this chapter; long-term liabilities will be covered in Chapters 13, 14, and 15.

liabilities the economic obligations of a firm; probable future sacrifices of economic benefits arising from present obligations of a particular entity to transfer assets or perform services to other entities in the future as a result of past transactions or events

LO1 Define current liabilities and identify common current liability accounts.

current liabilities economic obligations that are expected to be liquidated using current assets or refinanced by other current liabilities during the normal operating cycle or within one year of the balance sheet date, whichever is longer

 Critical Thinking: Why is it important to differentiate between long-term and current liabilities?

CHARACTERISTICS OF CURRENT LIABILITIES

All companies that present a classified balance sheet are required to provide a category for current liabilities. As defined in Chapter 1, **current liabilities** are economic obligations of a firm that are expected to be liquidated using current assets or refinanced by other current liabilities during the normal operating cycle or within one year of the balance sheet date, whichever is longer.[2] Note that the definition of a current liability is quite precise. It is not sufficient that a liability be due within one year. The liability must be expected to be retired by using a current asset (or by the incurrence of a current liability). Common current liabilities include accounts payable, notes payable within one year, dividends payable, advances from customers or collections received in advance, and accruals for items such as wages, salaries, commissions, rents, royalties, and other expenses.

Johnson Controls, Inc., an automotive industry supplier to Ford, presents a breakdown of current liabilities in Figure 12.1.

For most companies, the accounts payable category is the most substantial current liability. Johnson Controls is no exception, reporting $3,329.3 million in accounts payable at September 30, 2003, almost 60 percent of total current liabilities. The issues related to accounts payable have been discussed in Chapters 1 and 4 of the text. The remainder of this chapter concentrates on current liabilities for which particular accounting issues are evident.

INTERNATIONAL

The definition of current liabilities in international accounting standards is similar to that used in U.S. standards, with subtle differences. Until recently, international standards did not define current liabilities in conceptual terms, but instead listed the accounts or items that should be classified as current liabilities. In most cases, this approach led to the same result as U.S. standards. However, a recent revision of the international accounting standards should remove any remaining differences and result in uniformity between international and U.S. standards.[3] As a result, it is likely that the items listed as current liabilities on the balance sheets of U.S. companies will be the same as those listed by other companies.

LO2 Describe how to account for current liability accruals.

Critical Thinking: Why do you think it is important to record an expense that has been incurred but not yet paid?

ACCRUED LIABILITIES

Many of the current liabilities that appear on financial statements are the result of the accrual accounting process. As you recall from Chapter 1, the accrual accounting method requires the recording of adjustments to match expenses to revenue for the

---

2 "Restatement and Revision of Accounting Research Bulletins," *Accounting Research Bulletin No. 43* (New York: AICPA, 1953), Chap. 3, Sec. A.

3 "IASC-US Comparison Project" (Stamford, Conn.: FASB, 1996), p. 217.

Figure 12.1

Note on Current Liabilities—
Johnson Controls, Inc.

Johnson Controls

(In millions)	September 30,	
	2003	**2002**
Short-term debt	$ 150.5	$ 105.3
Current portion of long-term debt	427.8	39.9
Accounts payable	3,329.3	2,789.1
Accrued compensation and benefits	546.3	506.6
Accrued income taxes	58.7	182.7
Billings in excess of costs and earnings on uncompleted contracts	186.2	190.8
Other current liabilities	885.3	991.8
Current liabilities	$5,584.1	$4,806.2

period. Adjustments involving current liabilities can be included in one of two general categories:

1. To record expenses that have been incurred but have not yet been paid (accruals)

2. To adjust for amounts that have been previously received but have not been earned as of the end of the accounting period (deferrals)

accrued liabilities expenses that have been incurred but not yet paid

Accrued liabilities are expenses that have been incurred but not yet paid. Examples include salaries, interest, and income taxes. To record the accrual of these expenses, debit the appropriate expense account and credit the related payable account as follows:

Expense	xxx	
Payable		xxx

To illustrate, assume that a company's employees work during the last week of the fiscal year, but checks are not prepared and distributed until the following week. In this case, it is necessary to record a debit to Salaries Expense and a credit to Salaries Payable for the amount of one week's payroll. The payable recorded is a current liability, since the amount is to be paid within a week of the balance sheet date. As a general rule, most current liabilities are expected to be paid within one year of the balance sheet date.

Ford Motor Company included accrued liabilities totaling $32,171 million on its December 31, 2003 balance sheet. A breakdown of these accrued liabilities, taken from notes that accompany Ford's 2003 financial statements, is presented in Figure 12.2.

Figure 12.2

Note on Accrued Liabilities—
Ford Motor Company

Ford

Included in accrued liabilities at December 31 were the following (in millions):

	2003	2002
Accrued Liabilities (current):		
Dealer and customer allowances and claims	$ 16,098	$ 14,165
Deferred income taxes	2,996	2,614
Deferred revenue	2,587	2,423
Accrued interest	1,814	1,705
Employee benefit plans	1,732	1,360
Postretirement benefits other than pensions	1,397	1,302
Other	5,547	4,046
Total accrued liabilities	$ 32,171	$ 27,615

LO3 Describe how to account for current liability deferrals.

Critical Thinking: Can you identify situations in which a company should defer the recognition of revenues that it has received?

LIABILITIES FROM ADVANCE COLLECTIONS

In some cases, current liabilities involve amounts that have been received in advance and have not been earned as of year end. Advances from customers and refundable deposits are examples of such transactions. As indicated in Chapter 1, these amounts may be referred to as unearned income or deferrals.

Note the line item "Deferred revenue" in Figure 12.2. Deferred revenue arises from situations in which cash has been *received* in advance but *has not been earned*. Technically, this item is not an accrued liability, although Ford lists its deferred revenues as such. Statement readers should be careful to note the distinction between accrued liabilities and deferred revenue.

When advance payments are received, the transaction is recorded as follows:

| Cash | xxx | |
| Deferred Revenue (or Unearned Income) | | xxx |

At year end, it is necessary to record an adjusting entry for the amount earned during the period as follows:

| Deferred Revenue | xxx | |
| Income or Revenue | | xxx |

The balance of the Deferred Revenue account is generally presented as a current liability because it represents an amount that will be earned within one year of the balance sheet date.

LO4 Determine the liability for compensated employee absences.

Critical Thinking: As an employee, imagine that you have accrued 10 vacation days that you have not yet taken at year end. If you were to leave the company, you would be paid for any vacation days not taken. Why do you think your employer should account for this vacation pay owed to you?

compensated absences items such as vacation and sick pay that are expected to be paid out in future periods

vested benefits amounts that must be paid to an employee even if the company terminates the employment

EMPLOYEE-RELATED LIABILITIES

Unpaid employee compensation such as wages and salaries; payroll deductions for taxes, insurance premiums, or union dues; and bonuses are types of expenses that are often classified as current liabilities. These amounts are owed to employees or other entities as of the balance sheet date, but have not yet been paid. An accrual of wages or salaries would be reflected as a current liability, generally in a Salaries Payable or Wages Payable account. In addition, the company must consider whether an amount must be accrued for what are referred to as compensated absences.

COMPENSATED ABSENCES

Compensated absences are items such as vacation and sick pay that are expected to be paid out in future periods.[4] Compensated absences do not include pension costs or postretirement expenses because these items are covered by other accounting pronouncements. An employer *must* accrue a liability for compensated absences if *all* of the following conditions are met:[5]

1. The employee has already rendered the service required to earn the rights or benefits.

2. The obligation relates to rights that *accumulate* or *vest*. **Vested benefits** are amounts that must be paid to an employee even if the company terminates the employment. The benefits are not contingent on the employee's continuing to work for the company. For example, most companies allow employees to earn

4 "Accounting for Compensated Absences," *Statement of Financial Accounting Standards No. 43* (Stamford, Conn.: FASB, 1980), par. 1.

5 Ibid., par. 6.

accumulated rights unused rights that are carried over to a future period and can be used in a period subsequent to the period in which they were earned

vacation days and will pay them for those days even if they leave the company. **Accumulated rights** are unused rights that are carried over to a future period and can be used in a period subsequent to the period in which they were earned. Even when the company limits the amount that can be carried over to a future period, the rights are deemed to accumulate. For example, a company may allow an employee to earn 10 days of vacation pay per year. The employee may carry vacation days over to future periods until a maximum of 30 days has accumulated.

3. Payment of the compensation is probable.

4. The amount of the liability can be reasonably estimated.

❱ CALCULATING VACATION PAY ACCRUALS Assume that Nichols Company has 50 employees during 2005, and each employee earns 10 days of vacation pay per year. In estimating the amount of the liability, it is necessary to determine the applicable salary rate. Because the salary rate for future time periods is usually not known, the current year's salary rate must generally be used. Assume that each employee's salary rate during 2005 is $100 per day and that vacation days can accumulate and be used in future years. Nichols Company should accrue vacation pay at the 2005 year end with the following entry:

Payroll Expense (50 × 10 × $100)	50,000	
Vacation Payable		50,000

Assume that 10 of the employees use all of their vacation days in 2005. When they are paid their vacation pay, the following entry should be recorded:

Vacation Payable (10 × 10 × $100)	10,000	
Cash		10,000

Assume that the other 40 employees use all of their vacation days in 2006, when the salary rate is $105 per day. The following entry should be recorded when the vacation is taken by the employees:

Vacation Payable (40 × 10 × $100)	40,000	
Payroll Expense (40 × 10 × $5)	2,000	
Cash (40 × 10 × $105)		42,000

Note that the requirement that the company accrue for compensated absences introduces additional complexity into the payroll accounting system because the system requires determination of the amount of rights earned in previous periods and the rate at which rights were accrued during those periods.

❱ CALCULATING SICK PAY ACCRUALS The conditions for accrual of *sick pay* differ from those for accrual of pay for other compensated absences. If sick pay *vests* (the employee can be paid for unused days when he or she leaves the company), then the sick pay must be accrued. However, if the sick pay does not vest, the company is not required to accrue an amount as a current liability.[6] This difference exists because there is a conceptual difference between vacation pay and sick pay. Vacation pay is earned as the result of past service and should therefore be accrued. Sick pay, on the other hand, is dependent on the occurrence of a future event (the sickness) and therefore does not meet the accounting definition of a liability until the employee actually takes the sick days.

---

6 Ibid., par. 15.

LO5 Determine the proper classification for obligations that are expected to be refinanced.

obligations expected to be refinanced loans or obligations that are due within a year but that may not be paid off with current assets when they become due

Critical Thinking: Why do you think a company might prefer to classify debt as long-term, if possible, rather than short-term on its balance sheet?

SHORT-TERM OBLIGATIONS TO BE REFINANCED

Many companies carry loans or obligations that are due within a year but that may not be paid off with current assets when they become due. These loans are referred to as **obligations expected to be refinanced**. For example, a company may have a loan that is due within one year of the balance sheet date, but the loan is part of a *revolving credit* arrangement with the bank, under which the company has the ability to *refinance* the obligation when it becomes due. Should this loan be considered a current liability or a long-term liability? The answer to this question depends on the specific loan agreement. Under some agreements, accountants must view the sequence of events *after* the balance sheet date (but before the financial statements are issued) to determine the proper classification.

In general, most companies prefer not to treat these obligations as current liabilities because treating them as long-term liabilities results in a more favorable current ratio and amount of working capital, and thus a more favorable view of their liquidity. Authoritative guidance on this classification issue dictates that a short-term obligation that is expected to be refinanced can be excluded from the current liability category only in cases where the company has demonstrated the *intent* and the *ability* to refinance the obligation.[7]

DEMONSTRATING THE ABILITY TO REFINANCE

There are several ways in which a company may demonstrate its ability to refinance the obligation.

1. *Post–balance sheet issuance of a long-term obligation or equity securities.* After the balance sheet date, but before the financial statements are issued, a company may issue either another obligation or stock to replace the existing loan. This action demonstrates the ability to refinance.

2. *A financing agreement.* If a company has signed a financing agreement before the balance sheet date that clearly permits the refinancing of the existing short-term obligation, it can be used to demonstrate the intent to refinance, provided that all terms are readily determinable, there are no violations of the existing agreement, and both parties are financially capable of honoring the agreement.

If the ability to refinance is demonstrated by an actual refinancing after the balance sheet date (the first criterion just given), then the accountant should be aware of two additional guidelines. First, the amount of the obligation that is excluded from the current liabilities category of the balance sheet cannot exceed the actual amount of the refinancing. If the actual refinancing is less than the amount of the obligation that exists at the balance sheet date, then a portion of the actual obligation must be reported in the current liabilities category. Second, the funds from the refinancing must be available for the repayment of the short-term loan that exists at the balance sheet date. Thus, the refinancing must occur on a date *prior* to the due date of the existing loan. If the refinancing occurs after the due date of the existing loan (even by a few days), then clearly other funds were used to repay the short-term loan, and so the loan must be classified as a current liability on the balance sheet. We will illustrate the issues concerning short-term obligations with two examples.

EXAMPLE 1—A FINANCING AGREEMENT Assume that Diem Company has a loan of $1 million with First National Bank due on February 1, 2006. The company does not intend to repay the loan at that date, and on December 15, 2005, it enters into a refinancing agreement with First National Bank for a long-term refinancing of the $1 million. Also assume that there are no violations of the loan as of the balance sheet date

7 "Classification of Short-Term Obligations Expected to be Refinanced," *Statement of Financial Accounting Standards No. 6* (Stamford, Conn.: FASB, 1975), par. 10.

and that both parties have the ability to honor the refinancing agreement. Since Diem has signed a refinancing agreement before the balance sheet date, the company should present the following amounts on the balance sheet:

Diem Company Partial Balance Sheet December 31, 2005		
Current liabilities	$	0
Long-term liabilities		
Loan from First National		1,000,000

The notes to the financial statements should include a general description of the present loan agreement and the terms of the refinancing agreement of December 15, 2005.

If the refinancing agreement of December 15, 2005, had been for less than the existing loan amount, then a portion of the original loan would have to be shown as a current liability. For example, assume all of the facts in the previous example except that the refinancing agreement of December 15, 2005, was for $800,000. In that case, Diem should present the following amounts on the balance sheet:

Diem Company Partial Balance Sheet December 31, 2005		
Current liabilities		
Loan from First National	$200,000	
Long-term liabilities		
Loan from First National		800,000

❭ **EXAMPLE 2—ACTUAL REFINANCING**   Assume that Piet Company wishes to prepare a balance sheet at December 31, 2005. Because of the time involved in closing the books, obtaining an audit, and printing the report, the financial statements will be issued on March 1, 2006. As of December 31, 2005, the company has a loan of $1 million with Second National Bank due on February 1, 2006. On January 15, 2006, the company issued $1 million of stock at par value and used the proceeds to repay the loan. Since the company demonstrated the ability to refinance by issuing equity securities before the financial statements were issued, Piet should present the following amounts on its balance sheet:

Piet Company Partial Balance Sheet December 31, 2005		
Current liabilities	$	0
Long-term liabilities		
Loan from Second National		1,000,000

Since stock was issued to replace the loan from Second National, why was the loan presented as a liability at all? Remember that *as of the balance sheet date,* the amount in question was, in fact, a liability. After the balance sheet date, it was replaced by equity (stock). We have used that information to classify the loan as a long-term liability rather than a current liability. On the following year's balance sheet, at December 31, 2006, no liability will appear and the amount will be included in the stockholders' equity category. The notes to the financial statement of December 31, 2005, should indicate the terms of the loan agreement and the fact that the loan was repaid by the issuance of stock.

As in Example 1, if the amount of stock issued had been less than the amount needed to repay the loan, the difference would be reported as a current liability. Furthermore, the issuance of the stock must occur prior to the due date of the loan in order for any amount to be excluded from the current liability category. For example, assume in Example 2 that the stock had been issued on February 3, 2006. In that case, the entire amount of the loan to Second National Bank must be presented as a current liability on the balance sheet of December 31, 2005.

CHECK YOUR UNDERSTANDING

1. Describe the difference between an accrual and a deferral.

2. What journal entry is generally made when cash is received in advance but has not yet been earned?

3. Why do companies accrue current liabilities for vacation pay but not for sick pay that does not vest?

4. When a company carries a loan that it expects to refinance, how does it demonstrate the ability to refinance?

LO6 **Identify the proper accounting treatment for contingencies.**

contingency an existing condition, situation, or set of circumstances involving uncertainty that will be resolved when one or more future events occur

Critical Thinking: Do you think it is reasonable to expect companies to report on events that "might" occur in the future that would affect their financial standing? Explain potential criteria that you think should be considered.

Contingencies

One of the most difficult and controversial areas of accounting concerns whether a liability should be accrued for an uncertain, or contingent, item. A **contingency** is defined as an existing condition, situation, or set of circumstances involving uncertainty that will be resolved when one or more future events occur.[8] Thus, there are two important elements to the definition of a contingency:

1. As of the balance sheet date, an event must have occurred or a condition must be in existence.

2. The outcome of that event or condition must be dependent upon (or be contingent on) a future event.

A common example of a contingency is a lawsuit that has been filed but has not been settled as of the balance sheet date. The event that led to the lawsuit has already occurred, but the outcome is dependent upon a future event, who prevails in the lawsuit. Additional examples of contingencies include:

- Collectibility of receivables

- Obligations for product warranties or guarantees

- Threat of expropriation (takeover by a foreign government) of assets

- Pending or threatened litigation

- Guarantees of the indebtedness of others

- Actual or possible assessments or claims

---

8 "Accounting for Contingencies," *Statement of Financial Accounting Standards No. 5* (Stamford, Conn.: FASB, 1975), par. 1.

Figure 12.3

Note on Environmental Litigation—Johnson Controls

Johnson Controls

ENVIRONMENTAL LITIGATION AND PROCEEDINGS

The Company is involved in a number of proceedings relating to environmental matters. At September 30, 2003, the Company had an accrued liability of approximately $62 million relating to environmental matters compared with $32 million one year ago. The increase involves environmental matters related to the Varta acquisition. The Company's environmental liabilities do not take into consideration any possible recoveries of future insurance proceeds. Because of the uncertainties associated with environmental remediation activities, the Company's future expenses to remediate the currently identified sites could be considerably higher than the accrued liability. Although it is difficult to estimate the liability of the Company related to these environmental matters, the Company believes that these matters will not have a materially adverse effect upon its capital expenditures, earnings or competitive position.

When a contingency exists, the company must decide whether an amount should be recognized as a liability. Because of the conservative nature of accounting, the decision is influenced in part by whether the item in question is a loss contingency (contingent liability) or a gain contingency (contingent asset).

LOSS CONTINGENCIES

loss contingencies existing circumstances involving a potential loss that hinges on some future event

Loss contingencies are existing circumstances involving a potential loss that hinges on some future event. If a contingent item both is a loss contingency and is material, the amount of the loss should be accrued as a liability if *both* of the following conditions are met:

1. The loss is *probable*.

2. The amount of the loss can be *reasonably estimated*.

probable a future event or events are likely to occur

reasonably estimated using a professional judgment and taking reasonable steps to make estimates

The accounting guidelines do not require that the loss be a virtual certainty, but they do require that the loss be probable. The meaning of the term **probable** is subject to interpretation but implies "that [the] future event or events are likely to occur."[9] The meaning of **reasonably estimated** is also subject to interpretation. Often the amounts that will result from a future event (for example, the outcome of a lawsuit) are quite uncertain. But the guidelines clearly require accountants to exercise their professional judgment and take all "reasonable" steps to estimate an amount.

In some cases, it is difficult to specify an exact amount for the outcome of a future event, but a range of values may be determined. For example, it may be possible to estimate that a company stands to lose between $2 and $5 million as the result of a lawsuit. In this case, the accounting guidelines indicate that if the loss is probable and if all amounts within the range are equally likely, then the minimum value in the range should be accrued. The maximum value in the range should be disclosed in the notes to the financial statements.

Issues surrounding environmental damage are increasingly important to consider when assessing contingent liabilities. Figure 12.3 provides a portion of the note for Johnson Controls, a supplier to the auto industry. As you can see, the company has accrued liabilities related to environmental matters that are almost double the amount in the previous year.

In actual practice, companies are reluctant to accrue contingent liabilities, either because they consider the outcome of the event in question to be less than probable or

---

9 Ibid., par. 3.

Figure 12.4

Note on Contingent Liabilities—General Motors

> ## *General Motors*
>
> Litigation is subject to uncertainties and the outcome of individual litigated matters is not predictable with assurance. Various legal actions, governmental investigations, claims, and proceedings are pending against the Corporation, including those arising out of alleged product defects; employment-related matters; governmental regulations relating to safety, emissions, and fuel economy; product warranties; financial services; dealer, supplier, and other contractual relationships; and environmental matters. GM has established reserves for matters in which losses are probable and can be reasonably estimated. Some of the matters may involve compensatory, punitive, or other treble damage claims, or demands for recall campaigns, environmental remediation programs, or sanctions, that if granted, could require the Corporation to pay damages or make other expenditures in amounts that could not be estimated at December 31, 2003. After discussion with counsel, it is the opinion of management that such liability is not expected to have a material adverse effect on the Corporation's consolidated financial condition or results of operations.

because they claim that the amount cannot be reasonably estimated. Companies may be particularly hesitant to accrue a liability related to the outcome of a lawsuit or legal proceeding because it might be viewed as an admission of guilt or an acknowledgement that a liability does, in fact, exist. While that reluctance is understandable, the accounting guidelines clearly require accrual when a loss contingency is probable and can be reasonably estimated.

❱ DISCLOSURE OF LOSS CONTINGENCIES

❱ **PROBABLE**   When a contingent loss is probable and can be reasonably estimated, it should be accrued as a liability, and note disclosures should accompany the financial statements. Additionally, note disclosures should be provided in some cases even when the outcome is not considered probable.

❱ **REASONABLY POSSIBLE**   When the outcome of the loss contingency is deemed to be reasonably possible, the item should not be accrued as a liability but should be disclosed in the notes to the financial statements. The term **reasonably possible** indicates that "the chance of the future event occurring is more than remote but less than likely."[10] The note disclosure should include a description of the nature of the contingency and should include an estimate of the amount of the possible loss or range of loss.

reasonably possible the chance of the future event occurring is more than remote but less than likely

Just as Ford Motor disclosed contingent liabilities in regard to lawsuits as discussed in the Financial Reporting Case at the beginning of this chapter, nearly all major corporations are vulnerable to similar litigation and must therefore account for such potential liabilities. Figure 12.4 provides a portion of the note presented in **General Motors**'s 2003 annual report regarding contingent lawsuits for product liabilities and other legal matters.

❱ **REMOTE**   When the likelihood of a loss from a contingency is deemed to be **remote**, or the chance of future events occurring is slight, a company is not required to accrue a liability and in most cases is not required to disclose such events in the notes to the financial statements.

remote the chance of future events occurring is slight

In particular, the accounting guidelines do not require the disclosure of *unasserted* claims or assessments. For example, a company is normally not required to disclose a

10 Ibid.

lawsuit that *may* be filed or a governmental fine that *may* be assessed. Additionally, the guidelines indicate that it is normally not good practice to disclose general or unspecified business risks. In the past, some companies have disclosed an amount (or even recorded a liability) that has been reserved for contingencies or unexplained future events. While companies are free to disclose whatever information they deem appropriate, such disclosures are not required by the accounting guidelines.

On the other hand, some disclosures are required even when the likelihood of loss is deemed to be remote. Most notably, companies should present note disclosures regarding guarantees of the indebtedness of others. Consider a situation in which one party co-signs a loan for another party. Guarantees can arise in other ways, with one party assuming the liability if another party fails to perform its obligation. Even when the risk of loss is remote, the guarantor should disclose the nature of the agreement and the amount of the possible loss.

LO7 Determine the appropriate accounting treatment for warranties as contingent liabilities.

warranty an implied or expressed promise by the seller to compensate the buyer for a deficiency in the product

Critical Thinking: *If you purchase a car with a three-year warranty, do you think the seller should account for the possibility that you will have repair work done under warranty in the future? Explain your reasoning.*

❱ WARRANTIES

The vast majority of products sold in our economy carry a warranty or guarantee. A **warranty** is an implied or expressed promise by the seller to compensate the buyer for a deficiency in the product. In most cases, the warranty involves a promise to replace or repair the product if it is found to be deficient. In other cases, the warranty may involve a promise to pay a certain dollar amount if the product is deficient. A warranty is an important aspect of the purchase decision for many buyers and is often included in the price of the product. Automakers often tout their warranty as an important reason to purchase their auto rather than the auto of a competitor. A warranty is also extremely important for many other products ranging from computers to appliances.

A warranty represents a specific type of contingent liability in which the seller has made a promise and a liability has been incurred as a result of that promise. If the amount of the liability can be reasonably estimated at the time of the sale, then the amount meets the definition of a liability and should be recognized and reported as follows:

- The portion of the liability that is expected to be paid within one year of the balance sheet date should be included in the current liabilities category.

- The remainder should be included as a long-term liability.

- When the credit entry is made to record the liability, the debit is normally made to an expense account.

Thus, accounting for warranties can be viewed as an application of the matching principle. The expense must be accrued so that the expense related to the sale is recognized in the same period as the revenue.

To illustrate, assume that BigCar Company sells 100 cars for $30,000 each during 2005. Each car has a warranty that covers repairs for the first three years or 36,000 miles. Based on the past history of repairs, the company estimates that repairs are 2 percent of sales. BigCar should record warranty costs of $60,000 ($3,000,000 × 0.02) during 2005 with the following entry:

Warranty Expense	60,000	
Warranty Liability		60,000

Assume that during 2005, repair costs applicable to current-year sales were $26,000. The repair costs should be recorded as follows:

Warranty Liability	26,000	
Cash, Parts Inventory, or Accounts Payable		26,000

At December 31, 2005, the balance of the Warranty Liability account appears as shown on the following page.

Warranty Liability

	0	beg. bal.
	60,000	
26,000		
	34,000	**end. bal.**

→ Current $17,000

→ Long-term $17,000

As indicated by the T-account, one-half of the balance at December 31, 2005, should be considered a current liability and the other half should be treated as a long-term liability.

A review of the 2003 financial statements and notes for General Motors reveals that warranty costs make up a significant portion of the company's current liabilities. As of December 31, 2003, the company reported $8,674 million for policy, product warranty, and recall campaigns liability. Figure 12.5 provides a portion of the note related to these warranty liabilities.

It is important to note that whereas generally accepted accounting principles *require the accrual* of warranty costs, income tax rules do not allow for the same procedure. For income tax purposes, companies *are not allowed to accrue* warranty costs as an expense in the period of the sale. In other words, warranty costs cannot be taken as an income tax deduction until the costs are actually incurred or paid. Income tax rules require a form of cash-basis recording of warranty costs. The difference between financial accounting and income tax accounting for warranty costs results in an amount that must be recognized as deferred income tax. Refer to Chapter 16 for more on this issue.

❯ **WARRANTIES SOLD FOR CASH** As previously discussed, many product warranties are included in the purchase price of a new product. For example, when a new car is purchased, a standard warranty is often included in the purchase price. However, in some cases, a warranty is sold separately from the product, and a distinct cash amount is received for the warranty. For example, in addition to the basic three-year and 36,000-mile warranty available on many new autos, most dealers offer an *extended warranty* for an additional price. This extended warranty may begin after the basic warranty expires or may cover repair costs that are excluded from the basic warranty. Extended warranties are also commonly available for computer equipment and other technology products.

Figure 12.5

Note on Warranty Liability— General Motors

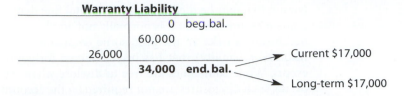

General Motors

	December 31,	
	2003	**2002**
Policy, product warranty and recall campaigns liability:		
Beginning balance	$8,850	$8,171
Payments	(4,435)	(4,182)
Increase in liability (warranties issued during period)	4,390	4,418
Adjustments to liability (pre-existing warranties)	(367)	323
Effect of foreign currency translation	236	120
Ending balance	$8,674	$8,850

Product-Related Expense

Provisions for estimated expenses related to product warranties are made at the time products are sold. These estimates are established using historical information on the nature, frequency, and average cost of warranty claims. Management actively studies trends of warranty claims and takes action to improve vehicle quality and minimize warranty claims.

When cash is received for an extended warranty, the amount should be deferred and recorded as revenue over the warranty period. Normally, the revenue should be recorded in a straight-line manner. For example, assume that BigCar Company sold 50 extended warranties in 2005 for $1,000 each. The extended warranty covers repair costs for two years after the basic three-year and 36,000-mile warranty has expired. During 2005, BigCar should record the sale of the warranties as follows:

Cash	50,000	
Extended Warranty Liability		50,000

At December 31, 2005, the Extended Warranty Liability account should be treated as a long-term liability on the balance sheet. Assume that in 2008, $20,000 of repair costs were incurred that were covered by the extended warranty agreements. The company should record the expense as follows:

Warranty Expense	20,000	
Cash, Parts Inventory, or Accounts Payable		20,000

One-half of the extended warranty amount should also be recorded as revenue on December 31, 2008:

Extended Warranty Liability ($50,000 $\times$ $\frac{1}{2}$)	25,000	
Warranty Revenue		25,000

Revenue generated from the sale of warranties may be of particular interest to financial statement users. In many cases, these sales provide a significant profit margin; they may even carry a higher profit margin than the sale of the product itself.

❯ PREMIUM OR COUPON OFFERS

Although warranties are prominent examples of contingent liabilities, premium or coupon offers also represent the creation of a contingent liability. For example, assume that ComputCo sells new computers and the sale price includes a coupon that allows the customer to buy certain software for the next year at 50 percent off the regular price. A contingent liability has been created because ComputCo has an obligation to sell software to the customer at less than the established price. At the end of each year, the company should develop an estimate of the number of coupons that will be redeemed and the cost of the software that will be sold. At year end, the company should record the following entry:

Expense for Coupons to Be Redeemed	xxx	
Estimated Liability for Coupons		xxx

Recording this contingent liability adheres to the matching principle, since the expense should be recorded in the period in which the sale occurs rather than the period in which the coupons are redeemed.

Another common example of a contingent liability occurs when airlines offer their customers frequent-flyer miles that may be redeemed for airline tickets in the future. A contingent liability must be recorded for the estimated cost of the airline tickets that will be redeemed in future periods.

GAIN CONTINGENCIES

gain contingencies uncertain situations that may result in a claim to an asset or a reduction in a liability

Accounting for gain contingencies is markedly different from that for loss contingencies. In general, **gain contingencies** are uncertain situations that may result in a claim to an asset or a reduction in a liability. They should not be recorded, because "to do

Illustration 12.1

Accounting Treatments for Contingencies

Contingency	Accounting Treatment
Liabilities/Losses	
If loss is probable, can be reasonably estimated, and is material in amount	• Record as liability and as a loss • Provide additional information in the notes
If loss is reasonably possible and is material in amount	• Do not record as liability or as a loss • Provide disclosure in the notes
If probability of loss is remote	• Do not record as liability or as a loss • Disclosure in the notes is not required
Assets/Gains	• Normally should not be recorded until the gain is received

so might be to recognize revenue prior to its realization."[11] This is an example of the conservatism principle evident in accounting. Loss contingencies are recorded in some cases, but gain contingencies are seldom recorded until they are realized. This practice of conservatism may cause difficulties in reporting. For example, refer to Figure 12.3. The Johnson Controls note indicates that a loss contingency for possible future environmental costs was accrued and recorded. It also indicates that potential liabilities accrued by the company "do not take into consideration possible recoveries of future insurance proceeds" because the insurance proceeds represent a gain contingency. Many accounting professionals feel that the restriction against recording the offsetting gain contingency results in an overstatement of the contingent liability and a presentation that is "overly conservative."

In this section, we have discussed the accounting for contingent losses and gains. Illustration 12.1 summarizes the proper accounting for contingencies.

CONTINGENT LIABILITIES—INTERNATIONAL DIFFERENCES

INTERNATIONAL

International accounting standards regarding contingent liabilities (*IAS 10* and *IAS 37*) are similar to U.S. standards (*SFAS No. 5*), but there are important differences. *IAS 37* holds that "provisions" should be recognized when:

> An enterprise has a present obligation (legal or constructive) as a result of a past event; it is probable (i.e. more likely than not) that an outflow of resources embodying economic benefits will be required to settle the obligation; and a reliable estimate can be made of the amount of the obligation.[12]

Although international standards use the same criteria of "probable" and "reasonably estimable," there are differences in the interpretation and application of the standards. First, international standards are less explicit about the meaning of the term *probable*. As a result, an enhanced level of judgment is involved in making the decision. Second, international accounting standards permit the *offsetting* of liabilities and assets in determining the amount of loss to be recognized. For example, if a large loss was probable, but it was expected that a portion of the loss would be covered by other sources (such as insurance), under international standards the *net* amount of the loss should be reported. Finally, U.S. standards provide more guidance concerning proper

---

11 Ibid., par. 17.

12 "Provisions, Contingent Liabilities and Contingent Assets," *International Accounting Standard No. 37* (London: IASC, 1998).

disclosure of items that are *not* probable losses (those referred to as reasonably possible). Under U.S. standards, these items are required to be disclosed in the notes.

The differences between accounting standards of specific countries and U.S. standards for contingent liabilities may be even more dramatic and have prompted one observer to note:

> The whole area of provisioning is notably significant, pervasive and lacking in relevant and comprehensive disclosures. In dealing with European companies wishing to register debt and equity securities on the U.S. capital markets, I often find that the most significant reconciling item between local GAAP financial statements and U.S. GAAP financial statements relates to the elimination of provisions allowed under local GAAP but not allowed under (FASB) Statement 5.[13]

CHECK YOUR UNDERSTANDING

1. Describe two important elements that define a contingency.

2. If a contingent loss is probable and can be reasonably estimated, how should it be recorded and disclosed?

3. What entry is generally made to record warranties included in product sales for a fiscal period?

4. How are gain contingencies accounted for?

LO8 Analyze how current liabilities affect the liquidity of a business.

Analysis of Current Liabilities

Current liabilities represent amounts that must be paid within one year (or the current operating cycle) of the balance sheet date. Evaluation of a company's ability to repay these current liabilities as they come due, or its liquidity, is therefore critical.

LIQUIDITY ANALYSIS

working capital a liquidity measurement that indicates the amount of current assets available to continue business operations; current assets minus current liabilities

current ratio a liquidity measurement that is calculated by dividing current assets by current liabilities

As you recall from Chapter 7, liquidity may be measured as the amount of **working capital**, defined as total current assets minus total current liabilities, or the amount of current assets available to continue business operations. Liquidity is more often measured as a financial ratio. The **current ratio**, another liquidity measurement, is calculated by dividing current assets by current liabilities.[14] The current ratio for Johnson Controls at September 30, 2003 and 2002, is provided in Illustration 12.2.

Illustration 12.2

Calculation of the Current Ratio for Johnson Controls

	2003	2002
Current assets (millions)	$5,620	$4,946
Current liabilities (millions)	$5,584	$4,806
Current ratio	1.01 to 1	1.03 to 1

---

13 Unidentified observer as quoted in "IASC-US Comparison Project," p. 179.

14 Ford Motor Company and General Motors do not present a classification of current assets and current liabilities on their financial statements. Thus it is difficult to calculate the current ratio and working capital.

Critical Thinking: *If a company chooses to pay off current liabilities with cash at the end of a fiscal period in an attempt to improve liquidity measurement, would you characterize this action as unethical or as creative financial management? Explain.*

Users of financial statements formerly used a 2-to-1 rule of thumb when evaluating a company's current ratio. That is, a company was deemed to have sufficient liquidity if it held twice as many current assets as current liabilities. This rule of thumb may not always be an accurate standard by which to judge a company's performance. For example, Illustration 12.2 reveals that the September 30, 2003 current ratio for Johnson Controls is 1.01 to 1, well below the 2-to-1 standard. Yet the company is well managed, uses its assets efficiently, and does not require high inventory levels. "Just-in-time" inventory techniques allow companies like Johnson Controls to reduce their inventory levels while still meeting customer demands. Companies with a current ratio that is "too high" may have a good liquidity level, but they may also not be using their current assets wisely. At the same time, it is still necessary use the current ratio to judge liquidity levels and to assess a company's ability to meet its obligations to pay its current liabilities. While the 2-to-1 standard may no longer be valid, the current ratio still provides important information when it is evaluated for a company over time or when one company is evaluated against another company in the same business or industry.

▶ WINDOW DRESSING AND ETHICS

 ETHICS

window dressing inappropriate actions that the management of a company may take at the end of the period to make the company's financial ratios appear more favorable

Because the current ratio is measured at a point in time (the balance sheet date), it is possible to manipulate the appearance of the ratio to a certain extent. The term **window dressing** refers to inappropriate actions that the management of a company may take at the end of the period to make the company's financial ratios appear more favorable than they actually are. In their effort to achieve financial targets, managers may be tempted to use various kinds of window dressing to satisfy the expectations of stockholders and boards of directors. In 2002, the famous investor Warren Buffett commented on the state of business ethics: "Today is significantly different from the 1950s. Back then there was less disclosure, but the disclosure you had was accurate. It's not like today, where too often otherwise high-grade companies start with a number of quarterly earnings and work backward. Situational ethics has reared its ugly head."[15]

To illustrate how companies may manipulate their accounts to present a more favorable picture of their financial condition, assume that Corky Company holds $100 million of current assets and $50 million of current liabilities near the end of a fiscal period. The calculation of working capital results in $50 million. The current ratio is 2 to 1 ($100 million ÷ $50 million). If the company wanted to improve its current ratio, it could simply pay some of its current liabilities with cash before the end of the period. Suppose the company paid $10 million of current liabilities on the last day of the accounting period. Current assets would decline to $90 million and current liabilities to $40 million. The amount of working capital would still be $50 million, but the current ratio would improve to 2.25 to 1 ($90 million ÷ $40 million). Readers of the statements should be vigilant in reviewing end-of-period activities for actions that artificially improve the appearance of liquidity.

Note that the use of window dressing to improve the current ratio is dependent on the level of current assets and current liabilities prior to taking action. In particular, the current ratio must be greater than 1 to 1 prior to the payment of the current liabilities at year end. If the ratio is less than 1 to 1, the opposite effect will occur; the ratio will actually decline as a result of the payment of the current liabilities.

CHECK YOUR UNDERSTANDING

1. How is the current ratio calculated? What does it reveal about a company's financial position?

2. How might a company use a window-dressing strategy to improve its current ratio?

15 "Dirty Rotten Numbers," *Fortune,* February 18, 2002, pp. 74–84.

LO9 Determine how current liabilities affect cash flow.

Critical Thinking: *Why do you think the activity in current liability accounts must be examined to determine cash flow for the period?*

Impact of Current Liabilities on Cash Flow

In most cases, current liabilities are related to the operating activities of the company. On the statement of cash flows, changes in these liabilities should be listed in the operating activities category in order to determine the amount of cash generated from operations. When the indirect method is used to develop the statement of cash flows, increases in current liabilities should appear as positive amounts, or as increases in cash from operating activities. Decreases should appear as negative amounts, or as decreases in cash from operating activities, because cash has been used to reduce the balance of the current liabilities.

Figure 12.6 shows the reconciliation of net income from continuing operations to cash flows from operating activities taken from Ford Motor Company's 2003 annual report. Note that in 2003, accounts payable and accrued and other liabilities decreased by $1,786 million. Thus, this amount appears as a negative amount on the reconciliation.

Normally, it should be assumed that all current liabilities are related to operating activities and thus should be shown in the operating activities category of the cash flow statement. However, there may be some exceptions. For example, assume that a company obtains a six-month loan and the loan is outstanding at the end of the accounting period. If the loan was obtained for operating purposes (for example, to purchase inventory), it should appear in the operating activities category. If, however, it was obtained as a source of financing (for example, if a short-term loan was taken out until long-term financing could be arranged), it should not be categorized under operating activities. Consider also the current maturities of long-term debt. While a portion of the debt should be classified as a current liability on the balance sheet, it should not be included in the operating activities category of the statement of cash flows.

ACCRUAL TO CASH FOR CURRENT LIABILITIES

In order to determine actual cash outflows for current liabilities, it is necessary to examine the balances of all current liability accounts. The balances of current liabilities

Figure 12.6

Note on Operating Cash Flows Before Securities Trading— Ford Motor Company (Automotive Division)

Ford

The reconciliation of net income/(loss) from continuing operations to cash flows from operating activities before securities trading is as follows (in millions):

	2003	2002	2001
Net income/(loss) from continuing operations	$(1,091)	$ (985)	$(6,152)
Depreciation and special tools amortization	5,472	4,896	4,997
Impairment charges (depreciation and amortization)	—	—	3,828
Amortization of goodwill and intangibles	24	21	296
Net losses/(earnings) from equity investments in excess of dividends remitted	(2)	134	845
Foreign currency adjustments	160	51	(201)
Loss on sale of business	—	519	—
Provision for deferred income taxes	785	(1,378)	(2,241)
Decrease/(increase) in accounts receivable and other current assets	(1,445)	2,568	1,225
Decrease/(increase) in inventory	(505)	(650)	1,125
Increase/(decrease) in accounts payable and accrued and other liabilities	(1,786)	3,928	4,707
Other	(430)	337	(989)
Cash flows from operating activities	$ 1,336	$ 9,481	$ 7,440

are the product of the accrual accounting system. They represent the receipts and payments made during the period, but also the adjusting entries made at the end of the period to reflect the accrual or deferral of income.

Assume that LP Company had the following account balances at the beginning and end of 2005:

Account	Beginning Balance	Ending Balance
Accounts Payable	$20,000	$40,000
Salaries Payable	60,000	50,000
Deposits in Advance	80,000	40,000

Also assume the following facts:

- The Accounts Payable account is used only for the purchase of inventory.

- Purchases of $100,000 occurred during 2004.

- Salaries expense for the year was $120,000.

- The Salaries Payable account is used to accrue salaries that will be paid in the following period.

- Deposits in advance represent cash received in advance from customers.

- The amount of deposits earned during the period and reflected on the income statement was $90,000.

The Accounts Payable and Salaries Payable accounts are accounts involving the payment of cash. To determine the amount of cash paid related to those accounts, perform the following computations:

	Accrual Amount	Cash Amount
Purchase of inventory	$100,000	
Less: Increase in accounts payable	(20,000)	
Cash paid for inventory		$ 80,000
Salaries expense	$120,000	
Add: Decrease in salaries payable	10,000	
Cash paid for salaries		$130,000

An increase in a current liability account indicates that *less* cash was paid and should be deducted to determine the amount of cash actually paid, as evidenced in the Accounts Payable account. A decrease in a current liability account indicates that *more* cash was paid and should be added to determine the amount of cash actually paid, as demonstrated in the Salaries Payable account. In either case, it is the *change* in the balance of the account that should be used to adjust the accrual amounts in order to determine the cash paid.

The Deposits in Advance account represents a receipt of cash, rather than a payment of cash. To determine the amount of cash received, perform the following computation:

	Accrual Amount	Cash Amount
Deposit revenue	$90,000	
Less: Decrease in deposits in advance	(40,000)	
Cash received for deposits		$50,000

In this case, a decrease in the balance of the account indicates that *less* cash was received than was earned and should be deducted to determine the amount of cash received. An increase in the balance of the account would indicate that *more* cash was received than was earned and would be added to determine the amount of cash received. Again, it is the *change* in the balance of the account, rather than the ending balance itself, that is important in determining the amount of cash received.

CHECK YOUR UNDERSTANDING

1. In preparing the statement of cash flows using the indirect method, how would a decrease in a current liability account be reflected?

2. Are current liabilities generally related to operating, financing, or investing activities?

Revisiting the Case

FIRESTONE TIRE RECALL AFFECTS FORD'S CONTINGENT LIABILITIES

1. A number of personal injury and class action lawsuits were filed against Ford Motor as a result of a tire recall and related Ford Explorer rollover accidents. The company also faced lawsuits from angry stockholders who felt that the company had breached its fiduciary duties by failing to act responsibly and misrepresenting its financial position.

2. Although Note 16 indicates that the company had established reserves for certain losses that were deemed probable, Ford could not reasonably estimate potential damages at December 31, 2000. The company did not reasonably expect that these claims would have a material effect on future financial statements.

3. Note 16 serves the interests of the company in that it provides a degree of transparency in reporting, protecting Ford against claims that it was not diligent in reporting any circumstances that might affect the company's financial standing. Investors have been provided with information about a potential issue that may entail large expenditures and thus may affect future earnings.

SUMMARY BY LEARNING OBJECTIVE

LO1 Define current liabilities and identify common current liability accounts.

Current liabilities are economic obligations that will require the use of a current asset (or the creation of another liability) within one year or the current operating cycle, whichever is longer. Examples of current liabilities include accounts payable, notes payable within one year, advances from customers, and accruals for items such as wages, salaries, rents, and royalties. On a classified balance sheet, current liabilities should be presented separately with a total for the category.

LO2 Describe how to account for current liability accruals.

Many of the current liabilities that appear on financial statements are the result of the accrual accounting process. It is necessary to record expenses that have been incurred but have not yet been paid (accruals).

LO3 Describe how to account for current liability deferrals.

When using the accrual method of accounting, it is necessary to adjust for amounts that have been previously received but have not been earned as of the end of the accounting period (deferrals). Liabilities resulting from advance collections often include refundable deposits or advances from customers.

LO4 Determine the liability for compensated employee absences.

A liability for a compensated employee absence, such as vacation pay, should be accrued if the employee's service has been rendered, the obligation to the rights vests or accumulates, the payment is probable, and the amount of the liability can be reasonably estimated. The liability should be recorded in the period in which it is earned. The liability for sick pay benefits should be accrued only if the amount of the benefit vests. Vesting means that the employee has the right to the benefit even if the employee leaves the company.

LO5 Determine the proper classification for obligations that are expected to be refinanced.

A short-term obligation that is expected to be refinanced can be excluded from the current liability category only if the company can demonstrate the intent and the ability to refinance the obligation. The ability to refinance can be demonstrated by the issuance of a long-term obligation or equity after the balance sheet date but before the issuance of the financial statements. It may also be demonstrated by a signed financing agreement before the balance sheet date that clearly permits the refinancing of the short-term obligation, provided that both parties to the agreement are capable of honoring the agreement.

LO6 Identify the proper accounting treatment for contingencies.

Contingent liabilities should be recorded as a liability on the balance sheet if the loss is probable and the amount can be reasonably estimated (and is a material amount). Contingent liabilities should not be recorded on the balance sheet but should be disclosed in the notes if the loss is reasonably possible. In most cases, contingent losses that are remote should not be recorded and need not be disclosed in the notes. An exception is guarantees of the indebtedness of others; these should be disclosed in the notes, even when the likelihood of loss is remote.

LO7 Determine the appropriate accounting treatment for warranties as contingent liabilities.

Under the accrual accounting process, warranties should be recorded as a liability in the same time period as that in which the sale of the product is recognized. At that time, the seller has made a promise, and a liability has been incurred as a result of that promise. In those cases where a warranty is sold separately from the product itself, the cash received should be recognized as a liability and should be earned over the life of the warranty agreement.

LO8 Analyze how current liabilities affect the liquidity of a business.

Current liabilities are an important aspect of the liquidity of a business. Companies must have enough current assets to be able to pay their current liabilities as they become due. Liquidity is sometimes measured as a dollar amount, referred to as working capital. It is more common to measure liquidity using the current ratio (total current assets divided by total current liabilities).

LO9 Determine how current liabilities affect cash flow.

Current liabilities should generally be presented in the operating activities section of the cash flow statement. When using the indirect method, an increase in a current liability should be presented as a source of cash and a positive amount on the statement of cash flows, and a decrease should be presented as a use of cash and a negative amount. The changes in the balances of current liability accounts are important elements of the company's cash flow from operating activities.

KEY TERMS

accrued liabilities (p. 547)
accumulated rights (p. 549)
compensated absences (p. 548)
contingency (p. 552)
current liabilities (p. 546)
current ratio (p. 559)
gain contingencies (p. 557)

liabilities (p. 546)
loss contingencies (p. 553)
obligations expected to be refinanced (p. 550)
probable (p. 553)
reasonably estimated (p. 553)
reasonably possible (p. 554)

remote (p. 554)
vested benefits (p. 548)
warranty (p. 555)
window dressing (p. 560)
working capital (p. 559)

EXERCISES

LO1, 2, 4, 5, 6, 7   EXERCISE 12-1   **Classify Current Liabilities**

Kivi Company is preparing its financial statements as of December 31, 2005, and reflects the following amounts or accounts:

A. Liability for payroll taxes withheld from employees.

B. Liability for vacation pay that accumulates and vests.

C. Liability for sick pay that accumulates but does not vest.

D. Note payable, due June 1, 2006, that Kivi has the intent and ability to refinance.

E. Liability for warranty for products sold during 2005. A basic two-year warranty accompanies all products sold and covers the cost of materials and labor for defective products.

F. Liability for extended warranty. During 2005, the company began to offer for cash an extended warranty to cover the costs after the expiration of the basic warranty.

G. Note payable, due July 1, 2007. The note requires annual payments of principal and interest.

H. Cash dividends declared but unpaid.

I. Stock dividends declared but unpaid.

J. A competitor may file suit against the company for patent infringement. As of December 31, 2005, a suit has not been filed, but the company's lawyers feel that such a suit is probable.

Required: For each situation, indicate (1) whether a liability should be recorded, (2) whether a note disclosure is required, and (3) whether the liability (if applicable) is classified as current or long-term.

LO3   EXERCISE 12-2   **Liability for Unearned Income**

Wego Bus Company allows its customers to purchase 30-ride bus passes. As of June 1, 4,000 passes had been purchased at $12 per pass. During the month of June, the price of a bus pass increased to $15 per pass. All outstanding passes will be honored at the price paid for them at the time of purchase. During June, 5,000 passes were purchased by customers at a cost of $15 per pass. In the month of June, the passes were accepted for 82,000 bus rides.

Required:

1. What amount of income should the company show on its monthly income statement for June?

2. What amount of liability should appear on the June 30 balance sheet?

LO7   EXERCISE 12-3   **Warranty Liability**

Fuzz and Static Company began to manufacture and sell cell phones in 2005. Each cell phone is sold with a basic two-year warranty against defects. During 2005, 280 phones were sold at $120 each. In addition, the company offers an extended warranty for $50 that covers repair costs for an additional two years after the basic warranty has expired. The company sold 100 extended warranties during the year. The company estimates that warranty costs will average $20 per unit during the first two years and $30 per unit during the extended-warranty period.

Required:

1. What amounts should be shown as warranty expense and warranty income on the annual income statement for 2005?

2. What amount should appear as a current liability related to warranty costs on the balance sheet at December 31, 2005?

3. What amount should appear as a long-term liability related to warranty costs on the balance sheet at December 31, 2005?

LO6 **EXERCISE 12-4** **Liability for Environmental Hazard** (CPA adapted)

During 2005, Supey Chemical Company discovered that it must pay an indeterminate amount for toxic waste cleanup on its land. The owner of the adjoining land, Gap Toothpaste, sold its property because of possible toxic water contamination by Supey and resulting potential adverse public reaction to its product. Gap sued Supey for damages. There is a reasonable possibility that Gap will prevail in the suit.

Required:

1. In its 2005 financial statements, how should Supey report the toxic waste cleanup? Why is this reporting appropriate?

2. In its 2005 financial statements, how should Supey report Gap's claim against it? Why is this reporting appropriate?

LO8 **EXERCISE 12-5** **Analysis of Liquidity and Current Liabilities**

ETHICS

Assume that you are the accountant for Window Company, which has a bank loan with National Bank. One of the provisions of the loan requires Window to maintain its liquidity at acceptable levels. The loan agreement specifies that the current ratio must be 2 to 1 at the end of the accounting period. It is near the end of the accounting year, and you are concerned about the company's ability to meet the liquidity requirements. In fact, shortly before year end, the accounts reflect total current assets of $200,000 and total current liabilities of $120,000.

The current liability total does not include a large invoice of $20,000 that was received for utilities. Since the amount will not be paid until the following year, you are considering recording the payment as an expense at that time. You are also considering making a payment of $40,000 on the accounts payable before year end. The president of the company has asked for a report on the company's liquidity and its ability to meet the loan provisions.

Required:

1. Consider the courses of action presented in this example. Do you consider either action to be unethical? Discuss your reasoning.

2. What is the impact of each action on the current ratio?

3. Write a short memo to the president that indicates the course of action that should be taken.

LO5 **EXERCISE 12-6** **Obligations to Be Refinanced**

Scott Company has the following obligations as of December 31, 2005, and wishes to present a classified balance sheet as of that date. The financial statements for the year 2005 will be issued on March 1, 2006.

A. A $100,000 loan payable to First State Bank, due January 15, 2006. On December 20, 2005, Scott signed an agreement to refinance the loan with First State on a long-term basis. Both parties have the ability to perform the refinancing.

B. A $150,000 loan payable to Second National Bank, due January 20, 2006. On January 18, 2006, Scott Company signed a three-year loan agreement in the amount of $170,000 and used the proceeds from the loan to repay the original loan.

C. A $170,000 loan payable to Third Avenue Bank, due February 1, 2006. On February 5, 2006, Scott negotiated an additional loan of $170,000 to replace the loan that had been paid a few days earlier.

D. A $200,000 loan payable to United Bank, due February 1, 2006. On January 21, 2006, the company issued stock in the amount of $180,000 and used the proceeds to aid in the repayment of the loan.

Required: For each of these loans, determine the amount that should be classified as a current liability as of December 31, 2005. If an amount is not classified as a current liability, indicate the proper presentation.

LO8 **EXERCISE 12-7** **Accrual to Cash for Current Liabilities**

Assume that Natalie Company recognized the following on its income statement for the year:

Interest Expense	$120,000
Salaries Expense	500,000
Rent Revenue	300,000

Also assume that the company had the following beginning and ending balances for the year 2005:

Account	Beginning Balance	Ending Balance
Interest Payable	$20,000	$30,000
Salaries Payable	45,000	40,000
Rent Collected in Advance	60,000	80,000

Required:

1. Determine the amount of cash paid for interest and salaries during the year.
2. Determine the amount of cash received for rent during the year.

LO8   EXERCISE 12-8   Cash to Accrual for Current Liabilities

Assume that Garnett Company paid the following amounts in cash for the current year:

Interest paid	$120,000
Salaries paid	500,000

Also assume that the company received $300,000 in cash as rent revenue. The company had the following beginning and ending balances for the year 2005:

Account	Beginning Balance	Ending Balance
Interest Payable	$20,000	$30,000
Salaries Payable	45,000	40,000
Rent Collected in Advance	60,000	80,000

Required:

1. Determine the amount of interest expense and salaries expense that should be recognized for the current year.
2. Determine the amount of rent revenue that should be recognized for the current year.

LO1, 2, 6   EXERCISE 12-9   Current Liabilities (CPA adapted)

Brite Corp. had the following liabilities at December 31, 2005:

Accounts Payable	$ 55,000
Unsecured Notes, 8%, due 7/1/06	400,000
Accrued Expenses	35,000
Contingent Liability	450,000
Senior Bonds, 7%, due 3/31/06	1,000,000

The contingent liability is an accrual for possible losses on a $1 million lawsuit filed against Brite. Brite's legal counsel expects the suit to be settled in 2007, and has estimated that Brite will be liable for damages in the range of $450,000 to $750,000.

Required: List the amounts that Brite should report in its December 31, 2005, balance sheet for current liabilities.

LO1, 2   EXERCISE 12-10   Current Liabilities (CPA adapted)

Mill Co.'s trial balance included the following account balances at December 31, 2005:

Accounts Payable	$15,000
Bonds Payable, due 2006	25,000
Discount on Bonds Payable, due 2006	3,000
Dividends Payable, 1/31/06	8,000
Notes Payable, due 2007	20,000

Required: List the amounts that should be included in the current liabilities section of Mill's December 31, 2005, balance sheet.

LO1, 2, 5   **EXERCISE 12-11   Liabilities and Refinancing**

At the financial statement date of December 31, 2005, the liabilities outstanding of Nyland Corporation included the following:

A. Cash dividends on common stock, $50,000, payable on January 15, 2006.

B. Note payable to Girard State Bank, $470,000, due January 20, 2006.

C. Serial bonds, $1,000,000, of which $200,000 mature during 2006.

D. Note payable to Third National Bank, $400,000, due January 27, 2006.

The following transactions occurred early in 2006:

Jan. 15   The cash dividends on common stock were paid.

   20   The note payable to Girard State Bank was paid.

   25   The corporation entered into a financing agreement with Girard State Bank, enabling it to borrow up to $500,000 at any time through the end of 2008. Amounts borrowed under the agreement would bear interest at 1 percent above the bank's prime rate and would mature three years from the date of the loan. The corporation immediately borrowed $470,000 to replace the cash used in paying its January 20 note to the bank.

   26   30,000 shares of common stock were issued for $300,000. The proceeds were used to liquidate the note payable to Third National Bank, with the remaining amount being paid in cash.

Feb. 1   The financial statements for 2005 were issued.

Required: Prepare a partial balance sheet for Nyland Corporation, showing the manner in which these liabilities should be presented at December 31, 2005. (You do not have to consider interest on the liabilities.) The liabilities should be properly classified between current and long-term. You do not need to provide the note disclosures.

LO4   **EXERCISE 12-12   Compensated Absences**

Ritter Company has 35 employees who work eight-hour days and are paid hourly. On January 1, 2005, the company began a program of granting its employees 10 days' paid vacation each year. Vacation days earned in 2005 may first be taken on January 1, 2006. Information relative to these employees is as follows:

Year	Hourly Wages	Vacation Days Earned by Each Employee	Vacation Days Used by Each Employee
2005	$17.20	10	0
2006	18.00	10	8
2007	19.00	10	10

Ritter has chosen to accrue the liability for compensated absences at the current rates of pay that are in effect when the compensated time is earned.

Required:

1. What is the amount of expense relative to compensated absences that should be reported on Ritter's income statements for 2005 and 2006?

2. What is the amount of the accrued liability for compensated absences that should be reported at December 31, 2006?

LO6   **EXERCISE 12-13   Contingencies** (CPA adapted)

Chester Company has the following contingencies:

A. A threat of expropriation exists for one of its manufacturing plants located in a foreign country. Expropriation is considered reasonably possible. Any compensation from the foreign government would be less than the carrying amount of the plant.

B. Potential costs exist as a result of the discovery of a safety hazard related to one of its products. These costs are probable and can be reasonably estimated.

C. One of its warehouses is located at the base of a mountain and can no longer be insured against rockslide losses. No rockslide losses have occurred.

Required:

1. How should Chester report the threat of expropriation of assets? Why?

2. How should Chester report the potential costs resulting from the safety hazard? Why?

3. How should Chester report the noninsurable rockslide risk? Why?

LO7, 9 **EXERCISE 12-14 Coupon Obligations and Cash Flows**

Imrie Co. includes one coupon in each bag of dog food it sells. In return for four coupons, customers receive a dog toy. The toys cost Imrie $2.00 each. Imrie estimates that 40 percent of the coupons will be redeemed. Data for 2004 follow:

Bags of dog food sold	200,000
Dog toys purchased for cash	16,000
Coupons redeemed	44,000

Required:

1. Calculate the amount of premium expense for 2004.

2. How much is the estimated premium liability at December 31, 2004?

3. Where are the amounts in questions 1 and 2 reported in Imrie's financial statements for the year ended December 31, 2004?

4. What type of liability is reported as a result of the coupons? Explain.

LO7, 9 **EXERCISE 12-15 Warranties and Cash Flows**

Holt Co. introduced a new product, sigits, during 2004. This product has a one-year warranty against defects. Warranty costs are estimated at 4 percent of sales. All sales are for cash. Cost of goods sold amounts to 45 percent of sales, all of which was paid during the year. Sales and actual warranty costs to repair products for the years ended December 31, 2004 and 2005, are as follows:

Year	Sales	Actual Warranty Costs
2004	$500,000	$19,000
2005	600,000	18,000

Required:

1. Prepare a partial income statement and balance sheet showing the results of the transactions for the year ended December 31, 2005.

2. How would your answer to question 1 differ if the warranty covered two years instead of one year? Explain.

3. Why is it necessary to accrue warranty costs?

LO5, 8 **EXERCISE 12-16 Obligation Expected to Be Refinanced and Liquidity**

Clinton Enterprises has a December 31 fiscal year end. Its 2004 financial statements were issued on March 15, 2005. Throughout 2004, borrowing rates hovered at 12 percent for unsecured debt and 8 percent for secured debt. Clinton provided the following information concerning an obligation held at December 31, 2004:

- 12 percent, four-year, unsecured $600,000 note with a maturity date of March 31, 2005, due to NationsBank.
- Accrued interest is paid quarterly on March 31, June 30, September 30, and December 31.

Clinton intended to obtain replacement financing at maturity. On March 3, 2005, the company issued stock with a par value of $50,000 for its market price of $560,000 and used the proceeds, along with $40,000 of its own cash from operating funds, to pay the NationsBank note at maturity. Total current assets and total current liabilities at December 31, 2004, excluding the note, are $2,400,000 and $1,200,000, respectively.

Required:

1. Evaluate the note in terms of the criteria for possible exclusion from the current liability category.

2. Show how the NationsBank note should be reported on Clinton's December 31, 2004, balance sheet.

3. What effect does the refinancing have on Clinton Enterprises' current ratio at December 31, 2004? Support your response with calculations.

LO4   EXERCISE 12-17   **Compensated Employee Absences**

Big Cheese Company has 32 employees, and each employee earns one day of vacation pay per month. Each employee earned $80 per day during 2005. There are 260 working days during 2005. Vacation days can accumulate and be used in future years. There were no accumulated days at the beginning of 2005. Terminated employees are paid accrued vacation along with their final paycheck. During 2005, a total of 290 vacation days were used by employees. The remainder of the employees will use their vacation during 2006, when the average rate of daily pay is expected to be $88.

Required:

1. Record the transactions related to employee vacations during 2005.

2. How much should Big Cheese Company report as Vacation Payable on December 31, 2005?

3. How would your answer to question 2 differ if this accrual related to sick pay instead of vacation pay?

LO3   EXERCISE 12-18   **Deferrals**

Bugs Away provides pest control services for 6,000 customers every month. Payment of the monthly fee of $40 is received from 40 percent of the customers at the time the service is rendered. Another 45 percent of customers pay annually on January 1, and the balance of customers pay during the month after the service is rendered. During the 2004–2005 holiday season, Bugs Away sold gift certificates to its customers for a total of $16,000. As of the end of the fiscal period, $9,000 of the certificates had been redeemed.

Required:

1. Determine how much should be reported as deferred revenue for Bugs Away at May 31, 2005, the end of its fiscal period.

2. How does deferred revenue differ from accrued liabilities?

LO1, 7   EXERCISE 12-19   **Premiums**

During May of 2004, Cable Com Company started a new program whereby customers could receive one free "pay-per-view" movie for every four movies ordered through the pay-per-view system. Cable Com's customers viewed 83,000 pay-per-view movies during May. Movies viewed during June totaled 86,000. About 30 percent of Cable Com's customers will be eligible for a free movie; however, it is estimated that only 20 percent of them will redeem. Cable Com has a normal charge of $3.95 per movie. Cable Com Company incurs licensing charges equal to $.65 per movie viewed by customers through the pay-per-view system. During May and June, there were 600 and 1,450 free movies viewed. The free viewing program expires December 31, 2004.

Required:

1. Calculate the total liability to be reported by Cable Com Company at June 30, 2004.

2. Describe how the cost of the remaining movies that have been "earned" by customers but not yet viewed is considered a liability.

LO2, 6, 7   **EXERCISE 12-20   Various Liabilities**

Adera, Inc. incurred several transactions, which are given in the following list. Adera began operations in January 2003. Its financial statements for the year ended December 31, 2004 were issued on March 1, 2005.

A. Adera borrowed $40,000 on November 1, 2004, by signing a 12-month note bearing interest at 12 percent. Interest is payable in full at maturity on October 31, 2005.

B. During 2004, Adera sold 8,000 ladders under a new marketing program. Each ladder carries one coupon, which entitles the customer to a $5.00 cash rebate. Adera estimates that 70 percent of the coupons will be redeemed, even though only 3,500 coupons had been processed during 2004.

C. In May of 2004, Adera became involved in a tax dispute with the IRS. At December 31, 2004, the tax attorney for Adera indicated that an unfavorable outcome to the dispute was probable. The additional taxes were estimated to be $300,000 but could be as high as $450,000. On March 15, 2005, Adera accepted an IRS settlement offer of $375,000.

Required: Prepare the current liabilities section of Adera, Inc.'s balance sheet at December 31, 2004.

LO2, 3, 9   **EXERCISE 12-21   Accruals, Deferrals, and Cash Flows**

Dapper Dan Clothing reported the following amounts at December 31, 2005 and 2004:

Account	December 31, 2005	December 31, 2004
Accounts Payable	$20,000	$40,000
Gift Certificate Obligations	9,000	15,000
Liability—Potential Lawsuit	90,000	0
Salaries Payable	60,000	50,000
Warranty Payable	8,800	8,200
Deposits in Advance	51,000	40,000

In addition, the following amounts appeared on Dapper Dan's income statement for the year ended December 31, 2005:

- Net income for the year was $65,000.
- Purchases during 2005 were $100,000.
- Salaries Expense, $216,000.
- Sales Revenue (earned during 2005), $687,000.
- Warranty Expense, $23,000.

Required:

1. How much cash was collected from customers during 2005?

2. How much cash was paid for salaries during 2005?

3. How much cash was paid for warranty costs during 2005?

4. What effect do the accruals and deferrals have on net income for 2005? (*Hint:* Determine cash-basis income.)

PROBLEMS

LO6   **PROBLEM 12-1   Contingencies**

Booker Company has the following contingent situations:

A. Booker has sued another company for damages of $2 million. Booker's attorneys believe it is probable that the company will win the lawsuit and be awarded $1.5 million.

B. On December 1, 2005, Jaron Company sued Booker Company for unfair competition. Booker's lawyers believe it is probable that the company will lose the lawsuit and be assessed an amount that may range from $3 million to $7 million.

C. Booker Company is not insured against lawsuits filed by customers for defective products. During the year the company had sales of $20 million. The company anticipates that lawsuits may be filed during 2006.

Required: How should Booker report the three contingencies on the balance sheet of December 31, 2005? Give your reasoning for your choices.

Analyze: Does the principle of conservatism play a role in reporting contingencies?

LO2, 3, 6, 7   PROBLEM **12-2**   **Current Liabilities** (CPA adapted)

Edge Company, a toy manufacturer, is in the process of preparing its financial statements for the year ended December 31, 2005. Edge expects to issue its 2005 financial statements on March 1, 2006. Consider the proper accounting treatment for each of the following items. You may ignore income tax effects in all cases.

A. Edge owns a small warehouse in which it stores inventory worth approximately $500,000. The warehouse is located on the bank of a river. Edge is not insured against flood losses. The river last overflowed 20 years ago.

B. Edge offers a warranty on its toys. Based on past experience, Edge estimates its warranty expense to be 1 percent of sales. Sales during 2005 were $10,000,000.

C. On October 30, 2005, a safety hazard related to one of Edge's toy products was discovered. It is considered probable that Edge will be liable for an amount in the range of $100,000 to $500,000.

D. On November 22, 2005, Edge initiated a lawsuit seeking $250,000 in damages for patent infringement.

E. On December 17, 2005, a former employee filed a lawsuit seeking $100,000 for unlawful dismissal. Edge's lawyers believe the suit has no merit. No court date has been set.

F. On December 15, 2005, Edge guaranteed a bank loan of $100,000 for its president's personal use.

G. On January 5, 2006, a warehouse containing a substantial portion of Edge's inventory was destroyed by fire. Edge expects to recover the entire loss, except for a $250,000 deductible, from insurance.

H. On February 4, 2006, the IRS assessed Edge an additional $400,000 for the 2001 tax year. Edge's tax attorneys and tax accountants have stated that it is likely that the IRS will agree to a $100,000 settlement.

Required:

1. If an adjustment is required, determine the proper amount and indicate the appropriate categorization on the income statement.

2. Determine whether additional disclosure is required, either on the face of the financial statements or in the notes.

Analyze: Why do you think Edge should disclose the fact that it has guaranteed a loan for the company's president?

LO8   PROBLEM **12-3**   **Effects on Liquidity**

A variety of business transactions that affect Peters Company's working capital are presented in the following list:

A. An accrual of $2,000 was made for salaries earned but unpaid at December 31, 2005.

B. On December 31, 2005, cash in the amount of $5,000 was received from a customer for a sale to be made in the following year.

C. Salaries of $800 that had been accrued in 2004 were paid in 2005.

D. A cash dividend of $12,000 was declared at year end, to be paid on January 15, 2006.

E. At December 31, 2005, the company signed a loan agreement of $40,000. The loan is for five years. Interest will be paid annually, and the principal will be repaid when the loan is due.

F. A customer brought in a defective product that requires parts and labor of $2,000. All products are sold with a one-year warranty.

G. It is reasonably possible that the company will be held liable in a lawsuit of $300,000.

H. The company co-signed for the loan of an officer. The loan is due in one year and is in the amount of $30,000.

I. A stock dividend of $9,000 was declared at year end, to be distributed on January 30, 2006.

Required: Assume that Peters Company had total current assets of $100,000 and total current liabilities of $50,000 before items A through I transpired. Calculate the amount of the company's working capital before and after each of the transactions. Consider each transaction independently. Assume a fiscal year end of December 31.

Analyze: Explain how the 2-to-1 rule of thumb has been used when evaluating a company's current ratio.

LO4, 5, 7   **PROBLEM 12-4   Compensated Absences, Warranties, Obligations to Be Refinanced**

Votaw Company is preparing a classified balance sheet as of December 31, 2005. The company's financial statements will be issued on February 20, 2006. Consider the following items:

A. The company has 100 employees who each work 40 hours per week and 50 weeks per year. The average salary rate is $10 per hour. Each employee earns two weeks of paid vacation per year and can accumulate up to a total of six months of vacation. An employee who leaves the company is paid for unused vacation pay; however, no employees retired or left during 2005. A total of 100 weeks of vacation were taken during 2005. As of January 1, 2005, the balance of the Vacation Payable account was $10,000.

B. Employees of the company are allowed 10 sick days per year. Employees may carry over unused sick days to the following year and accumulate a maximum of 60 sick days. An employee who leaves the company is not paid for unused sick days. During the year, employees took five sick days per employee.

C. The company sells a product that has a three-year warranty for defective parts and labor. The product sells for $1,000. During previous years, the company had estimated warranty costs at 2 percent of total sales. However, because of increases in the prices of parts and labor, the company determined that in 2005, warranty costs would be 4 percent. At January 1, 2005, the balance of the Warranty Liability account was $50,000. Sales for 2005 totaled $2 million. During the year, 100 customers brought their products in for repairs that averaged 3.5 percent of the sales cost.

D. At December 31, 2005, the company had a $500,000 loan with the local bank. The loan bears interest at 8 percent, with annual interest payable each October 1. The loan was due on February 15, 2006. On February 1, 2006, the company negotiated a new loan of $400,000 with the same bank. The proceeds, along with cash generated internally, were used to repay the loan when it came due on February 15.

Required:

1. Record all adjusting entries that are necessary for these items on December 31, 2005.

2. Assume there are no other current liabilities. Present the current liabilities section of the balance sheet as of December 31, 2005.

Analyze: If the company reported current assets of $202,000 at December 31, 2005, what is the current ratio? How does this compare to a competitor's ratio of 2.5 to 1?

LO8, 9   **PROBLEM 12-5   Liquidity Analysis and Cash Flows of Johnson Controls**

Johnson Controls supplies parts, including batteries and seats, to companies in the auto industry. The current liabilities portion of the company's balance sheets as of September 30, 2002 and 2003, follows.

Johnson Controls

(In millions)	2003	2002
Current Liabilities:		
Short-term debt	$ 150.5	$ 105.3
Current portion of long-term debt	427.8	39.9
Accounts payable	3,329.3	2,789.1
Accrued compensation and benefits	546.3	506.6
Accrued income taxes	58.7	182.7
Billings in excess of costs and earnings on uncompleted contracts	186.2	190.8
Other current liabilities	885.3	991.8
Total current liabilities	$5,584.1	$4,806.2

Required: Using the indirect method, determine how these amounts will be disclosed on the statement of cash flows. For each item, indicate which category of the statement of cash flows will be affected, the dollar amount that will be disclosed, and whether the amount will be an increase or decrease in cash flows for the period.

Analyze: Johnson Controls reported total current assets of $5,620 million and $4,946 million at the beginning and end of 2003. Assume that you are an analyst and must evaluate the liquidity of Johnson Controls. What factors should be considered in evaluating the liquidity of this company?

LO2, 7 PROBLEM **12-6 Premium Offers**

Goodee Cereal Company began a coupon offer in 2005. If customers send in the proof of purchase from four cereal boxes and $2.00, they can receive a CD from a new music artist. The cereal sells for $4.00 per box. Goodee expects that 70 percent of the cereal boxes will be used by customers for the redemption. During 2005 and 2006 the following events occurred:

2005

A. Sold 150,000 boxes of cereal for cash.

B. Purchased 40,000 CDs at $2.50 each for cash.

C. Customers sent in 100,000 proofs of purchase to receive 25,000 CDs. Mailing and shipping costs were $.80 per CD.

2006

A. Sold 200,000 boxes of cereal for cash.

B. Purchased 80,000 CD's at $2.50 each for cash.

C. Customers sent in 120,000 proofs of purchase to receive 30,000 CD's. Mailing and shipping costs were $.80 per CD.

Required:

1. Prepare the journal entries in 2005 and 2006 to record these events.

2. Determine the amounts of estimated liability for coupons that should be reported on the balance sheets of December 31, 2005 and 2006. Indicate what amounts should be current and long-term liabilities.

Analyze: Discuss any implications you can identify if this company did not accrue for the redemption of coupons.

LO1, 5 PROBLEM **12-7 Obligations Expected to Be Refinanced, Definition of a Liability, Reporting**

Rosado, Inc. has $500,000 of 12 percent notes payable due to First Union Bank on March 1, 2006. Interest is paid annually at December 31. At December 31, 2005, Rosado arranged with First Union Bank to borrow $500,000 to refinance the notes over six years. Rosado closed on the loan on February 10, 2006; however, because the bank deducted $4,000 in closing costs, Rosado received only $496,000. On February 15, 2006, Rosado issued its financial statements.

Required:

1. List the criteria necessary for Rosado to reclassify the debt. Indicate which facts from the transaction support the assumption that Rosado meets these criteria.

2. Prepare the liabilities section of Rosado's balance sheet in classified format at December 31, 2005.

Critical Thinking: Using the definition of *current liability*, explain the accounting justification for a portion of Rosado's debt being classified as current.

Analyze: Assume that this transaction is the only one affecting current liabilities. What net change occurred in this category?

LO8   **PROBLEM 12-8   Contingent Liabilities, Disclosure, Impact on Liquidity**

Briarstone Corporation, a manufacturer of tires, is preparing its annual financial statements at December 31, 2005. Because of recently proven hazards associated with its tires, the government is requiring Briarstone to recall certain tires it manufactured during the last six months. At year end, Briarstone estimates that it will cost between $8 and $10 million in total to recall and replace the tires. Briarstone had incurred $3 million in replacement costs as of year end.

Required:

1. Why is this situation considered a contingent liability?

2. What difficulties are present in accounting for contingent liabilities?

3. What amount and type of expense should Briarstone report on its income statement related to the tires for the year ended December 31, 2005?

4. Show how the contingency should be reported on Briarstone's balance sheet as of December 31, 2005. Include the note disclosure necessary for the contingency.

Analyze: How does this transaction affect Briarstone's liquidity?

LO1, 2, 3, 8   **PROBLEM 12-9   Reporting Accruals and Deferrals, Liquidity**

Daboul, Inc.'s 2005 financial statements were issued on February 18, 2006. The company's fiscal year ends on December 31, 2005. Daboul provided the following information relating to possible liabilities at December 31, 2005:

A. Daboul shipped 20,000 rebate coupons in products sold during 2005. The coupons are redeemable for $5.00 each. Each product is sold for $120 and has a cost of $65. Daboul anticipates that 60 percent of the coupons will be redeemed. The coupons expire on December 31, 2006. There were 4,000 coupons redeemed in 2005.

B. On September 30, 2005, Daboul signed a 10-month, 9 percent note due to Wachovia Bank with a face amount of $70,000, secured by the company's plant assets.

C. Daboul collects 6 percent sales tax from customers for all sales and remits each month's collections to the state on the 20th of the month following the sale. December sales totaled $900,000 before adding sales tax for the month.

D. Daboul sold gift certificates to its customers during 2005 for a total of $12,000. During the year, $12,200 of the certificates had been redeemed. As of December 31, 2004, the gift certificates outstanding totaled $2,600.

Required:

1. For each transaction, determine the amount that should be reported as a current liability as of December 31, 2005.

2. Show how these items would be reported in the current liabilities section of Daboul's balance sheet as of December 31, 2005.

Analyze: What impact would submitting the payment of December's sales taxes on December 31 have on Daboul's liquidity at December 31, 2005? Explain.

Critical Thinking: Explain how the proposed payment of sales taxes on December 31 might be labeled as window dressing.

Spreadsheet: Use a spreadsheet application to make the computations required in question 1 and to prepare the partial balance sheet for question 2.

LO7,9   **PROBLEM 12-10**   **Reporting Product Warranties, Cash Flows**

Caffey Co. began operations in 2004. During 2005, Caffey Co. sold modulators for $400 each, all carrying a two-year warranty against defects. Caffey's cost for each modulator is $120. Caffey does not keep inventory on hand. Inventory purchases payable on account at the beginning and end of 2005, respectively, totaled $12,000 and $16,800. Warranty costs are estimated at $60 for each defective product. Caffey outsources repairs and is required to pay the subcontractor at the time of each repair. During 2005, Caffey's sales of modulators totaled $800,000 for cash. The company estimates that 5 percent of the units sold will be returned for repairs under warranty. Actual warranty expenditures on the modulators totaled $2,100 for the year.

Required:

1. How much will Caffey Co. report as warranty expense for 2005?

2. Determine the amount that should be reported on Caffey's balance sheet as Warranty Liability as of December 31, 2005.

3. Prepare a partial statement of cash flows for 2005, demonstrating how these costs will be reported using the indirect method.

Communicate: What accounting concept justifies the accrual of warranty costs? Explain.

Analyze: Does the accrual of warranty obligations make a company appear more or less liquid?

LO6,8   **PROBLEM 12-11**   **Contingencies**

Chelsea's Tropical Fun sells tropical clothing and accessories in Jacksonville, Florida. Several unexpected problems occurred during 2005:

A. A suit for breach of contract seeking damages of $1,000,000 was filed against Chelsea's on June 1, 2005. The company's legal counsel believes that an unfavorable outcome is probable. A reasonable estimate of the court's award to the plaintiff is in the range of $200,000 to $800,000. The company's legal counsel believes that the best estimate of potential damages is $350,000.

B. On January 2, 2005, Chelsea's discontinued collision, fire, and theft coverage on its delivery vehicles and became self-insured for these risks. Actual losses of $40,000 during 2005 were charged to Delivery Expense. All but $3,000 of this amount has been paid. The 2005 premium for the discontinued coverage would have amounted to $75,000. The controller had estimated that $50,000 to $60,000 of repairs would be incurred during 2005.

C. During December 2005, Chelsea's filed suit against a competitor for copyright infringement, claiming $600,000 in damages. In the opinion of company counsel, it is probable that damages will be awarded. The best estimate of potential damages is $175,000.

Required:

1. Prepare a partial income statement and balance sheet for Chelsea's Tropical Fun for the year ended December 31, 2005, showing the results of these three issues.

2. Prepare adequate note disclosure reflecting the contingencies for Chelsea's for its year ended December 31, 2005.

3. For any transaction that does not require accrual or disclosure, indicate why not.

Analyze: Why are companies reluctant to accrue contingent liabilities? What negative effect does the accrual have on liquidity?

Spreadsheet: Use a spreadsheet application to prepare the financial statements required in question 1.

CASES

LO4   **CRITICAL THINKING CASE 12-1   Liability for Compensated Absences** (CPA adapted)
Essex Company provides a compensation plan that includes vacation pay and sick pay.

Required:

1. What conditions must be met for Essex to accrue compensation for future vacation pay? What is the theoretical justification for accruing compensation for vacation pay?

2. What conditions must be met for Essex to accrue compensation for future sick pay? What is the theoretical justification for accruing compensation for sick pay?

LO6   **FINANCIAL REPORTING CASE 12-2   Contingent Liability for Ford Motor Company**
The following announcement was made during 2003 about **Ford Motor Company**:

> In May 2003, Ford Motor Company made an announcement that it was recalling about 185,000 pickup trucks and sport-utility vehicles to inspect a steering part that might not have been properly installed and could lead to a loss of steering. Ford said the safety recall covered the 1997 model-year Ford F-150 and F-250 pickup trucks and Ford Expedition SUVs. The company estimated that less than 1% of the recalled vehicles will need repair. Along with the National Highway Traffic Safety Administration, Ford identified three minor accidents with two alleged minor injuries in connection with the problem. If repairs are needed, the company stated, customers will not be charged.[16]

Required:

1. Under what circumstances should Ford Motor Company record a product recall as a liability?

2. What information should be disclosed on the financial statements for the year 2003 for this recall?

LO6   **ETHICS CASE 12-3   McDonald's Obligation and Ethical Dilemma**

ETHICS

During 2001, a **McDonald's** game promotion became the target of a fraud scheme. Chief Executive Jack Greenberg received news from the FBI that certain individuals were being investigated in connection with the crime. The FBI wanted McDonald's to continue the game promotion to aid its investigation. McDonald's faced a dilemma: Should the corporation cooperate with law enforcement at the expense of its customers, or should it honor its obligation to its customers by discontinuing the promotional games?

McDonald's chose to continue the game and aid the investigation. On August 21, the FBI arrested two women and six men, including an employee of Simon Marketing, a company that handled promotions for McDonald's, for allegedly rigging McDonald's promotions and defrauding the fast-food chain of more than $13 million. No McDonald's employees were implicated. One day after the fraud announcement, the first class action lawsuit was filed in Illinois state court for damages on behalf of customers who participated in the promotions. McDonald's and Simon Worldwide Inc., the parent of the company that ran the games, were named as defendants. The lawsuit alleged violations of state

---

16 "Ford Recalls F150, F250 Pickups & Expedition," ConsumerAffairs.com, May 24, 2003, available at: **www.consumeraffairs.com/news03/ford_trkrecall.html.** Accessed 3/20/04.

consumer fraud acts and unjust enrichment. It asked for the return of any extra sales that McDonald's received as a result of the promotion.[17]

Required:

1. What are McDonald's ethical responsibilities in this case? Is its primary responsibility to its stockholders?

2. How should McDonald's report and/or disclose the lawsuits that were filed against it in the financial statements for 2001?

LO6   FINANCIAL REPORTING CASE **12-4**   **Contingent Liabilities and Contingent Assets**

The following information about a patent-infringement lawsuit appeared in 2003:

> **PC-Tel Inc.** said Tuesday it filed a patent-infringement lawsuit against Agere Systems, Lucent Technologies Inc. and U.S. Robotics Corp. over modems they have manufactured. PC-Tel, which has largely exited the modem business as it pursues stronger growth potential in the wireless-networking sector, generated $5 million in licensing revenue last year from a variety of sources. For the year, overall revenue totaled $48.8 million. The Chicago-based company estimates it could recover about $400 million from patent-infringement suits against these and other companies. PC-Tel is trying to recoup fees allegedly owed it from when the technology for 56k modems commanded higher prices—back in the late 1990s.[18]

Required:

1. How should the companies being sued present the lawsuit on their 2003 financial statements?

2. How should PC-Tel present the lawsuit on its 2003 financial statements? Is the accounting for contingent assets and contingent liabilities consistent?

LO7   ETHICS CASE **12-5**   **Balancing Cost and Quality**

ETHICS

In January 2003, the California Supreme Court reaffirmed a $290 million punitive damage award against **Ford Motor Company** relating to a product liability suit involving several fatalities.[19] That same month, William Clay Ford Jr., CEO of Ford Motor Company, announced that the company had been able to decrease the cost of its vehicles by $240 and that it was intensifying its efforts to continue decreasing product and other costs.[20] On February 20, the *Wall Street Journal* reported Ford's intention of recalling all of its 1997 Ford Escorts and Mercury Tracers, approximately 441,000 cars, to install air bag motor shields.[21]

Recalls are costly and typically result from the discovery of a general manufacturing defect. While general recalls are costly, the costs of covering individual defects under warranties are also significant. In fact, the cost of a warranty is typically the most common contingent liability for a manufacturer. A continuing trend toward longer warranty periods and increasing demand by car buyers for more comprehensive coverage has made warranty costs a very significant cost associated with the sale of vehicles. Ford recently increased the warranty period on its new Ford Focus from three to five years. Overall, its average warranty cost per car is $1,000.[22]

---

17 David Bailey, Reuters Internet Report, August 29, 2001.

18 "PC-Tel Files 4 Patent-Infringement Suits," *Wall Street Journal*, May 27, 2003.

19 Carol McHugh Sanders, *Defense Counsel Journal*, Vol. 70 (1), January 2003, pp. 163–164. (Recited from recorder [San Francisco]).

20 Norihiko Shirouzu, "Ford CEO Promises Faster Cuts in Costs, Results Above Forecasts," *Wall Street Journal*, January 13, 2003, p. C7.

21 "Ford's 1997 Escorts, Tracers Are Recalling over Air-Bag Bug," *Wall Street Journal*, February 20, 2003, p. D4.

22 Jane Spencer, "The Best Car Deals Around: Never Paying for Repairs—New Longer Warranties Open Door to Car Hypochondriacs; Making the 'rrr' Go 'mmmm,' " *Wall Street Journal*, November 12, 2002, p. D1.

A number of factors affect the cost of warranties. Some are controllable by the company, while others are uncontrollable. One of the most important controllable factors influencing the cost of warranties is the quality of the product. However, the costs associated with increased quality also increase the total cost associated with a vehicle. Continuous efforts to improve quality and minimize costs represent a difficult challenge. Pressures to decrease costs persist, and additional cost cuts are favored by investors.[23] However, serious breakdowns in quality can cause catastrophic human as well as financial losses. Ethical dilemmas arise for manufacturers as they balance the cost of quality with the cost of warranties and potential safety hazards.

Required: Suppose you are the chief cost accountant at a company like Ford. The chief operating officer of your company has asked you to develop cost/benefit projections for the next three years. Your objective is to find the lowest overall cost that balances the costs of (1) quality, (2) warranties, and (3) potential legal remedies. You are also asked to find ways to support the company's cost-reduction efforts. Assume that your father was recently injured in an automobile accident caused by a product defect. You believe that safety must be achieved regardless of the cost.

1. What ethical dilemmas do you face?
2. Who will be affected by decisions that attempt to balance cost concerns, safety issues, and warranty liabilities?
3. What values and principles are likely to influence this kind of decision?
4. What alternative actions might you consider?
5. What would you do?
6. How does Ford Motor Company's trend toward longer warranty periods affect its financial statements?
7. How will the trade-off between high quality and potential future contingent liabilities affect the financial statements?

LO6

ETHICS

ETHICS CASE 12-6   Defining Likelihood

Anne Frankoni is the controller of Quitan Company, a manufacturer of electronic toys. Quitan Company's CFO recently learned of a potential defect in one of its newest electronic voice-activated toys. Engineers discovered that a significant portion of the toys suffer from voice distortion after a short period of use. One of Quitan's corporate customers, Terrific Toys, purchased 20,000 units of the toy and utilized it in a major promotional campaign that included the use of its own logo. A significant number of the toys were defective, and Terrific Toys has indicated that it will sue Quitan because of the potential damage to its reputation caused by the defective toy. Quitan's attorney informs the CFO that the outcome of such a lawsuit is uncertain and that the chances of losing and winning the lawsuit are approximately equal. The attorney suggests that Quitan consider offering a settlement to Terrific Toys.

Quitan's CFO believes that the attorney's assessment is overly pessimistic and instructs the controller to simply disclose the contingent liability. Anne, who would like to adhere to the principle of conservatism, recommends that the company accrue a contingent liability and recognize a loss. The CFO does not agree with her recommendation. He states that at a probability of 50 percent, the company can use its own judgment as to whether to accrue or not to accrue.

Required:

1. What are the accounting and ethical issues that Anne faces? Briefly outline the proper accounting treatment for a contingent liability.
2. Who will be affected by Anne's decision?
3. What ethical values and principles are likely to influence Anne's decision?
4. What alternative actions might she take?

---

23 Betsy Morris, "Can Ford Save Ford?" *Fortune,* vol. 146(10), November 18, 2002, pp. 53–63.

5. a. Of the parties you listed in question 2, whose interest is most important?
   b. Of the values and principles you listed in question 3, which one is most important?
   c. Of the actions you listed in question 4, which one will cause the least harm or do the most good?
   d. Of the items you identified in a, b, and c, which consideration is the most important?
6. What do you think Anne should do?

LO7   **ANALYSIS CASE 12-7**   **Impact of Warranty Agreements**

Two different warranty scenarios are provided here:

> Scenario A: Dale's Electronics sold 10,000 MP3 players for $155 each during 2005. Each MP3 player comes with a two-year warranty. Dale's estimates that the warranty cost per MP3 machine will be $9. As of December 31, 2005, Dale's had spent an average of $4 per MP3 machine repairing MP3 players that had been returned by customers for service.

> Scenario B: Bert's Tech Shop sold 5,000 extended warranty agreements during 2005. These warranty agreements are separate from the underlying product's warranties and cover a period of three years, starting with 2005. Each warranty is sold at a price of $30. During 2005, Bert's spent $40,000 fixing products covered under its extended warranties.

Required: Provide an analysis of how this information would affect each company's financial statements. Calculate the amount of liabilities outstanding at the end of 2005 with respect to each warranty agreement, and indicate how the agreements will affect income for 2005.

LO6   **ANALYSIS CASE 12-8**   **Assessing Contingent Losses**

The following two independent situations occurred in 2005 for Roundtable Manufacturing:

A. In August, an employee was injured in a factory accident. The accident was partially the result of his own negligence. The worker has sued the company for $800,000. Your attorney believes it is reasonably possible that the outcome of the suit will be unfavorable and that the settlement will cost the company between $250,000 and $500,000.

B. A suit for breach of contract seeking damages of $1,200,000 was filed by a competitor against the company on October 4, 2005. The company's legal counsel believes that an unfavorable outcome is probable. A reasonable estimate of the award to the plaintiff is between $600,000 and $900,000. No amount within this range is a better estimate of potential damages than any other amount.

Required: Provide a report to the board of directors of Roundtable Manufacturing discussing how the company should disclose the two contingencies. Discuss the proper accounting treatment, including any required journal entries or disclosures, for each situation. Provide reasons for your answers.

LO7   **ANALYSIS CASE 12-9**   **Liabilities and Promotions**

As the new director of finance for Jam's Music Store, you are responsible for accounting for the company's promotions. At the beginning of 2005, you suggest that Jam's Music Store begin a promotion in which it gives its customers coupons redeemable for a poster and a CD. Your recommendation is that one coupon is issued for each dollar of sales and that a customer will be able to exchange 100 coupons and $2.00 cash (for handling and shipping) for the poster and CD.

You estimate that 40 percent of all coupons issued will be presented for redemption at some point. Jam's sales are expected to be $800,000 in 2005 and $1,000,000 in 2006. In addition, you forecast that Jam's will give out 2,000 posters and CDs during 2005 and 3,000 during 2006. For the promotion, Jam's Music Store will need to purchase 10,000 posters at a cost of $1.50 per poster and 10,000 CDs at a cost of $4.50 per CD during 2005.

Required: Prepare a report analyzing how the promotion will affect the financial statements of Jam's Music Store. In your report, forecast the expected yearly expense of the promotion and any liability outstanding at each year end.

LO7   **ANALYSIS CASE 12-10**   **Liabilities and Sports Promotions**

During April 2004, **Upper Deck**, a worldwide sports and entertainment company, published the following press release:

> In 2004, Upper Deck Golf returns to the fairways, sand traps, and greens around the country with a 132-card set featuring all of last year's best moments and a national sweepstakes whereby golf enthusiasts can win an invitation to a clinic hosted by Tiger Woods. For the third consecutive year, Upper Deck will pair up with Tiger Woods to bring golf fans and collectors together for a unique once-in-a-lifetime experience. This year, 10 collectors who find the Tiger Woods Golden Ball Marker card will be given an opportunity to learn and enhance their golf skills from the number one ranked male golfer in the world—Tiger Woods.
>
> No need to fret if you don't find the Tiger Golden Ball Marker card—consumers successfully discovering the secret Tiger Silver Ball Marker bounty card can redeem it for $1,000. There are 20 total Tiger Silver Ball Marker bounty cards.

Required: Explain how Upper Deck should account for and disclose this promotion in its financial statements. Assume that the golf cards are all sold in 2004 and the promotions can be redeemed in 2005.

LO1,6   **RESEARCH CASE 12-11**   **Assessing Company Debt**

Isle of Capri Casinos, Inc. is a developer, owner, and operator of casinos and related lodging and entertainment facilities in growing markets in the United States. The company wholly owns and operates 13 casinos located throughout the United States.

Required: Go to the company's website (**www.islecorp.com**) and obtain the latest annual report through the investor relations link. Answer the following questions:

1. What is Isle of Capri's largest current liability?

2. What is the total of Isle of Capri's current liabilities?

3. Isle of Capri lists "Progressive jackpots and slot club awards" as a current liability. What do you think this liability represents?

4. Does Isle of Capri have any contingencies outstanding? If so, what do they involve?

ON THE WEB

The following exercises, activities, and problems are available on the *Intermediate Accounting* website. Use these resources to reinforce your understanding of the topics presented in this chapter.

- CPA-Adapted Simulations
- Interpreting the Accounting Standards
- Extending the Global Focus
- Extending the Ethics Discussion
- Mastering the Spreadsheet
- Career Snapshots
- Annual Report Project
- ACE Practice Tests
- Flashcards
- Glossary
- Check Figures for Text Problems
- PowerPoint Presentations

SOLUTIONS: CHECK YOUR UNDERSTANDING

Current Liabilities (p. 552)

1. An accrual records expenses that have been incurred but have not been paid. A deferral adjusts for amounts that have been previously received but have not yet been earned by the end of the accounting period.

2. When cash is received in advance but has not yet been earned, the Cash account is debited and the Deferred Revenue (or Unearned Income) account is credited.

3. Companies accrue for vacation pay because it is vested and is earned as a result of past service, whereas sick pay is dependent on the occurrence of a future event and therefore does not meet the definition of a liability.

4. A company may demonstrate its ability to refinance by (1) issuance of a long-term obligation or equity securities to replace the current debt after the balance sheet

date, but before the issuance of the financial statements, or (2) signing a financing agreement before the balance sheet date that permits the refinancing.

Contingencies (p. 559)

1. Two important elements that define a contingency are (1) as of the balance sheet date, an event must have occurred or a condition must be in existence, and (2) the outcome of that event or condition must be dependent upon (or contingent on) a future event.

2. If a contingent loss is probable and can be reasonably estimated, it should be accrued as a liability and note disclosure should be provided.

3. Warranties that accompany a product sale are recorded by debiting the Warranty Expense account and crediting the Warranty Liability account.

4. Gain contingencies are not recorded because to do so might be to recognize revenue prior to its realization.

Analysis of Current Liabilities (p. 560)

1. The current ratio is calculated by dividing current assets by current liabilities. It measures how well a company can cover its current liabilities with its current assets.

2. A company might improve its current ratio by using cash to pay off some of its current liabilities.

Impact of Current Liabilities on Cash Flow (p. 563)

1. A decrease in a current liability account would be shown as a negative amount on the statement of cash flows, or as a decrease in cash from operating activities, because cash has been used to reduce the balance of the current liabilities.

2. Current liabilities are generally related to operating activities.

CPA-ADAPTED SIMULATION

This simulation asks you to complete various tasks related to a company's annual financial statements. If your instructor has signed up for CPAexcel™, you can do the work online at **www.cpaexcel.com/hmco.** You may also do the simulation manually.

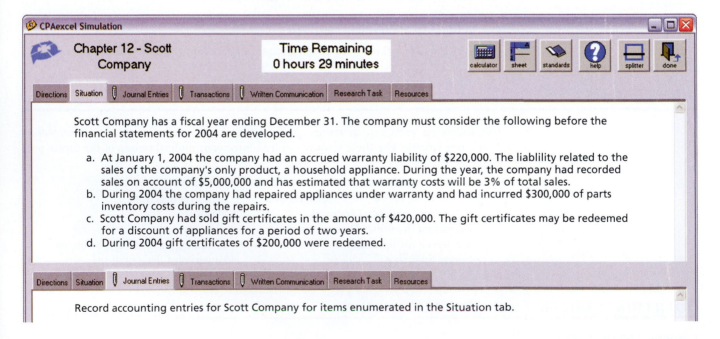

CPAexcel Simulation

Chapter 12 - Scott Company

Time Remaining
0 hours 29 minutes

calculator sheet standards help splitter done

Directions | Situation | Journal Entries | Transactions | Written Communication | Research Task | Resources

Scott Company has a fiscal year ending December 31. The company must consider the following before the financial statements for 2004 are developed.

a. At January 1, 2004 the company had an accrued warranty liability of $220,000. The liablility related to the sales of the company's only product, a household appliance. During the year, the company had recorded sales on account of $5,000,000 and has estimated that warranty costs will be 3% of total sales.
b. During 2004 the company had repaired appliances under warranty and had incurred $300,000 of parts inventory costs during the repairs.
c. Scott Company had sold gift certificates in the amount of $420,000. The gift certificates may be redeemed for a discount of appliances for a period of two years.
d. During 2004 gift certificates of $200,000 were redeemed.

Directions | Situation | Journal Entries | Transactions | Written Communication | Research Task | Resources

Record accounting entries for Scott Company for items enumerated in the Situation tab.

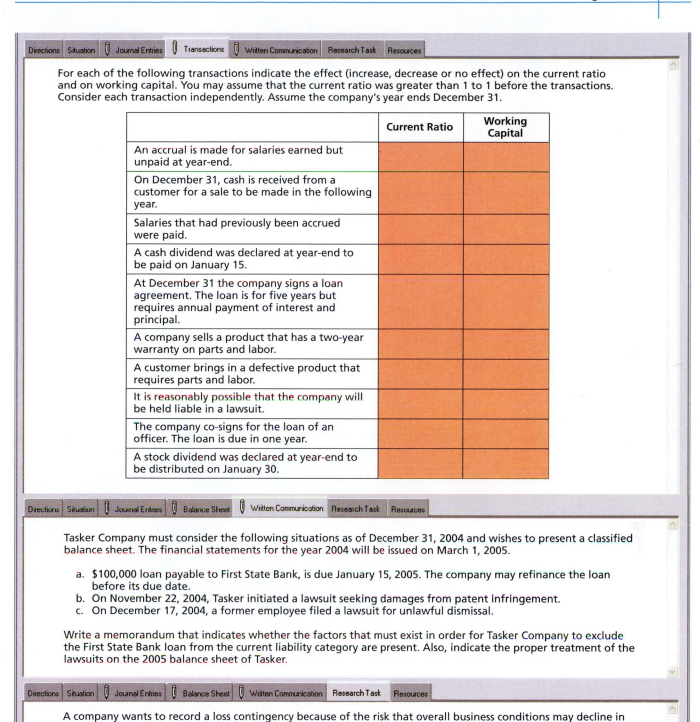

| Directions | Situation | Journal Entries | Transactions | Written Communication | Research Task | Resources |

For each of the following transactions indicate the effect (increase, decrease or no effect) on the current ratio and on working capital. You may assume that the current ratio was greater than 1 to 1 before the transactions. Consider each transaction independently. Assume the company's year ends December 31.

	Current Ratio	Working Capital
An accrual is made for salaries earned but unpaid at year-end.		
On December 31, cash is received from a customer for a sale to be made in the following year.		
Salaries that had previously been accrued were paid.		
A cash dividend was declared at year-end to be paid on January 15.		
At December 31 the company signs a loan agreement. The loan is for five years but requires annual payment of interest and principal.		
A company sells a product that has a two-year warranty on parts and labor.		
A customer brings in a defective product that requires parts and labor.		
It is reasonably possible that the company will be held liable in a lawsuit.		
The company co-signs for the loan of an officer. The loan is due in one year.		
A stock dividend was declared at year-end to be distributed on January 30.		

| Directions | Situation | Journal Entries | Balance Sheet | Written Communication | Research Task | Resources |

Tasker Company must consider the following situations as of December 31, 2004 and wishes to present a classified balance sheet. The financial statements for the year 2004 will be issued on March 1, 2005.

a. $100,000 loan payable to First State Bank, is due January 15, 2005. The company may refinance the loan before its due date.
b. On November 22, 2004, Tasker initiated a lawsuit seeking damages from patent infringement.
c. On December 17, 2004, a former employee filed a lawsuit for unlawful dismissal.

Write a memorandum that indicates whether the factors that must exist in order for Tasker Company to exclude the First State Bank loan from the current liability category are present. Also, indicate the proper treatment of the lawsuits on the 2005 balance sheet of Tasker.

| Directions | Situation | Journal Entries | Balance Sheet | Written Communication | Research Task | Resources |

A company wants to record a loss contingency because of the risk that overall business conditions may decline in the future. Management wants to establish an account for "general contingencies." What is the accounting stance on the use of general or unspecified contingencies?

Accounting for Long-Term Liabilities: Bonds and Notes Payable

LEARNING OBJECTIVES

After studying this chapter, you should be able to:

LO1 Explain the characteristics and advantages of long-term debt.

LO2 Determine the issue price of a bond.

LO3 Demonstrate how to amortize a bond premium or discount, using both the straight-line method and the effective interest method.

LO4 Determine the amount of gain or loss on a bond redemption.

LO5 Calculate imputed interest on notes payable.

LO6 Use ratio analysis to examine the effect of long-term liabilities on the financial statements.

LO7 Explain how long-term liabilities affect cash flow.

FINANCIAL REPORTING CASE

GEORGIA-PACIFIC'S LONG-TERM FINANCING NEEDS

Long-term debt is an important source of funding for companies like Georgia-Pacific that have a large amount of property, plant, and equipment and other long-term assets.

Georgia-Pacific Long-term assets play a significant role in Georgia-Pacific Corporation's operations. Because the company is in the paper packaging and building products business, it has large amounts of long-term assets in property, plant, and equipment. As of January 1, 2005, the company's long-term assets, net of accumulated depreciation, totaled nearly $8.4 billion. In addition, the company invests continually in new equipment and other long-term assets. It spent more than $713 million for plant and equipment in 2004.

Given its dependence on long-term assets, Georgia-Pacific must consider carefully how to finance its capital expenditures, and long-term debt is an important part of its financing strategy. The company's 2004 annual report shows long-term debt and other long-term liabilities of more than $11.6 billion as of January 1, 2005.

In the excerpt that follows from the Management Discussion and Analysis portion of the SEC filing, Georgia-Pacific discusses its overall approach to financing its operations. The company uses both debt and equity as a means of financing but relies heavily on borrowings and other forms of debt. When debt is used for financing, interest rate changes are an important risk factor, which the company has addressed with its strategy.

Georgia-Pacific

Liquidity and Capital Resources

We believe it is important to manage our debt and equity to keep our weighted average cost of capital low while retaining the flexibility needed to ensure that we can meet our financial obligations and finance capital spending and attractive business opportunities. We continuously review the appropriate level of debt to employ in our capital structure so that we have the necessary flexibility to finance future growth. Historically, we set debt targets based on our ability to generate cash under various business scenarios.

We maintain a high portion of our debt as long term at fixed interest rates. We intend to manage the maturities of our long-term debt (excluding bank debt) so that generally no more than $500 million matures in any one year, and if it does, so that the sum of the maturities in any two consecutive years does not significantly exceed $1 billion. Our current maturities are in substantial compliance with these guidelines. Generally, we seek to have 75% of our aggregate debt at fixed rates so as to minimize exposure to fluctuating interest rates. Currently, approximately 77% of our aggregate debt is at fixed rates....

We are focused on reducing the amount of debt that we carry and minimizing the interest costs on that debt. During 2004, our total debt level was reduced by $1,953 million using proceeds from asset sales and operating cash flows....[1]

EXAMINING THE CASE

1. What is Georgia-Pacific's overriding goal in financing its operations?

2. How does financing using fixed-rate debt minimize the risk of interest rate fluctuations?

3. How was the company able to reduce its overall debt level? Does it matter whether debt levels were reduced by asset sales rather than by operating cash flows?

---

1 Georgia-Pacific, 2004 Annual Report on Form 10-K.

LO1 **Explain the characteristics and advantages of long-term debt.**

long-term liability an obligation that will not be repaid within one year or the current operating cycle, whichever is longer

INTERNATIONAL

■ *Critical Thinking: Have you ever been faced with the need to raise extra cash in your personal finances? Did you consider selling off some assets or getting a loan? What advantages or risks can you identify for each option?*

loan covenants restrictions placed by lenders on a company's activities as a condition for lending

The Characteristics and Advantages of Debt and Equity

In their balance sheets, most companies divide their liabilities into two categories: current and long-term. A **long-term liability** is an obligation that will not be repaid within one year or the current operating cycle, whichever is longer. In this chapter, we examine long-term liabilities in the form of bonds payable or notes payable. In future chapters, we consider the accounting issues associated with other long-term liabilities, such as lease obligations, pension liabilities, and deferred taxes.

"Presentation of Financial Standards," *International Accounting Standard No. 1,* provides the requirements for the balance sheet presentations of international companies. It is similar to U.S. standards in that it recommends that companies distinguish between current and long-term liabilities in most cases. As a result, most international companies provide a breakdown of current and long-term liabilities, just as U.S. companies do.[2]

DEBT VERSUS EQUITY

Long-term liabilities are an important source of financing for many companies. Management must determine the most appropriate source of financing for each company activity, whether it be incurring additional long-term debt or issuing equity in the form of stock. While the use of debt provides several distinct advantages, it can also have disadvantages. Before choosing a source of financing, management must examine four key issues: tax advantages, control issues, effects on financial statements, and risk.

❱ TAX ADVANTAGES

The interest paid on debt is tax-deductible and can be used to reduce a corporation's tax liability. Dividends paid on stock, however, are not tax-deductible. Therefore, it is important for management to compare the after-tax costs of interest and dividends when choosing between debt and equity.

❱ CONTROL ISSUES

Because stock ownership usually carries voting privileges, the issuance of additional equity may reduce current stockholders' control of the company. Debt, in contrast, does not carry voting rights. Thus, existing owners may prefer to issue debt, based on the belief that doing so will enable them to maintain control. In actuality, the issuance of debt may also affect control. In many cases creditors place restrictions, called **loan covenants**, on a company's activities as a condition for lending. For example, a lender may require the company to maintain a specific level of liquidity as measured by the current ratio, a particular amount of cash on hand, or a predetermined minimum level of profitability. Such loan covenants do not involve voting rights but do limit a company's flexibility.

❱ EFFECTS ON FINANCIAL RATIOS

The issuance of stock negatively affects several important financial ratios. For example, a company's earnings are most commonly measured by the earnings per share (EPS) ratio (net income ÷ number of shares of common stock outstanding). The issuance of equity reduces EPS and, as a result, may make the company less attractive to investors and other financial statement users. On the other hand, the issuance of debt has a negative effect on the debt-to-equity ratio [total liabilities ÷ (total liabilities + stockhold-

---

2 "Presentation of Financial Statements," *International Accounting Standard No. 1* (London: IASB, 2005), sec. 1.60.

ers' equity)] and may be viewed negatively by credit-rating agencies and potential lenders.

RISK

The use of debt increases a company's risk in two ways. First, whenever a company borrows money, there is the potential for default. **Default risk** is the risk that the company may not be able to make the required interest payments on the debt and/or may not be able to repay the principal at maturity. Most large companies do not have significant default risk unless they suffer drastic changes in their economic fortunes. Second, when companies issue debt, they face the possibility that interest rates may change.

Interest-rate risk is the risk associated with changes in interest rates after a company borrows. Because interest rates in the financial markets change daily, all companies that borrow have significant levels of interest-rate risk. When interest rates fall, companies that have borrowed money at high rates of interest have an economic loss because they have agreed to pay interest at a rate that is higher than the current market rate of interest (of course, they "gain" if interest rates increase to a level higher than the amount they are paying). Most companies take steps to limit such risk. For example, **Weyerhaeuser**, another leading company in the paper and wood products industry, made the following disclosures about its financing strategy in the notes to its 2004 financial statements:

> The company is committed to the maintenance of a sound and conservative capital structure. This commitment is based on two considerations: the obligation to protect the underlying interests of its shareholders and lenders, and the desire to have access, at all times, to all major financial markets. The combination of maturing short-term debt and the structure of long-term debt will be managed judiciously to minimize risk.
>
> Weyerhaeuser Company and WRECO had 364-day and multi-year revolving lines of credit in the maximum aggregate amount of $2.5 billion as of December 26, 2004. The multi-year revolving line of credit expires in March 2007. WRECO can borrow up to $400 million under the 364-day facility.[3]

Ultimately, good corporate financial managers use *both* debt and equity. Their goal is to find the best combination of debt and equity that will minimize the overall cost of capital for their firm. As summarized in Illustration 13.1, they consider the advantages

default risk the risk that a company may not be able to make the required interest payments on its debt and/or may not be able to repay the principal at maturity

interest-rate risk the risk associated with changes in interest rates after a company borrows

Illustration 13.1

Characteristics and Advantages of Debt Versus Equity

Characteristic or Advantage	Equity	Debt
Tax considerations	Dividends are not tax deductible.	Interest on debt is tax deductible.
Control issues	Issuing stock may affect control of the company.	Bondholders do not have voting rights but may place loan covenant restrictions.
Effects on financial ratios	Issuing stock decreases the EPS ratio.	Issuing debt does not decrease EPS but does increase the debt-to-equity ratio.
Risk	There is risk that the market value of the stock may fluctuate.	Debt increases default risk and also has interest-rate risk (the risk of changes in interest rates).

---

3 Weyerhaeuser, 2004 Annual Report, p. 18.

leverage the use of debt to increase earning power

and characteristics of debt versus equity. When managers use debt effectively, they enhance the overall return on capital and thereby increase stockholders' wealth. The use of debt to increase earning power is referred to as **leverage**. When leverage is used wisely, long-term debt is an effective and important aspect of financial strategy. See "The Analysis of Long-Term Debt," later in this chapter, for further discussion of leverage.

DISTINGUISHING BETWEEN DEBT AND EQUITY

Over the past decade, a significant expansion in new financial instruments that blur the distinction between debt and equity has taken place. It has become difficult for accountants to determine whether such instruments should be classified in the balance sheet as long-term liabilities or as part of stockholders' equity. Some companies have issued shares of stock that *must* be redeemed at a future time, and accountants have questioned whether such instruments should be considered debt or equity. In past years, many such instruments were referred to as stock and were treated as part of stockholders' equity in the balance sheet. However, in 2004, the FASB issued "Accounting for Certain Financial Instruments with Characteristics of Both Liabilities and Equity," *Statement of Financial Accounting Standards No. 150*, which required that the following instruments be treated as liabilities:

1. A financial instrument issued in the form of shares that is mandatorily redeemable. The most common instrument is preferred stock that carries a mandatory redemption feature.

2. A financial instrument, such as stock, that includes an obligation to repurchase the shares or requires the issuer to transfer assets.

3. A financial instrument that embodies an unconditional obligation that the issuer must issue equity shares if the value of the obligation is fixed.[4]

This new position by the FASB has stirred controversy, eliciting opposition from many companies, especially small, closely held companies. Many of these companies have issued stock to their owners that carries a provision that the company will repurchase the stock at the time the owner retires or withdraws from the company. Previously, such stock was generally treated as part of stockholders' equity. The provisions of *SFAS No. 150* would require these instruments to be presented as a liability on the balance sheet. Because of the concerns raised by small companies, the FASB delayed the effective date of *SFAS No. 150* for *nonpublic* companies.[5] Although this delay will give small companies time to adjust to the new requirements, *SFAS No. 150* is the first step in an ongoing project undertaken by the FASB to develop a clearer distinction between debt and equity.

WHAT IS A LIABILITY? INSTRUMENTS SETTLED BY THE ISSUANCE OF STOCK

The stance taken by the FASB in *SFAS No. 150* required a change in what had been the basic definition of a liability. Prior to *SFAS No. 150*, a liability represented an item or

---

4 "Accounting for Certain Financial Instruments with Characteristics of Both Liabilities and Equity," *Statement of Financial Accounting Standards No. 150* (Stamford, Conn.: FASB, 2003).

5 "Effective Date, Disclosures, and Transition for Mandatorily Redeemable Financial Instruments of Certain Nonpublic Entities and Certain Mandatorily Redeemable Noncontrolling Interests Under FASB Statement No. 150, *Accounting for Certain Financial Instruments with Characteristics of Both Liabilities and Equity*," FASB Staff Position 150-3, issued November 7, 2003.

amount that would be paid in cash or with another asset. As defined in Chapter 1, the FASB has now stated that:

> Liabilities are probable future sacrifices of economic benefits arising from present obligations of a particular entity to transfer assets or provide services to other entities in the future as a result of past transactions or events.[6]

Although that definition can be applied to most situations, it is not easy to apply to several new types of financial instruments. Recently, some firms have issued instruments that clearly appear to be obligations, but that do not require payment in the form of cash or another asset. Instead, the obligations *require the issuance of stock* to settle the debt. Technically, the new instruments do not meet the FASB's definition of a liability; therefore, they are difficult to classify on the balance sheet.

As a result, the FASB signaled its intent to modify the definition of a liability by including the following addition:

> Certain obligations, primarily financial instruments or components of compound financial instruments, require or permit settlement by issuance of equity shares. If those financial instrument components establish a relationship between the issuer and the holder that is not an ownership relationship, they are liabilities.[7]

Unfortunately, the FASB has failed to issue a final statement on this issue and has chosen to address other issues related to distinguishing between debt and equity.

CLASSIFICATION OF LIABILITIES AND ETHICS

ETHICS As you can see, determining when an obligation is a liability can be difficult. Although this challenging issue has existed for years, cases like the one involving Enron, where liabilities were not disclosed in the company's balance sheet, have caused investors and statement users to question the overall picture presented in a company's balance sheet. Is the picture complete? Is it an accurate representation of the company's true assets and liabilities?

Substantial financial obligations can be carefully structured to evade the definition of a liability and therefore not be recognized as liabilities on the balance sheet. Ethical behavior on the part of accountants and corporate managers is required to ensure that proper disclosures are provided and that financial reporting is transparent. In addition, the FASB continues to shape the definition of a liability to make it more clear which obligations must be reported on the balance sheet.

> ### CHECK YOUR UNDERSTANDING
>
> 1. Describe the control issues associated with the issuance of stock versus the issuance of debt as a source of financing.
>
> 2. List and define the two types of risks associated with the issuance of debt.
>
> 3. Since the issuance of *SFAS No. 150*, how is stock that is mandatorily redeemable classified on the balance sheet?

---

6 "Elements of Financial Statements," *Statement of Financial Accounting Standards No. 6* (Stamford, Conn.: FASB, 1985), par. 35.

7 *Amendment to Statement of Financial Accounting Standards No. 6 to Revise the Definition of Liabilities*, October 27, 2000.

Bonds Payable

Bonds are a common source of long-term financing for companies. A **bond** is a contractual borrowing agreement in which the issuing party (the borrower) agrees to pay the investor (the lender or the party buying the bond) interest at a specified rate and agrees to repay the amount borrowed (the principal) at a specified maturity date. The **bond indenture** is an agreement that sets forth specific elements like the loan amount of the bond, the interest rate, and the maturity date. The loan amount is often referred to as the **face value**, or *par value*, of the bond.

In most cases, bonds are issued in denominations of $1,000, so the face value of each bond is $1,000. The interest on bonds is usually paid semiannually, even though bond indentures typically state the interest rate in annual terms. For example, a bond indenture might specify that the interest rate is 10 percent, paid semiannually. This means that the *annual rate* is 10 percent and that 5 percent will be paid after each six-month period. The total amount of a company's bond issue is usually very large—hundreds of thousands or even millions of dollars. A company may sell its entire bond issue to one investor, or it may sell its bonds through a brokerage firm or in an established market or bond exchange.

BOND CONTRACT TERMS

The bond indenture will also specify other aspects of the bond agreement. A bond contract is a flexible arrangement, and the terms of the contract can be modified to meet the needs of the issuing company and the investor. As a result, a variety of terms have developed to describe important aspects of bond agreements. The following list defines terms commonly used in bond contracts:

- **Debenture bonds** are bonds that are not backed by specific collateral but are based on the general creditworthiness of the company. These bonds may be referred to as *unsecured bonds*.

- **Mortgage bonds** are bonds that are backed by specific collateral. These bonds may be referred to as *secured bonds*. Often the collateral will be real estate (hence the term *mortgage bonds*), but the collateral may also be other assets with significant value. If the issuer defaults on the bond, the investor has first claim against the assets that have been used as collateral.

- **Coupon bonds** are bonds that bear a coupon for each interest payment. When an interest payment is due, the bondholder removes the applicable coupon and presents it to a bank for payment. Coupons allow bonds to be transferred between parties without notifying the issuer.

- **Zero-coupon bonds** do not require periodic interest payments, but instead promise to pay a fixed amount at the maturity date. Because a zero-coupon bond does not pay periodic interest, it sells at an amount significantly below its face value.

- **Convertible bonds** are bonds that may be converted into stock by the holder at a specified conversion rate. A holder of convertible bonds is entitled to a fixed rate of interest on the bonds but can exchange them for stock if the market price of the company's common stock rises.

- **Callable bonds** are bonds that can be retired by the issuer for a specified price before their maturity date. In most cases, the call price is higher than the face value and may be stated as a percentage. For example, if bonds are callable at 102, the issuer can retire the bonds by paying 102 percent of their face value.

- **Serial bonds** are bonds issued on the same date that have differing maturity dates. For example, if a company issues $1 million in bonds on a given date, it may retire

---

bond a contractual borrowing agreement in which the issuing party (the borrower) agrees to pay the investor (the lender or the party buying the bond) interest at a specified rate and agrees to repay the amount borrowed (the principal) at a specified maturity date

bond indenture an agreement that sets forth specific elements like the loan amount of the bond, the interest rate, and the maturity date

face value the loan amount of a bond; also called the *par value*

debenture bonds bonds that are not backed by specific collateral but are based on the general creditworthiness of the company; also called *unsecured bonds*

mortgage bonds bonds that are backed by specific collateral; also called *secured bonds*

coupon bonds bonds that bear a coupon for each interest payment

zero-coupon bonds bonds that do not require periodic interest payments, but instead promise to pay a fixed amount at the maturity date

convertible bonds bonds that may be converted into stock by the holder at a specified conversion rate

callable bonds bonds that can be retired by the issuer for a specified price before their maturity date

serial bonds bonds issued on the same date that have differing maturity dates

Illustration 13.2

Bond Terms and Terminology

Bond	A borrowing agreement in which the issuing party (the borrower) agrees to pay the investor (the lender or the party buying the bond) interest at a specified rate and agrees to repay the amount borrowed (the principal) at a specified maturity date.
Bond indenture	The bond contract that sets forth the specific elements of the agreement, including the loan amount, referred to as the face value, or par value, of the bond; the interest rate; and the maturity date.
Face value	The amount to be paid at maturity. Also called *par value*.
Debenture bonds	Bonds that are not backed by specific collateral but are based on the general creditworthiness of the company. These bonds may be referred to as *unsecured bonds*.
Mortgage bonds	Bonds that are backed by specific collateral. These bonds may be referred to as *secured bonds*.
Coupon bonds	Bonds that bear a coupon for each interest payment. When an interest payment is due, the bondholder removes the applicable coupon and presents it to a bank for payment.
Zero-coupon bonds	Bonds that do not require periodic interest payments, but instead promise to pay a fixed amount at the maturity date.
Convertible bonds	Bonds that the investor can convert into stock at a specified conversion rate.
Callable bonds	Bonds that can be retired by the issuer for a specified price before their maturity date.
Serial bonds	Bonds issued on the same date that have differing maturity dates.
Face rate of interest	The rate of interest to be paid to bondholders each period as specified in the bond indenture. Also called *coupon rate* or *stated rate*.
Market rate of interest	The rate of interest demanded by the bond market for bonds with the same characteristics as the bonds issued.
Issue price	The present value of the cash flows for the bond, calculated at the market rate of interest.
Discount on bonds	The excess of face value over issue price.
Premium on bonds	The excess of issue price over face value.

$200,000 of the bonds in 2010, $200,000 in 2011, and so forth. Serial bonds are advantageous for the issuer because the bonds are not all paid off at the same time.

The bond indenture may also spell out specific covenants, or restrictions. Covenants are used to provide an additional element of safety for the bondholders and to ensure that the issuer operates in ways that will ensure its profitability and the liquidity necessary to meet the periodic interest payments and to repay the principal. For example, the bond indenture may require that the issuer not exceed a maximum debt-to-equity ratio or that a minimum amount of working capital be maintained. In some cases, the bond indenture may limit dividends to a specified level (perhaps a maximum dollar amount of dividends, a per share amount, or a percentage of net income). Not only do bond covenants reduce the risk to investors, but they also benefit the issuing company by making the bonds more acceptable to the marketplace.

In the next section, you will learn how to determine the issue price of a bond. First, review the terms associated with bond transactions, presented in Illustration 13.2.

LO2 Determine the issue price of a bond.

🧩 *Critical Thinking: Because bonds rarely sell for an amount exactly equal to their face value, why is it important to correctly identify the issue price of a bond?*

face interest rate the rate of interest that will be paid to bondholders at each interest period as specified in the bond indenture; also referred to as *coupon rate* or *stated rate*

market interest rate the rate of interest demanded by the bond market at a particular time for bonds that have the same risk characteristics and maturity date as the bonds to be issued

issue price the present value of the cash flows for the bond, calculated at the market interest rate

DETERMINING A BOND'S SELLING PRICE

Bonds are simply a mechanism for a company to borrow money. The issuing company (the borrower) agrees to make interest payments over the life of the bond and to repay the principal at the maturity date (also referred to as the due date). The investor (the buyer of the bonds) is the lender. The investor will receive interest income over the life of the bonds and will receive the principal at the bonds' maturity date. Bonds may be sold to another company or financial institution or may be sold to the general public by using an underwriter or brokerage firm. It usually takes time for a company to develop the bond contract (bond indenture), obtain the necessary regulatory approval, make a public announcement of the bond offering, and then print the bond contracts. After completing the necessary steps, the company can issue the bonds at the selling price that is dictated by the market and the prevailing interest rates.

Bond prices are stated as a percentage of face value. For example, if you read that Avist Company bonds are selling at 102, it means that the bonds are selling at 102 percent of their face value. If Avist Company had issued bonds with a $200,000 face value, the current market price of the entire bond issue would be $204,000 ($200,000 × 1.02).

Two interest rates influence the selling price of bonds. The **face interest rate** (also referred to as *coupon rate* or *stated rate*) is the rate of interest that will be paid to bondholders at each interest period as specified in the bond indenture. For example, if the face value of the bonds is $200,000 and the face rate is 10 percent, paid semiannually, the issuing company must pay $10,000 ($200,000 × 10% × ½ year) at each interest payment date.

The **market interest rate** is the rate of interest demanded by the bond market at a particular time, in this case the time of issuance, for bonds that have the same risk characteristics and maturity date as the bonds to be issued.[8] The market interest rate is affected by general economic conditions, interest rate and monetary conditions, and the mood of potential investors about risk and return. Market conditions change daily, and so does the prevailing market interest rate.

In most cases, the market interest rate will differ from the face interest rate established by the issuer of the bonds. In some cases, the difference occurs because of the time lag between the printing of the bond indenture and the issuance of the bonds. For example, the bond indenture may specify interest payments of 8 percent, but the market interest rate may have risen to 8.2 percent by the time the bonds are issued. In other cases, the issuing company may intentionally establish a face interest rate that differs from the prevailing market interest rate. For example, when a company issues zero-coupon bonds, the face rate is set at zero, but market conditions will dictate the bonds' "true," or effective, rate of interest.

The **issue price** of a bond represents the present value of the cash flows for the bond, calculated at the market interest rate. Bonds produce two distinct cash flow streams: one from the interest payments and one from the principal. The interest payments represent an *ordinary annuity* that will be paid at each interest payment date until the maturity date. Thus, one element of a bond's issue price is the present value of that annuity. At the maturity date, the amount of principal must be repaid. Thus, the other element of the bond's issue price is the present value of the principal. The issue price of the bond is the total present value of all the future cash flows.[9]

For example, assume that on January 1, 2005, Sunny Devil Company issues bonds with a face value of $200,000 that pay 10 percent interest semiannually (5 percent per

---

8 The market rate of interest is also referred to as the *yield* on the bond. When the amount of premium or discount on the bond is taken into account, it is also referred to as the *effective rate of interest*. We will begin with the term *market rate of interest,* but you will see the other two terms when we actually record the interest amounts.

9 For calculations involving the time value of money, use the tables provided in Appendix A.

period) and mature in five years. Assume that the market interest rate at the date of issuance is 8 percent (4 percent per semiannual period). The issue price of the bonds is $216,222, calculated as follows:

Present Value Using a Calculator

Future Value = $200,000
Payments   = $10,000
N   = 10
I   = 4%
Present Value = $216,222

Present Value Using Tables

$10,000 × 8.1109	=	$ 81,109	
$200,000 × 0.6756	=	135,120	
Present Value		$216,229	(Difference due to rounding. We will use the present value calculated via the calculator.)

The bonds in this case would sell at a premium above face value.

premium on bonds the excess of the issue price of the bonds over their face value

A **premium on bonds** is the excess of the issue price of the bonds over their face value. The amount of the premium on the Sunny Devil bonds is $16,222:

$$\text{Premium} = \text{Issue Price} - \text{Face Value}$$
$$= \$216,222 - \$200,000$$
$$= \$16,222$$

Assume that Bruin Company also issues bonds with the same characteristics as Sunny Devil's bonds, except that the market interest rate was 12 percent (6 percent per semiannual period) at the time the bonds were issued. In that case, the issue price of the bonds is $185,280:

Present Value Using a Calculator

Future Value = $200,000
Payments   = $10,000
N   = 10
I   = 6%
Present Value = $185,280

Present Value Using Tables

$10,000 × 7.36009	=	$ 73,601	
$200,000 × 0.5584	=	111,680	
Present Value		$185,281	(Difference due to rounding. We will use the present value calculated via the calculator.)

The bonds in this case would sell at a discount below face value.

discount on bonds the excess of the face value of the bonds over their issue price

A **discount on bonds** is the excess of the face value of the bonds over their issue price. The amount of the discount on the Bruin Company bonds is $14,720:

$$\text{Discount} = \text{Face Value} - \text{Issue Price}$$
$$= \$200,000 - \$185,280$$
$$= \$14,720$$

Premiums and discounts are neither good nor bad. Once the issuing company has established the face interest rate on its bonds, it does not choose whether the bonds will sell at a premium or a discount. *The market dictates the selling price of a bond issue.* The existence of a premium or a discount depends solely on the relationship of the face interest rate and the market interest rate at the time of issuance. We can state the relationship as follows:

When market interest rate equals face interest rate ...	bonds sell at face value (issue price is equal to face value).
When face interest rate exceeds market interest rate ...	bonds sell at a premium (issue price is higher than face value).
When market interest rate exceeds face interest rate ...	bonds sell at a discount (issue price is less than face value).

RECORDING BOND ISSUANCE

When a company issues bonds, it records the face value of the bonds in a Bonds Payable account and records the difference between the issue price and the face value in a Premium on Bonds or Discount on Bonds account. The accounting entries on January 1, 2005, for Sunny Devil Company and Bruin Company for the two examples presented previously should be as follows:

Sunny Devil Company 10% Face Rate, 8% Market Rate Semiannual Payment		
Cash	216,222	
Premium on Bonds		16,222
Bonds Payable		200,000

Bruin Company 10% Face Rate, 12% Market Rate Semiannual Payment		
Cash	185,280	
Discount on Bonds	14,720	
Bonds Payable		200,000

Premium on Bonds is a balance sheet account and is presented in conjunction with the Bonds Payable account in the financial statements. If Sunny Devil developed a balance sheet on January 1, 2005, immediately after the issuance of the bonds at a premium, the following entries would appear in the long-term liabilities section:

Long-Term Liabilities

Bonds payable	$200,000	
Premium on bonds	16,222	$216,222

Because Premium on Bonds has a credit balance, it is *added to* the amount presented for Bonds Payable.

Likewise, the Discount on Bonds account is a balance sheet account that is presented in conjunction with the Bonds Payable account in the financial statements. However, Discount on Bonds has a debit balance and is *deducted* from the amount presented for Bonds Payable. If Bruin Company developed a balance sheet on January 1, 2005, immediately after the issuance of the bonds at a discount, the following entries would appear in the long-term liabilities section:

Long-Term Liabilities

Bonds payable	$200,000	
Discount on bonds	(14,720)	$185,280

RECORDING BONDS ISSUED BETWEEN INTEREST PAYMENT DATES

Bonds are often issued at a time other than the date on the bond indenture. When they are, the amount of the accrued interest is added to the purchase price of the bonds and is paid by investors. Assume, for example, that on March 1, 2005, Wildcat Company issues, at 103 plus accrued interest, 10-year bonds with a face value of $100,000 and a face interest rate of 6 percent. Interest is paid semiannually on June 30 and December 31. The bonds are dated January 1, 2005, and will be due on January 1, 2015. In this case, there will be $1,000 of accrued interest at the time the bonds are issued ($100,000 $\times$ 6% $\times$ 2/12), which represents the interest from January 1 to March 1, 2005.

The total amount received by Wildcat on March 1, 2005, is $104,000; it would be recorded as follows:

March 1, 2005		
Cash	104,000	
Interest Expense ($100,000 $\times$ 0.06 $\times$ 2/12)		1,000
Premium on Bonds		3,000
Bonds Payable		100,000

It may seem illogical to *credit* Interest Expense at the time of issuance, but this procedure enables Wildcat to record the first semiannual interest payment as follows:

June 30, 2005		
Interest Expense	3,000	
Cash		3,000

After the June 30 entry for interest, the Interest Expense account would appear as follows:

Interest Expense			
(6 months interest)	3,000	1,000	(less 2 months interest)
(equals 4 months interest incurred)			
bal.	**2,000**		

The balance of $2,000 is the amount of interest that was actually incurred for the four-month period that the bond was outstanding (March 1 through June 30). Thus, the initial credit is made to Interest Expense to reflect the proper amount of interest expense after the interest payment.

We will discuss amortization of premium or discount in a future section of the chapter. At this point it is important to note that any premium or discount related to bonds issued after the date on the bond indenture should be amortized over the time period from the *date of issuance* to the maturity date, as explained later in this chapter. The Wildcat bonds in this example may be referred to as 10-year bonds, but because they were issued two months after the date on the bond contract, they will not be outstanding for a full 10 years:

The Premium on Bonds account would be amortized over the period from the date of issuance, March 1, 2005, to the maturity date, January 1, 2015, or over a period of 118 months.

ACCOUNTING FOR BOND ISSUE COSTS

bond issue costs costs, such as legal fees, transfer fees, brokerage or underwriting costs, and taxes, that are incurred to issue bonds

An organization that issues bonds usually incurs some costs in the year of issuance—called **bond issue costs**—including legal fees, transfer fees, brokerage or underwriting costs, and, in some cases, taxes. The proper treatment of such costs is a matter of some debate. However, in general, bond issue costs should be treated as a deferred charge and amortized over the life of the bonds. As you learned in Chapter 4, a **deferred charge** results from a prepayment whose benefit will extend over a period of years from the time of incurrence and is carried forward to be expensed in future years. It must be treated as a balance sheet item until it is eliminated by amortization. It is similar in concept to a prepaid expense, except that prepaid expenses are typically classified as current assets and bond issue costs should be classified as a long-term asset because the length of time until the bonds' maturity date is usually longer than one year. Some companies classify bond issue costs as "other assets."

deferred charge a charge that results from a prepayment whose benefit will extend over a period of years from the time of incurrence and is carried forward to be expensed in future years; classified as "other assets" or "long-term assets"

Assume that a company issues bonds with a $100,000 face value at 100 and must pay $5,000 of costs associated with the issuance. The company records the following entry at the time the bonds are issued:

Cash	95,000	
Bond Issue Costs	5,000	
Bonds Payable		100,000

Assume that the life of the bond is five years and that the company amortizes bond issue costs on a straight-line basis each semiannual period. Thus, the same amount should be amortized in each period. The entry to record amortization of bond issue costs each period would be as follows:

Bond Issue Expense	500	
Bond Issue Costs		500

Bond issue costs *are not* treated as an adjustment of the amount of interest expense related to the bond. Amortized bond issue costs are charged to the Bond Issue Expense account rather than to the Interest Expense account.

ACCOUNTING FOR CHANGES IN MARKET INTEREST RATES AFTER ISSUANCE

As you have learned, the market interest rate reflects the risks associated with investing in a bond. The market considers the economic prospects of the issuing company and its ability to pay both interest and principal. The market also considers general economic conditions, the rate of inflation, government fiscal and monetary policies, and any other factors that may affect the company's future. As a result, the market interest rate changes daily.

You have also learned how market interest rates influence the issue price of bonds. If the market interest rate exceeds the face interest rate, the bond will sell at a discount. Conversely, if the market interest rate is less than the face interest rate, the bond will sell at a premium. In addition, the influence of market interest rates continues after bonds are issued. The daily fluctuations in market interest rates cause the selling prices of issued bonds to fluctuate daily as well.

Recall from earlier in the chapter that Sunny Devil Company issued bonds on January 1, 2005, with the following characteristics:

Date of bonds: January 1, 2005

Maturity date: January 1, 2010

Face value: $200,000

Face rate of interest: 10 percent paid semiannually (5 percent per period)

Market interest rate at the date of issuance: 8 percent (4 percent per semiannual period)

The issue price of the bonds was calculated as $216,222.

Assume that by January 1, 2006, a year after the issuance of the bonds, the market interest rate has increased to 10 percent (5 percent per semiannual period). The market price of the bond could be calculated as follows:

Present Value Using a Calculator

Future Value = $200,000
Payments   = $10,000
N   = 8
I   = 5%
Present Value = $199,992

Present Value Using Tables

$10,000 × 6.4632   = $ 64,632
$200,000 × 0.6768 = 135,360
Present Value $199,992

At the present time, accountants do not record changes in the market value of issued bonds. In effect, the market interest rate is not considered after the date of issuance. This treatment is consistent with the *historical cost* method. The amount of liability is recorded at the time of bond issuance based on the existing market rate. That amount is not intended to reflect interest-rate conditions after the date of issuance.

Some accountants have called for a form of *fair value* accounting, in which an interest rate that was current as of the date of the financial statements would be used to calculate the present value of the cash flows related to the bond liability. Although this form of accounting would provide relevant information about the current value of liabilities, it would add several complexities. One of the more controversial questions is how the unrealized gains or losses resulting from changes in the fair value of the liability would be treated. If a firm were to include those unrealized gains or losses as income, its income could fluctuate significantly from period to period. The FASB has been studying this issue and others related to fair value accounting for liabilities. Whereas the accounting model presently favors the historical cost method, in the future, some form of fair value (also called *current value*) accounting for liabilities may be embraced.

AMORTIZING A BOND PREMIUM OR DISCOUNT

LO3 Demonstrate how to amortize a bond premium or discount, using both the straight-line method and the effective interest method.

effective interest rate the interest rate paid after adjustments for any premium or discount resulting from market interest rates at the time of issue

amortization of a bond premium or discount the adjustment of interest expense for a bond premium or discount

straight-line method of amortization a method of amortization in which the same amount of premium or discount is allocated to each interest period over the life of the bond issue

A bond's face interest rate is the rate of interest paid to bondholders at each interest period, as specified in the bond indenture. A bond's **effective interest rate** is the interest rate paid after adjustments for any premium or discount resulting from market interest rates at the time of issue. Because a premium or discount affects interest expense each time interest is paid, the amount of the premium or discount must be reduced gradually over the life of the bond. Accountants' practice of adjusting interest expense for a premium or discount is called **amortization of a bond premium or discount**. When amortization occurs, the balance of the premium or discount account is systematically reduced and the amount is transferred to the Interest Expense account. If a discount is involved, as the unamortized discount amount decreases, the carrying value of the bond increases. If a premium is involved, as the unamortized premium amount decreases, the carrying value of the bond decreases. There are two ways of amortizing a bond premium or discount: the straight-line method and the effective interest method.

❯ THE STRAIGHT-LINE METHOD

When the **straight-line method of amortization** is used, the same amount of premium or discount is allocated to each interest period over the life of the bond issue. To

Critical Thinking: What underlying accounting concept calls for the allocation of a bond premium or discount over the life of the bond?

illustrate the amortization of premium and discount, we will return to the Sunny Devil and Bruin Company examples presented earlier:

Sunny Devil

Date of bonds: January 1, 2005
Maturity date: January 1, 2010
Face value: $200,000
Face interest rate: 10% paid semiannually (5% per period)
Market interest rate: 8% (4% per semiannual period)
Issue price: $216,222

Bruin

Date of bonds: January 1, 2005
Maturity date: January 1, 2010
Face value: $200,000
Face interest rate: 10% paid semiannually (5% per period)
Market interest rate: 12% (6% per semiannual period)
Issue price: $185,280

Sunny Devil Company has a Premium on Bonds account with a credit balance of $16,222 ($216,222 − $200,000), and Bruin Company has a Discount on Bonds account with a debit balance of $14,720 ($200,000 − $185,280):

Sunny Devil		**Bruin**	
Receives	$216,222	Receives	$185,280
At maturity repays	200,000	At maturity repays	200,000
Difference	$ 16,222	Difference	$ 14,720

Sunny Devil receives $216,222 at the time of borrowing but is obligated to repay only the principal of $200,000 at maturity. The premium of $16,222 represents a reduction of the effective interest rate on the bonds. Bruin, in contrast, receives only $185,280 at the time of borrowing but is also obligated to repay the principal of $200,000 at maturity. The discount of $14,720 represents an increase in the effective interest rate on the bonds.

Assume that both companies use the straight-line method of amortization and that they record amortization semiannually at each interest payment date. Both companies would record the interest payment as follows:

Sunny Devil		
Interest Expense	10,000	
Cash		10,000

Bruin		
Interest Expense	10,000	
Cash		10,000

In addition, Sunny Devil would amortize the premium and Bruin would amortize the discount as follows:

Sunny Devil		
Premium on Bonds	1,622	
Interest Expense		1,622
($16,222 ÷ 10 periods = $1,622)		

Bruin		
Interest Expense	1,472	
Discount on Bonds		1,472
($14,720 ÷ 10 periods = $1,472)		

We have used two journal entries to show that the amount of interest expense presented in the income statement is the result of (1) the amount of interest paid and (2) the amount of premium or discount amortized. In practice, however, one journal entry may be recorded that combines the effects as follows:

Sunny Devil		
Interest Expense	8,378	
Premium on Bonds	1,622	
Cash		10,000

Bruin		
Interest Expense	11,472	
Discount on Bonds		1,472
Cash		10,000

Illustration 13.3

Effects of Amortization

Amortization of Premium	Amortization of Discount
Decreases interest expense	Increases interest expense
Decreases bond carrying value	Increases bond carrying value
Increases net income	Decreases net income

The purpose of amortization is to change the amount of interest expense to reflect the fact that interest expense includes both the amount paid and the amount of premium or discount amortized. Each period the balance of the Premium on Bonds or Discount on Bonds account is reduced and transferred to Interest Expense:

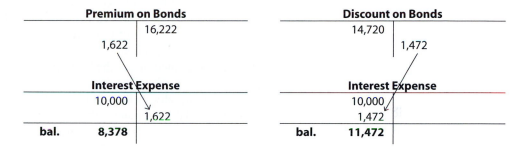

The effects of amortization are summarized in Illustration 13.3.

When straight-line amortization is used, the Premium on Bonds account or the Discount on Bonds account will be reduced by the same amount each period. By the maturity date of the bonds, the balance of the Premium on Bonds account or the Discount on Bonds account will be reduced to zero, and the entire balance of the premium or discount will have been used to adjust interest expense.

❯ THE EFFECTIVE INTEREST METHOD

The primary advantage of the straight-line method of amortization is its simplicity. Because the same amount of premium or discount is amortized each period, the calculation is not difficult. When the straight-line method is used to amortize a large amount of premium or discount, however, the results can be somewhat misleading. Under the straight-line method, the same *dollar amount* of interest expense is reported each period, even though the bond carrying value changes as amortization occurs. When a bond discount is amortized, the bond carrying value increases over time, and when a bond premium is amortized, the bond carrying value decreases over time. As a result, the effective interest rate on the bond (that is, interest expense divided by the carrying value of the bond) fluctuates. Conceptually, this is incorrect. The *interest rate* on the bond does not fluctuate and is a constant percentage of the bond's carrying value.

effective interest method of amortization a method of amortization in which a constant rate of interest is used to amortize a premium or discount over the life of a bond

The **effective interest method of amortization** is used to amortize a premium or discount at a *constant rate* of interest over the life of the bond. The dollar amount of interest expense changes each period, but the effective interest rate remains the same. In fact, the effective interest method is the method that is required in most bond situations. In actual practice, companies are allowed to use the straight-line method of amortization only if the results are not greatly different from those with the effective interest method (this would happen only if the amount of premium or discount was small or the amortization period was short).

To illustrate amortization using the effective interest method, we will return to the Sunny Devil and Bruin Company examples presented earlier. The two companies issued bonds with the provisions given on the following page.

Sunny Devil

Date of bonds: January 1, 2005

Maturity date: January 1, 2010

Face value: $200,000

Face interest rate: 10% paid semiannually (5% per period)

Market interest rate: 8% (4% per semiannual period)

Issue price: $216,222

Bruin

Date of bonds: January 1, 2005

Maturity date: January 1, 2010

Face value: $200,000

Face interest rate: 10% paid semiannually (5% per period)

Market interest rate: 12% (6% per semiannual period)

Issue price: $185,280

The purpose of amortization using the effective interest method is the same as that for the straight-line method. Over the life of the bond, Sunny Devil should reduce the balance of the Premium on Bonds account, and the amount transferred should reduce the amount of interest expense in each period. Bruin should reduce the balance of the Discount on Bonds account, and the amount transferred should increase the amount of interest expense in each period.

The amortization schedule for the bond premium for Sunny Devil is presented in Illustration 13.4.

The bond carrying value in Illustration 13.4 is the present value of the bond issued at a premium. At the date of issuance, the present value of the bond was the issue price of $216,222. The amounts in the Cash column are the interest payments made at the face rate of 10 percent (5 percent per semiannual period). Each period's interest expense is derived by multiplying the effective interest rate of 8 percent (4 percent per semiannual period) times the bond carrying value at the beginning of the period. The amount of premium amortized is the difference between the interest at the face rate (column A) and the interest at the effective rate (column B). Note that the amount of premium amortized differs in each period. However, over the life of the bond, a total

Illustration 13.4

Schedule of Bond Premium Amortization: Effective Interest Method

Face Rate: 10%, paid semiannually

Effective Rate: 8%, paid semiannually

Date	Column A Cash[a]	Column B Interest Expense[b]	Column C Premium Amortized[c]	Column D Bond Carrying Value[d]
1/1/05				$216,222
6/30/05	$10,000	$8,649	$1,351	214,871
12/31/05	10,000	8,595	1,405	213,466
6/30/06	10,000	8,539	1,461	212,005
12/31/06	10,000	8,480	1,520	210,485
6/30/07	10,000	8,419	1,581	208,904
12/31/07	10,000	8,356	1,644	207,260
6/30/08	10,000	8,290	1,710	205,550
12/31/08	10,000	8,222	1,778	203,772
6/30/09	10,000	8,151	1,849	201,923
12/31/09	10,000	8,077	1,923	200,000

[a] $200,000 × 0.10 × ½ year

[b] Bond Carrying Value × 0.08 × ½ year

[c] Column A − Column B

[d] Face Value + Unamortized Premium

Illustration 13.5

Schedule of Bond Discount Amortization: Effective Interest Method

Face Rate: 10%, paid semiannually

Effective Rate: 12%, paid semiannually

Date	Column A Cash[a]	Column B Interest Expense[b]	Column C Discount Amortized[c]	Column D Bond Carrying Value[d]
1/1/05				$185,280
6/30/05	$10,000	$11,117	$1,117	186,397
12/31/05	10,000	11,184	1,184	187,581
6/30/06	10,000	11,255	1,255	188,836
12/31/06	10,000	11,330	1,330	190,166
6/30/07	10,000	11,410	1,410	191,576
12/31/07	10,000	11,495	1,495	193,071
6/30/08	10,000	11,584	1,584	194,655
12/31/08	10,000	11,679	1,679	196,334
6/30/09	10,000	11,780	1,780	198,114
12/31/09	10,000	11,886	1,886	200,000

[a] $200,000 × 0.10 × ½ year
[b] Bond Carrying Value × 0.12 × ½ year
[c] Column B − Column A
[d] Face Value − Unamortized Discount

of $16,222 is amortized, and the bond's carrying value is reduced to its face value of $200,000 at the maturity date of January 1, 2010.

The bond amortization schedule in Illustration 13.4 is the basis for the journal entries that are recorded each period. Sunny Devil would record the following entries for the first two semiannual periods ended June 30, 2005, and December 31, 2005:

June 30, 2005		
Interest Expense	8,649	
Premium on Bonds	1,351	
Cash		10,000

December 31, 2005		
Interest Expense	8,595	
Premium on Bonds	1,405	
Cash		10,000

Note that the amortization of a premium reduces the effective interest on the bonds. Amortization is a noncash charge that is necessary to reflect the interest actually incurred on the bond obligation.

The amortization schedule for the bond discount for Bruin Company is presented in Illustration 13.5.

The bond carrying value in Illustration 13.5 is the present value of the bond issued at a discount. At the date of issuance, the present value of the bond was the issue price of $185,280. The amounts in the Cash column are the interest payments made at the face rate of 10 percent (5 percent per semiannual period). Each period's interest expense (column B) is derived by multiplying the effective interest rate of 12 percent (6 percent per semiannual period) times the bond carrying value at the beginning of the period. The amount of discount amortized is the difference between the interest at the face rate (column A) and the interest at the effective rate (column B). Note that when a discount exists, the amounts in column B exceed those in column A. Over the life of the bond, a total of $14,720 is amortized, and the bond's carrying value is increased to its face value of $200,000 at the maturity date of January 1, 2010.

The bond amortization schedule in Illustration 13.5 is the basis for the journal entries that are recorded each period. Bruin Company would record the following entries for the first two semiannual periods ended June 30, 2005, and December 31, 2005:

June 30, 2005		
Interest Expense	11,117	
Discount on Bonds		1,117
Cash		10,000

December 31, 2005		
Interest Expense	11,184	
Discount on Bonds		1,184
Cash		10,000

The amortization of a discount increases the effective interest on the bonds. It indicates that the actual rate of interest on the bonds is higher than the amount of the cash interest payments.

REDEMPTION OF BONDS

LO4 Determine the amount of gain or loss on a bond redemption.

extinguishment the retiring, refunding, or paying off of bonds

Critical Thinking: Do you think that gains or losses on bond redemptions should be considered extraordinary or unusual in nature? Explain your reasoning.

There are several ways in which bonds may be redeemed (or paid off). The FASB uses the general term **extinguishment** to refer to the retiring, refunding, or paying off of bonds. In the simplest case, bonds reach their maturity date and their principal is repaid. In such cases, there is ordinarily no gain or loss on the retirement of the bonds because they are retired at their face value. In other cases, bonds may be redeemed (retired or refunded) before their maturity date. Because all types of bond extinguishments are accounted for similarly, we will use the terms *redemption* or *retirement* of the bonds.

When bonds are retired before their maturity date, the issuing company must calculate and report any gain or loss that results. A gain is calculated as follows:

$$\text{Gain on Bond Retirement} = (\text{Bond Carrying Value} - \text{Unamortized Bond Issue Costs}) - \text{Bond Call Price}$$

where

$$\text{Bond Carrying Value} = \text{Bond Face Value} + \text{Unamortized Bond Premium}$$

or

$$\text{Bond Face Value} - \text{Unamortized Bond Discount}$$

bond call price an amount specified in the bond indenture; often stated as a percentage

The **bond call price** is an amount specified in the bond indenture, often stated as a percentage. For example, a call price of 102 means that the issuer must pay 102 percent of face value to retire the bonds before maturity. A gain occurs when the issuing party pays *less* to retire the bonds than the value of the bonds shown on the balance sheet at the time of redemption.

In contrast, a loss on bond retirement is calculated as follows:

$$\text{Loss on Bond Retirement} = \text{Bond Call Price} - (\text{Bond Carrying Value} - \text{Unamortized Bond Issue Costs})$$

where

$$\text{Bond Carrying Value} = \text{Bond Face Value} + \text{Unamortized Bond Premium}$$

or

$$\text{Bond Face Value} - \text{Unamortized Bond Discount}$$

A loss occurs when the issuing party pays *more* to retire the bonds than the value of the bonds on the balance sheet at the time of redemption.

The amount of gain or loss must be based on the bond carrying value *at the date of retirement* and is calculated *only for the portion of the bonds that will be retired*. To calculate a loss on bond retirement, let's look again at the bonds issued by Bruin Company. All of the basic information remains the same, but we will add bond issue costs of $5,000:

Date of bonds: January 1, 2005

Maturity date: January 1, 2010

Face value: $200,000

Face rate of interest: 10 percent paid semiannually (5 percent per period)

Market interest rate: 12 percent (6 percent per semiannual period)

Issue price of bond: $185,280, discount amortized semiannually using the effective interest method

Bond issue costs: $5,000, amortized semiannually using the straight-line method

Assume that on January 1, 2006, Bruin Company retires the bonds at 102. According to the schedule of amortization in Illustration 13.5, the bond carrying value as of January 1, 2006, is $187,581. The amount of unamortized bond issue costs as of January 1, 2006, is $4,000 ($5,000 ÷ 10 periods × 8 periods remaining). The *loss* on the bond retirement is calculated as follows:

$$\begin{aligned} \text{Loss on Bond Retirement} &= \text{Bond Call Price} - (\text{Bond Carrying Value} \\ &\quad - \text{Unamortized Bond Issue Costs}) \\ &= (\$200,000 \times 1.02) - (\$187,581 - \$4,000) \\ &= \$204,000 - \$183,581 \\ &= \underline{\$20,419} \end{aligned}$$

The company would record the following entry for the bond retirement:

January 1, 2006		
Bonds Payable	200,000	
Loss on Bond Redemption	20,419	
Discount on Bonds ($200,000 − $187,581)		12,419
Cash		204,000
Bond Issue Costs		4,000

❭ TREATMENT OF A GAIN OR LOSS

The gain or loss on bond retirement should be presented in the income statement. Prior to 2002, the applicable pronouncement, "Reporting Gains and Losses from Extinguishment of Debt," *Statement of Financial Accounting Standards No. 4*, said that all material gains and losses on bond redemptions should be considered extraordinary items and presented separately in the income statement in that category.[10] Although that pronouncement led to uniform reporting of bond gains and losses for all companies, it was inconsistent with the reporting of other types of gains and losses. To remedy the situation, in 2002 the FASB issued *SFAS No. 145*, which said that gains and losses on bond redemptions should be treated in the same way as other types of gains and losses. That is, if a material gain or loss on a bond redemption is both "unusual in nature" and "infrequent in occurrence," it should be treated as an extraordinary item and presented separately in the income statement in the extraordinary items section, net of tax.[11]

---

10 "Reporting Gains and Losses from Extinguishment of Debt," *Statement of Financial Accounting Standards No. 4* (Stamford, Conn.: FASB, 1975), par. 8.

11 "Rescission of SFAS 4, 44, and 64, Amendment of SFAS 13, and Technical Corrections," *Statement of Financial Accounting Standards No. 145* (Stamford, Conn.: FASB, April 2002).

In most cases, however, gains or losses on bond redemptions are not considered unusual and infrequent. Bond redemption transactions are not uncommon for companies, especially when interest-rate conditions change. Therefore, gains or losses on bond redemptions usually should *not* be treated as extraordinary items in the income statement. Most companies present gains or losses in the other income or expense section of the income statement. Because such gains or losses are not considered extraordinary, they are presented *before* tax, rather than net of tax. There may be some rare cases in which the gains or losses on bond redemptions are both unusual and infrequent in occurrence. In those cases, the gain or loss on bond redemption meets the criteria for an extraordinary item and should be shown, net of tax, in the extraordinary item section of the income statement.

❯ ACCRUED INTEREST WHEN RETIRING BONDS

In the previous example, the bonds were retired on a date immediately after the interest was due and paid. However, in some cases, bonds are retired at a time other than the interest payment date. For example, assume that Bruin Company retired its bonds on March 1, 2006, instead of on January 1, 2006.

First, Bruin Company's gain or loss on bond redemption must be based on the bond carrying value as of the date on which the bonds are redeemed. If a premium or discount is involved, it must be amortized up to the date of the redemption. The amount *unamortized* as of that date is used to calculate the bond carrying value. Similarly, if bond issue costs are involved, they must be amortized up to the date of the redemption. The amount unamortized as of that date is used to calculate the bond carrying value.

Second, the issuer of the bond must typically pay the call price of the bond plus the accrued interest at the time of the bond redemption. However, the amount of the accrued interest does not affect the amount of the gain or loss recognized on the bond redemption. The accrued interest should be charged to Interest Expense.

CHECK YOUR UNDERSTANDING

1. What is the difference between the face value of a bond and the issue price of a bond?

2. How is the premium on a bond issuance calculated?

3. If a bond was issued at a premium, how does the amortization of that premium affect net income?

4. How does the effective interest method of amortization differ from the straight-line method?

Long-Term Notes Payable

notes payable written promissory agreements to pay a set amount at some future date; usually require the payment of explicit interest in addition to the base obligation amount

Notes payable are written promissory agreements to pay a set amount at some future date. Notes also usually require the payment of explicit interest in addition to the base obligation amount. The accounting issues related to notes payable are similar to those for bonds payable. In fact, many companies do not distinguish between notes payable and bonds payable on their financial statements and report one line item for both amounts.

Figure 13.1

Note on Long-Term Debt—Georgia-Pacific

Georgia Pacific
NOTE 9.   INDEBTEDNESS

Our indebtedness includes:

In millions	January 1, 2005	January 3, 2004
Debentures and notes, average rate of 8.2% and 8.3%, payable through 2031	$6,324	$ 8,146
Credit facilities, average rates of 3.4% and 3.3%, payable through 2009	705	250
Revenue bonds, average rates of 5.3% and 5.4%, payable through 2031	785	755
Euro-denominated bonds, average rate of 4.75%, payable through 2004	—	378
Capital leases, average rates of 8.4% and 7.7%, payable through 2018	292	302
European debt, average rates of 3.7% and 3.6%, payable through 2031	44	77
Other loans, average rates of 3.1% and 2.9%, payable through 2005	10	11
Less: unamortized net discount	(33)	(56)
Total debt	8,127	9,863
Less: long-term portion of debt	8,070	9,074
Current portion of long-term debt	57	789
Secured borrowings and short-term notes, average rates of 2.8% and 2.1%	568	689
Total short-term debt	625	1,478
Total debt balance	$8,695	$10,552

Figure 13.1 presents the note from the 2004 annual report of **Georgia-Pacific Corporation** that details the company's long-term debt. At January 1, 2005, Georgia-Pacific had more than $8.1 billion in long-term debt that consisted of notes, bonds, and other loans. The interest rates on the long-term debt ranged from 2.9 percent to 8.4 percent because of variations in the provisions and maturity dates of these loans.

LO5 Calculate imputed interest on notes payable.

imputed interest rate an estimated interest rate based on the rate that an independent borrower and an independent lender would negotiate for a similar transaction under comparable terms and conditions

IMPUTED INTEREST ON NOTES PAYABLE

In most cases, the interest rate on a bond is readily apparent because it is stated in the bond indenture or the lending agreement. That rate, which was agreed upon between the borrower and the lender, is usually the best indicator of the interest rate to be applied to a transaction. However, in some cases, an accountant may need to use an **imputed interest rate**, which is an estimated interest rate based on the rate that an independent borrower and an independent lender would negotiate for a similar transaction under comparable terms and conditions. *Opinions of the Accounting Principles Board No. 21* requires interest to be imputed (1) when a note is non-interest-bearing or no interest rate is stated, and (2) when an interest rate is stated, but that interest rate is unrealistically low.[12] Both cases illustrate the importance of economic substance over

---

12 "Interest on Receivables and Payables," *Opinions of the Accounting Principles Board No. 21* (New York: AICPA, August 1971).

Critical Thinking: Explain how the accounting concept of "substance over form" is apparent in the process of imputing an interest rate.

form. That is, an accountant is required to view the substance of a lending transaction and cannot rely on the stated interest rate.

VALUING A NON-INTEREST-BEARING NOTE

Assume that on January 1, 2005, Buyborrow Company purchases a depreciable asset from Sellend Company in exchange for a five-year non-interest-bearing note. The principal of $100,000 will be paid at the maturity date of January 1, 2010. To place a fair value on the transaction, the accountant will impute an interest rate and use that rate to compute the *present value* of the note. Assuming that an 8 percent interest rate is applicable, the present value of the note would be $68,058:

Present Value Using a Calculator

Future Value = $100,000
N   = 5
I   = 8%
Present Value = $68,058

Present Value Using Tables

$100,000 × 0.6806
Present Value = $68,060   (Difference due to rounding. We will use the present value calculated via the calculator.)

The difference between the present value of the note and the face value of the note is treated as a discount on notes payable:

$$\text{Discount} = \text{Face Value} - \text{Present Value}$$
$$= \$100,000 - \$68,058$$
$$= \underline{\$31,942}$$

The best indicator of the value of the newly purchased depreciable asset is the present value of the non-interest-bearing note. Thus, Buyborrow Company would record the following transaction on January 1, 2005:

Asset	68,058	
Discount on Notes Payable	31,942	
Notes Payable		100,000

The Discount on Notes Payable account is a contra-liability account and is presented in the balance sheet as an adjustment of the Notes Payable account. Its balance represents the amount of interest that Buyborrow is in effect paying, even though the parties refer to the note as non-interest-bearing. The balance of the Discount on Notes Payable account is amortized using the effective interest method. Illustration 13.6 presents the amortization schedule for the note.

At each year end, Buyborrow will record an adjusting entry to amortize the Discount on Notes Payable account and recognize interest expense. At December 31, 2005, the following entry will be recorded:

Interest Expense	5,445	
Discount on Notes Payable		5,445

The process will continue until the note's maturity, when the discount will be fully amortized and the balance of the account will have been systematically transferred to Interest Expense over the life of the note.

Illustration 13.6

Schedule to Amortize Discount on Non-Interest-Bearing Note: Effective Interest Method

		Column A	*Column B* Interest Expense[b]	*Column C* Discount Amortized[c]	*Column D* Present Value
Date		Cash[a]			
1/1/05					$ 68,058
12/31/05		$0	$5,445	$5,445	73,503[d]
12/31/06		0	5,880	5,880	79,383
12/31/07		0	6,351	6,351	85,734
12/31/08		0	6,859	6,859	92,593
12/31/09		0	7,407	7,407	100,000

Imputed Interest Rate: 8%

[a] Zero because note is non-interest-bearing
[b] Present Value × 0.08
[c] Column B − Column A
[d] Previous Present Value + Discount Amortized

CHOOSING AN IMPUTED INTEREST RATE

In the previous example, we assumed that an 8 percent rate was applicable. In actual practice, the choice of applicable rate is often a matter of judgment. *APB No. 21* specifies that where possible, the rate should reflect the *fair value* of the asset, property, or service exchanged in the transaction. The difference between fair value and the face amount of the note should represent the discount applicable to the transaction. In many cases, however, it may be difficult to assess or determine the fair value of the asset, and the accountant must rely on other evidence to determine the applicable interest rate. *APB No. 21* specifies that the objective is to approximate the rate that would apply if an independent borrower and an independent lender had negotiated a similar transaction under comparable terms and conditions.[13] In all cases, the rate should at least equal the rate at which the *debtor* could obtain financing of a similar nature. Thus, the accountant must consider the credit standing of the debtor, any collateral specified, the terms of the note, and any other factors that may have a bearing on the interest rate.

Although the choice of interest rate is somewhat subjective, the rules requiring an imputation of interest are objective. The rules are intended to prevent two parties from engaging in transactions that will result in the overstatement of assets acquired and the misstatement of interest expense and net income.

▶ VALUING A NOTE WITH AN UNREALISTIC INTEREST RATE

If a note carries an interest rate that is unrealistically high or low, the accountant is required to impute an interest rate and record the present value based on that rate rather than the amount specified in the note agreement.

Assume, for example, that on January 1, 2005, Green Company purchases equipment from Blue Company. To finance the purchase, Green Company signs a five-year note to Blue Company that has a principal of $100,000 and calls for an annual interest rate of 2 percent, or $2,000 per interest period. Of course, an interest rate of 2 percent is unrealistic, so Green's accountant must determine what rate of interest truly applies to the transaction, given Green Company's credit history and other factors. Other factors would include current interest rates and economic considerations and conditions

---

13 Ibid., par. 106.

for the industry that Green Company is in. Assume that a 10 percent rate is applicable and should be used as the imputed rate of interest. The present value of the note is as follows:

Using a Calculator

Future Value	= $100,000
Annual Interest Payment	= $2,000
N	= 5
I	= 10%
Present Value	= $69,674

Using Tables

$100,000 × 0.62092 = $62,092
$2,000 × 3.7908 = 7,582
Present Value $69,674

The difference between the note's face value and its present value is treated as a discount on the note payable. Thus, the discount is $30,326:

$$\text{Discount} = \text{Face Value} - \text{Present Value}$$
$$= \$100,000 - \$69,674$$
$$= \$30,326$$

The asset purchased is recorded at the present value of the note. Thus, Green Company would record the following transaction on January 1, 2005:

Equipment	69,674	
Discount on Notes Payable	30,326	
Notes Payable		100,000

Green Company records interest for each period using the effective interest method. Illustration 13.7 presents the amortization schedule for this note.

Illustration 13.7

Amortization Schedule: Discount on Note with Unrealistic Interest Rate

Face Rate: 2%
Imputed Rate: 10%

Date	Column A Cash[a]	Column B Interest Expense[b]	Column C Discount Amortized[c]	Column D Present Value
1/1/05				$ 69,674
12/31/05	$2,000	$6,967	$4,967	74,641[d]
12/31/06	2,000	7,464	5,464	80,105
12/31/07	2,000	8,011	6,011	86,116
12/31/08	2,000	8,612	6,612	92,728
12/31/09	2,000	9,272	7,272	100,000

[a]$100,000 × 0.02
[b]Present Value × 0.10
[c]Column B − Column A
[d]Previous Present Value + Discount Amortized

At each year end, Green Company must record the interest payment and must also amortize a portion of the Discount on Notes Payable account and recognize interest expense. At December 31, 2005, the following entry would be recorded:

Interest Expense	6,967	
Cash		2,000
Discount on Notes Payable		4,967

The process will continue until maturity, when the entire discount will be amortized and the balance of the account will have been transferred to interest expense over the life of the note. Note that when the effective interest method is used, the process of amortizing a note payable with an unrealistic interest rate is identical to the process of amortizing a bond payable issued at a discount.

Theoretically, the rules for imputed interest apply to both discounts and premiums. However, premiums on notes requiring imputed interest are seldom, if ever, encountered. It is far more common to find a note with an unrealistically low interest rate, which requires a discount on notes payable, than to find a note with an unrealistically high interest rate, which requires a premium.

CHECK YOUR UNDERSTANDING

1. What is an imputed interest rate and why is one sometimes applied to notes payable transactions?

2. If a note carries an unrealistic interest rate, what kinds of factors would an accountant use to determine an imputed rate?

3. What account is debited if a note's face value is greater than its present value?

The Analysis of Long-Term Debt

LO6 Use ratio analysis to examine the effect of long-term liabilities on the financial statements.

Critical Thinking: *What financial amounts and existing agreements do you think a potential creditor may wish to review before extending credit to a company?*

debt-to-equity ratio a leverage ratio that indicates what percentage of a company's total assets is financed by creditors; Total Debt ÷ Total Assets (or Total Liabilities + Stockholders' Equity)

Debt plays an important role in the financial strategies of most companies. What distinguishes a successful debt strategy from an unsuccessful one, however, is the relative amount of a company's long-term debt and whether the company has successfully used debt to increase its return to stockholders.

DEBT, EQUITY, AND LEVERAGE

The most widely used measure of debt is the **debt-to-equity ratio**, which indicates what percentage of a company's total assets is financed by creditors. The higher the percentage of total assets represented by debt, the greater the risk that the company may be unable to meet its maturing obligations. The formula for the debt-to-equity ratio (also called *debt to total assets*) is computed as follows:

$$\text{Debt-to-Equity Ratio} = \text{Total Debt} \div \text{Total Assets}^{14} \text{ (or Total Liabilities} + \text{Stockholders' Equity)}$$

The debt-to-equity ratios for Georgia-Pacific and Weyerhaeuser for 2004 and 2003 are presented in Illustration 13.8. When we examine the ratios, we can see that the two

---

14 The debt-to-equity ratio measures total debt rather than only long-term debt. Some companies may adjust the ratio to consider only the long-term portion of debt. Another variation of this ratio is the debt-to-equity ratio that measures total liabilities divided by total stockholders' equity.

Illustration 13.8

Debt-to-Equity Ratios, 2003–2004—Georgia-Pacific and Weyerhaeuser

Georgia-Pacific (in millions)			
2004		**2003**	
Total Debt	*Total Assets*	*Total Debt*	*Total Assets*
$16,847	$23,072	$19,011	$24,405
Debt-to-Equity Ratio =		Debt-to-Equity Ratio =	
$16,847 ÷ $23,072 = 0.73		$19,011 ÷ $24,405 = 0.78	

Weyerhaeuser (in millions)			
2004		**2003**	
Total Debt	*Total Assets*	*Total Debt*	*Total Assets*
$20,699	$29,954	$21,490	$28,599
Debt-to-Equity Ratio =		Debt-to-Equity Ratio =	
$20,699 ÷ $29,954 = 0.69		$21,490 ÷ $28,599 = 0.75	

companies have a similar asset base, but Georgia-Pacific relies slightly more on debt as a source of financing. As mentioned earlier, companies in the timber and wood products industry must continually invest in long-term assets such as plant and equipment. Both of these companies have chosen to rely on long-term debt to finance those assets. Perhaps that reliance is explained in part by the low interests rates available. Many companies see debt as an effective source of financing. However, investors and creditors may become concerned if they believe that a company's debt-to-equity ratio is too high or if the debt-to-equity ratio increases year to year.

The debt-to-equity ratio is a rough indicator of a company's use of leverage. As discussed earlier, the term *leverage* refers to the use of borrowed funds to increase the profit from an investment. The *effective use of leverage* involves the use of debt to increase earning power. A company with a large amount of debt is considered highly leveraged. However, an analysis should not focus solely on a firm's amount of debt or its relative amount of debt as revealed by the debt-to-equity ratio. A more significant issue is whether the company has used debt effectively.

Two common measures of how effectively a company uses leverage are the return on assets ratio and the return on equity ratio. **Return on assets (ROA)** shows how efficiently a company uses its assets to produce income by expressing net income as a percentage of average total assets. A high return on assets ratio indicates that the company is using its assets effectively to generate income. The formula for return on assets is:

return on assets (ROA) a leverage ratio that shows how efficiently a company uses its assets to produce income by expressing net income as a percentage of average total assets; Net Income ÷ Average Total Assets

$$\text{Return on Assets} = \text{Net Income}[15] \div \text{Average Total Assets}$$

Return on stockholders' equity (ROE) shows how efficiently a company uses stockholders' investments to produce income by expressing net income as a percentage of average total stockholders' equity. The formula for return on stockholders' equity is:

return on stockholders' equity (ROE) a leverage ratio that shows how efficiently a company uses stockholders' investments to produce income by expressing net income as a percentage of average total stockholders' equity; Net Income ÷ Average Total Stockholders' Equity

$$\text{Return on Stockholders' Equity} = \text{Net Income} \div \text{Average Total Stockholders' Equity}$$

The use of *leverage is considered effective if the return on equity exceeds the return on assets*. Normally, the use of leverage is effective when a company can borrow at a fixed

---

15 Some analysts prefer to use net income before interest expense. If income is measured in this way, interest expense, net of the related tax effect, should be used to adjust the numerator of this ratio.

Illustration 13.9

Return on Assets and Return on Stockholders' Equity, 2004—Georgia-Pacific (in millions)

Return on assets (ROA)	
Net Income ($623) ÷ Average Total Assets ($23,739)	2.62%
Return on stockholders' equity (ROE)	
Net Income ($623) ÷ Average Total Stockholders' Equity ($5,810)	10.72%

rate of interest and invest in assets with returns that exceed the cost of the borrowed money. The amount by which the return on assets exceeds the cost of borrowing represents a benefit to the stockholders and an increase in their return.

Illustration 13.9 presents the return on assets and return on stockholders' equity for Georgia-Pacific for 2004. The company has a positive return, but the usefulness of the ratio could be enhanced by comparison with other companies in the industry.

The ratios show that the company has used leverage to its advantage because the return on stockholders' equity is larger than the return on assets. The company has been able to increase its return to stockholders through the effective use of long-term debt. It should be noted, however, that the negative effects of leverage can be equally dramatic. In economic downturns, highly leveraged companies will be burdened with greater fixed interest payments than companies with lower leverage, and their profitability will decline more rapidly.

INTEREST COVERAGE

times interest earned ratio a ratio that measures a company's ability to meet its interest payments as they come due by comparing income with interest expense; Income Before Interest and Taxes ÷ Interest Expense

Creditors are concerned about a borrower's ability to satisfy its obligations. The **times interest earned ratio** measures a company's ability to meet its interest payments as they come due by comparing income with interest expense. This ratio is calculated as follows:

Times Interest Earned = Income Before Interest and Taxes ÷ Interest Expense

When the times interest earned ratio is high, this indicates that the company can be expected to meet its future interest payments from future operations. When the ratio is low, it indicates that there is some question about the company's ability to meet future interest payments. The times interest earned ratio for Georgia-Pacific is given in Illustration 13.10.

Georgia-Pacific has 2.30 times as much in income before interest and taxes as it has in interest payments. Potential lenders may find the debt level to be high, but the associated interest payments do not appear to be worrisome. Current creditors appear to be safe, but future interest payments will be dependent on the company's ability to generate profits in the future.

Illustration 13.10

Times Interest Earned, 2004—Georgia-Pacific (in millions)

Net income	$ 623
Plus interest expense	706
Plus taxes	297
Numerator	$1,626
Denominator	÷$706
Times interest earned	2.30

1. How is the debt-to-equity ratio calculated?

2. What does the return on stockholders' equity ratio measure?

3. Explain what it means to say that a company is "highly leveraged."

LO7 Explain how long-term liabilities affect cash flow.

Critical Thinking: In regard to debt, what cash inflows or outflows do you think analysts and investors are likely to be interested in?

The Effects of Long-Term Debt on Cash Flow

The issuance of long-term debt is an important source of cash for most companies. Yet, the balance sheet reveals only the balances of the long-term debt accounts at the end of the period. The balances of these accounts do not reveal the amount of cash generated from long-term debt. Cash flow is indicated by the *change* in the long-term debt accounts as presented in the statement of cash flows. This statement reveals the amount of cash generated or used during the current period by long-term debt. The cash generated from long-term debt is presented on the statement of cash flows in the financing activities section. The financing activities section of Georgia-Pacific's statement of cash flows for 2004 is shown in Figure 13.2.

During 2004, Georgia-Pacific decreased its long-term debt position by repaying $6,801 million of long-term debt while adding $5,027 million of new debt. It is evident that during the year the company obtained nearly all of its financing from debt rather than from stock or other forms of equity.

In addition to knowing a company's cash flows from financing activities, analysts and other users of financial statements are often interested in particular cash flow amounts. One such amount is the interest paid during the year. In fact, interest and tax payments are often among the most important cash flow payments. Unfortunately, information about the amount of interest actually paid is very hard to discern from the statement of cash flows. Most companies use the indirect method to compile the statement of cash flows and report the amount of net income in the operating activities section. The amount of interest expense is hidden in the net income number, not disclosed as a separate line item within the operating activities section of the cash flow statement.[16] Because interest payments are of particular interest to analysts and statement users, the FASB requires that the amount of interest payments for the year be disclosed separately, either as additional information to accompany the cash flow statement or as information in the notes to accompany the annual report.

DETERMINING INTEREST PAID BY CONVERTING FROM ACCRUAL TO CASH

It is important to remember that the amount of interest expense reported on the income statement is based on accrual accounting and is not an indication of the amount of cash actually paid. To determine the actual cash flow amount, the income statement amount must be adjusted for any accruals or deferrals. We will use a hypothetical company to illustrate the conversion from accrual to cash.

---

16 Even if the direct method is used, there is some question about where interest payments should be disclosed. Many believe that it is conceptually incorrect to report interest as an operating activity. The FASB acknowledges this argument but requires interest to be reported as an operating activity for the sake of simplicity.

Figure 13.2

Excerpt from Statement of Cash Flows

Georgia-Pacific

Georgia-Pacific Corporation
For the Years Ended December 31, 2004, 2003, and 2002

(in millions)	2004	2003	2002
Cash flows from financing activities:			
Repayments and maturities of long-term debt	($6,801)	($8,090)	($5,030)
Additions to long-term debt	5,027	7,142	4,975
Fees paid to issue debt	(15)	(55)	(14)
Fees paid to retire debt	(52)	(0)	(0)
(Decrease) increase in bank overdrafts	(44)	(45)	71
Decrease in accounts receivable secured borrowings and short-term notes	(121)	(21)	(900)
Proceeds from option plan exercises	68	18	4
Proceeds from employee stock purchase plan	0	23	37
Cash dividends paid	(129)	(126)	(118)
Other, net	(0)	(1)	7
Cash used for financing activities	(2,067)	(1,155)	(968)

To convert from the accrual basis to the cash basis, we begin with the interest expense (the accrual number) and adjust for all balance sheet accounts related to interest. For example, the income statement of Iverson Company shows interest expense of $100,000 for the year 2005. In addition, the company had the following account balances at the beginning and end of the year 2005:

Account	Beginning Balance	Ending Balance
Interest Payable	$20,000	$35,000
Discount on Bonds	40,000	30,000

The $10,000 change in the Discount on Bonds Payable account is due to amortization of the discount. Because amortization is a noncash transaction, its amount must be deducted from the accrual-based amount of interest. Additionally, the increase in Interest Payable indicates that interest has been recorded as an expense but has not been paid. The amount of that noncash transaction must also be deducted from the accrual-based amount of interest. Thus, the amount of cash that Iverson actually paid for interest is as follows:

	Amount
Interest Expense	$100,000
Increase in Interest Payable	(15,000)
Decrease in Discount on Bonds	(10,000)
Interest paid	$ 75,000

All of the balance sheet accounts related to interest must be analyzed to determine the amount of interest paid. For example, some companies may have a Prepaid Interest account or a Premium on Bonds account in addition to the accounts in the preceding example. The balances of those accounts should be analyzed to determine the impact on cash flows. In each case, it is the *change* in the account balance, rather than the ending balance, that is used to adjust from the accrual-based amount of interest to the amount actually paid.

Revisiting the Case

GEORGIA PACIFIC'S LONG-TERM FINANCING NEEDS

1. Georgia-Pacific's expressed goal in its financing activities is to maintain a low overall average cost of capital while retaining its flexibility and financing its capital spending and business opportunities.

2. Georgia-Pacific indicates that the use of fixed-rate debt allows the company to avoid the exposure to fluctuating interest rates. However, that is only partially true because a company has interest rate risk even when using fixed-rate debt. For example, if a company has borrowed at a fixed rate and interest rates decline, the company will be paying a higher rate of interest than is necessary.

3. The company decreased its overall debt level by $1,953 million by a combination of sale of assets and operating cash flows. However, these two sources of cash are markedly different. If a company has reduced its debt by selling assets, it has reduced the size of the company and affected its potential in future periods. Sound companies generate cash from operating activities, which they can then use to reduce debt levels.

SUMMARY BY LEARNING OBJECTIVE

LO1 Explain the characteristics and advantages of long-term debt.

Long-term liabilities are obligations that will not be paid within one year or the current operating cycle, whichever is longer. They are an important source of financing because they offer a number of advantages. For example, interest on debt is tax-deductible, but a dividend on stock is not. Also, issuance of stock involves a change in control or ownership, but issuance of debt does not. And debt does not affect the earnings per share ratio in the same way that an issuance of stock would. Nonetheless, debt does involve a certain amount of risk. Interest rates may fluctuate, and interest and principal payments may not be met.

LO2 Determine the issue price of a bond.

A bond's issue price is determined by calculating the present value of the cash flows from its interest and principal. A bond pays interest at a fixed rate, called the face rate or coupon rate, and the periodic payments of that interest constitute an ordinary annuity. At maturity, the principal of the bond must be repaid as a single sum. The present value of the two kinds of cash flows is calculated using the market rate, or yield, on the bond. If a bond's face value is lower than its issue price, the bond sells at a premium. If a bond's face value is higher than its issue price, the bond sells at a discount.

LO3 Demonstrate how to amortize a bond premium or discount, using both the straight-line method and the effective interest method.

A premium or discount on a bond must be amortized over the life of the bond. The amount amortized affects the amount of interest expense recognized. When the straight-line method is used to amortize a premium or discount, the same dollar amount is amortized in each period. When the effective interest method is used to amortize a discount or premium, interest expense recognized is a constant percentage of the bond's carrying value. Under the effective interest method, the dollar amount of the premium or discount amortized varies each period, but the rate of interest is constant and represents the effective interest rate at the time of issuance.

LO4 Determine the amount of gain or loss on a bond redemption.

A company experiences a gain when the amount it pays to call bonds is less than the bonds' carrying value at the date of redemption. It experiences a loss when the amount it pays to call bonds is greater than the bonds' carrying value. A bond's carrying value is its face value plus any unamortized premium or minus any unamortized discount, plus unamortized issue costs. It is important to calculate bond carrying value at the date of the bond redemption and only for the portion of the bonds that is actually redeemed.

LO5 Calculate imputed interest on notes payable.

An imputed interest rate is an estimated interest rate based on the rate that an independent borrower and an independent lender would negotiate for a similar transaction under comparable terms and conditions. Interest must be imputed when a note payable is non-interest-bearing, when no interest rate is stated, or when the note's face interest rate is unrealistically low. Imputed interest should be treated as a discount on notes payable and should be amortized over the life of the note using the effective interest method of amortization.

LO6 Use ratio analysis to examine the effect of long-term liabilities on the financial statements.

The debt-to-equity ratio measures the relative importance of long-term debt as a source of financing. A company with a high debt-to-equity ratio is considered highly leveraged, meaning that it has a high amount of debt relative to its assets. The use of leverage is considered effective when the return on stockholders' equity exceeds the return on assets. This is an indication that a company has been able to borrow and earn a rate of return that is higher than its borrowing rate. The stockholders benefit through an increased return. It is also important to analyze a company's ability to meet its interest obligations. The times interest earned ratio is commonly used for that purpose.

LO7 Explain how long-term liabilities affect cash flow.

Debt is often a company's most important source of funds for financing assets. The cash flows generated from long-term liabilities are presented in the financing activities section of the statement of cash flows. Analysts and financial statement users are also interested in the amount of cash payments for interest during the period. That amount is not presented as a separate line item in the statement of cash flows when the indirect method is used. Furthermore, the amount of interest expense recognized in the income statement is based on the accrual method and does not represent the amount of cash paid for interest. To determine the amount of cash paid, interest expense must be adjusted for discount or premium amortized and for changes in any balance sheet accounts related to interest, such as interest payable or prepaid interest.

KEY TERMS

amortization of a bond premium or discount (p. 597)
bond (p. 590)
bond call price (p. 602)
bond indenture (p. 590)
bond issue costs (p. 595)
callable bonds (p. 590)
convertible bonds (p. 590)
coupon bonds (p. 590)
debenture bonds (p. 590)
debt-to-equity ratio (p. 609)
default risk (p. 587)
deferred charge (p. 596)

discount on bonds (p. 593)
effective interest method of amortization (p. 599)
effective interest rate (p. 597)
extinguishment (p. 602)
face interest rate (p. 592)
face value (p. 590)
imputed interest rate (p. 605)
interest-rate risk (p. 587)
issue price (p. 592)
leverage (p. 588)
loan covenants (p. 586)
long-term liability (p. 586)

market interest rate (p. 592)
mortgage bonds (p. 590)
notes payable (p. 604)
premium on bonds (p. 593)
return on assets (ROA) (p. 610)
return on stockholders' equity (ROE) (p. 610)
serial bonds (p. 590)
straight-line method of amortization (p. 597)
times interest earned ratio (p. 611)
zero-coupon bonds (p. 590)

EXERCISES

LO1 **EXERCISE 13-1** **Debt Versus Equity**

Assume that your client is a large company that needs $1 million to purchase additional assets for a planned expansion. Your client is considering whether to obtain the additional funds through additional debt or by issuing stock. The following data have been collected for your client:

Total debt	$1,000,000
Total assets	$5,000,000
Interest rate on debt	10%
Annual income before interest and taxes	$800,000
Tax rate	40%

Required:

1. What are the advantages and disadvantages of debt versus stock issuance?

2. How would debt issuance affect the debt-to-equity ratio? Calculate the ratio before and after the debt is issued. What other ratios or financial measures would be affected?

3. Your client has considered issuing debt that carries a provision allowing the lenders to convert their holdings to stock at a future time. Should such an instrument be considered to be debt or stock? Write a memo to advise your client on the proper accounting for this instrument.

4. Your client has considered issuing stock that pays interest based on the company's level of income. For example, if earnings were above a certain percentage, interest would be paid at 10 percent. But if the client's earnings were lower, the interest rate on the stock would be lowered also. Should such an instrument be considered to be debt or stock? Write a memo to advise your client on the proper accounting for this instrument.

LO2 **EXERCISE 13-2** **Issue Price of a Bond**

Assume that on January 1, 2005, a company issues bonds. The bonds are dated January 1, 2005, and have a face amount of $1,000,000. Interest will be paid at the rate of 8 percent semiannually for five years.

Required:

1. Calculate the issue price of the bonds and the amount of premium or discount on the bonds if the yield at the time of issuance is (a) 6 percent, (b) 8 percent, and (c) 10 percent.

2. Assume that the bonds are issued on January 1, 2005, to yield 10 percent. Also, assume that the market interest rate declines to 9 percent by January 1, 2006. Calculate the market value of the bonds as of January 1, 2006. How should the company account for the change in the market value of the bonds?

LO2 **EXERCISE 13-3** **Calculate the Yield on Bonds**

Assume that on January 1, 2005, a company issues bonds. The bonds are dated January 1, 2005, and have a face amount of $1,000,000. Interest will be paid at the rate of 8 percent semiannually for five years. The bonds are issued for $1,041,583.

Required:

1. Calculate the yield on the bonds.

2. Indicate how the bonds should be presented on the balance sheet immediately after issuance.

3. Assume that the market interest rate changes to 6.5 percent by January 1, 2006. Calculate the market value of the bonds as of January 1, 2006. How should the company account for the change in the market value of the bonds?

LO2 **EXERCISE 13-4** **Bonds Issued Between Payment Dates**

Assume that on March 1, 2005, a company issues bonds. The bonds are dated January 1, 2005, and have a face amount of $1,000,000. Interest will be paid at the rate of 8 percent semiannually on June 30 and December 31 for five years. The bonds are issued on March 1, 2005, for 102 plus accrued interest.

Required:

1. Calculate the total amount of cash received at the time the bonds are issued.
2. Prepare the journal entry for bond issuance on March 1, 2005.
3. Indicate the amount of interest that should be paid on June 30, 2005.
4. Indicate the amount of interest that should be paid on December 31, 2005.

LO3   EXERCISE 13-5   Effective Interest and Straight-Line Methods of Amortization

Refer to the facts in Exercise 13-3. Assume that the company amortizes premium or discount on bonds on each interest payment date of June 30 and December 31.

Required:

1. Calculate the amount of premium that should be amortized each period if the company uses the straight-line method.
2. Develop an amortization table that can be used to amortize the bond premium if the company uses the effective interest method. Prepare the journal entries that should be recorded on June 30, 2005, and December 31, 2005.
3. For each semiannual period over the life of the bonds, calculate interest as a percentage of bond carrying value (interest expense/bond carrying value) for the straight-line and effective interest methods. Explain why the effective interest method is considered to be the better method theoretically.

LO3   EXERCISE 13-6   Amortization—Straight-Line, Bonds Between Dates

Refer to the facts in Exercise 13-4. Assume that the company amortizes premium or discount on bonds on each interest payment date of June 30 and December 31. Assume that the company uses the straight-line method of amortization.

Required:

1. Calculate the amount of premium that should be amortized on June 30, 2005, and December 31, 2005.
2. Prepare the journal entries that should be recorded on June 30, 2005, and December 31, 2005.
3. Explain why investors/lenders are required to pay accrued interest when a bond is issued between interest payment dates.
4. Indicate how the bonds should be presented in the balance sheet on December 31, 2005.

LO4   EXERCISE 13-7   Gain or Loss—Redemption on an Interest Date

Refer to the facts in Exercises 13-3 and 13-5. Assume that the bonds are redeemed on December 31, 2005, at 102.

Required:

1. Determine the amount of gain or loss on bond redemption using both the straight-line and effective interest methods of amortization. (You may ignore income taxes.)
2. Prepare the journal entries necessary to record the bond redemption on December 31, 2005 for both the straight-line and effective interest methods.
3. Assume instead that the company redeems the bonds at 105. Determine the amount of gain or loss on bond redemption for both the straight-line and effective interest methods.
4. Assume that instead of redeeming all of the bonds on December 31, 2005, the company decides to redeem bonds with a face value of $400,000 at 102 on that date. Determine the amount of gain or loss on bond redemption and prepare the journal entries necessary to record the redemption on December 31, 2005 for both the straight-line and effective interest methods.

LO4   **EXERCISE 13-8   Gain or Loss—Redemption Not on an Interest Date**

Assume that on January 1, 2005, a company issues bonds. The bonds are dated January 1, 2005, and have a face amount of $800,000. Interest will be paid at the rate of 8 percent semiannually for five years. The bonds are issued at 98. The company uses the straight-line method of amortization and amortizes premium or discount on each interest date. Assume that the company redeems the bonds on April 1, 2006, for 102 plus accrued interest.

Required:

1. Determine the amount of gain or loss on bond redemption. (You may ignore income taxes.)

2. Prepare the journal entry necessary to record the bond redemption on April 1, 2006.

3. Assume that instead of redeeming all of the bonds on April 1, 2006, the company decides to redeem bonds with a face value of $200,000 at 102 plus accrued interest on that date. Determine the amount of gain or loss on bond redemption and prepare the journal entry necessary to record the redemption on April 1, 2006.

LO5   **EXERCISE 13-9   Imputed Interest on Note Payable**

Company A purchases equipment on January 1, 2005, from Seller Company and gives in exchange a five-year, non-interest-bearing note with a face amount of $150,000.

Company B purchases equipment on January 1, 2005, from Seller Company and gives in exchange a five-year note bearing interest at 2 percent annually with a face amount of $120,000. The payment of interest is due on December 31 of each year.

The market value of the equipment purchased cannot be easily determined. Company A must normally pay interest at the rate of 8 percent when borrowing; Company B, at the rate of 10 percent; and Seller Company, at the rate of 9 percent. You should assume that interest is compounded annually in all cases.

Required:

1. At what amounts should Company A and Company B record the equipment purchased?

2. Develop an amortization table for each company.

3. Prepare the necessary journal entries for Company A and Company B for December 31, 2005.

4. Draft a memo to the president of Company A that explains why interest must be recorded when the note is referred to as a non-interest-bearing note.

LO6   **EXERCISE 13-10   Analysis of Long-Term Debt**

International Paper is a large company that is in the same industry as Georgia-Pacific. The following information is available from International Paper's financial statements for the year ended December 31, 2003. All dollar amounts are in millions.

Total liabilities	$27,288
Assets, beginning balance	33,792
Assets, ending balance	35,525
Stockholders' equity, beginning balance	7,374
Stockholders' equity, ending balance	8,237
Net income	302
Interest expense	469
Tax benefit (a credit)	92

Required:

1. Compute the following for International Paper: debt-to-equity ratio, return on assets, return on stockholders' equity, and times interest earned ratio.

2. Would you consider International Paper to be "highly leveraged"? Indicate whether the company has used leverage effectively.

3. Compare the company's use of debt and its performance, as indicated by the ratios, to that of Georgia-Pacific. (Refer to the amounts calculated in this chapter.)

LO7   EXERCISE 13-11   **Accrual to Cash for Interest**

Assume that the income statement of Laker Company indicates interest expense of $100,000 for the year 2005. Also assume that the company had the following account balances at the beginning and end of the year 2005:

Account	Beginning Balance	Ending Balance
Interest Payable	$30,000	$15,000
Interest Paid in Advance	10,000	30,000
Premium on Bonds	40,000	30,000

You should assume that the change in the Premium on Bonds account represents amortization of the premium and that no bonds were redeemed during the period.

Required: Determine the amount of cash paid for interest during the year.

LO7   EXERCISE 13-12   **Cash to Accrual for Interest**

Assume that Shaq Company has made cash payments related to interest of $100,000 for the year 2005. Also, assume that the company had the following account balances at the beginning and end of the year 2005:

Account	Beginning Balance	Ending Balance
Interest Payable	$30,000	$15,000
Interest Paid in Advance	10,000	30,000
Premium on Bonds	40,000	30,000

You should assume that the change in the Premium on Bonds account represents amortization of the premium and that no bonds were redeemed during the period.

Required: Determine the amount of interest expense on the accrual basis for the year.

LO1, 2   EXERCISE 13-13   **Advantages of Bonds, Characteristics, Issue Price**

Swell Company's managers were debating whether to issue $50,000 of callable, term, debenture bonds for $45,200 or to issue 5,000 shares of $2 par value common stock that would generate the same amount of cash. Similar bonds had a yield of 10 percent on that date.

Required:

1. What are the advantages to Swell Company of issuing bonds instead of stock?
2. What is the significance of the "callable" feature?
3. Are the bonds that are being considered secured? How do you know?
4. At what percentage of face value or par would these bonds be quoted in the financial news on that date?

LO4   EXERCISE 13-14   **Bond Retirement**

Ricarder Company reported the following in its December 31, 2005 and 2004, balance sheet:

	December 31	
	2005	2004
Long-Term Debt		
Bonds, net of discount of $4,700 and $6,500, respectively	$163,300	$204,500

Bonds with a face amount of $80,000 were called during 2005 and retired at 102. During the year, new bonds were issued at 94 for cash. Bond discount totaling $1,300 was amortized during 2005.

Required:

1. Calculate the face amount of the bonds issued during 2005. At what discount were the new bonds issued?

2. Prepare the entry to record the new issuance of bonds during 2005.

3. Prepare the entry to record the bond retirement during 2005.

4. Why might a company call its bonds for retirement?

LO2 EXERCISE **13-15** **Issuance of Bonds**

On October 31, 2004, when the market rate of interest was 8 percent, the Mashni Company issued $40,000 of 6 percent, seven-year term bonds dated August 1, 2003, plus accrued interest. The bonds pay annual interest on July 31. Mashni has a December 31 year end. At December 31, 2004, the bonds were selling for 102.25.

Required:

1. When calculating the issue price of these bonds, why must you use six periods?

2. How much cash will Mashni Company receive upon the issuance of the bonds?

3. Briefly indicate the effect on the bond issue price if the bonds paid interest semiannually instead of annually. Do not calculate.

LO3 EXERCISE **13-16** **Bond Premium Amortization, Effective Interest Method**

On October 31, 2004, when the market rate of interest was 8 percent, the Moore Company issued $80,000 of 6 percent, seven-year term bonds dated August 1, 2003, for $72,604 plus accrued interest. The bonds pay annual interest on July 31.

Required:

1. Prepare an effective interest amortization table for the bond issue.

2. Calculate the book value of the bonds to be reported in Moore's balance sheet at December 31, 2004.

3. What is the nature of the balance in the Discount on Bonds account?

LO3 EXERCISE **13-17** **Effective Interest Amortization**

A bond amortization table prepared by the accountant for Data, Inc. appears below, without the column headings.

4/1/04				$86,798
10/1/04	$4,160	$3,125	$1,035	85,763
4/1/05	4,160	3,087	1,073	84,690
10/1/05	4,160	3,049	1,111	83,579
4/1/06	4,160	3,009	1,151	82,428
10/1/06	4,160	2,967	1,193	81,235
4/1/07	4,160	2,924	1,236	80,000*

*Rounded.

Required:

1. How long is the bond term?

2. Show how the interest payment is calculated. What is the annual stated rate of interest?

3. What is the annual effective interest rate?

4. Prepare two T-accounts, Bonds Payable and the related discount or premium account, and post all transactions through 2007.

5. What is the nature of the balance in the Premium on Bonds account?

LO2, 3   **EXERCISE 13-18   Bond Issuance, Effective Interest Amortization**

On November 30, 2004, the Galliher Company issued $80,000 of 10 percent term, three-year convertible bonds dated July 1, 2004, to Heflin Company, plus accrued interest. On that date, the market rate of interest was 7 percent. Bond issue costs amounted to $1,550 and were deducted by the broker before remitting the proceeds to Galliher. The bonds pay interest annually on July 1.

Required:

1. How much cash will Galliher receive upon the issuance of the bonds?
2. Prepare a partial balance sheet for Galliher at June 30, 2005, that shows the effects of the bond issuance.

LO5   **EXERCISE 13-19   Note Payable with Equal Payments, Unrealistic Rate**

Jones, Inc. prepared the following amortization schedule for an installment note:

Date	Payment	Interest	Principal Reduction	Present Value
7/1/2004				$5,247
9/30/2004	$500	$112	$388	4,859
12/31/2004	500	103	397	4,462
3/31/2005	500	95	405	4,057
6/30/2005	500	86	414	3,643
9/30/2005	500	77	423	3,220
12/31/2005	500	68	432	2,788
3/31/2006	500	59	441	2,347
6/30/2006	500	50	450	1,897
9/30/2006	500	40	460	1,437
12/31/2006	500	31	469	968
3/31/2007	500	21	479	489
6/30/2007	500	10	490	(1)*

*Rounded.

Required:

1. Calculate the annual interest rate on the loan.
2. Determine how much Jones will report in its balance sheet as of May 31, 2006, including the effects of any accruals.
3. Suppose the stated interest rate on the note is considered unrealistic. How would the amortization differ? Respond conceptually. Do not calculate.

LO7   **EXERCISE 13-20   Statement of Cash Flows**

On August 1, 2004, Patel Company issued $50,000 of 8 percent, three-year term bonds dated July 1, 2004, when the market rate of interest was 6 percent, plus accrued interest. The bonds pay interest semiannually on January 1 and July 1. Patel received $52,709 plus $333 for accrued interest upon the issuance of the bonds. Patel has no other debt obligations. Net income amounts reported for 2004 and 2005 are $23,500 and $24,000, respectively. Patel prepared the following amortization schedule for the bonds.

Date	Cash	Interest Expense	Amortization	Carrying Value
8/1/04				$52,709
1/1/05	$2,000	$1,581	$419	52,290
7/1/05	2,000	1,569	431	51,859
1/1/06	2,000	1,556	444	51,415
7/1/06	2,000	1,542	458	50,957
1/1/07	2,000	1,529	471	50,486
7/1/07	2,000	1,515	485	50,000

Required:

1. Prepare the operating activities section, assuming that the indirect method is used.

2. Why is an adjustment for amortization made in the operating activities section under the indirect method?

PROBLEMS

LO2, 3   **PROBLEM 13-1   Compute Missing Bond Values** (CPA adapted)

On January 1, 2005, North Company issued bonds payable with a face value of $480,000 at a discount. The bonds are due in 10 years, and interest is payable semiannually every June 30 and December 31. On June 30, 2005, and December 31, 2005, North made the semiannual interest payments due and recorded interest expense and amortization of bond discount. The amortization table given here has missing values.

Date	Cash	Interest Expense	Discount Amortization	Unamortized Discount	Bond Carrying Value
1/1/2005					(1)
6/30/2005	(2)	$18,000	$3,600	(3)	$363,600
12/31/2005	$14,400	(6)	(7)		

Annual stated interest rate (4)

Annual effective interest rate (5)

Required: Calculate the missing values 1–7.

Analyze: Why does the market interest rate often differ from the face interest rate of a bond?

LO3, 4   **PROBLEM 13-2   Comprehensive Bond Problem—Straight-Line Amortization**

On April 1, 2005, Fischer Company issued bonds with a face value of $800,000 at 98. The bonds pay semiannual interest on April 1 and October 1 at 8 percent (4 percent per semiannual period). The bonds are dated April 1, 2005, and are due in five years. At the time of issuance, Fischer paid $4,000 in legal costs and brokerage expenses associated with the bond issuance. The company uses the straight-line method of amortization for both issue costs and bond premium or discount and records amortization on each of the semiannual interest payment dates. Fischer Company's year ends December 31. On June 1, 2006, Fischer retired $200,000 of bonds at 103 plus accrued interest.

Required:

1. Record all entries necessary on October 1, 2005, related to the bonds.
2. Record all necessary adjusting entries on December 31, 2005.
3. Indicate the proper balance sheet presentation of all accounts related to the bonds in the balance sheet of December 31, 2005.
4. Determine the amount of gain or loss on the bonds redeemed on June 1, 2006.
5. Record the entries necessary for the bond redemption.
6. Determine the amount of discount on bonds payable and the amount of issue costs that should be amortized for the period ended October 1, 2006.

Analyze: What is the balance of the Discount on Bonds account at June 1, 2006 before the retirement of the bonds?

LO2, 3, 4   **PROBLEM 13-3   Comprehensive Bond Problem—Effective Interest**

On April 1, 2005, Horace Company issued bonds with a face value of $800,000. The bonds were issued at a price to yield a 10 percent return. The bonds pay semiannual interest on April 1 and October 1 at 8 percent (4 percent per semiannual period). The bonds are dated April 1, 2005, and are due in five years. At the time of issuance, Horace paid $4,000 for legal costs and brokerage expenses associated with the bond issuance. The company uses the straight-line method of amortization for issue costs and the effective interest method of amortization for bond premium or discount and records amortization on each of the semiannual interest payment dates. Horace Company's year ends December 31. On June 1, 2006, Horace retired $200,000 of bonds at 103 plus accrued interest.

Required:

1. Record all entries necessary on October 1, 2005, related to the bonds.
2. Record all necessary adjusting entries on December 31, 2005.
3. Indicate the proper balance sheet presentation of all accounts related to the bonds in the balance sheet of December 31, 2005.
4. Determine the amount of gain or loss on the bonds redeemed on June 1, 2006.
5. Record the entries necessary for the bond redemption.
6. Determine the amount of discount on bonds and the amount of issue costs that should be amortized for the period ended October 1, 2006.

Analyze: When a bond discount is amortized, does the bond carrying value increase or decrease over the period of amortization?

LO6   **PROBLEM 13-4   Boise Cascade's Long-Term Debt Note Disclosures**

A portion of **Boise Cascade**'s long-term debt note disclosure for the years ended December 31, 2003 and 2002, follows.

Boise Cascade

Long-term debt, almost all of which is unsecured, consists of the following:

	December 31	
Amounts in thousands	**2003**	**2002**
7.05% notes, due in 2005, net of unamortized discount of $65,000	$152,279	$153,264
9.45% debentures, due in 2009, net of unamortized discount of $108,000	149,869	149,846
7.35% debentures, due in 2016, net of unamortized discount of $65,000	124,935	124,930

Required:

1. Explain why the notes were all issued at a discount. What does this indicate about the market interest rate, or yield, at the time of issuance?

2. Assume that the market interest rate as of December 31, 2003, was 8 percent on the three bonds in the excerpt. Also, assume for simplicity that the bond interest is compounded annually and that all bonds mature on December 31 of the year indicated in the disclosures. Calculate the market value of each of the bonds as of December 31, 2003.

Analyze: Would the "market value" of the bonds be important information for readers of the financial statements?

LO6   **PROBLEM 13-5   International Paper's Long-Term Debt Note Disclosures**
The notes to **International Paper**'s 2002 annual report included the following paragraphs related to long-term debt.

International Paper

At December 31, 2002, International Paper's long-term debt was rated BBB by Standard & Poor's and Baa2 by Moody's Investor Services, both with a stable outlook, and International Paper's commercial paper was rated A-2 by Standard & Poor's and P-2 by Moody's Investor Services.

In October 2002, International Paper completed a private placement with registration rights of $1.0 billion aggregate principal amount of 5.85% notes due October 30, 2012. On November 15, 2002, the sale of an additional $200 million principal amount of 5.85% notes due October 30, 2012, was completed. The net proceeds of these sales were used to refinance most of International Paper's $1.2 billion aggregate principal amount of 8% notes due July 8, 2003, that were issued in connection with the Champion acquisition. The pretax early retirement cost of $41 million is included in Restructuring and other charges in the accompanying consolidated statement of earnings.

Required:

1. What is the meaning of the portion of the note disclosure that indicates "both with a stable outlook"? Would investors prefer a stable outlook or one that is fluctuating? Explain your answer.

2. How much is the annual interest cost savings as a result of refinancing the 8 percent notes related to the Champion acquisition?

Analyze: Why was International Paper willing to incur $41 million for the "early retirement" of debt?

LO5   **PROBLEM 13-6   Note Payable Transactions** (CPA adapted)

A. On April 1, 2005, Kern Company purchased a patent from Frey Corp. in exchange for a $100,000 non-interest-bearing note due April 1, 2007. There was no established price for the patent, and the note had no ready market. The prevailing interest rate for this type of note was 10 percent at April 1, 2005.

B. Kern has a $200,000 note payable to Cain Company dated December 31, 2002, which bears interest at 8 percent (annual compounding) and is due on December 31, 2007. Interest is payable annually on December 31, and all interest payments were made through December 31, 2005.

C. Kern has a $750,000 note payable to Able Company dated May 1, 2004, which bears interest at 9 percent. Principal payments of $250,000 plus interest are due annually beginning May 1, 2005. Kern made its first principal and interest payment on May 1, 2005.

Required:

1. Prepare a schedule showing the amount of interest expense and interest paid for 2005 and the amount of interest accrued at December 31, 2005.

2. Prepare the current and long-term liabilities portions of the balance sheet for Kern Company as of December 31, 2005. The transactions above reflect Kern's only liabilities.

Analyze: Kern Company's creditors are interested in the percentage breakdown of the current versus noncurrent liabilities. What percentage of total liabilities is composed of current liabilities? Of noncurrent liabilities?

LO7   PROBLEM 13-7   **Accrual to Cash—Two-Year Period**

Nathan Company began business on January 1, 2003. The amount of interest expense recorded by the company for 2004 and 2005 was $140,000 and $200,000, respectively. During 2004, a bond was issued at a discount of $45,000. The balance sheet of December 31, 2005, also revealed the following balances:

Account	December 31, 2005	December 31, 2004	December 31, 2003
Interest Payable	$40,000	$30,000	$23,000
Interest Paid in Advance	30,000	10,000	12,000
Discount on Bonds	30,000	40,000	0

Required: Determine the amount of cash paid for interest in 2005 and 2004.

Analyze: If the company earned income before taxes and interest of $480,000 in 2005, what is the times interest earned ratio?

LO6, 7   PROBLEM 13-8   **Analysis of the Statement of Cash Flows**

Lencioni Company has developed a statement of cash flows for the year ended December 31, 2005 using the indirect method. The operating activities portion appears as follows.

Lencioni Company
Partial Statement of Cash Flows
For the Year Ended December 31, 2005

Cash flows from operating activities:	
Net income	$500,000
Items in income not affecting cash:	
Depreciation	50,000
Amortization of bond premium	(20,000)
Deferred tax	5,000
Interest receivable	(10,000)
Prepaid interest	(7,000)
Inventory	(40,000)
Interest payable	25,000
Other	2,000
Net cash provided by operating activities	$505,000

Required: Lencioni's income statement for 2005 indicated that $90,000 of interest expense had been recognized. Determine the amount of cash paid for interest for the year. (You may assume no income taxes.)

Analyze: If Lencioni's average total assets are $3,500,000 in 2005, what is its ROA?

LO6   PROBLEM 13-9   **Research and Analysis of Companies Within an Industry**

The following information has been compiled for several companies within the same industry that may be considered competitors of one another in at least some product lines.

Data for Fiscal Year 2002	Boise Cascade	Georgia-Pacific	International Paper	United Stationers	Weyerhauser Company
Total assets, beginning of year	$4,933,968	$26,364,000	$37,717,000	$1,380,587	$18,293,000
Total assets, end of year	4,947,400	24,629,000	33,792,000	1,349,229	28,219,000
Total liabilities	3,547,869	20,069,000	26,418,000	790,345	21,596,000
Total stockholders' equity, beginning of year	1,578,353	4,905,000	10,291,000	538,681	6,695,000
Total stockholders' equity, end of year	1,399,531	4,560,000	7,374,000	558,884	6,623,000
Interest expense	118,494	841,000	783,000	16,960	874,000
Income before interest and taxes	119,499	333,000	1,154,000	113,329	1,245,000
Net income	11,340	(735,000)	(880,000)	60,228	241,000

Required: Calculate the following for each company: debt-to-equity ratio, return on assets, return on stockholders' equity, and times interest earned ratio.

Analyze: Write a report that compares the companies based on the ratios calculated.

LO2, 3 **PROBLEM 13-10** **Comprehensive Bond Problem—Issuance Between Interest Payment Dates, Effective Interest, Bond Issue Costs**

On June 1, 2005, Humer, Inc. issued five-year, $60,000, 10 percent bonds dated February 1, 2005. The bonds were sold on the open market to yield 8 percent. Interest is payable semi-annually on February 1 and August 1. Bond issue costs incurred and deducted by the broker were $1,500. Humer uses the effective interest method of amortizing discount and premium.

Required:

1. How much cash will Humer receive from the bond issuance on June 1, 2005?
2. Determine the impact the bond issue costs will have on Humer's income statement for the year ended December 31, 2005.
3. Identify three costs that might be included in "bond issue costs."
4. Amortize the bond premium, prepare the entries for 2005, and show how the bonds and any related amounts should be reported in Humer's balance sheet as of December 31, 2005.

Analyze: How does the concept of reporting bond issue costs differ from that of reporting prepaid expenses? Why does it differ?

LO3, 4 **PROBLEM 13-11** **Comprehensive Bond Problem—Straight-Line, Bond Issue Costs, Retirement**

On its December 31, 2004, balance sheet, Wallace Corp. reported 10-year bonds payable of $800,000. Interest is paid annually on March 1. The bonds had been issued at 102 on March 1, 2001, and the original bond issue costs totaled $21,000. Wallace uses straight-line amortization. On September 30, 2005, Wallace retired $200,000 of the outstanding bonds at 104. Wallace has a 30 percent income tax rate.

Required:

1. Determine the book value of the bonds on the date of retirement.
2. Show how Wallace will report the retirement results in its 2005 income statement.

Analyze: Would Wallace Corp. be more likely to retire the bonds if the market interest rate went up or down? Explain.

LO2, 3, 7   **PROBLEM 13-12   Comprehensive Bond Problem—Bond Issuance Between Interest Payment Dates, Effective Interest, Cash Flows**

Ragans Company issued $20,000 of three-year, 11 percent, bonds dated May 1, 2005, on June 30, 2005, for 110 1/2 plus accrued interest when the market interest rate was 7 percent. The bonds pay interest annually on April 30. Ragans Company's year end is December 31. Ragans uses the effective interest method of amortization.

Required:

1. Determine the amount of each cash interest payment.
2. Did these bonds sell at a premium or a discount? How do you know?
3. Prepare an amortization table for the bonds.
4. Show how the results of the bond transactions would be reported on Ragans's statement of cash flows for the year ended December 31, 2005, using the indirect method.

Analyze: Of what significance is the 7 percent interest rate to the issuer? What effect would an increase in the market interest rate one year after the issuance date have on the way in which interest is calculated?

LO2, 3   **PROBLEM 13-13   Comprehensive Bond Problem—Bond Issuance Between Interest Payment Dates, Effective Interest**

On June 1, 2004, Kimmel Company issued bonds. Information pertaining to the bonds is presented in the following amortization table.

6/1/04				$207,993
10/31/04	$8,500	$7,280	$1,220	206,773
4/30/05	8,500	7,237	1,263	205,510
10/31/05	8,500	7,193	1,307	204,203
4/30/06	8,500	7,147	1,353	202,850
10/31/06	8,500	7,100	1,400	201,449
4/30/07	8,500	7,051	1,449	200,000

Required:

1. Calculate the annual stated rate of interest on the bonds.
2. Determine the annual effective rate of interest on the bonds.
3. Did the bonds sell at a premium or a discount? Briefly explain why these bonds did not sell at par.
4. Are these bonds serial or term bonds? How do you know?
5. How much would be reported for interest expense for the year ended November 30, 2005?
6. How much will be reported as the net book value of the bonds on November 30, 2005?
7. How much cash did Kimmel Company receive on the issue date of the bonds?
8. At what "price" would you expect these bonds to be quoted in the financial news?
9. Prepare a partial balance sheet at November 30, 2005, for the bonds.

Analyze: Why is the amortization an adjustment of interest expense?

LO1, 6   **PROBLEM 13-14   Analysis of Long-Term Debt and Disclosure**

The information that appears on the following page is from Davis Company's note disclosure of December 31, 2005. At that time, Davis had total stockholders' equity of $120,000.

Davis Company has the following long-term obligations as of December 31, 2005:

Amounts due during the year ending:	10-Year Bonds	8-Year Note
December 31, 2006		$ 10,000
December 31, 2007		10,000
December 31, 2008		10,000
December 31, 2009	$100,000	10,000
December 31, 2010		10,000
Aggregate thereafter	0	20,000
Total	$100,000	$ 70,000
Less discount on bonds payable	(2,300)	
Less current portion		(10,000)
Long-term debt	$ 97,700	$ 60,000

The note is dated July 1, 2004, and carries an 8.5 percent interest rate. Principal and interest payments on the loan are due annually on July 1. Bond interest amortization during 2005 was $450. Davis's only other liabilities total $43,000; they consist of accounts payable and accrued obligations. Total assets declined by $30,000 from 2004 to 2005. Total liabilities have remained the same over the same period. Net income for 2005 was $54,000.

Required:

1. Prepare the liabilities section of the balance sheet for Davis Company as of December 31, 2005. Show proper classifications.

2. Calculate Davis Company's debt-to-equity ratio. What information does this provide?

Analyze: Calculate Davis's return on assets and return on stockholders' equity ratios. Is Davis using leverage effectively? Explain.

CASES

LO6   **FINANCIAL REPORTING CASE 13-1   Reading the Note Disclosures of Badger Paper Mills**
The following information is from the notes in Badger Paper Mills's 2002 annual report.

Long-term debt at December 31, 2002 and 2001, consists of the following:

(in thousands)	2002	2001
Revolving credit agreement	$ 19	$ 4,946
Term note	4,627	3,582
Variable-rate loan	1,675	—
Urban Development Action Grant ("UDAG")	1,646	1,680
	$7,967	$10,208
Less: Current maturities	590	414
	$7,377	$ 9,794

In November 2001, the Company obtained a revolving credit agreement with a commercial bank; the agreement expires in November 2004. The revolving credit agreement provides for maximum borrowings of $15 million, limited to certain percentages of receivables and inventory, and reduced by outstanding letters of credit. The revolving credit agreement bears interest at a variable rate based on alternative interest-rate bases, at the Company's option (4.25 percent at December 31, 2002). A facility fee of 0.25 percent is payable for unused amounts. At December 31, 2002, the revolving credit agreement required, among other items, the Company to maintain a fixed charge coverage ratio of 1.00, a minimum tangible net worth, as outlined in the agreement, and a limitation on capital expenditures.

Required:

1. What was the amount of debt for 2002 and 2001? What portion was classified as current and long-term for each year?

2. Comment on the purpose of the debt covenants referred to in the note.

3. What concerns about the company are raised by the note?

LO3, 4   FINANCIAL REPORTING CASE **13-2**   **Bond Amortization and Extinguishment** (CPA adapted)

On January 1, 2005, Drew Company issued 9 percent bonds dated January 1, 2005, at an effective rate (yield) of 10 percent. Drew uses the effective interest method of amortization. On July 1, 2007, the bonds were extinguished early when Drew acquired them in the open market for a price greater than their face amount.

Required:

1. Were the 9 percent bonds issued at face amount, at a discount, or at a premium? Why?

2. Would the amount of interest expense for the bonds using the effective interest method of amortization be higher in the first or second year of the life of the bond issue? Why?

3. How should the gain or loss on extinguishment of debt be determined? Does the early extinguishment of the bonds result in a gain or a loss? Why?

4. How should Drew report the early extinguishment of the bonds in its 2007 income statement?

LO3, 4   FINANCIAL REPORTING CASE **13-3**   **Bond Concepts** (CPA adapted)

On June 30, 2002, Corval Co. issued 15-year 12 percent bonds at a premium (yield of 10 percent). On November 30, 2005, Corval transferred both cash and property to the bondholders to extinguish the entire debt. The fair value of the transferred property equaled its carrying amount. The fair value of the cash plus property exceeded the bonds' carrying amount (ignore income taxes).

Required:

1. Explain the purpose of the effective interest method and the effect on Corval's bond premium of applying the method in 2002.

2. What would have been the effect on 2002 interest expense, net income, and the carrying amount of the bonds if Corval had incorrectly adopted the straight-line amortization method instead of the effective interest method?

3. How should Corval calculate and report the effects of the November 30, 2005, transaction in its 2005 income statement? Why is this presentation appropriate?

4. How should Corval report the effects of the November 30, 2005, transaction in its statement of cash flows using the indirect method?

LO1   FINANCIAL REPORTING CASE **13-4**   **Debt Versus Equity for International Paper**

Following are excerpts from the notes to the annual report of **International Paper** for 2002.

International Paper

In September 1998, International Paper Capital Trust III issued $805 million of International Paper-obligated mandatorily redeemable preferred securities. International Paper Capital Trust III is a wholly owned consolidated subsidiary of International Paper and its sole assets are International Paper 7 7/8% debentures. The obligations of International Paper Capital Trust III related to its preferred securities are fully and unconditionally guaranteed by International Paper. These preferred securities are mandatorily redeemable on December 1, 2038.

(continued)

In June 1998, IP Finance (Barbados) Limited, a non-U.S. wholly owned consolidated subsidiary of International Paper, issued $550 million of preferred securities with a dividend payment based on LIBOR. These preferred securities are mandatorily redeemable on June 30, 2008.

In March 1998, Timberlands Capital Corp. II, Inc., a wholly owned consolidated subsidiary of International Paper, issued $170 million of 7.005% preferred securities as part of the financing to repurchase the outstanding units of IP Timberlands, Ltd. These securities are not mandatorily redeemable and are classified in the consolidated balance sheet as a minority interest liability.

In the third quarter of 1995, International Paper Capital Trust (the Trust) issued $450 million of International Paper-obligated mandatorily redeemable preferred securities. The Trust is a wholly owned consolidated subsidiary of International Paper and its sole assets are International Paper 5 1/4% convertible subordinated debentures. The obligations of the Trust related to its preferred securities are fully and unconditionally guaranteed by International Paper. These preferred securities are convertible into International Paper common stock.

Distributions paid under all of the preferred securities noted above were $115 million, $129 million and $141 million in 2002, 2001 and 2000, respectively. The expense related to these preferred securities is shown in minority interest expense in the consolidated statement of earnings.

Required:

1. Discuss the factors that should be considered when deciding whether the securities detailed in the notes should be considered debt or equity.

2. Discuss the interest-rate risk, market risk, and credit risk that are present in the securities of International Paper.

LO1

ETHICS

ETHICS CASE 13-5 Determining a True Liability

Gregory Kluck is the chief accountant for Minger Company, a privately held company. Minger Company is planning to expand its operations by purchasing Meinzel Company, a small supplier, whose current owner and president is a personal friend of the president and founder of Minger Company. During the past decades, Minger has expanded several times by acquiring a small company and issuing mandatorily redeemable preferred stock to the previous owners. This preferred stock was classified as equity, and a relatively large issue currently is still outstanding. Minger's president, Carl Many, is planning to finance the newest acquisition in the same manner. Upon learning this, Gregory informs Carl that consistent with *SFAS No. 150*, any newly issued mandatorily redeemable preferred stock and the still outstanding issue will have to be classified as liabilities. *SFAS No. 150* requires that certain financial instruments that previously were classified as stockholders' equity will have to be reclassified as liabilities. Carl informs Gregory that the preferred stock will be issued without an express redeemable feature, but that an informal agreement between Carl and Meinzel's current president will allow the owner of Meinzel Company to redeem the stock during the next 10 years.

Gregory is troubled about this informal agreement and advises Carl to issue regular preferred stock without the informal agreement or to sign a note. Carl disagrees, however, and argues that regular preferred stock would have to carry a higher dividend and that a note would probably increase the company's cost of borrowing and would potentially lead to a violation of the loan covenant on an existing bank loan. The company proceeds with the acquisition and issues preferred stock with an informal oral agreement between Meinzel's and Minger's presidents that allows the stock to be redeemed within 10 years.

Required:

1. How do liabilities affect the perceived riskiness of the company? What ratios are affected, and what is the direction of the effect?

2. What are the accounting and ethical issues faced by the accountant?

3. Who will be affected by the decision made by the accountant? Does it matter that this is a privately held company?

4. What values and principles are likely to influence the accountant's decision?

5. What alternative actions can the accountant take?

6. a. Of the parties you identified in question 3, whose interest is most important?
   b. Of the values and principles you identified in question 4, which of them is the most important?
   c. Which of the possible actions you identified in question 5 will cause the least harm or do the most good?

7. What do you think the accountant should do?

LO1

ETHICS

ETHICS CASE 13-6 Acquisitions, Borrowing, and Risk

On December 9, 2003, **Office Max**, a well-known office supply retailer, became a wholly owned subsidiary of **Boise Cascade**. Boise Cascade paid $1.3 billion for its investment, paying 60 percent of the purchase price in stock and 40 percent in cash. Some of the cash was obtained by loans or other debt financing.[17] Subsequent to the investment and borrowing, Boise Cascade's debt rating was reduced. Reduced debt ratings typically indicate increased risk and may lead to a higher cost of borrowing and a lower potential return on assets.

The acquisition of Office Max is a major step in the company's long-term strategy to grow its distribution businesses.[18] In light of its increased debt and enhanced exposure to risk, a return to profitability will be important to Boise Cascade. A reduction in costs and enhanced sales revenue will tend to play an important role in achieving this goal.

The nature of Boise Cascade's business requires continuous investment in long-lived assets such as timberland. Deciding whether to finance such additional investments at a time when its debt rating has declined may create a conflict between long- and short-term objectives and lead to potential ethical dilemmas for executives involved in and affected by the decision.

Suppose you were the CEO of a company like Boise Cascade and also one of the key supporters of the recent acquisition of a major customer. Your employment contract with the company will be subject to renewal in less than one year. Negotiations on your new contract are likely to be influenced by the success of the recent major acquisition, as well as by the overall net income achieved by the company. Your operations manager recommends that additional capital expenditures be incurred during the current year, which will require additional financing. Your recommendations regarding capital expenditures and the type of financing (via debt or equity) will probably be followed. You believe that the capital expenditures are necessary for the long-run success of the company and that borrowing will be less costly than issuing equity. However, issuing equity would be in your own best interest until your contract negotiations are completed.

Required:

1. Describe the differing financial statement effects of borrowing and of issuing equity. What key ratios are affected?

2. What are the problems and issues that you face?

3. Who will be affected by your decision?

4. What values and principles are likely to influence your decision?

---

17 Boise Cascade, 2003 Annual Report, note 2.

18 Ibid.

5. What alternative actions might you consider?

6. What would you do?

LO3   FINANCIAL REPORTING CASE **13-7**   **Accounting for Bonds**

On January 1, 2005, Olivia's Diamonds issued $5,000,000 of 10 percent bonds dated January 1, 2005, and due December 31, 2009. Interest is payable semiannually on June 30 and December 31. The bonds were issued when the market yield was 9 percent, and Olivia's Diamonds uses the effective interest method to amortize discount or premium.

Required:

1. Using a spreadsheet, prepare an amortization schedule for Olivia's Diamonds.

2. At what amount would the bond obligation appear in Olivia's balance sheet for each year 2005 to 2008? Determine if the liability would be current or long-term.

3. What amount of interest would the company pay over the life of the bond?

4. What amount of interest expense would the company recognize over the life of the bond?

LO1   COMMUNICATION CASE **13-8**   **Capital Expansions and Financing**

Your company has a need for additional capital to expand the warehousing and distribution portion of its business. Many members of the board of directors are in favor of issuing new 10-year bonds, whereas others believe that the company should issue additional common stock. You suggest that a mix of the two ideas might be the best possible solution and suggest that the company issue convertible bonds. The board of directors asks you to write a memo detailing how convertible bonds work and identifying the advantages and disadvantages of issuing this type of security.

Required: Write a memo to the board of directors discussing how convertible bonds work and their effect on financial statements. In addition, examine any advantages and disadvantages that convertible bonds have over bonds and common stock.

LO6   RESEARCH CASE **13-9**   **Long-Term Debt Disclosures**

Best Buy Inc. is a leading specialty retailer of consumer electronics, personal computers, entertainment software, and appliances. The company operates over 750 retail stores in North America. The company's financial information, including its annual report, is found in the investor relations section of its website at **www.bestbuy.com**.

Required: Use Best Buy's most recent annual report to answer the following questions:

1. What amount of long-term debt did Best Buy report? What is the current portion of long-term debt reported?

2. What amount was reported in the company's statement of cash flows as the net proceeds from issuing long-term debt over each of the last three years?

3. What did Best Buy report in its debt note as the amount of debt maturing over the next five years?

LO6   ANALYSIS CASE **13-10**   **Analyzing Financial Position**

Select fiscal year 2003 financial information for **Wal-Mart** and **Costco** is provided here (all amounts in millions):

	Wal-Mart	Costco
Interest expense	$ 1,063	$ 29
Total debt	21,145	1,211
Total assets	94,685	11,620
Income before interest expense and tax	13,782	1,167

Required:

1. Use this information to calculate each company's times interest earned ratio.

2. Use this information to calculate each company's debt-to-equity ratio.

3. Based on the two ratios that you have just calculated, what conclusions can you draw about Wal-Mart and Costco?

ON THE WEB

The following exercises, activities, and problems are available on the *Intermediate Accounting* website. Use these resources to reinforce your understanding of the topics presented in this chapter.

- CPA-Adapted Simulations
- Interpreting the Accounting Standards
- Extending the Global Focus
- Extending the Ethics Discussion
- Mastering the Spreadsheet
- Career Snapshots
- Annual Report Project
- ACE Practice Tests
- Flashcards
- Glossary
- Check Figures for Text Problems
- PowerPoint Presentations

SOLUTIONS: CHECK YOUR UNDERSTANDING

The Characteristics and Advantages of Debt and Equity
(p. 589)

1. Stock ownership carries voting privileges and thus some degree of control of a company. Debt does not carry voting rights, but when debt is issued, loan covenants often restrict the activities of a business.

2. Default risk is the risk that a company may not be able to make the required interest payments on the debt and/or may not be able to repay the principal at maturity. Interest-rate risk is the risk associated with changes in interest rates after a company borrows.

3. Stock that is mandatorily redeemable is classified as a liability on the balance sheet.

Bonds Payable (p. 604)

1. The loan amount of a bond is often referred to as the face value, or par value. The issue price represents the present value of the cash flows for the bond calculated at the market interest rate.

2. The premium on a bond issuance is the excess of the issue price over the face value.

3. The amortization of a premium increases net income.

4. Under the straight-line method, the same dollar amount of interest expense is reported each period, even though the bond carrying value changes as amortization occurs. Under the effective interest method, the dollar amount of interest expense changes each period, but the effective interest rate remains the same.

Long-Term Notes Payable (p. 609)

1. An imputed interest rate is an estimated interest rate based on the rate that an independent borrower and an independent lender would negotiate for a similar transaction under comparable terms and conditions. *Opinions of the Accounting Principles Board No. 21 (APB No. 21)* requires interest to be imputed (1) when a note is non-interest-bearing or no interest rate is stated and (2) when an interest rate is stated but the interest rate is unrealistically low.

2. To determine an imputed interest rate, the accountant should approximate the rate that would apply if an independent borrower and an independent lender had negotiated a similar transaction under comparable terms and conditions. The credit standing of the debtor, any collateral specified, the terms of the note, and any other factors that may have a bearing on the interest rate should also be considered.

3. Discount on Notes Payable is debited if a note's face value is greater than its present value.

The Analysis of Long-Term Debt (p. 612)

1. Total debt is divided by total assets to arrive at the debt-to-equity ratio.

2. The return on stockholders' equity ratio measures how efficiently a company uses stockholders' investments to produce income by expressing net income as a percentage of average total stockholders' equity.

3. A company is highly leveraged if it has used a significant amount of borrowing to finance its activities.

The Effects of Long-Term Debt on Cash Flow (p. 614)

1. The cash flows from financing activities section reflects amounts used for or generated by long-term debt.

2. To convert from the accrual basis to the cash basis, one would begin with the interest expense (the accrual number) and adjust for all balance sheet accounts related to interest. Changes in the following accounts should be used to adjust to the actual amount paid for interest: Discount on Bonds, Interest Payable, Prepaid Interest, and Premium on Bonds.

CPA-ADAPTED SIMULATION

This simulation asks you to complete various tasks related to a company's annual financial statements. If your instructor has signed up for CPAexcel™, you can do the work online at **www.cpaexcel.com/hmco**. You may also do the simulation manually.

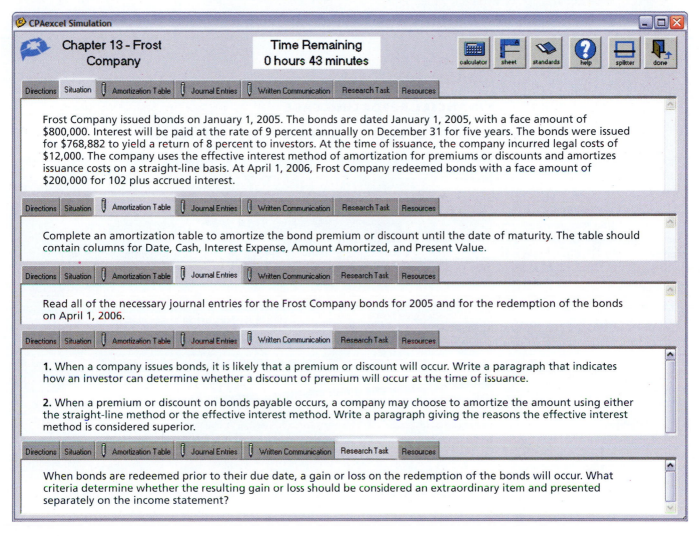

CPAexcel Simulation

Chapter 13 – Frost Company

Time Remaining
0 hours 43 minutes

calculator | sheet | standards | help | splitter | done

Directions | Situation | Amortization Table | Journal Entries | Written Communication | Research Task | Resources

Frost Company issued bonds on January 1, 2005. The bonds are dated January 1, 2005, with a face amount of $800,000. Interest will be paid at the rate of 9 percent annually on December 31 for five years. The bonds were issued for $768,882 to yield a return of 8 percent to investors. At the time of issuance, the company incurred legal costs of $12,000. The company uses the effective interest method of amortization for premiums or discounts and amortizes issuance costs on a straight-line basis. At April 1, 2006, Frost Company redeemed bonds with a face amount of $200,000 for 102 plus accrued interest.

Directions | Situation | Amortization Table | Journal Entries | Written Communication | Research Task | Resources

Complete an amortization table to amortize the bond premium or discount until the date of maturity. The table should contain columns for Date, Cash, Interest Expense, Amount Amortized, and Present Value.

Directions | Situation | Amortization Table | Journal Entries | Written Communication | Research Task | Resources

Read all of the necessary journal entries for the Frost Company bonds for 2005 and for the redemption of the bonds on April 1, 2006.

Directions | Situation | Amortization Table | Journal Entries | Written Communication | Research Task | Resources

1. When a company issues bonds, it is likely that a premium or discount will occur. Write a paragraph that indicates how an investor can determine whether a discount of premium will occur at the time of issuance.

2. When a premium or discount on bonds payable occurs, a company may choose to amortize the amount using either the straight-line method or the effective interest method. Write a paragraph giving the reasons the effective interest method is considered superior.

Directions | Situation | Amortization Table | Journal Entries | Written Communication | Research Task | Resources

When bonds are redeemed prior to their due date, a gain or loss on the redemption of the bonds will occur. What criteria determine whether the resulting gain or loss should be considered an extraordinary item and presented separately on the income statement?

Accounting for Leases

FINANCIAL REPORTING CASE

LEASED ASSETS ARE KEY AT AMR

AMR Corporation has made significant use of capital leases in acquiring its most important asset, its aircraft.

AMR AMR Corporation has identified six keys to success in the airline industry: safety, service, product, network, technology, and culture. Several of these issues depend directly on the acquisition and efficient use of assets. In particular, AMR has noted that modern travelers choose an airline largely on its ability to take them anywhere and everywhere they want to go. Thus, the company realized the importance of expansion of its route systems and the addition of the American Eagle feeder system. AMR has also made substantial investments in new and refurbished aircraft to improve the customer experience. This has enabled the company to advertise that its planes have been remodeled, with new seats and more legroom in passenger-class sections and even in-flight DVD video players in the first-class sections of some planes.

AMR has traditionally used a wide range of financing techniques to acquire its assets and invest in the future, including internally generated cash, secured debt arrangements, mortgages, and leases. Like other airlines, AMR has made significant use of leases to acquire its most important asset: aircraft. At December 31, 2003, the company had 398 in-service aircraft financed through either operating leases or capital leases. As you can see from the schedule taken from the company's 2003 annual report, 38 percent of the company's aircraft are leased.

Owned and leased aircraft operated by the Company at December 31, 2003 included:

Equipment Type	Seating Capacity	Owned	Capital Leased	Operating Leased	Total	Average Age (Years)
American Airlines Aircraft*						
Airbus A300-600R	266/267	10	—	24	34	14
Boeing 737-800	142	67	—	10	77	4
Boeing 757-200	168/176/188	84	9	47	140	9
Boeing 767-200 Extended Range	158	4	11	1	16	17
Boeing 767-300 Extended Range	212/213	40	7	11	58	10
Boeing 777-200 Extended Range	223/236/245	45	—	—	45	3
Fokker 100	87	14	—	24	38	11
McDonnell Douglas MD-80	129/131	148	72	142	362	15
Total		412	99	259	770	11
AMR Eagle Aircraft						
ATR 42	46	13	—	—	13	12
Bombardier CRJ-700	70	19	—	—	19	1
Embraer 135	37	39	—	—	39	4
Embraer 140	44	59	—	—	59	1
Embraer 145	50	52	—	—	52	4
Super ATR	64/66	40	—	2	42	9
Saab 340B/340B Plus	34	9	13	25	47	10
Total		231	13	27	271	7

As you will learn in this chapter, assets obtained through capital leases should be disclosed on the company's balance sheet. AMR's balance sheet for the year ended December 31, 2003, reported a net total of $1,371 million for leased flight equipment and property. The statement also reflected the lease obligations that accompany those assets: $1,225 million in long-term liabilities and $201 million in current liabilities. AMR's capital leases are shown on its balance sheet, but its operating lease transactions will not be found there. Investors must look to the income statement for aircraft rental amounts and to financial statement disclosures for information about the company's operating leases.

EXAMINING THE CASE

1. What methods of financing does AMR use to obtain its assets?

2. How are AMR's assets obtained through capital leases reflected on its financial statements?

3. How many of AMR's in-service aircraft are covered by capital leases? By operating leases?

LO1 Describe the characteristics and advantages of leases.

⊞ *Critical Thinking:* Have you ever considered leasing a car instead of purchasing it? What advantages or disadvantages contributed to your decision?

lease an agreement that secures the right to use property, plant, or equipment for a stated period of time in exchange for rent or some other form of compensation

lessor the party to a lease that conveys the right to use the property

lessee the party to a lease that acquires the right to use the property

An Overview of Leasing

Almost anyone who is in the market for a new car has been faced with the appeal of leasing. Nearly every auto advertisement touts the benefits of acquiring a new car by signing a lease and making lease payments instead of borrowing money to purchase the car and making loan payments. In fact, leasing now plays a significant role in the auto industry, and each year anywhere from 30 to 50 percent of new cars are acquired through lease transactions. Leasing has also gained importance in many other segments of our economy and the economies of the world.

THE ADVANTAGES OF LEASING

A **lease** is an agreement that secures the right to use property, plant, or equipment for a stated period of time in exchange for rent or some other form of compensation.[1] A lease always involves at least two parties: the **lessor**, which conveys the right to use the property, and the **lessee**, which acquires the right to use the property.[2] Leasing is a popular form of financing because it offers several advantages to the parties involved:

1. *Flexibility.* A lease contract may contain a wide array of provisions. Therefore, it can be structured to meet the needs of the parties involved. For example, both the length of a lease contract and the amount of the cash rental payments can be adjusted to suit the preferences of the lessee and the lessor.

2. *Financing benefits.* The financing benefits of a lease may take several forms.

   a. *100 percent financing.* Usually banks or lenders will finance only a portion of an asset in order to protect themselves in case of default. However, a lease may allow 100 percent of an asset to be financed, with little or no cash paid up front.

   b. *Financing at a fixed rate.* Many leases allow the lessee to pay a fixed interest rate for the duration of the contract. Of course, a locked-in interest rate is not always advantageous, and it usually benefits one party more than the other. For example, if interest rates rise after a fixed-rate lease is signed, the lessee benefits from having locked in a lower-than-market rate, but the lessor forgoes the income that would have been generated by a lease at the higher rate.

   c. *Financing at a lower rate.* Sometimes a lease agreement can offer a lower interest rate than a loan agreement. This is often due to the unique tax advantages available to one of the parties in the lease transaction. For example, if the parties are in different tax brackets, the party in the lower tax bracket cannot use the depreciation write-off from an asset as effectively as the party in the higher bracket. If the two make a leasing arrangement, the tax benefits can be passed to the party in the higher tax bracket.

3. *Reduction of risk.* A lease may allow the parties to reduce their risk. Often the greatest risk is obsolescence. For example, because of the rapid rate of change in computer technology, companies commonly lease their computers. If a leased computer becomes obsolete, the lessee is often allowed to return it at the end of the lease term. Of course, the return of obsolete equipment may not be an advantage to the lessor, who may compensate for the risk by charging a higher interest rate. In most cases, a lease contract can be structured so that all parties share the risks as effectively as possible.

---

1 "Accounting for Leases," *Statement of Financial Accounting Standards No. 13* (Norwalk, Conn.: FASB, 1976) as amended, par. 1.

2 In some cases, leases involve more than two parties; these are referred to as leveraged leases. We will not address the complexities of such leases in this text.

4. *Financial statement advantages.* One of the most controversial aspects of leasing is the way such agreements affect financial reporting. It is possible to structure a lease so that the lessee does not need to present the transaction in its balance sheet. When an asset is acquired through such a lease (called an *operating lease*), several key financial ratios will be more favorable than they would be if the asset were purchased with the proceeds of a loan. We will consider this advantage in more detail later in this chapter when we discuss operating leases.

PROVISIONS OF A LEASE CONTRACT

As discussed earlier, one of the greatest advantages that leasing offers is the flexibility to structure the transaction to meet the needs of the two parties. Such flexibility is a direct result of the variety of provisions, or terms, that can be built into a lease contract. Altering the provisions can drastically alter the basic nature of the lease and the relationship of the parties. To account for a lease correctly, the accountant must know its provisions. Among the more important provisions are:

1. *Term of the lease.* The contract should specify the term of the lease, usually in years or months. The term of the lease relative to the life of the asset is particularly significant. In some cases, a lease may allow an asset to be used for only a small portion of the asset's life. In other cases, the term of the lease may extend across the asset's entire useful life.

2. *Asset disposition at the end of the lease term.* A lease contract typically specifies which party will take possession of the asset at the end of the lease contract. Most contracts will specify one of the following two methods of disposition:

   a. *Asset reverts.* In this case, the asset reverts to the lessor at the end of the lease. Thus, the lessee has the right to use the asset only during the lease term and must return the asset when the lease expires.

   b. *Title passes.* In this case, both the possession of the asset and the legal title to the asset pass to the lessee at the end of the lease agreement. Thus, the lessee can ensure the use of the asset not only for the term of the lease, but also beyond it, until the end of the asset's useful life.

3. *Bargain purchase option.* In some cases, a lease contract may allow the lessee to purchase the asset at the end of the lease term. A **bargain purchase option** gives the lessee the right to purchase the asset at the end of the lease for a bargain price. A bargain price is assumed when the purchase price is significantly less than the expected fair value of the asset.[3] In most cases, the future price is set very low to encourage the lessee to exercise the purchase option.

4. *Residual value of the asset.* If the asset will revert to the lessor at the end of the lease agreement, the lease contract may address the **residual value of a leased asset**, which is the estimated fair market value of the asset at the termination of the lease. The residual value may be either guaranteed or unguaranteed.

   a. *Guaranteed residual value.* In some cases, the parties to a lease will agree on and specify a **guaranteed residual value**, a certain or determinable amount at which the lessor has the right to require the lessee to purchase the asset, or an amount that the lessee or a third party guarantees that the lessor will realize. At the end of the lease, if the asset's value is less than the specified amount, the lessee (or, in some cases, a third party) agrees to pay the difference to the lessor. A guaranteed residual value protects the lessor from unexpected decreases in the asset's value owing to wear and tear or obsolescence.

---

bargain purchase option an element of a lease contract that gives the lessee the right to purchase the asset at the end of the lease for a bargain price, i.e., one that is significantly less than the expected fair value of the asset

residual value of a leased asset the estimated fair market value of an asset at the termination of the lease

guaranteed residual value a certain or determinable amount at which the lessor has the right to require the lessee to purchase the asset, or an amount that the lessee or a third party guarantees that the lessor will realize

---

3 *SFAS No. 13* as amended, par. 5.

unguaranteed residual value an estimated residual value exclusive of any guaranteed amount; used in determining rental payments

executory costs annual costs associated with a leased asset, such as insurance, maintenance, taxes, and other annual costs

b. *Unguaranteed residual value.* Sometimes the two parties will agree on and specify an **unguaranteed residual value**, an estimated residual value exclusive of any guaranteed amount, for use in determining rental payments. At the termination of the lease, if the asset is worth less than the unguaranteed amount, the lessee is *not* required to pay the difference to the lessor. Thus, the lessor is not protected from the risk of unexpected changes in the asset's value.

5. *Executory costs.* A lease contract typically specifies which party is responsible for **executory costs**, such as insurance, maintenance, taxes, and other annual costs associated with the asset. In some cases, the lessee must pay such costs in addition to rental payments, and in other cases, the costs are borne by the lessor.

6. *Timing of payments.* The lease contract defines the timing of the lease payments. Some lease contracts specify that an annual payment is due at the end of each one-year period.[4] We will refer to this situation as an *ordinary annuity* and will calculate the present values accordingly. In other cases, the lessee is required to make payments at the beginning of each period. We will refer to this as an *annuity due* or an annuity in advance.

CONCEPTUAL ASPECTS OF LEASING

In considering a lease, it is important to distinguish between the *legal form* of the transaction and its *economic substance.* A lease is a legal contract that gives one party (the lessee) the right to use an asset in exchange for compensation to the other party (the lessor). Legally, the title to the asset is not transferred to the lessee when the lease is signed. The lessor is still the legal owner of the property. If the legal form of the transaction were the deciding factor, the asset would not appear on the lessee's balance sheet. However, from an accounting standpoint, it is more important to consider the actual economic substance of the transaction.

The proper accounting for leases is a matter of considerable controversy. Because a lease contract allows the lessee to *use* the property for a specified period of time, there are differing opinions about the true nature of the transaction. Some parties argue that because the lessee has the right to use the asset, the lessee should capitalize the asset. If that view is followed, the asset should be recognized on the lessee's balance sheet along with the associated liability. Other parties contend that merely having the right to use an asset does not meet the accounting definition of an asset, and thus a leased asset should not be capitalized or recognized on the lessee's balance sheet. At this time, the prevailing opinion is that *if a lease transfers substantially all of the benefits and risks of ownership*, the leased asset should be capitalized by the lessee along with the liability that is incurred.[5] That is, the economic substance of the transaction, rather than the legal form, should determine the proper accounting.

In practice, it has been difficult to develop accounting rules to determine when and in what circumstances substantially all of the benefits and risks of ownership have been transferred. As a result, there have been many accounting pronouncements that have attempted to provide specific guidelines for determining when a lease should be capitalized. In fact, in one survey of the best and worst accounting rules, "Accounting for Leases," *Statement of Financial Accounting Standards No. 13,* was judged to be the worst accounting rule. Respondents felt that *SFAS No. 13* has not improved the accounting for lease transactions and that the rules can be avoided or abused by reporting companies.[6] In 1999, the FASB declared its intention to restudy the entire area of lease accounting because the current rules have not led to the desired results.

---

4 In actual practice, lease payments may occur monthly or on some other periodic basis.

5 *SFAS No. 13* as amended, par. 59.

6 Cheri Reither, "What Are the Best and Worst Accounting Standards?" *Accounting Horizons,* September 1998, pp. 365–384.

Finally, it should be noted that there is a *lack of symmetry* in the accounting for lease transactions. In other business transactions, the accounting for one party in a transaction mirrors that for the other party. For example, if one party treats a transaction as a sale, the other party treats the transaction as a purchase. However, such symmetry is not always found in lease transactions. The lessee's accounting for a lease does not always mirror the lessor's accounting because the accounting rules are not always the same for both parties. The varying rules can lead to inconsistencies and, as a result, are frequently criticized by opponents of the current accounting standards. Because of this lack of symmetry, we will examine accounting for the lessee and the lessor in separate sections.

INTERNATIONAL

The international accounting rules concerning leases are similar to those in the United States. "Leases," *International Accounting Standard No. 17*, prescribes similar approaches to lease accounting based on whether a lease transfers substantially all of the risks and rewards of ownership.[7] In addition, *IAS No. 17* uses many of the same definitions and terms as *SFAS No. 13* to describe characteristics of leasing transactions and to provide accounting and reporting guidance. However, in 1996 the FASB joined with the International Accounting Standards Committee and standard-setting bodies of Canada, the United Kingdom, Australia, and New Zealand to publish a position paper that concluded that the distinctions currently used as guidance are arbitrary and unsatisfactory.[8] According to the position paper, the main deficiency is that existing standards do not provide for the recognition of "all material assets and liabilities arising from leases." The paper suggested that the comparability and usefulness of financial statements would be enhanced if the present approach were replaced by one that applied the same requirements to all leases.

CHECK YOUR UNDERSTANDING

1. Describe the two most commonly used methods of disposition of an asset specified in lease contracts.

2. What is a bargain purchase option?

3. What is the difference between ordinary annuity lease terms and annuity due lease terms?

4. What are the current FASB rules with regard to whether leased assets should be capitalized or not?

LO2 Explain the differences between an operating lease and a capital lease for the lessee.

Accounting for Leases as a Lessee

From the lessee's point of view, a lease must be accounted for as either an operating lease or a capital lease. Again, it is important to distinguish between the *legal form* of the transaction and its actual *economic substance*. Unfortunately, this is not easy to do, and the accountant must consider all the *risks and rewards of ownership* before deciding on the proper accounting.

In general, an **operating lease** is a financial arrangement in which the lessee does not assume the risks and rewards of ownership. As a result, the leased asset is not recorded as an asset in the lessee's balance sheet, and the obligation to make lease payments is not recorded as a liability. In fact, operating leases are often referred to as *off-balance-sheet financing*. Lease payments are treated as an expense.

operating lease a financial arrangement in which the lessee does not assume the risks and rewards of ownership, and thus the asset and the related liability are not recorded in the lessee's balance sheet

---

7 "Leases," *International Accounting Standard No. 17* (London: December 2003), par. 17.4.

8 Warren McGregor, "Accounting for Leases: A New Approach—Recognition by Lessees of Assets and Liabilities Arising Under Lease Contracts" (Norwalk, Conn.: FASB, 1996).

capital lease a financial arrangement in which the lessee assumes most of the risks and rewards of ownership, and thus the asset and a related liability are recorded in the lessee's balance sheet

🧩 *Critical Thinking: Why should a leased asset be listed on the balance sheet as an asset in some cases even though the company does not legally own the asset?*

In general, a **capital lease** is a financial arrangement in which the lessee assumes most of the risks and rewards of ownership. As a result, the leased asset is recorded (or capitalized) as an asset in the lessee's balance sheet, and the obligation to make lease payments is recorded as a liability. The lessee typically incurs interest and depreciation expense, which are reflected in the income statement.

LEASE CRITERIA FOR LESSEES

The FASB has developed specific criteria for distinguishing between an operating lease and a capital lease. To be classified as a capital lease, a lease must be noncancelable[9] and must meet *one or more* of the following criteria:

1. The lease transfers ownership of the property to the lessee at the end of the lease term.

2. The lease contains a bargain purchase option.

3. The lease term is equal to 75 percent or more of the estimated economic life of the leased property.[10]

4. The present value of the minimum lease payments (excluding executory costs) equals or exceeds 90 percent of the fair market value of the leased property.

It is clear that the FASB's intent was to develop an accounting rule that would classify most leases of assets to be capital leases that must be recorded in the lessee's balance sheet. For that reason, if a lease meets *any of the four criteria*, it must be classified as a capital lease. Only a lease that does not meet any of the four criteria can be classified as an operating lease. However, a considerable amount of judgment must be used in applying the criteria. For example, the fair market value of an asset at the inception of a lease must be estimated, and, when a purchase option is involved, the fair market value at lease termination must be estimated in order to identify a bargain purchase option. The third criterion requires that the economic life of the asset be carefully assessed. Complexities related to discount rate and minimum lease payments can also arise.

A further clarification is necessary at this point. The lease criteria specify that the lease be noncancelable. This is an important consideration in actual practice, but to simplify our presentation, we will discuss only leases that are noncancelable. None of the leases used in the examples throughout this chapter have cancellation clauses or similar complexities. Refer to the applicable FASB statements for information on leases with cancellation clauses.

▶ DISCOUNT RATE

incremental borrowing rate the interest rate that the lessee would have incurred to borrow a similar amount of money to purchase the leased asset at the inception of the lease

In applying the criteria, it is necessary to calculate the *present value* of the minimum lease payments. This requires the choice of an appropriate discount, or interest, rate. In most cases, the interest rate should be the lessee's **incremental borrowing rate**—the rate that, at the inception of the lease, the lessee would have incurred to borrow a similar amount of money to purchase the leased asset.[11] Establishing an incremental borrowing rate may require a degree of judgment because an actual loan was not in fact secured, a loan may not have been available, or loans may have been available from more than one source. Still, it is usually possible to determine an incremental borrowing rate with a reasonable degree of accuracy.

---

9 The lease literature contains many complexities beyond the scope of this text. We will not consider cancellation clauses or cancelable lease provisions.

10 If the beginning of the lease term falls within the last 25 percent of the total estimated economic life of the leased property, however, this criterion should not be used for classifying the lease.

11 *SFAS No. 13* as amended, par. 5, part L.

The accounting rules also specify that in some cases the implicit borrowing rate on the lease is a more appropriate measure than the incremental borrowing rate. The **implicit rate** is the rate that, when applied to the minimum lease payments, causes the total present value at the inception of the lease to be equal to the fair market value of the asset at that time.[12] In other words, the implicit rate is the rate that one can solve for if one knows the lease payments and the fair market value of the leased asset. The accounting rule for choosing between the incremental borrowing rate and the implicit rate can be summarized as follows:

> The incremental borrowing rate should be used in calculating the present value unless (a) the lessee *knows* the implicit rate of the lease, and (b) the implicit rate is less than the incremental borrowing rate.

This accounting rule may seem cumbersome, but it's intended to prevent the use of an artificially high rate. Remember, the higher the rate that is chosen, the lower the resulting present value. The accounting rule was an attempt to prevent a company from using an unrealistically high rate in an attempt to evade the fourth capitalization criterion. Unfortunately, companies have found ways to circumvent the intent of this rule.

> ### MINIMUM LEASE PAYMENTS

The fourth lease criterion refers to the present value of the minimum lease payments. Therefore, it is crucial to determine what amounts should be included as minimum lease payments. According to the FASB, **minimum lease payments** are the payments that the lessee is obligated to make or can be required to make in connection with the leased asset. Therefore, minimum lease payments include:

1. *Rental payments.* These are the annual rental payments called for in the lease contract. If the rental payments are the same amount in each period, they represent an annuity of payments.

2. *Bargain purchase option.* If the lessee is allowed to purchase the asset at less than market value, the amount of the bargain purchase option is included as a minimum rental payment. This amount is not an annuity. Instead, it is a one-time payment at the end of the lease term.

3. *Guaranteed residual value.* Any guarantee of the residual value by the lessee is included as a minimum rental payment. It is included because the lessor is assured that it will receive that amount at the termination of the lease. When the lessee agrees to make up any deficiency below a stated amount, the guaranteed residual value—rather than an estimate of the deficiency—is included in the minimum lease payments. This amount is a one-time payment at the end of the lease term.

The residual value is included as part of the minimum lease payments only if the lessee *guarantees* the amount. An *unguaranteed* residual value is not part of the minimum lease payments. The reasoning is that with an unguaranteed residual value, the lessor is not assured that it will receive this amount at the termination of the lease. If the leased asset is not worth the amount agreed upon as the residual value, the lessor must bear the loss.

Finally, it is important to understand that a lease contract is unlikely to contain *both* a bargain purchase option and a guaranteed residual value. A bargain purchase option is included in a contract to allow the lessee to purchase the asset at a favorable price at the end of the lease agreement. In contrast, a guaranteed residual value is included in the lease contract when the asset will revert to the lessor. A guaranteed residual value should be considered only when a bargain purchase option is not present.

implicit rate the interest rate that, when applied to the minimum lease payments, causes the total present value at the inception of the lease to be equal to the fair market value at that time

minimum lease payments the payments that the lessee is obligated to make or can be required to make in connection with a leased asset

---

12 Ibid., par. 5, part K.

Illustration 14.1

Characteristics of Operating Leases and Capital Leases

	Operating Lease	Capital Lease
Risks and rewards of ownership	Retained by the lessor.	Transferred to the lessee.
Lease criteria	Does not meet any of the four lease criteria.	Meets one or more of the four lease criteria.
Balance sheet impact	Leased asset and lease obligation do not appear on the lessee's balance sheet.	Leased asset and lease obligation appear on the lessee's balance sheet.
Income statement impact	Lease payments are treated as an expense.	Lessee will incur interest expense and depreciation expense.

Illustration 14.1 summarizes the differences between an operating lease and a capital lease for the lessee. We will illustrate the specific accounting transactions and their impact on the financial statements in the sections that follow.

LO3 Determine the rental payment for a lease.

CALCULATION OF LEASE PAYMENTS

One of the most important aspects of a lease is the lease payment or rental payment made by the lessee. In the examples that follow, we will generally assume that the rental payment is made annually. When the lessee and the lessor negotiate the lease arrangement, the two parties must agree on several elements of the lease contract, including the lease payment, the term (length) of the lease, and the residual value of the asset at the termination of the lease. Because the lease represents a series of payments into the future, present value techniques must be applied to determine the lease payments.[13] We will illustrate with two examples.

❭ **EXAMPLE 1** Assume that Rutowski Company wishes to lease an asset from Gable Company for five years and will make annual payments at the end of each lease year. Assume that the asset has a fair market value at lease inception of $500,000 and will have a residual value of $40,000 at lease termination. Assume that Gable Company wishes to achieve a 10 percent return on the leased asset.[14] The annual rental payment can be calculated using these steps:

Step 1: Determine the recoverable amount of the asset (Fair Market Value − Present Value of Residual).

Fair market value	$500,000	
Less: Present value of residual	24,836	($40,000 × 0.6209, the present value of $1 for 5 years, 10%)
Recoverable amount	$475,164	

Step 2: Determine the amount of the payments (Recoverable Amount ÷ Table Factor Representing the Present Value of an Annuity for 5 Years, 10%).

$475,164 ÷ 3.7908 (present value of ordinary annuity for 5 years, 10%) = $125,347

---

13 For calculations involving the time value of money, use the tables provided in Appendix A.

14 The desired return will be referred to as the *implicit rate of interest* in later sections of this chapter. Also, for purposes of determining the lease payments, the residual value is treated the same way, whether it is a guaranteed residual or is unguaranteed.

Thus, Gable must receive annual payments of $125,347 for five years in order to achieve a 10 percent return on the lease (and the asset must have a residual value of $40,000 at lease termination).

Solving for the lease payments using a financial calculator is somewhat easier. You must enter the following variables into the calculator, and the calculator will compute the annual payment:

Present value	$500,000
Future value	$ 40,000
N (number of payments)	5
I (interest rate)	10%

When the payment is computed, the calculator should indicate an amount of $124,345 (slight differences between table and calculator values may occur as a result of rounding).

In this example, Gable required that the lease payments be made at the end of each lease year. Thus, the first lease payment would be required one year after the inception of the lease. This is called an *ordinary annuity* (or annuity in arrears) of payments.

▶ EXAMPLE 2   Assume the same facts as provided in the previous example, except that Gable Company requires that the lease payments be made at the beginning of each lease year. The first lease payment will be due at the inception of the lease. In this case, the series of lease payments represents an *annuity due* (or annuity in advance). To determine the annual lease payments, we would perform the following steps:

Step 1: Determine the recoverable amount in the same manner as in the previous example (Fair Market Value − Present Value of Residual).

Fair market value	$500,000	
Less: Present value of residual	24,836	($40,000 × 0.6209, the present value of $1 for 5 years, 10%)
Recoverable amount	$475,164	

Step 2: Determine the amount of the payments (Recoverable Amount ÷ Table Factor Representing the Present Value of an Annuity for 5 Years, 10%), using the annuity factor representing an annuity due.

$475,164 ÷ 4.1699 (present value of annuity due for 5 years, 10%) = $113,951

Thus, Gable must receive smaller annual payments of $113,951 for five years in order to achieve a 10 percent return on the lease (and the asset must have a residual value of $40,000 at lease termination) if the payments will be received at the beginning of each lease year.

LO4 Account for an operating lease as the lessee.

H: *Critical Thinking: If you were the lessee in a lease arrangement, why do you think you might prefer to classify the lease as an operating lease?*

ACCOUNTING FOR AN OPERATING LEASE AS A LESSEE

When a lessee does not obtain substantially all the rights of ownership of an asset, the lease is classified as an operating lease. In such a case, the lessee treats the lease payments as rental payments, which are considered expenses as incurred. When rental payments are made, the accounting entry would ordinarily be

Lease Expense (or Rent Expense)	xxx	
Cash		xxx

Of course, if lease payments are made in advance, the balance sheet reflects the prepaid amount as of the balance sheet date. Adjusting entries would then be made to decrease the prepaid amount over the life of the lease.

Under an operating lease, the lessee obtains the right to use the asset but does not record the asset and the associated liability in the financial statements. This is often referred to as *off-balance-sheet financing*. Most companies that engage in lease transactions prefer to account for them as operating leases and will go to great lengths to structure their lease arrangements so that they achieve operating lease status. Their goal is to positively influence the financial ratios that analysts and statement users rely on to evaluate corporate performance. Because a leased asset and its related liability are not recognized on the lessee's financial statements, the ratios (such as the debt-to-equity ratio) may appear more favorable than they would if the asset and liability were recognized.

LEASE CLASSIFICATION ILLUSTRATED

Assume that Andrew Company wishes to lease equipment from Rezin Manufacturing Company. The two parties have agreed to the following lease arrangement:

Lease term	10 years
Useful life of asset	15 years
Annual rental payment at the beginning of each lease year	$100,000
Fair value of asset at lease inception	$800,000
Incremental borrowing rate	12%
Implicit borrowing rate (known by Andrew Company)	10%

The machine reverts to Rezin Manufacturing Company at lease termination. The parties have agreed that the residual value will be $321,880 at that time, but the amount is not guaranteed.

To determine the proper classification of this lease, the four criteria must be examined:

Criterion 1: Does title pass? *No*

Criterion 2: Is there a bargain purchase option? *No*

Criterion 3: Is the lease term equal to or greater than 75 percent of the asset's life?
10 years ÷ 15 years = 66.67% *No*

Criterion 4: Is the present value of the minimum lease payments equal to or greater than 90 percent of the asset's fair market value?

N = 10
I = 10%
Payments = $100,000 (annuity due)
PV = $675,902 (using calculator) or
$100,000 × 6.7590 = $675,900 (using table factors)
$675,900 ÷ $800,000 = 84.5% *No*

To be classified as a capital lease, a lease must meet one or more of the four criteria. Because the lease in question does not meet any of the criteria, it should be considered an operating lease.

OPERATING LEASE DISCLOSURES

Even though a leased asset and the related obligation do not appear in the lessee's balance sheet, the lessee is required to disclose information about the lease in the notes to the financial statements. The following information must be disclosed for an operating lease having an initial term in excess of one year:[15]

---

15 *SFAS No. 13* as amended, par. 16, part B.

1. The future minimum rental payments as of the balance sheet date, in aggregate and for each of the five succeeding fiscal years

2. The total of the minimum rental payments to be received in the future under subleases as of the balance sheet date

3. Rent expense for each period for which an income statement is presented, with separate amounts for minimum rentals, contingent rentals, and sublease rentals

4. A general description of the lessee's leasing arrangements, including the existence and terms of renewal or purchase options and any restrictions imposed by lease agreements

Figure 14.1 shows how **AMR Corporation** disclosed lease information in a note to its 2003 annual report. Note that AMR's future minimum payments for operating leases far exceed its future minimum payments for capital leases. This indicates that AMR has engaged in a significant amount of off-balance-sheet financing. In effect, the company's most important "assets," its aircraft, often are *not* recorded on the balance sheet as assets, and the obligations to make lease payments are often *not* recognized as liabilities. The users of AMR's financial statements must be aware of those facts if they are to interpret the financial statements correctly, and they must analyze the note information carefully to determine the effects of the leases.

Figure 14.1

Note on AMR Leases, 2003

AMR

AMR's subsidiaries lease various types of equipment and property, primarily aircraft and airport facilities. The future minimum lease payments required under capital leases, together with the present value of such payments, and future minimum lease payments required under operating leases that have initial or remaining noncancelable lease terms in excess of one year as of December 31, 2003, were (in millions):

Year Ending December 31,	Capital Leases	Operating Leases
2004	$ 325	$ 1,114
2005	256	1,056
2006	256	990
2007	187	968
2008	224	916
2009 and subsequent	1,111	8,387
	2,359	$13,431 (1)
Less: Amount representing interest	933	
Present value of net minimum lease payments	$1,426	

(1) As of December 31, 2003, included in Accrued liabilities and Other liabilities and deferred credits on the accompanying consolidated balance sheet is approximately $1.3 billion relating to rent expense being recorded in advance of future operating lease payments.

At December 31, 2003, the Company had 259 jet aircraft and 27 turboprop aircraft under operating leases and 99 jet aircraft and 13 turboprop aircraft under capital leases. The aircraft leases can generally be renewed at rates based on fair market value at the end of the lease term for one to five years. Some aircraft leases have purchase options at or near the end of the lease term at fair market value, but generally not to exceed a stated percentage of the defined lessor's cost of the aircraft or a predetermined fixed amount.

point ▶◀ counterpoint

Off-Balance-Sheet Financing

the controversy Off-balance-sheet financing comes into play when a firm enters into a transaction that obligates it to make future payments that are not recorded as actual liabilities on the balance sheet. Synthetic leases, securitizations, and unconsolidated entities are often at the root of such transactions. Although these off-balance-sheet transactions should be disclosed in the notes and in Management's Discussion and Analysis, they are ultimately not shown on the face of the balance sheet, and their amounts are often not included in total assets or total liabilities.

Since the highly publicized Enron case in which special-purpose entities (SPEs) were used to move liabilities away from Enron's balance sheet, any arrangement that resembles off-balance-sheet financing has been closely scrutinized. Perhaps this scrutiny is warranted. A study conducted by RateFinancials Inc. revealed that 75 percent of companies use complex financing devices to shift long-term financial obligations off their balance sheet.[1]

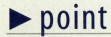 point

Herbert Birman

VP of finance and operations, MIS AG North America

on the point:

- **Greg Myers**
  CFO of Symantec Corporation
- **John Park**
  CFO, W.P. Carey & Co

▶ **Off-balance-sheet financing is a viable accounting technique when properly disclosed.**

In early 2003, a Webcast co-sponsored by CFO.com and the AICPA welcomed debate on the future of off-balance-sheet financing. Panelist Herbert Birman, VP of finance and operations at MIS AG North America, contended that the practice will remain a viable tool for securitizations, project finance structure, and synthetic leases. According to Birman, "The key to any off-balance-sheet transaction is transparent reporting."[2]

Many companies create off-balance-sheet arrangements in order to manage risk or take advantage of legitimate tax minimization opportunities. New rules issued by the FASB require that "all material off-balance-sheet transactions, arrangements, obligations (including contingent obligations), and other relationships of the issuer with unconsolidated entities or other persons, that may have a material current or future effect on financial condition, changes in financial condition, results of operations, liquidity, capital expenditures, capital resources, or significant components of revenues or expenses must be disclosed." The SEC has mandated that companies should provide a new section in Management's Discussion and Analysis to disclose off-balance-sheet arrangements if they are "reasonably likely" to be material to the company's financial condition.

"CFOs will tell you they need to do [off-balance-sheet financing] because rating agencies and banks penalize them if they don't," says Aram Kostoglian, a partner of BDO Seidman LLP, the national public accounting firm. "It's used very commonly."[3] These firms wish to move liabilities off the balance sheet so that their analysis ratios look favorable to credit rating agencies and banks. Cliff Griep, head of credit-ratings policy for Standard & Poor's says, "From a rating-agency perspective, we make adjustments. We will reflect the rate to what we believe to be economic reality."[4] Critics contend that financial statements should already reflect the reality of a company's situation without adjustment.

---

1 "One-Third of Publicly-Traded Companies Do Not Accurately Portray Their True Financial Condition, RateFinancials Study Finds," Business Wire, 6/18/04, available at: **http://www.forbes.com/businesswire/feeds/businesswire/2004/06/18/businesswire20040618005204r1.html**. Accessed 06/24/04.

2 "Webcast Debates the Future of Off-Balance-Sheet Financing," SmartPros.com, Jan. 22, 2003, available at **www.smartpros.com/x36787.xml**. Accessed 6/28/04.

3 Richard Gamble, "Shrewd (and Ethical) Tactics in Off-Balance-Sheet Financing," *Controller Magazine*, October 1997, p. 30.

4 "After the Fall," CFO.com, April 01, 2002, available at: **http://www.cfo.com/article/1,5309,6941|0|M|223|,00.html**. Accessed 06/30/04.

◀ counterpoint

Arthur Levitt Jr.

former SEC chairman

on the counterpoint:

- **Cisco Systems**
- **Leonard S. Hyman**
  senior associate R. J. Rudden Associates
- **Randy Casstevens**
  CFO of Krispy Kreme Doughnuts Inc.

◀ **Off-balance-sheet arrangements distort the financial statements of a company and lead to investors' mistrust in the investment community.**

Off-balance-sheet financing is considered by some to be a distortion tool. The former SEC chairman Arthur Levitt Jr. challenged: "Should companies still be allowed to leave billions of off-balance-sheet debt, such as lease financing, out of a company's reported liabilities? Off-balance-sheet debt persists, distorting the financial picture investors have been given of companies in many sectors. Markets will discipline themselves and their participants, but only if they have accurate financial information."[5] Leonard S. Hyman, a senior associate with R. J. Rudden Associates, believes that all material liabilities must be front and center. He also acknowledges that using off-balance-sheet financing as a strategy to "goose up the stock price" is often dishonest and will not be used in the future.[6]

Since the Enron fiasco, analysts and auditors now review off-balance-sheet transactions with a fine-tooth comb. Many companies have abandoned the practice for fear that investors will see the stunt as a means to hiding debt. Cisco Systems, for instance, announced that it would unwind all the leases it used to finance its headquarters and several manufacturing facilities. This act will put roughly $1.6 billion in real estate assets back on the balance sheet by the end of the current fiscal year. The debt related to those assets will also go on the balance sheet.[7]

In August 2002, chairman and CEO Sandy Weill announced that Citigroup would no longer perform material structured financings for clients that won't record them in their balance sheets unless the clients agree to publicly disclose the impact to investors. Citigroup will require "prompt disclosure of the details of the transaction, including management's analysis of the net effect the transaction has on the financial condition of the company, the nature and amount of the obligations, and a description of events that may cause an obligation to arise, increase, or be accelerated."[8]

Stephen G. Ryan, associate professor of accounting at New York University's Stern School of Business, advocates: "In the best of all worlds, companies would account for all the contractual rights and obligations in SPEs [special-purpose entities] and then tie the risks associated with them to items in the financial statements."[9]

Take a Position   Assume you are the controller for a large manufacturing company in North America. In the past, the company has structured its leases as off-balance-sheet arrangements. This year, the company is considering placing these obligations back in the balance sheet. What is your position? Explain.

Research   Locate the 2003 annual report for IBM on the company's website. What statements and disclosures were made on pages 59 and 65 regarding off-balance-sheet arrangements?

---

5 Steve Lim, Steven Mann, and Vassil Mihov, "Market Evaluation of off-balance sheet financing: You can run but you can't hide," Neeley School of Business, Texas Christian University, May 3, 2004, available at: **http://207.36.165.114/Zurich/Papers/180075.pdf**. Accessed 06/25/04.

6 "Webcast Debates the Future of Off-Balance-Sheet Financing."

7 "Lease Training Services: Off-Balance-Sheet Financing," Executive Caliber, available at **http://executivecaliber.ws/sys-tmpl/offbalancesheetfinancing/**. Accessed 06/25/04.

8 Tim Reason, "Reporting: See Through Finance," CFO.com., available at **www.cfo.com/article/1,5309,7775|0|BS|12|63,00.html**. Accessed 6/28/04.

9 "Reining in SPEs," CFO.com, Andrew Osterland, May 1, 2002, available at: **www.cfo.com/article/1%2C5309%2C7150|||2%2C00.html**. Accessed 06/28/04.

❱ LEASEHOLD IMPROVEMENTS

leasehold improvements additions or improvements made by the lessee to the leased asset

In some cases, a lessee will add to or improve a leased asset in its possession. These improvement or additions are called **leasehold improvements**. Leasehold improvements are considered an asset and are reported in the property, plant, and equipment category of the balance sheet, less the amount of the asset's accumulated depreciation or amortization. A leasehold improvement may be recognized as an asset even when an operating lease is involved. The result is somewhat strange in that the leased asset itself is not recorded as an asset in the balance sheet, but the leasehold improvement is recorded as an asset.

The straight-line method of depreciation is typically used for leasehold improvements. However, the time period used for depreciation purposes must be chosen carefully. Because the lessee will not retain the asset at the end of an operating lease agreement, a leasehold improvement will provide future benefit only over the time the leased asset is in the lessee's possession. Therefore, the general rule is that a leasehold improvement should be depreciated over the term of the lease or the life of the improvement, whichever is shorter.

For example, assume that on January 1, 2005, Zerull Company leased an office building for 30 years under an arrangement that will be treated as an operating lease. To make the building more accessible to its employees, Zerull resurfaced the parking lot at a cost of $100,000 on January 1, 2005, and estimated that the new pavement would last for 10 years. Because the lease is an operating lease, the office building will not appear as an asset in Zerull's balance sheet. However, the expenditure of $100,000 for a leasehold improvement should appear in the balance sheet as a long-term asset less depreciation. If the company uses the straight-line method of depreciation, the asset would appear as follows in the balance sheet of December 31, 2005:

Long-term assets (or Plant and equipment)

Leasehold improvement	$100,000
Less: Accumulated depreciation	(10,000)
	$ 90,000

The leasehold improvement will be depreciated over its useful life (10 years) because its useful life is shorter than the life of the lease (30 years).

A lessee discloses the depreciation periods used for leasehold improvements in the notes to the financial statements. Figure 14.2 presents AMR's accounting policy for leasehold improvements as disclosed in the notes to the company's 2003 financial statements.

ACCOUNTING FOR A CAPITAL LEASE AS A LESSEE

LO5 Account for a capital lease as the lessee.

🧩 *Critical Thinking: For the lessee in a lease agreement, what would be the impact on net income if a lease were classified as a capital instead of an operating lease?*

As discussed earlier, if a lease meets one or more of the four lease criteria, the lessee must treat it as a capital lease. Presumably, the lessee has acquired the rights of ownership of the asset; therefore, the asset is treated *as if* it had been purchased and an obligation had been incurred to finance the purchase.

❱ CAPITALIZING A LEASED ASSET

Once the lease agreement is signed, the lease is capitalized, or recognized, in the lessee's financial statements. The following journal entry would be recorded:

Leased Asset	xxx	
Lease Obligation		xxx

The asset is capitalized at the total present value of the minimum lease payments (excluding executory costs). However, the amount capitalized should not exceed the

Figure 14.2

AMR Accounting Policy for Leasehold Improvements

AMR

Equipment and Property The provision for depreciation of operating equipment and property is computed on the straight-line method applied to each unit of property, except that major rotable parts, avionics, and assemblies are depreciated on a group basis. The depreciable lives used for the principal depreciable asset classifications are as follows:

	Depreciable Life
American jet aircraft and engines	20–30 years
ATR 42 aircraft	2004[1]
Saab 340 aircraft	2005[1]
Other regional aircraft and engines	16–20 years
Major rotable parts, avionics, and assemblies	Life of equipment to which applicable
Improvements to leased flight equipment	Term of lease
Buildings and improvements (principally on leased land)	10–30 years or term of lease
Furniture, fixtures, and other equipment	3–10 years
Capitalized software	3–10 years

[1]Approximate final aircraft retirement date.

fair market value of the asset at the inception of the lease. In calculating the present value, the appropriate rate must be carefully chosen. (Refer to the earlier discussion of the lessee's incremental borrowing rate and the rate implicit in the lease agreement.) It is quite common in lease accounting to capitalize an amount that is not the fair market value of the asset. In fact, this is done whenever the lessee's borrowing rate is used to determine the present value.

Also, recall that the present value of the minimum lease payments includes not only the annual rental payments but also the price cited in any bargain purchase option or the guaranteed residual value.

DEPRECIATING A LEASED ASSET

A capitalized leased asset is a long-term asset and should be depreciated (or amortized) like other operating assets, such as plant and equipment. The time period over which a leased asset is depreciated depends on the terms of the lease contract and which party will acquire the asset at the termination of the agreement. If the leased asset will revert to the lessor at lease termination, the asset is depreciated *over the term of the lease.* The total amount depreciated (the depreciable basis) is the amount capitalized less the amount of any residual value specified in the lease contract.

In contrast, if the lessee will obtain the asset when the lease terminates, the asset is depreciated *over the useful life of the asset.* The total amount depreciated (the depreciable basis) is the capitalized amount less any residual value expected at the end of the asset's useful life. In some cases, the lessee will obtain the asset when the lease terminates because the lease contract specifies that title passes to the lessee at lease termination. If the title passes to the lessee, the asset is depreciated over its useful life. In other cases, the lease contract does not indicate that title passes but does specify a bargain purchase option. When the lease contract includes a bargain purchase option, the asset is also depreciated over its useful life. The reasoning is that in most cases the price cited in the bargain purchase option is quite favorable, so it is highly likely that the lessee will exercise the option and acquire the asset at the end of the lease agreement.

AMORTIZING A LEASE OBLIGATION

When a lease payment is made, one portion is allocated to interest and the other portion is allocated to principal. The amount allocated to interest is recognized as interest expense during the period in which the interest is incurred. The usual form of the journal entry is as follows:

Interest Expense	xxx	
Lease Obligation	xxx	
Cash or Payable		xxx

The amount of principal paid reduces the lease obligation liability. The *effective interest method* must be used to arrive at an amount of interest that is a constant percentage of the liability. The rate used in allocating interest and principal is the same rate that was used in calculating the capitalized amount for the lessee. That is, the lessee's borrowing rate is used unless the rate implicit in the lease agreement is lower than the borrowing rate and is known by the lessee.

Initially the leased asset and the lease obligation are recognized at the same amount, but after the initial recording, they are accounted for differently. The process of depreciation reduces the reported value of the leased asset. If the straight-line method is used, the value of the leased asset will be reduced evenly over the time period chosen. In contrast, the lease obligation is amortized using the effective interest method. The amount by which the principal is reduced will differ in each period. Therefore, after the initial recording, it is unlikely that the amount reported for the leased asset will be equal to the amount reported for the lease obligation.

▶ BALANCE SHEET PRESENTATION OF A CAPITAL LEASE

A leased asset that is treated as a capital lease is presented in the lessee's balance sheet, usually in the property, plant, and equipment category, net of accumulated depreciation. The lease obligation is presented as a liability in the lessee's balance sheet. In a classified balance sheet, the lease obligation is allocated between the current and long-term liabilities categories. The portion of the principal that will be reduced within one year of the balance sheet date is classified as current. The remaining portion is classified as long-term.

Figure 14.3 illustrates the disclosure of leases in the December 31, 2003, balance sheet of **Delta Air Lines, Inc.**, one of AMR's competitors in the airline industry. Note that as of the balance sheet date, Delta had $19 million of lease obligations that were current liabilities and an additional $78 million of lease obligations that were long-term liabilities.

▶ CAPITAL LEASE ILLUSTRATED—ANNUITY DUE

Assume that Verde Company wishes to lease equipment from Huskie Leasing Company. The two parties have agreed to the following lease arrangement:

Date of inception	January 1, 2005
Lease term	10 years
Useful life of asset	15 years
Annual rental payment due at the beginning of each lease year, including $5,000 for executory costs (insurance and taxes)	$105,000
Fair value of asset at lease inception	$675,902
Incremental borrowing rate	12%
Implicit borrowing rate (known by Verde)	10%

At the end of the lease term, title passes to the lessee.

▶ **CAPITALIZATION OF THE LEASE** One of the provisions of the lease contract states that at the termination of the lease, the lessee will retain possession of the asset and title will pass to the lessee. Thus, in effect, the economic substance of this transaction is identical to that of a purchase of the asset with installment payments made over

Figure 14.3

Lease Disclosure of Delta Air Lines, Inc.

Delta Airlines
LIABILITIES AND SHAREOWNERS' (DEFICIT) EQUITY

(in millions, except share data)	2003	2002
CURRENT LIABILITIES:		
Current maturities of long-term debt	$ 1,002	$ 666
Current obligations under capital leases	19	27
Accounts payable, deferred credits, and other accrued liabilities	1,759	1,921
Air traffic liability	1,308	1,270
Taxes payable	915	862
Accrued salaries and related benefits	1,285	1,365
Accrued rent	336	344
Total current liabilities	$ 6,624	$ 6,455
NONCURRENT LIABILITIES:		
Long-term debt	$10,962	$ 9,576
Long-term debt issued by Massachusetts Port Authority (Note 6)	498	498
Capital leases	78	100
Postretirement benefits	2,253	2,282
Accrued rent	701	739
Pension and related benefits	4,886	3,242
Other	204	93
Total noncurrent liabilities	$19,582	$16,530

a 10-year period. Because the lease arrangement meets at least one of the four lease criteria, Verde should treat it as a capital lease. Assuming that Verde Company wishes to prepare annual financial statements dated December 31, it would calculate the present value of the minimum lease payments and record the entry as follows:

Present value of the minimum lease payments calculated at 10 percent, where:

Payment = $100,000 (annuity due)

N = 10

I = 10%

$100,000 × 6.7590 = $675,900, using table factors

2005		
Jan. 1 Leased Equipment	675,900	
Lease Obligation		675,900

❱ **LEASE PAYMENTS**   The asset's present value is based on the annual lease payments ($100,000) and does not include executory costs ($5,000 for taxes and insurance). Note that in this lease, the asset's present value is equal to its fair value. That has occurred because (1) there is no residual value, and (2) the 10 percent rate was used to calculate both the payments of $100,000 and the present value. You will see that in many of the more complicated leases presented in this chapter, the present value recorded for the leased asset does not always equal the fair value of the asset.

2005		
Jan. 1 Executory Expense	5,000	
Lease Obligation	100,000	
Cash		105,000

Illustration 14.2

Schedule of Lease
Amortization for the Lessee—
Effective Interest Method for
Annuity Due Lease

Date	Cash	Interest Expense 10%	Reduction of Principal	Lease Obligation
1/1/05				$675,900
1/1/05	$100,000	$ 0	$100,000	575,900
1/1/06	100,000	**57,590**	**42,410**	533,490
1/1/07	100,000	53,349	46,651	486,839
1/1/08	100,000	48,684	51,316	435,523
1/1/09	100,000	43,552	56,448	379,075
1/1/10	100,000	37,908	62,092	316,983
1/1/11	100,000	31,698	68,302	248,681
1/1/12	100,000	24,868	75,132	173,549
1/1/13	100,000	17,354	82,646	90,903
1/1/14	100,000	9,090	90,910	0

Because the first payment is made at the signing of the lease, the payment is considered a reduction of the principal. No interest has accrued at that time.

❯ DEPRECIATION OF THE LEASED ASSET Assume that the asset will have a residual value of zero at the end of its useful life and that the company will use the straight-line method of depreciation. Because the lessee will retain the asset at the termination of the lease, the asset will be depreciated over a 15-year life. Thus, depreciation is $45,060 ($675,902 ÷ 15 years).

2005		
Dec. 31 Depreciation Expense	45,060	
Accumulated Depreciation—		
Leased Equipment		45,060

❯ ACCRUAL OF INTEREST At the end of the year, Verde Company must accrue the amount of interest that has been incurred but not yet paid. (Recall that this lease arrangement requires payments to be made each January 1.) An amortization schedule for this lease using the effective interest method is presented in Illustration 14.2. Based on that schedule, the amounts highlighted will be recorded in this 2005 adjusting entry:

Dec. 31 Interest Expense	57,590	
Interest Payable		57,590

On January 1, 2006, a lease payment will be made, and the accounting entry will be

2006		
Jan. 1 Executory Expense	5,000	
Interest Payable	57,590	
Lease Obligation	42,410	
Cash		105,000

Note that the January 1 transaction does not include interest expense because that amount was accrued as an adjusting entry at the close of the previous period.

❯ BALANCE SHEET PRESENTATION   As of December 31, 2005, the accounts for Leased Equipment, Accumulated Depreciation—Leased Equipment, and Lease Obligation appear as follows:

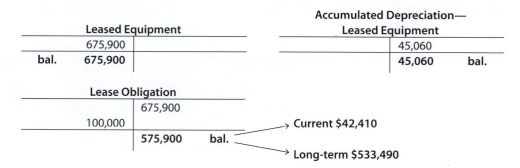

As a result, the presentation in Verde Company's balance sheet as of December 31, 2005, would be as follows:

Property, plant, and equipment

Leased equipment	$675,900	
Less: Accumulated depreciation	45,060	$630,840

Current liabilities

Lease obligation	$ 42,410

Long-term liabilities

Lease obligation	$533,490

❯ CAPITAL LEASE ILLUSTRATED—ORDINARY ANNUITY AND RESIDUAL VALUE

The previous example illustrated how a lessee would account for a rather straightforward lease agreement. We will now consider a lease that requires payments at the end of each lease term and involves a residual value. Assume that Bonds Company wishes to lease equipment from Lackey Company and that the two parties have agreed to the following lease arrangement:

Date of inception	January 1, 2005
Lease term	5 years
Useful life of asset	6 years
Annual rental payment due December 31 of each lease year, including $5,000 of executory costs (taxes and insurance)	$145,046
Fair value of asset at lease inception	$600,000
Incremental borrowing rate	10%
Implicit borrowing rate (unknown by Bonds)	8%

At the end of the lease term, the leased asset will revert to Lackey Company. The parties have agreed to a guaranteed residual value of $60,000 at the termination of the lease (end of year 5).

❯ CAPITALIZATION OF THE LEASE   This lease is a capital lease because it meets at least one of the four lease criteria (for example, 5 years ÷ 6 years = 83%). Therefore, Bonds Company (the lessee) should calculate the present value of the minimum lease payments, including both the annual rental payments (each of which, before executory costs, is $140,046) and the guaranteed residual value. Note that the appropriate

Illustration 14.3

Schedule of Lease Amortization for the Lessee—Effective Interest Method for Ordinary Annuity Lease

Date	Cash	Interest Expense 10%	Reduction of Principal	Lease Obligation
1/1/05				$568,140
12/31/05	$140,046	$56,814	$ 83,232	484,908
12/31/06	140,046	48,491	91,555	393,353
12/31/07	140,046	39,335	100,711	292,642
12/31/08	140,046	29,264	110,782	181,860
12/31/09	140,046	18,186	121,860	60,000
12/31/09	60,000	0	60,000	0

discount rate is the lessee's incremental borrowing rate of 10 percent. Bonds Company must use its borrowing rate because it does not know the implicit rate. The present value is computed as follows:

Payment = $140,046 (ordinary annuity)

FV = $60,000

N = 5

I = 10%

PV = $568,140 (using calculator) or

$140,046 × 3.7908   = $530,886

+ $60,000 × 0.6209   =   37,254

                       $568,140 (using table factors. Some rounding occurs when using tables.)

The following journal entry is then recorded:

Leased Equipment	568,140	
Lease Obligation		568,140

❯ LEASE PAYMENT   On December 31, Bonds Company will make the first payment of $145,046, which includes $5,000 of executory costs. An amortization schedule for this lease using the effective interest method is presented in Illustration 14.3. It shows what portions of each payment will be allocated to interest and principal. The highlighted amounts are those that will be recorded on December 31, 2005.

Based on the amortization schedule, the highlighted amounts will be recorded in this December 31, 2005 journal entry:

Executory Expense	5,000	
Interest Expense	56,814	
Lease Obligation	83,232	
Cash		145,046

❯ DEPRECIATION OF THE LEASED ASSET   Depreciation is recorded over the five-year period of the lease because the asset will revert to Lackey Company upon lease termination. Assuming straight-line depreciation, the amount of depreciation each year is calculated as ($568,140 − $60,000) ÷ 5 years = $101,628.

Depreciation Expense	101,628	
Accumulated Depreciation—Leased Equipment		101,628

) BALANCE SHEET PRESENTATION   As of December 31, 2005, the accounts for Leased Equipment, Accumulated Depreciation—Leased Equipment, and Lease Obligation appear as follows:

Leased Equipment			Accumulated Depreciation—Leased Equipment	
568,140			101,628	
bal. 568,140			101,628	bal.

Lease Obligation		
	568,140	
83,232		→ Current $91,555
	484,908 bal.	→ Long-term $393,353

As a result, the presentation in the lessee's balance sheet as of December 31, 2005, would be as follows:

Property, plant, and equipment

Leased asset	$568,140	
Less: Accumulated depreciation	101,628	$466,512

Current liabilities

Lease obligation		$ 91,555

Long-term liabilities

Lease obligation		$393,353

) RESIDUAL VALUE   The lease contract specifies that the equipment will revert to the lessor, Lackey Company, at the end of five years and that the lessee, Bonds Company, has guaranteed that the residual value will be $60,000 at that time. At the end of the five-year period, on December 31, 2009, Bonds Company's accounts will appear as follows before the guaranteed residual value is recorded:

Leased Equipment			Accumulated Depreciation—Leased Equipment	
568,140			101,628	
			101,628	
			101,628	
			101,628	
			101,628	
bal. 568,140			508,140	bal.

→ Book value $60,000 ←

Lease Obligation		
	568,140	
83,232		
91,555		
100,711		
110,782		
121,860		
	60,000 bal.	

If the value of the equipment on December 31, 2009, is at least $60,000, the lessee will make the entry shown on the next page.

Accumulated Depreciation—Leased Equipment	508,140	
Lease Obligation	60,000	
Leased Equipment		568,140

However, if the value of the asset on December 31, 2009, is only $40,000, the lessee will have to pay the difference in cash at that time. The following *additional* entry would then be recorded:

Loss on Leased Equipment	20,000	
Cash		20,000

CHECK YOUR UNDERSTANDING

1. With regard to the risks and rewards of ownership of an asset, how do operating and capital leases differ?

2. List the four criteria developed by the FASB to determine whether a lease must be capitalized.

3. If leasehold improvements are made to an asset covered by an operating lease, over what term should the improvements be depreciated?

4. If a lease has been classified as a capital lease, what accounts are affected when the initial lease is recorded?

5. What value is used to record an asset leased through a capital lease?

LO6 Explain how operating and capital leases affect a lessee's cash flow.

CASH FLOW

Critical Thinking: *Is there a difference in a company's cash flows if it classifies a lease as a capital lease rather than an operating lease? Explain.*

Analyzing Cash Flow: Operating Leases Versus Capital Leases

Whether a lease is an operating lease or a capital lease significantly affects the information that a company provides about the related cash flows. The cash outflows for an operating lease are reported as an operating activity in the cash flows from the operating activities section of the statement of cash flows. When a firm uses the indirect method for its statement of cash flows, as most firms do, the amount of lease expense (or rent expense) affects net income and would ordinarily not be disclosed separately in the statement.

For capital leases, the disclosure of cash flow effects is not as straightforward. Capital leases result in two expenses to the lessee. Depreciation on the leased asset is considered an operating activity and is disclosed in the cash flows from operating activities section of the statement of cash flows. Because depreciation is a noncash item and is not a cash flow, when the indirect method is used, its amount is added back to net income to eliminate any effect. When a lessee makes lease payments, the portion assigned to interest is also considered an operating activity. However, the portion of the lease payment that reduces the liability, the principal amount, is disclosed as a financing activity in the cash flows from financing activities section of the statement of cash flows. Given that the cash flows from leases are not disclosed as a single amount in the statement of cash flows, it is difficult to determine their effects. When lease-related amounts are disclosed in the statement of cash flows, they are divided between the operating activities and financing activities sections. Ultimately, the notes to the financial statements provide more reliable information about the cash flow effects of leases.

The statement of cash flows does disclose one other piece of lease information. When a lessee signs a capital lease agreement, it is considered a significant noncash

Figure 14.4

Consolidated Statements of Cash Flows

Continental Airlines

Continental Airlines, Inc.
Partial Consolidated Statements of Cash Flows

(In millions)

Year Ended December 31,	2003	2002	2001
Cash Flows from Financing Activities:			
Proceeds from issuance of long-term debt, net	$559	$596	$436
Payments on long-term debt and capital lease obligations	(549)	(383)	(367)
Purchase of common stock	—	—	(451)
Proceeds from issuance of common stock	5	23	241
Increase in restricted cash to collateralize letters of credit	(108)	(32)	(22)
Other	—	—	(11)
Net cash (used in) provided by financing activities	(93)	204	(174)

transaction and must be presented as a supplemental disclosure in the statement of cash flows.

Figure 14.4 shows a portion of **Continental Airlines**'s consolidated statements of cash flows for the year ended December 31, 2003. Note that Continental indicated a cash outflow for 2003 of $549 million for long-term debt and capital lease obligations.

CHECK YOUR UNDERSTANDING

1. For a capital lease, where would depreciation on a leased asset be found in the statement of cash flows?

2. For a capital lease, where would the cash paid to reduce the lease obligation be found in the statement of cash flows?

3. In which section of the statement of cash flows would cash outflows from an operating lease be reported?

LO7 Explain the differences between an operating lease, a direct financing lease, and a sales-type lease for the lessor.

H *Critical Thinking: For the lessor of an asset who provides the financing for the lease, what general types of income do you think might be derived from this arrangement?*

direct financing lease a form of capital lease in which the lessor transfers the risk and rewards of ownership to the lessee and serves as the financing agent

Accounting for Leases as a Lessor

The lessor in a lease agreement allows another party, the lessee, to use an asset in return for a series of payments. To account for a lease properly, the lessor must carefully consider the nature of the arrangement and the nature of the income to be recognized. It is also important to distinguish between the *legal form* of the transaction and its *economic substance*. For the lessor, a lease transaction must be accounted for as either an operating lease, a direct financing lease, or a sales-type lease.

As previously discussed, an operating lease is a financial arrangement in which the lessee does not assume the risks and rewards of owning the leased asset. In essence, the lessor rents the asset to the lessee. For that reason, the leased asset appears on the lessor's balance sheet, and the lessor accounts for it much like any other asset.

A **direct financing lease** is a form of capital lease in which the lessor transfers the risks and rewards of ownership to the lessee and serves as the financing agent. In essence, the lessor makes a loan to the lessee and receives payments of interest and principal in return. For that reason, the leased asset is removed from the lessor's balance sheet and replaced by a receivable for the future lease payments. The interest from the financing arrangement is recognized as interest income.

sales-type lease a form of capital lease in which the lessor is considered to be both selling an asset to the lessee and serving as the financing agent

A **sales-type lease** is a form of capital lease in which the lessor is considered to be both selling an asset to the lessee and serving as the financing agent. For that reason, the leased asset is removed from the lessor's balance sheet and replaced by a receivable for the future lease payments. In addition, the lessor recognizes two forms of income: a gross profit from in effect selling the asset and interest income resulting from the financing arrangement.

LEASE CRITERIA FOR LESSORS

The FASB has established specific criteria for classifying leases from the lessor's point of view. These criteria fall into two categories. The first category contains the same four criteria that are used by the lessee:

Type 1 Criteria

1. The lease transfers ownership of the property to the lessee at the end of the lease term.

2. The lease contains a bargain purchase option.

3. The lease term is equal to 75 percent or more of the estimated economic life of the leased property.[16]

4. The present value of the minimum lease payments (excluding executory costs) equals or exceeds 90 percent of the fair market value of the leased property.

However, two additional criteria are specified for the lessor:

Type 2 Criteria

1. The collectibility of the minimum lease payments is reasonably predictable.

2. There are no important uncertainties surrounding the amount of unreimbursable costs yet to be incurred by the lessor under the lease agreement.

The addition of these two criteria for the lessor is related to the conservative nature of the accounting discipline. Because the lessor records income (rather than expenses, as the lessee does), accountants need to be more assured that the income can be predicted and is reasonably certain. The two additional criteria specify that those conditions must exist before income can be recorded.

Illustration 14.4 indicates the differences between operating, direct financing, and sales-type leases for the lessor. We will illustrate the accounting transactions and the effects on the financial statements in the sections that follow.

LO8 Account for an operating lease as the lessor.

ACCOUNTING FOR AN OPERATING LEASE AS THE LESSOR

When the lessor does not transfer substantially all of the rights of ownership of an asset, the lease is classified as an operating lease. In this case, the lessor treats the lease payments as rental payments, which are considered income on the accrual basis. When rental payments are received, the accounting entry ordinarily appears as follows:

Cash	xxx	
Rent Revenue (or Lease Revenue)		xxx

Of course, if lease payments are received in advance, the balance sheet reflects the amount of unearned rent as of the balance sheet date. In addition, the leased asset

16 If the beginning of the lease term falls within the last 25 percent of the total estimated economic life of the leased property, however, this criterion should not be used for classifying the lease.

Illustration 14.4

Characteristics of Operating, Direct Financing, and Sales-Type Leases

	Operating Lease	Direct Financing Lease	Sales-Type Lease
Risks and rewards of ownership	Retained by the lessor.	Transferred to the lessee.	Transferred to the lessee.
Lease criteria	Does not meet any of the four Type 1 criteria and/or does not meet Type 2 criteria.	Meets one or more of the four Type 1 criteria and both of the Type 2 criteria.	Meets one or more of the four Type 1 criteria and both of the Type 2 criteria.
Balance sheet impact	Leased asset appears on lessor's balance sheet.	Lease Receivable and Unearned Interest Income appear on lessor's balance sheet.	Lease Receivable and Unearned Interest Income appear on lessor's balance sheet.
Income statement impact	Lease payments are treated as income.	The portion of the payments that represents interest is treated as income.	Gross profit is recorded in the year of sale. Interest income is recorded over the life of the lease.

remains on the lessor's balance sheet, and the lessor records depreciation on the asset as it does on other depreciable assets.

▶ INITIAL DIRECT COSTS

initial direct costs one-time up-front costs, such as legal fees, credit investigation costs, and document preparation fees, that are directly associated with negotiating and signing a lease agreement

The lessor must also account for **initial direct costs**, which are those costs that are directly associated with negotiating and signing the lease agreement.[17] Such costs include legal costs, costs of credit investigations, and costs of preparing documents. These costs are *one-time up-front costs* that are incurred in the year of the lease's inception. In that sense, they differ from executory costs, which are costs that are incurred annually in relation to a leased asset. The accounting for initial direct costs depends on the nature of the lease agreement. Initial direct costs incurred for an operating lease are deferred and amortized over the life of the lease in proportion to the recognition of rental income. At the time the costs are incurred, they are treated as a balance sheet account:

Initial Direct Costs	xxx	
Cash, Payable, etc.		xxx

When the costs are amortized, they are treated as expenses and matched against rental income:

Expense for Leased Asset	xxx	
Initial Direct Costs		xxx

If rental income is recognized on a straight-line basis, the initial direct costs are recorded as an expense on a straight-line basis. However, if rental income is recognized on some other pattern, the initial direct costs should be amortized (matched) in proportion to the income in each period.

---

17 *SFAS No. 13* as amended, par. 5, part M.

ACCOUNTING FOR DIRECT FINANCING AND SALES-TYPE LEASES AS THE LESSOR

If a lease meets *one or more of the Type 1 criteria* and meets *both of the Type 2 criteria*, it is not an operating lease. It is a capital lease, and the lessor must account for it as either a direct financing lease or a sales-type lease. Whether a lease is classified as a direct financing lease or a sales-type lease depends on the business purpose of the parties involved and the nature of the resulting profit.

It is important to note that symmetry is not always found between the accounting performed by the lessee and the accounting performed by the lessor. Dissimilarities can arise because the parties may apply different interest rates to their lease transactions. The lessee must consider two rates: the lessee's incremental borrowing rate and the rate implicit in the lease agreement. The lessor, however, must always use the rate implicit in the lease agreement. As a result, when accounting for the same transaction, the lessee may use one interest rate while the lessor uses another.

LO9 Account for a direct financing lease as the lessor.

▶ DIRECT FINANCING LEASE

When the lessor of a capital lease is a bank, a leasing company, or a financial institution that is operating only as a financing agent, the lease is a direct financing lease. Such a lease involves only one type of income: interest. The lessor, or financing agent, will use the effective interest method to recognize a portion of each payment as interest income over the life of the lease.

Assume that Binkert Company (the lessor) has leased an asset to Kearney Company (the lessee). The lease contract has the following features:

Date of inception	January 1, 2005
Lease term	5 years
Useful life of asset	6 years
Annual rental payments due December 31 of each lease year	$140,046
Fair value of asset at lease inception	$600,000
Implicit rate of interest	8%

At the end of the lease term, title to the leased asset will revert to Binkert Company. The parties have agreed to a guaranteed residual value of $60,000 at the termination of the lease. The collectibility of the minimum lease payments is reasonably predictable, and there are no important uncertainties about the lease agreement.

Because Binkert Company is not a manufacturer or dealer, and because the lease meets one or more of the Type 1 criteria and both of the Type 2 criteria, it is classified as a direct financing lease. Binkert Company will remove the asset from its books and will recognize a receivable account, Lease Receivable, for the amount of the payments to be received, known as the gross investment. **Gross investment** is the sum of the minimum lease payments, excluding executory costs, plus any amount of unguaranteed residual value. The gross investment is not calculated at present value. It is simply the undiscounted total of the cash flows specified in the lease contract.

gross investment the sum of the minimum lease payments, excluding executory costs, plus any amount of unguaranteed residual value

When determining gross investment, note that the minimum lease payments *include* any guaranteed residual value. If the residual value is unguaranteed, that amount is added to the minimum lease payments. As a result, all residual values, whether guaranteed or unguaranteed, are included in the receivable account called Lease Receivable. In this regard, residual values are treated differently by the lessee and the lessor and are another example of the lack of symmetry between the ways in which the two parties account for the same transaction.

unearned interest income the difference between the gross investment and the present value of the minimum lease payments plus the present value of the unguaranteed residual value of the asset

The lessor also records the lease's **unearned interest income**—the difference between the gross investment and the present value of the minimum lease payments

Illustration 14.5

Schedule of Lease Amortization for the Lessor— Effective Interest Method for an Ordinary Annuity Lease

Date	Cash	Interest Income 8%	Reduction of Principal	Net Lease Receivable
1/1/05				$600,000
12/31/05	$140,046	$48,000	$ 92,046	507,954
12/31/06	140,046	40,636	99,410	408,544
12/31/07	140,046	32,684	107,362	301,182
12/31/08	140,046	24,095	115,951	185,231
12/31/09	140,046	14,815*	125,231	60,000
12/31/09	60,000†	0	60,000	0

*Rounded.
†The final amount in the Cash column is the guaranteed residual value.

plus the present value of the unguaranteed residual value of the asset. The lessor uses the lease's implicit rate of interest and the effective interest method to amortize the amount in the Unearned Interest Income account to the Interest Income account over the life of the lease. An amortization schedule for this lease using the effective interest method is presented in Illustration 14.5.

The following entries would be recorded by Binkert Company:

Lease Inception

2005
Jan. 1 Lease Receivable [($140,046 × 5) + $60,000]   760,230
        Asset   600,000
        Unearned Interest Income   160,230

At the time the first payment is made, Binkert Company will record the following entries:

Lease Payment

2005
Dec. 31 Cash   140,046
        Lease Receivable   140,046
2005
Dec. 31 Unearned Interest Income   48,000
        Interest Income   48,000

net investment the balance of the Lease Receivable account less the balance of the Unearned Interest Income account

❯ **BALANCE SHEET PRESENTATION**   In its balance sheet, Binkert Company should report the **net investment,** which is the balance of the Lease Receivable account less the balance of the Unearned Interest Income account. The portion that is a current amount is presented in the current asset category, and the remainder is presented in the long-term asset category. As of December 31, 2005, the accounts appear as follows:

Lease Receivable		Unearned Interest Income	
760,230	140,046	48,000	160,230
bal. 620,184			112,230 bal.
Current Long-term		Current Long-term	
$140,046 $480,138		$40,636 $71,594	

Illustration 14.6

Accounting for Direct Financing Leases

Gross investment	The sum of the minimum lease payments, excluding executory costs, plus any amount of unguaranteed residual value
Unearned interest income	The difference between the gross investment and the present value of the minimum lease payments plus the present value of the unguaranteed residual value of the asset
Net investment	The balance of the Lease Receivable account less the balance of the Unearned Interest Income account

Therefore, the following amounts are presented in Binkert Company's balance sheet as of December 31, 2005:

Current assets

Net investment in lease $ 99,410
($140,046 − $40,636)

Long-term assets

Net investment in lease $408,544
($480,138 − $71,594)

The terms and calculations required for direct financing leases are summarized in Illustration 14.6.

❭ **TERMINATION OF THE LEASE**   The asset will revert to Binkert Company at the end of the lease term, and Kearney Company (the lessee) has guaranteed that the residual value will be at least $60,000 at that time. At the end of the lease term, but before the asset is returned, the Lease Receivable account will have a balance of $60,000, which is the amount owed by the lessee. If the asset is returned and its value is $60,000, Binkert Company will record the following transaction:

2009			
Dec. 31	Asset	60,000	
	Lease Receivable		60,000

Assume, however, that the asset has a value of only $45,000 when it is returned to Binkert Company. In that case, Kearney Company must pay the difference in cash, and Binkert Company will record the following transaction:

2009			
Dec. 31	Asset	45,000	
	Cash	15,000	
	Lease Receivable		60,000

A guaranteed residual value gives significant protection to the lessor and is important in many lease agreements.

LO10 Account for a sales-type lease as the lessor.

❭ **SALES-TYPE LEASE**

When the lessor of a capital lease is a manufacturer of or a dealer in the asset, the lease is a sales-type lease. Manufacturers and dealers use leases to facilitate sales and to attract potential customers who are not interested in making outright purchases. They also use leases to finance transactions. If an asset is purchased outright, the buyer may obtain funds from a bank or lending agency. If an asset is leased, however, the lessor is the financing agent. The lessor of a sales-type lease must thus recognize two distinct forms of income. One portion of each payment received represents gross profit on the "sale" of the asset to the lessee. The amount of gross profit on a lease transaction is the difference between the cost of the asset to the lessor and the sales price (or fair market value) of the asset. The other portion of each payment represents interest because the lessor is also the financing agent in the transaction.

For example, suppose that an auto dealer acquires a red car from its manufacturer (**General Motors** or **Ford**, for instance) for $15,000. The auto dealer knows that the fair market value of the car is $20,000 when it is sold to a customer. However, a customer wishes to lease the red car for a period of four years and is willing to make lease payments of $6,000 per year. For simplicity, we will assume that the lease payments are due annually and that the lease has met the Type 1 and Type 2 criteria. The arrangement is considered a sales-type lease because it involves two types of income, gross profit and interest:

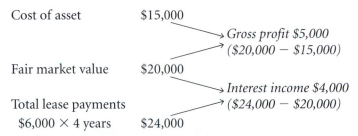

Cost of asset	$15,000
	Gross profit $5,000
	($20,000 − $15,000)
Fair market value	$20,000
	Interest income $4,000
Total lease payments	*($24,000 − $20,000)*
$6,000 × 4 years	$24,000

The lessor must treat the gross profit like the proceeds from the outright sale of an asset. The amount of gross profit is recognized as income in the year in which the lease is negotiated and signed. The lessor must also recognize the amount of interest income derived from financing the leased asset. Initially, the interest is recognized as unearned interest. The effective interest method of amortization is then used to record the interest income over the life of the lease.

Gross profit and interest income are often related. Thus, a lessor may be willing to adjust one type of income in order to increase the other. For example, it is quite common for auto dealers to advertise leases with very low interest rates. They do so not because they are eager to lend money to customers at low rates, but because offering low-rate leases enables them to sell more autos and increase their gross profit on sales. In effect, the financing division of an auto company often subsidizes the sales division to achieve the greatest overall profit. To account for a sales-type lease, the lessor removes the asset (inventory) from the books and recognizes a receivable account for the amount of the future payments to be received.

Assume that Tooltime Company is a dealer in heavy equipment for construction companies. Depending on a customer's preference, Tooltime will either sell the equipment outright or lease it. Tooltime purchases the equipment from Caterpillar at dealer rates and resells it to construction companies at a profit. Therefore, the equipment is a form of inventory to Tooltime and is carried in an inventory account until the time of sale. Tooltime and Urso Company have arranged the following lease agreement:

Date of inception	January 1, 2005
Lease term	5 years
Useful life of asset	6 years
Annual rental payments due December 31	
of each lease year	$140,046
Fair value of asset at lease inception	$600,000
Cost of asset to Tooltime	$500,000
Implicit rate of interest	8%

At the end of the lease term, title to the leased asset will revert to Tooltime Company. The parties have agreed to a guaranteed residual value of $60,000 at the termination of the lease. The collectibility of the minimum lease payments is reasonably predictable, and there are no important uncertainties regarding the lease agreement.

Illustration 14.7

Accounting for Sales-Type Leases

Lease receivable (gross investment)	The sum of the minimum lease payments, excluding executory costs, plus any amount of unguaranteed residual value
Unearned interest income	The difference between the gross investment and the present value of the minimum lease payments plus the present value of the unguaranteed residual value of the asset
Sales price of asset	The present value of the minimum lease payments
Cost of goods sold	The cost of the asset to the lessor less the present value of any unguaranteed residual value

Note that Tooltime's lease arrangement is nearly identical to Binkert Company's direct financing lease. The primary difference is that because Tooltime is a dealer in heavy equipment, the asset's cost to Tooltime ($500,000) is less than its selling price ($600,000). For that reason, Tooltime will recognize $100,000 of gross profit on the lease transaction. Assuming that the company records the cost of goods sold at the time of sale (the perpetual method of inventory), it will make the following entries:

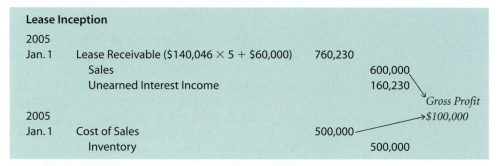

Lease Inception

2005			
Jan. 1	Lease Receivable ($140,046 × 5 + $60,000)	760,230	
	Sales		600,000
	Unearned Interest Income		160,230
			Gross Profit
2005			*→$100,000*
Jan. 1	Cost of Sales	500,000	
	Inventory		500,000

Tooltime would develop an amortization schedule for the lease using the effective interest method. That schedule would be identical to the amortization schedule for the direct financing lease in Illustration 14.5. Therefore, at the time of the first payment, Tooltime would record the following entries:

Lease Payment

2005			
Dec. 31	Cash	140,046	
	Lease Receivable		140,046
2005			
Dec. 31	Unearned Interest Income	48,000	
	Interest Income		48,000

❭ **BALANCE SHEET PRESENTATION**   The balance sheet presentation of the accounts related to sales-type leases is identical to that for direct financing leases. Refer to Binkert Company's balance sheet disclosures as of December 31, 2005.

Illustration 14.7 reviews the terms and calculations involved in sales-type leases.

CHECK YOUR UNDERSTANDING

1. Identify the differences between a sales-type lease and a direct financing lease.

2. For the lessor in an operating lease, how are initial direct costs treated?

3. Under a direct financing lease, what account is used to record a receivable for the amount of the payments to be received?

4. Under a sales-type lease, what two forms of income are generated?

Revisiting the Case

LEASED ASSETS ARE KEY AT AMR

1. AMR uses internally generated cash, secured debt arrangements, mortgages, and leases to obtain its assets.

2. Leased equipment under capital leases will appear as assets on the company's balance sheet, and the related lease obligations will appear as liabilities (classified appropriately between current and long-term).

3. There are 112 aircraft covered under capital leases and 286 aircraft covered under operating leases.

SUMMARY BY LEARNING OBJECTIVE

LO1 Describe the characteristics and advantages of leases.

A lease is the right to use property, plant, or equipment for a stated period of time in exchange for rent or some other form of compensation. A lease always involves at least two parties: the lessor, which conveys the right to use the property, and the lessee, which acquires the right to use the property. The advantages of leasing include the flexibility of the arrangement, the financing benefits, reduction of risk, and a more favorable financial statement presentation.

LO2 Explain the differences between an operating lease and a capital lease for the lessee.

An operating lease does not transfer substantially all of the risks of ownership to the lessee. A capital lease does transfer the risks of ownership and is similar in nature to a purchase of the asset. The FASB has established four criteria to determine whether a lease is an operating lease or a capital lease. If a lease meets any one of the four criteria, it must be treated as a capital lease by the lessee. The criteria establish a set of structured but arbitrary guidelines to determine the nature of a lease agreement.

LO3 Determine the rental payment for a lease.

The rental payments or lease payments generally represent an annuity of payments over the life of the lease. Present value techniques need to be applied to determine the amount of the payments. The critical variables are the fair market value of the asset, the term of the lease, and the residual value of the lease. Generally, it is necessary to determine the amount to be recovered by the lease arrangement as the fair market value minus the present value of the residual (or bargain purchase option). Then it is possible to determine the lease payment that will allow the lessor to achieve the desired return over the lease term.

LO4 Account for an operating lease as the lessee.

An operating lease should be treated as a rental arrangement by the lessee. When payments are made, the amount of the payments should be treated as an expense. The leased asset and the lease obligation do not appear in the lessee's balance sheet. The lessee is required to disclose in the notes the amount of future lease payments to be made under operating leases. If the lessee has improved the leased asset, the amount of the improvement should appear on the balance sheet as an asset and should be depreciated over the life of the lease.

LO5 Account for a capital lease as the lessee.

With a capital lease, the lessee should recognize the leased asset in the balance sheet as an asset and should recognize the lease obligation as a liability. The asset and liability should be recorded at the present value of the minimum lease payments, but not higher than the fair market value of the asset. Once it is capitalized, the asset should be reduced annually by depreciation (or amortization) like other operating assets. As the lessee makes payments, the balance of the lease obligation should be reduced, using the effective interest method of amortization. The portion of each payment that represents interest should be treated as interest expense, and the portion that represents principal should reduce the balance of the lease obligation.

LO6 Explain how operating and capital leases affect a lessee's cash flow.

The analysis of financial statements must consider the impact of leasing transactions. If a company that has leased assets is able to treat the transaction as an operating lease, its financial ratios may appear to be more favorable. The analyst must adopt methods to adjust for such effects in order to make companies comparable. The cash flow effects of operating leases are not shown separately on the cash flow statement. The cash flow effects of capital leases are difficult to discern because the interest and depreciation amounts are in the operating activities section of the cash flow statement, whereas the reduction of principal amount is disclosed in the financing activities section. The lease note is a better source of information on cash flows related to leases.

LO7 Explain the differences between an operating lease, a direct financing lease, and a sales-type lease for the lessor.

An operating lease does not transfer the risks and rewards of ownership to the lessee. If a lease meets any one of the Type 1 criteria and both of the Type 2 criteria, it is not an operating lease and must be treated as a direct financing lease or a sales-type lease. A direct financing lease is a form of capital lease in which the lessor serves as the financing agent. The lessor receives income in the form of interest income on the lease. A sales-type lease is used when the lessor is a manufacturer of or dealer in assets. The lessor receives income in the form of gross profit from the "sale" of the asset and receives interest income from the financing of the transaction.

LO8 Account for an operating lease as the lessor.

An operating lease should be treated as a rental arrangement, and the lessor should record income as it is earned. The leased asset should appear on the lessor's balance sheet and should be depreciated. If the lessor incurs any up-front costs related to the lease, these initial direct costs should be deferred and amortized over the life of the lease in proportion to the lease payments received.

LO9 Account for a direct financing lease as the lessor.

With a direct financing lease, the lessor should remove the leased asset from its balance sheet. A receivable should be established that indicates the total amount of the payments that will be received, including residual value. An Unearned Interest Income account should be established and amortized over the life of the lease by the effective interest method.

LO10 Account for a sales-type lease as the lessor.

With a sales-type lease, the lessor should remove the leased asset from its balance sheet. Gross profit should be recognized as the difference between the cost of the asset to the lessor and the fair market value of the asset at the time the lease is signed. A receivable should be established that indicates the total amount of the payments that will be received, including residual value. An Unearned Interest Income account should be established and amortized over the life of the lease by the effective interest method.

KEY TERMS

bargain purchase option (p. 639)
capital lease (p. 642)
direct financing lease (p. 659)
executory costs (p. 640)
gross investment (p. 662)
guaranteed residual value (p. 639)
implicit rate (p. 643)

incremental borrowing rate (p. 642)
initial direct costs (p. 661)
lease (p. 638)
leasehold improvements (p. 650)
lessee (p. 638)
lessor (p. 638)
minimum lease payments (p. 643)

net investment (p. 663)
operating lease (p. 641)
residual value of a leased asset
  (p. 639)
sales-type lease (p. 660)
unearned interest income (p. 662)
unguaranteed residual value (p. 640)

EXERCISES

LO2, 3, 5, 9   **EXERCISE 14-1   Lease for Lessee and Lessor**

Assume that Sosa Company purchased equipment on January 1, 2005, and has agreed to lease the equipment to McGuire Company. The lease arrangement contains the following provisions:

Date of inception of the lease	January 1, 2005
Lease term	6 years
Useful life of the asset	8 years
Annual rental payments due on December 31 of each lease year	
Fair value of asset at lease inception	$800,000
Incremental borrowing rate	12%
Implicit borrowing rate (known by lessee)	12%

At the end of the lease term, the equipment reverts to Sosa Company. The two parties have agreed that the asset will be worth $300,000, but McGuire Company has not guaranteed that amount.

Assume that the straight-line method of depreciation is used and that the asset will have zero residual value at the end of its useful life.

Required:

1. Calculate the amount of the annual lease payment.
2. What type of lease arrangement is this for McGuire Company? What type of lease arrangement is this for Sosa Company?
3. Record the necessary journal entries for McGuire Company for the year 2005.
4. Record the necessary journal entries for Sosa Company for the year 2005.

LO2, 3, 5   **EXERCISE 14-2   Capital Lease**

Symonds has agreed to lease a depreciable asset from another party. The provisions of the lease contract are as follows:

Date of inception of the lease	January 1, 2005
Lease term	6 years
Useful life of the asset	9 years
Fair value of asset at lease inception	$800,000
Incremental borrowing rate	14%
Implicit borrowing rate (known by lessee)	12%

Annual rental payments are due on December 31 of each lease year. At the end of the lease term, the equipment reverts to the lessor. The two parties have agreed that the asset will be worth $100,000, but Symonds has not guaranteed that amount.

Assume that the straight-line method of depreciation is used and that the asset will have zero residual value at the end of its useful life.

Required:

1. Calculate the amount of the annual lease payment.
2. What type of lease arrangement is this for Symonds?
3. Record the necessary journal entries for Symonds for the year 2005.
4. Prepare the lease disclosures that will appear on Symonds's balance sheet as of December 31, 2005. (You may exclude the note disclosures.)

LO2, 3, 5   **EXERCISE 14-3   Capital Lease**

Lambdin Company has agreed to lease a depreciable asset from another party. The provisions of the lease contract are as follows:

Date of inception of the lease	January 1, 2005
Lease term	6 years
Useful life of the asset	9 years
Fair value of asset at lease inception	$800,000
Incremental borrowing rate	14%
Implicit borrowing rate (known by lessee)	12%

Annual rental payments are due on January 1 of each lease year, with the first payment on January 1, 2005. At the end of the lease term, the equipment reverts to the lessor. The two parties have agreed that the asset will be worth $100,000, but Lambdin has not guaranteed that amount.

Assume that the straight-line method of depreciation is used and that the asset will have zero residual value at the end of its useful life.

Required:

1. Calculate the amount of the annual lease payment.
2. What type of lease arrangement is this for Lambdin?
3. Record the necessary journal entries for Lambdin for the year 2005.
4. Prepare the lease disclosures that will appear in Lambdin's balance sheet as of December 31, 2005. (You may exclude the note disclosures.)

LO3, 5 **EXERCISE 14-4** **Title Passes**

Assume that a lease agreement has the same provisions as those in Exercise 14-3 except that the title to the asset passes to the lessee at the end of the lease agreement.

Required:

1. Does the fact that the title passes affect the amount of the annual lease payments?
2. How does the fact that the title passes affect the depreciation of the asset?

LO3, 5 **EXERCISE 14-5** **Guaranteed Residual Value Lease**

Konercko Company has agreed to lease a depreciable asset from another party. The provisions of the lease contract are as follows:

Date of inception of the lease	January 1, 2005
Lease term	6 years
Useful life of the asset	9 years
Annual rental payments due on January 1 of each lease year, with the first payment on January 1, 2005	
Fair value of asset at lease inception	$800,000
Incremental borrowing rate	14%
Implicit borrowing rate (known by lessee)	12%

At the end of the lease term, the equipment reverts to the lessor. The two parties have agreed to a guaranteed residual value of $100,000 at the end of the lease.

Assume that the straight-line method of depreciation is used and that the asset will have zero residual value at the end of its useful life.

Required:

1. Calculate the amount of the annual lease payment.
2. What type of lease arrangement is this for Konercko?
3. Prepare an amortization schedule for the lease obligation for 2005 and 2006.
4. Record the necessary journal entries for Konercko for the year 2005.
5. Prepare the lease disclosures that will appear on Konercko's balance sheet as of December 31, 2005. (You may exclude the note disclosures.)
6. What effect is a guaranteed residual value likely to have on the rate of return (implicit borrowing rate) that is required by the lessor?

LO3, 5 **EXERCISE 14-6** **Guaranteed Residual Value Lease**

Valentin has agreed to lease a depreciable asset from another party. The provisions of the lease contract are as follows:

Date of inception of the lease	January 1, 2005
Lease term	4 years

Useful life of the asset	7 years
Annual rental payments due on December 31 of each lease year	
Fair value of asset at lease inception	$800,000
Incremental borrowing rate	10%
Implicit borrowing rate (unknown by lessee)	8%

At the end of the lease term, the equipment reverts to the lessor. The two parties have agreed to a guaranteed residual value of $100,000 at the end of the lease.

Assume that the straight-line method of depreciation is used and that the asset will have zero residual value at the end of its useful life.

Required:

1. Calculate the amount of the annual lease payment.
2. What type of lease arrangement is this for Valentin?
3. Prepare an amortization schedule for the lease obligation for 2005 and 2006.
4. Record the necessary journal entries for Valentin for the year 2005.
5. Prepare the lease disclosures that will appear on Valentin's balance sheet as of December 31, 2005. (You may exclude the note disclosures.)
6. Assume that you are an accountant for Valentin and that one of your duties is investor relations. A stockholder has questioned why the leased asset was not recorded at its fair market value. Draft a memo that explains the amount that was recorded.

LO3, 5   **EXERCISE 14-7   Bargain Purchase Option**

Romar has agreed to lease a depreciable asset from another party. The provisions of the lease contract are as follows:

Date of inception of the lease	January 1, 2005
Lease term	4 years
Useful life of the asset	7 years
Annual rental payments due on December 31 of each lease year	
Fair value of asset at lease inception	$800,000
Incremental borrowing rate	10%
Implicit borrowing rate (unknown by lessee)	8%

At the end of the lease term, Romar has the option to purchase the equipment for $100,000, an amount that is significantly less than the fair market value that will exist at that time.

Assume that the straight-line method of depreciation is used and that the asset will have zero residual value at the end of its useful life.

Required:

1. Calculate the amount of the annual lease payment.
2. What type of lease arrangement is this for Romar?
3. Prepare an amortization schedule for the lease obligation for 2005 and 2006.
4. Prepare the lease disclosures that will appear on Romar's balance sheet as of December 31, 2005. (You may exclude the note disclosures.)
5. Assume that you are an accountant for Romar and that one of your duties is investor relations. A stockholder has questioned why the leased asset was not recorded at its fair market value. Draft a memo that explains the amount that was recorded for the leased asset.

LO3, 5   **EXERCISE 14-8   Bargain Purchase Option**

Assume the same facts as stated in Exercise 14-7 except that Romar is aware that the lessor has established the implicit borrowing rate at 8 percent.

Required:

1. Explain why the lease in Exercise 14-7 would be recorded differently from the lease in this exercise.

2. Prepare an amortization schedule for the lease obligation for 2005 and 2006.

3. Record the necessary journal entries for the year 2005 for Romar.

LO6 EXERCISE 14-9 **Cash Flows for an Operating Lease**

Bert Company leases several assets using operating lease arrangements. For some leases, Bert Company is required to make advance lease payments. For other leases, the lessor bills Bert Company based on the amount of usage of the asset, and Bert must remit payment. For the year 2005, the following account balances are known:

	January 1	December 31
Prepaid Lease	$100,000	$130,000
Accrued Lease Liability	200,000	240,000
Lease Expense (Annual)		500,000

Required:

1. Calculate the amount of cash paid for lease payments for the year 2005.

2. How would the amount of lease payments be disclosed in Bert Company's statement of cash flows, assuming that the company uses the indirect method?

LO6 EXERCISE 14-10 **Cash Flows for a Capital Lease**

Ernie Company leases assets using capital lease arrangements. All its leases call for annual payments on December 31. For the year 2005, the following account balances are known:

	January 1	December 31
Leased Assets	$500,000	$500,000
Accumulated Depreciation—		
Leased Assets	100,000	168,000
Lease Obligation	500,000	428,000
Depreciation Expense—		
Leased Assets		68,000
Interest Expense		52,000

Required:

1. Calculate the amount of cash payments related to leased assets for the year 2005.

2. How would the information regarding leased assets be disclosed in Ernie's statement of cash flows for the year 2005, assuming that the company uses the indirect method?

LO7, 9 EXERCISE 14-11 **Lease for Lessor**

Gary Company wishes to acquire a large piece of equipment for its production process. It has determined that the equipment will cost $800,000 and has provided the equipment specifications to Andrew Leasing Company, and Andrew has purchased the asset. The two parties have entered into a lease agreement with the following contractual provisions:

Date of inception of the lease	January 1, 2005
Lease term	6 years
Useful life of the asset	9 years
Annual rental payments due on December 31 of each lease year	
Fair value of asset at lease inception	$800,000
Implicit borrowing rate	12%

At the end of the lease term, the equipment reverts to the lessor. The two parties have agreed that the asset will be worth $100,000, but the lessee has not guaranteed that amount.

Required:

1. Calculate the amount of the annual lease payment.
2. What type of lease arrangement is this for Andrew Leasing Company?
3. Prepare an amortization schedule for the lease for 2005 and 2006.
4. Record the necessary journal entries for Andrew Leasing Company for the year 2005.
5. Prepare the lease disclosures that will appear in Andrew's balance sheet as of December 31, 2005. (You may exclude the note disclosures.)

LO7, 9   **EXERCISE 14-12**   **Lease for Lessor**

Assume the same facts as given in Exercise 14-11 except that the lease payments occur on January 1 of each lease year, with the first lease payment on January 1, 2005.

Required:

1. Calculate the amount of the annual lease payment.
2. What type of lease arrangement is this for Andrew Leasing Company?
3. Prepare an amortization schedule for the lease for 2005, 2006, and 2007.
4. Record the necessary journal entries for Andrew Leasing Company for the year 2005.
5. Prepare the lease disclosures that will appear in Andrew's balance sheet as of December 31, 2005. (You may exclude the note disclosures.)

LO7, 10   **EXERCISE 14-13**   **Lease for Lessor**

Woody Ford, a new car dealership, has adopted a leasing program to stimulate sales of mid-sized new cars. It purchases this line of cars from the manufacturer at an invoice cost of $16,000 per car, and it sells the cars for $20,000 each (which represents their fair market value). The standard lease contract has the following requirements:

Term of the lease	60 months
Monthly payments due at the beginning of each month, with first payment due at the date of lease inception.	
Implied rate of interest	12% (or 1% per month)
Upon lease termination, the car reverts to Woody Ford, and the lessee guarantees that the asset will be worth $5,000 at that time.	

Assume that Woody Ford purchases a car on January 1, 2005, and leases it immediately.

Required:

1. Calculate the amount of the monthly lease payment.
2. What type of lease arrangement is this for Woody Ford?
3. Prepare an amortization schedule for the lease for 2005.
4. Record the necessary journal entries for Woody Ford for the year 2005.
5. Assume that the sales manager wishes to stimulate sales even further. She is concerned that the amount of the monthly payment may be a deterrent to some potential customers. However, Danielle Woody, who owns the company, is adamant that the dealership must be able to achieve a 12 percent return. Also, she is unwilling to reduce the selling price of the car below $20,000. What changes could be made in the lease contract to reduce the monthly payment without reducing the return?

LO7, 10   **EXERCISE 14-14**   **Lease for Lessor**

Dimlight Auto Company has instituted a leasing program to stimulate sales of one of its new car models. The invoice cost is $16,000 per car, and the selling price is $20,000 each (which represents fair market value). The lease contract has the following requirements:

Term of the lease	60 months
Monthly payments due at the beginning of each month, with first payment due at the date of lease inception.	

Implied rate of interest   12% (or 1% per month)

Upon lease termination, the title passes to the lessee, and the parties have agreed that the residual value of the asset will be $5,000 at that time.

Required:

1. Discuss the importance of the residual value in the lease agreement.

2. Calculate the amount of the monthly lease payment.

3. What type of lease arrangement is this for Dimlight?

4. Calculate the amount of the gross profit and the total interest on the lease contract.

LO1, 4, 5   **EXERCISE 14-15   Lessee Capital and Operating Leases**

Southwest Airlines reported total stockholders' equity of $5,052 million and total liabilities of $4,826 million at December 31, 2003. Its effective income tax rate is 35 percent. The average life of each aircraft is 20 years with negligible residual value. The following information appeared in Southwest's notes to its financial statements for the years ended December 31, 2003 and 2002:

Southwest Airlines

Note 8. LEASES

The Company had seven aircraft classified as capital leases at December 31, 2003. The amounts applicable to these aircraft included in property and equipment were:

(In millions)	2003	2002
Flight equipment	$171	$165
Less accumulated depreciation	114	106
	$ 57	$ 59

Total rental expense for operating leases charged to operations in 2003, 2002, and 2001 was $386 million, $371 million, and $359 million, respectively. The majority of the company's terminal operations space, as well as 89 aircraft, was under operating leases at December 31, 2003. Future minimum lease payments under capital leases and noncancelable operating leases with initial or remaining terms in excess of one year at December 31, 2003, were:

(In millions)	Capital Leases	Operating Leases
2004	$ 18	$ 283
2005	24	273
2006	14	219
2007	16	202
2008	13	190
After 2008	39	1,328
Minimum lease payments	$124	$2,495
Less amount of interest	33	
Present value of minimum lease payments	$ 91	
Less current portion	10	
Long-term portion	$ 81	

Required:

1. Prepare the liabilities section of Southwest Airlines's balance sheet to show how the leases would be reported at December 31, 2003.

2. Assume that $674 of the minimum operating lease payments is interest, of which $53 pertains to 2004. Prepare the liabilities section to show how the leases would be reported if all were treated as capital leases.

3. Calculate the debt-to-equity ratio assuming that the leases are treated as reported by Southwest Airlines. Then recalculate assuming that all leases are capitalized, based on the revised balance sheet in question 2.

LO2, 5, 7, 10   **EXERCISE 14-16**   **Type of Lease for Lessee and Lessor, Implicit and Incremental Rates**

On January 1, 2004, Daboul Enterprises leased a new piece of equipment from Adkins Leasing Company. Information concerning the lease is as follows:

A. Daboul signed a noncancelable lease that requires four equal annual payments of $21,400 each, due on January 1, beginning January 1, 2004.

B. The estimated useful life of the equipment is five years, at the end of which time it is expected to be worth $2,000.

C. The estimated residual value of the equipment at the end of the lease term is $9,000.

D. At lease inception, the fair value of the equipment is $83,000; its book value to the lessor is $76,000.

E. The interest rate used to calculate lease payments is 9 percent, which is known to both parties. Adkins's incremental borrowing rate is 7 percent; Daboul's incremental borrowing rate is 8 percent.

F. Under the lease terms, Daboul is obligated to pay an additional $100 per month (payable on the first day of each month) to Adkins for maintenance of the equipment.

G. The lease has a purchase option at the end of the lease term equal to $3,000.

H. Both parties use straight-line depreciation, and both parties have a fiscal year end of September 30.

I. Collectibility of the future lease payments is reasonably predictable, and no additional costs related to the lease are expected.

Required:

1. Apply the lease criteria and determine what type of lease this is for the lessee.
2. Apply the lease criteria and determine what type of lease it is for the lessor.
3. Why does the lessee use a different interest rate from that used by the lessor?

LO2, 5   **EXERCISE 14-17**   **Capital Lease for Lessee**

A lessee provided the following lease payment schedule. The expected residual value of the leased asset is $5,000 at the end of its 10-year useful life. The lease has no bargain purchase option, and ownership remains with the lessor at the end of the lease term. The fair value of the asset at inception is $46,000.

Date	Cash	Interest Expense	Reduction of Principal	Lease Obligation
3/1/04				$44,437
3/1/04	$6,800	$ 0	$6,800	37,637
3/1/05	6,800	3,387	3,413	34,223
3/1/06	6,800	3,080	3,720	30,504
3/1/07	6,800	2,745	4,055	26,449
3/1/08	6,800	2,380	4,420	22,029
3/1/09	6,800	1,983	4,817	17,212
3/1/10	6,800	1,549	5,251	11,961
3/1/11	6,800	1,077	5,723	6,238
3/1/12	6,800	562	6,238	0*

*Rounded.

Required:

1. Determine the implicit rate.
2. Identify the term of this lease
3. Calculate the annual depreciation amount for the lessee. Support your choice of amortization periods.
4. Does this lease have a guaranteed residual value stated in the lease? Briefly indicate how you know.

LO3, 7, 10   **EXERCISE 14-18**   **Lease Payment, Lessor Criteria, Purchase Option**

Talton Company leased a machine from Sona Corporation on July 31, 2005. The machine has a fair value of $30,000 and an original cost to Sona of $21,000. The lease agreement calls for four years of equal monthly payments on the last day of each month, with the first occurring on July 31, 2005. The useful life of the machine is expected to be four years with an estimated residual value of $8,000. Sona paid its attorney $1,000 to handle the lease closing. The lessor wants to earn a 12 percent return and to recover 100 percent, including its closing costs, by the end of the four-year lease term. The lease contains a bargain purchase option of $4,000 at the end of the lease term.

Required:

1. Determine the amount of each monthly lease payment.
2. What type of lease is this for the lessor?
3. What is the disposition of the leased asset, and what cash will change hands at the end of the lease term?

LO2, 5, 7, 9   **EXERCISE 14-19**   **Lessor and Lessee, Discount Rates**

On January 1, 2004, Kirby Enterprises leased a new piece of equipment from Mathews Leasing Company. Information concerning the lease is as follows:

A. Kirby signed a noncancelable lease that requires three equal annual payments of $14,000 each. The annual payments are due on January 1, beginning January 1, 2005.
B. The lease has an estimated value at the end of the lease term equal to $4,000. The lease requires the lessee to return the leased asset at this value at the end of the lease term.
C. The estimated useful life of the equipment is four years. At the end of this time, it is expected to be worth $1,000.
D. At lease inception, the fair market value of the equipment is $42,500; its book value is $42,500.
E. The interest rate used to calculate lease payments is 9 percent, which is known to both parties. Kirby's incremental borrowing rate is 7 percent; Mathews's incremental borrowing rate is 8 percent.
F. Both parties use straight-line depreciation, and both parties have a fiscal year end of March 31.
G. Collectibility of the future lease payments is reasonably predictable, and no additional costs related to the lease are expected.

Required:

1. What type of lease is this for the lessor? For the lessee?
2. At what amount will the leased equipment be recorded on the lessee's books on the lease inception date?
3. Identify the reason that Mathews's lease receivable and Kirby's lease liability are not equal.
4. What aspect of the lease other than the one that you identified in question 3 could cause the amounts in question 3 not to equal each other?

LO2, 3, 5, 7, 10   **EXERCISE 14-20**   **Lessor and Lessee**

Ganic Company leased a machine from Mendez Corporation on May 31, 2004. The machine has a fair value of $25,600 and an original cost to Mendez of $10,000. The lease agreement calls for four years of equal monthly payments on the last day of each month, with the first occurring on May 31, 2004. The useful life of the machine is five years with no residual value. Mendez paid its attorney $800 to handle the lease closing. The lease contains a guaranteed residual value of $3,000. The lessor wants to earn a 12 percent return and recover the asset's value, including closing costs, by the end of the four-year lease term.

Required:

1. Which company is the lessor?

2. What is the accounting name for the $800 cost?

3. Determine the amount of each of the following:

   a. Capitalized cost of the lease receivable for the lessor
   b. Gross profit that the lessor will report at lease inception
   c. Interest rate and number of periods to be used to determine the lease payment
   d. Present value of the minimum lease payments for the lessee
   e. Period of time over which the leased asset will be depreciated by the lessee
   f. Amount of each monthly lease payment
   g. The portion of the first payment that is interest

LO2, 4, 5   **EXERCISE 14-21   Lessee Capital and Operating Leases**

On March 1, 2004, Mitchell, Inc. leased equipment with a fair value of $28,000 to Chalk Company, with the first payment to be made at lease inception and annual payments thereafter. Each payment is $4,438. The equipment cost the lessor $20,000 and has an estimated life of eight years. The implicit borrowing rate for this lease is 10 percent. Mitchell's incremental borrowing rate is 9 percent, while Chalk's rate is 7 percent. The present value of the minimum lease payments is $26,500 for the lessee. The residual value at the end of the six-year lease term is expected to be $4,000. Mitchell expects no additional costs under the lease and is able to estimate any uncollectibles concerning the payments.

Required:

1. List the lessee criteria that are satisfied by this lease. Show calculations for the quantitative criteria.

2. How much should the lessee capitalize for the lease?

3. How much interest should the lessee recognize for its year ended December 31, 2004?

LO2, 4, 5   **EXERCISE 14-22   Lessee Capital and Operating Leases and Disclosure**

During 2004, Mendez signed two leases and properly accounted for both. The operating lease is for equipment with a fair value of $74,000 at inception and gross lease payments totaling $38,000 over the entire lease term. The capital lease is for equipment with a capitalized cost at lease inception of $134,600, a fair value of $145,000 at lease inception, and a book value to the lessee at the balance sheet date of $96,200. The lease payment dates and fiscal year-end dates are the same. Information from Mendez's note disclosure related to the leases follows:

NOTE 2—Lease Obligations: The company leases certain equipment used in its operations. As of December 31, the aggregate minimum rental commitments under noncancelable leases, net of interest, were approximately as follows:

Year Ended December 31,	Capital Lease	Operating Lease
2005	$ 13,000	$ 4,000
2006	14,100	4,300
2007	14,700	4,600
2008	15,000	5,100
2009	16,000	5,500
Thereafter	40,000	6,000
Net minimum lease payments	$112,800	$29,500

Required:

1. Prepare a partial classified balance sheet for Mendez, the lessee, at December 31, 2004, showing how the effects of the company's lease(s) would be reported.

2. List the primary disclosures concerning capital leases that must be made by the lessee in addition to the schedule given in note 2.

PROBLEMS

LO3, 5 **PROBLEM 14-1** **Capital Lease** (CPA adapted)

On January 2, 2005, Elsee Co. leased equipment from Grant, Inc. Lease payments are $100,000, payable annually every December 31 for 20 years. Title to the equipment passes to Elsee at the end of the lease term. The lease is noncancelable. The leased equipment has a $750,000 carrying amount on Grant's books. Its estimated economic life is 25 years on January 2, 2005. The rate implicit in the lease, which is known to Elsee, is 10 percent. Elsee's incremental borrowing rate is 12 percent. Elsee uses the straight-line method of depreciation.

Required: Prepare the necessary journal entries to be recorded by Elsee for:

1. Entering into the lease on January 2, 2005.

2. Making the lease payment on December 31, 2005.

3. Expenses related to the lease for the year ended December 31, 2005.

Analyze: What factors allowed you to determine the appropriate classification for this lease?

LO3, 5 **PROBLEM 14-2** **Capital Lease**

A lessee has entered into a lease agreement that has been classified as a capital lease, with the asset being returned to the lessor at the end of the lease term. The following information is part of the lease agreement:

A. The lease is initiated on January 1, 2005, for equipment with an expected useful life of three years. The equipment reverts to the lessor upon expiration of the lease agreement.

B. The fair market value of the equipment is $210,000.

C. Three payments in the amount of $74,000 per year beginning December 31, 2005 are due to the lessor. An additional sum of $2,000 is to be paid annually by the lessee for insurance.

D. The lessee guarantees a $20,000 residual value on December 31, 2007, to the lessor. Assume that the asset's actual residual value is zero on that date.

E. The lessee's incremental borrowing rate is 8 percent. (The lessor's implicit borrowing rate is unknown.)

Required:

1. Provide all necessary journal entries for the lessee for 2005.

2. Provide an amortization schedule for all years for the lessee.

3. Develop the proper balance sheet presentation for the lessee for a balance sheet dated December 31, 2005.

Analyze: Why might a company attempt to use as high an interest rate as possible when computing the present value of the minimum lease payments?

LO10 **PROBLEM 14-3** **Sales-Type Lease**

A lessor entered into a capital lease that has been classified as a sales-type lease. The following information is part of the lease agreement:

A. The lease term is 8 years. The estimated useful life of the asset is 10 years.

B. The lessor is to receive equal annual payments over the term of the lease. The leased property reverts to the lessor upon termination of the lease.

C. The lease is initiated on January 1, 2005. Payments are due on December 31 for the duration of the lease term.

D. The cost of the equipment is $160,000.

E. The selling price of the equipment for an outright purchase is $240,000.

F. The parties in the transaction have agreed that the equipment will have a residual value of $10,000 at the end of 8 years. The residual value is not guaranteed.

G. The lessor desires a return of 10 percent (the implicit borrowing rate).

Required:

1. Provide all necessary journal entries for the lessor for 2005.

2. Provide an amortization schedule for all years for the lessor.

3. Develop the proper balance sheet presentation for the lessor for a balance sheet dated December 31, 2005.

Analyze: Over the life of this lease, how much total interest income will be earned?

LO3, 5, 9   **PROBLEM 14-4   Lease for Both Parties**

Rodley Corp. enters into an agreement with Zilbeck Rentals Co. on January 1, 2005, for the purpose of leasing a machine to be used in its manufacturing operations. The following data pertain to the agreement:

A. The term of the noncancelable lease is three years with no renewal option. A payment of $78,443 is due on December 31 of each year.

B. The fair value of the machine on January 1, 2005, is $300,000. The machine has a remaining economic life of 10 years, with no residual value. The machine reverts to the lessor upon termination of the lease. Rodley guarantees a $100,000 residual value at the end of the lease term.

C. Rodley Corp. depreciates all machinery it owns on a straight-line basis. Rodley's incremental borrowing rate is 8 percent per year. Rodley does not have knowledge of the 5 percent implicit borrowing rate used by Zilbeck.

Required: On the basis of the information given, answer the following questions.

1. Record the entries required on Rodley's books for the inception of the lease on January 1, 2005.

2. Record the entry on Rodley's books on December 31, 2005, to record depreciation of the leased asset.

3. Record the first lease payment on Rodley's books.

4. Assume that the transaction is considered a direct financing lease for Zilbeck. Record the entries required on Zilbeck's books for the inception of the lease on January 1, 2005.

5. Record all entries necessary at the time of receipt of the first lease payment on Zilbeck Rentals's books.

Analyze: Describe the process by which you determined what type of lease this is from Rodley's viewpoint.

LO1, 2, 4, 5   **PROBLEM 14-5   Analysis of McDonald's Leases**

A note included in **McDonald's Corporation**'s 2003 annual report appears on the following page.

Required: Calculate the dollar amount that would have been used if McDonald's had treated the operating leases as capital leases. In calculating the present value, you may

McDonald's

Future minimum payments required under existing operating leases with initial terms of one year or more are:

(In millions)	Restaurant
2004	$ 930.9
2005	884.5
2006	831.2
2007	777.0
2008	725.9
Thereafter	6,358.8
Total minimum payments	$10,508.3

assume that a 10 percent discount rate is applicable and that the lease payments given in the note on the line referred to as "thereafter" will occur evenly over a 10-year time period after 2008.

Analyze: What information would be needed in order to make a more accurate estimate of the dollar amount of leases?

LO1, 2, 4, 5   **PROBLEM 14-6   Analysis of Starbucks's Leases**
The leasing note included in **Starbucks Coffee Company**'s 2003 annual report included the following information.

Starbucks

The Company leases retail stores, roasting and distribution facilities and office space under operating leases expiring through 2027. Most lease agreements contain renewal options and rent escalation clauses. Certain leases provide for contingent rentals based upon gross sales.

Rental expense under these lease agreements was as follows (in thousands):

Fiscal year ended	Sept. 28, 2003	Sept. 29, 2002	Sept. 30, 2001
Minimum rentals—Retail	$237,742	$200,827	$150,510
Minimum rentals—Other	22,887	19,143	16,033
Contingent rentals	12,274	5,415	4,018
Total	$272,903	$225,385	$170,561

Minimum future rental payments under noncancelable lease obligations as of September 28, 2003, are as follows (in thousands):

Fiscal year ending	
2004	$ 293,912
2005	284,401
2006	270,261
2007	253,944
2008	232,713
Thereafter	924,203
Total minimum lease payments	$2,259,434

Required: Calculate the dollar amount that would have been used if the operating leases had been treated as capital leases by Starbucks. In calculating the present value, you may assume that a 10 percent discount rate is applicable and that the lease payments given in the note on the line referred to as "thereafter" will occur evenly over a four-year time period after 2008.

Analyze: What information would be needed in order to make a more accurate estimate of the dollar amount of leases?

LO2, 4, 5   PROBLEM **14-7**   **Analysis of Operating Versus Capital Lease**
Tucker Company had the following simplified balance sheet as of December 31, 2005:

Current assets	$40,000	Current liabilities	$20,000
Long-term assets	50,000	Long-term liabilities	40,000
		Stockholders' equity	30,000
Total assets	$90,000	Total liabilities and stockholders' equity	$90,000

On January 1, 2005, Tucker signed a long-term lease agreement and has not recorded any transactions regarding the lease agreement. The lease is for 10 years, and the lease payments are $6,000 per year, payable each December 31. The implicit borrowing rate on the lease is 10 percent, which is equal to Tucker's incremental borrowing rate. Assume that the life of the leased asset is 10 years and that Tucker uses the straight-line method of depreciation and zero residual value for all assets. Also, Tucker's income statement for 2005 indicated a net income of $20,000 and a tax rate of 40 percent.

Required:

1. Calculate the revised net income for 2005 if the lease is treated as an operating lease and if it is treated as a capital lease.

2. Develop a revised balance sheet as of December 31, 2005, if the lease is treated as an operating lease and as a capital lease.

Analyze: Based on the revised income statement and balance sheet, calculate the current ratio, debt-to-equity ratio, and return on assets if the lease is treated as an operating lease and as a capital lease.

LO3, 7, 10   PROBLEM **14-8**   **Lease for Lessor, Payment Calculation**
Rooksberry Company leased a machine from Fowler Corporation on May 31, 2003. Fowler's original cost of the machine was $18,000, although the machine currently has a fair value of $24,000. The lease agreement calls for four years of equal monthly payments on the last day of each month, with the first occurring on May 31, 2003. The useful life of the machine is expected to be four years. Fowler paid its attorney $1,000 to handle the lease closing. The lease contains a bargain purchase option at the end of the lease term of $4,000. The lessor wants to earn a 12 percent return and recover 100 percent by the end of the four-year lease term, including closing costs. The lessor has no uncertain costs and feels that the lease payments will be collected with relative certainty.

Required:

1. Determine the amount of each monthly lease payment.

2. Determine which of the lease criteria are met and identify the type of lease that this arrangement is for Fowler.

3. Name the accounting term that should be assigned to the lease closing costs by the lessor. Briefly indicate the proper accounting treatment of the closing costs for Fowler Corporation.

Analyze: How and why are these costs accounted for differently from the way they would be if this arrangement qualified under the other two lease types for Fowler Corporation?

LO2, 7, 10   PROBLEM **14-9**   **Lease for Lessor and Lessee, Choice of Interest Rates**
On January 1, 2003, Roberts Enterprises leased a new piece of equipment from Gilpin Leasing Company. Information concerning the lease is given on the following page.

A. Roberts signed a noncancelable lease that requires three equal annual payments of $10,000 each. The annual payments are due on January 1, beginning January 1, 2004.

B. The lease has a guaranteed residual value at the end of the lease term equal to $3,000.

C. The estimated useful life of the equipment is five years, at the end of which time it is expected to be worth $1,000.

D. At lease inception, the fair value of the equipment is $30,000; its book value to the lessor is $22,000.

E. The interest rate used to calculate the lease payments is 10 percent, which is known to both parties. Gilpin's incremental borrowing rate is 7 percent; Roberts's incremental borrowing rate is 8 percent.

F. Both parties use straight-line depreciation, and both parties have a fiscal year end of March 31.

G. Collectibility of the future lease payments is reasonably predictable, and no additional costs related to the lease are expected.

Required:

1. What type of lease is this for the lessor? For the lessee? Support your answer with an analysis of the criteria.

2. At what amount will the leased equipment be recorded on the lessee's books on the lease inception date?

3. Prepare the amortization schedule for the lease for Roberts.

Analyze: Why will the capitalized lease amount for Gilpin differ from that for Roberts?

LO1, 2, 4, 5 **PROBLEM 14-10 Analysis of Lessee's Leases**

During 2001, Heltzel Company signed two leases and properly accounted for both. The capital lease is for equipment with a capitalized cost at lease inception of $100,000, a fair value of $110,000 at lease inception, and a book value to the lessee at December 31, 2003, of $82,500. The operating lease is for equipment with a fair value of $88,000 at inception and gross lease payments totaling $35,000 over the entire lease term. The lease payment date and fiscal year-end dates are the same. Information from Heltzel's note disclosure related to the leases follows.

NOTE 2—Lease Obligations: The company leases certain equipment used in its operations. As of December 31, 2003, the aggregate minimum rental commitments under noncancelable leases were approximately as follows:

	Capital Lease	Operating Lease
2004	$ 8,100	$ 2,100
2005	12,400	3,200
2006	15,200	4,300
2007	18,600	5,400
2008	10,000	6,000
Thereafter	30,000	6,600
Net minimum lease payments	$94,300	$27,600

Required: Prepare a partial *classified* balance sheet for Heltzel, the lessee, at December 31, 2003, showing how the effects of the company's lease(s) would be reported.

Analyze: Why might Heltzel prefer to account for its leases as operating leases instead of as capital leases? Explain.

LO7, 10 **PROBLEM 14-11 Lease for Lessor**

On April 1, 2003, Arendt Corporation leased equipment to Hew Company under an eight-year lease. Hew Company made the first payment of $4,500 on April 1, 2003. The equipment cost Arendt Corporation $22,000. The present value of the minimum lease payments is $26,400. The normal selling price of the leased equipment is $30,000. Arendt Corporation appropriately capitalizes this lease. The implicit borrowing rate in the lease is 10 percent, and both parties have an incremental borrowing rate of 8 percent. Both parties meet the lease criteria.

Required:

1. How do you know that Arendt should account for this lease as a sales-type lease?
2. How much interest will Arendt recognize on this lease during 2003?

Analyze: What interest rate should Hew use in recognizing the lease? Why does GAAP require that this rate be used?

LO2, 5   **PROBLEM 14-12**   **Analysis of Lessee's Leases**

An unlabeled lease amortization table prepared by Jix, Inc. (lessee) appears below. Title does not transfer to the lessee, and there is no bargain purchase option in the lease agreement. The asset has an expected economic life of 10 years. The estimated residual value at the end of the asset's useful life is $2,000. Both parties use straight-line depreciation. The fair value of the leased asset is $46,000 at inception. The lease is noncancelable.

10/1/03				$42,701
10/1/03	$6,445	$ 0	$6,445	36,256
10/1/04	6,445	2,900	3,545	32,711
10/1/05	6,445	2,617	3,828	28,883
10/1/06	6,445	2,311	4,134	24,749
10/1/07	6,445	1,980	4,465	20,284
10/1/08	6,445	1,623	4,822	15,462
10/1/09	6,445	1,237	5,208	10,254
10/1/10	6,445	820	5,625	4,629
10/1/11	5,000	370	4,630	0*

*Rounded.

Required:

1. Calculate the implicit interest rate for this lease.
2. What is the term of this lease? (How long is it?)
3. A payment occurs on October 1, 2011. What is this payment most likely for?
4. Suppose the lessee wants to pay off the lease as of September 30, 2007. How much is the payoff?
5. Prepare the asset section of the lessor's balance sheet as of March 31, 2005, assuming that the amortization table belongs to the lessor rather than the lessee.

Analyze: What is the book value of the leased asset as of March 31, 2005?

LO2, 5   **PROBLEM 14-13**   **Analysis of Lessee's Leases**

On March 1, 2003, Davis Co. and Mills Co. entered into a lease agreement that qualifies as a direct financing lease. The lessor's cost for the leased asset is $30,000. The lease contains a bargain purchase option of $6,000 that is exercisable at the end of the lease term. The expected economic life of the asset is 10 years. The lease term is 8 years. Payments are due annually on March 1. The asset is expected to have a residual value of $2,000 at the end of 10 years. Both parties use straight-line depreciation. The schedule for the lease, created by Mills's accountant, appears on the following page.

Year Ended	Amount
Dec. 31, 2004	$ 2,309
Dec. 31, 2005	2,539
Dec. 31, 2006	2,793
Dec. 31, 2007	3,073
Dec. 31, 2008	3,380
Aggregate thereafter	13,808
Total	$27,902
Less current	(2,309)
Long-term	$25,593

Required:

1. Is Mills the lessee or the lessor? How do you know?

2. Specifically *where* in an annual report would you expect to find this schedule?

3. How much would the lessee report as "long-term lease obligation" on its balance sheet at its fiscal year end, December 31, 2006, relative to this lease?

Analyze: The amounts reported on the schedule include no interest. Why not?

Communicate: What is the purpose of this schedule?

LO3, 5   **PROBLEM 14-14**   **Capitalizing Leases, Payment Calculation**

Rex Corporation leased a yacht to Lee Company under a noncancelable lease. The following information is available regarding the lease terms and the leased asset:

A. Rex's cost for the leased asset was $350,000. The asset was new at the lease inception date, January 1, 2003.

B. The eight-year lease requires annual payments each January 1, beginning January 1, 2004.

C. The estimated useful life of the leased asset is 10 years. The lease contains a guaranteed residual value at the end of the lease term in the amount of $40,000.

D. If Lee had purchased the yacht from Rex, the selling price would have been $460,000.

E. Rex incurred $1,000 of costs for lawyer's fees and other public recording costs associated with the lease.

F. Rex's implicit borrowing rate is 9 percent, which is known to Lee.

G. Lee's incremental borrowing rate is 10 percent; Rex's incremental borrowing rate is 8 percent.

H. Rex Corporation wishes to recover the amount it could have received had it sold the yacht and the initial direct costs it incurred.

I. Rex expects to collect all payments from Lee, and there are no material cost uncertainties.

Required:

1. Which interest rate will you use to calculate the lease payments? Why?

2. Compute the annual lease payments.

Analyze: Would the amount of the lease payments be the same, lower, or higher if you used a higher interest rate than you used in question 2? Explain.

Critical Thinking: What is the justification for capitalizing the leased asset on the lessee's books? Explain.

LO2, 7   **PROBLEM 14-15**   **Lease for Lessor and Lessee, Multiple Interest Rates**

On January 1, 2003, Beale Corporation leased equipment to Allen Company for 8 years. The equipment has an economic life of 12 years. The first payment was made on January 1,

2003, for $6,000. Thereafter, eight more annual payments of $10,000 are due on each subsequent January 1. Title is transferred to Allen Company at the end of the lease term. The purchase price of the leased equipment to Beale Corporation was $48,000, and no additional costs are expected under the terms of the lease. The normal selling price of the equipment is $65,000. Both companies use straight-line depreciation, and both use a 10 percent residual value. The implicit borrowing rate in the lease is 10 percent. The lessee's incremental borrowing rate is 11 percent. Beale expects to collect all payments from Allen.

Required: List all the criteria that must be evaluated by the lessee. Perform the necessary calculations and evaluate which criteria are met by the lease for the lessee.

Analyze: What type of lease is this for the lessee? For the lessor? Explain your selection.

LO2, 7, 10 | **PROBLEM 14-16   Lease for Lessor and Lessee**
On March 31, 2003, Mabardy Company leased a new piece of equipment from Olcott Company. Mabardy signed a noncancelable lease that requires six years of equal payments of $8,000 each. The first payment is due at the inception of the lease, and the remaining payments are due annually on March 31 of every year. The lease has a purchase option of $4,000 at the end of the lease term. The estimated economic life of the equipment is eight years. Olcott sells similar equipment for $45,000. On the lease inception date, the equipment had an inventory cost basis of $30,000 to Olcott. The implicit borrowing rate used in the lease agreement is 8 percent, which is known to Mabardy. Both parties depreciate all leased equipment by the straight-line method. The equipment is expected to be worth $9,000 at the end of the lease term and $3,000 at the end of its useful life. The lessor meets both of the additional lease criteria.

Required:

1. For how much should the leased equipment be recorded by the lessee on the lease inception date?

2. Which party will capitalize the leased equipment and why? Over how many years will the leased asset be depreciated?

3. Prepare the journal entry(ies) to record the lease on Olcott's books on the lease inception date.

4. What amounts will the lessor report on its income statement for the year ended December 31, 2003?

Analyze: What type of lease is this for the lessor? Explain.

LO2, 5, 7 | **PROBLEM 14-17   Lease for Lessee, Multiple Interest Rates, Income Statement**
On January 1, 2003, Expo Corporation (lessor) and Adco, Inc. (lessee) agree to an eight-year lease for equipment that has an economic life of 11 years. One up-front payment was made on January 1, 2003, for $6,000. Thereafter, seven more annual payments of $7,000 are due on each subsequent January 1, all of which Expo expects to collect. Title belongs to Expo Corporation at the end of the lease term. The purchase price of the leased asset to Expo Corporation was $32,000. The normal selling price is $44,000. Each party uses straight-line depreciation. The equipment is expected to be worth $10,000 at the end of the lease term and $3,000 at the end of its useful life. Expo satisfied its entire obligation under the terms of the lease on the inception day. The implicit borrowing rate in the lease is 10 percent, and this is known to both parties. Adco's incremental borrowing rate is 11 percent, and Expo's incremental borrowing rate is 8 percent.

Required:

1. Determine which of the lease criteria are satisfied by the lease terms for the lessee.

2. What type of lease is this for the lessee?

3. Prepare an amortization schedule for the lessee.

4. Over what time period should the lessee depreciate the equipment? Justify your response.

5. Prepare a partial multiple-step income statement for the year ended December 31, 2003, for the lessee, showing the amounts related to the lease.

Analyze: What type of lease is this for the lessor?

LO1, 5, 6 **PROBLEM 14-18** **Lease for Lessee, Analysis, Cash Flows**

Wiles Enterprises signed a noncancelable agreement to lease equipment from Lessor, Inc. The equipment has an estimated life of five years with an estimated residual value of $0 at the end of its useful life and of $4,000 at the end of the lease term. The lessee's incremental borrowing rate exceeds the interest rate implicit in the lease, which is known to both parties. Ownership belongs to the lessor at the end of the lease term. The fair value of the equipment at the inception date of the lease is $46,000. An unlabeled lease amortization table follows:

6/1/03				$43,153
6/1/03	$12,500	$ 0	$12,500	30,653
6/1/04	12,500	3,311	9,189	21,464
6/1/05	12,500	2,318	10,182	11,282
6/1/06	12,500	1,218	11,282	0

Required:

1. Determine the implicit rate of the lease.

2. Identify the term of the lease.

3. Identify the inception date of this lease.

4. Indicate the amounts that would be reported on the lessee's balance sheet at August 31, 2003, for the following:

   a. Lease obligation—current portion
   b. Accrued interest, if applicable
   c. Lease obligation—long-term portion
   d. Book value of the leased asset

5. Show the effects of the lease transaction on the statement of cash flows for 2003 for Wiles Enterprises if the company uses the indirect method.

Analyze: Does the lease have a bargain purchase option? How do you know?

CASES

LO3, 4, 9 **CRITICAL THINKING CASE 14-1** **Lack of Symmetry**

Clark Corporation, a lessor of equipment, purchased a new machine for $500,000 on January 1, 2005; it was delivered to Teryl Corporation, the lessee, on the same day. The following information relating to the lease is available:

A. The leased asset has a useful life of 10 years. The lease term is 7 years, with annual payments and the first payment due January 1, 2005.

B. At the termination of the lease, the equipment will revert to Clark. The residual value is expected to be $60,000, but this is not guaranteed by Teryl.

C. Teryl's incremental borrowing rate is 15 percent. The implicit borrowing rate on the lease is 12 percent, which is not known by Teryl.

D. Collectibility of the payments is reasonably predictable, and there are no important uncertainties surrounding the costs yet to be incurred by the lessor. Both the lessee and the lessor have an accounting year ended December 31.

Required:

1. Calculate the amount of the annual lease payment.

2. What type of lease arrangement is this for Clark? What type of lease arrangement is this for Teryl?

3. On whose books is the leased asset recorded? Do you think that the lease accounting rules should require a symmetry between the lessee's and the lessor's accounting?

LO2, 4, 5

ETHICS

ETHICS CASE 14-2   Creative Use of Lease Provisions

You are the accountant for a large company with several divisions. One of the divisional managers has asked for your help concerning a lease. The division has leased an asset with the following lease provisions:

Fair market value of the asset	$500,000
Present value of the minimum lease payments	$440,000
Life of the lease	7 years
Expected useful life of the asset	9 years

Asset reverts to the lessor at lease termination.

No bargain purchase option exists.

The division manager is interested in having the lease classified as an operating lease because his bonus is determined on the basis of the division's return on assets. You have indicated to the division manager that the lease must be treated as a capital lease because it meets the 75 percent rule.

Required: The division manager has asked that the useful life of the asset be changed from 9 years to 10 years in order to allow the lease to be classified as a capital lease. How should you respond?

LO3, 4, 5

ANALYSIS CASE 14-3   Financial Statement Analysis

The leasing note from the 2003 annual report of **United Airlines** follows.

United Airlines

At December 31, 2003, scheduled future minimum lease payments under capital leases (substantially all of which are for aircraft) and operating leases having initial or remaining noncancelable lease terms of more than one year were as follows:

(In millions)	Operating Leases		Capital Leases
	Aircraft	Nonaircraft	
Payable during			
2004	$ 768	$ 490	$ 256
2005	913	401	262
2006	799	370	262
2007	776	350	288
2008	766	340	206
After 2008	4,679	3,577	214
Total minimum lease payments	$8,701	$5,528	$1,488

As of December 31, 2003, we leased 280 aircraft, 58 of which were under capital leases. These leases have terms of 5 to 26 years, and expiration dates ranging from 2004 through 2018. Under the terms of all leases, we have the right to purchase the aircraft at the end of the lease term, in some cases at fair market value and in others at fair market value or a percentage of cost. Additionally, the above amounts include lease payments related to our UAX contracts for 46 aircraft under capital leases and 119 aircraft under operating leases as described in Note 2(i), "Summary of Significant Accounting Policies—United Express."

Required:

1. Assume that United Airlines makes all capital lease payments on December 31 and that a 6 percent rate is applicable to all lease agreements. In addition, assume that "after 2008" is a five-year period and that lease payments of the same amount will be made in each year after 2008. Determine the present value of the capital leases as of December 31, 2003.

2. Now consider the operating leases. Assume that "after 2008" is a five-year period and that lease payments of the same amount will be made in each year after 2008. Use the same interest rate you used for the capital leases. Calculate the present value of the future minimum lease payments. At December 31, 2003, UAL had total assets of $21,185 million and total liabilities of $14,084. How would total assets and liabilities have changed if the company had reclassified the operating leases as capital leases?

LO2

 ETHICS

ETHICS CASE 14-4 Classifying Leases

Albert Smith holds an accounting degree and the Certified Management Accounting (CMA) designation. He is the manager of the capital expenditures department at Tempo Delivery, Inc., a fast-growing regional delivery firm. Tempo leases all its delivery trucks and classifies most of these leases as capital leases. Since the business is rapidly expanding, Tempo's founder and president asks Albert to negotiate new lease contracts for an additional fleet of trucks.

In these negotiations, Albert has been instructed to negotiate leases that will not increase the company's reported debt. Albert knows that in order to avoid increasing reported debt, the leases must qualify as operating leases under *Statement of Financial Accounting Standards No. 13.*

Albert recently met Michael Elser while playing golf at the local golf course. Michael is the owner of a new truck-leasing company and is anxious to secure new leasing contracts. Albert discusses the company's plans with Michael and inquires about lease terms. Michael offers to structure the lease contracts so that the leases will qualify as operating leases. He suggests that he can exclude the standard bargain purchase option from the contract and lower the purchase price of the trucks. He explains that he will compensate for the price difference by adding a premium to a separate service contract. He assures Albert that the company will still be able to purchase the trucks for a verbally agreed-upon price at the end of the lease term. He points out that Tempo and everyone involved would benefit from these arrangements and offers to lease a new car to Albert, waiving the first year's lease payments.

Required:

1. What are the problems and issues faced by Albert?
2. Who will be affected by the decision that Albert makes?
3. What values and principles are likely to influence his decision?
4. What alternative actions might Albert take?
5. a. Of the parties you listed in your answer to question 2, whose interests are most important?
   b. Of the values and principles you listed in your answer to question 3, which is most important?
   c. Of the actions you listed in your answer to question 4, which will do the most good or cause the least harm?
   d. Consider your answers in a, b, and c. Which consideration is most important?
6. What should Albert do?

LO1, 2

 ETHICS

ETHICS CASE 14-5 Keeping Lease Liabilities Off the Books

The airline industry has been negatively affected by a number of adverse events in recent years. The events of September 11 reduced overall passenger demand and increased costs for such items as fuel and security. Many of the large carriers have since experienced perilous financial situations and have sought ways to reduce their expenses. Lease-related expenses constitute a significant part of **AMR**'s total expenses. In addition, capital leases, which consist primarily of long-term leases on passenger jets, significantly affect the company's financial position, its leverage, and its ability to borrow.

AMR's lease-related liabilities may soon become significantly higher. A new rule issued by the Financial Accounting Standards Board requires that airlines recognize liabilities related to airport terminal leasing in their balance sheets. This ruling is expected to increase AMR's liabilities by $2 billion and could adversely affect AMR's financial position.[18]

The way AMR's leases are structured could provide relief from the effects of the new FASB statement. By renegotiating existing leases so that the criteria for capital leases would not be met, the company could shift a large amount of its lease liabilities off its balance sheet. This could be accomplished, for example, by shortening the lease term, which would then qualify the leases as operating leases.

Suppose you are the CFO for a company like AMR that is experiencing serious financial problems. Your company is faced with the new FASB statement under which you must recognize billions in new debt related to airport terminal leasing. You are aware that the financial markets tend to react negatively to increases in debt. You know that by shifting your leases from capital to operating, you can decrease balance sheet debt. If you decrease the length of your lease terms, you will be able to reclassify the leases as operating leases. However, the chief operating officer informs you that the current lease period is optimal in terms of cost/benefit for your company.

Required:

1. How do operating leases affect the financial statements? How do capital leases affect the financial statements?

2. What ethical dilemma do you face?

3. Who will be affected by your decision?

4. What values and principles are likely to influence your decision?

5. What alternative actions might you take?

6. Would you ask the chief operating officer to establish a new policy that aims at avoiding classification as capital leases?

LO2   **CRITICAL THINKING CASE 14-6   Accounting for Leases**

As the chief accountant for Crescent Corporation, you are responsible for accounting for the company's leases. On July 1, 2005, Crescent leased office furniture to Luna Publishers. The furniture cost Crescent $35,000 and has a fair market value of $48,000. The term of the noncancelable lease is for four years, and payments are required at the beginning of each year starting with July 1, 2005. Crescent's fiscal year end is December 31.

Upon reading the lease, you find that the furniture, which has an economic life of nine years, is expected to have a residual value of $5,000 at the end of the lease. Crescent put a clause into the lease that allows Luna Publishers to purchase the furniture for $900. Collectibility of the lease payments is reasonably predictable, and Crescent has resolved all uncertainties with regard to the lease. Crescent Corporation desires a 9 percent return on its investment.

Required:

1. Determine how your company should account for this lease. Is the lease a capital lease or an operating lease? Is it a direct financing lease or a sales-type lease?

2. Calculate the rental payments needed for Crescent Corporation to recover its investment. Round your computations to the nearest dollar.

---

18 Elizabeth McDonald, "Dead Weight," *Forbes*, September 1, 2003, pp. 49–50.

3. Prepare the journal entries on Crescent's books to reflect the signing of the lease contract and to record the payments and revenues related to this lease for the years 2005 and 2006.

LO1 CRITICAL THINKING CASE 14-7 **Classification of Leases**

On January 2, 2005, Garbo Corporation signs a contract to lease film equipment from Paramount Inc. Garbo Corporation agrees to make lease payments of $32,000 per year and guarantees that the equipment will have a residual value of $22,500 at the end of the lease term.

The term of the noncancelable lease is five years, with no renewal option at the end of the lease term. Payments are due at the beginning of each year, beginning January 2, 2005. The fair value of the film equipment on January 2, 2005, is $150,000. In addition, the equipment has an economic life of nine years. The film equipment reverts to Paramount at the end of the lease term.

Garbo depreciates similar assets on the straight-line basis. Garbo's incremental borrowing rate is 10 percent per year; Garbo has no knowledge of Paramount's implicit borrowing rate.

Required:

1. Determine whether Garbo should classify this lease as a capital lease or an operating lease.

2. Prepare a lease amortization schedule for Garbo Corporation.

3. Prepare the journal entries on Garbo's books to reflect the signing of the lease contract and to record the payments and expenses related to this lease for the years 2005 and 2006.

LO1, 2 RESEARCH CASE 14-8 **Interpreting Financial Statements**

Albertsons operates grocery and drug stores throughout the United States. In addition, the company operates distribution centers and has recently started fuel stores. Although Albertsons owns a large portion of the real estate that it uses, it also enters into leases for stores and equipment. The company's website can be found at **www.albertsons.com** Go to the website and access the company's 2003 annual report to answer the following questions.

Required:

1. What was the amount of Land, Building and Equipment included in Albertsons' assets?

2. What amount of long-term debt and capitalized lease obligations did Albertsons report?

3. What is the value of Albertsons' real estate and equipment obtained through capital leases that is disclosed in its lease note?

4. What will be the amount of Albertsons' next year's payments for operating and capital leases?

LO2 COMMUNICATION CASE 14-9 **Lease Classification**

Assume that you are currently negotiating a lease transaction in the role of the lessee. Your managers are interested in determining whether the company should structure the lease as an operating lease or a capital lease.

Required:

Write a memo to management in which you discuss the financial statement effects of an operating lease versus those of a capital lease. Suggest to management how you would like to structure the lease agreement, and explain why. In addition, discuss the four capitalization criteria.

ON THE WEB

The following exercises, activities, and problems are available on the *Intermediate Accounting* website. Use these resources to reinforce your understanding of the topics presented in this chapter.

- CPA-Adapted Simulations
- Interpreting the Accounting Standards
- Extending the Global Focus
- Extending the Ethics Discussion
- Mastering the Spreadsheet
- Career Snapshots
- Annual Report Project
- ACE Practice Tests
- Flashcards
- Glossary
- Check Figures for Text Problems
- PowerPoint Presentations

SOLUTIONS: CHECK YOUR UNDERSTANDING

An Overview of Leasing (p. 641)

1. The two most commonly used methods of disposition are asset reverts and title passes. Under asset reverts, the asset reverts to the lessor at the end of the lease. Thus, the lessee has the right to use the asset only during the lease term and must return the asset when the lease expires. If title passes, both the possession of the asset and the legal title to the asset pass to the lessee at the end of the lease agreement. Thus, the lessee can ensure the use of the asset not only for the term of the lease but also beyond it, until the end of the asset's useful life.

2. A bargain purchase option is a provision that gives the lessee the right to purchase the asset at the end of the lease for a bargain price.

3. Some lease contracts specify that an annual payment is due at the end of each period (ordinary annuity). In other cases, the lessee is required to make payments at the beginning of each period (annuity due or annuity in advance).

4. If a lease transfers substantially all of the benefits and risks of ownership, the leased asset should be capitalized by the lessee along with the liability that is incurred.

Accounting for Leases as a Lessee (p. 658)

1. An operating lease is a financial arrangement in which the lessee does not assume the risks and rewards of ownership. A capital lease is a financial arrangement in which the lessee assumes most of the risks and rewards of ownership.

2. To be classified as a capital lease, a lease must be noncancelable and must meet one or more of the following criteria:

- The lease transfers ownership of the property to the lessee at the end of the lease term.
- The lease contains a bargain purchase option.
- The lease term is equal to 75 percent or more of the estimated economic life of the leased property.
- The present value of the minimum lease payments (excluding executory costs) equals or exceeds 90 percent of the fair market value of the leased property.

3. A leasehold improvement should be depreciated over the term of the lease or the life of the improvement, whichever is shorter.

4. The account Leased Asset is debited and the account Lease Obligation is credited.

5. The asset is capitalized at the total present value of the minimum lease payments (excluding executory costs).

Analyzing Cash Flow: Operating Leases Versus Capital Leases (p. 659)

1. Depreciation on a leased asset would be added back in the operating activities section of the statement of cash flows if the indirect method is used.

2. For a capital lease, the cash paid to reduce the lease obligation would be found in the financing activities section of the statement of cash flows.

3. Cash outflows from an operating lease would be reported in the operating activities section of the statement of cash flows.

Accounting for Leases as a Lessor (p. 666)

1. Under a direct financing lease, the lessor transfers the risks and rewards of ownership to the lessee and serves

as the financing agent. In essence, the lessor makes a loan to the lessee and receives payments of interest and principal in return. Thus, the leased asset is removed from the lessor's balance sheet and replaced by a receivable for the future lease payments. Under a sales-type lease, the lessor is considered to be both selling an asset to the lessee and serving as the financing agent. For that reason, the leased asset is removed from the lessor's balance sheet and replaced by a receivable for the future lease payments. In addition, the lessor recognizes two forms of income: a gross profit from in effect selling the asset and interest income resulting from the financing arrangement.

2. Initial direct costs incurred for an operating lease are deferred and amortized over the life of the lease in proportion to the recognition of rental income.

3. Lease Receivable (Gross Investment) is the account used to record a receivable for the amount of the payments to be received.

4. Under a sales-type lease, both gross profit on the "sale" of the asset and interest on the financing of the agreement are recognized.

CPA-ADAPTED SIMULATION

This simulation asks you to complete various tasks related to a company's annual financial statements. If your instructor has signed up for CPAexcel™, you can do the work online at **www.cpaexcel.com/hmco**. You may also do the simulation manually.

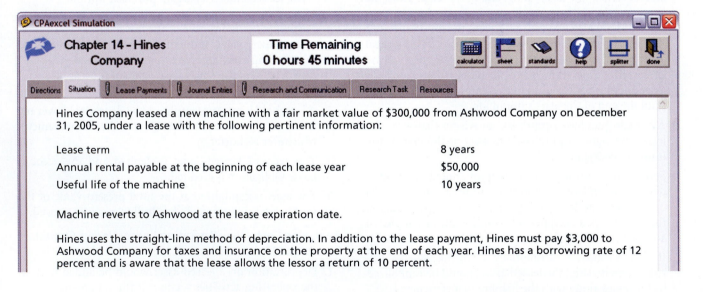

Hines Company leased a new machine with a fair market value of $300,000 from Ashwood Company on December 31, 2005, under a lease with the following pertinent information:

Lease term	8 years
Annual rental payable at the beginning of each lease year	$50,000
Useful life of the machine	10 years

Machine reverts to Ashwood at the lease expiration date.

Hines uses the straight-line method of depreciation. In addition to the lease payment, Hines must pay $3,000 to Ashwood Company for taxes and insurance on the property at the end of each year. Hines has a borrowing rate of 12 percent and is aware that the lease allows the lessor a return of 10 percent.

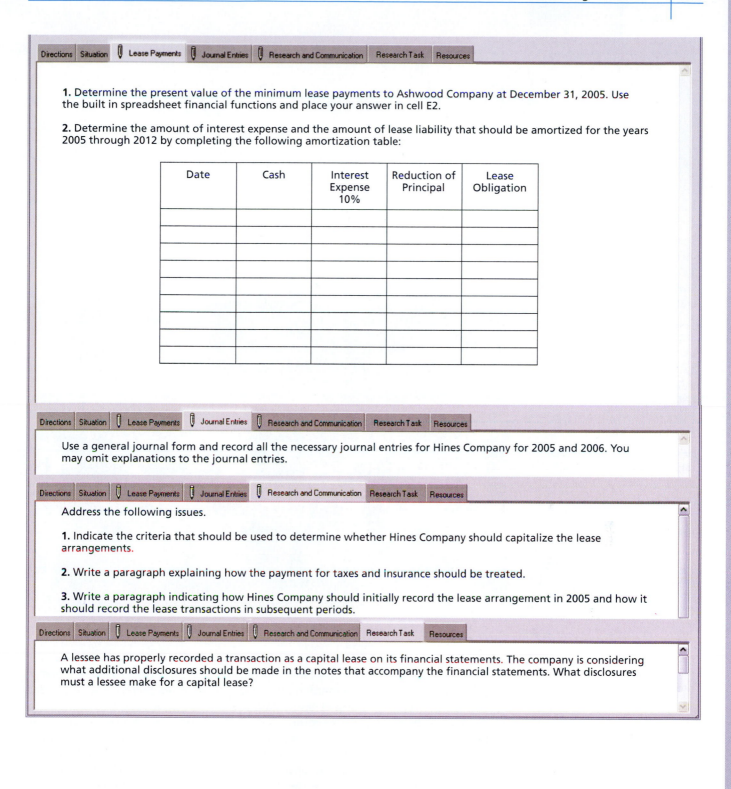

Directions   Situation   Lease Payments   Journal Entries   Research and Communication   Research Task   Resources

1. Determine the present value of the minimum lease payments to Ashwood Company at December 31, 2005. Use the built in spreadsheet financial functions and place your answer in cell E2.

2. Determine the amount of interest expense and the amount of lease liability that should be amortized for the years 2005 through 2012 by completing the following amortization table:

Date	Cash	Interest Expense 10%	Reduction of Principal	Lease Obligation

Directions   Situation   Lease Payments   Journal Entries   Research and Communication   Research Task   Resources

Use a general journal form and record all the necessary journal entries for Hines Company for 2005 and 2006. You may omit explanations to the journal entries.

Directions   Situation   Lease Payments   Journal Entries   Research and Communication   Research Task   Resources

Address the following issues.

1. Indicate the criteria that should be used to determine whether Hines Company should capitalize the lease arrangements.

2. Write a paragraph explaining how the payment for taxes and insurance should be treated.

3. Write a paragraph indicating how Hines Company should initially record the lease arrangement in 2005 and how it should record the lease transactions in subsequent periods.

Directions   Situation   Lease Payments   Journal Entries   Research and Communication   Research Task   Resources

A lessee has properly recorded a transaction as a capital lease on its financial statements. The company is considering what additional disclosures should be made in the notes that accompany the financial statements. What disclosures must a lessee make for a capital lease?

Pensions and Postretirement Plans

FINANCIAL REPORTING CASE

IBM's Employee Retirement Obligations Surpass the Half-Billion-Dollar Mark

With more than 319,000 employees, IBM's costs for pensions and postretirement benefits are staggering. Designing and managing these plans are critical to the company's business success.

IBM Step into the hallways of IBM as a new employee, and you'll find yourself in an environment where high performance is expected and rewarded accordingly. To attract and retain top-notch employees, this technology giant believes that competitive compensation and benefits packages are critical to its business strategy. IBM's compensation program seeks to offer competitive value that will attract the best talent to IBM, motivate individuals to perform at their highest levels, reward outstanding achievement, and retain those individuals with the leadership abilities and skills necessary for building long-term stockholder value.[1]

Many U.S. companies, like IBM, offer pension plans to their employees. These plans involve contributions by the employee and/or the employer and a promise by the employer to pay amounts to employees in the future. As the average age of the population increases and the "baby boomers" near retirement age, the costs associated with pension plans are increasing, especially for companies with a large pool of retired workers. Accounting for these plans requires accountants to address recogni-

---

1 IBM proxy statement, December 31, 2000.

IBM

RETIREMENT-RELATED BENEFITS

IBM offers defined benefit pension plans, defined contribution pension plans, as well as non-pension postretirement plans primarily consisting of retiree medical benefits. These benefits form an important part of the company's total compensation and benefits program that is designed to attract and retain highly skilled and talented employees. The following table provides the total retirement-related benefit plans' impact on income before income taxes.

(dollars in millions)

FOR THE YEAR ENDED DECEMBER 31:	U.S.			NON-U.S.			TOTAL		
	2003	2002	2001	2003	2002	2001	2003	2002	2001
Total retirement-related plans—cost/(income)	$ 67	$(154)	$(256)	$295	$(17)	$(181)	$362	$(171)*	$(437)*
Comprise:									
Defined benefit and contribution pension plans—(income)/cost	$(227)	$(478)	$(632)	$254	$(46)	$(209)	$ 27	$(524)	$(841)
Nonpension postretirement benefits—cost	294	324	376	41	29	28	335	353	404

Includes amounts for discontinued operations costs of $77 million and $56 million for 2002 and 2001, respectively.

tion issues (when should an expense and the related liability be recorded) and measurement issues (how should the expense and the related liability be valued).

As of December 2003, more than 319,000 individuals were employed at IBM worldwide. Designing an effective compensation strategy for such a work force is a huge task that must address elements like base salaries, pension plans, health care, and other postretirement benefits. The impact on income before income taxes can be substantial. The note disclosure on retirement-related benefits that appears above was taken from IBM's 2003 annual report. As you can see, the company reported costs of $362 million related to retirement benefit plans in 2003. Yet, in the two previous years, the company reported income of $171 million and $437 million, respectively.

EXAMINING THE CASE

1. What types of recognition and measurement issues are related to the accounting for retirement plans?
2. What types of retirement benefits does IBM offer to its employees, as mentioned in its note disclosure?
3. What income or expense was reported for U.S. defined benefit and defined contribution pension plans in 2003?

LO1 Understand the nature and types of pension plans used by companies.

pension plan a contract between a company and its employees under which the company agrees to pay benefits to the employees after they retire

🧩 *Critical Thinking: How do you think pension plans affect employee satisfaction?*

Types of Pension Plans

A pension plan is a contract between a company and its employees under which the company agrees to pay benefits to the employees after they retire. The exact nature of the pension agreement varies greatly from company to company. In most pension plans, the employer and/or the employee pay contributions into a pension fund. The legal statutes that govern pension plans generally require that the pension fund be managed by an entity that is independent of the company itself. The managers of the pension fund are entrusted with the fund's assets and are expected to invest those assets wisely. Consequently, the pension fund managers will invest the pension fund's assets to earn a return (in the form of interest, dividends, and capital appreciation) so that sufficient amounts are available to pay to the company's retirees at the time of retirement and for the years after retirement. Illustration 15.1 illustrates the parties and relationships involved in a pension plan.

It is important to identify the accounting entity that is the focus of our concern. The focus of this chapter is on the accounting for the *employer*. We will discuss the accounting entries that should be recorded to develop the employer's financial statements. We will also discuss the additional disclosures that should be presented in the notes that accompany those statements. Because the pension fund is an independent entity, we will not discuss in any detail the accounting presentation that must be made on the financial statements of the pension fund. The accounting for the *pension fund* is somewhat distinct from the accounting for the employer and must be treated separately.

There are many estimates and assumptions inherent in the accounting for a pension plan. For most employees, the time of retirement is many years in the future. The company must estimate how many employees will remain with the company until retirement, how much their retirement benefits will be at that time, what pension fund assets will be available to pay retirement benefits, and the length of time the employees will draw retirement benefits. Most large companies seek the assistance of actuaries to determine the appropriate estimates and assumptions and to establish the appropriate funding policies for the pension plan. **Actuaries** are certified individuals who are trained to determine future risk, estimate the probabilities of future events, make price decisions, and formulate investment strategies. The accountants and actuaries must jointly determine the proper financial presentation of pension plans. Although there are many types of pension plans that provide a variety of benefits, there are two general categories of plans: defined contribution plans and defined benefit plans.

actuaries certified individuals who are trained to determine future risk, estimate the probabilities of future events, make price decisions, and formulate investment strategies

DEFINED CONTRIBUTION PLANS

defined contribution plan a type of employee pension plan in which plan contributions are defined, but the amount that will be paid upon retirement is not known until retirement

A **defined contribution plan** is a type of employee pension plan in which plan contributions are defined, but the amount that will be paid upon retirement is not known

Illustration 15.1

Pension Fund Parties and Relationships

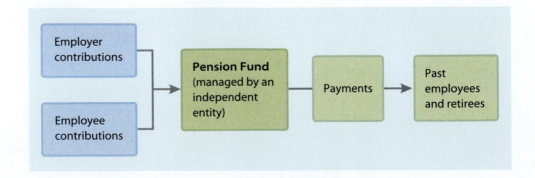

until retirement. Typically, an employer is required to contribute a specific amount to the plan every year; this amount is fixed by an agreement between the company and its employees or by a resolution of the board of directors. In most cases, the employee is also allowed to contribute to the plan. However, while the amount contributed to the plan is known, or defined, the amount that will be paid when an employee retires is not known or defined. There is no guarantee that the employee will get a certain amount upon retirement.

The most prominent examples of defined contribution plans are 401(k) plans and IRAs (individual retirement accounts). During the 1990s, 401(k) plans became enormously popular, and many companies eliminated their more traditional defined benefit plans, to be discussed in the next section. In a 401(k) plan, the employee pays an amount into a pension fund. Often, this amount is matched by a contribution from the employer. Employees are generally given a choice of investing strategies and funds. Through successful investing, the fund amount should grow and will be available to the employee at the time of retirement.

The 401(k)-type plans are popular with both employees and employers. Employees are allowed to tailor the pension plan to their own needs, investing their plan assets in investments with the risk and return characteristics that they prefer. This degree of control is attractive to employees. Employers are fond of this type of pension plan because *it shifts the risks* involved in retirement planning to the employee. The following excerpt was taken from a *Wall Street Journal* article in which the risks assumed by employees of **Enron Corporation** and **Morrison Knudsen Corporation** are discussed:

> Enron Corp. workers whose 401(k) balances have evaporated amid that company's bankruptcy may find valuable lessons in a continuing lawsuit brought by former Morrison Knudsen Corp. employees who found themselves in a similar situation. For one thing, they will learn that when companies fail, there are stark differences between [defined benefit] pension plans and [defined contribution plans such as] 401(k)s. [Defined benefit] pensions are protected, because companies must set aside money to pay the benefits workers have earned. And if the pension plan doesn't have enough money, the Pension Benefit Guaranty Corp., a federal agency, steps up to pay minimum pension benefits.
>
> There is no similar safety net for the 401(k)s, profit-sharing plans, and employee stock-ownership plans of companies that go bust. If money in the plan is lost because it was invested in employer stock that becomes worthless, that is tough luck.
>
> The only hope employees have of recovering their losses is if they can show that the company breached its fiduciary duty by not warning them that the stock was a poor investment. However, even if employees have a valid claim, they probably are still out of luck if the company slides into bankruptcy—as Morrison Knudsen did, and Enron has—because the bankruptcy proceedings ultimately could lead a trial court to dismiss the claim.
>
> The bottom line: To the extent possible, employees should diversify the investments in their retirement plans. Avoiding a concentrated stock position can be difficult when companies contribute their own stock to employee retirement plans. But in these situations, workers shouldn't add to their exposure by buying more company stock on their own, as many Enron employees did.[2]

During the stock market boom of the 1990s, employees were pleased with defined contribution–type plans because most investments performed well. When the stock market declined in 2001 and 2002, however, many employees found that the amount in their 401(k) plans also plummeted, leaving far less money available for retirement than

---

2 Ellen Schultz and Theo Francis, "Enron Workers in 401(k) Suit Can Learn from Precedent," *Wall Street Journal*, January 21, 2002.

they had anticipated. In some cases, the employer's contribution to the 401(k) plans came in the form of the company's own stock. If the company went out of business or went bankrupt, the employees lost twice—once because they lost their jobs and a second time because the value of their 401(k) plans suffered drastically.

Many of the problems with defined contribution plans came to light in the wake of the demise of Enron in early 2002, but warning signs had been evident earlier as the employees of **Morrison Knudsen**, **Rite Aid**, **Columbia HCA**, **McKesson**, and **Lucent Technologies** suffered from the decline of their retirement savings. As a result of these problems, there have been many calls for reform and additional legislation to protect employees, as discussed in this excerpt from a 2002 *Wall Street Journal* article:

> The question is whether pension law ought to be modified to include more protections for retirement savings plans, which many employees count on to fund retirement. In December, lawmakers introduced bills to make savings plans safer, and hearings are planned. Last week, President Bush said his administration is interested in examining the issue, and Treasury Secretary Paul O'Neill, Labor Secretary Elaine Chao and Commerce Secretary Don Evans said they were directing their staffs to begin evaluating the adequacy of retirement-plan rules.
>
> "We will take the necessary steps to ensure appropriate protection for the retirement nest eggs of millions of Americans," Mr. O'Neill said in a written statement.
>
> But if the past is any guide, change will be difficult. Employers say lawmakers are overreacting to views of participants and employers. Says James Delaplane, "Our general view is that the 401(k) system has been quite successful." Two important issues are whether employers ought to be allowed to contribute their own stock to employee retirement accounts, and whether employers should be allowed to lock employees into it.[3]

Although 401(k) plans have generated significant debate and potential legislation, the *accounting issues* related to defined contribution plans are not complex. In most cases, the employer should recognize an expense for any amount contributed to the pension fund. The employer should not recognize the pension fund assets on its balance sheet because the assets are separate from the company and controlled by the pension fund trustee. Similarly, the employer should not record a liability for pensions because the employer has no further obligation to the employees. For example, Wheatley Corporation contributes $80,000 to its defined contribution plan and records the transaction as follows:

Pension Expense	80,000	
Cash		80,000

DEFINED BENEFIT PLANS

The accounting issues for defined benefit pension plans are more challenging. "Employers' Accounting for Pensions," *Statement of Financial Accounting Standards No. 87*, is devoted to these types of pension plans. A **defined benefit plan** is a type of employee pension plan in which the amount of future benefits is fixed, but an employer's contributions vary depending on the assumptions about how much the fund will earn. The amount to be paid to employees at retirement is defined by a formula that may incorporate several variables. For example, the retirement pay may be based on a formula that combines the employee's age, years of service, and salary level

defined benefit plan a type of employee pension plan in which the amount of future benefits is fixed, but an employer's contributions vary depending on the assumptions about how much the fund will earn

---

3 Ellen Schultz, "Evaporation of Enron 401(K) Accounts Raises Question of Retirement Reform," *Wall Street Journal*, January 14, 2002.

over some time period. A common pension formula might define an annual retirement benefit as

$$2\% \times \text{Years of Service} \times \text{Final Year's Salary}$$

Using this formula, the annual benefits paid to an employee who retires after 20 years of service with a final salary of $120,000 would be $48,000 (2% × 20 years × $120,000).

The retirement amount is "defined" because each employee can determine the amount of his or her retirement pay using the pension formula and the applicable variables (such as age, years of service, and salary level). The amount of retirement pay is *not* determined by the amount of the employer's and employee's contributions and is not directly related to the investment performance achieved by the pension fund trustee. It is the duty of each employer that has a defined benefit pension plan to contribute sufficient assets and to ensure that those assets accumulate to a level that will allow the payments to retirees that are promised in the pension plan agreement.

When the assets of a pension plan are less than the future pension liability, the pension plan is referred to as **underfunded**. The employer is obligated to pay retirement benefits even if the plan has been underfunded. Thus, the employer assumes a large portion of the risk involved with the pension plan. However, the employee still carries a certain level of risk associated with the pension plan and the future retirement payments. There is always the risk that the sponsoring company may go out of business or become bankrupt, leaving employees and retirees without any funds for retirement benefits. Fortunately, this risk has been lessened by federal legislation and by the creation of the **Pension Benefit Guaranty Corporation (PBGC)**, a national insurer of pension plans. When a company becomes bankrupt and cannot meet its pension obligation or when a pension plan becomes insolvent for other reasons, the PBGC assumes the pension liability and will pay the retirement benefits (usually at a reduced level). The following excerpt taken from a *Chicago Tribune* article offers details on the insolvency of **Reliance Insurance Company** and the role of the PBGC:

> The Pension Benefit Guaranty Corp. assumed control of Reliance Insurance Co.'s pension plan and said the plan was underfunded by $124 million.
>
> The PBGC said in a news release that it was stepping in because the property-casualty insurance company was being liquidated by regulators, and that the company's pension plan, without government intervention, would have been unable to make payments to its retired former employees.
>
> Most of the 8,700 employees covered by the plan lost their jobs at some point during Reliance's rapid demise, which was capped by the Pennsylvania Insurance Department's order to liquidate the insurer in October. Some former Reliance staffers are working for the department to assist in the liquidation process.
>
> A spokeswoman for the Pennsylvania Insurance Department said there was no indication of wrongdoing related to the handling of Reliance's pension assets. Instead, Reliance became unable to continue making payments into the plan as its businesses moved closer to liquidation.
>
> Reliance's plan had assets of $143 million and benefit liabilities of $267 million. The PBGC said it would use the $143 million in assets, along with its own, to ensure that Reliance retirees will continue to receive monthly pension checks.[4]

The PBGC is funded by premiums that it collects from all defined benefit pension plans. In a sense, "healthy" pension plans are forced to cover the costs of "unhealthy"

underfunded the state of a pension plan when its assets are less than the future pension liability

Pension Benefit Guaranty Corporation (PBGC) a federally created agency that is responsible for insuring pension plans

---

4 "Retiree Benefits Aren't Ironclad; Bankruptcies Leave Some in the Lurch," *Chicago Tribune*, November 27, 2001.

plans. In recent years, the PBGC has increased the premiums it collects to cover the pension liability of an increasing number of bankrupt or insolvent pension plans. Companies that maintain healthy pension plans have expressed resentment at these increases, and some have eliminated their defined benefit pension plans in favor of defined contribution plans.

CHECK YOUR UNDERSTANDING

1. Explain the difference between a defined contribution plan and a defined benefit plan.

2. Why would a retirement plan that is underfunded be of concern to employees and investors?

3. What role does the Pension Benefit Guaranty Corporation (PBGC) play if a company defaults on its pension obligations?

LO2 **Determine how to account for a defined benefit pension plan.**

Critical Thinking: How do pension plans affect a company's expenses and liabilities?

Accounting for a Defined Benefit Plan

FUNDAMENTALS OF PENSION ACCOUNTING

Accounting for pensions and postretirement plans has been a difficult and controversial topic for the FASB. Fundamental judgments involving the *nature of the exchange* and the *measurement of the expense and liability* are involved. Illustration 15.2 summarizes the fundamental issues and corresponding FASB positions that have established the current accounting model. "Employers' Accounting for Pensions," *Statement of Financial Accounting Standards No. 87,* and subsequent pronouncements have significantly improved the accounting for defined benefit pension plans and the quality of the available financial disclosures.

Regarding the nature of the exchange, the FASB has adopted the position that a defined benefit pension plan involves the incurrence of a liability because a promise

Illustration 15.2

Fundamental Pension Issues/Positions

Issue	FASB Position
Nature of the exchange and existence of liability	A defined benefit pension plan involves the incurrence of a liability because a promise has been made to employees.
Recognition of expense	Pension expense should be recognized using accrual accounting procedures. The expense should be recorded when the pension is earned by the employees rather than when it is paid.
Distinction between expensing and funding	The funding decision is an actuarial decision. The expensing decision should be governed by accrual accounting procedures. The expense is not represented by the amount of cash put into the fund.
Measurement of expense	Pension expense should be measured based on a series of components. The combination of these components represents the amount of the expense to the employer.

has been made to employees. The liability of the employer exists even though a separate legal entity (the pension plan or trustee) is usually entrusted with the pension assets and the responsibility for making the payments to retirees.

Regarding the measurement of the expense, the FASB has adopted the stance that *accrual accounting* principles should be used to determine the expense. Prior to *SFAS No. 87*, some companies recognized the expense for pensions at the time the benefits were paid to employees, which was a form of cash-basis accounting rather than accrual accounting. The FASB position states that the employer incurs the expense at the time a promise has been made by the employer and the employee provides the services necessary to the firm. Thus, the expense for pensions should be recognized in the period in which the benefits are earned rather than in the period in which they are paid (accrual accounting rather than cash-basis accounting).

In addition, the FASB holds that there are two fundamental decisions involving pensions. The first is the *funding decision*, or the decision concerning how much should be paid into the pension fund by the employer. This is often referred to as an *actuarial decision* because the actuarial profession has developed highly sophisticated models to assist in the determination of proper funding levels. The second is the *expensing decision*, or the decision concerning the proper amount of expense that should be recognized. The FASB uses the term *net periodic pension cost*, and many firms use that term when referring to the amount of expense. In this text, we will use the term **pension expense**, defined as a composite of periodic changes that occur in both the pension obligation and the plan assets. Again, the FASB has relied on accrual accounting principles and has taken the stance that the funding decision is separate from the expensing decision. That is, under accrual accounting principles, the amount of pension expense differs from the amount of cash contributed to the pension fund by the employer. For example, suppose that for Wiley Company, the pension expense for the period is determined to be $40 million, but the company chooses to contribute $35 million cash to the fund. The entry would be recorded as follows:

pension expense a composite of periodic changes that occur in both the pension obligation and the plan assets

Pension Expense	40,000,000	
Accrued Pension Cost		5,000,000
Cash		35,000,000

If the company chooses to contribute more than the pension expense—say, $42 million for the preceding example—the entry would be recorded as follows:

Pension Expense	40,000,000	
Prepaid Pension Cost	2,000,000	
Cash		42,000,000

LO3 Explain the three methods used to value a pension obligation.

🧩 *Critical Thinking: How should the promise to fund employee retirements be valued as a liability on the financial statements of a company?*

THE PENSION OBLIGATION

As indicated earlier, the FASB states that a defined benefit pension plan involves the incurrence of a liability because a promise has been made to employees. Theoretically, the amount measured as the pension liability should represent the present value of the amounts that will be paid to retirees (including current employees who will retire) in all future periods. In order to determine this present value amount, it is necessary to make several assumptions about future events, including interest-rate conditions, inflation, years of service of employees, and the time period over which employees will draw retirement benefits. It is also necessary to develop an assumption about the amount of salary increases that employees will receive during their employment. Many pension plans base an employee's retirement benefit on the salary level that the employee has achieved at or near the time of retirement. For that reason, it is necessary to develop an assumption about *future salary levels* in order to calculate the present value of the pension obligation.

The pension obligation may be valued in one of three ways:

- Projected benefit obligation
- Accumulated benefit obligation
- Vested benefit obligation

Remember, the amount of this obligation is typically calculated by an actuary. But it is important for the accountant to understand how each measurement is derived.

❯ PROJECTED BENEFIT OBLIGATION

projected benefit obligation the present value as of a specific date of all benefits earned by an employee prior to that date

The **projected benefit obligation** is defined as the present value as of a specific date of all benefits earned by an employee prior to that date.[5] The projected benefit obligation is measured using assumptions concerning future salary increases if the pension benefit formula is based on future compensation levels. The company must make an explicit assumption concerning the rate of salary increases in order to calculate the projected benefit obligation. The assumption should incorporate such factors as the past salary and wage history of each category of employees, future hiring plans, union agreements, and any other factors affecting salaries and wages. The projected benefit obligation is the measure of the pension liability that should be used in the calculation of the interest cost component of pension expense. However, many critics of *SFAS No. 87* objected to the projected benefit obligation as a measure of the minimum liability that should be recorded. These objections were based on both theoretical and practical grounds.

The theoretical objections centered on the definition of a liability and whether amounts based on future salary increases were consistent with the accepted definition of a liability. Critics argued that a liability must be based on *known* events rather than unknown future events. In their view, a company *does not* have a liability for the portion of the pension payments that will be based on future salary levels until the employee actually works for the company and earns the salary increases. The critics pointed to other situations where the accountant is not required to anticipate future events in order to measure a liability.

The practical objections centered on the difficulty of estimating and measuring future salary increases. In many cases, salary increases are not assured and may take place many years in the future. A company's plans concerning salary increases are subject to change in response to changes in economic conditions or the profitability of the company. Because of the measurement difficulties, these critics argued that the minimum pension liability provision should not incorporate such amounts.

❯ ACCUMULATED BENEFIT OBLIGATION

accumulated benefit obligation the present value of benefits attributed by the pension benefit formula to employee service rendered before a specified date and based on employee service and compensation prior to that date

In order to achieve acceptance of *SFAS No. 87*, a compromise approach was reached, and the FASB defined another way to measure the pension liability. The **accumulated benefit obligation** is defined as the present value of benefits attributed by the pension benefit formula to employee service rendered before a specified date and based on employee service and compensation prior to that date.[6] The accumulated benefit obligation differs from the projected benefit obligation in that it includes no assumptions about future compensation levels. Essentially, the pension liability is computed based on each employee's *existing* salary level. Thus, the accumulated benefit obligation is a more conservative (lower) measure of the pension obligation. Companies are required to use this measure to determine the minimum pension liability.

---

5 "Employers' Accounting for Pensions," *Statement of Financial Accounting Standards No. 87* (Stamford, Conn.: FASB, 1985), par. 36.

6 Ibid.

Illustration 15.3

Measures of Pension Obligations

Vested benefit obligation   Accumulated benefit obligation   Projected benefit obligation

❱ VESTED BENEFIT OBLIGATION

vested benefit obligation the benefits for which the employee's right to receive a present or future pension benefit is no longer contingent on the employee's remaining in the service of the employer

SFAS No. 87 also offers a third measure of the liability for pensions. The **vested benefit obligation** is defined as the benefits for which the employee's right to receive a present or future pension benefit is no longer contingent on the employee's remaining in the service of the employer.[7] In other words, it is the amount that the employee is allowed to withdraw from the retirement fund if the employee leaves the company before retirement (for example, when an employee takes another job). Most pension plans provide vesting of benefits to employees in stages. For example, if an employee leaves the company after 5 years, the employee may withdraw 50 percent of the funds contributed by the employer; at 10 years, the employee may withdraw 75 percent of the funds contributed; and so forth.

❱ VALUATION METHODS COMPARED

The vested benefit obligation calculates the amount of the obligation if the employee leaves the company prior to retirement and therefore is a smaller amount than the accumulated benefit obligation. Furthermore, because the accumulated benefit obligation is calculated at existing salary levels, the amount of the obligation will be less than the projected benefit obligation. The relationship of the three measures of pension obligation is depicted in Illustration 15.3.

LO4 Identify the components of pension expense.

🕮 *Critical Thinking: Do you believe that the costs involved in providing pension plans to employees outweigh the benefits derived by the employer from those plans?*

PENSION EXPENSE

In addition to the measurement of pension liability, *SFAS No. 87* specifies a series of components that make up pension expense. Because the components are interrelated, *SFAS No. 87* requires that they be combined and refers to this as *netting* of these items. The net amount represents pension expense. Illustration 15.4 presents five components of pension expense. Service cost, past service cost, interest cost, and return on plan assets will be discussed in the following sections. A fifth component, gains and losses, will be introduced later in this chapter.[8]

❱ SERVICE COST

service cost the actuarial present value of benefits attributed by the pension benefit formula to services rendered by employees during that period

The **service cost** is the actuarial present value of benefits attributed by the pension benefit formula to services rendered by employees during that period.[9] Service cost

---

7 Ibid., Appendix C.

8 *SFAS No. 87* also discussed a sixth component, referred to as the *adoption amount* or the *transition amount*. The component was required for those companies that had a liability amount at the time *SFAS No. 87* was adopted. Because companies are many years beyond the year of adoption of *SFAS No. 87*, the adoption amount is no longer a concern.

9 *SFAS No. 87,* par. 264.

Illustration 15.4

Components of Pension Expense

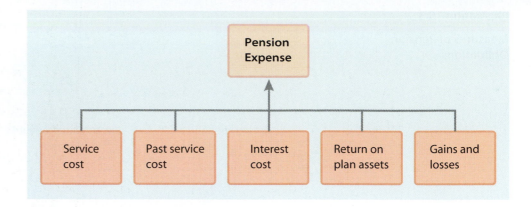

represents the amount of pension benefits that the employees have earned through their work during the current year. This is a present value amount because the retirement benefit will be paid many years in the future, at the time the employees retire. Therefore, it is necessary to estimate the amount of the retirement benefit that will be paid in the future and discount the amount to determine the present value of the future payments.

❱ PAST SERVICE COST

past service cost the cost of benefits granted for time periods prior to the adoption of the pension plan

The **past service cost** represents the cost of benefits granted for time periods prior to the adoption of the pension plan.[10] In most cases, when an employer develops a defined benefit plan, the employer tries to give some credit to those employees who were working for the company prior to the start of the plan. The present value of that credit granted to existing employees is the past service costs. *SFAS No. 87* holds that past service costs should not be treated as a prior period or retroactive adjustment. Rather, the amount of past service costs should be amortized as part of pension expense over some *future* time period. Thus, past service costs should initially be treated as *unrecognized* past service costs and amortized as a component of pension expense over a specified time period. Unrecognized past service costs should be amortized over the time period during which the employees will provide service to the employer. To reduce the complexity and detail of the computations, *SFAS No. 87* allows the use of straight-line amortization of the cost over the *average remaining service period* of employees who are expected to receive benefits under the plan.[11] It is important to understand, however, that unrecognized past service cost is not an account that appears on the employer's financial statements. It is one element of the computation of pension expense, not an account within the employer's accounting system.

❱ INTEREST COST

interest cost the increase in the pension liability (the projected benefit obligation) that occurs because of the passage of time

The **interest cost** represents the increase in the pension liability (the projected benefit obligation) that occurs because of the passage of time. A pension liability is similar to other liabilities in that if the liability is not paid, there is an interest cost. The amount of the interest that occurs on a pension liability is treated as one of the components of

---

10 The term *past service cost* refers to benefits prior to the adoption of the plan. The term *prior service cost* refers to benefits prior to the amendment of an existing plan. Because the two are handled in a similar manner, we will not distinguish between past and prior service costs.

11 *SFAS No. 87* indicates that the preferred method is to amortize over the years of service of the employees and refers to this method as the *benefits-years-of-service* approach. We will focus on the straight-line method of amortization. See *SFAS No. 87*, par. 27.

pension expense and increases the total pension expense to the employer. The interest cost component recognized in a period shall be determined as the increase in the *projected benefit obligation*. Measuring the projected benefit obligation as a present value requires accrual of an interest cost at a rate equal to the assumed discount rate. *SFAS No. 87* refers to this rate of interest as the discount rate or the settlement rate. The **settlement rate** is defined as the rate of interest that would be incurred if the employer took action to settle (pay off) the pension obligation. The interest cost component is measured as follows:

settlement rate the rate of interest that would be incurred if the employer took action to settle (pay off) the pension obligation

$$\text{Interest Cost} = \text{Projected Benefit Obligation at Beginning of the Period} \\ \times \text{Discount Rate}$$

❯ RETURN ON PLAN ASSETS

return on plan assets dividends and interest earned and unrealized and realized changes in the fair market value of the plan assets

The **return on plan assets** represents the dividends and interest earned and the unrealized and realized changes in the fair market value of the plan assets. The pension fund trustee is normally entrusted with investing the plan assets and earning interest and dividends on those assets in order to increase the funds available. To the extent that there is a return on the assets, the amount recognized as pension expense is *decreased*. Therefore, a return on plan assets is deducted when combining the components to calculate pension expense. *SFAS No. 87* holds that the *actual* return on plan assets shall be determined based on the fair value of plan assets at the beginning and the end of the period, adjusted for contributions and benefit payments. A reconciliation of the beginning and ending amount of plan assets would be as follows:

Beginning balance of plan assets	$xxxx
Plus: Contributions	xxxx
Actual return	xxxx
Less: Benefits paid to retirees	(xxxx)
Ending balance of plan assets	$xxxx

Because the accounting for the pension plan is separate from the accounting for the employer, the plan assets are *not* reflected on the employer's balance sheet. The employer is required to provide note disclosure of the amount of plan assets, and the return on the plan assets affects the amount of pension expense recorded by the employer, but the plan assets are not reflected on the balance sheet.

PENSIONS ILLUSTRATED

The following example illustrates a basic computation of pension expense. Additional complexities will be introduced in subsequent examples.

❯ **EXAMPLE 1** Assume the following amounts for ARN Company at January 1, 2005:

Projected benefit obligation	$1,000,000
Pension plan assets	750,000
Unrecognized past service costs	240,000

ARN and its actuaries have determined the following for 2005:

Service cost	$300,000
Actual (and expected) return on plan assets	$72,000
Discount (settlement) rate	10%
Average remaining service period of employees	12 years

ARN should determine pension expense for 2005 as follows:

Service cost	$300,000
Interest cost	100,000 ($1,000,000 × 0.10)
Return on assets	(72,000)
Amortization of past service costs	20,000 ($240,000 ÷ 12 years)
Total pension expense	$348,000

Assume that ARN Company decided to pay cash in the amount of $300,000 to the pension fund at December 31, 2005. The company should record the following journal entry:

Pension Expense	348,000	
Cash		300,000
Accrued Pension Cost		48,000

The Accrued Pension Cost account is a balance sheet account. A credit balance indicates that the amount funded (the credit to Cash) was *less* than the amount expensed. The balance of the account should be reflected in the long-term liabilities portion of the balance sheet.

) EXAMPLE 2 Assume the same facts as in Example 1, except that ARN decided to pay cash in the amount of $400,000 to the pension fund at December 31, 2005 (rather than $300,000 as in Example 1). The company should record the following journal entry on that date:

Pension Expense	348,000	
Prepaid Pension Cost	52,000	
Cash		400,000

The Prepaid Pension Cost account is also a balance sheet account. A debit balance indicates that the company has funded (the credit to Cash) *more* than the amount recorded as an expense. The balance of the account should be reflected in the long-term assets portion of the balance sheet. Note that the amount of pension assets and the amount of the projected benefit obligation are not reflected on the employer's balance sheet. Only the net amount of the difference between the amount expensed and the amount funded appears, either as a Prepaid Pension Cost account or as an Accrued Pension Cost account.

MINIMUM LIABILITY PROVISION

LO5 Describe and utilize the minimum liability provision for pension accounting.

Critical Thinking: *How can financial statement users be sure that companies sufficiently report their obligation to pay future retirement amounts?*

minimum pension liability the amount of the unfunded accumulated benefit obligation that should be recorded by a company with a defined benefit pension plan

Companies with a defined benefit plan must determine whether an amount beyond that recorded in the Prepaid Pension Cost or Accrued Pension Cost account must be recognized as a liability for the pension plan. This is referred to as the *minimum liability* provision.

The FASB believes that it is important for the company to record this liability if a pension plan is underfunded. A pension plan is underfunded if the pension plan assets are less than the pension plan liability. In order to determine the amount of underfunding, we must consider two alternative definitions or measurements of the pension liability.

● The **minimum pension liability** that should be recorded by a company with a defined benefit pension plan is the amount of the unfunded accumulated benefit obligation. It represents the amount by which the *accumulated benefit obligation exceeds the fair value of the assets* as of the end of the period. In other words, it is the amount by which the plan is underfunded based on existing salary levels.

additional minimum liability the amount of the unfunded accumulated benefit obligation after considering the Accrued Pension Cost (credit balance) or Prepaid Pension Cost (asset)

● The **additional minimum liability** is the amount of the unfunded accumulated benefit obligation after considering the Accrued Pension Cost (credit balance) or Prepaid Pension Cost (asset). If an additional minimum liability amount must be recorded, an equal amount should be recognized as an *intangible asset*. The amount of the additional liability and related intangible asset should be adjusted each year to reflect the amount of the underfunding of the pension plan. If a plan is overfunded, no additional liability or asset is recorded.

The following examples illustrate the minimum liability and additional liability concepts.

) EXAMPLE 3   Assume the same facts as in Example 1 with the following additional assumptions:

Accumulated benefit obligation December 31, 2005	$900,000
Plan assets, December 31, 2005	800,000
Balance of accrued pension (prior to entry in Example 1)	0

ARN Company should compute the minimum liability as follows:

Accumulated benefit obligation	$900,000
Plan assets	800,000
Minimum liability	$100,000

In Example 1, ARN Company recorded an entry resulting in a (credit) balance of $48,000 in the Accrued Pension Cost account. Because the company has already recognized a pension liability of $48,000, ARN should compute the additional minimum liability as follows:

Minimum liability	$100,000
Balance of Accrued Pension Cost	(48,000)
Additional liability	$ 52,000

ARN should record the following journal entry for the additional liability:

Intangible Pension Asset	52,000	
Additional Liability		52,000

ARN should present the following amounts on the financial statements for 2005. For information on note disclosure requirements, refer to pages 719–722.

Income Statement

Operating expenses:

Pension expense	$348,000

Balance Sheet

Intangible assets:

Intangible pension asset	$ 52,000

Long-term liabilities:

Pension liability	$100,000

Note that on the balance sheet, the balance of the Accrued Pension Cost account ($48,000) and the balance of the Additional Liability account ($52,000) are combined and presented as one amount in the long-term liabilities category ($100,000). This is the amount by which the pension fund is underfunded based on current salary levels and is important to users of the financial statements.

▶ EXAMPLE 4 To consider how the additional liability is calculated when a Prepaid Pension Cost account (debit balance) is present, assume the same facts as in Example 2 with the following additional assumptions:

Accumulated benefit obligation, December 31, 2005	$900,000
Plan assets, December 31, 2005	800,000
Balance of Prepaid Pension Cost (prior to entry in Example 2)	0

ARN Company should compute the minimum liability as follows:

Accumulated benefit obligation	$900,000
Plan assets	800,000
Minimum liability	$100,000

In Example 2, ARN recorded an entry resulting in a (debit) balance of $52,000 in the Prepaid Pension Cost account. Because an asset of $52,000 related to the pension plan has already been recorded, ARN should compute the additional minimum liability as

Minimum liability	$100,000
Balance of Prepaid Pension Cost	52,000
Additional liability	$152,000

ARN should record the following journal entry for the additional liability:

Intangible Pension Asset	152,000	
Additional Liability		152,000

ARN should present the following amounts on the financial statements for 2005. For information on note disclosure requirements, see pages 719–722.

Income Statement

Operating expenses:	
Pension expense	$348,000

Balance Sheet

Intangible assets:	
Intangible pension asset	$152,000
Long-term liabilities:	
Pension liability	$100,000

Note that on the balance sheet, the balance of the Prepaid Pension Cost account ($52,000 debit) and the balance of the Additional Liability account ($152,000 credit) are combined and presented as one amount in the long-term liabilities category ($100,000).

▶ MINIMUM LIABILITY AND COMPREHENSIVE INCOME

In most cases, an additional liability should be recognized by a journal entry crediting the Additional Liability account and debiting the Intangible Pension Asset account. The reasoning behind the use of an intangible asset account is based on the following logic. When underfunding has occurred, it is usually due to an amendment to the pension plan (past or prior service costs) that has not been funded. The FASB's thinking is that a plan amendment generally results in more satisfied and productive employees (an intangible asset to the company). Of course, the amount of the additional liability must be adjusted upward or downward each year to reflect the funding status of the pension plan. **Funding status** refers to whether the plan has sufficient assets to meet the future plan obligations. A pension plan is overfunded if the plan assets exceed the obligation and is underfunded if the obligation exceeds the plan assets.

funding status whether a pension plan has sufficient assets to meet future plan obligations

There is one exception to the recording procedures that we have described. *SFAS No. 87* provides that *the asset recognized shall not exceed the amount of unrecognized prior service cost.*[12] To the extent that the intangible asset would exceed the amount of unrecognized past or prior service cost, the excess should be reported as an element of comprehensive income.

Return to the facts in Example 4, but assume that ARN Company does not have any unrecognized prior service costs as of December 31, 2005. In that case, ARN Company should record the additional liability as follows:

Pension Adjustment—Other Comprehensive Income	152,000	
Additional Liability		152,000

The *change in the balance* of the Pension Adjustment—Other Comprehensive Income account should be treated as part of other comprehensive income on the statement of comprehensive income. The *balance* of the account should be treated as a contra–stockholders' equity item and presented on the balance sheet as follows:

Long-term liabilities:
    Pension liability $100,000 (credit balance)
Stockholders' equity:
    Pension adjustment—other
       comprehensive income $152,000 (debit balance)

LO6 **Explain and demonstrate the proper accounting treatment for pension gains and losses.**

Critical Thinking: *Does the performance of a pension fund affect the net income or loss of the sponsoring employer?*

PENSION GAINS AND LOSSES

The pension examples provided thus far have been relatively straightforward in that no gains or losses on the pension assets and liabilities were incurred. We will now consider cases in which such gains or losses occur. Pension gains and losses can originate from the following sources:

- Changes in the pension assets

- Changes in the projected benefit obligation

❱ GAINS OR LOSSES RESULTING FROM CHANGES IN PENSION ASSETS

Asset gains and losses are differences between the actual return on assets during a period and the expected return on assets for that period.[13] In some cases, the gain or loss may occur because the interest or dividends earned from investing the assets during the period were higher or lower than expected. Interest-rate conditions can change quite suddenly and affect the return on a large portfolio of invested assets. But the gain or loss may also be the result of unexpected changes in the market value of the assets. Since the pension fund assets are measured at market value, any fluctuations in market value affect the return on the assets for the period. Any *unexpected* fluctuations in market value would give rise to a gain or loss on the assets.

❱ **EXAMPLE 5** Assume the following amounts for BCX Company at January 1, 2005:

Projected benefit obligation	$1,000,000
Pension plan assets	$750,000
Unrecognized past service costs	$240,000
Expected return on plan assets	10%

---

12 *SFAS No. 87*, par. 37.

13 Ibid., par. 32.

BCX has determined the following for 2005:

Service cost	$300,000
Discount (settlement) rate	10%
Average remaining service period of employees	12 years
Actual return on plan assets	$80,000

In this case, BCX experienced a *gain* on plan assets of $5,000 because the actual return ($80,000) was larger than the expected return ($75,000).

ARN should determine pension expense for 2005 as follows:

Service cost	$300,000
Interest cost	100,000 ($1,000,000 × 0.10)
Amortization of past service costs	20,000 ($240,000 ÷ 12 years)
Actual return on assets	(80,000)
Difference between actual and expected return	5,000 ($80,000 − $75,000)
Amortization of gain/loss	?
Pension expense	$?

unrecognized gain or loss the total gain or loss on plan assets and pension liabilities that has not been amortized to pension expense

The gain on pension assets of $5,000 should be used to calculate an amount referred to as the unrecognized gain or loss. **Unrecognized gain or loss** represents the total gain or loss on plan assets and pension liabilities that has not been amortized to pension expense. We have entered a question mark in the preceding example because the unrecognized gain or loss is amortized only if it is a very large amount. This is referred to as the *corridor approach* and will be discussed on pages 711–713.

▶ GAINS OR LOSSES RESULTING FROM CHANGES IN THE PROJECTED BENEFIT OBLIGATION

Pension gains and losses can also result from fluctuations in the amount measured as the projected benefit obligation. These gains and losses are sometimes referred to as *actuarial gains and losses* because they usually result from changes in the assumptions that the actuaries must make when they estimate and calculate the pension amounts related to future periods. For example, if during the year the actuaries modify their assumptions concerning future interest rates (discount rates), the number of employees who will retire from the company, the number of years employees will draw retirement pay, inflation rates, or other economic factors, then a gain or loss will occur.

▶ **EXAMPLE 6** Assume the following amounts for Hopkins Company in 2005:

Projected benefit obligation, January 1, 2005	$ 800,000
Discount (settlement) rate	10%
Service cost for employee service of 2005	$100,000
Benefits paid to retirees	$50,000
Projected benefit obligation, December 31, 2005 (using updated actuarial assumptions)	$1,000,000

If the actuarial assumptions had not changed, we could calculate the ending amount of the projected benefit obligation as follows:

Projected benefit obligation, January 1, 2005	$800,000
Service cost	100,000
Interest	80,000 ($800,000 × 0.10)
Benefits paid	(50,000)
Expected ending projected benefit obligation	$930,000

The fact that the projected benefit obligation at year end was $1,000,000 indicates that there was a change in the actuarial assumptions used to calculate the pension liability. A *loss* occurs when the projected benefit obligation is *larger* than the expected obligation. A *gain* occurs when the projected benefit obligation is *less* than the expected obligation. In this case, the loss was $70,000 ($1,000,000 − $930,000). This loss is combined with any gain or loss on the pension assets to calculate the amount of the unrecognized gain or loss. However, the loss affects the amount calculated for pension expense only if it is a very large amount that exceeds the guidelines established by the corridor approach.

❱ CORRIDOR APPROACH TO GAINS AND LOSSES

During the deliberations preceding *SFAS No. 87*, the proper treatment of gains and losses associated with pension assets and liabilities generated a great deal of debate. To some extent, the concerns were a consequence of the decision to measure the fair value or market value of pension assets and liabilities. Fair value amounts fluctuate in response to market conditions and economic factors, and those fluctuations can give rise to gains or losses. Reporting companies were especially concerned because the dollar amount of assets and liabilities for many defined benefit pension plans of major, established companies is often very large. Even small changes in interest rates or stock prices or actuarial assumptions can cause dramatic gains or losses.

In the initial stages of its deliberations, the FASB indicated its preference for including all gains or losses in the calculation of pension expense. Reporting companies were alarmed at this proposed approach because it could have caused the amount of recognized pension expense to fluctuate wildly from period to period, resulting in increased volatility of reported profits. Companies argued vigorously that "the market" often perceives increased volatility of profits to be associated with increased risk. Many respondents to the FASB proposal were fearful that inclusion of *all* gains and losses in pension expense would affect their stock price adversely.

As a result, the FASB developed a compromise approach in an attempt to *smooth* the reporting of gains and losses. This approach allows a delayed recognition of gains and losses and was justified by the FASB as follows:

> This Statement provides for delayed recognition, in net periodic pension cost and in the related liability (accrued unfunded pension cost) or asset (prepaid pension cost), of certain changes in the present value of the obligation and the fair value of plan assets. Those changes (that is, gains and losses and the effects of plan amendments) are recognized in net periodic pension cost on a systematic basis over future periods. The Board concluded that it is not practical at this time to require accelerated recognition of those changes in financial statements as they occur, although certain of those changes are recognized in the statement of financial position through the minimum liability requirement of this Statement.
>
> The Board concluded that the difference between the actual return on assets and the expected return on assets could be recognized in net periodic pension cost on a delayed basis. Those effects include the gains and losses themselves. That conclusion was based on (a) the probability that at least some gains would be offset by subsequent losses and vice versa and (b) respondents' arguments that immediate recognition would produce unacceptable volatility and would be inconsistent with the present accounting model.[14]

corridor approach an approach in which gains and losses are included in pension expense only if they exceed established thresholds

The compromise approach is called the **corridor approach**. Under this approach, gains and losses are included in pension expense only if they exceed established

---

14 Ibid., par. 102, 121.

Illustration 15.5

The Corridor Approach

Corridor defined	10 percent of the greater of the projected benefit obligation or the market-related value of plan assets.
Market-related value of assets defined	Either the fair market value of the assets or a calculated value (such as an average) that recognizes changes in fair value in a systematic and rational manner over not more than five years.
What is compared	The cumulative unrecognized gain or loss is compared to the corridor amount.
If gains/losses are less than the corridor amount	Do not include any amount for gains/losses in the calculation of pension expense.
If gains/losses are greater than the corridor amount	Amortize the *excess* and include the amortized amount as a component of pension expense. The minimum amortization shall be that excess divided by the average remaining service period of active employees.

thresholds. Amortization of an unrecognized net gain or loss should be included as a component of net pension expense for a year if, *as of the beginning of the year*, unrecognized net gain or loss exceeds *10 percent of the greater of the projected benefit obligation or the market-related value of plan assets*. Illustration 15.5 summarizes the definitions and calculations necessary to apply the corridor approach.

The term **market-related value** means either the fair market value of the assets or a calculated value (such as an average) that recognizes changes in fair value in a systematic and rational manner over not more than five years.[15] If the unrecognized gain or loss exceeds the corridor amount, then a portion of the excess must be included as a component of pension expense. If amortization is required, the minimum amortization shall be that excess divided by the average remaining service period of active employees expected to receive benefits under the plan. The following example illustrates the use of the corridor approach.

market-related value either the fair market value of the assets or a calculated value (such as an average) that recognizes changes in fair value in a systematic and rational manner over not more than five years

❯ **EXAMPLE 7**   Assume that Bosio Company had no gains or losses on pension assets or liabilities prior to 2005. Assume the following for the years 2005, 2006, and 2007:

Year	Gain/Loss on Pension Assets During the Year	Gain/Loss on Pension Liability During the Year	Net
2005	$150,000 loss	$ 50,000 gain	$100,000 loss
2006	50,000 gain	120,000 loss	70,000 loss
2007	70,000 loss	70,000 loss	140,000 loss

Year	Projected Benefit Obligation, January 1	Market Value of Plan Assets, January 1	Average Remaining Service Period
2005	$700,000	$ 600,000	10 years
2006	800,000	700,000	10 years
2007	900,000	1,000,000	10 years

---

15 Ibid., par. 264. In our examples, we assume that market-related value is equal to fair value of assets in order to reduce the complexity of the calculations.

The amount of gain or loss that should be amortized in each of the years using the corridor approach should be determined as follows:

Year	Corridor Amount*	Unrecognized Gain/Loss at January 1	Excess	Amortized Amount†
2005	$ 70,000	$ 0	$ 0	$ 0
2006	80,000	100,000 loss	20,000	2,000
2007	100,000	168,000 loss‡	68,000	6,800

*10 percent of the greater of the projected benefit obligation or plan assets.
† Excess divided by average remaining service period of employees, 10 years in this example.
‡ $100,000 Loss + $70,000 Loss − $2,000 Amortized = $168,000 Unrecognized.

The corridor amount is based on the projected benefit obligation and plan assets at the beginning of the period and the gain or loss at the beginning of the period. Therefore, the amortized amount for 2005 is zero. In 2006, an amortized amount of $2,000 occurs, and this must be included as a component of pension expense. Because a loss amount is being amortized, the $2,000 amount will *increase* pension expense. In 2007, it is essential to calculate the *cumulative unrecognized* gain or loss. Gains and losses from all periods must be combined, but any amounts that have been amortized must be deducted, since those amounts have been recognized. The result for 2007 is a cumulative unrecognized loss of $168,000, or an excess (outside the corridor) of $68,000. This excess of $68,000 is amortized over the average remaining service period for employees (10 years in this case), and the result is $6,800 that must be recognized as a component of pension expense. Because the amount represents a loss, the $6,800 amount will *increase* pension expense.

❯ EVALUATION OF THE CORRIDOR APPROACH

In many cases, the FASB must make compromises in order to achieve acceptance of accounting pronouncements and to balance the costs and benefits of accounting information. The pronouncement of *SFAS No. 87* is no exception. The board sought to develop a method that would allow reporting firms to *smooth* the reporting of gains or losses associated with plan assets and liabilities. This determination is perhaps justified by the fact that these gains and losses may fluctuate from period to period, so that gains in one period will be offset by losses in another period and vice versa. It could be argued that the volatility introduced by the inclusion of the gains and losses in pension expense would be unnecessary and confusing and would affect the decisions of statement users. However, the corridor approach adopted in *SFAS No. 87* introduces an extreme form of smoothing.

Essentially, gains and losses are smoothed in three ways. First, gains and losses are recognized only if they are large enough to be outside the defined corridor. Second, if the gains and losses are outside of the corridor, only the excess amount is considered. Third, even the excess amount is smoothed by amortizing the amount over the average service period of employees.

Critics of the corridor approach argue that the method adopted in *SFAS No. 87* leads to unnecessary complexity as well as to pension information that is not useful for decision-making purposes. The pension expense recognized on the income statement is a combination of current events (employee service) and past events (delayed recognition of gains and losses). The pension amount recognized on the balance sheet (Accrued Pension Cost, Prepaid Pension Cost, and in some cases a Minimum Liability amount) does not accurately represent the employer's "true" liability for the defined benefit pension plan. While the critics may be correct, the pension note does provide important information concerning pensions and must be understood in order to develop an understanding of the status of any defined benefit pension plan. (See the "Note Disclosures" section in this chapter.)

Illustration 15.6

Components of Pension Expense

1. Service cost
2. + Interest component
    (interest rate × beginning balance of projected benefit obligation)
3. − Return on plan assets
4. + Past service cost amortized*
    Amortization method may be
    a. Remaining service life of employees (a declining amount per year)
    b. Straight-line over the average remaining service life of employees
5. − Gains amortized or + losses amortized using the corridor approach
    a. Recognize gain or loss that is greater than 10 percent of the larger of the projected benefit obligation or the market-related value of plan assets
    b. If recognized: Amortize the amount over the remaining service life of employees

*In most cases, when companies make an amendment to their pension plan, they do so to give employees more retirement benefits. The amendment will increase pension costs, and for that reason a plus sign has been used for past service costs amortized. There are some cases in which companies reduce employees' retirement benefits. In those cases, the amendment will reduce pension costs, and a negative sign should appear.

SUMMARY OF THE PENSION MODEL

Illustration 15.6 presents a summary of the components of pension expense used in the current pension model of *SFAS No. 87*.

CHECK YOUR UNDERSTANDING

1. How does the accumulated benefit obligation differ from the projected benefit obligation?
2. How is the vested benefit obligation for a pension plan measured?
3. In what instance should a minimum pension liability be recorded?
4. Pension gains and losses can originate from what two sources?

LO7 Identify the appropriate accounting treatment and disclosures for postretirement obligations and expenses.

■■■ Critical Thinking: *What implications might result if a company failed to properly measure postretirement benefit obligations like health-care costs for its retired employees?*

postretirement benefits benefits other than pensions that employees receive after retirement

Postretirement Obligations

During the deliberations on pension accounting, the FASB decided to limit the scope of the discussion to the accounting for pensions and tackle issues related to other postretirement benefits in another project. *SFAS No. 87* was issued to provide guidance on pension accounting, and it developed the pension accounting model that we examined in previous sections of this chapter. Later, "Employers' Accounting for Postretirement Benefits Other than Pensions," *Statement of Financial Accounting Standards No. 106,* was issued to provide guidance on the accounting for postretirement benefits.

Postretirement benefits are defined as benefits other than pensions that employees receive after retirement. Examples of such benefits may include an employer's promise to pay education benefits, legal aid, or relocation costs, but the most significant item is health-care benefits. Since it is the most significant item, we will center our discussion of postretirement costs on health-care costs. If an employer agrees to pay for some or all of the health-care costs of retired employees, the provisions of *SFAS No. 106* apply. Because of increased health-care costs in the United States, the costs to employers of such agreements have skyrocketed. In fact, in many cases, an employer's obligation for postretirement costs may exceed its obligation for pension benefits.

Prior to *SFAS No. 106*, many companies did not record the expense for postretirement costs prior to payment. Essentially, companies used a pay-as-you-go method, did not record the obligation for postretirement costs as a liability on their financial statements, and often did not even provide note disclosure of the obligation. Because of the large dollar amounts involved, users of the financial statements called for the FASB to require companies to recognize this liability. The FASB responded with the issuance of *SFAS No. 106*. However, the new accounting guidelines were met with considerable criticism from reporting firms, which argued that postretirement obligations did not meet the definition of a liability and argued that if a liability did exist, it should not be recognized because of the inability to reasonably measure the amounts of the future payments.

The accounting guidance provided in *SFAS No. 106* uses the pension accounting model with some modifications. In many ways, it is appropriate that the same accounting model be used because there are many similarities between pensions and postretirement benefits. Both involve a promise by the employer to pay amounts to retirees at a future time. Both involve payments far into the future and consequently require significant estimates and accounting judgments in order to measure the expense and the obligation. However, it is important to note that there are also differences between pensions and postretirement costs that may affect the accounting for such costs. The most important differences include the following:

- *Coverage.* Usually a pension covers only the employee, but some employee plans promise to cover the health care of employees *and their dependents.*

- *Ability to predict.* Pensions are usually a stable amount, but the amount of health-care costs incurred by a retiree may fluctuate from month to month. Government programs such as Medicare and Medicaid may also affect the costs incurred by the employer.

- *Funding issues.* Employers are required by federal legislation to pay amounts into a pension fund to cover pension costs. Employers are not legally required to fund postretirement obligations. In fact, until recently, many employers did not set aside funds specifically for postretirement costs.

- *Legal issues.* In most cases a promise by an employer to provide pension benefits is a legally binding contract. The legal status of a promise to provide postretirement benefits is much less clear. There have been many recent court cases involving companies that have terminated or reduced postretirement benefits to retirees or to existing employees who would become retired in the future. Whether a legally binding contract exists depends on a variety of factors, including the nature of the promise, the intent of the employer, and the understanding of the employees. In addition, if an employee leaves a company before retirement, the company generally has no obligation to provide these benefits in the future.

- *Tax considerations.* Companies are allowed a tax deduction for amounts paid to a pension fund, within defined limits. Generally, companies are not allowed a tax deduction for the funding of postretirement benefits.

MEASURING THE OBLIGATION

When discussing pensions, we introduced three methods of measuring the pension obligation: accumulated benefit obligation, projected benefit obligation, and vested benefit obligation. For postretirement benefits there are two ways to measure the obligation:

- Accumulated postretirement benefit obligation

- Expected postretirement benefit obligation

Illustration 15.7

Summary of Postretirement Terms

Accumulated postretirement benefit obligation	The present value of postretirement benefits attributed to employee service to date.
Expected postretirement benefit obligation	The present value of expected postretirement benefits to be received by employees.
Attribution period	The time period over which the employee earns the postretirement benefits. The period ends when the employee becomes eligible for benefits.

accumulated postretirement benefit obligation a measure of the present value of the postretirement benefits attributed to employee service up to the date of measurement

expected postretirement benefit obligation a measure of the present value of all postretirement benefits expected to be earned by employees by the time they retire

attribution period the time period over which an employee earns postretirement benefits

The **accumulated postretirement benefit obligation** is a measure of the present value of the postretirement benefits attributed to employee service up to the date of measurement. It does not consider any additional benefits that may be earned by employees for future service. The **expected postretirement benefit obligation** is a measure of the present value of all postretirement benefits expected to be earned by employees by the time they retire. In considering these measures of the liability, it was important for the FASB to consider the time period over which to record the postretirement expense. This time period is referred to as the **attribution period** and represents the time period over which the employee *earns* the benefits. The FASB has stated its belief that the benefits are earned over the time period beginning at the time of employment and ending when the employee is *eligible* for benefits:

> This Statement requires that an employer's obligation for postretirement benefits expected to be provided to or for an employee be fully accrued by the date that employee attains full eligibility for all of the benefits expected to be received by that employee, any beneficiaries, and covered dependents (the full eligibility date), even if the employee is expected to render additional service beyond that date.[16]

Some companies argued that the postretirement expense should be spread over a longer time period (the time until employees normally retire or the time until mandatory retirement age), but the FASB has taken the stance that the attribution period should be shorter (the time until the employee is eligible for benefits). A portion of the expected postretirement benefit obligation should be treated as an expense over this attribution period.

Illustration 15.7 summarizes key terms that are important to accounting for postretirement benefit plans.

COMPONENTS OF THE POSTRETIREMENT ACCOUNTING MODEL

In most respects, the calculation of postretirement expense is similar to that required in the pension accounting model. The detailed discussion of the areas in which the two are similar will not be repeated. Refer to Illustration 15.8 for an overview of the components of postretirement expense. Note, however, that the interest component of postretirement expense is based on the *accumulated* postretirement benefit obligation and measures the increase in that measure of the liability that occurs as a result of the passage of time. Also note that the amortization of past service costs associated with postretirement expense may be either a positive (increased expense) or a negative (decreased expense) amount. Past service costs often occur when a postretirement plan is amended. If the plan is amended to give *more* benefits to retirees, then a *loss* results,

---

16 "Employers' Accounting for Postretirement Benefits Other than Pensions," *Statement of Financial Accounting Standards No. 106* (Norwalk, Conn.: FASB, 1990), par. 43, 44.

Illustration 15.8

Components of Postretirement Expense

1.   Service cost

2.   + Interest component
     (interest rate × beginning balance of accumulated postretirement benefit obligation)

3.   − Return on plan assets (If the postretirement benefit plan is funded, an amount should be deducted representing the return on assets.)

4.   + or − Past service cost amortized*

     Amortization method may be

     a. Remaining service life of employees (a declining amount per year)

     b. Straight-line over the average time until eligible for benefits (attribution period)

5.   − Gains amortized or + losses amortized using the corridor approach

     a. Recognize gain or loss that is greater than 10 percent of the larger of:

         • Accumulated postretirement benefit obligation

         • Market-related value of plan assets

     b. If recognized: Amortize the amount over the remaining service period of employees

6.   + Transition amount (if amortized†)

     If amortized, over average remaining service period of employees or 20 years, if longer

* Past service cost amortized is added if additional benefits are given to employees and deducted if an amendment reduced benefits to employees.

† Companies were allowed to record the transition amount at the time of adoption of *SFAS No. 106* or may amortize the transition amount.

and the amount of the loss amortized *increases* postretirement expense. In recent years, however, many companies have taken action to reduce the amount of postretirement costs, particularly health-care costs. If the plan is amended to give *less* benefits to retirees, then a *gain* results, and the amount of the gain amortized *decreases* postretirement expense.

The following example illustrates the calculation of postretirement costs, excluding transition amounts.

❯ **EXAMPLE**   Assume the following amounts associated with postretirement benefits for Condon Company at January 1, 2005:

Accumulated postretirement benefit obligation	$1,000,000
Postretirement plan assets	50,000
Unrecognized past service costs	240,000

Condon has determined the following for 2005:

Service cost	$300,000
Actual (and expected) return on plan assets	$5,000
Interest rate (on liability)	10%
Average remaining service period of employees	12 years

Condon should determine postretirement expense for 2005 as follows:

Service cost	$300,000
Interest cost	100,000 ($1,000,000 × 0.10)
Amortization of past service costs	20,000 ($240,000 ÷ 12 years)
Return on assets	(5,000)
Total postretirement expense	$415,000

Companies are not required to contribute amounts to a postretirement fund, and most do not do so. Assume that Condon Company has decided to pay cash in the amount of $100,000 to the postretirement fund at December 31, 2005. The company should record the following journal entry:

Postretirement Expense	415,000	
Cash		100,000
Accrued Postretirement Cost		315,000

The Accrued Postretirement Cost account is a balance sheet account and should be presented as a long-term liability in Condon's balance sheet as of December 31, 2005.[17]

TRANSITION AMOUNTS

transition amount the excess of the accumulated postretirement benefit obligation over the fair value of plan assets (if any) as of the date of adoption of *SFAS No. 106*

One additional component of postretirement obligations may also be present for some companies. At the time of adoption of *SFAS No. 106*, many companies had a large liability for postretirement costs from previous periods that had not been recognized. This liability is referred to as the **transition amount** and is defined as the excess of the accumulated postretirement benefit obligation over the fair value of plan assets (if any) as of the date of adoption of *SFAS No. 106*. Companies were allowed to treat this transition amount in either of two ways: *immediate recognition* or *delayed recognition* over time.

If a company chose to recognize the transition amount immediately, the company was required to recognize the existing obligation as a change in accounting principle, and the cumulative effect was recognized on the income statement in the year of adoption. In spite of the rather drastic effect on reported earnings, many adopting companies chose the immediate recognition option. This required the companies to take a large hit to income in one period, but meant that the subsequent periods were not affected.

If delayed recognition was elected, the transition obligation was required to be amortized on a straight-line basis over the average remaining service period of active plan participants, except that (a) if the average remaining service period was less than 20 years, the employer was allowed to elect to use a 20-year period, and (b) if all or almost all of the plan participants were inactive, the employer was allowed to use the average remaining life expectancy of those plan participants.[18] Because most companies adopted *SFAS No. 106* in either 1989 or 1990, companies are near the end of the amortization period for transition amounts or have already reached the end of that period. For the few companies that are still amortizing a transition amount, the amortized amount should be a component of postretirement expense and should *increase* the amount of the expense recognized in each period.

MINIMUM LIABILITY PROVISION

One of the important differences between pensions and postretirement accounting concerns the need for a minimum liability provision. Under the pension accounting model, companies with an underfunded pension plan are required to recognize a liability for the unfunded accumulated benefit obligation. In the initial stages of the deliberations on *SFAS No. 106*, the FASB expressed its intent to require a minimum liability provision for postretirement costs. Since nearly all companies had underfunded postretirement plans at that time, there was a great deal of resistance to such a requirement. In an effort to reach a compromise solution that would be acceptable to all parties, the FASB eliminated the requirement for a minimum liability provision for postretirement costs. Its justification was stated as follows:

---

17 Ibid., par. 110.

18 Ibid., par. 112.

The Board concluded that this Statement should not require recognition of a minimum liability. The Board concluded that the transition provisions of this Statement that provide for the delayed recognition of an employer's obligation for postretirement benefits at the date this Statement is initially applied should not be overridden by a requirement to recognize a liability that would accelerate recognition of that obligation in the statement of financial position.

However, it is widely acknowledged that postretirement benefit plans are significantly or totally underfunded. As a result, recognition of a minimum liability for such plans would be commonplace rather than an exception.[19]

Because *SFAS No. 106* does not require a minimum liability to be recognized on the balance sheet, it is very important for statement users to use the note information to determine the "true" amount of the liability for postretirement costs. The next section considers the note disclosures required for pensions and postretirement costs.

CHECK YOUR UNDERSTANDING

1. What types of benefits might be considered postretirement benefits?

2. How did most companies handle the accounting for postretirement costs prior to *SFAS No. 106*?

3. What two methods are used to measure the obligation for postretirement benefits? Define both methods.

LO8 Analyze financial statements and disclosures related to pensions and postretirement costs.

Critical Thinking: What are the implications for potential investors if a company fails to properly disclose pension and postretirement benefit plan costs and obligations within its annual report?

Presentation and Analysis of Pensions and Postretirement Plans

NOTE DISCLOSURES

Our discussion of pension and postretirement costs has emphasized that the amounts recognized in the income statement and balance sheet for defined benefit plans do not present a complete picture of all the important aspects of pension and postretirement costs. It is important for any user of the financial statements to read and analyze the notes to the financial statements, where a wealth of information is provided. In particular, it is important to understand (a) the components that were used to calculate pension and postretirement expense and (b) the funding status of the plan. *SFAS No. 132* revised and expanded the required disclosures for both pensions and postretirement costs.[20] We will highlight the most important disclosures, but refer to *SFAS No. 132* for a complete listing of all the required disclosures.

Both pension expense and postretirement expense are based on the calculation of a series of components. *SFAS No. 132* outlines the following required disclosures related to the expense calculation:

An employer that sponsors one or more defined benefit pension plans or one or more defined benefit postretirement plans shall provide the following information:

- The amount of net periodic benefit cost recognized, showing separately the service cost component, the interest cost component, the

---

19 Ibid., par. 306, 307.

20 "Employers' Disclosures About Pensions and Other Postretirement Benefits," *Statement of Financial Accounting Standards No. 132* (Norwalk, Conn.: FASB, 1990), par. 5–11. This is a listing of the most important disclosures. Note that *SFAS No. 132* was revised in December 2003 and requires an expanded set of disclosures in addition to those listed here.

Illustration 15.9

Rates for Pension and Postretirement Costs

Discount rate for pensions	The rate used in calculating the interest component. Also referred to as the settlement rate.
Rate of return on pension assets	The rate that represents the expected return on assets invested in the pension plan.
Expected compensation rate	The rate that estimates the average amount of salary increases for employees in future periods. This rate is used in calculating the projected benefit obligation.
Discount rate for postretirement costs	The rate used in calculating the interest component for postretirement costs. (Similar to the discount rate for pension expense.) Also referred to as the settlement rate.
Rate of return on postretirement assets	The rate that represents the expected return on assets (if any) invested in the postretirement plan.
Health-care cost trend rate	The rate that is an estimate of the average increase in health-care costs that will occur in future periods.

expected return on plan assets for the period, the amortization of the unrecognized transition obligation or transition asset, the amount of recognized gains and losses, the amount of prior service cost recognized, and the amount of gain or loss recognized due to a settlement or curtailment.

- The amount included within other comprehensive income for the period arising from a change in the additional minimum pension liability recognized pursuant to paragraph 37 of Statement No. 87, as amended.

- On a weighted-average basis, the following assumptions used in the accounting for the plans: assumed discount rate, rate of compensation increase (for pay-related plans), and expected long-term rate of return on plan assets.

It is important to analyze the notes to determine whether the company has used reasonable assumptions in developing its pension and postretirement estimates and has applied those assumptions consistently from year to year. It is especially important to determine whether the various rates used in the projections are realistic. Illustration 15.9 summarizes the rates that have been discussed in this chapter and are presented in financial statement notes.

Statement users and analysts are particularly interested in the funding status of the plan. As defined earlier, funding status refers to whether the plan has sufficient assets to meet the future plan obligations. A pension plan is overfunded if the plan assets exceed the obligation and is underfunded if the obligation exceeds the plan assets. *SFAS No. 132* requires the following note disclosures to enable statement readers to assess the funding status of the plan:

An employer that sponsors one or more defined benefit pension plans or one or more defined benefit postretirement plans shall provide the following information:

a. A reconciliation of beginning and ending balances of the benefit obligation showing separately, if applicable, the effects during the period attributable to each of the following: service cost, interest cost, contributions by plan participants, actuarial gains and losses, foreign currency exchange rate changes, benefits paid, plan amendments, business combinations, divestitures, curtailments, settlements, and special termination benefits

b. A reconciliation of beginning and ending balances of the fair value of plan assets showing separately, if applicable, the effects during the period attributable to each of the following: actual return on plan assets, foreign currency exchange rate changes, contributions by the employer, contributions by plan participants, benefits paid, business combinations, divestitures, and settlements

c. The funded status of the plans, the amounts not recognized in the statement of financial position, and the amounts recognized in the statement of financial position, including:

(1) The amount of any unamortized prior service cost

(2) The amount of any unrecognized net gain or loss (including asset gains and losses not yet reflected in market-related value)

(3) The amount of any remaining unamortized, unrecognized net obligation or net asset existing at the initial date of application of Statement No. 87 or Statement No. 106

(4) The net pension or other postretirement benefit prepaid assets or accrued liabilities

(5) Any intangible asset and the amount of accumulated other comprehensive income recognized pursuant to paragraph 37 of Statement No. 87, as amended

Analysts are interested in both overfunded and underfunded pension and postretirement plans. If a plan is *overfunded*, this is a favorable indication of its status and may provide clues about future actions. In some cases, companies may see the overfunded plan as a source of cash and may access a portion of the overfunding to meet other financial needs. Employees and retirees should be quite concerned about such actions. Additionally, companies with an overfunded plan may be potential merger or takeover targets, as other companies may want to use the overfunding to finance their future activities. On the other hand, a plan that is *underfunded* is often viewed negatively by analysts and by employees. Employees and retirees have to be quite concerned about whether assets will be available to meet their retirement needs. It is important to analyze whether underfunding has occurred because the employer did not contribute sufficiently to the plan, because the return on assets was insufficient, or because of other factors.

The Financial Reporting Case at the beginning of this chapter introduced some of the pension issues facing large established companies such as **IBM**. Figure 15.1 contains a note disclosure regarding the funding status of IBM's pension plan at December 31, 2003 and 2002.[21]

IBM has some pension plans that are defined contribution plans and others that are defined benefit plans. When all of the pension plans are combined and presented in the aggregate, the pension plans appear to be reasonably well funded. For many years, IBM's pension plans were among the best-funded company pension plans in the United States. However, because of the stock market drop of 2001 and 2002, the value of plan assets declined, and the company's pension plan was no longer overfunded. In fact, at December 31, 2003, the fair value of the plan assets was less than the benefit obligation by about $425 million.

---

21 We have excerpted the information about IBM's U.S. pension plans. The company also disclosed information about its non-U.S. plans in the annual report.

Figure 15.1

Partial Pension Plan Note

IBM As of December 31,	2003	2002
	(Dollars in Millions)	
Change in benefit obligation:		
Benefit obligation at beginning of year	$ 38,357	$ 37,762
Service cost	576	650
Interest cost	2,518	2,591
Plan participants contributions	—	—
Acquisitions/divestitures, net	—	32
Amendments	—	18
Actuarial losses	3,472	47
Benefits paid from trust	(2,819)	(2,743)
Direct benefit payments	—	—
Foreign exchange impact	—	—
Plan curtailments/settlements/termination benefits	—	—
Benefit obligation at end of year	42,104	38,357
Change in plan assets:		
Fair value of plan assets at beginning of year	36,984	39,565
Actual return on plan assets	7,514	(3,801)
Employer contribution	—	3,963
Acquisitions/divestitures, net	—	—
Plan participants contributions	—	—
Benefits paid from trust	(2,819)	(2,743)
Foreign exchange impact	—	—
Fair value of plan assets at end of year	41,679	36,984
Fair value of plan assets in excess of benefit obligation	(425)	(1,373)

However, the funding status of the postretirement plans is quite different. Figure 15.2 presents the note from IBM's annual report of December 31, 2003, concerning its postretirement plans.

At December 31, 2003, IBM's projected obligation for postretirement costs was $6,181 million, and plan assets were $10 million. Therefore, the company has underfunded the obligation for postretirement costs by more than $6 billion. This is an indication that the company has a large future obligation that must be paid from funds generated in the future.

Figure 15.2

Partial Postretirement Obligation and Plan Note

IBM As of December 31,	2003	2002
(Dollars in Millions)		
Change in benefit obligation:		
Benefit obligation at beginning of year	$ 5,882	$ 6,148
Service cost	36	49
Interest cost	382	421
Actuarial losses/(gains)	419	(170)
Direct benefit payments	(538)	(566)
Benefit obligation at end of year	6,181	5,882
Change in plan assets:		
Fair value of plan assets at beginning of year	10	8
Accrued postretirement benefit liability recognized in the Consolidated Statement of Financial Position	$ (5,526)	$ (5,770)

EARNINGS MANAGEMENT AND ETHICS

ETHICS

The accounting for pensions and postretirement costs is based on a series of projections and estimates about future events. Each company must make assumptions regarding discount rates, projected salary increases, return on assets, health-care cost trends, and a variety of other economic events. Companies are given a great deal of latitude in making these estimates and judgments as long as the estimates are "reasonable" and reflect the environment and experience of the company. The ethical climate of an organization can play an important role in the range of reasonable estimates that the company makes. Because the dollar amounts involved with pensions and postretirement costs are large, a small change in an assumption can cause a large difference in the outcome. For example, as indicated in Figure 15.1, **IBM**'s projected benefit obligation for pensions was more than $42 billion as of December 31, 2003. This number is based on an assumed discount rate used to calculate the present value amount. If the company simply altered the discount rate by a small percentage, it would cause a large difference in the amount of pension expense for the company. The following excerpt, taken from a *Financial Executive* article, discusses assumed pension discount rates:

> When Fortune magazine editor Carol Loomis sat down for an interview with Warren Buffett late last year, the conversation could have led in many directions: the economy, the stock market or the tenets of value investing. Instead, it mostly led in just one: U.S. pension fund accounting and the current pension return assumptions underlying it. Buffett espoused in that interview (and has continued to espouse since) that pension accounting is likely to blossom into yet another scandal besmirching America's corporate boardrooms—and is a problem potentially far larger than the accounting shenanigans caused by companies such as Enron Corp. or Adelphia Communications. "I invite you to ask the CFO of a company having a large defined-benefit pension fund what adjustment would need to be made to the company's earnings if its pension assumptions were lowered to 6.5 percent," Buffett stated. "And then, if you want to be mean, ask what the company's assumptions were back in 1973 when both stocks and bonds had far higher prospective returns than they do now."
>
> Many corporations set this return assumption using a five-year moving average of recent annual returns, but the Financial Accounting Standards Board makes no explicit requirement to reveal what methodology is used—asking only that the approach be consistent over time.
>
> The "smoothed" accrual typically shows up either within the Gross Income line of the income statement or as a part of Sales and General Administration expense. Many Wall Street analysts bemoan this practice as a potential obfuscation of true operating earnings, but the accounting community has long since signed off on either treatment. But Buffett believes a 9.25 percent annual return assumption in today's world is just dead wrong, and to not admit that keeps corporate earnings artificially higher for a longer period of time—something potentially deceiving and dangerous. "Companies with return on asset assumptions above 6.5 percent are not facing reality, and anyone choosing not to lower assumptions—CEOs, auditors, actuaries all—is risking litigation for misleading investors," Buffett argues. "And directors who don't question [this] optimism simply won't be doing their job."[22]

Many analysts and accounting researchers have come to realize that it is possible for a company to "manage" its earnings by adjusting the important estimates higher or lower. The term **earnings management** is used when a company uses accounting

earnings management the purposeful use of accounting information, principles, or standards to smooth out ups and downs in the earnings process

22 Barclay T. Leib, "Questioning the Basic Assumptions," *Financial Executive*, September 2002, pp. 35–38.

Illustration 15.10

Summary of *IAS No. 19*—Defined Benefit Plans

- Current service cost should be recognized as an expense.
- All companies use the projected unit credit method (an accrued benefit method) to measure their pension expense and pension obligation.
- Projected benefit methods may not be used.
- The discount rate is the interest rate on high-quality corporate bonds with a maturity comparable to plan obligations.
- Plan assets and reimbursement rights are measured at fair value.
- Defined benefit obligations are presented net of plan assets.
- Reimbursement rights are presented as a separate asset.
- A net pension asset on the balance sheet may not exceed the present value of available refunds plus the available reduction in future contribution as a result of a plan surplus.
- If the net cumulative unrecognized actuarial gains and losses exceed the greater of (a) 10 percent of the present value of the plan obligation and (b) 10 percent of the fair value of plan assets, that excess must be amortized over a period no longer than the estimated average remaining working lives of employees participating in the plan.
- Faster amortization, including immediate income recognition for all actuarial gains and losses, is permitted if an enterprise follows a consistent and systematic policy.
- Past service cost should be recognized over the average period until the amended benefits become vested.
- The effect of termination, curtailment, or settlement should be recognized when the event occurs.

information, principles, or standards to smooth out the ups and downs in the earnings process. It is also possible to alter the apparent funding status of a company's pension and postretirement plans by adjusting the assumptions to make the plans appear more well funded. A variety of academic studies have been conducted to determine whether companies do in fact manage their earnings by adjusting pension and postretirement assumptions.[23] Although the results of these studies are not conclusive, there is some evidence to indicate that pension estimates are adjusted to alter a company's reported earnings and that the assumptions used by companies with well-funded plans differ from those used by companies with plans that are not as well funded. Analysts must be aware of the fact that companies may attempt to manage their earnings through their accounting for pensions and postretirement costs and need to carefully review the disclosures in the notes to the financial statements that indicate the assumptions used by the company.

INTERNATIONAL ISSUES

INTERNATIONAL

Pension and postretirement accounting is an area in which there are significant differences between the accounting guidance in U.S. generally accepted accounting principles and that in international accounting pronouncements. "Postemployment Benefits Including Pensions," *IAS No. 19,* and subsequent amendments and interpretations address pension and postretirement issues.[24] Illustration 15.10 provides a summary of portions of *IAS No. 19* pertaining to defined benefit pension and postretirement plans.

---

23 See, for example, G. Newell, J. Kreuze, and D. Hurtt, "Corporate Pension Plans: How Consistent Are the Assumptions in Determining Pension Funding Status," *Mid-American Journal of Business*, Fall 2002, pp. 23–29.

24 "Postemployment Benefits Including Pensions," *International Accounting Standard No. 19,* became effective in 1999, but amendments were made in 2000 and 2001. Additionally, an amendment concerning the "asset ceiling" provision of *IAS No. 19* is under consideration.

A comparison of *IAS No. 19* with the FASB standards reveals that there are many differences between the two. Most importantly, *IAS No. 19* covers both pensions and postretirement costs, whereas the FASB has issued separate pronouncements on pensions (*SFAS No. 87*) and postretirement costs (*SFAS No. 106*). Also, there are many differences in the way the components of the expense are calculated. For example, the interest cost component under *IAS No. 19* is calculated using the interest rate on high-quality corporate bonds, whereas the interest cost component in U.S. standards is based on the settlement rate. In addition, *IAS No. 19* does not require a minimum liability provision. Under U.S. standards, a minimum liability provision is required for underfunded defined benefit pension plans but is not required for postretirement obligations. For a full discussion of the other differences between U.S. and international standards on pension and postretirement accounting, refer to the IASB website.

CHECK YOUR UNDERSTANDING

1. What are the potential implications of an overfunded pension plan?

2. Under *IAS No. 19,* how should pension plan assets and reimbursement rights be measured?

3. The note disclosures required by *SFAS No. 132* include a reconciliation of beginning and ending balances of the benefit obligation. List the components that might be applicable to this reconciliation.

LO9 Determine how pensions and postretirement costs affect cash flow.

CASH FLOW $

 Critical Thinking: Which components of pension and postretirement plans require actual cash outflows?

Impact of Pension and Postretirement Costs on Cash Flow

PENSIONS IN THE STATEMENT OF CASH FLOWS

Pensions and postretirement costs are often a significant expense and are recognized in the income statement. However, it is also important to analyze the impact that pensions and postretirement costs have on the cash flows of the company. If a company presents the statement of cash flows using the indirect basis, the net income amount must be adjusted if the pension or postretirement expense amount does not represent the amount of cash actually paid. This is accomplished in the statement of cash flows by adjusting for the *change* in the Accrued Pension Cost and Accrued Postretirement Cost accounts. For example, assume that the Accrued Pension Cost account (a liability) increased during the period. That is an indication that the amount recorded as pension expense exceeds the amount of pension funding (the cash amount). Because pension expense was deducted in calculating net income, the increase in the Accrued Pension Cost should be *added* in the operating activities section of the statement of cash flows. On the other hand, assume that the Accrued Pension Cost account decreased during the period. That is an indication that the amount recorded as pension expense is less than the amount of pension funding. In that case, the decrease in the Accrued Pension Cost account should be deducted in the operating activities section of the statement of cash flows.

Figure 15.3 presents the operating activities portion of the statement of cash flows for **General Motors Corporation** for the year ended December 31, 2003. General Motors employs a large number of people and also has a large pool of retired employees for which the company has a defined benefit pension plan and a significant postretirement obligation. The operating activities section of the statement indicates an addition of $4,599 million for postretirement costs for the year 2003. This indicates that the cash outflow for postretirement costs for 2003 was less than the amount recognized as expense by $4,599 million. Additionally, the operating activities section

Figure 15.3

Partial Consolidated Statement of Cash Flows

General Motors

For The Years Ended December 31,	2003	2002	2001
Cash flows from operating activities	(dollars in millions)		
Income from continuing operations	$ 2,862	$ 1,975	$ 1,222
Adjustments to reconcile income from continuing operations to net cash provided by operating activities			
Depreciation and amortization expenses	13,978	11,865	11,764
Mortgage servicing rights amortization	1,602	3,871	948
Provision for financing losses	1,608	2,028	1,472
Other postretirement employee benefit (OPEB) expense	4,599	4,108	3,720
OPEB payments	(3,536)	(3,334)	(3,120)
VEBA (contributions)/withdrawals	(3,000)	(1,000)	1,300
Pension expense	3,412	1,780	540
Pension contributions	(18,168)	(5,156)	(317)
Retiree lump sum and vehicle voucher expense, net of payments	923	(254)	(136)
Net change in mortgage loans	456	(4,715)	(4,615)
Net change in mortgage securities	236	(656)	(777)
Change in other investments and miscellaneous assets	1,741	1,335	180
Change in other operating assets and liabilities (Note 1)	792	4,477	(234)
Other	95	(842)	233
Net cash provided by operating activities	$ 7,600	$15,482	$12,180

indicates an addition for the amount of pension expense of $3,412 million but a deduction for the amount of the cash contributions for pensions of $18,168 million. This reflects the effort that General Motors made during the year to increase the funding status of its very large pension plan.

ACCRUAL TO CASH ISSUES

The statement of cash flows provides important information about the *difference* between the amount of pension and postretirement expense and the amount of cash paid, but often it is important to determine the actual dollar amounts involved. That is, it is necessary to convert the accrual-based amounts (expense) to the cash amounts. For example, assume that Chester Company had the following amounts at the beginning and end of 2003:

Account	Beginning Balance	Ending Balance
Accrued Postretirement Cost	$400,000	$520,000

Also assume that the company recognized postretirement expense of $800,000 during 2003. The amount of the cash actually paid could be determined as follows:

$$\text{Postretirement Expense} \atop (\$800,000) \quad - \quad {\text{Increase in Accrued Postretirement} \atop \text{Cost } (\$120,000)} \quad = \quad {\text{Cash Paid} \atop (\$680,000)}$$

The amount of cash paid would represent the amount of cash used to fund the postretirement costs.

As a second example, assume that Hadley Company showed the following amounts related to pensions at the beginning and end of 2003:

	Beginning Balance	Ending Balance
Prepaid Pension Cost (debit balance)	$300,000	$380,000

Also assume that the company recognized pension expense of $700,000 during 2003. The amount of cash actually paid for pensions could be determined as follows:

$$\underset{(\$700{,}000)}{\text{Pension Expense}} + \underset{(\$80{,}000)}{\text{Increase in Prepaid Pension Cost}} = \underset{(\$780{,}000)}{\text{Cash Paid}}$$

It is important to remember that the amount of cash paid represents the amount of funding of the pension plan. It does not represent the amount of cash actually paid to retirees during the year.

CHECK YOUR UNDERSTANDING

1. In converting accrual to cash accounting for pension and postretirement expense, what accounts should be examined?

2. Since pension expense is deducted when calculating net income, how is the amount reflected on the statement of cash flows when using the indirect method?

Revisiting the Case

IBM's Employee Retirement Obligations Surpass the Half-Billion-Dollar Mark

1. Recognition issues related to retirement plans include when expenses and the related liabilities should be recorded. Measurement issues include how the expense and related liability should be valued.

2. IBM offers defined benefit pension plans, defined contribution pension plans, and nonpension postretirement plans, primarily consisting of retiree medical benefits.

3. In 2003, $227 million was reported for defined and benefit contribution plans in the United States.

SUMMARY BY LEARNING OBJECTIVE

LO1 Understand the nature and types of pension plans used by companies.

A pension plan is a promise by the employer to pay benefits to its employees upon retirement. Normally, the employer must pay a designated amount into a pension fund. The pension fund's trustee invests the funds so that they accumulate enough earnings to be able to pay the promised benefits to retirees. There are two primary categories of pension plans. A defined contribution plan is a pension plan in which the amount that is paid into the pension fund is known (or defined), but the amount that will be paid upon retirement is not known until retirement. The most prominent examples of defined contribution plans are 401(k) plans and IRAs (individual retirement accounts). A defined benefit plan is a plan in which the amount that will be paid to employees at retirement is defined. Usually, the amount of the employees' retirement pay is based on a formula that may incorporate several variables. For example, the retirement pay may be based on a formula that combines the employee's age, years of service, and salary level over some time period. The retirement amount is "defined" because each employee can determine the amount of his or her retirement pay if the employee is aware of the pension formula and the variables (such as age, years of service, and salary level) that he or she has achieved.

LO2 Determine how to account for a defined benefit pension plan.

SFAS No. 87 and subsequent pronouncements provide guidance on the accounting for defined benefit pension plans. The FASB states that a defined benefit pension plan involves the incurrence of a liability because a promise has been made to employees. Pension expense for the plan should be recognized using accrual accounting procedures. The expense should be recorded when it is earned by the employees rather than when it is paid. The FASB also holds that the determination of the funding of the pension plan is an actuarial decision, whereas the expensing decision should be governed by accrual accounting procedures. The expense is not represented by the amount of cash put into the fund. Instead, the pension expense should be measured based on a series of components. The combination of these components represents the amount of the expense to the employer.

LO3 Explain the three methods used to value a pension obligation.

The projected benefit obligation is defined as the present value as of a specific date of all benefits attributed by the pension benefit formula to employee service rendered prior to that date. The projected benefit obligation is measured using assumptions concerning future salary increases if the pension benefit formula is based on future compensation levels. The accumulated benefit obligation is defined as the present value of benefits attributed by the pension benefit formula to employee service rendered before a specified date and based on employee service and compensation prior to that date. The accumulated benefit obligation differs from the projected benefit obligation in that it includes no assumptions about future compensation levels. The vested benefit obligation is defined as the benefits for which the employee's right to receive a present or future pension benefit is no longer contingent on the employee's remaining in the service of the employer. In other words, it is the amount that the employee is allowed to withdraw from the retirement fund if the employee leaves the company before retirement (for example, when an employee takes another job).

LO4 Identify the components of pension expense.

Pension expense is made up of a series of components. Each of the components must be calculated, and the total represents the amount of pension expense for the period. The components include the service cost (the amount of benefits that the employees have earned through their work during the current year), interest cost (the increase in the obligation that occurs because of the passage of time), return on plan assets (the return on amounts invested in the pension fund), amortization of past service costs (the cost of benefits granted for time periods prior to the adoption of the pension plan), and amortization of any gains or losses on pension assets or liabilities if the amounts exceed a threshold referred to as the corridor amount.

LO5 Describe and utilize the minimum liability provision for pension accounting.

The minimum pension liability that should be recorded by a company with a defined benefit pension plan is the amount of the unfunded accumulated benefit obligation. This represents the amount by which the *accumulated benefit obligation exceeds the fair value of the assets* as of the end of the period. The additional minimum liability is the amount of the unfunded accumulated benefit obligation after considering the Accrued Pension Cost (credit balance) or Prepaid Pension Cost (debit balance). If an additional minimum liability amount must be recorded, an equal amount should be recognized as an *intangible asset* (or as a contra-equity item in some cases).

LO6 Explain and demonstrate the proper accounting treatment for pension gains and losses.

Pension gains and losses include gains or losses on both the pension assets and the pension liability. Gains and losses on the pension assets arise when the actual return on assets differs from the expected return. Gains and losses on pension liabilities occur as a result of changes in the actuarial assumptions used to estimate the liability. Pension gains and losses are amortized as a component of pension expense if the amounts are large enough to exceed the specified corridor amount.

LO7 Identify the appropriate accounting treatment and disclosures for postretirement obligations and expenses.

Postretirement benefits are defined as benefits *other than pensions* that employees receive after retirement. Examples of such benefits may include an employer's promise to pay education benefits, legal aid, or relocation costs, but the most significant item in most cases is health-care benefits. Postretirement expense is calculated using a series of components in a manner similar to the calculation of pension expense. However, a company is not required to recognize an amount for the minimum liability for postretirement obligations.

LO8 Analyze financial statements and disclosures related to pensions and postretirement costs.

It is important for any user of the financial statements to understand and analyze the note disclosures for pensions and postretirement obligations in order to determine the components that were used to calculate pension and postretirement expense and the funding status of the plan. Funding status refers to whether the pension plan is overfunded or underfunded. Overfunding occurs when the value of the pension assets is larger than the pension or postretirement obligation and is a favorable indication of the health of the plan. Underfunding occurs when the pension or postretirement obligation is larger than the assets available and is a negative indication of the health of the plan because it indicates that there is some doubt as to the ability of the employer to provide the benefits that have been promised.

LO9 Determine how pensions and postretirement costs affect cash flow.

Pension and postretirement expense are recognized in the income statement on the accrual basis. To determine the amount of cash paid during the period, it is important to use the information in the statement of cash flows. If a positive amount is presented in the operating activities section of the cash flow statement, this is an indication that the amount of cash paid for pensions or postretirement costs was less than the amount recognized as expense. If a negative amount is presented in the operating activities section of the cash flow statement, this is an indication that the amount of cash paid for pensions or postretirement costs was more than the amount recognized as expense.

KEY TERMS

accumulated benefit obligation (p. 702)
accumulated postretirement benefit obligation (p. 716)
actuaries (p. 696)
additional minimum liability (p. 707)
attribution period (p. 716)
corridor approach (p. 711)
defined benefit plan (p. 698)
defined contribution plan (p. 696)
earnings management (p. 723)

expected postretirement benefit obligation (p. 716)
funding status (p. 708)
interest cost (p. 704)
market-related value (p. 712)
minimum pension liability (p. 706)
past service cost (p. 704)
Pension Benefit Guaranty Corporation (p. 699)
pension expense (p. 701)

pension plan (p. 696)
postretirement benefits (p. 714)
projected benefit obligation (p. 702)
return on plan assets (p. 705)
service cost (p. 703)
settlement rate (p. 705)
transition amount (p. 718)
underfunded (p. 699)
unrecognized gain or loss (p. 710)
vested benefit obligation (p. 703)

EXERCISES

LO1, 2   **EXERCISE 15-1   Defined Contribution and Defined Benefit Plans**

Assume that you have recently started a new job and have been told that your employer offers a variety of benefit plans to its employees. The company provides a defined benefit pension plan and a defined contribution plan that can be used to supplement your retirement income.

Required:

1. Explain the differences between a defined benefit pension plan and a defined contribution plan. What factors would be important to you in choosing one of these plans?

2. Assume that you choose the defined contribution plan, but you want to calculate the present value of the retirement benefits that you will be paid upon retirement from your employer. Since you are still young, retirement is many years in the future. List the most important estimates and assumptions you must make in order to calculate the amount of your future retirement pay.

LO2, 3, 4, 5   **EXERCISE 15-2**   **Pension Expense**

The following information relates to the 2005 activity of the defined benefit pension plan of Linsey Corp., a company whose stock is publicly traded:

Service cost	$150,000
Expected and actual return on plan assets	40,000
Interest cost on pension benefit obligation	82,000
Amortization of actuarial loss	15,000
Fair value of plan assets at year end	800,000
Accumulated benefit obligation at year end	750,000
January 1 balance of Prepaid/Accrued Pension Cost	0
Employer contribution to plan during 2005	250,000

Required:

1. Determine the components of pension expense for 2005 and develop the accounting entry to record the pension expense.

2. Determine whether a minimum pension liability is necessary and, if it is, develop the accounting entry to record the minimum liability amount.

3. Indicate what amounts related to the pension would be shown in Linsey's 2005 income statement.

4. Indicate what amounts related to the pension would be shown in Linsey's balance sheet as of December 31, 2005. In what category of the balance sheet would the items be presented?

LO2, 3, 4, 5   **EXERCISE 15-3**   **Pension Expense and Accrued Pension Cost**

The following amounts are related to the defined benefit plan of Kane Company for 2005:

Prepaid pension cost, January 1, 2005	$ 2,000
Service cost	19,000
Interest cost	38,000
Expected and actual return on plan assets	22,000
Amortization of unrecognized prior service cost	52,000
Employer contributions	50,000

The fair value of plan assets exceeds the accumulated benefit obligation at December 31, 2005.

Required:

1. Determine the components of pension expense for 2005 and develop the accounting entry to record the pension expense.

2. Indicate what amounts related to the pension would be shown in Kane's 2005 income statement.

3. Indicate what amounts related to the pension would be shown in Kane's balance sheet as of December 31, 2005. In what category of the balance sheet would the items be presented?

LO2, 3, 4   **EXERCISE 15-4**   **Projected and Accumulated Pension Benefit Obligation**

The following information pertains to Seda Co.'s pension plan:

Actuarial estimate of projected benefit obligation at 1/1/05	$72,000
Assumed discount	10%

Service costs for 2005	$18,000
Pension benefits paid during 2005	$15,000

Required:

1. Develop a memo that explains the difference between the terms *accumulated benefit obligation* and *projected benefit obligation*. When calculating pension expense, which amount should be used? When calculating the minimum pension liability, which amount should be used?

2. Assuming that there were no changes in actuarial estimates during 2005, calculate Seda's projected benefit obligation at December 31, 2005.

3. Give an example of a change in actuarial estimate. How would such a change affect the projected benefit obligation?

LO2, 5   EXERCISE 15-5   Projected and Accumulated Benefit Obligation (CPA adapted)

On June 1, 2004, Ward Corp. established a defined benefit pension plan for its employees. The following information was available at May 31, 2005:

Projected benefit obligation	$14,500,000
Accumulated benefit obligation	12,000,000
Unfunded accrued pension cost	200,000
Plan assets at fair market value	7,000,000
Unrecognized prior service cost	2,550,000

Required:

1. Determine the amount of Ward's minimum pension liability at May 31, 2005.

2. Determine the amount of additional minimum liability that Ward should record at May 31, 2005. Give the journal entry to record the additional liability.

3. Indicate how the amounts related to Ward's pension liability should be presented in the balance sheet as of May 31, 2005. In what category of the balance sheet would the items be presented?

LO2, 3, 5   EXERCISE 15-6   Minimum Liability and Comprehensive Income

The following data relate to Alon Co.'s defined benefit pension plan as of December 31, 2005:

Projected benefit obligation	$280,000
Accumulated benefit obligation	240,000
Fair value of plan assets	100,000
Unrecognized prior service cost	45,000
Accrued pension cost	80,000

Required:

1. Determine the amount of Alon's minimum pension liability at December 31, 2005.

2. Determine the amount of additional minimum liability that Alon should record at December 31, 2005. Give the journal entry to record the additional liability.

3. Indicate how the amounts related to Alon's pension liability should be presented in the balance sheet as of December 31, 2005. In what category of the balance sheet would the items be presented?

LO4, 6   EXERCISE 15-7   Corridor Approach for Gains and Losses

The actuary for the pension plan for Fab Five calculated the following net gains and losses:

Unrecognized Net Gain or Loss

Year ended 2003	$1,200,000 gain
Year ended 2004	500,000 loss
Year ended 2005	800,000 gain

Other information about Fab Five's plan is as follows:

As of January 1	Projected Benefit Obligation	Plan Assets
2003	$6,000,000	$5,000,000
2004	6,600,000	5,600,000
2005	7,200,000	6,200,000

Fab Five has a stable work force of 200 employees. The total service years for all employees is 3,000.

Required: Determine the amount of gain or loss that should be amortized as a component of pension expense for each year 2003 to 2005.

LO4, 7 **EXERCISE 15-8 Postretirement Costs**

Foster Co. must determine the proper amounts related to its defined benefit postretirement plan. The following information pertains to Foster Co.'s postretirement plan for the year 2005:

Service cost	$120,000
Benefit payment	55,000
Interest on the accumulated postretirement benefit obligation	20,000
Unrecognized transition obligation (amortized over 20 years)	200,000
Funding payment by Foster to trustee	0

Required:

1. Develop a memo that indicates the most important differences between pensions and other postretirement costs. Also, indicate how the accounting is different for the two.

2. Determine the components of postretirement expense for 2005 and develop the accounting entry to record the postretirement expense.

3. Indicate what amounts related to the postretirement costs should be shown in Foster's 2005 income statement.

4. Indicate what amounts related to the postretirement costs would be shown in Foster's balance sheet as of December 31, 2005. In what category of the balance sheet would the items be presented?

LO9 **EXERCISE 15-9 Accrual to Cash**

Assume that Jalen Company has recognized $100,000 of pension expense and $200,000 of postretirement expense in its income statement for the year 2005. Also assume that the company had the following account balances at the beginning and end of the year 2005:

Account	Beginning Balance	Ending Balance
Prepaid Pension Cost	$35,000	$20,000
Accrued Postretirement Cost	44,000	50,000

Required: Determine the amount of cash paid (funding) for pensions and for postretirement benefits for 2005.

LO9 **EXERCISE 15-10 Cash to Accrual**

Assume that Weber Company has paid $800,000 in cash to a fund to cover pension and postretirement costs during 2005. Also assume that the company had the following account balances at the beginning and end of the year 2005:

Account	Beginning Balance	Ending Balance
Prepaid Pension Cost	$20,000	$48,000
Accrued Postretirement Cost	44,000	50,000

Required: Determine the combined amount of pension and postretirement expense recognized in Weber's income statement for the year 2005.

LO2, 4 **EXERCISE 15-11** **Pension Expense, Accrual**

Rocha Company has a defined benefit pension plan with the following account balances at January 1, 2005:

Projected Benefit Obligation	$2,300,000
Unrecognized Past Service Costs	350,000
Pension Plan Assets	1,500,000

Rocha Company's actuaries have determined that the service cost for the year ended December 31, 2005, is $420,000. Using a settlement rate of 8 percent, the actual and expected return on plan assets is determined to be $84,000. The average remaining service period of Rocha's employees is 14 years. Rocha made a pension payment of $460,000 during 2005.

Required:

1. Calculate pension expense for 2005.

2. Record the transaction to recognize pension expense for 2005.

3. What is the nature of the Accrued Pension Cost account and how is it reported in the financial statements?

LO2, 4, 5 **EXERCISE 15-12** **Pension Accrual, Minimum Liability**

Sorrenta, Inc. has a defined benefit pension plan with the following account balances at January 1, 2005:

Projected Benefit Obligation	$1,650,000
Unrecognized Past Service Costs	255,000
Pension Plan Assets	1,150,000
Accrued Pension Cost	227,500

Sorrenta's actuaries have determined that the service cost for the year ended December 31, 2005, is $287,000. The average remaining service period of Sorrenta's employees is 15 years. The actual and expected return on plan assets is determined to be $92,000. The expected settlement rate is 9 percent. Sorrenta made a pension payment of $456,000 during 2005. During 2005, $120,000 of benefits was paid to retirees. The accumulated benefit obligation at December 31, 2005, was $1,590,000.

Required:

1. Determine the pension expense for 2005 and prepare the journal entry.

2. Is the pension plan underfunded? Explain.

3. Determine the amounts to be reported in Sorrenta's December 31, 2005, balance sheet for the pension.

LO5 **EXERCISE 15-13** **Minimum Pension Liability—Comprehensive Income**

Conviser, Inc. has a defined benefit pension plan. The following amounts were determined for the year ended December 31, 2005:

Pension expense	$240,000
Average remaining employee service period	18 years
Expected and actual return on plant assets	$65,000
Expected settlement rate	6%
Pension funding payment	$210,000
Benefits paid to retirees	$72,000

The following account balances existed at January 1, 2005:

Projected Benefit Obligation	$960,000
Pension Plan Assets	390,000
Prepaid Pension Cost	80,000

The accumulated benefit obligation at December 31, 2005, was $810,000. The company has no unrecognized past service costs.

Required:

1. Show the effects of the pension in Conviser's balance sheet at December 31, 2005. Ignore income tax effects.
2. How does reporting for additional minimum pension liability differ when a company has no unrecognized past service cost from reporting when there is a balance in the unrecognized past service cost?

LO6 EXERCISE 15-14 **Pension Gains and Losses**

Herbert Company has a defined benefit pension plan and has determined the following amounts for the year ended December 31, 2005:

Expected settlement rate	7%
Service cost	$130,000
Benefits paid to retirees	$54,000

The projected benefit obligation at January 1, 2005, was $2,300,000.

Required:

1. Suppose an update in actuarial assumptions calculated the projected benefit obligation at December 31, 2005, to be $2,800,000. Determine whether an actuarial gain or loss exists and its amount, if any.
2. Identify the nature of any other gains or losses that may result in accounting for pensions. Explain how they might arise.

LO6 EXERCISE 15-15 **Gains and Losses, Corridor Approach**

B12 Company has a defined benefit pension plan and has determined the following amounts for the year ended December 31, 2005:

Expected settlement rate	8%
Service cost	$320,000
Benefits paid to retirees	$140,000
Average remaining service period	16 years

The projected benefit obligation and plan assets at January 1, 2005, were $1,840,000 and $1,630,000, respectively. An update in actuarial assumptions calculated the projected benefit obligation at December 31, 2005, to be $1,800,000. The unrecognized gain on pension assets as of January 1, 2005, was $80,000.

Required:

1. Determine the amount of the actuarial gain or loss.
2. Apply the corridor approach to the actuarial gain or loss. What effect does this amortization have on pension expense?
3. How does the corridor approach give rise to smoothing of pension gains and losses?

LO7 EXERCISE 15-16 **Postretirement Expense**

Ignito, Inc. has a defined benefit postretirement plan. The following information was determined for the postretirement plan for 2005:

Service cost	$86,000
Interest rate on obligation	8%
Actual and expected return on plan assets	$21,000
Fund contribution	$75,000
Average remaining service period of employees	10 years

The following amounts existed at January 1, 2005:

Accumulated Postretirement Benefit Obligation	$800,000
Plan Assets	450,000
Accrued Postretirement Cost	135,000
Unrecognized Past Service Costs	240,000

Required:

1. Calculate postretirement expense for 2005.

2. Prepare the journal entry to record the postretirement expense.

3. Show how the postretirement amounts will be reported in Ignito's 2005 income statement and the December 31, 2005, balance sheet.

4. How does the recognition of a minimum liability for postretirement accounting differ from that for pension accounting?

LO8   **EXERCISE 15-17   Disclosures Related to Pensions**

Dade, Inc. has a defined benefit pension plan. The following amounts were determined for the year ended December 31, 2005:

Service cost	$130,000
Interest cost	48,000
Pension funding payment	258,000
Actual return on plan assets	59,000
Benefits paid to retirees	84,000

The following account balances existed at January 1, 2005:

Projected Benefit Obligation	$880,000
Pension Plan Assets—fair value	350,000

The company has no unrecognized past service costs. The company began the creation of note disclosure related to its pensions as follows.

> **Note 4: Pension Benefits**
> Dade, Inc. offers defined benefit pension plans to its employees as a part of the company's total compensation and benefits program that is designed to attract and retain highly skilled employees. The discount rate for the year is 8.2%, and the expected long-term rate of return on plan assets is 7.5%. The assumed rate of compensation increase used to calculate the PBO is 8%.

Required: Complete the note disclosure for Dade, Inc.'s pension plan for the year ended December 31, 2005.

LO8   **EXERCISE 15-18   Pension Disclosure**

Hondo Car Parts, Inc. had an accumulated benefit obligation at December 31, 2005, of $1,060,000. The company's annual report included the following note related to pensions for 2005.

Note 6: Pension Benefits

Hondo Car Parts, Inc. offers defined benefit pension plans to its employees as a part of the company's total compensation and benefits program that is designed to attract and retain highly skilled employees. The company's pension expense for 2005 consisted of the following:

Service cost	$230,000
Interest cost	46,000
Return on plan assets	(55,000)
Net pension expense	$221,000

The following table describes the change in the projected benefit obligation for the year ended December 31, 2005:

Projected benefit obligation, January 1	$ 960,000
Service cost	230,000
Interest cost	46,000
Benefits paid to retirees	(72,000)
Projected benefit obligation, December 31	$1,164,000

The following table provides the changes in the fair value of the plan assets during 2005:

Fair value of the plan assets at January 1, 2005	$390,000
Actual return on plan assets	55,000
Employer contributions	256,000
Benefits paid	(72,000)
Fair value of the plan assets at December 31, 2005	$629,000

Projected benefit obligation in excess of the fair value of plan assets	$535,000

Required: Show what amounts Hondo Car Parts, Inc. will report in its financial statements for the year ended December 31, 2005.

LO9 **EXERCISE 15-19** **Cash Flow Effects of Pensions**

Eminem, Inc. has a defined benefit pension plan and has provided the following information for 2005:

Balances at January 1, 2005:

Projected pension benefit obligation, January 1, 2005	$1,230,000
Fair value of the plan assets	256,000
Accrued pension cost	45,000

Balances at December 31, 2005:

Accrued pension cost	$ 64,000
Fair value of the plan assets	232,000

Activity during 2005:

Pension benefits paid to employees	$142,000
Actual return on plan assets for the year	23,000

The average remaining service life of employees is 10 years.

Required:

1. Calculate the amount of cash paid for pension plan funding for 2005.
2. Show how the amount from question 1 will appear in the statement of cash flows under the indirect method.

LO5 **EXERCISE 15-20** **Minimum Pension Liability—Comprehensive Income**

Digital, Inc. has a defined benefit pension plan. The following amounts were determined for the year ended December 31, 2005:

Pension expense	$133,000
Actual return on plant assets	23,000
Pension funding payment	129,000
Benefits paid to retirees	88,000

The following account balances existed at January 1, 2005:

Pension Adjustment—Other Comprehensive Loss	$122,000
Pension Plan Assets	450,000
Accrued Pension Cost	134,000

The accumulated benefit obligation at December 31, 2005, was $834,000. The company has no unrecognized past service costs. The income tax rate for 2005 is 30 percent. Net income for 2005 was $165,000.

Required:

1. Show the effects of the pension in Digital's balance sheet at December 31, 2005.

2. Prepare a separate statement of comprehensive income for 2005.

PROBLEMS

LO2, 3, 4, 5, 6   PROBLEM **15-1**   **Comprehensive Pension Problem**

The Louisville Duke Company sponsors a defined benefit pension plan for its 200 employees. The company's actuary provided the following information about the plan:

	January 1, 2005	December 31, 2005
Projected benefit obligation	$3,000,000	$3,500,000
Accumulated benefit obligation	2,700,000	3,000,000
Plan assets (fair value)	1,800,000	2,200,000
Cumulative unrecognized net loss	0	360,000
Unrecognized past service cost	400,000	?
Expected asset return rate		10%
Discount rate (current settlement rate)		10%

The service cost component for employee services rendered for 2005 was computed as $400,000. The actual return on assets for 2005 was $200,000. The company expects the average remaining years of service for employees to be 10 years. Louisville Duke made a funding contribution to the pension plan of $550,000 on December 31, 2005 (which is reflected in the amounts given). Louisville Duke's 2004 balance sheet indicated an accrued pension cost amount of $800,000 and a balance in the Additional Liability account of $100,000.

Required:

1. Indicate the components of pension expense for 2005. Indicate whether the amounts increase or decrease the pension expense and indicate the total pension expense for 2005.

2. Prepare all necessary journal entries for 2005.

3. Indicate the amounts disclosed in the 2005 income statement for the pension plan.

4. Indicate the amounts related to the pension plan that are presented in the balance sheet as of December 31, 2005. In what category of the balance sheet would the items be presented?

Analyze: In what instances does the minimum liability provision apply?

LO3, 4, 5, 6   PROBLEM **15-2**   **Pension Expense and Pension Obligation**

The following is selected information about Flock Company's defined benefit pension plan.

	Year 2006	Year 2005
(in thousands)		
Interest cost	$210	$175
Service cost	190	170
Expected return on plan assets		180
Actual return on plan assets	160	170
Amortization of past service cost	20	20
Employer contributions	300	250
Pension expense	205	175
Benefits paid	190	174
Discount rate	7%	7%

Pension plan assets were $2,000 on 1/1/05. The prior service cost is amortized over 15 years, starting on 1/1/03.

Required:

1. Calculate the balance of the projected benefit obligation on 1/1/06.

2. Calculate the expected rate of return expressed in percent. Assume that the same rate was utilized for both years.

3. Calculate the balance of the unamortized past service cost on 12/31/06 before the amortization entry is made on 1/1/06.

4. Calculate the balance of the pension plan assets on 12/31/05.

5. Calculate the amortization of gains and losses for the year 2005.

Analyze: Calculate the expected return on plan assets for the year 2006 in dollars (round to the nearest thousand dollars).

LO2, 3, 4, 6   **PROBLEM 15-3   Comprehensive Pension Problem**

Consider the following information regarding Smith Company's defined benefit pension plan:

	2006	2005
(in thousands)		
Projected benefit obligation, 12/31	$10,500	$9,500
Accumulated benefit obligation, 12/31	8,500	8,000
Plan assets, 12/31	7,600	8,100
Pension expense	1,500	1,600
Employer contribution to pension plan	1,400	1,600
Unrecognized past service cost, 1/1	1,500	1,400
Accrued pension cost, 1/1		120

Required:

1. For each of the two years, show all journal entries that Smith Company made for its pension plan. Assume that the company contributed cash to its pension plan when the related expense was recognized.

2. Show the balance sheet presentation at 12/31/06, the end of the accounting period.

3. How would your answer to question 1 change if unrecognized past service cost on January 1 was $400 and $500 for the years 2006 and 2005, respectively? Assume that all other given information remained the same.

Analyze: Is an additional liability accrual necessary in 2005? Explain your answer.

LO2, 3, 4, 5, 6   **PROBLEM 15-4   Comprehensive Pension Problem** (CPA adapted)

The following information pertains to Sparta Co.'s defined benefit pension plan:

Discount rate	8%
Expected rate of return	10%
Average service life	12 years

At January 1, 2005:

Projected benefit obligation	$600,000
Fair value of pension plan assets	720,000
Unrecognized past service cost	240,000
Unamortized past pension gain	96,000

At December 31, 2005:

| Projected benefit obligation | $910,000 |
| Fair value of pension plan assets | 825,000 |

Service cost for 2005 was $90,000. There were no contributions made or benefits paid during the year. Sparta's unfunded accrued pension liability was $8,000 at January 1, 2005. Sparta uses the straight-line method of amortization over the maximum period permitted.

Required: For items 1 through 5, calculate the amounts to be recognized as components of Sparta's unfunded accrued pension liability at December 31, 2005. Amounts to be calculated:

1. Interest cost
2. Expected return on plan assets
3. Actual return on plan assets
4. Amortization of past service costs
5. Minimum amortization of unrecognized pension gain

Analyze: For items 6 through 10, determine whether the component increases or decreases Sparta's unfunded accrued pension liability. Items to be answered:

6. Service cost
7. Deferral of gain on plan assets
8. Actual return on plan assets
9. Amortization of past service costs
10. Amortization of unrecognized pension gain

LO5 PROBLEM 15-5 **Minimum Liability—Three Years**

Clark Company did not have a balance in Prepaid or Accrued Pension Cost prior to 2005. Prior to 2005, the company's pension plan had been overfunded, and as a result the company had not previously recorded a minimum liability provision. Assume that the company had the following amounts for the years 2005, 2006, and 2007:

	2005	2006	2007
Projected benefit obligation at year end	$8,000,000	$8,200,000	$7,800,000
Accumulated benefit obligation at year end	7,000,000	7,400,000	7,200,000
Fair value of pension assets at year end	6,500,000	6,700,000	7,250,000
Pension expense	1,200,000	1,220,000	1,240,000
Funding payment	1,000,000	1,110,000	1,140,000
Unrecognized past service cost	2,000,000	1,800,000	1,600,000

Required:

1. Determine the amount of the additional minimum liability that should be recognized in each period.

2. Determine the amounts that should be presented on the balance sheet as of December 31 of each year.

Analyze: How would your answers differ if there had been no unrecognized past service costs in any of the years?

LO5   PROBLEM 15-6   **Minimum Liability—Three Years**

Gary Company did not have a balance in Prepaid or Accrued Pension Cost prior to 2005. Prior to 2005, the company's pension plan had been overfunded, and as a result the company had not previously recorded a minimum liability provision. Assume that the company had the following amounts for the years 2005, 2006, and 2007:

	2005	2006	2007
Projected benefit obligation at year end	$8,000,000	$8,200,000	$7,800,000
Accumulated benefit obligation at year end	7,000,000	7,400,000	7,200,000
Fair value of pension assets at year end	6,500,000	6,700,000	7,250,000
Pension expense	1,000,000	1,110,000	1,140,000
Funding payment	1,200,000	1,220,000	1,240,000
Unrecognized past service cost	2,000,000	1,800,000	1,600,000

Required:

1. Determine the amount of the additional pension liability that should be recognized in each period.
2. Determine the amounts that should be presented in the balance sheet of December 31 of each year.

Analyze: How would your answers differ if there had been no unrecognized past service costs in any of the years?

LO7   PROBLEM 15-7   **Postretirement Obligation—Two Years**

Foster Company must determine the proper amounts related to its defined benefit postretirement plan. The following information pertains to Foster's postretirement plan for the years 2005 and 2006:

	2005	2006
Service cost	$120,000	$150,000
Accumulated benefit obligation, January 1	$700,000	$900,000
Unrecognized past service cost	$200,000	?
Discount rate	10%	10%
Actual and expected return on assets	8%	8%
Unrecognized gains and losses	0	0
Funding payment made December 31	$100,000	$100,000
Average attribution period for employees (in years)	12	12

Prior to 2005, Foster Company had not funded any amount for postretirement costs.

Required:

1. Determine the components of postretirement expense for 2005 and 2006.
2. Indicate what amounts related to the postretirement costs should be shown in Foster's 2005 and 2006 income statements.
3. Indicate what amounts related to the postretirement costs would be shown in Foster's balance sheet as of December 31, 2005 and 2006. In what category of the balance sheet would the items be presented?

Analyze: If the postretirement plan is amended in 2007 to give retirees more benefits, what effect will this action have on net income in that year? Explain your answer.

LO4, 7, 9   **PROBLEM 15-8   Pensions and the Statement of Cash Flows**

The following represents selected information from Hainz Company's statement of cash flows, direct format, for the year ended 12/31/05:

Cash paid to pension plan	$350,000
Cash paid for postretirement benefit plan	200,000

The reconciliation of net income to cash from operations shows the following:

Increase in accrued pension cost	$100,000
Increase in prepaid postretirement cost	40,000

A review of the notes to the financial statements shows that the funds paid $280,000 in pension benefits and $140,000 in postretirement benefits to retired employees.

Required:

1. Calculate pension expense.
2. Calculate postretirement expense.
3. Show the financial statement presentations in the company's statement of cash flows (indirect method) and income statement relating to pension and postretirement benefits. Indicate in what section of the financial statements these items are presented.
4. Can the changes in the accrued pension cost account and the prepaid postretirement cost account be combined or offset? Justify your answer.

Communicate: An employee of Hainz Company asks whether pension payments drain cash from the company in the year of the payments. What information should be contained in a memo that responds to this question?

LO2, 4, 5, 6   **PROBLEM 15-9   Comprehensive Pension Problem**

Consider the following selected information regarding Advanced Systems's defined benefit pension plan for the year 2005:

(in millions)	
Projected pension benefit obligation, 1/1	$110
Unamortized gain, 1/1, amortized over 10 years	20
Plan assets, 1/1	70
Pension benefits paid to employees	14
Pension expense for the year	18
Prepaid pension cost, 1/1	3 debit
Accrued pension cost, 12/31	2 credit
Actual return on plan assets for the year	6
Accumulated pension benefit obligation, 12/31	88

Required:

1. Calculate the contributions that were made to Advanced Systems's pension plan for the year 2005.
2. Calculate the amortization of gains or losses utilizing the corridor approach.
3. Calculate the ending balance of pension plan assets on 12/31/05.
4. Calculate the minimum liability and any potential additional minimum liability.

Analyze: Prior to the introduction of the corridor approach, what was the concern that companies had regarding the valuation of pension assets and liabilities at fair market values? If a corridor approach were not required, how would it affect the amounts companies recognize for pension expense?

LO2, 4, 5, 6 **PROBLEM 15-10 Comprehensive Pension Problem**

The following information relates to Milton Company's defined benefit pension plan for the year 2005:

Projected benefit obligation, 1/1	$1,800,000
Unrecognized past service cost, amortized over 10 years	1,200,000
Service cost for the year	900,000
Unrecognized gains or losses	0
Pension plan assets, 1/1	1,000,000
Pension benefits paid during the year	400,000
Employer contributions to the pension plan during the year	1,100,000
Actual return on plan assets	40,000
Accumulated benefit obligation, 12/31	2,300,000
Accrued pension cost, 1/1/05	150,000
Discount rate	8%
Expected rate of return on plan assets	10%

Required:

1. Compute the balance of the pension plan assets on 12/31/05.
2. Compute pension expense for the year.
3. Compute the minimum pension liability and additional minimum liability (if any).
4. Give the journal entry(ies) relating to the pension plan for the year 2005.
5. Compute the balance of the projected benefit obligation on 12/31/05.

Analyze: If Milton Company wished to decrease its pension liability, which estimates or assumptions might be altered? Explain your answer.

LO2, 3, 4, 5, 6, 8 **PROBLEM 15-11 Comprehensive Pension Problem**

Smith Corporation sponsors a defined benefit pension plan covering substantially all of its employees. The following information is available from the company's accounting system, the actuary, and the fund trustee for the year 2005:

Projected benefit obligation, 1/1	$100,000
Accumulated benefit obligation, 1/1	85,000
Vested benefits, 1/1	65,000
Pension plan assets, 1/1	83,000
Service cost for the year	12,000
Unrecognized past service costs, 1/1	30,000
Unamortized gain	20,000
Actual return on pension plan assets for the year	6,000
Employer contributions to pension plan	15,000
Benefits paid to employees	9,000
Average remaining service period	10 years

Smith discloses the following assumptions:

Discount rate	7%
Expected long-term ROR	8%
Expected compensation rate increase	3%

Required:

1. Calculate pension expense.
2. Calculate the balance of pension plan assets on 12/31/05.
3. Calculate the balance of the projected benefit obligation on 12/31/05.
4. Calculate the amount of the unamortized gain on 12/31/05 (after accrual of current-year expense).

Analyze: Describe the difference between the projected benefit obligation and the accumulated benefit obligation.

LO2, 3, 4, 5, 6, 8   **PROBLEM 15-12   Comprehensive Pension Problem**

The following selected information is taken from the financial statements of Adams Company for the year 2005:

Prepaid pension cost, 1/1/05	$ 50,000
Prepaid pension cost, 12/31/05	60,000
Additional minimum liability, 1/1/05	0
Additional minimum liability, 12/31/05	80,000
Pension expense	120,000
Pension adjustment—other comprehensive income	10,000
Unrecognized past service cost	70,000

Required:

1. Show all journal entries that Adams Company made related to its pension plan.
2. Calculate the minimum pension liability.
3. How is the pension plan reflected on the financial statements for 2005?

Analyze: Describe what the given information communicates to financial statement users regarding the funding status of the company's pension plan.

LO7   **PROBLEM 15-13   Comprehensive Postretirement Problem**

The following information relates to Weiss Company's postretirement benefit plan for the year 2005:

Accumulated postretirement benefit obligation, 1/1	$1,000,000
Unrecognized past service cost	300,000
Service cost for the year	100,000
Unrecognized losses	50,000
Plan assets, 1/1	800,000
Unamortized transition obligation, 1/1	0
Postretirement benefits paid to retirees during the current year	120,000
Employer contributions to the postretirement plan during the current year	110,000
Actual return on plan assets	(50,000)
Accrued postretirement liability, 1/1	10,000
Average remaining service period	15 years

Assumptions:

Discount rate	7%
Expected rate of return on plan assets	9%
Health-care trend rate	4%

Required:

1. Compute the postretirement expense for the year.
2. Compute the ending balance in postretirement plan assets on 12/31/05.
3. Show the journal entry(ies) made by the company relating to its postretirement benefit plan.

Analyze: When the Weiss Company adopted *SFAS No. 106* in 1992, it chose immediate recognition of its relatively large transition obligation. Suppose instead that the company had used the other alternative acceptable under *SFAS No. 106*. Describe how this would have affected the company's income and earnings per share for the current year.

CASES

LO1, 2, 4 **FINANCIAL REPORTING CASE 15-1** **Pension Components** (CPA adapted)

Essex Company has a single-employer defined benefit pension plan and a compensation plan for future vacations for its employees.

Required:

1. Define the interest cost component of pension expense for a period. How should Essex determine its interest cost component of pension expense for a period?

2. Define past service cost. How should Essex account for past service cost? Why?

LO2, 3, 4, 5, 6 **FINANCIAL REPORTING CASE 15-2** **Pension Components** (CPA adapted)

At December 31, 2005, as a result of its single-employer defined benefit pension plan, Bighorn Co. had an unrecognized net loss and an unfunded accrued pension cost. Bighorn's pension plan and its actuarial assumptions have not changed since it began operations in 2001. Bighorn has made annual contributions to the plan.

Required:

1. Identify the components of net pension cost that should be recognized in Bighorn's 2005 financial statements.

2. What circumstances caused Bighorn's
   a. unrecognized net loss?
   b. unfunded accrued pension cost?

3. How should Bighorn compute its minimum pension liability and any additional pension liability?

LO1, 2, 7 **CRITICAL THINKING CASE 15-3** **Postretirement Costs of Polaroid**

The following is an excerpt from a letter sent to the employees of **Polaroid Corporation** on October 12, 2001.

> Today, Polaroid Corporation took the painful but necessary step of voluntarily filing for reorganization under Chapter 11 of the U.S. Bankruptcy Code. This action became inevitable, particularly in recent weeks, as our revenues continued their sharp decline and our liquidity situation further deteriorated.
>
> As part of our need to reduce costs substantially, it is with great regret that we have terminated the retiree health and life insurance plans, as well as severance payments for former U.S. employees. It is important to note at this point that you have an option to continue your medical coverage in the Polaroid health plans under the Consolidated Omnibus Budget Reconciliation Act of 1985 (COBRA). If you choose this option you will pay the full unsubsidized premium plus a 2% administrative fee. For additional information about this option please call the Fidelity Benefits Connection at 1 800 210 4015. We are also notifying the Pension Benefit Guaranty Corporation (PBGC), a federal agency, about our Chapter 11 filing. We will cooperate with the PBGC as it assesses our pension status and outlook and continue to operate our plan in the normal manner. Retirees will be receiving a detailed information packet in the mail shortly.

The notes to the financial statements of December 31, 2000, contained the following disclosures:

(in millions)	
Net periodic postretirement benefit cost	$ 11.5
Net periodic pension cost/(benefit)	(18.0)
Projected benefit pension obligation	1,196.8
Fair value of pension plan assets at year end	1,388.5
Accumulated postretirement benefit obligation at year end	218.2
Fair value of postretirement plan assets at year end	0

Required:

1. Discuss the nature of the obligation for pensions and postretirement obligations. Do the obligations constitute *legal* obligations?

2. Why was the fair value of the postretirement plan assets at December 31, 2000, equal to zero?

3. Polaroid took the rather drastic action of eliminating health insurance and life insurance coverage for its employees and retirees. What amount of liability did the company eliminate as a result of that action?

4. Most companies have sought methods to limit their liability for postretirement obligations, especially health-care costs. Instead of eliminating the coverage for employees, what are examples of actions that companies have taken to reduce their exposure?

LO4, 7 **RESEARCH CASE 15-4** **Accounting for Transition Items**

The treatment of the transition item upon adoption of *SFAS No. 87*, "Employers' Accounting for Pensions," differed from that under *SFAS No. 106*, "Employers' Accounting for Postretirement Benefits Other than Pensions." Research these pronouncements and answer the following questions:

Required:

1. What is a transition item? How does it arise?

2. Describe the most significant differences between *SFAS No. 87* and *SFAS No. 106* in terms of the accounting treatment of the transition item.

3. Outline the potential financial statement implications of those differences.

4. What justification for those differences can be made?

LO4, 5, 7 **CRITICAL THINKING CASE 15-5** **Pension Estimates**

Accounting for defined benefit pensions and postretirement benefit plans other than pensions requires extensive estimates. These include employee turnover, longevity, and several rate estimates. In accounting for pensions and for postretirement benefit plans, companies must estimate a discount rate and an expected rate of return on plan assets. In addition, companies must estimate a compensation trend rate for pension plans and a health-care cost trend rate for postretirement benefit plans. Actuaries typically assist with this estimation process. However, it is ultimately the company that decides what rates it will use and which actuary it will hire. The rates chosen may significantly influence accounting accruals. In fact, for some companies with large plans, even a fractional change in these rates can significantly affect the company's expenses and obligations. Recent empirical studies suggest that companies may utilize the rate assumptions involved in accounting for pensions and postretirement benefits to manage their earnings. Earnings management generally represents an undesirable consequence of flexibility.

Required:

1. Briefly describe how each rate assumption may affect pension and postretirement benefit accruals and/or obligations.

2. Use an example to illustrate how a company could manage its earnings by choosing either a higher or a lower rate.

3. What factors facilitate earnings management with respect to defined benefit pension plans? Focus on (a) inherent characteristics of pension and other postretirement benefit plans and (b) accounting for pensions and other postretirement benefit plans.

LO4, 5 **ETHICS CASE 15-6** **Flexibility in Accounting for Pensions**

On December 9, 2003, the chief financial officer of Schoen Company enters the office of Maggie Flowers to share with her the news that the Dow Jones Industrial Average (DJIA) has just reached 10,000 points for the first time in 18 months. Maggie is the chief accountant for Schoen Company, a manufacturer of high-technology electronics components. Since 1958, Schoen Company has sponsored a defined benefit pension plan that covers substantially all of its full-time employees. Many of the company's current employees are nearing retirement. Thus, the company's accumulated and projected pension benefit obligations are very significant.

The CFO, Jerry Green, is very pleased about the positive stock market news. He asks Maggie to show him the company's pension plan numbers and disclosures for the upcoming reporting period. After reviewing the information, he tells Maggie that recent market and economic changes warrant some changes in the pension rate assumptions. He asks Maggie to increase the expected rate of return on plan assets from 8 percent to 8.75 percent, and the discount rate from 5.5 percent to 6 percent.

For the past few years, the actual returns on pension plan assets have been either negative or significantly below the 8 percent expected rate. Maggie asks why these changes are necessary. Jerry indicates that the increase in the expected rate of return is justified by the recent stock market gains and that the increase in the discount rate is justified because of rising interest rates and also to preserve conservatism. Jerry assures Maggie that he has already discussed the changes with the actuary and points out that the company's new rates will be well within the rate ranges set forth in the current edition of the AICPA's *Accounting Trends and Techniques*. He asks Maggie to recalculate the pension numbers utilizing the new assumptions and to take care of all necessary filings.

Maggie's calculations show that the increase in the rates will reduce pension expense slightly and that the increase in the discount rate will significantly reduce the reported pension obligations and the funding requirement and eliminate the necessity for an additional minimum liability accrual. Maggie is aware that the additional funding required under the current rates would cause cash flow problems for the company. Maggie, who worked in the Department of Labor's pension benefits division prior to joining the company, is concerned that the changes may not be justified.

Required:

1. Is Maggie faced with an ethical dilemma? If so, describe the issues.
2. Who will be affected by the decision that Maggie makes?
3. What values and principles are likely to influence her decision?
4. What alternative actions might Maggie consider?
5. a. Whose interest is most important?
   b. Which values and principles are most important?
   c. Which of the possible consequences will do the most good or cause the least harm?
   d. Which consideration is most important?
6. What would you do if you were Maggie?

LO8

ETHICS

ETHICS CASE 15-7   The Income-Generating Power of IBM's Pension Plan

On January 28, 2003, the new CEO of **IBM**, Samuel J. Palmisano, astounded his board members by announcing that he would cut his own bonus by 50 percent and share these funds with 20 of his top executives.[25] Bonus plans are a popular method of motivating and rewarding employees; however, typically they are not available to the majority of a company's employees. Employee-sponsored pension plans, on the other hand, typically are available to the majority of full-time employees.

There are two common types of pension plans: defined benefit and defined contribution pension plans. Accounting for defined contribution plans presents few accounting issues. However, accounting for defined benefit plans gives rise to complex accounting and business issues. Accounting issues include choosing appropriate pension rates (the discount rate, expected rate of return on pension plan assets, and rates of compensation increase), and business issues include selecting the amount of pension plan funding. The decisions that companies make regarding these issues can significantly affect their operating income and net income.

Pension plans typically add costs to a company's total compensation and tend to give rise to pension expense. When stock market returns are high, pension expense may be low;

---

25 Spencer E. Ante, "The New Blue," *BusinessWeek*, March 17, 2003, pp. 80–88.

in fact, the pension plan may even generate income. During extended periods of stock market declines, pension expense tends to increase. However, that is not always the case. During the past few years, IBM has consistently recognized income from its defined benefit pension plans. For example, IBM derived pretax income of $917 million, $1,025 million, $896 million, and $638 million from its U.S. plans during the years 2002, 2001, 2000, and 1999, respectively.[26],[27] In fact, approximately 10 percent of the company's income for the year 2001 was generated by pension plan income.

How is it possible for IBM to consistently recognize positive income from its pension plan, especially during years when actual returns are negative? There are two primary reasons: (1) Pension cost is calculated utilizing expected instead of actual returns, and (2) IBM utilized return rates between 8.5 and 10 percent during those years. Thus, while the actual return on IBM's pension plan assets was negative $2.405 billion during the year 2001, the company's pension cost calculation included a positive return of $4.202 billion.

Negative market (and pension plan) returns persisted. In its 10-K filing with the SEC, IBM announced that effective January 1, 2003, it had reduced its expected rate of return to 8 percent, which was expected to decrease income for the year 2003.[28] However, another pension-related action by IBM mitigated this effect. In December 2002, IBM announced that it would contribute $3.95 billion in cash and stock to its pension plan.[29] In contrast, in several prior years, IBM had contributed little or no funds to its plan. These additional funds created a significantly higher asset base to which the new lower expected return rate was applied, thus mitigating the effect of the decreased rate. So IBM still expects to derive positive income from its pension plan, continuing to boost its bottom line.

Required:

1. What are the ethical implications of relying on pension income to increase operating and net income?

2. Can accounting for defined benefit pension plans provide opportunities for earnings management?

3. Can the income-increasing effect of a positive expected rate of return continue to depress pension cost or generate income from pension plans? What provision of *SFAS No. 87* may prevent this from occurring?

4. Were pension plans intended to generate income for the sponsoring employer?

5. During the year 2000, IBM increased its expected rate of return from 9.5 to 10 percent and also decreased its discount rate from 7.75 to 7.25 percent. What effect do these two rate changes have?

LO1 **COMMUNICATION CASE 15-8   Pension Plan Choices**

As the chief financial officer for a company that is now profitable and stable, you are responsible for submitting a report to the board of directors concerning the effects of providing retirement benefits to employees. The board is choosing between a defined benefit plan and a defined contribution plan and would like to know how each of the plans will affect the company's financial statements.

Required: Prepare a written report comparing the financial statement effects of defined contribution and defined benefit plans.

LO7 **ANALYSIS CASE 15-9   Impact of Pension Assumptions**

One of the most difficult issues in pension accounting is understanding how changes in the underlying events and assumptions can affect the projected benefit obligation. The following table lists numerous events and changes in pension assumptions.

---

26 IBM, 2001 Annual Report.

27 IBM, 2002 10-K filing.

28 Ibid.

29 "IBM Contributes $3.95 Billion to Pension," January 1, 2003, available at:
   http://www.charlotte.com/mld/observer/business/4854266.htm?1c. Accessed 4/20/04.

Required: Complete the table by determining the impact on pension expense and projected benefit obligation for each change in assumption. The first row is completed as an example.

Change in Pension Assumption	Impact Change Would Have on Projected Benefit Obligation
1. Increase in discount (settlement) rate	Decrease PBO
2. Increase in expected return on plan assets	
3. Decrease in expected future compensation levels	
4. Increase in expected lifespan of retirees	
5. Increase in average remaining service life of employees	
6. Decrease in discount (settlement) rate	
7. Payment of benefits	
8. Increase in benefits because of plan amendment	
9. Increase in expected future compensation levels	

LO4, 7 COMMUNICATION CASE 15-10   Determining Pension Expense

As the controller for your company, you are asked to provide information to management concerning the company's pension plan.

Required: Prepare written responses to the following questions:

1. If your company decides to initiate a defined benefit pension plan and the company will recognize pension expense each period, what factors will determine each period's pension expense?

2. How will each element of pension expense affect total pension expense for the period (increase, decrease, or uncertain)?

3. What is the difference between the accumulated pension obligation and the projected pension obligation? What amount will appear in the balance sheet?

LO2 ANALYSIS CASE 15-11   Defined Benefit Pension Plans

As the controller for Rose Corp., you are required to account for the company's defined benefit pension plan. During January 2006, you are presented with the following information about the plan. On January 1, 2005, Rose Corp.'s projected benefit obligation was $4,300,000. On that date the fair value of plan assets was also $4,300,000. During 2005, Rose Corp. paid benefits to retirees of $285,000 and contributed an additional $326,000 to the pension plan. The service cost associated with the plan during 2005 was $210,000. Rose Corp. assumes a 6 percent settlement rate and expects a return of 8 percent on the plan assets. The actual return on plan assets during 2005 was $273,000.

Required:

1. Determine the projected benefit obligation at December 31, 2005.

2. Determine the fair value of plan assets at December 31, 2005.

3. Calculate pension expense for 2005.

ON THE WEB

The following exercises, activities, and problems are available on the *Intermediate Accounting* website. Use these resources to reinforce your understanding of the topics presented in this chapter.

- CPA-Adapted Simulations
- Interpreting the Accounting Standards
- Extending the Global Focus
- Extending the Ethics Discussion
- Mastering the Spreadsheet
- Career Snapshots

- Annual Report Project
- ACE Practice Tests
- Flashcards
- Glossary
- Check Figures for Text Problems
- PowerPoint Presentations

SOLUTIONS: CHECK YOUR UNDERSTANDING

Types of Pension Plans (p. 700)

1. A defined contribution plan is a type of employee pension plan in which plan contributions are defined, but the amount that will be paid upon retirement is not known until retirement. A defined benefit plan is a type of employee pension plan in which the amount of future benefits is fixed, but an employer's contributions vary depending on the assumptions about how much the fund will earn.

2. When the assets of a pension plan are less than the future pension liability, the pension plan is referred to as underfunded. This may be cause for concern by employees in that the employer may be at risk of not being able to meet the obligations of the plan. Investors may look poorly upon this situation in that it may indicate that the company has not planned sufficiently for its obligations to its employees.

3. The Pension Benefit Guaranty Corporation (PBGC) is a national insurer of pension plans. When a company becomes bankrupt and cannot meet its pension obligation or when a pension plan becomes insolvent for other reasons, the PBGC assumes the pension liability and will pay the retirement benefits (usually at a reduced level).

Accounting for a Defined Benefit Plan (p. 714)

1. The projected benefit obligation is measured using assumptions concerning future salary increases if the pension benefit formula is based on future compensation levels. The accumulated benefit obligation differs from the projected benefit obligation in that it includes no assumptions about future compensation levels.

2. Measurement of the vested benefit obligation is not based on the employee's remaining in the service of the employer. It is the amount that the employee is allowed to withdraw from the retirement fund if the employee leaves the company before retirement (for example, when an employee takes another job).

3. The FASB believes that it is important to record this liability if a pension plan is underfunded. A pension plan is underfunded if the pension plan assets are less than the pension plan liability.

4. Pension gains and losses can originate from changes in the pension assets or changes in the projected benefit obligation.

Postretirement Obligations (p. 719)

1. Education benefits, legal aid, relocation costs, and health-care benefits are examples of postretirement benefits.

2. Prior to *SFAS No. 106*, many companies did not record the expense for postretirement costs prior to payment. Essentially, companies used a pay-as-you-go method, did not record the obligation for postretirement costs as a liability on their financial statements, and often did not even provide note disclosure of the obligation.

3. The accumulated postretirement benefit obligation is a measure of the present value of the postretirement benefits attributed to employee service up to the date of measurement. It does not consider any additional benefits that may be earned by employees for future service. The expected postretirement benefit obligation is a measure of the present value of all postretirement benefits expected to be earned by employees by the time they retire.

Presentation and Analysis of Pensions and Postretirement Plans (p. 725)

1. Companies may see the overfunded plan as a source of cash and may access a portion of the overfunding to meet other financial needs. Companies with an overfunded plan may be potential merger or takeover targets, as other companies may want to use the overfunding to finance their future activities.

2. Under *IAS No. 19*, pension plan assets and reimbursement rights should be measured at fair value.

3. Service cost, interest cost, contributions by plan participants, actuarial gains and losses, foreign currency exchange rate changes, benefits paid, plan amendments, business combinations, divestitures, curtailments, settlements, and special termination benefits.

Impact of Pension and Postretirement Costs on Cash Flow (p. 727)

1. Accrued Postretirement Obligation, Postretirement Expense, Accrued Pension Cost, Prepaid Pension Cost, Pension Expense.

2. The increase in the accrued pension cost should be added in the operating activities section of the statement of cash flows under the indirect method.

CPA-ADAPTED SIMULATION

This simulation asks you to complete various tasks related to a company's annual financial statements. If your instructor has signed up for CPAexcel™, you can do the work online at **www.cpaexcel.com/hmco**. You may also do the simulation manually.

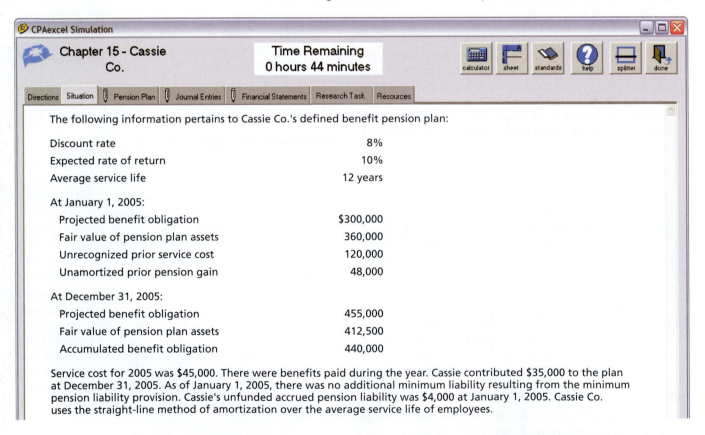

CPAexcel Simulation

Chapter 15 - Cassie Co.

Time Remaining
0 hours 44 minutes

calculator | sheet | standards | help | splitter | done

Directions | Situation | Pension Plan | Journal Entries | Financial Statements | Research Task | Resources

The following information pertains to Cassie Co.'s defined benefit pension plan:

Discount rate	8%
Expected rate of return	10%
Average service life	12 years
At January 1, 2005:	
Projected benefit obligation	$300,000
Fair value of pension plan assets	360,000
Unrecognized prior service cost	120,000
Unamortized prior pension gain	48,000
At December 31, 2005:	
Projected benefit obligation	455,000
Fair value of pension plan assets	412,500
Accumulated benefit obligation	440,000

Service cost for 2005 was $45,000. There were benefits paid during the year. Cassie contributed $35,000 to the plan at December 31, 2005. As of January 1, 2005, there was no additional minimum liability resulting from the minimum pension liability provision. Cassie's unfunded accrued pension liability was $4,000 at January 1, 2005. Cassie Co. uses the straight-line method of amortization over the average service life of employees.

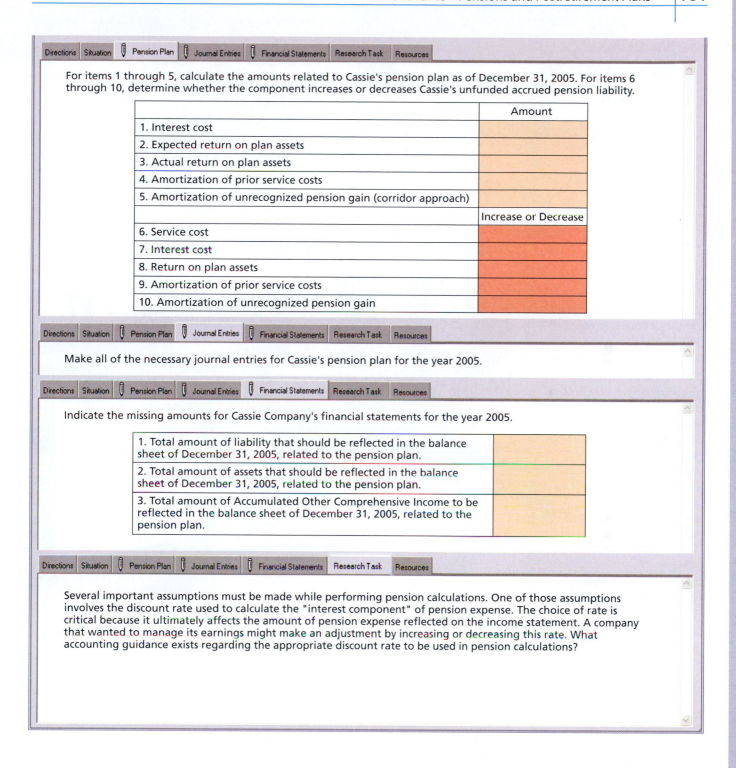

Directions Situation 🖉 Pension Plan 🖉 Journal Entries 🖉 Financial Statements Research Task Resources

For items 1 through 5, calculate the amounts related to Cassie's pension plan as of December 31, 2005. For items 6 through 10, determine whether the component increases or decreases Cassie's unfunded accrued pension liability.

	Amount
1. Interest cost	
2. Expected return on plan assets	
3. Actual return on plan assets	
4. Amortization of prior service costs	
5. Amortization of unrecognized pension gain (corridor approach)	
	Increase or Decrease
6. Service cost	
7. Interest cost	
8. Return on plan assets	
9. Amortization of prior service costs	
10. Amortization of unrecognized pension gain	

Directions Situation 🖉 Pension Plan 🖉 Journal Entries 🖉 Financial Statements Research Task Resources

Make all of the necessary journal entries for Cassie's pension plan for the year 2005.

Directions Situation 🖉 Pension Plan 🖉 Journal Entries 🖉 Financial Statements Research Task Resources

Indicate the missing amounts for Cassie Company's financial statements for the year 2005.

1. Total amount of liability that should be reflected in the balance sheet of December 31, 2005, related to the pension plan.	
2. Total amount of assets that should be reflected in the balance sheet of December 31, 2005, related to the pension plan.	
3. Total amount of Accumulated Other Comprehensive Income to be reflected in the balance sheet of December 31, 2005, related to the pension plan.	

Directions Situation 🖉 Pension Plan 🖉 Journal Entries 🖉 Financial Statements Research Task Resources

Several important assumptions must be made while performing pension calculations. One of those assumptions involves the discount rate used to calculate the "interest component" of pension expense. The choice of rate is critical because it ultimately affects the amount of pension expense reflected on the income statement. A company that wanted to manage its earnings might make an adjustment by increasing or decreasing this rate. What accounting guidance exists regarding the appropriate discount rate to be used in pension calculations?

Accounting for Income Taxes

FINANCIAL REPORTING CASE

PFIZER BENEFITS FROM TAX LAW

Understanding the difference between calculating income taxes for tax purposes and for financial reporting purposes can be critical in reducing the tax buden of large companies like Pfizer Inc.

Pfizer   If you were to review the financial statements of many U.S. companies with large annual revenues for a particular fiscal year, you might be surprised to learn that many of these companies paid little or no income tax to the Internal Revenue Service for the same period. There are instances of companies that actually had billions in earnings receiving tax refunds. A study published by the Institute on Taxation and Economic Policy titled "Corporate Income Taxes in the 1990s" found that Pfizer Inc., a major U.S. pharmaceutical company, reported earnings of nearly $1.2 billion in 1998, yet received a refund from the federal government of $197 million, a negative 16.5 percent tax rate.[1]

While it might make sense to think that U.S. companies that have significant amounts of revenue would pay equally significant amounts of taxes to the IRS each year, this is not always the case. This discrepancy results from the common practice of companies using one set of accounting rules for the financial statements provided to

---

1 "Pfizer: Greater Transparency in Tax Reporting," *Responsible Wealth*, available at: **www. responsiblewealth.org/shareholder/2003/Pfizer.html**. Accessed 6/18/03.

Pfizer

Consolidated Statement of Income
Pfizer Inc and Subsidiary Companies

	YEAR ENDED DECEMBER 31		
MILLIONS EXCEPT PER COMMON SHARE DATA	**2003**	**2002**	**2001**
Income from continuing operations before provision for taxes on income, minority interests and cumulative effect of change in accounting principles	3,263	11,796	9,984
Provision for taxes on income	1,621	2,609	2,433
Minority interests	3	6	14
Income from continuing operations before cumulative effect of change in accounting principles	1,639	9,181	7,537
Discontinued operations:			
Income from operations of discontinued businesses and product lines—net of tax	16	278	251
Gains on sales of discontinued businesses and product lines—net of tax	2,285	77	—
Discontinued operations—net of tax	2,301	355	251
Income before cumulative effect of change in accounting principles	3,940	9,536	7,788
Cumulative effect of change in accounting principles— net of tax	(30)	(410)	—
Net income	$ 3,910	$ 9,126	$ 7,788

Consolidated Statement of Cash Flows
Pfizer Inc and Subsidiary Companies

	YEAR ENDED DECEMBER 31		
MILLIONS OF DOLLARS	**2003**	**2002**	**2001**
Supplemental Cash Flow Information			
Non-cash transactions:			
Acquisition of Pharmacia, net of transaction costs	$55,871	$ —	$ —
Cash paid during the period for:			
Income taxes	$ 2,905	$ 1,480	$ 957
Interest	350	256	291

stockholders and analysts and a different set of accounting rules for their income tax calculations. Specifically, companies may be allowed certain deductions and credits under tax law that are not allowed under GAAP standards for financial reporting. In fact, the difference between the amount of income tax expense reflected on the income statement and the amount of income tax reported on the tax form can be staggering.

In this chapter, we will review the presentation of these amounts in Pfizer Inc.'s financial statements for 2003. Understanding the differences between the calculation of income taxes for tax purposes and their calculation for financial reporting purposes is critical to the accountant, the analyst, and the potential investor. Take a look at the above excerpt from Pfizer's 2003 consolidated statement of income. The provision for taxes on income was reported at $1,621 million for the year ended December 31, 2003. But if you review the consolidated statement of cash flows to find the amount of cash paid for taxes during the period, the amount is reported at $2,905 million. A review of the balance sheet for this period also reveals deferred taxes of $13,238 million. The calculations that underlie these amounts are based on different accounting rules—GAAP for financial reporting purposes and the tax codes for the various taxing authorities under which Pfizer divisions operate.

EXAMINING THE CASE

1. Why might a company's net income as reported on its income statement differ from its income as calculated for tax purposes?

2. What trend can you identify with regard to the actual cash payments made for taxes by Pfizer for 2001 through 2003? Express the trend in numeric terms.

Accounting for Tax Purposes Versus Accounting for Financial Reporting Purposes

By this point in your accounting studies, you have learned that the accounting used in issuing financial statements is not the same as the accounting used for tax purposes. In essence, most large companies keep two sets of books, one for financial accounting purposes (we will call this "per book") and the other for tax purposes ("per tax"). There is nothing unusual or unethical about keeping two sets of books. In large measure, the divergence of financial and tax accounting results from the different purposes of the bodies that develop the applicable governing rules. The accounting for financial statement purposes is governed by generally accepted accounting principles, or GAAP, as developed by the FASB and other organizations. The role of the FASB is to develop accounting rules that require companies to fairly present their financial activities in order to provide useful information to users of financial statements. The tax rules, on the other hand, are drafted by the U.S. government and administered by the Internal Revenue Service. The purpose of tax law is to raise the desired amount of money to finance government operations, to achieve certain economic objectives (such as inducing investment activities), and to promote desired social goals (such as fairness and equity in tax treatment).

INTERNATIONAL

The divergence of financial and tax accounting is not unique to the United States. Differences between the accounting for financial reporting purposes and the accounting for tax purposes exist in most countries. The FASB issued "Accounting for Income Taxes," *Statement of Financial Accounting Standards No. 109*, to address how to account for these differences.[2] The international accounting community addresses these issues in *International Accounting Standard No. 12*.[3] In most respects, the conclusions reached in the FASB and international statements are similar.

The most fundamental question concerning income tax accounting is whether companies should be required to account for the differences between income tax calculated using financial accounting rules and income tax calculated using tax rules. For many companies, the amount of this difference can be quite large. To account for the difference, it is necessary to "allocate" income tax from one time period to another. The next section discusses the need for interperiod allocation of income tax.

LO1 Explain why interperiod tax allocation is necessary.

THE NEED FOR INTERPERIOD ALLOCATION OF INCOME TAX

To illustrate why it is necessary to allocate tax from one time period to another, we will consider a simple example of a company for which depreciation amounts represent the

---

2 "Accounting for Income Taxes," *Statement of Financial Accounting Standards No. 109* (Norwalk, Conn.: FASB, 1992).

3 "Income Taxes," *International Accounting Standard No. 12* (London: IASC, 2000).

Illustration 16.1

Depreciation Amounts per Book and per Tax

Year	Book Depreciation	Tax Depreciation
1	$200,000	$250,000
2	200,000	250,000
3	200,000	250,000
4	200,000	250,000
5	200,000	0

⊞ Critical Thinking: *When companies compute income taxes owed to the IRS each year, do you think they use cash- or accrual-basis accounting? Why is this important? How does the recognition basis affect the amount of taxes owed?*

only difference between book and tax accounting. Assume that Noallocation Company will have the following revenue and expenses each year for the next five years:

Revenue	$700,000
Operating expenses (other than depreciation)	200,000

Also assume that Noallocation purchased an asset for $1 million at the beginning of Year 1. For book purposes, the asset will be depreciated over a five-year time period, using the straight-line method and zero residual value. However, for tax purposes, the company is allowed to depreciate the asset, using the straight-line method and zero residual value, over a four-year time period. The depreciation schedules for the two methods are provided in Illustration 16.1.

Some accountants have argued that tax allocation is not necessary. If tax allocation was not required, the amount of tax calculated using the tax rules would be the same as the amount recorded for financial reporting purposes. For our example, if we assume that the tax rate for IRS purposes is 40 percent, the result would be as shown in the following table. Each of Years 1 through 4 would be the same, with the results shown in the left-hand column. The result for Year 5 would be different because a different amount of tax would have to be paid to the IRS; this is shown in the right-hand column.

Noallocation
Income Statement
Annual Income Statement

	Years 1–4	Year 5
Revenue	$700,000	$700,000
Operating expense	200,000	200,000
Depreciation expense	200,000	200,000
Income before tax	$300,000	$300,000
Tax expense	100,000*	200,000†
Net income	$200,000	$100,000

*Tax as calculated on the tax return [($700,000 − $200,000 − $250,000) × 40%].
†Tax as calculated on the tax return ($700,000 − $200,000 − $0) × 40%.

Income statements based on no allocation of taxes are unsatisfactory for several reasons. First, the tax expense is based on the amount of tax paid and thus represents a form of cash-basis accounting rather than accrual-basis accounting. Financial accounting is based on the accrual accounting process, and so the amount of tax expense reported should reflect the amount *incurred* rather than the amount *paid*. Second, income statements based on no allocation do not reflect one of the cornerstones of the accrual accounting process, the *matching principle*. In the hypothetical example, the amount of revenue and expense is the same each year for five years. If that is the case, the amount of tax expense should be the same in each of the five years. Instead, Noallocation has reflected tax expense of $100,000 each year for Years 1 through 4 and $200,000 for Year 5. An accurate matching of revenue and expense has not occurred. Since the amount of revenue was the same in each period and the use of the asset was the same in each period, the amount of the expense matched against revenue should be the same in each period. In short, a portion of the $200,000 tax in Year 5 must be *allocated* to Years 1 through 4.

Of course, in actual business situations, the accounting for tax for book and tax purposes is not as straightforward as in this simple example. However, most financial accountants accept the idea that *some form of tax allocation is necessary to present useful financial information.* The controversy concerns exactly how to perform the allocation and the many procedural details involved. The next section considers these issues.

CHECK YOUR UNDERSTANDING

1. Explain why many companies keep two sets of books.

2. What is the purpose of tax law?

3. Why is it necessary to allocate tax from one time period to another for financial accounting purposes?

The Basics of Tax Allocation

Most accountants have concluded that some form of interperiod tax allocation is necessary to accurately record the current year's tax expense and future years' tax obligations. The FASB states that the objectives of accounting for income taxes are "to recognize (a) the amount of taxes payable or refundable for the current year and (b) deferred tax liabilities and assets for the future tax consequences of events that have been recognized in an enterprise's financial statements or tax returns."[4] In order to accomplish these objectives, a company must consider the reasons or the causes for the differences between the amount of **income tax payable** (the amount calculated using tax rules) and the amount of **income tax expense** (the amount calculated using GAAP accounting rules and reported on the income statement). Illustration 16.2 presents the terms that you will learn in this section.

income tax payable the amount of income tax calculated using tax rules and reported on the company's tax return

income tax expense the amount of income tax calculated using GAAP accounting rules and reported on the income statement

LO2 Identify permanent and temporary tax differences.

permanent differences amounts that are used to calculate tax expense for book purposes but not tax payable for tax purposes or vice versa (used to calculate tax payable for tax purposes but not tax expense for book purposes)

Critical Thinking: *Do you think the IRS allows certain deductions or credits that are not allowed by the FASB for financial reporting purposes? Does GAAP allow for certain expenses or income items that are not recognized by tax law?*

PERMANENT AND TEMPORARY DIFFERENCES

All differences between the amount of income tax payable and the amount of income tax expense can be classified as either permanent differences or temporary differences. **Permanent differences** are amounts used to calculate tax expense for book purposes but not tax payable for tax purposes or vice versa (used to calculate tax payable for tax purposes but not tax expense for book purposes).[5] These permanent differences may result from expenses or income items. Premiums paid for life insurance on corporate officers, fines levied by government agencies, and dividends received from other corporations are examples of permanent differences. Illustration 16.3 contains a list of several common permanent differences and their treatment.

The identification of permanent differences is important because current accounting rules indicate that interperiod allocation of taxes should occur for all *temporary* differences. That is, a deferred tax account should be established to allocate income tax differences. But the deferred tax account should reflect the tax impact only of temporary differences. *It should not reflect the impact of permanent differences* between the accounting done for book purposes and the accounting for tax purposes.

---

4 *SFAS No. 109*, par. 6.

5 It should be noted that *SFAS No. 109* contains a definition of temporary differences but not of permanent differences.

Illustration 16.2

Key Terms for Tax Accounting

Term	Definition
Income tax payable	The amount of income tax calculated using the IRS rules and reported on the company's tax return.
Income tax expense	The amount of income tax calculated using GAAP accounting rules and reported on the company's income statement.
Permanent differences	Amounts that affect the calculation of tax expense (books) but not tax payable (tax) or vice versa (amounts that affect the calculation of tax payable but not tax expense).
Temporary differences	Differences between tax expense (books) and tax payable (tax) that will affect future periods; also referred to as *timing differences.*
Originating temporary differences	Temporary differences when they first occur. An amount should be recognized as deferred tax at the time that the difference originates.
Reversing temporary differences	Temporary differences that occurred in a previous period, for which the opposite effect is occurring in the current period. An amount should be removed from deferred tax at the time the difference reverses.
Deferred tax liability	A liability for tax at a future time; also referred to as a *future taxable amount.* It represents a credit balance in a deferred tax account.
Deferred tax asset	A temporary difference where income has been reported for tax purposes but will be reported for book purposes in a future period or where an expense has been deducted for book purposes but will be deducted for tax purposes in a future period; also referred to as a *future deductible amount.* It represents a debit balance in a deferred tax account.

temporary differences items or amounts that are differences between the tax basis of an asset or liability and its reported amount in the financial statements that will result in taxable or deductible amounts in future years

Temporary differences are items or amounts that are "differences between the tax basis of an asset or liability and its reported amount in the financial statements that will result in taxable or deductible amounts in future years."[6] In other words, temporary differences represent amounts that will enter both the book and the tax calculations, but the *timing* of when these items enter the book and the tax calculations

Illustration 16.3

Permanent Differences and Treatments

Permanent Differences	Treatments
1. Premiums paid for life insurance on corporate officers	Deducted for book purposes. Not deductible for tax purposes.
2. Fines and penalties levied by government agencies	Deducted for book purposes. Not deductible for tax purposes.
3. Interest received on state and municipal obligations	Included as income for book purposes. Not included for tax purposes (tax-exempt income).
4. Proceeds from life insurance on corporate officers	Included as income for book purposes. Not included for tax purposes (tax-exempt income).
5. Dividends received from other corporations	Included as income for book purposes. A portion, usually 80 percent, is not included for tax purposes.

---

6 *SFAS No. 109,* par. 289.

Temporary Differences	Example
Expense items and deductions are taken for tax purposes before book purposes.	Accelerated depreciation is used for tax purposes and straight-line depreciation is used for book purposes.
Expense items and deductions are recorded for book purposes before tax purposes.	Warranty expense is reported on the accrual basis for book purposes, but the expense is deducted when paid for tax purposes.
Income is included for tax purposes before book purposes.	Rent income received in advance is included for tax purposes when received, but is recorded for book purposes when earned.
Income is recorded for book purposes before tax purposes.	The percentage-of-completion method is used for book purposes, and the completed-contract method is used for tax purposes.

differs. In some cases, an item may enter the calculation of tax expense before it enters the calculation of tax payable for tax purposes. Alternatively, an item may enter the calculation of tax payable before it enters the calculation of tax expense for book purposes. While the FASB prefers the use of the term *temporary differences,* for our purposes it may be easier to think of these items as *timing differences.*

) EXAMPLE 1 As an illustration, assume that Little & Sons Company has sales of $100,000 during 2004 and reports the amount as sales revenue on its income statement. Also, assume that the company wisely wishes to delay the reporting of a portion of that amount for tax purposes and is allowed to report revenue at the time the cash is collected. Assume that $30,000 of collections occurred during 2004 and the remainder will occur in 2005. In this example, a temporary difference exists because the total amount of revenue that will be recorded for both book and tax purposes is $100,000, but the timing of the revenue differs. For tax purposes, revenue of only $30,000 will be included in 2004. *The purpose of the deferred tax account is to reflect the timing differences.* That is, the deferred tax account is the mechanism for allocating tax between periods because of timing differences.

Timing differences can occur for both revenue and expense items. Also, timing differences occur when items enter book calculations first and tax calculations later, but they occur when the opposite happens—tax calculations first and book computations later—as well. Illustration 16.4 indicates the four cases that can give rise to temporary differences and some common examples of each.

) ORIGINATING AND REVERSING

originating temporary difference the initial difference between the book basis and the tax basis of an asset or liability in the current period

reversing temporary difference the removal of a temporary difference that originated in a previous period

For all temporary differences, it is important to identify whether a difference between book and tax occurred in the current period or in a past period. An **originating temporary difference** is the initial difference between the book basis and the tax basis of an asset or liability in the current period. A **reversing temporary difference** is the removal of a temporary difference that originated in a previous period.

To illustrate originating and reversing differences, review the data presented earlier in Example 1:

● 2004 sales: $100,000

● 2004 cash collections: $30,000

● 2005 cash collections: $70,000

● The company reports revenue for tax purposes when cash is collected.

The amount of originating and reversing differences would be calculated as follows:

Year 2004: Originating difference, $100,000 − $30,000 = $70,000

Year 2005: Reversing difference, $70,000

Note that *originating* and *reversing* refer to the amount of the *difference* between the book and tax amounts ($70,000) rather the total ($100,000 or $30,000).

It is important to identify originating and reversing differences because an originating difference indicates that an amount should *enter* the Deferred Tax account and a reversing difference indicates that an amount should *be removed from* the account. In simple situations (those that do not involve changes in tax rates), the amount of the entry to the deferred tax account should be calculated as follows:

$$\text{Temporary Difference} \times \text{Tax Rate} = \text{Entry to Deferred Tax Account}$$

If we assume a 30 percent tax rate for both 2004 and 2005, then

Year 2004: $70,000 × 30% = $21,000 enters the Deferred Tax account.

Year 2005: $70,000 × 30% = $21,000 is removed from the Deferred Tax account.

In Example 1, an item originated in one year and reversed in the next year. In other cases, the cycle of originating and reversing may extend over a longer period of time, as illustrated in the following example.

❭ EXAMPLE 2   Assume that on January 1, 2005, Rolf Company purchased an asset for $100,000 and will depreciate the asset over a four-year life with zero residual value. Assume that the company uses the straight-line method of depreciation for book purposes but uses an accelerated depreciation method for tax purposes, as outlined in the following chart:

Year	Straight-Line Depreciation	Accelerated Depreciation
2005	$25,000	$40,000
2006	25,000	30,000
2007	25,000	20,000
2008	25,000	10,000

As you can see, a temporary difference exists in this example because, although the total amount of depreciation taken over the asset's four-year life under either method is $100,000, the timing of the depreciation is different for book and tax purposes. We identify originating and reversing differences as follows:

Year	Straight-Line Depreciation	Accelerated Depreciation	Difference	Originating or Reversing
2005	$25,000	$40,000	$15,000	Originating
2006	25,000	30,000	5,000	Originating
2007	25,000	20,000	−5,000	Reversing
2008	25,000	10,000	−15,000	Reversing

Assume that the tax rate for all years is 40 percent. As a result, the impact on the Deferred Tax account is as shown on the following page.

Year 2005: $15,000 × 40% = $6,000 enters the Deferred Tax account.

Year 2006: $ 5,000 × 40% = $2,000 enters the Deferred Tax account.

Year 2007: $ 5,000 × 40% = $2,000 is removed from the account.

Year 2008: $15,000 × 40% = $6,000 is removed from the account.

The balance of the account at the end of 2008 equals zero.

The preceding example illustrates the theory that underlies accounting for deferred tax when no tax changes are involved and only one asset is involved. The theory can be stated as follows:

> *If* . . . only one asset or item is involved, if the tax rate is constant, and if amounts enter the deferred tax account when they originate and are removed when they reverse,
>
> *Then* . . . the balance of the Deferred Tax account will become zero after the items reverse. That is, the Deferred Tax account will account for the timing differences between book and tax amounts.

In practice, most companies encounter more than one item that causes differences between book and tax amounts. These situations add complexities to the process of determining the appropriate tax rate and applying it to current and future years.

LO3 Determine and record tax expense and tax payable.

future taxable amount a deferred tax liability; it represents a liability for income tax at a future time

future deductible amount a deferred tax asset; it results from a temporary difference that has been deducted for book purposes in the current period but will be deducted for tax purposes when it reverses

Critical Thinking: *How are future taxable amounts and future deductible amounts related to deferred tax assets and liabilities?*

▶ DEFERRED TAX LIABILITIES AND ASSETS

The Deferred Tax account appears on the balance sheet as either a deferred tax liability or a deferred tax asset. A deferred tax liability is referred to as a **future taxable amount** because it represents a liability for income tax at a future time period. That is, it results from a temporary difference that causes current tax payable to be *less* than the amount of tax expense recorded for book purposes and will cause future tax payable to *exceed* the amount recorded for book purposes when the item reverses. A deferred tax asset is referred to as a **future deductible amount** because it results from a temporary difference that has been deducted for book purposes in the current period but will be deducted for tax purposes when it reverses. That is, it will be deducted at a future time and is therefore a future benefit or asset to the company.

Whether an item is a deferred tax asset or a deferred tax liability is directly related to its effect on tax expense for book purposes and tax payable for tax purposes. If an item causes tax expense to exceed tax payable when it originates, then that item will be considered a deferred tax liability or future taxable amount. On the other hand, if the item causes tax payable to exceed tax expense when it originates, then that item will be considered a deferred tax asset or future deductible amount. Consider the four cases presented in Illustration 16.4. The applicable treatment of each case is outlined in Illustration 16.5.

To illustrate the application of the debit and credit rules for deferred taxes, review the data from Example 1 presented earlier:

- 2004 sales: $100,000

- 2004 collections: $30,000

- 2005 collections: $70,000

- Tax rate of 30 percent for both years.

- The company records income at the time of sale for book purposes and uses the installment sales method for tax purposes.

If we assume that the installment sales method is the only temporary difference between book and tax income for 2004, the following situation results:

	Book		Tax
Income Before Tax	>	Taxable Income
Tax Expense	>	Tax Payable

Therefore, the following entry is recorded:

Tax Expense	xxx	
Tax Payable		xxx
Deferred Tax Liability ($70,000 × 30%)		21,000

The balance of the Deferred Tax Liability account is a liability (rather than an asset) because the amount represents a future taxable amount. That is, the amount of the difference ($70,000 in this case) will be taxable when it is included for tax purposes in 2005.

In 2005, the difference will be included for tax purposes, requiring the following treatment:

Book		Tax
Income Before Tax	<	Taxable Income
Tax Expense	<	Tax Payable

This entry is thus recorded:

Tax Expense	xxx	
Deferred Tax Liability ($70,000 × 30%)	21,000	
Tax Payable		xxx

Illustration 16.5

Deferred Tax Assets and Liabilities Resulting from Temporary Differences

Case	Example	Debit or Credit Deferred Tax	Asset or Liability
Expense items and deductions are taken for tax purposes before book purposes.	Accelerated depreciation is used for tax purposes and straight-line depreciation is used for book purposes.	Credit when it originates; debit when it reverses	Deferred tax liability
Expense items and deductions are recorded for book purposes before tax purposes.	Warranty expense is reported on the accrual basis for book purposes, but the expense is deducted when paid for tax purposes.	Debit when it originates; credit when it reverses	Deferred tax asset
Income is included for tax purposes before book purposes.	Rent income received in advance is included for tax purposes when received, but is recorded for book purposes when earned.	Debit when it originates; credit when it reverses	Deferred tax asset
Income is recorded for book purposes before tax purposes.	The percentage-of-completion method is used for book purposes, and the completed-contract method is used for tax purposes.	Credit when it originates; debit when it reverses	Deferred tax liability

point ▶◀ counterpoint

Deferred Taxes

the controversy If you look at almost any company's tax expense for a fiscal year and compare it to the company's tax payable amount, you'll find the two numbers are not the same. In 2000, for instance, IBM reported a pretax profit of nearly $5.7 billion to its investors. But for the IRS, the company painted a different picture. At approximately $546 million, IBM's taxable profit for the year was a sliver of the earnings on display in its annual report.[1]

For many companies, the tax payable amount based on taxable profit seldom matches the tax expense estimated from pre-tax accounting profit. Why is this? The mismatch occurs because GAAP recognition criteria for items of income and expense differ from the recognition criteria of tax law. Future tax deductible amounts may be recorded as deferred tax assets on the books, whereas future taxable amounts are recorded as deferred tax liabilities. Some in the accounting profession contend that booking these deferred taxes provides a more accurate picture of the company; others believe that the amounts that arise from timing differences between "book" and "tax" do not represent the true liabilities of the company.

▶ point

Financial Accounting Standards Board

on the point:

- **Randolf Green**
  professional accounting fellow, Office of the Chief Accountant, SEC

▶ **Amounts that represent future tax deductions or future tax liabilities should be reflected on a company's balance sheet.**

Statement of Financial Accounting Standards No. 109 governs the accounting for temporary and permanent book-tax differences along with other aspects of accounting for income taxes. *SFAS No. 109* supports a balance-sheet approach in which future deductible amounts create deferred tax assets and future taxable amounts create deferred tax liabilities. The FASB believes that deferred taxes are true liabilities because they meet the definition of a liability established in *Statement of Financial Accounting Concepts No. 6* and because they are obligations for the consequences of taxable temporary differences that stem from the requirements of tax law. This position is supported by the accounting principle of matching. Those who practice the accrual basis of accounting, in which a variety of items are accrued, question why taxes would be any different. Supporters of this view believe that to accurately portray the financial condition of a company, deferred tax assets or tax liabilities must be included in the financial statements. Accounting professionals contend that the transactions or events that gave rise to the tax obligation occurred in the current period and therefore must be recognized.

◀ counterpoint

Dale Wettlaufer

senior financial analyst, The Motley Fool.com

on the counterpoint:

- **Dr. Lillian Mills**
  tax accounting professor

- **Kaye Newberry**
  associate professor

◀ **Inclusion of deferred tax liabilities and assets on the balance sheet can distort the valuation of a company and provide opportunities for earnings management.**

Accounting professionals and financial experts on the other side of this issue contend that deferred tax amounts are not *legal* liabilities at the time they are recog-

---

1 Jonathan Weisman, "At Firms, Dual Profit Pictures," WashingtonPost.com, October 10, 2002, available at: **http://www.washingtonpost.com/ac2/wp-dyn?pagename=article&contentId=A3551-2002Oct9&notFound=true.** Accessed 07/28/04.

nized in the sense that the company is not legally obligated to pay the amount that has been recognized as deferred tax. Users of financial statements, particularly financial analysts, often ignore deferred tax information in their assessments of solvency and corporate performance. Analysts exclude these amounts because they question whether these deferred tax assets or deferred tax liabilities will result in actual future resource inflows or outflows.

A variety of research projects have studied the effects of inclusion of deferred tax assets and liabilities in the valuation of a company as a whole.[2] Although many companies record deferred tax liabilities, these amounts are often carried on the books indefinitely and are sometimes ultimately not paid to any taxing authority. Dale Wettlaufer, a senior financial analyst with The Motley Fool.com states, "Certain liabilities mandated by GAAP (Generally Accepted Accounting Principles) reduce the amount of resources at the company's disposal in the ROE [return on equity] equation. Depending on the circumstances, though, these liabilities should not be counted as a reduction in the capital working for the benefit of shareholders."[3]

With regard to deferred tax assets, *SFAS No. 109* gives companies the opportunity to fully recognize amounts that are expected to be realized as a future tax allowance or deduction. The financial statement preparer must also establish a valuation allowance account if it is more likely than not that the asset will not be realized. An academic study completed by Mills and Newberry in 2001 argued that "managers typically have more discretion in financial reporting than in tax reporting and can exploit such discretion to manage income upwards in ways that do not affect current taxable income."[4] Many in the financial community have stated that this discretionary allowance account opens the door to earnings management. How do financial statement users determine whether the allowance account amount is reasonable? They can't—because the establishment of an allowance amount is a subjective task, there is no reliable way to analyze this estimate. Over the years, companies that use a valuation allowance account to smooth earnings have been the target of criticism from both investors and financial analysts.

Take a Position   Imagine that you are the controller for a major manufacturer of farming equipment and that your company has established a deferred tax liability account for tax amounts that are expected in future periods. How does this action affect net income for the current period? How would you answer criticisms against this action?

Research   Locate the 2003 annual report for Cendant Corporation. What amount did the company report for deferred income tax assets on its balance sheet? for deferred income tax liabilities?

---

2 David Guenther and Richard Sansing, "The valuation relevance of reversing deferred tax liabilities," August 2003, available at **http://mba.tuck.dartmouth.edu/pages/faculty/richard.sansing/GSreversal19AUG03.pdf**. Accessed 7/28/04.

3 Dale Wettlaufer, "A Look at ROIC," The Motley Fool.com, available at **http://www.fool.com/School/roic/roic01.htm**. Accessed 7/28/04.

4 L. Mills and K. Newberry, "The influence of tax and non-tax costs on book-tax reporting differences: Public and private firms," *Journal of the American Taxation Association*, Spring 2001.

The application of the debit and credit rules for deferred taxes can also be illustrated using the facts presented in Example 2:

- An asset is purchased on January 1, 2005, for $100,000.

- The straight-line method of depreciation is used for book purposes, resulting in depreciation of $25,000 per year.

- An accelerated method is used for tax purposes, resulting in depreciation of $40,000, $30,000, $20,000, and $10,000 over the four years.

- Assume the tax rate is 40 percent for all years.

If we assume that depreciation is the only temporary difference between book and tax, then the amount of the difference for 2005 and 2006 could be considered an originating difference and would have the following impact:

Year 2005			Year 2006		
Book		Tax	Book		Tax
Depreciation Expense $25,000	<	Depreciation Expense $40,000	Depreciation Expense $25,000	<	Depreciation Expense $30,000
Income Before Tax	>	Taxable Income	Income Before Tax	>	Taxable Income
Tax Expense	>	Tax Payable	Tax Expense	>	Tax Payable

Year 2005				Year 2006		
Tax Expense	xxx			Tax Expense	xxx	
Deferred Tax Liability ($15,000 × 40%)		6,000		Deferred Tax Liability ($5,000 × 40%)		2,000
Tax Payable		xxx		Tax Payable		xxx

The balance of the Deferred Tax Liability account represents a future taxable amount. As of December 31, 2006, the balance of the account appears as follows:

Deferred Tax Liability	
6,000	(15,000 × 40%)
2,000	(5,000 × 40%)
8,000	**bal.** Dec. 31, 2006

The temporary differences that occur in 2007 and 2008 for the depreciable asset are considered reversing differences and result in the following accounting entries:

Year 2007			Year 2008		
Book		Tax	Book		Tax
Depreciation Expense $25,000	>	Depreciation Expense $20,000	Depreciation Expense $25,000	>	Depreciation Expense $10,000
Income Before Tax	<	Taxable Income	Income Before Tax	<	Taxable Income
Tax Expense	<	Tax Payable	Tax Expense	<	Tax Payable

Year 2007				Year 2008		
Tax Expense	xxx			Tax Expense	xxx	
Deferred Tax Liability ($5,000 × 40%)	2,000			Deferred Tax Liability ($15,000 × 40%)	6,000	
Tax Payable		xxx		Tax Payable		xxx

Because the amounts in 2007 and 2008 represent a reversal of temporary differences, the Deferred Tax Liability account is debited to reduce the balance to zero as follows:

Deferred Tax Liability			
2007 (5,000 × 40%) 2,000	6,000	(15,000 × 40%) 2006
2008 (15,000 × 40%) 6,000	2,000	(5,000 × 40%) 2007
	0	**bal.** Dec. 31, 2008

Examples 1 and 2 are both situations that give rise to a deferred tax liability. When the temporary differences originated, the account was credited, and when the amounts reversed, the account was debited. However, in some cases, a temporary difference creates a deferred tax asset, as illustrated in Example 3.

▶ EXAMPLE 3 Assume that during 2005, you are notified that your company is being sued by another company. The suit alleges that a patent infringement has occurred as a result of your company's actions. A consultation with your attorney leads to the conclusion that it is *probable* that your company will be held liable in the lawsuit and that the amount of the loss can be *reasonably estimated* at $200,000. Because this is a contingent liability that meets the criteria for recognition, it must be recognized as an expense (or loss) for book purposes in 2005. However, this item is not deductible for tax purposes in 2005. It will be deductible when the lawsuit is actually settled. Assume that the tax rate for current and future time periods is 40 percent.

If we assume that the amount of the expense from the lawsuit is the only temporary difference between book and tax amounts for 2005, the following treatment is employed:

Book		Tax
Expense $200,000	>	Expense $0
Income Before Tax	<	Taxable Income
Tax Expense	<	Tax Payable

The following entry is recorded:

Tax Expense	xxx	
Deferred Tax Asset ($200,000 × 40%)	80,000	
Tax Payable		xxx

The balance of the Deferred Tax Asset account is an asset (rather than a liability) because the amount is considered a *future deductible amount.* In other words, the amount of the difference ($200,000 in this case) will provide a future benefit to the company, since taxes will be reduced at the time the amount becomes deductible for tax purposes.

CHECK YOUR UNDERSTANDING

1. Should a deferred tax account reflect the impact of temporary differences or permanent differences? Explain.

2. Why is it important to identify whether a difference is originating or whether it is reversing?

3. Briefly explain the difference between a deferred tax liability and a deferred tax asset.

Additional Aspects of Deferred Tax

Our examples thus far have been straightforward in the sense that each involves only one temporary difference and the tax rate for the current and future years is the same. In practice, accountants must consider additional issues that create complexities in the determination of deferred tax. These issues include

- Accounting for tax-rate changes

- Adjusting for new tax rates

- Accounting for valuation allowances for deferred tax assets

LO4 Determine deferred taxes when multiple tax rates or tax-rate changes are involved.

Critical Thinking: Do you think income tax–rate changes affect the operating income of a company in the year of the rate change? Explain your reasoning.

ACCOUNTING FOR TAX-RATE CHANGES

❯ DEFERRED METHOD

As you have learned, temporary differences can originate in one period and then reverse over a time span of several years. During that time, the applicable tax rate may change. Prior to *SFAS No. 109*, the accounting rules specified that companies should use the tax rate that existed at the time the temporary differences originated to calculate the amount entered in the Deferred Tax account. Further, the balance of the account was not adjusted if the tax rate changed in future periods. This method was often referred to as the *deferred method* of calculating deferred income taxes. It was also referred to as an *income statement–oriented approach* because the primary emphasis was placed on calculating the appropriate amount of income tax expense to be recognized on the income statement. However, when this method was applied over time, difficulties arose for some companies. In particular, it generally was not possible to determine whether the amount in the Deferred Tax account on the balance sheet accurately portrayed the tax consequences of the existing temporary differences. Over time, the balance of the Deferred Tax account grew, and users of financial statements questioned whether the amount really represented a liability (or in some cases an asset).

❯ LIABILITY METHOD

To remedy this difficulty, *SFAS No. 109* radically changed the accounting for deferred taxes by adopting what is called the *liability* method. This method is also referred to as a *balance sheet–oriented method* because the primary emphasis is placed on calculating the deferred tax asset or liability rather than on the amount of income tax expense on the income statement. Under this approach, a company uses the enacted tax rate that is applicable to the time periods in which the temporary differences will reverse or be settled.[7] With this approach, amounts for temporary differences should enter the Deferred Tax account (as originating differences) at the tax rate that will exist when the temporary differences reverse. However, it should be noted that a company should use a future tax rate only if it has been *enacted*. That is, if Congress or another taxing authority has passed legislation that has established a tax rate for future periods, then that tax rate should be used for the reversal of temporary differences.

To illustrate the accounting for a tax rate change, review the data presented in Example 1:

- Sales of $100,000 are recorded for book purposes in 2004.

- For tax purposes, the company uses the installment sales method, resulting in income of $30,000 in 2004 and $70,000 in 2005.

- A temporary difference of $70,000 originates in 2004 and reverses in 2005.

---

7 Ibid., par. 18.

Originally, we assumed that the tax rate was 30 percent for all periods. Instead, assume that the tax rate for 2004 is 30 percent, but the enacted tax rate for 2005 is 40 percent, and this rate has been enacted before the end of 2004. The amount of deferred tax should be calculated as follows:

Year 2004: $70,000 × 40% = $28,000 is credited to the Deferred Tax Liability account.

Year 2005: $70,000 × 40% = $28,000 is debited to the account.

The use of the future enacted tax rate is logical, and from a theoretical viewpoint it is consistent with a balance sheet emphasis. However, it should be noted that its use introduces an enormous amount of complexity and detail into the calculation of deferred taxes. It requires companies to develop schedules of their temporary differences that clearly define when the items are expected to reverse or be settled.[8]

In this text we will use a single, flat tax rate for each period. However, in actual practice, there are several additional complexities that must be considered in choosing the appropriate tax rate, including state and local taxes, the alternative minimum tax, and capital gains and losses. Further, *SFAS No. 109* requires that companies consider alternative tax-planning strategies that would affect future tax events and future tax rates.[9] These strategies might include plans to accelerate income or expense, capital gains and losses, and any tax loss carryforwards or carrybacks. While we will not address these issues, you should realize that the choice of an appropriate tax rate for calculation of deferred taxes is seldom a simple task.

ADJUSTING FOR NEW TAX RATES

The previous section considered how to select a tax rate when a future tax rate has been enacted. It emphasized that the future tax rate for the period of reversal should be used to establish the Deferred Tax account. If the future tax rate has in fact been enacted and is known at the time the Deferred Tax account is established, this procedure should be utilized. A different approach is used if the tax rate change occurs after the account has been established.

When a change in the enacted tax rate occurs, *SFAS No. 109* requires that the amount of the deferred tax asset or liability be adjusted for the effect of the new tax rate. The effect should be included in income from continuing operations during the time period that includes the enactment date.[10] As an example, review the data from Example 1:

● Sales of $100,000 are recorded for book purposes in 2004.

● For tax purposes, the company reports income when the cash is collected, resulting in income of $30,000 in 2004 and $70,000 in 2005.

● A temporary difference of $70,000 originates in 2004 and reverses in 2005.

In this case, assume that the applicable tax rate for 2004 was 30 percent. Early in 2005, new tax legislation was adopted that increased the company's tax rate to 40 percent. The treatment of deferred tax for each year should be as follows:

Year 2004: $70,000 × 30% = $21,000 is credited to the Deferred Tax Liability account.

---

8 Fortunately, the issue concerning future enacted tax rates is often a moot point. Congress and other taxing authorities seldom pass legislation that determines tax rates beyond the current year. Thus, in practice, it is quite common to use the current rate because future tax rates have not been enacted.

9 *SFAS No. 109*, par. 121.

10 Ibid., par. 27.

Year 2005: An increase in the Deferred Tax Liability account of $7,000 ($70,000 × 10 percent) should be recorded as follows:

Tax Expense	7,000	
Deferred Tax Liability		7,000

Note that the increase in the Deferred Tax Liability account must be based on the amount of the temporary difference of $70,000. It should not be based on the balance of the Deferred Tax Liability account. The balance of the Deferred Tax Liability account, after adjusting for the change in tax rate, is $28,000.

Year 2005: $70,000 × 40% = $28,000 is debited to the Deferred Tax Liability account.

Because the temporary difference has reversed, the balance of the Deferred Tax Liability account at December 31, 2005, should be zero.

LO5 Describe when and how a valuation allowance is recorded for a deferred tax asset.

Critical Thinking: What situations might require companies to adjust the value of a future tax benefit, or a Deferred Tax Asset account?

VALUATION ALLOWANCE FOR DEFERRED TAX ASSETS

As discussed earlier, deferred tax assets can arise from the two types of temporary differences shown in the following chart:

Case	Example	Debit or Credit Deferred Tax	Asset or Liability
Expense items and deductions are recorded for book purposes before tax purposes.	Warranty expense is recorded on the accrual basis for book purposes, but the expense is deducted when paid for tax purposes.	Debit when it originates; credit when it reverses	Deferred tax asset
Income is included for tax purposes before book purposes.	Rent income received in advance is included for tax purposes when received, but is recorded for book purposes when earned.	Debit when it originates; credit when it reverses	Deferred tax asset

In some cases, a deferred tax asset is recognized because *income* has been included for tax purposes prior to the time when it will be included for book purposes. In other cases, an asset is recorded because an *expense* has been recognized for book purposes before it will be deducted for tax purposes. For the latter type of temporary difference, the term *future deductible amount* applies because this term indicates that a deduction will be taken in a future period for tax purposes. When accounting for this type of temporary difference, the accountant should determine whether the deductible amount meets the definition of an asset and should therefore be recognized as such on the balance sheet.

As you recall, the accounting definition of an asset stresses that a *future benefit* must exist. The conservative nature of accounting dictates that an asset should not be recognized when the future benefit is not completely known at the present time and is dependent upon future events. In this case, the future benefit associated with a future deductible amount is dependent upon the existence of income in the future. Deductions are useful for tax purposes only if there is income to be reduced. Some would argue that if there is doubt about whether income will exist in the future, then there is doubt about whether the future deductible amounts represent a valid asset. Recall the following data from Example 3:

- A lawsuit was filed against your company in 2005, and $200,000 was recorded as an expense for book purposes for the contingent liability.

- The amount represents a temporary difference because it cannot be deducted for tax purposes until the lawsuit is settled.

- Assuming a 40 percent tax rate, a deferred tax asset of $80,000 was recognized.

Remember that a deferred tax asset is useful only if the company has income during the period in the future when the lawsuit is settled and a deduction can be taken for tax purposes. In this regard, the FASB has adopted a compromise stance in *SFAS No. 109*, requiring that a valuation allowance be recognized for a deferred tax asset if there is doubt about whether the company will be able to utilize the deduction in the future. The **Valuation Allowance account** is a contra-asset account and is an offset to the Deferred Tax Asset account. It is an indication that there is some doubt about whether the company will be able to utilize the future deductible amount that has been recorded as an asset.

Valuation Allowance account a contra-asset account that is an offset to the Deferred Tax Asset account; it indicates that there is some doubt about whether the company will be able to utilize the future deductible amount that has been recorded as an asset

Assume that your company believes that $40,000 of the $200,000 deduction will not be utilized in future periods. In this case, a valuation allowance of $16,000 ($40,000 × 40%) will be recorded as follows:

Tax Expense	16,000	
Valuation Allowance		16,000

After this is recorded, the impact of the temporary difference will appear on the balance sheet in the asset category as follows:

Asset

Deferred tax asset	$80,000	
Less: Valuation allowance	(16,000)	$64,000

The decision to record a valuation allowance is a matter of subjective judgment. *SFAS No. 109* indicates that if, based on the weight of available evidence, *it is more likely than not* (a likelihood of more than 50 percent) that some portion of the deferred tax asset *will not* be realized, then a Valuation Allowance account is necessary.[11]

In making this decision, accountants should consider all available evidence, including both positive and negative indications. The FASB has provided examples of possible indications for this decision. This critical decision can have a substantial impact on a company's financial results. When a future deductible amount exists, *each year* the company must analyze whether a Valuation Allowance account is necessary. If an account has been established, *each year* the company must consider whether the balance of the account should be increased or decreased. All changes in the account will affect the company's income for the current year.

DISCOUNTING

discounted for long-term assets and liabilities, represented at their present value amounts

Accounting rules generally maintain that long-term assets and liabilities must be **discounted**, or represented at their present value amounts.[12] The measurement of deferred taxes is an exception to these rules. Even though the effects of temporary

---

11 Ibid., par. 16.

12 "Interest on Receivables and Payables," *Opinions of the Accounting Principles Board No. 21* (New York: AICPA, 1971).

Illustration 16.6

Steps to Identify Deferred Tax Liability and Tax Expense

1. Calculate the amount of taxable income.	Book income must be reconciled to taxable income after considering all temporary and permanent differences.
2. Calculate the amount of tax payable.	This represents the amount of tax on the company's tax form (Taxable Income × Tax Rate).
3. Calculate the entry for deferred tax.	The entry for deferred tax should represent the temporary differences for the period multiplied by the appropriate tax rate.
4. Calculate the amount of tax expense.	This represents the amount reflected on the company's income statement. It is the amount of tax payable plus credits to Deferred Tax minus debits to Deferred Tax during the current year.
5. Record the journal entry.	The journal entry is based on the information in the previous steps.

differences often extend several years into the future, deferred taxes are not measured at their present value amounts. While this may seem inconsistent with other accounting rules, *SFAS No. 109* does not require discounting for the following reasons. First, certain conceptual issues related to the discounting of deferred taxes have not been resolved by the FASB, including what discount rate should be used and how to effectively incorporate risk into the measurement of present value. Second and more importantly, discounting of deferred taxes would introduce additional complexities, requiring a detailed scheduling of all temporary differences and an accounting for changes in cash flows and/or changes in discount rates. In an attempt to "simplify" the accounting for deferred taxes, the FASB does not require discounting.[13]

MULTIPLE TEMPORARY DIFFERENCES

Our examples thus far have dealt with the calculation of deferred tax when there is only one temporary difference between book and tax amounts. Illustration 16.6 presents the steps that should be taken when there are several differences between book and tax records. To illustrate this process, review the following example.

❭ **EXAMPLE 4**   Assume the following facts for Baylor Company in 2005:

● Book income before tax: $400,000. The following items were included in income:

   ❭ Interest income of $40,000 was received from investments in municipal bonds. This income is exempt for tax purposes.

   ❭ Rent income of $10,000 was collected in 2004 and included for tax purposes. For book purposes, it was reported as earned in 2005.

● The following items were deducted from income:

   ❭ An asset was purchased during 2005, and depreciation for book purposes was $20,000. Depreciation for tax purposes was $50,000.

   ❭ Warranty expense of $10,000 was recognized for book purposes, while $2,500 was recognized for tax purposes. (Assume a one-year warranty contract.)

● The balance of the Deferred Tax Asset account (debit) at January 1, 2005, was $4,000 as a result of the rent temporary difference.

---

13 *SFAS No. 109*, par. 198.

● The tax rate for all years was 40 percent.

Step 1: Calculate the amount of taxable income.

To do so, examine all differences (both permanent and temporary) between book income and taxable income. Taxable income is calculated as follows:

Book income	$400,000
Tax-exempt interest	(40,000)
Rent included for book purposes	(10,000)
Depreciation in excess of book depreciation	(30,000)
Warranty expense less than book	7,500
Taxable income	$327,500

Step 2: Calculate the amount of tax payable.

Tax Payable = Taxable Income × Tax Rate
Tax Payable = $327,500 × 40%
Tax Payable = $131,000

Step 3: Calculate the entry for deferred tax.

When the tax rate is constant and no other complexities exist, the deferred tax calculation can be based on the temporary differences that have occurred during the current year:

$10,000 × 40% = $4,000 credit to Deferred Tax Asset
$30,000 × 40% = $12,000 credit to Deferred Tax Liability
$ 7,500 × 40% = $3,000 debit to Deferred Tax Asset
Net entry to deferred tax = $13,000 credit

Note that the entry to deferred tax should be based only on the temporary differences. The interest amount of $40,000 is not included because it is a permanent difference.

The *balances* of the Deferred Tax Asset and Deferred Tax Liability accounts at the end of 2005 are shown by the following T-accounts:

Deferred Tax Asset

Beg. bal.	4,000		
		4,000	Entry for 2005 (reverses 2004 amount)
Entry for 2005 (originating item)	3,000		
bal. year end 2005	3,000		

Deferred Tax Liability

		0	Beg. bal.
		12,000	Entry for 2005 (originating item)
		12,000	bal. year end 2005

Alternatively, we could calculate the amount of deferred tax based on the *cumulative* temporary differences that exist at the beginning and end of the period as follows:

Beginning Balance
Deferred Tax Asset $10,000 × 40% = $ 4,000 debit ⌐

                                                            Entry
Ending Balance $13,000
Deferred Tax Liability $30,000 × 40% = $12,000 credit   → credit
Deferred Tax Asset   7,500 × 40% =   3,000 debit
Net balance $ 9,000 credit ⌐

Step 4: Calculate the amount of tax expense.

Note that tax expense cannot be calculated directly from the amount of income for book purposes before tax ($400,000 in this case). Rather, tax expense is calculated as follows:

$$\text{Tax Expense} = \text{Tax Payable} + \text{Net Entry to Deferred Tax (if credit)}$$

or

$$\text{Tax Expense} = \text{Tax Payable} - \text{Net Entry to Deferred Tax (if debit)}$$

$$\text{Tax Expense} = \$131,000 + \$13,000 = \$144,000$$

Step 5: Record the journal entry.

Tax Expense	144,000	
Tax Payable		131,000
Deferred Tax Asset ($4,000 − $3,000)		1,000
Deferred Tax Liability		12,000

CHECK YOUR UNDERSTANDING

1. If an expense has been recognized for book purposes before it will be deducted for tax purposes, does a deferred tax asset or a deferred tax liability result?

2. What criteria does the FASB provide for determining whether a valuation allowance should be established for a deferred tax asset?

LO6 Describe how tax expense, deferred tax liabilities, and deferred tax assets are presented in the financial statements.

Critical Thinking: *What role do you think conservatism plays in deciding how deferred tax liabilities and deferred tax assets should be reported?*

Financial Statement Presentation of Tax Amounts

Income tax expense, deferred tax liabilities, and deferred tax assets must be appropriately reflected on the financial statements of a company. We will demonstrate income statement and balance sheet disclosures for these items using the Baylor Company data from Example 4. Then, we will examine the income statement, balance sheet, and note disclosures for **Pfizer Inc**.

BALANCE SHEET

The Deferred Tax account may be presented in the asset and/or the liability category of the balance sheet. On the balance sheet, the total amount of deferred taxes must be separated into current and noncurrent amounts. For purposes of deferred tax classification, the FASB has developed a unique definition of current and noncurrent. *SFAS No. 109* indicates that the classification of deferred tax as current or noncurrent should generally be based on *the classification of the related asset or liability* that gave rise to the temporary difference.[14] In other words, if the asset or liability that caused the deferred tax is a long-term item, then the resulting deferred tax should be classified as long-term. On the other hand, if the related asset or liability is a current account, then the resulting deferred tax should be classified as current. The classification is generally *not* based on whether the temporary differences will reverse within a one-year time period.[15]

---

14 Ibid., par. 41.

15 *SFAS No. 109* notes that in a few cases the deferred tax is not related to a particular asset or liability. In those unusual cases, deferred tax should be classified according to whether the temporary differences will reverse within a one-year time period.

In Example 4, for Baylor Company, the balance of the Deferred Tax Asset account at the end of 2005 was $3,000 and the balance of the Deferred Tax Liability account was $12,000. The related assets or liabilities that gave rise to the deferred tax should be analyzed as follows:

Temporary Difference	Deferred Tax Amount	Related Asset or Liability	Classification of Deferred Tax
Depreciation difference of $30,000	$30,000 × 40%, or $12,000 credit	Equipment is long-term	Long-Term Deferred Tax Liability
Warranty Expense difference of $7,500	$7,500 × 40%, or $3,000 debit	Warranty liability is current	Current Deferred Tax Asset

Therefore the balances of the Deferred Tax Asset and Deferred Tax Liability accounts must be shown separately on the balance sheet as follows:

Current assets:
Deferred tax asset $3,000

Long-term liabilities:
Deferred tax liability $12,000

Remember that the FASB has chosen a unique distinction between current and noncurrent for deferred tax. The classification is based on whether the *related asset or liability* is current or noncurrent. It is *not* based on when the deferred tax items will reverse, and it is *not based on the amount of tax that will be paid within one year.* Therefore, this rule may not be consistent with the definitions of current and noncurrent that are used in other accounting applications; however, it was adopted to simplify the deferred tax calculation burden.

INCOME STATEMENT

According to *SFAS No. 109*, the significant components of income tax expense should be disclosed either within the income statement or in the notes that accompany the statement. The components displayed must disclose the amount of the **current tax expense** and the amount of **deferred tax expense**.[16]

current tax expense the amount of tax calculated and payable during the period for tax purposes (the amount of income tax payable)

deferred tax expense the amount of tax that has resulted from the current year's temporary differences

● The amount of the current tax expense is the amount of tax calculated and payable during the period for tax purposes (i.e., the amount of income tax payable).

● The amount of the deferred tax expense represents the amount of tax that has resulted from the current year's temporary differences.

In Example 4, the total amount of tax expense for 2005 was calculated as $144,000 and is analyzed as follows:

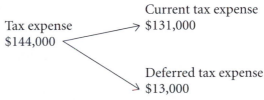

Tax expense
$144,000

Current tax expense
$131,000

Deferred tax expense
$13,000

---

16 Several other components must also be displayed if applicable. For example, any tax expense resulting from a change in tax rate must be disclosed, as must changes or adjustments to the Valuation Allowance account. See *SFAS No. 109*, par. 45, for a detailed listing of the required disclosures.

If the company chooses to disclose the amounts separately on the income statement, rather than in the notes, the amount of tax expense may appear as follows:

Income before tax		$ xxx
Income tax expense:		
Current	$131,000	
Deferred	13,000	
		144,000
Income from continuing operations		$ xxx

effective tax rate income tax expense divided by income before tax

The income statement amount can also be used to calculate the amount referred to as the effective tax rate. The **effective tax rate** is calculated as follows:

$$\text{Effective Tax Rate} = \text{Income Tax Expense} \div \text{Income Before Tax}$$

In Example 4, the effective tax rate would be calculated as the amount of income tax expense ($144,000) divided by the amount of income before tax. While the effective tax rate is often a useful number, it must be used carefully because it reflects not only the amount of tax payable to government entities for the current period but also the differences between book and tax accounting methods.

BALANCE SHEET DISCLOSURES AND RELATED NOTES FOR PFIZER

The impact of tax allocation and deferred taxes on asset and liability values can be substantial. Therefore, it is crucial that users of financial statements understand how to interpret the disclosures related to these items. Throughout this section, the balance sheet disclosures for Pfizer Inc. will be presented and discussed. Because of the size and scope of Pfizer's operations, the company's accountants must consider many differences between book and tax accounting. The noncurrent asset and long-term liabilities sections of the balance sheet for 2003 are provided in Figure 16.1.

As you recall, deferred tax may appear on the balance sheet as a deferred tax asset, a deferred tax liability, or both. Additionally, the deferred tax amounts must be classi-

Figure 16.1

Balance Sheet Excerpt

Pfizer

Pfizer Inc.
Partial Balance Sheet

(MILLIONS)	YEAR ENDED DECEMBER 31	
	2003	2002
Noncurrent assets:		
Long-term investments and loans	$ 6,142	$ 5,161
Property, plant and equipment, less accumulated depreciation	18,287	10,712
Goodwill	22,306	1,200
Identifiable intangible assets, less accumulated amortization	36,350	921
Other assets, deferred taxes and deferred charges	3,949	3,581
Long-term liabilities:	23,657	18,555
Long-term debt	5,755	3,140
Pension benefit obligations	2,861	1,327
Postretirement benefit obligations	1,451	623
Deferred taxes	13,238	364
Other noncurrent liabilities	4,436	2,397

Figure 16.2

Excerpt from Pfizer Note—Taxes on Income

Pfizer

Deferred tax assets and liabilities in the preceding table, netted by taxing location, are in the following captions in the consolidated balance sheet:

(MILLIONS OF DOLLARS)	2003	2002
Prepaid expenses and taxes	$ 1,907	$ 1,185
Other assets, deferred taxes and deferred charges	—	532
Deferred taxes on income	(13,238)	(364)
Net deferred tax asset/(liability)	$ (11,331)	$ 1,353

fied as current or long-term, using the definitions provided in *SFAS No. 109.* Pfizer's balance sheet for 2003 indicates a long-term liability for deferred tax of $13,238 million, highlighted in Figure 16.1

The note for 2003, as shown in Figure 16.2, reveals a net deferred tax liability for 2003 of $11,331 million, consisting of $1,907 million for deferred tax assets and $13,238 million for long-term deferred tax liabilities. Pfizer's note disclosure of deferred tax is comprehensive, allowing the statement user to tie the amounts in the notes to the amounts on the financial statements. The disclosures of many other companies often do not provide such comprehensive information.

SFAS No. 109 also requires companies to disclose the approximate tax effect of each type of temporary difference that gives rise to a significant portion of the deferred tax liabilities and assets.[17] Pfizer provided the note disclosure shown in Figure 16.3 as a breakdown of the temporary differences that make up the balances of the deferred tax asset and liability accounts.

Figure 16.3

Excerpt from Pfizer Note 10—Taxes on Income

Pfizer

The tax effects of the major items recorded as deferred tax assets and liabilities are:

	2003 DEFERRED TAX		2002 DEFERRED TAX	
(MILLIONS OF DOLLARS)	ASSETS	LIABILITIES	ASSETS	LIABILITIES
Prepaid/deferred items	$ 957	$ (592)	$ 931	$ (279)
Intangibles	257	(11,376)	13	(8)
Inventories	1,668	(343)	726	(137)
Property, plant and equipment	207	(1,541)	55	(813)
Employee benefits	2,022	(207)	601	(253)
Restructurings and other charges	428	(789)	186	(83)
Foreign tax credit carryforwards	153	—	253	—
Other carryforwards	92	—	53	—
Unremitted earnings	—	(2,837)	—	—
All other	1,033	(460)	385	(174)
Subtotal	6,817	(18,145)	3,203	(1,747)
Valuation allowance	(3)	—	(103)	—
Total deferred taxes	$ 6,814	$ (18,145)	$ 3,100	$ (1,747)
Net deferred tax asset/(liability)		$ (11,331)	$ 1,353	

---

17 *SFAS No. 109*, par. 43.

It is important to remember that the note shown in Figure 16.3 does not indicate the temporary differences that occurred during one particular time period. Rather, the note disclosure indicates the *cumulative temporary differences* at the end of the year that will reverse in future periods. Pfizer lists the primary cause of deferred tax *liabilities* in 2003 as intangibles ($11,376 million). This is a reflection of the new stance taken in *SFAS No. 142*, which does not allow certain intangibles to be amortized for financial reporting purposes. For tax purposes, a deduction for amortization has been taken, resulting in a deferred tax liability. The most substantial causes of deferred tax *assets* are listed as employee benefits ($2,022 million) and inventories ($1,668 million). This indicates that Pfizer recognized expenses related to these items for book purposes that cannot be deducted for tax purposes until a future time. Also, note that in some cases, there is doubt concerning whether future deductible amounts will be realized, as evidenced by the existence of a valuation allowance ($3 million) at the end of 2003.

INCOME STATEMENT DISCLOSURES AND RELATED NOTES FOR PFIZER

Income tax expense can have a sizable impact on a company's net income. A portion of Pfizer's income statement for the year ended December 31, 2003, is presented in Figure 16.4 and discussed in this section.

Pfizer recognized a provision for taxes on income (another term for income tax expense) on continuing operations of $1,621 million in 2003. Remember that this amount is based on the accounting for book purposes. *SFAS No. 109* requires companies to disclose separately the current portion and the deferred portion of income tax expense. Pfizer presented the note shown in Figure 16.5 to meet this disclosure requirement.

Figure 16.4

Income Statement Excerpt

Pfizer

Pfizer Inc., and Subsidiary Companies
Partial Consolidated Statement of Income

(MILLIONS, EXCEPT PER COMMON SHARE DATA)	YEAR ENDED DECEMBER 31		
	2003	2002	2001
Revenues	$ 45,188	$ 32,373	$ 29,024
Costs and expenses:			
Cost of sales	9,832	4,045	3,823
Selling, informational and administrative expenses	15,242	10,846	9,717
Research and development expenses	7,131	5,176	4,776
Merger-related in-process research and development charge	5,052	—	—
Merger-related costs	1,058	630	819
Other (income)/deductions—net	3,610	(120)	(95)
Income from continuing operations before provision for taxes on income, minority interests and cumulative effect of change in accounting principles	3,263	11,796	9,984
Provision for taxes on income	1,621	2,609	2,433
Minority interests	3	6	14
Income from continuing operations before cumulative effect of change in accounting principles	1,639	9,181	7,537

Figure 16.5

Excerpt from Pfizer Note—Taxes on Income

Pfizer

The provision for taxes on income from continuing operations before minority interests and the cumulative effect of change in accounting principles consists of the following:

(MILLIONS OF DOLLARS)	2003	2002	2001
United States:			
Taxes currently payable:			
Federal	$ 29	$ 1,403	$ 480
State and local	115	226	51
Deferred income taxes	502	(88)	974
Total U.S. tax provision	646	1,541	1,505
International:			
Taxes currently payable	1,581	1,265	810
Deferred income taxes	(606)	(197)	118
Total international tax provision	975	1,068	928
Total provision for taxes on income	$ 1,621	$ 2,609	$ 2,433

Additionally, *SFAS No. 109* requires a note disclosure for a "reconciliation using percentages or dollar amounts" of the reported amount of tax expense and the amount of tax expense that would result from applying the federal statutory rate to pretax income. The estimated amount and the nature of each significant reconciling item must be disclosed.[18] Pfizer provided the reconciliation in percentage form, as shown in Figure 16.6.

Notice that the reconciliation begins with the U.S. federal income tax rate of 35 percent and adjusts that rate to the effective tax rate reflected in the income statement. The reconciliation must consider the impact of tax rates in jurisdictions other than the United States. The reconciliation also describes the *permanent* differences that exist between book and tax for the company. Temporary differences affect the amount of the deferred tax account, but permanent differences are items that cause a difference between the statutory rate and the effective tax rate.

Figure 16.6

Excerpt from Pfizer Note 10—Taxes on Income

Pfizer

Reconciliation of the U.S. statutory income tax rate to our effective tax rate for continuing operations before the cumulative effect of change in accounting principles follows:

(PERCENTAGES)	2003	2002	2001
U.S. statutory income tax rate	35.0	35.0	35.0
Earnings taxed at other than U.S. statutory rate	(53.2)	(12.6)	(11.0)
U.S. research tax credit	(3.1)	(1.1)	(0.8)
Acquired IPR&D	54.2	—	—
Litigation settlement provisions	13.7	—	—
All other—net	3.1	0.8	1.2
Effective tax rate for income from continuing operations before cumulative effect of change in accounting principles	49.7	22.1	24.4

18 Ibid., par. 47.

CHECK YOUR UNDERSTANDING

1. Should deferred tax assets or liabilities be classified as current or long-term? Explain.

2. How is the effective tax rate for a company computed?

3. Based on Figure 16.5, what portion of Pfizer's provision for income tax of $1,621 million is identified as current for U.S. taxes?

LO7 Interpret income tax disclosures and their use in financial analysis.

Critical Thinking: As a potential investor in a company, why might you be interested in the activity of the Deferred Tax Liability, Deferred Tax Asset, and Valuation Allowance accounts?

Analyzing Income Tax Disclosures

In the previous section, we examined how income tax expense and deferred taxes are reflected in a company's financial statements and note disclosures. When reviewing these statements and disclosures, it is important to understand how they affect the representation of the company's financial condition.

DEFERRED TAXES AS TRUE LIABILITIES

As users of financial statements, we must examine whether the integrity of the company's assets and liabilities is intact. In essence, do these amounts represent *true* assets and liabilities? This is especially important with regard to deferred tax liabilities. Some analysts do not consider deferred taxes to be true liabilities. They *exclude* deferred tax liabilities when calculating debt-to-equity ratios and other ratios based on total liabilities. In their view, growing companies seldom see the balance of the deferred tax account decrease as a result of reversals of temporary differences. As we have seen, the dollar amount recognized can be quite large. Excluding deferred taxes from a computation of the debt-to-equity ratio can have a dramatic effect on the outcome.

On this issue, the FASB's stance is clear: The FASB adopts an asset-liability approach to deferred taxes and believes that the amount recognized as a deferred tax credit should be considered a liability on the balance sheet. It outlines three characteristics of liabilities as established in *Statement of Financial Accounting Standards No. 6*:[19]

1. Liabilities are probable future sacrifices of economic benefits arising from present obligations to transfer assets or provide services in the future as a result of past transactions.

2. The duty or obligation requires the entity to transfer its assets or perform a service, leaving it little or no discretion to avoid the future sacrifice.

3. The transaction or event obligating the entity has already happened.

The FASB believes that deferred taxes are true liabilities because the amounts recognized meet each of the three characteristics. Thus deferred taxes are "an obligation for the consequences of taxable temporary differences that stem from the requirements of the tax law"; "the only question is when, not whether, temporary differences will result in taxable amounts in future periods."[20]

Perhaps the reluctance on the part of some analysts to treat deferred taxes as a liability is a holdover from the accounting rules that preceded *SFAS No. 109*. Under those rules, the meaning of the deferred tax amounts recognized on the balance sheet was not clearly defined. The FASB has attempted to make the meaning of the balance sheet amounts more clear. It should be recognized that the nature of deferred tax amounts

---

19 See ibid., par. 75–79, for discussion.

20 Ibid., par. 76, 78.

differs from that of many other liabilities. Deferred tax amounts are not *legal* liabilities at the time they are recognized in the sense that the company is not legally obligated to pay the amount that has been recognized as deferred tax. If the amounts are future taxable amounts, they will become legal liabilities at a future time, when the temporary differences reverse and are recognized for tax purposes.

QUALITY OF EARNINGS ISSUES

Income tax disclosures and the related notes should be analyzed carefully because they may give important indications concerning the quality of the earnings reported by a company. First, it is important to determine the reasons for any large increases or decreases in the total amount of deferred tax. A large increase may be an indication of favorable factors, such as an accelerating pace of capital expenditures or expansion. But large increases in deferred tax may also be an indication that company management has made accounting changes in an effort to increase reported earnings. For example, a change in the estimated life of depreciable assets for book purposes would cause an increase in the balance of deferred tax. If such changes occur, analysts cannot rely on the quality of the earnings disclosures.

Second, deferred tax disclosures may help analysts compare the earnings quality of one company to that of another. The deferred tax note disclosures for all major companies contain a list of the temporary differences and whether those differences resulted in deferred tax assets or deferred tax liabilities (recall the Pfizer disclosures). Analysts often compare the temporary differences of companies that are in the same industry. If one company has more differences between tax and book amounts than other companies in the same industry, that company's accounting policy choices and the company's earnings disclosures may be called into question.

Third, deferred tax assets may be especially important indicators of the quality of earnings. Deferred tax assets often result when a company has recorded expenses, losses, or other deductions for book purposes *before* they have been deducted for tax purposes. For example, restructuring charges and contingent liabilities are often recorded for book purposes before they are allowed for tax purposes. In these cases, reported earnings have been reduced by a noncash charge that will have tax implications at a future date. Analysts usually believe that for good-quality earnings, the earnings from events should coincide with the cash consequences of those events. Deferred tax assets are an indication that the reported amount of earnings differs from the underlying cash flows.

EARNINGS MANIPULATION AND ETHICS

ETHICS In an earlier section, we presented the use of a Valuation Allowance account as an offset or contra account for a deferred tax asset. The valuation allowance is required when it is "more likely than not" that the deferred tax asset will not result in future benefits. This judgment provides an opportunity for smoothing and/or manipulation of earnings. When a Valuation Allowance account is established, income tax expense is increased and reported earnings are decreased. If management is attempting to smooth earnings over time, it is likely to establish or increase the Valuation Allowance account during periods of profitability. Once a Valuation Allowance account is established, additional judgment is needed at the end of each succeeding period to determine whether the account should be adjusted. If the account is reduced, income tax expense can be reduced and reported earnings increased. As you can see, management may be inclined to use this tool to increase earnings during periods in which the company has experienced downturns in profitability.

Admittedly, the judgments involved in deferred tax accounting are difficult, particularly the accounting for the Valuation Allowance account. However, the company's management, board of directors, and auditors must ensure that deferred tax judgments are made in a neutral and unbiased manner. Readers of financial statements must be vigilant to determine whether these judgments have been made in a manner that provides smoothing or manipulation of reported earnings.

> **CHECK YOUR UNDERSTANDING**
>
> 1. How do analysts generally view the quality of earnings of a company if earnings differ greatly from the cash consequences of the events of the period?
>
> 2. If a company wished to increase its profitability by manipulating a Valuation Allowance account, would the company increase or decrease the balance in that account?
>
> 3. Why are some analysts reluctant to treat deferred taxes as true liabilities?

LO8 Identify the effects of interperiod tax allocations on cash flow.

Critical Thinking: Given that the actual tax paid to the IRS is not reflected on a company's income statement or balance sheet, what accounts might you analyze to compute this amount?

Impact of Deferred Tax on Cash Flows

DEFERRED TAX ON THE STATEMENT OF CASH FLOWS

For any company, the changes in the deferred tax asset and liability accounts represent noncash amounts. The changes in these accounts must appear on the statement of cash flows when the indirect approach is used. The adjustment should appear in the operating activities section of the statement because the change in deferred tax affects the net income of the company for the period and represents an operating item.

The operating activities category of the 2003 statement of cash flows for Pfizer Inc. is provided in Figure 16.7. Note that the highlighted amount of ($104) million in 2003 represents a change in deferred taxes. Because it is a negative amount, it indicates that a deferred tax liability decreased (the most likely scenario for Pfizer) or a deferred tax asset increased, resulting in a negative influence on cash provided from operations. The following rules apply to the impact that changes in deferred tax have on the amount of cash provided:

If deferred tax liability increases ⟶ Positive

If deferred tax liability decreases ⟶ Negative

If deferred tax asset increases ⟶ Negative

If deferred tax asset decreases ⟶ Positive

ACCRUAL TO CASH

In some cases, the amount of income tax recognized on the accrual basis is known, but users may be interested in the amount of actual cash involved. Therefore, it is necessary to convert the accrual-basis records to a cash basis. For example, assume that Tiger Company recognized $100,000 of income tax expense on its income statement for 2005. Also, assume that the company had the following account balances at the beginning and end of 2005:

Account	Beginning Balance	Ending Balance
Deferred Tax Asset (Current)	$20,000	$35,000
Deferred Tax Liability (Long-Term)	40,000	44,000
Income Tax Payable	15,000	18,000

Figure 16.7

Operating Activities Section of the Statement of Cash Flows

Pfizer

Consolidated Statement of Cash Flows
Pfizer Inc. and Subsidiary Companies

	YEAR ENDED DECEMBER 31		
(MILLIONS OF DOLLARS)	2003	2002	2001
Operating Activities			
Net Income	$ 3,910	$ 9,126	$ 7,788
Adjustments to reconcile net income to net cash provided by continuing operating activities:			
Cumulative effect of change in accounting principles	30	410	—
Income from operations of discontinued businesses and product lines	(16)	(278)	(251)
Harmonization of accounting methodology	—	—	(175)
Merger-related in-process research and development charge	5,052	—	—
Charge for fair value mark-up of acquired inventory sold	2,820	—	—
Deferred taxes	(104)	(285)	1,092
Charges to write-down equity investments	16	45	—
Gains on sales of discontinued businesses and product lines	(3,885)	(117)	—
Gains on sales of products	(87)	(34)	
Depreciation and amortization	4,078	1,036	972
Other	604	(367)	176
Changes in assets and liabilities, net of effect of businesses acquired and divested:			
Accounts receivable	(904)	(963)	81
Inventories	(202)	(129)	(110)
Prepaid and other assets	(905)	(1,009)	(765)
Accounts payable and accrued liabilities	670	461	(412)
Income taxes payable	(550)	1,591	209
Other deferred items	1,198	377	256
Net cash provided by continuing operating activities	$ 11,725	$ 9,864	$ 8,861

To find the amount of cash actually paid for taxes during 2005, perform the following calculation:

	Accrual Amount	Cash Amount
Tax expense		$100,000
Increase in deferred tax asset		15,000
Increase in deferred tax liability		(4,000)
Increase in income tax payable		(3,000)
Tax paid		$108,000

All of the balance sheet accounts related to income tax must be analyzed in order to determine the amount of income tax paid. Note that it is the *change* in the account balance, rather than the ending balance of each account, that is important when adjusting from the accrual amount of tax to the amount actually paid.

1. In converting tax expense from an accrual basis to a cash basis to yield actual cash paid, how is a decrease in income tax payable treated in the computation?

2. If the balance in the Deferred Tax Asset account increases in a period, does this indicate a positive or a negative effect on cash flow?

Revisiting the Case

PFIZER BENEFITS FROM TAX LAW

1. Companies use GAAP for computing income for reporting purposes and use tax law for computing income for tax purposes.

2. Pfizer's actual cash paid for income taxes has dramatically increased over the last three years. From 2002 to 2003, the amount paid increased by 96.3 percent. From 2001 to 2002, the amount paid increased by 54.6 percent.

SUMMARY BY LEARNING OBJECTIVE

LO1 Explain why interperiod tax allocation is necessary.

Interperiod allocation of tax is necessary because of the differences between the accounting rules for financial statement purposes and those for income tax purposes. These differences arise because the objectives of financial accounting and tax accounting are different and because the regulatory bodies that develop the accounting rules are not the same. Although some accountants argue that the amount of tax computed by using the tax rules is the "true" amount of tax, most accountants recognize that interperiod allocation of tax is necessary to be consistent with the accrual basis of accounting. To match revenue and expense, it is necessary to report tax expense when it is incurred rather than when it is paid to the taxing authorities. Interperiod allocation of tax results in a more equitable reporting of income by companies.

LO2 Identify permanent and temporary tax differences.

Permanent differences are amounts that are used in the calculation of taxable income but not used in calculating book income, or vice versa (amounts used in the calculation of book income but not used in calculating taxable income). Permanent differences are not used in interperiod tax allocation and should not be reflected in the deferred tax account. Temporary differences are items that affect both book and taxable income, but not in the same time period. Often these items are referred to as timing differences (although there are a few technical differences between the terms *temporary* and *timing*). Timing differences should be reflected in the Deferred Tax account. The tax effect of the differences should enter the Deferred Tax account when the differences originate and should be removed when the differences have reversed.

LO3 Determine and record tax expense and tax payable.

Tax payable must be calculated using the tax rules. It represents the amount of tax based on the taxable income amount, after considering all income and deduction amounts allowed by the IRS. Tax expense is the amount reflected as expense on the income statement using the financial accounting rules. Tax expense represents the amount of income tax payable plus the amount of deferred tax credits for the current year and minus the amount of deferred tax debits for the current year.

LO4 Determine deferred taxes when multiple tax rates or tax-rate changes are involved.

SFAS No. 109 holds that when determining deferred tax amounts for temporary differences that extend over a period of years, companies should use the enacted tax rate that is applicable to the time periods in which the temporary differences will reverse or be settled. The future tax rate, if it is known, should be used to establish the Deferred Tax account. If the new rate was not known at the time the Deferred Tax account was established, the account should be adjusted for the effect of the new rate when the change occurs. The effect should be included in income from continuing operations during the time period that includes the enactment date.

LO5 Describe when and how a valuation allowance is recorded for a deferred tax asset.

When deferred tax assets are present, a company must consider whether a Valuation Allowance account is necessary. A deferred tax asset represents a future deductible amount for tax purposes. The benefit to be received from the future deductible amount is dependent upon the existence of future income that can be used to absorb the deduction. If it is more likely than not that some portion of the deferred tax asset will not be realized, a Valuation Allowance account should be established. The Valuation Allowance account is a balance sheet account and is a contra-asset account. It is shown on the balance sheet in conjunction with the Deferred Asset account.

LO6 Describe how tax expense, deferred tax liabilities, and deferred tax assets are presented in the financial statements.

Tax expense is recognized on the income statement. Two elements of tax expense must be reported (additional disclosures are necessary in some cases): the current provision and the deferred portion of the tax. The balance of the Deferred Tax account must be reported on the balance sheet and must be separated into its current and long-term components. The classification of deferred tax as current or long-term should be based on the classification of the related asset or liability that gave rise to the deferred tax amount. Deferred tax amounts related to long-term accounts should be classified as long-term for balance sheet purposes. The notes to the financial statements also provide important information regarding deferred tax. Companies are required to indicate the temporary differences that have led to the deferred tax amounts reflected on the balance sheet. Further, companies are required to report the causes of the differences between the federal statutory tax rate and the effective tax rate reported for financial statement purposes.

LO7 Interpret income tax disclosures and their use in financial analysis.

There are several analysis issues involving deferred tax and the related financial disclosures. First, users must consider carefully whether deferred tax credits actually represent liabilities or obligations of the firm. The FASB holds that the amounts do in fact represent liabilities because deferred tax credits are consistent with the accounting definition of the term *liabilities*. Second, income tax disclosures should be analyzed because they may give indications concerning the quality of a company's reported earnings as compared to that of other companies in the same industry. Third, deferred tax disclosures may be useful to analysts in detecting possible earnings manipulation or smoothing of earnings.

LO8 Identify the effects of interperiod tax allocations on cash flow.

Changes in the Deferred Tax account should be reflected in the statement of cash flows. Generally, they should be indicated in the operating activities category of the statement. An increase in a deferred tax liability is an addition to cash flow from operating activities, whereas an increase in a deferred tax asset is a deduction. In order to actually determine the cash flow impact of taxes during a period, an analyst must not only adjust the amount of tax expense for the change in the deferred tax asset or liability account, but also adjust for the change in any amount of tax payable or prepaid tax that existed at the beginning and end of the period.

KEY TERMS

current tax expense (p. 773)
deferred tax expense (p. 773)
discounted (p. 769)
effective tax rate (p. 774)
future deductible amount (p. 760)

future taxable amount (p. 760)
income tax expense (p. 756)
income tax payable (p. 756)
originating temporary difference (p. 758)

permanent differences (p. 756)
reversing temporary difference (p. 758)
temporary differences (p. 757)
Valuation Allowance account (p. 769)

EXERCISES

LO1 **EXERCISE 16-1 Allocation Versus Nonallocation**

Assume that Considine Company reports the following revenue and expense amounts for the years 2004, 2005, and 2006:

Revenue (other than construction revenue)	$700,000
Operating expenses	200,000

Considine also began a long-term construction project on January 1, 2004, that will result in a total gross profit of $420,000. The project will be completed evenly over a three-year time period. Considine uses the percentage-of-completion method for financial statement purposes but uses the completed-contract method for tax purposes. The tax rate is 40 percent in all periods.

Required:

1. Assume that no tax is allocated between periods for Considine's statements. The company records as tax expense the amount of tax paid, as calculated for tax purposes. Develop income statements for each of the three years 2004 to 2006. Calculate the effective tax rate for each period.

2. Assume that Considine allocates tax between periods using a deferred tax account. Develop income statements for each of the three years 2004 to 2006. Calculate the effective tax rate for each period.

3. Which income statements more fairly present Considine's financial performance? Explain your answer.

LO2 **EXERCISE 16-2 Permanent and Temporary Differences**

Andrew Company reports the following reasons for differences between its financial accounting and its tax amounts:

A. Premiums are paid for life insurance on corporate officers.

B. Accelerated depreciation is used for tax purposes, and straight-line depreciation is used for book purposes.

C. Fines and penalties have been levied by government agencies.

D. Warranty expense is recognized on the accrual basis for book purposes, but the expense is deducted when paid for tax purposes.

E. Straight-line depreciation is used for both book and tax purposes, but a 10-year life is used for book purposes and a 5-year life is used for tax purposes.

F. Interest is received on state and municipal obligations.

G. Proceeds from life insurance on corporate officers are received.

H. The percentage-of-completion method is used for book purposes, and the completed-contract method is used for tax purposes.

I. A contingent liability is recorded for book purposes before it is allowed for tax purposes.

J. The corporation receives a dividend from an investment in the stock of another company. For tax purposes, 80 percent of the dividend is excluded.

Required: Indicate whether the items should be considered temporary differences or permanent differences in calculating tax expense and deferred tax. Assume all items are independent scenarios.

LO3, 6 **EXERCISE 16-3 Tax Expense and Tax Payable, One Rate** (CPA adapted)

For the year ended December 31, 2005, Upham Co.'s books reflect income of $600,000 before provision for income tax expense. To compute taxable income for federal income tax purposes, the following items should be noted:

Income from exempt municipal bonds	$ 60,000
Depreciation deducted for tax purposes, in excess of depreciation recorded on the books	$120,000

Proceeds received from life insurance on death of officer $100,000
Enacted corporate tax rate   30%

Required:

1. Calculate taxable income and tax payable for tax purposes.

2. Calculate the amount of tax expense for 2005 and prepare an entry to record the deferred tax for the year.

3. Prepare the proper income statement presentation for the year 2005, beginning with the amount for income before tax. (Exclude earnings per share presentations.)

LO3, 4, 6   **EXERCISE 16-4   Tax Expense and Tax Payable, Two Rates**

For the year ended December 31, 2005, Mont Co.'s books showed income of $600,000 before provision for income tax expense. To compute taxable income for federal income tax purposes, the following items should be noted:

Income from exempt municipal bonds	$ 60,000
Depreciation deducted for tax purposes, in excess of depreciation recorded on the books	$120,000
Proceeds received from life insurance on death of officer	$100,000
Corporate tax rate for 2005	30%
Enacted tax rate for future periods	35%

Required:

1. Calculate taxable income and tax payable for tax purposes.

2. Calculate the amount of tax expense for 2005 and prepare an entry to record the deferred tax for the year.

3. Prepare the proper income statement presentation for the year 2005, beginning with the amount for income before tax. (Exclude earnings per share presentations.)

LO3, 4   **EXERCISE 16-5   Deferred Tax, Change in Rate**

Usalis, Inc. began operations on January 1, 2003. The company recognizes income from construction-type contracts under the percentage-of-completion method in its financial statements. Usalis appropriately uses the completed-contract method for income tax reporting. Reported income from construction-type contracts under each method is as follows:

Year	Percentage-of-Completion	Completed-Contract
2003	$ 600,000	$ —
2004	1,200,000	800,000
2005	1,700,000	1,400,000

Required:

1. The enacted income tax rate is 30 percent, and there are no other temporary differences. Calculate the balance of the deferred tax account at December 31, 2005.

2. Assume that the enacted tax rate changed to 40 percent on January 1, 2006. Usalis did not have knowledge of the new rate prior to its enactment. Record all entries necessary in 2006 because of the change in rates.

LO3, 5   **EXERCISE 16-6   Deferred Tax Asset**

Assume that Lane Company reports taxable income of $200,000 for 2005 and a tax rate of 35 percent. During 2005, Lane became the defendant in a lawsuit. The lawsuit has not been resolved at the end of the period, but Lane's lawyers believe that it is probable that the company will be held liable and have estimated that the amount of loss will be $80,000. As a result, the lawsuit has been recognized as a contingent liability for book purposes. However, the legal obligation is not deductible for tax purposes during 2005. The lawsuit represents the only difference between book and tax accounting for the year.

Required:

1. Assume that Lane Company has been quite profitable in past periods and expects to continue that pattern in the future. Record an entry to recognize tax expense, tax payable, and deferred tax for the year.

2. Assume that there is substantial doubt about whether Lane Company will be profitable in future periods. As a result, the company believes that one-half of the future deduction for legal costs will not be realized. Record an entry to recognize tax expense, tax payable, and deferred tax for the year.

3. Explain what circumstances require the utilization of a Valuation Allowance account when deferred tax is recognized. How should that account be presented on the financial statements?

LO2, 3, 6   **EXERCISE 16-7**   **Balance Sheet Presentation of Deferred Tax**

The Nall Company began operations in 2004. During the first two years, assume the following events:

A. In 2004 the company purchased a depreciable asset for $200,000. The company has used an accelerated method for tax purposes, resulting in depreciation of $80,000 and $60,000 for 2004 and 2005, respectively. For book purposes, the company has used the straight-line method with a five-year life and zero residual value.

B. On July 1, 2004, Nall received $100,000 for renting its excess office space. The rent agreement was for a one-year time period, beginning July 1. Rent income was taxable when received by Nall.

C. The company invested in bonds that produced tax-exempt interest of $10,000 in both 2004 and 2005. The amounts were treated as interest income for book purposes.

D. Beginning in 2005, Nall offered a one-year warranty on the product that it sold to customers. The company accrued warranty costs of $60,000 related to product sales. Actual warranty repair costs for the year totaled $20,000.

Required: Determine the amounts that should be reported as deferred tax on Nall's balance sheet as of December 31, 2005. Indicate whether each amount should be reflected in the current or long-term section of the balance sheet. Assume a 40 percent tax rate.

LO8   **EXERCISE 16-8**   **Accrual to Cash**

Assume that Forsberg Company recognized $100,000 of income tax expense on its income statement for the year 2005. Also assume that the company had the following account balances at the beginning and end of 2005:

Account	Beginning Balance	Ending Balance
Deferred Tax Asset (Current)	$35,000	$20,000
Deferred Tax Liability (Long-Term)	44,000	40,000
Income Tax Payable	18,000	15,000

Required: Determine the amount of cash paid for taxes during 2005.

LO8   **EXERCISE 16-9**   **Cash to Accrual**

Assume that Hutchinson Company paid $94,000 for income taxes in the year 2005. Also assume that the company had the following account balances at the beginning and end of 2005:

Account	Beginning Balance	Ending Balance
Deferred Tax Asset (Current)	$35,000	$20,000
Deferred Tax Liability (Long-Term)	44,000	40,000
Income Tax Payable	18,000	15,000

Required: Determine the amount of tax expense recognized on Hutchinson's income statement for the year 2005.

LO8   **EXERCISE 16-10   Deferred Tax on the Statement of Cash Flows**

In 2005, the operating activities portion of the statement of cash flows for Lambdin Company appeared as follows:

Cash Flows from Operating Activities:	
Net income (after tax expense of $400,000)	$600,000
Adjustments to reconcile net earnings to cash flows:	
Depreciation	xxx
Increase in deferred tax liability	20,000
Losses on sale of equipment	xxx
Changes in assets and liabilities:	
Increase in current assets	(xxx)
Increase in tax payable	10,000
Increase in other current liabilities	xxx
Net Cash Flows from Operating Activities	$ xxxxx

Required: Calculate the amount of cash paid by Lambdin for taxes during 2005.

LO2   **EXERCISE 16-11   Permanent and Temporary Differences**

All differences between the amount of income tax payable and the amount of income tax expense can be classified as either permanent differences or temporary differences. A number of items that may give rise to differences are as follows:

A. Season tickets are sold in advance by the Jacksonville Jaguars football team.

B. Available-for-sale securities decreased in value during the year.

C. A company accrues interest on a note receivable in the period before the borrower pays.

D. Subsequent expenditures related to depreciable assets are expensed for tax purposes and capitalized for accounting purposes.

E. A company applies the matching concept in accounting for expected warranty costs.

F. A company acquires a business and recognizes goodwill. Tax laws require goodwill to be amortized over 15 years.

G. Patents are amortized over a longer period for GAAP than for tax purposes.

H. The direct write-off method is used to account for bad debts for GAAP purposes.

I. Customers pay amounts due in the period after the sale is recognized.

J. A company complies with the LIFO conformity rule.

K. A company receives proceeds from a life insurance policy on which it is the beneficiary.

L. A company is assessed a late fee for submitting its payroll taxes after the due date.

M. A company pays commissions related to the purchase of municipal bonds.

Required: For each of the items listed, indicate whether the type of difference is permanent (P), temporary (T), or neither (X), and whether the item will create a deferred tax asset (DTA), a deferred tax liability (DTL), or neither (X).

LO5, 6   **EXERCISE 16-12   Presentation in Financial Statements and Valuation Allowance**

Larsen Company reported the following selected account balances in its adjusted trial balance at December 31, 2004:

Deferred Tax Liability (relates to a fair value adjustment for trading securities)	$14,000
Deferred Tax Asset (relates to a contingent lawsuit from 2003 to be settled in 2006 or after)	32,000
Deferred Tax Liability (relates to depreciation that is expected to reverse from 2005 through 2007)	15,000

Income Tax Payable	$62,000
Income Tax Expense ($12,000 relates to an extraordinary loss)	80,000
Deferred Tax Asset (relates to uncollectible accounts, which are written off when they are eight months past due)	12,000

It is "more likely than not" that the company will benefit from only 60 percent of any future tax benefits.

Required: Show how the results of these income tax effects should be reported in the respective sections of Larsen's balance sheet at December 31, 2004.

LO2, 3, 4   EXERCISE 16-13   **Temporary Differences with Multiple Tax Rates**

Patterson Corporation began operations during 2004. Other information provided by Patterson for 2004 and 2005 follows:

2004:

Depreciation costs are written off for income tax purposes on a different basis from that used for accounting purposes, resulting in a $60,000 additional expense for tax purposes as compared to accounting purposes that will reverse at an equal amount per year for each of the next three years.

2005:

- The depreciation difference from 2004 reverses as expected.
- Patterson collected $45,000 for rent under operating leases that will be earned equally during 2005, 2006, and 2007.
- Penalties incurred amounted to $3,000, but they will not be paid until 2006.
- Entertainment expenses reported on the income statement totaled $4,000. The amount allowed for tax purposes is 50 percent.
- Patterson accrued interest revenue of $5,000 on municipal bonds. Interest will be received during 2006.

The enacted tax rates are 26 percent for 2004, 30 percent for 2005, 35 percent for 2006, and 32 percent for 2007 and thereafter.

Required:

1. Determine the amounts that will be reported on the December 31, 2005, balance sheet as deferred tax assets or liabilities for each item given.

2. Which items will produce permanent differences? What is meant by the description of the differences produced by these items as "permanent"?

LO2, 3, 4   EXERCISE 16-14   **Temporary Differences with Multiple Tax Rates**

Plumbing Below Enterprises began operations during 2004. Other information provided for 2004 and 2005 follows:

2004:

- Pretax financial income is $76,000.
- Depreciation costs are written off for income tax purposes on a different basis from that used for accounting purposes, resulting in a $57,000 additional expense for tax purposes as compared to accounting purposes that will reverse at an equal amount per year for each of the next three years.

2005:

- Pretax financial income is $181,800.
- The depreciation difference from 2004 reverses as expected.
- Penalties incurred amounted to $2,400, but they will not be paid until 2006.
- Entertainment expenses reported on the income statement totaled $8,000. The amount allowed for tax purposes is 50 percent.
- Plumbing Below accrued interest revenue of $7,000 on municipal bonds. Interest will be received during 2006.

The enacted tax rates are 26 percent for 2004, 30 percent for 2005, 35 percent for 2006, and 32 percent for 2007 and thereafter.

Required:

1. Determine any deferred tax amounts at December 31, 2005.
2. Calculate taxable income for 2005.
3. Calculate income tax payable at December 31, 2005.
4. Why is it important to distinguish permanent from temporary differences?

LO5, 6 **EXERCISE 16-15** **Presentation in Financial Statements and Valuation Allowance**

Burns Company reported the following selected account balances in its adjusted trial balance at December 31, 2004:

Deferred Tax Liability (relates to reporting installment revenue in the accounting records; one-third is expected to reverse during 2005 and the balance equally during 2006 and 2007)	$15,000
Income Tax Expense	34,000
Deferred Tax Asset (relates to a rent received in advance for 2006)	11,000
Deferred Tax Liability (relates to a depreciation difference that is expected to reverse equally over the next four years)	24,000
Income Tax Payable	32,300
Deferred Tax Asset (relates to accounting for inventory costing method differences)	9,000

It is "more likely than not" that the company will benefit from only 80 percent of any income tax benefits.

Required: Show how the effects of each of these items would be reported in Burns Company's balance sheet at December 31, 2004, by preparing a partial balance sheet.

LO3, 4 **EXERCISE 16-16** **Income Tax Expense and Income Tax Payable with Multiple Rates**

O'Neal Corporation's income statement for the year ended December 31, 2005, shows pretax income of $300,000. The following items are treated differently on the tax return and in the accounting records:

Account	Tax Return	Accounting Records
Warranty expense	$120,000	$180,000
Depreciation expense	840,000	660,000
Tax-exempt interest revenue	0	24,000

O'Neal's tax rate for 2005 is 30 percent, and the enacted rate for both 2006 and 2007 is 40 percent. The remaining $60,000 of warranty costs will be incurred in 2006. Depreciation recorded in the accounting records will exceed tax return depreciation by $70,000 in 2006.

Required:

1. How much deferred tax liability does O'Neal have at December 31, 2005?
2. How much deferred tax asset does O'Neal have at December 31, 2005?
3. How much is income tax payable at December 31, 2005?
4. How much is income tax expense for 2005?
5. How much is net income for 2005?

LO3 **EXERCISE 16-17** **Tax Expense and Tax Payable**

Crews Company began operations during 2004. Enacted tax rates are 28 percent for 2004, 30 percent for 2005, 34 percent for 2006, and 38 percent for 2007 and thereafter. Pretax financial income for 2005 is $80,000.

On January 2, 2004, equipment costing $150,000 was purchased. The equipment had a life of four years and a $10,000 residual value. The straight-line method of depreciation is used for book purposes. Tax depreciation each year is as follows: 2004, $65,000; 2005, $33,000; 2006, $27,000; and 2007, $15,000.

Required:

1. Draw a tax T-account with the correct account title that will be used in interperiod tax allocation for the equipment. Post all amounts to this T-account through December 31, 2007. Label each posting by date and calculate the balance at each fiscal year end.

2. Calculate taxable income for 2005.

3. How much cash will be due for income taxes for 2005?

LO7   EXERCISE 16-18   Tax Disclosures

The note that appears on the opposite page is from the 2003 annual report of **Southwest Airlines**.

The following amounts appeared on Southwest Airlines financial statements for the years ended December 31, 2003 and 2002:

(in millions)	2003	2002
Income taxes refund receivable	$51	$ 0
Income taxes paid	51	3
Unrealized gain (loss) on derivative instruments, net of deferred taxes of $43 and $56	66	88

Required: Reconstruct the summary journal entries that Southwest Airlines prepared to accrue income taxes, pay taxes, and receive its refund for 2003. Assume that income taxes payable at December 31, 2003 and 2002, were $15 and $12 million, respectively.

LO3, 8   EXERCISE 16-19   Income Tax Expense and Cash Flows

The following accounts appeared on Doogle Donuts's adjusted trial balance for 2005 and 2004:

	12/31/05	12/31/04
Deferred Tax Asset—Current	$ 9,200	$ 8,600
Deferred Tax Asset—Long-Term	11,300	12,200
Deferred Tax Liability—Long-Term	25,600	21,600
Deferred Tax Liability—Current	6,700	9,800
Income Tax Payable	22,800	35,100
Valuation Allowance	3,800	5,100

The following income statement was prepared by Doogle Donuts's accountant for 2005:

Doogle Donuts
Income Statement
For the Year Ended December 31, 2005

Sales	$2,910,000
Cost of sales	1,410,000
Gross profit	$1,500,000
Operating expenses	980,000
Income before taxes	$ 520,000
Income taxes	182,000
Income from operations	$ 338,000
Extraordinary loss from hurricane, net of $24,000 taxes	56,000
Net income	$ 282,000

Southwest Airlines

Note 15. INCOME TAXES

Deferred income taxes reflect the net tax effects of temporary differences between the carrying amounts of assets and liabilities for financial reporting purposes and the amounts used for income tax purposes. The components of deferred tax assets and liabilities at December 31, 2003 and 2002, are as follows:

(In millions)	2003	2002
DEFERRED TAX LIABILITIES:		
Accelerated depreciation	$ 1,640	$ 1,440
Scheduled airframe maintenance	77	71
Fuel hedges	79	35
Other	19	26
Total deferred tax liabilities	1,815	1,572
DEFERRED TAX ASSETS:		
Deferred gains from sale and leaseback of aircraft	89	96
Capital and operating leases	73	77
Accrued employee benefits	108	86
State taxes	47	43
Other	40	37
Total deferred tax assets	357	339
Net deferred tax liability	$ 1,458	$ 1,233

The provision for income taxes is composed of the following:

(In millions)	2003	2002	2001
CURRENT:			
Federal	$ 73	$ (19)	$ 99
State	10	1	10
Total current	83	(18)	109
DEFERRED:			
Federal	170	157	187
State	13	13	21
Total deferred	183	170	208
	$ 266	$ 152	$ 327

For the year 2002, Southwest Airlines Co. had a tax net operating loss of $163 million for federal income tax purposes. This resulted in a federal tax refund due to utilization of this net operating loss as a carryback to prior taxable years. This refund, estimated at $51 million at December 31, 2002, was included in "Accounts and other receivables" in the Consolidated Balance Sheet at December 31, 2002 and was collected in 2003. The effective tax rate on income before income taxes differed from the federal income tax statutory rate for the following reasons:

(In millions)	2003	2002	2001
Tax at statutory U.S. tax rates	$ 247	$ 138	$ 290
Nondeductible items	7	6	7
State income taxes, net of federal benefit	15	9	20
Other, net	(3)	(1)	—
Total income tax provision	$ 266	$ 152	$ 317

Required:

1. Determine the net amount of income tax expense for 2005.

2. How much "cash paid for income taxes" is to be reported on Doogle Donuts's statement of cash flows for 2005?

3. Show what amounts related to income taxes will appear on the statement of cash flows in the operating activities section using the indirect method for 2005.

LO1, 2, 3, 4 **EXERCISE 16-20 Income Tax Expense, Income Tax Payable, Multiple Tax Rates**

Epic, Inc. prepared the following recap of the information needed for income taxes for 2005:

A. Pretax financial income is $100,000.

B. Epic incurred $10,000 for entertainment expenses; however, only $7,000 had been paid as of year end. The amount allowed for tax purposes is 50 percent.

C. Epic collected $50,000 for magazine subscriptions, of which $15,000 were produced and delivered during 2005, and the balance will be produced and delivered during 2006.

D. Epic wrote off $12,000 of trade receivable bad debts. At year end, Epic estimated bad debts expense in the amount of $18,000.

E. The enacted tax rates are 30 percent for 2005, 34 percent for 2006, and 33 percent for 2007 and thereafter.

Required:

1. Determine the amount that will be reported in Epic's December 31, 2005, balance sheet as deferred tax asset.

2. How much is taxable income for 2005?

3. How much cash will be paid for taxes for 2005?

4. How much is Epic's income tax expense for 2005? Record the journal entry to accrue income taxes for 2005.

5. Explain why interperiod tax allocation is necessary.

PROBLEMS

LO2, 3 **PROBLEM 16-1 Book to Tax Differences**

Assume that on January 1, 2005, the balance of the Deferred Tax account for Zerull Company was zero. Zerull company calculated the amount of income before tax for the year 2005 as $160,000. The company has the following differences between book and tax amounts for the year:

Interest on municipal bonds	$10,000
Depreciation on tax return in excess of books	25,000
Fines and penalties deducted on books	5,000
Installment sales income recorded for books (assume sales are collected within one year)	8,000
Contingent loss recorded for book purposes (assume the amount involved will be paid in 2007)	12,000

Zerull's tax rate for current and future periods is 40 percent.

Required: Develop a reconciliation that calculates the amount of taxable income for 2005.

Analyze: Indicate which of these differences are temporary and which are permanent. Indicate which of these differences are originating and which are reversing.

LO2, 3   PROBLEM **16-2**   **Tax to Book Differences**

Assume that on January 1, 2005, the balance of Deferred Tax for Hart Company was zero. The company calculated the amount of taxable income for its tax return for the year 2005 as $120,000. The company has the following differences between book and tax amounts for the year:

Interest on municipal bonds	$10,000
Depreciation on tax return in excess of books	25,000
Fines and penalties deducted on books	5,000
Installment sales income recorded for books (assume sales are collected within one year)	8,000
Contingent loss recorded for book purposes (assume the amount involved will be paid in 2007)	12,000

Hart's tax rate for current and future periods is 40 percent.

Required: Develop a reconciliation that calculates the amount of income before tax per books for 2005.

Analyze: Indicate which of the differences between book and tax amounts are temporary and which are permanent. In addition, indicate which of these differences are originating and which are reversing.

LO2, 3, 6   PROBLEM **16-3**   **Tax Expense, Tax Payable and Financial Disclosures**

Refer to the information for Zerull Company in Problem 16-1 for the year 2005.

Required:

1. Develop an accounting entry to recognize tax expense, tax payable, and deferred tax for 2005.

2. Beginning with the amount of income before tax, develop Zerull's income statement for 2005. (Exclude earnings per share amounts.)

3. Determine the amounts that should be disclosed for deferred tax on Zerull's balance sheet as of December 31, 2005. Indicate whether the amounts are assets or liabilities and whether they are current or long-term. You may assume that a Valuation Allowance account is not necessary for any of the deferred tax items.

Analyze: What is Zerull's effective tax rate for 2005?

LO2, 3, 6   PROBLEM **16-4**   **Tax Expense, Tax Payable, and Financial Disclosures**

Refer to the information for Hart Company in Problem 16-2 for the year 2005.

Required:

1. Develop an accounting entry to recognize tax expense, tax payable, and deferred tax for 2005.

2. Beginning with the amount of income before tax, develop Hart's income statement for the year 2005. (You should exclude earnings per share amounts.)

3. Determine the amounts that should be disclosed for deferred tax on Hart's balance sheet as of December 31, 2005. Indicate whether the amounts are assets or liabilities and whether they are current or long-term. You may assume that a Valuation Allowance account is not necessary for any of the deferred tax items.

Analyze: What is Hart's effective tax rate for 2005?

LO3, 7   PROBLEM **16-5**   **Interpreting Home Depot's Note Disclosures**

On the following page are excerpts from the notes in **Home Depot**'s annual report for the year ended February 2, 2003.

Home Depot

Note 3. Income Taxes

The provision for income taxes consisted of the following (in millions):

| | Fiscal Year Ended | | |
	Feb. 2, 2003	Feb. 3, 2002	Jan. 28, 2001
Current:			
Federal	$1,679	$1,594	$1,267
State	239	265	216
Foreign	117	60	45
	2,035	1,919	1,528
Deferred:			
Federal	174	(12)	98
State	1	(1)	9
Foreign	(2)	7	1
	173	(6)	108
Total	$2,208	$1,913	$1,636

The Company's combined federal, state and foreign effective tax rates for fiscal years 2002, 2001 and 2000, net of offsets generated by federal, state and foreign tax incentive credits, were approximately 37.6%, 38.6% and 38.8%, respectively.

The tax effects of temporary differences that give rise to significant portions of the deferred tax assets and deferred tax liabilities as of February 2, 2003, and February 3, 2002, were as follows (in millions):

	Feb. 2, 2003	Feb. 3, 2002
Deferred Tax Assets:		
Accrued self-insurance liabilities	$ 305	$ 220
Other accrued liabilities	92	138
Net loss on disposition of business	31	31
Total gross deferred tax assets	428	389
Valuation allowance	(31)	(31)
Deferred tax assets, net of valuation allowance	397	358
Deferred Tax Liabilities:		
Accelerated depreciation	(571)	(492)
Accelerated inventory deduction	(149)	—
Other	(39)	(55)
Total gross deferred tax liabilities	(759)	(547)
Net deferred tax liability	$(362)	$(189)

A valuation allowance existed as of February 2, 2003, and February 3, 2002, due to the uncertainty of capital loss utilization. Management believes the existing net deductible temporary differences comprising the deferred tax assets will reverse during periods in which the Company generates net taxable income.

Required:

1. Assuming that there were no other events that affected deferred taxes (such as sales of assets) during the year ended February 2, 2003, develop an accounting entry to recognize the amount of tax expense, tax payable, and deferred tax for the year ended February 2, 2003.

2. What is meant by the term *accrued self-insurance liabilities*? Explain how the accounting for such items results in deferred tax.

Analyze: What percentage of total deferred tax assets was deducted as a valuation allowance in 2003?

LO7   **PROBLEM 16-6   Lowe's Tax Disclosures**
The following excerpts are taken from the note disclosures of **Lowe's** 2002 annual report.

Lowe's	Note 13. Income Taxes		
	Jan. 31, 2003	Feb. 1, 2002	Feb. 2, 2001
(In Millions)	Components of Income Tax Provision		
Current			
Federal	$597	$490	$398
State	83	69	50
Total Current	680	559	448
Deferred			
Federal	173	35	19
State	35	7	4
Total Deferred	208	42	23
Total Income Tax Provision	$888	$601	$471

The tax effect of cumulative temporary differences that gave rise to the deferred tax assets and liabilities at January 31, 2003 and February 1, 2002 is as follows (in millions):

	January 31, 2003			February 1, 2002		
	Assets	Liabilities	Total	Assets	Liabilities	Total
Excess Property and Store Closing Costs	$ 24	$ —	$ 24	$ 28	$ —	$ 28
Self-Insurance	58	—	58	63	—	63
Depreciation	—	(498)	(498)	—	(331)	(331)
Vacation Accrual	5	—	5	27	—	27
Allowance for Sales Returns	26	—	26	9	—	9
Other, Net	6	(41)	(35)	12	(20)	(8)
Total	$119	$(539)	$(420)	$139	$(351)	$(212)

Required:

1. What were the most significant causes of Lowe's deferred tax assets and liabilities? How do they compare with those of Lowe's competitor, Home Depot, in Problem 16-5?

2. What are the possible reasons that Home Depot recognized an amount as a valuation allowance when Lowe's did not? Which of the two companies has acted more conservatively?

Analyze: Lowe's eliminated its Valuation Allowance account in the year ended January 30, 2000. What was the impact of this elimination on the company's earnings? What does this indicate about the quality of the company's earnings?

Research: What amounts are reflected on Lowe's current-year statement of cash flows that relate to deferred or current taxes? How can these amounts be used to analyze the quality of Lowe's earnings?

LO3, 7   **PROBLEM 16-7   Abbott Laboratories's Tax Disclosures**
Abbott Laboratories is a large company in the pharmaceutical industry. On the following page are the disclosures concerning income taxes that appear as notes to Abbott's financial statements of December 31, 2003.

Abbott Laboratories

Note 6. Taxes on Earnings (in thousands)

	2003	2002	2001
Current:			
U.S. Federal and Possessions	$ 578,407	$442,891	$ 633,684
State	29,662	19,324	74,087
Foreign	409,773	324,250	388,950
Total current	1,017,842	786,465	1,096,721
Deferred:			
Domestic	26,911	111,429	(741,213)
Foreign	(63,221)	(16,260)	(21,563)
Enacted tax rate changes	(348)	(1,924)	(1,187)
Total deferred	(36,658)	93,245	(763,963)
Total	$ 981,184	$879,710	$ 332,758

The temporary differences that give rise to deferred tax assets and liabilities were as follows (in thousands):

	2003	2002	2001
Compensation and employee benefits	$ 539,668	$ 544,148	$ 434,549
Trade receivable reserves	252,559	209,899	219,387
Inventory reserves	163,492	127,173	140,762
Deferred intercompany profit	380,854	240,463	254,276
State income taxes	68,489	91,140	100,265
Depreciation	(203,019)	(183,410)	(168,499)
Other, primarily acquired in-process research and development and other accruals and reserves not currently deductible, and the excess of book basis over tax basis of intangible assets	226,200	435,397	504,649
Total	$1,428,243	$1,464,810	$1,485,389

Valuation allowances for deferred tax assets were not significant.

Required:

1. Reconstruct a journal entry to recognize tax expense, tax payable, and deferred tax for the year 2003.

2. Is tax expense higher or lower than tax payable for the year? How will that affect the company's cash flow for the year?

3. What were the most important causes of deferred tax assets and liabilities for the company?

4. Explain why the company has deferred tax assets.

Analyze: Review the breakdown of tax provisions for Pfizer in Figure 16.5. How does this presentation differ from the Abbott Laboratories note offered in this problem?

Critical Thinking: Do you believe that Abbott Laboratories has used conservative accounting treatments in developing its financial statements? Explain your reasoning.

LO2, 3, 4, 6   **PROBLEM 16-8   Calculate Tax Expense, Tax Payable, Deferred Tax**

In 2005, the accountant for Pacter Co. developed the following list of items causing differences between pretax accounting income and taxable income:

A. Beginning in 2005, the company sold merchandise on an installment contract basis. Pacter elected, for tax purposes, to report the gross profit from these sales in the years in which the receivables are collected. However, for financial statement purposes, Pacter reported the gross profit at the time of sale. These procedures created a difference between book and taxable income of $80,000. Pacter anticipates collection of the receivables in 2006 and classifies Installments Receivable as a current asset.

B. For the last several years, Pacter has used an accelerated method of depreciation of equipment for tax purposes and straight-line for book purposes. Relevant depreciation information is as follows:

Asset	Date Purchased	Life	Cost	2005 Tax Depreciation	2005 Book Depreciation
Equipment A	1/2/02	5 years	$150,000	$20,000	$30,000
Equipment B	1/2/05	5 years	90,000	30,000	18,000

Tax depreciation for equipment A for 2002, 2003, 2004, and 2006 amounts to $50,000, $40,000, $30,000, and $10,000, respectively. Tax depreciation for equipment B for 2006, 2007, 2008, and 2009 amounts to $24,000, $18,000, $12,000, and $6,000, respectively.

C. Pacter leased part of its building to ABC Company on July 1, 2004. The lease covered 12 months, and the monthly rental was $10,000. Pacter received the year's rent in advance and included the entire amount on its 2004 tax return. This resulted in a $60,000 difference between book and taxable income in 2004, and an amount had been entered in deferred tax in that year to reflect the difference.

D. Pacter owns $20,000 of long-term bonds issued by the State of Illinois upon which 10 percent interest is paid annually. In 2005, Pacter showed $2,000 of income from the bonds on its income statement but did not show any of this amount on its tax return.

E. In 2005, Pacter insured the lives of its chief executives. The premiums paid amounted to $8,000, and this amount was shown as an expense on the income statement. However, this amount was not deducted on the tax return. The company is the beneficiary.

F. Additional data:

Income tax rates prior to 2005	40%
Income tax rate in 2005 and all future years	40%
Balance in Deferred Taxes 1/1/05 (the result of items B and C)	$12,000 debit
Pretax accounting income for 2005	$500,000

Required:

1. Starting with pretax accounting income, calculate the amount of taxable income for 2005.

2. Make the entry necessary to record tax expense, tax payable, and deferred tax for 2005. Indicate which differences are originating and which are reversing.

3. Present the income statement amounts for 2005 beginning with income before tax.

Analyze: What is the balance of current deferred taxes on the 12/31/05 balance sheet? What is the balance of long-term deferred taxes on the 12/31/05 balance sheet?

LO2, 3, 4, 6   **PROBLEM 16-9   Balance Sheet Presentation of Deferred Tax, Choosing Tax Rates**
Sealy Company depreciates its machinery using an accelerated method of depreciation for income tax reporting and the straight-line method for financial statement reporting. For the 2005 calendar year, depreciation of machinery totaled $650,000 under the accelerated method and $435,000 under the straight-line method. This temporary difference will reverse over the next two years, with straight-line being greater by $90,000 and $125,000 in 2005 and 2006, respectively. Also in 2005, Sealy received interest on state and local bonds of $80,000. Sealy's accounting income in 2005 was $40,000. Sealy's income tax rates are 40 percent in 2005, 35 percent in 2006, and 30 percent in 2007.

Required:

1. Calculate the amount that should be reported as a deferred tax asset or liability at December 31, 2005, 2006, and 2007. Show these amounts on a partial comparative balance sheet for the same dates.

2. Indicate why the amounts you calculated in question 1 are reported as a deferred tax asset or as a deferred tax liability.

Communicate: Is a deferred tax amount created from a permanent difference? Explain your answer.

LO1, 2, 3, 4, 6

PROBLEM 16-10 Deferred Tax Amounts, Book to Taxable Income, Multiple Rates, Financial Reporting

Bailey Corporation recognized revenue of $290,000 on its 2005 income statement that was related to the performance of services, but only $260,000 had to be recognized for tax purposes on the basis of the installment sales method. The remaining collections are expected to be $20,000 in 2006 and $10,000 in 2007. The tax rate in 2005 was 25 percent, and the enacted tax rates for 2006 and 2007 are 30 percent and 35 percent, respectively. Financial income before taxes for Bailey for 2005 is $80,000.

Required:

1. Calculate taxable income for 2005.
2. Calculate income tax expense for 2005. What journal entry will be recorded?
3. Determine the amount of net income Bailey Corporation will report for the year ended December 31, 2005.
4. Prepare a partial classified balance sheet for Bailey Corporation showing all tax amounts that will be reported as of December 31, 2005.

Analyze: What distortion in net income would result if Bailey did not allocate income taxes? Justify your response.

Spreadsheet: Use a spreadsheet to perform the calculations required in questions 1, 2, and 3. Prepare the partial classified balance sheet using a spreadsheet.

LO2, 3, 4, 6

PROBLEM 16-11 Deferred Tax Amounts, Book to Taxable Income, Multiple Rates, Financial Reporting

Dopple Dogs began operations in January 2003. Dopple sells hot dog franchises in the southwestern United States. For financial reporting purposes, the franchise fee is recognized in the year in which the franchise is sold. In 2003, $4,800,000 of franchise fee revenue was recognized for financial reporting purposes. For tax purposes, only $1,200,000 was recognized in 2003. In 2004, 2005, and 2006, the amounts recognized for tax purposes will be $1,400,000, $1,400,000, and $800,000, respectively. Pretax financial income for 2003 was $4,200,000, which included proceeds from a life insurance policy relating to the death of a key officer of the corporation, of which the corporation is the beneficiary, in the amount of $200,000. The enacted tax rates for 2003, 2004, 2005, and 2006 were 30 percent, 35 percent, 40 percent, and 40 percent, respectively.

Required:

1. Determine the amount of taxable income for 2003.
2. Prepare a partial balance sheet and partial income statement showing the tax effects at the end of 2003.

Analyze: Why is the determination of permanent differences important, given that no deferred tax amount is calculated for them?

LO1, 2, 3, 4, 6

PROBLEM 16-12 Multiple Deferred Tax Amounts, Reversal of Deferred Tax Amounts, Book to Taxable Income, Multiple Rates, Financial Reporting

Morales Construction began operations during 2002. The following information is provided by Morales for 2002 and 2003:

2002: Pretax financial income is $460,000.

- Depreciation for accounting purposes was based on straight-line with no residual value, and depreciation for income tax purposes was based on MACRS. The machinery being depreciated cost $200,000 and had a five-year life. MACRS was calculated as follows for each of the consecutive years of the machinery's life: $60,000, $38,000, $36,000, $33,000, and $33,000.

- Morales accrued interest revenue on municipal bonds of $8,000. Interest will be received during 2003.

2003: Pretax financial income is $430,000.

- Depreciation differences from 2002 reverse as expected.
- Bond interest was received as expected.
- Morales estimated bad debts expense in the amount of $22,000 during 2003, and wrote off $2,000. The remainder will be written off during 2004.
- During 2003, Morales collected $80,000 of magazine subscriptions, of which $30,000 were produced and delivered during 2003. The balance will be produced and delivered during 2004.

The enacted tax rates are as follows:

- 26 percent for 2002
- 32 percent for 2003
- 35 percent for 2004
- 37 percent for 2005 and years thereafter

Required:

1. Determine the amounts that will be reported on the December 31, 2003, balance sheet as deferred tax items.
2. Calculate income tax payable at December 31, 2003.
3. How much is income tax expense for 2003?
4. How much total cash must be paid for taxes related to income for 2003?

Analyze: What amount would have been paid had no tax allocation occurred? Explain your answer.

LO2, 3, 4, 6   **PROBLEM 16-13   Multiple Deferred Tax Amounts, Reversal of Deferred Tax Amounts, Book to Taxable Income, Multiple Rates, Financial Reporting**

Brown Company began operations during 2004. The enacted tax rates are 26 percent for 2004, 28 percent for 2005, 32 percent for 2006, and 35 percent for 2007 and years thereafter. Pretax financial income is $200,000 for 2004, $65,000 for 2005, and $120,000 during 2006.

On January 2, 2004, heavy equipment costing $280,000 was purchased. The equipment had a life of four years and no residual value. The straight-line method of depreciation is used for book purposes, and the tax depreciation taken each year is

2004: $100,000
2005:   65,000
2006:   60,000
2007:   55,000

On January 2, 2005, $120,000 was collected in advance for rental of a building for a three-year period. For accounting purposes, the rent will be earned as follows: $40,000 during 2005, $40,000 during 2006, and $40,000 during 2007. The estimated warranty liability related to 2005 sales totaled $14,000. Repair costs under warranties during 2005 were $10,000. The remainder of the costs will be paid in 2006. Penalties and fines incurred during 2005 totaled $9,000.

Required:

1. Label the name of the tax T-account that will be used in interperiod tax allocation for the heavy equipment. Post all amounts to the T-account through December 31, 2007. Label each posting by date.
2. How much is taxable income for 2005?
3. How much is income tax payable at the end of 2005?
4. Calculate income tax expense for 2005.

Analyze: Classify each deferred tax item as current or long-term. Briefly justify why you classified each item the way you did.

LO2, 3, 4, 6   PROBLEM 16-14   **Multiple Deferred Tax Amounts, Reversal of Deferred Tax Amounts, Book to Taxable Income, Multiple Rates, Financial Reporting**

Information for Njomba Company for 2004 and 2005, its first two years of operations, follows. Enacted income tax rates are 30 percent for 2004, 34 percent for 2005, 32 percent for 2006, and 26 percent for 2007 and years after. It is "more likely than not" that the company will benefit from all future deductible amounts.

2004: Pretax financial income is $123,000.

- Depreciation for accounting purposes was based on the straight-line method with no residual value, and MACRS was used for income tax purposes. The equipment has an original cost of $120,000 and an estimated five-year life. MACRS was calculated as follows for each year of the equipment's four-year tax life: $60,000, $22,000, $20,000, $18,000. (*Hint:* The depreciation period can be different.)
- Njomba accrued interest revenue on municipal bonds totaling $3,800. Interest will be received during 2005.

2005: Pretax financial income is $160,000.

- Depreciation differences from 2004 reverse as expected.
- Bond interest was received as expected.
- Njomba sold $120,000 of concert tickets; half of the performances took place during 2005 and the other half during 2006.
- Njomba purchased shares of Nolan Company common stock for $46,000 and accounted for it under the cost method.
- Njomba received cash dividends totaling $5,000 from its investment in Nolan Company; these qualify as 80 percent domestic dividends.
- A late tax payment was made for payroll, and Njomba was assessed $1,000 penalty and $500 interest as a result.

Required:

1. Calculate taxable income for 2005.
2. How much is income tax expense for 2005?
3. Prepare a partial income statement for 2005 for Njomba, beginning with income before taxes.

Analyze: What is Njomba's effective tax rate for 2005?

Communicate: Assume that you are the accountant for Njomba Company. Your boss has questioned why deferred taxes are not presented at present value. In a memo, explain the FASB's position on discounting and deferred taxes.

LO2, 4, 5, 6, 7   PROBLEM 16-15   **Financial Reporting, Valuation Allowance**

Dockins, Inc. reported pretax income of $480,000 and the following account balances from its accounting records as of the end of 2005:

Deferred Tax Asset (relates to a contingent loss from 2002)	$ 32,000
Deferred Tax Liability (relates to depreciation that will reverse equally over the next four years)	48,000
Income Tax Payable	25,000
Income Tax Expense	168,000
Deferred Tax Asset (relates to accounting for uncollectible trade receivables)	15,000
Deferred Tax Liability (relates to inventory reporting differences)	4,000

Additional information:

- It is "more likely than not" that the company will benefit from only 80 percent of any income tax benefits.

• Tax benefits from the contingent loss are expected to occur several years in the future.
• During 2005, Dockins submitted estimated taxes amounting to $130,000.

Required:

1. Briefly state the two distinct reasons why income tax expense is not equal to income taxes payable for Dockins.

2. Show how the effects of the items listed in the problem (including the effects of question 1) would be reported by Dockins, Inc. at December 31, 2005, by preparing a partial balance sheet that reflects the *proper reporting* and *balance sheet classifications*.

Analyze: Determine the company's effective income tax rate. What does this rate tell you?

LO5, 8   **PROBLEM 16-16   Cash Flow Effects, Valuation Allowance**

The following is selected information from Dove, Inc.'s accounting records for the year ended December 31, 2005. All accounts have normal balances.

Income Statement

Sales	$620,000
Cost of sales	320,000
Gross profit	$300,000
Operating expenses	160,000
Income before taxes	$140,000
Income taxes	42,000
Income from operations	$ 98,000
Extraordinary loss, net	11,200
Net income	$ 86,800

Accounts and Balances	12/31/05	12/31/04
Deferred Tax Liability—Current	$14,600	$ 9,600
Deferred Tax Liability—Long-Term	12,000	15,000
Income Tax Payable	37,200	35,500
Deferred Tax Asset—Current	5,000	6,600
Deferred Tax Asset—Long-Term	21,500	14,000
Valuation Allowance	3,000	5,000

During 2005, Dove incurred a casualty loss (extraordinary) in the amount of $16,000. The valuation allowance pertains to a portion of the long-term amounts.

Required:

1. How much cash did Dove *pay* for income taxes during 2005?

2. Determine total income tax expense for 2005. Explain your answer.

3. From an accounting perspective, what is Dove's effective income tax rate?

Analyze: Why are the changes in the balances of the income tax accounts used in determining the amount of cash paid for income taxes instead of the ending balance of each of the income tax accounts? Explain.

LO5, 6, 7   **PROBLEM 16-17   Financial Reporting, Valuation Allowance**

Burns Company reported the following selected account balances in its adjusted trial balance at December 31, 2005:

Deferred Tax Liability (relates to reporting installment revenue in the accounting records; one-third is expected to be collected during 2006 and the balance during 2007)	$15,000
Income Tax Expense	34,000

Deferred Tax Liability (relates to using percentage-of-completion for book purposes and completed-contract for tax purposes for project to be completed in 2006)	$11,000
Deferred Tax Liability (relates to a depreciation difference that is expected to reverse equally over the next four years)	24,000
Income Tax Payable	25,000
Deferred Tax Asset (relates to accounting for inventory using the lower-of-cost-or-market valuation)	9,000

It is "more likely than not" that the company will benefit from only 80 percent of any income tax benefits, which are expected to occur after the economic slump ends, probably during 2007 or 2008.

Required: Show how the effects of the items listed above would be reported in Burns Company's balance sheet at December 31, 2005, by preparing a partial classified balance sheet that reflects the *proper reporting*. Show no more detail on the balance sheet than is required by GAAP.

Analyze: What would be the impact on assets and income if a company failed to establish a Valuation Allowance account?

LO1, 2, 3, 4, 6   **PROBLEM 16-18   Multiple Deferred Tax Amounts, Book to Taxable Income, Multiple Rates, Financial Reporting**

Brown Company began operations during 2004. The enacted tax rates are 26 percent for 2004, 28 percent for 2005, 32 percent for 2006, and 35 percent for 2007 and years thereafter.

2004: Pretax financial income is $300,000. Depletion costs are written off for income tax purposes on a different basis, resulting in a $30,000 additional expense for tax purposes as compared to accounting purposes. This amount will reverse at an equal amount per year for each of the next two years.

2005: Pretax financial income is $200,000. The temporary difference related to depletion from 2004 reverses as expected. Uncollectible accounts of $20,000 are expensed for financial reporting purposes but will not be deductible in the income tax computations until 2006. Penalties incurred and accrued amounted to $1,000 (these will be paid in 2006). Total entertainment expenses reported on the company's income statement amounted to $4,000, although the amount allowed for tax purposes is only 50 percent. Life insurance premiums in the amount of $3,000 were paid and expensed on the income statement.

Required:

1. List the *individual* deferred tax assets and deferred tax liabilities and their respective account balances as of December 31, 2005, using a three-column table with the following headings: Deferred Tax Asset or Deferred Tax Liability, Item Causing Difference, and 12/31/05 Balance. (Do not net deferred tax amounts for reporting purposes.)

2. Calculate these amounts:
   - Taxable income for 2004
   - Income tax payable at December 31, 2004
   - Taxable income for 2005
   - Income tax payable at December 31, 2005

3. How much income tax expense should be reported for the year ended December 31, 2005?

Analyze: If Brown Company wished to reduce reported earnings, what actions might it take with regard to deferred tax assets?

Communicate: Suppose that you are the accounting manager for Brown Company and that you are training a new accountant. Explain to your trainee why interperiod tax allocation is necessary.

CASES

LO1, 6   **CRITICAL THINKING CASE 16-1   Explain Deferred Tax, Determine Balance Sheet Disclosure** (CPA adapted)

The following differences enter into the reconciliation of the financial accounting income and taxable income of A.P. Baxter Corp. for the current year:

A. Tax depreciation exceeds book depreciation by $30,000.

B. Estimated warranty costs of $6,000 applicable to the current year's sales have not been paid. Baxter expects to pay half of the warranty costs in the following year, and the remainder in subsequent years.

C. Percentage depletion deducted on the tax return exceeds cost depletion by $45,000.

D. Unearned rent of $25,000 was deferred on the books but appropriately included in taxable income. Baxter expects to earn the rent within the following year.

E. A book expense of $2,000 for life insurance premiums on officers' lives is not allowed as a deduction on the tax return.

Required:

1. Describe the objective of accounting for income taxes on an accrual basis.

2. Consider each reconciling item independently of all the others and explain whether each item would enter into the calculation of deferred taxes. For any items that are included in the calculation, explain the effect of the item on the current year's income tax expense and how the amount would be reported on the balance sheet. (Calculations are not required.)

LO1, 2, 3, 4, 6   **COMMUNICATION CASE 16-2   Explain Deferred Tax, Change in Rate** (CPA adapted)

Chris Green, CPA, is auditing the 2004 financial statements for Rayne Company. The controller, Barbara Dunn, has provided Green with the following information:

For the year ended December 31, 2004, Dunn has prepared a schedule of all differences between financial statement income and income tax return income. Dunn believes that as a result of pending legislation, the enacted tax rate at December 31, 2004, will be increased for 2005. Dunn is uncertain which differences to include and which rates to apply in computing deferred taxes under *SFAS No. 109*. Dunn has requested an overview of *SFAS No. 109* from Green.

Required:

Prepare a brief memo to Dunn from Green to:

- Identify the objective of accounting for income taxes.
- Define temporary differences.
- Explain how to measure deferred tax assets and liabilities.
- Explain how to measure deferred income tax expense or benefit.
- Explain how the change in tax rate affects the calculation of deferred tax.

LO5   **ETHICS CASE 16-3   A Matter of Judgment**

ETHICS

Robert Kuhn is the accounting supervisor at Klinger Development Inc., a new pharmaceutical research company that specializes in developing home testing kits. The company successfully introduced its first product to the market in 2004 and expects to market its second product by the end of 2006. In 2005, Klinger Inc. reported a small profit, and the company also expects to report a profit for the current year, 2006.

During March of 2006, Robert prepares a projected balance sheet and income statement for the current year. The company's president is planning to use these statements to request an increased line of credit from the bank. The projected balance sheet shows a deferred tax asset related to R&D supplies, which were purchased on an extended credit agreement with the supplier and will be paid in February of 2007. The R&D supplies were expensed during the current year and are tax-deductible in 2007, when they will be paid. Robert knows that the realization of this deferred tax asset depends on the availability of income. Based on his projections, Robert is concerned that the company may not be able to generate sufficient income next year to offset the deferred tax asset. He discusses this with Jim Schneider, the company's controller, and suggests that a valuation allowance of $40,000 should be recorded. Jim does not agree and argues that (1) in his opinion, sales will increase sharply next year, generating more than sufficient income, (2) the increased line of credit is crucial to the company's success, and it is important to present a positive projected balance sheet to the chairman of the bank, and (3) the company's current and future products will benefit hundreds of thousands of individuals. Robert brings up the issue that deferred tax assets should be recognized only to the extent that they are expected to be realized. He refers to *SFAS No. 109*, "Accounting for Income Taxes," which requires companies to evaluate this expectation by determining whether it is "more likely than not" that the asset will be realized. Jim argues that projections are just estimates and do not fall under the same stringent rules as published financial statements, and that "more likely than not" is a term that is open to interpretation. He reminds Robert that both their positions depend on the company's survival and instructs him to omit the valuation allowance.

Required:

1. What are the financial reporting issues in this situation? How will addressing these issues affect the company's financial statements?

2. What are the ethical issues faced by Robert?

3. Who will be affected by his decision?

4. What values and principles are likely to influence his decision?

5. What alternative actions can Robert consider?

6. What do you think Robert should do?

LO6, 7, 8

ETHICS ⚖️

ETHICS CASE 16-4   Tax Manipulation or Strategy?

Glaxo, a global pharmaceutical company and the creator and distributor of widely used medications, is having difficulties with the Internal Revenue Service (IRS). The IRS claims that the company has understated its profits and underpaid its taxes for nearly a decade. Specifically, the IRS asserts that Glaxo's U.S. subsidiary has overpaid for its purchases of drugs from its U.K. parent company, resulting in inflated costs of goods sold and lower taxable income. Glaxo contends that the high price was justified because of the valuable and extensive research efforts by the parent company. The IRS maintains that the price paid by the U.S. company should have been lower because the U.S. company's product promotion also contributed a significant part of the value of the products.[21]

Research and development costs are a highly significant portion of the costs of new medications. However, the allocation of these costs to specific products involves considerable judgment. Thus, the issues are not clear-cut, and prolonged litigation between the IRS and Glaxo is expected to ensue. A tax court judgment against Glaxo may result in a potentially significant tax liability and required cash payment. In addition, it may significantly affect the company's financial statements, causing increases in tax expense, which will reduce current- and prior-year income and require financial statement restatements. This could affect the company's profitability for years to come.

Many representatives of the company are likely to be affected by this tax dispute, including tax accountants, attorneys, and cost and financial accountants, as well as top executives. Glaxo's dispute with the IRS and its resolution may involve difficult decisions and create ethical dilemmas for those involved in the situation.

Suppose you are a member of the tax accounting staff for Glaxo. You are responsible for supplying the IRS with extensive documentation regarding this tax issue. Your superior has instructed you to cooperate with the IRS only to the extent necessary, without volunteering any additional information. Suppose you are aware of the existence of documents that you believe could support the IRS's case for higher taxes. You feel very loyal to your company, but you also feel a public duty. On the one hand, you are considering "dropping

---

21 Glenn R. Simpson, "Glaxo in Major Battle with IRS over Taxes on Years of U.S. Sales," *Wall Street Journal*, June 11, 2002, p. A1.

a hint," but on the other hand, you are considering misfiling the documents in order to make discovery less likely.

Required:

1. What issues do you face?
2. Who will be affected by your decision?
3. What values and principles are likely to influence your decision?
4. What alternative actions should you consider?
5. Review the values and principles you identified in question 3 and the people or entities you identified in question 2. What is the most important goal in this situation?
6. What would you do?

LO3   **COMMUNICATION CASE 16-5   Deferred Tax Assets**

As the controller for LightSpan, Inc., you are asked to explain to management why the company is recording a deferred tax asset. Based on your analysis of the financial records, you determine that the items giving rise to deferred tax assets are the allowance for doubtful accounts, accrued expenses, and vacation accrual.

Required: Prepare a memo to management that explains what a deferred tax asset is and how the items named create a deferred tax asset. In addition, include in your memo an explanation of the situations in which financial statement income will be greater than taxable income as a result of these transactions.

LO5   **ANALYSIS CASE 16-6   Valuation Allowances**

TiVo, Inc. provides television services for digital video recorders on a subscription basis. The company has been in business for a number of years; however, as of the end of its 2004 fiscal year, the company had incurred significant losses, had a substantial negative cash flow, and recognized limited revenue. Examining the company's tax note, you discover that TiVo has reported the following information.

TiVo

The tax effects of temporary differences that give rise to significant portions of the Company's deferred tax assets are presented below:

(In thousands)	Fiscal Year Ended January 31	
	2004	2003
Deferred tax assets:		
Net operating loss carryforwards	$ 165,758	$ 154,616
Deferred revenue and rent	33,131	25,446
Capitalized research	12,253	7,596
Convertible notes payable	1,912	1,964
Prepaid marketing expense	1,861	17,926
Other	2,589	3,497
Gross deferred tax assets before valuation allowance	217,504	211,045
Less: Valuation allowance	(217,504)	(211,045)
Net deferred tax assets	$ 0	$ 0

Required:

1. Why do you think that TiVo has established a valuation allowance for its deferred tax asset?
2. In general, when should a company establish a valuation allowance for a deferred tax asset?

3. What journal entry would TiVo have made to establish the valuation allowance?

4. If TiVo becomes profitable in the future, what do you think will happen to the valuation allowance?

LO6 **ANALYSIS CASE 16-7   Presentation of Tax Assets and Liabilities**

As the chief financial officer of a manufacturing company, you are responsible for the company's financial statements. The company currently recognizes a current deferred tax asset and a long-term deferred tax liability. At a recent board of directors meeting, a number of directors were concerned about these amounts because of the upcoming presidential election and the potential changes in corporate tax laws. One political party is in favor of raising federal corporate tax rates, while the other party promotes reducing federal corporate tax rates.

Required:

1. Discuss how changes in the federal corporate tax rate will affect the company's deferred tax asset and deferred tax liability.

2. Discuss how changes in the federal corporate tax rate will affect the company's income statement and statement of cash flows.

LO7 **RESEARCH CASE 16-8   Interpreting Financial Statements**

Johnson Outdoors, Inc. designs, manufactures, and markets outdoor recreation products. Johnson Outdoors produces kayaks, paddleboats, scuba gear, tents, backpacks, and other related goods. The company is based in Wisconsin, but manufactures and sells its goods worldwide.

Required: Go to the company's website (**www.johnsonoutdoors.com**) and obtain the company's 2003 annual report through the investor relations link. Answer the following questions:

1. Where does Johnson Outdoors report information about its income taxes?

2. What is the amount reported as gross deferred tax asset? Does the company reduce the gross amount with a valuation allowance? If so, by what amount?

3. How much current and deferred income tax expense does Johnson Outdoors report?

4. What are the company's statutory U.S. federal income tax rate and effective tax rate?

ON THE WEB

The following exercises, activities, and problems are available on the *Intermediate Accounting* website. Use these resources to reinforce your understanding of the topics presented in this chapter.

- CPA-Adapted Simulations
- Interpreting the Accounting Standards
- Extending the Global Focus
- Extending the Ethics Discussion
- Mastering the Spreadsheet
- Career Snapshots

- Annual Report Project
- ACE Practice Tests
- Flashcards
- Glossary
- Check Figures for Text Problems
- PowerPoint Presentations

SOLUTIONS: CHECK YOUR UNDERSTANDING

Accounting for Tax Purposes Versus Accounting for Financial Reporting Purposes (p. 756)

1. Many companies keep two sets of books because they follow two sets of rules for accounting—one for financial accounting purposes ("per book") and the other for tax purposes ("per tax"). The accounting for financial statement purposes is governed by generally accepted accounting principles, or GAAP, as developed by the FASB and other organizations. The tax rules, on the other hand, are drafted by the U.S. government and administered by the Internal Revenue Service.

2. The purpose of tax law is to raise the desired amount of money to finance government operations, to achieve certain economic objectives (such as inducing investment activities), and to promote desired social goals (such as fairness and equity in tax treatment).

3. Financial accounting is based on the accrual accounting process, so the amount of tax expense reported should reflect the amount *incurred* rather than the amount *paid*. Allocation is necessary to accurately record the current year's tax expense and future years' tax obligations.

The Basics of Tax Allocation (p. 765)

1. A deferred tax account should reflect the impact of temporary differences. Temporary differences are a result of timing (or accrual processes). Permanent differences are items that are deductible for tax purposes, but not for book purposes (or vice versa); thus, they will never affect the other set of books and should not be recorded as a deferral of any kind.

2. An originating temporary difference is the initial difference between the book basis and the tax basis of an asset or liability in the current period; it will be entered into a deferred tax account. A reversing temporary difference is the removal of a temporary difference that originated in a previous period from a deferred tax account.

3. A deferred tax liability represents a liability for income tax at a future time period. It results from a temporary difference that causes current tax payable to be *less* than the amount of tax expense recorded for book purposes and will cause future tax payable to *exceed* the amount recorded for book purposes when the item reverses. A deferred tax asset results from a temporary difference that has been deducted for book purposes in the current period but will be deducted for tax purposes when it reverses and is thus a future benefit.

Additional Aspects of Deferred Tax (p. 772)

1. If an expense has been recognized for book purposes before it will be deducted for tax purposes, a deferred tax asset results.

2. The decision to record a valuation allowance is a matter of subjective judgment, but the FASB indicates that if, based on the weight of available evidence, *it is more likely than not* (a likelihood of more than 50 percent) that some portion of the deferred tax asset *will not* be realized, then a Valuation Allowance account is necessary.

Financial Statement Presentation of Tax Amounts (p. 778)

1. The FASB has indicated that the classification of deferred tax as current or noncurrent should generally be based on *the classification of the related asset or liability* that gave rise to the temporary difference.

2. The effective tax rate is calculated by dividing income tax expense by income before taxes.

3. U.S. taxes of $29 million (federal) and $115 million (state and local), are classified as current.

Analyzing Income Tax Disclosures (p. 780)

1. If earnings differ greatly from the cash consequences of the events of the period, analysts may question the quality of earnings, since this may indicate a large amount of deferrals.

2. A company would decrease the balance of a Valuation Allowance account if it wished to increase its profitability for the period.

3. Some analysts are reluctant to treat deferred taxes as true liabilities because deferred tax amounts are not *legal* liabilities at the time they are recognized in the sense that the company is not legally obligated to pay the amount that has been recognized as deferred tax.

Impact of Deferred Tax on Cash Flows (p. 782)

1. A decrease in income tax payable would be added to the tax expense reported on the income statement for the period, or the decrease would be deducted from net income using the indirect method.

2. If the balance in the Deferred Tax Asset account increases in a period, cash flows from this transaction have been negatively affected.

CPA-ADAPTED SIMULATION

This simulation asks you to complete various tasks related to a company's annual financial statements. If your instructor has signed up for CPAexcel™, you can do the work online at **www.cpaexcel.com/hmco**. You may also do the simulation manually.

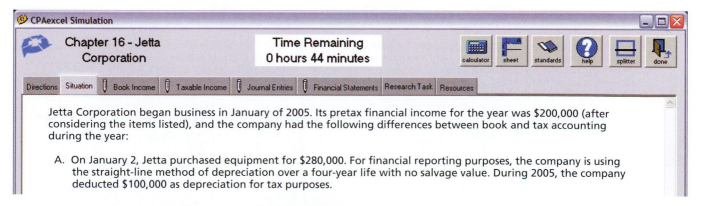

B. On January 2, Jetta received two years' rent in advance, for a total of $60,000. For tax purposes, rent is included when received.

C. During 2005, Jetta invested $80,000 in tax-exempt bonds and received interest of $3,000.

D. The company's product carries a two-year warranty. Based on the accrual method, the company has estimated the warranty cost for 2005 on all products sold to be $20,000. The actual cost incurred to repair products under warranty during 2005 was $12,000.

E. Jetta began a long-term constuction contract during 2005 that will be completed in 2006. The company will use the completed-contract method for tax purposes and will use the percentage-of-completion methods for financial reporting purposes. The estimated gross profit on the project for 2005 was $50,000.

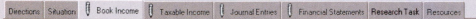

Directions | Situation | Book Income | Taxable Income | Journal Entries | Financial Statements | Research Task | Resources

For each of the five differences between book and tax income, determine whether the item should be treated as a temporary or a permanent difference. For those items that are temporary differences, indicate whether they will result in a deferred tax asset or a deferred tax liability. Double click the shaded cells to view a list of selection choices.

Difference	Temporary or Permanent	Deferred Tax Asset or Deferred Tax Liability
A. Equipment		
B. Rent		
C. Bond interest		
D. Warranty		
E. Long-term contract		

Directions | Situation | Book Income | Taxable Income | Journal Entries | Financial Statements | Research Task | Resources

1. Use the form provided to calculate the amount of taxable income for Jetta Corporation for 2005. For each difference (A through E), indicate whether the difference will be added, subtracted, or excluded when determining the taxable income.

2. Assume that the tax rate for 2005 is 35 percent and that a tax rate of 40 percent has been enacted for all future years. Determine the amount of federal tax liability for 2005.

Financial income	$200,000
A. Equipment	
B. Rent	
C. Bond interest	
D. Warranty	
E. Long-term contract	
Taxable income	
Federal tax liability	

Directions | Situation | Book Income | Taxable Income | Journal Entries | Financial Statements | Research Task | Resources

Record the journal entries for income tax expense, income tax payable, and deferred tax for Jetta Corporation for 2005.

Directions | Situation | Book Income | Taxable Income | Journal Entries | Financial Statements | Research Task | Resources

Indicate the proper balance sheet presentation of deferred tax (you may omit the footnote disclosures) for Jetta Corporation as of December 31, 2005.

Directions | Situation | Book Income | Taxable Income | Journal Entries | Financial Statements | Research Task | Resources

During 2006, Jetta is sued by another company for $300,000. At the conclusion of the year, Jetta's lawyers believe it is probable that the company will be held liable for an amount between $150,000 and $200,000. The company's chief accountant is unsure how this item should be treated when determining deferred tax. In particular, the company has asked for your input about whether a Valuation Allowance account should be established for the deferred tax related to this lawsuit.

Under what circumstances should a Valuation Allowance account be established as a contra-account to a deferred tax asset?

PART FOUR

Stockholders' Equity and Cash Flows

I n Part Three, we examined balance sheet elements that represent the liabilities of a company. Now we will turn our attention to the accounts that represent the ownership interests of the shareholders of a corporation. Chapters 17 and 18 bring into focus the way in which investments by stockholders affect the company and how corporations account for money that they retain on behalf of their stockholders. In Chapter 19, we will return to the statement of cash flows for a final look at how this statement fills in the financial information gaps that are not covered by the income statement, the balance sheet, or the statement of stockholders' equity.

17 Stockholders' Equity

The number of active U.S. corporations is nearing 5 million, and they account for over $17 trillion in annual revenue. While most of the accounting for partnerships and sole proprietorships is similar to that for corporations, Chapter 17 examines the treatment of various stockholders' equity elements that differentiate this form of business organization from the others. Corporations must account for different classes of stock, convertible securities, and treasury stock, and must reflect these transactions properly in their financial statements.

18 Dilutive Securities and Earnings per Share

If you're interested in the financial performance of a company, you'll probably use earnings per share as a key analysis measure. While calculating a company's earnings per share of common stock might seem simple, variables like convertible securities, stock options, and capital structure can affect this important ratio. In Chapter 18, you will learn how to compute and analyze earnings per share in complex and simple capital structures and how to factor in the presence of securities that might dilute the interests of common stockholders.

19 Revisiting the Statement of Cash Flows

In Chapter 5, we discussed the basic structure of the statement of cash flows and examined how cash is used for or generated from operating, financing, and investing activities. In this chapter, we will revisit this important financial statement to understand how to prepare the statement using both the direct and indirect methods and how to use the statement for further analysis purposes.

Stockholders' Equity

FINANCIAL REPORTING CASE

MICROSOFT INTRODUCES NEW DIVIDEND POLICY

Business owners like Bill Gates of Microsoft Corporation choose the corporate form of organization because the liability of owners is limited to the amount that stockholders have invested in the business.

Microsoft When Microsoft wants to raise a little cash, the investment community delivers. With more than 10.8 billion shares of stock outstanding, stockholders have participated in creating a market value for Microsoft stock of more than $280 billion as of March 2004. The world's number one software maker's stock is held by private investors, employees, and institutional investors, but large pension plans have become its largest class of stockholder. Of course, the company's founders, Bill Gates and Paul Allen, own enough shares to be among the richest individuals in the world.

Microsoft investors seek some of that same wealth through appreciation in the stock's price and, recently, through modest dividends. Prior to 2003, Microsoft had not paid dividends to its stockholders. In 2003, however, the company announced and paid a small dividend of eight cents per share. In 2004, the company declared a very large, special dividend of $3 per share. Microsoft's decision to offer dividends may have been spurred by the decline in its stock price. Or perhaps the move was in response to a change in the way dividends are taxed when they are received by

Microsoft

STOCKHOLDERS' EQUITY STATEMENTS
(in millions)

Year Ended June 30	2002[1]	2003[1]	2004
Common stock and paid-in capital			
Balance, beginning of period	$ 28,390	$ 41,845	$ 49,234
Cumulative SFAS 123 retroactive adjustments	6,560	—	—
Common stock issued	1,655	2,966	2,815
Common stock repurchased	(676)	(691)	(416)
Stock-based compensation expense	3,784	3,749	5,734
Stock option income tax benefits/(deficiencies)	1,596	1,365	(989)
Other, net	536	—	18
Balance, end of period	41,845	49,234	56,396
Retained earnings			
Balance, beginning of period	18,899	12,997	15,678
Cumulative SFAS 123 retroactive adjustments	(5,062)	—	—
Net income	5,355	7,531	8,168
Other comprehensive income:			
Net gains/(losses) on derivative instruments	(91)	(102)	101
Net unrealized investment gains/(losses)	5	1,243	(873)
Translation adjustments and other	82	116	51
Comprehensive income	5,351	8,788	7,447
Common stock dividend	—	(857)	(1,729)
Common stock repurchased	(6,191)	(5,250)	(2,967)
Balance, end of period	12,997	15,678	18,429
Total stockholders' equity	$ 54,842	$ 64,912	$ 74,825

[1]June 30, 2002 and 2003 stockholders' equity statements have been restated for retroactive adoption of the fair value recognition provisions of SFAS 123, *Accounting for Stock-Based Compensation,* as discussed in Note 13.

investors. Regardless of the motivation, it is likely that investors will continue to look to the performance of the stock price as the primary source of shareholder value.[1]

Microsoft's stockholders' equity statements for 2002, 2003, and 2004, presented here, detail the activity in accounts such as Common Stock and Paid-in Capital, and Retained Earnings. The issuance of common stock dividends in 2004 reduced Retained Earnings by $1,729 million, yet the balance of the account still exceeded $18.4 billion in 2004.

EXAMINING THE CASE

1. What amount was received for stock issued during 2004?

2. What other types of transactions, besides dividend payments, affected retained earnings in 2004?

3. What were possible motives for Microsoft's decision to pay a dividend to its stockholders?

---

1 Bill Parrish, "Feeding Many Mouths," *Barron's Online*, April 21, 2003.

LO1 **Describe the advantages and disadvantages of the corporate form of organization.**

Critical Thinking: If you were starting a new business, what issues do you think you would consider when choosing a form of organization?

Corporate Form of Organization

Companies may be organized in several alternative legal forms, of which the main ones are sole proprietorships, partnerships, and corporations. While most of the accounting procedures for these various forms of organization are similar, the accounting for ownership interests is different. In this chapter, you will learn how to account for the ownership interests of the corporation, the dominant form of organization in our economy. Though the total number of partnerships and sole proprietorships in the United States exceeds the number of corporations, the sizes of corporations and their contributions to the gross domestic product of the United States are greater. The dominance of this type of organization results from several advantages that are available only to the corporate form of organization.

ADVANTAGES OF THE CORPORATE FORM

❯ LIMITED LIABILITY

The most important reason why business owners choose the corporate form of organization is that the corporation is considered a separate legal entity and the liability of its owners is limited to the amount that they have invested in the business. This advantage is known as **limited liability.** This means that if a company is organized as a corporation, the personal assets of its owners are not at risk. When a company is organized as a partnership or a sole proprietorship, the owners of the company are personally liable for the actions and debts of the company. For example, if a partnership or sole proprietorship is held liable in a lawsuit or other legal proceeding, the owners may lose their personal assets as well as the assets of the business.

limited liability the principle that the liability of the owners of a corporation is limited to the amount that they have invested in the business

❯ EASE OF FUNDING

Another important advantage of the corporate form of organization is the ability to raise capital efficiently. A corporation can obtain financing by selling shares of stock to the public. The issuance of stock is attractive because shares can be easily sold, transferred, and purchased, and these transactions do not change the legal basis of the corporation. Stockholders typically share in the financial success of the company either through dividends or through stock appreciation. Conversely, partnerships and sole proprietorships can obtain new financing only by borrowing money (debt) or by seeking additional invested capital from new partners. In the case of a partnership, any change in the number of partners results in a new legal basis—it is essentially a new company, and a new partnership agreement must be developed. For that reason, the ownership rights of partners cannot be transferred easily.

❯ TAX CONSIDERATIONS

The corporate form of organization carries unique tax considerations. Whereas the profits of a partnership or a sole proprietorship are taxed as income of the individual owners, the corporation is deemed to be a separate entity and is taxed separately. Corporations must file a tax return and pay income tax based on the income of the corporation. Owners (stockholders) are then taxed on dividends received from the corporation. This may be an advantage, depending on the corporation's income and the tax situation of the owners.

DISADVANTAGES OF THE CORPORATE FORM

❯ AGENCY RELATIONSHIP

One of the most important consequences of the corporate form of organization is that the owners of the company are usually removed from the day-to-day management of the company. In large corporations, professional managers are hired to operate the company. This creates an agency relationship in which the managers operate as the agents of the owners in attempting to maximize the owners' profits. In some cases, managers may develop their own personal goals and operate the company in a manner that meets those goals, and a lack of goal congruence may result. In other words, the goals of the managers may not be consistent with the goals of the owners (the stockholders). Therefore, it is important that corporations develop a reward system, using salaries, bonuses, and stock options, that allows managers to achieve their own personal goals and rewards them for operating the company in a manner that is consistent with the stockholders' goals.

Accountants and auditors play an important role in monitoring the owner-management relationship. Auditors ensure that the information provided by company management is credible and fairly presents the financial condition of the company. External parties rely on that information in making investment decisions.

❯ LEGAL RESTRICTIONS

When a company chooses to organize as a corporation, it faces a myriad of legal restrictions and requirements. Corporations are subject to the laws of the state in which they are incorporated and to federal laws and restrictions. They are also subject to the requirements of the SEC if they are publicly traded and listed on a U.S. stock exchange. All of these legal requirements are intended to ensure that corporations operate in a manner that is consistent with society's goals. Because of these legal requirements, corporations often face greater costs for compliance and reporting. In many cases, the accounting for stockholders' equity is influenced by these legal requirements, discussed in upcoming sections of this chapter.

❯ DOUBLE TAXATION

Although it is true that corporate income is taxed separately from the dividends paid to stockholders, this income is essentially the same income and thus is taxed twice. This consequence is referred to as *double taxation*. A tax law change in 2003 has lessened the impact of this double taxation.

Illustration 17.1 summarizes the advantages and disadvantages of corporations.

Illustration 17.1

Advantages and Disadvantages of the Corporate Form of Organization

Advantages	
Limited liability	The liability of the owners (stockholders) is limited to the amount of their investment in the business.
Ease of financing	Shares of stock can be easily transferred, bought, and sold without changing the legal basis of the corporation.
Tax considerations	A corporation is deemed to be a separate entity and is taxed separately. Owners are taxed only on the dividends they receive from the corporation.
Disadvantages	
Agency relationship	The owners of the company are usually not involved in day-to-day management of the company. Professional managers are hired to operate the company.
Legal restrictions	Corporations are subject to the laws of the state in which they are incorporated. If a corporation is considered a public company, it is also subject to the requirements of the SEC and a myriad of federal rules and regulations.
Double taxation	Stockholders may be subject to some level of double taxation. Income is taxed as profits to the corporation and then taxed again when it is distributed to the stockholders as dividends.

OTHER FORMS OF ORGANIZATION

When business owners are considering the different legal forms of organization, they may also choose a form of organization that has some of the characteristics of both partnerships and corporations. These options include

- S corporations
- Limited liability partnerships (LLPs)

S CORPORATIONS

The owners of an S corporation are liable for an amount that is limited to their investment in the business. However, an S corporation is not subject to income tax as a corporation. Instead, the income of the corporation is taxed as personal income to the owners in a manner somewhat similar to the way partnerships are treated. This is advantageous in some cases because the double taxation of profits is avoided.

LIMITED LIABILITY PARTNERSHIPS

Another form of organization that has become quite popular is called the limited liability partnership, or LLP. An LLP is organized as a partnership and is treated as such for tax purposes. The income of the company is treated as income of the individual partners and is taxed on their personal tax returns. However, an LLP allows some of the limited liability features of a corporation. In an LLP, a partner is liable for his or her own actions, but his or her liability for the actions of other partners is limited to the amount invested in the business. Most large accounting firms were previously organized as partnerships but have changed the form of their organizations to LLPs to take advantage of this limited liability feature.

CHECK YOUR UNDERSTANDING

1. What is the most important reason that business owners choose the corporate form of organization?

2. How does an S corporation differ from a regular corporation?

3. Explain how double taxation relates to the corporation.

LO2 Present the stockholders' equity section of the balance sheet in the proper format.

Critical Thinking: What key components of stockholders' equity do you think should be reported on a company's balance sheet?

Stockholders' Equity Overview

As you recall from your early studies of accounting principles, stockholders' equity is equal to the total assets of a business minus its total liabilities. Stockholders' equity is generated from two sources: amounts invested by shareholders (contributed capital) and amounts earned by the corporation (retained earnings). A variety of legal and reporting requirements govern the accounting for and disclosure of these equity transactions. In the following sections, we will examine the individual components that make up the stockholders' equity section of the balance sheet.

FINANCIAL REPORTING FOR STOCKHOLDERS' EQUITY

There is a good deal of flexibility allowed in the manner in which the stockholders' equity category of the balance sheet is presented. The proper reporting is usually influenced by both accounting and legal requirements. As we discuss the components of

Illustration 17.2

Stockholders' Equity Section of Balance Sheet

Hang Corporation December 31, 2005 (in thousands)			
Capital Stock:			
Preferred stock, $10 par, 8%, cumulative, 100,000 shares authorized, 50,000 shares issued		$500	
Common stock, $1 par, 500,000 shares authorized, 200,000 shares issued		200	
Common stock distributable		10	
Additional Paid-in Capital:			
Paid-in capital in excess of par—preferred		100	
Paid-in capital in excess of par—common		600	
Paid-in capital from treasury stock		50	
Paid-in capital from stock options		300	
Total contributed capital			$1,760
Retained Earnings:			
Unappropriated retained earnings		$800	
Appropriated retained earnings		80	
Total retained earnings			880
Accumulated other comprehensive income			400
Treasury stock, 1,000 shares common			(11)
Total stockholders' equity			$3,029

stockholders' equity in the coming pages, refer to Illustration 17.2, the stockholders' equity section of Hang Corporation's balance sheet.

LO3 Explain the distinctions between different classes of stock.

contributed capital the owners' investments in a business; also called *paid-in capital*

❱ CONTRIBUTED CAPITAL

When the stockholders' equity section of the balance sheet is prepared, it is important to first provide details on **contributed capital**, also called *paid-in capital,* which is defined as the owners' investments in a business. Within the contributed capital portion of stockholders' equity, each class of stock should be presented separately. Actual companies may have more than two classes, each with distinct voting rights and other privileges. Companies develop different classes of stock to appeal to the different risk and return preferences of potential investors. The Model Business Corporation Act, which is the basis for most state laws governing issuance of stock, no longer uses the terms *preferred stock* and *common stock.* Yet many companies still present stock of these two general types. As you can see in Illustration 17.2, Hang Corporation lists three separate categories of capital stock: preferred stock, common stock, and common stock distributable.

common stock a class of corporate stock that carries voting rights and entitles owners to share in the firm's profits through dividends, if issued

dividends distributions to shareholders of cash or property that has been earned through profitable operations

shares authorized the total number of shares that can be issued at any time, as indicated in the corporate charter

❱ **COMMON STOCK**   **Common stock** is a class of corporate stock that carries voting rights and entitles owners to share in the firm's profits through dividends, if they are issued. Common stockholders are not guaranteed dividends, but they generally profit greatly if the company is successful. As you learned in Chapter 1, **dividends** are distributions to shareholders of cash or property that has been earned through profitable operations.

For each class of stock, the company must disclose the number of shares of stock that are authorized, issued, and outstanding. **Shares authorized** is the total number of shares that can be issued at any time, as indicated in the corporate charter. At the time of its incorporation, a company must apply to the state authorities and must request authorization to issue shares. Usually, companies will request authorization of a very large number of shares to cover any possible future need for financing. **Shares issued** is the number of shares that have been issued, or sold, to the stockholders. **Shares outstanding** is the number of shares that are owned by stockholders as of the balance sheet date. As shown in Illustration 17.2, Hang Corporation has issued 200,000 shares of common stock and has 500,000 shares authorized.

shares issued the number of shares that have been issued, or sold, to the stockholders

shares outstanding the number of shares that are owned by stockholders as of the balance sheet date

The numbers of shares issued and outstanding differ because of the number of shares held as treasury stock. Treasury stock is included in the number of shares issued but is not considered to be outstanding because it is stock that has been repurchased by the company. Thus, for Hang Corporation, the number of shares of common stock issued and outstanding is as follows:

Shares issued	200,000
Less: Shares held as treasury stock	1,000
Shares outstanding	199,000

stock distributable a stock dividend that has been declared by the company but for which the shares of stock have not been issued to stockholders as of the balance sheet date

Hang Corporation also has an account titled Common Stock Distributable. **Stock distributable** represents a stock dividend that has been *declared* by the company but for which the shares of stock have not been issued to stockholders as of the balance sheet date.

preferred stock a class of capital stock that has preference over common stock in terms of receipt of dividends and of assets in the event of liquidation but usually does not carry voting rights

) PREFERRED STOCK **Preferred stock** is a class of capital stock that has some form of preference over common stock but usually does not carry voting rights. Generally, preferred stock has a preference in one or both of the following areas:

1. Dividends on preferred stock must be declared before dividends on common stock. This does not mean that the board of directors has a legal obligation to declare a dividend on preferred stock. It only means that if a dividend is declared, preferred stockholders must receive a dividend before common stockholders.

2. In the event that a corporation is liquidated or dissolved, preferred stockholders have a right to the company's assets before the common stockholders.

Critical Thinking: If you were presented with the opportunity to purchase common or preferred stock in your favorite company, which class of stock would you purchase? Why?

The following additional terms and features may be associated with preferred stock:

1. *Convertible.* Preferred stock may allow stockholders the right to convert the stock into common stock.

2. *Redeemable.* Preferred stock may allow stockholders to redeem their stock at a specified price.

3. *Callable.* Preferred stock may be callable at the option of the company. In this case, the company can choose to pay a specified amount to the stockholders in order to redeem or retire the stock.

4. *Cumulative.* The dividend on preferred stock is often cumulative. If this is the case, dividends that are not paid are considered to be *in arrears*. Before a dividend on common stock can be declared in a subsequent period, the dividends in arrears as well as the current year's dividend must be paid to the preferred stockholders.

5. *Participating.* If preferred stock carries a participating feature, it allows the preferred stockholders to receive a dividend in excess of the regular rate when the firm has been particularly profitable and declares an abnormally large dividend.

Because preferred stock can have a variety of terms and features, it is important for potential investors to read the financial statement notes and accompanying disclosures and understand the nature of the stock before investing in it.

❱ ADDITIONAL PAID-IN CAPITAL

The contributed capital portion of stockholders' equity in the balance sheet should also contain any amounts received in excess of the par value of the stock when stock was issued. As you can see in Illustration 17.2, Hang Corporation uses accounts titled Paid-in Capital in Excess of Par—Preferred, Paid-in Capital in Excess of Par—Common, Paid-in Capital—Treasury Stock, and Paid-in Capital—Stock Options. Alternative account titles include Additional Paid-in Capital or Premium on Stock.

❱ RETAINED EARNINGS

retained earnings the accumulated earnings of a firm since its inception less dividends or other distributions to owners

Retained earnings are the accumulated earnings of a firm since its inception less dividends or other distributions to owners. The presentation of this category within the stockholders' equity section of the balance sheet is usually straightforward. In the Hang Corporation example (Illustration 17.2), the company lists two categories of retained earnings: appropriated and unappropriated. Unappropriated retained earnings are the amount that is available for the payment of dividends. An appropriation of retained earnings indicates that a portion of retained earnings has been designated for a specific purpose.

❱ ACCUMULATED OTHER COMPREHENSIVE INCOME

accumulated other comprehensive income amounts that are not treated as income on the traditional income statement and are not included in the net income figure, but are included in the broader definition of income known as comprehensive income

Two other presentation issues involving the stockholders' equity section of the balance sheet should be noted. First, companies must disclose the amount of accumulated other comprehensive income. **Accumulated other comprehensive income** represents amounts that are not treated as income on the traditional income statement and are not included in the net income figure, but *are* included in the broader definition of income known as comprehensive income. At this time, there are four particular items that are included as accumulated other comprehensive income:

1. Foreign currency translation adjustments

2. The adjustment for the minimum pension liability (in some cases)

3. Unrealized gains or losses on investments in available-for-sale securities

4. Unrealized gains or losses on derivative financial instruments that involve cash flow hedging strategies

In each case, the amounts related to these items are not included in the calculation of net income but are included in comprehensive income. Note that the balance sheet amount does not represent the amount for the current year, but rather represents the *total amount* or the accumulated amount. Typically, accumulated other comprehensive income appears near the bottom of the stockholders' equity section.

Second, note that treasury stock is presented in the stockholders' equity section of the balance sheet. Treasury stock is a deduction from equity and is treated as a *contra-equity* account. The nature of treasury stock will be discussed later in this chapter. Normally, it is presented near the bottom of the stockholders' equity section.

❱ STOCKHOLDERS' EQUITY FOR NIKE

As noted earlier, the existence of different classes of stock may have important implications for the voting rights of stockholders. The stockholders' equity section of **Nike**'s consolidated balance sheet and the related notes are presented in Figure 17.1. Financial statement users should examine the notes to determine the voting rights of each class of stock.

As you can see from Figure 17.1, Nike has authorized and issued two classes of common stock. The first class, referred to as Class A common stock, is convertible. The number of shares outstanding at May 31, 2004, is 77.6 million shares. The second class of stock, referred to as Class B common stock, does not have a par value but like Class

Figure 17.1

Shareholders' Equity Section of the Balance Sheet

Nike

Nike Corporation
May 31, 2003 and 2004
(in millions)

	May 31,	
	2004	2003
Shareholders Equity:		
Common Stock at stated value (Note 10):		
Class A convertible—77.6 and 97.8 shares outstanding	$ 0.1	$ 0.2
Class B—185.5 and 165.8 shares outstanding	2.7	2.6
Capital in excess of stated value	887.8	589.0
Unearned stock compensation	(5.5)	(0.6)
Accumulated other comprehensive loss (Note 13)	(86.3)	(239.7)
Retained earnings	3,982.9	3,639.2
Total shareholders' equity	$4,781.7	$3,990.7

Note 10—Common Stock

The authorized number of shares of Class A Common Stock, no par value, and Class B Common Stock, no par value, are 110 million and 350 million, respectively. Each share of Class A Common Stock is convertible into one share of Class B Common Stock. Voting rights of Class B Common Stock are limited in certain circumstances with respect to the election of directors.

A stock has a stated value. The balance sheet indicates that the number of shares of Class B stock outstanding at May 31, 2004, is 185.5 million shares.

The notes indicate that the Class A common stock can be converted into Class B common stock, but that the voting rights of the Class B common stock are restricted when electing members to the board of directors.

INTERNATIONAL ISSUES REGARDING STOCKHOLDERS' EQUITY

While international accounting standards have been issued on a variety of accounting topics, the IASC has released no standards that pertain directly to the proper presentation of the stockholders' equity section of the balance sheet. As a result, the accounting standards of each country prevail, creating differences in reporting. For example, Japanese accounting standards do not require a statement of changes in equity to be provided in the annual report. The accounting standards of the United Kingdom require treasury stock to be shown as an asset rather than as a reduction of stockholders' equity.[2] In the future, international accounting standards may be issued that will bring uniformity to the reporting of stockholders' equity.

> **CHECK YOUR UNDERSTANDING**
>
> 1. What is the difference between common stock and preferred stock?
>
> 2. What are amounts that have been received from external sources called on the statement of stockholders' equity?
>
> 3. Explain how shares outstanding, shares issued, and shares authorized differ.

---

2 For more detail, refer to *GAAP 2000: A Survey of National Accounting Rules in 53 Countries.* PriceWaterhouseCoopers, December 2000.

Issuance of Stock

Companies may issue stock in a variety of ways. The most common method is the issuance of stock for cash, either directly or through a brokerage. In some cases, two classes of stock may be issued for a lump-sum amount. Finally, stock may be issued in return for consideration other than cash. We will examine the accounting treatment for each type of issuance in the sections that follow.

ISSUANCE OF STOCK FOR CASH

When a company issues stock with a par value, it must account for the par value of the stock separately from the amount received in excess of par. For example, if Shalnour, Inc. issues 10,000 shares of common stock with a par value of $5 per share at an issue price of $15 per share, the following entry should be recorded:

Cash	150,000	
Common Stock		50,000
Paid-in Capital in Excess of Par—Common		100,000

The account Paid-in Capital in Excess of Par—Common may also have a title such as Additional Paid-in Capital—Common. It represents the amount received at the time of issuance that is in excess of the par value of the stock. Since both the Common Stock account and the Paid-in Capital in Excess of Par—Common account are presented in the stockholders' equity category, the distinction between the two is important only because of a legal requirement. Specifically, if stock were to be issued for less than the par value (at a discount), the company could, at a later time, ask the stockholders to remit the amount of the discount if the company is unable to meet its financial obligations. For that reason, companies set the par value at a very low level so that the stock will always sell at an amount higher than par. In fact, most states do not allow stock to be sold at less than par value.

Some states allow companies to sell no-par stock. In that case, the entire amount received from issuance should be recorded in the stock account. In the previous example, the entry would simply be recorded as follows:

Cash	150,000	
Common Stock		150,000

ISSUANCE OF STOCK FOR A LUMP SUM

In some cases, both preferred and common stock are issued for a lump-sum dollar amount. This may occur because companies wish to obtain financing at the lowest possible cost. In other instances, investors may be hesitant to buy preferred stock because its market value is difficult to determine, so companies offer a combination of common and preferred stock for a lump sum. On the other hand, there may also be cases in which common stock is not attractive to stockholders. Generally, preferred stock is more stable, and the dividend on preferred stock may be more reliable than that on the common stock. In some cases, investors may be more willing to purchase the common stock if they can also purchase preferred stock at the same time.

To illustrate, assume that Jen Company issues 10,000 shares of $5 par common stock and 5,000 shares of $1 par preferred stock for a lump sum of $72,000. The company wishes to allocate the purchase price between the preferred stock and the common stock. In this case, the proper procedure is to allocate the purchase price *according to the proportion of the total fair market value of the two classes of stock at the date of issuance represented by each class.* Assume that if the stock had been sold separately, the market value of the common stock would have been $6 per share and that

Illustration 17.3

Lump-Sum Allocation of Stock Issuance

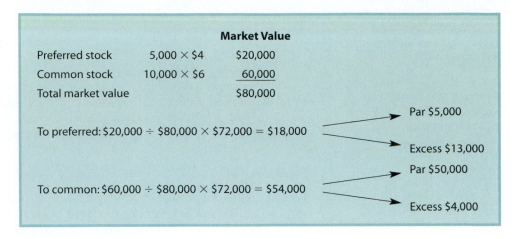

		Market Value
Preferred stock	5,000 × $4	$20,000
Common stock	10,000 × $6	60,000
Total market value		$80,000

To preferred: $20,000 ÷ $80,000 × $72,000 = $18,000 → Par $5,000 / Excess $13,000

To common: $60,000 ÷ $80,000 × $72,000 = $54,000 → Par $50,000 / Excess $4,000

of the preferred stock would have been $4 per share. The allocation is shown in Illustration 17.3.

Based on this allocation, the company should record the following journal entry for the lump-sum issuance:

Cash	72,000	
Preferred Stock		5,000
Paid-in Capital in Excess of Par—Preferred		13,000
Common Stock		50,000
Paid-in Capital in Excess of Par—Common		4,000

Occasionally, if the stock is not widely traded, the determination of its market value may be difficult. However, every effort should be made to develop a reasonable estimate of the market value as the basis for the allocation.

ISSUANCE OF STOCK FOR NONCASH CONSIDERATION

When stock is issued for a consideration other than cash (nonmonetary exchange), an appropriate value must be determined at which to record the transaction. The general rule in such cases is that the exchange should be recorded *at the fair market value of the consideration given or the fair market value of the consideration received, whichever is more reliable.* For large companies with stock that is actively traded on the stock exchange, the fair market value of the stock will be easily determined and will be more reliable. For example, assume that the Tan Company issues 10,000 shares of $5 par common stock to obtain a parcel of land at a time when the stock is trading on the stock market for $20 per share. The company should record the following transaction:

Land	200,000	
Common Stock		50,000
Paid-in Capital in Excess of Par—Common		150,000

In some cases, stock is issued in exchange for services, rather than for an asset as in this example. The same procedure should be followed: The services should be valued at the fair market value of the consideration given (the stock) or the consideration received (the services), whichever can be more readily determined. Smaller companies may have stock that is not actively traded, and so the fair market value of the stock may not be easy to determine. In such cases, it may be necessary to determine the fair market value of the asset received (or services received) in the exchange as the basis for recording the transaction. Fair market value may be determined by the assessed value or by reference to similar transactions that the company may have engaged in in past periods.

1. If a company issues common stock with a par value for cash, what account is used to account for any amount received in excess of par value?

2. If a company issues both preferred stock and common stock for a lump-sum price, how is the cost allocated?

3. If stock is issued by a company in exchange for services, how should the exchange be valued?

LO5 Explain the accounting for treasury stock.

treasury stock stock that has been issued to stockholders, then repurchased by the company and is being held by the company for a purpose

🧩 *Critical Thinking: What role do you think the dynamic of supply and demand plays in a company's decision to buy back its own stock?*

Treasury Stock

Treasury stock is stock in the corporation that (1) has been issued to stockholders, (2) has been repurchased by the company, and (3) is being held by the company for a purpose and has not been retired. Note that treasury stock is the company's own stock that has been repurchased. If the stock of another company is purchased, it is considered an investment, not treasury stock.

Companies may choose to purchase treasury stock for the following reasons:

1. *To improve financial ratios.* A purchase of treasury stock reduces the number of shares of stock outstanding. This has the effect of increasing important financial ratios, including the widely tracked earnings per share (EPS) ratio.

2. *To maintain control and prevent takeover attempts.* A purchase of treasury stock may allow the company to maintain better control of the ownership of the stock. This may be one tool used to prevent a takeover attempt or a hostile bid for the stock.

3. *To use it for employee compensation.* Treasury stock is very commonly used by companies that provide stock to their employees as part of a compensation plan, as a bonus, or through an employee stock purchase plan.

4. *To use excess cash.* When a company has excess cash, it must decide among a variety of available financial options. Sometimes the most profitable option is to buy treasury stock and thereby reduce the amount of dividends paid and increase the stock price per share.

During the stock downturn of 2001 and 2002, the repurchase of stock became especially prevalent. When stock prices are at depressed levels, companies may be aggressive in purchasing their own stock because it helps restore investors' confidence in the company, as expressed in the following excerpt from an article titled "Tech Companies Go on Buyback Binge," published in *TechWeb* magazine.

> In a move intended to rescue plummeting stock values and improve shareholder confidence, a flood of tech companies have revealed plans to buy back their own securities, potentially spending billions of dollars in the process.
>
> On Monday, Intel, the world's largest chipmaker, said it would add another 300 million shares to buybacks already under way, bringing the total value of its repurchased stock to more than $7 billion. Customer-relationship-management software maker Siebel Systems Inc. said it would repurchase up to $500 million of its common stock. And content-delivery company Akamai Technologies Inc. said it might spend up to $20 million. The announcements come on the heels of a number of other initiatives disclosed last week: Cisco Systems said it may repurchase 3%, or roughly $3 billion of its stock; software

maker BEA Systems may spend up to $100 million; and wireless services company Dobson Communications may buy back up to $80 million. Analysts say the buybacks are a good way to reassure investors, assuming businesses follow through.

"The announcements might shore up some confidence," says William Schaff, chief investment officer for Bay Isle Financial Corp., "but just because they announce doesn't mean they'll actually implement." Schaff says that buybacks may help some companies improve their stock value, but if they don't improve their fundamentals, it'll be a worthless gesture: "The market will go where the fundamentals lead it."[3]

PURCHASE OF TREASURY STOCK

When a company purchases treasury stock, the cost of the treasury stock should be recorded in the Treasury Stock account.[4] The Treasury Stock account has a normal debit balance, but it is not an asset account. As indicated earlier in this chapter, Treasury Stock should be presented as a contra–stockholders' equity account and represents a reduction in total stockholders' equity. Note that the purchase of treasury stock does not alter the total number of shares of common stock *issued*, but it does decrease the total number of shares *outstanding*. For example, assume that Nicholson Company purchased 1,000 shares of its own $2 par common stock at a price of $15 per share on January 1, 2005. The company should record the following transaction:

Treasury Stock	15,000	
Cash		15,000

REISSUANCE OF TREASURY STOCK

In some cases, treasury stock may be held for a time and then reissued or resold to stockholders. Whenever a reissuance of treasury stock occurs, there is one general guideline for proper accounting treatment: *The reissuance of stock should not result in a gain or loss that is reported on the income statement.* Instead, all reissuances of treasury stock affect accounts within the stockholders' equity section of the balance sheet.

❱ REISSUE FOR MORE THAN PURCHASE PRICE

Assume that Nicholson Company reissues 300 shares (purchased at $15 per share) for $20 per share on February 1, 2005. The company should record this journal entry:

Cash	6,000	
Treasury Stock (300 × $15)		4,500
Paid-in Capital from Treasury Stock (300 × $5)		1,500

In an economic sense, the company gained because stock was purchased at $15 per share and resold for $20 per share. However, no gain is presented on the income statement. Instead, the account Paid-in Capital from Treasury Stock is treated as an element of contributed capital within the stockholders' equity section.

❱ REISSUE FOR LESS THAN PURCHASE PRICE

When a company reissues treasury stock for less than the purchase price, the difference between the amount received and the purchase price of the treasury stock should be

---

3 "Tech Companies Go on Buyback Binge," *TechWeb News*, September 17, 2001, available at: **www.techweb.com**. Accessed on 5/9/04.

4 Although there are two methods of recording treasury stock, the cost method is the more common method and is the one presented in this text. The par value method may also be used.

used to reduce the Paid-in Capital from Treasury Stock account from previous transactions. If the amount of the difference exceeds the balance of the Paid-in Capital from Treasury Stock account, the remainder is treated as a reduction of Retained Earnings. For example, assume that on March 1 Nicholson Company reissued an additional 300 shares of treasury stock (originally purchased at $15 per share) for $8 per share. The company should record the following journal entry:

Cash	2,400	
Paid-in Capital from Treasury Stock (300 × $5)	1,500	
Retained Earnings (300 × $2)	600	
Treasury Stock		4,500

Again, note that in an economic sense, the company has experienced a loss, since treasury stock was purchased at $15 per share and reissued for $8 per share. But the loss is not presented on the income statement. Also, note that the Paid-in Capital from Treasury Stock account may have a credit balance or a zero balance, but the journal entry is made in a manner that does not create a debit balance in the account. Instead, the Retained Earnings account is used to absorb any amount remaining after the Paid-in Capital from Treasury Stock account has been reduced to zero.

RETIREMENT OF TREASURY STOCK

There may be a few unusual cases in which a company retires treasury stock. This signals a change in the company's intentions because treasury stock is generally repurchased from stockholders and held for a specific purpose. When that purpose changes and the company decides to retire the stock, it must adhere to all legal requirements in reducing the company's legal capital.

Refer to our previous example for Nicholson Company. When the company purchased treasury stock and then reissued the stock, the Common Stock account and the Paid-in Capital in Excess of Par—Common account were not affected. However, if the company chooses to *retire* stock held as treasury stock, the Common Stock account and the Paid-in Capital in Excess of Par—Common account must be reduced.

Assume that on April 1, 2005, Nicholson Company wishes to retire the 200 shares of treasury stock. Also assume that the stock (with a $2 par value) had originally been issued to stockholders at $12 per share (and had been purchased as treasury stock for $15 per share). The company should record the following journal entry to record the retirement:[5]

Common Stock (200 × $2)	400	
Paid-in Capital in Excess of Par—Common (200 × $10)	2,000	
Retained Earnings (200 × $3)	600	
Treasury Stock (200 × $15)		3,000

Interestingly, total stockholders' equity is not affected when a retirement of treasury stock occurs. All of the affected accounts are within the stockholders' equity section, and the journal entry simply rearranges amounts in those accounts.

> **CHECK YOUR UNDERSTANDING**
>
> 1. List reasons why a company might repurchase its own stock from the market.
>
> 2. How does the Treasury Stock account affect total stockholders' equity?
>
> 3. Gains on the resale of treasury stock are recorded in which account?

---

5 The accounting guidance concerning the retirement of treasury stock is somewhat unclear. We will assume that if Paid-in Capital from Treasury Stock exists as a result of previous transactions, it should be reduced to zero, and any remaining amount should be a reduction of Retained Earnings.

Critical Thinking: In what ways do companies provide returns to their investors?

Dividends

Many investors look to the price appreciation of their stock as the primary source of income. However, dividends may also be an important element of the total return on an investment in stock. In the following sections, we will examine the various types of dividends that can be declared and paid by corporations, beginning with cash dividends. Property dividends are used less frequently, but their impact on stockholders' equity is also examined. The section ends with a discussion of the accounting for stock dividends.

CASH DIVIDENDS

It is important to note that there are no legal provisions that require companies to declare a cash dividend.[6] This is true even if the stock is cumulative. The liability for dividends is created at the time the dividend is declared. Assume that Kristen Company has outstanding 100,000 shares of $8 par common stock and 40,000 shares of 8 percent preferred stock with a par value of $10 per share. If the company declares the dividend on preferred stock and a $1 per share dividend on common stock on July 1, the following entry should be made:

Retained Earnings	132,000	
Dividends Payable—Preferred (40,000 × $10 × 8%)		32,000
Dividends Payable—Common		100,000

Cash dividends should be declared and paid based on the number of shares of stock *outstanding* as of a given date specified by the board of directors. In other words, cash dividends cannot be paid on treasury stock, since the company declaring the dividend is holding these shares. With regard to dividends, there are three important dates:

- *Date of declaration.* The date on which the company declares the dividend. Retained earnings should be reduced on this date.

- *Date of record.* Stockholders who own the stock as of the date of record will receive the dividend. Stockholders who purchase stock after this date will not.

- *Date of payment.* The date on which the company actually pays the dividend to the stockholders.

When a cash dividend is paid, the company should simply reduce (debit) the Dividends Payable account or accounts and reduce (credit) cash.

Most companies attempt to maintain a consistent pattern of cash dividends because their stockholders expect it. Most state laws allow the payment of dividends even when the company has not been profitable for the most recent fiscal year. It is not uncommon for companies that have declared a net loss to continue to pay dividends to stockholders in order to maintain their consistent dividend pattern. In unusual cases, a company may declare a liquidating dividend. A **liquidating dividend** occurs when the amount of the dividend exceeds the balance of the Retained Earnings account. Any portion of the dividend that exceeds the balance of Retained Earnings represents a return of the stockholders' invested capital and should be debited to Additional Paid-in Capital rather than to Retained Earnings.

liquidating dividend a dividend whose amount exceeds the balance of the Retained Earnings account

---

6 There may be financial considerations that make it wise to declare a dividend. Also, there may be tax consequences when a dividend is not paid and the balance in the Retained Earnings account accumulates.

Illustration 17.4

Dividend When Participating Preferred Stock Is Present

	Preferred	Common
1. Dividends in arrears to preferred:		
40,000 × $10 × 8% × 1 year	$32,000	
2. Current year's dividend to preferred:		
40,000 × $10 × 8%	32,000	
3. An equal percentage to common:		
100,000 × $8 × 8%		$ 64,000
4. Remainder allocated on basis of par value:		
To preferred—		
$400 ÷ $1,200 × $72,000	24,000	
To common—		
$800 ÷ $1,200 × $72,000		48,000
Totals	$88,000	$112,000
Per share for preferred:		
$88,000 ÷ 40,000	$2.20	
Per share for common:		
$112,000 ÷ 100,000		$1.12

❱ PARTICIPATING PREFERRED STOCK

Sometimes companies must consider how to allocate dividends between the classes of stock that have been issued. In all cases, the terms and provisions of the stock agreements dictate the allocation of dividends. A particular difficulty arises when preferred stock carries a participating feature. Participating preferred stock allows the preferred stockholders to share in the good fortune of the company when an especially large dividend is declared. The extra dividend is divided between the preferred and common stock based on the total par values of the classes of stock.

For example, assume that Kristen Company has 100,000 shares of $8 par common stock and 40,000 shares of 8 percent cumulative, participating preferred stock with a par value of $10 per share. Assume that the preferred stock dividend is in arrears for one year prior to the current year, and that the company wishes to declare a dividend of $200,000 on December 1, 2005. The preferred stock must first receive the dividends in arrears and an 8 percent dividend for the current period. The common stock should then receive a dividend that is also equal to 8 percent of the par value. The remainder should be allocated between preferred and common based on the proportion of total par value represented by each of the two classes. Illustration 17.4 indicates the amount that should be declared for preferred and common stockholders in this scenario.

PROPERTY DIVIDENDS

property dividend a distribution of an asset other than cash to the stockholders; also called a nonmonetary transfer to owners

A **property dividend** is a distribution of an asset other than cash to the stockholders. In order to conserve cash, a company may issue land, inventory, or a security to the stockholders. This is also referred to as a *nonmonetary transfer to owners*. When a property dividend is declared, the distribution should be recorded at the fair market value of the asset on the date of declaration, and a gain or loss should be recorded for the difference between the cost and the market value of the asset at that date.

For example, assume that on July 1, 2005, Robinson Company declared its intention to distribute bonds of Baggs Company that it has held as an investment. The property dividend will be distributed on August 10, 2005. Assume that the bonds were purchased at face value of $200,000 and were treated as an element of the held-to-maturity portfolio. Because of a change in interest-rate conditions, the fair market value of the bonds is currently $220,000. On July 1, Robinson Company should record the following entries:[7]

Investment in Bonds—Held to Maturity	20,000	
Gain on Investment		20,000
Retained Earnings	220,000	
Dividends Payable		220,000

The Gain on Investment account should be considered a realized gain and presented on the income statement. In most cases, the gain will not be considered an extraordinary item and should be presented in the other income category of the income statement.

On August 10, when the property dividend is distributed, Robinson should record the following entry:

Dividends Payable	220,000	
Investment in Bonds—Held to Maturity		220,000

STOCK DIVIDENDS AND STOCK SPLITS

stock dividend the issuance of shares of a company's own stock to its stockholders

The nature of a stock dividend is markedly different from that of cash or property dividends. A **stock dividend** occurs when a company issues shares of its own stock to its stockholders. A company may issue a stock dividend because it wishes to declare a dividend and does not have cash available. More often, stock dividends occur because the company wishes to decrease the price per share at which its stock trades in the stock market. Most companies want their stock to sell in a certain price range so that it appeals to certain types of stockholders (for example, individual investors or institutional investors). Since a stock dividend represents additional shares of ownership, the effect is to decrease the selling price of the stock. The accounting for stock dividends depends on the *size* of the dividend and its *legal* basis. However, in all cases stock dividends *do not* represent an expense to the corporation and *do not* result in income to the recipients.

▶ SMALL STOCK DIVIDENDS

The accounting for stock dividends is based on accounting guidance that most accountants view as rather archaic. Accountants recognize that stock dividends do not change a company's total assets and do not alter the proportionate ownership of the company by each of the stockholders. However, many recipients of stock dividends look upon them as distributions of corporate earnings, usually in an amount equivalent to the fair value of the additional shares. Based on that reasoning, the accounting guidance requires an amount equal to the *fair market value* of the additional shares as of the date of declaration to be transferred from retained earnings to the permanent capital of the company.

For example, assume that on July 1, 2005, Johnson Company declared and distributed a 10 percent stock dividend to common stockholders at a time when the market price of the stock was $50 per share and there were 100,000 shares of stock outstanding

---

7 We have used an example involving the held-to-maturity portfolio to simplify the presentation. It should be noted, however, that companies are ordinarily expected to hold such securities to maturity, not to distribute them as dividends. Also, it should be noted that if a property dividend involves securities treated as available-for-sale or as trading securities, the amount of gain or loss previously recorded as unrealized must be considered and a "reclassification" entry may be necessary.

with a par value of $10 per share.[8] Johnson Company should record the following accounting entry:

Retained Earnings (100,000 × 10% × $50)	500,000	
Common Stock		100,000
Paid-in Capital in Excess of Par—Common		400,000

Note that a stock dividend does not alter *total* stockholders' equity. Most stockholders look favorably upon stock dividends because they see them as an indication of a positive future outlook for the company. However, stock dividends also involve a reduction in the Retained Earnings account and a transfer of that amount to the permanent capital (contributed capital) of the company. Since future dividends are taken from retained earnings, a stock dividend reduces the ability of the company to declare cash dividends in the future. In that sense, a stock dividend is a reduction in the dividend-paying ability of the company and serves as a signal to stockholders that the company has financial needs other than the payment of dividends.

❱ LARGE STOCK DIVIDENDS

The accounting described in the previous section is based on the assumption in the accounting guidance that small stock dividends do not have a material impact on the per share market value of the stock. When a large stock dividend is involved, it will affect the stock price, and the accounting should be altered. The accounting guidance indicates that "there is no need to capitalize retained earnings other than to the extent occasioned by legal requirements."[9] However, legal requirements often dictate that an amount of retained earnings equal to the *par value* of the additional number of shares issued be transferred. Therefore, the entry for large stock dividends should be made based on the par value of the stock.

What is the distinction between a large and a small stock dividend? The accounting guidance indicates that when a stock dividend exceeds *20 to 25 percent* of the number of shares of stock outstanding, it should be considered a large stock dividend. The reasoning is based on the belief that stock dividends that are smaller than that level do not affect stock price in a material way. Research concerning the behavior of stock prices that has been conducted since the issuance of the accounting guidance suggests that stock prices respond to all but the very smallest (perhaps 2 percent) stock dividends. In effect, the research indicates that the 20 to 25 percent rule is not a proper distinction. In spite of this research, the accounting for stock dividends continues to be based on the 20 to 25 percent cutoff.

For example, assume that Johnson Company declared and distributed a 100 percent stock dividend to the common stockholders when there were 100,000 shares of stock outstanding with a par value of $10 per share. The following entry should be recorded:

Retained Earnings (100,000 × 100% × $10)	1,000,000	
Common Stock		1,000,000

A large stock dividend has many of the characteristics of a stock split. In fact, the accounting guidance suggests that such dividends be referred to as a stock split effected in the form of a dividend. This is the language that companies often use when they declare a large stock dividend.

---

8 It is not entirely clear whether stock dividends should be based on the number of shares of stock outstanding. State law may dictate the basis of the stock dividend. In all of our examples, we will assume that stock dividends are declared and distributed on the basis of the stock outstanding.

9 "Restatement and Revision of Accounting Research Bulletins," *Accounting Research Bulletin No. 43* (FASB, 1953), par. 11.

Illustration 17.5

History of Microsoft Common Stock Splits

Split	Payable Date	Type of Split*	Closing Price Before/After
First	Sept. 18, 1987	2 for 1	Sept. 18— $114.50 Sept. 21—$53.50
Second	Apr. 12, 1990	2 for 1	Apr. 12—$120.75 Apr. 16—$60.75
Third	June 26, 1991	3 for 2	June 26—$100.75 June 27—$68.00
Fourth	June 12, 1992	3 for 2	June 12—$112.50 June 15—$75.75
Fifth	May 20, 1994	2 for 1	May 20—$97.75 May 23—$50.63
Sixth	Dec. 6, 1996	2 for 1	Dec. 6—$152.875 Dec. 9—$81.75
Seventh	Feb. 20, 1998	2 for 1	Feb. 20—$155.13 Feb. 23—$81.63
Eighth	Mar. 26, 1999	2 for 1	Mar. 26—$178.13 Mar. 29—$92.38
Ninth	Feb. 14, 2003	2 for 1	Feb. 14—$48.30 Feb. 18—$24.96

*Type of split:
2 for 1 = one additional share for every share held (multiply number by 2 for new total)
3 for 2 = one additional share for every two shares held (multiply number by 1.5 for new total)[10]

❱ STOCK SPLITS

From an economic perspective, a stock split is very similar to a stock dividend. Both result in additional shares of stock being issued to the stockholders. In fact, in the previous section, we noted that large stock dividends are often referred to as stock splits effected in the form of a dividend. However, under some state laws there is a legal distinction between a large stock dividend and a stock split. Specifically, a stock split does not require the transfer of retained earnings into permanent capital, but it does result in a change in the par value per share of the stock. For example, if a company declares a 2-for-1 stock split on its $10 par stock, the par value per share is adjusted to $5 per share after the split. No formal journal entry is made, but a memorandum entry is made to note that the company has twice as many shares of stock after the stock split. Companies may declare different types of splits (2 for 1, 3 for 2), as shown in Illustration 17.5 for **Microsoft**.

❱ SUMMARY OF STOCK DIVIDENDS AND SPLITS

The accounting for stock dividends and stock splits is based on both accounting and legal considerations. The economic impact of small stock dividends, large stock dividends, and stock splits is similar, but the accounting in each case is different. It is important for users of financial statements to understand that in all cases stock dividends and stock splits do not alter the total amount of stockholders' equity, but they do alter the number of shares of stock issued and outstanding.

---

10 Investor Relations, Microsoft website, available at: **www.microsoft.com.** Accessed 4/2002.

Illustration 17.6

Stock Dividends and Stock Splits

	Small Stock Dividend	Large Stock Dividend	Stock Split
Treatment	Record at fair market value	Record at par value	No entry required
Journal entry	Debit Retained Earnings; Credit Stock; Credit Paid-in Capital in Excess of Par	Debit Retained Earnings; Credit Stock	No entry required
Change in par value per share	No change	No change	Reduces par value per share

Illustration 17.6 summarizes the accounting treatment for small stock dividends, large stock dividends, and stock splits.

CHECK YOUR UNDERSTANDING

1. What three dates are important with regard to dividends?

2. What does it mean when preferred stock carries a participating feature?

3. How should the distribution of a property dividend be recorded?

4. Discuss the similarities and differences between a large stock dividend and a stock split.

LO7 Describe how convertible securities affect stockholders' equity.

Critical Thinking: How do you think the interests of stockholders are affected by securities that can be converted into stock?

Convertible Securities

When considering stockholders' equity, it is important to consider not only the stock that currently exists, but also the events and transactions that could affect the interests of the stockholders in the future. In this section, two instruments that have potential implications for stockholders will be examined: convertible bonds and convertible preferred stock.

CONVERTIBLE BONDS

convertible bonds a fixed obligation that pays interest similar to other bond issuances, but that has a clause that allows the bonds to be converted into stock

Convertible bonds are a fixed obligation. They pay interest similar to other bond issuances, but they have a clause that allows the bonds to be converted into stock. Often, there are sound financial reasons for companies to issue convertible bonds. For investors, convertible bonds are attractive because they have a lower level of risk than stock and a more stable return in the form of interest payments. But investors also have the potential to receive a higher return by converting the bonds into stock when they believe the company's future is favorable. For issuing companies, convertible bonds are often attractive because the interest rate on these bonds is less than that on bonds without a conversion feature. This allows companies to obtain financing at a reduced cost.

When convertible bonds are issued, the bonds should be treated as a liability and presented in the long-term liabilities section of the balance sheet. If the bonds are issued at an amount that differs from their face value, the premium or discount should be *amortized over the time from issuance to maturity date*. Premium or discount amortization should not reflect the possibility that the bonds may be converted before the maturity date.

Assume that Diehl Company issued 5 percent convertible bonds with a face value of $500,000 at 98 on January 1, 2005. Each $1,000 bond can be converted into eight shares of common stock that has a $10 par value per share. Interest is paid semiannually on June 30 and December 31. The bonds are due in five years, and the discount is amortized on a straight-line basis. When the bonds are issued on January 1, 2005, the company should record the following entry:

Cash	490,000	
Discount on Bonds	10,000	
Bonds Payable		500,000

When interest is paid on June 30 and December 31, the company should record interest and amortization of the discount as follows:

Interest Expense	13,500	
Discount on Bonds ($10,000 ÷ 5 years × ½)		1,000
Cash ($500,000 × 0.05 × ½ year)		12,500

Assume that the bondholders convert bonds with a face value of $100,000 into common stock on January 1, 2006. When the bonds are converted, Diehl must transfer an amount from the long-term liabilities category to the stockholders' equity category. The amount transferred should represent the *book value* (carrying value) of the bonds as of the date of the conversion.[11] The book value of the bond is calculated as follows:

Bond issue price	$490,000
Plus discount amortized for 2005	2,000
Bond carrying value on $500,000 of bonds	$492,000
Bond carrying value of bonds converted	$ 98,400
[$492,000 × ($100,000 ÷ $500,000)]	

Diehl should record the conversion with the following entry on January 1, 2006:

Bonds Payable	100,000	
Discount on Bonds ($100,000 − $98,400)		1,600
Common Stock (100 bonds × 8 × $10)		8,000
Paid-in Capital in Excess of Par—Common		90,400

There is some debate about the nature of the exchange of convertible bonds into stock. If the economic position of the company has changed as a result of the conversion, then it could be argued that a gain or loss should be recorded on the exchange. The book value method (used in this text) takes the position that the legal form of the instruments is altered by the conversion, but the economic status of the company has not been altered.

After portions of the bonds are converted, the amortization of premium or discount should be calculated based on the *remaining* bonds. For example, on June 30, 2006, Diehl should record amortization of $800, calculated as follows:

$$(\$10,000 \div 5 \text{ years}) \times (6 \text{ months} \div 12 \text{ months}) \times (\$400,000 \div \$500,000) = \$800$$

CONVERTIBLE PREFERRED STOCK

convertible preferred stock a class of stock distinct from common stock that carries a provision allowing it to be converted into common stock

Convertible preferred stock is a class of stock distinct from common stock that carries a provision allowing it to be converted into common stock. The financial motiva-

11 We will illustrate the method referred to as the book value method. Under this approach, no gain or loss is recorded on the conversion. Another, less common method is referred to as the fair value method.

tions for issuing convertible preferred stock may vary. In some cases, convertible preferred stock is used to convey voting rights to certain stockholders. In many other cases, such stock may be issued because it represents the most effective means of obtaining additional financing at the lowest cost. Investors find convertible preferred stock attractive because it often provides a more stable return at a lower risk level than common stock but still provides the opportunity to receive a higher return if the stock is converted to common stock.

Convertible preferred stock is treated as preferred stock until the time of conversion. That is, it should be presented in the stockholders' equity section of the balance sheet and labeled as preferred stock. When the stock is converted, an accounting entry is made to eliminate the preferred stock and transfer the book value (par value plus paid-in capital) to common stock within the stockholders' equity section. For example, assume that Nall Company has 1,000 shares of $10 par convertible preferred stock, originally issued at $50 per share. Each share of preferred can be converted into five shares of $4 par common stock. When the stock is converted, the following transaction should be recorded:

Preferred Stock	10,000	
Paid-in Capital in Excess of Par—Preferred	40,000	
Common Stock (1,000 × 5 × $4)		20,000
Paid-in Capital in Excess of Par—Common		30,000

Unlike the case of convertible bonds, there is little debate about the accounting for convertible preferred stock. The conversion of preferred stock into common stock does not result in a gain or loss that should be presented on the income statement. The conversion is, however, an important event and does affect the number of shares of common stock outstanding.

CHECK YOUR UNDERSTANDING

1. What are convertible bonds and how are they treated in the accounting records when they are issued?

2. If a company has issued convertible preferred stock and it has not yet been converted, where would its value be reflected in the financial statements?

LO8 Calculate and interpret key analysis measurements related to stockholders' equity.

🧩 *Critical Thinking: If you were considering the purchase of stock in a particular company, what financial data would be of interest to you?*

dividend payout ratio the portion of the current year's income that is paid out to the stockholders; calculated by dividing dividends by net income or dividing dividends per share by earnings per share

Analysis of Stockholders' Equity

The analysis of stockholders' equity is centered on three key measurements: the dividend payout ratio, the return on stockholders' equity, and earnings per share. In the following sections we will discuss the dividend payout ratio and the return on stockholders' equity. Earnings per share will be covered in Chapter 18.

DIVIDEND PAYOUT RATIO

The **dividend payout ratio** is calculated by dividing cash dividends by net income or by dividing dividends per share by earnings per share. If there is preferred stock outstanding, the ratio is computed for common stockholders by dividing cash dividends paid to common stockholders by net income minus any dividends paid to preferred stockholders. The dividend payout ratio measures the portion of the current year's income that is paid out to the stockholders. Since many companies do not pay dividends at all, this ratio, when used comparatively, may vary widely. The following table presents the dividend payout ratio for Microsoft and several other technology companies in 2003.

Company	Dividend Payout
Microsoft	9.1 %
Intel	17.0
Sun MicroSystems	0.0
Red Hat	0.0

Note that in the technology industry, payment of dividends is not always the norm. Several of Microsoft's competitors have never paid dividends to their stockholders. It is also important to remember that dividends are only one element of the total return to stockholders. Appreciation of the stock price is another important element. When stock prices were increasing rapidly during the 1990s, some investors overlooked the stable return available from dividends. But as stock prices took a downturn in 2001 and 2002, there was a renewed interest in dividends and dividend policy on the part of investors, as evidenced by the following excerpt from the article titled "Turbocharging with Dividends," from *Better Investing*:

> Thinking of venerable blue chips as stodgy and old-fangled, it can sometimes be easy to ignore companies such as Ford, Verizon, J.P. Morgan Chase, Kellogg and Chevron. But companies like these pay out generous dividends. At the time of this writing, Ford's dividend yield (annual dividend divided by share price) is 4.8 percent, Verizon's is 2.9 percent, Kellogg's, 3.7 percent; Chevron's 2.7 percent.
>
> Why should you consider a stock that pays a dividend? Well consider a market downturn. (It's actually not so hard to imagine these days is it?) Consider a year, or several years, of little or no stock appreciation, perhaps even depreciation of the prices of your stock. If you bought shares of Ford when the dividend yield was 4.8 percent, that means as long as the company remains healthy, you're pretty much guaranteed a piece of total return every year, regardless of what happens to stock price.[12]

Dividend payout ratios are important, but anticipating *changes* in dividend patterns may be more important. Stock prices reflect the market's expectation of current and future dividends. If a firm unexpectedly decreases the amount of dividends it pays, this will have a negative impact on the stock price. For that reason, firms attempt to keep a stable dividend pattern even when profits are declining or are negative.

RETURN ON STOCKHOLDERS' EQUITY

return on stockholders' equity
a measure of the return to common stockholders; calculated by dividing net income by average stockholders' equity for a fiscal period

Since stockholders contribute capital for the purpose of generating income, they are interested in the amount of income earned on each dollar they invest. **Return on stockholders' equity** is defined as net income divided by the average stockholders' equity for a period. Normally, this ratio is intended to measure the return to the common stockholders. If preferred stock is involved, the ratio is calculated as follows:

$$\text{Return on Stockholders' Equity} = \frac{\text{Net Income} - \text{Preferred Dividends}}{\text{Average Common Stockholders' Equity}}$$

Common stockholders' equity is calculated by subtracting preferred stock (Preferred Stock account and additional paid-in capital on preferred stock) from stockholders' equity. To compute average common stockholders' equity, use the following equation:

$$\text{Average Common Stockholders' Equity} = \frac{(\text{Beginning Common Stockholders' Equity} + \text{Ending Common Stockholders' Equity})}{2}$$

12 Selena Maranjian, "Turbocharging with Dividends," *Better Investing*, November 2001, p. 20.

A high return on stockholders' equity is always a positive indication about a company's profitability, but the ratio should be interpreted with care. Highly leveraged companies can achieve a high return on stockholders' equity (see the discussion of leverage in Chapter 13), but they also hold more debt obligations and carry more risk.

The following table provides the return on stockholders' equity ratios for Microsoft and other firms in the technology industry for 2003.

Company	Return
Microsoft	17.65%
Intel	15.39
Red Hat	(1.98)
Sun MicroSystems	(42.09)

As you can see, Microsoft provided a higher return on stockholders' equity than many of its competitors. In fact, many companies experienced large net losses during the same time period.

CHECK YOUR UNDERSTANDING

1. How is the return on stockholders' equity ratio calculated if preferred stock is involved, and what does it tell an investor?

2. How is the dividend payout ratio calculated?

LO9 Determine how stockholders' equity transactions affect cash flow.

Critical Thinking: *How do you think stock and dividend transactions affect cash flow?*

Cash Flow Issues Related to Stockholders' Equity

STOCKHOLDERS' EQUITY TRANSACTIONS ON THE STATEMENT OF CASH FLOWS

Transactions involving stockholders' equity are important events and should be presented in the financing activities section of the statement of cash flows. When stock is issued, it should appear as an addition to the cash provided by financing activities. Also, dividends paid should appear as a reduction in the financing activities section.

Figure 17.2 provides the financing activities category of the statement of cash flows for Microsoft for the year ended June 30, 2004. This section of Microsoft's statement of cash flows is somewhat unique because it does not display any debt activities for the three-year period; Microsoft did not borrow in the 2002–2004 period. All of its financing activities were related to stock transactions. Throughout the period, the company repurchased more stock than it issued. This has become a common practice

Figure 17.2

Microsoft Statement of Cash Flows

Microsoft	Microsoft Corporation Partial Statement of Cash Flows (in millions)		
Year Ended June 30	**2002**	**2003**	**2004**
Financing Activities			
Common stock issued	$1,497	$2,120	$2,748
Common stock repurchased	(6,069)	(6,486)	(3,383)
Common stock dividends	—	(857)	(1,729)
Net cash used for financing	(4,572)	(5,223)	(2,364)

for many large firms that have seen their stock price decline and their other investment alternatives curtailed.

Some transactions affecting the stockholders' equity category do not affect cash and should not be presented on the statement of cash flows. For example, the issuance of stock for noncash consideration should not be included, since no cash is involved. Also, the conversion of bonds does not affect cash directly. Both of these examples are known as *significant noncash transactions*. While they do not affect actual cash, they should be reported separately in a schedule that accompanies the statement of cash flows. See Chapter 19 for additional discussion of this topic.

CASH VERSUS ACCRUAL ISSUES

In most cases, stockholders' equity transactions involve the receipt or payment of cash, and there is not a large discrepancy between cash and accrual-based amounts. There are some exceptions, however, when changes in stockholders' equity accounts are not accompanied by changes in cash. Earlier in this chapter, we noted that stock dividends and stock splits do not involve cash but do involve the issuance of additional shares of stock. For that reason, stock dividends and stock splits are not presented on the statement of cash flows.

It is also important to distinguish between the *declaration* of dividends and the actual *cash payment* of dividends. Assume, for example, that the McClure Company had the following amounts at the beginning and end of the period:

Account	Beginning Balance	Ending Balance
Dividends Payable	$ 40,000	$ 55,000
Retained Earnings	320,000	500,000

Assume that the company's net income was $300,000 and that only net income and dividends affected the Retained Earnings account. The amount of cash dividends declared for the period could be calculated as follows:

Retained Earnings beginning balance	$320,000
Plus: Net income	300,000
Less: Retained Earnings ending balance	(500,000)
Dividends declared	$120,000

The actual amount of cash dividends paid should reflect both the dividends declared and the change in the Dividends Payable account. We could calculate dividends paid as follows:

Dividends declared	$120,000
Less: Increase in Dividends Payable	(15,000)
Dividends paid	$105,000

Remember that dividends are deducted from Retained Earnings when they are declared, but dividends are often paid to stockholders at a date later than the declaration date.

> **CHECK YOUR UNDERSTANDING**
>
> 1. Stock transactions are reflected in which section of the statement of cash flows?
>
> 2. Why are stock dividend transactions not reflected on the statement of cash flows?
>
> 3. Are dividends deducted from Retained Earnings when they are declared or when they are paid?

Revisiting the Case

MICROSOFT INTRODUCES NEW DIVIDEND POLICY

1. The company received $2,815 million from the issuance of stock during 2004.

2. Gain on derivative instruments, net income for 2004, net unrealized investment gains, translation adjustments, and the repurchase of common stock also affected retained earnings.

3. Microsoft may have been motivated to pay a dividend by the recent decline in its stock price or by changes in the way dividends are taxed when they are received by investors.

SUMMARY BY LEARNING OBJECTIVE

LO1 Describe the advantages and disadvantages of the corporate form of organization.

Although there are more partnerships and sole proprietorships than there are corporations in the United States, the corporate form is the preferred form of legal organization for large companies with many owners. The primary advantages of the corporate form of organization are the limited liability of stockholders for the actions of the company and the ability to raise capital efficiently. A corporation is considered a separate legal entity and must pay taxes on its income. The primary disadvantage of the corporate form is that the owners (stockholders) are often not directly involved in the activities of the company and must rely on managers to operate the company profitably. Corporations are also subject to many more legal restrictions than other forms of organization.

LO2 Present the stockholders' equity section of the balance sheet in the proper format.

The two distinct categories in the stockholders' equity section of the balance sheet are contributed capital and retained earnings. Contributed capital (also called *paid-in capital*) consists of amounts raised from external sources on the sale of the different classes of stock. Retained earnings are income that the corporation has earned and has not paid out as dividends. Stockholders' equity should also include a negative (debit) balance account for treasury stock held by the company. Additionally, stockholders' equity may include a category for the company's accumulated other comprehensive income. This represents amounts that have not been included in the net income calculation but have been included in the broader definition of income known as comprehensive income.

LO3 Explain the distinctions between different classes of stock.

Common stock carries voting rights but is ranked below preferred stock in terms of dividends and of distribution of assets in the event of liquidation. Common stockholders are not guaranteed dividends, but they generally profit greatly if the company is successful. Many companies have several classes of common stock, each with specific features. Preferred stock has a preference over common stock in some specific aspect of performance, generally with regard to either dividends or assets in the event of liquidation, or both. In addition, preferred stock may have a conversion feature or may be callable, cumulative, redeemable, or participating.

LO4 Demonstrate the proper accounting treatment for the issuance of stock.

When stock is issued for cash, the amount of the par value should normally be kept separate from the amount received in excess of par. When two classes of stock are issued for a lump-sum amount, the issuance price should be allocated between the two classes on the basis of their proportionate fair market values. When stock is issued for noncash consideration, the transaction should be valued based on the fair market value of either the consideration given or the consideration received, whichever is more reliable.

LO5 Explain the accounting for treasury stock.

Treasury stock is stock that the company has issued and then repurchased from the stockholders. It is often used as a means of distributing a small number of shares to employees as an element of compensation. In some cases, the purchase is used to increase the stock's market price. Treasury stock represents a contra–stockholders' equity account with a debit balance. When treasury stock is purchased, it reduces total stockholders' equity and the total number of shares outstanding. When treasury stock is reissued, it increases stockholders' equity. If it is reissued for more than the purchase price, the difference represents additional paid-in capital. If it is reissued for less than the purchase price, the difference is deducted from additional paid-in capital if such an account exists or, if it does not or if the amount in that account is insufficient, from retained earnings.

LO6 Demonstrate how to account for stock splits and cash, property, and stock dividends.

The amount paid for cash dividends is based on the number of shares of stock outstanding as of the date of declaration. The dividends reduce retained earnings and total stockholders' equity. Care must be taken to distribute the dividends correctly when both preferred and common stock are present. A stock dividend is the issuance of additional shares of stock to the company's stockholders. It reduces retained earnings but does not decrease total stockholders' equity. A small stock dividend transfers from retained earnings to contributed capital an amount equal to the fair market value of the stock distributed as of the date of declaration. For a large stock dividend, the amount transferred is equal to the par value of the stock. A stock split is very similar to a stock dividend, but it is not accounted for in the same manner. No accounting entry is made for a stock split, but the par value per share of the stock is reduced.

LO7 Describe how convertible securities affect stockholders' equity.

Convertible securities are instruments that can result in the issuance of additional shares of stock at a future time. Convertible bonds should be treated as a liability until the point of conversion. When the bonds are converted, an amount equal to the carrying value (book value) of the bonds should be transferred to stockholders' equity. Normally, no gain or loss is recorded on the conversion of the bonds. Convertible preferred stock should be treated as preferred stock until it is converted. When the stock is converted, the amount attributable to the converted preferred stock should be transferred to the common stock accounts. No gain or loss should be recorded on the conversion of preferred stock.

LO8 Calculate and interpret key analysis measurements related to stockholders' equity.

The dividend payout ratio represents the portion of net income that has been distributed to stockholders. This ratio varies widely among companies, and many companies do not distribute any dividends. It is also important to analyze any changes in a company's dividend policy. An increase in dividends may indicate a particularly profitable period, and a decrease may indicate that the company has financial needs other than dividends. The return on stockholders' equity ratio is the amount of net income earned for each dollar invested by stockholders; it is calculated by dividing net income by the average stockholders' equity for a period. A high return on equity is desirable but may also mean that the company is highly leveraged.

LO9 Determine how stockholders' equity transactions affect cash flow.

The cash flow effects of stockholders' equity transactions are normally presented in the financing activities section of the statement of cash flows. Most stockholders' equity events involve cash receipts or payments, but there are some notable exceptions, such as stock dividends, stock splits, and the issuance of stock for noncash consideration. When cash dividends are involved, it is important to distinguish between the amount of dividends declared and the amount actually paid. Dividends paid should reflect both dividends declared and the change in the Dividends Payable account.

KEY TERMS

accumulated other comprehensive
   income (p. 817)
common stock (p. 815)
contributed capital (p. 815)
convertible bonds (p. 829)
convertible preferred stock (p. 830)
dividend payout ratio (p. 831)
dividends (p. 815)

limited liability (p. 812)
liquidating dividend (p. 824)
preferred stock (p. 816)
property dividend (p. 825)
retained earnings (p. 817)
return on stockholders' equity
   (p. 832)

shares authorized (p. 815)
shares issued (p. 816)
shares outstanding (p. 816)
stock distributable (p. 816)
stock dividend (p. 826)
treasury stock (p. 821)

EXERCISES

LO1   **EXERCISE 17-1   Corporate Form of Organization**

On January 1, 2005, three individuals plan to start a business. They are confused about whether the business should be organized as a partnership or as a corporation and have asked for your opinion. The three expect the business to earn a profit of $300,000 during 2005 (with the partners sharing equally in the profits), and they wish to withdraw $80,000 each from the business for their living expenses.

Required:

1. Discuss the tax issues that must be considered when deciding whether the company should be organized as a partnership or a corporation.

2. Write a paragraph that summarizes the issues other than taxes that the individuals should consider when deciding on the proper legal form for the company.

LO2, 3, 4, 5   **EXERCISE 17-2   Stock Issuance and Stockholders' Equity**

Arial Company had the following transactions in the first year of its operations.

A. On January 10, 2005, the company issued 100,000 shares of its $5 par common stock for $8 per share and 20,000 shares of its $40 par, 6 percent preferred stock for $48 per share.

B. On March 1, the company issued 10,000 shares of common and 4,000 shares of preferred for $330,000. The market value of the common stock and the preferred stock on March 1 was $10 and $50, respectively.

C. On June 1, the company issued 8,000 shares of common stock to its legal counsel as payment for legal services. The legal counsel had billed for 1,000 hours of service, and the normal billing fee is $100 to $120 per hour. The market price of the common stock on June 1 was $11 per share.

D. On July 1, 5,000 shares of common stock were purchased as treasury stock at $14 per share.

E. On December 15, the board of directors voted to pay the annual cash dividend to preferred stockholders on January 20, 2006.

F. On December 31, the company determined that its income for the year was $405,000.

Required:

1. Record journal entries for these transactions for 2005.

2. Develop the stockholders' equity section of the balance sheet as of December 31, 2005.

LO5, 6   **EXERCISE 17-3   Stock Dividends and Splits**

The following events occurred for Randolph and Co. in 2005:

A. Declared and issued a 30 percent stock dividend

B. Declared and issued a 10 percent stock dividend

C. Issued a stock split

   D. Made the entry (if any) for dividends in arrears on cumulative preferred stock

   E. Declared a cash dividend

   F. Paid a cash dividend

   G. Purchased treasury stock

Required: For each event, indicate whether the event caused an increase or a decrease or had no effect on total stockholders' equity, retained earnings, and (for items A, B, and C) par value per share.

LO2, 5, 6   **EXERCISE 17-4   Stock Dividends and Cash Dividends** (CPA adapted)

Brady Company has 30,000 shares of $10 par value common stock authorized and 20,000 shares issued and outstanding. On August 15, 2005, Brady purchased 1,000 shares of treasury stock for $12 per share. Brady uses the cost method to account for treasury stock. On September 14, 2005, Brady sold 500 shares of the treasury stock for $14 per share. In October 2005, when the market value of the common stock was $16 per share, Brady declared and distributed a stock dividend of 2,000 unissued shares. On December 20, 2005, Brady declared a $1 per share cash dividend, payable on January 10, 2006, to shareholders of record on December 31, 2005.

Required: Draft a written response to the following questions:

1. How should Brady account for the purchase and sale of the treasury stock, and how should the treasury stock be presented in Brady's balance sheet at December 31, 2005?

2. How many shares of stock will be distributed for the stock dividend? How should Brady account for the stock dividend, and how will it affect Brady's stockholders' equity at December 31, 2005?

LO3, 6   **EXERCISE 17-5   Cash Dividend to Preferred and Common**

Par Corp. wishes to declare and distribute a dividend on December 31, 2005. The outstanding capital stock at December 31, 2005, consists of 30,000 shares of 5 percent preferred stock, par value $10 per share, and 200,000 shares of common stock, par value $1 per share. Dividends have not been paid for two years prior to the current year.

Required:

1. Determine the amount of the dividends that should be paid to the preferred and common stockholders if the preferred stock is cumulative and nonparticipating and the total amount available for dividends is (a) $45,000, (b) $75,000, and (c) $125,000.

2. Determine the amount of the dividends that should be paid to the preferred and common stockholders if the preferred stock is cumulative and participating and the total amount available for dividends is (a) $45,000, (b) $75,000, and (c) $125,000.

LO7   **EXERCISE 17-6   Convertible Bonds**

Vargo Company issued convertible bonds on January 1, 2005, that were due in 10 years. On January 1, 2006, the bonds, which had a face amount of $500,000 and unamortized discount on bonds payable of $7,500, were converted to common stock. Each $1,000 bond is convertible into 12 shares of common stock with a par value of $50 per share.

Required:

1. How should the bonds be presented on the balance sheet at December 31, 2005?

2. What entry should be recorded on January 1, 2006, for the bond conversion?

3. What effect does the bond conversion have on the number of shares of stock and on total stockholders' equity?

LO7   **EXERCISE 17-7   Convertible Bonds**

Wang Company issued convertible bonds on January 1, 2005. The bonds had a face value of $1,000,000, paid interest at 8 percent semiannually (4 percent per semiannual period), were issued to yield 10 percent, and are due in 10 years. Assume that the company uses the effective interest method of amortization. On January 1, 2006, bonds with a face amount of

$600,000 were converted into common stock. Each $1,000 bond is convertible into 12 shares of common stock with a par value of $40 per share.

Required:

1. How should the bonds be presented on the balance sheet at December 31, 2005?

2. What entry should be recorded on January 1, 2006, for the bond conversion?

3. What effect does the bond conversion have on the number of shares of stock and on total stockholders' equity?

LO7 **EXERCISE 17-8 Convertible Preferred Stock**

In 2005, Starr, Inc. issued 10,000 shares of $100 par value convertible preferred stock for $105 per share. One share of preferred stock can be converted into three shares of Starr's $20 par value common stock at the option of the preferred stockholder. In August 2006, all of the preferred stock was converted into common stock. The market value of the common stock at the date of the conversion was $30 per share.

Required:

1. How should the preferred stock be presented on the balance sheet at December 31, 2005?

2. What entry should be recorded in August 2006 for the conversion of the preferred stock?

3. Explain the effect of the conversion on the number of shares of preferred stock, the number of shares of common stock, and total stockholders' equity.

LO8 **EXERCISE 17-9 Analysis of Stockholders' Equity**

Python Systems provided the following financial information for its fiscal years 2003 through 2005:

(Dollars in thousands except per share amounts)	2005	2004	2003
Total stockholders' equity	$298,550	$340,697	$354,527
Net income (loss) per share	($1.54)	($.26)	$1.29
Dividends per share	$.12	$.12	$.12
Weighted-average shares outstanding (in thousands)	27,291	27,040	26,793

Required:

1. Calculate the return on stockholders' equity and the dividend payout ratio for 2005, 2004, and 2003. Assume that total stockholders' equity for 2002 was $244,996,000.

2. The dividend payout ratio is an indication of the company's dividend policy. Do you consider Python's policy to be stable from period to period?

LO9 **EXERCISE 17-10 Stockholders' Equity and the Statement of Cash Flows**

Assume that Franks Company has the following balances in its stockholders' equity accounts at the beginning and end of the period:

	Beginning Balance	Ending Balance
Common Stock	$100,000	$150,000
Paid-in Capital in Excess of Par—Common	500,000	600,000
Treasury Stock	50,000	80,000
Retained Earnings	820,000	980,000

Assume that there are no retirements of stock during the period and that the only transactions involving the Retained Earnings account are cash dividends declared and the net income of $200,000.

Required: Develop the financing activities category of the statement of cash flows for Franks Company for the period.

LO9 **EXERCISE 17-11   Cash Amounts for Stockholders' Equity**
Assume that Phillips Company has the following account balances at the beginning and end of the period:

	Beginning Balance	Ending Balance
Retained Earnings	$500,000	$420,000
Dividends Payable	40,000	80,000
Treasury Stock	90,000	45,000
Paid-in Capital from Treasury Stock	20,000	35,000

Assume that the only transactions affecting the Retained Earnings account during the period were a stock dividend of $320,000, net income of $400,000, and a cash dividend declared. No treasury stock was purchased during the period.

Required:

1. Determine the amount of cash paid for dividends during the period.
2. Determine the amount of cash received from the sale of treasury stock during the period.

LO2, 4, 5, 6 **EXERCISE 17-12   Stock Transactions and Stockholders' Equity Reporting**
The following are amounts for selected accounts from Fane's Fries, Inc.'s accounting records at July 1, 2004:

Paid-in Capital in Excess of Par—Common	$54,000
Paid-in Capital in Excess of Par—Preferred	26,000
Treasury Stock, 800 common shares	6,000
Common Stock, $.20 par, 100,000 shares authorized	5,000
Preferred Stock, 5%, cumulative, $2.50 par, 18,000 shares authorized	40,000
Retained Earnings	45,000

The following transactions occurred during the year ended June 30, 2005:

A. The State of Florida authorized Fane's Fries to sell 8,000 additional shares of its preferred stock.
B. 4,000 preferred shares were sold to investors for $24 each.
C. 6,000 common shares were sold to investors for $4 each.
D. The company declared a cash dividend totaling $35,000 to common and preferred shareholders.
E. The company purchased 400 additional shares of its own stock at the same price as those already reacquired.
F. Net income reported on Fane's Fries's income statement was $72,000 for the year ended June 30, 2005. Revenues for the same period totaled $460,000.

Required: Prepare the stockholders' equity section of the balance sheet at June 30, 2005, after considering the effects of the current period transactions.

LO2, 3, 4, 5, 8 **EXERCISE 17-13   Interpreting Number of Shares and Issue Price**
Haltern, Inc. reported net income totaling $42,000 and $36,000 during the years ended December 31, 2005 and 2004, respectively. Total common stockholder's equity at December 31, 2003, was $136,000. The stockholders' equity sections of Haltern, Inc.'s balance sheets are as follows. No dividends are in arrears.

Stockholders' Equity	Dec. 31, 2005	Dec. 31, 2004
Preferred stock, ___?___ par, 5%, 10,000 shares authorized, 3,000 and ___?___ shares issued	$ 60,000	$ 50,000
Common stock, $.50 par value; 40,000 shares authorized, ___?___ shares issued	12,000	12,000
Paid-in capital in excess of par—preferred	60,000	56,000
Paid-in capital in excess of par—common	50,000	30,000
Retained earnings	99,000	65,000
Other accumulated comprehensive income/(loss)	3,000	(2,400)
Total	$284,000	$210,600
Common treasury stock (400 shares at 12/31/05)	(7,200)	(3,060)
Total stockholders' equity	$276,800	$207,540

Required: Answer each of the independent questions that follow.

1. Show how the balance in the Common Stock account as of December 31, 2005, was calculated.
2. What is the par value of each share of preferred stock?
3. How many more shares of common stock is Haltern able to issue as of December 31, 2005, under its current corporate charter?
4. How many shares of common stock are outstanding as of December 31, 2005?
5. At December 31, 2005, what is the average price at which each share of preferred stock was originally sold?
6. Assuming that all treasury shares have the same cost, how many shares of treasury stock were purchased during 2005?
7. Evaluate the return on stockholders' equity for the years presented.

LO6   **EXERCISE 17-14   Stock Splits, Stock Dividends and Cash Dividends**

The stockholders' equity accounts and balances from Forbess, Inc.'s accounting records are given here. No dividends were paid during 2004 or 2005, during which time the number of outstanding shares was the same as for 2006. The preferred stock is cumulative.

Stockholders' Equity	Dec. 31, 2007	Dec. 31, 2006
Preferred Stock, $2 par value, 6%, 5,000 shares authorized	$ 9,000	$ 7,500
Common Stock, 50,000 shares authorized	4,000	3,600
Paid-in Capital in Excess of Par—Common	40,000	30,000
Paid-in Capital in Excess of Par—Preferred	16,000	10,000
Retained Earnings	28,000	21,000
Treasury Stock, Common ($11 per share cost)	4,950	2,750

Required: Answer each of the independent questions that follow.

1. If Forbess declares a 15 percent preferred stock dividend at the end of 2007, how many preferred shares will be outstanding immediately after the declaration?
2. If Forbess declared cash dividends totaling $12,000 and paid dividends totaling $10,000 during 2007, how much was its 2007 net income?
3. If Forbess declares a 2-for-1 preferred stock split at the end of 2007, how many preferred shares will be outstanding immediately after the declaration?
4. How much are dividends in arrears as of December 31, 2006, if no cash dividends were declared or paid during 2006?
5. How is the nature of a stock dividend different from that of cash and property dividends? Explain.

LO6 **EXERCISE 17-15   Dividend Preferences**

The stockholders' equity accounts and balances from Hop, Inc.'s accounting records are given here. No dividends were paid during 2004 and 2005. Hop declared a $15,660 cash dividend to shareholders of record on 12/31/06.

Stockholders' Equity	Dec. 31, 2006	Dec. 31, 2005
Preferred Stock, 8%, 5,000 shares authorized, 3,000 shares issued	$ 9,000	$ 9,000
Common Stock, $.80 par value; 40,000 shares authorized	18,000	14,000
Paid-in Capital in Excess of Par—Preferred	30,000	30,000
Paid-in Capital in Excess of Par—Common	66,000	30,000
Retained Earnings	44,000	24,000
Treasury Stock, Common ($4 per share cost)	7,200	1,800

Required:

1. Determine the total dividends to be given to each class of shareholders if the preferred stock is:

   a. Cumulative, but not participating
   b. Participating, but not cumulative
   c. Cumulative and participating

2. Under what dividend preferences does a preferred shareholder benefit the most?

3. Explain why dividends in arrears are not liabilities.

LO2, 4, 5, 9 **EXERCISE 17-16   Stock Transactions and Cash Flow**

The stockholders' equity accounts and balances for Ting, Inc. are as follows:

Stockholders' Equity	Dec. 31, 2005	Dec. 31, 2004
Preferred Stock, $4 par value, 6%, 8,000 shares authorized, 2,000 shares issued	$ 8,000	$ 8,000
Common Stock, $2 par value; 50,000 shares authorized	20,000	12,000
Paid-in Capital in Excess of Par—Preferred	40,000	40,000
Paid-in Capital in Excess of Par—Common	50,000	34,000
Retained Earnings	90,000	60,000
Treasury Stock, Common ($24 per share cost)	7,200	1,800

During 2005, the company sold 50 shares of treasury stock for $28 per share and acquired some additional shares on the open market.

Required:

1. Prepare journal entries for all stock transactions that occurred during the year.

2. Show how the transactions would be presented on a statement of cash flows for 2005.

3. For what reasons might a company buy treasury shares?

LO6, 9 **EXERCISE 17-17   Stock Dividends and Cash Flow**

The stockholders' equity accounts for Berg, Inc. are as follows:

Stockholders' Equity at December 31, 2004

Preferred Stock, $5 par value, 6%, 12,000 shares authorized, 2,000 shares issued	$10,000
Common Stock, $1 par value; 40,000 shares authorized	14,000
Paid-in Capital in Excess of Par—Preferred	56,000
Paid-in Capital in Excess of Par—Common	58,000
Retained Earnings	72,000

The following transactions occurred during 2005. No other stock transactions occurred during 2005.

July 1   Berg, Inc. declared and distributed a 10 percent stock dividend to common stock-holders when the market price of the stock was $40 per share.

Aug. 1   Berg declared a 30 percent stock dividend to preferred shareholders.

Dec. 1   Berg declared a $.30 per share cash dividend to shareholders of record on December 15.

Required:

1. Record the effects of each of the transactions.
2. Why are the 10 percent and the 30 percent stock dividends accounted for differently?
3. What are the effects of the three transactions on the statement of cash flows?

LO2   **EXERCISE 17-18   Comprehensive Income Presentation**

Selected account balances for Nolan Company as of December 31, 2005 and 2004 are given here.

Accounts	Dec. 31, 2005	Dec. 31, 2004
Unrealized Gain/(Loss) on Trading Securities	$ 3,200	$4,000
Unrealized Gain/(Loss) on Available-for-Sale Securities	(11,000)	3,500
Foreign Currency Translation Gain/(Loss)	(4,200)	(7,000)
Minimum Pension Liability Adjustment—credits	1,600	1,300
Unrealized Gains/Losses on Cash Flow Hedging Derivatives	4,000	8,800

Net income for 2005 was $32,500. The income tax rate is 30 percent.

Required:

1. Determine the amount of accumulated other comprehensive income to be reported as part of stockholders' equity on Nolan Company's balance sheet at December 31, 2005.
2. How does the amount reported as other comprehensive income differ from what is reported in question 1?
3. Are the items included as part of comprehensive income really considered part of income? Explain.

LO7, 9   **EXERCISE 17-19   Convertible Securities and Cash Flow**

On November 30, 2004, the Galliher Company issued $80,000 of 10 percent, four-year term convertible bonds dated November 30, 2004. Each $1,000 bond is convertible into 50 shares of $2 par value common stock. On March 31, 2005, bondholders converted 60 percent of the bonds. On that date, the carrying value of the bonds was $81,600, the bonds had a fair market value of $82,500, and the stock was selling for $25 per share.

Required:

1. When the bonds were issued on November 30, 2004, what was the proper accounting for the conversion feature of the bonds?
2. What is the significance for the accounting records of the conversion feature of con-vertible preferred stock?
3. Record the conversion of the bonds on March 31, 2005.
4. How is the conversion reported on the statement of cash flows for 2005?

LO3, 6, 8   **EXERCISE 17-20   Dividend and Preferences**

Single, Inc. reported net income totaling $66,000 and $45,000 during the years ended December 31, 2005 and 2004, respectively. Total stockholders' equity at December 31, 2003, was $186,000. The stockholders' equity section of Single, Inc.'s financial statements follows. No dividends were declared or paid during 2004.

Stockholders' Equity	Dec. 31, 2005	Dec. 31, 2004
Preferred stock, 5%, 10,000 shares authorized, 3,000 shares issued	$ 60,000	$ 60,000
Common stock, $.10 par value; 400,000 shares authorized	12,000	12,000
Paid-in capital in excess of par—preferred	60,000	56,000
Paid-in capital in excess of par—common	50,000	30,000
Retained earnings	99,000	65,000
Other accumulated comprehensive income/(loss)	3,000	(2,400)
Total	$284,000	$220,600
Treasury stock (400 common shares at 12/31/05)	(7,200)	(3,060)
Total stockholders' equity	$276,800	$217,540

Required:

1. If Single declares a 10 percent preferred stock dividend on January 1, 2006, how many shares will be outstanding immediately after the declaration?

2. How much were cash dividends declared for 2005?

3. If the preferred stock is cumulative and nonparticipating, how much will the common shareholders receive if the total dividend declared is $32,000 for 2005? Include the effects of question 1.

4. If the preferred stock was convertible, would the dividend allocation in question 3 differ? Why or why not?

PROBLEMS

LO2, 6 PROBLEM **17-1** **Stockholders' Equity Missing Values**

The stockholders' equity section of the balance sheet of **Outback Steakhouse** at December 31, 2003, is presented here. Some numbers have been removed.

Outback

(all amounts in thousands)	12/31/03	12/31/02
STOCKHOLDERS' EQUITY		
Common Stock, $0.01 par value, 200,000 shares authorized; _____ and _____ shares issued; and _____ and _____ outstanding as of December 31, 2003 and 2002, respectively	$ 788	$ 788
Additional paid-in capital	254,852	236,226
Retained earnings	934,516	902,910
Other comprehensive loss	(2,078)	—
	1,188,078	1,139,924
Treasury Stock, 4,471 shares and 2,870 shares at December 31, 2003 and 2002, respectively, at cost	(161,808)	(86,948)
Total stockholders' equity	??	??

Required:

1. Determine the missing values in the stockholders' equity section of the balance sheet.

2. Determine the average issue price of the common stock, assuming that all paid-in capital was from stock issuances.

3. Determine the average purchase price of treasury stock.

Analyze: Assume that the company was considering a 3-for-2 stock split. What effect would the split have on the stockholders' equity accounts?

LO2, 3, 4, 5, 6, 8   **PROBLEM 17-2   Stockholders' Equity Transactions** (CPA adapted)

Min Co. is a publicly held company whose shares are traded in the over-the-counter market. The stockholders' equity accounts at December 31, 2004, were as follows:

Preferred stock, $100 par, 6% cumulative, 5,000 shares authorized, 2,000 shares issued and outstanding	$ 200,000
Common stock, $1 par, 150,000 shares authorized, 100,000 shares issued and outstanding	100,000
Additional paid-in capital	800,000
Retained earnings	1,586,000
Total stockholders' equity	$2,686,000

Transactions during 2005 were as follows:

A. February 1: Issued 13,000 shares of common stock to Ram Co. in exchange for land. On the date it was issued, the stock had a market price of $11 per share. The land had a carrying value on Ram's books of $135,000 and an assessed value for tax purposes of $90,000.

B. March 1: Purchased 5,000 shares of common stock to be held as treasury stock for $14 per share.

C. May 1: Declared a property dividend of securities held by Min to common stockholders. The securities had a carrying value of $600,000. The fair value of the securities was $720,000 on the date of declaration, $758,000 on the date of record, and $736,000 on the date of distribution.

D. October 1: Reissued 2,000 shares of treasury stock at $16 per share.

E. November 4: Declared the annual cash dividend to preferred stockholders. The dividend was paid on January 5, 2006.

F. November 4: Declared a cash dividend of $1.50 per share to common stockholders of record November 15. The cash dividend was paid on January 5, 2006.

G. Net income for 2005 was $838,000.

Required:

1. Record the necessary journal entries for 2005.

2. Develop the stockholders' equity section of the balance sheet as of December 31, 2005.

Analyze: What is the dividend payout ratio for 2005?

Spreadsheet: Use a spreadsheet to create the stockholders' equity section of the balance sheet for December 31, 2005.

LO7   **PROBLEM 17-3   Convertible Bonds**

Beech Company had 20,000 shares of common stock issued and outstanding and an additional paid-in capital balance of $50,000 as of January 1, 2005. Beech Company issued five-year convertible bonds on January 1, 2005. The bonds had a face value of $1,000,000, paid interest at 8 percent semiannually (4 percent per semiannual period) on June 30 and December 31, and were issued at 102. Assume that the company uses the straight-line method of amortization and amortizes a premium or discount on each interest payment date. Each $1,000 bond is convertible into 12 shares of common stock with a par value of $40 per share. On March 31, 2006, bonds with a face value of $200,000 were converted to common stock. On June 30, 2006, additional bonds with a face value of $300,000 were converted to common stock.

Required:

1. How should the bonds be presented on the balance sheet of December 31, 2005?

2. What entry should be recorded on March 31, 2006, for the bond conversion?

3. What entry should be recorded on June 30, 2006, for the bond conversion?

4. Determine the amount of premium or discount that should be amortized on June 30, 2006, and December 31, 2006.

5. Determine the number of shares of stock outstanding and total stockholders' equity on June 30, 2006, and December 31, 2006.

Analyze: By what amount did the Common Stock account change as a result of the bond conversions?

LO5   PROBLEM 17-4   **Treasury Stock**

On January 1, 2005, Yang Company had the following balances in its stockholders' equity accounts:

Common Stock, $5 par	$100,000
Additional Paid-in Capital	500,000
Retained Earnings	800,000

On March 1, the company purchased 2,000 shares as treasury stock at $40 per share. On April 1, the company resold 500 shares of treasury stock at $42 per share. In addition, on May 1, the company resold 1,000 shares of treasury stock at $35 per share. The company retired the remaining treasury stock on July 1.

Required:

1. Calculate the number of shares issued and the number of shares outstanding on January 1, March 1, April 1, May 1, and July 1.

2. Record the entries necessary for the treasury stock transactions.

Analyze: What impact did the March 1 transaction have on total stockholders' equity?

LO8, 9   PROBLEM 17-5   **Wendy's Statement of Cash Flows**

The financing activities category of the statement of cash flows for **Wendy's International** is as follows.

Wendy's

Wendy's International, Inc. and Subsidiaries
Consolidated Statements of Cash Flows

(in thousands)	Dec. 28, 2003	Dec. 29, 2002	Dec. 30, 2001
Cash flows from financing activities			
Proceeds from issuance of senior notes, net of issuance costs	$ 39,985	$223,037	$197,138
Proceeds from employee stock options exercised	46,720	77,737	40,207
Repurchase of common stock	(56,992)	(49,401)	(287,308)
Principal payments on long-term obligations	(5,966)	(4,274)	(5,078)
Dividends paid on common and exchangeable shares	(27,322)	(27,076)	(26,824)
Net cash provided by (used in) financing activities	$ (3,575)	$220,023	$ (81,865)

Over a 12-year period, Wendy's earnings per share increased steadily from $.04 to $2.07 per share. The dividend remained constant at $.24 per share over that period.

Required:

1. What are possible reasons why the company repurchased common stock in each of the three years?

2. Comment on Wendy's dividend policy. What are possible reasons that the company has consistently paid a dividend to stockholders when many other companies in the restaurant industry have not done so? What has happened to the dividend payout ratio during the company's history? What is the impact of this change in the dividend payout ratio?

Analyze: What does it mean to investors when the company uses cash for financing activities? What is the source of the cash used to repurchase stock and make dividend payments?

Research: Locate the current year's annual report for Wendy's International. Did the company repurchase any stock? Describe the repurchase details.

LO2, 6 PROBLEM 17-6 **Stock Dividends and Splits**

The following excerpt was taken from the balance sheets of Oakless, Inc. at December 31, 2005:

Contributed capital:	
Preferred stock, 5%, 200,000 shares at $1 par	$ 200,000
Common stock, 400,000 shares issued at $2 par	800,000
Paid-in capital in excess of par—preferred	2,500,000
Paid-in capital in excess of par—common	5,000,000
Retained earnings	9,000,000
Treasury stock, common, 4,000 shares at cost	(48,000)
Total stockholders' equity	$17,452,000

During 2006, the following events and transactions occurred:

A. On April 4, a 30 percent stock dividend was declared and distributed to the common stockholders. The market value of the stock was $14 per share.

B. On July 1, a 3 percent common stock dividend was declared and distributed when the market value was $12 per share. The state in which the company operates provides that stock dividends are based on the number of shares outstanding.

C. On December 1, the board of directors declared a 5 percent cash dividend to preferred stockholders, payable on December 20 to stockholders of record on December 10.

D. On December 2, the board of directors declared a cash dividend of $.50 per share to common stockholders, payable on December 20 to stockholders of record on December 10.

Required:

1. Record all journal entries necessary for the events of 2006. After each entry, determine the number of shares of common stock issued and the number of shares of common stock outstanding.

2. Prepare the stockholders' equity section of the balance sheet for Oakless, Inc. at December 31, 2006. Net income for the year was $900,000.

Analyze: By what percentage did total stockholders' equity change from 2005 to 2006?

LO1, 2 PROBLEM 17-7 **Presentation, Corporate Form**

Lantuna, Inc. presented the following partial balance sheet at December 31, 2005 and 2004.

Lantuna, Inc.
Stockholders' Equity Section of Balance Sheet
December 31, 2005 and 2004

Stockholders' Equity	12/31/05	12/31/04
Cumulative preferred stock, 6%, $5 par value, 10,000 shares authorized; shares issued _____	$ 22,000	$ 15,000
Common stock, $2 par value, 60,000 shares authorized; shares issued: 2005, 14,000; 2004, 12,000	28,000	24,000
Paid-in capital in excess of par—preferred	65,000	32,000
Paid-in capital in excess of par—common	25,000	11,000
Retained earnings	42,000	40,000
Accumulated other comprehensive income	6,000	3,400
Treasury stock, common, (400 and 550 shares at cost)	(12,000)	(16,000)
Total stockholders' equity	$176,000	$109,400

Required:

1. How many additional shares of preferred stock can Lantuna issue as of December 31, 2005, under its current corporate charter?

2. How many shares of preferred stock were issued during 2005?

3. How many shares of common stock are outstanding as of December 31, 2005?

4. Explain the concept of limited liability as it applies to the common stockholders of Lantuna, Inc. Why do you think that this is the most important reason that companies choose the corporate form?

5. How much is total contributed capital at December 31, 2005?

6. How does contributed capital differ from the "earned" capital of a corporation?

Analyze: If Lantuna authorizes another 10,000 shares of common stock, what does this mean to existing stockholders? Explain.

LO2, 3 PROBLEM 17-8   **Presentation and Stock Issuances**

The partial balance sheet for Michel, Inc. at December 31, 2005 is presented here. Some figures have been removed.

Michel, Inc.
Stockholders' Equity Section of Balance Sheet
December 31, 2005 and 2004

Stockholders' Equity	12/31/05	12/31/04
Cumulative $2.50 par, 6% preferred stock, 30,000 shares authorized; shares issued _____	$ 31,000	$ 28,000
Common stock, _____ par value, 80,000 shares authorized; shares issued: 2005, _____; 2004, 15,000	38,000	30,000
Paid-in capital in excess of par—preferred	44,000	34,000
Paid-in capital in excess of par—common	33,000	15,000
Retained earnings	21,000	16,000
Accumulated other comprehensive income	2,000	800
Treasury stock, common (shares at cost)	(3,000)	(2,000)
Total stockholders' equity	$166,000	$121,800

Required:

1. Determine the number of shares of preferred stock issued as of the following dates:
   a. December 31, 2005
   b. December 31, 2004

2. Reconstruct the journal entry prepared by Michel, Inc. during 2005 to issue the preferred stock.

3. Determine the number of shares of common stock issued as of December 31, 2005.

4. Why is accounting for the par value separately from the amount received over par important?

Analyze: What was the average issue price per share of the preferred stock during 2005?

LO2, 6 PROBLEM 17-9   **Presentation, Cash, and Stock Dividends**

Big Gun manufactures defense weapons for the federal government. The company's accountant presented the following account balances at the beginning of 2005:

Common Stock, $2 par value, 80,000 shares authorized, 14,200 shares issued	$ 28,400
Paid-in Capital in Excess of Par—Common	144,000
Retained Earnings	35,000
Treasury Stock, Common (1,500 shares at cost)	7,500

During 2005, Big Gun reported net earnings of $98,000. Its stock was selling for $15 per share on November 16 and $17 per share on December 31, 2005.

The following transactions occurred during 2005:

A. Big Gun declared a 10 percent common stock dividend on November 16, 2005, to be distributed on January 16, 2006.

B. Big Gun declared cash dividends totaling $32,000 on December 21, 2005, to be paid on January 5, 2006.

Required:

1. Prepare the journal entries to record transactions A and B.

2. Prepare the stockholders' equity section of the balance sheet at December 31, 2005, reflecting the transactions and account balances provided.

3. From a business perspective, what differences will investors see from receiving a stock dividend as compared to a stock split?

Critical Thinking: In what way are stock splits and stock dividends similar from an economic perspective?

Analyze: Why would the declaration of stock dividends have the potential to reduce a company's ability to pay cash dividends in the future?

LO3, 6, 7   **PROBLEM 17-10   Cash Dividends to Preferred and Common, Stock Dividend, Convertible Preferred Stock**

Gill Corporation reported the following account balances at December 1, 2005:

Convertible Preferred Stock, $1.50 par, 8%, 12,000 shares issued	$18,000
Common Stock, $.50 par, 24,000 shares issued and outstanding	12,000
Paid-in Capital in Excess of Par—Preferred	64,000
Paid-in Capital in Excess of Par—Common	80,000
Retained Earnings	30,000

No dividends were declared or paid during the year ended December 31, 2004. The following transactions occurred during December of 2005 and are not reflected in the balances given:

A. December 2: A 10 percent common stock dividend was declared. It will be distributed on December 12.

B. December 12: The stock dividend was distributed.

C. December 15: A total cash dividend of $9,200 was declared to shareholders of record on December 31.

Required: Calculate the total cash dividend (December 15) for each class of stock, assuming that the preferred stock is

1. Cumulative and nonparticipating

2. Cumulative and participating

Analyze: If the preferred stock was *not* convertible, what difference would this make in your answer? Explain.

Communicate: Assume that you are the investor relations officer for the Gill Corporation. You have been asked to explain the nature of cumulative participating preferred stock at a meeting of new investors. Draft an outline of your presentation.

LO5, 9   **PROBLEM 17-11   Treasury Stock, Cash Flows**

The stockholders' equity section of Lewis, Inc.'s financial statements appears on the following page. No dividends were paid during 2005. Lewis acquired additional shares of treasury stock during the year and reissued shares with an original cost of $2,000. No shares were reissued in the past.

Stockholders' Equity	Dec. 31, 2005	Dec. 31, 2004
Preferred stock, $2 par value, 5%, 40,000 shares authorized, 30,000 and 26,000 shares issued	$ 60,000	$ 52,000
Common stock, $.50 par value, 40,000 shares authorized	12,000	12,000
Paid-in capital in excess of par—preferred	60,000	56,000
Paid-in capital in excess of par—common	50,000	30,000
Paid-in capital from treasury stock	5,500	0
Retained earnings	99,000	65,000
Accumulated other comprehensive income/(loss)	3,000	(2,400)
Total	$289,500	$212,600
Treasury stock, common (400 and 300 shares at cost)	(7,200)	(3,060)
Total stockholders' equity	$282,300	$209,540

Required:

1. Prepare the journal entry to record the reissuance of the treasury shares during 2005.

2. Assuming that all treasury shares have the same cost, determine the cost per share of the treasury stock purchased during 2005.

3. Prepare the journal entry to record the acquisition of the new treasury shares during 2005.

4. How many shares of common stock are outstanding at December 31, 2005?

5. Show how the treasury stock transactions that occurred during 2005 should be reported on the statement of cash flows.

Analyze: If Lewis, Inc. decides to retire all treasury stock, which accounts will be reduced?

LO2, 6, 7   PROBLEM 17-12   **Stockholders' Equity, Cash Dividends, Stock Split, Conversion of Stock**

Alabassi Corporation reported the following tentative account balances at the beginning of 2005:

Preferred Stock (6%, convertible, cumulative, nonparticipating, $2 par, 75,000 shares issued)	$150,000
Common Stock ($.50 par, 60,000 shares issued and outstanding)	30,000
Paid-in Capital in Excess of Par—Preferred	120,000
Paid-in Capital in Excess of Par—Common	72,000
Retained Earnings	34,000
Dividends Payable	10,000

Each share of preferred stock is convertible into five shares of common stock. The company's common stock was trading at $8 per share on December 31, 2005. Its preferred stock had a market price of $13 and $12 per share at April 30 and December 31, 2005, respectively. All shares of stock reported as of the beginning of 2005 were issued at the same price. The following transactions occurred during 2005 and are not reflected in the balances provided:

A. January 16: Paid the cash dividends from the previous year.

B. March 1: A 2-for-1 common stock split occurred.

C. April 30: Shareholders owning 3,000 shares of the preferred stock exercised the conversion feature. The conversion feature was adjusted at the time of the split to allow conversion of preferred stock into ten shares of common stock.

D. December 15: Declared a total cash dividend of $12,000 to shareholders of record on December 30, to be paid on January 30, 2006.

The company reported net income of $51,000 for 2005.

Required:

1. Prepare the journal entries for transactions A through D.

2. Prepare the stockholders' equity section of the balance sheet for Alabassi Corporation as of December 31, 2005.

Analyze: What is the effect of a stock split on the income statement? Explain.

LO6, 8, 9 PROBLEM 17-13 **Cash Flow Effects of Dividends, Stock Split, Dividend Payout Ratio**

Darnell Corporation reported the following account balances at the beginning of 2005:

Preferred Stock (6%, noncumulative, nonparticipating, $1 par, 32,000 shares issued)	$32,000
Common Stock ($.90 par, 75,000 shares issued and outstanding)	67,500
Paid-in Capital in Excess of Par—Preferred	80,000
Paid-in Capital in Excess of Par—Common	65,000
Retained Earnings	37,000
Dividends Payable	12,000

The company's common stock was trading at $9 per share on March 8, 2005. Its preferred stock had a market price of $18 and $19 at June 12 and December 31, 2005, respectively. The following transactions occurred during 2005 and are not reflected in the balances provided:

A. January 31: Paid the cash dividends from the previous year.

B. March 8: A 3-for-1 common stock split occurred.

C. June 12: Declared a 10 percent preferred stock dividend.

D. December 15: Declared a full dividend to preferred shareholders and $.08 per share to common shareholders of record on December 30, to be paid on January 16, 2006.

The company reported net income of $98,000 for 2005.

Required:

1. Record the journal entries for transactions A through D.

2. Prepare a partial statement of cash flows that reflects the transactions for Darnell Corporation for the year ended December 31, 2005.

Analyze: Determine Darnell's dividend payout ratio for 2005. Suppose Darnell's payout ratio for 2004, 2003, and 2002 was 16.3, 15.8, and 16.6, respectively. What would be the reaction of shareholders as a result of the ratio for 2005?

CASES

LO5 CRITICAL THINKING CASE 17-1 **Stock Buy-Backs**

The following excerpt was taken from **Wendy's International** Form 8-K, released to the SEC on September 21, 1999:

Wendy's

Wendy's International, Inc. announced that its Board of Directors has approved a $250 million increase to the Company's share repurchase program, for the repurchase of common stock over the next 18 to 24 months. The Company also announced that it has nearly completed, ahead of schedule, the initial $350 million repurchase program originally announced in 1998.

Required:

1. What is a stock repurchase? What journal entry is needed to record a stock repurchase? What journal entries are needed to record the sale of repurchased stock?

2. Why would companies want to repurchase their own stock? What factors limit the amount of a stock repurchase and the conditions under which repurchases can occur?

3. How does a stock repurchase affect the company's financial statements?

4. Discuss the effect of the stock repurchase and the sale of repurchased stock on net income and earnings per share.

LO6, 9 **RESEARCH CASE 17-2** **Dividend Policy**

The following excerpt was taken from a **Xerox Corporation** press release, published in July of 2001:

> ## *Xerox*
>
> The Board of Directors of Xerox Corporation today decided to eliminate the payment of dividends on its common stock. The decision was made in line with the company's turn-around objective to strengthen Xerox's liquidity and to restore long-term value to share-holders and bondholders. Previously the company had paid a quarterly dividend of 5 cents per share.
>
> "After serious deliberation, the Board of Directors chose to eliminate the dividend—a decision that contributes to the progress Xerox is making in restoring its financial strength and helps to provide the flexibility required to build on the effective execution of its turn-around plan," said Paul A. Allaire, chairman and chief executive officer. "As Xerox returns to profitability, the Board will consider the reinstatement of dividends."
>
> Today's announcement will reduce the company's cash requirement by approximately $140 million on an annualized basis.

Required:

1. How does the elimination of the dividend to common stockholders "contribute to the progress" the company is making in restoring its financial strength?
2. What reaction to the company's decision would you expect from stockholders?
3. Research the stock price performance of Xerox in the month before and after the announcement of the dividend cut. Can you determine how the stock price responded to the press release?

LO5, 6 **ETHICS CASE 17-3** **Stock Transactions**

Company A's stock usually trades in the $15–$25 per share range, but because of a business downturn, the stock has declined below that range. To bolster the selling price of the stock, the company purchased a large block of its stock as treasury stock. The company undertook the repurchase of stock while it was in private negotiations with another party who may sign an agreement to purchase large quantities of a new product that Company A will produce. The CFO of Company A believes that the contract will be signed and that the stock price will experience a major jump as a result, so the treasury stock can be sold at that time for a large profit. However, he is somewhat concerned that these actions may not be in the best interests of the stockholders. After all, if the treasury stock had not been purchased, it would be the stockholders, rather than Company A, that would profit from the rebound in the stock.

Company B's stock usually trades in the $20–$25 per share range, but because of the company's profitable history, it has begun to sell well above that range. To bring the stock back to the desired selling range, the company plans to issue a stock split to the stockhold-ers. Since the split will result in additional shares of stock outstanding, the market price per share of the stock will decline.

Required: Present your views concerning whether Company A and Company B have acted ethically in their stock transactions. Are the actions of one company more ethical than those of the other? Explain your reasoning.

LO6 **ETHICS CASE 17-4** **Insider Information**

Albert Kuhn is the controller of Margit Corporation, a manufacturer of heavy machinery. In the past, a considerable part of the company's revenue was earned on government contracts. This helped the company maintain its slow but steady growth. During the past ten years, the company has paid steadily increasing quarterly dividends to its stockholders. These factors have made the company's stock a favorite among conservative investors.

Recent spending cuts in the state's budget have led to a sharp decrease in the government contracts awarded to Margit Corporation, and the company has not been able to secure sufficient private contracts to make up for this loss in revenue. Because of this situation and the resulting cash constraints, the CEO and CFO of the company have decided to ask the board of directors to significantly reduce dividends for the next few years. Albert has just learned about this decision during an executive meeting.

Albert's grandmother owns a considerable amount of Margit Corporation's common stock. She depends on the quarterly dividends as a source of income. As her only grandchild, Albert will inherit the stock in the future. He knows that the value of the stock is likely to drop when the dividend cut is announced, and he is aware that because of the recent reduction in the tax rate for dividends, his grandmother was counting on higher income from her stock.

Required:

1. What are the problems and issues that Albert faces?

2. Who will be affected by his actions?

3. What values and principles are likely to influence his decision?

4. What alternative actions might Albert take?

5. What should Albert do?

LO1

ETHICS

ETHICS CASE 17-5   Shareholders and Consumers—Competing Interests?

On January 16, 2004, the *Wall Street Journal* reported that according to the U.S. Department of Justice, Microsoft had again violated its antitrust settlement agreement.[13] As part of this settlement, Microsoft had agreed to allow users of its software to disable the Internet Explorer and utilize a competitor's Internet program. However, according to the report, Microsoft's Windows XP software was overriding the disabling option when users selected the "Shop for Music Online" option. Microsoft did not admit that it had violated the agreement but decided to comply with the Justice Department for "business reasons."[14]

A few days later, the *Wall Street Journal* reported that while Microsoft's revenue had increased, its deferred revenue was continuing to decline. Decreases in deferred revenue indicate a reduction in the number of new multiyear licensing agreements.[15] Consistent declines in multiyear licensing agreements may curtail future growth, which is essential for enhancing stockholders' wealth. Thus, strategies to ensure extensive use of its software may support future growth and potentially benefit investors by increasing stock values.

Consumers, however, generally will not benefit from enhanced monopoly power of a global giant. Instead, consumers tend to benefit from enhanced competition. Thus, the interests of consumers and those of stockholders may not coincide, and this may create ethical dilemmas for decision makers.

Suppose you were one of the major decision makers at Microsoft and were responsible for signing new multiyear licensing agreements. Also suppose that you hold a large amount of the company's stock.

Required:

1. How do you think multiyear software licensing agreements are accounted for in accordance with GAAP? How do these agreements affect growth in future periods?

2. What are the problems and issues that you face?

3. Who will be affected by your decisions?

---

13 John R. Wilke, "Microsoft Changes Browser to Comply with Settlement," *Wall Street Journal*, January 16, 2004, p. A8.

14 Ibid.

15 Robert A. Guth, "Microsoft Rides Increasing Demand," *Wall Street Journal*, January 23, 2004, p. A3.

4. What values and principles are likely to influence your decision?

5. What alternative actions might you take?

6. What would you do?

LO1 COMMUNICATION CASE **17-6** **Organizing as a Corporation**

After graduating, you join a small family-owned company as the assistant controller. The company has been in business for twelve years and has been profitable for the last seven years. The company is looking to expand its operations, but it will need to raise additional funds in order to pay for the expansion. Currently the company is operated as a partnership, with the partners being the members of the founding family and three managers. The company has been approached by an investment banking firm to discuss changing its structure to a corporation and selling shares to the public through an initial public offering. Management asks you to evaluate the investment banker's offer.

Required:

Write a memo to management analyzing the advantages and disadvantages of the company's changing its organizational form from a partnership to a corporation and selling shares to the public.

LO8 ANALYSIS CASE **17-7** **Dividend Payout Ratio and Return on Stockholders' Equity**

Graham Railways, Inc. operates railroads in a number of southern cities. The company is evaluating its operations and provides you with the following information:

	2005	2004	2003	2002
Net income	$ 62,854	$ 45,852	$ 35,456	$14,750
Total assets at year end	381,500	246,250	145,490	71,268
Weighted-average number of shares outstanding	52,500	47,500	41,000	75,888
Total liabilities at year end	206,100	117,800	52,690	17,623
Dividends paid	42,000	27,500	19,750	17,000
Common stockholders' equity at year end	175,400	128,450	92,800	53,645

Required: For each of the years 2003 through 2005, calculate Graham Railways's dividend payout ratio and its return on stockholders' equity. The company has no preferred stock outstanding.

LO2, 4, 5, 6 FINANCIAL STATEMENT PREPARATION CASE **17-8** **Stockholders' Equity**

Microbee Honey Corporation is a honey distribution company that was incorporated during 2004. The following list includes all of the transactions that have affected Microbee's stockholders' equity section since the company was incorporated.

In 2004, 40,000 shares of 9 percent, $100 par value cumulative preferred stock were authorized. On February 25, 2004, the corporation issued 30,000 shares of preferred at $108 per share. On March 10, 2005, the corporation exchanged 5,000 shares of preferred for a parcel of land appraised at $550,000. At that date, the preferred stock was actively traded on the New York Stock Exchange and had a quoted price of $114 per share.

The articles of incorporation authorized Microbee for 200,000 shares of $1 par value common stock. Since the authorization, the following common stock transactions have taken place:

A. 1/30/04: Issued 40,000 shares at a price of $22 per share.

B. 12/1/04: Declared and distributed a 10 percent stock dividend; the market price on that date was $26.

C. 3/15/05: Repurchased 6,000 shares for the treasury at a price of $33 per share.

D. 11/5/05: Reissued 3,000 shares from the treasury at a price of $45 per share.

E. 6/30/06: Declared and distributed a 50 percent stock dividend; the market price on that date was $46.

Microbee has earned a total of $2,800,000 after income taxes over the three-year period. In addition to the stock dividends listed, Microbee has declared and paid all required preferred stock dividends in 2004, 2005, and 2006. Microbee has not paid common stock dividends over the three-year period.

Required: Prepare the stockholders' equity section of the balance sheet for Microbee Honey Corporation at December 31, 2006. Account for treasury stock using the cost method. Microbee does issue stock dividends on shares in the treasury.

LO3 **RESEARCH CASE 17-9** **Classes of Stock**

Dow Jones & Company, Inc. is a global provider of business and financial news and information through newspapers and other media. Most notably, it publishes the *Wall Street Journal.* Its 2003 10-K provides the following data about stockholders' equity:

Dow Jones

Stockholders' Equity:

	2003	2002
Common stock, par value $1.00 per share; authorized 135,000,000 shares; issued 81,493,687 shares in 2003 and 81,404,677 shares in 2002	$ 81,494	$ 81,405
Class B common stock, convertible, par value $1.00 per share; authorized 25,000,000 shares; issued 20,687,333 shares in 2003 and 20,776,344 shares in 2002	20,687	20,776
	$102,181	$102,181

Required: The Dow Jones & Company website can be found at **www.dowjones.com**. Go to the company's website and obtain the latest annual report through the investor relations link. Answer the following questions:

1. How do Dow Jones's two classes of common stock differ?
2. What types of investors own each class of common stock?
3. Which class of common stock is used to calculate earnings per share?

On the Web

The following exercises, activities, and problems are available on the *Intermediate Accounting* website. Use these resources to reinforce your understanding of the topics presented in this chapter.

- CPA-Adapted Simulations
- Interpreting the Accounting Standards
- Extending the Global Focus
- Extending the Ethics Discussion
- Mastering the Spreadsheet
- Career Snapshots

- Annual Report Project
- ACE Practice Tests
- Flashcards
- Glossary
- Check Figures for Text Problems
- PowerPoint Presentations

Solutions: Check Your Understanding

Corporate Form of Organization (p. 814)

1. The most important reason that business owners choose the corporate form of organization is limited liability (the corporation is considered a separate legal entity, and the liability of owners is limited to the amount that they have invested in the business).

2. Like the owners of a regular corporation, the owners of an S corporation are liable for an amount limited to their investment in the business. However, the S corporation is not subject to income tax as a corporation, whereas the regular corporation is subject to corporate income tax.

3. Double taxation refers to the fact that the earnings of a corporation are taxed, then dividends that are paid to the corporation's owners are taxed. Thus, the income is

taxed twice: once at the corporate level and once at the individual level.

Stockholders' Equity Overview (p. 818)

1. Common stock is a class of stock that ranks below preferred stock with regard to some factors, usually receipt of dividends and distribution of assets in the event of liquidation. Preferred stock may be given preference in a variety of ways: dividend payment, distribution of assets if the company is liquidated, conversion rights, or redemption rights.

2. Amounts that have been received from external sources, primarily from the sale of stock to stockholders, are called contributed capital.

3. Shares authorized is the total number of shares that can be issued at any time, as indicated in the corporate charter. Shares issued is the number of shares that have actually been issued, or sold, to the stockholders. Shares outstanding is the number of shares that are owned by stockholders as of the balance sheet date.

Issuance of Stock (p. 821)

1. Paid-in Capital in Excess of Par—Common or Additional Paid-in Capital—Common.

2. The purchase price is allocated according to the proportion of the total fair market value of the two classes of stock at the date of issuance.

3. The services should be valued at the fair market value of the consideration given (the stock) or the consideration received (the services), whichever can be more readily determined.

Treasury Stock (p. 823)

1. Companies might repurchase their own stock to improve their financial ratios, to maintain control and prevent takeover attempts, to use the stock for employee compensation, or as a use of excess cash.

2. Treasury Stock is presented as a contra–stockholders' equity account and represents a reduction of total stockholders' equity.

3. Paid-in Capital from Treasury Stock.

Dividends (p. 829)

1. The date of declaration is the date on which the company declares the dividend. Retained earnings should be reduced on this date. The date of record dictates who will receive the dividend. Stockholders who purchase stock after this date will not. The date of payment is the date on which the company actually pays the dividend to the stockholders.

2. Participating preferred stock allows the preferred stockholders to share in the good fortune of the company when an especially large dividend is declared. The extra dividend is divided between the preferred and common stock based on the total par values of the classes of stock.

3. When a property dividend is declared, the distribution should be recorded at the fair market value of the asset on the date of declaration, and a gain or loss should be recorded for the difference between cost and market value at that date.

4. Both a large stock dividend and stock split result in additional shares of stock being issued to stockholders. Some state laws draw a legal distinction between a large stock dividend and a stock split. A stock split does not require the transfer of retained earnings into permanent capital, but it does result in a change in the par value per share of stock. No formal journal entry is made, but a memorandum entry is made to note that the company has twice as many shares of stock after the 2 for 1 stock split as it did before. A large stock dividend requires an entry to debit Retained Earnings and credit the Stock account. There is no change in the par value of the stock.

Convertible Securities (p. 831)

1. Convertible bonds are a fixed obligation; they pay interest similar to other bond issuances, but they have a clause that allows the bonds to be converted into stock. When convertible bonds are issued, the bonds should be treated as a liability and presented in the long-term liabilities section of the balance sheet. If the bonds are issued at an amount that differs from their face value, the premium or discount should be *amortized over the time from issuance to maturity date.*

2. If a company has issued convertible preferred stock that has not yet been converted, it is treated as preferred stock until the time of conversion. That is, it should be presented in the stockholders' equity section of the balance sheet and labeled as preferred stock.

Analysis of Stockholders' Equity (p. 833)

1. Net Income − Preferred Dividends ÷ Average Common Stockholders' Equity, where Common Stockholders' Equity = Total Stockholders' Equity − Preferred Stock. It tells an investor the amount of income earned for each dollar invested.

2. Dividends ÷ Net Income.

Cash Flow Issues Related to Stockholders' Equity (p. 834)

1. Stock transactions are reflected in the financing activities section of the statement of cash flows.

2. Stock dividends do not involve cash.

3. Dividends are deducted from Retained Earnings when they are declared.

CPA-ADAPTED SIMULATION

This simulation asks you to complete various tasks related to a company's annual financial statements. If your instructor has signed up for CPAexcel™, you can do the work online at **www.cpaexcel.com/hmco**. You may also do the simulation manually.

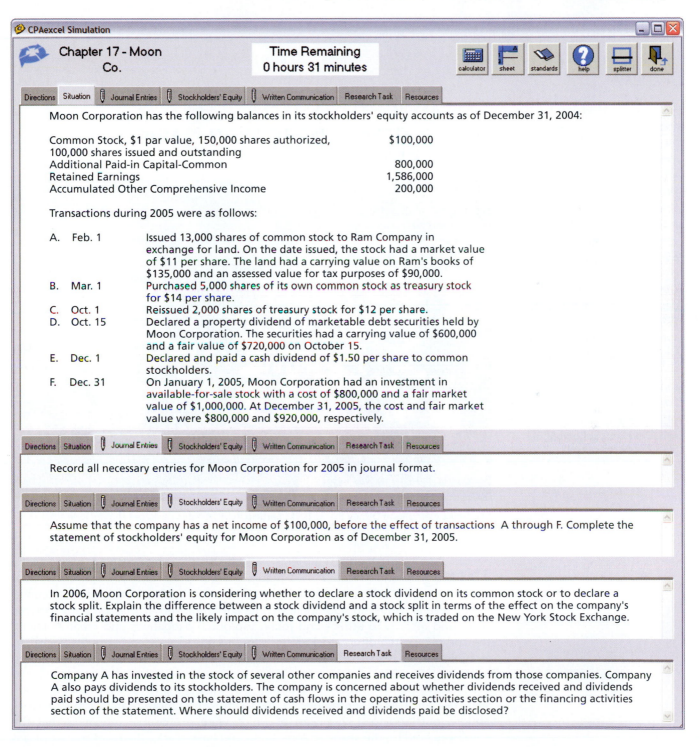

CPAexcel Simulation

| Chapter 17 - Moon Co. | Time Remaining 0 hours 31 minutes | calculator | sheet | standards | help | splitter | done |

Directions | Situation | Journal Entries | Stockholders' Equity | Written Communication | Research Task | Resources

Moon Corporation has the following balances in its stockholders' equity accounts as of December 31, 2004:

Common Stock, $1 par value, 150,000 shares authorized, 100,000 shares issued and outstanding	$100,000
Additional Paid-in Capital-Common	800,000
Retained Earnings	1,586,000
Accumulated Other Comprehensive Income	200,000

Transactions during 2005 were as follows:

A. Feb. 1   Issued 13,000 shares of common stock to Ram Company in exchange for land. On the date issued, the stock had a market value of $11 per share. The land had a carrying value on Ram's books of $135,000 and an assessed value for tax purposes of $90,000.

B. Mar. 1   Purchased 5,000 shares of its own common stock as treasury stock for $14 per share.

C. Oct. 1   Reissued 2,000 shares of treasury stock for $12 per share.

D. Oct. 15   Declared a property dividend of marketable debt securities held by Moon Corporation. The securities had a carrying value of $600,000 and a fair value of $720,000 on October 15.

E. Dec. 1   Declared and paid a cash dividend of $1.50 per share to common stockholders.

F. Dec. 31   On January 1, 2005, Moon Corporation had an investment in available-for-sale stock with a cost of $800,000 and a fair market value of $1,000,000. At December 31, 2005, the cost and fair market value were $800,000 and $920,000, respectively.

Directions | Situation | Journal Entries | Stockholders' Equity | Written Communication | Research Task | Resources

Record all necessary entries for Moon Corporation for 2005 in journal format.

Directions | Situation | Journal Entries | Stockholders' Equity | Written Communication | Research Task | Resources

Assume that the company has a net income of $100,000, before the effect of transactions A through F. Complete the statement of stockholders' equity for Moon Corporation as of December 31, 2005.

Directions | Situation | Journal Entries | Stockholders' Equity | Written Communication | Research Task | Resources

In 2006, Moon Corporation is considering whether to declare a stock dividend on its common stock or to declare a stock split. Explain the difference between a stock dividend and a stock split in terms of the effect on the company's financial statements and the likely impact on the company's stock, which is traded on the New York Stock Exchange.

Directions | Situation | Journal Entries | Stockholders' Equity | Written Communication | Research Task | Resources

Company A has invested in the stock of several other companies and receives dividends from those companies. Company A also pays dividends to its stockholders. The company is concerned about whether dividends received and dividends paid should be presented on the statement of cash flows in the operating activities section or the financing activities section of the statement. Where should dividends received and dividends paid be disclosed?

CHAPTER EIGHTEEN

Dilutive Securities and Earnings per Share

FINANCIAL REPORTING CASE

DISNEY OFFERS MORE THAN MAGIC TO EXECUTIVES

Many cast members at Disney theme parks participate in benefits packages that include stock purchase plans so that they may become "owners" of the company.

Disney More than just a theme park, the Walt Disney Company reigns as the world's number two media conglomerate and employs more than 100,000 individuals throughout the world. During peak summer hours, several thousand additional people are employed at the company's theme parks and resorts. To attract and retain top-notch executives and creative talent, the company often offers stock options as part of its salary and benefits packages, as indicated in Note 10 from the company's annual report for the year ended September 30, 2004.

A stock option represents the right to buy the company's stock, usually at a very attractive price. As of September 30, 2004, Disney had more than 221 million stock options outstanding, 132 million of which were exercisable (meaning that the employee holding the stock options could purchase stock).[1] Many of these options were granted to the CEO, Michael Eisner. As one of the nation's most highly compen-

---

1 The Walt Disney Company annual report, 2004, p. 70.

Disney

NOTE 10. STOCK INCENTIVE PLANS

Under various plans, the Company may grant stock options and other equity-based awards to executive, management and creative personnel at exercise prices equal to or exceeding the market price at the date of grant. Effective in January 2003, options granted for common stock become exercisable ratably over a four-year period from the grant date, while options granted prior to January 2003 generally vest ratably over a five-year period from the grant date. All options expire 10 years after the date of grant. At the discretion of the Compensation Committee, options can occasionally extend up to 15 years after date of grant. Shares available for future option grants at September 30, 2004 totaled 57 million.

sated CEOs, Eisner set a record in December 1997 by exercising $570 million in stock options.

While stock options often result in significant profits for executives, they present difficult accounting issues for the granting company. In fact, the accounting for stock options and other dilutive securities has been one of the most controversial issues faced by the FASB in recent years. Stock options are considered to be dilutive securities because they have the potential to reduce (or dilute) the earnings per share for common stockholders. While it is important to understand how to account for these securities, it is equally critical for users of financial statements to understand how earnings per share are affected by these transactions.

EXAMINING THE CASE

1. What are stock options?

2. Why are stock options considered dilutive securities?

3. According to Note 10, if you were a manager at Disney and you were granted stock options in 2003, how long would it take for your options to vest? When would your option to buy stock expire?

LO1 Understand how to account for dilutive securities.

dilutive securities financial instruments that do not represent common stock when they are issued but could become common stock at a future time and have the potential to affect earnings per share

🧩 *Critical Thinking: Define the term* dilutive *as you think it applies to the value of an investor's holdings. What events might dilute the value of a common stock investment?*

Accounting for Dilutive Securities

Dilutive securities are financial instruments that do not represent common stock when they are issued but could become common stock at a future time. They are called "dilutive" because of their potential impact on the company's earnings per share. If the securities were to become stock, earnings per share would be decreased (diluted) because there would be additional shares of stock outstanding. Dilutive securities may take any of the following financial instrument forms:

- Convertible bonds
- Convertible preferred stock
- Warrants
- Stock options

Illustration 18.1 defines each type of dilutive security and describes its potential impact on common stock. We will discuss these securities in the coming pages.

CONVERTIBLE BONDS AND CONVERTIBLE PREFERRED STOCK

Convertible bonds and convertible preferred stock were introduced in Chapter 17. As you recall, convertible bonds are a *liability* at the time of issuance but carry a provision that allows the bondholder to convert the bonds into common stock. If the bonds are converted, additional shares of common stock will be outstanding and the reported earnings per share will therefore be decreased (diluted). Likewise, convertible preferred stock is a preferred stock instrument at issuance but carries a provision that allows the holder to convert the preferred stock into common stock. Again, if the preferred stock is converted, the number of shares of common stock outstanding will increase and the reported earnings per share will be diluted.

There are sound financial reasons for the issuance of both convertible bonds and convertible preferred stock. The instruments are often an efficient means of raising capital at a low cost and present an attractive risk-reward combination for the buyer. The procedures related to accounting for convertible bonds and convertible preferred stock were presented in the previous chapter. Later in this chapter, you will learn how these financial instruments should be considered when calculating earnings per share.

WARRANTS

stock warrants financial instruments that represent the right to purchase additional shares of common stock at an established price (the exercise price)

exercise price the price at which the holder of a warrant or an option has the right to buy or sell

Stock warrants represent the right to purchase additional shares of common stock at an established price, usually referred to as the **exercise price**. The exercise price is the price at which the holder of a warrant or an option has the right to buy or sell.

Stock warrants may be issued in several ways. In some cases, warrants may be given to existing stockholders so that they can purchase additional stock at an attractive price. Usually stockholders have the right to maintain their proportionate ownership of a company; this is referred to as the preemptive right. If a company issues a large block of stock to one class of stockholders, it may give stock warrants to the other stockholders so that they can maintain their proportionate ownership of the company by purchasing additional shares.

detachable warrants warrants that are issued in conjunction with other securities

Warrants may be issued in conjunction with other securities. These warrants are referred to as **detachable warrants**. Accounting for detachable warrants gives rise to the following questions:

- Should the warrants be treated separately from the accompanying security?
- How is the value of the warrants determined?

Illustration 18.1

Summary of Dilutive Securities

Dilutive Security	Defined	Impact
Convertible bonds	Bonds that can be converted into common stock	Will result in additional shares of common stock when converted
Convertible preferred stock	Preferred stock that can be converted into common stock	Will result in additional shares of common stock when converted
Warrants	The right to purchase shares of common stock at an established price	Will result in additional shares of common stock when the right is exercised
Stock options	The right of an employee to purchase additional shares of common stock at an established price	Will result in additional shares of common stock when the right is exercised

Consider the following example. Assume that Meredith Company issues 10-year bonds with detachable warrants for $106,000 on January 1, 2007. The bonds have a face value of $100,000 and pay interest at 8 percent semiannually (4 percent per semi-annual period). Each $1,000 bond has five warrants attached, and each warrant allows the holder to purchase one share of common stock for the next two years at $50 per share.

When a company issues a bond with detachable warrants, it has issued two distinct instruments: a bond that will pay a fixed rate of interest, and a warrant that will allow the holder to purchase additional shares of common stock. *The issue price should be allocated to the two instruments according to the proportionate fair market values of the two instruments as of the issue date.* Assume that the fair market value of the bonds (without warrants attached) is 104 on January 1, 2007, and the warrants could be sold for $8 per warrant. The allocation of cost between the warrant and the bond is provided in Illustration 18.2.

Illustration 18.2 indicates that the amount of the issue price that should be allocated to the bonds is $102,074. In other words, a bond premium account should be established for the difference between the issue price and the face value, or $102,074 − $100,000 = $2,074. The following accounting entry should be recorded on January 1, 2007, for the issuance of the bonds with detachable warrants:

Cash	106,000	
Bonds Payable		100,000
Premium on Bonds		2,074
Paid-in Capital from Warrants		3,926

Because warrants are treated as a separate instrument, a separate account should be established for them. The Paid-in Capital from Warrants account appears within the

Illustration 18.2

Allocation of Issue Price for Detachable Warrants

Market value of bonds	$104,000
Market value of warrants	4,000 (500 × $8)
Total market value	$108,000

Allocated to bonds: $104,000 ÷ $108,000 × $106,000 = $102,074

Allocated to warrants: $4,000 ÷ $108,000 × $106,000 = $3,926

Per warrant: $3,926 ÷ 500 = $7.85

contributed capital portion of stockholders' equity on the balance sheet. It indicates to statement users that some warrants are outstanding that could be exercised by the holders to purchase additional shares of stock.

Assume that on July 1, 2007, the warrants are exercised to purchase additional common stock (with a par value of $10 per share). The exercise price is $50 per share. Meredith Company should record the following transaction:

Cash	25,000	
Paid-in Capital from Warrants	3,926	
Common Stock (500 shares × $10 par)		5,000
Paid-in Capital in Excess of Par—Common		23,926

Note that when the warrants are exercised, the Paid-in Capital from Warrants account should be eliminated (debited). Essentially, the buyer of the stock has given consideration of $50 per share in cash but has also given warrants that had been assigned a value of $3,926. The cost per share (or basis) for the buyer should be $57.85 ($28,926 ÷ 500 shares).

When a company has issued a large block of warrants, a ready market exists for the warrants. In some cases, the holders of the warrants may choose to sell their warrants to another party rather than exercise them to purchase stock. In other cases, the warrants are not exercised before the end of the exercise period; instead, they lapse or expire. Often this happens because the market price of the stock is *less* than the exercise price. In our example, if the market price of the stock is less than $50 per share, the holders of the warrants will not exercise the warrants that require purchase at $50 per share. These types of warrants are referred to as *out-of-the-money* or *underwater* warrants. When warrants lapse or expire, the amount should be removed from the Paid-in Capital from Warrants account and placed in another stockholders' equity account, such as Paid-in Capital from Expired Warrants.

EMPLOYEE STOCK OPTIONS

stock options a financial instrument that gives an employee the right to purchase shares of common stock at an established price, referred to as the exercise price or the option price

Stock options represent the right of an employee to purchase shares of stock at an established price, referred to as the exercise price or the option price. Options are similar to warrants in that a right to purchase additional shares of common stock has been conveyed to the option holders. The accounting for stock options is considered in *SFAS 123,* as revised in 2004.[2] The FASB uses the term *share-based payments* to denote any arrangement in which stock is issued or a liability is incurred in exchange for employee services. We will use the more common term of *stock options* and limit our discussion to arrangements in which an employee has the right to purchase shares of stock.

As discussed in the Financial Reporting Case presented at the beginning of this chapter, companies often establish stock option plans for their employees. The exact nature of such a plan varies greatly from company to company. In some cases, the stock options are made available to large numbers of employees to allow them to share in the good fortune of the company. More commonly, stock options are available to a more restricted group of top-level employees whose actions as managers can influence the direction of the company and the company's stock price. The company's goal in developing a stock option plan is to achieve some level of *goal congruence.* That is, a stock option plan is intended to motivate the executives of the company to manage the company in a way that increases the stock price. If this happens, the managers benefit because they can exercise their stock options at a profit. Stockholders benefit because the stock price increases.

Stock options became extremely prevalent in the 1990s as boards of directors developed new benefit models that involved the use of stock options to sweeten com-

---

2 "Share-Based Payment," *Statement of Financial Accounting Standards No. 123* (revised 2004) (Stamford: Conn: FASB, 2004).

pensation packages for executives. Technology and Internet companies that did not have much cash available for compensation were known for their generous use of options as a way to attract employees. Indeed, many analysts feel that stock options were an essential element of the explosive growth that occurred during the decade of the 1990s, characterized by unprecedented levels of employment and productivity. Notably, accounting for stock options has been a controversial issue centered on the following questions:

1. Do stock options result in salary expense or compensation expense to the granting company?

2. If stock options result in compensation expense, how should the amount be measured?

3. Over what period of time should the compensation be recorded as an expense?

The FASB has addressed these questions in several pronouncements over the years. We will first discuss the traditional method, which is referred to as the *intrinsic value method,* to present the deficiencies of that approach. Since the issuance of *SFAS 123* as revised in 2004, companies are now required to use a method called the *fair value method.* We will present the fair value approach and discuss the information that must be disclosed for companies that offer employee stock option plans.

LO2 Understand how to account for stock options.

Critical Thinking: *If an employee has the option to purchase stock in the future, what impact do you think this arrangement has on the financial condition of the offering company?*

intrinsic value method a method of measuring compensation through stock options in which the compensation is measured as the difference between the exercise price and the quoted market price of the stock as of the measurement date

measurement date the first date on which the number of shares of stock that can be purchased and the option price or exercise price are known

date of grant the date on which a company develops a formal stock option plan

service period the period of time for which the employee must work in order to be eligible for the stock option plan

INTRINSIC VALUE METHOD

The **intrinsic value method** was the accepted accounting practice for many years and was detailed in *APB No. 25.*[3] Using this method, *compensation is measured as the difference between the exercise price and the quoted market price of the stock as of the measurement date.* The **measurement date** is defined as the first date on which the number of shares of stock that can be purchased and the option price or exercise price are known. In most cases, the measurement date is the **date of grant**, usually the date on which the company develops a formal stock option plan.

The total compensation from a stock option plan is recognized as an expense over the service period. The **service period** is defined as the period of time for which the employee must work in order to be eligible for the stock option plan. Ordinarily, compensation should be allocated evenly over the service period (for example, one-half in each period if it is a two-year period, or one-third in each period if it is a three-year period).

DEFICIENCIES OF THE INTRINSIC VALUE METHOD The FASB rejected the intrinsic value method in the revision of *SFAS 123.* The FASB determined this method to be deficient in several important aspects, including the following:

1. *Determination of compensation expense.* Under the intrinsic value method, the accounting for compensation expense is generally based on the assumption that the expense is related to the granting of the stock options, and that the employees' decisions to exercise or not exercise the options should not affect the amount of the expense. The FASB had allowed one exception to the general rule, however. If employees fail to satisfy a requirement for the award of the stock options, compensation expense should not be reported.[4] For example, if an employee leaves the company before the option has been earned, compensation expense is not recorded. However, under the intrinsic value method, *compensation expense is recorded even if the employee does not exercise the options.* The FASB believes that the employee's decision to exercise or not exercise should not affect the amount of compensation expense.

---

3 "Accounting for Stock Issued to Employees," *Accounting Principles Board Opinion No. 25* (Norwalk, Conn.: APB, 1972).

4 *SFAS No. 123,* par 26.

2. *Use of market value at the date of grant.* The intrinsic value method bases compensation on the difference between the exercise price specified in the stock option plan and the market value of the stock at the date of grant. But the price on the exercise date may differ greatly from the price at the date of grant. The actual value conveyed to the employee is based on the price at the time of exercise. Yet that fact was not recognized under the accounting of *APB No. 25*.

The intrinsic value method led most companies to introduce noncompensatory stock option plans. A **noncompensatory plan** has an exercise price *equal* to the market price at the date of grant. For this type of plan, *no compensation expense* is ever recorded by the company. If a company is profitable, its stock price often increases significantly over time, and when the employees exercise the options, the market price is often much higher than the exercise price. Employees could gain significantly in economic terms, but with a noncompensatory plan, the employer did not record any of this amount as an expense.

3. *Measurement of the value of the stock option.* As just stated, the intrinsic value method measures the value of the stock option as the difference between the exercise price and market price on the date of grant and does not adjust this value for subsequent changes in the price of the stock. This does not lead to an accurate measurement of the "true value" of the stock option. The FASB has acknowledged that a more detailed and complex model is necessary to accurately measure the value of the stock option that is given to employees.

The intrinsic value method of accounting for stock options came under severe criticism in the post-Enron era of 2002. The method was characterized as misleading because it allowed companies to grant stock options to their employees without recording the corresponding expense. When the stock price of many technology companies fell drastically during this period, a call for accounting methods that more "truly reflected" corporate activities resounded.

The alternative approach to the recording of stock options is referred to as the fair value method. For several years, companies were allowed to use *either* the intrinsic value method or a fair value method to account for stock options. In 2004, however, the FASB stated that companies are required to use a fair value method to account for stock options. In doing so, the FASB has clearly acknowledged the deficiencies of the intrinsic value method that were cited earlier.

FAIR VALUE METHOD

The **fair value method** was developed by the FASB in *SFAS No. 123*, which was later revised in 2004. It requires *public entities* to measure compensation of employees based on the fair value of the option at the date of grant. The objective is to estimate the fair value of the stock that the entity is obligated to issue when employees have rendered the service and have satisfied all of the requirements of the stock option plan. All of the unique features and terms of the plan should be considered in determining the fair value. In most cases companies will find it necessary to use a so-called option pricing model that takes into consideration all of the estimates and assumptions of the plan to determine the fair value.

The material that accompanies *SFAS 123* discusses two particular types of valuation techniques: a lattice or binomial model and a closed form model. The most widely known model is the Black–Scholes–Merton model. It is used by valuation professionals to estimate the fair value of options and other financial instruments. The workings of the option pricing models are beyond the scope of this discussion.

FORFEITURES
In some cases, stock options are not exercised, because employees fail to satisfy a requirement specified for the award of the stock options. For example, an employee may leave the company before meeting the time period required to be eligible for stock options. These situations are referred to as **forfeitures**. Under the intrinsic value

---

noncompensatory plan a stock option plan that has an exercise price equal to the market price at the date of grant

fair value method a method of measuring compensation through stock options in which the compensation is measured as the fair value of the option on the date of grant

forfeiture Stock options that are not exercised, because employees fail to satisfy a requirement specified for the award of the stock options

Illustration 18.3

Fair Value Method of Calculating Compensation

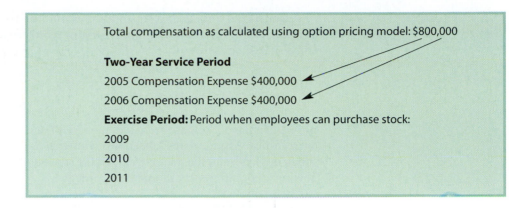

Total compensation as calculated using option pricing model: $800,000

Two-Year Service Period

2005 Compensation Expense $400,000

2006 Compensation Expense $400,000

Exercise Period: Period when employees can purchase stock:

2009

2010

2011

method, compensation expense was adjusted at the time of the forfeiture. However, *SFAS 123* as revised requires entities to estimate the number of instruments that will be forfeited at the date of grant and incorporate that estimate into the determination of the fair value of the options.

❱ ALLOCATION TO SERVICE PERIODS   Once the fair value of the compensation is determined, it must be allocated to expense. In this regard *SFAS 123* as revised is similar to the previous accounting rules. Compensation should be recognized as an expense over the service period. Because the estimation of compensation is based on a series of estimates and assumptions, it may be necessary to adjust the estimate if new information indicates that the original estimates are no longer valid. This revision should be treated as a change in estimate and recorded in the current period and future periods of the stock option plan.[5]

❱ REQUIREMENTS FOR NONPUBLIC ENTITIES   The accounting for stock options is difficult and complex. It may be particularly difficult and costly for small companies and companies that do not have stock that is traded actively on a stock exchange or other market mechanism. As a result, *SFAS 123* as revised allows *nonpublic* entities some concessions. Nonpublic entities are required to use a fair value approach to account for stock options, unless it is not possible to estimate fair value because the expected volatility of the shares cannot be determined (for example, when the stock is not traded actively).[6] In those cases, the nonpublic entity must still use a fair value approach, but may determine the value of the compensation by substituting the volatility of an industry sector index instead of the expected volatility of its stock.

❱ AN EXAMPLE   To illustrate the fair value method, consider the following simplified stock option plan. On January 1, 2007, Baxter Company, a public entity, grants to its employees the right to purchase 50,000 shares of $5 par common stock at $40 per share. Employees earn the right to participate in the stock option plan by working for the two years ending in 2008. Eligible employees can purchase stock during the three-year time period ending December 31, 2011. The company does not estimate any forfeiture will occur as a result of employees leaving the company.

Using a fair value approach, the market price of $50 per share would *not* be the basis for determining compensation. Assume that an option pricing model was applied and it was determined that the fair value of the options at the date of grant was $800,000. Illustration 18-3 identifies the exercise period and service period for this stock option plan.

---

5 *SFAS No. 123*, revised, par. 39.

6 *SFAS 123*, revised, par. iv, part b.

Under *SFAS No. 123,* compensation should be recorded as an expense over the service period. Thus the accounting entry to record compensation expense in 2007 and 2008 should be as follows:

Compensation Expense	400,000	
Paid-in Capital from Stock Options		400,000

When the options are exercised, the receipt of cash and the issuance of stock must be recorded. Assume that 40,000 options are exercised on January 1, 2010, the common stock is issued, and the market value of the stock on that date is $62 per share. The following accounting entry should be recorded:

Cash ($40 × 40,000 options)	1,600,000	
Paid-in Capital from Stock Options		
(40,000 ÷ 50,000 × $800,000)	640,000	
Common Stock		200,000
Paid-in Capital in Excess of Par—Common		2,040,000

When the options are exercised, the balance of the Paid-in Capital for Stock Options account should be reduced. In this case, the balance should be reduced by $640,000. At the end of the exercise period (three years in this case), if options have not been exercised, the balance of the Paid-in Capital from Stock Options account should be transferred to the Paid-in Capital from Expired Options account.

In some cases, stock options are not exercised because employees do not have sufficient cash to purchase stock. In many more cases, options are not exercised because the market price of the stock has fallen below the exercise price. During the stock downturn of 2000 and 2001, these *underwater* stock options became a problem for many companies. When stock prices fell below the stock options' exercise price, many companies realized that stock options were no longer an incentive for their employees. They sought to reduce the exercise price to a more realistic level. This is referred to as *repricing* stock options.

❯ THE ACCOUNTING DEBATE

The accounting for stock options has been the subject of heated debate. Even before revising *SFAS 123* in 2004, the FASB had viewed the fair value method as conceptually superior, as it provides a more accurate measure of compensation. This position has met with fierce opposition from reporting firms for many years. The opponents based their arguments on several grounds. They believed that the fair value method was too subjective and complex. Objections were based on the belief that use of the fair value method would significantly increase compensation expense and reduce income for many companies. The opponents also feared that reporting firms would reduce or eliminate stock option plans and therefore would be unable to attract and retain high-quality employees. Intense lobbying of Congress and the White House ensued. The Senate Banking Committee held hearings on the stock option issue in 1993, and legislation was introduced in Congress that would have nullified the requirements of the FASB.

Some companies began to accept the fair value method even before the requirements of the revised *SFAS 123* were finalized. **Coca-Cola** voluntarily adopted the fair value method in reaction to the severe criticism of stock option accounting in the post-Enron era. Other companies have sought to replace stock options with other forms of employee compensation. **Microsoft** announced that it will discontinue the use of stock options as a way to compensate employees because of the accounting issues involved, and also because most of its outstanding stock options are underwater as a result of the long downturn in the company's stock price.[7] The **Walt Disney**

---

7 "Microsoft Ushers Out Era of Options," *Wall Street Journal*, July 9, 2003, p. 1. Also see several related articles in the *Wall Street Journal*, July 10, 2003.

Figure 18.1

Stock Option Note—Walt Disney Company

Disney

The following table summarizes information about stock option transactions:

(shares in millions)	2004		2003		2002	
	Shares	Weighted Average Exercise Price	Shares	Weighted Average Exercise Price	Shares	Weighted Average Exercise Price
Outstanding at beginning of year	219	$26.44	216	$27.48	188	$29.54
Awards forfeited	(8)	24.40	(14)	44.41	(14)	33.64
Awards granted	27	24.61	30	17.34	50	21.99
Awards exercised	(11)	18.77	(3)	14.57	(2)	18.02
Awards expired	(6)	33.56	(10)	47.73	(6)	34.72
Outstanding at September 30	221	$26.50	219	$26.44	216	$27.48
Exercisable at September 30	132	$28.39	109	$27.86	88	$26.89

Company, referred to earlier in the chapter, did not adopt the fair value method for its 2004 financial statements, but does provide expanded disclosures in the notes to its annual report detailing what impact the fair value method would have had if it had been used.

▶ DISCLOSURE OF STOCK OPTIONS

Regardless of the method used to account for stock options, the following note disclosures are among those required by *SFAS No. 123*:[8]

1. A description of the plan, including the general term of awards.

2. The number and weighted-average exercise prices of options, classified by those outstanding at the beginning of the period, those outstanding at the end of the period, those exercisable, and those granted, exercised, forfeited, and expired.

3. The weighted-average grant-date fair value of options granted during the year. Disclosure should be made separately for options whose price equals, exceeds, or is less than market price.

4. A description of the methods and significant assumptions used in estimating fair value.

5. Total compensation cost recognized in income for the period.

6. The terms of significant modifications of outstanding awards.

7. For options outstanding at the end of the period, the range of exercise prices and the weighted-average remaining contractual life of the options.

The Walt Disney Company Financial Reporting Case presented at the opening of this chapter indicates that the company uses stock options extensively to remunerate its top-level executives. Disney used the intrinsic value method in 2004 but disclosed the required information about fair value in the notes. Figure 18.1 provides a portion of the stock option note from Walt Disney Company's annual report dated September 30, 2004.

Figure 18.1 indicates that 221 million stock options were outstanding at September 30, 2004. A portion of these (132 million) were exercisable at the balance sheet

---

8 *SFAS No. 123* as revised in 2004. See additional disclosure requirements in the appendix to the standard.

point ▶◀ counterpoint

The Impact of Stock Option Expensing

the controversy In 2004 the FASB issued *SFAS No. 123,* as revised, with guidelines that require the expensing of stock options. A stock option gives the recipient the right to buy a certain number of shares in the granting company at a fixed price for a certain number of years. Stock options have been used both in private and public companies to recruit and retain employees. Long-standing controversies over this particular accounting treatment were finally settled in December 2004, but new discussions emerged on the impacts to employee benefits, stock prices, and investor interest in companies that continue to issue stock options.

▶ point

Dennis Powell

CFO of Cisco

on the point:

- **George Scalise**
  Semiconductor Industry Association
- **Many Cisco employees**
- **Mark Heesen**
  President, National Venture Capital Association

▶ **The FASB's decision to require expensing of stock options has caused a downturn in stock option grants and has erased billions of dollars in profits for companies that continue to issue stock options.**

The new requirement of expensing equity compensation has caused additional controversy and concern to companies that provide stock options. Many believe this to be the final blow to broad-based equity plans. They fear that if companies continue to offer stock options to their employees and now have to expense them, the impact to their bottom line will cause stockholders to abandon ship for companies that use other forms of compensation.

In fact, many comanies *are* looking into other forms of compensation. Microsoft has shifted away from stock options to restricted stock. Other companies are cutting back on who gets equity stock or reducing the amounts provided. A survey conducted by Mercer HR in 2005 revealed that firms that changed their equity plans usually reduced stock option participation and/or the number of shares granted. About 45 percent of companies surveyed will either eliminate awards to non-management employees for stock options or change their plans so they will have little appeal to these workers.[1]

Dennis Powell, CFO of Cisco, laments the loss of stock options as a major recruitment tool as the expensing rule becomes a reality. The company's broad-based options program will likely be drastically reduced due to the billions of dollars that would now impact the income statement's bottom line. He categorizes this major change in company culture as a loss of employee ownership and fears that this will impact employee loyalty and innovation.

A 2005 Top Five survey of 42 major technology companies in Silicon Valley reported that 74 percent are considering replacing some of their options with other long-term incentive vehicles, with the same number considering reducing the size of their grants. Half of the companies are also considering reducing eligibility. Restricted stock is the most common substitute, being looked at by 55 percent of the companies.[2]

Mark Heesen, president of the National Venture Capital Association, also believes that stock options have been a critical factor in fueling entrepreneurial fires and spurring economic growth. He believes start-up companies that cannot lure new employees with stock options because of the stock options' cost to the bottom line will be seriously crippled in their ability to compete against established firms.

---

1 Sam Shah, "Examining the Future of Broad-Based Options," *CPA Journal Online,* available at: **http://www.nysscpa.org/cpajournal/2005/605/perspectives/p10.htm**. Accessed 8/4/05.

2 Aubrey Bout, Top Five, "The Changing Landscape of Equity Compensation in Technology Companies," *WorkSpan Magazine,* April 2005.

◀ counterpoint

Corey Rosen

*Executive Director of the
National Center for Employee
Ownership*

on the counterpoint:

- **Consumers Union**
- **Alan Greenspan**
  *Federal Reserve System
  Chairman*
- **Consumer Federation of
  America**
- **U.S. Public Interest Research
  Group**

◀ *SFAS No. 123* **does not prevent companies from issuing stock options to employees, and companies that choose to continue to offer broad-based stock options plans will reap the rewards in employee productivity and satisfaction.**

Alan Greenspan, a proponent of stock option expensing, reminds critics of *SFAS No. 123*, as revised, that the rule in no way inhibits a comany's legal authority to grant options. It just means that the company must show the cost of those options. He and others, such as Warren Buffett and former SEC Chairman, Arthur Levitt, believe that these costs should not be indefinitely buried in the notes to financial statements. When faced with the idea that expensing will make it more difficult for some companies to attract talent because of a restated bottom line, individuals in the camp are likely to retort, "Isn't it better to present an honest picture of the company to the market and to the potential employee than to recruit under false pretenses?"

Because companies must show the cost of stock options, does this mean these plans should be dumped? Corey Rosen, executive director of the National Center for Employee Ownership, says no. He cites a Rutgers University study in which companies that granted options to a broad base of employees yielded a 17 percent improvement in productivity over what would have been expected had the companies not set up such plans. Return on assets increased by 2.3 percent per year over what would have been expected, while stock performance was either better or about the same than comparable companies, depending on how performance was measured.[3] Thus, proponents of stock option plans believe that the benefits of the plans to corporate performance can still outweigh the expenses.

Mark Sullivan, a compensation practice leader at RSM McGladrey, recently completed a survey of compensation practices at small and mid-market companies. Though he thought the new rule would cause the granting of options to fall off steeply, the decrease has not been as much as he expected.[4]

For companies that have decided to veer away from stock options, a variety of other plans are available. The first choice for alternative forms of long-term, equity-based incentives among public companies surveyed was time-vested restricted stock (52 percent), followed by performance-vested restricted stock (40 percent). The first choice among private companies continues to be time-vested stock options (39 percent), followed by performance-vested stock options (33 percent).

Compensation experts agree that bonuses and salary bumps will likely play a more significant role in the future. Although the number of options awarded at Maryland's largest companies fell by 40 percent in 2004, bonuses and salaries climbed more than 12 percent. Companies will also be more strategic about which employees receive equity compensation.

Take a Position   Assume you are the chief financial officer of a major U.S. corporation that has used stock options as compensation for executives and middle managers in the past. What is your opinion regarding the use of stock options in the future? Explain your answer.

Research   Locate Cisco's 2005 annual report online and find any discussion regarding the expensing of stock options therein. Compare the company's annual earnings for 2003, 2004, and 2005. How has *SFAS No. 123*, as revised, impacted the company's bottom line?

---

3 Corey Rosen, "Who Should Get Options? What Research, Not Theory, Tells Us," May 2003, available at: **http://www.nceo.org/library/who_should_get_options.html**. Accessed 8/2/04.

4 Mark Reilly, "Stock Options Play Large Role in CEO's Compensation," *The Business Journal*, July 22, 2005, available at: **http://twincities.bizjournals.com/twincities/stories/2005/07/25/focus5.html**. Accessed 8/5/05.

Figure 18.2

Fair Value Method Disclosures—Walt Disney Company

Disney

The following table reflects pro forma net income (loss) and earnings (loss) per share had the Company elected to record an expense for the fair value of employee stock options pursuant to the provisions of *SFAS 123:*

	Year Ended September 30,		
(in millions, except for per share data)	**2004**	**2003**	**2002**
Net income (loss) attributed to Disney common stock:			
As reported	**$2,345**	$1,267	$1,236
Pro forma after stock option expense	**2,090**	973	930
Diluted earnings (loss) per share attributed to Disney common stock:			
As reported	**1.12**	0.62	0.60
Pro forma after stock option expense	**1.00**	0.48	0.45

date. If the options were exercised, the number of shares of stock outstanding would increase and earnings per share would decrease. Disney offers fair value method notes to indicate the potential impact on net income, as shown in Figure 18.2.

Walt Disney reported net income of $2,345 million using the intrinsic value method, but would have reported net income of $2,090 if it had used the fair value method. Earnings per share would have dropped from $1.12 to $1.00. As you can see, the way stock options are accounted for can make a large difference in income and earnings per share.

❱ INTERNATIONAL PERSPECTIVE ON STOCK OPTIONS

INTERNATIONAL

Stock options are not unique to U.S. companies. Many companies in other countries use stock option plans to remunerate their employees. Likewise, the accounting bodies in other countries have struggled to develop the proper accounting for stock options. The International Accounting Standards Board moved to a fair value method of accounting for stock options earlier than the FASB did. The IASB issued *International Financial Reporting Standard (IFRS) No. 2* in 2004; it requires that stock options, referred to as share-based payments in the standard, be recognized as an expense. This expense will be measured as the fair value of the equity instruments (options) issued, determined on the date of grant. The issuance of *IFRS No. 2* placed a great deal of pressure on the FASB to make the accounting in the United States consistent with the international standard.

Predictably, those who oppose the fair value method endorsed by the FASB also oppose the standards proposed by the IASB. The Financial Executives International (previously Financial Executives Institute) stated its belief that the IASB should not revisit the issues studied by the FASB concerning stock options and should not adopt a standard based on a fair value approach as follows:

> We encourage the IASB to adopt the current U.S. model. This alone would further international convergence and harmony and would be a significant improvement for many countries around the world. Taking this action quickly and decisively would enhance the IASB's credibility, recognize that stock option accounting in the U.S. is not going to change and move ahead the one-global accounting standards agenda.
>
> If the IASB does not heed this advice, we urge Congress to exercise its oversight responsibility and ensure that the current U.S. employee stock

option accounting rules remain intact. We would also encourage Congress to ensure that the U.S. FASB remains strong and preeminent. The goal of one set of global accounting standards will still be a valid and laudable objective. A goal that the FASB may need to achieve, should the IASB fail.[9]

CHECK YOUR UNDERSTANDING

1. What are convertible bonds?

2. If detachable warrants are issued with a bond, how are costs allocated to the transaction?

3. What information, at a minimum, must a stock option plan specify?

4. Under the fair value method, how would stock option compensation be measured?

Earnings per Share

In the preceding portions of this chapter and in the previous chapter, the accounting issues related to the issuance of dilutive securities and their conversion to common stock were discussed. In the following pages, we discuss how dilutive securities affect the calculation of earnings per share.

No other piece of financial information is more important than the earnings per share ratio. **Earnings per share (EPS)**, at a basic level, is defined as the amount of earnings associated with each common share of a company's stock. When a company reports its earnings in the financial press, it reports the earnings per share ratio as a summary of its activities. Analysts and investors develop sophisticated models to predict the EPS for the following quarters and for the future annual periods. Any change in EPS or any unexpected fluctuations in past or projected EPS cause the stock price to respond immediately, and often quite drastically. Reactions to EPS changes are often inappropriate because of improper analysis of the ratio or uninformed use of the financial statement data. Many financial experts have lamented that this fixation on EPS leads to a short-term orientation on the part of management because the company is constantly judged on its short-term results, as indicated by its EPS. If a company does not meet its EPS goals or the expectations of the market, its stock price will be driven downward. Although it is unfortunate that there is such an emphasis on this one piece of financial information, the trend is likely to continue.

Because EPS is an important financial measurement, the accounting rules for its calculation are detailed and specific. Currently *SFAS No. 128* indicates how EPS should be calculated and presented for both a simple and a complex capital structure.[10] One of the reasons that the FASB issued new guidance on EPS was to make the accounting guidance similar to the international accounting pronouncements. In fact, the FASB pursued its project on EPS concurrently with the IASC (which has become the IASB) project on EPS. Consequently, the U.S. and international guidelines for accounting for EPS are very similar.

earnings per share (EPS) the amount of earnings associated with each common share of a company's stock

---

9   Financial Executives International website, "Stock Options: What Does History Tell Us?" *Financial Executive,* October 2001.

10 "Earnings per Share," *Statement of Financial Accounting Standards No. 128* (Stamford, Conn.: FASB, 1997).

LO3 Calculate the earnings per share in a simple capital structure.

simple capital structure a structure in which no dilutive securities are present, although there may be more than one class of stock

basic EPS the amount of net income associated with each outstanding share of a firm's common stock; net income minus preferred stock dividends divided by the weighted-average number of common shares outstanding

⊞ Critical Thinking: *As a stockholder, what factors do you think might affect earnings per share?*

weighted-average number of shares outstanding the number of shares outstanding during a period weighted by the fraction of the period during which they are outstanding

COMPUTING EPS—SIMPLE CAPITAL STRUCTURE

A **simple capital structure** is a structure in which no dilutive securities are present. Dilutive securities include the four instruments discussed earlier: convertible bonds, convertible preferred stock, warrants, and stock options. Note that a simple capital structure may have more than one class of stock. For example, a company that has both common stock and preferred stock will still have a simple capital structure as long as there are no dilutive securities.

A company with a simple capital structure is required to present an earnings per share amount referred to as basic EPS. **Basic EPS** is calculated as follows:

$$\frac{\text{Net Income} - \text{Preferred Stock Dividends}}{\text{Weighted-Average Shares of Common Stock Outstanding}}$$

It is important to remember that the focus of the EPS calculation is on the *common* stockholders. Thus, EPS measures the rights of common stockholders to the income of the company. In the next sections, we will discuss issues concerning both the numerator and the denominator of the EPS fraction as well as presentation issues.

❯ NUMERATOR OF EPS

The numerator of the EPS fraction should represent the amount of income that is available to the common stockholders. Therefore, preferred stock dividends that have been *declared* during the current period should be deducted. If preferred stock dividends have not been declared, the terms of the preferred stock become important. If the preferred stock is *cumulative*, the dividend for the current period should be deducted even if it has not been declared, because preferred stockholders must receive that dividend at some time in the future before common stockholders can receive a dividend. However, if the preferred stock is not cumulative, the dividend should be deducted only if it has been declared.[11]

❯ DENOMINATOR OF EPS

The denominator of the EPS ratio should *not* be simply the number of shares of common stock outstanding as of the end of the period. Rather, it should reflect a **weighted-average number of shares outstanding** during the period. This means that shares that are issued during a period are weighted by the fraction of the period during which they are outstanding. In actual practice, some firms calculate the weighted average based on the number of days the stock was outstanding. For illustration purposes, we will use a less precise method and calculate the weighted average based on the number of months involved.[12] For example, assume that Earnford Company had 12,000 shares of common stock outstanding on January 1, 2007. The following transactions occurred during the fiscal year:

March 1: Issued 6,000 shares for cash

April 1: Purchased 3,000 shares as treasury stock

September 1: Issued 9,000 shares for cash

Illustration 18.4 provides a calculation of the weighted-average number of shares of common stock outstanding for the year ended December 31, 2007.

The calculation is based on the weighted-average number of shares *outstanding*. Thus, issuances of stock increase the denominator and purchases of treasury stock reduce the denominator.

---

11 Ibid., par. 9.

12 Ibid., par. 45 notes that many firms base the weighted average on the number of days involved but does allow "less-precise" averaging methods.

Illustration 18.4

Calculation of Weighted Average

Date	Total Shares		Weighting		
January 1–March 1	12,000	×	2/12	=	2,000
March 1–April 1	18,000	×	1/12	=	1,500
April 1–September 1	15,000	×	5/12	=	6,250
September 1–December 31	24,000	×	4/12	=	8,000
			Weighted average		17,750

When the number of shares of stock is changed as a result of a *stock dividend or stock split*, the procedure is altered somewhat. If the number of shares of stock increases as a result of a stock dividend or a stock split, the weighting should treat the increase as though it occurred at the beginning of the period.[13] Essentially, shares issued as a result of a stock dividend or split are weighted for the entire period, regardless of when they were issued during the period. For example, assume that Manning Company had 12,000 shares of common stock outstanding on January 1, 2007. The following transactions occurred during the period:

March 1: Issued 6,000 shares for cash

April 1: Purchased 3,000 shares as treasury stock

July 1: Declared and issued a 2-for-1 stock split

September 1: Issued 9,000 shares for cash

Note that the transactions are the same as those in the previous example, except for the July 1 stock split. Illustration 18.5 provides a calculation of the weighted-average number of shares of common stock outstanding for the year ended December 31, 2007.

If a company presents comparative financial statements and has had a stock dividend or split in the current period, the weighted-average number of shares of common stock outstanding must be restated retroactively for past statements presented for comparison purposes.

PRESENTATION OF EARNINGS PER SHARE

Even for a simple capital structure, EPS must be calculated and presented for the net income amount. EPS should also be presented for income from continuing operations (if that line item exists) on the *face* of the income statement. In addition, the company must present EPS for discontinued operations and extraordinary items, *either on the face of the income statement or in the notes to the financial statements*. Illustration 18.6

Illustration 18.5

Calculation of Weighted Average, Including Stock Split

Date	Total Shares		Weighting			
January 1–March 1	12,000	×	2/12	× 2	=	4,000
March 1–April 1	18,000	×	1/12	× 2	=	3,000
April 1–July 1	15,000	×	3/12	× 2	=	7,500
July 1–September 1	30,000	×	2/12		=	5,000
September 1–December 31	39,000	×	4/12		=	13,000
			Weighted average			32,500

---

13 Ibid., par. 54.

Illustration 18.6

Presentation of EPS

Net sales	xxx
Cost of sales	xxx
Gross profit	xxx
Operating expenses	xxx
Income from operations	xxx
Other income or expense	xxx
Income from continuing operations before income taxes	xxx
Income taxes	xxx
Income from continuing operations	xxx ⟶ EPS*
Discontinued operations (net of tax):	
Income or loss from operations (net of tax)	xxx ⟶ EPS†
Gain or loss from disposal (net of tax)	xxx ⟶ EPS†
Income before extraordinary items	xxx ⟶ EPS†
Extraordinary items (net of tax)	xxx ⟶ EPS†
Net income	xxx ⟶ EPS*

*EPS is required on the face of the statement.
†EPS is required either on the face of the statement or in the notes.

indicates the line items on a hypothetical income statement for which EPS should be presented.

LO4 Calculate the earnings per share in a complex capital structure.

complex capital structure a capital structure in which dilutive securities are present

diluted EPS what EPS would be if all of the dilutive securities were converted into common stock or were exercised and resulted in common stock

🧩 *Critical Thinking: What types of securities do you think exist in a complex capital structure? Why do these securities add to the complexity of the structure?*

COMPUTING EPS—COMPLEX CAPITAL STRUCTURE

A **complex capital structure** is a structure in which dilutive securities are present. These securities could become common stock, thus altering EPS. When a company has a complex capital structure, it must present two earnings per share amounts: basic earnings per share, calculated in the same manner as discussed for a simple capital structure, and diluted earnings per share.

The purpose of the **diluted EPS** amount is to indicate what EPS would be if all of the dilutive securities were converted into common stock (in the case of convertible debt and convertible preferred stock) or if they were exercised and resulted in common stock (in the case of warrants or stock options). Thus, the calculation of diluted EPS is, to a certain extent, a calculation of the "worst-case scenario," or what would happen to EPS if all of the instruments representing potential increases in common stock were in fact to become common stock. Diluted earnings per share could be described as follows:

$$\frac{\text{Net Income} - \text{Preferred Stock Dividends} + \text{Effect of Dilutive Securities}}{\text{Weighted-Average Shares of Common Stock Outstanding} + \text{Effect of Dilutive Securities}}$$

To determine the impact of dilutive securities, a series of assumptions should be considered, as discussed in *SFAS No. 128*. We will illustrate the calculation of diluted EPS for different types of dilutive securities in the sections that follow.

▶ DILUTED EPS FOR CONVERTIBLE BONDS OR CONVERTIBLE PREFERRED STOCK

If a company has convertible bonds outstanding, both the numerator and the denominator of the diluted EPS calculation are affected.[14] It is necessary to calculate the

---

14 Ibid., par. 11.

Illustration 18.7

If-Converted Method

Before-tax interest: $600,000 \times 0.10 = $60,000$

Impact on numerator (interest after tax):
$60,000 \times (1 - 0.4) = $36,000$

Impact on denominator (number of additional shares):
$600,000 \div $1,000 \times 20 = 12,000$ shares

Diluted earnings per share should be calculated as:

$$\frac{$500,000 + $36,000}{100,000 + 12,000} = $4.79 \text{ (rounded)}$$

if-converted method calculation of the impact on EPS as if the bonds had been converted to common stock as of the beginning of the period (if the bonds were issued prior to the beginning of the period) or as of the issue date (if the bonds were issued during the current period)

impact on EPS *as if* the bonds had been converted to common stock as of the beginning of the period (if the bonds were issued prior to the beginning of the period) or as of the issue date (if the bonds were issued during the current period). This approach is referred to as the **if-converted method**. Note that the purpose of the if-converted method is to calculate the *potential impact* of the convertible bonds if they were to be converted into common stock. An amount representing the additional number of shares of common stock that would have been issued if the bonds had been converted should be added to the denominator. The numerator is adjusted to add back the *after-tax* amount of interest that would have been avoided if the bonds had been converted. In other words, if the bonds had been converted to stock, the company would not have incurred interest on the bonds, and net income would have increased.

For example, assume that Freefall Company has a basic EPS for the year ended December 31, 2007, of $5 per share, based on a net income of $500,000 and 100,000 shares of common stock. The company does not have any preferred stock but has convertible bonds outstanding during the year. Prior to January 1, 2007, the company issued at face value $600,000 of convertible bonds that pay interest of 10 percent. Each $1,000 bond can be converted into 20 shares of common stock. Assume that the company is subject to a 40 percent tax rate and that no bonds were actually converted into common stock during the period. Even though the bonds were not converted, we must determine the impact on earnings per share that would occur *if* the bonds were converted into stock. The impact of the convertible bonds on diluted EPS can be calculated as shown in Illustration 18.7.

The calculation of diluted EPS when convertible preferred stock has been issued is similar. An amount should be added to the *denominator* that represents the additional number of shares of common stock that would have been issued if the preferred stock had been converted to common stock. An amount should be added to the *numerator* that represents the preferred stock dividend that would have been avoided if the preferred stock had been converted to common stock. However, you should note that with preferred stock, it is not necessary to consider the tax impact. Dividends on preferred stock are not deductible in determining net income, so it is not necessary to calculate a net-of-tax amount for preferred stock dividends.

antidilutive securities securities whose assumed exercise would create an increase in earnings per share; these securities are generally excluded from the computation of earnings per share

❭ **ANTIDILUTIVE SECURITIES**   The procedure described for convertible bonds and convertible preferred stock should be followed unless the security is antidilutive.[15] **Antidilutive securities** are those whose inclusion would cause EPS to increase rather than decrease. For convertible bonds and convertible preferred stock, the if-converted method alters both the numerator and the denominator of the EPS calculation. Therefore, it is possible that the inclusion of a security in the calculation would actually cause EPS to increase. *Antidilutive securities are not included in the calculation of EPS.* This is consistent with the idea that the diluted EPS figure is intended to present a worst-case scenario. Dilutive securities are included, but antidilutive securities are not included.

---

15 Ibid., par. 13.

❱ **CHANGES IN CONVERSION RATES** In some cases, the conversion rate for a convertible security may not be the same over the life of the security. For example, a convertible bond may be convertible into 10 shares of stock before a specified date and convertible into 20 shares of stock after that date. How should such securities be treated when calculating diluted EPS? *SFAS No. 128* specifies that the diluted EPS amount should be based on the conversion rate that is the most advantageous to the bondholders (or the most unfavorable to the issuing company).[16] Again, this manner of calculating diluted EPS is consistent with the idea that it is intended to convey the worst-case scenario or the most unfavorable EPS that could result from the dilutive securities.

❱ **DILUTED EPS FOR OPTIONS OR WARRANTS**

The impact of outstanding stock options and warrants must also be considered when calculating diluted EPS. In most cases, options and warrants do not affect the numerator of the EPS calculation. The focus is on how options and warrants affect the denominator of the calculation. In order to determine the effect, the **treasury stock method** is applied. The treasury stock method assumes that outstanding options or warrants are exercised at the beginning of the period (or at the time of issuance, if that is later) and common stock is issued at the exercise price. The proceeds (hypothetically) received from the exercise of the options are assumed to be used to purchase common stock as treasury stock; hence the name *treasury stock method*. It is assumed that treasury stock is purchased at the average market price of the common stock during the period. The *net increase*, or the difference between the number of shares of stock assumed to have been issued upon exercise and the number of shares of stock assumed to have been purchased as treasury stock, is the amount included in the denominator when calculating diluted EPS.

> **treasury stock method** a method of computing EPS that assumes that outstanding options or warrants are exercised at the beginning of the period (or at the time of issuance, if that is later) and common stock is issued at the exercise price, and that the proceeds received from the exercise are used to purchase treasury stock

For example, assume that Freefall Company has a basic EPS for the year ended December 31, 2007, of $5 per share, based on a net income of $500,000 and 100,000 shares of common stock. The company does not have any preferred stock but has 20,000 options outstanding. Each option can be exercised to purchase one share of common stock. Assume that the options were issued prior to January 1, 2007, and allow the holder to purchase stock at $20 per share. The average market price of the common stock during 2007 was $25 per share.

Illustration 18.8 presents the results of applying the treasury stock method for the company for 2007.

Illustration 18.8

Treasury Stock Method

	Number of Shares
Assumed exercise of options	20,000
Proceeds = 20,000 × $20 = $400,000	
Assumed purchase of treasury stock	
$400,000 ÷ $25	(16,000)
Net increase	4,000

The first step results in an increase in number of shares of common stock of 20,000, and the second step results in a decrease of 16,000 shares. The net increase of 4,000 shares is the amount included in the denominator of the diluted EPS calculation.

Diluted earnings per share should be calculated as:

$$\frac{\$500,000}{100,000 + 4,000} = \$4.81 \text{ (rounded)}$$

---

16 Ibid., par. 12.

Warrants and options should be treated in the same manner when calculating EPS.

❭ ANTIDILUTIVE SECURITIES   Options and warrants that are antidilutive should not be included in the calculation of EPS. Again, antidilutive securities are instruments whose inclusion would cause EPS to increase rather than decrease. Because options and warrants do not affect the numerator of the EPS fraction, it should be easier to determine when a security is antidilutive. If the treasury stock method is applied and the result is a net decrease in shares instead of a net increase, the security is antidilutive. An even more straightforward way to determine whether the securities are antidilutive is to compare the exercise price of the option or warrant to the average market value of the stock for the period. *If the exercise price is higher than the average market price of the stock, the option or warrant is antidilutive and should not be included in the EPS calculation.* There is some logic to this approach, since holders of warrants or options are very unlikely to exercise the warrants or options and purchase stock at the exercise price when the exercise price exceeds the market value of the stock.

DILUTED EARNINGS PER SHARE WHEN MULTIPLE DILUTIVE SECURITIES ARE PRESENT

In the examples presented thus far, we have dealt with situations in which only one dilutive security is present. We will now illustrate the calculation of EPS when there is more than one dilutive security.

Assume that Freefall Company has a basic EPS for the year ended December 31, 2007, of $5 per share, based on a net income of $500,000 and 100,000 shares of common stock. The company does not have any preferred stock but does have 20,000 options outstanding. Each option can be exercised to purchase one share of common stock. Assume that the options were issued prior to January 1, 2007, and allow the holder to purchase stock at $20 per share. The average market price of the common stock during 2007 was $25 per share. The company also has convertible bonds outstanding during the year. Prior to January 1, 2007, the company issued at face value $600,000 of convertible bonds that pay interest of 10 percent. Each $1,000 bond can be converted into 20 shares of common stock. Assume that the company is subject to 40 percent tax and that no bonds were actually converted into common stock during the period.

Earnings per share would be calculated as indicated in Illustration 18.9.[17]

❭ TESTING FOR ANTIDILUTION

When several securities are involved, there may be some question as to how to determine whether a security is antidilutive. In such cases, each security or each class of securities should be considered separately rather than considering all securities in the aggregate. Furthermore, in complex situations, securities may be dilutive on their own but antidilutive when included with other potential securities. Therefore, the order in

Illustration 18.9

Calculation of Diluted Earnings per Share

	Numerator	Denominator	
Basic EPS	$500,000	100,000	$5.00 per share
Options	0	4,000	(see Illustration 18.8)
Subtotal	$500,000	104,000	$4.81
Convertible bonds	36,000	12,000	(see Illustration 18.7)
Total	$536,000	116,000	**Diluted EPS $4.62**

---

17 The example is patterned after Illustration 4 in *SFAS No. 128*.

which the securities are tested for dilution affects the outcome. In such cases, *SFAS No. 128* specifies that the securities should be ranked according to their earnings per incremental share.[18] **Earnings per incremental share** is defined as the *change* in the numerator divided by the *change* in the denominator that occurs when the security is included in the earnings per share calculation. Thus, the following steps should be taken to calculate diluted earnings per share when more than one dilutive security is present:

earnings per incremental share
a ratio used to rank EPS by the change in the numerator divided by the change in the denominator that occurs when the security is included in the earnings per share calculation

1. Calculate basic EPS.

2. Calculate earnings per incremental share for each of the dilutive securities.

3. Rank the securities from smallest to largest effect per share. That is, rank from most dilutive to least dilutive.

4. Include the securities in the EPS calculation in that order *if* their inclusion causes EPS to decline.

5. If a security's inclusion causes EPS to increase, then the security is considered antidilutive and is not included in the calculation of diluted EPS.

Note that the *change* in the numerator is zero for options and warrants. Therefore, as in the previous example, options and warrants are always included in the calculation before convertible bonds or convertible preferred stock. In this example, the convertible bonds were included because their inclusion caused EPS to decline (from $4.81 before inclusion to $4.62 after inclusion). If their inclusion had caused EPS to increase to an amount above $4.81, the convertible bonds would have been considered antidilutive and excluded from the calculation of diluted earnings per share.

ADDITIONAL DISCLOSURE REQUIREMENTS

The presentation of EPS on the income statement was shown in Illustration 18.6. The following additional disclosures must be made for each period for which an income statement is presented:[19]

1. A reconciliation of the numerator and denominator of the basic and diluted earnings per share computations for income from continuing operations.

2. The effect that has been given to preferred dividends in arriving at income available to common stockholders.

3. Securities that could potentially dilute EPS in the future that were not included in the computation of EPS because doing so would have been antidilutive.

Figure 18.3 presents the disclosures concerning EPS presented on the face of the income statement for the Walt Disney Company for the years ended September 30, 2004, 2003, and 2002.

A review of the information presented in Figure 18.3 shows an increasing trend in the EPS figures, which is encouraging and may indicate that a recovery is under way. To complete a meaningful analysis, though, statement users should also understand how EPS was calculated. Earlier in this chapter, we indicated that the Walt Disney Company had a large number of stock options outstanding at year end that must be treated as a dilutive security for EPS calculations. You might expect that as a result, the company would exhibit a rather large difference between basic and diluted EPS. However, as of September 30, 2004, basic EPS was $1.14 per share and diluted EPS was at $1.12 per share. The note information provided in Figure 18.4 states that the difference between basic and diluted EPS in the previous years was solely attributable to stock options. The

---

18 *SFAS No. 128*, Illustration 4.

19 Ibid., par. 40.

Figure 18.3

EPS Disclosures—Walt Disney Company

Disney

Results of Operations (in millions, except per share data)	2004	2003	2002
Earnings per share before the cumulative effect of accounting change:			
Diluted	$ 1.12	$ 0.65	$ 0.60
Basic	$ 1.14	$ 0.65	$ 0.61
Cumulative effect of accounting changes per share	—	$ (0.03)	$—
Earnings per share:			
Diluted	$ 1.12	$ 0.62	$ 0.60
Basic	$ 1.14	$ 0.62	$ 0.61
Average number of common and common equivalent shares outstanding:			
Diluted	2,106	2,067	2,044
Basic	2,049	2,043	2,040

Figure 18.4

Note Disclosures of EPS—Walt Disney Company

Disney

Earnings Per Share

The Company presents both basic and diluted earnings per share (EPS) amounts. Basic EPS is calculated by dividing net income by the weighted average number of common shares outstanding during the year. Diluted EPS is based upon the weighted average number of common and common equivalent shares outstanding during the year, which is calculated using the treasury stock method for stock options and assumes conversion of the company's convertible senior notes (see Note 6). Common equivalent shares are excluded from the computation in periods in which they have an antidilutive effect. Stock options for which the exercise price exceeds the average market price over the period have an antidilutive effect on EPS and, accordingly, are excluded from the calculation.

company did not have any convertible bonds, convertible preferred stock, or warrants that affected EPS. Furthermore, although there were a large number of stock options in 2004, many of the stock options did not affect the diluted EPS calculation because they were antidilutive. That is an indication that Walt Disney had a significant number of stock options outstanding for which the exercise price of the options exceeded the average market price during the period. As a result, those stock options did not have much of an effect on the EPS calculation.

CHECK YOUR UNDERSTANDING

1. How is basic earnings per share calculated? Does the numerator include preferred dividends that have been declared, but are unpaid?

2. If a company has a simple capital structure, how should EPS be presented for income from continuing operations? For extraordinary items? For discontinued operations?

3. Why do companies present diluted EPS?

LO5 Understand the analysis issues related to earnings per share.

Critical Thinking: *What controversial issues do you think exist with regard to the computing and reporting of EPS?*

Analysis Issues for Earnings per Share

The EPS ratio is one of the most essential analysis tools used by investors, managers, and financial analysts. It is important to understand which EPS number has been reported by a company and how the EPS was calculated.

PRO FORMA EARNINGS PER SHARE AND ETHICAL CONSIDERATIONS

Recently, many companies have been publishing an amount referred to as **pro forma earnings per share**. The exact meaning of pro forma earnings per share varies from company to company. Usually, it represents an attempt to exclude nonrecurring items, write-offs, restructuring charges, and similar negative amounts from EPS. Analysts need to know about costs or expenses that are one-time items so that they can more accurately predict future earnings. Also, it should be noted that companies are free to report financial information in addition to the required information concerning EPS. Additional disclosures about company results are often provided and even encouraged.

Many financial analysts and accounting professionals feel that companies have used the reporting of pro forma earnings to improve the appearance of their financial status. Company press releases may emphasize pro forma EPS amounts to such an extent that the basic or diluted EPS numbers are buried, thereby misleading the investing public. In some cases, a negative EPS has been reported as a positive one on a pro forma basis. In other cases, the divergence between the actual number and the pro forma disclosure has been substantial. In 2001, **Cisco Systems, Inc.** reported a quarterly loss of $2.7 billion but also reported a pro forma income of $230 million. Yahoo turned a $1.39 per share loss into an $.08 pro forma per share loss for the second quarter.[20]

ETHICS

pro forma earnings per share a term that varies from company to company but usually represents an attempt to exclude nonrecurring items, write-offs, restructuring charges, and similar negative amounts from EPS

Because no rules exist for what should be included in pro forma EPS, many have become skeptical, as indicated in this excerpt from a *Business Week* article:

> Amazon.com Inc. can't even settle on a single definition of pro forma. In its Apr. 24 results announcement, it reported a "pro forma operating" loss of $49 million in the first quarter of this year. Confusingly, it also reported a "pro forma net" loss of 21 cents a share, equivalent to $76 million. Investors had to pick carefully among a slew of numbers to see that Amazon actually had a net loss of $234 million, or 66 cents a share, using GAAP. Among the items excluded from pro forma operating losses were a net interest expense of $24 million and a $114 million charge for restructuring costs, such as closing a warehouse. "The pro forma numbers are how we think about our business" and how Wall Street analysts follow it, says Amazon spokesman Bill Curry, emphasizing that the GAAP numbers are included.
>
> The spread of pro forma earnings has plunged investors into an Alice-in-Wonderland world. SEC Chief Accountant Lynn E. Turner calls pro forma results "EBS earnings"—for Everything but Bad Stuff. "Way too often, they seem to be used to distract investors from the actual results," Turner says. Wall Street, of course, is happy to play along: First Call's Hill says more than 260 companies have persuaded a majority of top financial analysts to abandon GAAP when making earnings estimates.[21]

---

20 Justin Gillis, "Corporate America's New Math: Investors Now Face Two Sets of Numbers in Figuring a Company's Bottom Line," *Washington Post*, July 22, 2001.

21 "The Numbers Game: The Latest Abuse, Pro Forma Earnings," *Business Week*, May 14, 2001.

In fact Lynn Turner, the SEC's chief accountant, stated that "people are using the pro forma earnings to present a tilted, biased picture to investors that I don't believe necessarily reflects the reality of what's going on in business."[22] The SEC has asked industry groups to develop voluntary guidelines that would encourage companies to make clear how their pro forma numbers were calculated.

The SEC, as required by the Sarbanes-Oxley Act, has begun to develop rules for the disclosure of pro forma earnings disclosure.[23] Those guidelines require companies to clearly present and reconcile the differences between pro forma earnings and the GAAP-based results. It requires that press releases and communications about earnings contain a tabular presentation of the reconciliation of pro forma earnings and GAAP-based earnings. In addition, it stresses the need for consistency from period to period in the manner in which pro forma earnings are calculated. While companies can attempt to present their results in the best possible light, the use of pro forma amounts should not detract from or diminish the amounts that have been calculated based on carefully constructed generally accepted accounting principles.

> **CHECK YOUR UNDERSTANDING**
>
> 1. What does pro forma earnings per share generally represent?
>
> 2. How could pro forma earnings per share be used to mislead investors?
>
> 3. What guidance, as required by the Sarbanes-Oxley Act, is the SEC proposing on the disclosure of pro forma earnings?

LO6 Understand the cash flow presentation of earnings.

Critical Thinking: Why do you think companies are not allowed to present cash flow per share amounts in their earnings announcements?

CASH FLOW $

Cash Flow Issues Related to EPS

Whereas earnings are based on the accrual process and are reflected on the income statement, the *cash impact* of earnings is presented on the statement of cash flows. Earnings are the major source of cash flows from operating activities and are presented in that category of the statement of cash flows. Transactions related to stockholders' equity are presented in the financing activities category of the statement of cash flows.

Figure 18.5 presents the financing activities category of the statement of cash flows of Walt Disney Company for the year ended September 30, 2004. The statement reveals that Disney paid $2,479 million to reduce borrowings and received $201 million from the exercise of stock options. In fact, borrowings and stock options were the largest *sources* of cash from financing activities for 2004. This is an indication of the importance Disney placed on stock options as an element of its financial strategy.

As we have indicated in this chapter, a great deal of emphasis is placed on EPS amounts by the financial community. Note, however, that companies are not allowed to present an amount of cash flow per share, as specified by *SFAS No. 95*. Neither cash flow nor any component of it is an alternative to net income as an indicator of an enterprise's performance.[24] In the board's view, a major problem with reporting cash

---

22   Gillis, "Corporate America's New Math."

23   Proposed Rule: "Conditions for Use of Non-GAAP Financial Measures," SEC, Release No. 33–8145.

24   "Statement of Cash Flows," *Statement of Financial Accounting Standards No. 95* (Norwalk, Conn.: FASB, 1987), par. 33.

Figure 18.5

Statement of Cash Flows, Financing Activities Section— Walt Disney Company

Figure 18.5

Statement of Cash Flows, Financing Activities Section— Walt Disney Company

Disney

(in millions)	Year Ended September 30		
	2004	**2003**	**2002**
Financing Activities			
Borrowings	**$176**	$1,635	$4,038
Reduction of borrowings	**(2,479)**	(2,059)	(2,113)
Commercial paper borrowings, net	**100**	(721)	(33)
Dividends	**(430)**	(429)	(428)
Exercise of stock options and other	**201**	51	47
Repurchases of common stock	**(335)**	—	—
Hong Kong Disneyland minority interest capital contributions	**66**	—	—
Cash (used) provided by financing activities	**(2,701)**	(1,523)	1,511

flow data is investor understanding. Investors over the years have become accustomed to seeing only EPS amounts. "To report other data on a per share basis invites the danger that investors, creditors, and others may confuse those measures with the conventional accounting measure of earnings per share."[25]

CHECK YOUR UNDERSTANDING

1. Where in the statement of cash flows will the exercise of stock options appear?

2. What is the FASB's rationale for not allowing companies to present an amount of cash flow per share as an indicator of performance?

Statement of Stockholders' Equity

LO7 Develop a statement of stockholders' equity.

Critical Thinking: *As a potential investor, what types of financial information would you be interested in with regard to stockholders' equity? Where might you find this information?*

The statement of retained earnings provides details on changes that have occurred in the Retained Earnings account during a particular period. As you have learned, the ending balance of Retained Earnings must be calculated, based on the net income for the period as well as dividends and other changes in the account. The balance of Retained Earnings is presented on the balance sheet.

While a statement of retained earnings is useful, large public companies are required by the SEC to provide a more complete picture of the changes in stockholders' equity by presenting a statement of stockholders' equity, sometimes called the *statement of shareholders' equity* or the *statement of changes in stockholders' equity*. The purpose of the statement of stockholders' equity is to present all of the items that changed the balance of each of the stockholders' equity accounts. For most companies, there are only a few transactions that affect stockholders' equity during a given period, but these transactions are important.

The statement of shareholders' equity for the Walt Disney Company at September 30, 2004, is presented in Figure 18.6.

Figure 18.6 provides the beginning and ending balances of each of the stockholders' equity accounts and the transactions affecting these accounts for 2004. In this year, significant items include net income of $2,345 million (increase in Retained Earnings)

---

25 Ibid., par. 123.

Figure 18.6

Statement of Shareholders' Equity—Walt Disney Company

Disney

(in millions, except per share data)	Shares	Common Stock	Retained Earnings	Accumulated Other Comprehensive Income (Loss)	Treasury Stock	Total Shareholders' Equity
Balance at September 30, 2003	2,044	$12,154	$13,817	$(653)	$(1,527)	$23,791
Exercise of stock options and issuance of restricted stock	11	293	—	—	—	293
Common stock repurchases	(15)	—	—	—	(335)	(335)
Dividends ($0.21 per share)	—	—	(430)	—	—	(430)
Other comprehensive income (net of tax $245 million)	—	—	—	417	—	417
Net income	—	—	2,345	—	—	2,345
Balance at September 30, 2004	2,040	$12,447	$15,732	$(236)	$(1,862)	$26,081

and dividends of $430 million (decrease in Retained Earnings). Note that the statement also includes a column devoted to accumulated other comprehensive income. In 2004, the other comprehensive income (net of tax) of $417 million increased total stockholders' equity. However, the total accumulated comprehensive amount at September 30, 2004 was a loss of $653 million. Examples of items that affect accumulated other comprehensive income are

1. Unrealized gains or losses on available-for-sale securities

2. Foreign currency translation adjustments

3. The minimum pension liability adjustment (in certain cases)

4. Unrealized gains or losses on cash flow hedges

These items are not included in the computation of net income. A careful analysis of the statement of stockholders' equity can provide investors and creditors with important information that is not available on the other financial statements.

> **CHECK YOUR UNDERSTANDING**
>
> 1. What is the purpose of the statement of stockholders' equity? Why is this statement more useful than the balance sheet?
>
> 2. What types of items affect accumulated other comprehensive income but are not included in the computation of net income?

Revisiting the Case

DISNEY OFFERS MORE THAN MAGIC TO EXECUTIVES

1. Stock options represent the right to buy the company's stock, usually at a very attractive price.

2. Stock options are considered to be dilutive securities because they have the potential to reduce (or dilute) the earnings per share for common stockholders.

3. Options on common stock vest over a five-year period from the grant date and expire 10 years after the grant date.

SUMMARY BY LEARNING OBJECTIVE

LO1 Understand how to account for dilutive securities.

Dilutive securities are instruments that are not common stock when issued but can become common stock in the future. Stock warrants, stock options, convertible bonds, and convertible preferred stock are examples of dilutive securities. The accounting for convertible bonds and convertible preferred stock was discussed in Chapter 17. When stock warrants are issued with another security, a portion of the purchase price must be allocated to the warrants; this becomes part of contributed capital in the stockholders' equity section of the balance sheet. If the warrants are exercised, this account is eliminated and common stock is issued at the exercise price. If the warrants are not exercised, this account is eliminated and a new account is established to indicate the end of the exercise period. The accounting for stock options is similar to that for warrants. An account is established in contributed capital for stock options outstanding. If the stock options are exercised, the account is eliminated and common stock is issued at the exercise price.

LO2 Understand how to account for stock options.

The intrinsic value method was the traditional approach to accounting for stock options. Under the intrinsic value method, the total amount of compensation was measured as the difference between the option price and the market price on the measurement date, which is usually the date of grant. Compensation was allocated to expense over the service period, the period during which the employee provides service and earns the stock options. The fair value method is now required to account for stock options. When using this method, the total amount of compensation is measured as the fair value of the options. Fair value is determined by an option-pricing model or some other more complex measure of fair value. Compensation is allocated to expense over the service period in a manner similar to that used in the intrinsic value approach.

LO3 Calculate the earnings per share in a simple capital structure.

Earnings per share in a simple capital structure is calculated as net income less preferred stock dividends divided by the weighted-average number of shares of common stock outstanding for the period. It is a measure of the earnings of the common stockholder and is referred to as basic EPS. EPS must be presented for the net income amount and must also be presented for other numbers on the income statement, beginning with the line for income from continuing operations.

LO4 Calculate the earnings per share in a complex capital structure.

For a complex capital structure, two earnings per share figures must be presented. Basic EPS should be calculated in the same manner as for a simple capital structure. In addition, diluted EPS must be calculated and presented. Diluted EPS is the EPS that would result if all of the dilutive securities were converted to common stock at the beginning of the period. For convertible preferred stock or convertible bonds, an amount representing the interest or dividends that would have been avoided if the securities had been converted must be added to the numerator. The denominator should be adjusted to reflect the additional number of shares that would be issued. For stock options and warrants, an amount should be added to the denominator that represents the additional number of shares that would have been issued upon exercise of the securities.

LO5 Understand the analysis issues related to earnings per share.

EPS is the most important means of analysis of company performance and is widely used by analysts and investors. Recently, companies have issued alternative measures of EPS, which they have referred to as pro forma EPS amounts. Generally, pro forma EPS calculations exclude nonrecurring expenses, losses, and restructuring charges, but each company computes the amounts differently. Attempts are underway to develop guidelines for the reporting of pro forma EPS.

LO6 Understand the cash flow presentation of earnings.

Earnings information is presented in the operating activities section of the statement of cash flows. Net income must be adjusted for many noncash items in order to determine the amount of cash flow from operations. Transactions affecting stockholders' equity are presented in the financing activities section and represent significant sources of cash to finance the company's operations. The FASB does not allow cash flow per share to be presented in the financial statements because it fears that statement users will be confused by such a presentation.

LO7 Develop a statement of stockholders' equity.

Large public companies are required by the SEC to provide a more complete picture of the changes in stockholders' equity by presenting a statement of stockholders' equity. The purpose of the statement of stockholders' equity is to present all of the items that changed the balance of each of the stockholders' equity accounts.

KEY TERMS

antidilutive securities (p. 875)
basic EPS (p. 872)
complex capital structure (p. 874)
date of grant (p. 863)
detachable warrants (p. 860)
diluted EPS (p. 874)
dilutive securities (p. 860)
earnings per incremental share (p. 878)

earnings per share (EPS) (p. 871)
exercise price (p. 860)
fair value method (p. 864)
forfeitures (p. 864)
if-converted method (p. 875)
intrinsic value method (p. 863)
measurement date (p. 863)
noncompensatory plan (p. 864)
pro forma earnings per share (p. 880)

service period (p. 863)
simple capital structure (p. 872)
stock options (p. 862)
stock warrants (p. 860)
treasury stock method (p. 876)
weighted-average number of shares outstanding (p. 872)

EXERCISES

LO1 EXERCISE 18-1 Convertible Preferred Stock

In 2006, Starr, Inc. issued 10,000 shares of $100 par value convertible preferred stock for $103 per share. One share of preferred stock can be converted into three shares of Starr's $20 par value common stock at the option of the preferred stockholder. In August 2007, all of the preferred stock was converted into common stock. The market value of the common stock at the date of the conversion was $30 per share.

Required:

1. How should the stock issue appear on the balance sheet at December 31, 2006?
2. What is the journal entry that should be recorded in August 2007 when the stock is converted?
3. What amount of gain or loss should be recorded on the conversion?

LO1 EXERCISE 18-2 Warrants

On December 31, 2007, Jason Company issued 200 of its 9 percent, $1,000 bonds at 105. Attached to each bond was one detachable stock warrant entitling the holder to purchase 10 shares of Jason's $10 par common stock at $90 per share. On December 31, 2007, the market value of the bonds, without the stock warrants, was 102, and the market value of each stock purchase warrant was $50. On January 15, 2008, 120 warrants were exercised. The remaining warrants expired on December 31, 2008.

Required:

1. What is the journal entry that should be recorded when the bonds are issued on December 31, 2007?
2. How should the bonds and the warrants appear on the balance sheet at December 31, 2007?
3. What is the journal entry that should be recorded on January 15, 2008, when the warrants are exercised? Is total stockholders' equity increased or decreased as a result of the exercise of the warrants? What is the cost of the stock purchased on January 15, 2008?
4. What entry should be recorded when the warrants expire?

LO1 EXERCISE **18-3** **Warrants**

On December 31, 2007, West Corporation issued $600,000 of 8 percent nonconvertible bonds at 102, which are due on December 31, 2017. Each $1,000 bond was issued with 25 detachable stock warrants, each of which entitled the bondholder to purchase one share of West common stock, par value $25, for $50. The bonds without the warrants would normally sell at 98. On December 31, 2007, the fair market value of West's common stock was $40 per share and the fair market value of the warrants was $2.00. On January 25, 2008, the warrants were exercised to purchase stock when the market price was $55 per share.

Required:

1. Prepare the journal entry that should be recorded when the bonds are issued on December 31, 2007.

2. How should the bonds and the warrants appear on the balance sheet at December 31, 2007?

3. Prepare the journal entry that should be recorded on January 25, 2008, when the warrants are exercised. Is total stockholders' equity increased or decreased as a result of the exercise of the warrants? What is the cost of the stock purchased on January 25, 2008?

LO2 EXERCISE **18-4** **Stock Options, Fair Value Method**

On January 1, 2006, Usalis Company granted employee options to purchase 20,000 shares of $1 par common stock. The option price was $15 per share throughout the exercise period of January 1, 2008 to January 1, 2010. In order to be eligible for the stock options, the employees must provide service for a two-year period beginning in 2006. Usalis is unsure about the proper method to account for stock options but has tentatively decided to use a fair value approach. The company has also estimated that 2,000 of the stock options will be forfeited because of employees leaving the company before they are eligible. An option-pricing model has estimated the total fair value of the options to be $360,000. During 2008, a total of 4,000 options were exercised to purchase stock.

Required:

1. Determine the amount of compensation expense that should be reported for the years 2006 and 2007 using the fair value method.

2. Record the journal entry to recognize compensation expense in 2006 and 2007.

3. Record the journal entry necessary when options are exercised in 2008.

4. What is the impact of the stock options that are forfeited? At what point should forfeitures be recorded?

LO2 EXERCISE **18-5** **Stock Options, Fair Value Method**

On January 1, 2006, Jenna Corporation granted employees options to purchase 10,000 shares of $10 par stock. The option price was $12 per share, and the options could be exercised during the period January 1, 2008, to January 1, 2010. An option-pricing model was used to determine that the fair value of the option plan was $100,000. The options were considered to be additional employee compensation for a two-year service period beginning in 2006. During 2008, 6,000 of the options were exercised. By January 1, 2010, no other options had been exercised. The market price of the stock on January 1 was as follows:

2006	2007	2008
$15	$16	$17

Required:

1. Determine the amount of compensation expense that should be reported for the years 2006 and 2007 using the fair value method.

2. How would the stock options appear on the balance sheet at December 31, 2006?

3. Record all journal entries necessary for the years 2006 to 2009.

4. When the market price of the stock increased to $16 in 2007 and $17 in 2008, how did this affect the amount of compensation expense?

LO3, 4 EXERCISE **18-6 EPS Presentation**

Sun Devil Company has disclosed the following amounts on its income statement and balance sheet for 2007:

Income Statement

Income from continuing operations before income taxes	$520,000
Income taxes	208,000
Income from continuing operations	$312,000
Discontinued operations:	
Loss on disposal of division, less tax of $18,000	(36,000)
Income before extraordinary item	$276,000
Extraordinary loss, less tax of $30,000	(76,000)
Net income	$200,000

Balance Sheet

Cumulative preferred stock, 6%, $50 par, 100,000 shares authorized, 80,000 shares outstanding	$ 4,000,000
Common stock, $5.00 par, 1,000,000 shares authorized, 600,000 shares outstanding	3,000,000
Additional paid-in capital	5,000,000
Retained earnings	3,000,000
Total stockholders' equity	$15,000,000

Required: Assume that there was no change in the stock accounts during the year. Calculate all required earnings per share amounts for 2007.

LO3, 4 EXERCISE **18-7 Weighted-Average Calculation**

The 2007 balance sheet and other information for Hoops Galore revealed the following information:

Common stock, $10 par, 50,000 shares issued and outstanding as of January 1, 2007

Preferred stock, $100 par, 6%, cumulative, 1,000 shares issued and outstanding as of January 1, 2007, and December 31, 2007

Stock transactions during 2007 consisted of the following:

March 1: Issued 10,000 shares of common stock for cash

April 1: Purchased 2,000 shares of common stock as treasury stock

August 1: Resold 1,000 shares of treasury stock for cash

September 1: Declared and issued a 50 percent stock dividend on common stock

Required:

1. Does Hoops Galore have a simple or a complex capital structure? Why?

2. Calculate the weighted-average number of shares of stock outstanding that should be used to calculate EPS for the 2007 income statement.

LO4 EXERCISE **18-8 EPS with Convertible Bonds**

Keys Company had net income of $100,000 for the year ended December 31, 2007. The company had 10,000 shares of common stock outstanding at all times during the year. On January 1, 2007, the company issued 10-year convertible bonds with a face value of $200,000 at 105. Each $1,000 bond can be converted to 50 shares of common stock. The bonds pay interest annually at 8 percent. The company uses the straight-line method of amortization and has a 40 percent tax rate.

Required:

1. Calculate the required EPS figures for 2007.

2. Calculate the required EPS figures for 2007 assuming that the convertible bonds were issued on July 1, 2007, instead of January 1, 2007.

LO4 **EXERCISE 18-9 EPS for Convertible Bonds with Changing Conversion Rate**

Tag Company had net income of $200,000 for the year ended December 31, 2007. The company had 20,000 shares of common stock outstanding at all times during the year. On January 1, 2007, the company issued 10-year convertible bonds with a face value of $200,000 at 105. For the first two years, each $1,000 bond can be converted to 25 shares of common stock. After that time, the bonds can be converted to 30 shares of common stock. The bonds pay interest annually at 8 percent. The company uses the straight-line method of amortization and has a 40 percent tax rate.

Required:

1. Calculate the required EPS figures for 2007.

2. Calculate the required EPS figures for 2007 assuming that the convertible bonds were issued on July 1, 2007, instead of January 1, 2007.

LO4 **EXERCISE 18-10 EPS with Stock Options**

Keys Company had net income of $100,000 for the year ended December 31, 2007. The company had 10,000 shares of common stock outstanding at all times during the year. On January 1, 2007, the company issued 10,000 stock options. Each option can be used to purchase one share of common stock at $10 per share. The average market price of the common stock during 2007 was $20 per share, and the closing price at December 31, 2007, was $25 per share.

Required:

1. Calculate the required EPS figures for 2007.

2. Calculate the required EPS figures for 2007 assuming that the options were issued on April 1, 2007. (Assume that the average market price of the common stock was $20 and the closing price was $25.)

3. Calculate the required EPS figures for 2007, assuming that the average market price of the common stock was $8 per share and the closing price was $9.

LO1 **EXERCISE 18-11 Stock Warrants**

On June 1, 2007, Walton Company issued $54,000 of 7 percent, six-year term bonds for $56,656. Other information relating to the bonds is as follows:

A. Each $1,000 bond has five detachable warrants. Each warrant entitles the investor to purchase one share of $2 par value common stock for $30.

B. Immediately after the issuance, the stock was selling for $37 per share, the bonds were quoted at 101, and the warrants were selling for $15.20 each.

Required:

1. How much will Walton record in the stockholders' equity section of its balance sheet for the warrants?

2. What are the three possibilities for the disposition of the stock warrants by the party holding the warrants?

LO1 **EXERCISE 18-12 Stock Warrants**

On July 30, 2007, Roberts Company issued $120,000 of 8 percent, four-year term bonds to Kirkland Company for $128,961. Each $1,000 bond has four detachable warrants attached.

A. Each warrant entitles the investor to purchase one share of $3 par value common stock for $40.

B. Immediately after the issuance, the bonds were quoted at 94⅔, the stock was selling for $84 per share, and the warrants were selling for $30 each.

Required:

1. Prepare the journal entry to record the exercise of the warrants.

2. What accounting entries must be made if the warrants lapse before they are exercised?

LO3 **EXERCISE 18-13 Basic EPS Presentation**

Venus Board Shorts reported the following information about its stock at the end of December 31, 2007:

Preferred stock, $2 par, 5%, cumulative, 300,000 shares authorized, 120,000 shares outstanding	$240,000
Common stock, $1 par, 500,000 shares authorized, 240,000 shares outstanding	240,000

Amounts from Venus Board Shorts's income statement for 2007 were as follows:

Income from continuing operations before taxes	$680,000
Income tax expense	204,000
Income from continuing operations	$476,000
Extraordinary gain, less tax of $25,000	80,000
Net income	$556,000

The only stock issued during 2007 was 80,000 shares of common stock on June 30. No dividends were declared during 2007.

Required:

1. Calculate all required earnings per share amounts for 2007.

2. Are dividends on cumulative preferred stock deducted from the numerator even if they are not declared? If so, why?

LO4 **EXERCISE 18-14 EPS with Convertible Bonds**

Undersold Company reported net income of $44,000 for 2007. The company has 10,000 shares of common stock and no preferred stock. During 2006, the company issued $400,000 of 8 percent convertible bonds at face value. Each $1,000 bond can be converted into 24 shares of common stock. No bonds were converted during the year. The company's tax rate is 30 percent. No additional stock was issued during 2007.

Required:

1. Calculate basic EPS.

2. Calculate diluted EPS.

3. How will the calculations of EPS differ if the convertible bonds are antidilutive?

LO4, 5 **EXERCISE 18-15 EPS and Analysis Issues**

Eminem, Inc. had 50,000 shares of $.50 par value common stock and 10,000 shares of $1 par value, 8 percent, convertible preferred stock outstanding during 2007. Each share of preferred stock can be converted into two shares of common stock. No preferred shares were converted during the year. The company's tax rate is 30 percent. The following partial income statement was drafted by the corporate accounting department and provided to the CFO for the annual earnings announcement:

Income from continuing operations before taxes	$221,000
Income tax expense	66,000
Income from continuing operations	$155,000
Discontinued operations:	
Loss on disposal of division, less tax of $11,000	(31,000)
Income before extraordinary loss	$124,000
Extraordinary loss, less tax of $8,000	(18,000)
Net income	$106,000

Required:

1. Calculate the pro forma EPS amount(s) that will probably be used by the CFO for the annual earnings announcement.

2. Calculate the EPS amounts that are required by GAAP.

3. Will the pro forma EPS clearly present the company's performance for the year? What changes related to pro forma announcements are being made by the SEC? Explain.

LO7 EXERCISE 18-16 **Statement of Stockholders' Equity**

The following account balances appeared in RM, Inc.'s adjusted trial balance at December 31, 2007 and 2006:

	12/31/07	12/31/06
Common Stock, $1 par, 80,000 shares authorized	$ 40,000	$ 32,000
Paid-in Capital in Excess of Par—Common	730,000	620,000
Unrealized Gain/(Loss) on Cash Flow Hedges	(12,000)	5,000
Minimum Pension Liability Adjustment—(debit)/credit	(15,000)	(31,000)
Foreign Currency Translation Adjustments—(debit)/credit	7,000	4,000
Preferred Stock, 6%, cumulative	60,000	58,000
Retained Earnings	140,000	128,000
Dividends Payable	24,000	29,000
Paid-in Capital in Excess of Par—Preferred	220,000	184,000
Treasury Stock (at cost)	24,000	14,000

No tax effects are included in the comprehensive income account balances. The company's income tax rate is 30 percent. During the year, treasury stock was acquired, and both preferred and common stock were issued for cash. Net income for 2007 was $135,000.

Required:

1. Prepare a statement of stockholders' equity for RM, Inc. for the year ended December 31, 2007.

2. What is the purpose of the statement of stockholders' equity?

LO6 EXERCISE 18-17 **Cash Flows Related to Stockholders' Equity**

The following account balances appeared in Daboul, Inc.'s adjusted trial balance at December 31, 2007 and 2006:

	12/31/07	12/31/06
Common Stock, $1 par, 80,000 shares authorized	$ 30,000	$ 22,000
Paid-in Capital in Excess of Par—Common	256,000	216,000
Unrealized Gain/(Loss) on Cash Flow Hedges	(12,000)	5,000
Preferred Stock, 6%, cumulative	40,000	34,000
Retained Earnings	87,000	83,000
Dividends Payable	14,000	19,000
Paid-in Capital from Treasury Stock	5,400	0
Paid-in Capital in Excess of Par—Preferred	157,000	125,000
Treasury Stock (at cost)	16,000	7,000

The company's income tax rate is 30 percent. During the year, treasury stock with an original cost of $6,000 was sold, and additional treasury shares were acquired. Both preferred and common stock were issued for cash. Net income for 2007 was $65,000.

Required:

1. Show how the effects of these items will be reflected in the financing activities section of the statement of cash flows for 2007.

2. Why is cash flow per share not reported? Justify your answer.

LO6   **EXERCISE 18-18   Cash Flow Effects of Stockholders' Equity**

OutKast Music Company began 2007 with 16,000 shares of $.50 par value common stock outstanding, no shares of treasury stock, $23,000 of retained earnings, $14,000 of dividends payable, and total stockholders' equity of $126,000. The following transactions occurred during 2007:

Jan. 16   Paid cash dividends declared during previous year.
Mar. 1   Sold 8,000 common shares for $45,000.
May 31   Declared a 2-for-1 stock split.
July 1   Issued a 10 percent stock dividend.
Oct. 31   Repurchased 5,000 shares on the open market for $25,000.
Dec. 1   Resold 3,000 of the treasury shares for $21,000.
       1   Declared cash dividends of $.50 per share to shareholders of record on December 12.
      31   Net income for the year was $62,000.

Required:

1. Prepare the financing activities section of the statement of cash flows for 2007.

2. Calculate the number that will be used in the statement of cash flows when the dividends declared on December 1 are paid.

3. Why do stock splits and stock dividends not appear in the financing activities section of the statement of cash flows?

LO2, 6   **EXERCISE 18-19   Stock Options and Cash Flows**

On January 1, 2007, Selectric Company granted its employees the right to purchase 20,000 shares of $1 par common stock at $28 per share through December 31, 2012. To be eligible for the plan, employees must remain employed through 2008. The market price of the common stock at January 1, 2007, was $38 per share. The Black-Scholes option-pricing model was applied, and the fair value of the options was determined to be $120,000. On January 1, 2009, when the market value of the stock was $45 per share, the employees exercised the options, and common stock was issued.

Required:

1. Record annual compensation expense as it relates to the issuance of the options for 2007 and 2008, using the intrinsic value method.

2. Record the exercise of the options on January 1, 2009.

3. Show the effects of the stock options on the statement of cash flows for the years ended December 31, 2007, 2008, and 2009, assuming that the indirect method is used.

LO6, 7   **EXERCISE 18-20   Statement of Stockholders' Equity and Cash Flows**

The following account balances appeared in Rosenberg, Inc.'s adjusted trial balance at December 31, 2006:

Dividends Payable	$ 13,000
Common Stock, $1 par, 80,000 shares authorized	16,000
Unrealized Gain/(Loss) on Available-for-Sale Investments	(2,000)
Paid-in Capital in Excess of Par—Preferred	88,000
Treasury Stock (500 shares at cost)	3,000
Paid-in Capital in Excess of Par—Common	136,000
Preferred Stock, $3 par value, 6%	22,000
Retained Earnings	45,000

The following are transactions from Rosenberg, Inc.'s accounting records that occurred during 2007:

A. The company declared a 2-for-1 common stock split.

B. One thousand preferred shares were sold to investors for $16 each.

C. Five thousand common shares were sold to investors for $8 each. This transaction occurred after the common stock split in item A.

D. The company purchased 400 additional shares of its own stock at the same price it had paid for those already reacquired.

E. Net income reported on Rosenberg, Inc.'s income statement was $44,000 for the year ended December 31, 2007. (The company's tax rate is 30 percent.)

F. An adjustment was made to increase the value of the available-for-sale investments by $6,000.

Required:

1. Prepare a statement of stockholders' equity for the year ended December 31, 2007.

2. What is the difference between what is reported in the stockholders' equity section of the balance sheet and what is reported in the statement of stockholders' equity?

PROBLEMS

LO3, 4 **PROBLEM 18-1** **EPS for Complex Capital Structure**

Assume the following information concerning Tulley Company for 2007:

A. Net income: $200,000.

B. Common stock, $5 par, 40,000 shares issued and outstanding as of January 1, 2007

C. Two stock transactions occurred during 2007. On March 1, 20,000 shares were issued for cash. On July 1, 24,000 shares were issued for cash.

D. Tulley Company has issued 10 convertible bonds with a $1,000 face amount. Each bond is convertible into 100 shares of common stock at the present date and for the next 10 years. Tully's interest expense for 2007 was $700. No bonds were converted during the year.

E. On April 1, 2007, stock options were issued to purchase 1,000 shares of common stock at $15 per share. None of the options were exercised during 2007.

F. Warrants to purchase common stock, Series B: 800 warrants to purchase shares at $45 per share. It takes one warrant to buy one share of stock. As of December 31, no warrants had been exercised.

G. Income tax rate: 40 percent.

H. Average market price per share of common stock during the entire year was $30. Closing market price per share at year end was $25.

Required: Determine basic and diluted earnings per share for 2007.

Analyze: If there were preferred shares outstanding and preferred stock dividends had been declared for the year, how would basic EPS be affected?

LO2 **PROBLEM 18-2** **Stock Options**

On November 1, 2004, Colombo Corporation adopted a stock option plan that granted options to key executives to purchase 30,000 shares of the company's $10 par value stock. The options were granted on January 1, 2006, and were exercisable during the years 2006 to 2008, if the grantee was still an employee; the options expire at the end of that time period. The market price of the stock on January 1, 2006, was $45. The service period is two years beginning in 2006. The option price was set at $40, and the fair value option-pricing model determined the total compensation expense to be $450,000.

During 2008, all remaining options were exercised when the market value was $67.

Required:

1. Calculate the amount of compensation expense that should be recorded in each of the years using the fair value method.

2. Record all necessary journal entries for 2006 to 2008, assuming that the company uses the fair value method.

Analyze: If the market price of the stock had been $32 in 2008 (instead of $67), what situation would exist?

LO2, 4, 5   **PROBLEM 18-3   Note Presentation of Earnings and Stock Options**

The following disclosures are taken from the notes of **Intel Corporation** for the year ended December 25, 2004, concerning stock options:

Intel

Note 2: Accounting Policies

The company has employee equity incentive plans, which are described more fully in Note 11: Employee Equity Incentive Plans. Intel accounts for its equity incentive plans under the intrinsic value recognition and measurement principles of APB Opinion No. 25, Accounting for Stock Issued to Employees, and related interpretations. The exercise price of options is equal to the market price of Intel common stock (defined as the average of the high and low trading prices reported by the NASDAQ Stock Market) on the date of grant. Accordingly, no stock-based compensation, other than acquisition-related compensation, is recognized in net income. The following table illustrates the effect on net income and earnings per share as if the company had applied the fair value recognition provisions of *Statement of Financial Accounting Standards (SFAS) No. 123,* Accounting for Stock-Based Compensation, as amended, to options granted under the stock option plans and rights to acquire stock granted under the company's Stock Participation Plan, collectively called options. For purposes of this pro-forma disclosure, the value of the options is estimated using a Black–Scholes option pricing model and amortized ratably to expense over the options vesting periods. Because the estimated value is determined as of the date of grant, the actual value ultimately realized by the employee may be significantly different.

(In Millions—Except Per Share Amounts)	2004	2003	2002
Net income, as reported	$ 7,516	$ 5,641	$ 3,117
Less: Total stock-based employee compensation expense determined under the fair value method for all awards, net of tax	1,271	991	1,170
Pro-forma net income	$ 6,245	$ 4,650	$ 1,947
Reported basic earnings per common share	$ 1.17	$ 0.86	$ 0.47
Pro-forma basic earnings per common share	$ 0.98	$ 0.71	$ 0.29
Reported diluted earnings per common share	$ 1.16	$ 0.85	$ 0.46
Pro-forma diluted earnings per common share	$ 0.97	$ 0.71	$ 0.29

Note 11: Employee Stock Benefit Plans

(Shares in Millions)	Shares Available for Grant	Number of Shares	Weighted-Average Exercise Price
December 27, 2003	526.9	850.1	$25.54
Grants	(114.7)	114.7	$26.23
Exercises	—	(48.4)	$10.89
Cancellations	11.5	(32.5)	$30.00
Expiration of 1984 Stock Option Plan	(143.2)	—	—
Cancellation of 1997 Stock Option Plan	(300.1)	—	—
Adoption of 2004 Equity Incentive Plan	240.0	—	—
December 25, 2004	220.4	883.9	$26.26
Options exercisable at:			
December 28, 2002		274.0	$16.57
December 27, 2003		327.5	$20.53
December 25, 2004		397.5	$23.83

Required:

1. What is the number of stock options outstanding at the end of the year? At what price were the options exercisable?

2. What accounting method was used to account for the stock options? Explain why the use of the fair value method would have reduced EPS.

Analyze: What impact did the stock options have on net income and EPS for the company?

Research: Locate the current-year annual report for Intel. How many options are exercisable at year end?

LO3, 4 PROBLEM 18-4 **EPS with Convertible Preferred Stock**

Nat Company reported net income of $100,000 for the year ended December 31, 2007. The company had 10,000 shares of common stock outstanding at all times during the year. On January 1, 2007, the company issued 10,000 shares of $10 par, 8 percent preferred stock. No preferred stock dividends were declared or paid during 2007.

Required:

1. Assume that the preferred stock is not convertible and is noncumulative. Calculate EPS for the year 2007.

2. Assume that the preferred stock is not convertible and is cumulative. Calculate EPS for the year 2007.

3. Assume that the preferred stock is cumulative and convertible into common stock. Each share of preferred stock can be converted into one share of common stock. Calculate EPS for the year 2007.

4. Assume that the preferred stock is cumulative and convertible into common stock. During 2007, every two shares of preferred stock could be converted into one share of stock. Calculate EPS for the year 2007.

Analyze: Assume that Rand Company, a competitor of Nat, reported EPS of $12. Compare this amount to the amount computed in question 1. What does this comparison tell you?

LO3, 4, 5 PROBLEM 18-5 **Note Presentations of AOL Time Warner**

Time Warner Inc. is a major media and entertainment industry giant and a competitor of Walt Disney Company. Disclosures from the company's notes that accompany the financial statements for the year ended December 31, 2004, appear on the facing page.

Required:

1. How did the company calculate basic and diluted earnings per share? What were the numerator and the denominator in each case?

2. What types of dilutive securities did the company have during 2004? What dilutive securities were present in 2002? How did they affect EPS?

3. What does the note mean when it refers to antidilutive securities? How were the antidilutive securities treated when calculating EPS?

Analyze: By what percentage did the average number of common shares outstanding (diluted) change between 2003 and 2004?

LO4 PROBLEM 18-6 **Earnings per Share**

Consider the following information regarding Schon Corporation for the year 2007:

Common Stock

January 1, 2007	360,000 shares outstanding
July 1, 2007	Sold 200,000 additional shares
July 8, 2007	Declared and issued a 50 percent stock dividend
September 1, 2007	Sold 240,000 additional shares
October 1, 2007	Purchased 60,000 shares on the open market to be held as treasury shares

Time Warner Inc.

Excerpt from Consolidated Statement of Operations

	Years Ended December 31 (millions, except per share amounts)		
	2004	**2003**	**2002**
Net income (loss)	$ 3,364	$ 2,639	$(97,217)
Basic net income (loss) per common share	$ 0.74	$ 0.59	$ (21.82)
Average basic common shares	4,560.2	4,506.0	4,454.9
Diluted net income (loss) per common share	$ 0.72	$ 0.57	$ (21.82)
Average diluted common shares	4,694.7	4,623.7	4,454.9

Income (Loss) per Common Share

Income (Loss) Per Common Share Before Discontinued Operations and Cumulative Effect of Accounting Change

Set forth below is a reconciliation of basic and diluted income (loss) per common share before discontinued operations and cumulative effect of accounting change:

	Years Ended December 31		
	2004	**2003**	**2002**[a]
			(restated)
	(millions, except per share amounts)		
Income (loss) before discontinued operations and cumulative effect of accounting change—basic and diluted	$ 3,209	$ 3,146	$(41,970)
Average number of common shares outstanding— basic	4,560.2	4,506.0	4,454.9
Dilutive effect of stock options and restricted stock	57.4	55.2	—
Dilutive effect of mandatorily convertible preferred stock	77.1	62.5	—
Average number of common shares outstanding— diluted	4,694.7	4,623.7	4,454.9
Income (loss) per common share before discontinued operations and cumulative effect of accounting change:			
Basic	$ 0.70	$ 0.70	$ (9.42)
Diluted	$ 0.68	$ 0.68	$ (9.42)

---

[a]2002 basic and diluted loss per common share are the same because the effect of Time Warner's stock options and convertible debt was antidilutive.

Schon Corporation has the following securities and options outstanding throughout the entire year:

Preferred Stock

Nonconvertible cumulative preferred stock, 8%, $100 par, issued at par	$200,000
Convertible cumulative preferred stock, 6%, $100 par, issued at $105, convertible into 20,000 shares of common stock	400,000
Paid-in capital in excess of par—preferred	20,000

Bonds

$1,000 convertible bonds, 6%, issued at par, convertible into 25,000 shares of common stock	$500,000

All preferred stock dividends are one year in arrears. Additional information:

Stock options, exercisable for	120,000 shares
Option price	$25 per share
Average market price	$32
Year-end market price	$36

Net income for the year is $640,000. The company's tax rate is 40 percent. No actual conversions occurred, and no options were exercised during 2007.

Required:

1. Calculate Schon's basic earnings per share.
2. Calculate Schon's diluted earnings per share.
3. For each item that was included in diluted earnings per share, explain the reason for its inclusion.

Analyze: If no preferred stock were involved, calculate Schon's basic earnings per share.

Communicate: Assume that you are the CFO for Schon Corporation. You are interviewing a CPA for a position in the company, and you ask the applicant to describe the financial statement disclosures necessary for EPS, other than the EPS numbers themselves. What answer would be correct?

LO1 PROBLEM 18-7 **Warrants, Convertible Bonds**

On January 1, 2007, Gruen Corporation has the following bonds outstanding:

> 500, 5 percent, semiannual, $1,000 par bonds, each with a detachable stock warrant. Each warrant authorizes the holder to purchase 10 shares of $1 par common stock at $8 per share.

> 400, 5 percent, semiannual, $1,000 par value convertible bonds; each bond is convertible into 50 shares of common stock.

On July 2, 2007, one-quarter of the bond warrants are exercised and one-half of the convertible bonds are converted to common stock. The company already has properly accrued its semiannual interest and amortization and paid the interest that was due on July 1.

Review of the company's ledger on July 1 shows the following information relating to the bonds:

Bonds with Detachable Warrants

Bonds Payable	$500,000
Unamortized Premium on Bonds	20,000
Unamortized Bond Issue Cost	30,000
Paid-in Capital from Stock Warrants	9,000

Convertible Bonds

Bonds Payable	$400,000
Unamortized Premium on Bonds	30,000
Unamortized Bond Issue Cost	25,000

Required:

1. Prepare the journal entry to record the exercise of the warrants.
2. Prepare the journal entry to record the conversion of the bonds.
3. How do detachable warrants and convertible bonds differ with respect to the account-ing treatment? How are they similar? What role does the market value at the day of exercise or conversion play?

Communicate: Discuss how bond conversions should be treated under international accounting standards.

Analyze: What effect did (a) the exercise of warrants and (b) the bond conversion have on the financial statements?

LO3, 4   **PROBLEM 18-8   Weighted-Average Calculation**

The following transactions occurred with respect to Alt Corporation's common stock:

Common stock outstanding on January 1, 2007	700,000 shares
February 1, 2007, additional shares were sold	180,000 shares
March 1, 2007, options were exercised	20,000 shares
July 1, 2007, additional shares were sold	200,000 shares
August 1, 2007, a 10 percent stock dividend was declared	
September 1, 2007, additional shares were sold	240,000 shares
October 1, 2007, the company's stock split 2 for 1	
November 1, 2007, shares were purchased on the open market	120,000 shares

Required:

1. Calculate the weighted-average shares outstanding for 2007.
2. Calculate the number of shares outstanding at 12/31/07.

Analyze: If income for the year was $460,000, calculate basic EPS.

LO3, 5   **PROBLEM 18-9   Earnings per Share, Analysis**

Adams Corporation's statement of changes in stockholders' equity revealed the following transactions that affected stockholders' equity during 2007. The company has no preferred shares.

Feb.	1	40,000 shares were sold.
Mar.	1	A 10 percent stock dividend was issued.
July	1	46,000 additional shares were sold.
Aug.	1	20,000 shares were repurchased on the open market.
Nov.	1	The company's stock split 2 for 1.
Dec.	1	40,000 of the treasury shares were resold.
	31	Income for the year was $250,000.
	31	Total cash dividends declared were $200,000, or $.50 per share to all shareholders of record on December 2.

Required:

1. Calculate the total number of shares that Adams Corporation had outstanding on December 31, 2007.
2. Calculate the total number of shares that Adams Corporation had outstanding on January 1, 2007.

3. Explain how each transaction affects (a) the earnings per share of this company and (b) the total earnings of a particular stockholder who held stock during the entire year 2007, did not purchase additional shares, and did not sell any shares.

Analyze: Explain how each transaction affects the proportional ownership of a stockholder who held stock in Adams Corporation during the entire year 2007 and did not purchase or sell any shares.

LO7   **PROBLEM 18-10   Retained Earnings**

The following selected information relates to Neu Corporation's stockholders' equity on December 31, 2007:

Common Stock, 500,000 shares, $1 par	$ 500,000
Paid-in Capital in Excess of Par—Common	1,500,000
Preferred Stock, 6%, cumulative	200,000
Retained Earnings	500,000
Treasury Stock (at cost)	400,000

The following represent transactions that occurred during 2008 and may or may not have affected Neu Corporation's retained earnings.

Feb. 1   Treasury stock costing $100,000 was sold for $95,000.

15   An error in counting the prior-year ending inventory was discovered. The error resulted in overstated ending inventory at December 31, 2007, of $30,000.

Apr. 1   Treasury stock costing $250,000 was sold for $280,000.

Oct. 30   A 30 percent stock dividend was declared and issued; the market value on that date was $6.20 per share.

Dec 2   Cash dividends of $100,000 were declared.

Preferred stock dividends were one year in arrears.

Effective January 1, the company changed its accounting for depreciable property, plant, and equipment from the double-declining-balance method of depreciation to the straight-line method. The pretax difference between the two depreciation methods for the current year was $20,000 and was included in the calculation of the current year's net income.

The average corporate tax rate is 40 percent. Neu Corporation's net income for the year was $190,000.

Required:

1. Calculate Neu Corporation's retained earnings balance at December 31, 2008; separately list each transaction that affected retained earnings and include an appropriate reference.

2. If a particular transaction does not affect retained earnings, indicate what account and financial statement would instead be affected by the transaction.

Analyze: How does the purchase of treasury stock provide a quick improvement in earnings per share?

LO3, 4, 5   **PROBLEM 18-11   Earnings per Share**

Consider the partial income statement for Dunn Company for the year 2007 that appears at the top of the facing page.

Required: Show the detailed earnings per share presentation that would appear on Dunn Company's income statement for the year ended 12/31/07. Assume that Dunn Company has no equity contracts or potentially dilutive securities and that it had 20,000 weighted-average shares outstanding.

Analyze: Suppose that Dunn Company had potentially dilutive securities that are dilutive for some income statement line items and antidilutive for others. Which income statement

Income from operations		$150,000
Other income:		
Interest expense	$(10,000)	
Interest revenue	5,000	
Gain on disposal of equipment	7,000	2,000
Income from continuing operations (before tax)		$152,000
Income taxes		(60,800)
Income from continuing operations		$ 91,200
Discontinued operation:		
Loss on discontinued operations		(12,000)
Extraordinary gain (net of tax obligation of $4,000)		6,000
Net income		$ 85,200

line items should be used to decide whether the effect of these securities should be included or excluded?

LO3, 4, 5   **PROBLEM 18-12   Earnings per Share, Analysis**

Morgan Company had net income of $350,000 for the year ended December 31, 2007. The company had 50,000 shares of common stock outstanding at all times during the year. Also outstanding on that date were 2,000 shares of 8 percent cumulative convertible preferred stock, $100 par, that were issued at 105. Each two shares of preferred stock can be converted into three shares of common stock. No other potentially dilutive securities were outstanding.

Required:

1. Calculate earnings per share for 2007.

2. Calculate earnings per share for 2007, assuming that half of the preferred stock shares were converted at the beginning of the year.

Analyze: Compare the two sets of results and explain any differences and similarities.

LO5, 6   **PROBLEM 18-13   Cash Flows Related to Stockholders' Equity**

Axel Company included the following account on the balance sheet for the year ended December 31, 2007:

	2007	2006
Dividend Payable	$40,000	$20,000

The financing activities section of the statement of cash flows included the following amounts:

	2007
Financing Activities:	
Repurchases of stock	($15,000)
Exercise of stock options	5,000
Dividends	(80,000)

Additional information:

A. During 2006, 500 options had been issued, allowing common stock with a $2 par value to be purchased at an exercise price of $10 per share. The market price on the date of grant was $10 per share. All options were exercised in 2007.

B. The company's common stock has a par value of $2 per share, had been issued in 2005 for $10, and had a market value of $15 per share when it was repurchased and retired.

Required:

1. Calculate the dollar amount of dividends declared during 2007.

2. Prepare the journal entry that was made at the time the stock options were exercised. Assume that the company uses the fair value method.

3. Prepare the journal entry made to repurchase the stock.

Analyze: What was the net cash effect of questions 1 through 3?

CASES

LO4, 5   **CRITICAL THINKING CASE 18-1   Earnings per Share** (CPA adapted)

Columbine Company's 10-year convertible bonds were issued and dated October 1, 2007. Each $1,000 bond is convertible, at the holder's option, into 20 shares of Columbine's common stock. Columbine, a public company, had a net loss for the year. There was no change in the number of shares outstanding during the year.

Required:

1. Describe and distinguish between basic and diluted earnings per share. Include in your discussion the meaning of dilutive securities.

2. Determine whether to include the convertible bonds in computing 2007 diluted earnings per share.

LO1   **CRITICAL THINKING CASE 18-2   Convertible Securities**

A recent article in the business press contained the following information:

> More and more companies seem to be converting to convertible bonds and preferred stock.
>
> **Nortel Networks Corp.** announced its plans to sell $1 billion of convertible senior notes, while **Lucent Technologies** enjoyed a rousing reception for its $1.9 billion convertible preferred shares.[26]

Required:

1. What are convertible bonds, and what are some reasons why they may be gaining in popularity?

2. How do convertible bonds and convertible preferred stock affect the earnings per share calculation?

3. What is the difference between convertible bonds and convertible preferred stock? Are they treated differently on the income statement? Are they treated differently when calculating EPS?

LO5   **ETHICS CASE 18-3   Pro Forma Earnings**

 ETHICS

The following report concerned the upcoming 2001 first-quarter earnings announcement of **Amazon.com**.

> Amazon.com Inc. said Monday it will report somewhat better-than-expected first-quarter results. The online retailing bellwether said it expects revenue of $695 million, and a pro forma loss per share of 22 cents. Analysts surveyed by earnings tracker First Call had forecast revenue of $669.6 million and a pro forma loss of 30 cents a share in the period ended March 31. The news sent shares of Amazon sharply higher in Monday trading, helping to lift the tech-heavy Nasdaq

---

26 Amanda Lang, "Convertibles Court Market," *CNN Money,* August 14, 2001, available at: **http://money.cnn.com/2001/08/14/investing/v_bonds/index.htm.** Accessed June 29, 2004.

composite index. Pro forma results exclude stock-based compensation costs, amortization of goodwill and other intangibles and any restructuring charges, and is the number followed by analysts.

Although it is the largest online retailer, the company has never shown a profit. Jeff Bezos, the company's chief executive, told CNNfn in January that he expects Amazon to post an operating profit by the end of this year. When it reported fourth-quarter results in January, Amazon disclosed a broad restructuring plan under which it laid off roughly 15 percent of its work force and consolidated its distribution and customer service center network. Including an estimated $150 million charge against earnings related to the restructuring, Amazon said it expects to post a net loss below $255 million.[27]

Required:

1. What is the meaning of pro forma earnings as used by Amazon.com?

2. In your opinion, was the use of pro forma earnings in the company's announcement misleading? Do you believe the company acted ethically?

3. Find the company's results for the year 2001. Did Bezos's expectation of an operating profit by year end turn out to be true?

LO2, 5   **CRITICAL THINKING CASE 18-4   Impact of Stock Options**

The following news report appeared on the CNN/Money website concerning the accounting for stock options by technology companies. The news report and other similar reports led to the issuance of *SFAS 123* as revised in 2004.

As U.S. technology companies reported soaring growth and record profits in recent years, the complex accounting methods they used made for a wide disparity between what they actually earned and what they highlighted in their reports, a study from Merrill Lynch shows. The report, by Merrill analysts Gary Schieneman and Steven Milunovich, shows that if non-operating items and one-time charges and credits as well as imputing stock option expenses had been included, the reported earnings of the 37 leading technology companies it studied would have been an average of 25 percent lower in 2000.

In the report, which measures the performance of leading tech outfits across all sectors from 1997 through 2000, the analysts point out that all of them had significant stock option plans and adopted the "intrinsic value" approach to accounting for the options. Under that approach, no compensation expense is reported for options, which results in an overstatement of profits, the report says. Had these companies used the "fair value" approach—paying most of their compensation in cash and reporting the entire amount as an expense as their non-U.S. counterparts are required to do—their reported earnings would have been decreased by 60 percent, the report shows.

"The press writes about questionable practices such as excluding option expense from the income statement and the use of pro forma earnings, but few calculate the earnings impact," Milunovich writes in the report.[28]

Required:

1. Explain the accounting for stock options under the intrinsic value and fair value methods.

2. Why did the intrinsic value method lead to the reporting of no compensation expense by technology companies?

---

27 "Amazon to beat 1Q Targets," *CNN Money,* April 9, 2001, available at: **http://money.cnn.com/2001/04/09/technology/amazon/index.htm.** Accessed June 29, 2004.

28 "Tech Earnings Questioned," *CNN Money,* June 19, 2001, available at: **http://money.cnn.com/2001/06/19/technology tech_earnings/index.htm.** Accessed June 29, 2004.

LO5   ANALYSIS CASE **18-5**   **Capital Structure**

The following shows Bernd Company's calculations of earnings per share. Bernd Company had no antidilutive securities outstanding during the year.

Basic EPS:
$$\frac{\$208,000 - \$8,000}{40,000} = \$5.00 \text{ per share}$$

Diluted EPS:
$$\frac{\$200,000 - \$8,000 + \$8,000 + \$10,000\,(1 - 0.4)}{40,000 + 3,000^* + 2,000 + 5,000} = \$4.28 \text{ per share}$$

*Supportive calculation:

9,000 shares $\times$ \$10.00 = \$90,000 (\$90,000 $\div$ \$15 = 6,000 shares)

− 6,000 shares assumed repurchased

= 3,000 incremental shares issued

Required: Based on the information given, describe the company's capital structure. Include as much detail as can reasonably be deduced.

LO2   RESEARCH CASE **18-6**   **Stock Options**

On August 6, 2002, **General Motors Corporation** announced that on January 1, 2003, it would begin expensing the value of any newly granted stock options. Previously, the company had applied the intrinsic value method, as did most companies that granted stock options.

Required:

1. What is the method that General Motors Corporation adopted as of January 1, 2003, called?

2. Retrieve the company's 10-Q as of October 31, 2002, and investigate what effect the adoption of this method was expected to have on earnings and earnings per share amounts.

3. How did this decision affect the company's financial statements for 2003 and 2004?

4. Refer to the company's 10-Q as of October 31, 2002, and investigate whether GM's stock options were dilutive. State any reasons given by GM for not including stock options in the EPS calculations.

LO5   ANALYSIS CASE **18-7**   **Earnings per Share**

Laser International produces semiconductors. The company has 15,000 shares of $40 par value 8 percent cumulative preferred stock issued and outstanding. Laser International also has 400,000 shares of $1 par value common stock issued and outstanding, 300,000 of which were outstanding at the beginning of the year and 100,000 of which were issued on September 1. In addition, Laser International also issued at par 250, $1,000 par value, 9 percent convertible bonds; each bond is convertible into 50 shares of common stock. The bonds have been outstanding the entire year. Laser has a 34 percent tax rate.

The income statement of Laser International showed the following information on December 31, 2007:

Income before income taxes	$1,593,200
Income tax expense (34% tax rate)	541,688
Income before extraordinary gain	$1,051,512
Extraordinary gain (net of taxes)	532,975
Net income	$1,584,487

Required: Calculate earnings per share for Laser International and prepare the earnings per share information that Laser would present in its income statement.

ON THE WEB

The following exercises, activities, and problems are available on the *Intermediate Accounting* website. Use these resources to reinforce your understanding of the topics presented in this chapter.

- CPA-Adapted Simulations
- Interpreting the Accounting Standards
- Extending the Global Focus
- Extending the Ethics Discussion
- Mastering the Spreadsheet
- Career Snapshots

- Annual Report Project
- ACE Practice Tests
- Flashcards
- Glossary
- Check Figures for Text Problems
- PowerPoint Presentations

SOLUTIONS: CHECK YOUR UNDERSTANDING

Accounting for Dilutive Securities (p. 871)

1. Convertible bonds are a liability at the time of issuance but carry a provision that allows the bondholder to convert the bonds into common stock.

2. The issue price should be allocated to the two instruments according to the proportionate fair market values of the two instruments as of the issue date.

3. Stock option plans must specify the number of shares of stock that may be purchased by the employee, the option price or exercise price that the employee must pay, and the time period over which the employee is allowed to purchase the stock.

4. Under the fair value method, stock option compensation should be measured as the fair value of the options on the date of grant.

Earnings per Share (p. 879)

1. Basic earnings per share is calculated by dividing net income minus preferred stock dividends by the weighted-average shares of common stock outstanding. Preferred dividends on cumulative preferred stock should be deducted in the numerator regardless of whether they have been declared or not declared. Preferred dividends on noncumulative preferred stock should be deducted only if the dividend has been declared.

2. EPS should be presented for income from continuing operations (if that line item exists) on the *face* of the income statement. In addition, the company must present EPS for discontinued operations and extraordinary items, *either on the face of the income statement or in the notes.*

3. Companies present diluted EPS to indicate what EPS would be if the dilutive securities were converted to common stock.

Analysis Issues for Earnings per Share (p. 881)

1. Pro forma earnings per share generally represents an attempt to exclude nonrecurring items, write-offs, restructuring charges, and similar negative amounts from EPS.

2. Company press releases may emphasize pro forma EPS amounts to such an extent that the basic or diluted EPS numbers are buried, thereby misleading the investing public. In some cases, a negative EPS has been reported as a positive one on a pro forma basis.

3. This guidance requires companies to clearly present and reconcile the differences between pro forma earnings and GAAP-based results. It requires that press releases and communications about earnings contain a tabular presentation of the reconciliation of pro forma earnings and GAAP-based earnings. Further, it stresses the need for consistency from period to period in the manner in which pro forma earnings are calculated.

Cash Flow Issues Related to EPS (p. 882)

1. The exercise of stock options will appear in the financing activities section.

2. The FASB believes that reporting data other than earnings on a per share basis invites the danger that investors, creditors, and others may confuse those measures with the conventional accounting measure of earnings per share.

Statement of Stockholders' Equity (p. 883)

1. The purpose of the statement of stockholders' equity is to present all of the items that changed the balance of each of the stockholders' equity accounts. While the balance sheet presents the balance of many of the stockholders' equity accounts, it does not detail the changes in those accounts.

2. Unrealized gains or losses on available-for-sale securities, foreign currency translation adjustments, the minimum pension liability adjustment (in certain cases), and unrealized gains or losses on cash flow hedges.

CPA-ADAPTED SIMULATION

This simulation asks you to complete various tasks related to a company's annual financial statements. If your instructor has signed up for CPAexcel™, you can do the work online at **www.cpaexcel.com/hmco**. You may also do the simulation manually.

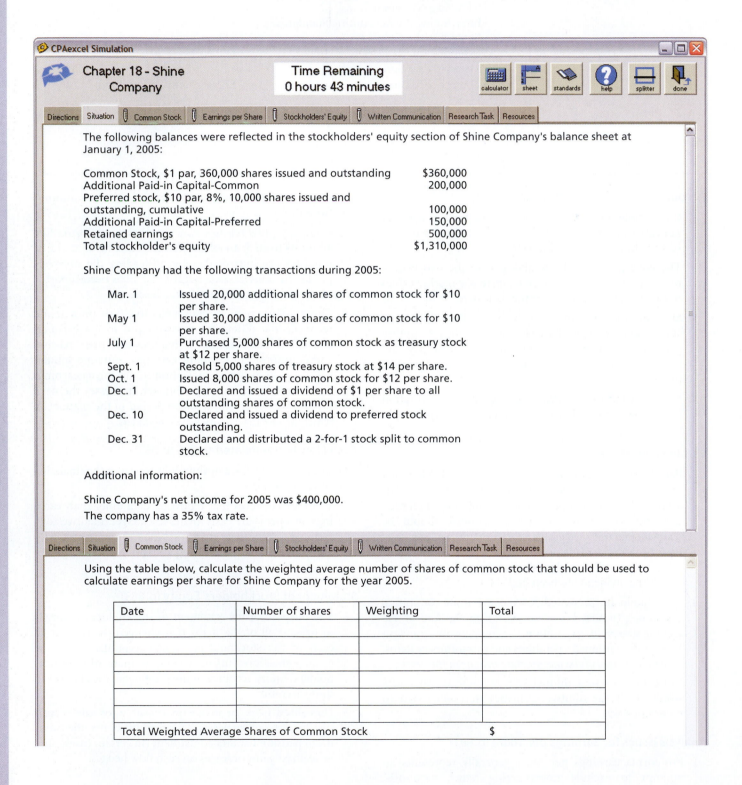

CPAexcel Simulation

Chapter 18 – Shine Company

Time Remaining
0 hours 43 minutes

calculator | sheet | standards | help | splitter | done

Directions | Situation | Common Stock | Earnings per Share | Stockholders' Equity | Written Communication | Research Task | Resources

The following balances were reflected in the stockholders' equity section of Shine Company's balance sheet at January 1, 2005:

Common Stock, $1 par, 360,000 shares issued and outstanding	$360,000
Additional Paid-in Capital-Common	200,000
Preferred stock, $10 par, 8%, 10,000 shares issued and outstanding, cumulative	100,000
Additional Paid-in Capital-Preferred	150,000
Retained earnings	500,000
Total stockholder's equity	$1,310,000

Shine Company had the following transactions during 2005:

Mar. 1	Issued 20,000 additional shares of common stock for $10 per share.
May 1	Issued 30,000 additional shares of common stock for $10 per share.
July 1	Purchased 5,000 shares of common stock as treasury stock at $12 per share.
Sept. 1	Resold 5,000 shares of treasury stock at $14 per share.
Oct. 1	Issued 8,000 shares of common stock for $12 per share.
Dec. 1	Declared and issued a dividend of $1 per share to all outstanding shares of common stock.
Dec. 10	Declared and issued a dividend to preferred stock outstanding.
Dec. 31	Declared and distributed a 2-for-1 stock split to common stock.

Additional information:

Shine Company's net income for 2005 was $400,000.

The company has a 35% tax rate.

Directions | Situation | Common Stock | Earnings per Share | Stockholders' Equity | Written Communication | Research Task | Resources

Using the table below, calculate the weighted average number of shares of common stock that should be used to calculate earnings per share for Shine Company for the year 2005.

Date	Number of shares	Weighting	Total
Total Weighted Average Shares of Common Stock			$

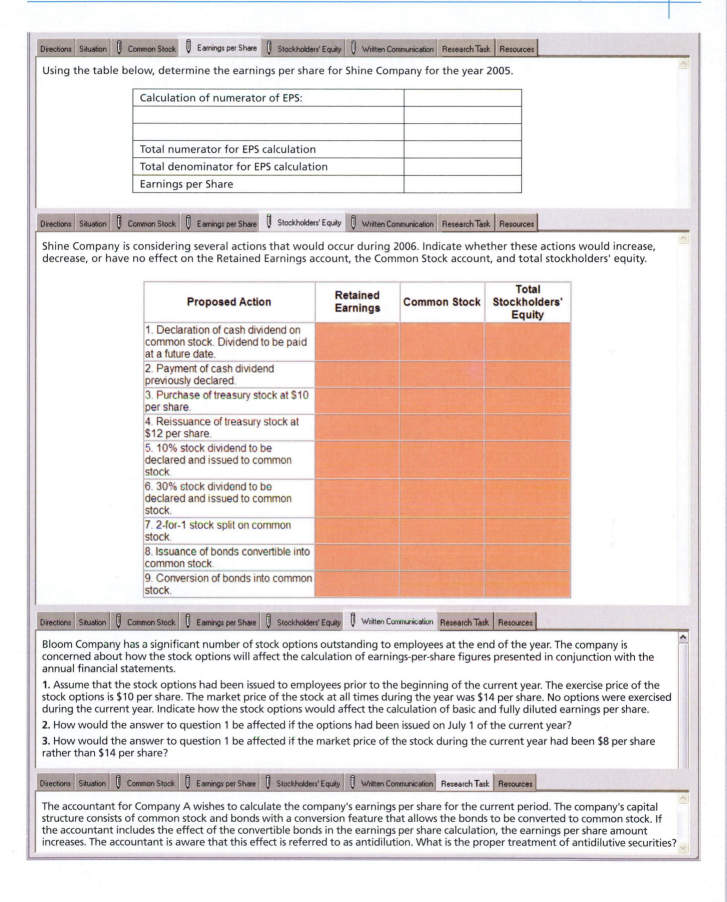

| Directions | Situation | Common Stock | Earnings per Share | Stockholders' Equity | Written Communication | Research Task | Resources |

Using the table below, determine the earnings per share for Shine Company for the year 2005.

Calculation of numerator of EPS:	
Total numerator for EPS calculation	
Total denominator for EPS calculation	
Earnings per Share	

| Directions | Situation | Common Stock | Earnings per Share | Stockholders' Equity | Written Communication | Research Task | Resources |

Shine Company is considering several actions that would occur during 2006. Indicate whether these actions would increase, decrease, or have no effect on the Retained Earnings account, the Common Stock account, and total stockholders' equity.

Proposed Action	Retained Earnings	Common Stock	Total Stockholders' Equity
1. Declaration of cash dividend on common stock. Dividend to be paid at a future date.			
2. Payment of cash dividend previously declared.			
3. Purchase of treasury stock at $10 per share.			
4. Reissuance of treasury stock at $12 per share.			
5. 10% stock dividend to be declared and issued to common stock.			
6. 30% stock dividend to be declared and issued to common stock.			
7. 2-for-1 stock split on common stock.			
8. Issuance of bonds convertible into common stock.			
9. Conversion of bonds into common stock.			

| Directions | Situation | Common Stock | Earnings per Share | Stockholders' Equity | Written Communication | Research Task | Resources |

Bloom Company has a significant number of stock options outstanding to employees at the end of the year. The company is concerned about how the stock options will affect the calculation of earnings-per-share figures presented in conjunction with the annual financial statements.

1. Assume that the stock options had been issued to employees prior to the beginning of the current year. The exercise price of the stock options is $10 per share. The market price of the stock at all times during the year was $14 per share. No options were exercised during the current year. Indicate how the stock options would affect the calculation of basic and fully diluted earnings per share.

2. How would the answer to question 1 be affected if the options had been issued on July 1 of the current year?

3. How would the answer to question 1 be affected if the market price of the stock during the current year had been $8 per share rather than $14 per share?

| Directions | Situation | Common Stock | Earnings per Share | Stockholders' Equity | Written Communication | Research Task | Resources |

The accountant for Company A wishes to calculate the company's earnings per share for the current period. The company's capital structure consists of common stock and bonds with a conversion feature that allows the bonds to be converted to common stock. If the accountant includes the effect of the convertible bonds in the earnings per share calculation, the earnings per share amount increases. The accountant is aware that this effect is referred to as antidilution. What is the proper treatment of antidilutive securities?

Revisiting the Statement of Cash Flows

LEARNING OBJECTIVES

After studying this chapter, you should be able to:

LO1 Describe how the activities of a business are reflected and categorized in the statement of cash flows.

LO2 Distinguish between the direct and indirect methods of preparing the cash flows from operating activities section of the statement of cash flows.

LO3 Prepare a full statement of cash flows using both the indirect and the direct methods.

LO4 Describe how the statement of cash flows can be used to analyze liquidity and risk, and explain how product life cycles affect cash flows.

FINANCIAL REPORTING CASE

MOTOROLA DOUBLES ITS CASH BALANCE YET REPORTS NET LOSSES

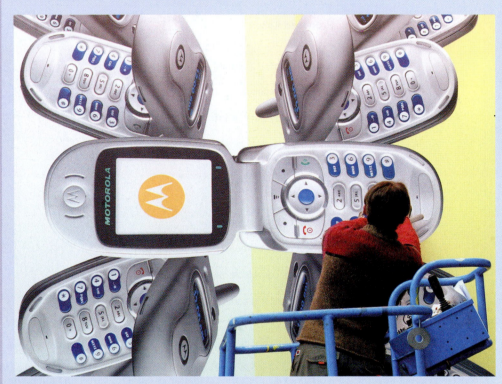

Investors must look to the statement of cash flows to determine how companies like Motorola are able to maintain positive cash flows while reporting large net losses.

Motorola Is it possible for a company to report net losses, yet increase its cash balance and generate millions of dollars from operations? Motorola, a global leader in providing communications solutions, did just that in 2001 and 2002. During these years, the company reported combined losses on its income statement of almost $6.4 billion. During that same two-year period, Motorola's core operations generated $3.3 billion in cash, and the company's cash balance almost doubled, from $3.3 billion to $6.5 billion.

What caused these divergent results? In 2000, Motorola undertook a massive restructuring program to cut costs, reduce payrolls, initiate efficiency improvements, and exit from unprofitable markets. While some of the restructuring charges involved cash payments, most of the charges were noncash items that decreased net income without decreasing cash flows. As you can see from the graph presented here, Motorola's net income took a significant dive in 2001, while its cash balance

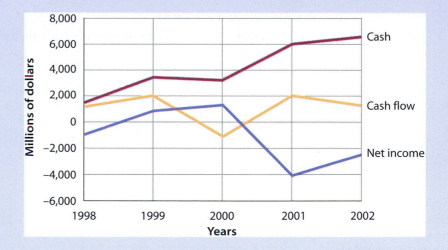

increased. Cash flows from operating activities remained positive, even with the dip in net income.

In order to provide information on the effect of certain items on income and cash flows, companies are required to prepare a statement of cash flows. The statement provides a reconciliation of the Cash account from the beginning of the accounting period to the end of the accounting period and allows users to understand which activities provided cash and which activities used cash. The charges for reorganization (highlighted) that affected Motorola's net income can be seen on the company's consolidated statement of cash flows ($2,627 million in 2002 and $4,786 in 2001). Since these charges did not involve cash, they were added back to net income in order to arrive at cash flows from operating activities.

Motorola

Motorola, Inc.
Operating Activities Section of the Consolidated Statements of Cash Flows

(In millions) Years Ended December 31	2002	2001	2000
OPERATING			
Net earnings (loss)	$ (2,485)	$ (3,937)	$ 1,318
Adjustments to reconcile net earnings (loss) to net cash provided by (used for) operating activities:			
Depreciation and amortization	2,108	2,552	2,527
Charges for reorganization of businesses and other charges	2,627	4,786	1,483
Gains on sales of investments and businesses, net	(96)	(1,931)	(1,570)
Deferred income taxes	(1,570)	(2,273)	239
Investment impairments and other	1,391	1,252	332
Change in assets and liabilities, net of effects of acquisitions and dispositions:			
Accounts receivable	155	2,445	(1,471)
Inventories	(102)	1,838	(2,305)
Other current assets	39	249	(532)
Accounts payable and accrued liabilities	(980)	(3,030)	(666)
Other assets and liabilities	252	25	(519)
Net cash provided by (used for) operating activities	1,339	1,976	(1,164)

EXAMINING THE CASE

1. If Motorola had not booked noncash "charges for reorganization of businesses and other charges" in 2002, what net income or loss would the company have reported? (Ignore any income tax calculations.)

2. If a company reports positive cash flows from operating activities on its statement of cash flows and net losses on its income statement, describe potential factors that may be responsible for these results.

3. What goals does Motorola hope to accomplish with its restructuring program?

LO 1 Describe how the activities of a business are reflected and categorized in the statement of cash flows.

statement of cash flows a financial statement that shows the amount of cash collected and disbursed by a firm over a specified period for operating activities, investing activities, and financing activities

operating activities the transactions required to produce revenues and run the business

investing activities the transactions that involve spending on productive assets or investments in order to achieve the objectives of the business

financing activities transactions that involve the receipt or payment of cash related to liabilities and owners' equity (other than through operations)

Classification of Business Activities

As you recall from Chapter 5, the **statement of cash flows** is a financial statement that shows the amount of cash collected and disbursed by a firm over a specified period for operating activities, investing activities, and financing activities. It provides financial statement users with the information necessary to reconcile the change in a company's cash and cash equivalents.

● **Operating activities** are the transactions that are required to produce revenues and run the business. As you can see from Illustration 19.1, operating activities may include the receipt of cash from the sale of goods and services, the receipt of interest and dividends, and the payment of cash for salaries, inventory, taxes, and other expenses.

● **Investing activities** are those transactions that involve spending on productive assets or investments in order to achieve the objectives of the business. Some of the activities found in this category are cash inflows from the sale of property, investments, or marketable securities and cash outflows from the purchase of investments or property, as depicted in Illustration 19.2.

● **Financing activities** are transactions that involve the receipt or payment of cash related to liabilities and owners' equity (other than through operations). They include obtaining resources from owners and providing those owners with a return on their investment and borrowing money from creditors and repaying those obligations. Illustration 19.3 depicts the activities commonly associated with financing activities: sale of capital stock, issuance of debt, repayment of debt, purchase of treasury stock, and payment of dividends.

Illustration 19.1

Types of Cash Inflows and Outflows from Operating Activities

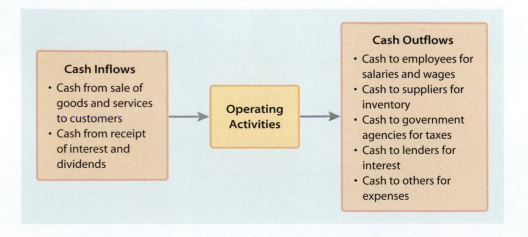

Illustration 19.2

Types of Cash Inflows and Outflows from Investing Activities

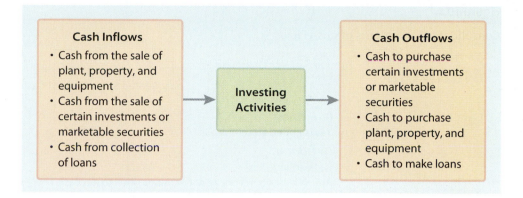

Cash Inflows
- Cash from the sale of plant, property, and equipment
- Cash from the sale of certain investments or marketable securities
- Cash from collection of loans

Investing Activities

Cash Outflows
- Cash to purchase certain investments or marketable securities
- Cash to purchase plant, property, and equipment
- Cash to make loans

Critical Thinking: Why do you think it might be important to group cash inflows and outflows from certain types of business activities or kinds of transactions?

significant noncash transactions and events transactions not involving cash that are not part of the actual statement of cash flows but should be reported in an accompanying schedule or note

As you can see in Figure 19.1 (page 910), **Motorola**'s consolidated statements of cash flows have operating, investing, and financing activities sections. The last portion of the statement reconciles the beginning cash balance to the ending cash balance for each period.

In addition to the statement of cash flows, companies must provide information concerning two important items. First, companies must disclose the amount of cash paid for interest and taxes. This information may be provided along with the statement of cash flows or in an accompanying schedule or note. Second, companies must also disclose **significant noncash transactions and events**. These transactions and events are not part of the actual statement of cash flows but should be reported in an accompanying schedule or note. Transactions that would be reported as significant noncash transactions include:

- Acquisition of assets by issuing equity securities or issuing debt
- Exchanges of nonmonetary assets
- Refinancing of long-term debt
- Retirement of long-term debt by issuing equity
- Conversion of debt or preferred stock into common stock

CHECK YOUR UNDERSTANDING

1. If a company spent cash to purchase some of its own capital stock, how would this activity be classified in the statement of cash flows?

2. How might the exchange of nonmonetary assets be reflected in a company's financial statements?

3. Describe the types of activities that might be found in the financing activities section of a statement of cash flows.

Illustration 19.3

Types of Cash Inflows and Outflows from Financing Activities

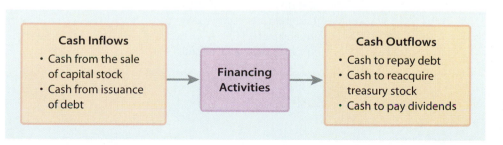

Cash Inflows
- Cash from the sale of capital stock
- Cash from issuance of debt

Financing Activities

Cash Outflows
- Cash to repay debt
- Cash to reacquire treasury stock
- Cash to pay dividends

Figure 19.1

Consolidated Statements of Cash Flows

Motorola

Motorola, Inc.
Consolidated Statements of Cash Flows

(In millions) Years Ended December 31	2002	2001	2000
OPERATING			
Net earnings (loss)	$ (2,485)	$ (3,937)	$ 1,318
Adjustments to reconcile net earnings (loss) to net cash provided by (used for) operating activities:			
Depreciation and amortization	2,108	2,552	2,527
Charges for reorganization of businesses and other charges	2,627	4,786	1,483
Gains on sales of investments and businesses, net	(96)	(1,931)	(1,570)
Deferred income taxes	(1,570)	(2,273)	239
Investment impairments and other	1,391	1,252	332
Change in assets and liabilities, net of effects of acquisitions and dispositions:			
Accounts receivable	155	2,445	(1,471)
Inventories	(102)	1,838	(2,305)
Other current assets	39	249	(532)
Accounts payable and accrued liabilities	(980)	(3,030)	(666)
Other assets and liabilities	252	25	(519)
Net cash provided by (used for) operating activities	1,339	1,976	(1,164)
INVESTING			
Acquisitions and investments, net	(94)	(512)	(1,912)
Proceeds from sale of investments and businesses	96	4,063	1,433
Capital expenditures	(607)	(1,321)	(4,131)
Proceeds from sale of property, plant and equipment	143	14	174
Sales of short-term investments	23	233	345
Net cash provided by (used for) investing activities	(439)	2,477	(4,091)
FINANCING			
Net proceeds from (repayment of) commercial paper and short-term borrowings	(180)	(5,688)	3,884
Net proceeds from issuance of debt	64	4,167	1,190
Repayment of debt	(299)	(305)	(5)
Issuance of common stock	401	362	383
Debt redemption payment	(106)	—	—
Payment of dividends	(364)	(356)	(333)
Net cash provided by (used for) financing activities	(484)	(1,820)	5,119
Effect of exchange rate changes on cash and cash equivalents	9	148	(100)
Net increase (decrease) in cash and cash equivalents	425	2,781	(236)
Cash and cash equivalents, beginning of year	6,082	3,301	3,537
Cash and cash equivalents, end of year	$ 6,507	$ 6,082	$3,301
CASH FLOW INFORMATION			
Cash paid during the year for:			
Interest, net	$ 569	$ 844	$ 529
Income taxes, net of refunds	83	676	130

LO 2 Distinguish between the direct and indirect methods of preparing the cash flows from operating activities section of the statement of cash flows.

Critical Thinking: *How do you think the statement of cash flows helps users correlate the economic activities of a business with its cash inflows and outflows?*

Cash Flows from Operating Activities—The Indirect Method Versus the Direct Method

The statement of cash flows is a reconciliation of the cash balance from the beginning of the period to the end of the period. The statement begins by presenting the cash provided or used by each of the three business activities and finishes with the ending cash balance. When preparing the statement, the following information must be gathered:

● The most recent income statement

● The two most recent balance sheets

● Additional data from the general ledger that relate to cash inflows or outflows

Before beginning the preparation of the statement of cash flows, managers must determine whether the operating activities section (the first section of the statement) should be prepared using the direct method or the indirect method. Accounting standards permit the operating activities section to be presented using either method. It is important to recognize that the decision to use the direct or the indirect method affects only the operating activities section of the statement. Both the financing activities section and the investing activities section are prepared using a standard format.

USING THE DIRECT METHOD

direct method the method of preparing the cash flows from operating activities section in which each item within the income statement's "income from continuing operations" is converted into its cash equivalent

Under the **direct method** of preparing the cash flows from operating activities section, each item within the income statement's "income from continuing operations" is converted into its cash equivalent. For example, sales revenue is converted into cash received from customers and salaries expense is converted into cash paid to employees. This process results in converting income from continuing operations into cash flow from operating activities.

Two of the main advantages of the direct method are:

1. The direct method shows the full amount of the cash inflows and outflows arising from the operating activities. Thus, the statement of cash flows provides evidence of all of the company's actual cash inflows and cash outflows, which is more consistent with the objective of the statement.

2. The direct method also provides information about the amount of sales that have actually resulted in cash inflows. This can be helpful in evaluating the economic value of the sales shown in the income statement.

USING THE INDIRECT METHOD

indirect method the method of preparing the cash flows from operating activities section in which net income is adjusted for items that do not affect cash flows, such as depreciation, amortization, depletion, gains, losses, and changes in current assets and current liabilities

Under the **indirect method**, net income is adjusted for items that *do not* affect cash flows, such as depreciation, amortization, depletion, gains, losses, and changes in current assets and current liabilities. When the indirect method is used, net income, as determined in the income statement, is listed first and then reconciled to net cash provided or used by operating activities by making adjustments for certain noncash items.

Most companies prepare their statements of cash flows using the indirect method for a number of reasons. One important reason is simplicity. If a company prepares its report using the direct method, it must also provide a reconciliation of net income to operating cash flows, like that prepared using the indirect method, as a separate schedule in the notes to the financial statements.

Two of the main advantages of the indirect method are:

1. The reconciliation of net income and the cash provided or used by operating activities is important to understand, since it demonstrates the connection between economic activities and the generation and use of cash.

2. The use of the direct method may involve significant costs compared to the indirect method. This is especially true when the level of detail of cash inflows and outflows includes such items as sensitive segment information or information about strategic suppliers and employees.

CHECK YOUR UNDERSTANDING

1. What advantages to using the indirect method of preparing the operating activities section of the statement of cash flows can you identify?

2. Describe the difference in the way a statement of cash flows prepared using the direct method and one prepared using the indirect method looks.

3. If a statement of cash flows starts out with net income (or net loss) and adds or subtracts noncash items, has the indirect method or the direct method been used?

LO 3 Prepare a full statement of cash flows using both the indirect and the direct methods.

Critical Thinking: *How might the statement of cash flows be used to explain how a company is financing an expansion strategy?*

Preparing the Operating Activities Section of the Statement of Cash Flows

To illustrate the preparation of the statement of cash flows, we will use the financial statements of Graham Products. Illustration 19.4 presents the income statement for 2005 and the balance sheets at December 31, 2005 and 2004. It also provides transaction data relevant to preparing the company's statement of cash flows.

Illustration 19.4

Financial Statements and Transaction Data

Graham Products
Income Statement
For the Year Ended December 31, 2005

Sales	$147,000	
Cost of sales	84,000	
Gross profit		$63,000
Operating expenses		
Depreciation expense	$ 9,000	
Bad debt expense	3,000	
Salaries expense	14,600	
Insurance expense	600	
Rent expense	10,000	
Total operating expenses		37,200
Income from operations		$25,800
Other revenues and gains		
Gain on sale of equipment	$ 1,500	
Unrealized gain on trading securities	2,000	3,500
Other expenses and losses		
Interest expense		(4,200)
Income from continuing operations before tax		$25,100
Income tax expense		6,900
Net income		$18,200

Illustration 19.4 (*cont.*)

Graham Products
Balance Sheet

	December 31, 2005	December 31, 2004
Assets		
Current assets:		
Cash and cash equivalents	$ 41,900	$ 25,000
Trading securities	3,000	1,000
Accounts receivable	24,500	7,000
Less: Allowance for doubtful accounts	(3,500)	(1,750)
Inventory	28,000	35,000
Prepaid insurance	2,000	1,000
Total current assets	$ 95,900	$ 67,250
Property and equipment:		
Equipment	42,000	38,500
Less: Accumulated depreciation	(14,000)	(7,000)
Land	25,000	10,000
Total assets	$148,900	$108,750
Liabilities and Stockholders' Equity		
Current liabilities:		
Accounts payable	$ 17,500	$ 21,000
Accrued salaries payable	5,500	8,000
Rent payable	5,000	1,000
Income tax payable	6,900	4,000
Total current liabilities	$ 34,900	$ 34,000
Long-term notes payable	50,000	35,000
Less: Discount on notes payable	(2,800)	(3,500)
Total liabilities	$ 82,100	$ 65,500
Stockholders' equity:		
Common stock	45,000	30,000
Retained earnings	24,800	13,250
Less: Treasury stock	(3,000)	0
Total liabilities and stockholders' equity	$148,900	$108,750

Additional Information:

• Graham Products sold equipment during the period that originally cost $5,000. The equipment had a carrying amount of $3,000 and was sold for $4,500.

• Graham Products purchased land during the period by issuing $15,000 of notes payable.

• Graham Products wrote off $1,250 of accounts receivable as uncollectible during the period.

• There were no purchases of trading securities during the period. The increase in the account is a result of an unrealized gain.

• Graham Products issued $15,000 of common stock during the year and repurchased $3,000 of treasury stock; the company uses the cost method.

• Graham Products declared and paid dividends of $6,650 during the period.

Throughout the following pages, we will examine how each section of the statement of cash flows is prepared, using data from Graham Products's balance sheet, income statement, and relevant general ledger accounts.

The first step in the preparation of the statement of cash flows is to prepare the operating activities section. As you learned earlier, this section provides information about the activities that a company normally engages in when producing revenues. These activities include the selling of goods and services and the expenses related to producing those revenues.

When preparing this section of the statement of cash flows, the first decision to be made is whether to use the direct or the indirect method. Because the indirect method is most commonly used in practice, we illustrate this approach first and then discuss and illustrate the direct method.

THE INDIRECT METHOD OF PREPARING THE OPERATING ACTIVITIES SECTION

The indirect method requires that three general types of adjustments be made to net income to arrive at cash provided or used by operating activities. The three types of adjustments can be summarized as follows:

1. Adjustments for noncash income items

2. Adjustments for realized gains and losses recognized in the income statement

3. Adjustments for changes in current operating asset and liability accounts, excluding the Cash account

▶ ADJUSTMENTS FOR NONCASH OPERATING ITEMS

In order to transform accrual-based net income into cash flows from operating activities, noncash items must be identified and reversed. When net income was calculated in the income statement, certain items that did not actually affect cash were deducted or added. Examples of noncash operating items that need to be added back to net income in the statement of cash flows are:

● Depreciation expense

● Amortization expense

● Losses due to impairment

● Compensation expense related to stock option plans

● Amortization of discount on notes or bonds payable

● Unrealized losses on trading security investments

● Net loss from investments accounted for under the equity method

When net income was calculated, certain items were added to income that did not actually affect cash. Examples of noncash items that need to be subtracted from net income in the statement of cash flows are:

● Amortization of premium on notes or bonds payable

● Unrealized gain on trading securities

● Net revenue from investments accounted for under the equity method

Refer to the financial statements for Graham Products that are presented in Illustration 19.4 to determine if the company included any of the above items. As you can see from the income statement, the company recognized depreciation expense and an unrealized gain on trading securities. Also note on the balance sheet that a portion of the discount on notes payable has been amortized. All of these items will need adjustment in the statement of cash flows. As you can see, depreciation expense, amortization expense, salaries expense, and an unrealized gain on trading securities are items that will need adjustment. Also, because Graham Products uses the equity method of accounting for investments, an adjustment will be required for any revenue that is recognized.

❯ DEPRECIATION   By examining Graham Products's income statement, balance sheet, and additional data, it can be determined that depreciation expense for the period is $9,000. To confirm this amount, review the beginning and ending balances of the Accumulated Depreciation account along with the equipment sales transaction information to perform the following calculation:

Ending balance of Accumulated Depreciation	$14,000
Plus: Accumulated depreciation related to assets sold	2,000
Less: Beginning balance of Accumulated Depreciation	(7,000)
Depreciation expense	$ 9,000

The amount of $9,000 should be added back to net income.

❯ AMORTIZATION OF DISCOUNT ON NOTES PAYABLE   Graham Products will also need to add back the portion of the notes payable discount that was amortized during the period ($700). This adjustment is made because amortization of the notes payable discount represents the noncash portion of interest expense for the period. A company with a notes payable premium would need to subtract any premium amortization, as this represents the amount by which cash interest paid exceeds interest expense.

❯ COMPENSATION EXPENSE RELATED TO STOCK OPTIONS   Although Graham Products does not have any of this type of compensation expense, it is important to highlight this item due to the magnitude of stock option compensation. Stock option compensation expense reduces income, but because it does not require a cash payment to employees, it must be added back to net income.

❯ UNREALIZED GAIN   Changes in the value of trading securities also result in noncash charges in the income statement. The company's trading securities portfolio increased in value from $1,000 to $3,000 during 2005. To recognize this change, Graham Products recorded an unrealized gain and an increase in its trading investment asset account; however, the unrealized gain did not result in any cash being received by the company. For this reason, the unrealized gain of $2,000 would be subtracted from net income to arrive at cash flows from operating activities. If an unrealized loss had been recorded, it would be added back to net income.

It is important to note that the adjustment for unrealized gains and losses relates only to investments accounted for as trading securities. Because unrealized gains and losses from investments classified as available for sale do not affect net income, no adjustment is needed.

❯ REVENUE RECOGNIZED UNDER THE EQUITY METHOD OF ACCOUNTING FOR INVESTMENTS   The equity method of accounting for investments also creates a need for an adjustment for noncash items. The equity method results in recognition of revenue and an increase in the investment account equal to the investor's share of the investee's net income or net loss. In addition, the equity investment account is decreased (and the Cash account is increased) for any dividends received from the investee.

For example, assume that Company A owned 30 percent of Company B and accounted for its investment using the equity method. Suppose Company B reported net income of $10,000 and paid $2,000 in dividends. Company A would record the following entries to recognize its share of income and dividends:

Equity Investment in Company B ($10,000 × 30%)	3,000	
Revenue from investment in Company B		3,000
Cash ($2,000 × 30%)	600	
Equity Investment in Company B		600

To calculate the amount of the adjustment required in the operating activities section of the statement of cash flows, Company A would subtract the revenue from its investment in Company B less its share of the dividends ($3,000 − $600 = $2,400).

> **BAD DEBT EXPENSE**   Bad debt expense creates a unique problem in the preparation of the operating activities section of the statement of cash flows. Bad debt expense is a noncash charge, but unlike depreciation and the other charges we have discussed, it also affects the Accounts Receivable account by increasing the Allowance for Doubtful Accounts account. For this reason, bad debt expense is not added back at this point; instead, the change in net accounts receivable is added or subtracted later in the operating activities section.

> ### ADJUSTMENTS FOR REALIZED GAINS AND LOSSES

Realized gains and losses require adjustments in the operating activities section of the statement of cash flows. Recall that the sale of capital equipment is reported in the investing activities section of the statement of cash flows. Graham Products sold equipment with an original cost of $5,000 and accumulated depreciation of $2,000 for $4,500. This transaction resulted in a realized gain of $1,500, reported in the income statement, and an increase in cash of $4,500.

The $4,500 cash received by Graham Products is reported in the investing activities section of the statement of cash flows. However, the net income amount used to begin the operating activities section includes the $1,500 gain. So that we do not count both the cash received from the transaction and the gain, the indirect method requires that the amount of the gain be subtracted from net income when calculating cash flows from operating activities. If the transaction had resulted in a loss, then the amount of the loss would be added back to net income when calculating cash flows from operating activities.

> ### ADJUSTMENTS FOR CHANGES IN CURRENT OPERATING ASSETS AND LIABILITIES

The last type of adjustment needed to convert net income to cash flows from operating activities is for changes in current operating asset and liability accounts. Current operating accounts are those that are generally used in the normal operations of the business to make sales and pay suppliers and vendors. These accounts represent the difference between cash received or paid during the period and accrual-basis revenue and expense.

For example, a sale on credit results in an increase in income during the period without an equivalent increase in cash. A prepayment of next period's rent expense results in an immediate reduction in cash without an equivalent decrease in this period's income. Current operating asset and liability accounts hold the difference between cash-basis accounting and accrual-basis accounting, and adjustments for changes in these accounts must be made when calculating cash flows from operating activities.

The adjustment to net income differs depending on whether the account is a current operating asset or a current operating liability and whether the balance of the account has increased or decreased.

- Increases in current operating asset accounts must be subtracted in the operating activities section, as these increases require the use of cash.

- Decreases in current operating asset accounts are added back in the operating activities section, as these decreases are a source of cash.

Examining the current assets section of Graham Products's balance sheet in Illustration 19.4, we see that the changes in the Trading Securities, Accounts Receivable,

Inventory, and Prepaid Insurance accounts must be adjusted in the statement of cash flows.

❯ TRADING SECURITIES

Trading securities are investments that are expected to be held for only a short period; for this reason, cash flows related to purchasing and selling trading securities are included in the operating activities section. The change in this account was due to an increase in the market value of the securities and not to any cash effects; for this reason, no adjustment is made for the increase in this account. Recall that the unrealized holding gain related to the trading securities was treated as an adjustment of a noncash operating item.

❯ ACCOUNTS RECEIVABLE

Examining Graham Products's balance sheet, we see that Accounts Receivable increased on a net basis by $15,750 during the year. This increase in Accounts Receivable means that revenue on an accrual basis was higher than that on a cash basis and that not all of the sales resulted in cash being received immediately.

❯ INVENTORY AND PREPAID INSURANCE

Graham Products's two other current operating asset accounts are Inventory and Prepaid Insurance. Inventory decreased by $7,000 during the period, whereas Prepaid Insurance increased by $1,000. These changes result in adding back $7,000 and subtracting $1,000 to arrive at net cash flows from operating activities.

Changes in current operating liability accounts are treated in an opposite manner from changes in current operating asset accounts.

- An increase in a current operating liability should be added back in the operating activities section.

- A decrease in a current operating liability account should be subtracted in the operating activities section.

❯ ACCOUNTS PAYABLE

For Graham Products, the Accounts Payable account decreased by $3,500 during the period; thus, this amount was deducted from net income in the operating activities section of the statement of cash flows. The decrease in Accounts Payable is a result of the accrual expense being less than the cash payments during the period. In other words, more cash was paid to suppliers than expense was recognized.

❯ OTHER CURRENT OPERATING LIABILITIES

Other current operating liability accounts that changed during the period for Graham Products were as follows:

- Accrued Salaries Payable decreased by $2,500

- Rent Payable increased by $4,000

- Income Tax Payable increased by $2,900

To arrive at cash flows from operating activities, the increases in both Rent Payable and Income Tax Payable would be added back to net income, whereas the decrease in Accrued Salaries Payable would be subtracted from net income.

These adjustments complete the steps necessary to transform net income to cash flows from operating activities using the indirect method. Illustration 19.5 provides a summary of the additions and deductions made when adjusting net income to cash flows.

Illustration 19.6 presents the statement of cash flows for Graham Products prepared using the indirect method.

Illustration 19.5

Preparing the Operating Activities Section of the Statement of Cash Flows— Indirect Method

Additions
Depreciation expense
Amortization of intangibles
Amortization of discount on notes or bonds payable
Increase in deferred tax liability or decrease in deferred tax asset
Loss on sale of assets

Deductions
Amortization of premium on notes or bonds payable
Decrease in deferred tax liability or increase in deferred tax asset
Gain on sale of assets

Analysis of Current Assets/Liabilities
Decrease/increase in current assets (Inventory, Receivables, Prepaid Expenses, etc.)
Decrease/increase in current liabilities (Accounts Payable, Salaries Payable, etc.)

Illustration 19.6

Statement of Cash Flows (Indirect Method)

Graham Products
Statement of Cash Flows (Indirect Method)
For the Year Ended December 31, 2005

Cash Flows from Operating Activities:		
Net income		$18,200
Adjustments to reconcile net income to net cash provided by operating activities:		
Depreciation expense	$ 9,000	
Amortization of notes payable	700	
Unrealized gain on trading securities	(2,000)	
Gain on sale of equipment	(1,500)	
Increase in accounts receivable (net)	(15,750)	
Decrease in inventory	7,000	
Increase in prepaid insurance	(1,000)	
Decrease in accounts payable	(3,500)	
Decrease in accrued salaries payable	(2,500)	
Increase in rent payable	4,000	
Increase in income tax payable	2,900	(2,650)
Net cash provided by operating activities		$15,550
Cash Flows from Investing Activities:		
Purchase of equipment	($8,500)	
Sale of equipment	4,500	
Net cash used by investing activities		(4,000)
Cash Flows from Financing Activities:		
Sale of common stock	$15,000	
Purchase of treasury stock	(3,000)	
Payment of dividends	(6,650)	
Net cash provided by financing activities		5,350
Net increase in cash and cash equivalents		$16,900
Cash and cash equivalents at January 1, 2005		25,000
Cash and cash equivalents at December 31, 2005		$41,900
Supplemental Cash Flow Disclosures:		
Cash paid for interest	$ 3,500	
Cash paid for income taxes	4,000	
Noncash Investing and Financing Activities:		
Land valued at $15,000 was purchased by issuance of notes payable		

THE DIRECT METHOD OF PREPARING THE OPERATING ACTIVITIES SECTION

To prepare the operating activities section of the statement of cash flows using the direct method, we will need the income from continuing operations section of the income statement and the two most recent balance sheets. Each line of the income statement has one or more related balance sheet accounts that are used to account for accruals or deferrals for that line. For example, the income statement line Salaries Expense relates to the balance sheet account Accrued Salaries Payable. To determine the amount of cash paid for salaries, the change in the Accrued Salaries Payable account must be examined. Using Graham Products's balance sheet information, each item in the income from continuing operations section of the income statement will be transformed into its related cash flows, illustrated as follows.

❯ SALES TRANSFORMED TO CASH COLLECTED FROM CUSTOMERS

To transform sales into cash collected from customers, we will need the sales information and the beginning and ending balances for the related balance sheet account, Accounts Receivable. Cash collected from customers is then calculated as follows:

Beginning balance of Accounts Receivable	$xxx
Plus: Sales	xxx
Cash available for collection	$xxx
Less: Ending balance of Accounts Receivable	(xxx)
Accounts receivable written off as uncollectible	(xxx)
Cash collected from customers	$xxx

Recall that under the indirect method of calculating cash flows from operating activities, accounts receivable net of the allowance was used. However, under the direct method, accounts receivable is examined by itself because it shows cash collections.

Because Graham Products has written off accounts receivable during the period, the change in Accounts Receivable must be adjusted to arrive at cash collected from customers. Therefore, the transformation of sales to cash collected from customers is calculated as follows:

Beginning balance of Accounts Receivable	$ 7,000
Plus: Sales	147,000
Cash available for collection	$154,000
Less: Ending balance of Accounts Receivable	(24,500)
Accounts receivable written off as uncollectible	(1,250)
Cash collected from customers	$128,250

What calculation should be made if customers prepay for goods or services, so that the related balance sheet account is a liability, such as Deferred Revenue? For example, an insurance company collects payment prior to the period in which insurance is effective. When it receives a prepayment, it makes the following journal entry:

Cash	XXX	
Deferred Revenue		XXX

In cases where payment is made before revenue is recognized, the method for transforming revenue to cash collected from customers is as follows:

Ending balance of Deferred Revenue (liability account)	$xxx
Plus: Revenue for the period	xxx
Less: Beginning balance of Deferred Revenue (liability account)	(xxx)
Cash collected from customers	$xxx

❱ COST OF SALES TRANSFORMED TO CASH PAID FOR INVENTORY

To determine how much cash was paid for inventory during an accounting period, two balance sheet accounts must be examined: Accounts Payable and Inventory. Accounts Payable reflects the amount owed on inventory purchases, and the Inventory account is needed to determine how much inventory is still on hand and has not yet been sold. Using this information, cash paid for inventory is calculated as follows:

Ending balance of Inventory	$xxx
Plus: Cost of sales	xxx
Available inventory	$xxx
Less: Beginning balance of Inventory	(xxx)
Inventory purchased	$xxx
Plus: Beginning balance of Accounts Payable	xxx
Inventory obligations outstanding	$xxx
Less: Ending balance of Accounts Payable	(xxx)
Cash paid for inventory	$xxx

The amount that Graham Products paid for inventory in 2005 is calculated as follows:

Ending balance of Inventory	$ 28,000
Plus: Cost of sales	84,000
Available inventory	$112,000
Less: Beginning balance of Inventory	(35,000)
Inventory purchased	$ 77,000
Plus: Beginning balance of Accounts Payable	(21,000)
Inventory obligations outstanding	$ 98,000
Less: Ending balance of Accounts Payable	(17,500)
Cash paid for inventory	$ 80,500

❱ EXPENSES TRANSFORMED TO CASH PAID

To convert expenses to cash paid during the period, we must first determine whether the expense is an accrued one, in which case the cash payment is made after incurring it, or a prepaid one, in which case the payment was made prior to incurring it.

❱ **ACCRUED EXPENSES** Accrued expenses have related balance sheet accounts that are liabilities. For example, Graham Products recorded accrued expenses that include salaries expense, rent expense, and income tax expense. To determine the cash paid associated with accrued expenses, the expense must be examined in association with the change in the related liability account. Examining Graham Products's salary information, we see that the company recorded salaries expense of $14,600 and had a liability at year end of $5,500 for Accrued Salaries Payable. This liability represents salaries expense that has been incurred, but not yet paid.

In order to transform accrued expenses to the amount of cash paid for the expense, begin with the liability account's beginning balance and add the expense for the period, then subtract the beginning balance of the liability account. Graham Products had a beginning balance in the Accrued Salaries Payable account of $8,000 and recorded $14,600 of salaries expense. However, $5,500 remained in the liability account at the end of the period. Cash paid for salaries is calculated as follows:

Beginning balance of Accrued Salaries Payable	$ 8,000
Plus: Salaries expense	14,600
Less: Ending balance of Accrued Salaries Payable	(5,500)
Cash paid for salaries	$17,100

The accountant would perform the same analysis for rent expense and income tax espense to determine the cash paid for rent and income during the period.

❯ PREPAID EXPENSES   To transform prepaid expenses to the amount of cash paid during the period, begin with the ending balance of the related asset account, add the expense for the period, then subtract the ending balance of the asset account. Graham Products's Prepaid Insurance account had an ending balance of $2,000 at the end of 2005 and a beginning balance of $1,000. In addition, Graham Products reported insurance expense of $600 during the period. The amount of cash paid for insurance during 2005 is determined as follows:

Ending balance of Prepaid Insurance	$2,000
Plus: Insurance expense	600
Less: Beginning balance of Prepaid Insurance	(1,000)
Cash paid for insurance	$1,600

❯ INTEREST EXPENSE TRANSFORMED TO CASH PAID FOR INTEREST

To obtain the amount of cash paid for interest, the expense must be adjusted for the amount of premium or discount amortized during the period. This adjustment is made because the amortization represents the difference between cash paid and interest expense. Amortization of a discount represents the amount by which interest expense exceeds cash interest for the period, whereas amortization of a premium represents the amount by which cash interest is greater than interest expense.

For Graham Products, the $700 of discount amortized during the period is subtracted from interest expense to obtain cash paid for interest.

These steps allow users to calculate cash flows from operating activities using the direct method. Illustration 19.7 provides a summary of how each item in the income statement is converted to cash flows. Illustration 19.8 presents Graham Products's 2005 statement of cash flows using the direct method.

Illustration 19.7

Preparing the Operating Activities Section of the Statement of Cash Flows— Direct Method

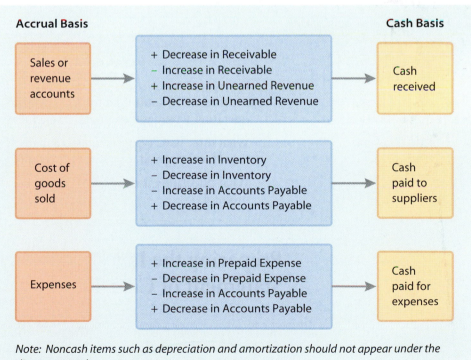

Note: Noncash items such as depreciation and amortization should not appear under the direct approach.

Illustration 19.8

Statement of Cash Flows (Direct Method)

Graham Products
Statement of Cash Flows (Direct Method)
For the Year Ended December 31, 2005

Cash Flows from Operating Activities:		
Cash collected from customers		$128,250
Cash paid for inventory		(80,500)
Cash paid for salaries		(17,100)
Cash paid for insurance		(1,600)
Cash paid for interest		(3,500)
Cash paid for rent		(6,000)
Cash paid for taxes		(4,000)
Net cash provided by operating activities		$ 15,550
Cash Flows from Investing Activities:		
Purchases of equipment	($8,500)	
Sale of equipment	4,500	
Net cash used by investing activities		(4,000)
Cash Flows from Financing Activities:		
Sale of common stock	$15,000	
Purchase of treasury stock	(3,000)	
Payment of dividends	(6,650)	
Net cash provided by financing activities		5,350
Net increase in cash and cash equivalents		$ 16,900
Cash and cash equivalents at January 1, 2005		25,000
Cash and cash equivalents at December 31, 2005		$ 41,900
Supplemental Cash Flow Disclosures:		
Cash paid for interest		$ 3,500
Cash paid for income taxes		4,000
Noncash Investing and Financing Activities:		
Land valued at $15,000 was purchased by issuance of notes payable		

CHECK YOUR UNDERSTANDING

1. If Prepaid Insurance has increased during the fiscal period, will the amount of the increase be subtracted from or added to net income (or net loss) in the operating activities section of the statement of cash flows?

2. What three basic types of adjustment are needed to convert net income to cash flows for the period using the indirect method?

3. What calculation is required to convert cost of goods sold to cash paid for inventory?

Preparing the Investing Activities Section of the Statement of Cash Flows

As you recall, the investing activities section of the statement of cash flows provides information about what management is doing with the capital assets of the firm. These activities involve the firm's operating assets, marketable securities, investments, and notes receivables.

The preparation of the investing activities section of the statement of cash flows requires an analysis of the accounts associated with investing activities—typically, accounts like Equipment, Accumulated Depreciation, Land, and Available-for-Sale Securities. Note that cash proceeds and payments should be shown independently in the investing activities section. Returning to the transaction information provided for Graham Products in Illustration 19.4, we see that the company both sold equipment and purchased equipment. Therefore, the Equipment and Accumulated Depreciation accounts and the Land account should be reviewed.

❭ EQUIPMENT AND ACCUMULATED DEPRECIATION   Recall that Graham Products sold equipment that had an original cost of $5,000 and a remaining book value of $3,000 for $4,500 in cash. This transaction resulted in a gain for Graham Products of $1,500. It is important to recognize that the full amount of the cash proceeds of a sale of equipment is reported in the investing activities section, which also required that we subtract the gain in the operating activities section.

Graham Products also purchased $8,500 of equipment during the period; this is reported as a cash payment. This can be determined by examining the change in the Equipment account:

Ending balance of Equipment	$42,000
Less: Beginning balance of Equipment	(38,500)
Plus: Sale of equipment	5,000
Purchase of equipment	$ 8,500

❭ LAND   A further analysis of the balance sheet for Graham Products shows a $15,000 increase in the Land account. A purchase of land would normally be reported in the investing activities section; however, Graham Products purchased the land by issuing long-term notes payable and no cash was involved. Noncash transactions that are significant to investors' understanding of the financial statements should be reported in an accompanying schedule or report. Graham Products has elected to report its significant noncash transactions in a schedule at the end of the statement.

❭ INVESTMENTS   The purchase or sale of investments should also be reported in the investing activities section. Investments include available-for-sale and held-to-maturity investments, and also investments accounted for under the equity method. Transactions involving trading securities (including unrealized holding gains and losses and purchases and sales) should be part of operating activities. When reporting transactions involving investments, it is important to include only the cash proceeds from sales of investments and any cash payments made to acquire investments.

The final activities reported in the investing activities section are loans made by the company to others. Normally companies would report such loans as notes receivable in the balance sheet.

This completes the analysis of balance sheet accounts related to investing activities. Return to Illustration 19.6 or 19.8 to review the investing activities section of the statement of cash flows for Graham Products.

CHECK YOUR UNDERSTANDING

1. What general ledger accounts should generally be reviewed for transactions that affect the investing activities section of the statement of cash flows?

2. Would proceeds from the sale of an investment be reflected as a positive amount or a negative amount in the investing activities section?

3. When analyzing activity in securities accounts, what types of transactions would be included in the statement of cash flows?

Preparing the Financing Activities Section of the Statement of Cash Flows

The financing activities section of the statement of cash flows provides information about transactions between the company and its owners and creditors. These activities involve the firm's debt and equity accounts and its payment of dividends.

The preparation of the financing activities section of the statement of cash flows requires an analysis of the accounts associated with financing activities. For Graham Products, these accounts include the Long-Term Notes Payable account, the Common Stock account, and the Retained Earnings and Treasury Stock accounts. As in the investing activities section, cash proceeds and payments should be shown independently in the financing activities section.

Let's review each account that we have just mentioned to find the company's cash flows from financing activities.

❯ **LONG-TERM NOTES PAYABLE** The increase in Graham's Long-Term Notes Payable account is due to the purchase of land, not the receipt of cash, and is disclosed as a significant noncash transaction.

❯ **COMMON STOCK** Graham Products's Common Stock account increased by $15,000 during the year. Based on the additional information, common stock was issued, and this is a source of cash provided by financing activities.

❯ **TREASURY STOCK** The company repurchased $3,000 of its own stock during the year. The reacquisition of a company's own shares qualifies as a financing cash outflow.

❯ **DIVIDENDS** The final financing activity for Graham Products is the payment of dividends. The amount of dividends paid during the period can be determined by analyzing the Retained Earnings account.

For Graham Products, the following information is available for the Retained Earnings account:

Retained Earnings		
	13,250	Beg. bal.
Dividends 6,650	18,200	Net income
	24,800	End. bal.

This completes the analysis of the balance sheet accounts related to financing activities for Graham Products. Review Illustration 19.6 or 19.8 to see how each amount discussed is reflected in the statement of cash flows.

CHECK YOUR UNDERSTANDING

1. Describe a transaction affecting the Treasury Stock account that would result in a cash outflow.

2. How would the repayment of a long-term note be reflected in the financing activities section of the statement of cash flows?

3. To determine the amount of cash paid for dividends in a period, which general ledger account should be reviewed?

Using the Statement of Cash Flows for Analysis

LO 4 Describe how the statement of cash flows can be used to analyze liquidity and risk, and explain how product life cycles affect cash flows.

CASH FLOW

product life cycle the stages a product goes through from concept to use to eventual withdrawal from the marketplace

🧩 *Critical Thinking: How do you think the launch of a new product line might affect a company's cash flows from operating activities?*

PRODUCT LIFE CYCLES AND CASH FLOW

Analysts examine many aspects of a company's statement of cash flows. The first issue to examine is a firm's cash flows in relation to the **product life cycle**, or the stages that a product goes through from concept to use to eventual withdrawal from the marketplace. A company's products normally go through four phases: introduction, growth, maturity, and decline. Normally, companies do not rely on only one product, but rather have many products at various stages. However, this analysis is useful when thinking about a company's main cash flow generator.

During a product's introduction phase, net income is usually negative, and the company's cash flows from operating activities are negative because of the costs of developing and introducing the product. In addition, the acquisition of physical assets to manufacture the product results in negative cash flows from investing activities. At this point, the company must fund its operations by engaging in financing activities. Because of the risk and the lack of capital assets that can be used as collateral, most of the financing proceeds will come from issuing equity.

As the company's product enters the growth phase and sales of the product begin to accelerate, the company's net income turns positive and operating activities begin to generate positive cash flows. However, the company will still have negative cash flows from investing activities because it will need to make investments in order to increase capacity. Normally, a company that is in the growth stage will still require cash from financing activities; however, the company is becoming less risky as its product is becoming accepted, and this allows the company to begin issuing debt.

The third stage of the product life cycle is maturity, during which net income is positive and is reaching its peak. In this stage, the company's product is reaching its maximum sales, and the company does not need any additional manufacturing capacity. During the maturity stage, the company's operations are generating enough positive cash flows to pay for investing activities. The company does not need to obtain cash from financing activities and may begin to pay dividends or repurchase treasury stock.

The final stage of the product life cycle is decline. During this stage, the company's net income is beginning to decline and the company has excess manufacturing capacity. Cash flows from operating activities are still positive, but are declining. Because the company has excess manufacturing capacity, it does not need to invest in additional physical assets and may even begin to sell off its excess plant and equipment. Financing activities to repay debt and pay dividends to stockholders use cash. Illustration 19.9 shows the trend of financing, investing, and operating activities in relation to the life cycle of a firm's products.

LIQUIDITY AND RISK

ANALYSIS

Elements taken from the statement of cash flows can also be used to assess a company's liquidity and risk. Previously, you learned that the current ratio and the quick ratio can be used to assess a company's liquidity. These ratios provide a measure of assets available at a specific point in time to meet current liabilities.

The cash flow measure of liquidity is a ratio that measures resources generated *over a period of time* that are available to meet current liabilities. The **operating cash flow ratio** is calculated in the following manner:

operating cash flow ratio a liquidity ratio that measures resources generated over a period of time that are available to meet current liabilities; calculated by dividing cash flows from operating activities by current liabilities

$$\text{Operating Cash Flow Ratio} = \frac{\text{Cash Flows from Operating Activities}}{\text{Current Liabilities}}$$

Illustration 19.9

Product Life Cycles and Cash Flows from Financing, Operating, and Investing Activities

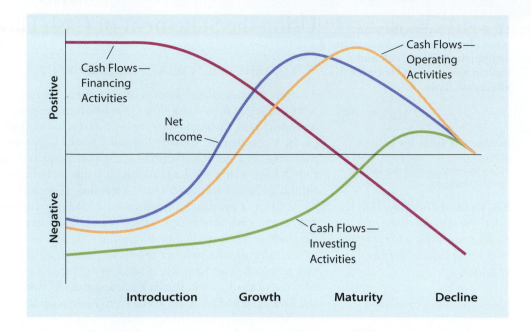

Using the figures for Graham Products, the operating cash flow ratio is calculated as follows:

$$\frac{\$15,550}{\$34,900} = 0.45$$

This ratio tells analysts that the company generated a little less than half of the cash needed to settle its current liabilities in one year's operating cycle. For Motorola, this ratio was 0.136 for the 2002 fiscal year, indicating that the company generated approximately 14 cents from operating activities during the year for every dollar of current liabilities. This ratio provides a more dynamic measurement of the resources available for meeting current obligations.

Another cash flow ratio that analysts use to assess risk is the cash current debt coverage ratio. The **cash current debt coverage ratio** is calculated in the following manner:

cash current debt coverage ratio a liquidity ratio used to asses risk; calculated by subtracting current dividends from cash flows from operating activities and dividing the result by current interest-bearing debt

$$\text{Cash Current Debt Coverage Ratio} = \frac{\text{Cash Flows from Operating Activities} - \text{Current Dividends}}{\text{Current Interest-Bearing Debt}}$$

The numerator of this ratio provides the amount of cash flows from operating activities that remains after paying dividends to shareholders. This amount is available to repay debt. When comparing ratios from two companies, a higher ratio indicates that the company faces less risk.

CHECK YOUR UNDERSTANDING

1. What measurement does the operating cash flow ratio provide?

2. Would you expect cash flows from investing activities to be positive or negative during a product's introduction phase? Explain.

3. What operating, investing, and financing activities may take place during a product's maturity stage?

Revisiting the Case

MOTOROLA DOUBLES ITS CASH BALANCE YET REPORTS NET LOSSES

1. If Motorola had not booked noncash "charges for reorganization of businesses and other charges" in 2002, it would have reported net income of $142 million. (Add back $2,627 million in charges to a net loss of $2,485 million.)

2. If a company reports positive cash flows on its statement of cash flows and net losses on its income statement, noncash income statement items should be investigated. Noncash items such as depreciation and amortization and restructuring charges are common items that cause a reduction in net income but do not reduce cash flows.

3. Motorola's restructuring program is intended to cut costs, reduce payrolls, initiate efficiency improvements, and exit from unprofitable markets.

SUMMARY OF LEARNING OBJECTIVES

LO1 Describe how the activities of a business are reflected and categorized in the statement of cash flows.

Business activities are divided into three categories in the statement of cash flows. Operating activities are the transactions required to produce revenues and run the business. These include the receipt of cash from the sale of goods and services, the receipt of interest and dividends, and the payment of cash for salaries, inventory, taxes, or other expenses. Investing activities are those transactions that involve spending on productive assets or investments in order to achieve the objectives of the business. Cash inflows from the sale of property, investments, or marketable securities and cash outflows from the purchase of investments or property fall into this category. Financing activities are transactions that involve the receipt or payment of cash related to liabilities and owners' equity (other than through operations). They include obtaining resources from owners and providing those owners with a return on their investment and borrowing money from creditors and repaying those obligations.

LO2 Distinguish between the direct and indirect methods of preparing the cash flows from operating activities section of the statement of cash flows.

Under the direct method of preparing the operating activities section of the statement of cash flows, each item within the income statement's income from continuing operations is converted into its cash equivalent, providing evidence of all of the company's actual cash inflows and cash outflows. In contrast, the indirect method begins with the net income (or loss) for the period and adjusts it for items that *do not* affect cash flows, including depreciation, amortization, depletion, gains, losses, and changes in current assets and current liabilities. When the indirect method is used, net income, as determined in the income statement, is listed first and then reconciled to net cash supplied to or used by operating activities by making the adjustments for the noncash items previously listed.

LO3 Prepare a full statement of cash flows using both the indirect and the direct methods.

To prepare the statement of cash flows, the operating activities section is completed first, followed by the investing activities and financing activities sections. The statement shows users the cash used by or generated from each type of business activity. The final portion of the statement reconciles the beginning cash balance with the ending cash balance. The operating activities section may be completed using the indirect or the direct method. When the indirect method is used, net income (or loss) is listed first, followed by adjustments for noncash items like depreciation, amortization, gains, losses, and changes in current assets and liabilities. When the direct method is used, all items from the income from continuing operations section of the income statement are translated into their cash equivalents. The investing and financing sections are presented using one standard format. Cash inflows and outflows in these sections are listed independently.

LO4 Describe how the statement of cash flows can be used to analyze liquidity and risk, and explain how product life cycles affect cash flows.

Analysis of a company's product life cycles can yield insight into the related cash flows from operating, investing, and financing activities. The four phases of a product's life cycle—introduction, growth, maturity, and decline—affect a variety of business decisions. Investing in additional capital assets, paying off debt, and paying dividends are a few of the activities affecting cash flows that may be delayed or accelerated depending on the stage of development. In addition, analysts may use elements found in the statement of cash flows to assess liquidity or risk. The operating cash flow ratio measures resources generated *over a period of time* that are available to meet current liabilities. It is calculated by dividing cash flows from operating activities by current liabilities. The cash current debt coverage ratio is calculated by dividing cash flows from operating activities less dividends by current interest-bearing debt.

KEY TERMS

cash current debt coverage ratio (p. 926)
direct method (p. 911)
financing activities (p. 908)

indirect method (p. 911)
investing activities (p. 908)
operating activities (p. 908)
operating cash flow ratio (p. 925)

product life cycle (p. 925)
significant noncash transactions and events (p. 909)
statement of cash flows (p. 908)

EXERCISES

LO2   **EXERCISE 19-1   Direct Method—Operating Activities**

The following information was taken from Cape Row Company's accounting records for 2004:

Accounts Receivable, gross, January 1, 2004	$ 34,500
Accounts Receivable, gross, December 31, 2004	30,400
Sales	400,000
Uncollectible accounts written off	1,200
Current-year estimate of uncollectible accounts	6,500

Required:

1. If Cape Row uses the direct method in its 2004 statement of cash flows, how much should it report as cash collected from customers?

2. Show how this amount will be reported in the statement of cash flows.

LO1,3   **EXERCISE 19-2   Investing Activities**

During the current year, Rang Company had the following account balances and information available:

	Ending Balance	Beginning Balance
Land	$ 77,000	$ 65,000
Building and Equipment	280,000	200,000
Accumulated Depreciation	46,000	50,000
Dividends Payable	15,000	10,000
Retained Earnings	200,000	150,000

Additional information:

A. Land with a carrying value of $38,000 was sold at a loss of $8,000.

B. Equipment with an original cost of $20,000 that had a book value of $4,000 was written off as obsolete.

C. During the year, a building with an original cost of $60,000 and accumulated depreciation of $25,000 was sold at a $23,000 gain.

D. Depreciation expense for the period was recorded.

E. Net income for the year was $80,000.

    F. Additional plant assets were purchased during the year.

    G. Rang Company has no notes payable in the liability section of its balance sheet.

Required: Prepare the investing activities section of the statement of cash flows.

LO1   **EXERCISE 19-3   Reporting of Noncash Items**

The following is the intangible assets section of Corps, Inc.'s comparative balance sheets:

Intangible Assets	Dec. 31, 2005	Dec. 31, 2004
Patent, net of amortization, $22,000 and $18,000	$130,000	$106,000

Additional information: One new patent was purchased on June 30, 2005, by issuing 200 shares of $10 par value common stock, which was selling for $140 per share at June 30, 2004, and $150 at December 31, 2005.

Required:

1. Why will the effects of the patent acquisition not appear in the investing activities section of the statement of cash flows?

2. Show how the effects of the patent acquisition would appear in the company's financial statements.

LO1   **EXERCISE 19-4   Reporting of Noncash Items, Indirect Method**

The following is the intangible assets section of Titolini, Inc.'s comparative balance sheet:

Intangible Assets	Dec. 31, 2005	Dec. 31, 2004
Trademarks, net of amortization, $125,000 and $100,000	$652,000	$600,000

The 2005 income statement disclosed a $42,000 loss on the impairment of a trademark. An additional trademark was purchased during 2005 by issuing 1,000 shares of $1 par value common stock that was currently selling for $20 per share plus an additional cash payment. Titolini reported net income for the year ended December 31, 2005 of $215,000.

Required: Show how the effects of all transactions relating to the trademarks would be reported in the statement of cash flows for 2005 if the indirect method is used.

LO1, 2   **EXERCISE 19-5   Categories of Cash Flow Transactions**

Certain cash flows are reported differently under the direct and indirect methods of preparing the statement of cash flows. Several options are as follows:

    A. Indirect method—operating activities section—add to net income

    B. Indirect method—operating activities section—subtract from net income

    C. Direct method—operating activities section—a separate cash inflow

    D. Direct method—operating activities section—a separate cash outflow

    E. Investing activity

    F. Financing activity

    G. Significant noncash disclosure

    H. Not reported

Required: Identify the proper reporting in the statement of cash flows for each transaction that follows by selecting the letters of *all* correct choices from the list of reporting options (A through H).

1. Permanent impairment of value of $10,000 recognized on patent.

2. Successful defense of patent costing $50,000 in attorney's fees.

3. Amortization expense recognized.

4. Acquisition of trademark by issuing stock.

5. Trade of patent with a fair value of $60,000 and a book value of $24,000 to another company in exchange for a copyright with a fair value of $80,000. Cash difference paid.

6. Payment of wages to employees.

7. Capitalization of interest related to construction of a new ship.

8. Accrual of income taxes due.

9. Cash payment for costs to develop a process to manufacture a new computer disk.

10. Accrual of costs incurred for quality control on newly introduced products.

LO2 **EXERCISE 19-6** **Operating Activities—Indirect Method**

Sikes, Inc. had a net loss of $12,000 for 2005. The increases or decreases in selected accounts during 2005 are as follows:

Accounts

Receivable (net)	$16,000 Decrease
Inventory	4,500 Increase
Prepaid Insurance	2,900 Increase
Accounts Payable	8,000 Increase
Dividends Payable	7,200 Decrease

Required:

1. How much cash was provided by operations during 2005?

2. Explain how a company could report a net loss for the year and still have cash flows generated from operations.

LO1, 2 **EXERCISE 19-7** **Categories of Cash Flow Transactions**

Cash flows are reported in one of the three sections of the statement of cash flows. Several treatment options are as follows:

A. An adjustment in the operating activities section that must be added

B. An adjustment in the operating activities section that must be subtracted

C. Investing activity

D. Financing activity

E. Reported only as a significant noncash disclosure

F. Not reported separately in the statement of cash flows using the indirect method

Required: Identify the proper reporting of each of the following transactions in the statement of cash flows by selecting the letters of the correct choices from the list of reporting options (A through F). Assume that the indirect approach is used.

1. Stock issued in exchange for equipment

2. Increase in Interest Receivable

3. Purchase of land for speculative purposes

4. Payment of dividends to shareholders

5. Gain on the sale of long-lived assets no longer needed in the production process

6. Retirement of long-term debt

7. Amortization of copyright

8. Receipt of dividends on common stock

9. Purchase of available-for-sale securities

10. Purchase of treasury stock from investors

LO1, 3 **EXERCISE 19-8** **Statement of Cash Flows—Direct Method**

The following information is available from Blue Corporation's accounting records for the year ended December 31, 2005:

Cash collected from customers	$360,000
Repayment of long-term debt and interest ($5,000 is interest)	21,000
Cash paid for inventory	140,000

Cash paid for salaries	$120,000
Gain from sale of equipment	3,000
Purchase of long-term bond investment	40,000
Cash from sale of equipment	54,000
Cash dividends declared	38,000
Income taxes paid	16,000
Treasury stock acquired for cash	15,000
Rent collected	6,000
Purchase of land	78,000
Portion of land purchase financed with long-term debt	65,000
Cash paid for research and development costs	23,000
Cash dividends paid	22,000
Beginning Cash balance	18,500

Required: Prepare a statement of cash flows for 2005 for Blue Corporation.

LO1, 2 **EXERCISE 19-9 Direct Method—Operating Activities**

Ippso, Inc. has the following account balances for the beginning and end of the current year:

	Ending Balance	Beginning Balance
Cash	$17,000	$1,500
Accounts Receivable	7,500	3,500
Inventory	3,500	8,000
Plant and Equipment, net	11,500	7,000
Accounts Payable	6,700	1,000
Salaries Payable	0	1,800
Dividends Payable	1,800	1,200
Income Tax Payable	5,500	1,000
Common Stock	3,000	2,000
Additional Paid-in Capital	9,000	5,500
Retained Earnings	13,500	7,500

The company released the following income statement for the current year:

Ippso, Inc.
Income Statement
For the Current Year

Sales	$70,500
Sales returns and allowances	(1,000)
Net sales	$69,500
Cost of sales	(16,000)
Gross profit	$53,500
Salaries expense	(19,000)
Interest expense	(5,000)
Depreciation expense	(2,000)
Income tax expense	(11,000)
Net income	$16,500

Required: Using the direct method, prepare the operating activities section of Ippso's statement of cash flows for the year. All amounts owed to creditors pertain to merchandise.

LO1 **EXERCISE 19-10 Categories of Cash Flow Transactions**

Various cash flow categories in which transactions are reported are as follows:

A. Inflow of cash from an investing activity

B. Outflow of cash for an investing activity

C. Inflow of cash from a financing activity

D. Outflow of cash for a financing activity

E. Operating activities

F. Reported as significant noncash disclosure only

Required: Identify the proper reporting in the statement of cash flows of each transaction that follows by selecting the letters of the correct choices from the list of reporting options (A through F). For any transaction that would be reported differently under the indirect method and the direct method, indicate how it would be reported under each method.

1. Sell preferred stock to new stockholders
2. Purchase treasury stock
3. Issue a long-term note in exchange for a building acquired
4. Repay principal borrowed from bank
5. Pay interest on bank loan
6. Sell investment in real estate
7. Lend money to a subsidiary
8. Pay salaries previously accrued
9. Purchase a trading security
10. Pay cash dividends to stockholders

LO2 **EXERCISE 19-11 Cash Received from Customers**

At December 31, 2005 and 2004, Hall, Inc. reported the account balances that follow. During 2005, Hall, Inc. wrote off $2,100 of uncollectible accounts.

	12/31/05	12/31/04
Accounts Receivable	$ 42,000	$ 42,500
Sales	799,000	965,000
Bad Debt Expense	2,800	2,000
Unearned Revenue	4,200	5,000
Dividends	15,000	12,600
Allowance for Uncollectible Accounts	3,000	2,300
Accounts Payable	34,800	35,000

Required:

1. Calculate "cash collected from customers" to be reported in the 2005 statement of cash flows, assuming Hall uses the direct method of calculating cash flows from operations.
2. Why does Bad Debt Expense create a unique situation when determining cash flows from operations using the indirect method of calculating cash flows from operations?

LO1, 3 **EXERCISE 19-12 Reporting Investing and Financing Activities**

Information from Chingy Web Development's comparative balance sheets follows:

	Dec. 31, 2005	Dec. 31, 2004
Land	$100,000	$ 40,000
Equipment	600,000	500,000
Notes Payable	92,000	0
Retained Earnings	95,000	120,000
Additional Paid-in Capital	85,000	20,000
Common Stock, $1 par value	90,000	50,000

Additional information:

A. New equipment purchased during 2005 totaled $100,000 in exchange for a $92,000, 12 percent, five-year term note and the balance in cash.

B. Land appraised at $60,000 was acquired in exchange for website development services.

C. During 2005, a stock dividend was declared and distributed.

D. Net income for 2005 was $80,000.

Required: Show how these items are reported in the investing and financing activities sections of the 2005 statement of cash flows; include disclosure of significant noncash items.

LO1, 2   **EXERCISE 19-13   Operating Activities and Cash Equivalents**
The following transactions occurred for Solamia Company during 2005:

A. Purchased trading securities for $600 cash on June 1, 2005. Sold the same securities on July 16 for a gain of $100.

B. On September 30, 2005, collected cash from the maturity of a $10,000, 90-day Treasury bill. Immediately used part of the cash to buy an $8,000, 120-day certificate of deposit.

C. Purchased a $20,000, 60-day certificate of deposit for cash.

D. Reimbursed the $800 petty cash account for $125 for postage and other miscellaneous expenses. The account has been active for several years.

Required: Show how these items will appear in the statement of cash flows for the year ended December 31, 2005, under the indirect method. For any transactions that do not directly appear in the statement of cash flows, explain why. Solamia Company reported net income of $72,000 for 2005.

LO1, 2   **EXERCISE 19-14   Categories of Cash Flow Transactions**
GAAP requires certain transactions to be reported within each of the three sections of the statement of cash flows. Several transactions for Winkler Corporation are as follows:

A. Paid off a portion of long-term debt that was not due until the next fiscal period

B. Paid interest on a long-term note payable

C. Paid a short-term nonoperating note

D. Paid sales taxes collected from customers

E. Paid salaries that were accrued in the previous fiscal period

F. Issued stock in exchange for the purchase of a new building

G. Paid dividends to shareholders of record

H. Paid cash for a new generator that will be a backup energy source for a new building

I. Made an adjustment to cash as a result of an error in recording an expense found during a bank reconciliation

J. Factored receivables to a finance company

Required: For each of these transactions, indicate in which section of the statement of cash flows the amount will be reported under the direct method, and whether the transaction is a cash outflow or inflow.

LO2   **EXERCISE 19-15   Operating Activities—Taxes and Cash Equivalents**
Selected account balances at December 31, 2005 and 2004, for Sollee, Inc. are as follows:

	12/31/05	12/31/04
60-day Treasury Bill	$ 70,000	$ 20,000
6-month Certificate of Deposit	25,000	0
Cash	19,400	25,400
Deferred Tax Asset, Current	14,600	10,200
Investment in Trading Securities	84,000	101,300
Income Tax Payable	22,000	32,000
Deferred Tax Liability, Noncurrent	7,600	15,800
Unrealized Holding Gain—Trading Securities	3,200	4,800
Dividend Income	1,100	500
Income Tax Expense	156,000	129,000
Valuation Allowance	4,000	2,500

The 60-day Treasury bills are dated October 3, 2005, and November 23, 2004. The CD matures on February 4, 2006.

Required:

1. How much is the change in cash and cash equivalents for 2005?

2. How much cash was paid for income taxes during 2005?

3. During what stage of the company's product life cycle will cash flows paid for income taxes be largest?

LO2   EXERCISE **19-16**   **Trading Securities**

Selected account balances for Guarantee, Inc. are presented here:

	12/31/05	12/31/04
120-day Treasury Bill	$70,000	$ 20,000
6-month Certificate of Deposit	25,000	0
Cash	19,400	25,400
Investment in Trading Securities	84,000	101,300
Realized Loss on Sale of Trading Securities	1,300	3,400
Unrealized Holding Gain—Trading Securities	3,200	4,800
Dividend Income	1,100	500

During 2005, Guarantee sold trading securities with an original cost of $58,000. Additional trading securities were purchased during the year. Guarantee reported net income of $97,000 for the year ended December 31, 2005.

Required:

1. Prepare journal entries for all transactions relating to the trading securities that occurred during 2005.

2. Show how the effects of the trading securities are reported in the statement of cash flows for 2005 under both the direct and indirect methods.

3. Why do you think trading securities are reported differently from other investments in the statement of cash flows?

LO2   EXERCISE **19-17**   **Operating Activities—Indirect Method**

The following is information from Light, Inc. at December 31, 2005 and 2004.

Accounts	12/31/05	12/31/04
Accounts Receivable, net	$ 20,400	$ 23,300
Inventories	16,000	14,500
Patent	28,000	15,000
Investment in Dark Company	16,000	22,000
Equipment	214,000	211,000
Accounts Payable	8,700	10,000
Income Tax Payable	3,000	2,500
Accumulated Depreciation	35,000	33,000

Light's income statement for the year ended December 31, 2005 appears at the top of the facing page.

The investment in Dark Company is accounted for using the equity method. All acquisitions of long-term assets were for cash unless otherwise stated. The plant assets were sold for $12,000 and had an original cost of $45,000.

Required:

1. Compute the net cash flows from the operating activities section of Light Inc.'s statement of cash flows for 2005, using the indirect method.

Light, Inc.
Income Statement
For the Year Ended December 31, 2005

Sales	$380,000
Cost of sales	225,000
Gross profit	$155,000
Bad debt expense	(2,200)
Amortization of patent	(800)
Other operating expenses	(69,000)
Investment earnings (Dark Company)	4,000
Loss on sale of plant assets	(3,000)
Income tax expense	(33,000)
Net income	$ 51,000

2. Both the income statement and the statement of cash flows contain operating activities. How does the presentation of operating activities in the statement of cash flows differ from the presentation in the income statement?

LO4   EXERCISE 19-18   **Analysis of Cash Flows**

Following are totals from the statement of cash flows and the amount of net income/(loss) for Markum Corporation for two different accounting periods:

	Case X	Case Y
Cash flows from (for) operating activities	$165,000	($ 45,000)
Cash flows from (for) investing activities	(20,000)	(135,000)
Cash flows from (for) financing activities	(25,000)	168,000
Net increase (decrease) in cash flows	$120,000	($ 12,000)
Net income/(loss)	$213,000	($ 35,000)

Required: Identify which phase of the life cycle of Markum Corporation's product each of these cases most likely represents. Elaborate on what occurs in each of the phases that you identify.

LO4   EXERCISE 19-19   **Analysis of Cash Flows**

Following are totals from the statement of cash flows and the amount of net income/(loss) for Sharl Corporation for two different accounting periods:

	Case X	Case Y
Cash flows from (for) operating activities	$50,000	$14,000
Cash flows from (for) investing activities	(32,000)	21,000
Cash flows from (for) financing activities	20,000	(46,000)
Net increase (decrease) in cash flows	$38,000	($11,000)
Net income/(loss)	$45,000	$13,000

Required: Identify which phase of the life cycle of Sharl Corporation's product each of these cases most likely represents. Elaborate on what occurs in each of the phases that you identify.

LO4   EXERCISE 19-20   **Analysis of Cash Flows**

Totals from selected financial statements of Gill Corporation for the years ended December 31, 2005 and 2004 are given on the top of the next page.

	12/31/05	12/31/04
Cash flows from (for) operating activities	$102,000	$ 12,000
Cash flows from (for) investing activities	16,000	33,000
Cash flows from (for) financing activities	(40,000)	(25,000)
Net increase (decrease) in cash flows	$ 78,000	$ 20,000
Net income/(loss)	$ 60,000	$ 24,000
Current assets	$256,000	$244,000
Total assets	960,000	850,000
Current liabilities	120,000	86,000
Dividends	34,000	10,000

Of the current liabilities, 30 percent are interest-bearing.

Required:

1. Calculate the operating cash flow ratio for the years ended December 31, 2005 and 2004. What information does this provide?

2. Calculate the cash current debt coverage ratio for the years ended December 31, 2005 and 2004. What information does this provide?

PROBLEMS

LO1, 2, 3   PROBLEM **19-1**   **Statement of Cash Flows—Direct Method**

Conviser Company's income statement for the year ended December 31, 2005, appears below. Its comparative balance sheets at December 31, 2005 and 2004, appear on the facing page.

Conviser Company
Income Statement
For the Year Ended December 31, 2005

Sales		$285,600
Cost of sales		156,000
Gross profit		$129,600
Operating expenses:		
General and administrative expenses	$78,400	
Salaries expense	27,000	
Rent expense	2,800	
Depreciation expense	5,100	
Total operating expenses		(113,300)
Other revenue and expenses:		
Gain on sale of equipment	$ 700	
Interest revenue	300	
Interest expense	(2,000)	(1,000)
Income from continuing operations before income taxes		$ 15,300
Income tax expense		5,800
Net income		$ 9,500

Additional information:

A. The company declared dividends in the amount of $9,100 during the year.

B. Additional land and equipment were purchased for cash.

Conviser Company
Comparative Balance Sheets
December 31, 2005 and 2004

	December 31, 2005	December 31, 2004
Assets		
Current assets:		
Cash	$ 13,000	$ 32,200
Accounts receivable	15,400	17,500
Inventory	19,400	21,500
Prepaid rent	300	2,700
Total current assets	$ 48,100	$ 73,900
Property and equipment:		
Land	53,600	28,000
Equipment	48,200	35,600
Less: Accumulated depreciation	(6,300)	(3,900)
Total assets	$143,600	$133,600
Liabilities and Stockholders' Equity		
Current liabilities:		
Accounts payable	$ 12,400	$ 24,500
Salaries payable	1,700	2,600
Interest payable	1,900	3,000
Income tax payable	5,500	3,200
Dividends payable	2,900	—
Total liabilities	$ 24,400	$ 33,300
Long-term notes payable	8,000	30,000
Stockholders' equity:		
Common stock, $1 par	20,000	18,000
Preferred stock, $4 par	26,000	12,000
Additional paid-in capital	55,000	30,500
Retained earnings	10,200	9,800
Total current liabilities and stockholders' equity	$143,600	$133,600

C. Equipment that had originally cost $8,000 was sold for $6,000 cash. The book value at the time of the sale was $5,300.

D. All accounts payable are related to merchandise purchases.

E. The company uses a perpetual LIFO inventory system and uses straight-line depreciation for all depreciable assets.

Required: Prepare a statement of cash flows using the direct method and include a reconciliation of net income to net cash from operating activities.

Analyze: What are the main advantages of preparing the statement of cash flows using the direct method?

LO1, 2, 3   PROBLEM **19-2   Statement of Cash Flows—Indirect Method**
Use the information from Problem 19-1 for Conviser Company for the year ended December 31, 2005.

Required: Prepare a statement of cash flows using the indirect method.

Analyze: Identify the major advantages of using the indirect method of preparing the statement of cash flows.

LO1, 2, 3, 4 PROBLEM 19-3 **Statement of Cash Flows—Direct Method**

Provided here are the comparative balance sheets for First Coast, Inc. at December 31, 2005 and 2004:

First Coast, Inc.
Comparative Balance Sheets
December 31, 2005 and 2004

	Dec. 31, 2005	Dec. 31, 2004
Assets		
Current assets:		
Cash	$135,000	$115,000
Certificate of deposit, 90-day	20,000	15,000
Trading securities	48,000	23,000
Accounts receivable	45,400	62,400
Less: Allowance for uncollectible accounts	(2,900)	(2,200)
Inventory	27,600	26,200
Prepaid insurance	5,500	4,000
Total current assets	$278,600	$243,400
Property and equipment:		
Land	56,000	30,000
Equipment	122,000	65,000
Accumulated depreciation	(24,000)	(16,000)
Total assets	$432,600	$322,400
Liabilities and Stockholders' Equity		
Current liabilities:		
Accounts payable	$ 45,000	$ 83,000
Customer advances	15,000	4,000
Income taxes payable	3,500	2,600
Dividends payable	18,000	16,000
Total current liabilities	$ 81,500	$105,600
Bonds payable	100,000	70,000
Less: Discount on bonds	(3,300)	(2,600)
Stockholders' equity:		
Common stock	80,000	50,000
Additional paid-in capital	120,000	80,000
Retained earnings	54,400	19,400
Total liabilities and stockholders' equity	$432,600	$322,400

The company's income statement for the year ended December 31, 2005, appears at the top of the facing page.

Additional information is as follows:

A. Land and additional equipment were purchased for cash.

B. Trading securities were purchased during the year. None were sold.

C. A piece of equipment that had originally cost $12,000, with accumulated depreciation in the amount of $7,200, was sold. This was the only equipment sold during the year.

D. The company declared dividends in the amount of $25,000 during the year.

E. Bonds were issued at 95 percent of the face value.

First Coast, Inc.
Income Statement
For the Year Ended December 31, 2005

Sales		$895,000
Cost of sales		(656,000)
Gross profit		$239,000
Operating expenses:		
General and administrative expenses	$123,500	
Bad debt expense	3,000	
Insurance expense	3,600	
Depreciation expense	15,200	
Total operating expenses		(145,300)
Other revenues and expenses:		
Dividend revenue	$ 1,000	
Interest expense	(8,200)	
Loss on sale of equipment	(500)	(7,700)
Income from continuing operations before income taxes		$ 86,000
Income tax expense		26,000
Net income		$ 60,000

Required: Prepare a statement of cash flows for First Coast, Inc. using the direct method.

Analyze: Evaluate where this company is obtaining its funds and for what purpose it is using the funds.

LO1, 2, 3   PROBLEM **19-4**   **Statement of Cash Flows—Indirect Method**
Use the information provided in Problem 19-3.

Required: Prepare a statement of cash flows for First Coast, Inc. for the year ended December 31, 2005, using the indirect method.

Analyze: Which section(s) of the statement differ when the statement of cash flows is prepared using the indirect method as opposed to using the direct method?

LO1, 2, 3   PROBLEM **19-5**   **Operating Cash Flows—Indirect Method**
Information from Chimney Repairs Inc.'s financial statements for the years ended December 31, 2005 and 2004, is as follows:

Chimney Repairs Inc.
Income Statement
For the Year Ended December 31, 2005

Sales	$500,000
Cost of sales	200,000
Gross profit	$300,000
Amortization of bond issue costs	(1,000)
Interest expense	(29,000)
Other operating expenses	(100,000)
Unrealized gain from trading securities	4,000
Realized loss on trading securities	(8,000)
Income tax expense	(60,000)
Net income	$106,000

Chimney Repairs Inc.
Balance Sheet Amounts
December 31, 2005 and 2004

	12/31/05	12/31/04
Accounts receivable, net	$40,000	$38,000
Inventory	16,000	21,000
Salaries payable	6,000	12,000
Deferred bond issue costs	17,500	18,500
Bonds payable, net of discount	80,000	60,000
Deferred tax liability—long-term	2,000	9,000
Accounts payable	18,000	4,000
Income tax payable	57,000	45,000
Deferred tax asset—current	8,000	12,600
Trading securities	17,000	40,000
Fair value adjustment—trading securities	4,000	0

Additional information: Of the total amount of interest expense, $5,000 is bond discount amortization. During 2005, a portion of the trading securities was sold. No trading securities were purchased. All acquisitions were for cash unless otherwise stated. Bad debt expense included with operating costs was $500.

Required: Compute net cash flows from operating activities to be shown on Chimney's statement of cash flows for 2005, using the indirect method.

Analyze: What are the types of adjustments that must be made when preparing the operating activities section of the statement of cash flows using the indirect method? Why are these adjustments necessary?

LO1, 2, 3   PROBLEM 19-6   **Operating Cash Flows—Direct Method**

Rickets uses the direct method to prepare its statement of cash flows. The following are selected accounts from Rickets's trial balances at December 31, 2005, and December 31, 2004. All accounts have normal balances.

	Dec. 31, 2005	Dec. 31, 2004
Cash	$ 35,000	$ 32,000
Accounts Receivable	53,000	50,000
Inventory	31,000	47,000
Cost of Sales	250,000	380,000
90-day Treasury Bill	40,000	55,000
Interest Expense	4,300	2,600
Trading Securities	30,000	16,000
Customer Deposits	14,000	12,000
Sales Discounts	400	300
Income Tax Expense	40,400	61,200
4-month CD, matures 1/8/06	25,000	0
Allowance for Uncollectible Accounts	3,000	2,600
Accumulated Depreciation	16,500	15,000
Accounts Payable	25,000	17,500
Income Tax Payable	21,000	27,100
Deferred Tax Liability	14,000	12,000
Interest Payable	5,300	4,600
Sales	830,000	770,000
Bad Debt Expense	3,200	2,700

Rickets wrote off $2,900 of receivables during the year.

Required:

1. Determine cash collected from customers during 2005.
2. Determine the amount of cash paid for interest during 2005.
3. Determine the amount of cash paid for inventory during 2005.
4. Determine the amount of cash paid for income taxes during 2005.
5. What is the nature of the operating activities section of the statement of cash flows?

Analyze: Determine the net increase or decrease in cash and cash equivalents for 2005.

LO1, 2, 3   **PROBLEM 19-7**   **Investing and Operating Activities**

During 2005, Nutrition Connections sold a building with a book value of $40,000 and an original cost of $280,000. Also during 2005, Nutrition Connections purchased a new building by signing a mortgage for $350,000 and paying the balance in cash. The following information is taken from the accounting records of Nutrition Connections for the years ended December 31, 2005 and 2004.

	Dec. 31, 2005	Dec. 31, 2004
Accumulated Depreciation—Building	$150,000	$250,000
Net Income (Loss)	450,000	240,000
Accounts Payable	280,000	230,000
Building	720,000	620,000
Dividends Payable	60,000	80,000
Retained Earnings	400,000	300,000
Depreciation Expense	140,000	150,000
Loss on Sale of Building	10,000	—

Required:

1. Prepare the investing and financing activities sections of the statement of cash flows and any related supplemental disclosure needed for the year ended December 31, 2005.
2. Prepare a partial operating activities section of the statement of cash flows to show the effects of the plant asset transactions for 2005.

Communicate: Describe the nature of the items reported as part of investing activities.

Analyze: In examining the balance sheet, in which accounts do you normally look to find investing activities?

LO1, 2, 4   **PROBLEM 19-8**   **Operating Activities and the Product Life Cycle**

The following data are taken from the accounts of Epic Company at December 31, 2005 and 2004:

	Dec. 31, 2005	Dec. 31, 2004
Cash	$64,000	$53,000
Accounts Receivable	28,000	25,000
Trading Securities	15,000	4,000
Unrealized Gain on Trading Securities	0	1,000
Accounts Payable	6,500	10,000
Inventory	37,500	40,000
30-day Certificate of Deposit	22,000	35,000

Epic Company paid $42,000 in dividends, recognized a gain of $13,000 on the sale of some of its production equipment, incurred $7,000 of depreciation expense and $2,100 of patent amortization, and purchased trading securities during the year. Epic reported $65,000 of net income for 2005.

Required:

1. Calculate Epic's cash flows from operating activities for 2005.

2. Calculate the amount that Epic would report as "Net increase/decrease in cash and cash equivalents" for the year ended December 31, 2005.

3. Which method of preparing the statement of cash flows is preferred by the FASB? Why do you think the FASB prefers this method?

Analyze: In which of the four phases of the company's life cycle do you think Epic is operating? Explain.

LO1,3   **PROBLEM 19-9   Investing Activities and Supplemental Disclosure**

Solano Company had the following account balances and information available for 2005:

	December 31	January 1
Land	$ 85,000	$ 45,000
Building and Equipment	180,000	100,000
Accumulated Depreciation	36,000	50,000
Investment in Available-for-Sale Securities	29,000	16,000
Patents, net	15,000	10,000
Unrealized Gain from Available-for-Sale Securities	2,300	500
Retained Earnings	200,000	150,000

Land with a carrying value of $35,000 was sold at a loss of $6,000. Equipment with an original cost of $20,000 that had a book value of $4,000 was written off as obsolete. During the year, a building with an original cost of $60,000 and accumulated depreciation of $25,000 was sold at a $23,000 gain. Depreciation expense for the period was recorded. Net income for the year was $60,000. A patent was acquired during the year in exchange for issuing 1,200 shares of common stock with a par value of $1 per share and a market value of $26 per share. Additional marketable securities were purchased during the year. Solano Company has no notes payable in the liabilities section of its balance sheet.

Required:

1. Prepare the investing activities section of the statement of cash flows for the year ended December 31, 2005.

2. Prepare the disclosure for significant noncash transactions for the statement of cash flows for the year ended December 31, 2005.

3. What transactions in addition to those reported in question 2 are required to be reported as supplemental disclosures for the statement of cash flows?

Analyze: By what net amount did the Land account change during 2005?

LO1,3   **PROBLEM 19-10   Financing Activities**

Green Light Company presented the following account balances for 2005:

	Dec. 31, 2005	Jan. 1, 2005
Dividends Payable	$ 6,000	$10,000
Additional Paid-in Capital	98,000	40,000
Retained Earnings	128,000	96,000
Treasury Stock, 200 and 350 shares, respectively	21,500	7,000
Machinery	78,000	53,000
Accumulated Depreciation—Machinery	14,200	19,000
Common Stock	42,000	30,000
Investment in Trading Securities	15,000	65,000

Additional information:

A. Cash dividends of $21,000 were declared on December 15, 2005, payable January 15, 2006.

B. An old machine that had an original cost of $12,000 and was 60 percent depreciated was sold for a gain of $4,000.

C. A fully depreciated office machine that cost $4,500 was written off.

D. The company issued 1,200 shares of its common stock (par value $10) on June 15, 2005.

E. A loan was acquired in the amount of $40,000 cash.

F. Trading securities were sold during the year.

G. Some items appearing in Green Light's income statement of 2005 were sales revenues of $236,000, interest income from investments of $1,400, depreciation expense, interest expense of $2,400, an unrealized loss on trading securities of $600, a realized gain on the sale of trading securities of $2,300, and miscellaneous cash expenses of $7,300.

H. Net income was $53,000.

Required:

1. How much would be reported as "cash paid for dividends" in the statement of cash flows for the year ended December 31, 2005?

2. How much would be reported as "cost of machinery purchased" in the statement of cash flows for the year ended December 31, 2005?

3. How much would be reported as "proceeds from issuance of stock" in the statement of cash flows for the year ended December 31, 2005?

4. How would the effects of the treasury stock be shown in the statement of cash flows for 2005?

5. Prepare the operating activities section of the statement of cash flows for 2005, using the indirect method.

Analyze: If the company had not sold trading securities in this period, what would the net increase in cash flows from operating activities have been?

LO1, 2, 3   **PROBLEM 19-11   Cash Flows for Investments**

At December 31, 2005 and 2004, Starter Company had the following account balances:

	2005	2004
Cash	$ 70,000	$120,000
90-day Treasury Bill, dated October 3, 2005	100,000	0
Certificate of Deposit, due November 4, 2008	130,000	100,000
Available-for-Sale Securities	60,000	10,000
Fair Value Adjustment—Available-for-Sale Securities	3,800 cr.	2,400 cr.
Trading Securities	60,000	100,000
Unrealized Gain—Trading Securities	2,000 dr.	0
Realized Loss on Sale of Trading Securities	2,700	0
Realized Loss on Sale of Available-for-Sale Securities	1,600	0
Dividend Income	23,000	26,000

During 2005, trading securities were sold. During the year, the company purchased available-for-sale securities; then it sold some of those securities that had a cost of $40,000.

Required:

1. Calculate the cash flows related to the available-for-sale securities.

2. Calculate the cash flows related to the trading securities.

Analyze: Why are unrealized gains and losses on available-for-sale securities treated differently from those on trading securities investments?

LO1, 2, 3   **PROBLEM 19-12   Financing Activities**

Shown at the top of the next page are selected account balances at December 31, 2005 and 2004, provided by Allen Company.

	2005	2004
Accounts Payable	$ 4,000	$ 3,000
Dividends Payable	9,000	15,000
Treasury Stock	10,000	0
Notes Payable	41,200	0
Retained Earnings	108,000	54,000

The following additional information is available:

A. Net income for the year as reported in the income statement was $144,000.

B. Allen acquired a four-year loan at 10 percent on January 1, 2005, in the amount of $46,000.

C. One loan payment during 2005 totaled $9,400 and was made on December 31, 2005. The payment included both accrued interest and principal.

D. Dividends of $90,000 were declared during 2005.

E. Treasury stock was acquired.

Required: Prepare the financing activities section of the statement of cash flows for Allen Company for the year ended December 31, 2005.

Analyze: What might you expect to find in the financing activities section of the statement of cash flows if a company is in the growth stage of product development? Explain.

LO1, 2, 4 PROBLEM 19-13 **Operating Activities—Indirect Method**

The following information was selected from Save, Inc.'s accounting records and financial statements for 2005. Save uses the indirect method to prepare its statement of cash flows.

Increase in noncurrent deferred income tax liability	$ 4,000
Current-year depreciation of plant assets	1,400
Decrease in Income Tax Payable	11,000
Increase in Deferred Tax Asset—Current	3,000
Interest Expense	20,000
Interest capitalized during the period	6,500
Increase in Unrealized Loss on Available-for-Sale Investments	5,000
Bonds payable (net) issued in exchange for land	46,000
Cash dividends paid	6,500
Amortization of Discount on Bonds	2,000
Decrease in Interest Payable	4,900
Income Tax Expense	33,000
Recognizing an unrealized loss on trading securities	2,800
Net income	120,000

Required: Using the information given, calculate the amount to report as cash flows from operating activities for Save, Inc.

Analyze: Explain the effects on operating activities of the four stages of a product's life cycle.

LO1, 2, 3 PROBLEM 19-14 **Operating Activities—Indirect Method**

Use the following selected financial information for Amberly Corp. for the years ended December 31, 2005 and 2004, to answer the questions that follow.

	12/31/05	12/31/04
Accounts Receivable	$ 36,000	$ 42,000
Accounts Payable	28,000	25,000
Certificates of Deposit	12,000	4,000
Patent	16,000	15,000

	12/31/05	12/31/04
Equipment	$160,000	$140,000
Accumulated Depreciation	30,000	34,000
Note Payable, due in 10 months	19,000	20,000
Trading Securities	7,000	5,000
Retained Earnings	65,000	40,000
Other current accrued liabilities	12,000	12,000
Sales	420,000	400,000
Cost of Sales	280,000	272,000
Patent Amortization Expense	1,000	1,000
Gain (Loss) on Sale of Equipment	1,800	(400)
Interest Expense (includes bond amortization)	9,600	7,600
Unrealized Loss on Trading Securities	1,400	1,600
Other operating expenses	84,000	90,000
Net income	45,900	27,400

Additional information:

A. Equipment with a cost of $21,000 and a book value of $3,000 was sold during 2002. Additional equipment was purchased.

B. Information on the CDs is as follows: $4,000, 120-day CD dated and acquired November 15, 2004; $12,000, 180-day CD maturing on January 4, 2006, and acquired on November 30, 2005.

C. Depreciation expense is included in "other operating expenses."

D. Bond premium amortization for 2005 was $800 and for 2004 was $1,300.

E. Trading securities with a cost of $5,000 were sold for their book value.

Required: Prepare the operating activities section of the statement of cash flows for 2005, using the indirect method.

Analyze: Calculate the operating cash flow ratio for 2005. Indicate what information is provided by this ratio.

CASES

LO3   **FINANCIAL REPORTING CASE 19-1   Preparing the Statement of Cash Flows**

Starting Line Corporation has provided the following income statement and balance sheet:

Starting Line Corporation
Income Statement
For the Year Ended December 31, 2006

Revenues	$ 210,600	
Cost of sales	126,360	
Gross profit		$84,240
Operating expenses		
Depreciation expense	$ 2,550	
Salary expense	31,590	
Insurance expense	25,272	
Rent expense	10,530	
Interest expense	3,974	
Total operating expenses		73,916
Income from operations		$10,324
Income tax expense		3,097
Net income		$ 7,227

Starting Line Corporation
Balance Sheet
December 31, 2006 and 2005

	2006	2005
Assets		
Current assets:		
Cash and cash equivalents	$ 38,880	$ 35,880
Accounts receivable	71,280	52,440
Inventory	51,840	41,400
Total current assets	$162,000	$129,720
Property and equipment:		
Equipment	$109,350	$ 96,600
Less: Accumulated depreciation	(21,870)	(19,320)
Equipment—net	$ 87,480	$ 77,280
Land	$ 74,520	$ 69,000
Total assets	$324,000	$276,000
Liabilities and Stockholders' Equity		
Current liabilities:		
Accounts payable	$ 38,880	$ 27,600
Salaries payable	18,101	27,600
Rent payable	16,200	13,800
Income tax payable	6,480	5,520
Total current liabilities	$ 79,661	$ 74,520
Long-term note payable	97,200	66,240
Total liabilities	$176,861	$140,760
Stockholders' equity:		
Common stock	64,800	57,960
Retained earnings	82,339	77,280
Total liabilities and stockholders' equity	$324,000	$276,000

Additional data for 2006:

A. Starting Line paid dividends of $2,168 in 2006.

B. Starting Line purchased $12,750 of equipment and $5,520 of land in 2006.

C. Starting Line borrowed an additional $30,960 during 2006.

Required: Prepare Starting Line's statement of cash flows using the indirect method.

LO3 FINANCIAL REPORTING CASE **19-2** **Sources and Use of Cash**

Branson Enterprises is a market leader in the retail industry. Selected financial information about Branson Enterprises is listed here:

A. Purchased real estate for $675,000 in cash. The cash was borrowed from a bank.

B. Sold investments for $170,000.

C. Paid dividends of $330,000.

D. Issued shares of common stock for $150,000.

E. Purchased machinery and equipment for $120,000 cash.

F. Repaid a $360,000 bank loan.

G. Reduced accounts receivable by $180,000.

H. Increased accounts payable by $70,000.

Required: Use the information given to calculate the following for Branson Enterprises:

1. Cash provided or used by investing activities.

2. Cash provided or used by financing activities.

LO3   COMMUNICATION CASE **19-3**   **Cash Projections**

The following is information about three different companies.

A. Gaming Technology Corporation is a developer of computer software for the X-Box gaming system. The company recently launched its first software title. The company is expanding its operations by hiring additional developers and administrative staff. Gaming Technology is not yet profitable, but it expects to show a profit within two to three years. Investors view the company as being on the cutting edge with its technology and have been happy to keep investing in the company. Gaming Technology has not borrowed money yet, but is considering doing so in the future.

B. Midwest Corporation is a furniture manufacturing company. The company is experiencing its 20th year of profitability. Management is concerned by the recent economic downturn in the furniture business, which has hurt sales in the three most recent fiscal years. For this reason, the company is only replacing fully depreciated equipment. Midwest prides itself in paying dividends and having no debt on its balance sheet.

C. Wired Inc. is a technology manufacturing company. The company has just introduced its tenth new product and is the leader in market share for its industry. The company continues to invest in new equipment and property and to expand by purchasing its competitors. The company has yet to pay dividends, but it is considering doing so in the future. The company's largest current asset is cash, which is a result of its high profit margin. Because of this, the company has no need for external sources of cash.

Required: For each company, prepare a report examining whether you think the company's cash flows from each activity (operating, investing, and financing) will be positive (the activity provides cash) or negative (the activity uses cash). Provide support for your answers.

LO2, 3   RESEARCH CASE **19-4**   **Sources and Uses of Cash**

Ethan Allen Interiors Inc. is a manufacturer and retailer of home furnishings and accessories. The company is vertically integrated in that it manufactures furniture and sells it directly to consumers through an exclusive network of 309 retail stores. The company's website can be found at **www.ethanallen.com.** Go to the company's website and access the company's 2003 annual report to answer the following questions:

Required:

1. Does Ethan Allen use the direct or the indirect method to calculate cash flows from operations?

2. How much cash did Ethan Allen's operating activities generate in 2003?

3. What items used the largest amount of Ethan Allen's cash flows during the period?

4. What was the amount of cash provided or used by 2003 financing activities?

LO4   ANALYSIS CASE **19-5**   **Cash Flows from Operations**

As a new financial analyst for an investment firm, you have the task of evaluating the cash flows from operating activities of two possible investments, Harry Company and Sally Company, which are in the same industry. Your manager suggests that even though both companies had the same amount of net income and cash flows provided by operations, there might be important differences between the two. The following table presents cash flows from operations for each company for the year ended December 31, 2005.

	Harry Company	Sally Company
Net income	$55,000	$55,000
Depreciation expense	25,000	10,000
Amortization expense—patent	5,000	0
Change in accounts receivable	(7,000)	2,000
Change in inventory	(5,000)	5,000
Change in accounts payable	7,000	6,000
Change in salaries payable	(5,000)	(3,000)
Cash provided by operations	$75,000	$75,000

Required: Write a report examining the operating activities section of the cash flow statements for Harry Company and Sally Company. Include in your report a recommendation of which company would be a better investment based on cash flow from operations.

LO1, 4

ETHICS ⚖

ETHICS CASE 19-6   Cash Versus Accrual Accounting

Motorola is a globally known communications technology company. In the 1980s, the company was best known for its innovation in cell phone technology and became the world leader in cell phone sales. However, in the mid-1990s, the company lost this position to Nokia. During the past few years, Motorola has undertaken a major restructuring effort, which included reducing its work force by 40 percent.[1] The company has been unable to regain its lost market share. In 2003, after several years of significant losses, Motorola finally was able to report positive income. In fact, for the year ended December 31, 2003, the company reported net income of $893,000.[2] In contrast, for the year 2002, the company reported a net loss of $2,485,000, and for the year 2001, it reported a net loss of $3,937,000. However, during the same two years (2001 and 2002), the company's cash flows from operations were positive, totaling $1,339,000 in 2002 and $1,976,000 in 2001.[3]

As set forth in the chapter discussion, a large portion of the discrepancy between cash flows and accrual income can result from special nonrecurring items, particularly restructuring charges. Interestingly, during 2003, Motorola's special nonrecurring items increased income.

Although special nonrecurring items contribute to the discrepancy between cash and accrual income, depreciation—an "ordinary" recurring expense—also contributes very significantly to this discrepancy. For example, for 2002, Motorola's depreciation was $2,108,000, and during 2001, depreciation was $2,552,000.

Achieving positive income after two consecutive years of losses was very important to Motorola. Investors would like to see the company increase its profitability in future years. Flexibility in accounting for depreciation could help achieve this objective. For example, the company could change its estimates of the depreciable assets' useful life. This strategy would decrease depreciation, increase income, and reduce the discrepancy between cash and accrual income.

Suppose you are the CFO of a company similar to Motorola. You are aware that key company executives and investors would like the company to continue to achieve earnings growth, which would also indicate that the reorganization had been successful. Would you be willing to change accounting estimates, such as the useful life of long-lived assets, in order to help achieve this growth and reduce the discrepancy between cash and accruals?

Required:

1. Why does depreciation cause a discrepancy between cash from operations and accrual income? How does it affect the statement of cash flows?

2. If you were the CFO of a company like Motorola, what ethical issues would you face when considering a change in accounting estimates?

3. Who will be affected by the decision you make?

4. What values and principles are likely to influence your decision?

5. What alternative actions might you consider?

6. a. Whose interest is most important?
    b. Which values and principles are most important?
    c. Which of the possible consequences will do the most good or cause the least harm?
    d. Which consideration is most important?

---

1 Jesse Drucker and Joann S. Lublin, "Leading the News: Motorola Searches for a New CEO; Glavin's Resignation Came as Board Lost Confidence in His Decision Making," *Wall Street Journal,* September 22, 2003, p. A3.

2 Source of information: Motorola Reports Fourth-Quarter and Full-Year 2003 Financial Results. Motorola 2004, available at: **www.motorola.com.** Accessed 07/18/04.

3 Source of information: Yahoo Finance, available at: **http://finance.yahoo.com/q/cf?s=MOT&annual.** Accessed 07/18/04.

7. Does changing accounting estimates violate GAAP?

8. What would you do?

LO1

ETHICS

ETHICS CASE 19-7   Cash or Noncash Transactions

Martin is the capital expenditure and operations manager of Abad Company, a company specializing in deliveries in remote rural areas. Abad Company is planning to purchase several new delivery trucks to replace an aging fleet. The truck distributor, with which the company has a good business relationship, has offered to finance the acquisition. Abad Company is trying to expand its operations and currently is seeking to merge with a larger company. Employee (and outside) owners expect a significant appreciation in the value of their ownership interest if the merger occurs on favorable terms. A stable or even increasing stock price would support this objective. During an executive meeting, the CEO mentioned that it would be helpful if the company were perceived as a growing company.

During lunch, Martin discusses the potential merger and the new trucks with Richard, a junior accounting staff member. Martin mentions to Richard that the purchase of the new trucks will look favorable in the statement of cash flows, as it will show that the company is growing. Richard, however, reminds him that this transaction will be considered a noncash financing and investing activity and will be disclosed as such.

After returning from lunch, Martin calls the distributor and indicates that the company will obtain outside financing for the trucks and pay for them in cash. Martin manages to arrange a loan with the bank. However, because of the urgency of completing the transaction, he accepts an interest rate that is 1 percent higher than the rate offered by the distributor. Martin believes that the 1 percent difference is not material, and that the positive impression of the transaction in the company's statement of cash flows will more than compensate for the higher rate. Suppose you were in Richard's position and you learned about the change in the transaction after it had already been executed.

Required:

1. How are the original and the revised transactions treated in a statement of cash flows?

2. What is the accounting issue surrounding these transactions?

3. What are the ethical problems and issues faced by Richard?

4. Who will be affected by Richard's decision?

5. What values and principles are likely to influence the decision?

6. What alternative actions can Richard take?

7. a. Whose interest is most important?
   b. Which values and principles are most important?
   c. Which of the possible consequences will do the most good or cause the least harm?

8. What would you do?

ON THE WEB

The following exercises, activities, and problems are available on the *Intermediate Accounting* website. Use these resources to reinforce your understanding of the topics presented in this chapter.

- CPA-Adapted Simulations
- Interpreting the Accounting Standards
- Extending the Global Focus
- Extending the Ethics Discussion
- Mastering the Spreadsheet
- Career Snapshots
- Annual Report Project
- ACE Practice Tests
- Flashcards
- Glossary
- Check Figures for Text Problems
- PowerPoint Presentations

SOLUTIONS: CHECK YOUR UNDERSTANDING

Classification of Business Activities (p. 909)

1. If a company spent cash to purchase its own capital stock, this would be classified as a financing activity.

2. The exchange of nonmonetary assets would not be reflected in the statement of cash flows, but rather would be shown in an accompanying schedule or report.

3. Cash paid to settle debt, to reacquire capital stock, or to pay dividends. Cash received from the sale of capital stock or from the issuance of debt.

Cash Flows from Operating Activities—The Indirect Method Versus the Direct Method (p. 912)

1. There are two main advantages of the indirect method: (1) the reconciliation of net income and the cash provided or used by operating activities is important because it shows the connection between economic activities and the generation and use of cash, and (2) using the indirect method may be less costly, especially when the level of detail of cash inflows and outflows includes such items as sensitive segment information or information about strategic suppliers and employees.

2. When the indirect method is used, the statement begins with net income or loss and adds or subtracts noncash items, realized gains and losses recognized in the income statement, and changes in current operating asset and liability accounts, excluding the Cash account. When the direct method is used, the first line item is not operating loss or income. Instead, each item in the income statement is converted to its cash equivalent and listed accordingly. The total is the net cash provided by operating activities.

3. Indirect method.

Preparing the Operating Activities Section of the Statement of Cash Flows (p. 922)

1. If the Prepaid Insurance account has increased during the fiscal period, the amount of the increase will be subtracted from net income (or net loss) in the operating activities section of the statement of cash flows.

2. Adjustments for noncash income items; adjustments for realized gains and losses recognized in the income statement; and adjustments for changes in current operating asset and liability accounts, excluding the Cash account.

3. To convert cost of goods sold to cash paid for inventory:

Ending balance of Inventory	$xxx
Less: Cost of goods sold	(xxx)
Available inventory	$xxx
Less: Beginning balance of Inventory	(xxx)
Inventory purchased	$xxx
Plus: Beginning balance of Accounts Payable	xxx
Inventory obligations outstanding	$xxx
Less: Ending balance of Accounts Payable	(xxx)
Cash paid for inventory during the year	$xxx

Preparing the Investing Activities Section of the Statement of Cash Flows (p. 923)

1. The following general ledger accounts should generally be reviewed for transactions that affect the investing activities section of the statement of cash flows: operating asset accounts, marketable securities accounts, any investment-related accounts, and notes receivable.

2. Proceeds from the sale of an investment would be reflected as a positive amount (cash inflow) in the investing activities section.

3. Cash proceeds from sales and any cash payments made to acquire investments would be included in the statement of cash flows.

Preparing the Financing Activities Section of the Statement of Cash Flows (p. 924)

1. The purchase of a company's own capital stock would constitute a cash outflow.

2. The repayment of a long-term note with cash would be reflected in the financing activities section of the statement of cash flows as a cash outflow (negative amount).

3. The Retained Earnings account should be reviewed to determine the amount of cash paid for dividends in a period.

Using the Statement of Cash Flows for Analysis (p. 926)

1. The operating cash flow ratio provides a measure of resources generated over a period of time that are available to meet current liabilities.

2. Cash flows from investing activities would likely be negative during a product's introduction phase because manufacturing the product may require the acquisition of operating assets.

3. During the maturity stage of a product, cash flows from operating activities may still be positive, but they have reached their peak. Because sales are probably at their peak, there is likely to be no need for capital expenditures. Cash flow from operations may be providing enough cash to pay off debt, pay dividends, or repurchase treasury stock—cash outflows in the financing activities section.

CPA-ADAPTED SIMULATION

This simulation asks you to complete various tasks related to a company's annual financial statements. If your instructor has signed up for CPAexcel™, you can do the work online at **www.cpaexcel.com/hmco.** You may also do the simulation manually.

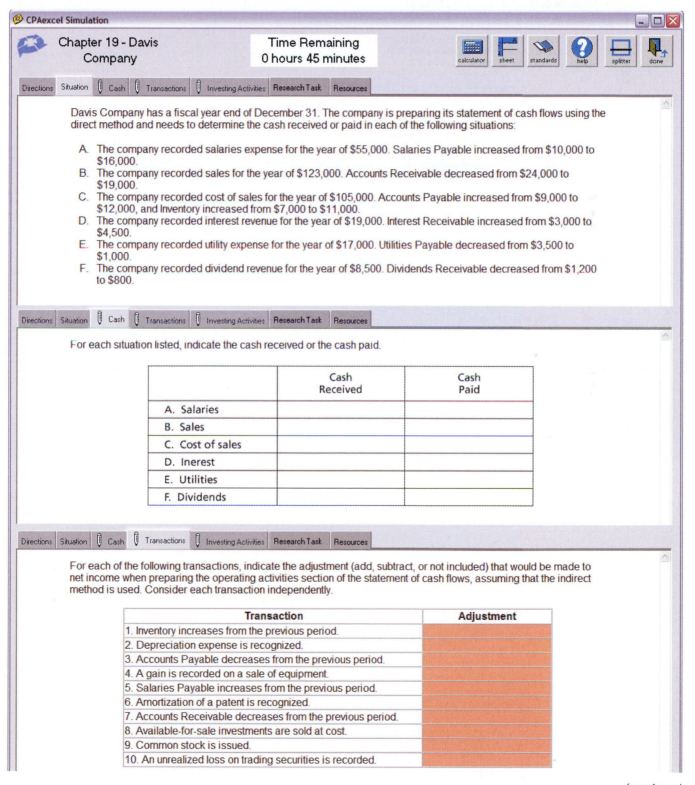

CPAexcel Simulation

Chapter 19 - Davis Company

Time Remaining
0 hours 45 minutes

calculator   sheet   standards   help   splitter   done

Directions | Situation | Cash | Transactions | Investing Activities | Research Task | Resources

Davis Company has a fiscal year end of December 31. The company is preparing its statement of cash flows using the direct method and needs to determine the cash received or paid in each of the following situations:

A. The company recorded salaries expense for the year of $55,000. Salaries Payable increased from $10,000 to $16,000.
B. The company recorded sales for the year of $123,000. Accounts Receivable decreased from $24,000 to $19,000.
C. The company recorded cost of sales for the year of $105,000. Accounts Payable increased from $9,000 to $12,000, and Inventory increased from $7,000 to $11,000.
D. The company recorded interest revenue for the year of $19,000. Interest Receivable increased from $3,000 to $4,500.
E. The company recorded utility expense for the year of $17,000. Utilities Payable decreased from $3,500 to $1,000.
F. The company recorded dividend revenue for the year of $8,500. Dividends Receivable decreased from $1,200 to $800.

Directions | Situation | Cash | Transactions | Investing Activities | Research Task | Resources

For each situation listed, indicate the cash received or the cash paid.

	Cash Received	Cash Paid
A. Salaries		
B. Sales		
C. Cost of sales		
D. Inerest		
E. Utilities		
F. Dividends		

Directions | Situation | Cash | Transactions | Investing Activities | Research Task | Resources

For each of the following transactions, indicate the adjustment (add, subtract, or not included) that would be made to net income when preparing the operating activities section of the statement of cash flows, assuming that the indirect method is used. Consider each transaction independently.

Transaction	Adjustment
1. Inventory increases from the previous period.	
2. Depreciation expense is recognized.	
3. Accounts Payable decreases from the previous period.	
4. A gain is recorded on a sale of equipment.	
5. Salaries Payable increases from the previous period.	
6. Amortization of a patent is recognized.	
7. Accounts Receivable decreases from the previous period.	
8. Available-for-sale investments are sold at cost.	
9. Common stock is issued.	
10. An unrealized loss on trading securities is recorded.	

(continues)

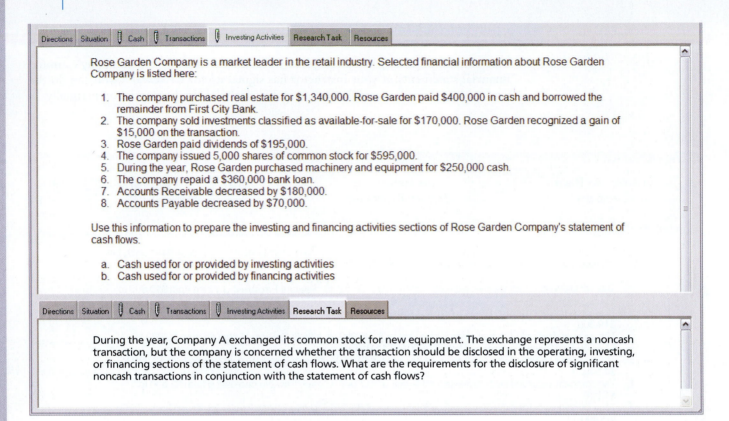

Directions | Situation | Cash | Transactions | Investing Activities | Research Task | Resources

Rose Garden Company is a market leader in the retail industry. Selected financial information about Rose Garden Company is listed here:

1. The company purchased real estate for $1,340,000. Rose Garden paid $400,000 in cash and borrowed the remainder from First City Bank.
2. The company sold investments classified as available-for-sale for $170,000. Rose Garden recognized a gain of $15,000 on the transaction.
3. Rose Garden paid dividends of $195,000.
4. The company issued 5,000 shares of common stock for $595,000.
5. During the year, Rose Garden purchased machinery and equipment for $250,000 cash.
6. The company repaid a $360,000 bank loan.
7. Accounts Receivable decreased by $180,000.
8. Accounts Payable decreased by $70,000.

Use this information to prepare the investing and financing activities sections of Rose Garden Company's statement of cash flows.

a. Cash used for or provided by investing activities
b. Cash used for or provided by financing activities

Directions | Situation | Cash | Transactions | Investing Activities | Research Task | Resources

During the year, Company A exchanged its common stock for new equipment. The exchange represents a noncash transaction, but the company is concerned whether the transaction should be disclosed in the operating, investing, or financing sections of the statement of cash flows. What are the requirements for the disclosure of significant noncash transactions in conjunction with the statement of cash flows?

The Time Value of Money

Introduction of Time Value Concepts

One of the most important tools that an accountant needs is a strong understanding of the time value of money. For example, investment decisions involve understanding the idea that an investor will invest a particular dollar amount today with the expectation of receiving a larger amount in the future. In order to evaluate the investment, an accountant must be able to understand how future amounts relate to today's invested amount. Will the investor receive enough of a return to justify the risk taken? Is the investment providing enough of a return compared to other investment opportunities?

Likewise, borrowing decisions are based on understanding how much money will be received today versus how much will need to be paid back in the future. Am I borrowing so much today that I will not have the future funds to pay back the loan? How does the amount that I will need to pay on the loan compare to the amount I would need to pay on other loans for different lengths of time?

In both cases, the cash flows of today and future cash flows are separated by time. In order to compare these cash flows, they all must be put on the same footing, using time value of money computations. In order to determine that the right decision is being made today, the accountant must be able to compare future cash flows with the cash amount received or paid today.

We will first examine the concept of interest and then investigate how to calculate present and future values.

LO1 Explain the difference between simple and compound interest.

interest the cost of borrowing money or the return (amount earned) from lending money

Interest

Interest is the cost of borrowing money or the return (amount earned) from lending money. It is the cost associated with the use of money for a specific period of time. The amount of money that is invested or borrowed and on which interest is calculated is called the principal amount. When computing interest, it is important to understand whether the interest is calculated on a simple or a compound basis.

SIMPLE INTEREST

simple interest method the method of calculating interest in which the interest for each period is computed only on the principal amount; commonly expressed as Interest = Principal × Rate × Time (Number of Periods)

When interest is calculated under the **simple interest method**, the principal amount on which the interest is computed remains the same each period. Under a simple interest assumption, the interest for each period will be the same as long as the principal amount does not change.

For example, assume that an investor puts $1,000 into a bank account and wants to know how much money she will have in three years, given that the bank pays interest at a rate of 8 percent per year using the simple interest method. In this situation, the investor would calculate the interest earned each period using the following formula:

$$\text{Interest} = \text{Principal} \times \text{Rate} \times \text{Time, or } I = P \times R \times T$$

The investor would receive $80 of interest for each yearly period ($80 = $1,000 × 8% × 1). At the end of the three years, the investor would have three years of interest plus the principal amount, or $1,240 [$1,000 + 3($80)].

COMPOUND INTEREST

compound interest method the method of calculating interest in which interest is computed not only on the principal amount, but also on interest previously earned

Under the **compound interest method**, the interest for each period is computed not only on the principal amount, but also on interest previously earned. Returning to the previous example of putting $1,000 into a bank account that pays interest at a rate of 8 percent per year, what amount would be received at the end of the three years if interest were to be compounded yearly? In this case, interest would be calculated as follows:

Year 1: Interest = $1,000 × 8% × 1 = $80

Year 2: Interest = ($1,000 + $80) × 8% × 1 = $86.40

Year 3: Interest = ($1,000 + $80 + $86.40) × 8% × 1 = $93.31

Total amount received at the end of three years:

Principal	$1,000.00
Year 1 interest	80.00
Year 2 interest	86.40
Year 3 interest	93.31
	$1,259.71

The compound interest method always results in a greater amount of interest than the simple interest method because interest is earned on previous interest. In order to aid in finding present and future values, financial formulas have been used to develop time value of money tables that allow for quick calculation. We will examine the use of these tables in the next section.

One important thing to remember when calculating interest is that the interest rate and the time period must be consistent. In the previous examples, the interest rate was 8 percent per year and the time period over which interest was calculated was yearly. When a time period of less than a year is used—for example, when interest is compounded semiannually or quarterly—the interest rate must be adjusted so that it is consistent with the number of interest periods per year.

For instance, if $1,000 was deposited in a bank account that paid interest quarterly at a rate of 8 percent per year, the interest earned in each quarterly period and in one year using the simple interest method would be as follows:

Quarterly Interest

I = P × R × T
I = $1,000 × (8%/4) × 1 period
I = $20

Annual Interest

I = P × R × T
I = $1,000 × (8%/4) × 4 periods
I = $80

Under the compound interest method, quarterly and annual interest would be:

First-Quarter Interest

I = P × R × T
I = $1,000 × (8%/4) × 1 period
I = $20

Second-Quarter Interest

$I = P \times R \times T$

$I = (\$1{,}000 + \$20) \times (8\%/4) \times 1 \text{ period}$

$I = \$20.40$

Third-Quarter Interest

$I = P \times R \times T$

$I = (\$1{,}000 + \$20 + \$20.40) \times (8\%/4) \times 1 \text{ period}$

$I = \$20.81$

Fourth-Quarter Interest

$I = P \times R \times T$

$I = (\$1{,}000 + \$20 + \$20.40 + \$20.81) \times (8\%/4) \times 1 \text{ period}$

$I = \$21.22$

Total interest for the year $= \$20 + \$20.40 + \$20.81 + \$21.22 = \$82.43$

Present and Future Values

Now that we have mastered calculating interest using the simple interest and compound interest methods, we will concentrate on understanding present and future values. In each instance, we will look at two situations. The first situation is one in which there is only one amount in the future or in the present for the investor or borrower to consider. These problems are called single-amount problems. In the second situation, we will consider the case in which the investor or borrower has to evaluate a series of equal cash flows, equally spaced in time. These series of cash flows are called annuities.

Finally, since most situations in accounting call for calculating interest using the compound interest method, our discussions will focus on that method. In order to solve these problems, we can use financial formulas, time value of money tables, or a financial calculator. In our discussion of present values and future values, we will illustrate each of the methods.

LO2 Determine the present and future value of a single amount.

PRESENT VALUE OF A SINGLE AMOUNT

The present value of a single amount is the value today of a single amount to be paid or received in the future. For the investor, it is the amount that must be invested today at a given rate of interest to produce a given future value. For example, an investor may be interested in determining how much money would need to be invested today at 6 percent interest in order to have enough money to purchase a new piece of equipment that is expected to cost $25,000 two years from today. The financial formula used to calculate the present value is as follows:

$$PV = FV \times (1 + I)^{-N}$$

where:

PV = present value amount

FV = future value amount

I = interest rate

N = number of periods

With this formula, we can calculate the present value of $25,000 two years from today given an interest rate of 6 percent per year as follows:

PV = $25,000 × $(1 + 0.06)^{-2}$

PV = $25,000 × (0.8900)

PV = $22,250

Time value of money tables have been developed to aid in the calculation of present and future value amounts. For this example, we can use Table A.1 on page 969. This table gives the present value factors for a single amount. These factors are also referred to as discount factors when calculating present values. To find the proper present value factor to use in this example, read across the row for two periods to the column for 6 percent interest, which provides the present value factor of 0.8900. By multiplying the present value factor by the principal amount of $25,000, we again obtain the present value of $22,250:

PV = $25,000 × Present Value Factor (2 periods, 6 percent)

PV = $25,000 × (0.8900)

PV = $22,250

FUTURE VALUE OF A SINGLE AMOUNT

The future value of a single amount is the amount that an investment will be worth at a future date if it is invested at a given interest rate. From the perspective of an investor or manager, it is the amount that he or she will have in the future if he or she invests a known amount at a given rate today. For example, assume that the board of directors of a company wants to declare a special dividend five years from today. In order to fund this special dividend, the manager puts $150,000 in a bank account earning 4 percent per year. How much money will be available to pay the special dividend?

The financial formula for the future value of a single amount is

$$FV = PV \times (1 + I)^N$$

where:

FV = future value amount

PV = present value amount

I = interest rate

N = number of periods

Returning to our example, given an interest rate of 4 percent per year and a present value of $150,000, in five years the board of directors would be able to declare the following special dividend:

FV = $150,000 × $(1 + 0.04)^5$

FV = $150,000 × 1.2167

FV = $182,505

To find the future value, we could also use the time value of money tables. Table A.2 on page 970 provides the future value factors for a single amount. To determine the future value factor, go to the row for five periods and move across to the column for 4 percent. You find that the factor for the future value of a single amount is 1.2167. This factor is multiplied by the present value to obtain the future value of $182,505.

LO3 Determine the present and future value of an ordinary annuity or an annuity due.

ANNUITIES

Now that you have analyzed single-amount time value problems, we will discuss annuities. An **annuity** is a or series of fixed payments of equal amount. An annuity can

annuity a series of fixed payments of equal amount

take either of two forms: an ordinary annuity or an annuity due. An ordinary annuity is one in which each payment is made or received at the end of the period. Interest payments are normally considered ordinary annuities because the payments come at the end of the interest period. For example, assume that you have invested $10,000 in a bank account on which interest is paid monthly. The following time line illustrates the payments.

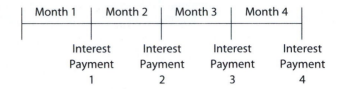

Even though interest is accruing over the entire interest period, the payment arrives at the end of the interest period. For this reason, this investment is an ordinary annuity.

annuity due an annuity in which each payment is made or received at the beginning of the period

An **annuity due** is an annuity in which each payment is made or received at the beginning of the period. For example, insurance payments and rent payments take the form of annuities due, since the payments are made at the beginning of the coverage period or rental period. Think about your rent payments with regard to the following time line:

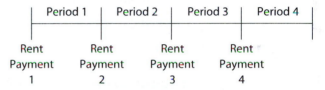

The rent payment covers the entire rental period; however, it is made at the beginning of the period, making it an annuity due. Both types of annuities are common in accounting and finance.

▶ PRESENT VALUE OF AN ORDINARY ANNUITY

Many times accountants need to determine the present value of a series of future cash flows. Interest payments, impairment testing, and lease payments are just a few examples that call for the accountant to determine the present value of an annuity. When those cash flows come at the end of each period, as interest payments do, the annuity is an **ordinary annuity**.

ordinary annuity an annuity in which each payment is made or cash received at the end of the period

▶ **EXAMPLE 1**   *Assume that you must pay $2,000 per year for four years, with payments to be made at the end of each year. What is the present value of the series of payments if a 5 percent interest rate, compounded annually, is applicable?*

The process of calculating a present value can be thought of as a process of discounting. The present value of an amount is less than the future amount that will be received because of the time value of money. These future amounts must be discounted to calculate the present value. For Example 1, the time line could be depicted as follows:

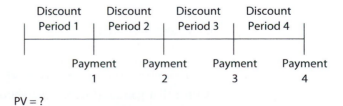

Note that in Example 1, there will be

Four payments

Four discount periods

) PRESENT VALUE OF AN ANNUITY DUE

Many times annuity payments will be made at the beginning of each period, in which case the annuity is called an annuity due.

) **EXAMPLE 2**   *Assume that you must pay $2,000 per year for four years with payments to be made at the beginning of each year. What is the present value of the series of payments if a 5 percent interest rate, compounded annually, is applicable?*

For Example 2, the time line could be depicted as follows:

Note that in Example 2, there will be

Four payments

Three discount periods

Because the first payment will be received at the present time, it is not necessary to discount this payment.

) CALCULATIONS FOR AN ORDINARY ANNUITY AND AN ANNUITY DUE

We can calculate the present value of an annuity using the tables provided in this appendix.

For Example 1, we should use Table A.3 as follows:

$$\$2,000 \times 3.5460 = \$7,092$$

where 3.5460 is the table factor for N = 4 and I = 5 percent.

For Example 2, we should use Table A.4 as follows:

$$\$2,000 \times 3.7232 = \$7,446.40$$

where 3.7232 is the table factor for N = 4 and I = 5 percent.

Note that there is a relationship between an ordinary annuity and an annuity due. Specifically, an annuity due involves *one less discount period* than an ordinary annuity. We could calculate the present value of an annuity due by first calculating the present value of an ordinary annuity and then multiplying the result by 1 + I. For Example 2, we could calculate the future value as follows:

$$\$7,092 \times 1.05 = \$7,446.60$$

(Difference from the previously calculated figure is due to rounding.)

) ADDITIONAL EXAMPLES OF PRESENT VALUE

Assume that you need to rent warehouse space for the next three years and the landlord offers you two options. The first option is to make traditional rental payments of $25,000 at the beginning of each of the three years. The second choice is to make one payment of $70,000 up front covering the entire three-year period. You know that your normal borrowing rate is 9 percent per year. In order to evaluate the two competing offers, it is necessary to calculate the present value of the rental payments, which take the form of an annuity due, and compare it to the $70,000 single-payment amount.

Table A.4 on page 972 provides the discount factors to use when calculating the present value of an annuity due. For this example, go to the row for three periods and the column for 9 percent per year, which provides a discount factor of 2.7591. Calculate the present value of the rental payments as follows:

> PV Annuity Due = Annuity Amount × Table Factor (3 periods, 9%)
> PV Annuity Due = $25,000 × 2.7591
> PV Annuity Due = $68,977.50

The present value of the three rental payments is $68,977.50. In this case, given an interest rate of 9 percent, you would be better off making three rental payments over the three-year period than paying $70,000 initially.

❯ FUTURE VALUE OF AN ORDINARY ANNUITY

Accountants are also concerned about determining the future value of a series of set cash flows. Bond sinking funds and investment funds each require knowledge of how to calculate the future value of an annuity. When the payments are made or received at the end of the period, the resulting cash flows create an ordinary annuity, and when the cash flows occur at the beginning of each period, the result is an annuity due.

❯ **EXAMPLE 3**   *Assume that you are a landlord who will receive rent payments of $1,000 per year for four years. Unlike most landlords, you allow the renters to pay the rent at the end of each period. You can invest all rent received at a rate of 8 percent, compounded annually. How much will you have accumulated at the end of Year 4?*

A time line would illustrate the payments as follows:

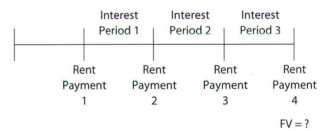

Because the rent payments will be received at the end of each period, no interest will accrue in the first period. As a result, in this example, there will be

Four rental payments

Three interest periods

For this reason, the example has the form of an ordinary annuity.

❯ FUTURE VALUE OF AN ANNUITY DUE

An annuity due is an annuity in which each payment is made or received at the beginning of the period.

❯ **EXAMPLE 4**   *Assume that you are a landlord who will receive rent payments of $1,000 per year for four years. Renters must pay the rent at the beginning of each period. You can invest all rent received at a rate of 8 percent, compounded annually. How much will you have accumulated at the end of Year 4?*

A time line would illustrate the payments as shown on the following page.

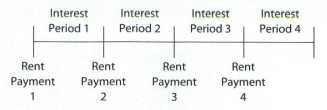

Because the first rental payment is received at the beginning of the first period, interest will accrue on that payment when it is invested for the year. As a result, there will be

Four rental payments

Four interest periods

For this reason, the example takes the form of an annuity due.

▶ CALCULATIONS FOR AN ORDINARY ANNUITY AND AN ANNUITY DUE

We can calculate the future value of an annuity using the tables provided in this appendix. For Example 3, we should use Table A.5 as follows:

$$\$1,000 \times 4.5061 = \$4,506.10$$

where 4.5061 is the table factor for $N = 4$ and $I = 8$ percent.
    For Example 4, use Table A.6 as follows:

$$\$1,000 \times 4.8666 = \$4,866.60$$

where 4.8666 is the table factor for $N = 4$ and $I = 8$ percent.
    Note the relationship between an ordinary annuity and an annuity due. Specifically, an annuity due involves *one more interest period* than an ordinary annuity. We could calculate the future value of an annuity due by first calculating the future value of an ordinary annuity and then multiplying the result by $1 + I$. For Example 4, we could calculate the future value as follows:

$$\$4,506.10 \times 1.08 = \$4,866.59$$

(Difference from the previously calculated figure is due to rounding.)

▶ ADDITIONAL EXAMPLES OF FUTURE VALUE

Suppose that you decide to invest $100,000 at the end of each of the next five years in order to accumulate enough cash to retire a bond that will be coming due at the end of the five years. The financial institution in which you invest the money guarantees an interest rate of 7 percent per year. This is a future value problem because we need to determine how much money would be accumulated at the end of the five years.
    A time line would illustrate the investments as follows:

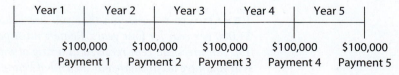

Table A.5 on page 973 provides the factors for calculating the future value of an ordinary annuity. By reading across the five-period line to the 7 percent column, a time value factor of 5.7507 is obtained. This factor can be used to determine the future value of the annuity by multiplying it by the annuity cash flow:

FV Ordinary Annuity = Annuity Amount × Table Factor (5 periods, 7%)

FV Ordinary Annuity = $100,000 × 5.7507

FV Ordinary Annuity = $575,070

It is important to recognize that when we make five payments of $100,000, or $500,000 in total, we accumulate more than $500,000. This is because the payments are earning interest prior to the end of the five-year period.

When annuity cash flows occur at the beginning of each period, the annuity becomes an annuity due. Thinking about our last example, if we assume that we make each payment at the beginning of the period rather than at the end of the period, how much cash will be available to retire the bonds at the end of the five years?

In this case, the time line would illustrate the investments as follows:

FV = ?

Determine the future value of an annuity due from Table A.6. Using five periods and 7 percent, we find a future value factor of 6.1533. Use this factor to obtain the future value of the annuity due as follows:

FV Annuity Due = Annuity Amount × Table Factor (5 periods, 7%)

FV Annuity Due = $100,000 × 6.1533

FV Annuity Due = $615,330

At the end of the five years, $615,330 will be available to retire the debt. Why is this amount larger than the amount in the previous example, where the investments were made at the end of each period? The future value of an annuity due is larger than that for an ordinary annuity because each cash flow investment earned interest for one additional period, since it was made at the beginning of the period rather than at the end of the period.

LO4 Explain how to use the expected cash flow approach to determine present values.

Time Value of Money in Accounting Situations

Statement of Financial Accounting Concepts No. 7, "Using Cash Flow Information and Present Value in Accounting Measurements," provides a basis for determining future cash flows when approximating the fair value of an asset or liability. In many cases, there may only be one future cash flow amount to value, and in these cases the methods previously examined apply.[1]

However, *SFAC No. 7* provides guidance about cases in which future cash flows are uncertain. For example, assume that a manager is trying to determine the future cash flows from a piece of equipment in order to test for impairment. The machine is

---

1 "Using Cash Flow Information and Present Value in Accounting," *Statement of Financial Accounting Concepts No. 7* (Norwalk, Conn.: FASB, 2000).

expected to provide one more year of service, and the cash flow will come one year from today. The manager estimates the following cash flows along with their probabilities:

Probability	Cash Flow from Machine
25%	$ 300,000
50	800,000
25	1,500,000

When a manager can only estimate a range of future cash flows, *SFAC No. 7* suggests that the manager should calculate the present value by discounting the expected cash flow. The expected cash flow is found by multiplying each cash flow estimate by its relevant probability estimate and then summing the amounts. In this example, the expected cash flow would be calculated as follows:

Probability		Cash Flow from Machine		Expected Amount
25%	×	$ 300,000	=	$ 75,000
50	×	800,000	=	400,000
25	×	1,500,000	=	375,000
		Expected Cash Flow	=	$850,000

The expected cash flow would then be discounted at the risk-free rate of interest. The FASB concludes that the risk-free rate of interest should be used because uncertainty has already been taken into account when calculating the expected cash flow.

LO5 Solve for an unknown variable in a time value of money scenario.

SOLVING FOR UNKNOWNS

Many times, time value of money problems will require a manager to solve for an interest rate or time period, as opposed to a present amount or future amount. For example, a company that needs to retire $1,500,000 in bonds in five years may decide to invest $931,350 today in a fund that will grow large enough to retire the bonds. What interest rate is necessary if the $931,350 is to grow to $1,500,000?

A time diagram would illustrate the problem as follows:

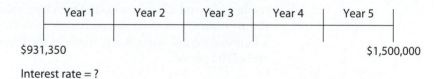

	Year 1	Year 2	Year 3	Year 4	Year 5	

$931,350 $1,500,000

Interest rate = ?

To solve this problem using the time value tables, the present value formula is

$$PV = FV \times \text{Present Value Factor (5 periods, ?\%)}$$
$$\$931,350 = \$1,500,000 \times \text{Present Value Factor (5 periods, ?\%)}$$

In this case, both the present value amount and the future value amount are known, so the present value factor can be calculated:

$$PV \div FV = \text{Present Value Factor (5 periods, ?\%)}$$
$$\$931,350 \div \$1,500,000 = \text{Present Value Factor (5 periods, ?\%)}$$
$$0.6209 = \text{Present Value Factor (5 periods, ?\%)}$$

The value of 0.6209 is the present value of a single amount factor from Table A.1. The interest rate can be solved for by reading across the five periods row until the value 0.6209 is found. This factor represents an interest rate of 10 percent. So if $931,350 is invested for five years at 10 percent, it will grow to $1,500,000 and the company will be able to retire its bonds.

The same methodology can be used for situations in which it is necessary to solve for the number of periods. For example, assume that you invest $130,000 at 12 percent today, and you want it to grow to $1,000,000. How many periods will it take? Again, we can use the present value formula in order to solve the problem:

$$
\begin{aligned}
\text{PV} \quad &= \quad \text{FV} \quad \times \text{Present Value Factor (? periods, 12\%)} \\
\$130,000 &= \$1,000,000 \times \text{Present Value Factor (? periods, 12\%)}
\end{aligned}
$$

Because both the present value and the future value amounts are known, we can solve for the present value factor:

$$
\begin{aligned}
\text{PV} \quad \div \quad \text{FV} \quad &= \text{Present Value Factor (? periods, 12\%)} \\
\$130,000 \div \$1,000,000 &= \text{Present Value Factor (? periods, 12\%)} \\
0.1300 &= \text{Present Value Factor (? periods, 12\%)}
\end{aligned}
$$

The value of 0.1300 is the present value of a single amount factor from Table A.1. To find the number of periods, read down the 12 percent column until the value 0.1300 is found. This factor represents 18 periods. So if $130,000 is invested for 18 years at 12 percent, it will grow to $1,000,000.

USING A CALCULATOR TO SOLVE TIME VALUE OF MONEY PROBLEMS

Many times it is easier to use a financial calculator to solve time value of money problems than to use financial formulas or turn to a time value of money table. To illustrate how to solve time value of money problems with a calculator, we can use the Hewlett-Packard 10 B Business calculator to solve the examples given earlier.

Financial calculators normally have seven keys or inputs that are used in determining present and future values:

N: Number of payments

I/YR: Interest rate per year

PV: Present value

FV: Future value

PMT: Annuity payment

P/YR: Number of payments per year

BEG/END: Type of annuity

It is important to note that not every key or input is needed for every present or future value problem. In addition, financial calculators assume that one of the cash flows will be a cash outflow and one will be a cash inflow, so a result may come up as negative. Finally, remember to hit the "clear all" key before calculating a new time value of money problem.

❯ PRESENT VALUE OF A SINGLE AMOUNT

Our example looked at how much an investor would have to invest today in order to have $25,000 two years from today, given an interest rate of 6 percent. To solve this problem with a financial calculator, input the following information:

N: 2

I/YR: 6

FV: 25,000

After entering this information, press the PV key to receive a result of −22,249.91. The negative amount represents a cash outflow today. Note that the time value of money results obtained with a financial calculator may differ slightly from the results obtained using the tables because of rounding.

❱ FUTURE VALUE OF A SINGLE AMOUNT

Our future value of a single amount problem asked how large a special dividend a company could pay in five years if it invested $150,000 in a bank account today earning 4 percent per year. To solve this problem with the financial calculator, input the following information:

N: 5

I/YR: 4

PV: −150,000 (negative because this represents a current cash outflow)

After entering this information, press the FV key to receive a result of $182,497.94. This amount differs slightly from the result obtained using the time value of money table ($182,505.00) because of rounding.

❱ PRESENT VALUE OF AN ANNUITY

To calculate the present value of an ordinary annuity using the calculator, the annuity payment will need to be input. It is also important to ensure that the calculator is performing an ordinary annuity and not an annuity due calculation. When calculating ordinary annuities, ensure that the calculator is in the END mode. For the Hewlett-Packard 10 B, this is the default mode. In our example, we found the present value of four interest payments of $2,000 each, discounted at 5 percent per year.

N: 4

P/YR: 1

I/YR: 5

PMT: −2,000 (negative because the interest represents a cash outflow)

After entering this information, press the PV key to receive a result of $7,091.90.

To solve an annuity due problem with a calculator, you need to ensure that an annuity due and not an ordinary annuity will be calculated by selecting the BEG mode on the calculator. To determine the present value of three rental payments of $25,000 each, occurring at the beginning of each period, when the interest rate is 9 percent, enter the following information:

BEG mode

N: 3

I/YR: 9

PMT: −25,000

Pressing the PV key results in the rental payments having a present value of $68,977.78.

❱ FUTURE VALUE OF AN ANNUITY

When determining the future value of an ordinary annuity and an annuity due, we looked at an example in which a manager invested $100,000 each year for five years at an interest rate of 7 percent. The problem involves an ordinary annuity when the investments are made at the end of each period. To calculate this future value using the calculator, enter the following information:

N: 5

I/YR: 7

PMT: −100,000 (negative because each investment is a cash outflow)

By pressing the FV key, we obtain a future value of $575,073.90.

Assume that the investments are made at the beginning of each year. This becomes an annuity due problem. Remember to switch the annuity mode to BEG. Enter the same information as before:

BEG mode

N: 5

I/YR: 7

PMT: −100,000 (negative because each investment is a cash outflow)

The future value is found by pressing the FV key, which results in an answer of $615,329.07.

KEY TERMS

annuity (p. 957)
annuity due (p. 957)

compound interest method (p. 954)
interest (p. 953)

ordinary annuity (p. 957)
simple interest method (p. 953)

EXERCISES

LO1, 2   **EXERCISE A-1   Present Value of Single Amounts**

The following situations represent future single amounts to be received at specified interest rates after a specified number of time periods.

	Future Amount	Interest Rate	Number of Periods
A.	$25,000	5%	5
B.	17,000	10	10
C.	10,000	12	3
D.	30,000	7	7

Required: Determine the present value of these single amounts.

LO1, 2   **EXERCISE A-2   Present Value of Single Amounts**

The following situations represent future single amounts to be received at specified interest rates after a specified number of time periods, with interest compounded quarterly or semiannually.

	Future Amount	Interest Rate	Number of Years	Interest Compounded
A.	$25,000	16%	5	Quarterly
B.	17,000	10	10	Semiannually
C.	10,000	12	3	Quarterly
D.	30,000	8	7	Semiannually

Required: Determine the present value of these single amounts, assuming that interest is compounded quarterly or semiannually.

LO1, 2   EXERCISE A-3   **Future Value of Single Amounts**

Assume that interest is compounded annually for the following scenarios.

	Present Amount	Interest Rate	Number of Periods
A.	$22,000	6%	8
B.	32,000	12	5
C.	50,000	8	10
D.	3,000	4	18

Required: Determine the future value of these single amounts.

LO1, 2   EXERCISE A-4   **Future Value of Single Amounts**

The following situations represent present single amounts invested at a specified interest rate for a specified number of time periods.

	Present Amount	Interest Rate	Number of Periods	Interest Compounded
A.	$22,000	6%	8	Semiannually
B.	32,000	12	5	Quarterly
C.	50,000	8	10	Semiannually
D.	3,000	8	4	Quarterly

Required: Determine the future value of these single amounts, assuming that interest is compounded quarterly or semiannually.

LO3   EXERCISE A-5   **Present Value of Annuity**

A 10-year annuity pays $10,000 at the end of each year and is discounted at a rate of 5 percent.

Required: Determine the present value of the 10-year annuity.

LO3   EXERCISE A-6   **Present Value of Annuity**

Refer to the annuity in Exercise A-5. Assume that payments were made at the beginning of the year.

Required: Determine the present value of the annuity.

LO3   EXERCISE A-7   **Future Value of Annuity**

Assume that you invest $3,000 in an IRA account at the beginning of each year at an interest rate of 8 percent.

Required: How much money will you have at the end of 20 years?

LO3   EXERCISE A-8   **Future Value of Annuity**

Refer to the IRA account described in Exercise A-7. Assume that you make your payment at the end of each year, instead of the beginning of each year.

Required: How much would the value of the account be after 20 years?

LO4 EXERCISE A-**9** **Expected Cash Flow**

The following two scenarios present probabilities of cash flows:

	Probability	Cash Flows
Scenario 1:	10%	$ 5,000
	30	15,000
	40	25,000
	20	50,000
Scenario 2:	30%	$ 5,000
	30	25,000
	40	50,000

Required: Calculate the expected cash flow for each of the two scenarios.

LO3 EXERCISE A-**10** **Future Value of Annuity**

Olivia Rose can invest $5,000 each year for five years at 12 percent annual interest with the following potential variables:

A. Assume that the investment earns simple interest.

B. Assume that the investment compounds interest annually.

C. Assume that the investment compounds interest semiannually.

D. Assume that the investment compounds interest quarterly.

Required: How much money would Olivia Rose have at the end of five years with each assumption?

PROBLEMS

LO2 PROBLEM A-**1** **Future Value of Single Amount**

Tom Hanks is shipwrecked on January 1, 2005. At that time, he had $3,200,000 in his bank account. Tom is found five years later and returns home.

Required: How much money will Tom have if his bank has been paying 8 percent per year?

LO3 PROBLEM A-**2** **Future Value of Annuity**

Kelly Smith just had her first child and wants to start saving for the child's college education. She puts $2,500 into her child's bank account, starting with the day of the child's birth.

Required: If the investment returns 7 percent per year, how much money will be available for the child's college education in 18 years?

LO3 PROBLEM A-**3** **Present Value of Annuity**

On May 1, 2005, Davis Corp. purchases a new machine requiring eight annual payments of $75,000, starting on the purchase date. The interest rate in the purchase agreement is 9 percent per year.

Required: At what amount should Davis record the equipment?

LO3 PROBLEM A-**4** **Present Value of Annuity**

On January 1, 2005, Branson leases a warehouse. The lease has a term of 10 years and requires annual payments of $30,000 beginning on the date the lease is signed. The lease has an implicit interest rate of 6 percent.

Required: At what amount should Branson record the lease liability on January 1, 2005, before any lease payments are made?

LO5   PROBLEM A-5   **Solving for Unknown Interest Rate**

John Hewitt purchases a new automobile on July 1, 2005, that has a current price of $28,500. John agrees to make 30 monthly payments of $1,093.40, starting today.

Required: What monthly interest rate has John agreed to?

LO5   PROBLEM A-6   **Solving for Unknown Interest Rate**

Lisa Sendek purchases 20 new computer servers for $22,800 on November 1, 2005, and agrees to make three annual payments of $8,847.15 starting one year from today.

Required: What interest rate has Lisa agreed to?

LO5   PROBLEM A-7   **Solving for Period of Investment**

Amy Hardee wants to accumulate $250,000 for retirement.

Required: If Amy invested $97,732.60 today at an interest rate of 11 percent per year, how many years would it take her to reach her goal?

LO2   PROBLEM A-8   **Comparing Future and Present Value Options**

Pete Gillem enters into a new contract with his employer and is given the option of receiving an up-front bonus of $25,000 or a bonus of $40,000 three years from today.

Required: If the interest rate in the economy is 10 percent, which bonus is more attractive?

LO3   PROBLEM A-9   **Future Value of Annuity**

Jane Tew agrees to donate $50,000 per year for 10 years, starting on January 1, 2005.

Required: If the interest rate is 9 percent, what is the future value of Jane's donations?

LO2, 3   PROBLEM A-10   **Present Value of Bonds**

Stricker Industries, Inc. issued $2,000,000 of 9 percent bonds on January 1, 2005. The bonds pay interest annually on December 31. The maturity date on these bonds is December 31, 2014 (10 years). The bonds were sold to yield an effective interest rate of 10 percent. Stricker Industries has a December 31 year end.

Required: Determine the price of the bonds on January 1, 2005.

LO4   PROBLEM A-11   **Valuation of Loss Contingency**

Rehage Corporation is involved in a lawsuit with a vendor and believes that it is probable that the company will lose. The president of Rehage believes that the case will be decided in two years and estimates the following cash flow loss probabilities:

Probability	Estimated Cash Flow Loss
25%	$ 800,000
30	1,100,000
40	1,400,000
5	5,000,000

Required: If the risk-free interest rate is 4 percent per year, how much should Rehage record as a loss contingency?

TABLE A.1

Present Value Factors for a Single Amount

Period(s)	1%	2%	2.5%	3%	4%	5%	6%	7%	8%	9%	10%	11%	12%
1	0.9901	0.9804	0.9756	0.9709	0.9615	0.9524	0.9434	0.9346	0.9259	0.9174	0.9091	0.9009	0.8929
2	0.9803	0.9612	0.9518	0.9426	0.9246	0.9070	0.8900	0.8734	0.8573	0.8417	0.8264	0.8116	0.7972
3	0.9706	0.9423	0.9286	0.9151	0.8890	0.8638	0.8396	0.8163	0.7938	0.7722	0.7513	0.7312	0.7118
4	0.9610	0.9238	0.9060	0.8885	0.8548	0.8227	0.7921	0.7629	0.7350	0.7084	0.6830	0.6587	0.6355
5	0.9515	0.9057	0.8839	0.8626	0.8219	0.7835	0.7473	0.7130	0.6806	0.6499	0.6209	0.5935	0.5674
6	0.9420	0.8880	0.8623	0.8375	0.7903	0.7462	0.7050	0.6663	0.6302	0.5963	0.5645	0.5346	0.5066
7	0.9327	0.8706	0.8413	0.8131	0.7599	0.7107	0.6651	0.6227	0.5835	0.5470	0.5132	0.4817	0.4523
8	0.9235	0.8535	0.8207	0.7894	0.7307	0.6768	0.6274	0.5820	0.5403	0.5019	0.4665	0.4339	0.4039
9	0.9143	0.8368	0.8007	0.7664	0.7026	0.6446	0.5919	0.5439	0.5002	0.4604	0.4241	0.3909	0.3606
10	0.9053	0.8203	0.7812	0.7441	0.6756	0.6139	0.5584	0.5083	0.4632	0.4224	0.3855	0.3522	0.3220
11	0.8963	0.8043	0.7621	0.7224	0.6496	0.5847	0.5268	0.4751	0.4289	0.3875	0.3505	0.3173	0.2875
12	0.8874	0.7885	0.7436	0.7014	0.6246	0.5568	0.4970	0.4440	0.3971	0.3555	0.3186	0.2858	0.2567
13	0.8787	0.7730	0.7254	0.6810	0.6006	0.5303	0.4688	0.4150	0.3677	0.3262	0.2897	0.2575	0.2292
14	0.8700	0.7579	0.7077	0.6611	0.5775	0.5051	0.4423	0.3878	0.3405	0.2992	0.2633	0.2320	0.2046
15	0.8613	0.7430	0.6905	0.6419	0.5553	0.4810	0.4173	0.3624	0.3152	0.2745	0.2394	0.2090	0.1827
16	0.8528	0.7284	0.6736	0.6232	0.5339	0.4581	0.3936	0.3387	0.2919	0.2519	0.2176	0.1883	0.1631
17	0.8444	0.7142	0.6572	0.6050	0.5134	0.4363	0.3714	0.3166	0.2703	0.2311	0.1978	0.1696	0.1456
18	0.8360	0.7002	0.6412	0.5874	0.4936	0.4155	0.3503	0.2959	0.2502	0.2120	0.1799	0.1528	0.1300
19	0.8277	0.6864	0.6255	0.5703	0.4746	0.3957	0.3305	0.2765	0.2317	0.1945	0.1635	0.1377	0.1161
20	0.8195	0.6730	0.6103	0.5537	0.4564	0.3769	0.3118	0.2584	0.2145	0.1784	0.1486	0.1240	0.1037
25	0.7798	0.6095	0.5394	0.4776	0.3751	0.2953	0.2330	0.1842	0.1460	0.1160	0.0923	0.0736	0.0588
30	0.7419	0.5521	0.4767	0.4120	0.3083	0.2314	0.1741	0.1314	0.0994	0.0754	0.0573	0.0437	0.0334

TABLE A.2

Future Value Factors for a Single Amount

Periods	1%	2%	2.5%	3%	4%	5%	6%	7%	8%	9%	10%	11%	12%
1	1.0100	1.0200	1.0250	1.0300	1.0400	1.0500	1.0600	1.0700	1.0800	1.0900	1.1000	1.1100	1.1200
2	1.0201	1.0404	1.0506	1.0609	1.0816	1.1025	1.1236	1.1449	1.1664	1.1881	1.2100	1.2321	1.2544
3	1.0303	1.0612	1.0769	1.0927	1.1249	1.1576	1.1910	1.2250	1.2597	1.2950	1.3310	1.3676	1.4049
4	1.0406	1.0824	1.1038	1.1255	1.1699	1.2155	1.2625	1.3108	1.3605	1.4116	1.4641	1.5181	1.5735
5	1.0510	1.1041	1.1314	1.1593	1.2167	1.2763	1.3382	1.4026	1.4693	1.5386	1.6105	1.6851	1.7623
6	1.0615	1.1262	1.1597	1.1941	1.2653	1.3401	1.4185	1.5007	1.5869	1.6771	1.7716	1.8704	1.9738
7	1.0721	1.1487	1.1887	1.2299	1.3159	1.4071	1.5036	1.6058	1.7138	1.8280	1.9487	2.0762	2.2107
8	1.0829	1.1717	1.2184	1.2668	1.3686	1.4775	1.5938	1.7182	1.8509	1.9926	2.1436	2.3045	2.4760
9	1.0937	1.1951	1.2489	1.3048	1.4233	1.5513	1.6895	1.8385	1.9990	2.1719	2.3579	2.5580	2.7731
10	1.1046	1.2190	1.2801	1.3439	1.4802	1.6289	1.7908	1.9672	2.1589	2.3674	2.5937	2.8394	3.1058
11	1.1157	1.2434	1.3121	1.3842	1.5395	1.7103	1.8983	2.1049	2.3316	2.5804	2.8531	3.1518	3.4785
12	1.1268	1.2682	1.3449	1.4258	1.6010	1.7959	2.0122	2.2522	2.5182	2.8127	3.1384	3.4985	3.8960
13	1.1381	1.2936	1.3785	1.4685	1.6651	1.8856	2.1329	2.4098	2.7196	3.0658	3.4523	3.8833	4.3635
14	1.1495	1.3195	1.4130	1.5126	1.7317	1.9799	2.2609	2.5785	2.9372	3.3417	3.7975	4.3104	4.8871
15	1.1610	1.3459	1.4483	1.5580	1.8009	2.0789	2.3966	2.7590	3.1722	3.6425	4.1772	4.7846	5.4736
16	1.1726	1.3728	1.4845	1.6047	1.8730	2.1829	2.5404	2.9522	3.4259	3.9703	4.5950	5.3109	6.1304
17	1.1843	1.4002	1.5216	1.6528	1.9479	2.2920	2.6928	3.1588	3.7000	4.3276	5.0545	5.8951	6.8660
18	1.1961	1.4282	1.5597	1.7024	2.0258	2.4066	2.8543	3.3799	3.9960	4.7171	5.5599	6.5436	7.6900
19	1.2081	1.4568	1.5987	1.7535	2.1068	2.5270	3.0256	3.6165	4.3157	5.1417	6.1159	7.2633	8.6128
20	1.2202	1.4859	1.6386	1.8061	2.1911	2.6533	3.2071	3.8697	4.6610	5.6044	6.7275	8.0623	9.6463
25	1.2824	1.6406	1.8539	2.0938	2.6658	3.3864	4.2919	5.4274	6.8485	8.6231	10.8347	13.5855	17.0001
30	1.3478	1.8114	2.0976	2.4273	3.2434	4.3219	5.7435	7.6123	10.0627	13.2677	17.4494	22.8923	29.9599

TABLE A.3

Present Value Factors for an Ordinary Annuity

Pay at end of month

Periods	1%	2%	2.5%	3%	4%	5%	6%	7%	8%	9%	10%	11%	12%
1	0.9901	0.9804	0.9756	0.9709	0.9615	0.9524	0.9434	0.9346	0.9259	0.9174	0.9091	0.9009	0.8929
2	1.9704	1.9416	1.9274	1.9135	1.8861	1.8594	1.8334	1.8080	1.7833	1.7591	1.7355	1.7125	1.6901
3	2.9410	2.8839	2.8560	2.8286	2.7751	2.7232	2.6730	2.6243	2.5771	2.5313	2.4869	2.4437	2.4018
4	3.9020	3.8077	3.7620	3.7171	3.6299	3.5460	3.4651	3.3872	3.3121	3.2397	3.1699	3.1024	3.0373
5	4.8534	4.7135	4.6458	4.5797	4.4518	4.3295	4.2124	4.1002	3.9927	3.8897	3.7908	3.6959	3.6048
6	5.7955	5.6014	5.5081	5.4172	5.2421	5.0757	4.9173	4.7665	4.6229	4.4859	4.3553	4.2305	4.1114
7	6.7282	6.4720	6.3494	6.2303	6.0021	5.7864	5.5824	5.3893	5.2064	5.0330	4.8684	4.7122	4.5638
8	7.6517	7.3255	7.1701	7.0197	6.7327	6.4632	6.2098	5.9713	5.7466	5.5348	5.3349	5.1461	4.9676
9	8.5660	8.1622	7.9709	7.7861	7.4353	7.1078	6.8017	6.5152	6.2469	5.9952	5.7590	5.5370	5.3282
10	9.4713	8.9826	8.7521	8.5302	8.1109	7.7217	7.3601	7.0236	6.7101	6.4177	6.1446	5.8892	5.6502
11	10.3676	9.7868	9.5142	9.2526	8.7605	8.3064	7.8869	7.4987	7.1390	6.8052	6.4951	6.2065	5.9377
12	11.2551	10.5753	10.2578	9.9540	9.3851	8.8633	8.3838	7.9427	7.5361	7.1607	6.8137	6.4924	6.1944
13	12.1337	11.3484	10.9832	10.6350	9.9856	9.3936	8.8527	8.3577	7.9038	7.4869	7.1034	6.7499	6.4235
14	13.0037	12.1062	11.6909	11.2961	10.5631	9.8986	9.2950	8.7455	8.2442	7.7862	7.3667	6.9819	6.6282
15	13.8651	12.8493	12.3814	11.9379	11.1184	10.3797	9.7122	9.1079	8.5595	8.0607	7.6061	7.1909	6.8109
16	14.7179	13.5777	13.0550	12.5611	11.6523	10.8378	10.1059	9.4466	8.8514	8.3126	7.8237	7.3792	6.9740
17	15.5623	14.2919	13.7122	13.1661	12.1657	11.2741	10.4773	9.7632	9.1216	8.5436	8.0216	7.5488	7.1196
18	16.3983	14.9920	14.3534	13.7535	12.6593	11.6896	10.8276	10.0591	9.3719	8.7556	8.2014	7.7016	7.2497
19	17.2260	15.6785	14.9789	14.3238	13.1339	12.0853	11.1581	10.3356	9.6036	8.9501	8.3649	7.8393	7.3658
20	18.0456	16.3514	15.5892	14.8775	13.5903	12.4622	11.4699	10.5940	9.8181	9.1285	8.5136	7.9633	7.4694
25	22.0232	19.5235	18.4244	17.4131	15.6221	14.0939	12.7834	11.6536	10.6748	9.8226	9.0770	8.4217	7.8431
30	25.8077	22.3965	20.9303	19.6004	17.2920	15.3725	13.7648	12.4090	11.2578	10.2737	9.4269	8.6938	8.0552

TABLE A.4

Present Value Factors for an Annuity Due   *Pay at Beginning of month*

Periods	1%	2%	2.5%	3%	4%	5%	6%	7%	8%	9%	10%	11%	12%
1	1.0000	1.0000	1.0000	1.0000	1.0000	1.0000	1.0000	1.0000	1.0000	1.0000	1.0000	1.0000	1.0000
2	1.9901	1.9804	1.9756	1.9709	1.9615	1.9524	1.9434	1.9346	1.9259	1.9174	1.9091	1.9009	1.8929
3	2.9704	2.9416	2.9274	2.9135	2.8861	2.8594	2.8334	2.8080	2.7833	2.7591	2.7355	2.7125	2.6901
4	3.9410	3.8839	3.8560	3.8286	3.7751	3.7232	3.6730	3.6243	3.5771	3.5313	3.4869	3.4437	3.4018
5	4.9020	4.8077	4.7620	4.7171	4.6299	4.5460	4.4651	4.3872	4.3121	4.2397	4.1699	4.1024	4.0373
6	5.8534	5.7135	5.6458	5.5797	5.4518	5.3295	5.2124	5.1002	4.9927	4.8897	4.7908	4.6959	4.6048
7	6.7955	6.6014	6.5081	6.4172	6.2421	6.0757	5.9173	5.7665	5.6229	5.4859	5.3553	5.2305	5.1114
8	7.7282	7.4720	7.3494	7.2303	7.0021	6.7864	6.5824	6.3893	6.2064	6.0330	5.8684	5.7122	5.5638
9	8.6517	8.3255	8.1701	8.0197	7.7327	7.4632	7.2098	6.9713	6.7466	6.5348	6.3349	6.1461	5.9676
10	9.5660	9.1622	8.9709	8.7861	8.4353	8.1078	7.8017	7.5152	7.2469	6.9952	6.7590	6.5370	6.3282
11	10.4713	9.9826	9.7521	9.5302	9.1109	8.7217	8.3601	8.0236	7.7101	7.4177	7.1446	6.8892	6.6502
12	11.3676	10.7868	10.5142	10.2526	9.7605	9.3064	8.8869	8.4987	8.1390	7.8052	7.4951	7.2065	6.9377
13	12.2551	11.5753	11.2578	10.9540	10.3851	9.8633	9.3838	8.9427	8.5361	8.1607	7.8137	7.4924	7.1944
14	13.1337	12.3484	11.9832	11.6350	10.9856	10.3936	9.8527	9.3577	8.9038	8.4869	8.1034	7.7499	7.4235
15	14.0037	13.1062	12.6909	12.2961	11.5631	10.8986	10.2950	9.7455	9.2442	8.7862	8.3667	7.9819	7.6282
16	14.8651	13.8493	13.3814	12.9379	12.1184	11.3797	10.7122	10.1079	9.5595	9.0607	8.6061	8.1909	7.8109
17	15.7179	14.5777	14.0550	13.5611	12.6523	11.8378	11.1059	10.4466	9.8514	9.3126	8.8237	8.3792	7.9740
18	16.5623	15.2919	14.7122	14.1661	13.1657	12.2741	11.4773	10.7632	10.1216	9.5436	9.0216	8.5488	8.1196
19	17.3983	15.9920	15.3534	14.7535	13.6593	12.6896	11.8276	11.0591	10.3719	9.7556	9.2014	8.7016	8.2497
20	18.2260	16.6785	15.9789	15.3238	14.1339	13.0853	12.1581	11.3356	10.6036	9.9501	9.3649	8.8393	8.3658
25	22.2434	19.9139	18.8850	17.9355	16.2470	14.7986	13.5504	12.4693	11.5288	10.7066	9.9847	9.3481	8.7843
30	26.0658	22.8444	21.4535	20.1885	17.9837	16.1411	14.5907	13.2777	12.1584	11.1983	10.3696	9.6501	9.0218

TABLE A.5

Future Value Factors for an Ordinary Annuity

Periods	1%	2%	2.5%	3%	4%	5%	6%	7%	8%	9%	10%	11%	12%
1	1.0000	1.0000	1.0000	1.0000	1.0000	1.0000	1.0000	1.0000	1.0000	1.0000	1.0000	1.0000	1.0000
2	2.0100	2.0200	2.0250	2.0300	2.0400	2.0500	2.0600	2.0700	2.0800	2.0900	2.1000	2.1100	2.1200
3	3.0301	3.0604	3.0756	3.0909	3.1216	3.1525	3.1836	3.2149	3.2464	3.2781	3.3100	3.3421	3.3744
4	4.0604	4.1216	4.1525	4.1836	4.2465	4.3101	4.3746	4.4399	4.5061	4.5731	4.6410	4.7097	4.7793
5	5.1010	5.2040	5.2563	5.3091	5.4163	5.5256	5.6371	5.7507	5.8666	5.9847	6.1051	6.2278	6.3528
6	6.1520	6.3081	6.3877	6.4684	6.6330	6.8019	6.9753	7.1533	7.3359	7.5233	7.7156	7.9129	8.1152
7	7.2135	7.4343	7.5474	7.6625	7.8983	8.1420	8.3938	8.6540	8.9228	9.2004	9.4872	9.7833	10.0890
8	8.2857	8.5830	8.7361	8.8923	9.2142	9.5491	9.8975	10.2598	10.6366	11.0285	11.4359	11.8594	12.2997
9	9.3685	9.7546	9.9545	10.1591	10.5828	11.0266	11.4913	11.9780	12.4876	13.0210	13.5795	14.1640	14.7757
10	10.4622	10.9497	11.2034	11.4639	12.0061	12.5779	13.1808	13.8164	14.4866	15.1929	15.9374	16.7220	17.5487
11	11.5668	12.1687	12.4835	12.8078	13.4864	14.2068	14.9716	15.7836	16.6455	17.5603	18.5312	19.5614	20.6546
12	12.6825	13.4121	13.7956	14.1920	15.0258	15.9171	16.8699	17.8885	18.9771	20.1407	21.3843	22.7132	24.1331
13	13.8093	14.6803	15.1404	15.6178	16.6268	17.7130	18.8821	20.1406	21.4953	22.9534	24.5227	26.2116	28.0291
14	14.9474	15.9739	16.5190	17.0863	18.2919	19.5986	21.0151	22.5505	24.2149	26.0192	27.9750	30.0949	32.3926
15	16.0969	17.2934	17.9319	18.5989	20.0236	21.5786	23.2760	25.1290	27.1521	29.3609	31.7725	34.4054	37.2797
16	17.2579	18.6393	19.3802	20.1569	21.8245	23.6575	25.6725	27.8881	30.3243	33.0034	35.9497	39.1899	42.7533
17	18.4304	20.0121	20.8647	21.7616	23.6975	25.8404	28.2129	30.8402	33.7502	36.9737	40.5447	44.5008	48.8837
18	19.6147	21.4123	22.3863	23.4144	25.6454	28.1324	30.9057	33.9990	37.4502	41.3013	45.5992	50.3959	55.7497
19	20.8109	22.8406	23.9460	25.1169	27.6712	30.5390	33.7600	37.3790	41.4463	46.0185	51.1591	56.9395	63.4397
20	22.0190	24.2974	25.5447	26.8704	29.7781	33.0660	36.7856	40.9955	45.7620	51.1601	57.2750	64.2028	72.0524
25	28.2432	32.0303	34.1578	36.4593	41.6459	47.7271	54.8645	63.2490	73.1059	84.7009	98.3471	114.4133	133.3339
30	34.7849	40.5681	43.9027	47.5754	56.0849	66.4388	79.0582	94.4608	113.2832	136.3075	164.4940	199.0209	241.3327

TABLE A.6

Future Value Factors for an Annuity Due

Periods	1%	2%	2.5%	3%	4%	5%	6%	7%	8%	9%	10%	11%	12%
1	1.0100	1.0200	1.0250	1.0300	1.0400	1.0500	1.0600	1.0700	1.0800	1.0900	1.1000	1.1100	1.1200
2	2.0301	2.0604	2.0756	2.0909	2.1216	2.1525	2.1836	2.2149	2.2464	2.2781	2.3100	2.3421	2.3744
3	3.0604	3.1216	3.1525	3.1836	3.2465	3.3101	3.3746	3.4399	3.5061	3.5731	3.6410	3.7097	3.7793
4	4.1010	4.2040	4.2563	4.3091	4.4163	4.5256	4.6371	4.7507	4.8666	4.9847	5.1051	5.2278	5.3528
5	5.1520	5.3081	5.3877	5.4684	5.6330	5.8019	5.9753	6.1533	6.3359	6.5233	6.7156	6.9129	7.1152
6	6.2135	6.4343	6.5474	6.6625	6.8983	7.1420	7.3938	7.6540	7.9228	8.2004	8.4872	8.7833	9.0890
7	7.2857	7.5830	7.7361	7.8923	8.2142	8.5491	8.8975	9.2598	9.6366	10.0285	10.4359	10.8594	11.2997
8	8.3685	8.7546	8.9545	9.1591	9.5828	10.0266	10.4913	10.9780	11.4876	12.0210	12.5795	13.1640	13.7757
9	9.4622	9.9497	10.2034	10.4639	11.0061	11.5779	12.1808	12.8164	13.4866	14.1929	14.9374	15.7220	16.5487
10	10.5668	11.1687	11.4835	11.8078	12.4864	13.2068	13.9716	14.7836	15.6455	16.5603	17.5312	18.5614	19.6546
11	11.6825	12.4121	12.7956	13.1920	14.0258	14.9171	15.8699	16.8885	17.9771	19.1407	20.3843	21.7132	23.1331
12	12.8093	13.6803	14.1404	14.6178	15.6268	16.7130	17.8821	19.1406	20.4953	21.9534	23.5227	25.2116	27.0291
13	13.9474	14.9739	15.5190	16.0863	17.2919	18.5986	20.0151	21.5505	23.2149	25.0192	26.9750	29.0949	31.3926
14	15.0969	16.2934	16.9319	17.5989	19.0236	20.5786	22.2760	24.1290	26.1521	28.3609	30.7725	33.4054	36.2797
15	16.2579	17.6393	18.3802	19.1569	20.8245	22.6575	24.6725	26.8881	29.3243	32.0034	34.9497	38.1899	41.7533
16	17.4304	19.0121	19.8647	20.7616	22.6975	24.8404	27.2129	29.8402	32.7502	35.9737	39.5447	43.5008	47.8837
17	18.6147	20.4123	21.3863	22.4144	24.6454	27.1324	29.9057	32.9990	36.4502	40.3013	44.5992	49.3959	54.7497
18	19.8109	21.8406	22.9460	24.1169	26.6712	29.5390	32.7600	36.3790	40.4463	45.0185	50.1591	55.9395	62.4397
19	21.0190	23.2974	24.5447	25.8704	28.7781	32.0660	35.7856	39.9955	44.7620	50.1601	56.2750	63.2028	71.0524
20	22.2392	24.7833	26.1833	27.6765	30.9692	34.7193	38.9927	43.8652	49.4229	55.7645	63.0025	71.2651	80.6987
25	28.5256	32.6709	35.0117	37.5530	43.3117	50.1135	58.1564	67.6765	78.9544	92.3240	108.1818	126.9988	149.3339
30	35.1327	41.3794	45.0003	49.0027	58.3283	69.7608	83.8017	101.0730	122.3459	148.5752	180.9434	220.9132	270.2926

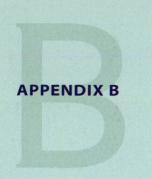

Official Accounting Pronouncements

TABLE B.1

Accounting Research Bulletins (ARBs), Committee on Accounting Procedures, AICPA

Date Issued	Number	Title
June 1953	No. 43	Restatement and Revision of Accounting Research Bulletins Nos. 1–42, and Accounting Terminology Bulletin No. 1 (originally issued 1939–1953)
Oct. 1954	No. 44	Declining-Balance Depreciation; Revised July 1958 (amended)
Oct. 1955	No. 45	Long-Term Construction-Type Contracts (unchanged)
Feb. 1956	No. 46	Discontinuance of Dating Earned Surplus (unchanged)
Sept. 1956	No. 47	Accounting for Costs of Pension Plans (superseded)
Jan. 1957	No. 48	Business Combinations (superseded)
April 1958	No. 49	Earnings per Share (superseded)
Oct. 1958	No. 50	Contingencies (superseded)
Aug. 1959	No. 51	Consolidated Financial Statements (amended and partially superseded)

TABLE B.2

Accounting Terminology Bulletins, Committee on Terminology, AICPA

Date Issued	Number	Title
Aug. 1953	No. 1	Review and Résumé (of the eight original terminology bulletins) (amended)
Mar. 1955	No. 2	Proceeds, Revenue, Income, Profit, and Earnings (amended)
Aug. 1956	No. 3	Book Value (unchanged)
July 1957	No. 4	Cost, Expense, and Loss (amended)

TABLE B.3

Accounting Principles Board (APB) Opinions, AICPA

Date Issued	Number	Title
Nov. 1962	No. 1	New Depreciation Guidelines and Rules (amended)
Dec. 1962	No. 2	Accounting for the "Investment Credit" (amended)
Oct. 1963	No. 3	The Statement of Source and Application of Funds (superseded)
Mar. 1964	No. 4	Accounting for the "Investment Credit" (amending No. 2)
Sept. 1964	No. 5	Reporting of Leases in Financial Statements of Lessee (superseded)
Oct. 1965	No. 6	Status of Accounting Research Bulletins (partially superseded)
May 1966	No. 7	Accounting for Leases in Financial Statements of Lessors (superseded)
Nov. 1966	No. 8	Accounting for the Cost of Pension Plans (superseded)
Dec. 1966	No. 9	Reporting the Results of Operations (amended and partially superseded)
Dec. 1966	No. 10	Omnibus Opinion—1966 (amended and partially superseded)
Dec. 1967	No. 11	Accounting for Income Taxes (superseded)
Dec. 1967	No. 12	Omnibus Opinion—1967 (partially superseded)
Mar. 1969	No. 13	Amending Paragraph 6 of APB Opinion No. 9, Application to Commercial Banks (unchanged)
Mar. 1969	No. 14	Accounting for Convertible Debt and Debt Issued with Stock Purchase Warrants (unchanged)
May 1969	No. 15	Earnings per Share (amended)
Aug. 1970	No. 16	Business Combinations (amended)
Aug. 1970	No. 17	Intangible Assets (amended)
Mar. 1971	No. 18	The Equity Method of Accounting for Investments in Common Stock (amended)
Mar. 1971	No. 19	Reporting Changes in Financial Position (amended)
July 1971	No. 20	Accounting Changes (amended)
Aug. 1971	No. 21	Interest on Receivables and Payables (amended)
April 1972	No. 22	Disclosure of Accounting Policies (amended)
April 1972	No. 23	Accounting for Income Taxes—Special Areas (superseded)
April 1972	No. 24	Accounting for Income Taxes—Equity Method Investments (unchanged)
Oct. 1972	No. 25	Accounting for Stock Issued to Employees (unchanged)
Oct. 1972	No. 26	Early Extinguishment of Debt (amended)
Nov. 1972	No. 27	Accounting for Lease Transactions by Manufacturer or Dealer Lessors (superseded)
May 1973	No. 28	Interim Financial Reporting (amended and partially superseded)
May 1973	No. 29	Accounting for Nonmonetary Transactions (unchanged)
June 1973	No. 30	Reporting the Results of Operations (amended)
June 1973	No. 31	Disclosure of Lease Commitments by Lessees (superseded)

TABLE B.4

Statements of Financial Accounting Standards (SFASs) , Financial Accounting Standards Board (FASB)

Date Issued	Number	Title
Dec. 1973	No. 1	Disclosure of Foreign Currency Translation Information (superseded)
Oct. 1974	No. 2	Accounting for Research and Development Costs
Dec. 1974	No. 3	Reporting Accounting Changes in Interim Financial Statements
Mar. 1975	No. 4	Reporting Gains and Losses from Extinguishment of Debt (amended)
Mar. 1975	No. 5	Accounting for Contingencies (amended)
May 1975	No. 6	Classification of Short-Term Obligations Expected to Be Refinanced
June 1975	No. 7	Accounting and Reporting by Development Stage Enterprises
Oct. 1975	No. 8	Accounting for the Translation of Foreign Currency Transactions and Foreign Financial Statements (superseded)
Oct. 1975	No. 9	Accounting for Income Taxes—Oil and Gas Producing Companies (superseded)
Oct. 1975	No. 10	Extension of "Grandfather" Provisions for Business Combinations
Dec. 1975	No. 11	Accounting for Contingencies—Transition Method
Dec. 1975	No. 12	Accounting for Certain Marketable Securities
Nov. 1976	No. 13	Accounting for Leases (amended, interpreted, and partially superseded)
Dec. 1976	No. 14	Financial Reporting for Segments of a Business Enterprise (amended)
June 1977	No. 15	Accounting by Debtors and Creditors for Troubled Debt Restructurings
June 1977	No. 16	Prior Period Adjustments
Nov. 1977	No. 17	Accounting for Leases—Initial Direct Costs
Nov. 1977	No. 18	Financial Reporting for Segments of a Business Enterprise—Interim Financial Statements
Dec. 1977	No. 19	Financial Accounting and Reporting by Oil and Gas Producing Companies (amended)
Dec. 1977	No. 20	Accounting for Forward Exchange Contracts (superseded)
April 1978	No. 21	Suspension of the Reporting of Earnings per Share and Segment Information by Nonpublic Enterprises
June 1978	No. 22	Changes in the Provisions of Lease Agreements Resulting from Refundings of Tax-Exempt Debt
Aug. 1978	No. 23	Inception of the Lease
Dec. 1978	No. 24	Reporting Segment Information in Financial Statements That Are Presented in Another Enterprise's Financial Report
Feb. 1979	No. 25	Suspension of Certain Accounting Requirements for Oil and Gas Producing Companies
April 1979	No. 26	Profit Recognition on Sales-Type Leases of Real Estate
May 1979	No. 27	Classification of Renewals or Extensions of Existing Sales-Type or Direct Financing Leases
May 1979	No. 28	Accounting for Sales with Leasebacks
June 1979	No. 29	Determining Contingent Rentals
Aug. 1979	No. 30	Disclosure of Information about Major Customers
Sept. 1979	No. 31	Accounting for Tax Benefits Related to U.K. Tax Legislation Concerning Stock Relief
Sept. 1979	No. 32	Specialized Accounting and Reporting Principles and Practices in AICPA Statements of Position and Guides on Accounting and Auditing Matters (amended and partially superseded)
Sept. 1979	No. 33	Financial Reporting and Changing Prices (amended and partially superseded)
Oct. 1979	No. 34	Capitalization of Interest Cost (amended)
Mar. 1980	No. 35	Accounting and Reporting by Defined Benefit Pension Plans (amended)
May 1980	No. 36	Disclosure of Pension Information
July 1980	No. 37	Balance Sheet Classification of Deferred Income Taxes

TABLE B.4

Statements of Financial Accounting Standards (SFASs) , Financial Accounting Standards Board (FASB) *(continued)*

Date Issued	Number	Title
Sept. 1980	No. 38	Accounting for Preacquisition Contingencies of Purchased Enterprises
Oct. 1980	No. 39	Financial Reporting and Changing Prices: Specialized Assets—Mining and Oil and Gas
Nov. 1980	No. 40	Financial Reporting and Changing Prices: Specialized Assets—Timberlands and Growing Timber
Nov. 1980	No. 41	Financial Reporting and Changing Prices: Specialized Assets—Income-Producing Real Estate
Nov. 1980	No. 42	Determining Materiality for Capitalization of Interest Cost
Nov. 1980	No. 43	Accounting for Compensated Absences
Dec. 1980	No. 44	Accounting for Intangible Assets of Motor Carriers
Mar. 1981	No. 45	Accounting for Franchise Fee Revenue
Mar. 1981	No. 46	Financial Reporting and Changing Prices: Motion Picture Films
Mar. 1981	No. 47	Disclosure of Long-Term Obligations
June 1981	No. 48	Revenue Recognition When Right of Return Exists
June 1981	No. 49	Accounting for Product Financing Arrangements
Nov. 1981	No. 50	Financial Reporting in the Record and Music Industry
Nov. 1981	No. 51	Financial Reporting by Cable Television Companies
Dec. 1981	No. 52	Foreign Currency Translation
Dec. 1981	No. 53	Financial Reporting by Producers and Distributors of Motion Picture Films
Jan. 1982	No. 54	Financial Reporting and Changing Prices: Investment Companies
Feb. 1982	No. 55	Determining Whether a Convertible Security Is a Common Stock Equivalent
Feb. 1982	No. 56	Designation of AICPA Guide and SOP 81-1 on Contractor Accounting and SOP 81-2 on Hospital-Related Organizations as Preferable for Applying APB Opinion 20
Mar. 1982	No. 57	Related Party Disclosures
April 1982	No. 58	Capitalization of Interest Cost in Financial Statements That Include Investments Accounted for by the Equity Method
April 1982	No. 59	Deferral of the Effective Date of Certain Accounting Requirements for Revision Plans of State and Local Governmental Units
June 1982	No. 60	Accounting and Reporting by Insurance Enterprises (amended)
June 1982	No. 61	Accounting for Title Plant
June 1982	No. 62	Capitalization of Interest Cost in Situations Involving Certain Tax-Exempt Borrowings and Certain Gifts and Grants
June 1982	No. 63	Financial Reporting by Broadcasters
Sept. 1982	No. 64	Extinguishment of Debt Made to Satisfy Sinking-Find Requirements
Sept. 1982	No. 65	Accounting for Certain Mortgage Bank Activities
Oct. 1982	No. 66	Accounting for Sales of Real Estate
Oct. 1982	No. 67	Accounting for Costs and Initial Rental Operations of Real Estate Projects
Oct. 1982	No. 68	Research and Development Arrangements
Nov. 1982	No. 69	Disclosures About Oil and Gas Producing Activities
Dec. 1982	No. 70	Financial Reporting and Changing Prices: Foreign Currency Translation
Dec. 1982	No. 71	Accounting for the Effects of Certain Types of Regulation
Feb. 1983	No. 72	Accounting for Certain Acquisitions of Banking or Thrift Institutions
Aug. 1983	No. 73	Reporting a Change in Accounting for Railroad Track Structures
Aug. 1983	No. 74	Accounting for Special Termination Benefits Paid to Employees
Nov. 1983	No. 75	Deferral of the Effective Date of Certain Accounting Requirements of Pension Plans of State and Local Governmental Units
Nov. 1983	No. 76	Extinguishment of Debt

TABLE B.4

Statements of Financial Accounting Standards (SFASs) , Financial Accounting Standards Board (FASB) *(continued)*

Date Issued	Number	Title
Dec. 1983	No. 77	Reporting by Transferors for Transfers of Receivables with Recourse
Dec. 1983	No. 78	Classifications of Obligations That Are Callable by the Creditor
Feb. 1984	No. 79	Elimination of Certain Disclosures for Business Combinations by Nonpublic Enterprises
Aug. 1984	No. 80	Accounting for Futures Contracts
Nov. 1984	No. 81	Disclosure of Postretirement Health Care and Life Insurance Benefits
Nov. 1984	No. 82	Financial Reporting and Changing Prices: Elimination of Certain Disclosures
Mar. 1985	No. 83	Designation of AICPA Guides and Statement of Position on Accounting by Brokers and Dealers in Securities, by Employee Benefits Plans, and by Banks as Preferable for Purposes of Applying APB Opinion 20
Mar. 1985	No. 84	Induced Conversions of Convertible Debt
Mar. 1985	No. 85	Yield Test for Determining Whether a Convertible Security Is a Common Stock Equivalent
Aug. 1985	No. 86	Accounting for the Costs of Computer Software to Be Sold, Leased, or Otherwise Marketed
Dec. 1985	No. 87	Employers' Accounting for Pensions
Dec. 1985	No. 88	Employers' Accounting for Settlements and Curtailments of Defined Benefit Pension Plans and for Termination Benefits
Dec. 1986	No. 89	Financial Reporting and Changing Prices
Dec. 1986	No. 90	Regulated Enterprises—Accounting for Abandonments and Disallowances of Plant Costs
Dec. 1986	No. 91	Accounting for Nonrefundable Fees and Costs Associated with Originating or Acquiring Loans and Initial Direct Costs of Leases
Aug. 1987	No. 92	Regulated Enterprises—Accounting for Phase-in Plans
Aug. 1987	No. 93	Recognition of Depreciation by Not-for-Profit Organizations
Oct. 1987	No. 94	Consolidation of All Majority-Owned Subsidiaries
Nov. 1987	No. 95	Statement of Cash Flows
Dec. 1987	No. 96	Accounting for Income Taxes
Dec. 1987	No. 97	Accounting and Reporting by Insurance Enterprises for Certain Long-Duration Contracts and for Realized Gains and Losses from the Sale of Investments
June 1988	No. 98	Accounting for Leases: Sale-Leaseback Transactions Involving Real Estate; Sales-Type Leases of Real Estate; Definition of Lease Term; Initial Direct Costs of Direct Financing Leases
Sept. 1988	No. 99	Deferral of the Effective Date of Recognition of Depreciation by Not-for-Profit Organizations
Dec. 1988	No. 100	Accounting for Income Taxes—Deferral of the Effective Date of FASB Statement No. 96
Dec. 1988	No. 101	Regulated Enterprises—Accounting for the Discontinuation of Application of FASB Statement No. 71
Feb. 1989	No. 102	Statement of Cash Flows—Exemption of Certain Enterprises and Classification of Cash Flows from Certain Securities Acquired for Resale
Dec. 1989	No. 103	Accounting for Income Taxes—Deferral of the Effective Date of FASB Statement No. 96
Dec. 1989	No. 104	Statement of Cash Flows—Net Reporting of Certain Cash Receipts and Cash Payments and Classification of Cash Flows from Hedging Transactions
Mar. 1990	No. 105	Disclosure of Information About Financial Instruments with Off-Balance-Sheet Risk and Financial Instruments with Concentrations of Credit Risk
Dec. 1990	No. 106	Employers' Accounting for Postretirement Benefits Other than Pensions
Dec. 1991	No. 107	Disclosures About Fair Value of Financial Instruments

TABLE B.4

Statements of Financial Accounting Standards (SFASs) , Financial Accounting Standards Board (FASB) *(continued)*

Date Issued	Number	Title
Dec. 1991	No. 108	Accounting for Income Taxes—Deferral of the Effective Date of FASB Statement No. 96
Feb. 1992	No. 109	Accounting for Income Taxes
Aug. 1992	No. 110	Reporting by Defined Benefit Pension Plans of Investment Contracts
Nov. 1992	No. 111	Rescission of FASB Statement No. 32 and Technical Corrections
Nov. 1992	No. 112	Employers' Accounting for Postemployment Benefits
Dec. 1992	No. 113	Accounting and Reporting for Reinsurance of Short-Duration and Long-Duration Contracts
May 1993	No. 114	Accounting by Creditors for Impairment of a Loan
May 1993	No. 115	Accounting for Certain Investments in Debt and Equity Securities
June 1993	No. 116	Accounting for Contributions Received and Contributions Made
June 1993	No. 117	Financial Statements of Not-for-Profit Organizations
Oct. 1994	No. 118	Accounting by Creditors for Impairments of a Loan—Income Recognition and Disclosures
Oct. 1994	No. 119	Disclosure About Derivative Financial Instruments and Fair Value of Financial Instruments
Jan. 1995	No. 120	Accounting and Reporting by Mutual Life Insurance Enterprises
Mar. 1995	No. 121	Accounting for the Impairment of Long-Lived Assets
May 1995	No. 122	Accounting for Mortgage Servicing Rights
Oct. 1995	No. 123	Accounting for Stock-Based Compensation
Nov. 1995	No. 124	Accounting for Certain Investments Held by Not-for-Profit Organizations
June 1996	No. 125	Accounting for Transfers and Servicing of Financial Assets and Extinguishment of Liabilities
Dec. 1996	No. 126	Exemption from Certain Required Disclosures About Financial Instruments for Certain Nonpublic Entities
Dec. 1996	No. 127	Deferral of the Effective Date of Certain Provisions of FASB Statement No. 125
Feb. 1997	No. 128	Earnings per Share
Feb. 1997	No. 129	Disclosure of Information About Capital Structure
June 1997	No. 130	Reporting Comprehensive Income
June 1997	No. 131	Disclosures About Segments of an Enterprise and Related Information
Feb. 1998	No. 132	Employers' Disclosures About Pensions and Other Postretirement Benefits, An Amendment of FASB Statements No. 87, 88, and 106
June 1998	No. 133	Accounting for Derivative Instruments and Hedging Activities
Oct. 1998	No. 134	Accounting for Mortgage-Backed Securities Retained After the Securitization of Mortgage Loans Held for Sale by a Mortgage Banking Enterprise, An Amendment of FASB Statement No. 65
Feb. 1999	No. 135	Rescission of FASB Statement No. 75 and Technical Corrections
June 1999	No. 136	Transfers of Assets to a Not-for-Profit Organization or Charitable Trust That Raises or Holds Contributions for Others
June 1999	No. 137	Accounting for Derivative Instruments and Hedging Activities—Deferral of the Effective Date of FASB Statement No. 133, An Amendment of FASB Statement No. 133
June 2000	No. 138	Accounting for Certain Derivative Instruments and Certain Hedging Activities, An Amendment of FASB Statement No. 133
June 2000	No. 139	Rescission of FASB Statement No. 53 and Amendments to FASB Statements No. 63, 89, and 121
Sept. 2000	No. 140	Accounting for Transfers and Servicing of Financial Assets and Extinguishments of Liabilities, A Replacement of FASB Statement No. 125

TABLE B.4

Statements of Financial Accounting Standards (SFASs) , Financial Accounting Standards Board (FASB) *(continued)*

Date Issued	Number	Title
June 2001	No. 141	Business Combinations
June 2001	No. 142	Goodwill and Other Intangible Assets
June 2001	No. 143	Accounting for Asset Retirement Obligations
Aug. 2001	No. 144	Accounting for the Impairment or Disposal of Long-Lived Assets
April 2002	No. 145	Rescission of FASB Statements No. 4, 44, and 64, Amendment of FASB Statement No. 13, and Technical Corrections
June 2002	No. 146	Accounting for Costs Associated with Exit or Disposal Activities
Oct. 2002	No. 147	Acquisitions of Certain Financial Institutions, An Amendment of FASB Statements No. 72 and 144 and FASB Interpretation No. 9
Dec. 2002	No. 148	Accounting for Stock-Based Compensation—Transition and Disclosure, An Amendment of FASB Statement No. 123
April 2003	No. 149	Amendment of Statement 133 on Derivative Instruments and Hedging Activities
May 2003	No. 150	Accounting for Certain Financial Instruments with Characteristics of both Liabilities and Equity
Rev. Dec. 2003	No. 132R	Employers' Disclosures About Pensions and Other Postretirement Benefits, An Amendment of FASB Statements No. 87, 88, and 106
Nov. 2004	No. 151	Inventory Costs, An Amendment of ARB No. 43, Chapter 4
Dec. 2004	No. 152	Accounting for Real Estate Time-Sharing Transactions, An Amendment of FASB Statements No. 66 and 67
Dec. 2004	No. 153	Exchanges of Nonmonetary Assets, An Amendment of APB Opinion No. 29
Rev. Dec. 2004	No. 123R	Share-Based Payment
May 2005	No. 154	Accounting Changes and Error Corrections, A Replacement of APB Opinion No. 20 and FASB Statement No. 3

TABLE B.5

Financial Accounting Standards Board (FASB), Interpretations

Date Issued	Number	Title
June 1974	No. 1	Accounting Changes Related to the Cost of Inventory (APB Opinion No. 20)
June 1974	No. 2	Imputing Interest on Debt Arrangements Made Under the Federal Bankruptcy Act (APB Opinion No. 21) (superseded)
Dec. 1974	No. 3	Accounting for the Cost of Pension Plans Subject to the Employee Retirement Income Security Act of 1974 (APB Opinion No. 8)
Feb. 1975	No. 4	Applicability of FASB Statement No. 2 to Purchase Business Combinations
Feb. 1975	No. 5	Applicability of FASB Statement No. 2 to Development State Enterprises (superseded)
Feb. 1975	No. 6	Applicability of FASB Statement No. 2 to Computer Software
Oct. 1975	No. 7	Applying FASB Statement No. 7 in Statements of Established Enterprises
Jan. 1976	No. 8	Classification of a Short-Term Obligation Repaid Prior to Being Replaced by a Long-Term Security (FASB Standard No. 6)
Feb. 1976	No. 9	Applying APB Opinions No. 16 and 17 when a Savings and Loan or Similar Institution Is Acquired in a Purchase Business Combination (APB Opinion No. 16 and 17)
Sept. 1976	No. 10	Application of FASB Statement No. 12 to Personal Financial Statements (FASB Standard No. 12)
Sept. 1976	No. 11	Changes in Market Value After the Balance Sheet Date (FASB Standard No. 12)
Sept. 1976	No. 12	Accounting for Previously Established Allowance Accounts (FASB Standard No. 12)
Sept. 1976	No. 13	Consolidation of a Parent and Its Subsidiaries Having Different Balance Sheet Dates (FASB Standard No. 12)
Sept. 1976	No. 14	Reasonable Estimation of the Amount of a Loss (FASB Standard No. 5)
Sept. 1976	No. 15	Translation of Unamortized Policy Acquisition Costs by Stock Life Insurance Company (FASB Standard No. 8) (amended and partially superseded)
Feb. 1977	No. 16	Clarification of Definitions and Accounting for Marketable Equity Securities That Become Nonmarketable (FASB Standard No. 12)
Feb. 1977	No. 17	Applying the Lower of Cost or Market Rule in Translated Financial Statements (FASB Standard No. 8) (superseded)
Mar. 1977	No. 18	Accounting for Income Taxes in Interim Periods (APB Opinion No. 28)
Oct. 1977	No. 19	Lessee Guarantee of the Residual Value of Leased Property (FASB Standard No. 13)
Nov. 1977	No. 20	Reporting Accounting Changes Under AICPA Statements of Position (APB Opinion No. 20)
April 1978	No. 21	Accounting for Leases in a Business Combination (FASB Standard No. 13)
April 1978	No. 22	Applicability of Indefinite Reversal Criteria to Timing Differences (APB Opinion No. 11 and 23)
Aug. 1978	No. 23	Leases of Certain Property Owned by a Governmental Unit or Authority (FASB Standard No. 13)
Sept. 1978	No. 24	Leases Involving Only Part of a Building (FASB Standard No. 13)
Sept. 1978	No. 25	Accounting for an Unused Investment Tax Credit (APB Opinion No. 2, 4, 11, and 16)
Sept. 1978	No. 26	Accounting for Purchase of a Leased Asset by the Lessee During the Term of the Lease (FASB Standard No. 13)
Nov. 1978	No. 27	Accounting for a Loss on a Sublease (FASB Standard No. 13 and APB Opinion No. 30)
Dec. 1978	No. 28	Accounting for Stock Appreciation Rights and Other Variable Stock Option or Award Plans (APB Opinion No. 15 and 25) (amended)
Feb. 1979	No. 29	Reporting Tax Benefits Realized on Disposition of Investments in Certain Subsidiaries and Other Investees (APB Opinion No. 23 and 24)
Sept. 1979	No. 30	Accounting for Involuntary Conversions of Nonmonetary Assets to Monetary Assets (APB Opinion No. 29)

TABLE B.5

Financial Accounting Standards Board (FASB), Interpretations *(continued)*

Date Issued	Number	Title
Feb. 1980	No. 31	Treatment of Stock Compensation Plans in EPS Computations (APB Opinion No. 15 and Interpretation 28)
Mar. 1980	No. 32	Application of Percentage Limitations in Recognizing Investment Tax Credit (APB Opinion No. 2, 4, and 11)
Aug. 1980	No. 33	Applying FASB Statement No. 34 to Oil and Gas Producing Operations (FASB Standard No. 34)
Mar. 1981	No. 34	Disclosure of Indirect Guarantees of Indebtedness of Others (FASB Standard No. 5)
May 1981	No. 35	Criteria for Applying the Equity Method of Accounting for Investments in Common Stock (APB Opinion No. 18)
Oct. 1981	No. 36	Accounting for Exploratory Wells in Progress at the End of Period
July 1983	No. 37	Accounting for Translation Adjustments upon Sale of Part of an Investment in a Foreign Entity (Interprets FASB Statement No. 52)
Aug. 1984	No. 38	Determining the Measurement Date for Stock Option, Purchase, and Award Plans Involving Junior Stock (Interprets APB Opinion No. 25)
Mar. 1992	No. 39	Offsetting of Amounts Related to Certain Contracts (Interprets APB Opinion No. 10 and FASB Statement No. 105)
Apr. 1993	No. 40	Applicability of Generally Accepted Accounting Principles to Mutual Life Insurance and Other Enterprises (Interprets FASB Statements No. 12, 60, 97, and 113)
Dec. 1994	No. 41	Offsetting of Amounts Related to Certain Repurchase and Reverse Repurchase Agreements
Sept. 1996	No. 42	Accounting for Transfers of Assets in Which a Not-for-Profit Organization Is Granted Variance Power
June 1999	No. 43	Real Estate Sales (Interprets FASB Statement No. 66)
Mar. 2000	No. 44	Accounting for Certain Transactions Involving Stock Compensation (Interprets APB Opinion No. 25)
Nov. 2002	No. 45	Guarantor's Accounting and Disclosure Requirements for Guarantees, Including Indirect Guarantees of Indebtedness of Others (Interprets FASB Statements No. 5, 57, and 107 and rescission of FASB Interpretation No. 34)
Jan. 2003	No. 46	Consolidation of Variable Interest Entities (Interprets ARB No. 51)
Rev. Dec. 2003	No. 46R	Consolidation of Variable Interest Entities (Interprets ARB No. 51)
Mar. 2005	No. 47	Accounting for Conditional Asset Retirement Obligations, An Interpretation of FASB Statement No. 143

TABLE B.6

Statements of Financial Accounting Concepts (SFACs), Financial Accounting Standards Board (FASB)

Date Issued	Number	Title
Nov. 1978	No. 1	Objectives of Financial Reporting by Business Enterprises
May 1980	No. 2	Qualitative Characteristics of Accounting Information
Dec. 1980	No. 3	Elements of Financial Statements of Business Enterprises
Dec. 1980	No. 4	Objectives of Financial Reporting by Nonbusiness Organizations
Dec. 1984	No. 5	Recognition and Measurement in Financial Statements of Business Enterprises
Dec. 1985	No. 6	Elements of Financial Statements
Feb. 2000	No. 7	Using Cash Flow Information and Present Value in Accounting Measurements

TABLE B.7

Financial Accounting Standards Board (FASB), Technical Bulletins

Date Issued	Number	Title
Dec. 1979	No. 79-1	Purpose and Scope of FASB Technical Bulletins and Procedures for Issuance
Dec. 1979	No. 79-2	Computer Software Costs
Dec. 1979	No. 79-3	Subjective Acceleration Clauses in Long-Term Debt Agreements
Dec. 1979	No. 79-4	Segment Reporting of Puerto Rican Operations
Dec. 1979	No. 79-5	Meaning of the Term "Customer" as It Applies to Health Care Facilities Under FASB Statement No. 14
Dec. 1979	No. 79-6	Valuation Allowances Following Debt Restructuring
Dec. 1979	No. 79-7	Recoveries of a Previous Writedown Under a Troubled Debt Restructuring Involving a Modification of Terms
Dec. 1979	No. 79-8	Applicability of FASB Statements 21 and 33 to Certain Brokers and Dealers in Securities
Dec. 1979	No. 79-9	Accounting in Interim Periods of Changes in Income Tax Rates
Dec. 1979	No. 79-10	Fiscal Funding Clauses in Lease Agreements
Dec. 1979	No. 79-11	Effect of a Penalty on the Term of a Lease
Dec. 1979	No. 79-12	Interest Rate Used in Calculating the Present Value of Minimum Lease Payments
Dec. 1979	No. 79-13	Applicability of FASB Statement No. 13 to Current Value Financial Statements
Dec. 1979	No. 79-14	Upward Adjustment of Guaranteed Residual Values
Dec. 1979	No. 79-15	Accounting for Loss on a Sublease Not Involving the Disposal of a Segment
Dec. 1979	No. 79-16	Effect of a Change in Income Tax Rate on the Accounting for Leveraged Leases
Dec. 1979	No. 79-17	Reporting Cumulative Effect Adjustment from Retroactive Application of FASB No. 13
Dec. 1979	No. 79-18	Transition Requirements of Certain FASB Amendments and Interpretations of FASB Statement No. 13
Dec. 1979	No. 79-19	Investor's Accounting for Unrealized Losses on Marketable Securities Owned by an Equity Method Investee
Dec. 1980	No. 80-1	Early Extinguishment of Debt Through Exchange for Common or Preferred Stock
Dec. 1980	No. 80-2	Classification of Debt Restructuring by Debtors and Creditors
Feb. 1981	No. 81-1	Disclosure of Interest Rate Futures Contracts and Forward and Standby Contracts
Feb. 1981	No. 81-2	Accounting for Unused Investment Tax Credits Acquired in a Business Combination Accounted for by the Purchase Method
Feb. 1981	No. 81-3	Multiemployer Pension Plan Amendments Act of 1980
Feb. 1981	No. 81-4	Classification as Monetary or Nonmonetary Items
Feb. 1981	No. 81-5	Offsetting Interest Cost to Be Capitalized with Interest Income
Nov. 1981	No. 81-6	Applicability of Statement 15 to Debtors in Bankruptcy Situations

TABLE B.7

Financial Accounting Standards Board (FASB), Technical Bulletins *(continued)*

Date Issued	Number	Title
Jan. 1982	No. 82-1	Disclosure of the Sale or Purchase of Tax Benefits Through Tax Leases
Mar. 1982	No. 82-2	Accounting for the Conversion of Stock Options into Incentive Stock Options as a Result of the Economic Recovery Tax Act of 1981
July 1983	No. 83-1	Accounting for the Reduction in the Tax Basis of an Asset Caused by the Investment Tax Credit (ITC)
Mar. 1984	No. 84-1	Accounting for Stock Issued to Acquire the Results of a Research and Development Arrangement
June 1984	No. 79-1	Purpose and Scope of FASB Technical Bulletins and Procedures for Issuance (Revised)
Sept. 1984	No. 84-2	Accounting for the Effects of the Tax Reform Act of 1984 on Deferred Income Taxes Relating to Domestic International Sales Corporations
Sept. 1984	No. 84-3	Accounting for the Effects of the Tax Reform Act of 1984 on Deferred Income Taxes of Stock Life Insurance Enterprises
Oct. 1984	No. 84-4	In-Substance Defeasance of Debt
Mar. 1985	No. 85-1	Accounting for the Receipt of Federal Home Loan Mortgage Corporation Participating Preferred Stock
Mar. 1985	No. 85-2	Accounting for Collateralized Mortgage Obligations (CMOs)
Nov. 1985	No. 85-3	Accounting for Operating Leases with Scheduled Rent Increases
Nov. 1985	No. 85-4	Accounting for Purchases of Life Insurance
Dec. 1985	No. 85-5	Issues Relating to Accounting for Business Combinations
Dec. 1985	No. 85-6	Accounting for a Purchase of Treasury Shares
Oct. 1986	No. 86-1	Accounting for Certain Effects of the Tax Reform Act of 1986
Dec. 1986	No. 86-2	Accounting for an Interest in the Residual Value of a Leased Asset
April 1987	No. 87-1	Accounting for a Change in Method of Accounting for Certain Postretirement Benefits
Dec. 1987	No. 87-2	Computation of a Loss on an Abandonment
Dec. 1987	No. 87-3	Accounting for Mortgage Servicing Fees and Rights
Dec. 1988	No. 88-1	Issues Relating to Accounting for Leases
Dec. 1988	No. 88-2	Definition of a Right of Setoff
Dec. 1990	No. 90-1	Accounting for Separately Priced Extended Warranty and Product Maintenance Contracts
April 1994	No. 94-1	Application of Statement 115 to Debt Securities Restructured in a Troubled Debt Restructuring
Dec. 1997	No. 97-1	Accounting Under Statement 123 for Certain Employee Stock Purchase Plans with a Look-Back Option
July 2001	No. 01-1	Effective Date for Certain Financial Institutions of Certain Provisions of Statement 140 Related to the Isolation of Transferred Financial Assets

TABLE B.8

Financial Accounting Standards Board (FASB), FASB Staff Positions (FSP)

Date Issued	Number	Title
April 2003	FAS 140-1	Accounting for Accrued Interest Receivable Related to Securitized and Sold Receivables Under FASB Statement 140, Accounting for Transfers and Servicing of Financial Assets and Extinguishments of Liabilities
Sept. 2003	FAS 146-1	Determining Whether a One-Time Termination Benefit Offered in Connection with an Exit or Disposal Activity Is, in Substance, an Enhancement to an Ongoing Benefit Arrangement
Oct. 2003	FAS 150-1	Issuer's Accounting for Freestanding Financial Instruments Composed of More Than One Option or Forward Contract Embodying Obligations Under FASB Statement No. 150, Accounting for Certain Financial Instruments with Characteristics of Both Liabilities and Equity
Oct. 2003	FAS 150-2	Accounting for Mandatorily Redeemable Shares Requiring Redemption by Payment of an Amount That Differs from the Book Value of Those Shares, Under FASB Statement No. 150, Accounting for Certain Financial Instruments with Characteristics of Both Liabilities and Equity
Nov. 2003	FAS 150-3	Effective Date, Disclosures, and Transition for Mandatorily Redeemable Financial Instruments of Certain Nonpublic Entities and Certain Mandatorily Redeemable Noncontrolling Interests Under FASB Statement No. 150, Accounting for Certain Financial Instruments with Characteristics of Both Liabilities and Equity
Nov. 2003	FAS 150-4	Issuers' Accounting for Employee Stock Ownership Plans Under FASB Statement 150, Accounting for Certain Financial Instruments with Characteristics of Both Liabilities and Equity
Nov. 2003	FAS 144-1	Determination of Cost Basis for Foreclosed Assets Under FASB Statement No. 15, Accounting by Debtors and Creditors for Troubled Debt Restructurings, and the Measurement of Cumulative Losses Previously Recognized Under Paragraph 37 of FASB Statement No. 144, Accounting for the Impairment or Disposal of Long-Lived Assets
Jan. 2004	FAS 106-1	Accounting and Disclosure Requirements Related to the Medicare Prescription Drug, Improvement and Modernization Act of 2003
April 2004	FAS 129-1	Disclosure Requirements Under FASB Statement No. 129, Disclosure of Information About Capital Structure, Relating to Contingently Convertible Securities
April 2004	FAS 141-1 and FAS 142-1	Interaction of FASB Statements No. 141, Business Combinations, and No. 142, Goodwill and Other Intangible Assets, and EITF Issue No. 04-2, Whether Mineral Rights Are Tangible or Intangible Assets
May 2004	FAS 106-2	Accounting and Disclosure Requirements Related to the Medicare Prescription Drug, Improvement and Modernization Act of 2003
June 2004	FAS 97-1	Situations in Which Paragraphs 17(b) and 20 of FASB Statement No. 97, Accounting and Reporting by Insurance Enterprises for Certain Long-Duration Contracts and for Realized Gains and Losses from the Sale of Investments, Permit or Require Accrual of an Unearned Revenue Liability
Sept. 2004	FAS 142-2	Application of FASB Statement No. 142, Goodwill and Other Intangible Assets, to Oil- and Gas-Producing Entities
Dec. 2004	FAS 109-1	Application of FASB Statement No. 109, Accounting for Income Taxes, to the Tax Deduction on Qualified Production Activities Provided by the American Jobs Creation Act of 2004
Dec. 2004	FAS 109-2	Accounting and Disclosure Guidance for the Foreign Earnings Repatriation Provision Within the American Jobs Creation Act of 2004
April 2005	FAS 19-1	Accounting for Suspended Well Costs
June 2005	FAS 143-1	Accounting for Electronic Equipment Waste Obligations
June 2005	FAS 150-5	Issuers' Accounting Under FASB Statement 150 for Freestanding Warrants and Other Similar Instruments on Shares That Are Redeemable
Rev. Aug. 2005	FAS 123R-1	Classification and Measurement of Freestanding Financial Instruments Originally Issued in Exchange for Employee Services Under FASB Statement No. 123(R)
Oct. 2005	FAS 13-1	Accounting for Rental Costs Incurred During a Construction Period
Rev. Oct. 2005	FAS 123R-2	Practical Accommodation to the Application of Grant Date as Defined in FASB Statement No. 123(R)

TABLE B.8

Financial Accounting Standards Board (FASB), FASB Staff Positions (FSP) *(continued)*

Date Issued	Number	Title
June 2003	FIN 45-1	Accounting for Intellectual Property Infringement Indemnifications Under FASB Interpretation No. 45, Guarantor's Accounting and Disclosure Requirements for Guarantees, Including Indirect Guarantees of Indebtedness of Others
Dec. 2003	FIN 45-2	Whether FASB Interpretation No. 45, Guarantor's Accounting and Disclosure Requirements for Guarantees, Including Indirect Guarantees of Indebtedness of Others, Provides Support for Subsequently Accounting for a Guarantor's Liability at Fair Value
Rev. Feb. 2004	FIN 46R-1	Reporting Variable Interests in Specified Assets of Variable Interest Entitles as Separate Variable Interest Entities Under Paragraph 13 of FASB Interpretation No. 46 (revised December 2003), Consolidation of Variable Interest Entities (This FSP replaces FIN 46-2 for any entity to which Interpretation 46 [revised December 2003][FIN 46(R)] is applied.)
Rev. Feb. 2004	FIN 46R-2	Calculation of Expected Losses Under FASB Interpretation No. 46 (revised December 2003), Consolidation of Variable Interest Entities (This FSP replaces FIN 46-5 for any entity to which Interpretation 46 [revised December 2003][FIN 46(R)] is applied.)
Rev. Feb. 2004	FIN 46R-3	Evaluating Whether as a Group the Holders of the Equity Investment at Risk Lack the Direct or Indirect Ability to Make Decisions About an Entity's Activities Through Voting Rights or Similar Rights Under FASB Interpretation No. 46 (revised December 2003), Consolidation of Variable Interest Entities (This FSP replaces FIN 46-8 for any entity to which Interpretation 46 [revised December 2003][FIN 46(R)] is applied.)
Rev. April 2004	FIN 46R-4	Technical Correction of FASB Interpretation No. 46 (revised December 2003), Consolidation of Variable Interest Entities, Relating to Its Effects on Question No. 12 of EITF Issue No. 96-21, Implementation Issues in Accounting for Leasing Transactions Involving Special-Purpose Entities
Rev. Mar. 2005	FIN 46R-5	Implicit Variable Interests Under FASB Interpretation No. 46 (revised December 2003), Consolidation of Variable Interest Entities (This FSP is applicable to both nonpublic and public reporting enterprises. This issue commonly arises in leasing arrangements among related parties and in other types of arrangements involving related parties and previously unrelated parties.)
July 2005	APB 18-1	Accounting by an Investor for Its Proportionate Share of Accumulated Other Comprehensive Income of an Investee Accounted for Under the Equity Method in Accordance with APB Opinion No. 18 upon a Loss of Significant Influence
Sept. 2004	EITF 03-1-1	Effective Date of Paragraphs 10 and 20 of EITF Issue No. 03-1, The Meaning of Other-Than-Temporary Impairment and Its Application to Certain Investments
Mar. 2005	EITF 85-24-1	Application of EITF Issue No. 85-24, Distribution Fees by Distributors of Mutual Funds That Do Not Have a Front-End Sales Charge, When Cash for the Right to Future Distribution Fees for Shares Previously Sold Is Received from Third Parties
May 2005	EITF 00-19-1	Application of EITF Issue No. 00-19 to Freestanding Financial Instruments Originally Issued as Employee Compensation
July 2005	SOP 78-9-1	Interaction of AICPA Statement of Position 78-9 and EITF Issue No. 04-5

TABLE B.9

International Accounting Standards (IAS), International Accounting Standards Committee (IASC)

Number	Title	Last Revised
No. 1	Presentation of Financial Statements (revised)	Dec. 2003
No. 2	Inventories (revised)	Dec. 2003
No. 3	Consolidated Financial Statements (superseded)	—
No. 4	Depreciation Accounting (withdrawn, superseded)	—
No. 5	Information to Be Disclosed in Financial Statements (superseded)	—
No. 6	Accounting Responses to Changing Prices (superseded)	—
No. 7	Cash Flow Statements	1992
No. 8	Accounting Policies, Changes in Accounting Estimates, and Errors	Dec. 2003
No. 9	Accounting for Research and Development Activities (superseded)	—
No. 10	Events After the Balance Sheet Date	1999
No. 11	Construction Costs	1993
No. 12	Income Taxes	2000
No. 13	Presentation of Current Assets and Current Liabilities (superseded)	—
No. 14	Segment Reporting	1997
No. 15	Information Reflecting the Effects of Changing Prices	Dec. 2003
No. 16	Property, Plant and Equipment	Dec. 2003
No. 17	Leases	Dec. 2003
No. 18	Revenue	1993
No. 19	Employee Benefits	2002
No. 20	Accounting for Government Grants and Disclosure of Government Assistance	1983
No. 21	The Effects of Changes in Foreign Exchange Rates	Dec. 2003
No. 22	Business Combinations (superseded)	1998
No. 23	Borrowing Costs	1993
No. 24	Related Party Disclosures	Dec. 2003
No. 25	Accounting for Investments (superseded)	—
No. 26	Accounting and Reporting by Retirement Benefit Plans	1987
No. 27	Consolidated and Separate Financial Statements	Dec. 2003
No. 28	Investments in Associates	Dec. 2003
No. 29	Financial Reporting in Hyperinflationary Economies	1989
No. 30	Disclosures in the Financial Statements of Banks and Similar Financial Institutions	1990
No. 31	Interests in Joint Ventures	Dec. 2003
No. 32	Financial Instruments: Disclosures and Presentation	Dec. 2003
No. 33	Earnings per Share	Dec. 2003
No. 34	Interim Financial Reporting	1998
No. 35	Discontinuing Operations (superseded)	1998
No. 36	Impairment of Assets	Mar. 2004
No. 37	Provisions, Contingent Liabilities and Contingent Assets	1998
No. 38	Intangible Assets	Mar. 2004
No. 39	Financial Instruments: Recognition and Measurement	Dec. 2005
No. 40	Investment Property	Mar. 2004
No. 41	Agriculture	2001

TABLE B.10

International Financial Reporting Standards (IFRS), International Accounting Standards Board (IASB)

Number	Title	Last Revised
No. 1	First-Time Adoption of International Financial Reporting Standards	June 2003
No. 2	Share-Based Payment	Feb. 2004
No. 3	Business Combinations	Mar. 2004
No. 4	Insurance Contracts	Mar. 2004
No. 5	Non-Current Assets and Presentation of Discontinued Operations	Mar. 2004
No. 6	Exploration for and Evaluation of Mineral Resources	Aug. 2005
No. 7	Financial Instruments: Disclosure	Aug. 2005

National Accounting Boards and Organizations

American Accounting Association (AAA)

www.aaahq.org

American Institute of Certified Public Accountants (AICPA)

www.aicpa.org

Association of Government Accountants (AGA)

www.agacgfm.org

Financial Accounting Standards Board (FASB)

www.fasb.org

Financial Executives International (FEI)

www.fei.org

Governmental Accounting Standards Board (GASB)

www.gasb.org

Institute of Internal Auditors (IIA)

www.theiia.org

Institute of Management Accountants (IMA)

www.imanet.org

Securities and Exchange Commission (SEC)

www.sec.gov

Index

Note: **Boldface** type indicates real-world companies.

Analysis Ratios and Measures

Ratio or Measure	Calculation	Type	Chapter
Accounts Receivable Turnover Ratio	Net Sales ÷ Average Net Accounts Receivable	Activity	7
Asset Turnover Ratio	Net Sales ÷ Average Net Operating Assets	Activity	9
Average Useful Life of Operating Assets	Average Operating Assets ÷ Depreciation Expense	Performance	9
Benchmarking	Compares a company's financial results with results from other companies or with an industry average	Comparative	4
Cash Current Debt Coverage Ratio	Cash Flows from Operating Activities − Current Dividends ÷ Current Interest-Bearing Debt	Adequacy	19
Cash Debt Coverage Ratio	Cash Flows from Operating Activities ÷ Average Total Debt	Adequacy	5
Cash Dividend Coverage Ratio	Cash Flows from Operating Activities ÷ Total Dividends Paid	Adequacy	5
Cash Dividend Payout Ratio	Total Dividend Paid ÷ Cash Flows from Operating Activities	Adequacy	5
Cash Flow per Share	Cash Flows from Operating Activities ÷ Number of Issued Shares	Performance	5
Cash Flow Return on Assets	(Cash Flows from Operating Activities + Interest Paid + Taxes Paid) ÷ Average Total Assets	Performance	5
Cash Flow Return on Equity	(Cash Flows from Operating Activities − Preferred Dividends Paid) ÷ Average Common Stockholders' Equity	Performance	5
Cash Flow to Net Income	Cash Flows from Operating Activities ÷ Net Income	Performance	5
Cash Flow to Operating Income	Cash Flows from Operating Activities ÷ Operating Income	Performance	5
Cash Interest Coverage Ratio	(Cash Flows from Operating Activities + Interest Paid + Taxes Paid) ÷ Cash Interest Payments	Adequacy	5
Current Ratio	Current Assets ÷ Current Liabilities	Liquidity	7
Days in Inventory	365 ÷ Inventory Turnover Ratio	Activity	8
Days in Receivables	365 ÷ Accounts Receivable Turnover Ratio	Activity	7
Debt-to-Equity Ratio	Total Debt ÷ Total Stockholders' Equity	Leverage	13
Defensive Ratio	(Cash + Investments + Receivables) ÷ Average Daily Operating Cash Outflow	Liquidity	7
Dividend Payout Ratio	Cash Dividends ÷ Net Income, or Dividends Per Share ÷ Earnings Per Share	Adequacy	17